OFFICE FOR
**NATIONAL
STATISTICS**

D1628260

Guide to

Official
Statistics

2000 edition

Editorial Team:	Andrew Corris
	Brian Yin
	Claire Ricketts
Consultant Statistician:	James Denman
Production Team:	Dave Pike
	Kim Slater
Design:	Shain Bali

London: The Stationery Office

About the Office for National Statistics

The Office for National Statistics (ONS) is the Government Agency responsible for compiling, analysing and disseminating many of the United Kingdom's economic, social and demographic statistics, including the retail prices index, trade figures and labour market data, as well as the periodic census of the population and health statistics. The Director of ONS is also Head of the Government Statistical Service (GSS) and Registrar-General in England and Wales and the agency carries out all statutory registration of births, marriages and deaths there.

Editorial policy statement

The Office for National Statistics works in partnership with others in the Government Statistical Service to provide Parliament, government and the wider community with the statistical information, analysis and advice needed to improve decision-making, stimulate research and inform debate. It also registers key life events. It aims to provide an authoritative and impartial picture of society and a window on the work and performance of government, allowing the impact of government policies and actions to be assessed.

Information services

For general enquiries about official statistics, please contact the National Statistics Public Enquiry Service:

Telephone	-	020 7533 5888
Textphone (Minicom)	-	01633 812399

Alternatively write to the National Statistics Public Enquiry Service, Zone DG/18, 1 Drummond Gate, London, SW1V 2QQ. Fax 020 7533 6261 or e-mail **info@ons.gov.uk**.

Most National Statistics publications are published by The Stationery Office and can be obtained from The Publications Centre, P.O. Box 276, London, SW8 5DT. Tel 0870 600 5522 or fax 0870 600 5533.

National Statistics can also be contacted on the Internet at **http://www.ons.gov.uk**

ISBN 0 11 621161 X

369 0023077

369 0023077

Contents

15 Environment

Sources and Analyses

Products

16 Civic Affairs, Culture, Sport and Leisure

Sources and Analyses

Products

17 Government and Public Sector

18 Government Statistics - General

The Guide to Official Statistics

Introduction

The Guide to Official Statistics is published by the Office for National Statistics on an occasional, or ad hoc basis and is designed to answer the following questions:

- What sort of statistics does the government produce ?
- What subject matters do these statistics cover ?
- Who produces them ?
- How, and when, were they obtained ?
- In what form are the statistics produced ?
- How, and where, can users find them ?

It provides a comprehensive Directory of all the statistical censuses, surveys, administrative systems, press releases, publications, databases, CD-ROMs, and other services which are managed by statisticians working in the Government Statistical Service (GSS), in the Northern Ireland Statistics and Research Agency and in a range of other complementary organisations. The GSS embraces the Office for National Statistics (ONS) itself as well as each of the statistical divisions within over 30 other Government Departments and Agencies, and is the major provider of official statistics in the United Kingdom.

The information presented in the Guide, which is often referred to as 'metadata' (or 'information about data'), represents a small selection of the much more extensive metadata made available via another GSS information service called StatBase which is accessible via the World Wide Web. Anyone with an Internet connection can access StatBase, free of charge, through the following address.

http://www.statistics.gov.uk

The ONS has overall responsibility for both the Guide and StatBase but depends on all those within the GSS and other organisations who devote time and effort to providing the necessary content.

Structure of the Guide

The Guide to Official Statistics employs the same classification system as StatBase by linking every GSS statistical resource to one of seventeen 'Themes', each of which covers a major aspect of national life. Each of the chapters in the Guide equates to a single StatBase Theme and, within each chapter, each of the paragraphs equates to a single StatBase Subject-Area (within each Theme). A brief description of the contents of each Chapter (or Theme) is given after this introduction. The Guide differs from StatBase in one respect, however, by including a chapter devoted specifically to 'Web Services'.

Terminology used

The Guide also uses the same terminology as StatBase by describing each of the GSS's statistical resources as either a 'Source', 'Analysis', 'Product', or 'Contact'. A short definition of each of these concepts is given below:-

Sources - defined as any statistical system or procedure for collecting raw data, be it a Census, a postal survey, a telephone inquiry, an administrative system, or whatever. The decennial Population Census would be a typical example of a 'Source'.

Analyses - defined as any 'value-added' secondary statistics derived from the raw data gathered from any Source or combination of Sources which have been deemed to be sufficiently important to merit a special mention - the Retail Price Index would a typical example of an 'Analysis'.

Products - defined as any physical 'output' or service, be it a Press Release, hardcopy publication, Database, CD-ROM, Diskette, Enquiry Service, or whatever - the annual publication entitled 'Social Trends' would be a typical example of a 'Product'.

Contacts - defined as the 'owners' or 'managers' of any statistical resource, or their nominated information/enquiry agents - in other words, the person or persons from whom more information can be obtained.

Information provided

The details provided for each of the statistical resources described in the Guide are only a small selection of the more detailed information which is provided within StatBase. Explanatory definitions of each of the fields used within the Guide are given below:-

Sources and Analyses

Besides a 'Title', a 'Description', and a 'Statistician' or other 'Contact Point' the following details are given for each Source or Analysis, where possible:

Organisation: the name of the Government Department, Agency or other organisation which owns or sponsors each Source/Analysis.

Status: the operational status of the Source. This field indicates whether the resource is ongoing or not.

Collection Method: the methodological basis of the Source. This field indicates whether the Source is a census, sample survey, or whatever.

Frequency: Frequency of collection or compilation of the data.

Reference Period: the standard period of time to which the data collected via this Source or Analysis refers.

Timeliness: the interval of time which normally elapses between the collection/compilation of data and its release.

Earliest Available Date: the earliest point in time (or reference period) to which the data collected via this resource refers.

National Coverage: indicates whether the statistical coverage is for the UK as a whole, or for one or more of its constituent countries.

Sub-National: an indicator of whether the geographical coverage is full, sampled or partial.

Disaggregation: shows the range of spatial units or administrative areas for which data from this Source/Analysis can be disaggregated.

Products

Besides a 'Title', a 'Description', and a 'Contact Point', the following details are given for each Product, where possible:

Organisation: the name of the Government Department, Agency or other organisation which owns or sponsors each Product.

Delivery: the type of Product - is it a Press Release, hardcopy publication, DataBase, etc ?

Frequency: the frequency with which the Product is released.

Price: the price or range of prices charged to buyers of, or subscribers to, this Product.

ISBN: where applicable, the 'International Standard Book Number' of the Product (see Note below on 'Timeliness').

ISSN: where applicable, the 'International Standard Serial Number' of the Product.

Coverage / Completeness / Timeliness

A gap of several months can elapse between the publication of a Guide such as this, and the period of time when its contents were originally gathered and assembled for inclusion. Moreover, the contents of this Guide were extracted from StatBase during a period when the latter was still in its infancy. Since then considerable efforts have been made to ensure that StatBase obtains full coverage of all the GSS's statistical resources and that each of the metadata fields in StatBase have been fully completed. It may be the case, therefore, that entries in this Guide are not as complete or up-to-date as those held in StatBase. Readers with access to the Word Wide Web who want more information about a particular entry, or want to know whether there have been any significant changes to some of the details included in the Guide (e.g. the ISBNs, or the listed 'Owners') are advised to log onto StatBase in order to obtain the most recent information about each Source, Analysis or Product.

A quick guide to the contents of each chapter (or StatBase THEME)

1. Website and Electronic Services

This Chapter describes some of the individual Departmental Websites and Databanks through which users can access official statistics as well as a range of other national and international metadata and data systems which complement official sources of information.

2. Compendia and Reference

This Chapter brings together all those statistical products and services which don't fit neatly into any one single Chapter because they include a whole hotch-potch of information and statistics taken from a whole range of statistical Themes. This is where you will find references to any material (e.g. The Annual Abstract) which covers the complete range of responsibilities covered by the Government Statistical Service.

3. Population, Census, Migration and Vital Events

This Chapter brings together information and statistics about the individuals and families who populate this country including those who arrive in the country as immigrants, and those who leave as emigrants. It covers statistics about their numbers, now and in the future, their personal characteristics and their lifestyles, and also brings together information and statistics which describe the major 'vital' events which affect their lives and lifestyles - their births, marriages, divorces and deaths. The material referred to in this Chapter provides useful background material to the material referred to in all the other Chapters.

4. Health and Care

This Chapter brings together information and statistics about the National Health Service and the other services which provide for the more vulnerable members of our society. It covers statistics about Hospitals, GPs, Dental Clinics, Residential Homes, and Care Centres and the services they provide; statistics about the medical, dental, opthalmic and other staff who deliver these services; statistics about the patients and other persons they care for; and statistics about the social, mental, medical, dental and other conditions they deal with. Some of the subject matters covered by this Chapter relate to others covered by the Education and Training and Labour Market Chapters.

5. Education and Training

This Chapter brings together information and statistics about nurseries, schools, colleges and universities, and the academic, educational and vocational training services they provide; statistics about the teachers and academics who work in these institutions; statistics about the pupils and students enrolled in them; and statistics about the pay or funding they receive. Some of the subject matters covered by this Chapter relate to others covered by the Crime, Health, and Labour Market Chapters.

6. Labour Market

This Chapter brings together information and statistics about our working lives. It covers statistics about the personal characteristics and work experience of those people who have a job, as well as those who don't; statistics about the sort of occupations and industries in which people work; statistics about their travel-to-work arrangements and statistics about their productivity and their pay and earnings from employment. It also covers statistics about employers, their demand for labour, their employment costs, statistics about industrial relations between employers and employees, and statistics about the arrangements for achieving Health and Safety at work. Some of the subject matters covered by this Chapter relate to others covered by the Education, Health and Population Themes.

7. Housing

This Chapter brings together information about the domestic living arrangements of individuals and families and covers statistics on the provision, improvement, purchase, and sale of housing within the UK, whether owner-occupied or rented, and its corollary - homelessness.

8. Crime and Justice

This Chapter brings together information and statistics about 'Crime and Justice', and 'Law and Order' in the UK. It covers statistics about the Police Force and their work; statistics about criminals and the crimes they commit; statistics about the activities of the Courts when dealing with those who either seek justice or face justice; and statistics about the operations of the Prison and Probationary Service when dealing with those who break the law. Some of the subject matters covered by this Chapter relate to others covered by the Education Theme.

9. Household Finances

This Chapter brings together information about the financial arrangements of individuals and families and covers statistics about households' income (whether from work, pensions, benefits, etc), statistics about households' expenditure (whether on goods and services, taxation, leisure, etc) and statistics on households' assets and liabilities.

10. The Economy

This Chapter brings together information and statistics about the management of the country's Economy. It covers statistics about the country's overall economic performance and our national wealth - measured by the 'National

Economic Accounts' - and statistics about our economic relations with other countries, whether in terms of our international trade in goods and services, or inward and outward investment - measured by the 'Balance of Payments Accounts'. It also covers information and statistics about Prices and Inflation - measured by indices such as the Retail Price Index. Some of the subject matters covered by this Chapter relate to others covered by the Agriculture, Commerce and Industry, and Government Themes.

11. Banking and Finance
This Chapter brings together information and statistics about the Bank of England, Pension Funds, the High Street Banks, Insurance Companies, Unit and Investment Trusts, Building Societies, etc. Some of the subject matters covered in this chapter relate to others covered in the Economy Chapter.

12. Commerce, Construction, Energy and Industry
This Chapter brings together information and statistics about the manufacturing, mining and quarrying, and building and construction industries, the energy and utility sectors (e.g. oil, gas, electricity, water, etc) and the wholesaling, retailing, and other service industries. It covers statistics about the management and administration of commerce and industry in this country and detailed statistics about the economic activity of each sector - i.e. statistics about their output, sales, stocks, purchases, expenditures, exports, employees, etc. Some of the subject matters covered by this Theme relate to others covered by the Economy and Labour Market Themes.

13. Transport, Travel and Tourism
This Chapter brings together information and statistics about those people, whether UK citizens or overseas visitors, who travel within the UK, or abroad, and perhaps visit tourist attractions, or stay in tourist accommodation. It also includes information about travellers' means of transport, and the amount of passengers or goods carried by either air, road, rail, or sea. Some of the subject matters covered in this Chapter relate to others covered by the Labour Market Theme.

14. Agriculture, Fishing, Food and Forestry
This Chapter covers statistics about the economic management and use of the nation's land, rivers and marine resources for cultivating crops, fruit or vegetables, rearing livestock and poultry, breeding and catching fish, or growing timber. It also covers statistics about the Animal Feed, Dairy, Food, Drink, and other 'agro-industries' which depend on these primary industries, the human and other resources engaged in each activity, and statistics about animal health and food safety. Some of the subject matters covered by this Chapter relate to others covered by the Economy, Environment , Health and Labour Market Themes.

15. The Environment
This Chapter covers statistics about the Environment in which we live. It covers statistics about wildlife and the natural world, the air we breathe, the water around us, the land we live on, and the way we use these and other natural resources. It also covers statistics about waste, pollution and environmental damage and efforts to reduce their impact through recovery and recycling. Some of the subject matters covered by this Theme relate to others covered by the Agriculture Theme.

16. Civic Affairs, Culture, Sport and Leisure
This Chapter brings together statistics about the provision of civic and community services such as the Fire Brigade Service, Electoral Registration and Gaming and Liquor Licensing and statistics about peoples' cultural and leisure activities and participation in sport.

17. Government and Public Sector
This Chapter brings together information and statistics about Central Government (whether in England, Northern Ireland, Scotland or Wales), Local Government, Government Agencies and the Armed Forces. It covers statistics on the number of people working in each area of Government, statistics on Government income (from borrowing, taxation, etc), and Government expenditure, whether at home or abroad (e.g. on Foreign Aid). Some of the subject matters covered by this Theme relate to others covered by the Economy Theme and Labour Market Theme.

18. Government Statistics - General
This is where you will find reports and products concerned with the management and administration of 'Government Statistics' in this country e.g. the GSS Annual Report, Codes of Practice, methodological material, etc.

Economy

Education

Housing

Crime & justice

Population

Income

Websites and Electronic Services

The statistics described in this Guide are collected, administered and disseminated by a number of separate Departments, Agencies and organisations who together comprise the Government Statistical Service (GSS). The basic data are generated from a number of separate information 'Sources' and the resultant statistics are disseminated through a whole range of statistical 'Analyses' and 'Products', all of which are described in the following chapters. Some of these data are also made available on-line via the whole range of individual Departmental Websites or GSS databanks described in this Chapter.

Users who want on-line access to the 'metadata' contained within this Guide, or who want to obtain some of the data described in this Guide are advised, in the first instance, to visit the GSS Website (http://www.statistics.gov.uk (http://www.statistics.gov.uk)). Later this year, this site will be expanded to become the 'National Statistics' website. In addition to its other metadata and data facilities, the GSS site also provides access to a range of other Departmental Websites. The GSS Website also provides free access to **StatBase** which incorporates two linked services: a metadata service called **StatSearch** and a data service called **StatStore.**

A click on the 'StatSearch' button will give you free access to a comprehensive and up-to-date directory of official statistics which, amongst other things, tells you sort of statistics are collected and published by the GSS, when they were produced, who produced them, how they can be obtained, and in what form. A click on the 'StatStore' button will give you free access to a wide selection of the data collected and disseminated by the GSS. The available data are presented in the form of either multi-dimensional datasets or time-series datasets, and can either be viewed on screen or downloaded to the user's own PC.

Users who want to obtain the complete histories of the economic time-series published by the Office for National Statistics on behalf of the GSS, whether it be in First Releases or in compendia volumes such as *Economic Trends* or *Financial Trends*, may wish to consider becoming a subscriber to the **DataBank** service. Users who only want to select a limited number of these time-series from across a whole range of publications may find it more economical to use the **TimeZone** service. This is a self-selection version of the DataBank service and it can be accessed from within StatBase, via the GSS Website.

I

Websites and Electronic Services - *Products*

1.1 Compendia & Reference - United Kingdom

(The) Data Archive
http://dawww.essex.ac.uk

The Data Archive (sponsored by the University of Essex) holds the largest collection in the UK of computer-readable data on social and economic topics. Data are acquired from academic, commercial and government sources and preserved and made available for further analysis by the research community. The Archive holds over 4,000 datasets. Most relate to post-war Britain, although an increasing number of historical studies pertaining to earlier periods are now becoming available. Data are made available over the network, on CD-ROM, and on a variety of other media according to the wishes of the user. Access to the Archive's holdings is provided to all researchers and teachers unless restrictions have been required by the owners. The Archive also provides information on the location and availability of data and sponsors various activities - including workshops, user groups and regular newsletters - designed to improve the quality of data and their secondary analysis. The data available extend across the full range of the social sciences and humanities and contain information about most areas of social and economic life. In addition to British cross sectoral studies from academic, government and commercial sources, the Archive holds time series data, major longitudinal studies, panel surveys and major cross-sectional studies. Data holdings include: UK Census data; General Household Surveys; Family Expenditure Surveys; ONS DataBank; Labour Force Surveys; British Crime Surveys; British Social Attitudes; etc. The Data Archive will endeavour to locate and obtain relevant research data for any interested enquirer.

Available from
User Services
The Data Archive
University of Essex
Colchester
CO4 3SQ.
Tel: 01206 872001;
Email: archive@essex.ac.uk

The Government Statistical Service (GSS) Website – The Source
www.statistics.gov.uk

The Source is a Government website, which aims to provide users with the information they need to access statistics, easily and quickly. It is the home site for the Government Statistical Service (GSS), and is managed on its behalf by the Office for National Statistics (ONS).

The GSS provides the United Kingdom with most of its official statistics. Statistics on many aspects of national life are collected, analysed and published by government statisticians and their staff located in over 30 departments and agencies. In this way the GSS is 'decentralised'. This allows GSS staff to work closely with Ministers and policy makers in departments, providing statistics and advising on their use, and ensuring that statistics play an important role in shaping and monitoring government policy.

This site provides access to a selection of the vast range of statistics which the GSS produces covering themes such as the environment, health, transport, crime, the economy and population. It has a link to the Scottish Executive website and provides a home for StatBase (both of which are described in more detail in their own entries).

With the advent of National Statistics in May 2000 (see the Introduction to this book for further details), this website, and the ONS website will merge under the '*www.statistics.gov.uk*' web address.

Support e-mail addresses
the.source@ons.gov.uk (for feedback and other enquiries)
info.gssweb@ons.gov.uk (for technical enquiries)

Inforoute
www.inforoute.hmso.gov.uk

Inforoute is a new UK Government website which has been set up to provide a gateway and central information point to guide and direct a route through the maze of official government information and materials. Inforoute will provide direct access to the Government Information Asset Registers (IARs) which individual departments will

be setting up. Each IAR will concentrate on sources of unpublished information in the sense that it is not formally published, eg datasets/databases and other significant information resources, which may currently only be made available on request. Individual departments will have primary responsibility for putting in place their own IARs which they will maintain on their own Web sites. Inforoute will eventually contain a complete subject index and hypertext links to the individual IARs.

London Research Centre
www.london-research.gov.uk/ds/dshome.htm

This site gives access to, and information about, a wealth of data for London. The Demographic and Statistical Studies Department, at the London Research Centre, has an international reputation for its expertise and research in: the UK Census of Population; demographic projections and estimates; economic data; the application of mapping and geographic information systems in local government; London election statistics; statistics sources for London; and school roll projection. The department carries out research and provides information for all the London local authorities. It also undertakes commissioned work for, and sells products to, a wide range of other clients, including government departments, local authorities outside London, Training and Enterprise Councils, health authorities, and universities and colleges.

Support e-mail address
dsinfo@london-research.gov.uk

NISRA
www.nisra.gov.uk

The website for the Northern Ireland Statistics and Research Agency contains details of the statistics, products and services available from the Agency. These include 'Key Statistics' for the region, publication information, press releases, surveys, and contact details for NISRA staff.

The site also contains detailed information on the products and services available from Census Office for Northern Ireland as well as news of progress towards the 2001 Census.

Information on the registration of births, marriages, adoptions and deaths in Northern Ireland is available from the General Register Office section of the site.

Support e-mail address
nisra.rreb@dfpni.gov.uk

Northern Ireland Office
www.nio.gov.uk

This site provides background information on the current political and security situation in Northern Ireland together with a comprehensive list of all Northern Ireland Department Press Releases.

Support e-mail address
press.nio@nics.gov.uk

Office for National Statistics
www.ons.gov.uk

The Office for National Statistics (ONS) is a Government Agency created in April 1996 by the merger of Central Statistical Office and the Office of Population Censuses and Surveys. The work of ONS affects everyone; it produces and disseminates social, health, economic, demographic, labour market and business statistics. It also conducts the Census and a whole range of social surveys. It is responsible for the registration of births, marriages and deaths and the National Health Service Central Register.

The ONS website provides links to a wealth of statistical information. Their latest press releases and bulletins, covering the whole range of the organisation's work, are available. Information is also given on the variety of other ways ONS data can be obtained including books, CD-ROMS and the Databank service for macro-economic statistics. A link can also be found to the Government Statistical Service (GSS) website *'www.statistics.gov.uk'* produced by the ONS on behalf of the Government Statistical Service, which also includes StatBase (please see the separate entries for both the GSS website and StatBase for fuller details).

With the advent of National Statistics in May 2000 (see the Introduction to this book for further details), this website, and the GSS website will merge under the *'www.statistics.gov.uk'* web address.

Support e-mail addresses
feedback@ons.gov.uk (please use this address for technical queries only)
info@ons.gov.uk (please use this address to request additional information)

Scottish Executive
http://194.247.69.28/stats/default.htm

The Scottish Executive (SE) Statistics Home Page gives access to a wide range of data about Scotland, using pillar subject categories. All SE hardcopy publications are available on the site, which also links to StatBase to provide a comprehensive set of sources for the statistics. Some topics offer downloadable datasets for further analysis. Links to other organisations which produce statistics on Scotland, such as the Scottish Health Service and the Scottish Funding Councils for Higher and Further Education, are also featured.

Support e-mail address
statistics.enquiries@scotland.gov.uk

SOSIG – The Social Science Information Gateway
www.sosig.ac.uk

SOSIG provides a browsable and searchable catalogue of thousands of high quality Internet resources of relevance to anyone involved in teaching, learning or research in the social sciences. Users can browse and search for particular types of information in over 200 subject areas, including statistical data and supporting materials. All of the resources that appear in the catalogue have been selected and catalogued by subject specialists. The Gateway offers a number of additional services such as an automatically generated index of a further 50,000 social science Web pages, a database of UK social science departments and an online thesaurus. SOSIG is a national service funded by the Economic and Social Research Council (ESRC) and the Joint Information Systems Committee (JISC) as part of the UK Resource Discovery Network (RDN).

Support e-mail address
sosig-info@bristol.ac.uk

StatBase
www.statistics.gov.uk

StatBase is an on-line information resource accessible via the web which has two main components - StatSearch and StatStore. StatSearch lies at the heart of the system and contains a comprehensive catalogue with an associated Search Directory. It is a vital reference tool for anyone seeking detailed information about official statistics - i.e. information gathered and disseminated by the Government Statistical Service and other official organisations within the UK. It provides detailed 'metadata' about all the 'Sources' (i.e. censuses, surveys and administrative systems) used to gather

official statistics about each subject-area, and all the more important 'Secondary Analyses' derived from these Sources. In addition, StatSearch provides metadata about all the 'Products' associated with official statistics such as publications, databases, statistical services etc. In each case, StatSearch also provides the names and locations of the relevant 'Contacts'. A subset of the detailed metadata held within StatSearch provides the content for the 'Guide to Official Statistics'. However, the Guide is not updated with the same frequency as StatSearch.

The 'discovery metadata' within StatSearch allows users to discover the existence, location, collection and release arrangements of any Source, Analysis or Product; any relevant Contact details; and any links between each of them. The 'evaluation metadata' within StatSearch allows potential users to ascertain whether or not a particular Source or Product meets their needs in terms of timeliness, subject coverage, geographical coverage, disaggregation, quality, etc. The Information Directory within Statbase is based on a three-level hierarchy of Themes, Subject-Areas (within Themes) and Topics (within Subject-Areas) provides users with easy-to-read signposts to the contents of the database. This allows users to locate any Source, Analysis or Product which is relevant to whichever Theme, Subject-area or Topic interests them.

StatStore contains an extensive range of statistics covering a wide spectrum of social, economic and socio-economic affairs. These are presented in the form of either time-series or cross-sectional analyses, some of which are free and some chargeable.

With the advent of National Statistics in April 2000 (see the Introduction to this book for further details), the Government Statistical Service website (of which StatBase is presently a part) and the Office for National Statistics website will merge under the *'www.statistics.gov.uk'* web address.

Support e-mail address
idb.dataunit@ons.gov.uk

United Kingdom Standard Geographic Base (UKSGB)
www.ngdf.org.uk/uksgb/homepage.htm

The United Kingdom Standard Geographic Base (UKSGB) aims to provide users and suppliers of geographic information with a standard and consistent approach to commonly used geographical units in the UK. These are known as the UKSGB core spatial units and currently include administrative

Products

and postal geographies. To help you understand these core spatial units and how they link together, the online UKSGB Directory identifies and describes each core spatial unit, and provides information about the available datasets containing information such as up to date names, codes, boundaries, and grid co-ordinates for each of the core spatial units. A contact is given for each supplier of these datasets.

Support e-mail address
uksgb@ons.gov.uk

1.2 Compendia & Reference-International

Eurostat
www.europa.eu.int/en/comm/eurostat/serven/home.htm

The Statistical Office of the European Communities (Eurostat) has a website that contains a large amount of statistical and related information. It has an area that looks at all the publications and CD-ROMs the office produces. European indicators, catalogues and press releases can all be viewed online. There is also access to a Data Shop where specific requests for data can be formulated online.

Support e-mail address
info.desk@eurostat.cec.be

NESSTAR – Networked Social Science Tools and Resources
www.nesstar.org

The NESSTAR project is being developed by three partners - the UK Data Archive at the University of Essex, the Norwegian Data Archive and the Danish Data Archive. By taking advantage of developments in computer networking and data and text browsing tools, NESSTAR should become a world leading resource enabling users to identify, browse and acquire relevant national data across international and internal boundaries. The final version of the system should be Available from January 2000.

There are four main components to the proposed NESSTAR system: An enhanced version of the Integrated Data Catalogue will enable users to search for relevant data across several countries in one action, allowing the searching of the study descriptions of identified data sets; a text search system will enable searches by individual field names or variable names within data sets. This will include the ability to search for similar themes across data sets; a data browsing and visualisation system will enable users to

conduct simple data analysis on-line (this will include simple tabulations and graphics); and an authentication system will facilitate access to more sensitive data sets.

Project manager's e-mail address
peterl@essex.ac.uk

Organisation for Economic Cooperation and Development (OECD)
www.oecd.org/statlist.htm

The OECD statistics page lists all its links to data split by broad themes, which include: OECD statistics; economic statistics; agriculture; energy; development and co-operation; public management; education, labour and social affairs; science, technology and industry; health; and transport. These themes are then broken down into more detailed subjects.

r-cade – Resource Centre for Access to Data on Europe
www.r-cade.dur.ac.uk

This website has been developed by the r.cade project at the University of Durham. The r.cade site provides access to European and international data sets covering a wide range of topics from unemployment and the environment to finance and industry. Customers from any sector, from anywhere in the world, can use the r·cade services to gain access to data. Services include online access to a database via the Internet, customised data extractions, consultancy and special academic concessions. It is an official Eurostat datashop and also disseminates data produced by UNIDO, ILO and UNESCO. The r.cade website can be used to preview r·cade's data holdings, to find the services best suited to your requirements and which may be relevant to research, policy and business needs. r.cade also provide a comprehensive guide to other data sources on Europe found on the Internet.

United Nations
www.un.org/depts/unsd

The UN Statistics Division provides a wide range of statistical outputs and services for producers and users of statistics worldwide. By increasing the global availability and use of official statistics, this work facilitates national and international policy formulation, implementation and monitoring. This website provides access to various statistics and statistical indicators; plus information on statistical methods, sources and references, and international cooperation in statistics.

Support e-mail address
statistics@un.org

1.3 Population, Census, Migration and Vital Events

General Register Office for Scotland
www.open.gov.uk/gros/library.htm

The Data Library at the GRO(S) website is where their statistics can be found. It has information on population and vital events (births, marriage and deaths). Files can be downloaded free of charge, but copyright conditions apply.

Support e-mail address
webmaster@gro-scotland.gov.uk

1.4 Health and Care

Department of Health Statistics Home Page
www.doh.gov.uk/public/stats1.htm

This website contains information on all Department of Health statistical publications, covering both health and personal social services. Many of these are also available in full on the site, including all new Statistical Bulletins. In addition, information about an increasing number of statistical returns is available. For further detail, the site contains:

• Statistics Division of the Department of Health (www.doh.gov.uk/public/stats5.htm) An introduction to statistics in the Department of Health.
• Statistics on the Web (www.doh.gov.uk/public/stats3.htm) Actual statistical publications, categorised under Public Health; Health Care; Social Care; Workforce; and Expenditure.
• Surveys (www.doh.gov.uk/public/england.htm) Links to Health Survey documents and provides details of other health related surveys sponsored by the Department of Health.
• Statistical Returns on the Web (www.doh.gov.uk/public/statret.htm) Links to a number of actual returns and their guidance.
• Developments in Statistical Collections (www.doh.gov.uk/barker1.htm) Details of a number of developments that the Department of Health is undertaking.
• Recent Publications (www.doh.gov.uk/public/recpub.htm) A list of those statistical publications that have been published in the last six months and those that have been pre-

announced for the coming month. Links made to documents, if available, or to a Statistical Press Notice, if one is issued.
• Full List of Publications (www.doh.gov.uk/public/hpssspub.htm) A full list of statistical publications categorised under Public Health; Health Care; Social Care; Workforce; and Expenditure. Links made to documents, if available, or to a Statistical Press Notice, if one is issued.
• Obtaining Information (www.doh.gov.uk/public/pubinfo.htm) Details of how further information can be obtained, including statistical contacts.

Support e-mail address
Individual documents/pages contain contact details where appropriate.

Department of Health & Social Services (NI)
www.dhssni.gov.uk/hpss/statistics/index.html

The web pages of Regional Information Branch provide links to a variety of publications, bulletins and reports. The branch is part of the Information and Analysis Unit. Regional Information Branch is responsible for the collection, quality assurance, primary analysis and publication of timely and accurate information derived from a wide range of statistical data supplied by the Health and Personal Social Services (HPSS).

Support e-mail address
shaun.mccann@dhssni.gov.uk

Department of Social Security
www.dss.gov.uk/asd/online.html

The home page for the Analytical Services Division within the DSS provides links to a small list of statistical documents including Households Below Average Income, Research Reports and other information about people on benefits. The site will be undergoing major changes in the near future which should include a significant increase in the statistical information provided.

Support e-mail address
scottb@asdlondon.dss-asd.gov.uk

1.5 Education and Training

Department for Education and Employment
www.dfee.gov.uk/sfr.htm

This page within the Department for Education and Employment's website contains links to all their latest statistical first releases.

Support e-mail address
info@dfee.gov.uk

Department of Education for Northern Ireland
www.nics.gov.uk/deni/statistics/index.htm

These pages have links to DENI's Statistical Press Release Library, Research Briefings and a PDF version of the Compendium of Northern Ireland Educational Statistics.

Support e-mail address
deni@nics.gov.uk

1.6 Labour Market

Nomis®
Electronic service provided by the University of Durham on behalf the Office for National Statistics

A database of labour statistics run on behalf of the Office for National Statistics by the University of Durham. Contains a comprehensive range of official statistics relating to the labour market including: unemployment; employment; earnings; vacancies; training; Labour Force Survey and the Census of Population. Nomis contains the following key datasets: Labour Force Survey; Claimant Count; Annual Employment Survey / Census of Employment; Vacancies handled by Jobcentres; and 1991 Census of Population. Nomis data can be analysed using an extensive range of geographies including: Government Office regions; Travel-to-Work areas; Counties; Unitary Authorities; Local Authorities; TECS and LECS; Parliamentary constituencies; Postcode sectors; Jobcentre areas; and Wards.

Available from
Ann Blake
Room B3/02
Office for National Statistics
I Drummond Gate
London
SWIV 2QQ
Tel: 020 7533 6130
Email: ann.blake@ons.gov.uk

1.7 Crime and Justice

(The) Home Office RDS Website
www.homeoffice.gov.uk/rds/index.htm

The Research Development and Statistics Directorate (RDS) is an integral part of the Home Office. The HO website provides links to the Directorate's Publications, Research Programme and Statistical Programme. This year, for the first time, the

Digest (containing information on the Criminal Justice System in England and Wales) will be made available on-line.

Support e-mail address
rds.ho@gtnet.gov.uk

(The) Lord Chancellor's Department
www.open.gov.uk/lcd/research/introfr.htm

Website containing links to research papers produced by the Lord Chancellor's Department.

Support e-mail address
enquiries.lcdhq@gtnet.gov.uk

Northern Ireland Office
www.nio.gov.uk

This site provides background information on the current political and security situation in Northern Ireland together with a comprehensive list of all Northern Ireland Department Press Releases.

Support e-mail address
press.nio@nics.gov.uk

Royal Ulster Constabulary
www.ruc.police.uk/press/statistics

The RUC statistics page contains links to data on the Province's security situation, road accidents and other crime statistics.

Support e-mail address
press@ruc.police.uk

1.8 The Economy

Databank
Electronic service provided by the Office for National Statistics

An electronic and chargeable publication series which provides Office for National Statistics time-series statistics 'in bulk'. Contains official statistics published by the ONS, including major series such as GDP, PSBR, RPI, Balance of Payments (ONS Pink Book), National Accounts (ONS Blue Book), Index of Production, and Claimant Count. Time series are available on disk or by internet download. Payment can be made by various subscription charges and one-off payments.

Available from
ONS Customer & Electronic Services Unit,
Room B1/05,
Office for National Statistics,
I Drummond Gate,

London,
SW1V 2QQ
Tel: 020 7533 5675.

http://www.ons.gov.uk/dbank_f.html

1.9 Banking and Finance

(The) Bank of England
www.bankofengland.co.uk/mfsd/index.htm

The Monetary & Financial Statistics Division ("MFSD") pages of the Bank of England website aim to give some background to the division's work and the data they collect and publish. The site contains links to all MFSD's recent Statistical releases and publications; interest and exchange rate data; information about MFSD itself; and links to other useful statistical websites. The aim is to develop the site further, as better ways are found to present the statistical data in a more accessible way.

Support e-mail address
mfsd_ibs@bankofengland.co.uk

1.10 Commerce, Construction, Energy and Industry

Department of Trade and Industry
www.dti.gov.uk/public/frame8.html

These web pages are produced by the DTI's Statistics Directorate which is responsible for the development of statistical policy and classifications and for providing support and advice to the Department, its ministers and the business community covering a wide range of core Trade and Industry-related statistics. A small list of currently available information is accessed via a link.

Support e-mail address
joe.ewins@esdv.dti.gov.uk

1.11 Transport, Travel and Tourism

Civil Aviation Authority
www.caaerg.co.uk/adu/home.htm

The Aviation Data Unit collects and disseminates statistics and market information about the UK aviation industry. In addition to regularly published material, special analyses of data may be commissioned within certain confidentiality constraints. There are three main types of

data: UK Airport Statistics covering all traffic into and out of the United Kingdom; UK Airline Statistics covering UK carriers activity worldwide; and Punctuality Statistics measuring the punctuality of passenger services at ten UK airports. Publications covering the above three subjects are now available free of charge from this website.

Support e-mail address
mcleans@caaerg.co.uk

Department of the Environment, Transport and the Regions
www.detr.gov.uk

The homepage for the Department of the Environment, Transport and the Regions has a large array of links out to information covering its diverse areas of interest. There is a specific link for transport statistics which takes you to a page of recent reports and bulletins put out by the department. Further statistical material can be found by exploring the other links on the home page.

Support e-mail address
webmaster.detr@gtnet.gov.uk

1.12 Agriculture, Fishing, Food and Forestry

Forestry Commission
www.forestry.gov.uk

This site contains links to the latest forestry statistics in "Facts & Figures", "Forestry Industry Handbook", and "Wood Supply & Demand". Access can also be gained to the National Inventory of Woodland regional reports for Scotland, with county reports for England and Wales to follow. Other statistics reports, such as "Public Opinion of Forestry", "Sawmill Survey", and "Timber price index for conifer standing sales" are also available. Most of these are available to view and download as PDF files.

Support e-mail address
statistics@forestry.gov.uk

Ministry of Agriculture, Fisheries and Food
www.maff.gov.uk/esg/default.htm

The Economics and Statistics Group of the Ministry of Agriculture, Fisheries and Food produces a wide range of statistics covering much of the agriculture, fishing and food industries. All main releases of statistics are shown on the site in the form of pdf files and many detailed statistics are made

available in spreadsheet format. In many cases statistics cover the whole of the UK and data is combined from surveys run by the other agricultural departments (Scottish Executive Agriculture, Environment and Fisheries department, Department of Agriculture Northern Ireland and the National Assembly for Wales).

Support e-mail address
webmaster@inf.maff.gov.uk

1.13 Environment

Countryside Agency
www.countryside.gov.uk

This website provides access to the Agency's research notes, some of which contain statistical material.

Support e-mail address
richard.baldelli@countryside.gov.uk

Countryside Information System
http://mwnta.nmw.ac.uk/ceh/cis/ciscat.htm

The Countryside Information System (CIS) is a Microsoft Windows-based program for PC's giving easy access to spatial information about the British countryside which can assist policy development at national scales. It combines, analyses and presents a comprehensive range of environmental data sets for each one kilometre square of the National Grid in Great Britain.

Data supplied with CIS include counties and administrative regions, land cover information from satellite, and national field surveys in 1978, 1984, 1990 and 1998 which document the changes in the ecological characteristics of the British countryside. Other data sets are available such as Designated Areas (e.g. SSSI's), Ordnance Survey topography and geographical reference, and flora and fauna. Details on data available for use in CIS are given in the CIS Environmental Catalogue, a hypertext database regularly updated and downloadable from the World Wide Web at http://mwnta.nmw.ac.uk/ceh/cis/ciscat.htm.

The CIS allows users to (1) combine, analyse and present environmental data, (2) characterise geographical regions, (3) select areas with different environmental features and (4) produce maps, tables of statistics and charts.

Support e-mail address
timothy.moffat@ite.ac.uk

Department of Environment (NI)
www.doeni.gov.uk/core.htm

The Central Statistics & Research Branch are part of the core of the Department of the Environment (NI). The Branch has responsibility for compiling and disseminating statistics on some of the Department's key areas of responsibility, these include: Housing & Construction, Transport and Urban Regeneration. This website has links to recent reports produced by the Branch, which include; Housing Statistics 1997/98; Quarterly Housing & Construction Bulletin; Transport Statistics 1997/98; Road and Rail Transport Statistics Bulletin; Belfast Residents Survey; and Londonderry Residents Survey

Support e-mail address
CSRB@doeni.gov.uk

Department of the Environment, Transport and the Regions
www.detr.gov.uk

The homepage for the Department of the Environment, Transport and the Regions has a large array of links out to information covering its diverse areas of interest. There is a specific link for transport statistics which takes you to a page of recent reports and bulletins put out by the department. Further statistical material can be found by exploring the other links on the home page.

Support e-mail address
webmaster.detr@gtnet.gov.uk

(The) Environment Agency
www.environment-agency.gov.uk/envinfo/index.htm

This site provides access to an on-line version of the State of the Environment. This contains over 30 chapters and hundreds of graphs and charts about the State of the Environment in England and Wales. Includes the latest bathing water quality and other sample datasets.

Support e-mail address
webmaster@environment-agency.gov.uk

National Air Quality Archive: Internet Site
www.aeat.co.uk/netcen/airqual

This site gives access to a queriable database of concentration and emissions statistics. There is also the on-line version of the annual report of the DETR's automatic monitoring networks called Air Pollution in

the UK; a queriable database of statistics updated daily from the monitoring networks; and access to active maps of estimated pollutant concentrations and emissions, bulletins of the latest hours data from the automatic networks, a forecast of air pollution levels for the next 24 hours, and access to an archive of all air pollution data gathered from National Networks.

Support e-mail address
aqinfo@aeat.co.uk

Scottish Environment Protection Agency (SEPA)
www.sepa.org.uk

SEPA is charged with preventing the pollution of land, air and water, and the protection of Scotland's environment. The SEPA website contains information and data on the state of Scotland's environment, press releases and copies of publications.

Support e-mail address
info@sepa.org.uk

1.14 Government and Public Sector

Defence Analytical Services Agency
www.mod.uk/dasa

The Defence Analytical Services Agency (DASA) is part of the Government Statistical Service. It is a small Defence Agency of around 130 staff in the administration and statistical grades, which provides professional statistical and other analytical services to the UK Ministry of Defence (MoD). The Agency is spread over six sites in the southern half of the country - Bath, Bristol, Gloucester, Portsmouth, Upavon (near Swindon), and Whitehall, London.

The site contains news and corporate information about DASA itself. There are also links to downloadable versions of some of the statistical products they produce, including UK Defence Statistics, the annual statistical compendium of the Ministry of Defence. The majority of the products are made available in Adobe PDF format, though UK Defence Statistics is also available in HTML format.

Support e-mail addresses
General information: info@dasa.mod.uk
Personnel & recruitment personnel@dasa.mod.uk
Support: webmaster@dasa.mod.uk

Department for International Development
www.dfid.gov.uk

This site includes extracts from the latest edition of Statistics on International Development (formerly British Aid Statistics). It is intended to make the whole publication available online in the future.

Support e-mail address
enquiry@dfid.gov.uk

Her Majesty's Customs and Excise
www.hmce.gov.uk

Information on this site is split into two areas relating to the public and businesses. Statistical information is not kept specifically in one location, but is more likely to be in the Information for Business area and can be found by browsing the site. Subjects in the Information for Business area include VAT, Intrastat, Customs, Excise, and Regions.

HM Customs and Excise - UK Tariff and Statistical Office
www.hmce.gov.uk/bus/tso/index.htm

Information on this site relates to the work of the UK Tariff and Statistical Office (TSO), an Executive Unit within HM Customs and Excise, which provides information on UK trade in goods, the Tariff, and services related to facilitating and supporting trade within the global market.

The site includes summary tables of UK Overseas Trade Statistics. They contain:

- statistics of UK imports from and exports to countries outside the European Community (EC) which have been compiled from declarations made to HM Customs and Excise by importers, exporters and their agents, and;

- statistics of UK arrivals from and dispatches to other Member States of the EC compiled from Intrastat returns sent by traders and their agents to the TSO.

Support e-mail address
statistics.tso@hmce.gov.uk

1.15 Government Statistics – General

The Government Statistical Service (GSS) Website – The Source
www.statistics.gov.uk

Products

The Source is a Government website, which aims to provide users with the information they need to access statistics, easily and quickly. It is the home site for the Government Statistical Service (GSS), and is produced on its behalf by the Office for National Statistics (ONS).

The GSS provides the United Kingdom with most of its official statistics. Statistics on many aspects of national life are collected, analysed and published by government statisticians and their staff located in over 30 departments and agencies. In this way the GSS is 'decentralised'. This allows GSS staff to work closely with Ministers and policy makers in departments, providing statistics and advising on their use, and ensuring that statistics play an important role in shaping and monitoring government policy.

This site provides access to a selection of the vast range of statistics which the GSS produces covering themes such as the environment, health, transport, crime, the economy and population. It has a link to the Scottish Executive website and provides a home for StatBase (both of which are described in more detail in their own entries).

With the advent of National Statistics in April 2000 (see the Introduction to this book for further details), this website, and the ONS website will merge under the *'www.statistics.gov.uk'* web address.

Support e-mail addresses
the.source@ons.gov.uk (for feedback and other enquiries)
info.gssweb@ons.gov.uk (for technical enquiries)

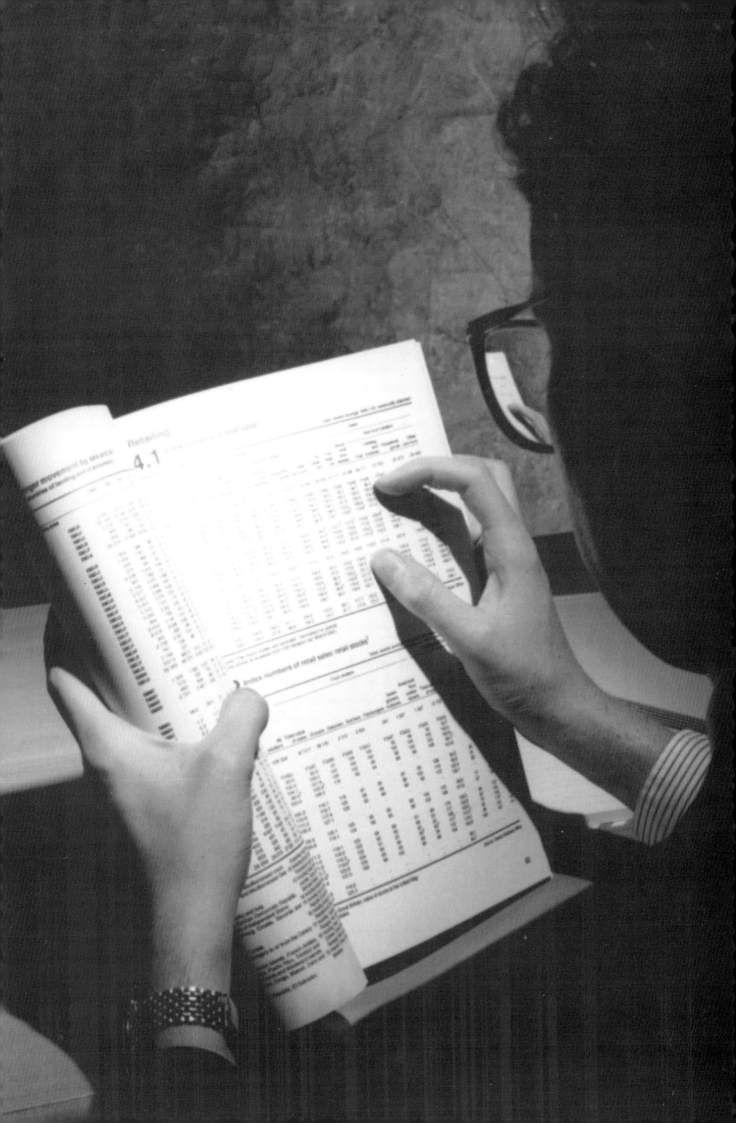

2

Compendia and Reference

Compendia and Reference volumes are disseminated by a number of separate Departments, Agencies and organisations including the **Office for National Statistics, Scottish Executive, the National Assembly for Wales**, and **the Northern Ireland Statistics and Research Agency** and embrace all of the Themes and Subject Areas included within this Guide.

Users looking for a cross-section of reference material and statistics may find the following compendium products useful:

On-line Databases (See Chapter 1):

StatBase – StatSearch (for metadata)
StatBase – StatStore (for all types of data)
StatBase –TimeZone (for individual time-series)
DataBank (for time-series 'batched' as complete publications)

Hardcopy Compendia (UK Coverage):

Annual Abstract of Statistics
Britain 2000: The Official Yearbook of the United Kingdom
Monthly Digest of Statistics
Regional Trends (annual publication)
Social Trends (annual publication)

Hardcopy Compendia (Country Specific Coverage)

Digest of Welsh Statistics (annual publication)
Northern Ireland Annual Abstract of Statistics (annual publication)
Scottish Abstract of Statistics (annual publication)

Users may also find what they need on the various Departmental Websites. These are listed in Chapter 1.

2 Compendia and Reference - *Sources and Analyses*

2.1 United Kingdom

British Social Attitudes Survey (BSA) Series

National Centre for Social Research; the BSA is sponsored by the Gatsby Charitable Foundation (one of the Sainsbury Family Charitable Trusts), government departments, quasi-governmental bodies and other grant-giving organisations.

The National Centre for Social Research, an independent non-profit research institute, carries out a series of annual surveys charting continuity and change in British social, economic, political and moral values in relation to other changes in society. Each year up to 3,600 respondents are asked about their attitudes and opinions on a wide range of issues, some of which are covered every year, others less often. For example, questions can cover such topics as newspaper readership, political parties and trust, public spending, welfare benefits, health care, childcare, poverty, the labour market and the workplace, education, charitable giving, the countryside, transport and the environment, Europe, economic prospects, race, religion, civil liberties, immigration, sentencing and prisons, fear of crime and the portrayal of sex and violence in the media.

The surveys began in 1983. Between 1984 and 1986, the ESRC funded the introduction of a panel element so that changes in the attitudes of individuals could be tracked. Between 1989 and 1996 the National Centre for Social Research collaborated with the Policy Planning and Research Unit (PPRU) of the Northern Ireland Statistics and Research Agency and the Queen's University, Belfast, on the linked Northern Ireland Social Attitudes Survey, and some of the findings from this survey have been included in BSA reports. In 1994 and 1998 young people (aged 12-19) living in adult respondents' households were also interviewed (Young People's Social Attitudes Survey). Since 1985, the questionnaires have contained questions asked in up to 25 countries, as part of the National Centre's participation in the International Social Survey Programme (ISSP).

Some discontinuities (apply to BSA team at the National Centre for Social Research for details)

Status: Ongoing
Collection Method: Household/Person (Sample) Survey
Frequency: Annually
Reference Period: Fieldwork takes place in spring or early summer each year
Timeliness: 18 months (data publicly released on publication of Annual Report)
Earliest Available Data: March-April 1983
National Coverage: Great Britain
Sub-National: South of the Caledonian Canal
Disaggregation: See Technical Reports on the BSA surveys, published by SCPR

Statistician
Katarina Thomson
National Centre for Social Research
Tel: 020 7250 1866;
Email: k.thomson@natcen.ac.uk

Products that contain data from this source
British Social Attitudes Reports; The Data Archive

Continuous Household Survey - Northern Ireland

Northern Ireland Statistics and Research Agency

The Northern Ireland Statistics and Research Agency carries out a survey on characteristics of households. The sample consists of 4,500 addresses per year. Data are available by household size, tenure, availability of consumer durables, health, income, smoking, drinking and contraception. Data cover Northern Ireland and are available at regional level. The survey has been carried out continuously since 1983. Before April 1989 it was carried out on calendar-year basis but since then it has been carried out each financial year. The main results are available within four months of the end of fieldwork.

Status: Ongoing
Collection Method: Household/Person (Sample) Survey
Frequency: Annually
Reference Period: April to March
Timeliness: Within four months of the end of fieldwork
Earliest Available Data: 1983
National Coverage: Northern Ireland

Statistician
Kevin Sweeney
Department of Finance and Personnel - Northern Ireland
Central Survey Unit
Tel: 028 9025 2490

Products that contain data from this source
Cigarette smoking among people aged 16 or over: by gender, 1996-97: regional dataset; Cigarettes smoked by smokers aged 16 or over: by gender, 1996-97: regional dataset; Consultations with an NHS GP and reports of limiting long-standing illness, 1996-97: regional dataset; Continuous Household Survey (PPRU Monitor); Households with selected durable goods, 1996-97: regional dataset; Northern Ireland Annual Abstract of Statistics; Participation in selected leisure and sporting activities, 1996-97: regional dataset; Participation in the National Lottery, 1996-97: regional dataset; Regional Trends; Social Trends; The Data Archive

---

General Household Survey - GB

Office for National Statistics; sponsored by Department of Health, DETR and other government departments.

The Office for National Statistics carries out the General Household Survey (GHS), a multi-purpose sample survey on approximately 9,000 households and about 16,000 adults aged 16 and over. Data are collected on five core topics, namely education, employment, health, housing, and population and family information. Other areas such as leisure, household burglary, smoking and drinking are covered periodically. Data cover Great Britain and some regional tabulations are available. The Survey began in 1971 and the five core topics have been included continuously. Special topics are added and changed from year to year. The Survey began reporting on a financial-year basis after 1988, instead of a calendar year, and data are published annually each spring. No data collection in 1997/8 financial year. Moved to computer-assisted interviewing in 1995.

Status: Ongoing
Collection Method: Computer-assisted personal interviewing
Frequency: Continuously
Reference Period: Financial year
Earliest Available Data: 1971
National Coverage: Great Britain

Statistician
Dr Ann Bridgwood
Office for National Statistics
Tel: 020 7533 5303

Products that contain data from this source
Cigarettes smoked by smokers aged 16 or over: by gender, 1996-97: regional dataset; Consultations with an NHS GP and reports of limiting long-standing illness, 1996-97: regional dataset; Health Inequalities Decennial Supplement; House Property and Inheritance in the UK; Housing Equity Withdrawal; Living in Britain (results from the 1998 General Household Survey,) Negative Equity; Occupational Health Decennial Supplement; Statistical Bulletin on Smoking; The Data Archive; The Health of Adult Britain 1841 - 1994, Decennial Supplement, Volumes 1 and 2

(The) ONS Omnibus Survey - GB
Office For National Statistics

The Office for National Statistics carries out the Omnibus Survey; a multi-purpose survey based on interviews with a sample of about 1,900 adults per survey month, with one adult selected from each household. The Survey is a vehicle providing quick results from relatively short and simple sets of questions. Questions on particular topics can be added for one month or for longer if required. Over 100 question modules have been included to date covering a very wide range including contraception, unused medicines, mortgage arrears, organ transplants, retirement income, fire safety, daycare for the under fives, sunburn and time use. The Survey covers Great Britain and data are available at standard region level. The Survey began in October 1990 and has been carried out monthly since then. Standard tables and data are available to customers within four weeks of the completion of fieldwork (that is eight weeks after the final date for commissioning questions). The survey does not always take place in each month of any year.

Status: Ongoing
Collection Method: Computer-aided personal interviewing
Frequency: Monthly
Reference Period: Varies according to topic
Earliest Available Data: 1990

National Coverage: Great Britain

Statistician
Olwen Rowlands
Office for National Statistics
Social Survey Division
Tel: 020 7533 5308;
Email: olwen.rowlands@ons.gov.uk

Products that contain data from this source
Cooking: Attitudes and Behaviour; Drinking: adults' behaviour and knowledge; Food safety in the home; National Fire Safety Week and Domestic Fire Safety; Residual Medicines; Smoking-related behaviour and attitudes; The Data Archive; The ONS Omnibus GB; The Prevalence of Back Pain in Great Britain

Scottish Household Survey
Scottish Executive

A continuous sample survey of households, covering the whole of Scotland. Sample size around 15,000 households per annum. The survey will cover a range of topics, but will focus particularly on transport, local government services and social exclusion topics.

Status: Ongoing
Collection Method: Household/Person (Sample) Survey
Frequency: Continuous
Reference Period: Survey will be continuous, with interviews taking place each month. Summary results will be published quarterly, and more detailed results annually.
Timeliness: First bulletin, on the first quarter of 1999, will be published in July 1999
Earliest Available Data: The survey started early in 1999.
National Coverage: Scotland
Disaggregation: Data will be available down to local authority level (after 2 years of fieldwork)

Statistician
Louise Finlayson
Scottish Executive
Central Research Unit
2J Victoria Quay
Edinburgh EH6 6QQ
Tel: 0131 244 7557;
Email: shs@scotland.gov.uk

Products that contain data from this source
A series of quarterly bulletins; the first of these was called the Scottish Household Survey: Bulletin 1.

2

Compendia and Reference - *Products*

2.2 United Kingdom

Annual Abstract of Statistics
Office for National Statistics

This product contains a comprehensive collection of statistics covering the nation. It contains statistics on the United Kingdom's economy, industry, society and demography presented in easy to read tables and backed up with explanatory notes and definitions. It is compiled from 100 sources and has more than 10,000 series. It is a comprehensive reference tool, which can be used to build a picture of the United Kingdom, provide support for a business case or be used for its range of index numbers. It covers the following areas: area; parliamentary elections; overseas aid; defence; population and vital statistics; education; labour market; personal income, expenditure and wealth; health; social protection; crime and justice; lifestyles; environment, water and housing; transport and communications; national accounts; prices; government finance; external trade and investment; research and development; agriculture, fisheries and food; production; banking and insurance etc; and services industry.

Delivery: Periodic Release
Frequency: Annually
Price: £39.50
ISBN: 0 11 621068 0
ISSN: 0072 5730

Available from
TSO Publications Centre and Bookshops
Please see Annex B for full address details.

(A) Brief Guide to Gender Statistics
Office for National Statistics and Equal Opportunities Commission

The Guide aims to indicate the main sources of statistics on gender-related topics for the United Kingdom and includes both official and non-government sources. It is not intended to be a comprehensive reference work and is aimed primarily at those who need to use statistics on gender-related topics but who may not have detailed knowledge of statistical sources. Such users may be initially interested in statistics available in published analyses, so most references are to publications. However, for those wishing to look further, electronic datasets and databases are also referred to where appropriate. Guidance on further sources of information is contained in the Guide. The Guide has four sections: a brief discussion of the main official and non-official data sources by broad topic area; a listing of the main sources of data in alphabetical order; guidance and contacts for further information; and finally, an index of topics (or keywords), cross-referring to the data sources described in Sections 1 and 2. The Guide has 68 pages A5 size.

Delivery: Hardcopy publication
Frequency: One-off 1998
Price: £7.00
ISBN: 1 85774 263 X

Available from
National Statistics Sales Office
Please see Annex B for full address details.

Briefings on Women and Men in Britain
Equal Opportunities Commission

A new series of briefings on a range of gender-related themes are to be published from October 1999. Each briefing consists of one page discussing current policy issues, plus seven pages of graphics and commentary covering the latest statistical information on women and men.

All of the data in this product are disaggregated by gender.

Frequency: Ad-hoc
Price: Free

Available from
Customer Contact Point
Equal Opportunities Commission
Please see Annex B for full address details

Britain 2000: The Official Yearbook of the United Kingdom
Office for National Statistics

The annual 'Britain Yearbook' gathers together in a single volume a complete range of official information about the structure and organisation of the United Kingdom (England, Northern Ireland, Scotland and Wales), and the government policies that underpin 'how Britain works'. The 2000 edition is the 51st in an annual series dating back to the 1940s. It has become a widely used work of reference, both in the UK itself and overseas, where it is an important element of the information service provided by British diplomatic posts.

Delivery: Periodic Release
Frequency: Annually
Price: The 2000 edition costs £37.50 (hardback)
ISBN: 0-11-621098-2

Available from
TSO Publications Centre and Bookshops
Please see Annex B for full address details.

British Social Attitudes Reports
National Centre for Social Research

A series of annual reports each looking at a different aspect of social attitudes in Britain. The most recent editions are "British - and European - Social Attitudes: the 15th BSA Report" and "The End of Conservative Values?: the 14th BSA Report".

Delivery: Periodic Release
Frequency: Annually
Price: £25.00
ISBN: 1 84014 046 1
ISSN: 0267 6869

Available from
Ashgate Publishing Ltd
Please see Annex for full address details

Continuous Household Survey (PPRU Monitor)
Department of Finance and Personnel - Northern Ireland

A selection of tables giving the latest information and indicating where changes have taken place. The most recent monitor (PPRU Monitor 1/92) contains data on household composition, tenure, consumer durables, health, opinions on the most important problem facing Northern Ireland, income, sports and leisure, smoking and patterns of alcohol consumption.

Frequency: Occasional,
Price: Free

Available from
Kevin Sweeney
Department of Finance and Personnel –
Northern Ireland
Londonderry House
21–27 Chichester Street
Belfast
Tel: 028 9025 2490

Digest of Welsh Local Area Statistics
National Assembly for Wales

Contains latest statistics mainly at Unitary Authority level on topics such as population, economics, education and training, health and personal social services, housing and local government finance, agriculture and forestry, transport, environment and law and order.

Delivery: Periodic Release
Frequency: Annually
Price: £15.00 - postage free within the UK
ISBN: 0 7504 2251 3
ISSN: 1362-3583

Available from
Publications Unit, Statistical Directorate
National Assembly for Wales
Please see Annex B for full address details

or

Clive Lewis
Room 2-002
National Assembly for Wales
Crown Building
Cathays Park
Cardiff CF10 3NQ
Tel: 029 2082 3220;
Email: clive.lewis@wales.gsi.gov.uk

Digest of Welsh Statistics
National Assembly for Wales

A compendium of statistics covering all aspects of Welsh life - data at the Wales level only, since 1996. The digest contains data on population, vital statistics, health and personal social services, social security, law, order and protective services, housing and planning, Welsh language, electorate, recreation, schools, higher and further education, labour, industrial production, energy, construction and investment, agriculture, forestry, fishing, transport and communication, national income, personal incomes, expenditure, and environment.

Frequency: Annually
Price: £15.00 postage paid within the UK
ISBN: 0 7504 2249 1
ISSN: 0262-8295

Available from
Publications Unit, Statistical Directorate
National Assembly for Wales
Please see Annex B for full address details

Sources from which data for this product are obtained
Building Societies; Drug Offenders - UK; Grant and Group Repair Schemes - Wales; Homelessness; Hospital Bed Use - Wales; Index of Production and Construction - Wales; Labour Dispute Statistics; Local Authority Budget Requirement - Wales; Local Authority Capital Forecast - Wales; Local Authority Capital Outturn - Wales; Local Authority Capital Payments - Wales; Local Authority General Fund Revenue Account - Wales; Local Authority Revenue Outturn - Wales; Notifiable Offences - England and Wales; Road Accidents - Wales; Road Lengths - Wales; Sales of Local Authority Dwellings

Facts about Women and Men in Great Britain
Equal Opportunities Commission

Handy, pocket-size summary of statistics giving a broad picture of the relative position of women and men in Great Britain. Contains sex-disaggregated data covering a range of topics, for example, population, education and training, economic activity, employment, and earnings.

All of the data in this product are disaggregated by gender.

Delivery: Periodic Release
Frequency: Annually
Price: Free

Available from
Customer Contact Point
Equal Opportunities Commission
Please see Annex B for full address details

Facts about Women and Men in Scotland
Equal Opportunities Commission

Handy, pocket-size summary of statistics giving a broad picture of the relative position of women and men in Scotland. Contains sex-disaggregated data covering a range of topics, for example, population, education and training, economic activity, employment, and earnings.

All of the data in this product are disaggregated by gender.

Delivery: Periodic Release
Frequency: Annually
Price: Free

Available from
Customer Contact Point
Equal Opportunities Commission
Please see Annex B for full address details

Facts About Women and Men in Wales / Ffeithiau Am Fenywod a

Dynion Yng Nghymru
Equal Opportunities Commission

Handy, pocket-size summary of statistics giving a broad picture of the relative position of women and men in Wales. Contains sex-disaggregated data covering a range of topics, for example, population, education and training, economic activity, employment, and earnings.

All of the data in this product are disaggregated by gender

Delivery: Periodic Release
Frequency: Annually
Price: Free

Available from
Customer Contact Point
Equal Opportunities Commission
Please see Annex B for full address details

Focus on London
Office for National Statistics. Government Office for London, and the London Research Centre

Focus on London is the result of a unique partnership between the Office for National Statistics, the Government Office for London and the London Research Centre. It draws together data from a wide range of sources to present a rounded portrait of London today. Containing a wealth of demographic, social, industrial and economic statistics and commentary, it looks at changes over recent years and highlights differences between the boroughs, the Inner and Outer London areas and the country as a whole. It is aimed both at the specialist user and the general reader including: Research officers in local government and health authorities, TECs, chambers of commerce and charities; Academics, researchers and teachers of economic, social and urban studies and geography; Marketing professionals and businesses in London; Community relations officers and students. Focus on London's 12 chapters contain commentary, tables, charts and maps covering the following topics: The evolution of London; Population; Environment; Housing; The Economy; Labour Market; Education and Training; Living in London; Tourism and Leisure; Travel and Communications; Public Services; and London Government. It includes a further 40 pages of detailed statistics, with much of the data presented at borough level. Also included is a CD-ROM containing the data for further analysis and a full electronic copy of the publication. There is also a references and further reading section plus useful contact points in key organisations.

Delivery: Periodic Release
Frequency: Annually
Price: £45.00
ISBN: 0-11-621159-8
ISSN: 1367-4617

Available from
TSO Publications Centre and Bookshops
Please see Annex B for full address details.

Focus on Northern Ireland
Northern Ireland Statistics and Research
Agency

A regional statistical profile of Northern
Ireland. Contains statistical information and
comment relating to most aspects of life in
Northern Ireland, including population, the
environment, the labour market, living
standards, health, education, and crime. It
also provides comparisons with the United
Kingdom as a whole and other regions of
the European Union, including the Republic
of Ireland.

Delivery: First Release
Frequency: Ad hoc
Price: £30.00
ISBN: 0 11 620772 8

Available from
TSO Publications Centre and Bookshops
Please see Annex B for full address details.

Focus on the East Midlands
Office for National Statistics

Published in 1995, Focus on the East
Midlands was a pilot publication aimed at
meeting the increasing demand for more
easily accessible regional statistics. It brings
together statistical information about the
East Midlands from across the Government
Statistical Service in the form of
commentary, tables, charts and maps. It
provides an intriguing insight into most
aspects of life within the region and how it
has changed. Comparisons are made
between the counties and districts of the
region and between the region and the
country as whole. It is aimed at all who live,
work or have an interest in the region,
whether as a general reader or as a specialist.
Focus on the East Midlands contains
commentary, tables, charts and maps
covering the following topics: The Land and
Environment; Population; The Economy;
The Labour Market; Housing; Education
and Training; Household and family
characteristics; Living Standards; Health;
and Crime

Delivery: Ad hoc/One-off Release
Frequency: Ad-hoc
Price: £19.95
ISBN: 0 11 620718 3

Available from
Electronic Sales Unit or TSO Publications Centre
and Bookshops
Please see Annex B for full address details.

Focus on the South East
Office for National Statistics and
Government Office for the South East

Stretching from Dover to Didcot and from
Banbury to Brighton, the South East region
(the administrative area covered by the
Government Office for the South East) is
the United Kingdom's gateway to the
markets of Continental Europe. But just how
is Britain's most populated region
performing in the 1990s compared with the
rest of the United Kingdom? What are the
latest trends in its economy and labour
market? How does life in Surrey differ from
life in Sussex? The answers to these and a
host of other questions can be found in Focus
on the South East, produced jointly by the
Office for National Statistics and the
Government Office for the South East. It is
designed as a reference work for anyone
with an interest in today's Britain, from
planners and researchers to students,
teachers, business people and the general
reader. Local authorities, companies and
other agencies can use it to research
investment, marketing and recruitment
decisions. Schools and universities will find
it useful for project work and research. The
South East described in this publication
comprises the nine "counties" of Berkshire,
Buckinghamshire, East Sussex, Hampshire,
Isle of Wight, Kent, Oxfordshire, Surrey and
West Sussex. It excludes London. Focus on
the South East's seven chapters contain
commentary, tables, charts and maps
covering the following topics: The South
East: an overview; Population; The
Economy; Labour Market; Education and
Training; Transport and the Environment;
and Living in the South East. It includes a
further 14 pages of detailed statistics, with
much of the data presented at "county" and
local authority district level. There is also a
references and further reading section plus
useful contact points in key organisations.

Delivery: Ad hoc/One-off Release
Price: £30.00
ISBN: 0-11-620921-6

Available from
Electronic Sales Unit or TSO Publications Centre
and Bookshops
Please see Annex B for full address details.

Focus on the South West
Office for National Statistics and
Government Office for the South West

Stretching from Poole to Penzance, from
Torquay to Tewkesbury, the South West is
the largest Government Office Region in
England. As the Millennium approaches,
what are the long-term trends in its
population, economy, labour market and
environment? How does its performance
compare with the rest of the United
Kingdom? How does life in Cornwall differ
from life in Gloucestershire? The answers
to these and a host of other questions can
be found in Focus on the South West,
produced jointly by the Office for National
Statistics and the Government Office for
the South West and published in October
1998. The South West described in the
publication is the administrative area
covered by the Government Office for the
South West. Over the past few years there
have been many changes to the region's
internal boundaries. For the purposes of the
book, data relate where possible to the
boundaries established after the local
government reorganisation on 1 April 1998.
Where data are not available for the Unitary
Authorities or the new counties, figures
relating to the former counties are shown.
For detail of content see *Focus on the South
West*.

Delivery: Ad hoc/One-off Release
Price: £30.00
ISBN: 0 11 621064 8

Available from
Electronic Sales Unit or TSO Publications Centre
and Bookshops
Please see Annex B for full address details..

Living in Britain
Office for National Statistics

This report, based on the results of the 1998
General Household Survey (GHS) contains
up-to-date information on a wide range of
socio-demographic topics and provides a
comprehensive picture of how people live,
and the social change they experience, in
Britain today. It also shows a number of
trends and changes measured by the survey
since it began in 1971. In addition to the
topics covered by the GHS each year -
population characteristics, households and
families, marriage, cohabitation and fertility,
health, pensions and housing - the 1998
report updates information on: smoking,
drinking, contraception and day care,
subjects which have been included in
selected years only.

Frequency: Annually
Price: £39.50
ISBN: 0 11 621254 3

Available from
TSO Publications Centre and Bookshops
Please see Annex B for address details.

Monthly Digest of Statistics
Office for National Statistics

This product contains the latest monthly and quarterly data for a wide range of business, economic and social statistics, keeping you briefed on developments. It gives the user a monthly economic and social update on the United Kingdom. It gives the latest figures for 130 tables within 20 themes. It can, for example, provide the latest figures for a combination of indexes, which could be used to index-link contracts. It covers the following subject areas: national accounts; population and vital statistics; social services; law enforcement; agriculture, food, drinks and tobacco; production, labour market, output and costs; energy; chemicals; metals, engineering and vehicles; textiles and other manufactures; construction; transport; retailing (including Retail Sales Index); external trade in goods; overseas finance; home finance; prices and wages (including Retail Prices Index, Producer Price Index and Average Earnings Index). It also contains 'Britain Update'. This provides an economic and social overview of the nation, compiled from Government Statistical Service releases in the previous month. It has commentary in executive summary form, and includes tables and charts. The target market is those who require the latest business, economic and social data from a broad mix of topics. Also, those who want a monthly update on economic and social developments.

Delivery: Periodic Release
Frequency: Monthly
Price: £15.00
Annual subscription including Annual Supplement and postage £150.00
ISSN: 0308-6666

Available from
TSO Publications Centre and Bookshops
Please see Annex B for full address details.

Databank
Please see Annex B for full address details.

NDAD - The UK National Digital Archive of Datasets
Public Record Office

The United Kingdom National Digital Archive of Datasets (NDAD) is the most recent addition to the Public Record Office (PRO). Its function is to preserve and, where possible, provide access to public records whose primary form is that of a dataset. In this context, dataset means any form of structured, computer-based data and encompasses survey files, databases and geographical information systems as well as other forms of data. NDAD produces on-line catalogues for all material in its archive,

covering all aspects of the datasets from a broad view of their administrative and historical background to detailed descriptions of each field in each dataset together with the attributes of such fields. The archive also contains documentation on the context, provenance and use of the datasets. This documentation is also catalogued and available on-line. For open datasets the service concentrates on providing access to the data rather than allowing manipulation of it. Thus, one may subset datasets in a number of ways and perform complex queries to identify certain elements in the data. NDAD can also supply copies of datasets and documentation, either in whole or in part, in digital or paper formats. The service is designed for access via the web (http://ndad.ulcc.ac.uk/); facilities are available, by appointment only, at the University of London Library for use by those without web access. NDAD is operated by ULCC in conjunction with the University of London Library, acting as agents of the Public Record Office. The NDAD holdings comprise computer datasets which were used, or are in use, in government departments and other similar bodies subject to the Public Records Act 1958. As well as holding the data itself, NDAD provides essential metadata which describes the relationship between data items, helps the system present data on-screen to users, and allows for export of data to modern software systems. NDAD also contains documents relating to the datasets, covering such areas as system design and uses made of the data. Extensive catalogue information is provided for each holding. This information covers the administrative history of the department concerned and of the dataset itself, as well as information on the computing systems and software used to produce and process it, the ways in which the data was collected and used, and the dates of collection and use. The more detailed elements of the catalogue describe data down to the level of the individual field, and the relations between data elements.

Delivery: Periodic Release
Frequency: Ad hoc
Price: Free for access; copies may be purchased

Available from
National Digital Archive of Datasets
Please see Annex B for full address details

(The) New Councils: Statistical Report
Scottish Executive

This publication was published in May 1995 and contains key statistics for the new councils in Scotland. It is a collection of those figures which were available at the

time of going to press. Many of the statistics that have been presented have been reworked to the new boundaries, but where this has not been possible, the figures have been estimated by pro-rating on the basis of population, households or other means. This publication begins with two sections that describe the new council areas and provide notes that facilitate comparisons between the old local authority boundaries with those for the new councils. These sections are followed by a further 9 sections which contain data on: Population; Households and Families; Education; Industry; Recorded Crime; Social Work; Transport; Agriculture; and Environment. The final section 'Annexes' provides information on statistical assumptions, population, household, and land area matrices, and the effects of local government reform on the administrative structure of services to the public.

Delivery: Ad hoc/One-off Release
Price: £10.00
ISBN: 0 7480 1267 2

Available from
TSO Publications Centre and Bookshops
Please see Annex B for full address details.

Northern Ireland Annual Abstract of Statistics
Northern Ireland Statistics and Research Agency

Digest of Northern Ireland Statistics. Contains data on population, households, health and social services, justice and security, education and childcare, housing, environment and climate, transport and communications, tourism, fires, labour, earnings and income, production and energy, agriculture forestry and fishing, regional accounts, public finance, and banking.

Delivery: Periodic Release
Frequency: Annually
Price: £16.50
ISBN: 1 899203 24 9
ISSN: 0267 6044

Available from
Annual Abstract Sales
Northern Ireland Statistics and Research Agency
Please see Annex B for full address details

Programme for the Valleys Statistical Profile
National Assembly for Wales

This publication presents data for the Programme for the Valleys area and compares them with data for Wales as a whole. Data describing the population, health, housing, education and industry of the Programme for the Valleys area.

Products

Delivery: Ad hoc/One-off Release
Price: £5.00
ISBN: 0 7504 0527 9

Available from
Gaynor Williams
National Assembly for Wales
Please see Annex B for full address details

Regional Competitiveness Indicators
Department of Trade and Industry

The bi-annual Indicators provide 13 statistics which illustrate the factors determining the regional competitiveness of the English Regions (as defined by the Government Offices) as well as of Scotland, Wales and Northern Ireland. The 48 pages cover 13 charts and 25 tables providing information on regional competitiveness and cover economic variables such as GDP per head, productivity, the labour market, education & training, investment, transport infrastructure and property costs. It is aimed at regional organisations such as Government Offices, TECs and Chambers of Commerce.

Delivery: Periodic Release
Frequency: Bi-annually
Price: £10.00 per year (2 issues)

Available from
General Enquiries on Regional Statistics
Department of Trade and Industry
Please see Annex B for full address details

Region in Figures
Office for National Statistics

The Region in Figures series provides the perfect solution for anyone with an interest in a specific Government Office Region. Similar in style and layout to Regional Trends, each of the nine GORs are covered in a separate volume providing a more in depth look at a region than Regional Trends ever can. A wealth of trend and sub-regional data is contained covering a wide range of demographic, social, industrial and economic statistics. Region in Figures provides essential information for policy-makers, marketing professionals, researchers, students and teachers, journalists and anyone with an interest in their region. The chapters covered are - population, the economy, the labour market, education and training, transport and the environment and living in the region. Region in Figures is available both on paper in a convenient comb bound format and electronically.

Delivery: Periodic Release
Frequency: Annually
Price: £15.00 each, £30.00 for 3 or £75.00 for a full set of nine or a full electronic dataset

Available from
ONS Direct
Please see Annex B for full address details.

Regional Trends
Office for National Statistics

Regional Trends is the most comprehensive annual source of official statistics about the twelve statistical regions of the United Kingdom (Government Office Regions within England). It includes a wide range of demographic, social, industrial and economic statistics, covering most aspects of life in the regions. Regional Trends provides essential information for a wide range of people: policy-makers, marketing professionals, researchers, students and teachers, journalists and anyone with general regional interests. Regional Trends contains profiles of each of the regions and data, allowing comparisons to made across the regions, on population, households, education and training, the labour market, housing, health, lifestyles, crime and justice, transport, the environment, regional accounts, and industry and agriculture. It also contains key data for the sub-regions of the United Kingdom covering area and population, vital and social statistics, education, housing and households, labour market, deprivation and economic statistics, and regional accounts. There is also a chapter on European Union regional statistics.

Delivery: Periodic Release
Frequency: Annually
Price: £39.50
ISBN: 0 11 621158 X
ISSN: 0261-1783

Available from
Electronic Sales Unit or TSO Publications Centre and Bookshops
Please see Annex B for full address details.

Regional Trends (First 30 Years) CD-ROM
Office for National Statistics

Regional Trends CD-ROM provides a complete archive of the first 30 years of publication of Regional Trends (1965-1995). Combining the original text and graphical material with the ease of access and storage capacity of CD-ROM, this package provides a powerful and convenient method of comparing statistics for the regions over the entire 30 year period and for more recent years, county and local authority districts. It includes a wide range of demographic, social, industrial and economic statistics, covering most aspects of life in the regions. Regional Trends CD-ROM contains data, allowing comparisons to made across the regions, on population,

households, education and training, the labour market, housing, health, lifestyles, crime and justice, transport, the environment, regional accounts, and industry and agriculture. It also contains profiles of each of the regions, and key data for the sub-regions of the United Kingdom covering area and population, vital and social statistics, education, housing and households, labour market and economic statistics, and regional accounts. There are also sections on European Union regional statistics.

Delivery: Ad Hoc/One-off Release
Price: £99.00 + VAT
£49.00 + VAT for public libraries and academia
ISBN: 0 11 525031 X

Available from
Electronic Sales Unit or TSO Publications Centre and Bookshops
Please see Annex B for full address details.

Scottish Abstract of Statistics
Scottish Executive

The Scottish Executive Abstract of Statistics is designed to be the major reference volume for statistics in life in Scotland. The publication is produced with the assistance of a number of government departments and other organisations. The 1998 publication is the 26th edition of Scottish Abstract of Statistics. This publication contains fifteen chapters, many of which show series for a number of years whilst others give information at local authority level. Scottish Abstract of Statistics contains data on: Population, Vital Statistics and Elections; Health; Social Work; Housing; Education and Training; Labour Market; Household Income and Expenditure; Industry; Agriculture, Fisheries and Forestry; Environment; Transport; Crime and Justice; Social Security; Finance; and Leisure & Tourism. Further information about any of the information contained in the Scottish Abstract of Statistics is available from the source of the information. Contact telephone numbers are provided at the rear of the publication.

Delivery: Periodic Release
Frequency: Annually
Price: £25.00
ISBN: 0 7480 7186 5

Available from
TSO Publications Centre and Bookshops
Please see Annex B for full address details.

Scottish Statistics Fact Card
Scottish Executive

At a glance pocket breakdown of statistics relating to life in Scotland. Data is provided for a UK comparison. This guide contains fourteen sections, which provide information on Scotland both for the last two years and a ten year comparison. Comparable UK figures are also provided for the latest year. Scottish Statistics: Fact card contains data on: Population and Vital Statistics; Housing; Health; Law; Social Security; Employment; Income and Expenditure; Gross Domestic Product; Agriculture, Forestry and Fisheries; Education; Social Work; Environment and Conservation; Transport and Communication; and Finance. A section providing additional information is located at the rear of the guide.

Delivery: Periodic Release
Frequency: Annually
Price: Free

Available from
David Burman
Scottish Executive
Central Statistics Unit
1B Victoria Quay
Edinburgh EH6 6QQ
Tel: 0131 244 0442;
Email: statistics.enquiries@scotland.gov.uk

Social and Community Planning Research (SCPR) Reports and Publications 1988
(SCPR changed its name in May 1999 to the National Centre for Social Research)

Catalogue of reports and publications based on research carried out by Social and Community Planning Research. The (now the National Centre for Social Research) list gives details of the British Election Study Series, the British Social Attitudes Survey Series, the England and Wales Youth Cohort Studies, the Scottish School Leavers Survey Series, the British Crime Survey Series, the Family Resources Survey Series, the Health Survey for England, the Workplace Employee Relations Survey Series, the European Union Household Panel, and Deliberative Polls. There are also details of many other studies on a range of topics including Training and Education, Employment and the Workplace, Health and Lifestyles, Welfare Provision and Care, Housing, Transport, Ethnic and other Minority Groups. The list also gives details of publications by the Centre for Research into Elections and Social Trends (CREST), an ESRC Research Centre linking the National Centre with updates and Nuffield College, Oxford, and of the National Centre's Survey Methods Centre.

Delivery: Ad hoc/One-off Release
Price: Free
ISBN: none

Available from
Sue Johnson

National Centre for Social Research
35 Northampton Square
London EC1V 0AX
Tel: 020 7250 1866;
Email: s.johnson@natcen.ac.uk

Social Focus on Children
Office for National Statistics

Published in 1994, Social Focus on Children was the first in a new series of publications aimed at complementing the policy approach of Social Trends, by providing a new perspective - that of different groups in society. Social Focus on Children looks at what it is like to be a child in the United Kingdom. Contains data which look at children as a part of family life, their health, education, home environment, welfare and other aspects of lifestyle. Social Focus on Children contains commentary, tables, charts and maps covering the following topics: The characteristics of children; Births and survival; Family life; Health; Nutrition; Life at school; The home environment; Care and welfare; Children as victims of crime; Children's spending power; Getting about; and Use of free time.

Delivery: Ad Hoc/One-off Release
Price: Hardcopy: £25.00
Floppy disk: free on completion of readership survey form
ISBN: 0-11-620655-1
ISSN: 1355-5987

Available from
TSO Publications Centre and Bookshops
Please see Annex B for full address details.

Social Focus on Ethnic Minorities
Office for National Statistics

Social Focus on Ethnic Minorities was published in 1996 as the third in a series of publications which bring together statistics from a wide variety of sources to paint a picture of different groups of people in contemporary society. Social Focus on Ethnic Minorities looks at what it is like to be a member of an ethnic minority group in Great Britain by comparing and contrasting the characteristics of the main ethnic groups. There are often bigger differences between the individual ethnic minority groups than between ethnic minorities as a whole and the White population. This publication therefore focuses on comparisons between ethnic minority groups. Social Focus on Ethnic Minorities contains commentary, tables, charts and maps covering the following topics: The ethnic minority population; Families, homes and crime; Education; Economic characteristics; and Health and lifestyles.

Delivery: Ad Hoc/One-off Release
Price: Hardcopy: £25.00
Floppy disk £15.00 (available to purchasers of the book)
ISBN: 0-11-620793-0
ISSN: 1355-5987

Available from
TSO Publications Centre and Bookshops
Please see Annex B for full address details.

Social Focus on Families
Office for National Statistics

Social Focus on Families was published in 1997 as the fourth in a series of publications which brings together statistics from a wide variety of sources to paint a picture of different groups of people in contemporary society. In looking at the family we have a broader canvas than the previous titles in the Social Focus series. The book examines trends in family life, to look at dynamics, investigates the real everyday changes that affect individual families, and explores changing attitudes. Social Focus on Families gives a broad overview of a subject on which much in-depth research and analysis has already been done by others. Social Focus on Families contains commentary, tables, charts and maps covering the following topics: Family structure and change; Cohabitation, marriage and divorce; Family building; Parenting; Economic activity; Income; Expenditure; Homes; Lifestyles; and Relationships.

Delivery: Ad Hoc/One-off Release
Price: Hardcopy: £30.00;
Floppy disk £15.00 (available to purchasers of the book)
ISBN: 0-11-620919-4

Available from
TSO Publications Centre and Bookshops
Please see Annex B for full address details.

Social Focus on Older People
Office for National Statistics

Social Focus on Older People was published in 1999 and is the seventh in a series of publications which brings together statistics from a wide variety of sources to paint a picture of different groups of people in contemporary society. This edition looks at the experiences, lifestyles and attitudes of people aged 50 and over in the United Kingdom today, as well as illustrating changes over time. Social Focus on Older People contains commentary, tables, charts and maps covering the following topics: Population structure; Family life; Living arrangements; Geographical distribution; Housing; Labour market; Education and training; Leisure activities; Religious activities; Participation in voluntary work;

Personal safety; Travel; Income; Income distribution; Wealth; Health; Health behaviour; Daily living; Social care; Caring; and Health care.

Delivery: Ad-hoc/One-off Release
Price: Hardcopy: £30.00
Floppy disk: £10.00 (available to purchasers of the book)
ISBN: 0-11-621168-7

Available from
TSO Publications Centre and Bookshops
Please see Annex B for full address details.

Social Focus on the Unemployed
Office for National Statistics

Social Focus on the Unemployed was published in 1998 as the fifth in a series of publications which brings together statistics from a wide variety of sources to paint a picture of different groups of people in contemporary society. This edition looks at unemployed people in the United Kingdom and the experience of unemployment, both economically and socially, for the individual, their household and their family. Social Focus on the Unemployed contains commentary, tables, charts and maps covering the following topics: Structure; Focus groups; Households; Macro risks and solutions; Micro risks and solutions; Unemployment experiences; Income; Expenditure; Homes; Social impact of unemployment; and Health.

Delivery: Ad Hoc/One-off Release
Price: Hardcopy: £30.00
Floppy disk: £15.00 (available to purchasers of the book)
ISBN: 0-11-621039-7
ISSN: 0306 7742

Available from
TSO Publications Centre and Bookshops
Please see Annex B for full address details.

Social Focus on Women
Office for National Statistics and Equal Opportunities Commission

Published in 1995, Social Focus on Women was the second in a series of publications which paint a picture of different groups of people in contemporary society. This edition complemented the United Kingdom report which was prepared by the DfEE at the request of the United Nations for the Fourth World Conference on Women which was held in Beijing in September 1995. Social Focus on Women looks at what it is like to be a woman in the United Kingdom, and also sets this in context by looking at changes in the lives of women in recent years and providing some comparisons with men. Social Focus on Women contains

commentary, tables, charts and maps covering the following topics: Women as partners; Women as mothers; Women as carers; Economic activity; Employment; Earnings; Women's access to resources; Health and well-being; Women as criminals; Women as victims; Women in society; Use of free-time; and Women on the move.

Delivery: Ad Hoc/One-off Release
Price: Hardcopy: £25.00
Floppy disk: £15.00 (available to purchasers of the book)
ISBN: 0-11-620713-2
ISSN: 1355 5987

Available from
TSO Publications Centre and Bookshops
Please see Annex B for full address details.

Social Focus on Women and Men
Office for National Statistics

Social Focus on Women and Men was published in 1998 as the sixth in a series of publications which brings together statistics from a wide variety of sources to paint a picture of different groups of people in contemporary society. Social Focus on Women and Men was produced in partnership with the Equal Opportunities Commission (EOC). This edition looks at the relative status, experiences, lifestyles and attitudes of women and men in the United Kingdom today, as well as illustrating changes over the years. By focusing on gender comparisons, this report provides a different perspective to Social Focus on Women which was published in 1995 and acts as a successor to the EOC's Women and Men in Britain 1995: The Life Cycle of Inequality. Social Focus on Women and Men contains commentary, tables and charts covering the following topics: Population; Households and families; Homes; Education and qualifications; Training; Economic activity; Type of job; Unemployment; Trade unions and industrial tribunals; Work and family; Income; Earnings; Expenditure; Wealth; Health; Disability and caring; Health behaviour; Activities; Travel; Crime; Political participation; and Beliefs.

Delivery: Ad-hoc/One-off Release
Price: Hardcopy: £30.00
Floppy disk: £10.00 (available to purchasers of the book)
ISBN: 0-11-621069-9
ISSN: 1355 5987

Available from
TSO Publications Centre and Bookshops
Please see Annex B for full address details.

Social Trends
Office for National Statistics

Social Trends is an established reference source of official statistics. It draws together social and economic data from a wide range of government departments and other organisations to paint a broad picture of British society today, and how it has been changing. Social Trends is aimed at a very wide audience: policy makers in the public and private sectors; market service providers; lawyers; people in government; journalists and other commentators; academics and students; schools; and the general public. Social Trends contains 13 chapters each focusing on a different social policy area, described in tables, charts and explanatory text. Social Trends contains data on: Population; Households and families; Education and training; Labour market; Income and wealth; Expenditure; Health; Social protection; Crime and justice; Housing; Environment; Transport; and Lifestyles and Social Participation. In addition some editions contain special report(s) on specific topics. To preserve topicality, over half of the tables and charts in the chapters of Social Trends are new compared with the previous edition.

Delivery: Periodic Release
Frequency: Annually
Price: Hardcopy: £39.50
Floppy disk: £15.00 (available to purchasers of the book).
CD-ROM (compilation of editions 1-25): £99.00 + VAT
ISBN: 0-11-621242 X
ISSN: 0306 7742

Available from
TSO Publications Centre and Bookshops
Please see Annex B for full address details.

Social Trends 28 Pocketbook 1998 edition
Office for National Statistics

Social Trends Pocketbook is a new venture. It presents an authoritative picture of UK society today in a handy, accessible and compact booklet. As the name suggests, it is a mini version of Social Trends 28, the annual report which gives a comprehensive picture of social change in the United Kingdom. The contents of the Pocketbook have been selected from Social Trends 28 to give an overview of the key aspects of life in Britain today and how it has been changing. The purpose of the Pocketbook is to make the information contained in Social Trends more widely available. Its format means that now this information can be readily available from the pocket, briefcase, bag or rucksack. It is invaluable for anyone who would like their own quick reference guide to life in modern Britain. The Social Trends 28 Pocketbook contains 13 chapters each focusing on a different social policy area, described in tables, charts and explanatory text. The Pocketbook contains data on: Population; Households and families; Education and training; Labour market; Income and wealth; Expenditure; Health; Social protection; Crime and justice; Housing; Environment; Transport; and Lifestyles.

Delivery: Ad-hoc/One-off Release
Price: £3.00 (including postage and packing)
£12.50 for 10 copies to schools (including postage and packing)
ISBN: 1-85774-270-2

Available from
ONS Direct
Please see Annex B for full address details.

Social Trends Pocketbook 1999 edition
Office for National Statistics

This second edition of the Social Trends Pocketbook follows on from the successful pilot edition produced in 1998. It has been produced as part of an ONS initiative to make statistics more accessible to schools and colleges at an affordable price. It is specifically aimed at students, but its handy, quick reference style will make it invaluable to anyone who would like their own pocket-sized guide to life in modern Britain. The contents of the Pocketbook have been selected from the latest edition of Social Trends. The Social Trends Pocketbook 1999 edition contains 13 chapters each focusing on a different social policy area, described in tables, charts and explanatory text. The Pocketbook contains data on: Population; Households and families; Education and training; Labour market; Income and wealth; Expenditure; Health; Social protection; Crime and justice; Housing; Environment; Transport; and Lifestyles.

Delivery: Ad-hoc/One-off Release
Frequency: Annually
Price: £3.00 (including postage and packing)
£12.50 for 10 copies to schools (including postage and packing)
ISBN: 1-85774-316-4

Available from
ONS Direct
Please see Annex B for full address details.

Spatial Information Enquiry Service (SINES)
Ordnance Survey

Enquiry service providing details on several hundred spatially referenced datasets held by government departments. Contains information about datasets on agriculture, commerce and industry, education, employment, environment, geology, health, law enforcement, marine, meteorology, property, survey and mapping, taxation, and transport. SINES can provide information on specific datasets in one of three ways: Printout: containing title, purpose, sources, date of collection and frequency of update, method of spatial referencing, indication of geographical extent, contact details and topics included; Floppy disk: Details as for Printout, in a DOS format text file; E-mail: Details as for floppy disk. Small files only.

Delivery: Ad-hoc/One-off Release
Price: On request

Available from
SINES HelpLine
Room N285
Ordnance Survey
Romsey Road
Southampton, SO16 4GU
Tel: 023 8079 2711; Fax: 023 8079 2452.
E-mail: sines@ordsvy.govt.uk (Monday - Friday 8.30am - 5.00pm)

(A) Statistical Focus on Wales
National Assembly for Wales

A publication providing a first point of reference for anyone wanting to know more about Wales. It offers a descriptive introduction to key official statistics, painting an objective and factual picture. The Statistical Focus starts by answering the most basic questions: Where is Wales? How big is it? What is the population? To these fundamentals it adds information on the society, economy and environment. Readers wishing to explore in greater depth are guided by coloured reference markers to two sections on coloured pages, one which gives technical explanations of certain statistics and one which provides a bibliography of statistical sources. Finally, there are addresses for obtaining publications and telephone contact points for statistical enquiries.

Delivery: Ad hoc
Price: £10.00 - postage free within the UK
ISBN: 0 7504 1681 5
ISSN: 1362-3575

Available from
Alan Jackson
National Assembly for Wales
Crown Building
Cathays Park
Cardiff CF10 3NQ
Tel: 029 2082 5088;
Email: alan.jackson@wales.gsi.gov.uk

Statistical Publications Information Leaflet
Scottish Executive

The Statistical Publications Information Leaflet provides details of the statistical bulletins that are published by the Scottish Executive. The publication of statistical bulletins enables statistical information about Scotland to be made available quickly and economically. Some bulletins are issued at regular intervals and update standard statistics, whilst others are occasional and are intended to provide a more detailed analysis of a specific topic. The Statistical Publications Information Leaflet also provides useful information about regularly produced statistical volumes, how to order publications and useful contact points for information.

Delivery: Periodic Release
Frequency: Ad hoc
Price: Free

Available from
David Burman
Scottish Executive
Central Statistics Unit
1B Victoria Quay
Edinburgh EH6 6QQ
Tel: 0131 244 0442;
Email: statistics.enquiries@scotland.gov.uk

Statistics for Assembly Constituency Areas
National Assembly for Wales

Contains data on population and vital statistics, the economy, education and training, health and personal local services, housing, agriculture and forestry, and transport and environment.

Delivery: Ad hoc
Price: £15.00 postage paid within the UK.
ISBN: 0 7504 2303 X

Available from
Publications Unit, Statistical Directorate
National Assembly for Wales
Please see Annex B for full address details

Tracking People: A Guide to Longitudinal Social Sources
Office for National Statistics

This booklet covers data sources which draw on government and non-government data sources. The information has been gathered together order to increase awareness of longitudinal data sources and encourage their use. A wide range of topic areas are covered by the entries in this guide, with data being collected from both administrative sources and surveys. The guide covers a wide range of topic areas including: education, health,

Products

family formation, crime, benefit claimants and employment.

Delivery: Ad hoc/One-off Release
Price: £10.00
ISBN: 1 85774 301 6

Available from
National Statistics Sales Office
Please see Annex B for full address details

25 Years of Social Trends
Office for National Statistics

Social Trends on CD-ROM provides a complete archive of the first 25 years of publication of Social Trends. Combining the original text and graphical material with the ease of access and storage capacity of CD-ROM, this package provides a powerful and convenient method of comparing statistics and trends over the entire 25 year period.

Delivery: Ad Hoc/One-off Release
Price: CD-ROM (compilation of editions 1-25): £99.00 + VAT

Available from
ONS Direct
Please see Annex B for full address details.

Wales in Figures Fact Card
National Assembly for Wales

Key figures on a variety of subject areas for Wales: It summarises the information given in more detail in the publication 'Digest of Welsh Statistics'.

Delivery: Periodic Release
Frequency: Annually
Price: Free

Available from
Claire Owen
National Assembly for Wales
Crown Building
Cathays Park
Cardiff CF10 3NQ
Tel: 029 2082 5044;
Email: claire.owen@wales.gsi.gov.uk

Welsh Social Trends
National Assembly for Wales

Tables and diagrams presenting information on the characteristics of the people of Wales, their lifestyle and living conditions. Contains data on population, social characteristics, health and personal social services, housing, justice and crime, education and training, economic characteristics and finance. Where possible, data are contrasted over time, across the counties of Wales and with the corresponding picture for the rest of Britain.

The publication consists of approximately 90 A4 (landscape style) pages and includes text, tables, charts and maps. The publication is divided into chapter each of which contains text, charts and maps outlining trends in the data tables. Chapters include Population, Social Characteristics, health and Personal Social Services, Housing, Justice and Crime, Education and Training, Economic Characteristics and finance.

Delivery: Discontinued in 1993
Frequency: Ad-hoc
Price: £10.00 inclusive of postage within the UK
ISBN: 0 7504 0528 7
ISSN: 0140-9018

Available from
Claire Owen
National Assembly for Wales
Crown Building
Cathays Park
Cardiff CF10 3NQ
Tel: 029 2082 5044;
Email: claire.owen@wales.gsi.gov.uk

See also:

In the Websites and Electronic Services chapter
(The) Data Archive
The Government Statistical Service (GSS) Website – The Source
Inforoute
London Research Centre
NISRA
Northern Ireland Office
Office for National Statistics
Scottish Executive
SOSIG – The Social Science Information Gateway
StatBase
United Kingdom Standard Geographic Base

2.3 International

Europe in Figures
Eurostat

Part of Eurostat's General Statistics theme, Theme 1. This publication contains the essential socio-economic information needed for a good understanding of the European Union. It contains reference work giving details of finance, international trade, key figures for agriculture, industry, population, employment and much more. Simple and attractive, this publication gives a panoramic view of the EU today (425 pages).

Some of the data in this product is disaggregated by gender.

Delivery: Periodic Release
Frequency: Ad hoc
Price: £10.00
ISBN: 92 827 0075 5

Available from
TSO Publications Centre and Bookshops
Please see Annex B for full address details.

Eurostat Yearbook 1997 - A Statistical Eye on Europe 1986-1996
Eurostat

This publication is divided into five main chapters for the consultation and comparison of key statistical data from the different EU Member States for 1986 to 1996. These are: the people, the land and the environment, national income and expenditure, enterprises and activities in Europe, and the European Union. It offers a comprehensive statistical presentation supplemented by comparative data for the EU's main trading partners.

Some of the data in this product is disaggregated by gender.

Delivery: Periodic Release
Frequency: Annually
Price: £26.00
ISBN: 92-828-2133-1

Available from
TSO Publications Centre and Bookshops
Please see Annex B for full address details.

Facts Through Figures, 1997
Eurostat

Facts through figures covers the following principal themes: day to day life, environment, demography, economy and various socio-cultural data for quick reference and easy comparison of facts and figures on the 15 EU countries.

Delivery: Periodic Release
Frequency: Ad hoc
Price: Free
ISBN: 92 828 4948 1

Available from
Bob Dodds
Office for National Statistics
See Annex B for full address details

(A) Social Portrait of Europe - 1998 Edition
Eurostat

Part of Eurostats Population and social conditions theme (Theme 3), series A: Yearbooks and yearly statistics. This edition gives full, precise and comparable information on population, work, living standards and conditions and daily life in the 15 member states.

Delivery: Ad hoc/One-off Release
Frequency: Annual
Price: £15.25
ISBN: 92 827 9093 2

Available from
TSO Publications Centre and Bookshops
Please see Annex B for full address details.

See also:

In the Websites and Electronic Services
chapter
Eurostat
NESSTAR – Networked Social Science
Tools and Resources
Organisation for Economic Cooperation and
Development (OECD)
r-cade – Resource Centre for Access to Data
on Europe
United Nations

**Other Products which may be of interest,
but are not featured in this book due to
lack of details:**

Eurostat Catalogue - Mini-guide - Eurostat

3

Population, Census, Migration and Vital Events

Population and Vital Statistics are collected, administered and disseminated by a number of separate Departments, Agencies and organisations including **the Office for National Statistics, the Home Office, the Government Actuary's Department, the General Register Office for Scotland, the National Assembly for Wales and the Northern Ireland Statistics and Research Agency.** The available statistics embrace a number of subject areas including: **Births and Fertility, Deaths and Stillbirths, Divorce, Emigration, Immigration and Migration, First Names and Surnames Registered, Marriage and Cohabitation, Population and Housing, and Population Estimates and Projections.**

The basic data are generated from a number of separate information 'Sources' and the resultant statistics are disseminated through a whole range of statistical 'Analyses' and 'Products', all of which are described in the following chapter. Users looking for a cross-section of UK-wide statistics on **Population and Vital Statistics** may find the following products useful:

> **Population Trends** (quarterly publication)
> **Key Population and Vital Statistics** (annual publication)
> **Vital Statistics** (annual publication)

Users interested in a wider range of official statistics including **Population and Vital Statistics** may like to refer to the following compendia:

> On-line Databases (See Chapter 1):
> > **StatBase - StatStore**

> Hardcopy Compendia (See Chapter 2):
> > **Annual Abstract of Statistics**
> > **Britain 2000: The Official Yearbook of the United Kingdom**
> > **Monthly Digest of Statistics**
> > **Regional Trends**
> > **Social Trends**

Users may also find what they need on the various Departmental Websites. These are listed in Chapter 1.

3

Population, Census, Migration and Vital Events - *Sources and Analyses*

3.1 Abstracts, Compendia, A-Z Catalogues, Directories and Reference Material

(The) ONS Longitudinal Study
Office for National Statistics

The ONS Longitudinal Study (LS) is a representative one per cent sample of the population of England and Wales containing linked Census and vital events data. The LS was begun in the early 1970's by selecting everyone born on one of four particular days who was enumerated at the 1971 Census. Subsequent samples have been drawn and linked from the 1981 and 1991 Censuses. Population change is reflected by the addition of new sample members born on LS dates, together with the recording of exits via death or emigration. Routinely collected data on mortality, fertility, cancer registration, infant mortality, widowerhoods and the migration of LS members are linked into the sample. Continuous collection since 1971.

Status: Ongoing
Collection Method: Longitudinal Study
Frequency: Continuously
Reference Period: 1971 Census onwards.
Timeliness: There is a short time lag between collection and release of Census and vital event data to the LS.
Earliest Available Data: 1971
National Coverage: England and Wales
Disaggregation: Ward; Enumeration District (ED); Local Authority District (LAD)/Unitary Authority (Eng); London Borough; Registration District (births/marriages/deaths); Unitary Authority; County (E&W)/Unitary Authority (Eng)

Statistician
Jillian Smith
Office for National Statistics
Health & Demography; Longitudinal Study
Tel: 020 7533 5184;
Email: jillian.smith@ons.gov.uk

Products that contain data from this source
Longitudinal Study 1971-1991 History, Organisation and Quality of Data; Longitudinal Study, Housing Deprivation and Social Change; Longitudinal Study, Socio-demographic Differences in Cancer Survival Rates; Health Inequalities Decennial Supplement; Health Statistics Quarterly No: 1 - Spring 1999; Occupational Health Decennial Supplement

3.2 Births and Fertility

Births - Scotland
General Register Office for Scotland

The General Register Office for Scotland has responsibility for the registration of births in Scotland. Birth statistics include sex of child, age of mother, marital status of parents, area of residence and fertility rates. Data are available for Scotland, local authority and health board areas, registration districts, and areas defined in terms of postcodes. Birth statistics have been published since 1855 and detailed tabulations are available from 1969. Data are collected continuously and are first available in summary form four weeks after the reference period. Final annual data are available after six to seven months.

Status: Ongoing
Collection Method: Administrative Records
Frequency: Continuously
Timeliness: Six to seven months (annual data)
Earliest Available Data: 1855
National Coverage: Scotland
Disaggregation: local authority and health board areas, registration districts, and areas defined in terms

Statistician
Graham Jackson
General Register Office for Scotland
Tel: 0131 314 4229;
Email: graham.jackson@gro-scotland.gov.uk

Products that contain data from this source
1994-based National Population Projections; 1996-based National Population Projections first release; Annual Abstract of Statistics; Annual Report of the Registrar General for Scotland; General Register Office for Scotland (GRO(S)) Site on the World Wide Web; Mid-year Population Estimates, Scotland; National Population Projections; Population Projections, Scotland; Population Trends; Regional Trends; Registrar General's Preliminary Return; Registrar General's Quarterly Return; Social Trends

Births Registration - Northern Ireland
Department of Finance and Personnel - Northern Ireland

Births by residence, age of mother, age of father, marital status, social class and occupation.

Status: Ongoing
Collection Method: Administrative Records
Frequency: Continuously
Reference Period: 1st January to 31st December
Timeliness: within six months
Earliest Available Data: 1922
National Coverage: Northern Ireland
Disaggregation: District Council Area (Northern Ireland); Health and Social Services Board (NI)

Statistician
John Gordon
Department of Finance and Personnel - Northern Ireland
GRO-NI
Tel: 028 9025 2032

Products that contain data from this source
Annual Report of the Registrar General for Northern Ireland; Quarterly Return of the Registrar General for Northern Ireland

British Cohort Study
Centre for Longitudinal Studies

The first survey, called the British Births Survey, was carried out by the National Birthday Trust Fund in association with the Royal College of Obstetricians and Gynaecologists. Its aims were to look at the social and biological characteristics of mothers in relation to neonatal morbidity, and to compare the results with those of the 1958 National Child Development Survey (NCDS). Since its inception the scope of the survey has broadened from a strictly medical focus at birth to encompass physical and educational development at the age of 5, physical, educational and social development at the ages of 10 and 16, and physical, educational, social and economic development at 26 years.

Status: Ongoing
Collection Method: Cohort Study
Frequency: Full Sweep - 1970, 1975, 1980, and 1996. Sub-sample - 1972, 1973, 1977, 1991
Earliest Available Data: 1970 (British Births Survey) 1975, 1980 (Child Health and Education Study) 1986 (Youthscan)
National Coverage: Great Britain

Statistician
John Bynner
Centre for Longitudinal Studies
Tel: 020 7612 6900 - Ext. 6901;
Email: http://www.cls.ioe.ac.uk

Conceptions - England and Wales
Office for National Statistics

The Office for National Statistics compiles conception statistics from the records of birth registration and of legal abortions.

Data are available by date of event, mother's age, outcome (maternity or abortion), occurrence inside/outside marriage and area of usual residence with summary rates. The data cover England & Wales, England, and Wales and are produced at standard region, county, regional and district health authority, and local authority levels.

Status: Ongoing
Earliest Available Data: 1969
National Coverage: England and Wales
Disaggregation: Government Office Regions; Metropolitan Counties; Regional (Health) Office Areas; Local Authority District (LAD) / Unitary Authority (Eng); London Borough; Ward.

Statistician
Liz Kirby
Office for National Statistics
Tel: 020 7533 5137

Products that contain data from this analysis
Birth Statistics; Key Population and Vital Statistics (Series VS); Population Trends; Health Statistics Quarterly; Conceptions in England and Wales (on disk)

Registration of Births - England and Wales
Office for National Statistics

The Office for National Statistics (ONS) compiles demographic and social statistics on births derived from the records of live birth and stillbirth registration within England and Wales. By law, a birth should be registered within forty two days of its occurrence.

Data on live birth and stillbirth counts are available by date of event, mother's age, father's age, occurrence inside/outside marriage, duration of marriage, social class, place of confinement, cohort analysis,

country of birth, previous liveborn children within marriage, multiple maternities and area of usual residence with summary rates. Quarterly national figures (including rates) are seasonally adjusted in some tables. The data are also used to produce conception statistics. The birth statistics series cover England and Wales. Statistics are produced at government office region, county, regional and district health authority, local authority and ward levels.

Status: Ongoing
Collection Method: Administrative Records
Reference Period: Calendar year
Timeliness: Annually in May after extract of previous year's data.
Earliest Available Data: 1962 (as computer files)
National Coverage: England and Wales
Disaggregation: District Health Authority (DHA)/Health Authority (E&W); Government Office Region (GOR); Local Authority District (LAD)/Unitary Authority(Eng); London Borough; Postcode Sector; Registration District (births/marriages/deaths); Regional Health Authority (RHA)/Regional (Health) Office Area; Unitary Authority; Ward; County (E&W)/Unitary Authority (Eng)

Statistician
Tim Devis
Office for National Statistics
Population and Vital Statistics; Vital Statistics Outputs
Tel: 01329 813339;
Email: tim.devis@ons.gov.uk

Products that contain data from this source
Annual Abstract of Statistics; Birth Statistics; Births and Deaths Extracts; Conceptions in England and Wales (on disk); Demographic Statistics (Eurostat); Health Inequalities Decennial Supplement; Health Statistics Quarterly No: 1 - Spring 1999; Key Population and Vital Statistics (Series VS); Live birth: age of mother and occurrence within/outside of marriage, 1986-1996 (a. numbers); Live births: occurrences within/outside marriage and sex, 1986-1996; Live births: occurrence within/outside marriage and sex, 1986; Live births: within/outside marriage and sex, 1986-1996; Mean age of all mothers at live birth 1986-1996; Mid-year Population Estimates for England and Wales; Mortality Statistics: Childhood infant and perinatal; Occupational Health Decennial Supplement; Population Trends; Public Health Births File; Regional Trends; Social Trends; Vital Statistics Tables

See also:
In this chapter:
Deaths Registration - Northern Ireland *(3.3)*

In other chapters:
Congenital Anomalies - England and Wales *(see the Health and Care chapter)*

3.3 Deaths and Stillbirths

Childhood and Infant Mortality - England and Wales
Office for National Statistics

The Office for National Statistics compiles data on childhood and infant mortality. The information is collected at death registration by the registration service. Some infant mortality statistics also make use of linked birth registrations. Data are collected for England and Wales.

Status: Ongoing
Frequency: Continuously
Timeliness: Data on deaths registered in a particular calendar year are available in the following June. Data on deaths which occurred during a calendar year are available the following August.
Earliest Available Data: 1840
National Coverage: England and Wales
Disaggregation: Standard region, county, health authority and local authority district

Statistician
Nirupa Dattani
Office for National Statistics
Children & Families; Child Health
Tel: 020 7533 5205;
Email: nirupa.dattani@ons.gov.uk

Products that contain data from this analysis
Annual Abstract of Statistics; Health Statistics Quarterly No: 1 - Spring 1999; Infant & Perinatal Mortality - social & biological factors; Infant and Perinatal Mortality: (DHAs and RHAs) Monitor; Key Population and Vital Statistics (Series VS); Mortality Statistics: Childhood infant and perinatal; Population Trends; Regional Trends; Social Trends; Sudden Infant Deaths; Vital Statistics Tables

Childhood and Infant Mortality - Scotland
General Register Office for Scotland

The General Register for Scotland has responsibility for the registration of deaths. Data include numbers and rates of stillbirths, and perinatal, neonatal, postneonatal and infant deaths. Variables used include sex of child, age of child, cause of death, marital status of parents and social class. Data are available for Scotland and for local authority and health board areas, registration districts, and areas defined in terms of postcodes.

Frequency: Continuously
Earliest Available Data: 1855
National Coverage: Scotland
Disaggregation: Postcode Unit

Statistician
Graham Jackson
General Register Office for Scotland
Tel: 0131 314 4229;
Email: graham.jackson@gro-scotland.gov.uk

Products that contain data from this analysis
Annual Report of the Registrar General for Scotland; Registrar General's Quarterly Return; Registrar General's Preliminary Return; GRO(s) Website; Regional Trends; Social Trends

Deaths Registration - Northern Ireland
Northern Ireland Statistics and Research Agency

Deaths by age, sex, cause, area of residence, occupation and social class.

Status: Ongoing
Collection Method: Administrative Records
Frequency: Continuously
Reference Period: 1st January to 31st December
Timeliness: Within six months
Earliest Available Data: 1922
National Coverage: Northern Ireland
Disaggregation: Health and Social Services Board (NI); District Council Area (Northern Ireland)

Statistician
John Gordon
Department of Finance and Personnel - Northern Ireland
GRO-NI
Tel: 028 9025 2032

Products that contain data from this source
Annual Report of the Registrar General for Northern Ireland; Quarterly Return of the Registrar General for Northern Ireland

Deaths Reported to Coroners, England and Wales
Home Office

The Home Office compiles data on deaths reported to coroners in England and Wales in accordance with Section 28 of the Coroners Act 1988. Data are available by deaths reported to coroners, post-mortem examinations, inquests held, and verdicts returned at inquests.

Status: Ongoing
Collection Method: Administrative Records
Frequency: Annually
Reference Period: Calendar year
Timeliness: Report published in April of following year
Earliest Available Data: 1980 (in this form)
National Coverage: England and Wales
Disaggregation: Coroners districts (on request)

Statistician
Ann Barber
Home Office
Tel: 020 7273 2712

Products that contain data from this source
Annual Home Office Statistical Bulletin on Deaths Reported to Coroners

Linked Births and Infant Deaths - England & Wales
Office for National Statistics

Infant death records which have been linked to their corresponding birth records. This enables analysis of infant deaths by various social and biological factors recorded only at birth.

Status: Ongoing
Frequency: Continuously
Timeliness: Provisional data for a calendar year are available the following June.
Earliest Available Data: 1975
National Coverage: England and Wales

Statistician
Nirupa Dattani
Office for National Statistics
Children & Families; Child Health
Tel: 020 7533 5205;
Email: nirupa.dattani@ons.gov.uk

Products that contain data from this analysis
Infant & Perinatal Mortality - social & biological factors; Mortality Statistics: Childhood infant and perinatal; Sudden Infant Deaths

Mortality - Scotland
General Register Office for Scotland

The General Register Office for Scotland has responsibility for the registration of deaths. Data include numbers and rates of deaths. Variables used include sex, age and cause of death. Data are available for Scotland and for local authority and health board areas, registration districts, and areas defined in terms of postcodes.

Status: Ongoing
Collection Method: Administrative Records
Frequency: Continuously
Earliest Available Data: 1855
National Coverage: Scotland
Disaggregation: Postcode unit

Statistician
Graham Jackson
General Register Office for Scotland
Tel: 0131 314 4229;
Email: graham.jackson@gro-scotland.gov.uk

Products that contain data from this source
1994-based National Population Projections; 1996-based National Population Projections first release; Annual Abstract of Statistics; General Register Office for Scotland (GRO(S)) Site on the World Wide Web; National Population Projections; Population Projections, Scotland; Population Trends; Regional Trends; Registrar General's Preliminary Return; Registrar General's Quarterly Return; Social Trends; Mid-year Population Estimates, Scotland

Registration of Deaths - England and Wales
Office for National Statistics

The Office for National Statistics (ONS) compiles mortality statistics which are based on registrations of deaths. These registrations are made by local registrars of births and deaths, and in most cases are required within five days of the death occurrence. Registrars supply details of all deaths to ONS each week. ONS processes and tabulates the data, publishing figures weekly, monthly, quarterly and annually. Main analyses of mortality data are by age, sex, area of residence and cause of death.

Mortality statistics cover registrations of deaths in England and Wales and are available for Government Office Regions, standard regions, counties (England and Wales), regional health authorities, district health authorities, counties, local authority districts, wards and postcode sectors.

Status: Ongoing
Collection Method: Administrative Records
Reference Period: Calendar year
Timeliness: Annually in May after extract of previous years' data (of death registrations), a second extract (of death occurrences) is taken in the following September
Earliest Available Data: 1959 (As computer file)
National Coverage: England and Wales
Disaggregation: District Health Authority (DHA)/Health Authority (E&W); Government Office Region (GOR); Local Authority District (LAD)/Unitary Authority(Eng); London Borough; Postcode Area; Regional Health Authority (RHA)/ Regional (Health) Office Area; Registration District (births/marriages/deaths); Unitary Authority; Ward; County (E&W)/Unitary Authority (Eng)

Statistician
Tim Devis
Office for National Statistics
Population and Vital Statistics; Vital Statistics Outputs
Tel: 01329 813339;
Email: tim.devis@ons.gov.uk

Products that contain data from this source
20th Century Mortality (England & Wales 1901-1995) CD-ROM; 20th Century Mortality: 1996-97 Update disk; Accuracy of Rolled-forward Population Estimates in England and Wales, 1981-91; Annual Abstract of Statistics; Births and Deaths Extracts; Death Counts; Health Inequalities Decennial Supplement; Health Statistics Quarterly No: 1 - Spring 1999; Infant and Perinatal Mortality: (DHAs and RHAs) Monitor; Key Population and Vital Statistics (Series VS); Local Mortality Datapack; Mid-year Population Estimates for England and Wales; Monthly News Release on Weekly Deaths; Mortality Statistics: Cause; Mortality Statistics: Childhood infant and perinatal; Mortality Statistics: General; Mortality Statistics: Injury and Poisoning; Occupational Health Decennial

Supplement; Population Projections: Trends, Methods and Uses; Population Trends; Public Health Mortality File; Regional Trends; Social Trends; Sub-national Population Projections - England Series PP3; The Health of Adult Britain 1841 - 1994, Decennial Supplement, Volumes 1 and 2; The Health of Adult Britain 1841-1994, Decennial Supplement, Volume 1; The Health of Adult Britain 1841-1994, Decennial Supplement, Volume 2; Vital Statistics Tables

See also:
In this chapter:
Registration of Births - England and Wales *(3.2)*

In other chapters:
Congenital Anomalies - England and Wales *(see the Health and Care chapter)*

3.4 Demographic including Census, Economic and Social Characteristics of Population

Census of Population - Northern Ireland
Northern Ireland Statistics and Research Agency

The Northern Ireland Statistics and Research Agency is responsible for carrying out the Population Census on the entire population of Northern Ireland. Data are available by area, population, households, age, sex, marital status, birthplace, religion, dwelling type, tenure, household size, occupational density, amenities, cars, economically active persons, long-term illness, term-time students' addresses, academic qualifications and Irish language. Data cover the whole province and are also available for local government districts, wards, enumeration districts, postcode sectors, grid squares, health and social services boards, education and library boards, and parliamentary constituencies. The Census, carried out every ten years, was established in Northern Ireland in 1926 and last took place in 1991. Reports are published one to three years after the Census date.

Status: Ongoing
Frequency: Decennial
Timeliness: Reports are published between one and three years after the Census
Earliest Available Data: 1926
National Coverage: Northern Ireland
Disaggregation: Local government districts, wards, enumeration districts, postcode sectors, grid squares, health and social services boards, education and library boards, and parliamentary constituencies

Statistician
Jacquie Hyvart
Census Office for Northern Ireland
Northern Ireland Statistics and Research Agency
Tel: 028 9052 6942

Products that contain data from this source
Labour Force Survey Religion Report; Northern Ireland Census: Economic Activity Report; Northern Ireland Census: Education Report; Northern Ireland Census: Housing and Household Composition Report; Northern Ireland Census: Irish Language Report; Northern Ireland Census: Migration Report; Northern Ireland Census: Summary Report; Northern Ireland Census: Workplace and Transport to Work Report; Population Trends; The 1991 Census Users' Guide

Census of Population - Scotland
General Register Office for Scotland

The Office for National Statistics and the General Register Office for Scotland carry out the National Census of Population and Housing which is conducted every ten years, the most recent being 1991. Questions were asked on population by age, sex, marital status, ethnic group, social group, socio-economic group, country of birth, economic activity, travel to work, migration, limiting long-term illness, household size, tenure and amenities. The responses to those questions which are easiest to code are fully processed (100 per cent sample). Whether the respondents were in households or in communal establishments such as hospitals or hotels. Responses to other questions which are harder to code are processed only for a 10 per cent sample of household forms and a 10 per cent sample of persons returned on forms for communal establishments.

Status: Ongoing
Collection Method: Census
Frequency: Decennial
Reference Period: As at April 1991
Earliest Available Data: 1801
National Coverage: Scotland
Disaggregation: Region and District, Council Area, Postcode Sector, Health Board Area, New Town, Regional Electoral Division, District Ward, Parliamentary Constituency, Locality, Civil Parish, Output Area, Inhabited Islands

Statistician
Garnett Compton
General Register Office for Scotland
Tel: 0131 314 4298; Email: garnett.compton@gro-scotland.gov.uk

Products that contain data from this source
1991 Census Economic Activity - Scotland; 1991 Census Gaelic Language Scotland (bilingual); 1991 Census Housing and Availability of Cars Scotland; 1991 Census Inhabited Islands Monitor - Scotland; 1991 Census Key Statistics for Localities in Scotland; 1991 Census Parliamentary Constituencies -Scotland (New); 1991 Census Parliamentary Constituencies-

Scotland; 1991 Census Postcode Sector Monitors Scotland; 1991 Census Preliminary Report for Scotland; 1991 Census Regional Reports Scotland; 1991 Census Report for New Towns Scotland; 1991 Census Report for Scotland; 1991 Census Scotland Summary Monitor; 1991 Census Workplace and Transport to Work - Scotland; 1991 Local Base Statistics (LBS); 1991 Small Area Statistics (SAS); Census Historical Tables: Great Britain; Mid-year Population Estimates, Scotland; Population Projections, Scotland

Census of Population and Housing - Great Britain - 1991
Office for National Statistics

The Office for National Statistics and the General Register Office for Scotland carry out the National Census of Population and Housing which is conducted every ten years, the most recent being 1991. Questions were asked on population by age, sex, marital status, ethnic group, social group, socio-economic group, country of birth, economic activity, travel to work, migration, limiting long-term illness, household size, tenure and amenities.

Data are collected for Great Britain and are available for several other geographic levels including standard region, county (England and Wales), regional health authority, district health authority, parliamentary constituency, European constituency, postcode sector, local government district, ward, civil parish, enumeration district and urban/rural areas. For Scotland the geographic breakdowns used include local government region, district and islands area, health board area, regional electoral divisions, inhabited islands, localities and output areas.

Status: Ongoing
Collection Method: Census
Frequency: Decennial
Reference Period: as at April 1991
Earliest Available Data: 1801
National Coverage: Great Britain
Disaggregation: Local Authority District (LAD)/ Unitary Authority(Eng), standard region, county (England and Wales), regional health authority, district health authority, parliamentary constituency, European constituency, postcode sector, local government district, ward, civil parish, enumeration district and urban/rural areas

Statistician
Census Customer Services - ONS
Office for National Statistics
Census Division; Census Marketing
Tel: 01329 813800;
Email: census.marketing@ons.gov.uk

Products that contain data from this source
1991 Census Children and Young Adults; 1991 Census Commissioned Tables - England and Wales; 1991 Census Commissioned Tables - Scotland; 1991 Census Communal Establishments; 1991 Census County Monitors; 1991 Census County Reports; 1991 Census Definitions Great

Sources and Analyses

Britain; 1991 Census Economic Activity; 1991 Census Ethnic Group and Country of Birth; 1991 Census European Constituency Monitor; 1991 Census Gaelic Language Scotland (bilingual); 1991 Census Great Britain Monitor; 1991 Census Great Britain Summary and Review Monitor: Local Authorities; 1991 Census Health Area Monitors; 1991 Census Household and Family Composition (10%); 1991 Census Household Composition; 1991 Census Housing and Availability of Cars; 1991 Census Key Facts on Electronic Fiche; 1991 Census Key Statistics for Local Authorities - Great Britain; 1991 Census Key Statistics for Localities in Scotland; 1991 Census Key Statistics for New Health Areas; 1991 Census Key Statistics for Urban and Rural Areas - Great Britain; 1991 Census Limiting Long-term Illness; 1991 Census Local Base Statistics (LBS); 1991 Census Migration; 1991 Census New Parliamentary Constituency Monitors; 1991 Census Parliamentary Constituency Monitors; 1991 Census People and Households in Postcode; 1991 Census Persons Aged 60 and Over; 1991 Census Postcode Sector Monitors; 1991 Census Preliminary Report for England and Wales; 1991 Census Qualified Manpower; 1991 Census Regional Migration Statistics; 1991 Census Regional Reports Scotland; 1991 Census Report for England, Regional Health Authorities; 1991 Census Report for Great Britain; 1991 Census Report for Scotland; 1991 Census Report for Wales (Adroddiad Cymru); 1991 Census Samples of Anonymised Records; 1991 Census Scotland Summary Monitor; 1991 Census Sex, Age and Marital Status; 1991 Census Small Area Statistics (SAS); 1991 Census Special Migration Statistics (SMS) - Scotland; 1991 Census Special Workplace Statistics; 1991 Census Supplementary Monitor on People Sleeping Rough; 1991 Census Table 100; 1991 Census Topic Monitors; 1991 Census Topics Report for Health Areas; 1991 Census Usual Residence; 1991 Census Welsh Language / Cymraeg; 1991 Census Workplace and Transport to Work; Census Historical Tables: Great Britain; Census News; Ethnicity in the 1991 Census, Volume 1 : Demographic characteristics of the ethnic minority populations; Ethnicity in the 1991 Census, Volume 2 : The ethnic minority populations of Great Britain; Ethnicity in the 1991 Census, Volume 3 : Social geography and ethnicity in Britain: geographical spread, spatial concentration and internal migration; Ethnicity in the 1991 Census, Volume 4 : Employment, education and housing among the ethnic minority populations of Britain; Health Inequalities Decennial Supplement; Occupational Health Decennial Supplement; Population Trends; Population, Household and Dwellings in Europe - Main Results of the 1990/91 Censuses; The 1991 Census Table 100; The 1991 Census Users' Guide; Ward and Civil Parish Monitors (England) Ward and Community Monitors (Wales)

Ethnic Group and Birthplace - GB
Office for National Statistics

The Office for National Statistics compiles statistics of the population analysed by ethnic group. Estimates of various individual ethnic groups, countries of birth and nationalities

are produced using Labour Force Survey data together with results from the 1991 Census of Population. Data are available on ethnicity by age, sex, birthplace, region of residence, nationality, family and household type.

National Coverage: Great Britain
Disaggregation: Standard regional and metropolitan county level. Non-metropolitan counties, regional and district health authorities, local authorities districts, wards, enumeration districts and postcode sector level data are only available for the 1991 Census

Statistician
Census Customer Services - ONS
Office for National Statistics
Census Division; Census Marketing
Tel: 01329 813800;
Email: census.marketing@ons.gov.uk

Products that contain data from this analysis
1991 Census Ethnic Group and Country of Birth; 1991 Census Topics Report for Health Areas; Labour Market Trends; Population Trends; Regional Trends; Social Trends; Statistical News

National Health Service Central Register
General Register Office for Scotland

The General Register Office for Scotland collates data on behalf of the health service in Scotland on the registration of patients with their general practitioners (GPs) and is informed of any moves between GPs.

Status: Ongoing
Collection Method: Administrative Records
Frequency: Continuously
National Coverage: Scotland

Statistician
Graham Jackson
General Register Office for Scotland
Tel: 0131 314 4229;
Email: graham.jackson@gro-scotland.gov.uk

Products that contain data from this source
1994-based National Population Projections; 1996-based National Population Projections first release; Inter-regional migration: Regional Dataset; Mid-year Population Estimates, Scotland; National Population Projections; Population Projections, Scotland; Population Trends; Regional Trends

Survey of Register of Electors in England and Wales
Office for National Statistics

Annual survey of all Electoral Registration Officers in England and Wales carried out by ONS on behalf of the Home Office. This survey collects electoral registration data by local authority district.

Status: Ongoing
Collection Method: Census
Frequency: Annually
Reference Period: February 16th annually
Timeliness: One month
National Coverage: England and Wales
Sub-National: Full geographical coverage
Disaggregation: Local Authority District (LAD)/ Unitary Authority (Eng)

Statistician
Roma Chappell
Office for National Statistics
Population and Vital Statistics; Population Estimates Unit
Tel: 01329 813262;
Email: roma.chappell@ons.gov.uk

Products that contain data from this source
Electoral Statistics; Population Estimates, England and Wales; Population Trends; Regional Trends; Social Trends

---

See also:
In other chapters:
Child Benefit *(see the Household Finances chapter)*
Household Survey - Wales *(see the Housing chapter)*
Lone Parent Cohort *(see the Labour Market chapter)*
Northern Ireland Labour Force Survey Religion Report *(see the Labour Market chapter)*

3.5 Divorce

Divorces - England and Wales
Office for National Statistics; sponsored by Lord Chancellor's Department

The Office for National Statistics compiles divorce data collected from courts by the Lord Chancellor's Department. The data cover England & Wales, England, Wales. The series began in 1974. Data are published annually approximately eighteen to twenty months after the year to which it refers and provisional data are produced on a quarterly basis.

Status: Ongoing
Collection Method: Administrative Records
Frequency: Annual
Reference Period: Calendar year
Timeliness: Annually approximately eighteen months after extract of the data
Earliest Available Data: 1974
National Coverage: England and Wales

Statistician
Tim Devis
Office for National Statistics
Population and Vital Statistics; Vital Statistics Outputs
Tel: 01329 813339;
Email: tim.devis@ons.gov.uk

Products that contain data from this source
Demographic Statistics (Eurostat); Marriage, divorce and adoption statistics; Population Trends; HSQ; Regional Trends; Social Trends

Divorces - Scotland
General Register Office for Scotland

The General Register Office for Scotland (GRO(S)) has responsibility for compiling data on divorces collected from the courts.

Status: Ongoing
Collection Method: Administrative Records
Frequency: Continuously
Earliest Available Data: 1855
National Coverage: Scotland
Disaggregation: Council Area

Statistician
Garnett Compton
General Register Office for Scotland
Tel: 0131 314 4298;
Email: garnett.compton@gro-scotland.gov.uk

Products that contain data from this source
Annual Report of the Registrar General for Scotland; General Register Office for Scotland (GRO(S)) Site on the World Wide Web; Population Trends; Regional Trends; Registrar General's Preliminary Return; Registrar General's Quarterly Return; Scottish Abstract of Statistics; Social Trends

3.6 Emigration, Immigration and Migration

Applications for Entry Clearance Made in the Indian Subcontinent
Home Office

The Home Office compiles data on applications for entry clearance made at British High Commissions in the Indian subcontinent, both for settlement in the UK and for temporary visits. Data are available by type of applicant, waiting times and the outcomes of applications and cover applications made in India, Pakistan and Bangladesh. Administrative data on applications for entry clearance made in the Indian subcontinent has been collected in its current form since 1977.

Status: Ongoing
Collection Method: Administrative records
Frequency: Continuous
Reference Period: Quarterly
Timeliness: Approx. 6 months after end of period
Earliest Available Data: 1977
National Coverage: Bangladesh, India, Pakistan

Statistician
Keith Jackson
Home Office
Research, Development and Statistics Directorate

Room 1305
Apollo House
36 Wellesley Road
Croydon Surrey CR9 9RR
Tel: 020 8760 8307

Products that contain data from this source
Bulletin 'Control of Immigration Statistics, United Kingdom' Command Paper 'Control of Immigration Statistics, United Kingdom'

Immigration and Nationality Administrative Systems
Home Office

Systems, continuously updated, containing data on passenger admissions (excluding EEA nationals) and refusals, asylum applications, after-entry applications, enforcement action and applications for British citizenship, in the UK - in respect of the Home Office administration of the control of immigration and granting of citizenship.

Minor discontinuities have resulted from changes in the immigration rules. Larger discontinuities have reflected the enlargement in stages of the European Community/Union, and the formation of the European Economic Area in 1994. Details are given in the annual Command Paper "Control of Immigration, Statistics, United Kingdom". The British Nationality Act 1981, which came into operation on 1 January 1983, affected the numbers of citizenship applications in the period 1981-7.

Status: Ongoing
Collection Method: Administrative Records
Frequency: Continuously
Reference Period: Month
Timeliness: 6 months (approx)
Earliest Available Data: Varies. Some series go back to 1963 on the current basis.
Disaggregation: None

Statistician
Keith Jackson
Home Office
Immigration and Community Unit; Immigration Research and Statistics Service
Tel: 020 8760 8307

Products that contain data from this source
Bulletin "Asylum Statistics, United Kingdom"; Bulletin "Control of Immigration: Statistics, United Kingdom"; Bulletin "Persons Granted British Citizenship, United Kingdom"; Command Paper "Control of Immigration: Statistics, United Kingdom"; Leaflet "Key Statistics of Immigration and Citizenship"

Internal Migration
Office for National Statistics

The Office for National Statistics produces estimates of internal migration within the

United Kingdom which are based on the movement of NHS doctors' patients between Family Health Service Authorities (FHSAs) in England and Wales, Area Health Boards in Scotland and Northern Ireland. Data are available on flows within the UK and England and Wales, by age and sex. Quarterly figures are adjusted to account for differences in recorded cross-border flows between England and Wales, Scotland and Northern Ireland. Migration flows are available at standard regional, metropolitan county and Family Health Service Authority Levels. The series is available on an annual basis from 1975.

Status: Ongoing
Frequency: Weekly
Reference Period: Rolling year
Timeliness: Quarterly
Earliest Available Data: 1975
National Coverage: United Kingdom
Disaggregation: Family Health Service Authority (FHSA); London Borough; Government Offices regions (GORs) and Standard Statistical Regions (SSRs)

Statistician
Lucy Vickers
Office for National Statistics
Population and Vital Statistics; Migration and Subnational Population Projections Unit
Tel: 01329 813799

Products that contain data from this analysis
Key Population and Vital Statistics (Series VS); Nomis®; Population Trends; Regional Trends; Social Trends

International Migration
Office for National Statistics

The Office for National Statistics produces estimates of international migration which are primarily derived from the International Passenger Survey (IPS).

The IPS covers the principal air and sea routes between the UK and countries outside the British Isles. The routes between the UK and the Irish Republic are excluded, as is all movement of diplomats and armed forces. Also it is highly likely that the data exclude short-term visitors who are subsequently granted an extension of stay for a year or more (for example, as students, on the basis of marriage or because they applied for asylum after entering the country). The adjustment needed to give better estimates of actual net migration is derived from the Irish Labour Force Survey, NHS Central Registers and the administration of immigration control. The main groups of data available are migration by last/next residence abroad, citizenship, country of birth, destination/ origin within the UK and also by age, sex, occupation prior to migration and reason for migration.

IPS figures are subject to sampling and non-sampling errors. The sampling errors are relatively large where the estimates are based on very small numbers of contacts. The series covers the UK (Great Britain, England and Wales, individual UK countries, standard regions of England and Greater London), and the rest of world (Europe, old and new Commonwealth, Indian sub-continent, African and Caribbean Commonwealths, Middle East, and other countries of interest). Please note that data for continents and countries of the world are currently supplied to international organisations only.

Status: Ongoing
Frequency: Quarterly
Reference Period: Rolling Year
Timeliness: Quarterly
Earliest Available Data: 1975
National Coverage: United Kingdom
Disaggregation: Government Office Region (GOR); Standard Statistical Region (SSR)

Statistician
Lucy Vickers
Office for National Statistics
Population and Vital Statistics; Migration and Subnational Population Projections Unit
Tel: 01329 813799

Products that contain data from this analysis
A Review of Migration Data Sources; Annual Abstract of Statistics; Command Paper "Control of Immigration: Statistics, United Kingdom"; Demographic Statistics (Eurostat); Key Population and Vital Statistics (Series VS); Population Trends; Regional Trends; Social Trends; Welsh Social Trends

Migration - Scotland
General Register Office for Scotland

The General Register Office for Scotland compiles estimates of migration based on a number of sources including the National Health Service Central Register, electoral registers, the Population Census, and the International Passenger Survey. Estimates are available by age and sex for moves between health board areas and moves between Scotland and the rest of the UK.

Frequency: Annually
National Coverage: Scotland

Statistician
Garnett Compton
General Register Office for Scotland
Tel: 0131 314 4298;
Email: garnett.compton@gro-scotland.gov.uk

Products that contain data from this analysis
Annual Report of the Registrar General for Scotland; Mid-year Population Estimates, Scotland; Population Trends; Regional Trends; Scottish Abstract of Statistics

Migration Series - Northern Ireland
Northern Ireland Statistics and Research Agency

Inward and Outward migration flows to Northern Ireland

Status: Ongoing
Frequency: Annually
Reference Period: 1st July to 30th June
Timeliness: One year later
National Coverage: Northern Ireland

Statistician
Robert Beatty
Northern Ireland Statistics and Research Agency
Demography and Methodology Branch
Tel: 028 9052 6907;
Email: robert.beatty@dfpni.gov.uk

See also:
In other chapters:
International Passenger Survey - UK (*see the Transport, Travel and Tourism chapter*)

3.7 First Names and Surnames Registered

First Names - England and Wales
Office for National Statistics

The Office for National Statistics compiles information on the frequencies of the most popular first names recorded on the National Health Service Central Register for England and Wales. The information has been compiled for 1944, 1954, 1964, 1974, 1984 and 1994. Statistics are also available for each standard region and Wales for 1994.

Status: Ongoing
Frequency: Annually
Reference Period: Year
Timeliness: 2 weeks
Earliest Available Data: 1944
National Coverage: England and Wales
Sub-National: Regions for 1994 only

Statistician
Adrian Read
Office for National Statistics
Tel: 0151 471 4203

Products that contain data from this analysis
First Names: The Definitive Guide to Popular Names in England and Wales

Personal Names - Scotland
General Register Office for Scotland

The General Register Office for Scotland compiles data on the frequencies of forenames and surnames appearing in the registers of births, marriages and deaths. The information covers Scotland and

summary statistics are available for local authority areas. The surveys were carried out in 1855-58, 1935, 1958 and 1976. Since 1990 computerisation has meant that data can be produced annually three months after the end of the year; and computerisation of the Church of Scotland parish registers means that analysis of names is possible back to 1553.

Status: Ongoing
Frequency: Continuously
National Coverage: Scotland

Statistician
Graham Jackson
General Register Office for Scotland
Tel: 0131 314 4229;
Email: graham.jackson@gro-scotland.gov.uk

Products that contain data from this analysis
General Register Office for Scotland (GRO(S)) Site on the World Wide Web; Personal Names in Scotland.

3.8 Marriage and Cohabitation

Marital Status Projections
Government Actuary's Department

The Government Actuary's Department compiles Marital Status Projections. These are projections of the future numbers in the population by age, sex and legal marital status. The mid-1996 based projections also include projections by heterosexual cohabitation. The data cover England and Wales. Projections are made on an ad hoc basis. As Marital Status Projections are forward looking each new set supersedes the previous set.

Frequency: Every 3-5 years
Reference Period: 25 years forward from the projection base year
National Coverage: England and Wales

Statistician
Chris Shaw
Government Actuary's Department
B2
Tel: 020 7211 2662;
Email: chris.shaw@gad.gov.uk

Products that contain data from this analysis
Population Trends 95, Projections of Households in England to 2016

Marriage Registration - Northern Ireland
Northern Ireland Statistics and Research Agency

Marriages by age, method of celebration, previous marital status and month.

Status: Ongoing
Collection Method: Administrative Records
Frequency: Continuously
Reference Period: 1st January to 31st December
Timeliness: within six months
Earliest Available Data: 1922
National Coverage: Northern Ireland
Sub-National: Area Health Boards and District Councils

Statistician
John Gordon
Department of Finance and Personnel - Northern Ireland
GRO-NI
Tel: 028 9025 2032

Products that contain data from this source
Annual Report of the Registrar General for Northern Ireland; Quarterly Return of the Registrar General for Northern Ireland

Marriages - Scotland
General Register Office for Scotland

The General Register Office for Scotland has responsibility for registration of marriages. Variables used for marriages include age at marriage, country of birth and method of celebration. Data are available for Scotland and for local authority and health board areas. Selected data are available for registration districts.

Status: Ongoing
Frequency: Continuously
Earliest Available Data: 1855
National Coverage: Scotland
Disaggregation: Postcode unit

Statistician
Graham Jackson
General Register Office for Scotland
Tel: 0131 314 4229;
Email: graham.jackson@gro-scotland.gov.uk

Products that contain data from this source
Annual Report of the Registrar General for Scotland; General Register Office for Scotland (GRO(S)) Site on the World Wide Web; Population Trends; Regional Trends; Registrar General's Preliminary Return; Registrar General's Quarterly Return; Social Trends

Registration of Marriages - England and Wales
Office for National Statistics

The Office for National Statistics compiles data on marriages from churches and registrars. The data cover England & Wales, England, Wales. They are available at government office region, standard statistical region, county, registration district, metropolitan (and non-metropolitan) county and London borough levels.

Status: Ongoing
Collection Method: Administrative Records
Reference Period: Calendar year
Timeliness: Annually approximately eighteen to twenty months after the reference year
National Coverage: England and Wales
Disaggregation: Government Office Region (GOR); London Borough; Standard Statistical Region (SSR); Registration District (births/marriages/deaths); Unitary Authority; County (E&W)/Unitary Authority (Eng)

Statistician
Tim Devis
Office for National Statistics
Population and Vital Statistics; Vital Statistics Outputs
Tel: 01329 813339;
Email: tim.devis@ons.gov.uk

Products that contain data from this source
Demographic Statistics (Eurostat); Marriage, Divorce and Adoption Statistics; Marriages per 1,000 population, 1985-1995 first marriage rates; Marriages per 1,000 population, 1985-1995 remarriage rates; Mean age of all women at marriage 1986-1995; Population Trends; Regional Trends; Social Trends; HSQ

3.9 Population and Housing - General

Household Estimates and Projections
Department of the Environment, Transport and the Regions

Every two or three years the DETR produces household projections for future years. ONS's population projections are split by marital status using the Government Actuary's Department's marital status projections, and an estimate of the institutional population subtracted to give the private household population. These population figures split by age, sex and marital status, are multiplied by projected 'household representative rates' (which represent the projected portion of the population in that category who are household representatives) to give the numbers of households. The household representative rates are based on the 1971, 1981, 1991 Censuses and 1992 Labour Force Survey data.

Status: Ongoing
Timeliness: Mid-year estimates are produced in the autumn of the year following the year in question. Projections are produced every two or three years.
Earliest Available Data: 1981
National Coverage: England

Statistician
Dorothy Anderson
Department of the Environment, Transport and the Regions
Housing Data and Statistics (HDS); HDS4
Tel: 020 7890 3265

Products that contain data from this analysis
Projections of Households in England to 2016

Life Tables - Scotland
General Register Office for Scotland

Scottish Life Tables based on the mortality experience of three years centred on a census year (e.g. 1990-92) are prepared by the Government Actuary's Department on behalf of the General Register Office for Scotland (GRO(S)). Abridged life tables for Scotland are prepared and published each year by GRO(S) with related information about expectation of life. Life tables cover Scotland with abridged life tables for local authority and health board areas.

Status: Ongoing
National Coverage: Scotland

Statistician
Garnett Compton
General Register Office for Scotland
Tel: 0131 314 4298;
Email: garnett.compton@gro-scotland.gov.uk

Products that contain data from this analysis
Annual Abstract of Statistics; Annual Report of the Registrar General for Scotland; Scottish Abstract of Statistics

Life Tables - United Kingdom
Government Actuary's Department

The Government Actuary's Department compiles data on life expectancy from data derived from Registrars General on population and deaths. Data are available in the form of life tables on both a period and a cohort basis. The data cover the United Kingdom, Great Britain, England & Wales, England, Scotland, Wales and Northern Ireland. Graduated Life Tables for England & Wales or Scotland are published every ten years based on the three years around a census date, ungraduated tables are produced each year. Historical life tables dating back to 1851 are available for England & Wales.

Status: Ongoing
Frequency: Annually
National Coverage: United Kingdom

Statistician
Steve Smallwood
Government Actuary's Department
B2
Tel: 020 7211 2667;
Email: steve.smallwood@gad.gov.uk

Products that contain data from this analysis
Annual Abstract of Statistics; English Life tables; Population Trends; Scottish Life tables; Social Trends

Sources and Analyses

Sub-National Household Projections - Wales
National Assembly for Wales

Household projections in Wales are compiled first at the national level and then for each county (unitary authority level). They are derived using the same model and are based on the same assumptions for marital status and household formation as the projections for England.

Status: Ongoing
Frequency: Every 2 or 3 years
Reference Period: Varies
Timeliness: Varies
National Coverage: Wales
Sub-National: By local authority

Statistician
Ed Swires-Hennessy
National Assembly for Wales
Cardiff
Wales
Tel: 029 2082 5087; Fax: 029 2082 5350;
Email: ed.swires-hennessy@wales.gsi.gov.uk

See also:
In this chapter:
Census of Population - Northern Ireland *(3.4)*
(The) ONS Longitudinal Study *(3.1)*

In other chapters:
Household Survey - Wales *(see the Housing chapter)*

3.10 Population Estimates and Projections

Mid-Year Population Estimates - Northern Ireland
Northern Ireland Statistics and Research Agency

The General Register Office for Northern Ireland compiles data based on the official Census, modified to include births, deaths and migration up to 30 June. Results also allow for changes in Her Majesty's Forces stationed throughout the province. Data available for Northern Ireland totals from 1922. Age and sex distributions for Northern Ireland are available from 1971 onwards. Age and sex distributions for Health Boards are available from 1981. Age and sex distributions for Local Government Districts are available from 1991.

Status: Ongoing
Frequency: Annually
Reference Period: 1st July to 30th June (one year lapsed)
Earliest Available Data: 1922
National Coverage: Northern Ireland

Disaggregation: District Council Area (Northern Ireland); Health and Social Services Board (Northern Ireland)

Statistician
George King
Northern Ireland Statistics and Research Agency
GRO-NI
Tel: 028 9025 2027;
Email: george.king@dfpni.gov.uk

Products that contain data from this analysis
Annual Report of the Registrar General for Northern Ireland; Quarterly Return of the Registrar General for Northern Ireland, Annual Report of the Chief Medical Officer for Northern Ireland, Northern Ireland Annual Abstract of Statistics, Population Trends, Regional Trends, Population Estimates - England and Wales

---

Population Estimates - England and Wales
Office for National Statistics

The Office for National Statistics compiles annual (mid-year) population estimates for England and Wales based on the latest Census of Population, with allowance for under-enumeration, and updated to reflect subsequent births, deaths, migration and ageing. Estimates of the national population are available by sex and single year of age, with corresponding data at standard region, county, local authority district/London borough, health region and health district levels.

Status: Ongoing
Frequency: Annually
Reference Period: Mid-year to mid-year
Timeliness: 14 month interval
Earliest Available Data: 1981 (electronically)
National Coverage: United Kingdom
Disaggregation: England & Wales, Standard Statistical Regions, Government Office Regions, current and former counties, Unitary Authorities and local government districts, health authorities (E&W).

Statistician
Roma Chappell
Office for National Statistics
Population and Vital Statistics; Population Estimates Unit
Tel: 01329 813262;
Email: roma.chappell@ons.gov.uk

Products that contain data from this analysis
Accuracy of Rolled-forward Population Estimates in England and Wales, 1981-91; Annual Abstract of Statistics; Birth Statistics; Key Population and Vital Statistics (Series VS); Making a Population Estimate in England and Wales; Mid-year Population Estimates for England and Wales; Mortality Statistics: Cause; Mortality Statistics: General; Mortality Statistics: Injury and Poisoning; Nomis®; Population Trends; Regional Trends; Social Trends

---

Population Estimates - Scotland
General Register Office for Scotland

The General Register Office for Scotland compiles the mid-year population estimates for Scotland. Data are available by sex, single year of age, and administrative areas of Scotland. The estimated population of an area includes all those usually resident whatever their nationality. Students are treated as being resident at their term-time address. Members of HM and non-UK armed forces stationed in Scotland are included. The estimates are based on the 1991 Census, adjusted for under-enumeration, and take account of subsequent births, deaths and migration. The data cover Scotland and estimates are available for local authority and health board areas.

Status: Ongoing
Frequency: Annually
Reference Period: Mid-year to mid-year
Earliest Available Data: 1855 - Scotland
National Coverage: Scotland
Disaggregation: Council area, Health board areas

Statistician
Garnett Compton
General Register Office for Scotland
Tel: 0131 314 4298; Email: garnett.compton@gro-scotland.gov.uk

---

Products that contain data from this analysis
Annual Abstract of Statistics; Annual Report of the Registrar General for Scotland; General Register Office for Scotland (GRO(S)) Site on the World Wide Web; Mid-year Population Estimates, Scotland; Nomis®; Population Trends; Regional Trends; Scottish Abstract of Statistics; Scottish Health Statistics; the Scottish Environment Statistics

---

Population Projections
Government Actuary's Department

The Government Actuary's Department (GAD) compiles National Population Projections which are available by age and sex. Results are based on the latest available mid-year population estimates and future assumptions for fertility, mortality and migration are made, based on the examination of the statistical evidence available at the time. Data are available for the United Kingdom, Great Britain, England & Wales, England, Scotland, Wales and Northern Ireland.

Population projections have been made by the Government Actuary's Department since the 1920s. However, as they are forward looking each new set supersedes the previous set. Projections based on a full-scale review of the underlying long-term assumptions have been carried out every two years since 1979. Exceptionally a 1992-based projection was made as it was required to update the next round of long- term sub-national projections. The latest set of projections are 1996-based.

Frequency: Bi-annually
Reference Period: 40 years forward from the projection base year for the component countries of the UK, 70 years forward for GB and UK.
National Coverage: England, Wales, Scotland, Northern Ireland, England and Wales, GB, UK

Statistician
Steve Smallwood
Government Actuary's Department
B2
Tel: 020 7211 2667;
Email: steve.smallwood@gad.gov.uk

Products that contain data from this analysis
1994 Based Household Projections for Wales (1997); 1994-based National Population Projections; 1996-based National Population Projections first release; Annual Abstract of Statistics; National Population Projections; Population Trends; Social Trends

---

Sub-National Population Projections - England
Office for National Statistics

The Office for National Statistics compiles sub-national population projections for England. They are based on the latest population estimates and recent data on births, deaths and migration. The projections control to the national projections for England produced by the Government Actuary's Department. The results are available by sex and various age groups. Data cover England and are available for Government office regions, unitary authorities, metropolitan and shire counties, London boroughs, metropolitan and county districts, and health authorities.

Status: Ongoing
Frequency: Three to Five years
Reference Period: 25 years projected on basis of 3-5 years worth of local data, mid-year population estimates and national projections.
Timeliness: Two years
Earliest Available Data: 1996
National Coverage: England
Disaggregation: London Boroughs, Metropolitan and County districts; Health Authority areas

Statistician
Lucy Vickers
Office for National Statistics
Population and Vital Statistics; Migration and Subnational Population Projections Unit
Tel: 01329 813799

Products that contain data from this analysis
Nomis®; Population Projections: Trends, Methods and Uses; Population Trends; Regional Trends; Sub-national Population Projections - England Series PP3; Sub-national Population Projections for local and health authority areas in England, (1996-based)

Sub-National Population Projections - Scotland
General Register Office for Scotland

The Government Actuary's Department (GAD) in consultation with the Registrars General prepares population projections for the four countries of the United Kingdom. Sub-national population projections consistent with the GAD totals are prepared by the General Register Office for Scotland. The projections cover a fifteen-year period and are available by sex, single year of age and administrative area. Data are available for Scotland and local authority and health board areas.

Status: Ongoing
National Coverage: Scotland
Disaggregation: Council Area (Scot)/District and Islands Area (Scotland)

Statistician
Garnett Compton
General Register Office for Scotland
Tel: 0131 314 4298;
Email: garnett.compton@gro-scotland.gov.uk

Products that contain data from this analysis
General Register Office for Scotland (GRO(S)) Site on the World Wide Web; National Population Projections; Nomis(R); Population Projections, Scotland; Regional Trends; Scottish Abstract of Statistics; Scottish Health Statistics

---

Sub-National Population Projections - Wales
National Assembly for Wales

Status: Ongoing
Frequency: Every 2 or 3 years
Reference Period: Varies
Timeliness: Varies
Earliest Available Data: The year in the title of the publication is the earliest "projection" year e.g. "1994 - based population projections for Wales" covers projections from a base of 1994 onwards.
National Coverage: Wales
Disaggregation: By local authority

Statistician
Clive Lewis
National Assembly for Wales
Tel: (+44) 029 2082 3220;
Email: clive.lewis@wales.gsi.gov.uk

Products that contain data from this analysis
Household Projections for Wales; Digest of Welsh Local Area Statistics; Regional Trends

---

Other Sources & Analyses which may be of interest, but are not featured in this book due to lack of details:

Migration - Northern Ireland - Northern Ireland Statistics and Research Agency

Population, Census, Migration and Vital Events - *Products*

Annual Report of the Registrar General for Northern Ireland
Northern Ireland Statistics and Research Agency

Vital statistics on population, births, deaths, stillbirths and infant deaths, births, deaths and marriages in Northern Ireland. The report contains a comprehensive range of statistics comprising of both base data and associated ranges.

Delivery: Periodic Release
Frequency: Annually
Price: £25.00
ISBN: 1 899203 23 0

Available from
John Gordon
2nd Floor
GRO(NI)
Northern Ireland Statistics and Research Agency
Oxford House
49-55 Chichester Street
Belfast BT1 4HL
Tel: 028 9025 2032

Sources from which data for this product are obtained
Births Registration - Northern Ireland; Deaths Registration - Northern Ireland; Marriage Registration - Northern Ireland; Mid year population estimates - Northern Ireland; Population Estimates - Northern Ireland

Annual Report of the Registrar General for Scotland
General Register Office for Scotland

Annual statistics for vital events and related topics such as population and divorce. The report contains a wide range of tables covering population, births, stillbirths and infant deaths, deaths, deaths by cause, marriages, divorces and adoptions.

Frequency: Annually
Price: £15.00
ISBN: 1 874451 54 0
ISSN: 0080-7869

Available from
Carole Welch
Room 1/2/9
General Register Office for Scotland
Ladywell House
Ladywell Road
Edinburgh EH12 7TF
Tel: 0131 314 4243; Email: carole.welch@gro-scotland.gov.uk

Sources from which data for this product are obtained
Births - Scotland; Childhood and Infant Mortality - Scotland; Divorces - Scotland; Life Tables - Scotland; Marriages - Scotland; Migration - Scotland; Population Estimates - Scotland

Births and Deaths Extracts
Office for National Statistics

Annual extract of births and deaths individual records, for health authorities only. Used for a variety of applications e.g. monitoring local trends, preparing annual reports, outcome linkage, quality checking local statistics. Individual records are extracted from the births and deaths registrations datasets.

Delivery: Periodic Release
Frequency: Annually
Price: £60.00 + VAT for own health authority £17.50 + VAT for subsequent other health authorities

Available from
Helen Booth
Room 2300
Office for National Statistics
Segensworth Road
Titchfield
Fareham
Hampshire PO15 5RR
Tel: 01329-813323

Sources from which data for this product are obtained
Registration of Births - England and Wales; Registration of Deaths - England and Wales; Deaths by Occurrence - England and Wales

1991 Census Children and Young Adults
Office for National Statistics

Figures on 'children and young adults' from the 1991 Census, Great Britain. Contains eight tables (five covering 100 per cent variables and three 10 per cent tables) each down to regional level and giving breakdowns by age (up to 29 years of age), covering: total numbers, migrants and long-term illness; marital status; economic activity; ethnic group; housing; family status of the child or young adult; social class of families; and higher educational qualification by ethnic group. All tables relate to Great Britain, England and Wales, England, regions, metropolitan counties, Inner London, Outer London, regional remainders, Wales, Scotland.

Frequency: Decennial
Price: £47.00
ISBN: 0 11 691525 0

Available from
TSO Publications Centre and Bookshops
Please see Annex B for full address details

Sources from which data for this product are obtained
Census of Population and Housing - Great Britain -1991

Demographic Statistics (Eurostat) 1998 Edition
Eurostat

This publication contains all of the principal series of demographic statistics, namely population by sex and age group, births, deaths, migration, marriages, divorces, fertility, life expectancy and population projections. It uses both absolute numbers and rates which are given in considerable detail for each country in the Union.

Delivery: Periodic
Frequency: Annual
Price: £22.50
ISBN: 92 828 5992 4

Available from
TSO Publications Centre and Bookshops
Please see Annex B for full address details.

Sources from which data for this product are obtained
Divorces - England and Wales; International Migration; Registration of Births - England and Wales; Registration of Marriages - England and Wales

Health Statistics Quarterly
Office for National Statistics

This quarterly publication covers health information. It contains commentary on the latest findings, topical articles on relevant subjects illustrated with colour charts and diagrams, regularly updated statistical tables and graphs, showing trends and the latest quarterly information: on deaths, childhood mortality, cancer survival, abortions, congenital anomalies, morbidity etc. Articles in issue Number 1 (Spring 1999) included: socio-economic differentials in health; prescribing for patients with asthma by general practitioners in England and Wales; death certification and the epidemiologist; trends in mortality of young adults; and weekly deaths in England and Wales. HSQ also includes as appropriate, reports on annual data for births, deaths and input to childhood mortality - these replace the former monitors.

Delivery: Periodic Release
Frequency: Quarterly
Price: Annual 4 editions - £75.00 including postage; Individual - £20.00; Annual subscription of £135.00 (including postage) for both Health Statistics Quarterly and Population Trends (i.e. 8 editions)
ISSN: 1465-1645

Available from
TSO Publications Centre and Bookshops
Please see Annex B for full address details.

Sources from which data for this product are obtained
Cancer Registrations - England & Wales; Childhood and Infant Mortality - England and Wales; Congenital Anomalies - England and Wales; Registration of Births - England and Wales; Registration of Deaths - England and Wales; The ONS Longitudinal Study

Key Population and Vital Statistics (Series VS)
Office for National Statistics

Selection of primarily annual population and vital statistics for local authority and health areas. Contains population estimates for Government Office Regions, local administrative areas, and health authorities in England and Wales, Scotland and Northern Ireland together with statistics on births and deaths in these areas and on movements of population between family health service authorities in reference year.

Delivery: Periodic Release
Frequency: Annually
Price: £35.00 - 1997
ISBN: 0 11 621046 X (Series VS)

Available from
TSO Publications Centre and Bookshops
Please see Annex B for full address details.

Sources from which data for this product are obtained
Childhood and Infant Mortality - England and Wales; Conceptions - England and Wales; Internal Migration; International Migration; Population Estimates - England and Wales; Registration of Births - England and Wales; Registration of Deaths - England and Wales

Longitudinal Study 1971-1991 History, Organisation and Quality of Data
Office for National Statistics

A reference source containing methodological, quality and linkage details for the LS.

Delivery: Ad Hoc/One-off Release
Frequency: Ad-hoc
Price: £27.30
ISBN: 0116916370

Available from
Jillian Smith
Office for National Statistics
Health & Demography; Longitudinal Study
Tel: 020 7533 5184;
Email: jillian.smith@ons.gov.uk

Marriage, Divorce and Adoption Statistics
Office for National Statistics

Review of the Registrar General on marriages and divorces in England and Wales. Contains a variety of statistics on marriages solemnised, and dissolutions and annulments of marriages granted in England and Wales for a particular year. Marriage tables cover, for example, age, previous marital condition and manner of solemnisation. Divorce statistics cover age, duration of marriage and number and age of children involved. Summary tables of adoption orders from 1975 are included.

Delivery: Periodic Release
Frequency: Annually
Price: £25.00
ISBN: 0 11 620930 5

Available from
TSO Publications Centre and Bookshops
Please see Annex B for full address details.

Sources from which data for this product are obtained
Divorces - England and Wales; Registration of Marriages - England and Wales

Population Trends
Office for National Statistics

This quarterly publication covers population and demographic information. It contains commentary on the latest findings, topical articles on relevant subjects such as one parent families, cohabitation, fertility differences, international demography, population estimates and projections for different groups, illustrated with colour charts and diagrams, regularly updated statistical tables and graphs, showing trends and the latest quarterly information: on conceptions, births, marriages, divorces, internal and international migration, population estimates and projections, etc

Coverage: England and Wales, and in many instances United Kingdom as a whole and constituent countries.

Delivery: Periodic Release
Frequency: Quarterly
Price: Annual 4 editions £75.00 including postage Individual £20.00

Annual subscription of £135.00 including postage, for both Health Statistics Quarterly and Population Trends publications (i.e. 8 editions)
ISSN: 0307-4436

Available from
TSO Publications Centre and Bookshops
Please see Annex B for full address details.

Sources from which data for this product are obtained
Registration of births, deaths & marriages, and divorces granted in the constituent countries; Abortion notifications in England and Wales for conception statistics; Censuses of Population in Great Britain and Northern Ireland ; International Passenger Survey for international migration and National Health Service Centre Registers for internal migration, population estimates and sub-national projections; National projections and life expectancies from the Government Actuary.

Postcode Sector Lineprints
General Register Office for Scotland

Total Births by postcode sector and District by age of mother, sex of parents and their social class and previous number of children. Total Deaths by postcode sector and District by age and sex and list by cause of death

Frequency: Annually
Price: Various

Available from
Carole Welch
Room 1/2/9
General Register Office for Scotland
Ladywell House
Ladywell Road
Edinburgh EH12 7TF
Tel: 0131 314 4243;
Email: carole.welch@gro-scotland.gov.uk

Sources from which data for this product are obtained
Postcode boundaries - Scotland

Postcode Unit Counts
General Register Office for Scotland

The postcode unit count gives a list of each postcode in Scotland where a birth or death was recorded and gives the total of births and deaths by sex. Subsets of postcodes.

Frequency: Annually
Price: Various

Available from
Carole Welch
Room 1/2/9
General Register Office for Scotland
Ladywell House
Ladywell Road
Edinburgh EH12 7TF
Tel: 0131 314 4243;
Email: carole.welch@gro-scotland.gov.uk

Sources from which data for this product are obtained
Postcode boundaries - Scotland

Quarterly Return of the Registrar General for Northern Ireland
Northern Ireland Statistics and Research Agency

A quarterly return of births, deaths and marriages. Some of the data in this product is disaggregated by gender.

Delivery: Periodic Release
Frequency: Quarterly

Available from
John Gordon
Room 2nd Floor
GRO(NI)
Northern Ireland Statistics and Research Agency
Oxford House
49-55 Chichester Street
Belfast BT1 4HL
Tel: 028 9025 2032

Sources from which data for this product are obtained
Births Registration - Northern Ireland; Deaths Registration - Northern Ireland; Marriage Registration - Northern Ireland; Mid year population estimates - Northern Ireland

---

Registrar General's Preliminary Return
General Register Office for Scotland

Provisional annual statistics for vital events. The preliminary return contains a selection of provisional data on births, deaths, cause of death, and marriages.

Frequency: Annual
Price: £1.00

Available from
Carole Welch

Room 1/2/9
General Register Office for Scotland
Ladywell House
Ladywell Road
Edinburgh EH12 7TF
Tel: 0131 314 4243; Email: carole.welch@gro-scotland.gov.uk

Sources from which data for this product are obtained
Births-Scotland; Divorces-Scotland; Marriages-Scotland; Mortality-Scotland

---

Registrar General's Quarterly Return
General Register Office for Scotland

Provisional quarterly statistics for vital events. The quarterly return contains a selection of provisional data on births, deaths, cause of death, and marriages.

Frequency: Quarterly
Price: £1.00

Available from
Carole Welch
Room 1/2/9
General Register Office for Scotland
Ladywell House
Ladywell Road
Edinburgh EH12 7TF
Tel: 0131 314 4243;
Email: carole.welch@gro-scotland.gov.uk

Sources from which data for this product are obtained
Births - Scotland; Divorces - Scotland; Marriage Registration - Northern Ireland; Marriages - Scotland; Mortality - Scotland

---

Scottish Health Statistics
The Scottish Executive

Presents the latest available and trend statistics on a comprehensive range of health topics to assist planning, policy, performance measurement and research.

Delivery: Periodic Release
Frequency: Annually
Price: £25.00 outside NHS, free on website

Available from
Customer help desk
Room B037
Information and Statistics Division, NHS in Scotland
Trinity Park House
South Trinity Road
Edinburgh EH5 3SQ
Tel: 0131 551 8899

Sources from which data for this product are obtained
Cancer screening; Notification of an abortion; Population Estimates - Scotland; Record linkage - linked dataset; Sub-national Population Projections - Scotland

---

Visitors to the Public Search Room
Office for National Statistics

Report of a survey for the Registration Division of OPCS carried out in March 1994. (This publication is probably obsolete now that the Public Search Room has moved to Myddleton Place. New information will be available soon). The report contains information about the number and type of user of the Public Search Room and the service provided at St Catherine's House (OPCS) where birth, marriage and death indexes can be consulted by the public and certificates ordered. This updates information in the Attitudes to the Public Search Room survey which was carried out in January 1989.

Frequency: Ad hoc
Price: £6.00
ISBN: 1 85774 191 9

Available from
General Manager (PSR)
Office for National Statistics
1 Myddleton Place
London EC1R 1UW
Tel: 020 7533 6402

Vital Statistics Tables
Office for National Statistics

Tables of annual data on vital statistics for local and health authority areas in England and Wales. The five sets of detailed vital statistics available cover: vital statistics summary; birth statistics; mortality statistics; vital statistics and deaths from selected causes by wards; and infant mortality.

Delivery: Periodic Release
Frequency: Annually
Price: £30.00 / £40.00 + VAT

Available from
E&W Births Enquiries
Room 2300
Office for National Statistics
Segensworth Road
Titchfield
Fareham
Hampshire PO15 5RR
Tel: 01329 813758

Sources from which data for this product are obtained
Childhood and Infant Mortality - England and Wales; Registration of Births - England and Wales; Registration of Deaths - England and Wales

---

3.12 Births and Fertility

Birth Statistics - FM1
Office for National Statistics

Review of the Registrar General on births and patterns of family building in England and Wales. Contains a wide range of statistics (for England and Wales) for births occurring in a particular year and for women born in particular years. The tables cover counts of births and rates, analysed by, for example, age and marital status of parents, place of confinement, area of residence of mother, social class of father (as defined by occupation). Conception data are also shown, analysed for example by age of woman at conception and outcome (maternity or abortion). Some historical data (last ten years) are included and a summary of the main patterns and trends.

Delivery: Periodic Release
Frequency: Annually
Price: £25.00
ISBN: ISBN 0 11 621092 3

Available from
TSO Publications Centre and Bookshops
Please see Annex B for full address details.

Sources from which data for this product are obtained
Abortion notification forms (HSA4); Conceptions - England and Wales; Population Estimates - England and Wales; Registration of Births - England and Wales

Births in Scotland 1976-95
The Scottish Executive

Presents trend statistics on a range of maternity topics to assist planning, policy, performance measurement and research.

Delivery: Ad hoc/One-off Release

Available from
Customer help desk
Room B037
Information and Statistics Division, NHS in Scotland
Trinity Park House
South Trinity Road
Edinburgh EH5 3SQ
Tel: 0131 551 8899

Conceptions in England and Wales (on Disk)
Office for National Statistics

Conceptions for each ward in England and Wales. Conceptions which led to maternities or legal abortions under the 1967 Act. They do not include conceptions resulting in spontaneous miscarriages during the first 23 weeks of gestation nor any illegal abortions.

Delivery: Periodic Release
Frequency: Annually
Price: £40.00 + VAT

Available from
E&W Births Enquiries
Room 2300
Office for National Statistics
Segensworth Road
Titchfield
Fareham
Hampshire
PO15 5RR
Tel: 01329 813758

Sources from which data for this product are obtained
Registration of Births - England and Wales
Abortion Notification Forms (HSA4) - England and Wales

Congenital Anomaly Statistics 1997
Office for National Statistics

Annual review of notifications of congenital anomalies received as part of the England and Wales National Congenital Anomaly System. Contains statistics of notifications of congenital anomalies received as part of the ONS monitoring system for England and Wales in the reference year. Data are given for standard regions, government office regions and regional and district health authorities.

Frequency: Annually
Price: £25.00
ISSN: 011 621 1563

Available from
TSO Publications Centre and Bookshops
Please see Annex B for full address details.

Sources from which data for this product are obtained
Congenital Anomalies - England and Wales

New Perspectives on Fertility in Great Britain
Office for National Statistics

Academic papers on fertility (Britain and Europe). A collection of papers examining various current key methodological issues and the relationship between fertility and recent changes in the pattern of marriage. Recent trends in British fertility are compared with those in other European countries.

Frequency: Ad hoc
Price: £14.20
ISBN: 0 11 691552 8 (SMPS No 55)

Available from
TSO Publications Centre and Bookshops
Please see Annex B for full address details.

Public Health Births File
Office for National Statistics

Individual records for health authorities.

Delivery: Periodic Release
Frequency: Monthly
Price: £850.00 monthly or £1000.00 weekly. Ex. VAT

Available from
Helen Booth
Room 2300
Office for National Statistics
Segensworth Road
Titchfield
Fareham
Hampshire PO15 5RR
Tel: 01329-813323;
Email: helen.booth@ons.gov.uk

Sources from which data for this product are obtained

Registration of Births - England and Wales

See also:
In this chapter:
Annual Report of the Registrar General for Northern Ireland *(3.11)*
Annual Report of the Registrar General for Scotland *(3.11)*
Births and Deaths Extracts *(3.11)*
Demographic Statistics (Eurostat) *(3.11)*
Infant and Perinatal Mortality: (DHAs and RHAs) Monitor *(3.13)*
Key Population and Vital Statistics (Series VS) *(3.11)*
Mortality Statistics: Childhood Infant and Perinatal *(3.13)*
Population Trends *(3.11)*
Postcode Sector Lineprints *(3.11)*
Postcode Unit Counts *(3.11)*
Quarterly Return of the Registrar General for Northern Ireland *(3.11)*
Registrar General's Preliminary Return *(3.11)*
Registrar General's Quarterly Return *(3.11)*
Vital Statistics Tables *(3.11)*

In other chapters:
Abortion Statistics Annual Reference Volume *(see the Health and Care chapter)*
Health and Personal Social Services Statistics for England *(see the Health and Care chapter)*
Legal Abortions Quarterly Monitors *(see the Health and Care chapter)*

3.13 Deaths and Stillbirths

Death Counts
Office for National Statistics

A video designed to assist doctors in completing the medical certificate of cause of death.

Delivery: On receipt of order
Frequency: Ad-hoc

Price: £40.00 for video and training pack. Additional training pack £10.00: contains exercises in deaths certification.

Available from
E&W Deaths Enquiries
Room 2300
Office for National Statistics
Segensworth Road
Titchfield
Fareham
Hampshire PO15 5RR
Tel: 01329 813758

Sources from which data for this product are obtained
Registration of Deaths - England and Wales

Death Statistics for Funeral Directors
Office for National Statistics

A bespoke service for Funeral Directors giving numbers of deaths by registration district

Frequency: Monthly
Price: On application

Available from
E&W Deaths Enquiries
Room 2300
Office for National Statistics
Segensworth Road
Titchfield
Fareham
Hampshire PO15 5RR
Tel: 01329 813758

Sources from which data for this product are obtained
Registration of Deaths - England and Wales

Deaths Reported to Coroners - England and Wales
Home Office

The Home Office compiles data on deaths reported to coroners in England and Wales in accordance with Section 28 of the Coroners Act 1988. Data are available by deaths reported to coroners, post-mortem examinations, inquests held, and verdicts returned at inquests. Administrative data on the work of coroners has been collected since the late 18th century. The Home Office has published statistical bulletins on deaths reported to coroners since 1981. The data are collected annually and published every April.

Delivery: Periodic Release
Frequency: Annually
Price: Free
ISSN: 0143 6384

Available from
Information and Publications Group
Home Office
Tel: 020 7273 2084

Sources from which data for this product are obtained
Coroners in England and Wales

English Life Tables
Government Actuary's Department

Graduated life tables constructed from the mortality experience of the population of England and Wales during the three years 1990, 1991 and 1992. They are the 15th in a series known as the English Life tables which are associated with decennial population censuses, beginning with the census of 1841. As well as the English Life Table, the volume contains a description of the calculations, including the graduation process, and comparisons with previous English Life Tables. Some of the data in this product is disaggregated by gender.

Delivery: Periodic Release
Frequency: Every 10 years
Price: £25.00
ISBN: 0-11-620925-9

Available from
TSO Publications Centre and Bookshops
Please see Annex B for full address details.

Sources from which data for this product are obtained
Life Tables - United Kingdom

Infant and Perinatal Mortality: (DHAs and RHAs) Monitor
Office for National Statistics

Provisional numbers of annual occurences of infant and perinatal deaths.

Contains provisional statistics of live births, stillbirths and infant deaths which occurred in the reference year, for regional and district health suthorities in England and Wales.

Note: In future this information will be published in Health Statistics Quarterly.

Delivery: First Release
Frequency: Annually
Price: £4.00
ISSN: 0953 3397

Available from
Tim Devis
Room 1300
Office for National Statistics
Segensworth Road
Titchfield
Fareham
Hampshire PO15 5RR
Tel: 01329 813339;
E-mail: tim.devis@ons.gov.uk

Sources from which data for this product are obtained
Childhood and Infant Mortality - England and Wales; Registration of Births - England and Wales; Registration of Deaths - England and Wales

Local Mortality Datapack
Office for National Statistics

Populations and Deaths from selected causes, sex and 5 year age groups by area for 1979 - 1992.

Delivery: On receipt of order
Frequency: Ad-hoc
Price: £99.00

Available from
E&W Deaths Enquiries
Room 2300
Office for National Statistics
Segensworth Road
Titchfield
Fareham
Hampshire PO15 5RR
Tel: 01329 813758

Sources from which data for this product are obtained
Registration of Deaths - England and Wales

Monthly News Release on Weekly Deaths
Office for National Statistics

Estimated weekly death registrations in England and Wales, for the past 4 weeks and cumulative 52 week totals. Deaths for certain selected causes are also given

Delivery: News/Press Release
Frequency: Monthly
Price: Free

Available from
ONS Press Office
Office for National Statistics
1 Drummond Gate
London SW1V 2QQ
Tel: 020 7533 6363/6364

Sources from which data for this product are obtained
Registration of Deaths - England and Wales

Mortality Statistics: Cause - DH2
Office for National Statistics

Annual review of the Registrar General on deaths by cause in England and Wales. Contains statistics of deaths in England and Wales analysed by cause of death, sex, and age group for the reference year. Deaths are classified according to the 9th revision of the International Classification of Diseases (ICD9). Latest year published 1997.

Delivery: Periodic Release
Frequency: Annually
Price: £35.00
ISBN: 0 11 6210958

Available from
TSO Publications Centre and Bookshops
Please see Annex B for full address details.

Sources from which data for this product are obtained
Population Estimates - England and Wales;
Registration of Deaths - England and Wales

Mortality Statistics: Childhood Infant and Perinatal - DH3
Office for National Statistics

Annual review of the Registrar General on childhood, infant and perinatal deaths: social and biological factors, in England and Wales. Contains statistics produced from stillbirth records, and from the linkage of childhood and infant death records to the corresponding birth records for the reference year, in England and Wales. From 1993, this volume has been combined with Mortality Statistics: Childhood (Series DH6). Latest year published 1997.

Delivery: Periodic Release
Frequency: Annually
Price: £35.00
ISBN: 0 11 621048-6

Available from
TSO Publications Centre and Bookshops
Please see Annex B for full address details.

Sources from which data for this product are obtained
Childhood and Infant Mortality - England and Wales; Linked Births and Infant Deaths - England & Wales; Registration of Births - England and Wales; Registration of Deaths - England and Wales

Mortality Statistics: General - DH1
Office for National Statistics

DH1 - Annual review of the Registrar General on deaths in England and Wales. Contains key statistics of deaths and death rates in England and Wales by age, sex, marital status, place of death, birthplace and coroner involvement for the reference year. Since 1993 this volume has included some tables previously included in Mortality Statistics: Area (Series DH5).

Delivery: Periodic Release
Frequency: Annually
Price: £25.00
ISBN: 0 11 621094 X

Available from
TSO Publications Centre and Bookshops
Please see Annex B for full address details.

Sources from which data for this product are obtained
Population Estimates - England and Wales;
Registration of Deaths - England and Wales

Mortality Statistics: Injury and Poisoning - DH4
Office for National Statistics

Review of the Registrar General on deaths attributed to injury and poisoning in England and Wales. Contains a detailed analysis of deaths attributed to accidents, poisoning and violence in England and Wales. These deaths are analysed by age, sex, cause and place of occurrence for each of the main types of accident for the reference year.

Delivery: Periodic Release
Frequency: Annually
Price: £30.00
ISBN: 0 11 621070-2

Available from
TSO Publications Centre and Bookshops
Please see Annex B for full address details.

Sources from which data for this product are obtained
Population Estimates - England and Wales;
Registration of Deaths - England and Wales

Public Health Mortality File
Office for National Statistics

Individual Records for Health Authorities

Delivery: Periodic Release
Frequency: Monthly
Price: £3,000.00 monthly or £3,300.00 weekly Ex. VAT

Available from
Helen Booth
Room 2300
Office for National Statistics
Segensworth Road
Titchfield
Fareham
Hampshire PO15 5RR
Tel: 01329-813323;
Email: helen.booth@ons.gov.uk

Sources from which data for this product are obtained
Registration of Deaths - England and Wales

Scottish Life Tables
General Register Office for Scotland

This set of Scottish Life tables, 1990-92, together with the associated tables and commentary, were prepared by the Government Actuary, at the invitation of the Registrar General for Scotland. The tables are based on mortality experience in

Scotland during the years 1990, 1991 and 1992 and this volume forms the First Supplement to the Registrar General's Annual Report 1996. It is similar in form to its predecessor, Life Tables 1980-82, Supplement to the 1987 Annual Report. Some of the data in this product is disaggregated by gender.

Frequency: Ad-hoc
Price: £4.50
ISBN: 1 874451 53 2

Available from
Carole Welch
Room 1/2/9
General Register Office for Scotland
Ladywell House
Ladywell Road
Edinburgh EH12 7TF
Tel: 0131 314 4243;
Email: carole.welch@gro-scotland.gov.uk

Sources from which data for this product are obtained
Life Tables - United Kingdom

Sudden Infant Deaths
Office for National Statistics

Mortality statistics on sudden infant deaths. Contains provisional statistics of sudden infant deaths in England and Wales which occurred in the reference year. Deaths are analysed by various social and biological factors. Some data are given for the latest five years. Report in 'Health Statistics Quarterly' (Autumn Edition)

Delivery: Periodic Release
Frequency: Annually
Price: £20.00
ISSN: 0953-4415

Available from
Nirupa Dattani
Room B5/10
Office for National Statistics
1 Drummond Gate
London SW1P 2QQ
Tel: 020 7533 5205;
E-mail: nirupa.dattani@ons.gov.uk

Sources from which data for this product are obtained
Childhood and Infant Mortality - England and Wales; Linked Births and Infant Deaths - England & Wales

Twentieth Century Mortality (England & Wales 1901 - 1995) CD-ROM
Office for National Statistics

The Twentieth Century Mortality Files are a record of mortality in England and Wales between 1901 and 1995. The files consist of an aggregated database of deaths by age-group, sex, year and underlying cause. Also included are the International Classification of Diseases (ICD) dictionaries and populations for England and Wales. The CD-ROM contains four file formats: Access v2.0, Access 95, dBase III, and comma separated variables.

Delivery: Periodic Release
Frequency: Five-yearly
Price: £50.00 (£58.75 inc.VAT)
ISBN: 1-875774-239-7

Available from
ONS Direct
Please see Annex B for full address details.

Sources from which data for this product are obtained
Registration of Deaths - England and Wales

Twentieth Century Mortality: 1996-97 Update Disk
Office for National Statistics

1997 deaths by age, sex and underlying cause, and populations for England and Wales. The update disk contains deaths by sex and age, coded to the fourth digit of the International Classification of Diseases Ninth Revision along with population data by age and sex. Some of the data in this product is disaggregated by gender.

Frequency: Ad-hoc
Price: £20.00 (free to CD-ROM purchasers).

Available from
ONS Direct
Please see Annex B for full address details.

Sources from which data for this product are obtained
Registration of Deaths - England and Wales

See also:
In this chapter:
Annual Report of the Registrar General for Northern Ireland *(3.11)*
Annual Report of the Registrar General for Scotland *(3.11)*
Birth Statistics *(3.12)*
Births and Deaths Extracts *(3.11)*
Health Inequalities Data Diskette *(3.11)*
Health Inequalities Decennial Supplement *(3.14)*
Key Population and Vital Statistics (Series VS) *(3.14)*
Population Trends *(3.11)*
Postcode Sector Lineprints *(3.11)*
Postcode Unit Counts *(3.11)*
Quarterly Return of the Registrar General for Northern Ireland *(3.11)*
Registrar General's Preliminary Return *(3.11)*

Registrar General's Quarterly Return *(3.11)*
Vital Statistics Tables *(3.11)*

In other chapters:
(The) Health of Adult Britain 1841 - 1994, Decennial Supplement, Volumes 1 and 2 *(see the Health and Care chapter)*
(The) Health of Our Children *(see the Health and Care chapter)*
Indicators of Sustainable Development - United Kingdom *(see the Environment chapter)*
Longitudinal Study: Socio-Demographic Differences in Cancer Survival 1971-83 *(see the Health and Care chapter)*
TENDON *(see the Health and Care chapter)*

3.14 Demographic including Census, Economic and Social Characteristics of Population

Attitudes to Charitable Giving
Office for National Statistics; sponsored by Home Office

A small qualitative study, carried out in 1991, which looked at peoples attitudes to giving to charities, reasons why people donated money and the different patterns of donation.

Frequency: Ad hoc
Price: £3.20
ISBN: 0 11 691678 8

Available from
ONS Direct
Please see Annex B for full address details.

(The) 1991 Census Area Master File
Office for National Statistics

Provides the constitution of the different area levels (in England and Wales) used for both planning the area base of the 1991 Census and for processing output. The file defines areas in terms of the smallest real unit necessary to provide a comprehensive constitution and gives the codes used by ONS to identify each area.

Frequency: Decennial
Price: price varies

Available from
Census Customer Services - ONS
Please see Annex B for full address details.

1991 Census Commissioned Tables - England and Wales
Office for National Statistics

Statistical tables containing 1991 Census data for Great Britain independently commissioned by customers. In addition to the standard tables prepared for the Local Statistics Reports and abstracts, and Topics Reports, it is possible for tables to be independently commissioned, and paid for, by customers. Commissioned output may take the form of either extension tables (that is, standard tables for smaller areas than those presented in published reports, or for expanded versions of standard distributions of variables), or new tables (that is, tables to be specified by customers themselves). Hardcopy printout customised for requirements. Dependent on customer specification.

Frequency: Decennial
Price: Varies according to individual requirements

Available from
Census Customer Services - ONS
Please see Annex B for full address details.

Sources from which data for this product are obtained
Census of Population and Housing - Great Britain - 1991.

1991 Census Commissioned Tables - Scotland
General Register Office for Scotland

The General Register Office for Scotland can produce customer defined tables from the 1991 Census. The tables can include extensions to standard variables, new combinations of standard variables or customised variables. Customised and extension variables may only be available at Region and District level. Some of the data in this product is disaggregated by gender.

Frequency: Decennial
Price: Variable

Available from
Peter Jamieson
Room 1/2/9
General Register Office for Scotland
Ladywell House
Ladywell Road
Edinburgh EH12 7TF
Tel: 0131 314 4254;
Email: peter.jamieson@gro-scotland.gov.uk

Sources from which data for this product are obtained
Census of Population and Housing - Great Britain - 1991.

1991 Census Communal Establishments
Office for National Statistics

Figures on people in 'communal establishments' from the 1991 Census, Great Britain. Covers people not in households on Census night but present in establishments such as hospitals, hotels and prisons. The 100 per cent tables are mainly at regional level and cover the sex, age, marital condition, ethnic group, economic position, and long-term illness of the people in each type of establishment, together with figures on the number and size of each type of establishment. The tables cover: present and resident population; age and marital status; type of establishment, migrants and long-term illness; ethnic group; economic position; establishment size (number of persons); number of establishments; and hotels and boarding houses.

Frequency: Decennial
Price: £33.40
ISBN: 0 11 691513 7

Available from
Census Customer Services - ONS or TSO Publications Centre and Bookshops
Please see Annex B for full address details.

Sources from which data for this product are obtained
Census of Population and Housing - Great Britain - 1991.

1991 Census County Monitors
Office for National Statistics

A series of 56 booklets, one for each county in England and Wales and Inner and Outer London, presenting summary statistics taken from the 1991 Census. Contains statistics from the 1991 Census for each county in England and Wales (and Inner and Outer London). These are 100 per cent Local Base Statistics covering: population present 1981-91, hectares, resident population, age, economic characteristics, tenure and amenities, dwellings, selected characteristics of household composition (including long-term illness), ethnic group, selected characteristics of young adults and pensioners, Welsh language (in Wales only), and giving some figures on percentage change between 1981-91.

Frequency: Decennial
Price: £2.00 each
ISBN: Various
ISSN: 0261-2216 (series CEN 91 CM xx)

Available from
Census Customer Services - ONS or TSO Publications Centre and Bookshops
Please see Annex B for full address details.

Sources from which data for this product are obtained
Census of Population and Housing - Great Britain - 1991

1991 Census County Reports
Office for National Statistics

Statistical tables on all topics covered by the 1991 Census at county level for England and Wales. A series of 56 reports (each published in two parts), one for each county in England and Wales and Inner and Outer London based on the 1991 Census. Each county report presents the full range of output from the Local Base Statistics (the 100 per cent tables in Part 1 and the 10 per cent in Part 2), for each local authority district).

Frequency: Decennial
ISBN: Various

Available from
Census Customer Services - ONS or TSO Publications Centre and Bookshops
Please see Annex B for full address details.

Sources from which data for this product are obtained
Census of Population and Housing - Great Britain - 1991.

1991 Census Definitions Great Britain
Office for National Statistics

Presents the definitions and general explanatory notes in a single comprehensive volume. Comprises eight chapters covering: brief description of the legal aspects, how the Census was conducted and processed, confidentiality measures and the topics that have been included; population bases constructed from the Census questions; the population groups that make up the composition of the bases; Communal establishments; classifications of household spaces and dwelling types; details relating to the 100 and 10 per cent samples respectively for each topic processed; and describes with the use of maps, standard area levels for which the local and topic statistics are available. Additional information is provided in the form of classifications for ethnic group, country of birth, family unit, SOC and Industry codes.

Delivery: Ad Hoc/One-off Release
Frequency: Decennial
Price: £13.80
ISBN: 0 11 691361 4

Available from
Census Customer Services - ONS or TSO Publications Centre and Bookshops
Please see Annex B for full address details.

1991 Census Economic Activity
Office for National Statistics

Figures on 'economic activity' from the 1991 Census. Published in separate volumes for Great Britain and for Scotland, each contain twenty tables (mostly at 10 per cent) plus three subsidiary tables, at regional or national level and covering: economic position and employment status; occupation (Standard Occupational Classification); industry; hours worked; and social class and socio-economic group.

Frequency: Decennial
Price: £33.40 - for Great Britain - £39.00 for Scotland
ISBN: 0 11 691521 8

Available from
Census Customer Services - ONS or TSO Publications Centre and Bookshops
Please see Annex B for full address details.

Sources from which data for this product are obtained
Census of Population and Housing - Great Britain - 1991.

1991 Census Economic Activity - Scotland
General Register Office for Scotland

Figures on 'economic activity' from the 1991 Census. Published in separate volumes for Scotland and for Great Britain, each contain twenty tables (mostly at 10 per cent) plus three subsidiary tables, at regional or national level and covering: economic position and employment status; occupation (Standard Occupational Classification); industry; hours worked; and social class and socio-economic group.

Frequency: Decennial
Price: £39.00
ISBN: 0 11 691521 8

Available from
TSO Publications Centre and Bookshops
Please see Annex B for full address details.

Sources from which data for this product are obtained
Census of Population - Scotland

Sources from which data for this product are obtained
Census of Population and Housing - Great Britain - 1991

Products

1991 Census Enumeration District / Postcode Directory
Office for National Statistics

A directory linking postcodes to the 1991 Census geography of enumeration districts (EDs) in England and Wales is available both at the national level and for individual counties. It is the first directory based on postcodes enumerated in a census, and is designed to help overcome the differences between postcode and census geography. The directories contain the following information for each postcode wholly within a single ED or for each part postcode in two or more EDs: ED identity, Special Enumeration District indicator (where applicable,) pseudo ED identity, National Grid centroid, number of resident households, and number of resident households with imputed postcode. The first version of the national directory contains all the individual county directories and incorporates the re-classification of those unit postcodes that cross county boundaries. A second version of the national directory also containing postcodes not enumerated in the Census (such as large user postcodes) is also available.

Frequency: Decennial
Price: price on application

Available from
Census Customer Services - ONS
Please see Annex B for full address details.

1991 Census European Constituency Monitor
Office for National Statistics

A single booklet presenting the same statistics covered in the Parliamentary Constituency Monitors, for each European constituency with boundaries defined at the time of the 1994 EC elections in Great Britain. The various tables cover: population present 1971 - 1991; resident population - 1981 base; resident population and area; residents by age; economic characteristics; tenure and amenities; dwellings; household composition; ethnic group of residents; young adults; pensioners; born in Wales/Welsh speakers, born in Scotland/Gaelic speakers, born in Northern Ireland/Irish language speakers; and residents.

Frequency: Decennial
Price: £2.80
ISBN: 1 85774 167 6
ISSN: series CEN 91 EPCM

Available from
Census Customer Services - ONS or TSO Publications Centre and Bookshops
Please see Annex B for full address details.

Sources from which data for this product are obtained
Census of Population and Housing - Great Britain - 1991

1991 Census Gaelic Language Scotland (Bilingual)
General Register Office for Scotland

Figures on 'Gaelic language in Scotland' from the 1991 Census. Contains nine tables (five 100 per cent and four 10 per cent sample tables), mainly for Scotland and the major Gaelic-speaking districts in Scotland, covering: trends since 1891; speaking, reading and writing Gaelic by age group; Gaelic-speaking migrants and other migrants; Gaelic-speakers by household and family composition; and Gaelic-speakers by economic position, occupation, social class and higher qualifications.

Frequency: Decennial
Price: £46.00
ISBN: 0 11 495255 8

Available from
TSO Publications Centre and Bookshops
Please see Annex B for full address details.

Sources from which data for this product are obtained
Census of Population - Scotland; Census of Population and Housing - Great Britain - 1991

1991 Census General Report
Office for National Statistics

An overview of the 1991 Census covering the administration, fieldwork, processing and statistical assessment of the data collected.

Delivery: Ad Hoc/One-off Release
Price: £9.00
ISBN: 0 11 691330 4

Available from
Census Customer Services - ONS or TSO Publications Centre and Bookshops
Please see Annex B for full address details.

1991 Census Great Britain Monitor
Office for National Statistics

A summary booklet showing key population and housing statistics for Great Britain taken from the 1991 Census. Contains statistics from the 1991 Census for Great Britain and the constituent Regional Health Authority areas of England. These are 100 per cent Local Base Statistics covering: population present 1891-1991, hectares, resident population, age, economic characteristics,

tenure and amenities, dwellings, selected characteristics of household composition (including long-term illness), ethnic group, selected characteristics of young adults and pensioners, Welsh language (in Wales only), and giving some figures on percentage change between 1981-91. Monitors for the Welsh counties are published bilingually in English and Welsh.

Frequency: Decennial
Price: £2.00
ISBN: 1 85774 073 4
ISSN: 0261-2216 (series CEN 91 CM 56)

Available from
Census Customer Services - ONS or TSO Publications Centre and Bookshops
Please see Annex B for full address details.

Sources from which data for this product are obtained
Census of Population and Housing - Great Britain - 1991.

1991 Census Great Britain Summary and Review Monitor: Local Authorities
Office for National Statistics

A summary booklet showing key statistics on population and housing for local authority districts in Great Britain taken from the 1991 Census. Contains statistics from the 1991 Census for the 459 local authority districts in Great Britain (including the London boroughs and the three island areas of Scotland). These are 100 per cent Local Base Statistics covering: population present 1891-1991, hectares, resident population, age, economic characteristics, tenure and amenities, dwellings, selected characteristics of household composition (including long-term illness), ethnic group, selected characteristics of young adults and pensioners, Welsh language (in Wales only), and giving some figures on percentage change between 1981-91. Monitors for the Welsh counties are published bilingually in English and Welsh. A summary Monitor for Scotland (figures for Scottish Regions) has been produced by GRO(S).

Frequency: Decennial
Price: £2.00
ISBN: 1 85774 077 7
ISSN: 0261-2216 (series CEN 91 CM 57)

Available from
Census Customer Services - ONS or TSO Publications Centre and Bookshops
Please see Annex B for full address details.

Sources from which data for this product are obtained
Census of Population and Housing - Great Britain - 1991.

1991 Census Health Area Monitors
Office for National Statistics

Summary statistics from the 1991 Census at the Regional and District Health Authority level. A series of 16 booklets, one for each Regional Health Authority in England and Wales, and separately for Great Britain, presenting statistics from the 1991 Census. These Monitors present most of the same statistics covered by the County Monitors (but excluding 1981-91 change figures) for each District Health Authority. The various tables cover: population and area; residents by age; economic characteristics; tenure and amenities; dwellings; household composition; ethnic group of residents; young adults; and pensioners.

Frequency: Decennial
Price: £2.00 each
ISBN: Various
ISSN: 1350-214X (series CEN 91 HAM)

Available from
Census Customer Services - ONS or TSO Publications Centre and Bookshops
Please see Annex B for full address details.

Sources from which data for this product are obtained
Census of Population and Housing - Great Britain - 1991.

Census Historical Tables: Great Britain
Office for National Statistics

Selected data from 1801 to 1991 Censuses. Contains six 100 per cent tables which show: persons present and intercensal changes for Great Britain, England, Wales and Scotland for all Censuses from 1801 to 1991; persons present down to county/region level from 1891 to 1991, the proportion of the total population in each area at each Census, and intercensal change; and sex, age and marital status at national level from 1891 to 1991.

Frequency: Decennial
Price: £7.60
ISBN: 0 11 691509 9

Available from
Census Customer Services - ONS or TSO Publications Centre and Bookshops
Please see Annex B for full address details.

Sources from which data for this product are obtained
Census of Population - Scotland; Census of Population and Housing - Great Britain - 1991.

1991 Census Household and Family Composition (10%)
Office for National Statistics

Figures on 'household and family composition' from the 1991 Census, Great Britain. Major report with 31 tables plus six subsidiary tables (all at 10 per cent), primarily at Great Britain/National level. The results on households are extended to cover the 10 per cent variables such as social class, or are presented in combination with statistics on families covering, for example, children in families, couples and lone-parent families, multi-family households by ethnic group, and 'earners' and dependants in families. The 31 tables cover: residents; rooms; tenure; amenities; earners; age, sex and ethnic group; economic activity; social class and socio-economic group; economic activity and dependent children; dependants; limiting long-term illness; pensioners; Dependent and non-dependent children; Children in families; Families with dependent children; Couple families: age and marital status; couple families: economic position; couple families: social class; couple families: mothers; couple families: ethnic group; lone parent families: age and marital status; lone parent families: economic position and hours worked; lone parent families: social class; lone parent families: ethnic group; household structure: dependent children; household structure: ethnic group; household structure: age; dependants in families; households, families and dependants; 'earners' and dependants in families. The six subsidiary tables cover: relationship to household head; number of family units in household; number of persons in family unit; families and no-family persons; household heads; residents: economic position; lone parent families: economic position and children.

Frequency: Decennial
Price: £29.00
ISBN: 0 11 691523 4

Available from
Census Customer Services - ONS or TSO Publications Centre and Bookshops
Please see Annex B for full address details.

Sources from which data for this product are obtained
Census of Population and Housing - Great Britain - 1991.

1991 Census Household Composition
Office for National Statistics

Figures on 'household composition' from the 1991 Census, Great Britain. Contains 18 tables (all at 100 per cent) including seven at regional level covering: dependant children; household spaces and housing; housing and tenure; rooms and tenure; density and tenure; household space type; tenure; housing; rooms; density; 'earners'; economic position and age of head of household; ethnic group of household head; household dependant type; household dependant type and housing; 'carers'; 'earners' and dependants; and floor level.

Frequency: Decennial
Price: £27.40
ISBN: 0 11 691560 9

Available from
Census Customer Services - ONS or TSO Publications Centre and Bookshops
Please see Annex B for full address details.

Sources from which data for this product are obtained
Census of Population and Housing - Great Britain - 1991

1991 Census Housing and Availability of Cars
Office for National Statistics

Figures on 'housing and the availability of cars' from the 1991 Census, Great Britain. Contains 22 tables (all at 100 per cent), some down to district or county level, but most at regional or national level, which cover tenure, amenities and number of rooms, cross-tabulated by characteristics such as households with children and/or pensioners. Number of cars available to a household is similarly cross-tabulated. There are also figures on household spaces and dwellings.

Frequency: Decennial
Price: £30.40
ISBN: 0 11 691512 9

Available from
Census Customer Services - ONS or TSO Publications Centre and Bookshops
Please see Annex B for full address details.

Sources from which data for this product are obtained
Census of Population and Housing - Great Britain - 1991.

1991 Census Housing and Availability of Cars Scotland
General Register Office for Scotland

Figures on 'housing and the availability of cars' from the 1991 Census, Scotland. Contains 22 tables (all at 100 per cent), some down to Region level but most at Scotland level.

Frequency: Decennial
Price: £33.00
ISBN: 0 11 495255 8

Available from
TSO Publications Centre and Bookshops
Please see Annex B for full address details.

Sources from which data for this product are obtained
Census of Population - Scotland.

1991 Census Inhabited Islands Monitor - Scotland
General Register Office for Scotland

1991 Census, summary of statistics on the population and households of the inhabited islands of Scotland.

Frequency: Decennial
Price: £3.00
ISBN: 1 874451 44 3

Available from
Peter Jamieson
Room 1/2/8
General Register Office for Scotland
Ladywell House
Ladywell Road
Edinburgh EH12 7TF
Tel: 0131 314 4254;
Email: peter.jamieson@gro-scotland.gov.uk

Sources from which data for this product are obtained
Census of Population - Scotland.

1991 Census Key Facts on Electronic Fiche
Office for National Statistics

Delivery: Ad Hoc/One-off Release
Price: price on application

Available from
Census Customer Services - ONS
Please see Annex B for full address details.

Sources from which data for this product are obtained
Census of Population and Housing - Great Britain - 1991.

1991 Census Key Statistics for Local Authorities - Great Britain
Office for National Statistics

Contains tables covering: population present on Census night; resident population and area; age structure; communal establishments, long term illness and migrants; birthplace and ethnic group (and Welsh/Gaelic language); male and female economic activity; household spaces and tenure; rooms, amenities, central heating and cars; household and family composition; social class

(based on occupation); travel to work and hours worked; occupation groups and higher qualification; and Industry of employment.

Frequency: Decennial
Price: £27.00
ISBN: 0 11 6915773

Available from
Census Customer Services - ONS or TSO Publications Centre and Bookshops
Please see Annex B for full address details.

Sources from which data for this product are obtained
Census of Population and Housing - Great Britain - 1991.

1991 Census Key Statistics for Localities in Scotland
General Register Office for Scotland

Key Statistics from the 1991 Census at the locality level in Scotland. A single report presenting a selection of over 170 key statistics, derived mainly from the 1991 Census Small Area Statistics, for 448 localities (urban areas) in Scotland with a population of 1,000 or more and rural parts of Regions. The report includes Ordnance Survey maps showing the boundaries of localities.

Frequency: Decennial
Price: £29.00
ISBN: 0 11 495736 3

Available from
TSO Publications Centre and Bookshops
Please see Annex B for full address details.

Sources from which data for this product are obtained
Census of Population - Scotland; Census of Population and Housing - Great Britain - 1991.

1991 Census Key Statistics for New Health Areas
Office for National Statistics

Key statistics from the 1991 Census for Health Areas. A single report presenting a selection of key statistics for each of the new Health Authorities in England and Wales and Health Boards in Scotland. Around 140 key statistics similar to those covered in the report for local authorities (but excluding the 1981-91 change variables) are given for each of the new health authorities in England and Wales, and for each Health Board in Scotland. Corresponding national figures are given on each page for ready comparison. The tables included cover: population present on Census night; age structure; communal establishments; birthplace and ethnic group; male economic activity; female economic activity; household spaces

and tenure; rooms amenities; household composition; family composition; social class; travel to work and hours worked; occupation groups and higher qualifications; Industry of employment; and area and population density.

Frequency: Decennial
Price: £20.00
ISBN: 0 11 691699 0

Available from
Census Customer Services - ONS or TSO Publications Centre and Bookshops
Please see Annex B for full address details.

Sources from which data for this product are obtained
Census of Population and Housing - Great Britain - 1991.

1991 Census Key Statistics for Urban and Rural Areas - Great Britain
Office for National Statistics

Key statistics from the 1991 Census for urban areas. A set of reports presenting the same selection of 140 or so key statistics for urban areas. These comprise of: a single volume covering over 300 urban areas in Great Britain with a population of 20,000 or more and rural parts of counties, and separate 'regional' reports presenting the same data, additionally, for 2,200 smaller urban areas, grouped geographically into Scotland, the North, the Midlands, the South East, the South West and Wales. The reports will include Ordnance Survey maps showing the boundaries of urban areas.

Frequency: Decennial
ISBN: 0 11 691679 6

Available from
Census Customer Services - ONS or TSO Publications Centre and Bookshops
Please see Annex B for full address details.

Sources from which data for this product are obtained
Census of Population and Housing - Great Britain - 1991.

1991 Census Limiting Long-Term Illness
Office for National Statistics

Figures on 'limiting long-term illness' from the 1991 Census, Great Britain. Contains seven 100 per cent tables, giving results from information collected for the first time in the 1991 Census - mainly at the national level - each giving results by age groups on the long-term ill in: households; communal establishments by type; ethnic groups; and by economic activity, housing tenure and amenities, and household type.

Frequency: Decennial
Price: £16.90
ISBN: 0 11 691515 3

Available from
Census Customer Services - ONS or TSO Publications Centre and Bookshops
Please see Annex B for full address details.

Sources from which data for this product are obtained
Census of Population and Housing - Great Britain - 1991.

1991 Census Local Base Statistics (LBS)
Office for National Statistics

Standard statistical abstracts comprising a dataset of around 20,000 counts (cells) covering the complete range of topics from the 1991 Census. The LBS are the largest dataset on the population in Great Britain available for academic research. LBS are available for the following areas: wards in England and Wales, postcode sectors in Scotland, local authority districts, regional health authorities in England, district health authorities in England and Wales, Health Boards in Scotland, parliamentary and European constituencies, counties/Scottish Regions, standard regions of England, Wales, England & Wales, Scotland and Great Britain.

Frequency: Decennial
Price: Cost varies according to individual requirements. Estimates can be provided on request

Available from
Census Customer Services - ONS
Please see Annex B for full address details.

Sources from which data for this product are obtained
Census of Population and Housing - Great Britain - 1991.

1991 Census Migration
Office for National Statistics

Figures on 'national migration' from the 1991 Census, Great Britain. Published as two separate parts. Part 1 contains twelve 100 per cent tables, including tables of origins and destination and giving distance of moves down to the level of the region and main urban centres. Other tables are at national level and cover the characteristics of migrants and wholly moving households. These are tabulated by type of move, such as moves within (local government) district. In Part 2, the eight 10 per cent tables cover

the socio-economic groups, occupation and industry of migrants, and also tabulate these variables by distance of move. Tables included within Part 1 cover: origins and destinations; age and sex; marital status and age; single years of age and marital status; economic position; migrant households; migrants in households; composition of wholly moving households; migrants in wholly moving households; distance of move; ethnic group; and communal establishments. Tables included within Part 2 cover: origin and SEG (socio-economic group); age and SEG; economic position and employment status; occupation; industry; distance of move and SEG; distance of move and occupation; and distance of move and industry.

Frequency: Decennial
Price: Part 1 £45.40
Part 2 £12.40

ISBN: Pt 1: 0 11 691519 6 Pt 2: 0 11 691585 4

Available from
Census Customer Services - ONS or TSO Publications Centre and Bookshops
Please see Annex B for full address details.

Sources from which data for this product are obtained
Census of Population and Housing - Great Britain - 1991.

1991 Census New Parliamentary Constituency Monitors
Office for National Statistics

Each of the twelve booklets presents similar tables to those appearing in the County Monitor series, plus some additional statistics taken from the 10 percent Local Base Statistics, for each new parliamentary constituency. The booklets cover: resident population and area; residents by age; economic characteristics; tenure and amenities (selected categories); dwellings; household composition (selected categories); ethnic group of residents; young adults (selected categories); pensioners (selected categories); residents (social class); industry and qualifications; Annex A; and the Parliamentary Constituency Index.

Frequency: Periodic
Price: £4.00

Available from
Census Customer Services - ONS
Please see Annex B for full address details.

Sources from which data for this product are obtained
Census of Population and Housing - Great Britain - 1991.

Census News
Office for National Statistics

This product is a newsletter which is published approximately four times during a year. The newsletter provides information on many aspects of the 1991 Census and developments towards the 2001 Census, including details of relevant publications and Census-related activities. The newsletter is a major source of information about the availability of Census results and also reports on the main findings from evaluations of the coverage and quality of the data.

Frequency: Several times a year
Price: Free of charge

Available from
Census Customer Services - ONS
Please see Annex B for full address details.
Census Customer Services - GRO(s)

Sources from which data for this product are obtained
Census of Population and Housing - Great Britain - 1991.

1991 Census Parliamentary Constituencies -Scotland (New)
General Register Office for Scotland

1991 Census, summary figures on population and households in the new parliamentary constituencies in Scotland with effect from General Election 1997. The tables cover: population present 1971 -1991; resident population -1981 base; resident population and area; residents by age; economic characteristics; tenure and amenities; dwellings; household composition; ethnic group of residents; young adults; pensioners; and residents by social class, industry and qualifications. Annex A covers the Parliamentary Constituency Index.

Frequency: Decennial
Price: £4.00
ISBN: 1 85774 215 X

Available from
Peter Jamieson
Room 1/2/9
General Register Office for Scotland
Ladywell House
Ladywell Road
Edinburgh EH12 7TF
Tel: 0131 314 4254;
Email: peter.jamieson@gro-scotland.gov.uk

Sources from which data for this product are obtained
Census of Population - Scotland.

1991 Census Parliamentary Constituencies - Scotland
General Register Office for Scotland

The tables cover: population present 1971 - 1991; resident population -1981 base; resident population and area; residents by age; economic characteristics; tenure and amenities; dwellings; household composition; ethnic group of residents; young adults; unemployed; pensioners; and residents by social class, industry and qualifications. Annex A covers the Parliamentary Constituency Index.

Frequency: Decennial
Price: £2.80
ISBN: 1 874451 40 0

Available from
Peter Jamieson
Room 1/2/9
General Register Office for Scotland
Ladywell House
Ladywell Road
Edinburgh EH12 7TF
Tel: 0131 314 4254;
Email: peter.jamieson@gro-scotland.gov.uk

Sources from which data for this product are obtained
Census of Population - Scotland.

1991 Census Parliamentary Constituency Monitors
Office for National Statistics

Statistics from the 1991 Census for each parliamentary constituency in England (grouped in standard regions), and separately for Wales and Scotland. Each of the ten booklets presents similar tables to those appearing in the County Monitor series, plus some additional statistics taken from the 10 per cent Local Base Statistics, for each parliamentary constituency in Great Britain. The booklets cover: population present 1971 -1991; resident population -1981 base; resident population and area; residents by age; economic characteristics; tenure and amenities; dwellings; household composition; ethnic group of residents; young adults; pensioners; born in Wales/Welsh speakers; and residents by social class, industry and qualifications. Annex A covers the Parliamentary Constituency Index.

Frequency: Decennial
Price: £2.80
ISBN: Various
ISSN: 0144-5537 (series CEN 91 PCM)

Available from
Census Customer Services - ONS or TSO
Publications Centre and Bookshops
Please see Annex B for full address details.

Sources from which data for this product are obtained
Census of Population and Housing - Great Britain - 1991.

1991 Census People and Households in Postcode
Office for National Statistics

Postcode headcounts are available for every postcode in England and Wales. These counts for Households and Population have been extracted from the Enumeration District to Postcode Directory.

Frequency: Ad-hoc
Price: Price on application

Available from
Census Customer Services - ONS
Please see Annex B for full address details.

Sources from which data for this product are obtained
Census of Population and Housing - Great Britain - 1991

1991 Census Persons Aged 60 and Over
Office for National Statistics

Selected data on 'people aged 60 and over' from the 1991 Census, Great Britain. Contains six 100 per cent tables, mostly down to regional level, covering: population, sex, age and marital status; sex, age and long-term illness; persons not in households; 'earners' in households with elderly people; long-term illness in communal establishments; and housing.

Frequency: Decennial
Price: £16.90
ISBN: 0 11 691511 0

Available from
Census Customer Services - ONS or TSO
Publications Centre and Bookshops
Please see Annex B for full address details.

Sources from which data for this product are obtained
Census of Population and Housing - Great Britain - 1991.

1991 Census Postcode Sector Monitors
Office for National Statistics

Summary statistics from the 1991 Census for each postcode town or group of postcode towns. Each of the nineteen booklets presents a selection of a dozen statistics taken from the Small Area Statistics, for each postcode sector throughout Great Britain. Postcode area map included.

Frequency: Decennial
Price: £4.00
ISBN: various
ISSN: 1352-0377 (series CEN 91 PSM)

Available from
Census Customer Services - ONS or TSO
Publications Centre and Bookshops
Please see Annex B for full address details.

Sources from which data for this product are obtained
Census of Population and Housing - Great Britain - 1991.

1991 Census Postcode Sector Monitors Scotland
General Register Office for Scotland

Summary statistics from the 1991 Census for each town or group of postcode towns. Each of the twelve booklets presents a selection of a dozen statistics taken from the Small Area Statistics, for each postcode sector for Regions and their constituent districts.

Frequency: Decennial
Price: Various
ISBN: various

Available from
Peter Jamieson
Room 1/2/9
General Register Office for Scotland
Ladywell House
Ladywell Road
Edinburgh EH12 7TF
Tel: 0131 314 4254;
Email: peter.jamieson@gro-scotland.gov.uk

Sources from which data for this product are obtained
Census of Population - Scotland.

1991 Census Preliminary Report for England and Wales
Office for National Statistics

Initial (unprocessed) figures of the population present on Census night. Contains preliminary population figures for local authority district, London borough, county, and region, and in England and Wales as a whole. Comparative populations for 1961, 1971 and 1981 are included, as well as the hectares in each area in 1991 and an initial count of the number of household spaces. Further tables give: the population of the country and intercensal change for every Census since 1801, and the population of the UK and constituent parts, and for the Isle of Man, Jersey and Guernsey for each Census since 1851, together with intercensal changes.

Frequency: Decennial
Price: £8.00
ISBN: 0 11 691347 9

Available from
Census Customer Services - ONS or TSO
Publications Centre and Bookshops
Please see Annex B for full address details.

Sources from which data for this product are obtained
Census of Population and Housing - Great Britain - 1991.

1991 Census Preliminary Report for Scotland
General Register Office for Scotland

Initial (unprocessed) figures of the population present on Census night in Scotland.

Frequency: Decennial
Price: £3.80
ISBN: 0 11 494180 7

Available from
TSO Publications Centre and Bookshops
Please see Annex B for full address details.

or

Peter Jamieson
Room 1/2/9
General Register Office for Scotland
Ladywell House
Ladywell Road
Edinburgh EH12 7TF
Tel: 0131 314 4254;
Email: peter.jamieson@gro-scotland.gov.uk

Sources from which data for this product are obtained
Census of Population - Scotland.

1991 Census Qualified Manpower
Office for National Statistics

Figures on 'qualified manpower' from the 1991 Census, Great Britain. Contains nineteen tables (all 10 per cent sample) mainly at Great Britain level but with some at regional level, analysing the population aged 18 or over by higher qualifications. The qualified population is grouped into three levels of qualification and further analysed by such topics as occupation, subject of qualification, economic activity and industry. A further set of tables analyses men and women by subject of qualification by current occupation and industry. The tables cover: age and sex; economic position; economic position and age; occupation; industry; subject and age; level of qualification and subject; economic position, subject and age; occupation and subject; occupation, subject and age; industry and subject; industry, subject and age; occupation, industry and subject; occupation and industry, education;

occupation and industry, health, medicine and dentistry; occupation and industry, technology and engineering; occupation and industry, social, administrative and business studies; occupation and industry, science; and occupation and industry: all subjects.

Frequency: Decennial
Price: £37.90
ISBN: 0 11 691586 2

Available from
Census Customer Services - ONS or TSO
Publications Centre and Bookshops
Please see Annex B for full address details.

Sources from which data for this product are obtained
Census of Population and Housing - Great Britain - 1991.

1991 Census Regional Reports Scotland
General Register Office for Scotland

Statistical tables on all topics covered by the 1991 Census at Region level for Scotland. A series of twelve reports (each published in two parts), one for each Region and its constituent Districts based on the 1991 Census. Each regional report presents a full range of output from the Local Base Statistics (the 100 per cent tables in Part 1 and the 10 per cent in Part 2), for each local authority district.

Frequency: Decennial
ISBN: Various

Available from
TSO Publications Centre and Bookshops
Please see Annex B for full address details.

or

Peter Jamieson
Room 1/2/9
General Register Office for Scotland
Ladywell House
Ladywell Road
Edinburgh EH12 7TF
Tel: 0131 314 4254;
Email: peter.jamieson@gro-scotland.gov.uk

Sources from which data for this product are obtained
Census of Population - Scotland; Census of Population and Housing - Great Britain - 1991.

1991 Census Report for England, Regional Health Authorities
Office for National Statistics

Summary statistics for England from 1991 Census. Contains statistical tables for England and Regional Health Authorities in England from the 1991 Census. Part 1 gives the full range of Census statistics taken from

100 per cent of Census returns. Part 2 gives socio-economic characteristics based on a 10 per cent sample of Census returns. Because of processing difficulties encountered in translating migration flows between local authority district-based areas to flows between health authority district-based areas, this Report was produced without tables 15,16 and 96 from the standard set of LBS. Inclusion of these tables, which show migrant flows for residents, wholly moving households and members of the armed forces, would have seriously delayed the publication of this Report. Instead, these three tables were produced around Spring 1994 and published as a supplement to the Report. (A companion Monitor is available from ONS, priced £2.00.)

Frequency: Decennial
Price: Part 1 £47.00, Part 2 £31.00
ISBN: 0 11 691558 7 (Part 1), 0 11 691559 5 (Part 2)

Available from

Census Customer Services - ONS or TSO
Publications Centre and Bookshops
Please see Annex B for full address details.

Sources from which data for this product are obtained
Census of Population and Housing - Great Britain -1991.

1991 Census Report for Great Britain
Office for National Statistics

Summary statistics for Great Britain from the 1991 Census. Part 1 contains results based on 100 per cent Census returns. Part 2 contains further analysis of a 10 per cent sample of returns. Contains 1991 Census summary statistics for Great Britain for the following main topics in Part 1: demographic and economic characteristics, housing, households and household composition, household spaces and dwellings, Welsh language (in Wales only) and Gaelic (Scotland only). Part 2 covers economic and employment status, occupation, industry, travel to work, qualified manpower, family type (based on a 10 per cent sample of Census returns). Results are given for standard regions, metropolitan counties and regional remainders in England, Scotland and Wales.

Frequency: Decennial
Price: Part 1 £85.00, Part 2 £40.00
ISBN: 0 11 691536 6 (Part 1), 0 11 691526 9 (Part 2)

Available from
Census Customer Services - ONS or TSO
Publications Centre and Bookshops
Please see Annex B for full address details.

Sources from which data for this product are obtained
Census of Population and Housing - Great Britain - 1991.

1991 Census Report for New Towns Scotland
General Register Office for Scotland

Statistical tables on all topics covered by the 1991 Census for New Towns in Scotland. This report (published in two parts) presents a full range of output from the Local Base Statistics (the 100 per cent tables in Part 1 and the 10 per cent in Part 2) for each of the five New Towns in Scotland.

Frequency: Decennial
Price: £53.00 (Parts 1 and 2 not sold separately)
ISBN: 0 11 495224 8

Available from

TSO Publications Centre and Bookshops
Please see Annex B for full address details.

Sources from which data for this product are obtained
Census of Population - Scotland.

1991 Census Report for Scotland
General Register Office for Scotland

Statistical tables on all topics covered by the 1991 Census for Scotland. This report (published in two parts) presents a full range of output from the Local Base Statistics (the 100 per cent tables in Part 1 and the 10 per cent in Part 2) for each local authority region.

Frequency: Decennial
Price: Part 1 £65.00, Part 2 £33.00
ISBN: 0 11 495119 5 (Part 1), 0 11 495120 9 (Part 2)

Available from
TSO Publications Centre and Bookshops
Please see Annex B for full address details.

Sources from which data for this product are obtained
Census of Population - Scotland; Census of Population and Housing - Great Britain - 1991.

1991 Census Report for Wales (Adroddiad Cymru)
Office for National Statistics (then OPCS)

Summary statistics for Wales from 1991 Census covering demographic, social & economic data including tables on ethnicity, limiting long-term illness, lone parents and the Welsh language. Part 1 gives the full range of Census statistics taken from 100 per cent of Census returns. Part 2 gives socio-economic characteristics based on a 10 per cent sample of Census returns. Information in both volumes is produced for Wales and the former eight counties.

Frequency: Decennial
Price: Part 1 £40.00, Part 2 £29.00
ISBN: 0 11 691554 4 (Part 1), 0 11 691562 5 (Part 2)

Available from
TSO Publications Centre and Bookshops
Please see Annex B for full address details.

Sources from which data for this product are obtained
Census of Population and Housing - Great Britain - 1991.

1991 Census Residents and Workers
Office for National Statistics

This dataset is a sub-set of the Special Workplace Statistics (SWS) for England and Wales. The counts extracted show those resident and working in the same zone, residents travelling out of the zone to work and workers travelling into the zone to work.

Frequency: Ad-hoc
Price: Price on application

Available from
Census Customer Services - ONS
Please see Annex B for full address details.

Sources from which data for this product are obtained
Census of Population and Housing - Great Britain - 1991.

Records
Office for National Statistics

Samples of Anonymised Records (SARs), known more commonly in other countries as Census Microdata or Public Use Samples, are abstracts of individual Census records (confidentiality of individuals and households is protected). SARs from the 1991 Census of Great Britain database are available in two forms: a 2 per cent sample of individuals in households and communal establishments; and a 1 per cent hierarchical sample of households and individuals in those households. The 2 per cent SAR contain some 1.12 million individual records, selected from the population base which lists persons at their place of enumeration. Details indicate whether or not the person was a usual resident, and, if in a household, whether they were present or absent on Census night. The following other information is given for each sampled individual: details on the full range of Census characteristics from sex/age/marital status through ethnic group, economic position and limiting long-term illness to so-called derived variables such as social class and socio-economic group; details about the accommodation in which the individual was enumerated (such as tenure and availability of amenities/car) or, if they were in a communal establishment, the type of establishment; information about the sex, economic position and social class of the individual's family head; and limited information about other members of the individual's household (such as the number of persons with long-term illness and number of pensioners). The 1 per cent SAR contain some 240,000 household records together with sub-records - one for each person in a selected household. Information is available about the household's accommodation together with information (similar to that in the 2 per cent sample) about each individual in the household and how they are related to the head of the household.

Frequency: Decennial
Price: Cost varies according to individual requirements

Available from
Census Customer Services - ONS
Please see Annex B for full address details.

Sources from which data for this product are obtained
Census of Population and Housing - Great Britain - 1991.

1991 Census Scotland Summary Monitor
General Register Office for Scotland

A summary booklet showing key statistics on population and housing for Regions in Scotland taken from the 1991 Census.

Frequency: Decennial
Price: £2.00
ISBN: 1 874451 12 5

Available from
Peter Jamieson
Room 1/2/9
General Register Office for Scotland
Ladywell House
Ladywell Road
Edinburgh EH12 7TF
Tel: 0131 314 4254;
Email: peter.jamieson@gro-scotland.gov.uk

Sources from which data for this product are obtained
Census of Population - Scotland; Census of Population and Housing - Great Britain - 1991.

1991 Census Sex, Age and Marital Status
Office for National Statistics

Figures from the 1991 Census for sex, age and marital status, Great Britain. Contains three 100 per cent tables giving: marital status by sex and age in single years of age; similar figures with quinary age groups down to county/Scottish Region level; and sex by single year of age 0-24 down to county/Scottish Region level.

Frequency: Decennial
Price: £19.00
ISBN: 0 11 691508 0

Available from
Census Customer Services - ONS or TSO Publications Centre and Bookshops
Please see Annex B for full address details.

Sources from which data for this product are obtained
Census of Population and Housing - Great Britain - 1991.

1991 Census Small Area Statistics (SAS)
Office for National Statistics

Statistical abstracts - an abbreviated version of the Local Base Statistics (see above) comprising more than 9,000 counts, available for the same areas as LBS for some smaller areas. 1991 Census data available for the same areas as the LBS but also for the following smaller areas: enumeration districts in England and Wales, output areas in Scotland, civil parishes (in England and Scotland), communities in Wales, Scottish localities, inhabited islands, new towns, regional electoral divisions, postcode sectors in England and Wales.

Frequency: Decennial
Price: Varies according to individual requirements. Estimates can be provided on request.

Available from
Census Customer Services - ONS
Please see Annex B for full address details.

Sources from which data for this product are obtained
Census of Population and Housing - Great Britain - 1991.

1991 Census Special Migration Statistics (SMS)
Office for National Statistics

Customised analysis of the Census questions on 'usual address one year before the Census' which provides information on

migrants within and between local areas. SMS are available for local authority districts for most counts, and for wards (in England and Wales) and postcode sectors (in Scotland) for the less detailed counts. The tables cover: all migrants by age by sex; wholly moving households and residents in wholly moving households; all migrants: age (5 year groups) by sex; all migrants: marital status by sex; all migrants: ethnic group; all migrants: whether resident in households by whether suffering limiting long-term illness; all migrants aged 16+: economic position; wholly moving households: tenure; wholly moving households: sex and economic position of head; residents in wholly moving households: sex and economic position of head; and all migrants: Gaelic or Welsh speakers. Machine-readable media only.

Frequency: Decennial
Price: Varies according to individual requirements. Estimates can be provided on request.

Available from
Census Customer Services - ONS
Please see Annex B for full address details.

Sources from which data for this product are obtained
Census of Population and Housing - Great Britain - 1991.

1991 Census Special Migration Statistics (SMS) - Scotland
General Register Office for Scotland

Customised analysis of the Census question on 'usual address one year before the Census' which provides information on migrants within and between local areas. Some of the data in this product is disaggregated by gender.

Frequency: Decennial
Price: Standard Charge £274, then varying costs per area

Available from
Peter Jamieson
Room 1/2/8
General Register Office for Scotland
Ladywell House
Ladywell Road
Edinburgh EH12 7TF
Tel: 0131 314 4254;
Email: peter.jamieson@gro-scotland.gov.uk

Sources from which data for this product are obtained
Census of Population and Housing - Great Britain - 1991.

1991 Census Special Workplace Statistics
Office for National Statistics

Customised analysis of the Census questions on 'usual address one year before the Census' (10 per cent sample only). Special Workplace Statistics provide information on workforces in area workplace and residence for customer-defined zones, and on journeys from areas of residence to workplace between zones. Customers may specify zones in terms of enumeration districts or postcodes, in England and Wales, and Output Areas, in Scotland. The tables cover: economic position and age; hours worked and family position; type of workplace i.e. working within zone, workplace at home; distance to work; transport to work i.e. car, bus etc; cars available in household; occupation (sub-major group); social class and socio-economic group; and Industry divisions and classes (Sets A & B); Industry divisions (Set C). Machine-readable media only.

Frequency: Decennial
Price: Varies according to individual requirements. Estimates can be provided on request.

Available from
Census Customer Services - ONS
Please see Annex B for full address details.

Sources from which data for this product are obtained
Census of Population and Housing - Great Britain - 1991.

1991 Census Supplementary Monitor on People Sleeping Rough
Office for National Statistics

Booklet presenting preliminary counts of the numbers of people sleeping rough on Census night for local authority areas in England and Wales. A wide range of abstracts of Census data can be obtained direct from the Census Offices, rather than through the published reports described above. These abstracts are produced and made available by the Census Offices to customers on request and for a charge, under Section 4.2 of the 1920 Census Act.

Frequency: Decennial
Price: £2.00
ISBN: 0 90 495269 X

Available from
Census Customer Services - ONS or TSO Publications Centre and Bookshops
Please see Annex B for full address details.

Sources from which data for this product are obtained
Census of Population and Housing - Great Britain - 1991.

1991 Census Table 100
Office for National Statistics

At the date of the 1991 Census (21st April) not all residential schools and colleges were in term-time and many students resident in such establishments were enumerated at their home address. A complete GB matrix of districts of students' usual residence by the district of term-time address, by sex and age produced as two separate tables: 1. a base of resident students for every local authority district (LGD)1; and 2. a base of present students who are resident outside GB for every LGD.

Frequency: Ad-hoc
Price: price on application

Available from
Census Customer Services - ONS
Please see Annex B for full address details.

Sources from which data for this product are obtained
Census of Population and Housing - Great Britain - 1991

1991 Census Topic Monitors
Office for National Statistics

Most Topic Statistics Reports are preceded by the publication of corresponding Topic Monitors, which present the key findings for each topic, illustrated with maps and charts. Topic Monitors cover Great Britain, the contents vary according to topic.

Frequency: Decennial
Price: £2.00 per monitor
ISSN: 0969-0204

Available from
Census Customer Services - ONS or TSO Publications Centre and Bookshops
Please see Annex B for full address details.

Sources from which data for this product are obtained
Census of Population and Housing - Great Britain - 1991.

1991 Census Topics Report for Health Areas
Office for National Statistics

The report contains 21 tables at the English regional health authority area level, plus Scotland and Wales, covering a range of 100 per cent topics. The tables cover: sex, age and marital status; persons aged 60 and over; under 16s; students and schoolchildren; economic position; ethnic group (full and summary classifications); ethnic group and age; ethnic group, long-term illness and economic position; ethnic group of migrants to UK; distance of move of migrants; long-term illness of residents in households; long-term illness and ethnic group; long-term illness and household composition; communal establishment size (number of persons); type of communal establishment; long-term illness in communal establishments; tenure and age of residents; tenure and amenities; cars and pensioners; household composition and housing; and household space type and dwellings. All the tables are to be published for the following areas: Great Britain, England, Regional Health Authority Areas, Wales, Scotland.

Frequency: Decennial,
Price: £45.00
ISBN: 0 11 691567 6

Available from
Census Customer Services - ONS or TSO Publications Centre and Bookshops
Please see Annex B for full address details.

Sources from which data for this product are obtained
Census of Population and Housing - Great Britain - 1991; Ethnic Group and Birthplace - GB.

(The) 1991 Census User Guides
Office for National Statistics

Documentation to assist Census users to obtain and better understand the wide range of Census outputs. These are generally issued on request from Customer Services free of charge. A catalogue of current User Guides is also available. User Guides take the form of prospectuses, file specifications and area constitutions. Constitution User Guides are available on electronic media.

Frequency: Ad hoc
Price: Free

Available from
Census Customer Services - ONS
Please see Annex B for full address details.

(The) 1991 Census Users' Guide
Office for National Statistics

This definitive introduction to the 1991 Census covers all aspects of Census activities, from enumeration and data collection through to the newest forms of output available for analysis. Edited by Angela Dale and the late Catherine Marsh, the Guide also explains fully the geography of the Census and includes a discussion of developments over time. The volume provides some historical background to census-taking and gives a consideration of the ethical and confidentiality issues. Intended as a source book for anyone with an interest in using Census statistics, the Guide will be particularly helpful to teachers and students in the social sciences. It also forms a well-indexed manual for research workers.

Frequency: Ad hoc
Price: £19.80
ISBN: 0 11 691527 7

Available from
Census Customer Services - ONS
Please see Annex B for full address details.

Sources from which data for this product are obtained
Census of Population - Northern Ireland; Census of Population and Housing - Great Britain - 1991.

1991 Census Usual Residence
Office for National Statistics

Figures on area of 'usual residence' from the 1991 Census. Contains six 100 per cent tables down to local government district level which show the usual resident counts on which the 1991 Census results are based, together with figures of students and schoolchildren by area of usual residence and term-time address, and visitors by country of usual residence.

Frequency: Decennial
Price: £22.80
ISBN: 0 11 691510 2

Available from
Census Customer Services - ONS or TSO Publications Centre and Bookshops
Please see Annex B for full address details.

Sources from which data for this product are obtained
Census of Population and Housing - Great Britain - 1991.

1991 Census Validation Survey: Coverage Report
Office for National Statistics

This report assesses the coverage of the 1991 Census (i.e. the proportion of the population who were successfully enumerated) as shown by the Census Validation Survey (CVs). CVs findings are compared to Census results and preliminary estimates of net under-coverage are given. As well as the coverage results, it contains information on the Census Validation Survey methodology, and an account of the way the Census population figures were adjusted to arrive at the official mid-year population estimates made by the Registrar General.

Frequency: Ad hoc
Price: £11.60
ISBN: 0 11 691591 9 (series SS 1334)

Available from
TSO Publications Centre and Bookshops
Please see Annex B for full address details.

1991 Census Welsh Language
Office for National Statistics

Figures on 'Welsh language in Wales' from the 1991 Census. Contains nine tables (five 100 per cent and four 10 per cent sample tables), mainly at Wales or county level, covering: trends since 1921; speaking, reading and writing Welsh by age group; Welsh-speaking migrants and other migrants; Welsh speakers by household and family composition; and Welsh speakers by economic position, occupation, social class and higher qualifications.

Frequency: Decennial
Price: £19.70
ISBN: 0 11 691575 7

Available from
Census Customer Services - ONS
Please see Annex B for full address details.

Sources from which data for this product are obtained
Census of Population and Housing - Great Britain - 1991.

1991 Census Workplace and Transport to Work
Office for National Statistics

Figures on 'workplace and transport to work' from the 1991 Census. Published in separate volumes for Great Britain and Scotland, each containing eight tables with the same outlines but, while some tables in the Great Britain report are at regional level, all tables in the Scotland report go down to (local government) district level. Figures are also given for city centres and other major centres of employment. The tables cover: resident and working populations; area of workplace by area of residence; area of residence by area of workplace; means of travel to work; distance and travel to work; and car availability by means of travel to work.

Frequency Decennial
Price: £75.00
ISBN: 0 11 691522 6

Available from
Census Customer Services - ONS or TSO Publications Centre and Bookshops
Please see Annex B for full address details.

Sources from which data for this product are obtained
Census of Population and Housing - Great Britain - 1991.

1991 Census Workplace and Transport to Work - Scotland
General Register Office for Scotland

1991 Census topic report (10% sample) on Workplace and Transport to work. All tables give data for each Region and District in Scotland. Data includes: Area of Workplace and Residence, Occupation and Industry, Social class and socio-economic group, Distance and transport to work and car availability of Residents and workers.

Frequency Decennial
Price: £41.00
ISBN: 0 11 495264 7

Available from
TSO Publications Centre and Bookshops
Please see Annex B for full address details.

Sources from which data for this product are obtained
Census of Population - Scotland

Disabled Persons Statistical Data - Second Edition
Eurostat

This forms part of Eurostat's Population and Social Conditions theme (Theme 3), Series D: Studies and research. This study aims to provide the reader with statistics for a better understanding of the situation of the disabled with a view to fulfilling their needs and thus contributing to an improvement in the forming of policies in their favour. Additionally it can serve as a basis from improving the methods of statistical collection as well as the content of the data, leading to a better statistical tool.

Frequency Ad hoc
ISBN: 92 826 9652 9

Available from
TSO Publications Centre and Bookshops
Please see Annex B for full address details.

Ethnicity in the 1991 Census, Volume 1 : Demographic Characteristics of the Ethnic Minority Populations
Office for National Statistics

This book is the first of a four-volume series which records the results of a significant innovation in the British census - the introduction of a direct question on ethnic origin. Edited by leading specialists in the

field, and with contributions from a wide range of researchers and academics, the series provides comprehensive analyses on a variety of aspects of the different ethnic minority populations. The theme of this first volume is the demographic characteristics of the ethnic minority populations: their size and growth, immigration patterns, age structure and ageing, marriage patterns, and household and family structure. There is a separate chapter on the indigenous and older minorities. Other chapters review the development of the ethnic group question and its effectiveness in identifying the main ethnic minority groups, and the effect of non-response to the 1991 Census on ethnic group enumeration.

Frequency One-off
Price: £25.00
ISBN: 0 11 691655 9

Available from
TSO Publications Centre and Bookshops
Please see Annex B for full address details.

Sources from which data for this product are obtained
Census of Population and Housing - Great Britain - 1991.

Ethnicity in the 1991 Census, Volume 2 : The Ethnic Minority Populations of Great Britain
Office for National Statistics

This book is the second of a four-volume series which records the results of a significant innovation in the British census - the introduction of a direct question on ethnic origin. Edited by leading specialists in the field, and with contributions from a wide range of researchers and academics, the series provides comprehensive analyses on a variety of aspects of the different ethnic minority populations. This second volume presents a collection of ten profiles of the main ethnic minority groups, and the Irish-born, identified by the 1991 Census of Great Britain. The profiles describe the demographic and geographic structure of each group, and their social and economic characteristics.

Frequency One-off
Price: £24.00
ISBN: 0 11 691656 7

Available from
TSO Publications Centre and Bookshops
Please see Annex B for full address details.

Sources from which data for this product are obtained
Census of Population and Housing - Great Britain - 1991.

Ethnicity in the 1991 Census, Volume 3 : Social Geography and Ethnicity in Britain: Geographical Spread, Spatial Concentration and Internal Migration
Office for National Statistics

This book is the third of a four-volume series which records the results of a significant innovation in the British census - the introduction of a direct question on ethnic origin. Edited by leading specialists in the field, and with contributions from a wide range of researchers and academics, the series provides comprehensive analyses on a variety of aspects of the different ethnic minority populations. This third volume examines the ethnic geography of Great Britain. Part 1 describes the broad national patterns of ethnic settlement. Part 2 looks in detail at the three major areas of ethnic minority settlement. Some of the policy implications of spatial segregation and concentration on the basis of ethnicity or 'race' are also discussed. The book will be of particular interest to social scientists and policy analysts wishing to understand the changing ethnic geography of contemporary Britain.

Frequency One-off
Price: £27.50
ISBN: 0 11 691657 5

Available from
TSO Publications Centre and Bookshops
Please see Annex B for full address details.

Sources from which data for this product are obtained
Census of Population and Housing - Great Britain - 1991

Ethnicity in the 1991 Census, Volume 4 : Employment, Education and Housing Among the Ethnic Minority Populations of Britain
Office for National Statistics

This book is the fourth of a four-volume series which records the results of a significant innovation in the British census - the introduction of a direct question on ethnic origin. Edited by leading specialists in the field, and with contributions from a wide range of researchers and academics, the series provides comprehensive analyses on a variety of aspects of the different ethnic minority populations. This fourth volume explores the relative situations of the different minority ethnic groups in respect of their patterns of education, employment and housing - three inter-related factors which contribute considerably to the material quality of life. The book will be of

particular interest to social scientists and policy makers.

Frequency One-off
Price: £29.95
ISBN: 0 11 691658 3

Available from
TSO Publications Centre and Bookshops
Please see Annex B for full address details.

Sources from which data for this product are obtained
Census of Population and Housing - Great Britain - 1991.

Health Inequalities Data Diskette
Office for National Statistics

Diskette containing population and mortality data from the volume Health Inequalities Decennial Supplement, with some additional and extended datasets. The diskette contains a set of data tables providing supplementary information on health inequalities. Includes deaths data for men and women aged 20-64, by five year age group and social class, for years 1991-93; population data by five year age group for men and women by social class for mid-1991.

Delivery: First Release
Frequency: Ad-hoc
Price: £25.00

Available from
ONS Direct
Please see Annex B for full address details.

Sources from which data for this product are obtained
Census of Population and Housing - Great Britain - 1991; General Household Survey - GB; Health Survey for England; Registration of Births - England and Wales; Registration of Deaths - England and Wales; The ONS Longitudinal Study

---

Health Inequalities Decennial Supplement
Office for National Statistics

Health Inequalities is a comprehensive volume of analysis and commentary which presents a picture of current patterns and recent trends in ill health and death in England and Wales by measures of socio-economic status. People living in different socio-economic environments face very different risks of ill health and death. In general, those at the bottom of the social scale have much poorer health than those higher up. The volume covers inequalities in expectation of life, mortality, morbidity, and health-related behaviours amongst both adults and children, and for different migrant groups as well as presenting historical and

international findings. The volume draws on a wide range of data sources to present a picture of patterns and trends in ill-health and death. The 16 chapters combine both summary and detailed commentary with tables and figures, and comprehensive references for further reading. Some of the data in this product are disaggregated by gender.

Frequency Ten yearly (decennial)
Price: £35.00
ISBN: 0 11 620942 9

Available from
TSO Publications Centre and Bookshops
Please see Annex B for full address details.

Sources from which data for this product are obtained
Census of Population and Housing - Great Britain - 1991; General Household Survey - GB; Health Survey for England; Registration of Births - England and Wales; Registration of Deaths - England and Wales; The ONS Longitudinal Study

---

Key Population Statistics 1991-1994: Welsh Unitary Authorities
Office for National Statistics and the National Assembly for Wales

A publication providing a selection of 140 key statistics derived from the 1991 Census together with population estimates and key vital statistics for the period 1991-1994 for the unitary authorities of Wales - which came into effect on 1 April 1996 under the Local Government (Wales) Act 1994. The tables cover: population present on Census night and resident population; age structure; communal establishments, long-term illness and migrants; birthplace, ethnic group and Welsh language; male economic activity; female economic activity; household spaces and tenure; rooms, amenities, central heating and cars; household composition; family composition; social class (based on occupation); travel to work and hours worked; occupation groups and higher qualifications; Industry of employment; estimated resident population by sex and age group; population change 1991-92 to 1993-94; fertility; and mortality.

Delivery: One off
Price: £25.00
ISBN: 0 11 691659 1

Available from
Census Customer Services - ONS
Please see Annex B for full address details.

Sources from which data for this product are obtained
Census of Population and Housing - Great Britain - 1991

1991 Local Base Statistics (LBS)
General Register Office for Scotland

Standard statistical abstracts comprising a dataset of around 20,000 counts (cells) covering the complete range of topics from the 1991 Census. Some of the data in this product is disaggregated by gender.

Delivery: Ad Hoc/One-off Release
Frequency: Decennial
Price: Standard charge £59.00 then £4.27 per area

Available from
Peter Jamieson
Room 1/2/8
General Register Office for Scotland
Ladywell House
Ladywell Road
Edinburgh EH12 7TF
Tel: 0131 314 4254;
Email: peter.jamieson@gro-scotland.gov.uk

Sources from which data for this product are obtained
Census of Population - Scotland.

New Local Government Area Monitor Key Population Statistics 1991-1996
Office for National Statistics

Covers unitary authorities and two-tier counties in England coming into effect on 1 April 1998. This monitor contains a selection of 1991 Census statistics and estimates of the mid-year population and some summary vital event statistics for the years 1991-1996, for those reorganised English local authorities which came into effect on 1 April 1998 under the terms of the Local Government Act 1992. The tables cover: population and area; residents by age; economic characteristics; tenure and amenities: selected categories; dwellings; household composition: selected categories; ethnic group of residents; young adults: selected categories; pensioners: selected categories; estimated resident population; fertility; and mortality.

Frequency One-off
Price: £5.50
ISSN: 1462 4893

Available from
Census Customer Services - ONS
Please see Annex B for full address details.

Sources from which data for this product are obtained
Census of Population and Housing - Great Britain - 1991

New Local Government Area Monitor Key Population Statistics 1991-1994
Office for National Statistics

Covers unitary authorities and two-tier counties in England coming into effect on 1 April 1996. This monitor contains a selection of 1991 Census statistics and estimates of the mid-year population and some summary vital event statistics for the years 1991-1994 for those re-organised English local authorities which came into effect on 1 April 1996 under the terms of the Local Government Act 1992. The tables cover: population and area; residents by age; economic characteristics; tenure and amenities: selected categories; dwellings; household composition: selected categories; ethnic group of residents; young adults: selected categories; pensioners: selected categories; estimated resident population; fertility; and mortality.

Delivery: Ad Hoc/One-off Release
ISSN: 1363 1462

Available from
Census Customer Services - ONS
Please see Annex B for full address details.

Sources from which data for this product are obtained
Census of Population and Housing - Great Britain - 1991

New Local Government Area Monitor Key Population Statistics 1991-1995
Office for National Statistics

Covers unitary authorities and two-tier counties in England coming into effect on 1 April 1997. This monitor contains a selection of 1991 Census statistics and estimates of the mid-year population and some summary vital event statistics for the years 1991-1995, for those re-organised English local authorities which came into effect on 1 April 1997 under the terms of the Local Government Act 1992. The tables cover: population and area; residents by age; economic characteristics; tenure and amenities: selected categories; dwellings; household composition: selected categories; ethnic group of residents; young adults: selected categories; pensioners: selected categories; estimated resident population; fertility; and mortality.

Delivery: Ad Hoc/One-off Release
Frequency: One-off
ISSN: 1363 1462

Available from
Census Customer Services - ONS
Please see Annex B for full address details.

Sources from which data for this product are obtained
Census of Population and Housing - Great Britain - 1991

Northern Ireland Census: Economic Activity Report
Northern Ireland Statistics and Research Agency

Topic report of the Northern Ireland Population Census with socio-economic details. Contains data on economically active and inactive populations. The former is analysed by industry and occupational groupings divided into age, marital status, employment status, socio-economic groups and areas of workplace. Some local government district data are available.

Frequency Decennial
Price: £16.25
ISBN: 0 337 07752 5

Available from
TSO Publications Centre and Bookshops
Please see Annex B for full address details.

Sources from which data for this product are obtained
Census of Population - Northern Ireland.

Northern Ireland Census: Education Report
Northern Ireland Statistics and Research Agency

Topic report of the Northern Ireland Population Census with socio-economic details. The report contains educational, professional and vocational qualifications by age, sex, occupation and industry.

Frequency Decennial
Price: £8.00
ISBN: 0 337 07756 8

Available from
TSO Publications Centre and Bookshops
Please see Annex B for full address details.

Sources from which data for this product are obtained
Census of Population - Northern Ireland.

Northern Ireland Census: Housing and Household Composition Report
Northern Ireland Statistics and Research Agency

Topic report of the Northern Ireland Population Census with socio-economic details. The report contains data on the composition, social and economic characteristics of households by tenure, housing density, car availability, sex, age and marital status.

Frequency Decennial
Price: £19.25
ISBN: 0 337 07754 1

Available from
TSO Publications Centre and Bookshops
Please see Annex B for full address details.

Sources from which data for this product are obtained
Census of Population - Northern Ireland.

Northern Ireland Census: Irish Language Report
Northern Ireland Statistics and Research Agency

Topic report of the Northern Ireland Population Census with socio-economic details. The report contains tables on spoken, written and reading knowledge with cross-tabulations by age, sex, marital status, occupation, industry and socio-economic group.

Frequency Decennial
Price: £8.00
ISBN: 0 337 07757 6

Available from
TSO Publications Centre and Bookshops
Please see Annex B for full address details.

Sources from which data for this product are obtained
Census of Population - Northern Ireland.

Northern Ireland Census: Migration Report
Northern Ireland Statistics and Research Agency

Topic report of the Northern Ireland Population Census with socio-economic details. The report contains data on migrant characteristics by age, sex and marital status. There are flow matrices for local government districts showing current residence by residence one year ago detailing intra-local government district moves and migrants from outside Northern Ireland. Civilian and military moves are not distinguished.

Frequency Decennial
Price: £8.75
ISBN: 0 337 07755 X

Available from
TSO Publications Centre and Bookshops
Please see Annex B for full address details.

Sources from which data for this product are obtained
Census of Population - Northern Ireland.

Northern Ireland Census: Summary Report
Northern Ireland Statistics and Research Agency

Topic report of the Northern Ireland Population Census with socio-economic details. The report contains data on population change, age distribution, sex, marital status, birthplace, religion, households, tenure, amenities, density of occupation and private vehicles for Northern Ireland and each district council. Data are available by wards, total population, long-term illness, students, private households, unoccupied dwellings, rooms, and towns with a minimum population of 1,000.

Frequency Decennial
Price: £16.25
ISBN: 0337 077495

Available from
TSO Publications Centre and Bookshops
Please see Annex B for full address details.

Sources from which data for this product are obtained
Census of Population - Northern Ireland.

Northern Ireland Census: Workplace and Transport to Work Report
Northern Ireland Statistics and Research Agency

Topic report of the Northern Ireland Population Census with socio-economic details. The report contains data on the economically active population by area of residence and area of workplace. The main workplace movements are given at the level of local government district and include means of transport to work, socio-economic group, occupation and industrial classifications.

Frequency Decennial
Price: £8.00
ISBN: 0 337 07753 3

Available from
TSO Publications Centre and Bookshops
Please see Annex B for full address details.

Sources from which data for this product are obtained
Census of Population - Northern Ireland.

ONS Classification of Wards
Office for National Statistics

The Ward classification was created in the same way as the published Local and Health Authority Classification by using selected Local Base variables from the 1991 Census.

A complete list of the variables is available on request. Available only on electronic media. Supplied electronically in spreadsheet format. Each Ward/Postcode Sector has been allocated a Group and Cluster name and these are listed in the electronic file, together with the values from each of the variables used to determine into which Group/Cluster each Ward/PS belongs.

Frequency Ad-hoc
Price: on application

Available from
Census Customer Services - ONS
Please see Annex B for full address details.

Portrait of the Islands
Eurostat

This publication provides information on all inhabited islands of the EU. It shows where they all are and describes their special living conditions and economic situations.

Frequency Ad hoc
Price: £21.00

Available from
Bob Dodds.
Please see Annex B for full address details.

1991 Small Area Statistics (SAS)
General Register Office for Scotland

Statistical abstracts - an abbreviated version of Local Base Statistics comprising more than 9,000 counts,

Delivery: Ad Hoc/One-off Release
Frequency: decennial
Price: Standard charge £59.00 then £2.28 per area for lower levels and £3.03 for higher levels

Available from
Peter Jamieson
Room 1/2/9
General Register Office for Scotland
Ladywell House
Ladywell Road
Edinburgh EH12 7TF
Tel: 0131 314 4254;
Email: peter.jamieson@gro-scotland.gov.uk

Sources from which data for this product are obtained
Census of Population - Scotland.

1991 Special Workplace Statistics (SWS)
General Register Office for Scotland

Customised analysis of the Census questions on 'usual address one year before Census (10% sample). Special Workplace Statistics provide information on workforces in area of workplace and residence for customer defined zones, and on journeys from areas of residence to workplace between zones.

Delivery: Ad Hoc/One-off Release
Frequency: Decennial
Price: Standard charge of £520.00, then varying costs per area

Available from
Peter Jamieson
Room 1/2/8
General Register Office for Scotland
Ladywell House
Ladywell Road
Edinburgh EH12 7TF
Tel: 0131 314 4254;
Email: peter.jamieson@gro-scotland.gov.uk

Urban Areas Analysis
Department of the Environment, Transport and the Regions

Analysis of census data by urban area. Target market: Department of the Environment, Transport and the Regions, Government Offices for the Regions, researchers undertaking work for the Department. Contains summaries of census variables by size of urban area, in tables or maps.

Frequency Ad-hoc

Available from
Stephen Hall
DETR
Room E3/J10
Eland House
Bressenden Place
London
Tel: 020 7890 5514;
Email: shall.detr@gtnet.gov.uk

Sources from which data for this product are obtained
Urban areas analysis

Ward and Civil Parish Monitors (England) Ward and Community Monitors (Wales)
Office for National Statistics

Summary statistics from the 1991 Census at ward and civil parish level in England and Wales. A series of 54 booklets, one for each county, presenting some 30 statistics taken from the 1991 Census Small Area Statistics (mainly expressed as percentages but with some counts) for each Ward and Civil Parish within England, and Community for Wales. Each monitor contains statistics for Great Britain, the relevant County and Local Government District supplementary to the Wards and Civil Parishes. Counts are provided for the following: persons present - 1981 and 1991, area in Hectares, residents by sex, households. Percentage counts are provided for the following: percentage

increase/decrease 81-91, residents aged under 16, pensionable age to 75yrs, 75 & over, limiting long-term illness, ethnic groups other than white, migrants, women aged 16-59 in employment, owner occupied households, rented from a local authority, pensioner only households, single person households, households with one person aged 16 & over with child(ren) aged 0-15, with no car, with 2 or more cars.

Frequency Decennial
Price: £2.40
ISBN: various
ISSN: 0144-5537 (series CEN 91 WCP)

Available from
Census Customer Services - ONS
Please see Annex B for full address details.

Sources from which data for this product are obtained
Census of Population and Housing - Great Britain - 1991.

Ward and Civil Parish Monitors Scotland
General Register Office for Scotland

Summary statistics from the 1991 Census at ward and parish level in Scotland. A series of twelve booklets, one for each Region, presenting some statistics taken from the 1991 Census Small Area Statistics (mainly expressed as percentages but with some counts) for each ward and civil parish. Each monitor contains statistics for Great Britain, the relevant County and Local Government District supplementary to the Wards and Civil Parishes. Counts are provided for the following: persons present - 1981 and 1991, area in hectares, residents by sex, households. Percentage counts are provided for the following: percentage increase/decrease 81-91, residents aged under 16, pensionable age to 75yrs, 75 & over, limiting long-term illness, ethnic groups other than white, migrants, women aged 16-59 in employment, owner occupied households, rented from a local authority, pensioner only households, single person households, households with one person aged 16 & over with child(ren) aged 0-15, with no car, with 2 or more cars.

Frequency Decennial
Price: £2.40 each
ISBN: various

Available from
Peter Jamieson
Room 1/2/9
General Register Office for Scotland
Ladywell House
Ladywell Road
Edinburgh EH12 7TF
Tel: 0131 314 4254;
Email: peter.jamieson@gro-scotland.gov.uk

Sources from which data for this product are obtained
Census of Population - Scotland

1992 Welsh Social Survey: Report on the Welsh Language
National Assembly for Wales

A summary of the findings from the questionnaire on the Welsh language issued as part of the 1992 Welsh Social Survey. Although the main interview survey has been conducted at approximately five yearly intervals the Welsh language questionnaire was a one off. The survey inquired into the ability of the population to speak Welsh and the degree to which the language was used. Information was collected from almost 28,000 individuals. The publication summarises the results of the survey and supplements the information available from the 1991 Census. The bi-lingual publication examines, through tables, charts and text, the numbers and distribution of Welsh speakers in Wales and provides information on the use of the language in everyday situations. It looks at the use of Welsh in the home, school and work and in social situations and the audiences and readerships of the Welsh media.

Delivery: Ad hoc/One-off Release
Frequency: One-off
Price: £7.00 - postage free within the United Kingdom.
ISBN: 07504 1226 7

Available from
Henry Small
National Assembly for Wales
Crown Building
Cathays Park
Cardiff CF10 3NQ
Tel: 029 2082 5063;
Email: henry.small@wales.gsi.gov.uk

Sources from which data for this product are obtained
Household Survey - Wales.

Women and Men in the European Union
Eurostat

This publication, issued on the eve of the fourth World Women's Conference in Beijing, presents the situation of women living in the EU at the beginning of the 1990s and compares it with that of men. Some of the data in this product is disaggregated by gender.

Delivery: Ad hoc/One-off Release
Frequency: Ad hoc
Price: £10.25
ISBN: 92 826 9619 7

Available from
TSO Publications Centre and Bookshops
Please see Annex B for full address details.

Young Carers and their Families
Office for National Statistics; sponsored by
Department of Health

A qualitative study of young carers
identified in the ONS Omnibus Survey from
September to November 1994. The report
examines the attitudes and characteristics of
young carers.

Frequency Ad hoc
Price: £9.95
ISBN: 0 11 691 6850

Available from
TSO Publications Centre and Bookshops
Please see Annex B for full address details.

Sources from which data for this product are
obtained
Omnibus Survey

See also:
In this chapter:
Births in Scotland 1976-95 *(3.12)*
1991 Census Children and Young Adults
(3.11)
1991 Census Ethnic Group and Country of
Birth (3.16)
Demographic Statistics (Eurostat) *(3.11)*
Population Trends *(3.11)*

In other chapters:
Adult Literacy in Britain *(see the Education
and Training chapter)*
General Household Survey: Participation in
Sport *(see the Civic Affairs, Sport and
Leisure chapter)*
Occupational Health Decennial Supplement
(see the Labour Market chapter)
1993 Welsh House Condition Survey
(Report 1994) *(see the Housing chapter)*

3.15 Divorce

Please see:
In this chapter:
Annual Report of the Registrar General for
Northern Ireland *(3.11)*
Annual Report of the Registrar General for
Scotland *(3.11)*
Demographic Statistics (Eurostat) *(3.11)*
Marriage, Divorce and Adoption Statistics
(3.11)
Population Trends *(3.11)*
Registrar General's Quarterly Return *(3.11)*

3.16 Emigration, Immigration and Migration

Bulletin "Asylum Statistics, United Kingdom"
Home Office

Annual detailed statistics analysed by
nationality on asylum applications, including
historical statistics. 50 pages, 42 tables and
charts, commentary and explanatory notes on
asylum applications received and decided -
also appeals, cases outstanding and applicants
detained or removed from the country.

Delivery: First Release
Frequency: Annually
Price: Free
ISSN: 0143 6384

Available from
Information and Publications Group
Room 201
Home Office
50 Queen Anne's Gate
London SW1H 9AT

Sources from which data for this product are
obtained
Immigration and nationality administrative
systems

Bulletin "Control of Immigration: Statistics, United Kingdom"
Home Office

Bi-annual summary statistics on the main
aspects of immigration control, including
asylum, giving data for the latest 3 years
and 8 quarters. 36 pages, 26 tables and
charts, commentary and explanatory notes
on entry clearance applications overseas,
selected categories of port admissions,
asylum applications, settlement and
enforcement action.

Delivery: First Release
Frequency: Bi-annually
Price: Free
ISSN: 0143 6384

Available from
Information and Publications Group
Room 201
Home Office
50 Queen Anne's Gate
London SW1H 9AT

Sources from which data for this product are
obtained
Immigration and nationality administrative
systems

Bulletin "Persons Granted British Citizenship, United Kingdom"
Home Office

Annual statistics on applications for British
citizenship, including historical statistics. 20
pages, 9 tables and charts, commentary and
explanatory notes on applications received,
granted and refused, with grants analysed
by category and previous nationality; also,
grants in Hong Kong and renunciations.

Delivery: First Release
Frequency: Annually
Price: Free
ISSN: 0143 6384

Available from
Information and Publications Group
Room 201
Home Office
50 Queen Anne's Gate
London SW1H 9AT

Sources from which data for this product are
obtained
Immigration and nationality administrative
systems

1991 Census Ethnic Group and Country of Birth
Office for National Statistics

Figures on 'ethnic group and country of
birth' from the 1991 Census, Great Britain.
Contains twenty tables (thirteen covering
100 per cent variables and seven 10 per cent
tables), mainly at national level, but also
with six at regional level, giving - in the case
of ethnic group - results from information
collected for the first time in a British
Census. There is also a table giving counts
of the full classification of ethnic groups,
that is the 'written in' answers to the
question. Country of birth tables cover:
marital status; age; birthplace of household
head; migrants to UK; country of birth; age
and marital status; age and birthplace;
communal establishments; migrants in UK;
economic position; housing characteristics;
household space type; occupation (10%
sample); industry (10% sample); hours
worked (10% sample); social class and
socio-economic group (10% sample);
qualified persons (10% sample); household
family type (10% sample); families (10%
sample). Ethnic group is tabulated by sex,
age and marital status, birthplace, migration,
economic position, housing characteristics,
occupation, industry, social class and
socio-economic group, higher qualification,
and family composition. Tables produced for
the statistical office of the European
community cover country of birth by: age;
economically active; population in

employment; employees; unemployed; industry (10% sample); and household size.

Some of the data in this product is disaggregated by gender.

Frequency Decennial
Price: £45.00
ISBN: 0 11 6915 18 8

Available from
Census Customer Services - ONS or TSO Publications Centre and Bookshops
Please see Annex B for full address details.

Sources from which data for this product are obtained
Census of Population and Housing - Great Britain - 1991; Ethnic Group and Birthplace - GB.

1991 Census Regional Migration Statistics
Office for National Statistics

Analysis of the Census questions on 'usual address one year before the Census'. Dataset available on machine-readable media only, presented in two parts for each Standard Region of England, Wales and Scotland. Each part has topic coverage similar to the tables in the Migration Topic Report includes some figures down to (local government) district level. Machine-readable media only.

Available from
Census Customer Services - ONS
Please see Annex B for full address details.

Command Paper "Control of Immigration: Statistics, United Kingdom"
Home Office

Annual detailed statistics analysed by nationality on the various aspects of immigration control, together with summary statistics on asylum applications, including historical statistics. 127 pages, 53 tables and charts, commentary and explanatory notes on entry clearance applications overseas, port admissions (excluding EEA nationals) and refusals, asylum applications, after-entry applications including settlement, enforcement action and immigration appeals.

Delivery: Periodic Release
Frequency: Annually
Price: £18.40 (1997 Edition)
ISBN: 0-10-140332-1 (1997 Edition)

Available from
TSO Publications Centre and Bookshops
Please see Annex B for full address details.

Sources from which data for this product are obtained
Immigration and nationality administrative systems; International Migration

---

International Migration (Series MN)
Office for National Statistics

Presents the latest figures on migrants entering or leaving the United Kingdom and England and Wales, based primarily on data from the International Passenger Survey. Contains statistics on the flows of international migrants to and from the United Kingdom and England and Wales during the reference year and also for the last ten years. Provides detailed information on characteristics of migrants including sex, age, citizenship, country of last or next residence, country of birth, reason for migration, occupation and marital status. Tables of the number of individuals accepted for settlement in the UK and those granted British citizenship are also included using figures supplied by the Home Office.

Delivery: Periodic Release
Frequency: Annually
Price: £30.00 - 1996
ISBN: 0 11 6916541 (series MN No 20)

Available from
TSO Publications Centre and Bookshops
Please see Annex B for full address details.

Sources from which data for this product are obtained
International Passenger Survey - UK

Key Statistics Immigration and British Citizenship - Leaflet
Home Office

Brief statistics on the various aspects of immigration control, including asylum, including data for previous year and 10 years earlier. Folded leaflet, 10 tables and charts on entry clearance applications overseas, passenger arrivals and refusals, asylum applications, after-entry applications including settlement, enforcement action and grants of citizenship.

Delivery: Periodic Release
Frequency: Annually
Price: Free
ISBN: 1 84082 2805

Available from
Information and Publications Group
Room 201
Home Office
50 Queen Anne's Gate
London SW1H 9AT

Sources from which data for this product are obtained
Immigration and nationality administrative systems

National Population Projections: A New Methodology for Determining Migration Assumptions
Government Actuary's Department

Methodology paper by the Government Actuary's Department on the assumptions made for future migration and their effect on population projections in the United Kingdom. Historical data are analysed for net migration into the United Kingdom as well as internal migration between countries of the United Kingdom. This paper contains the derivation of a model used to assist in the setting of the migration assumptions for the national population projections.

Frequency Ad hoc
Price: £4.00
ISBN: 1 85774 181 1

Available from
ONS Direct
Please see Annex B for full address details.

(A) Review of Migration Data Sources
Office for National Statistics

An Occasional Paper on data sources for estimating migration. Contains a full description and appraisal of the data sources currently used, and makes a number of recommendations for improvement in their utilisation. A number of possible sources are described, and there are suggestions for harnessing some of these.

Frequency Ad Hoc
Price: £4.50
ISBN: 0 904952 74 6 (Occasional Paper No 39)

Sources from which data for this product are obtained
International Migration

See also:
In this chapter:
Annual Report of the Registrar General for Scotland *(3.11)*
1991 Census Children and Young Adults *(3.11)*
Demographic Statistics (Eurostat) *(3.11)*
Key Population and Vital Statistics (Series VS) *(3.11)*
Population Trends *(3.11)*
Sub-National Population Projections *(3.20)*

In other chapters:
Nomis® (*See the Websites and Electronic Services chapter*)

3.17 First Names and Surnames Registered

First Names: The Definitive Guide to Popular Names in England and Wales
Office for National Statistics

This publication contains information about the changing popularity of first names over fifty years taken from the National Health Service Register for England and Wales, at ten-yearly intervals since 1944, with regional analyses for 1994.

Frequency Ad hoc
Price: £4.95
ISBN: 0 11 691 6338

Available from
TSO Publications Centre and Bookshops
Please see Annex B for full address details.

Sources from which data for this product are obtained
First Names - England and Wales

(A) Guide to Popular First Names in Northern Ireland
Northern Ireland Statistics and Research Agency - GRO(NI)

Frequency of first names in Northern Ireland in 1995. Some comparisons with earlier years are also given.

Price: £4.00

Available from
George King
GRO-NI
Northern Ireland Statistics and Research Agency
Tel: 028 9025 2027

Personal Names in Scotland
General Register Office for Scotland

Frequency of forenames and surnames in Scotland. Contains tables giving the frequency and regional distribution of forenames and surnames in Scotland in 1990. Some comparisons with earlier surveys are also given. Updates for later years data is also available.

Price: £2.95

Available from
Carole Welch
Room 1/2/9
General Register Office for Scotland
Ladywell House
Ladywell Road
Edinburgh EH12 7TF
Tel: 0131 314 4243;
Email: carole.welch@gro-scotland.gov.uk

Sources from which data for this product are obtained
Personal Names - Scotland

3.18 Marriage and Cohabitation

Please see:
In this chapter:
Annual Report of the Registrar General for Northern Ireland *(3.11)*
Annual Report of the Registrar General for Scotland *(3.11)*
Demographic Statistics (Eurostat) *(3.11)*
Marriage, Divorce and Adoption Statistics *(3.11)*
Population Trends *(3.11)*
Quarterly Return of the Registrar General for Northern Ireland *(3.11)*
Registrar General's Quarterly Return *(3.11)*

3.19 Population and Housing - General

1994 Based Household Projections for Wales (1997)
National Assembly for Wales

Household projections and household estimates for Wales are produced and published every two to three years by the Department. They are based on the population projections produced by the Department whose foundation is the Registrar General's Mid-Year Estimate of population in the specified year. The latest projections take 1994 as their base and provide estimates of numbers of households by unitary authority, type of household and head of household up to 2016. The projection method is trend based considering changes in household formation (derived from the Censuses of 1971, 1981 and 1991 and from the annual Labour Force Surveys.), in marital status and cohabitation. The publication consists of approximately 20 A4 pages and includes text, tables and charts. The text gives a brief introduction followed by methodology and results. The tables show a Wales summary, a unitary authority summary plus projections by age and sex of household for both Wales and unitary authorities. The appendix give details of definitions and unitary authority contacts.

Delivery: Periodic Release
Frequency: Ad-hoc
Price: £10.00 inclusive of postage within the UK
ISBN: 0 7504 1687 4
ISSN: 0269 - 204x

Available from
Fiona Leadbitter
National Assembly for Wales
Crown Building
Cathays Park
Cardiff CF10 3NQ
Tel: 029 2082 5055;
Email: fiona.leadbitter@wales.gsi.gov.uk

Sources from which data for this product are obtained
Population Projections

Household Projections for Scotland
The Scottish Executive

A Scottish Executive Statistical Bulletin containing projections of the numbers of different types of households in Scotland and individual local authorities up to the year 2010.

Delivery: Periodic Release
Frequency: Biennial
Price: £2.00
ISSN: 0264 1143

Available from
TSO Publications Centre and Bookshops
Please see Annex B for full address details.

Sources from which data for this product are obtained
Household Projections

Projections of Households in England to 2016
Department of the Environment, Transport and the Regions

Gives summary results of the DETR's household projections and estimates for England, the regions, counties, met districts and London boroughs, for the years 1981, 1991, 1996, 2001, 2006, 2011, and 2016. It includes a description of the method of calculation.

Frequency: Every two or three years
Price: £45.00

Available from
TSO Publications Centre and Bookshops
Please see Annex B for full address details.

Sources from which data for this product are obtained
Household Estimates and Projections

1993 Welsh House Condition Survey (Report 1994)
National Assembly for Wales

A summary volume containing tables, charts and explanatory text covering the key findings of the 1992 Welsh Social Survey and the 1993 Welsh House Condition Survey. The publication gives information on the numbers of unfit homes in Wales and estimates of the costs of repair together with information about the dwelling stock and the households who occupy it. The publication is most likely to be of interest to housing practitioners and researchers. Approximately 110 pages aimed at those with an interest in housing conditions in Wales. The publication contains information on the incidence of unfit dwellings, the reasons for unfitness, the costs of making fit and other repair costs and changes since the previous survey (1986). There are also sections on households and the type of accommodation they occupy. The report also gives technical details on the methodology used in the surveys.

Frequency Periodic
Price: £7.00 (including p&p).
ISBN: 0 7504 1037 X
ISSN: 0263 - 9629

Available from
Henry Small
National Assembly for Wales
Crown Building
Cathays Park
Cardiff CF10 3NQ
Tel: 029 2082 5063;
Email: henry.small@wales.gsi.gov.uk

Sources from which data for this product are obtained
House Condition Survey - Wales; Household Survey - Wales

See also:
In this chapter:
Population Trends *(3.11)*

In other chapters:
General Household Survey: Voluntary Work 1987 *(see the Health and Care chapter)*
Housing and Construction Statistics Annual Volume *(see the Housing chapter)*

3.20 Population Estimates and Projections

Accuracy of Rolled-Forward Population Estimates in England and Wales, 1981-91
Office for National Statistics

Methodology paper comparing the Registrar General's rolled-forward population estimates for areas within England and Wales with the final revised estimates rebased using 1991 Census results. Analysis and results are given for errors in age groups by area. Percentage errors in rolled-forward estimates are given for standard regions, counties, county districts/London boroughs, and regional and district health authorities.

Frequency One-off
Price: £5.00
ISBN: 1 85774 197 8 (OPCS Occasional Paper No 44)

Sources from which data for this product are obtained
Population Estimates - England and Wales; Registration of Deaths - England and Wales.

Annual Report of the Chief Medical Officer for Northern Ireland
Department of Health and Social Services - Northern Ireland

Frequency: Annual

Available from
Dr M Boyle
Department of Health and Social Services
Castle Buildings
Stormont
Belfast
Tel: 028 90520713

Sources from which data for this product are obtained
Population Estimates - Northern Ireland

1994-Based National Population Projections for Wales
National Assembly for Wales

Delivery: Periodic Release
Frequency: Ad hoc
Price: £5.00 - inclusive of postage within the United Kingdom
ISBN: 0 7504 1228 3
ISSN: 0269 204X

Available from
Clive Lewis
National Assembly for Wales
Crown Building
Cathays Park
Cardiff CF10 3NQ
Tel: 029 2082 3220;
Email: clive.lewis@wales.gsi.gov.uk

1996-Based National Population Projections
Government Actuary's Department

1996-based national population projections series PP2 no21. Contains details of the Government Actuary's population projections by age and sex for the United Kingdom and constituent countries, and explains the methodology and assumptions used. United Kingdom projections are made 70 years forward while projections for the constituent countries of the UK cover 40 years. The publication contains an order form to obtain an electronic presentation of the projection results direct from the Government Actuary's Department.

Some of the data in this product is disaggregated by gender.

Delivery: Periodic Release
Frequency: Normally every two years
Price: £30.00
ISBN: 0-11-621160-1

Available from
TSO Publications Centre and Bookshops
Please see Annex B for full address details

Sources from which data for this product are obtained
Births - Scotland; International Passenger Survey - UK; Mortality - Scotland; National Health Service Central Register; Population Projections

1996 - Based National Population Projections First Release
Government Actuary's Department

Mid-1996 based principal population projections for United Kingdom and constituent countries. The First release was published on 27 November 1997. The release contains a brief summary of the Government Actuary's principal population projections by age and sex for the United Kingdom and constituent countries. The detail of the projection is available direct from GAD on paper and/or disk.

Frequency: Normally every two years
Price: First release is free
(Available from ONS press office)
Up to 20 pages from the projections are available free from GAD. Complete paper copies are £20 a country. A CD containing all the countries plus textual information and graphs is also available from GAD priced £40.00 +VAT. If the reference volume PP2 no 21 is purchased the CD is priced at £15.00 +VAT.

Available from
ONS Press Office
Office for National Statistics
1 Drummond Gate
London SW1V 2QQ
Tel: 020 7533 6363/6364

Sources from which data for this product are obtained
Births - Scotland; International Passenger Survey - UK; Mortality - Scotland; National Health Service Central Register; Population Projections.

Mid-year Population Estimates for England and Wales
Office for National Statistics

Population estimate statistics for England and Wales (mid-1997). National population by sex and single year of age, together with estimated total population of each local and health authority, at the reference date.

Delivery: Periodic Release
Frequency: Annually
Price: £4.00
ISSN: 0953-3419

Available from
Brett Leeming
Room 2300
Office for National Statistics
Segensworth Road
Titchfield
Fareham
Hampshire PO15 5RR
Tel: 01329 813318

Sources from which data for this product are obtained
Population Estimates - England and Wales, Scotland, Northern Ireland; Registration of Births - England and Wales; Registration of Deaths - England and Wales; Electoral Statistics

---

Mid-year Population Estimates, Scotland
General Register Office for Scotland

Summary of mid-year estimates of the population of Scotland and its administrative areas; explanatory notes and details of other related GRO(S) products. Contains estimates of the population of Scotland by single year of age and sex, and by five-year age group and sex for the administrative areas. Other items covered are components of population change, and land area and population density.

Frequency Annual
Price: £4.00
ISBN: 1 874451 55 9

Available from
Peter Jamieson
Room 1/2/8
General Register Office for Scotland
Ladywell House
Ladywell Road
Edinburgh EH12 7TF
Tel: 0131 314 4254;
Email: peter.jamieson@gro-scotland.gov.uk

Sources from which data for this product are obtained
Births - Scotland; Census of Population - Scotland; Migration - Scotland; National Health Service Central Register; Population Estimates - Scotland.

Population Projections - Northern Ireland
Northern Ireland Statistics and Research Agency

The Government Actuary's Department produces population projections for Northern Ireland as it does for the other countries of the United Kingdom. The Northern Ireland Statistics and Research Agency produces sub-national population projections at Health Board level, the totals of which are constrained to the Northern Ireland totals produced by the Government Actuary's Department.

Frequency Every 2 years

Available from
Robert Beatty
Northern Ireland Statistics and Research Agency
Demography and Methodology Branch
Tel: 028 9052 6907;
Email: robert.beatty@dfpni.gov.uk

Sources from which data for this product are obtained
Annual Report of the Registrar General for Northern Ireland

Population Projections, Scotland
General Register Office for Scotland

Summary of population projections for Scotland and its administrative areas; explanatory notes and methodological information and details of other GRO(S) products. Contains population projections for Scotland and its administrative areas by selected age groups and sex; components of population change by region and health board areas; projected births by standard area; assumed fertility and mortality rates for Scotland; fertility and mortality local scaling factors and migration assumptions by standard area.

Frequency Ad hoc
Price: £4.00
ISBN: 1 874451 50 8

Available from
Peter Jamieson
Room 1/2/8
General Register Office for Scotland
Ladywell House
Ladywell Road
Edinburgh EH12 7TF
Tel: 0131 314 4254;
Email: peter.jamieson@gro-scotland.gov.uk

Sources from which data for this product are obtained
Births - Scotland; Census of Population - Scotland; Mortality - Scotland; National Health Service Central Register; Sub-national Population Projections - Scotland.

Population Projections: Trends, Methods and Uses
Office for National Statistics

Collection of papers presented at British Society for Population Studies conference 1990. Covers four main themes: the production and usage of national projections; projections at the local level; how national projections are used to explore possible effects of population change on three sectors of the economy (labour market, transportation, financial services); and a review of methods, sources of data, and assumptions.

Frequency Ad hoc
Price: £7.00
ISBN: 0 904952 61 4 (Occasional Paper No 38)

Available from
Lucy Vickers
Population and Vital Statistics; Migration and Subnational Population Projections Unit
Room 2300
Office for National Statistics
Segensworth Road
Titchfield
Fareham
Hampshire PO15 5RR
Tel: 01329 813799

Sources from which data for this product are obtained
Registration of Deaths - England and Wales; Sub-national Population Projections - England.

Sub-National Population Projections
Department of the Environment, Transport and the Regions

Consultation with English local and health authorities on migration assumptions within draft sub-national population projections. Includes consultation package and planning pages of DETR website, evaluation of authority responses, liaison with Office for National Statistics and Department of Health. Representation for the Department, Government Offices for the Regions and local authorities on matters relating to population projections.

Some of the data in this product is disaggregated by gender.

Delivery: Periodic Release

Available from
Lucy Vickers
Population and Vital Statistics; Migration and Subnational Population Projections Unit
Room 2300
Office for National Statistics
Segensworth Road
Titchfield
Fareham
Hampshire PO15 5RR
Tel: 01329 813799

Sub-National Population Projections - England Series PP3
Office for National Statistics

Sub-national Population projections for England. Contains long-term population projections by sex and age for the government office regions, unitary authorities, counties, London boroughs, metropolitan and shire districts, and regional and district health authorities of England for the base year and approximately 25 years ahead, and explains briefly the methodology and assumptions used. Reference volume for subnational population projection contains tables, maps and text (Series PP3). The 1993-based sub-national projections (Series PP3 no 9) are now superseded, and the 1996-based volume (series PP3 no 10) to be published in August 1999. CD ROM was published in February 1999. Data can be requested from Sub-national Population Projections Unit.

Delivery: Periodic Release
Frequency: Every Three to Five Years
Price: £30.00 (expected)
ISBN: 0 11 691635 4 (Series PP3)

Available from
TSO Publications Centre and Bookshops
Please see Annex B for full address details.

Sources from which data for this product are obtained
Registration of Deaths - England and Wales; Sub-national Population Projections - England

---

Sub-National Population Projections for Local and Health Authority Areas in England, (1996-Based) - Monitors
Office for National Statistics

Population projections for local government and health authority areas in England (1996-based). The ONS monitor contains summary results, and a brief description of methods and assumptions, for projections of local government and health authority areas in England. Long-term projections (25 years) are published about every three to five years, and short-term projections in other years. The latest monitor contains 1996-based long term projections. The 1993 -based sub-national projections (Series PP3 no 9) are now superseded, and the 1996 based volume

(series PP3 no 10) to be published in August 1999. CD ROM published February 1999.

Delivery: Periodic Release
Frequency: every three to five years
Price: £4 (PP3 98/1)
ISSN: 0953-3435 (Series PP3)

Available from
TSO Publications Centre and Bookshops
Please see Annex B for full address details.

Sources from which data for this product are obtained
Sub-national Population Projections - England

Sub-National Population Projections for Wales
National Assembly for Wales

Summary tables of projected population for local authorities and health authorities in Wales. By unitary and health authority and Wales, analyses of population projections (for the following 20 years) by age and gender including details of projected components of population change. Details include a description of methodology.

Delivery: News/Press Release
Frequency: Generally bi-annual
Price: £5.00 postage paid within the UK
ISBN: 0 7504 1228 3
ISSN: 0269 204X

Available from
Publications Unit, Statistical Directorate
National Assembly for Wales
Crown Building
Cathays Park
Cardiff CF10 3NQ
Tel: 029 2082 5044;
Email: claire.owen@wales.gsi.gov.uk

Sources from which data for this product are obtained
National Population Projections (Government Actuary's Department)
ONS Population Estimates
ONS Components of Change

See also:
In this chapter:
Annual Report of the Registrar General for Northern Ireland *(3.11)*
Key Population and Vital Statistics (Series VS) *(3.11)*
National Population Projections: A New Methodology for Determining Migration Assumptions (3.16)
Population Trends *(3.11)*
Twentieth Century Mortality (England & Wales 1901 - 1995) CD-ROM *(3.13)*
Twentieth Century Mortality: 1996-97 Update Disk *(3.13)*

In other chapters:
Housing and Construction Statistics Annual Volume *(see the Housing chapter)*
Nomis(®) *(see the Websites and Electronic Services chapter)*
(The) Scottish Environment Statistics *(see the Environment chapter)*

Other Products which may be of interest, but are not featured in this book due to lack of details:
Women's Migration: Marriage Fertility and Divorce - Office for National Statistics
Socio Demographic Mortality Differentials - Office for National Statistics
Department of the Environment, Transport and the Regions Census Unit - DETR
Social Class and Occupational Mobility - Office for National Statistics
Social Distribution of Cancer - Office for National Statistics
Longitudinal Study, Housing Deprivation and Social Change - Office for National Statistics

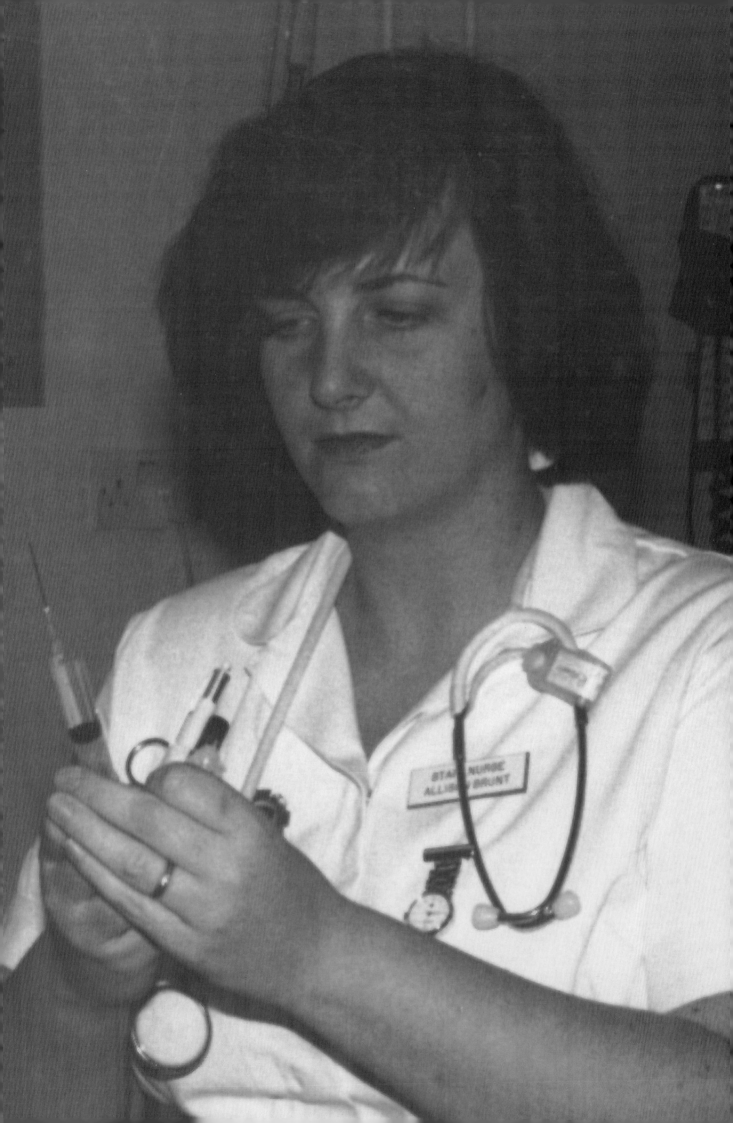

4   Health and Care

Statistics covering **Health and Care** are collected, administered and disseminated by a number of separate Departments, Agencies and organisations including the **Office for National Statistics, the Department of Health,** the **NHS Executives, Scottish Executive, the NHS in Scotland, the National Assembly for Wales, the Northern Ireland Department of Health and Social Services, the Office of Manpower Economics** and **the Health and Safety Executive.** The available statistics embrace a number of subject areas including: **Abortions, Ambulance Service, Childcare Services, Community Health Services, Community Social Services, Cost of Healthcare and Social Services, Daycare Facilities for Children, Demand and Supply of Healthcare Staff, Dental Health, Diet and Nutrition, Disability, Drug Abuse etc, Employment/Staffing, Family Planning, GMPs, Hospital Services, Incidence and Prevention of Disease Etc, Mental Health, Opthalmic Services, Pharmaceutical Services, and Private Healthcare.**

The basic data are generated from a number of separate information 'Sources' and the resultant statistics are disseminated through a whole range of statistical 'Analyses' and 'Products', all of which are described in the following chapter. Users looking for a cross-section of UK-wide statistics on **Health and Care** may find the following products useful:

> **Health Statistics Quarterly** (quarterly publication)
> **Health and Personal Social Services Statistics** (annual publications)

Users interested in a wider range of official statistics including **Health and Care** statistics may like to refer to the following compendia:

> On-line Databases (See Chapter 1):
> > **StatBase – StatStore**
>
> Hardcopy Compendia (See Chapter 2):
> > **Annual Abstract of Statistics**
> > **Britain 2000: The Official Yearbook of the United Kingdom**
> > **Regional Trends**
> > **Social Trends**

Users may also find what they need on the various Departmental Websites. These are listed in Chapter 1.

4

Health and care - *Sources and Analyses*

4.1 Abstracts, Compendia, A-Z Catalogues, Directories, Reference Material

General and Personal Medical Services Census
Department of Health

A register of general medical practitioners who are in contract with Health Authorities in England and Wales. Each census provides up-to-date details relating to all aspects of General Practice such as partnership structure, doctors' lists, GP Registrars and Assistants, practice staff, services offered by doctors and target achievements.

Status: Ongoing
Collection Method: Census
Frequency: Annually
Reference Period: 1 October
Timeliness: October collection May release
Earliest Available Data: 1991
National Coverage: England and Wales
Disaggregation: Family Health Services Authority (FHSA) /Health Authority (E&W)

Statistician
Dr Andy Sutherland
Department of Health
Stats (W)GMS
Tel: 0113 25 45905;
Email: asutherl@doh.gov.uk

Key Statistics KS1
Department of Health

Key statistics is intended to collect the most important pieces of currently available information on personal social services on a fast track basis. Information covers data on children's services, adults services, services for the elderly, unit cost data, and expenditure and budget data.

Status: Ongoing
Collection Method: Census
Frequency: Annually
Reference Period: 31 March
Earliest Available Data: 1998
National Coverage: England
Disaggregation: County (E&W) / Unitary Authority (England)

Statistician
Nazeema Momin
Department of Health
Statistics Division 3; Statistics Division 3C
Tel: 020 7972 5599;
Email: nmomin@doh.gov.uk

Personal Social Services - Northern Ireland
Department of Health and Social Security - Northern Ireland

The Department of Health and Social Services (NI) collates personal social services statistics for Northern Ireland. Data are collected in respect of the following specific groups: children, elderly, learning disability, mentally ill, physically disabled, and sensorially impaired. Activities monitored include residential accommodation, children in care, child abuse, clients in contact with the Board, home help service, and meals-on-wheels. Data are available since 1988-89 on electronic database, however data from 1974 are stored in a manual format. Data are collected annually at the end of March; the majority are not published but information is available to the public, on request, six months after the reference period.

Frequency: Annually
Timeliness: Information available, by request, six months after the reference period
Earliest Available Data: Data is available from 1947 stored in a manual format and from 1988-89 electronically
National Coverage: Northern Ireland

Statistician
Dr Linda Bradley
Department of Health and Social Security - Northern Ireland
Tel: 028 9052 0726

Products that contain data from this source
Health and Personal Social Services Statistics (NI); Regional Trends; Social Focus on Children; Social Trends

Welsh Office Core Indicators
National Assembly for Wales

A fast track quarterly collection to monitor a broad spectrum of NHS performance. Includes indicators on activity, waiting lists, patients charter, complaints, community health, mental health, continuing health care, and financial information. The information collected is held in an executive information system (the WOCI EIS).

Data for around 100 indicators is collected (including activity, waiting lists, patients charter, complaints, community health, mental health, continuing health care, clinical effectiveness and financial information). For most indicators, the data forming the numerator and denominator of the indicator is collected as well as the value of the indicator itself (this enables all Wales values to be calculated).

The indicators cover a broad spectrum of NHS performance and, as a 'fast track' system, are used to monitor performance in these areas - for instance, Patients Charter objectives and changes in waiting lists. Summary information is published in the National Assembly for Wales quarterly statistical release 'NHS Wales Hospital Activity' and in the annual publication 'Health Statistics Wales'. It may also be used in answering Parliamentary Questions, preparing briefing for ministers and in response to ad hoc requests.

The individual indicators collected can change over time as new, more relevant indicators are introduced and indicators which are no longer relevant are removed.

Status: Ongoing
Collection Method: Census
Frequency: Mostly quarterly, but some are annually
Timeliness: Around 2 months of the end of the quarter.
Earliest Available Data: The quarter April to June 1994
National Coverage: Wales
Disaggregation: District Health Authority (DHA)/Health Authority (E&W);

Statistician
Graham Davies
National Assembly for Wales
Statistical Directorate; Health Statistics Analysis Unit (3)
Tel: (029) 2082 5086;
Email: graham.davies@wales.gsi.gov.uk

Products that contain data from this source
Health Statistics Wales; NHS Wales Hospital Activity

See also:
In this chapter:
Staff of Social Services Departments in Wales (STF 1,2,3 + 4) *(4.15)*

In other chapters:
(The) ONS Longitudinal Study (see the Population, Census, Migration and Vital Events chapter)

4.2 Abortions

Abortion Notification Forms (HSA4)
Office for National Statistics; sponsored by Department of Health and National Assembly for Wales

The Office for National Statistics has responsibility for compiling data on legal abortions. Data relate to the number of abortions taking place in England and Wales under the Abortion Act 1967 which are notified (by the practitioner terminating the pregnancy) to the Chief Medical Officers.

Data are available by country and health region of termination, maternal age, marital status, previous live and stillborn children, statutory grounds, gestational age, purchaser (NHS, non-NHS and agency) and country of residence. In addition, annual data give national and regional abortion rates, numbers by method of termination, complications, duration of stay, regional and district health authority of residence and (from 1992) local authority area levels. The legal abortion series covers abortions performed in England and Wales to residents of any country and data are available at regional health authority, district health authority and (from 1992) local authority area levels.

Abortion data have been collected since the Abortion Act 1967, which came into effect on 27 April 1968. Section 37 of the Human Fertilisation and Embryology Act 1990 made changes to the Abortion Act 1967. These changes came into effect on 1 April 1991. This made changes to some of the Statistics collected before and after April 1991. Summary of the changes are in the OPCS publication 'Abortion Statistics 1991' series AB no. 18.

Status: Ongoing
Collection Method: Administrative Records
Frequency: Continuously
Reference Period: Notification forms received by CMOs forwarded to ONS twice a week
Timeliness: Quarterly data published within 5 months after the end of quarter. Provisional annual data published within 6 months and final annual data within 12 months of the end of the year.
Earliest Available Data: 1968
National Coverage: England and Wales

Disaggregation: District Health Authority (DHA) / Health Authority (E&W); Local Authority District (LAD) / Unitary Authority (England); Regional Health Authority (RHA) / Regional (Health) Office Area

Statistician
Lyn Watmore
Office for National Statistics
Population and Vital Statistics, Morbidity Statistics
Tel: 01329 813618;
Email: lyn.watmore@ons.gov.uk

Products that contain data from this source
Health Statistics Quarterly; Abortion Statistics Annual Reference Volume; Congenital Anomaly Statistics

Abortion Statistics
National Assembly for Wales

Details of termination of pregnancy performed in Wales and of terminations of pregnancy performed on Welsh residents in England. The information is used by the National Assembly for Wales to monitor terminations in Wales and for Welsh residents and is also provided to health authority Directors of Public Health on request.

Aggregate summary data for England and Wales is published by ONS in the annual publication 'Abortion Statistics'. More detailed information for women living in Wales is included in the annual National Assembly for Wales publication 'Health Statistics Wales' and in an annual statistical brief prepared by HSA, circulated within the National Assembly for Wales, to Directors of Public Health, to gynaecologists and to other people on request. The information is also used in answering Parliamentary Questions, preparing briefing for ministers and in response to ad hoc requests, although because of the sensitivity of the information each request is scrutinised carefully to ensure there is no risk of individuals being identified from the information provided. Summary data is available from around the early 1970s, with a detailed database being held since 1995 by Health Statistics and Analysis Unit. The Office for National Statistics have data for additional earlier years going back to around 1970.

Status: Ongoing
Collection Method: Administrative Records
Frequency: Annually
Earliest Available Data: 1970
National Coverage: Wales
Sub-National: Health Authority

Statistician
Adrian Crompton
National Assembly for Wales
Statistical Directorate; Health Statistics and Analysis Unit (4)
Tel: 029 2082 5033
Email: statswales@gtnet.gov.uk

Notification of an Abortion
Information and Statistics Division, NHS in Scotland

Provides information on abortions performed under the abortion act 1967.

Status: Ongoing
Collection Method: Administrative Records
Frequency: Continuously
Reference Period: 1968 to date
Earliest Available Data: 1968
National Coverage: Scotland
Sub-National: Health Board

Statistician
Peter Knight
Information and Statistics Division, NHS in Scotland
Hospital & community information
Tel: 0131 551 8739

Products that contain data from this source
Scottish Health Statistics

4.3 Ambulance Service

Ambulance Services - England
Department of Health

The Department of Health compiles data on ambulance services provided by the NHS in England. Data are collected for: emergency, urgent and special/planned patient journeys; and emergency calls, including the proportion where the response time was within set targets. Performance figures are provided for each individual service together with comparative information for earlier years.

Status: Ongoing
Collection Method: KA34, KA34 (New) returns from each ambulance service.
Frequency: Annually
Reference Period: Financial year
Timeliness: Three months
Earliest Available Data: 1987-88
National Coverage: England
Sub-National: Ambulance NHS Trust

Statistician
Lesz Lancucki
Department of Health
Tel: 020 7972 5533;
Email: llancuck@doh.gov.uk

Products that contain data from this source
DH Statistical Bulletin - Ambulances Services, England; Health and Personal Social Services Statistics for England

Patient Transport - Northern Ireland
Department of Health and Social Services - Northern Ireland

The Department of Health and Social Services (NI) collates patient transport statistics covering ambulance journeys in Northern Ireland. Data, submitted by the NI Ambulance Service, are collected about the number and type of ambulance journeys and activation/response times for emergency journeys in HSS Boards. Response times are collected quarterly and the number of journeys annually at the end of March. Data are published annually, approximately one month after the reference period and are available on spreadsheet since 1988-89.

Status: Ongoing
Collection Method: Return from Northern Ireland Ambulance Service
Frequency: Quarterly
Timeliness: One month after reference period
Earliest Available Data: 1988-89
National Coverage: Northern Ireland
Sub-National: Full
Disaggregation: Health and Social Services Boards

Statistician
Jenny Orr
Department of Health and Social Services - Northern Ireland
Tel: 028 9052 2580;
Email: jenny.orr@dhssni.gov.uk

Products that contain data from this source
Patient Transport Statistics

Patient Transport Services (KA34) - Wales
National Assembly for Wales

Aggregate quarterly information on patient transport services, including details of the timeliness of emergency and urgent ambulance services for each ambulance division and summary information on the number of patient journeys. KA34 is used by the National Assembly for Wales to monitor ambulance response times, including patients charter standards. A quarterly statistical brief summarising the information is prepared and circulated within the National Assembly for Wales and to the Welsh Ambulance Services NHS trust. It is also available to anyone else on request. An annual summary brief (including trends in numbers of calls and journeys as well as information on response times) is also prepared.

Summary information from the returns is published in the annual publication 'Health Statistics Wales'. It may also be used in answering Parliamentary Questions, Assembly Questions, preparing briefing for

and in response to ad hoc requests. KA34 provides details of the total number of patient journeys, and this information is used to project growth in the expenditure on patient transport services for PES purposes.

Status: Ongoing
Collection Method: Survey
Frequency: Quarterly
Reference Period: The quarters ending in March, June, September and December
Earliest Available Data: 1990/91
National Coverage: Wales
Disaggregation: NHS Ambulance Trust, Unitary Authority

Statistician
Dr Gwyneth Thomas
National Assembly for Wales
Statistical Directorate; Health Statistics and Analysis Unit (1)
Tel: 029 2082 5039.
Email: gwyneth.thomas@wales.gsi.gov.uk

Products that contain data from this source
Health Statistics Wales; Patient Transport Statistics - Annual statistical brief to National Assembly for Wales and Ambulance Trust; Patient Transport Statistics - Quarterly Statistical Brief to National Assembly for Wales and Ambulance Trust

See also:
In this chapter:
Community Activity (4.6)

4.4 Attitudes to, and experience of, National Health Service (NHS)

NHS Patients' Complaints - England
NHS Executive HQ

The NHS Executive HQ collect data on written complaints made by or on behalf of patients about hospital and community services, and family health services from all HAs and NHS Trusts in England. Data are collected on number of written complaints made, the nature of the complaint and investigatory action taken.

Status: Ongoing
Collection Method: Administrative records
Frequency: Annual
Reference Period: Financial year
Timeliness: December
Earliest Available Data: 1990-91
National Coverage: England
Sub-National: NHS Trusts, HAs

Statistician
Jolly Arif
NHS Executive HQ
Performance Analysis Branch

NHS Performance (League) Tables, England
National Health Service Executive Headquarters; sponsored by Department of Health

Information collected from health authorities and NHS Trusts for performance monitoring. These returns have changed over time - for further information please contact Jolly Arif on 0113 2545440

Collection Method: Administrative Records
Frequency: Annually / Quarterly
Reference Period: Financial Year
Timeliness: Around autumn
Earliest Available Data: 1993/94
National Coverage: England
Sub-National: NHS Trusts, Health Authorities, Regions

Statistician
Jolly Arif
National Health Service Executive Headquarters Performance Analysis Branch
Tel: 0113 25 45440. Email: jarif@doh.gov.uk

Products that contain data from this source
Performance (League) Tables

Patients' Complaints - Wales
National Assembly for Wales

The returns of written complaints by or on behalf of patients are compiled by the National Assembly for Wales on the numbers of complaints by patients in the NHS from NHS Trust and district health authorities. Data are available by the numbers of complaints against purchasers and providers, the nature of the complaint and investigatory action. Complaints are classified as wholly or partly clinical and other, and hospital or community. The survey has covered Wales since 1985-86 and is carried out annually.

Collection Method: Survey
Frequency: Annual
Earliest Available Data: 1985-86
National Coverage: Wales

Statistician
Cath Roberts
National Assembly for Wales
Statistical Directorate; Health Statistics and Analysis Unit 2 (HSA2)
Tel: (029) 2082 5033;
Email: cath.roberts@wales.gsi.gov.uk

Products that contain data from this source
Social Services Statistics for Wales

4.5 Childcare Services

Child Protection - England
Department of Health

The Department of Health compiles data on the numbers of children and young people on the Child Protection Registers of local authorities. Returns are submitted from each local authority in England for the year ending 31 March. Data are collected on form CPR1. Data are collected on the numbers of children on the Register by category of abuse, sex, and age group, by legal status and, if looked after, by type of placement, registrations during the year by category of abuse, sex and age group, first registrations, children who were the subject of initial child protection conferences, and deregistrations by sex and length of time on the Register. Figures are published annually for England, local authorities and for Audit Commission and Inspectorate regions.

Status: Ongoing
Collection Method: Census
Frequency: Annually
Reference Period: 31 March
Timeliness: Between 6-8 months
Earliest Available Data: 31 March 1989
National Coverage: England
Disaggregation: Local authority metropolitan districts and shire counties; Unitary Authority; London Borough

Statistician
Michael Cornish
Department of Health
Statistics Division 3; Statistics Division 3A
Tel: 0171 972 5573;
Email: mcornish@doh.gov.uk

Products that contain data from this source
Children and Young Persons on Child Protection Registers; Health and Personal Social Services Statistics for England; Key Indicators Expert System: Monitoring Services for Children; Key Indicators Graphical System

---

Child Protection MIS Survey (SWS FORM CP1, CP2, CP3 & CP4)
Scottish Executive

The Scottish Executive Home Department conducts the Child Protection Management Information System Survey. Data are collected on details of Child Protection Referral, basic personal details on the child involved, case conference details and case conference review details. It is an annual survey which began in 1992.

Status: Ongoing
Collection Method: Census
Frequency: Event based unit return
Timeliness: Bulletin produced within 12 months of receipt of data. Provisional tables for use internally, within a few months of receipt of data.
Earliest Available Data: 1993
National Coverage: Scotland
Disaggregation: Local Government Region (Scotland); Council Area (Scotland)/District and Islands Area (Scotland)

Statistician
Jill Alexander
Scottish Executive
Economics Advice and Statistics; 6
Tel: 0141 242 5459;
Email: jill.alexander@scotland.gov.uk

Products that contain data from this source
Child Protection Management Information

Children and Young Persons Accommodated in Secure Units - England and Wales
Department of Health

The Department of Health compiles data on children and young persons accommodated in secure units maintained by local authority Social Services departments in England. Returns completed annually by each secure unit provide information on the type of establishment in England, and the number of places available at 31 March. For each child accommodated during the year, their sex, date of birth, legal status on entry, date placed in secure accommodation, re-admission during the year, date discharged and the incare authority is recorded. The returns are collected on a financial-year basis and results published annually for individual secure units, child care authorities and England. This data has been collected in its present form since year ending 31 March 1985.

Status: Ongoing
Collection Method: Census
Frequency: Annually
Reference Period: 31 March
Timeliness: 6 - 8 months
Earliest Available Data: 31 March 1985
National Coverage: England and Wales
Disaggregation: Local authority metropolitan districts and shire counties; Unitary Authority; London Borough

Statistician
Michael Cornish
Department of Health
Statistics Division 3; Statistics Division 3A
Tel: 020 7972 5573;
Email: mcornish@doh.gov.uk

Products that contain data from this source
Children Accommodated in Secure Units; Health and Personal Social Services Statistics for England; Key Indicators Expert System: Monitoring Services for Children; Key Indicators Graphical System

---

Children and Young Persons on the Child Protection Register (SSDA 908)
National Assembly for Wales

Status: Ongoing
Collection Method: Administrative Records
Frequency: Annually
Reference Period: 31 March
Timeliness: 6 - 8 months
Earliest Available Data: 1988
National Coverage: Wales
Disaggregation: Local Authority District (LAD) / Unitary Authority (England)

Statistician
Robin Jones
National Assembly for Wales
Statistical Directorate; Health Statistics and Analysis Unit 2 (HSA2)
Tel: 029 2082 3625.

Products that contain data from this source
Child Protection Register Wales - Statistical Release
Social Services Statistics Wales

Children Looked After (SSDA 903) - Wales
National Assembly for Wales

Data are compiled on each episode of care for children looked after by local authorities. The main topics covered are age, gender, legal status, reason for being looked after and placement.

Status: Ongoing
Collection Method: Administrative Records
Frequency: Annually
Reference Period: 1 April - 31 March
Timeliness: Results published within 12 months
Earliest Available Data: 1976
National Coverage: Wales
Disaggregation: Local Authority District (LAD) / Unitary Authority (England)

Statistician
Robin Jones
National Assembly for Wales
Statistical Directorate; Health Statistics and Analysis Unit 2 (HSA2)
Tel: 029 2082 3625;
Email: robin.jones@wales.gsi.gov.uk

Products that contain data from this source
Social Services Statistics Wales

Children Looked After (SWS FORM CH1) - Scotland
Scottish Executive

The Scottish Executive Home Department conducts two annual surveys on children in care: The Children-in-Care Survey collects data on admissions, discharges, and changes in accommodation or statute and reviews/hearings. General details are available on the

Sources and Analyses

children, whether they are on the Child Protection Register and if they have any disabilities. This quarterly Survey first began in 1991 and covers the whole of Scotland. Results are published annually. Collection reduced from quarterly to six monthly.

Status: Ongoing
Collection Method: Census
Frequency: Bi-annually
Timeliness: Bulletin produced within 12 months of receipt of data. Provisional tables for use internally, within a few months of receipt of data.
Earliest Available Data: 1978
National Coverage: Scotland
Disaggregation: Council Area (Scotland)/ District and Islands Area (Scotland); Council Area (Scotland)/District and Islands Area (Scotland)

Statistician
Carol Calvert
Scottish Executive
2; Statistics Branch
Tel: 0131 244 5366;
Email: carol.calvert@scotland.gov.uk

Products that contain data from this source
Children Under Supervision Orders

Children Looked After (SWS INTERIM Return)
Scottish Executive

The interim collection collects data on gender, agebank and accommodation of children looked after. A more comprehensive return will be introduced from April 1999.

Status: Ongoing
Collection Method: Census
Frequency: Annually
Reference Period: 1 April - 31 March
Timeliness: Information Note within 12 months of receipt of data
National Coverage: Scotland
Disaggregation: Council Area (Scotland)/ District and Islands Area (Scotland)

Statistician
Carol Calvert
Scottish Executive
2; Statistics Branch
Tel: 0131 244 5366;
Email: carol.calvert@scotland.gov.uk

Children Looked After - England
Department of Health

The Department of Health compiles data on children looked after (i.e. in the care of local authorities or provided with accommodation by Social Services departments). Results from the database are available from the implementation of the children Act 1989 in October 1991 and reflect definitions, procedures and classifications introduced by the Act, published annually for England,

local authorities and Audit Commission and Inspectorate regions. Until 31 March 1991, figures were compiled from a similar annual survey on Children in Care of Local Authorities. This did not include placement change or linkage between years.

The main topics covered are age, gender and duration of children who ceased to be looked after during the year ending 31 March; Days of accommodation for placements during the year to 31 March; Date of birth and Legal status.

Status: Ongoing
Collection Method: Census
Frequency: Annually
Reference Period: March 1992
Timeliness: 8 months and over
Earliest Available Data: 31 March 1992
National Coverage: England
Disaggregation: Unitary Authority; Local authority metropolitan districts and shires; London Borough

Statistician
Michael Cornish
Department of Health
Statistics Division 3; Statistics Division 3A
Tel: 020 7972 5573;
Email: mcornish@doh.gov.uk

Products that contain data from this source
Children Looked After by Local Authorities; Children Looked after in England: 1997/98; Health and Personal Social Services Statistics for England; Key Indicators Expert System: Monitoring Services for Children; Key Indicators Graphical System

Children Subject to Supervision Orders - England (Up to 31 March 1998)
Department of Health

The Department of Health compiles data on children who are subject to Supervision Orders. This feedback publication, 'Supervision Orders Year ending 31 March 1997 England', contains detailed statistics on children placed under the supervision of local authorities in England. The data were compiled from information collected on the Department of Health statistical return SSDA906, submitted by local authorities. The form seeks information on the number of children subject to supervision orders during the year and at 31 March. It also requests details about certain conditions attached to supervision orders. Only supervision orders made to the local authority are included on the form (irrespective of who carries out the supervision); supervision orders made to the Probation Service are not included. As from the 1997-98 year, information on Children Act Supervision Orders will cease to be collected.

Status: Ceased (Discontinued after 1997/98 Bulletin)
Collection Method: Census
Frequency: Annually
Reference Period: 31 March
Timeliness: 6 - 8 months
Earliest Available Data: 31 March 1991
National Coverage: England
Sub-National: Local Authority
Disaggregation: Unitary Authority; Local authority metropolitan districts and shire counties; London Borough

Statistician
Michael Cornish
Department of Health
Statistics Division 3; Statistics Division 3A
Tel: 020 7972 5573;
Email: mcornish@doh.gov.uk

Products that contain data from this source
Children Under Supervision Orders; Health and Personal Social Services Statistics for England; Key Indicators Expert System: Monitoring Services for Children; Key Indicators Graphical System

Children's Day Care Facilities (SSDA 503) - Wales
National Assembly for Wales

The National Assembly for Wales compiles data on day care provision for children (under 8 years) in each local authority. Data are collected on day nurseries, childminders, playgroups, family centres, out-of-school clubs and holiday schemes. Figures relate to 31 March and are collected on the number of providers and places, and on the number of children receiving local authority provision.

Status: Ongoing
Collection Method: Administrative Records
Frequency: Annually
Reference Period: 31 March
Timeliness: 9-12 months
Earliest Available Data: 1974
National Coverage: Wales
Disaggregation: Local Authority District (LAD) / Unitary Authority (England)

Statistician
Robin Jones
National Assembly for Wales
Statistical Directorate; Health Statistics and Analysis Unit 2 (HSA2)
Tel: 029 2082 3625.

Products that contain data from this source
Social Services Statistics Wales

Children's Homes
Department of Health

The Department of Health collates data on children's homes, and produces the publication 'Children's Homes at 31 March

England'. This publication contains statistics on children's homes in England at 31 March. The figures are compiled from information on each home submitted either to the Statistics Division of the Department of Health (Branch SD3A) by local authorities on form CH1 or obtained from information provided directly to the Department of Health by voluntary and assisted homes. From year ending 31 March 1998 and onwards, the publication will be published triennially.

The types of home covered by the form sent to local authorities are: local authority maintained homes; homes controlled by local authorities; private children's homes registered under Part VIII of the Children Act 1989; residential care homes accommodating children and registered under the Registered Homes Act 1984; schools dual registered under Section 63 of the Children Act 1989 and under the Education Act, 1944 or 1993. For each home included, the following information was sought: location; type of home; registration status; facilities; age limits for those accommodated; age criteria used on entry; and maximum number accommodated overnight

Status: Ongoing
Collection Method: Census
Frequency: Triennial
Reference Period: 31 March
Timeliness: 6 - 8 months
Earliest Available Data: 31 March 1995
National Coverage: England
Disaggregation: Unitary Authority; Local authority metropolitan districts and shire counties; London Borough

Statistician
Michael Cornish
Department of Health
Statistics Division 3; Statistics Division 3A
Tel: 020 7972 5573;
Email: mcornish@doh.gov.uk

Products that contain data from this source
Children's Homes; Health and Personal Social Services Statistics for England; Key Indicators Expert System: Monitoring Services for Children; Key Indicators Graphical System

---

Fostering Services (SSDA 904)
National Assembly for Wales

The National Assembly for Wales compiles data on the number of approved foster parents and places and the number of private fostering arrangements and children in private fostering arrangements in each local authority.

Status: Ongoing
Collection Method: Administrative Records
Frequency: Annually
Reference Period: 31 March

Timeliness: 9-12 months
Earliest Available Data: 1977
National Coverage: Wales
Disaggregation: Local Authority District (LAD) / Unitary Authority (England)

Statistician
Robin Jones
National Assembly for Wales
Statistical Directorate; Health Statistics and Analysis Unit 2 (HSA2)
Tel: 029 2082 3625.

Products that contain data from this source
Social Services Statistics Wales

Residential Care Homes for Children (SWS FORM R1-C)
Scottish Executive

The Residential Establishment for Children/ Young People Survey collects data on the type of home, bed complement, staffing, admissions and discharges, and details on the residents.

Status: Ongoing
Collection Method: Census
Frequency: Annually
Timeliness: Bulletin produced within 12 months of receipt of data.
Earliest Available Data: 1989
National Coverage: Scotland
Disaggregation: Council Area (Scotland)/ District and Islands Area (Scotland)

Statistician
Jill Alexander
Scottish Executive
Economics Advice and Statistics; 6
Tel: 0141 242 5459;
Email: jill.alexander@scotland.gov.uk

Products that contain data from this source
Children Under Supervision Orders

Return of Particulars for Voluntary/Assisted Childrens Homes
National Assembly for Wales

Status: Ongoing
Collection Method: Administrative Records
Frequency: Annually
National Coverage: Wales

Statistician
Robin Jones
National Assembly for Wales
Statistical Directorate; Health Statistics and Analysis Unit 2 (HSA2)
Tel: 029 2082 3625

Secure Accommodation (SSDA 912)
National Assembly for Wales

The National Assembly for Wales compiles data on children placed in and discharged from secure units. Data are collected on sex, date of birth, legal status and care authority.

Status: Ongoing
Collection Method: Administrative Records
Frequency: Annually
Reference Period: 31 March
Timeliness: 9-12 months
Earliest Available Data: 1988
National Coverage: Wales
Disaggregation: Local Authority District (LAD) / Unitary Authority (England)

Statistician
Robin Jones
National Assembly for Wales
Statistical Directorate; Health Statistics and Analysis Unit 2 (HSA2)
Tel: 029 2082 3625

Products that contain data from this source
Social Services Statistics Wales
Children Accommodated in Secure Units England and Wales

Statistics of Adoption Applications Survey (SWS FORM A2 & A3)
Scottish Executive

The Scottish Executive Home Department conducts the Statistics of Adoption Applications Survey. Data are collected on the child, adopters, outcome and agreement of parents, court decisions, whether the child was brought from overseas, and type of adoption agency. They also carry out the Statistics of Adoption Applications for the Making and Revocation of Freeing Orders Survey. This collects the child's birth date, application date and the outcome of parental agreement and court proceedings.

Status: Ongoing
Collection Method: Census
Frequency: Quarterly
Timeliness: Bulletin produced every 3 years.
Earliest Available Data: 1983
National Coverage: Scotland
Disaggregation: Council Area (Scotland)/ District and Islands Area (Scotland); Sheriff Courts

Statistician
Carol Calvert
Scottish Executive
2; Statistics Branch
Tel: 0131 244 5366;
Email: carol.calvert@scotland.gov.uk

Products that contain data from this source
Adoptions Applications in Scotland

Supervision Orders (SSDA 06)
National Assembly for Wales

The National Assembly for Wales collects data on the numbers of children placed under supervision orders during each year, by legal status.

Status: Ongoing
Collection Method: Administrative Records
Frequency: Annually
Reference Period: 31 March
Timeliness: 9-12 months
Earliest Available Data: 1978
National Coverage: Wales
Disaggregation: Local Authority District (LAD) / Unitary Authority (England)

Statistician
Robin Jones
National Assembly for Wales
Statistical Directorate; Health Statistics and Analysis Unit 2 (HSA2)
Tel: 029 2082 3625

Products that contain data from this source
Social Services Statistics Wales

See also:
In this chapter:
Children's Daycare Facilities - England *(4.9)*
Key Statistics KS1 *(4.1)*

In other chapters:
Children Order Proceedings - Northern Ireland (see the Crime and Justice chapter)

4.6 Community Health Services

Chiropody Services - Wales (SBL 618)
National Assembly for Wales

The National Assembly for Wales compiles data on chiropody services in Wales. The data provide a summary of the number of people receiving NHS chiropody treatment in the community and schools. Data are available for NHS Trusts and Directly Managed Units of health authorities. Similar information dates back to the early 1970s. Data are collected each financial year and published annually. The return was completed for the last time for the year ending March 31 1997 and has now been discontinued.

Status: Ceased completely
Frequency: Annually
Reference Period: 1 April 1996 to 31 March 1997
Earliest Available Data: 1991/92
National Coverage: Wales
Disaggregation: NHS Trusts

Statistician
Dr Gwyneth Thomas
National Assembly for Wales
Statistical Directorate; Health Statistics and Analysis Unit (1)
Tel: 029 2082 5039.
Email: gwyneth.thomas@wales.gov.uk

Products that contain data from this source
Health Statistics Wales

Community and Cross Sector Activity
Department of Health

DH collects information about community and cross sector activity. Data are collected on the childhood immunisation programmes (DH form ICC 50); the cervical (KC53 and KC61) and breast (KC62 and 63) screening programmes; community nursing including maternity services (midwife clinics and domiciliary units) (KC54); health visitors (KC55); district nurses (KC56); psychiatric nurses (KC57); learning difficulty nurses (KC58) and other specialist nurses (KC59).

Cross sector data includes chiropody services (KT23); clinical psychology (KT24); occupational therapy (KT26); physiotherapy (KT27) and speech therapy services (KT29). Data is also available about the services provided by NHS family planning clinics (KT3). (Information about Sexually Transmitted Diseases is now collected by the Public Health Laboratory Service - Communicable Disease Surveillance Centre (KC60).

Status: Ongoing
Collection Method: Returns from NHS Trusts, Health Authorities
Frequency: Annually
Reference Period: Financial year
Timeliness: 8/10 months
Earliest Available Data: 1988-89
National Coverage: England
Disaggregation: NHS Trusts

Statistician
Lesz Lancucki
Department of Health
Tel: 020 7972 553;
Email: llancuck@doh.gov.uk

Products that contain data from this source
Statistical summaries and bulletins are available for all the activities described.

Community Health Services - Northern Ireland
Department of Health and Social Services - Northern Ireland

The Department of Health and Social Services (NI) collates Community Services statistics about activity in Community Health Services in Northern Ireland. Data cover immunisation, child health surveillance, community nursing, cervical cytology, genito-urinary medicine, breast screening, community dental service, and infectious disease notifications. Results were first collected in 1988-89, although results for breast screening and dental

services are only available from 1992-93 and 1993-94 respectively. Collection of information on community nursing, child health surveillance and community dental services was discontinued in 1997. The immunisation and genito-urinary medicine data exists in a different format from 1974. Data are collected annually (at the end of March) and quarterly but can sometimes be restricted by incomplete returns. Data are available about six months after the reference period although the majority are not formally published.

Status: Ongoing
Collection Method: Returns from Health and Social Services Trusts
Frequency: Annually
Reference Period: Financial year
Timeliness: Six months after reference period
Earliest Available Data: 1988-89
National Coverage: Northern Ireland
Sub-National: Full
Disaggregation: Health and Social Services Trusts

Statistician
Jenny Orr
Department of Health and Social Services - Northern Ireland
Tel: 028 9052 2580;
Email: jenny.orr@dhssni.gov.uk

Products that contain data from this source
Community Health Services; Health and Personal Social Services Statistics (NI); Community Statistics; Regional Trends; Social Focus on Children; Social Trends

---

Paramedical Services - Northern Ireland
Department of Health and Social Services - Northern Ireland

The Department of Health and Social Services (NI) collates data on Professions Allied to Medicine (PAMS) concerning the paramedical services in Northern Ireland. Data cover activity in chiropody, clinical psychology, dietetics, occupational therapy, physiotherapy, orthoptics, and speech therapy. Data are available quarterly from 1988-89 six months after each reference period but can be restricted by incomplete returns. Since 1993-94 the data has been stored on a spreadsheet system.

Status: Ongoing
Collection Method: Returns from Health and Social Services Trusts
Frequency: Quarterly
Timeliness: Six months after reference period
Earliest Available Data: 1988-89
National Coverage: Northern Ireland
Sub-National: Partial
Disaggregation: Health and Social Services Trusts

Statistician
Jenny Orr
Department of Health and Social Services -
Northern Ireland
Tel: 028 9052 2580;
Email: jenny.orr@dhssni.gov.uk

Products that contain data from this source
Paramedical Statistics

Patient Care in the Community - District Nurses and Other Nurses (KC55)
National Assembly for Wales

The National Assembly for Wales compiles data on patient contacts with NHS community nursing staff: health visitors, district nurses and other nurses. Data are available by the number of patients seen during the year by community nurses, and the number of contacts between patients and nurses, including where these took place. The data cover Wales and are available for NHS Trusts. Some information dates back to 1991-92, although the details collected were restructured in 1995. Data are collected each financial year and published annually.

Status: Ongoing
Collection Method: Survey
Frequency: Annually
Reference Period: 1 April to 31 March
Timeliness: Health Statistics and Analysis Unit send forms out in March for completion, with a target date for their return of mid May, the timeliness of the return of forms is improving and progress is being made towards it. HSA aim for key summary data for all of Wales to be available by the end of September, but this is dependent on the timely return of forms and resolution of queries.
Earliest Available Data: 1991/92
National Coverage: Wales
Disaggregation: NHS Trust

Statistician
Dr Gwyneth Thomas
National Assembly for Wales
Statistical Directorate; Health Statistics and Analysis Unit (1)
Tel: 029 2082 5039.
Email: gwyneth.thomas@wales.gov.uk

Products that contain data from this source
Health Statistics Wales

Patient Care in the Community: CPNs and CMHNS (KC57)
National Assembly for Wales

The National Assembly for Wales compiles data on psychiatric and mental handicap nurses in the Welsh NHS. Data are available on the number of patients seen during the year by community psychiatric and mental handicap nurses, for NHS Trusts.

Status: Ongoing
Collection Method: Survey
Frequency: Annually
Reference Period: 1 April to 31 March
Timeliness: Health Statistics and Analysis Unit send forms out in March for completion, with a target date for their return of mid May, the timeliness of the return of forms is improving and progress is being made towards it. The aim is for key summary data for all of Wales to be available by the end of September, but this is dependent on the timely return of forms and resolution of queries.
Earliest Available Data: Some information dates back to 1990-91, although the details collected were restructured in 1995.
National Coverage: Wales
Disaggregation: NHS Trust

Statistician
Dr Gwyneth Thomas
National Assembly for Wales
Statistical Directorate; Health Statistics and Analysis Unit (1)
Tel: 029 2082 5039.
Email: gwyneth.thomas@wales.gov.uk

Products that contain data from this source
Health Statistics Wales

Register of People with Disabilities (SSDA900)
National Assembly for Wales

The National Assembly for Wales collects information on the number of people with physical and visual disabilities included on, or added to in the last year, the registers maintained by Local Authority Social Services departments under Section 29 of the National Assistance Act 1948

Status: Ongoing
Collection Method: Administrative Records
Frequency: Annually
Reference Period: 31 March
Timeliness: 9-12 months
Earliest Available Data: 1980
National Coverage: Wales
Disaggregation: Local Authority District (LAD) / Unitary Authority (England)

Statistician
Robin Jones
National Assembly for Wales
Statistical Directorate; Health Statistics and Analysis Unit 2 (HSA2)
Tel: 029 2082 3625

Products that contain data from this source
Social Services Statistics Wales

See also:
In this chapter:
Day Centres Information *(4.9)*

Adult Services: Assessments, Placements and Waiting Lists (AS1)
National Assembly for Wales

Assessments, outcome arrangements and waiting lists for adult services, by client group

Status: Ongoing
Collection Method: Administrative Records
Frequency: Quarterly
Reference Period: Quarters ending 31 March, 30 June, 30 September, 31 December
Timeliness: 3 months
Earliest Available Data: 1995
National Coverage: Wales
Disaggregation: Local Authority District (LAD)/ Unitary Authority

Statistician
Robin Jones
National Assembly for Wales
Statistical Directorate; Health Statistics and Analysis Unit 2 (HSA2)
Tel: 029 2082 3625

Products that contain data from this source
Social Services Statistics Wales
Quarterly Statistical Brief - Local Authority Community and Residential Care

Adult Services: Numbers of Residential and Other Clients (AS2)
National Assembly for Wales

Placements in residential and nursing homes, respite care, day care, home care services for adults - by client group

Status: Ongoing
Collection Method: Administrative Records
Frequency: Annually
Reference Period: 31 March
Timeliness: 9-12 months
Earliest Available Data: 1995
National Coverage: Wales
Disaggregation: Local Authority District (LAD) / Unitary Authority (England)

Statistician
Robin Jones
National Assembly for Wales
Statistical Directorate; Health Statistics and Analysis Unit 2 (HSA2)
Tel: 029 2082 3625

Products that contain data from this source
Social Services Statistics Wales

Adult Services: Volume of Day and Domiciliary Services (AS3)
National Assembly for Wales

Home care, day care, meals, respite care and other services - volumes

Status: Ongoing
Collection Method: Administrative Records
Frequency: Annually
Reference Period: 31 March
Timeliness: 9-12 months
Earliest Available Data: 1995
National Coverage: Wales
Disaggregation: Local Authority District (LAD) / Unitary Authority (England)

Statistician
Robin Jones
National Assembly for Wales
Statistical Directorate; Health Statistics and Analysis Unit 2 (HSA2)
Tel: 029 2082 3625

Products that contain data from this source
Social Services Statistics Wales

Day and Domiciliary Personal Social Services for Adults
Department of Health

The information is taken from a survey week in September and is collected from all Local Authorities at England level using the Department of Health statistical returns HH1 (on home help and home care), MS1 (on meals service) and DC3 (day centres). These forms were introduced in 1992 in response to the need for information to monitor and evaluate the community care changes. Previously the Department of Health collected less detailed information on day centres and meals (on forms DC1 and DC2, and SSDA302). Information on home help and home care was previously collected by CIPFA. The purpose of the community care reforms of 1993 was to enable more people to continue to live in their own homes as independently as possible. New Statistical returns were introduced in 1992 to monitor and evaluate these changes. Note: the returns DC3 and MS1 will not be collected from 1999.

Status: Ongoing
Collection Method: Census
Frequency: Annually
Reference Period: Survey week in Autumn
Earliest Available Data: Autumn 1992
National Coverage: England
Disaggregation: Unitary Authority; Local Authority / Metropolitan Districts / Shire Counties

Statistician
Tracie Kilbey
Department of Health
Statistics Division; SD3B
Tel: 020 7972 5582;
Email: tkilbey@doh.gov.uk

Products that contain data from this source
Day and Domiciliary Personal Social Services for

Adults, England; Day and domiciliary Personal Social Services for Adults, Detailed statistics; Key Indicators Graphical System

Day Centres Information
National Assembly for Wales

The National Assembly for Wales collects data on local authority day centres client groups and the number of half day sessions available per week.

Status: Ongoing
Collection Method: Administrative Records
Frequency: Annually
Reference Period: 31 March
Timeliness: 9-12 months
Earliest Available Data: 1980
National Coverage: Wales
Disaggregation: Local Authority

Statistician
Robin Jones
National Assembly for Wales
Statistical Directorate; Health Statistics and Analysis Unit 2 (HSA2)
Tel: 029 2082 3625

Products that contain data from this source
Social Services Statistics Wales

Day Services for Adults (SWS FORM D-1B)
Scottish Executive

The Scottish Executive Home Department conducts annual surveys on care centres in Scotland. The Day Care Centres Survey collects data on numbers of local authority and voluntary day centres for the mentally and physically handicapped and elderly, and adult training centres in Scotland. Data have been collected continuously since 1980 and are published annually. Data are also collected on income and expenditure on tasks relating to the registration and inspection of residential homes and daycare centres for both adults and children. Data are available on request for the last two years. Revised form introduced 1998

Status: Ongoing
Collection Method: Census
Frequency: Annually
Reference Period: as at 31 March
Timeliness: Bulletin produced within 12 months of receipt of data.
Earliest Available Data: 1976
National Coverage: Scotland
Disaggregation: Council Area (Scotland)/ District and Islands Area (Scotland); Health Board Area (Scotland); Local Government Region (Scotland)

Statistician
Jill Alexander
Scottish Executive
Economics Advice and Statistics; 6

Tel: 0141 242 5459;
Email: jill.alexander@scotland.gov.uk

Products that contain data from this source
Community Care Bulletin

Home Care Statistical Return (SWS FORM H1)
Scottish Executive

The Scottish Executive Home Department conducts annual surveys on home helps and meals-on-wheels in Scotland. Home Helps Survey collects data on clients receiving home help services and on numbers of staff. Data have been collected continuously for the past ten years and are published annually. Form revised February 1998

Status: Ongoing
Collection Method: Census
Frequency: Annually
Reference Period: Week containing the 31st March
Timeliness: Bulletin produced within 12 months of receipt of data.
Earliest Available Data: 1986
National Coverage: Scotland
Disaggregation: Council Area (Scotland)/ District and Islands Area (Scotland)

Statistician
Jill Alexander
Scottish Executive
Economics Advice and Statistics; 6
Tel: 0141 242 5459;
Email: jill.alexander@scotland.gov.uk

Products that contain data from this source
Community Care Bulletin

Local Authority and Independent Residential Homes (RA)
National Assembly for Wales

Covers Local authority and independent registered homes. Data are collected on client groups, places, residents, and source of residents finding (independent homes), and for dual registered homes the number of nursing beds.

Status: Ongoing
Collection Method: Administrative Records
Frequency: Annually
Reference Period: 31 March
Timeliness: 9-12 months
Earliest Available Data: 1980
National Coverage: Wales
Disaggregation: Local Authority; Postcode Area

Statistician
Robin Jones
National Assembly for Wales
Statistical Directorate; Health Statistics and Analysis Unit 2 (HSA2)
Tel: 029 2082 3625

Products that contain data from this source
Social Services Statistics Wales

Lunch Clubs (SWS FORM D3)
Scottish Executive

The Scottish Executive Home Department conducts Financial Provision, Material Provision, and Lunch Club Provision Surveys. Data are collected on provisions made for groups such as the elderly and handicapped in the community in financial, material and other support areas.

Status: Ongoing
Collection Method: Census
Frequency: Annually
Reference Period: as at 31st March
Timeliness: Bulletin produced within 12 months of receipt of data.
Earliest Available Data: 1986
National Coverage: Scotland
Disaggregation: Council Area (Scotland)/ District and Islands Area (Scotland)

Statistician
Jill Alexander
Scottish Executive
Economics Advice and Statistics; 6
Tel: 0141 242 5459;
Email: jill.alexander@scotland.gov.uk

Products that contain data from this source
Community Care Bulletin

Material Provision (SWS FORM M1)
Scottish Executive

The Scottish Executive Home Department conducts Financial Provision, Material Provision, and Lunch Club Provision Surveys. Data are collected on provisions made for groups such as the elderly and handicapped in the community in financial, material and other support areas.

Status: Ongoing
Collection Method: Census
Frequency: Annually
Reference Period: as at 31st March
Timeliness: Bulletin produced within 12 months of receipt of data.
Earliest Available Data: 1986
National Coverage: Scotland
Disaggregation: Council Area (Scotland) / District and Islands Area (Scotland)

Statistician
Jill Alexander
Scottish Executive
Economics Advice and Statistics; 6
Tel: 0141 242 5459;
Email: jill.alexander@scotland.gov.uk

Products that contain data from this source
Community Care Bulletin

Meals-On-Wheels (SWS FORM H2)
Scottish Executive

The Scottish Executive Home Department conducts annual surveys on home helps and meals-on-wheels in Scotland. Meals-on-Wheels Survey collects data on the number of clients and meals delivered.

Status: Ongoing
Collection Method: Census
Frequency: Annually
Reference Period: as at 31st March
Timeliness: Bulletin produced within 12 months of receipt of data.
Earliest Available Data: 1986
National Coverage: Scotland
Disaggregation: Council Area (Scotland)/ District and Islands Area (Scotland)

Statistician
Jill Alexander
Scottish Executive
Economics Advice and Statistics; 6
Tel: 0141 242 5459;
Email: jill.alexander@scotland.gov.uk

Products that contain data from this source
Community Care Bulletin

NHS Day Care Survey: Availability and Use of Facilities - Wales
National Assembly for Wales

The NHS Day Care Survey: Availability and Use of Facilities is compiled by the National Assembly for Wales on the availability of daycare facilities under the NHS for Wales for the elderly, mentally ill or handicapped. Data are collected from NHS daycare facilities on the numbers of patient attendances by speciality and function of the clinic. Numbers of patients who are regular day attendees or those using a hospital bed are collected for attendance or re-attendance. The Survey is carried out annually and results can be obtained for NHS Trusts or Directly Managed Units of treatment from 1988-89 to the current year.

Frequency: Annually
Earliest Available Data: 1988-89
National Coverage: Wales

Statistician
Adrian Crompton
National Assembly for Wales
Statistical Directorate; Health Statistics and Analysis Unit (4)
Tel: 029 2082 5033.
Email: statswales@gtnet.gov.uk

Private Hospitals, Homes and Clinics
Department of Health

This information is based on the RH(N) form (previously KO36 form) completed annually via all Health Authorities. Statistics collected are on registration details, registered and occupied beds and qualified nursing staff recorded at the date of routine inspection between 1 October and 31 March for private hospitals, homes and clinics registered under Section 23 of the Registered Homes Act 1984.

Status: Ongoing
Collection Method: Census
Frequency: Annually
Reference Period: As at 31 March or at date of inspection
Timeliness: 10 months
Earliest Available Data: December 1985
National Coverage: England
Disaggregation: Unitary Authority; Local Authority / Metropolitan Districts / Shire Counties

Statistician
Tracie Kilbey
Department of Health
Statistics Division; SD3B
Tel: 020 7972 5582;
Email: tkilbey@doh.gov.uk

Products that contain data from this source
Day and domiciliary Personal Social Services for Adults, Detailed statistics; Health and Personal Social Services Statistics for England; Key Indicators Graphical System; Residential Personal Social Services for Adults, Detailed statistics on residential and nursing care homes and local authority supported residents

Referrals, Assessments and Packages of Care
Department of Health

Work has been in progress to develop a coherent set of national statistics related to adult community care. The project is currently in dress rehearsal stage, but full implementation will take place from 1 April 2000. The new data collection will provide details of Referrals to Social Services Departments in Local Authorities, Assessments and Packages of Care for individuals. This project will replace the DC3 and MS1 data collections and collects data for a calendar year 1 April - 31 March and for 31 March

Status: New collection
Collection Method: Census
Frequency: Annually
Reference Period: 1 April to 31 March
Timeliness: To be determined
Earliest Available Data: 2000/2001 but rehearsal started 1 Jan 1999 - 31 March 1999
National Coverage: England
Disaggregation: Unitary Authority; Local Authority / Metropolitan Districts / Shire Counties

Statistician
Tracie Kilbey
Department of Health
Statistics Division; SD3B
Tel: 020 7972 5582;
Email: tkilbey@doh.gov.uk

Products that contain data from this source
To be determined

Registered Establishments (SWS FORM RE1 (AH), (AD), (CH), (CD)
Scottish Executive

These annual forms are statements of income and expenditure relating to Local Authority administration of residential and day care establishments.

Status: Ceased temporarily
Collection Method: Census
Frequency: Annually
Reference Period: Whole year
National Coverage: Scotland
Disaggregation: Council Area (Scotland)/ District and Islands Area (Scotland)

Statistician
Jill Alexander
Scottish Executive
Economics Advice and Statistics; 6
Tel: 0141 242 5459;
Email: jill.alexander@scotland.gov.uk

Products that contain data from this source
Community Care Bulletin

Residential Establishment Census Return (SWS FORM R1)
Scottish Executive

The Scottish Executive Home Department conducts annual surveys on care homes in Scotland. The Residential Care Home Survey collects data on elderly, physically and mentally handicapped and mentally ill people in local authority and private homes, including numbers of homes, beds, residents and staff, length of stay and handicap of resident. Data have been collected continuously since 1980 and are published annually. Data are also collected on income and expenditure on tasks relating to the registration and inspection of residential homes and daycare centres for both adults and children. Data are available on request for the last two years.

Status: Ongoing
Collection Method: Census
Frequency: Annually
Reference Period: as at 31st March
Timeliness: Bulletin produced within 12 months of receipt of data.
Earliest Available Data: 1978
National Coverage: Scotland

Disaggregation: Council Area (Scotland)/ District and Islands Area (Scotland); Health Board Area (Scotland); Postcode Area; Postcode District; Postcode Sector

Statistician
Jill Alexander
Scottish Executive
Economics Advice and Statistics; 6
Tel: 0141 242 5459;
Email: jill.alexander@scotland.gov.uk

Products that contain data from this source
Community Care Bulletin; Vacancy Monitoring Report

Residential Personal Social Services for Adults
Department of Health

The information is derived from a number of annual statistical returns submitted by, or through, local authorities to the Department of Health - RA Forms A, B and C (residential care homes). A new return was introduced for the year ending 31 March 1997 to collect information on residential homes, replacing the returns RAC5 and RAC5S. The new return collects aggregate data for each local authority on the number of homes and places on local authority registers at 31 March, by primary client group and type of accommodation (LA, voluntary, private, small homes and dual registered homes). SR1 form (Local authority supported residents). The SR1 return introduced for the 1993/94 collection year, collects information on local authority supported residents in staffed homes or other accommodation. Data are collected by type of care, age group, type of accommodation, type of stay and location. Data on short stay admissions of supported residents are also collected.

Status: Ongoing
Collection Method: Census
Frequency: Annually
Reference Period: 31 March (places etc), financial year (admissions)
Timeliness: nine months
Earliest Available Data: March 1995
National Coverage: England
Disaggregation: Unitary Authority; Local authority/Metropolitan Districts /Shire Counties; Local Authority/Metropolitan Districts/Shire Counties

Statistician
Tracie Kilbey
Department of Health
Statistics Division; SD3B
Tel: 020 7972 5582;
Email: tkilbey@doh.gov.uk

Products that contain data from this source
Health and Personal Social Services Statistics for England; Key Indicators Graphical System; Residential Personal Social Services for Adults,

Detailed statistics on residential and nursing care homes and local authority supported residents; Residential Personal Social Services for Adults, England

Supported Accommodation (SWS FORM SA-1)
Scottish Executive

The Scottish Executive Home Department conducts annual surveys on care homes in Scotland. The survey on Supported Accommodation collects details on homes which provide some form of support, but are not registered. Data have been collected continuously since 1980 and are published annually. Data are also collected on income and expenditure on tasks relating to the registration and inspection of residential homes and daycare centres for both adults and children.

Status: Ongoing
Collection Method: Census
Frequency: Annually
Reference Period: as at 31st March
Timeliness: Bulletin produced within 12 months of receipt of data. Provisional tables for use internally, within a few months of receipt of data.
Earliest Available Data: 1980
National Coverage: Scotland
Disaggregation: Council Area (Scotland)/ District and Islands Area (Scotland)

Statistician
Jill Alexander
Scottish Executive
Economics Advice and Statistics; 6
Tel: 0141 242 5459;
Email: jill.alexander@scotland.gov.uk

Products that contain data from this source
Community Care Bulletin

Vacancy Monitoring Return (SWS FORM VM-1)
Scottish Executive

The Scottish Executive Home Department conducts annual surveys on care homes in Scotland. The Vacancy Monitoring Survey collects data on capacity and occupancy of private/voluntary and local authority residential care homes every six months. Data are also collected on income and expenditure on tasks relating to the registration and inspection of residential homes and daycare centres for both adults and children. Data are available on request for the last two years.

Status: Ongoing
Collection Method: Census
Frequency: Annually
Reference Period: year to 31st March
Earliest Available Data: 1995
National Coverage: Scotland

Disaggregation: Council Area (Scotland)/ District and Islands Area (Scotland); Health Board Area (Scotland); Local Government Region (Scotland); Postcode Area; Postcode Sector; Postcode District

Statistician
Jill Alexander
Scottish Executive
Economics Advice and Statistics; 6
Tel: 0141 242 5459;
Email: jill.alexander@scotland.gov.uk

Products that contain data from this source
Vacancy Monitoring Report

4.8 Cost of Healthcare and Social Services

Cost Book Data System
Information and Statistics Division, NHS in Scotland

To provide a database of comparative costs broken down to patient type within speciality for analytical purposes.

Status: Ongoing
Collection Method: Administrative Records
Frequency: Annually
Reference Period: Financial year
Timeliness: 3 months after year end
Earliest Available Data: 1960/61
National Coverage: Scotland
Disaggregation: Health Board; Hospital

Statistician
Graham Mitchell
Information and Statistics Division, NHS in Scotland
Tel: 0131 551 8022

Products that contain data from this source
Scottish Key Indicators for Performance (SKIPPER)

Dental Expenditure
Department of Health

The information is available annually for gross and net payments. The gross payments are the total amounts spent on General Dental Service, Emergency Dental Service and Salaried Dental Service dental activity, whereas the net expenditure excludes revenue generated from payments from patients.

Status: Ongoing
Collection Method: Administrative Records
Frequency: Annually
Timeliness: 3 months
Earliest Available Data: 1978/79
National Coverage: United Kingdom

Statistician
Billy Burns
Department of Health
Tel: 020 7972 5388

Financial Provision (SWS FORM F1)
Scottish Executive

The Scottish Executive Home Department conducts Financial Provision, Material Provision, and Lunch Club Provision Surveys. Data are collected on provisions made for groups such as the elderly and handicapped in the community in financial, material and other support areas. Form revised February 1998

Status: Ongoing
Collection Method: Census
Frequency: Annually
Reference Period: 1st April-31st March
Timeliness: Bulletin produced within 12 months of receipt of data.
Earliest Available Data: 1987
National Coverage: Scotland
Disaggregation: Council Area (Scotland)/ District and Islands Area (Scotland)

Statistician
Jill Alexander
Scottish Executive
Economics Advice and Statistics; 6
Tel: 0141 242 5459;
Email: jill.alexander@scotland.gov.uk

Products that contain data from this source
Community Care Bulletin

Health Costing Returns - Wales
National Assembly for Wales

Information on speciality and programme costs is collected from trusts on the financial return TFR2. This is collected annually by the National Assembly for Wales. The forms support the annual accounts, and similar forms are collected in England. Some aggregate information from the returns is used for the PES process. The information may also be used in answering Parliamentary Questions, Assembly Questions and requests, and brief details are published in 'Health Statistics Wales'. Until and including 1991/92, an annual booklet of detailed information was produced by the National Assembly for Wales for circulation to trusts, health authorities, within the National Assembly for Wales and to anyone else on request. This has been discontinued with summary figures published in the annual Health Statistics Wales volume.

Status: Ongoing
Collection Method: Aggregate return
Frequency: Annually
Reference Period: 1 April to 31 March
Timeliness: NHS Finance Division of the National Assembly for Wales carry out this survey with other financial returns, with a return date of 31 July.
Earliest Available Data: 1986/87
National Coverage: Wales

Disaggregation: NHS Trust

Statistician
Dr Gwyneth Thomas
National Assembly for Wales
Statistical Directorate; Health Statistics and Analysis Unit (1)
Tel: 029 2082 5039.
Email: gwyneth.thomas@wales.gov.uk

Products that contain data from this source
Health Statistics in Wales

Research into Changes in Hospital Consultants Work
Office of Manpower Economics

Qualitative research and survey of 4,000 hospital consultants.

Collection Method: Small-scale (Sample) Survey
Frequency: Ad hoc
Earliest Available Data: Autumn 1997
National Coverage: Great Britain

Statistician
Grant Whitfield
Office of Manpower Economics
Tel: 020 7467 7231

Products that contain data from this source
Report of the Review Body on Doctors' and Dentists' Remuneration 1998

RO3
Department of Health; sponsored by DETR

Detailed information for local authorities in England on income and expenditure for Personal Social Services.

Status: Ongoing
Collection Method: Census
Frequency: Annually
Reference Period: Financial year
Earliest Available Data: 1994-5
National Coverage: England
Disaggregation: Local Authority District (LAD) / Unitary Authority (England)

Statistician
Brian Allen
Department of Health, 452C,
Statistics Division 3; Statistics Division 3C
Tel: 020 7972 5595;
Email: ballen@doh.gov.uk

Products that contain data from this source
Personal Social Services Current and Capital Expenditure in England: 1997-98 (Bulletin)

See also:
In this chapter:
General Dental Service - Monthly Scheduled Payments to Dentists *(4.11)*
General Dental Service - Treatments Data *(4.11)*

Sources and Analyses

Key Statistics KS1 *(4.1)*
Residential Establishment Census Return
(SWS FORM R1) *(4.7)*

4.9 Daycare Facilities for Children

Children's Daycare Facilities - England
Department of Health

The Department of Health compiles data on daycare provision for young children (aged under eight) in each local authority in England. Data are collected on day nurseries, childminders, playgroups, and family centres and on out-of-school clubs and holiday schemes for children aged five to seven. Figures relate to 31 March each year and are collected on the number of providers and places, and on the number of children receiving local authority provision, where possible provision for children aged under five is separately identified. Since 1994, information on sessions operated by playgroups has been collected. Figures are published annually for England, local authorities and for Audit Commission and Inspectorate Regions.

The publication for year ending 31 March 1997 is the last one to be produced by the Department of Health, and responsibility for the statistics relating to Children's Day Care Facilities is being transferred to the Department for Education and Employment. Data is collected on form SSDA 503. The data has been collected in its present form since year ending 31 March 1986.

The last publication of 'Children's Day Care Facilities' is for 31 March 1997, and responsibility for statistics relating to children's day care facilities has now moved to the Department of Education and Employment.

Status: Ceased completely
Collection Method: Census
Frequency: Annually
Reference Period: 31 March
Timeliness: 6 - 8 months
Earliest Available Data: 31 March 1986
National Coverage: England
Disaggregation: Unitary Authority; Local authority metropolitan districts and shire counties; London Borough

Statistician
Michael Cornish
Department of Health
Statistics Division 3; Statistics Division 3A
Tel: 020 7972 5573;
Email: mcornish@doh.gov.uk

Products that contain data from this source
Children's Day Care Facilities (up to 31 March 1997); Health and Personal Social Services Statistics for England; Key Indicators Expert System: Monitoring Services for Children; Key Indicators Graphical System

Facilities for the Daycare and Education of Children and Support to the Families Survey (SWS FORM D1-C)
Scottish Executive

The Scottish Executive Home Department carries out the Facilities for the Day Care and Education of Children and Support to the Families Survey, completed every three years. Data are collected on numbers of local authority and registered voluntary day nurseries, pre-school playgroups, registered childminders with numbers of places available, sources of funding, and number of children attending. The Survey has been conducted for over ten years although the format was slightly modified in 1994. Form revised November 1998

Status: Ongoing
Collection Method: Census
Frequency: Every 3 years
Reference Period: as at 31 March
Timeliness: Bulletin produced within 12 months of receipt of data.
Earliest Available Data: 1976
National Coverage: Scotland
Disaggregation: Council Area (Scotland)/ District and Islands Area (Scotland); Local Government Region (Scotland)

Statistician
Jill Alexander
Scottish Executive
Economics Advice and Statistics; 6
Tel: 0141 242 5459;
Email: jill.alexander@scotland.gov.uk

Products that contain data from this source
Services for Children

4.10 Demand for, and Supply of, Healthcare staff

Please see:
In this chapter:
Staff of Social Services Departments in Wales (STF 1) - HQ, Social Work, Domiciliary *(4.15)*

4.11 Dental Health

Adult Dental Health Survey - UK
Department of Health

The Adult Dental Survey is a periodic survey, the latest of which was carried out in 1988, to establish the current state of dental health of adults and compare the results with similar surveys carried out in the 1960s and 1970s. The survey was conducted by the Office of Population Censuses and Surveys, (now the Office for National Statistics) on behalf of the UK Health Departments. In 1988, 6825 adults were examined and 4331 were dentally examined. Results of the corresponding 1998 survey are due to be published by the end of 1999.

Status: Ongoing
Collection Method: Large-scale (Sample) Survey
Frequency: Decennial
Reference Period: 1988
Timeliness: 3 years
Earliest Available Data: 1968
National Coverage: United Kingdom

Statistician
Mr W. Burns
Department of Health
Tel: 020 7972 5389

Products that contain data from this source
Adult Dental Health Survey 1988

Children's Dental Health Survey - UK
Department of Health

The Children's Dental Health Survey has been carried out every ten years since 1973 by the Office of Population Censuses and Surveys (now the Office for National Statistics) on behalf of the UK Health Departments. The latest survey in 1993 involved the examination of the teeth of 17,000 children aged between five and fifteen years attending state schools in the United Kingdom.

Status: Ongoing
Collection Method: Large-scale (Sample) Survey
Frequency: Decennial
Reference Period: January - May 1993
Timeliness: 1 year
Earliest Available Data: 1973
National Coverage: United Kingdom

Statistician
Mr W. Burns
Department of Health
Tel: 020 7972 5389

Products that contain data from this source
Children's Dental Health in the United Kingdom 1993

Community Dental Service Treatment Record
Information and Statistics Division, NHS in Scotland

To provide community dental departments with data for contracting purposes/ monitoring of service provision at Trust and national level.

Status: Ongoing
Collection Method: Administrative Records
Frequency: Continuously
Reference Period: Annual
Earliest Available Data: 1990
National Coverage: Scotland
Disaggregation: NHS Trust

Statistician
Susan Burney
Information and Statistics Division, NHS in Scotland
Tel: 0131 551 8542

Products that contain data from this source
Annual Report of the Dental Practice Board, Scotland; Scottish Health Statistics

Community Health Services - Dental Services (KC64)
National Assembly for Wales

The National Assembly for Wales compiles data on Community Dental Services. Data are available on screening and preventive programmes, details of the number of patients seen by the Community Dental Service, the number of contacts between patients and community dentists - including the type of care and treatment provided, and details of the amount of time (and travelling time) spent on a number of service activities. Data cover Wales and are available for NHS Trusts. Similar information goes back to 1991-92, although the details collected were restructured in 1994. Earlier data are available on a different basis. The data are collected each financial year and results are published annually.

A project is being conducted to identify the data requirements of the Community Dental Service, to provide an assessment and evaluation of the data process and to make recommendations for future collection, collation, analysis and presentation of information in Wales. This will have implications for central collection of data via KC64 in that recommendations will be made relating to what should be collected and how that should be derived from existing systems locally.

Status: Ongoing
Collection Method: Aggregate return
Frequency: Annually
Reference Period: 1 April to 31 March

Timeliness: Forms are sent out for completion in March, with a target date for their return of mid May. The aim is for key summary data for all of Wales to be available by the end of September, but this is dependent on the timely return of forms and resolution of queries.
Earliest Available Data: 1991-92
National Coverage: Wales
Disaggregation: NHS Trust

Statistician
Dr Gwyneth Thomas
National Assembly for Wales
Statistical Directorate; Health Statistics and Analysis Unit (1)
Tel: 029 2082 5039.
Email: gwyneth.thomas@wales.gov.uk

Products that contain data from this source
Health Statistics Wales

Emergency Dental Service
Department of Health

A Health Authority may make arrangements with any dentist whose name is included in the HA dental list, for the provision of treatment in urgent cases at a health centre, when dentists in the locality or parts of its locality, are not normally available to provide general dental services. "Urgent cases" are those patients the dentist considers need immediate treatment for an acute condition. This annual survey monitors the levels of Emergency Dental Service available in each Health Authority area in England and Wales.

Status: Ongoing
Collection Method: Census
Frequency: Annually
National Coverage: England and Wales
Disaggregation: Health Authority

Statistician
Billy Burns
Department of Health
Tel: 020 7972 5388

General Dental Service - Manpower
Department of Health

The number of GDS dentists quarterly in the United Kingdom, and by Health Authority/Health Board for England, Wales and Scotland. This data is broken down into: Principals - A dentist whose name appears on an HA dental list as a GDS principal. This is not an indication of how much work is carried out in the GDS; Assistants - a GDS assistant is a dentist working under the supervision of a GDS principal who is responsible for the quality of the assistants work. An assistant cannot hold a contract with a HA or appear on a HA list; and Vocational Trainees - those dentists working

for the mandatory 1 year period under the guidance of a qualified dentist after completing the five year degree course. Vocational training was voluntary when first introduced in 1978/88, but became compulsory on 1 October 1993.

Status: Ongoing
Collection Method: Administrative Records
Frequency: Quarterly
National Coverage: United Kingdom

Statistician
Billy Burns
Department of Health
Tel: 020 7972 5388

General Dental Service - Monthly Scheduled Payments to Dentists
Department of Health

Data by main category of expenditure is available from the monthly payments schedule. Registrations - number of adult and child patients registered with a GDS dentist and payments. Number and cost of courses of treatment processed for payment in the month. Gross cost - the total cost scheduled to be paid out to the dentist. This covers all fee payments for courses of treatment and registrations.

Status: Ongoing
Collection Method: Administrative Records
Frequency: Monthly
Timeliness: 3 months
Earliest Available Data: October 1990
National Coverage: Great Britain
Disaggregation: By HA for England and Wales

Statistician
Billy Burns
Department of Health
Tel: 020 7972 5388

General Dental Service - Treatments Data
Department of Health

This data is collated quarterly on the numbers and costs of individual GDS treatments scheduled for payment in the period. This information is available for England and Wales, for ages under 18 and 18 and over. It is based on a 5% sample of patients.

Status: Ongoing
Collection Method: Administrative Records
Frequency: Quarterly
Timeliness: 3 Months
Earliest Available Data: 1990
National Coverage: England and Wales

Statistician
Billy Burns
Department of Health
Tel: 020 7972 5388

General Dental Service Datasets
Information and Statistics Division, NHS in
Scotland

To provide information on general dental
practitioners including registrations,
treatments and earnings

Status: Ongoing
Collection Method: Administrative Records
Frequency: Continuously
Reference Period: Annual
Timeliness: Monthly in arrears
Earliest Available Data: 1987
National Coverage: Scotland
Disaggregation: Health Board

Statistician
Susan Burney
Information and Statistics Division, NHS in
Scotland
Tel: 0131 551 8542

**KC64 - Community Care Dental
Survey**
Department of Health

This annual survey collects information on
the main activities of the Community Dental Service. These include: Screening
Programmes - the process of covering a
large population using the simplest possible tests to identify those individuals in need
of dental care including, examinations in a
dental surgery and counselling and advice.
Preventative Programmes - where a defined
target group receive some prophylactic or
protection measure designed to reduce the
levels of oral disease in that target group.
Patient Care - all activities carried out on a
one to one basis by registered CDS staff for
the treatment of established oral disease or
the prevention of oral disease.
Episodes of Care - this is where there is a
series of face to face contacts with CDS staff
needed to complete a patient treatment plan.
It may extend over a short or long period.

Status: Ongoing
Collection Method: Small-scale (Sample)
Survey
Frequency: Annually
Reference Period: Financial Year
Earliest Available Data: 1990/91
National Coverage: England

Statistician
Billy Burns
Department of Health
Tel: 020 7972 5388

See also:
In this chapter:
Community Health Services - Northern
Ireland *(4.6)*

4.12 Diet and Nutrition

Diet and Nutrition
Department of Health

The National Diet and Nutrition Survey is a
programme designed to provide a
comprehensive picture of the dietary habits
and nutritional status of the population. The
first part of the programme was a survey of
children aged one and a half to four and a
half years carried out by the former Office
of Population Censuses and Surveys on
behalf of the Department of Health and
Ministry of Agriculture, Fisheries and Food
during 1991 and 1993. Further surveys will
cover other age groups.

Status: Ongoing
Collection Method: Large-scale (Sample)
Survey
Frequency: As necessary
Reference Period: July 1992-June 1993
Timeliness: 2 years
Earliest Available Data: 1967/8

Statistician
Anthony Boucher
Department of Health
Tel: 020 7972 5389

Infant Feeding - UK - 1995
Department of Health

The Infant Feeding Survey is a survey of
mothers in the UK carried out by the Office
for National Statistics on behalf of UK
Health Departments. The Survey has been
carried out every five years since 1975. The
Survey interviews mothers on how they feed
their babies from birth to nine months, and
on weaning practices. Data are analysed by
the age of infant (one, two and six weeks;
four, six and nine months) and, in some
cases, by age of mother, but not by sex of
infant. Data are analysed by broad
geographical area. Socio-economic analysis
is by main occupation of mother and by
social class of husband or partner. Data are
not analysed by ethnic group.

Status: Ongoing
Collection Method: Large-scale (Sample)
Survey
Frequency: Every 5 years
Reference Period: August-October
Timeliness: 2 years
Earliest Available Data: 1975
National Coverage: United Kingdom

Statistician
Anthony Boucher
Department of Health
Tel: 020 7972 5389

Products that contain data from this source
Infant Feeding in 1995

4.13 Disability

**Congenital Anomalies - England
and Wales**
Office for National Statistics

The Office for National Statistics runs the
National Congenital Anomaly System.
Congenital anomalies are voluntarily
notified by district health authorities. Data
on anomalies are available for a number of
variables including by mother's age, month
of birth, sex, birthweight, multiplicity. Data
cover England and Wales and are available
at district health authority and postcode
level. The System has been in operation for
all malformations since 1964 although an
exclusion list was introduced on 1 January
1990. Before 1 January 1995 notifications
were requested for anomalies identified at
or within ten days of birth; this limit was
removed on 1 January 1995. The data are
published annually by the end of the year
following the reference year.

Status: Ongoing
Collection Method: Voluntary Notification
Frequency: Continuously
Reference Period: Annual
Timeliness: The data are published annually by
the end of the year following the reference year.
Earliest Available Data: 1964
National Coverage: England and Wales
Disaggregation: Standard Regions, Government
Office Regions; Health Authority

Statistician
Beverley Botting
Office for National Statistics
Tel: 020 7533 5195;
Email: bev.botting@ons.gov.uk

Products that contain data from this source
Congenital Anomaly Statistics 1997; The ONS
Monitoring Scheme for Congenital
Malformations

Congenital Malformations
National Assembly for Wales

A new project holding information on
congenital anomalies detected during
pregnancy, at birth or during the first year
of life. Individual records, including details
of the foetus / infant, anomalies detected,
and parental details, are held.

Status: Ongoing

Statistician
Adrian Crompton
National Assembly for Wales
Statistical Directorate; Health Statistics and
Analysis Unit (4)
Tel: 029 2082 5033.
Email: statswales@gtnet.gov.uk

Persons on Learning Disability Register (SSDa 901)
National Assembly for Wales

Status: Ongoing
Collection Method: Administrative Records
National Coverage: Wales
Disaggregation: Local Authority District (LAD) / Unitary Authority (England)

Statistician
Robin Jones
National Assembly for Wales
Statistical Directorate; Health Statistics and Analysis Unit 2 (HSA2)
Tel: 029 2082 3625

Register of the Deaf and Hard of Hearing
Department of Health

This information is obtained from return SSDA910 and related to the register of deaf or heard of hearing people maintained by Local Authority Social Services Departments under Section 29 of the National Assistance Act 1948. The form seeks information on the numbers of persons on the register at the end of the year.

Status: Ongoing
Collection Method: Census
Frequency: Triennial
Earliest Available Data: 1983
National Coverage: England
Disaggregation: Unitary Authority; Local Authority / Metropolitan Districts / Shire Counties

Statistician
Tracie Kilbey
Department of Health
Statistics Division; SD3B
Tel: 020 7972 5582;
Email: tkilbey@doh.gov.uk

Products that contain data from this source
Day and Domiciliary Personal Social Services for Adults, Detailed statistics; Health and Personal Social Services Statistics for England; Key Indicators Graphical System; Residential Personal Social Services for Adults, Detailed statistics on residential and nursing care homes and local authority supported residents. Publication - People Registered as Deaf of Hard of Hearing.

Registered Blind and Partially Sighted People
Department of Health

This information is obtained from return SSDA902 and relates to the register of blind and partially sighted persons maintained by Local Authority Social Services Departments under Section 29 of the National Assistance Act 1948. The form seeks information on the numbers of persons on the register at the end of the year and the number of new

registrations during the year. Data are also requested on the number of registered blind persons who have an additional disability by age. Since 1979/80 complete data have normally been collected every third year, commencing with the data for 1981/82. This restriction was imposed in order to reduce the form filling burden on local authorities. The return for 1984/85 was however, postponed for a year in order to coincide with the collection cycle for the BD8 return on which data on causes of blindness and partial sight are collected. Data on new registrations of children under 16 have continued to be collected on an annual basis.

Status: Ongoing
Collection Method: Census
Frequency: Triennial
Reference Period: As at 31 March
Earliest Available Data: 1972
National Coverage: England
Disaggregation: Unitary Authority; Local Authority / Metropolitan Districts / Shire Counties

Statistician
Tracie Kilbey
Department of Health
Statistics Division; SD3B
Tel: 020 7972 5582;
Email: tkilbey@doh.gov.uk

Products that contain data from this source
Health and Personal Social Services Statistics for England; Key Indicators Graphical System. Publication - Registered Blind and Partially Sighted People

Registers of People with Physical Disabilities
Department of Health

This information is obtained from return SSDA911 and relates to the register of people with physical disabilities maintained by Local Authority Social Services Departments under Section 29 of the National Assistance Act 1948. The form seeks information on the numbers of persons on the register at the end of the year.

Status: Ongoing
Collection Method: Census
Frequency: Triennial
Earliest Available Data: 1981
National Coverage: England
Disaggregation: Unitary Authority; Local Authority/ Metropolitan Districts/Shire Counties

Statistician
Tracie Kilbey
Department of Health
Statistics Division; SD3B
Tel: 020 7972 5582;
Email: tkilbey@doh.gov.uk

Products that contain data from this source
Health and Personal Social Services Statistics for England; Key Indicators Graphical System; Registered Blind and Partially Sighted People Publication - Registers of People with Physical Disabilities

Registration of Blind Persons and Partially Sighted Persons (SWS FORM SWB)
Scottish Executive

This return, which is completed by Societies for the Blind in some cases, gives numbers of people registered blind as at the census date, by sex and age-group. There are separate tables for numbers who have various additional disabilities and for those first registered during the year up to the census date. Similar tables ask for details of those registered partially sighted.

Status: Ongoing
Collection Method: Census
Frequency: Annually
Reference Period: as at 31st March
Timeliness: Bulletin produced within 12 months of receipt of data. Provisional tables for use internally, within a few months of receipt of data.
Earliest Available Data: 1986
National Coverage: Scotland
Disaggregation: Council Area (Scotland)/ District and Islands Area (Scotland)

Statistician
Carol Calvert
Scottish Executive
2; Statistics Branch
Tel: 0131 244 5366;
Email: carol.calvert@scotland.gov.uk

Products that contain data from this source
Community Care Bulletin

Survey of Disability - Northern Ireland
Department of Finance and Personnel - Northern Ireland

The Policy Planning and Research Unit of the Northern Ireland Statistics and Research Agency surveyed 6,500 disabled adults and children in private households and communal establishments during 1989-90. Data were collected on the estimated number of disabled people and the type and severity of their disabilities. Information on economic activity, employment, mobility and use of transport, special educational needs of disabled children and the financial circumstances of adults with disabilities and families with disabled children was also collected. The final report was published early in 1996.

Statistician
Bernie Duffy
Social Policy Branch
Tel: 028 9052 6080

Products that contain data from this source
PPRU Surveys of Disability Report 1: The Prevalence of Disability Among Adults in Northern Ireland; PPRU Surveys of Disability Report 2: The Prevalence of Disability Among Children in Northern Ireland; PPRU Surveys of Disability Report 3: Disability and Employment in Northern Ireland; PPRU Surveys of Disability Report 4: Disabled Adults in Northern Ireland, Services and Transport

---

Vehicle Badges for Physically or Visually Disabled (SSDA 310)
National Assembly for Wales

Status: Ongoing
Collection Method: Administrative Records
Frequency: Annually
Reference Period: 31 March
Timeliness: 9-12 months
Earliest Available Data: 1987
National Coverage: Wales
Disaggregation: Local Authority

Statistician
Robin Jones
National Assembly for Wales
Statistical Directorate; Health Statistics and Analysis Unit 2 (HSA2)
Tel: 029 2082 3625

Products that contain data from this source
Social Services Statistics Wales

Wheelchairs and Artificial Limbs, England - KO73
National Health Service Executive Headquarters; sponsored by Department of Health

Number of wheelchairs, special seating and artificial limbs issued in England. Number of attendances for assessment, fitting or maintenance of a new or existing artificial limb in England. The KH09, one of the Körner returns, was introduced for the financial year 1987/88.

Status: Ceased completely
Collection Method: Census
Frequency: Annually
Reference Period: Financial Year
Timeliness: Ceased collecting
Earliest Available Data: 1987/88
National Coverage: England
Disaggregation: NHS Hospital Trust; Regional Health Authority (RHA)/Regional (Health) Office Area

Statistician
Ian Mills
National Health Service Executive Headquarters
FPA-PA
Tel: 0113 254 5522.
Email: jclark@doh.gov.uk

Products that contain data from this source
Wheelchairs and artificial limbs, England

See also:
In this chapter:
Material Provision (SWS FORM M1) *(4.7)*

In other chapters:
Labour Force Survey (see the Labour Market chapter)

4.14 Drug abuse, Misuse of Alcohol, Smoking

Drug Misuse Database
Department of Health

Database of bi-annual returns from Regional Drug Database Managers in England. Some data also available for Scotland and Wales. Provides data on new drug agency episodes (people presenting to services for problem drug misuse for the first time, or for the first time for six months). Includes details of age, gender, details of up to five drugs misused, information regarding injecting and sharing equipment, together with the type of agency attended and Health Authority of treatment. The returns for each six month period from 1 October 1992 to 31 March 1996 were compiled from Dept of Health form KO71. This collected total numbers, rather than information about individuals, as is now the case.

Status: Ongoing
Collection Method: Administrative Records
Frequency: Bi-annually
Reference Period: 6 month periods, ending March and September
Timeliness: Approximately 11 months
Earliest Available Data: Six months ending March 1993
National Coverage: England
Disaggregation: Regional (Health) Office Area, Health Authority

Statistician
Patsy Bailey
Department of Health
SD2; SD2D
Tel: 020 7972 5551;
Email: pbailez@doh.gov.uk

Products that contain data from this source
Statistical Bulletin on Drug Misuse

Drug Misuse Database
Information and Statistics Division, NHS in Scotland

To gain an objective picture of aspects of drug misuse across Scotland for service provision etc.

Status: Ongoing
Collection Method: Administrative Records
Frequency: Continuously
Timeliness: 3 months in advance
Earliest Available Data: 1990
National Coverage: Scotland
Disaggregation: Health Board

Statistician
Peter Knight
Information and Statistics Division, NHS in Scotland
Hospital & community information
Tel: 0131 551 8739

Products that contain data from this source
Drug Misuse Statistics - Scotland 1998/99

Smoking Among Secondary School Children 1996 - GB
Department of Health; sponsored by Office for National Statistics

A survey of smoking among secondary school children has been carried out by the Office for National Statistics on behalf of the Health Departments of Great Britain every two years since 1982. Children completed a questionnaire about current smoking behaviour and a diary recording all cigarettes smoked in the previous week. In addition, since 1988, saliva specimens were tested for traces of cotinine (a metabolite of nicotine) to provide an independent assessment of exposure to tobacco smoke. Data are analysed by age, sex and region. A further survey covering England alone was carried out in 1993.

Status: Ongoing
Collection Method: Large-scale (Sample) Survey
Frequency: Annually
Reference Period: 1996
Timeliness: Every 2 years
Earliest Available Data: 1982
National Coverage: Great Britain

Statistician
Patsy Bailey
Department of Health
Tel: 020 7972 5551

Products that contain data from this source
Smoking among secondary school children; Young Teenagers and alcohol in 1996 Vols 1 & 2

Smoking and Misuse of Alcohol
Department of Health

The Department of Health compiles data on smoking and misuse of alcohol from a variety of sources. Occasional publications on trends are also prepared.

Status: Ongoing
Earliest Available Data: Most topics: 1972 (smoking), 1986 (misuse of alcohol).
National Coverage: Great Britain
Disaggregation: Regional Health Authority (RHA)/Regional (Health) Office Area

Statistician
Patsy Bailey
Department of Health
SD2; SD2D
Tel: 020 7972 5551;
Email: pbailez@doh.gov.uk

Products that contain data from this analysis
Statistical Bulletin on Smoking

4.15 Employment and Staffing - Healthcare and Social Services

Medical and Dental Staff Census - Wales
National Assembly for Wales

A Census of all directly employed medical and dental staff involved in clinical work in NHS Wales. Data are available by grade, speciality of staff, and at NHS Trust and health authority level. Information on vacant posts is also available. Although data are available since the early 1970s, definitions have changed over time so that exact comparisons may not be possible.

Status: Ongoing
Collection Method: Census
Frequency: Annually
Reference Period: 30 September each year
Timeliness: The target is for provisional summary information to be available from the census by January of the following year, with final results and more detailed information available by March.
Earliest Available Data: Some information on a slightly different base is available for the early 1970s
National Coverage: Wales
Disaggregation: Trust; Health Authority (E&W).

Statistician
Graham Davies
National Assembly for Wales
Statistical Directorate; Health Statistics Analysis Unit (3)
Tel: 029 2082 5086.
Email: graham.davies@wales.gov.uk

Products that contain data from this source
Health Statistics Wales; Regional Trends

Medical and Dental Staff Database
Information and Statistics Division, NHS in Scotland

To provide a file of medical and dental staff

engaged in clinical work. To give statistical advice, data and analysis.

Status: Ongoing
Collection Method: Administrative Records
Frequency: Continuously
Timeliness: 6 months in arrears
Earliest Available Data: 1981
National Coverage: Scotland
Disaggregation: NHS hospitals

Statistician
Graham Mitchell
Information and Statistics Division, NHS in Scotland
Tel: 0131 551 8022

Products that contain data from this source
Consultant's directory (Scotland); WEBS

Medical and Dental Workforce Census
Department of Health

NHS Hospital and Community Health Services (HCHS) medical and dental staff in England.

Status: Ongoing
Collection Method: Census
Frequency: Annually
Reference Period: 30 September
Timeliness: Collected September released Summer
Earliest Available Data: 1987
National Coverage: England
Disaggregation: Regional Health Authority (RHA)/Regional (Health) Office Area; Trust level

Statistician
John Bates
Department of Health
Stats(W)A
Tel: 0113 25 45878

Products that contain data from this source
Hospital, Public Health and Community Health Service Medical and Dental Staff in England

Non-Medical Staff Census - Wales
National Assembly for Wales

Details about non-medical staff-in-post, directly employed in the NHS are collected as an annual snapshot (at June 30, September 30, December 31). Data is submitted for each non-medical member of staff (nurses, therapeutic and technical staff, administrative staff, etc,). Medical and dental staff involved in clinical work are collected separately in an annual census as an individual record.

This method of collecting non-medical staffing information (and the use of free-standing occupation codes to group staff) is relatively recent. In the past, non-medical

staffing information was obtained from the central Standard Payroll System and staff were grouped according to payscale codes. However, with the decentralisation of pay systems, the spread of local payscales and the consequent need for information maintained on personnel rather than pay systems, an alternative approach was developed. Information from the old system is available from around 1980 - 1996; information from the new system is available from around 1996 (some retrospective estimates for the new occupation groups have also been made dating back to around 1993).

Status: Ongoing
Collection Method: Census
Frequency: Annual
Reference Period: Annual at 30 September, quarterly historically
Timeliness: The target is for information to be available within 6-8 weeks of the snapshot date (more detailed information may take a little longer).
Earliest Available Data: 1996
National Coverage: Wales
Disaggregation: District Health Authority (DHA)/Health Authority (E&W); Health Authority (E&W)

Statistician
Graham Davies
National Assembly for Wales
Statistical Directorate; Health Statistics Analysis Unit (3)
Tel: 029 2082 5086.
Email: graham.davies@wales.gov.uk

Products that contain data from this source
Health Statistics Wales; Regional Trends; Social Services Statistics for Wales

Non-Medical Workforce Census - England
Department of Health

The Department of Health compiles data on NHS Hospital and Community Health Services non-medical staff. The results help to establish trends in the number of non-medical staff employed. Data cover England. Results were most recently published for the period 1987-97. 1982-1994 non-medical workforce staff data collected by payscale. 1995 collected by occupation code. Data not comparable.

Status: Ongoing
Collection Method: Census
Frequency: Annually
Reference Period: 30 September
Timeliness: Collection September. Released May
Earliest Available Data: 1982
National Coverage: England
Disaggregation: District Health Authority (DHA)/Health Authority (E&W); Regional Health Authority (RHA)/Regional (Health) Office Area; NHS Trust

Statistician
Richard Reed
Department of Health
Stats(W)B
Tel: 0113 2545 891

Personnel Information Management System (PIMS) - Northern Ireland
Department of Health and Social Security - Northern Ireland

Status: Ongoing
Collection Method: Administrative source
Frequency: Quarterly
Timeliness: One month
Earliest Available Data: March 1990
National Coverage: Northern Ireland
Disaggregation: Trust

Statistician
Tracy Power
Department of Health and Social Security - Northern Ireland
Tel: 028 9052 2008

Research into the Work and Responsibilities of Consultants in Public Health Medicine

A survey of 300 consultants. Office of Manpower Economics

Status: Ceased completely
Collection Method: Small scale (sample) survey
Frequency: Ad hoc
Reference Period: May 1998
National Coverage: Great Britain

Statistician
Grant Whitfield
Office of Manpower Economics
Tel: 020 7467 7231

Products that contain data from this source
Report of the Review Body on Doctors' and Dentists' Remuneration 1999

Research into the work and responsibilities of hospital consultants

A survey of 4,000 consultants. Office of Manpower Economics

Status: Ceased completely
Collection Method: Small scale (sample) survey
Frequency: Ad hoc
Reference Period: May 1998
National Coverage: Great Britain

Statistician
Grant Whitfield
Office of Manpower Economics
Tel: 020 7467 7231

Products that contain data from this source
Report of the Review Body on Doctors' and Dentists' Remuneration 1999

Research into the Workload and Intensity of Work of Hospital Consultants

Qualitative research and small scale survey of consultants, junior doctors and trust managers. Office of Manpower Economics

Status: Ceased completely
Collection Method: Small scale (sample) survey and focus groups
Frequency: Ad hoc
Reference Period: Summer 1998
National Coverage: United Kingdom

Statistician
Grant Whitfield
Office of Manpower Economics
Tel: 020 7467 7231

Products that contain data from this source
Report of the Review Body on Doctors' and Dentists' Remuneration 1999

SSDS 001
Department of Health

Detailed information for local authorities in England on staff of social services departments.

Status: Ongoing
Collection Method: Census
Frequency: Annually
Reference Period: 30 September
Earliest Available Data: 1993
National Coverage: England
Disaggregation: Local Authority District (LAD) / Unitary Authority (England)

Statistician
Brian Allen
Department of Health, 452C,
Statistics Division 3; Statistics Division 3C
Tel: 020 7972 5595;
Email: ballen@doh.gov.uk

Products that contain data from this source
Personal Social Services Staff of Social Services Departments at 30 Sept 1998 (Bulletin)

Staff of Social Services Departments (STF 1) - HQ, Social Work, Domiciliary
National Assembly for Wales

Annual collection of directly employed staff of social services departments. Details of numbers of full and part time staff, qualified staff, Welsh speaking staff and whole time equivalents by grade and setting.

Status: Ongoing
Collection Method: Administrative Records
Frequency: Annually
Reference Period: 30 September
Timeliness: 6-9 months
Earliest Available Data: 1975

National Coverage: Wales
Disaggregation: Local Authority District (LAD) / Unitary Authority (England)

Statistician
Robin Jones
National Assembly for Wales
Statistical Directorate; Health Statistics and Analysis Unit 2 (HSA2)
Tel: 029 2082 3625

Products that contain data from this source
Social Services Statistics Wales

Staff of Social Services Departments (STF 2) - Residential Services
National Assembly for Wales

Annual collection of directly employed staff of social services departments. Details of numbers of full and part time staff, qualified staff, Welsh speaking staff and whole time equivalents by grade and setting.

Status: Ongoing
Collection Method: Administrative Records
Frequency: Annually
Reference Period: 30 September
Timeliness: 6-9 months
Earliest Available Data: 1975
National Coverage: Wales
Disaggregation: Local Authority District (LAD) / Unitary Authority (England)

Statistician
Robin Jones
National Assembly for Wales
Statistical Directorate; Health Statistics and Analysis Unit 2 (HSA2)
Tel: 029 2082 3625

Products that contain data from this source
Social Services Statistics Wales

Staff of Social Services Departments (STF 3) - Day Services
National Assembly for Wales

Annual collection of directly employed staff of social services departments. Details of numbers of full and part time staff, qualified staff, Welsh speaking staff and whole time equivalents by grade and setting.

Status: Ongoing
Collection Method: Administrative Records
Frequency: Annually
Reference Period: 30 September
Timeliness: 6-9 months
Earliest Available Data: 1975
National Coverage: Wales
Disaggregation: Local Authority District (LAD) / Unitary Authority (England)

Statistician
Robin Jones
National Assembly for Wales

Sources and Analyses

Statistical Directorate; Health Statistics and Analysis Unit 2 (HSA2)
Tel: 029 2082 3625

Products that contain data from this source
Social Services Statistics Wales

Staff of Social Services Departments (STF 4) - Management Qualifications
National Assembly for Wales

Annual collection of directly employed staff of social services departments. Details of numbers of full and part time staff, qualified staff, Welsh speaking staff and whole time equivalents by grade and setting.

Status: Ongoing
Collection Method: Administrative Records
Frequency: Annually
Reference Period: 30 September
Timeliness: 6-9 months
Earliest Available Data: 1975
National Coverage: Wales
Disaggregation: Local Authority District (LAD) / Unitary Authority (England)

Statistician
Robin Jones
National Assembly for Wales
Statistical Directorate; Health Statistics and Analysis Unit 2 (HSA2)
Tel: 029 2082 3625

Products that contain data from this source
Social Services Statistics Wales

Staffing of Social Work Departments (SWS FORM, SSR, SLA1, SLA2, SLA3 & OT1)
Scottish Executive; sponsored by Social Work Services Group Statistics Group

These annual forms are used to collect details of Local Authority Social Work Department staffing by grade and type of location, with details of main qualifications and terms of appointment. Current training and turnover are included along with a projection of numbers of Occupational Therapists over a 6-year period. SSR Forms used 2 out of every 3 years.

Status: Ongoing
Collection Method: Census
Frequency: Every 3 years
Reference Period: 1st October
Timeliness: Bulletin produced within 12 months of receipt of data.
Earliest Available Data: 1978
National Coverage: Scotland
Disaggregation: Council Area (Scotland)/ District and Islands Area (Scotland)

Statistician
Jill Alexander
Scottish Executive

Economics Advice and Statistics; 6
Tel: 0141 242 5459;
Email: jill.alexander@scotland.gov.uk

Products that contain data from this source
Staff of Scottish Social Work Departments

See also:
In this chapter:
General Dental Service - Manpower *(4.11)*
Home Care Statistical Return (SWS FORM H1) *(4.7)*
Residential Establishment Census Return (SWS FORM R1) *(4.7)*

4.16 Family Planning

Summary of Family Planning Services (KT31)
National Assembly for Wales

The National Assembly for Wales compiles data on family planning services. Data are collected on the number of clients seen in NHS family planning clinics and the method of contraception chosen. The data cover Wales and are available for NHS Trusts. Some information dates back to 1990-91, although the details collected were restructured in 1995. Data are collected each financial year and published annually. Some information dates back to 1990-91, although the details collected were restructured in 1995.

Status: Ongoing
Collection Method: Survey
Frequency: Annually
Reference Period: 1 April to 31 March
Timeliness: Health Statistics and Analysis Unit send out forms in March for completion, with a target date for their return of mid May, the timeliness of the return of forms is improving and progress is being made towards it. The aim is for key summary data for all of Wales to be available by the end of September, but this is dependent on the timely return of forms and resolution of queries.
Earliest Available Data: Some information dates back to 1990-91
National Coverage: Wales
Disaggregation: NHS Trust

Statistician
Dr Gwyneth Thomas
National Assembly for Wales
Statistical Directorate; Health Statistics and Analysis Unit (1)
Tel: 029 2082 5039.
Email: gwyneth.thomas@wales.gov.uk

Products that contain data from this source
Family Planning Service in Wales - Annual statistical brief; Health Statistics Wales

GP and Practice Database
Information and Statistics Division, NHS in Scotland

Data on principals in general medical practices, their patients, claims and incomes.

Status: Ongoing
Collection Method: Administrative Records
Frequency: Continuously
Timeliness: 6 months in arrears
National Coverage: Scotland
Disaggregation: Health Board

Statistician
Susan Burney
Information and Statistics Division, NHS in Scotland
Hospital & community information
Tel: 0131 551 8542

Products that contain data from this source
GP Directory

General Medical Practitioners Out-Of-Hours Work
Office of Manpower Economics

Qualitative research and survey of 4,000 general medical practitioners.

Status: Ceased completely
Collection Method: Small-scale (Sample) Survey
Frequency: Ad hoc
Earliest Available Data: Autumn 1996
National Coverage: Great Britain

Statistician
Grant Whitfield
Office of Manpower Economics
Tel: 020 7467 7231

Products that contain data from this source
Report of the Review Body on Doctors' and Dentists' Remuneration 1997

General Practice Research Database - UK
Department of Health (Medicines Control Agency)

The Medicines Control Agency manages the General Practice Research Database. Anonymised patient-based morbidity, prescribing and referral data are available, collected from a sample of several hundred general practices in the National Health Service (NHS). Data cover the UK and are available at country and district health authority level. The database was started in 1987 with data collected about every six weeks. First practice recruited June 1987.

Peak recruitment during 1988 and 1989. Practices have therefore been supplying data for varying periods of time. In January 1999 there were 419 participating practices covering approximately 3 million patients. Recruitment of practices is continuing.

Status: Ongoing
Collection Method: Administrative Records
Frequency: Periodic
Reference Period: Either full record, or since last collection (approximately 6 weeks)
Timeliness: Data are entered by GP, or other practice staff, either during consultation, or after receipt from another source (e.g. hospital). Data are collected by MCA from practices every 6 weeks on average. After quality checking, data are stored until next update of the database. The most recent update of the "frozen" database was early in 1999. An additional "live" database will be introduced in summer 1999. This will be updated after the data from each practice are quality checked.
Earliest Available Data: 1987
National Coverage: United Kingdom
Disaggregation: Regional Health Authority (RHA)/Regional (Health) Office Area; District Health Authority (DHA)/Health Authority (E&W); Individual (anonymised) practice; Office for National Statistics Area Classifications

Statistician
Louise Wood
General Practice Research Database
Medicines Control Agency
Tel: 020 7273 0698;
Email: gprd@mca.gov.uk

Products that contain data from this source
General Practice Research Database (authorised users only); Key Health Statistics from General Practice 1996 (Series MB6 No. 1); Key Health Statistics from General Practice, (Studies on Medical and Population Subjects No. 60); Regional Trends; Social Trends

Research into Changes in GMPs Work
Office of Manpower Economics

Qualitative research and survey of 4,000 GMPs.

Collection Method: Small-scale (Sample) Survey
Frequency: Ad hoc
Earliest Available Data: Autumn 1997
National Coverage: Great Britain

Statistician
Grant Whitfield
Office of Manpower Economics
Tel: 020 7467 7231

Products that contain data from this source
Report of the Review Body on Doctors' and Dentists' Remuneration 1998

4.18 Hospital Services (other than for the mentally disordered)

Accident & Emergency Waiting Times Survey
Scottish Executive

Information on waiting times for patients who attend accident & emergency (A&E) departments.

Status: Ongoing
Collection Method: Large-scale (Sample) Survey
Frequency: Bi-annually
Timeliness: 9 months in arrears
Earliest Available Data: 1994
National Coverage: Scotland
Sub-National: NHS Trusts

Statistician
Peter Knight
Scottish Executive
Tel: 0131 551 8739

Products that contain data from this source
Accident & Emergency: various bulletins and health briefings

Bed Availability and Occupancy, England - KH03
National Health Service Executive Headquarters; sponsored by Department of Health

This annual return, collected from every NHS hospital in England (Trusts, directly managed units and hospitals), is one of the Körner returns. The return collects information on the type of facilities available at each Trust and the number of bed-days available and occupied in each type of ward throughout the year in question. The Körner return KH03 was introduced for the financial year 1987/88, and replaced form SH3, which had been run in various forms since 1949. The major differences between the two are that: KH03 is based on a financial year while the SH3 was based on a calendar year; KH03 data is collected by ward classification whereas the SH3 was collected by clinical speciality/department; and the KH03 collects some extra information, namely on beds in wards open day only and neonatal cots in maternity wards. Some further changes were made to the KH03 in 1996/97. Full details can be found in the product/book "Bed availability and occupancy".

Status: Ongoing
Collection Method: Census
Frequency: Annually
Reference Period: Financial Year

Timeliness: The information is usually published in the Autumn following the end of the financial year
Earliest Available Data: 1966
National Coverage: England
Disaggregation: NHS Hospital Trust; Regional Health Authority (RHA)/Regional (Health) Office Area

Statistician
Ian Mills
National Health Service Executive Headquarters
FPA-PA
Tel: 0113 254 5522.
Email: jclark@doh.gov.uk

Products that contain data from this source
Bed availability and occupancy, England; Statistical Bulletin: NHS hospital activity statistics, England

Chronically Sick and Disabled Persons Act 1970 - Return Under Section 17(2), England - SBH179
National Health Service Executive Headquarters; sponsored by Department of Health

The SBH179 recorded the number of chronically sick and disabled persons aged under 65 who were inappropriately admitted to, or resident in, wards using wholly or mainly for the care of elderly persons, therefore not conforming to Section 17(1) of the Act. Until 1987/88, the information was collected over the period 1 July to 30 June. From 1987/88 to 1996/97, the information was collected over the financial year.

Status: Ceased completely
Collection Method: Census
Frequency: Annually
Reference Period: Financial year
National Coverage: England
Disaggregation: NHS Hospital Trust

Statistician
Ian Mills
National Health Service Executive Headquarters
FPA-PA
Tel: 0113 254 5522.
Email: jclark@doh.gov.uk

Products that contain data from this source
Chronically sick and disabled persons act 1970 England

Consultant Outpatient Attendance Activity and Accident and Emergency Services Activity, England - KH09
National Health Service Executive Headquarters; sponsored by Department of Health

This annual return, collected from every NHS hospital in England (Trusts, directly managed units and hospitals), is one of the Körner returns. The return collects information on the number of first and subsequent attendances by patients at consultant outpatient clinics, and the number of written GP referrals and private patient attendances by speciality, and the number of first and subsequent attendances by patients at accident and emergency departments. The KH09, one of the Körner returns, was introduced for the financial year 1987/88.

Status: Ongoing
Collection Method: Census
Frequency: Annually
Reference Period: Financial Year
Timeliness: The information is usually published in the Autumn following the end of the financial year
Earliest Available Data: 1987/88
National Coverage: England
Disaggregation: NHS Hospital Trust; Regional Health Authority (RHA)/Regional (Health) Office Area

Statistician
Ian Mills
National Health Service Executive Headquarters
FPA-PA
Tel: 0113 254 5522.
Email: jclark@doh.gov.uk

Products that contain data from this source
Outpatients and Ward Attendees, England; Statistical Bulletin: NHS hospital activity statistics, England

Health Authority, Hospital Trust and Ambulance Trust Performance - Wales
National Assembly for Wales

The National Assembly for Wales compiles NHS performance tables. Information is obtained from Trusts/hospitals, ambulance authorities and Health Authorities relating to their performance, linking this where appropriate to Patient's Charter targets and standards. The majority of data is already collected via other sources (cancelled operations, accident and emergency assessment, waiting in clinics, emergency ambulance response times, breast and cervical screening and vaccination and immunisation rates) but data on outpatients' appointments, day-case surgery, inpatient waiting times and outpatient appointment waiting times are collected specifically for this purpose. The information for the tables was first collected in 1994. The data are collected annually during April and May and usually published in June or July. The 1998 tables were published on December 8th.

Status: Ongoing
Collection Method: Census
Frequency: Annual
Reference Period: April and May

Timeliness: To date, Summer after reference period although the 1998 tables will be out in December.
Earliest Available Data: 1994
National Coverage: Wales
Disaggregation: Health Authority and Trust level

Statistician
Graham Davies
National Assembly for Wales
Statistical Directorate; Health Statistics Analysis Unit (3)
Tel: 029 2082 5086.
Email: graham.davies@wales.gov.uk

Hospital Activity Statistics
Information and Statistics Division, NHS in Scotland

Monitoring and reporting NHS hospital activity and resource use including bed availability and usage.

Status: Ongoing
Collection Method: Administrative Records
Frequency: Quarterly
Reference Period: To date
Timeliness: 6 weeks in arrears
Earliest Available Data: 1974
National Coverage: Scotland
Disaggregation: Health Board

Statistician
Peter Knight
Information and Statistics Division, NHS in Scotland
Hospital & community information
Tel: 0131 551 8739

Products that contain data from this source
Scottish Health Statistics

Hospital Bed Use - Wales
National Assembly for Wales

The Hospital Bed Use Survey, carried out by the National Assembly for Wales, collects data on hospital bed use in terms of occupancy by speciality for NHS Trusts. The unit is the death or discharge. Data are compiled by and collected from each hospital site and returned to the Welsh Health Common Services Authority. Results are available on inpatients and day cases, and outpatient attendances, and show various performance indicators such as duration of stay, bed-use factor, the ratio of new outpatient attendances to total outpatient attendances by speciality and out-patient non attendances by speciality. The Survey is carried out quarterly and results are available since 1949, however information for new outpatients is not available for 1992-93 and 1993-94. Information is used in the PES process. It is also used in answering Parliamentary Questions, preparing briefing for ministers and in response to ad hoc requests.

Status: Ongoing
Collection Method: Administrative Records
Frequency: Quarterly
Timeliness: The data is due to be submitted to HMIS within 4 weeks of the end of the quarter - the timeliness of information for Wales as a whole depends on the slowest data provider, however it should usually be available within around 2 months (sometimes as provisional data). It can be some months before data is available for the whole of Wales.
Earliest Available Data: 1949
National Coverage: Wales
Disaggregation: Health Authority / Trust

Statistician
Graham Davies
National Assembly for Wales
Statistical Directorate; Health Statistics Analysis Unit (3)
Tel: 029 2082 5086.
Email: graham.davies@wales.gov.uk

Products that contain data from this source
Digest of Welsh Statistics; Health Statistics Wales

Hospital Episode Statistics
Department of Health

The Department of Health compiles the hospital episode statistics database. It contains all patient-based records of finished consultant episodes (ordinary admissions and day cases) by diagnosis, operation and speciality from NHS hospitals in England. Data are adjusted to allow for incomplete recording and episodes without a valid diagnosis.

Data on diagnostics cover: ordinary admissions, day cases and bed-days of ordinary admissions by broad diagnosis (ICD9 Diagnostic H List) at region of treatment; ordinary admissions by broad diagnosis and length of stay; episodes (including day cases) by broad diagnosis, age group and sex; episodes (including day cases) by detailed diagnosis (3-digit ICD9) and region of treatment. Operations include: ordinary admissions, day cases and bed-days of ordinary admissions by principal operation (OPCS4R short list) at region of treatment; all finished consultant episodes (including day cases) involving an operation by principal operation (OPCS4R 3-digit classification) for region of treatment and age group.

Administrative data, considered by speciality, covers ordinary admissions, day cases, bed-days of ordinary admissions, mean and median duration of stay by treatment region and age group. Results are also given for ordinary admissions, day cases and bed-days for all specialities by age group, sex and region of residence, indicating the rate per 10,000 population. Totals for ordinary admissions and day cases are also analysed by age group, sex, treatment region and method of assessment. The data cover waiting

Sources and Analyses

list and booked cases treated by diagnostic and operation short list by waiting time, and injury and poisoning episodes by diagnostic short list and external cause.

Before the introduction of HES in 1988-89 there was the Hospital in-patient enquiry (HIPE). HIPE relates to discharges and deaths which is not directly comparable to HES data. HIPE finished in 1985.

Collection Method: Administrative Records
Frequency: Annually
Reference Period: The Financial Year
Timeliness: 18 months
Earliest Available Data: 1988-89
National Coverage: England
Disaggregation: District Health Authority (DHA)/Health Authority (E&W); Enumeration District (ED); Postcode Area; Postcode District; Regional Health Authority (RHA)/Regional (Health) Office Area; Ward

Statistician
Linda Shurlock
Department of Health
SD2; SD2 HES
Tel: 020 7972 5567

Products that contain data from this source
Health and Personal Social Services Statistics for England; Hospital Episode Statistics Vol 1: Finished consultant episodes by diagnosis and operative procedure, injury, poisoning by external causes - England

---

Hospital Inpatient System - Northern Ireland
Department of Health and Social Services - Northern Ireland

The Department of Health and Social Services (NI) maintains the Hospital Inpatient System (HIS) which holds data on all inpatients stays in acute hospitals in Northern Ireland. Data are derived from the Patient Administration Scheme (PAS) resident in hospital sites throughout Northern Ireland. Data, collected continually, are available from 1968. Until 1987 data were stored on annual files containing activity data on all hospital inpatients (70 per cent coverage). The HIS was set up in 1988-89 and contains all activity data from 1988 to the current year. Files are created annually six months after the end of the financial year.

Status: Ongoing
Collection Method: Computerised extracts from hospital administrative records
Frequency: Annual
Reference Period: Financial year
Timeliness: Six months after reference period
Earliest Available Data: 1968
National Coverage: Northern Ireland
Sub-National: Full
Disaggregation: Postcode area, ward, district council, parliamentary constituency, Health Board of residence and treatment.

Statistician
Pauline Sheals
Department of Health and Social Services - Northern Ireland
Tel: 028 9052 2925;
Email: pauline.sheals@dhssni.gov.uk

Products that contain data from this source
Health and Personal Social Services Statistics (NI); Hospital Inpatients System (HIS); Hospital Inpatients System (HIS) Standard Analyses; Regional Trends; Social Trends

---

Imaging and Radiodiagnostic Examinations or Tests, England - KH12
National Health Service Executive Headquarters; sponsored by Department of Health

This annual return, collected from every NHS hospital in England (Trusts, directly managed units and hospitals), is one of the Körner returns. The return collects information on the number of imaging and radiodiagnostic examinations or tests carried out by imaging departments or other departments in NHS hospitals in England. The KH12, one of the Körner returns, was introduced for the financial year 1987/88. The KH12 was substantially revised for 1995-96 and several Trusts had difficulty supplying data in the new format. Care needs to be taken in interpreting the figures and in attempting comparison with other years.

Status: Ongoing
Collection Method: Census
Frequency: Annually
Reference Period: Financial Year
Timeliness: The information is usually published in the Autumn following the end of the financial year
Earliest Available Data: 1987/88
National Coverage: England
Disaggregation: NHS Hospital Trust; Regional Health Authority (RHA)/Regional (Health) Office Area

Statistician
Ian Mills
National Health Service Executive Headquarters
FPA-PA
Tel: 0113 254 5522.
Email: jclark@doh.gov.uk

Products that contain data from this source
Imaging and radiodiagnostics, England

Inpatient Waiting Lists - England
Department of Health

The Department of Health compiles data on the number of patients waiting to be admitted to NHS hospitals in England and the numbers of English residents waiting to be admitted to NHS hospitals in England and the numbers of English residents

waiting to be admitted to hospital. Data are available monthly on the number of patients waiting for elective admission and how long they have been waiting. In addition, once a quarter information is also collected by main consultant speciality and by type of admission (inpatient or day case). Data are collected from NHS Trusts and Health Authorities in England, via a central collection exercise - forms are completed by hand or electronically.

Information is published every month. Data are available around five weeks after the end of the month, except where the month coincides with a quarter, when they are available around six weeks after the end of the month.

From April 1999, information from Health Authorities is being collected on a "responsible population" basis, not on a resident basis.

Status: Ongoing
Collection Method: Census
Frequency: Monthly
Reference Period: 'Snapshot' of position at month end
Timeliness: Data is published around 5 or 6 weeks after the month end
Earliest Available Data: December 1949
National Coverage: England
Disaggregation: NHS Region, NHS Trusts and Health Authorities

Statistician
Martin Campbell
National Health Service Executive Headquarters
FPA-PA; Waiting Times
Tel: 0113 254 5455;
Email: mcampbel@doh.gov.uk

Products that contain data from this source
Health and Personal Social Services Statistics for England; Hospital Waiting List Statistics: England; NHS Quarterly Review; Regional Trends; Social Trends

---

Körner Aggregate Hospital Returns - Northern Ireland
Department of Health and Social Services - Northern Ireland

The Department of Health and Social Services (NI) collates Körner Aggregate Hospital Returns (KARS) on hospital services and activities in Northern Ireland. The data are derived from the Patient Administration System (PAS) used in Health Service hospitals and cover inpatient and outpatient activity. Information is available from 1981. Data from 1988-89 are stored on a database system and are collected quarterly, except for a Census of hospital services which is conducted annually at 31 March. Data are published annually on a financial-year basis and an ad hoc query facility is also available to the public.

Status: Ongoing
Collection Method: Returns from Health and Social Services Trusts
Frequency: Quarterly
Reference Period: Quarter
Timeliness: Six months after reference period
Earliest Available Data: 1988-89
National Coverage: Northern Ireland
Sub-National: Full
Disaggregation: Health and Social Services Trusts

Statistician
Jim McColgan
Department of Health and Social Services - Northern Ireland
Tel: 028 9052 2580;
Email: jim.mccolgan@dhssni.gov.uk

Products that contain data from this source
Hospital Statistics; Körner Aggregate Hospital Returns (KARS); Northern Ireland Waiting List Statistics; Regional Trends; Social Focus on Children; Social Trends

Laboratory Statistics
Information and Statistics Division, NHS in Scotland

To provide information for managing laboratories to provide information for planning staff and workload.

Status: Ongoing
Collection Method: Administrative Records
Frequency: Quarterly
Timeliness: 1 year
Earliest Available Data: 1975
National Coverage: Scotland
Disaggregation: Health Board

Statistician
Peter Knight
Information and Statistics Division, NHS in Scotland
Hospital & community information
Tel: 0131 551 8739

NHS Day Care: Availability and Use of Facilities, England - KH14
National Health Service Executive Headquarters; sponsored by Department of Health

This annual return, collected from every NHS hospital in England (Trusts, directly managed units and hospitals), is one of the Körner returns. This return collects information on the number of attendances at NHS day care centres in England. The KH14, one of the Körner returns, was introduced for the financial year 1987/88.

Status: Ongoing
Collection Method: Census
Frequency: Annually
Reference Period: Financial Year
Timeliness: The information is usually published in the Autumn following the end of the financial year
Earliest Available Data: 1987/88
National Coverage: England
Disaggregation: NHS Hospital Trust; Regional Health Authority (RHA)/Regional (Health) Office Area

Statistician
Ian Mills
National Health Service Executive Headquarters
FPA-PA
Tel: 0113 254 5522.
Email: jclark@doh.gov.uk

Products that contain data from this source
Health Statistics Wales; NHS day care facilities, England

Patient Episode Database for Wales (PEDW)
National Assembly for Wales; sponsored by NHS Wales

The National Assembly for Wales and the NHS Wales record patient throughput for hospitals in Wales in the Patient Episode Database for Wales (PEDW). Data on each inpatient and day-case finished consultant episode are drawn from hospital patient administration systems. Data are available from administrative records which cover speciality of treatment, length of stay, waiting times, diagnosis and surgical procedure, health authority of residence, district health authority of treatment, and postcode sector.

NHS and National Assembly for Wales are main customers for PEDW data. PEDW is the principal source of patient based data on hospital activity in Wales and has a variety of uses, including supporting the management and planning of services and the evaluation of NHS performance and trends. It is a valuable source of epidemiological data at the national and local level, and also contributes to the cancer registration process. Information from PEDW is used in the resource allocation process. It is also used in answering Parliamentary Questions, preparing briefing for ministers and in response to ad hoc requests and research. It has recently been used in the new set of clinical outcome indicators being developed by Department of Health and the National Assembly for Wales.

PEDW replaced the Hospital Activity Analysis in 1991-92. There have been some coverage problems in the first year and with the completeness of clinical information

throughout. There has been some improvement in data completeness and quality, although there are still problems (particularly for clinical data). Coding levels vary widely between trusts and between specialities, which may further affect the usefulness of the data for some purposes.

Status: Ongoing
Frequency: Monthly
Timeliness: In the past PEDW has been criticised in terms of timeliness of information. This is improving, and many records are now submitted within a month or two of the end of the consultant episode (although the records are not necessarily complete at this stage and amendments including more detail - particularly clinical details - may be made). However the timeliness of information for Wales as a whole depends on the slowest data provider and the time needed to undertake analyses - some information for a full (financial) year is generally available within around 6 months.
Earliest Available Data: 1991-92 (replacing the Hospital Activity Analysis)
National Coverage: Wales
Disaggregation: NHS trusts

Statistician
Graham Davies
National Assembly for Wales
Statistical Directorate; Health Statistics Analysis Unit (3)
Tel: 029 2082 5086.
Email: graham.davies@wales.gov.uk

Products that contain data from this source
Health Statistics Wales

Scottish Record Linkage - Linked Dataset
Scottish Executive

Used as a basis for most of CRAG clinical outcome indicators; readmission rates; patient and stay based trends in admissions, bed use and lengths of stay. Links hospital discharge records, RG deaths and cancer registrations for individual patients.

Status: Ongoing
Frequency: Quarterly
Reference Period: 1981 onwards
Timeliness: 3 months in arrears
Earliest Available Data: 1968
National Coverage: Scotland
Disaggregation: Health Board

Statistician
Mary Smalls
Scottish Executive
Tel: 0131 551 8167

Products that contain data from this analysis
CRAG Clinical outcome indicators; Scottish Health Statistics

Summary of Patient Activity Return, England - KP70
National Health Service Executive Headquarters; sponsored by Department of Health

This annual return, collected from every NHS hospital in England (Trusts, directly managed units and hospitals), is one of the Körner returns. This return collects information on inpatient activity in NHS hospitals in England. Activity is recorded in terms of finished consultant episodes (FCEs) for ordinary admissions and day case admissions, by speciality. Well babies are also counted. The Körner return KP70 was introduced for the financial year 1987/88, and replaced form SH3, which had been run in various forms since 1949. The Körner reforms introduced the concept of the finished consultant episode on a financial year basis. Prior to this, the SH3 collected details about deaths in, and discharges from, hospitals on a calendar year basis.

Status: Ongoing
Collection Method: Census
Frequency: Annually
Reference Period: Financial year
Timeliness: The information is usually published in the Autumn following the end of the financial year
Earliest Available Data: 1949
National Coverage: England
Disaggregation: NHS Hospital Trust; Regional Health Authority (RHA)/Regional (Health) Office Area

Statistician
Ian Mills
National Health Service Executive Headquarters
FPA-PA
Tel: 0113 254 5522.
Email: jclark@doh.gov.uk

Products that contain data from this source
Ordinary and day case admissions, England; Statistical Bulletin: NHS hospital activity statistics, England

Summary of Ward Attendees, England - KH05
National Health Service Executive Headquarters; sponsored by Department of Health

This annual return, collected from every NHS hospital in England (Trusts, directly managed units and hospitals), is one of the Körner returns. This return collects information on the number of attendances by ward attendees throughout the year at each NHS Hospital Trust in England. The KH05, one of the Körner returns, was introduced for the financial year 1987/88.

Status: Ongoing
Collection Method: Census
Frequency: Annually
Reference Period: Financial Year
Timeliness: The information is usually published in the Autumn following the end of the financial year
Earliest Available Data: 1987/88
National Coverage: England
Disaggregation: NHS Hospital Trust; Regional Health Authority (RHA)/Regional (Health) Office Area

Statistician
Ian Mills
National Health Service Executive Headquarters
FPA-PA
Tel: 0113 254 5522.
Email: jclark@doh.gov.uk

Products that contain data from this source
Outpatients and Ward Attendees, England; Statistical Bulletin: NHS hospital activity statistics, England

Waiting List Census
Information and Statistics Division, NHS in Scotland

To allow local and central monitoring of waiting lists, including time on waiting lists in relation to Patients Charter commitments.

Status: Ongoing
Collection Method: Administrative Records
Frequency: Quarterly
Reference Period: 1992 onwards
Timeliness: 6 weeks in advance
Earliest Available Data: 1992
National Coverage: Scotland
Disaggregation: NHS Trust, Health Board of treatment

Statistician
Peter Knight
Information and Statistics Division, NHS in Scotland
Hospital & community information
Tel: 0131 551 8739

Waiting Time for First Outpatient Appointments - England
Department of Health

The Department of Health compiles data on waiting times for first out-patient appointments. Data are available on the length of time patients waited for their first consultant outpatient appointment following a written referral from their GP by main consultant speciality for each NHS provider (i.e. individual NHS Trust) and Health Authority. Data on the number of referrals and on the number of attendances for first outpatient appointment are available for England and at regional level and by NHS Trust and Health Authority.

From June 1999, information from Health Authorities is being collected on a 'responsible population' basis, rather than a resident basis.

Information is published quarterly around eight weeks of the end of the quarter. Information on selected specialities is published annually in the NHS Performance Guide. Data was first collected for the quarter ended September 1993, from NHS Trusts, by speciality. Since the quarter ending June 1997, outpatient data was also collected from Health Authorities, by speciality also.

Status: Ongoing
Collection Method: Census
Frequency: Quarterly
Reference Period: Events occurring during the quarter
Timeliness: Data is published around 8 weeks after the quarter end
Earliest Available Data: September 1993
National Coverage: England
Disaggregation: NHS Region, NHS Trusts and Health Authorities

Statistician
Martin Campbell
National Health Service Executive Headquarters
FPA-PA; Waiting Times
Tel: 0113 254 5455;
Email: mcampbel@doh.gov.uk

Products that contain data from this source
NHS Quarterly Review; Performance (League) Tables; Waiting Times for First Outpatient Appointments in England; Waiting Times for First Outpatient Appointments in England: Detailed Statistics

4.19 Incidence and Prevention of Disease, Illness and Injury

Adult Screening Programmes - Cervical Cytology (KC53)
National Assembly for Wales

Aggregate annual information about the cervical screening status of health authority residents, covering the whole of Wales. The National Assembly for Wales uses information from these returns to monitor the cervical screening programme. Summary information from the returns is published in 'Health Statistics Wales'. More detailed information is available from HSA on request. Following the recommendations of the Expert Advisory Group on Cervical Screening in Wales, detailed data are being fed back to the NHS in the form of annual reports. Summary information on the percentage of women screened in the last 5 years is calculated using KC53 data and subsequently used in NHS performance tables. Information may also be used in answering Parliamentary Questions, preparing briefing for ministers and in response to ad hoc requests. The form has recently been brought into line with that collected by Department of Health in England (in part because it is produced by an England and Wales computer system, which is updated in line with changes to the English form).

Status: Ongoing
Collection Method: Survey of all eligible women
Frequency: Annually
Reference Period: I April to 31 March
Timeliness: HSA send out forms in March for completion by health authorities. The forms are due for return by mid May. The aim is for key summary data for all of Wales to be available by the end of September, but this is dependent on the timely return of forms and resolution of queries.
Earliest Available Data: 1989/90
National Coverage: Wales
Disaggregation: Health Authority

Statistician
Dr Gwyneth Thomas
National Assembly for Wales
Statistical Directorate; Health Statistics and Analysis Unit (1)
Tel: 029 2082 5039.
Email: gwyneth.thomas@wales.gov.uk

Products that contain data from this source
Cervical Screening Programme, Wales - Annual Report; Cervical Screening Programme, Wales - Annual Statistical brief; Health Statistics Wales

Cancer Intelligence Unit Ad Hoc Request and Analysis
Information and Statistics Division, NHS in Scotland

To analyse, interpret and present information from the Scottish Cancer registry and related databases.

Status: Ongoing
Collection Method: Administrative Records
Frequency: Continuously
Timeliness: I year in advance
Earliest Available Data: 1968
National Coverage: Scotland
Sub-National: Health Board

Statistician
Roger Black
Information and Statistics Division, NHS in Scotland
Scottish Cancer Intelligence Unit
Tel: 0131 551 8053

Cancer Registration - Northern Ireland
Department of Health and Social Security - Northern Ireland

The Cancer Registry, formerly maintained by the Department of Health and Social Services (NI), contains data on cancer registrations in Northern Ireland. Data are available from 1959 to 1992, for individual hospitals only, but are no longer collected by the Department (transferred to Queen's University, Belfast). However, an ad hoc query facility is available to the public for this period.

Status: Ceased completely
Collection Method: Returns from hospitals
Frequency: Continuous
Reference Period: Annual
Earliest Available Data: 1959
National Coverage: Northern Ireland
Sub-National: Full
Disaggregation: Hospitals

Statistician
Jenny Orr
Department of Health and Social Services - Northern Ireland
Tel: 028 9052 2580;
Email: jenny.orr@dhssni.gov.uk

Products that contain data from this source
CRAG Clinical outcome indicators

Cancer Registrations - England and Wales
Office for National Statistics

The Office for National Statistics compiles data on the occurrence and characteristics of malignant neoplasms and certain non-malignant tumours. Cancer registration is conducted by ten independent regional cancer registries which collect data on cancers incident in residents of their regions. Information is available by regional health authority; data below this level may be available from the relevant regional cancer registry. Data have been collected since 1971 on a continuous basis and are published annually, three to four years after the year in which the cancer was diagnosed. The data are held in the national cancer registration database, which is continually being updated. Information is published in annual volumes, monitors, and on CD-ROM. Estimates of cancers diagnosed in years for which data are not yet available, but for which deaths information has been published, are made available in a monitor by ONS. Information on the diagnosis of new cases of cancer has been collected since the late 1940s. Whilst complete geographical national coverage was achieved in 1962, ascertainment (the completeness of registration) continued to vary. It improved throughout the 1970s across the regional cancer registries.

In 1996, the person-based national database went 'live'. It currently contains around 6 million records of cancers diagnosed in 1971 and onwards. It is continuously updated as the regional registries submit their data sets and as amendments are made as a result of the many quality checks built into the system. A large amount of data enhancement has been done to improve the quality of information held. Since January 1993, it has been mandatory for the NHS, including trusts, to provide data according a stated list of core items, known as the cancer registration minimum data set. These items, together with more detailed background on the collection of cancer registrations, can be found in the annual reference volumes for years 1990 and 1992, 'Cancer statistics - registrations.' Series MB1 no.23 - 25.

Status: Ongoing
Collection Method: Administrative Records
Frequency: Continuously
Earliest Available Data: 1971
National Coverage: England and Wales
Disaggregation: Regional Health Authority (RHA)/Regional (Health) Office Area

Statistician
Penny Babb
Office for National Statistics
Demography & Health; Epidemiology & Fertility
Tel: 020 7533 5266;
Email: penny.babb@ons.gov.uk

Products that contain data from this source
Cancer 1971-1997; Cancer Statistics - Registration, 1990, England & Wales; Cancer Statistics - Registration, 1991, England & Wales; Cancer Statistics - Registration, 1992, England & Wales; Cancer Statistics: 1989 Registrations; Cancer survival in England and Wales: 1981 and 1989 registrations; Cancer survival trends in England and Wales, 1971-1995; deprivation and NHS Region; CRAG Clinical outcome indicators; Estimates of newly diagnosed cases of cancer, England and Wales, 1993-1997; Health Statistics Quarterly No: 1 - Spring 1999; Incidence of and mortality from cancers of the lung, skin, breast and cervix - England; Occupational Health Decennial Supplement; Registrations of Cancer Diagnosed in 1990, England and Wales; Registrations of cancer diagnosed in 1991, England & Wales; Registrations of cancer diagnosed in 1992, England and Wales; Review of the National Cancer Registration System; Scottish Cancer Intelligence Unit Annual Report; Trends in Cancer Survival

Cancer Registrations - Wales
National Assembly for Wales

The National Assembly for Wales and NHS Wales holds responsibility for data on the registrations of the occurrence of new cancers which is derived mainly from the Patient Episode Database for Wales and death certificates. Data are available by site of the cancer, age, sex, and at health authority level and are used for monitoring trends in the disease, epidemiological work and clinical studies. Data are collected and compiled continually by the Wales Cancer Registry and published every two years. The Registry covers Wales since 1974 and continues to be updated some time after initial registration, so it is likely that figures will differ between sources and within the same source over time.

Frequency: Published every two years
Earliest Available Data: 1974
National Coverage: Wales

Statistician
Adrian Crompton
National Assembly for Wales
Statistical Directorate; Health Statistics and Analysis Unit (4)
Tel: 029 2082 5033.
Email: statswales@gtnet.gov.uk

Products that contain data from this source
Cancer Registrations in Wales; CRAG Clinical outcome indicators; Social Services Statistics for Wales

---

Cervical Cytology Screening
Information and Statistics Division, NHS in Scotland

Collection of local and national statistics and monitoring of the performance of the clinical screening programme

Status: Ongoing
Collection Method: Administrative Records
Frequency: Annually
Timeliness: 9 months in arrears
Earliest Available Data: 1994
National Coverage: Scotland
Disaggregation: Health Board

Statistician
Peter Knight
Information and Statistics Division, NHS in Scotland
Hospital & community information
Tel: 0131 551 8739

Child Health System Pre School
Information and Statistics Division, NHS in Scotland

To facilitate the surveillance of child health in the local and national population.

Status: Ongoing
Collection Method: Administrative Records
Frequency: Quarterly
Timeliness: Quarterly in arrears
Earliest Available Data: 1997
National Coverage: Scotland
Disaggregation: Health Board

Statistician
Peter Knight
Information and Statistics Division, NHS in Scotland
Hospital & community information
Tel: 0131 551 8739

Communicable Diseases
National Assembly for Wales

Statistician
Adrian Crompton
National Assembly for Wales
Statistical Directorate; Health Statistics and Analysis Unit (4)
Tel: 029 2082 5033.
Email: statswales@gtnet.gov.uk

Congenital Anomalies
Information and Statistics Division, NHS in Scotland

To provide baseline data for use in the local surveillance of the first year prevalence congenital anomalies.

Status: Ongoing
Collection Method: Administrative Records
Frequency: Continuously
Timeliness: 1994
National Coverage: Scotland
Disaggregation: Health Board

Statistician
Peter Knight
Information and Statistics Division, NHS in Scotland
Hospital & community information
Tel: 0131 551 8739

Continuous Morbidity Recording (CMR)
Information and Statistics Division, NHS in Scotland

To provide a picture of activity and morbidity in general practice.

Status: Ongoing
Collection Method: Cluster sample - 10% population
Frequency: Continuously
Timeliness: Monthly in arrears
Earliest Available Data: 1994
National Coverage: Scotland
Disaggregation: Health Board, GP Practice

Statistician
James Urquhart
Information and Statistics Division, NHS in Scotland
Tel: 0131 551 8109

Firework Injuries Survey
National Assembly for Wales; sponsored by Department of Trade and Industry

An annual survey of injuries treated in A&E departments which were caused by fireworks (but not bonfires) during a 4 week period around bonfire night. The information collected includes (for each case) the date of treatment, age of patient, place where the injury occurred, type of firework, type of injury (which area of the body), outcome of injury (including

transfers between hospitals). Department of Trade and Industry are in the lead in running the database (and decide what information should be collected), supported by National Assembly for Wales. Collection of the Welsh data is done by Health Statistics and Analysis Unit, funded internally.

Status: Ongoing
Collection Method: Survey: of all firework injuries in the period of highest risk
Frequency: Annually
Reference Period: 4 week period around bonfire night.
Timeliness: Data is available from December but it is not released until the end of October in the following year.
Earliest Available Data: Data for Wales from 1990
National Coverage: England and Wales

Statistician
Graham Davies
National Assembly for Wales
Statistical Directorate; Health Statistics Analysis Unit (3)
Tel: 029 2082 5086.
Email: graham.davies@wales.gov.uk

Health Status - Wales
National Assembly for Wales

The National Assembly for Wales has completed a postal survey using a sample of 50,000 of the adult population drawn from the Electoral Register. The survey covered people's views of the NHS and the areas they would most like to see improved, illnesses or disabilities they might have, how they go about their everyday lives and about their circumstances and lifestyle. The survey covers Wales and is available at new district health authority levels.

Collection Method: Probability sample from Electoral Register
Frequency: Periodic
Reference Period: Previous year
National Coverage: Wales

Statistician
Adrian Crompton
National Assembly for Wales
Statistical Directorate; Health Statistics and Analysis Unit (4)
Tel: 029 2082 5033.
Email: statswales@gtnet.gov.uk

Products that contain data from this source
Health Statistics Wales

Health Survey for England
Department of Health

The Health Survey for England comprises a series of annual surveys, of which the 1997 survey is the seventh. Since 1994, the Health Survey for England has been carried out by the Joint Health Surveys Unit of Social and

Community Planning Research (SCPR) and the Department of Epidemiology and Public Health at University College, London (UCL).

Since 1995 the surveys have included children aged 2-15 as well as adults. This report is concerned solely with the health and growth of children and young adults aged 2-24, and combines data from the 1995-1997 surveys. Key findings relating to all adults in the 1997 survey are summarised in a separate set of reference tables to be published early in 1999.

The Health Survey series was designed to achieve the following aims:

1. To provide annual data for nationally representative samples to monitor trends in the nation's health.
2. To estimate the proportion of people in England who have specified health conditions.
3. To estimate the prevalence of certain risk factors associated with these conditions.
4. To examine differences between subgroups of the population (including regional populations) in their likelihood of having specified conditions or risk factors.
5. To assess the frequency with which particular combinations of risk factors are found, and in which groups these combinations most commonly occur.
6. To monitor progress towards selected health targets.
7. (From 1995) to measure the height of children at different ages, replacing the National Study of Health and Growth.

Each survey in the series consists of core questions and measurements (for example, anthropometric and blood pressure measurements and analysis of blood and saliva samples), plus modules of questions on specific issues that change periodically. The surveys have involved nurse visits as well as interviews.

The 1997 Survey

In order to increase the number of children available for analysis in the 1997 survey, the design was modified from previous years. In part of the sample the procedure was the same as in the two preceding years: all adults in the selected households were surveyed, and up to two children were surveyed. In the other part of the sample, only children were surveyed, not adults (though a household questionnaire collected a certain amount of information about the household and its members).

'Core' topics, repeated every year for both adults and children, were blood pressure,

anthropometry, cigarette smoking, alcohol consumption and self-assessed general health. Saliva samples were obtained from those aged 4-17. Blood samples were obtained from those aged 18-24.

For children, the special topics in 1997 were respiratory conditions (asthma and asthma-related symptoms), lung function, non-fatal accidents, physical exercise and eating habits. The Strengths and Difficulties Questionnaire was completed by parents, describing the behaviour of each surveyed child. A telephone follow-up survey examined children's use of sun protection and the prevalence of sunburn. It also examined parents' and childrens' attitudes toward sun protection.

For those aged 16-24, the special topics in 1997 were respiratory problems, lung function, physical activity and diet. The General Health Questionnaire (GHQ12) was administered to those aged 13 and over.

Status: Ongoing
Collection Method: Household/Person (Sample) Survey
Frequency: Continuously
Timeliness: Annual
National Coverage: England

Statistician
Anthony Boucher
Department of Health
Tel: 020 7972 5389

Products that contain data from this source
Health Survey for England: The Health of Young People 1995-97.

Immunisation & Vaccination Activity (KC50)
National Assembly for Wales

Most information on immunisation and vaccination is derived from the Child Health System. However, a small amount of additional information (including for adults) is collected on the annual KC50 aggregate returns. Information is collected annually, on an all Wales basis, by NHS Trust. KC50 data is not routinely published, but it is available on request. It may be used when vaccinations given to the wider population (rather than just children) is of interest.

Status: Ongoing
Collection Method: Survey
Frequency: Annually
Reference Period: 1 April to 31 March
Timeliness: HSA send out KC50 forms in March for completion, with a target date for their return of mid May, the timeliness of the return of forms is improving and progress is being made towards it. The aim is for key summary data for all of Wales to be available by the end of September, but this is dependent on the timely return of forms

and resolution of queries.
Earliest Available Data: 1989/90
National Coverage: Wales
Disaggregation: NHS Trust

Statistician
Dr Gwyneth Thomas
National Assembly for Wales
Statistical Directorate; Health Statistics and Analysis Unit (1)
Tel: 029 2082 5039.
Email: gwyneth.thomas@wales.gov.uk

Products that contain data from this source
Health Statistics Wales

Morbidity Statistics from General Practice - England and Wales
Office for National Statistics; sponsored by Department of Health

Following on from a small pilot study in 1951-54, surveys of morbidity in General Practice have taken place about every ten years since 1955-56. The latest study was carried out in 1991-92 by the then Office of Population Censuses and Surveys on behalf of the Department of Health and the Royal College of General Practitioners. The study covered approximately 1 per cent of the population of England and Wales on the list of 60 volunteer GP practices. Socio-economic data were also collected by interview for 83 per cent of the patients involved. No decision has been taken on any prospective "MSGP5".

Status: Ceased temporarily
Collection Method: Large-scale (Sample) Survey
Frequency: Studies held approximately every ten years
Reference Period: Studies held 1955-56; 1970-76; 1981-82, 1991-92.
Timeliness: Interval between collection and release varies with the studies, the publication of the 1991-92 results in 1995 being earlier than the previous studies due to increased computerisation in general practice and the collection of socio-economic data within the practices.
Earliest Available Data: Report on first study published in 3 volumes in 1960: second study reports published 1979/1982; third study reports published 1986/1989
National Coverage: England and Wales
Disaggregation: General Practice patient catchment area

Statistician
John Cloyne
Office for National Statistics
Demography and Health Division; General Practitioner Research Database
Tel: 020 7533 5215;
Email: gprd@ons.gov.uk

Products that contain data from this source
Morbidity Statistics from General Practice 1991-92; Morbidity Statistics from General Practice 1991-92 on CD-ROM

Morbidity Statistics from General Practice 1991-92 (MSGP4)
Office for National Statistics; sponsored by Department of Health

The Office of Population Censuses and Surveys (now part of the Office for National Statistics), jointly with the Royal College of General Practitioners and the Department of Health, conducted the fourth of a series of studies of Morbidity Statistics from General Practice in 1991-92. The study examines the pattern of disease seen by GPs by the age, sex and socio-economic characteristics of patients. Data are available for three main regions: the North, the Midlands and Wales and the South. The series, which is carried out approximately every ten years, was first compiled for 1955-56.

A nationally-representative sample of general practitioners' and practice nurses' recorded details of every face-to-face contact with their patients over the course of a year, in order to examine the pattern of disease seen by GPs. 502,493 patients at some time during the study year, representing 468,042 person years at risk (socio-economic data collected for 83% of patients). Over 1.3m contacts recorded with study doctors, an average of 3.8 contacts by each person who consulted. Data collection by computer and floppy disk. An evaluation exercise suggested that 96% of contacts with a doctor in the surgery and 95% in patients' homes were reported. However, only an estimated 61% of referrals to outpatient departments were reported. A sample comparison suggested that 93% of diagnoses were correctly reported. Three previous national studies - 1955-56; 1970-76; 1981-82: data for these studies available on request.

Status: Ceased completely
Collection Method: Large-scale (Sample) Survey
Frequency: Periodic
Reference Period: 1 September 1991 - 31 August 1992
Timeliness: Data collected 1991-92; publication 1995 being earlier than the previous studies due to increased computerisation in general practice and the collection of socio-economic data within the practices. CDs issued 1998.
Earliest Available Data: 1995
National Coverage: England and Wales
Disaggregation: General Practice patient catchment area

Statistician
John Cloyne
Office for National Statistics
Demography and Health Division; General Practitioner Research Database
Tel: 020 7533 5215;
Email: gprd@ons.gov.uk

Products that contain data from this source
Morbidity Statistics from General Practice 1991-92; Morbidity Statistics from General Practitioners - Fourth national study 1991-1992; The Health of Adult Britain 1841 - 1994, Decennial Supplement, Volumes 1 and 2

Pathology Laboratories - Cervical Cytology and Biopsies (KC61)
National Assembly for Wales

Information on cervical smears and biopsies examined by pathology laboratories. Collected annually. Contains data at all Wales, Health Authority and Trust level. Other information collected includes the number of smears subdivided by their source (GPs, NHS community clinics, GUM clinics, etc) and the number of these which were inadequate specimens. The results of smears are shown broken down by women's age groups. For laboratories having a histopathology department on site, information is collected relating the result of biopsy to the result of cytology test. Pathology laboratories use a variety of computer systems (most commonly TELEPATH, an England and Wales system), but the information required to complete KC61 cannot always be readily extracted from these systems. The Welsh KC61 form has recently been realigned with that collected in England (there were previously slight differences), which should make the information easier to extract for laboratories using the TELEPATH computer system.

Status: Ongoing
Collection Method: Survey
Frequency: Annually
Reference Period: 1 April to 31 March
Timeliness: KC61 forms are sent out to pathology laboratories examining cervical smears in NHS trusts. They are due to be completed and returned by mid May. The timeliness of the return of forms is improving and progress towards meeting the target is being made. The Health Statistics and Analysis Unit aim for key summary data for all of Wales to be available by the end of September, but this is dependent on the timely return of forms and resolution of queries.
Earliest Available Data: 1989/90
National Coverage: Wales
Disaggregation: NHS Trust

Statistician
Dr Gwyneth Thomas
National Assembly for Wales
Statistical Directorate; Health Statistics and Analysis Unit (1)
Tel: 029 2082 5039.
Email: gwyneth.thomas@wales.gov.uk

Products that contain data from this source
Cervical Screening Programme, Wales - Annual Report; Cervical Screening Programme, Wales - Annual Statistical brief; Health Statistics Wales

---

Primary Immunisation
Information and Statistics Division, NHS in Scotland

Information on the levels of immunity against childhood diseases: note areas which require increased resources to boost programme; monitor health boards against targets.

Status: Ongoing
Collection Method: Administrative Records
Frequency: Quarterly
Timeliness: 3 months in arrears
Earliest Available Data: 1984
National Coverage: Scotland
Disaggregation: Health Board

Statistician
Peter Knight
Information and Statistics Division, NHS in Scotland
Hospital & community information
Tel: 0131 551 8739

Products that contain data from this source
Scottish Health Statistics

Scottish Breast Screening Data
Information and Statistics Division, NHS in Scotland

Activity, monitoring data for Breast Screening Programme

Status: Ongoing
Collection Method: Administrative Records
Frequency: Continuously
Timeliness: Quarterly in arrears
Earliest Available Data: 1987
National Coverage: Scotland
Disaggregation: Health Board

Statistician
Jan Warner
Information and Statistics Division, NHS in Scotland
Central co-ordinating unit for screening
Tel: 0131 551 8626

Scottish Cancer Registry
Information and Statistics Division, NHS in Scotland

To monitor trends in cancer incidence and survival

Status: Ongoing
Collection Method: Administrative Records
Frequency: Continuously
Timeliness: Concurrent
National Coverage: Scotland
Disaggregation: Health Board

Statistician
Roger Black
Information and Statistics Division, NHS in Scotland
Scottish Cancer Intelligence Unit
Tel: 0131 551 8053

Products that contain data from this source
Scottish Cancer Intelligence Unit Annual Report; Scottish Health Statistics; Trends in Cancer Survival

Scottish Morbidity Record (SMR)
Information and Statistics Division, NHS in Scotland; sponsored by ISD

To provide information on inpatients and day cases, outpatients, maternity patients, psychiatric and learning disability patients, cancer registration, community, dentistry, cardiac surgery and drug misuse.

Status: Ongoing
Collection Method: Administrative Records
Frequency: Continuously
Reference Period: 1996 onwards
Timeliness: Monthly in arrears
Earliest Available Data: 1961 - 1996 (major revision)
National Coverage: Scotland
Disaggregation: Health Board, NHS Trust, speciality, patient

Statistician
Peter Knight
Information and Statistics Division, NHS in Scotland
Hospital & community information
Tel: 0131 551 8739

Products that contain data from this source
Scottish Record Linkage Database; Scottish Health Statistics

Sexually Transmitted Diseases - England
The Public Health Laboratory Service - Communicable Disease Surveillance Centre (CDSC)

CDSC compiles data on the number of new cases of sexually transmitted diseases identified and treated at NHS genito-urinary medicine (GUM) clinics. Figures, obtained quarterly from each clinic, are available for each of the major diseases.

Status: Ongoing
Collection Method: Returns for NHS GUM clinics
Frequency: Annually
Reference Period: Financial year
Timeliness: One year
Earliest Available Data: 1988-89
National Coverage: England
Disaggregation: Health Authority

Statistician
Mike Catchpole
PHLS - CDSC
Tel: 0181 200 6868

Products that contain data from this source
Health and Personal Social Services Statistics for England; CDR Supplement

Sexually Transmitted Diseases - Wales (KC60)
National Assembly for Wales

The National Assembly for Wales compiles data on genito-urinary medicine clinic cases of sexually transmitted diseases. Details are used in the Communicable Diseases Surveillance Centre (Wales) for monitoring changes in infection rates. Data are available by the number of cases of specific sexually transmitted diseases seen at genito-urinary medicine hospital clinics, for NHS Trusts, and, in some cases, individual hospital clinics. Some information dates back to the early 1970s, although the details collected were restructured in 1995. Data are collected quarterly and published on an annual basis.

KC60 data may be used for STD surveillance. In particular, part of the KC60 data allows a more comprehensive view of HIV, allowing high risk behaviour to be related to HIV trends. Selected data are integrated into a quarterly bulletin on HIV surveillance produced by PHLS CDSC Welsh unit for health authority consultants in communicable disease control, National Assembly for Wales, Blood Transfusion Service, laboratories and GUM physicians. Summary all Wales information from KC60 is included in the National Assembly for Wales publication 'Health Statistics Wales'. It may also be used to answer Parliamentary and Assembly Questions. Ad hoc requests for information are rare, but because of the sensitive nature of the information would be considered individually. Some information dates back to the early 1970s, although the details collected were restructured in 1995.

Status: Ongoing
Collection Method: Survey
Frequency: Quarterly
Reference Period: the quarters ending March, June, September and December
Timeliness: Forms are due to be returned within around 4-6 weeks of the end of the quarter (however it is not uncommon for all Wales data to be held up while waiting for outstanding data from one or two clinics.
Earliest Available Data: Some information dates back to the early 1970s
National Coverage: Wales
Disaggregation: NHS Trust

Statistician
Dr Gwyneth Thomas
National Assembly for Wales
Statistical Directorate; Health Statistics and Analysis Unit (1)
Tel: 029 2082 5039.
Email: gwyneth.thomas@wales.gov.uk

Products that contain data from this source
Health Statistics Wales

See also:
In this chapter:
Community Health Services - Northern Ireland *(4.6)*

In the Labour Market chapter:
Asbestosis Register - Great Britain
Central Index of Dose Information (CIDI)
Continuing Increase in Mesothelioma Mortality in Great Britain
Diseases Reported Under the Reporting of Injuries, Diseases and Dangerous Occurrences Regulations (RIDDOR)
Employment Data from Employer Surveys and the Labour Force Survey
Industrial Injuries - Prescribed Diseases
Information on Enforcement Under the Health and Safety at Work Etc Act from Health and Safety Executive Enforcing Authorities and Local Authorities
Injuries and Dangerous Occurrences Reported Under the Reporting of Injuries, Diseases and Dangerous Occurrences Regulations (RIDDOR)
Lead Workers Under Medical Surveillance
Mesothelioma Register - Great Britain
Musculoskeletal Occupational Surveillance Scheme (MOSS)
Occupational Physicians Reporting Activity (OPRA) Surveillance Scheme
Occupational Skin Disease Surveillance Scheme (EPIDERM) - UK
Occupational Surveillance for Audiologists (OSSA)
Pesticide Incidents Appraisal Panel
Self-Reported Work-Related Illness Survey 1995 (SWI95)
Surveillance Scheme for Infectious Diseases at Work (SIDAW)
Surveillance Scheme for Occupational Stress and Mental Illness (SOSMI)
Surveillance Scheme for Work-Related and Occupational Respiratory Disease Survey (SWORD)
Work-Related Accidents Survey (Labour Force Survey)

4.20 Mental Health Services

Census of Patients in Mental Illness and Learning Disability Units in Wales
National Assembly for Wales; sponsored by National Assembly for Wales Statistical Directorate

The Welsh Health Common Services Authority, on behalf of the National Assembly for Wales, holds an annual Census of patients in mental illness and learning disability units in Wales. The Census covers patients in all hospitals and units with learning disabilities or a mental illness and collects details of their place of residence, length of stay, and where applicable, the section of the Mental Health Act under which they are detained. A form is sent out to each hospital / unit to be completed in respect of every patient resident on 31 March each year. The information is used to monitor the use of the Mental Health Act and to monitor the Mental Illness and Learning Disabilities strategies. It is also used to respond to Parliamentary Questions. Census was undertaken every two years from 1979 and annually from 1992

Status: Ongoing
Collection Method: Census
Frequency: Annually
Reference Period: 31 March each year
Timeliness: Data available around 6 months after census date.
Earliest Available Data: 1979
National Coverage: Wales
Disaggregation: Unitary Authority, Health Authority and Trust level

Statistician
Graham Davies
National Assembly for Wales
Statistical Directorate; Health Statistics Analysis Unit (3)
Tel: 029 2082 5086.
Email: graham.davies@wales.gov.uk

Products that contain data from this source
Census of Patients in Mental Handicap Hospitals and Units in Wales; Health Statistics Wales; Social Services Statistics for Wales

Guardianship Under the Mental Health Act (1983) - England
Department of Health

This information is based on the collection of return SSDA 702. It holds the latest information available on the numbers of people subject to guardianship under sections 7 and 37 of the Mental Health Act 1983.

Status: Ongoing
Collection Method: Census
Frequency: Annually
Reference Period: As at 31 March
Earliest Available Data: 1984
National Coverage: England
Disaggregation: Local Authority / Metropolitan Districts / Shire Counties; Unitary Authority

Statistician
Tracie Kilbey
Department of Health
Statistics Division; SD3B
Tel: 020 7972 5582;
Email: tkilbey@doh.gov.uk

Products that contain data from this source
Guardianship Under the Mental Health Act (1983); Health and Personal Social Services Statistics for England; Key Indicators Graphical System

KH15
Department of Health

From 1 April 1987, following the Körner review of health service information, statistics on patients detained under the Mental Health Act, admitted to NHS facilities and NHS patients using non-NHS facilities under contractual arrangements (as authorised under Section 23 of the NHS Act 1977) were collected on the aggregate return KH15 on a financial year basis.

Status: Ceased completely
Collection Method: Census
Frequency: Annually
Reference Period: Financial Year
Earliest Available Data: 1987-88

Statistician
Drew Hird
Department of Health
Tel: 020 7972 5604;
Email: dhird@doh.gov.uk

Products that contain data from this source
Inpatients Formally Detained in Hospitals Under the Mental Health Act 1983 and Other Legislation - Bulletin; Inpatients Formally Detained in Hospitals Under the Mental Health Act 1983 and Other Legislation, NHS trusts, high security hospitals and private facilities - Booklet

KH16
Department of Health

From 1 April 1987, following the Körner review of health service information, statistics on changes in legal status of patients detained under the Mental Health Act were collected on this return.

Status: Ceased completely
Collection Method: Census
Frequency: Annually
Reference Period: Financial Year
Earliest Available Data: 1987-88

Statistician
Drew Hird
Department of Health
Tel: 020 7972 5604;
Email: dhird@doh.gov.uk

Products that contain data from this source
Inpatients Formally Detained in Hospitals Under the Mental Health Act 1983 and Other Legislation - Bulletin; Inpatients Formally Detained in Hospitals Under the Mental Health Act 1983 and Other Legislation, NHS trusts, high security hospitals and private facilities - Booklet

KO37
Department of Health

This form was used to collect numbers of patients detained under the Mental Health Act and admissions to private mental nursing homes registered to detain patients.

Status: Ceased completely
Collection Method: Census
Frequency: Annually
Reference Period: Financial Year
Earliest Available Data: 1987-88

Statistician
Drew Hird
Department of Health
Tel: 020 7972 5604;
Email: dhird@doh.gov.uk

Products that contain data from this source
Inpatients Formally Detained in Hospitals Under the Mental Health Act 1983 and Other Legislation - Bulletin; Inpatients Formally Detained in Hospitals Under the Mental Health Act 1983 and Other Legislation, NHS trusts, high security hospitals and private facilities - Booklet

Körner Return KP90, Informal Patients and Patients Detained Under the Mental Health Act 1983
National Assembly for Wales

Aggregate information on formal and informal admissions of psychiatric patients to NHS units for people with a mental illness or learning disability and to registered private mental nursing homes. Information is also collected on changes in the legal status of patients in such facilities, and on the number of psychiatric patients resident at 31 March. The return is collected annually from NHS hospitals & units for people with a mental illness or learning disability and registered private mental nursing homes. Information is collected on the number of admissions of psychiatric patients during the year (subdivided by the section of the Mental Health Act 1983 under which they were detained, the mental category and sex of the patient - although for informal admissions, only the number of patients by sex is collected). Details of changes in the legal status of patients are collected (including information on the use of supervised discharge under the Mental Health (Patients in the Community) Act 1995), and finally the number of psychiatric patients resident at 31 March (by sex and (for detained patients) by mental category).

Information from the return is used by the National Assembly for Wales to monitor the use made of the Mental Health Act 1983 and the use of supervised discharge under the Mental Health (Patients in the Community)

Act 1995. It may also be in consideration of policy options regarding care of people with mental illness or learning disability (including formulation of new legislation). Information is also used to respond to Parliamentary Questions and requests for information from the National Assembly for Wales, NHS and other sources. Summary information is included in the annual National Assembly for Wales publication 'Health Statistics Wales' and also in a Statistical Brief. The Körner mental health returns were last reviewed in 1995/96, as a result of which the 3 returns collected at the time (KH15, KH16, KO37) were replaced by a single revised form (the new KP90) from 1996/97.

Status: Ongoing
Collection Method: Census
Frequency: Annually
Reference Period: Financial year
Timeliness: The aim is for key summary data for all of Wales to be available by the end of September, but this is dependent on the timely return of forms and resolution of queries.
National Coverage: Wales
Disaggregation: Trust level

Statistician
Graham Davies
National Assembly for Wales
Statistical Directorate; Health Statistics Analysis Unit (3)
Tel: 029 2082 5086.
Email: graham.davies@wales.gov.uk

Products that contain data from this source
Admission of patients to mental health facilities in Wales (including patients detained under the Mental Health Act 1983); Health Statistics Wales

KP90
Department of Health

Following a review by the Department of requirements for information on patients detained under the Mental Health Act 1983, a new return, KP90, was introduced for 1996-97. This return replaced returns KH15 and KH16, previously completed by NHS trusts, and KO37, completed by the health authorities on behalf of private hospitals in their area. It is also completed by the three Special Health Authorities managing the high security hospitals.

Status: Ongoing
Collection Method: Census
Frequency: Annually
Reference Period: Financial Year
Timeliness: Aim is for data to be available by end of September, but this is dependent on timely return of forms and resolution of queries.
Earliest Available Data: 1996-97
National Coverage: England
Sub-National: Full
Disaggregation: Trust level

Statistician
Drew Hird
Department of Health
Tel: 020 7972 5604;
Email: dhird@doh.gov.uk

Products that contain data from this source
Inpatients Formally Detained in Hospitals Under the Mental Health Act 1983 and Other Legislation - Bulletin; Inpatients Formally Detained in Hospitals Under the Mental Health Act 1983 and Other Legislation, NHS trusts, high security hospitals and private facilities - Booklet

Learning Disabilities - Wales
National Assembly for Wales

The National Assembly for Wales compiles a survey on health and social care for people with a learning disability. A sample of 4,000 people with a learning disability was drawn from the Social Services Client Record System. The survey covered people's illnesses and disabilities, how they go about their everyday lives, and questions on their circumstances and lifestyle. The survey covers Wales and results are available at new district health authority and county levels.

Statistician
Adrian Crompton
National Assembly for Wales
Statistical Directorate; Health Statistics and Analysis Unit (4)
Tel: 029 2082 5033.
Email: statswales@gtnet.gov.uk

Mental Health Enquiry (MHE)
Department of Health

Up to 1986, statistics on formal admissions to NHS hospitals and units were collected by the Mental Health Enquiry (MHE) from all psychiatric hospitals, including special hospitals, on a calendar year basis.

Status: Ceased completely
Collection Method: Census
Frequency: Annually
Reference Period: Calendar Year

Statistician
Drew Hird
Department of Health
Tel: 020 7972 5604;
Email: dhird@doh.gov.uk

Products that contain data from this source
Inpatients Formally Detained in Hospitals Under the Mental Health Act 1983 and Other Legislation - Bulletin; Inpatients Formally Detained in Hospitals Under the Mental Health Act 1983 and Other Legislation, NHS trusts, high security hospitals and private facilities - Booklet

Mental Health Inpatients System - Northern Ireland
Department of Health and Social Services - Northern Ireland

The Mental Health Inpatients System (MHIS) is maintained by the Department of Health and Social Security and holds hospital activity and Census data. Data are collected on all individual inpatient stays in mental illness and learning disability hospitals and units derived from hospital administrative records. A census of all long-stay and detained inpatients is also conducted as at 31 March each year. Data, collected continuously, are available from 1960 to 1994-95 from annual files with activity data recorded for all mental illness patients. From 1989-90 they were held on the Mental Health Records Scheme (database system) containing data on all mental illness inpatients and outpatients and learning disability inpatients and Census data for 1989-98. This was updated to the current system, MHIS, in 1993-4. The latest published information relates to 1994-95.

Status: Ongoing
Collection Method: Returns and computerised extracts from hospitals
Frequency: Continuous
Reference Period: Financial year
Earliest Available Data: 1960
National Coverage: Northern Ireland
Sub-National: Full
Disaggregation: Hospitals

Statistician
Tony O'Brien
Department of Health and Social Services - Northern Ireland
Tel: 028 9052 2504;
Email: tony.obrien@dhssni.gov.uk

Products that contain data from this source
Health and Personal Social Services Statistics (NI); Mental Health Inpatients System (MHIS); Mental Health Standard Analyses; Northern Ireland Mental Illness Statistics; Northern Ireland Psychiatric Census Data; Social Trends

Mental Illness/Learning Disability Patients - Northern Ireland
Department of Health and Social Services - Northern Ireland

The Department of Health and Social Services (NI) collates Mental Illness/Learning Disability Census data, derived from hospital administrative records. The data cover inpatients resident in mental illness and learning disability hospitals and units in Northern Ireland as at 17 February. Data are available to the public on request comprising an age by length of stay breakdown for hospitals and Health and Social Services Boards only. The Census began in 1991. Before 1994 data were collected as at 17 December. Results are published annually, four months after the reference period.

Status: Ongoing
Collection Method: Returns from hospitals
Frequency: Annual
Reference Period: At 17 February each year
Timeliness: Four months after census date
Earliest Available Data: 1991
National Coverage: Northern Ireland
Sub-National: Full
Disaggregation: Hospitals

Statistician
Tony O'Brien
Department of Health and Social Services - Northern Ireland
Tel: 028 9052 504;
Email: tony.obrien@dhssni.gov.uk

Products that contain data from this source
Development of Services for People with a Mental Handicap or Mental Illness in Northern Ireland; Mental Illness/Learning Disability Census Tables

Number of Persons Admitted to Local Authority Guardianship (SSDA 702) - Wales
National Assembly for Wales

Status: Ongoing
Collection Method: Administrative Records
Frequency: Annually
Reference Period: 31 March
Timeliness: 9-12 months
Earliest Available Data: 1980
National Coverage: Wales
Disaggregation: Local Authority District (LAD) / Unitary Authority (England)

Statistician
Robin Jones
National Assembly for Wales
Statistical Directorate; Health Statistics and Analysis Unit 2 (HSA2)
Tel: 029 2082 3625

Products that contain data from this source
Social Services Statistics Wales

Psychiatric Morbidity in Great Britain
Department of Health

The OPCS psychiatric morbidity reports present data on four surveys carried out during 1993 and 1994. Private household survey of 10,000 adults aged 16-64. Supplementary sample of 350 people aged 16-64 with psychosis living in private households identified via GPs and Mental Health Teams and residents of group homes or recognised lodgings who were classified as having schizophrenia or affective psychosis.

Institutions - 1,200 people aged 16-64 living in institutions specifically catering for people with mental illnesses.
Homeless people - 1,100 people aged 16-64 living in hostels for the homeless and other such institutions.

Reports 1-3 cover: the prevalence of psychiatric disorders among people living in private households, physical complaints of people with psychiatric disorders and their use of services, the receipt of treatments, and how people with a neurotic disorder differ from those without one (e.g. their economic activity, social functioning, their use of alcohol, drugs and tobacco).

Reports 4-6: reports on the prevalence of psychiatric morbidity in different sorts of institutions and presents data on residents with various disorders and their difficulties with social functioning etc.

Report 7: presents data on, among other things, the prevalence of psychiatric disorders, the physical health of the homeless, their economic, social and financial circumstances and their use of alcohol, drugs and tobacco.

Report 8: Presents data on the first three surveys and identifies characteristics associated with differences in the circumstances and health related behaviour of adults with psychosis.

Earliest Available Data: 1995
National Coverage: Great Britain

Assistant Statistician
Drew Hird
Department of Health
Tel: 020 7972 5604

See also:
In this chapter:
Residential Establishment Census Return (SWS FORM R1) *(4.7)*

4.21 Ophthalmic Services

General Ophthalmic Services - England and Wales
Department of Health

The NHS Executive compiles Ophthalmic Statistics for England and Wales relating to the General Ophthalmic Services and other ophthalmic data. Data are collected from Health Authorities and are used to monitor trends and forecast volumes and costs of sight testing activity and vouchers towards the cost of spectacles and in the deliberations of the group considering the sight test fee for opticians. Data are available for sight tests

and vouchers paid for by Health Authorities and general ophthalmic expenditure by year. Ophthalmic workforce statistics are also collated. The names of each practitioner holding a contract with a Health Authority are collected and used to monitor the availability of practitioners to carry out NHS sight tests. Data on optometrists cover England and Wales; data on ophthalmic medical practitioners cover Great Britain. General ophthalmic and workforce data are available at Health Authority level. Workforce statistics are collected annually in December and data on sight tests and vouchers are collected twice a year, in March and September. A statistical bulletin covering general ophthalmic and workforce data is published annually in November.

Status: Ongoing
Collection Method: Data collected from all Health Authorities; some data sample-based.
Frequency: Workforce: Annually Sight tests and vouchers: Twice a year
Reference Period: Workforce: as at 31 December. Activity: April to September and October to March.
Timeliness: 4-5 months
National Coverage: England and Wales
Disaggregation: Health Authority

Statistician
Sheila M. Dixon
Department of Health
Statistics Division; General Opthalmic Services Statistics
Tel: 020 7972 5507/9; Email: s.dixon@doh.gov.uk

Products that contain data from this source
General Ophthalmic Services Activity Statistics; General Ophthalmic Services Workforce Statistics; Health and Personal Social Services Statistics for England; Ophthalmic Services Statistical Bulletin; Regional Trends

General Ophthalmic Services - Vouchers - GB
Department of Health

The NHS Executive conducts the optical Voucher Survey on a sample of approximately 30 Health Authorities. The authorities send the NHS Executive all the vouchers they have paid for in July and a sample of these vouchers is analysed in order to monitor the performance of the Voucher Scheme. The Survey covers England, Wales and Scotland and has been carried out annually since 1989. Results for Great Britain are published annually in April or May.

Status: Ongoing
Collection Method: Sample
Frequency: Annually
Reference Period: July
Timeliness: 10 months
Earliest Available Data: 1989
National Coverage: Great Britain

Statistician
Sheila M. Dixon
Department of Health
Statistics Division; General Opthalmic Services
Statistics
Tel: 020 7972 5507/9;
Email: s.dixon@doh.gov.uk

Products that contain data from this source
Voucher Survey

Sight Tests Volume and Workforce Survey - GB
Department of Health

The NHS Executive conducts a survey of ophthalmic practitioners, to report on the workforce and the total volume of NHS and private sight tests.

Status: Ongoing
Collection Method: Sample of Optometrists and Ophthalmic Medical Practitioners.
Frequency: Annually
Reference Period: Year April to March
Timeliness: 8 months
Earliest Available Data: 1993-94
National Coverage: Great Britain

Statistician
Sheila M. Dixon
Department of Health
Statistics Division; General Opthalmic Services
Statistics
Tel: 020 7972 5507/9;
Email: s.dixon@doh.gov.uk

Products that contain data from this source
Sight Tests Volume and Workforce Survey

4.22 Pharmaceutical Services

Pharmaceutical Services Form PHS1
National Health Service Executive

The NHS Executive compiles data on community pharmacies in contract with Health Authorities in England and Wales. Data is collected using NHS pharmaceutical services form PHS1. Information is collected on openings and closures of community pharmacies, disposal of unwanted medicines, applications to hold pharmaceutical contracts and pharmacies that receive payments under the essential small pharmacy scheme, or are paid to provide additional hours of service and advice to residential and nursing homes. Form PHS1 covers all health authorities in England and Wales, and is collected bi-annually. The need for this data was identified during a strategic review of departmental requirements for information in the Family Health Service business area.

Status: Ongoing
Collection Method: data collection from all HAs
Frequency: Annually
Reference Period: Financial year ending 31st March
Timeliness: 4 months
Earliest Available Data: March 1994
National Coverage: England and Wales
Disaggregation: Health Authorities (HAs)

Statistician
Phil Massey
National Health Service Executive
SD1; SD1C
Tel: 020 7972 5504

Products that contain data from this source
Community Pharmacies in England and Wales;
General Pharmaceutical Services in England

Prescription Cost Analysis System
Department of Health

The Department of Health compiles data on all prescriptions dispensed in the community in England. The data are from the Prescription Cost Analysis System which is part of prescription pricing and information systems managed by the Prescription Pricing Authority. Data are available on the trends in numbers and costs of prescriptions dispensed including analyses by therapeutic group, category of exemption (for example children, young people and elderly people) and generic prescribing.

All prescription statistics are based on information systems at the Prescription Pricing Authority (PPA). Statistics from 1991 are based on the new Prescription Cost Analysis (PCA) system which was introduced in January 1991. The new PCA system is based on an analysis of all prescriptions dispensed in the community by community pharmacists and appliance contractors, dispensing doctors, and prescriptions submitted by doctors for items personally administered. Prior to 1991 statistics were based on a sample of 1 in 200 prescriptions dispensed in the community by community pharmacists and appliance contractors only. Volume statistics are in terms of number of items as opposed to the number of fees used in data prior to 1991. Quarterly data are available from 1991 onwards.

Status: Ongoing
Frequency: Quarterly
Reference Period: The quarters ending March, June, September, December
Timeliness: 3 months
Earliest Available Data: 1980 (Annual) 1991 (Quarterly)
National Coverage: England
Disaggregation: Family Health Service Authority (FHSA)

Statistician
Ann Custance
Department of Health
Statistics Division 1; Statistics Division 1E (Prescription Statistics and Analysis)
Tel: 020 7972 5513; Email: acustanc@doh.gov.uk

Products that contain data from this source
Health and Personal Social Services Statistics for England; Prescription Cost Analysis; Regional Trends; Social Trends; Statistics of Prescriptions Dispensed in the Community, England

Prescription Pricing Authority - Chemists' Particulars
National Health Service Executive

Data is obtained annually from the Prescription Pricing Authority as a by product of the systems they use to pay pharmacies. It covers numbers of prescriptions dispensed, net ingredient cost and type for each pharmacy and appliance contractor in England in contract with a health authority to dispense NHS prescriptions. Prior to 1991 the data collated by the Prescription Pricing Authority was based on a sample of 1 in 200 and was grossed up, it is now based on the whole population.

Status: Ongoing
Collection Method: Electronic Link
Frequency: Annually
Reference Period: the financial year.
Timeliness: 4 months
Earliest Available Data: 1991-92
National Coverage: England
Disaggregation: Health Authorities (HAs)

Statistician
Neil Higginbottom
National Health Service Executive
SD1; SD1C
Tel: 020 7972 5501;
Email: kchilds@doh.gov.uk

Products that contain data from this source
General Pharmaceutical Services in England

Prescriptions - Wales
National Assembly for Wales

Quarterly extract of data held by the Prescribing Information and Pricing Services providing details of all prescriptions dispensed in the community (mostly but not exclusively written by GP's).

Status: Ongoing
Collection Method: Survey
Frequency: Quarterly
Reference Period: The quarters ending March, June, September and December.
Timeliness: Monthly payment schedules are compiled from the information and passed to health authorities to enable them to make payments to pharmacies, appliance and oxygen contractors, dispensing doctors and doctors who personally administer items. Quarterly data is returned to HSA.

Earliest Available Data: 1973
National Coverage: Wales
Disaggregation: GP Practice; Health Authority

Statistician
Dr Gwyneth Thomas
National Assembly for Wales
Statistical Directorate; Health Statistics and
Analysis Unit (1)
Tel: 029 2082 5039.
Email: gwyneth.thomas@wales.gov.uk

Products that contain data from this source
Health Statistics Wales; NHS Prescription Items
Prescribed by Dentists - Annual statistical brief;
Statistics of Prescriptions Dispensed in Wales -
Annual Report; Statistics of Prescriptions
Dispensed in Wales - Annual statistical brief

4.23 Private Healthcare, Homes and Hospitals

Information on Small Registered Residential Care Homes
National Assembly for Wales

Status: Ongoing
Collection Method: Administrative Records
Frequency: Annually
National Coverage: Wales
Disaggregation: Postcode Area

Statistician
Robin Jones
National Assembly for Wales
Statistical Directorate; Health Statistics and
Analysis Unit 2 (HSA2)
Tel: 029 2082 3625

Private Homes, Hospitals and Clinics (KO36) - Wales
National Assembly for Wales

The National Assembly for Wales compiles
data on private homes, hospitals and clinics
registered under Section 23 of the Registered
Homes Act 1984. Data are available on the
registration status of the home, facilities,
length of stay and residential costs, source
of funds, residents by admission and age,
and the numbers of qualified staff.

Status: Ongoing
Collection Method: Census
Frequency: Annual
Reference Period: 1 April - 31 March
Timeliness: Within 12 months of receipt
Earliest Available Data: 1985 - 86
National Coverage: Wales
Disaggregation: Local Authority

Statistician
Robin Jones
National Assembly for Wales
Statistical Directorate; Health Statistics and
Analysis Unit 2 (HSA2)
Tel: 029 2082 3625;
Email: robin.jones@wales.gsi.gov.uk

Products that contain data from this source
Social Services Statistics for Wales
Health Statistics Wales

See also:
In this chapter:
Residential Establishment Census Return
(SWS FORM R1) *(4.7)*

Health and Care - *Products*

Consultant's Directory (Scotland)
Scottish Executive

Lists all hospital, community and public health medicine consultants based on a snap shot of the ISD Scotland database.

Frequency: Monthly - Only available in NHS

Available from
Customer help desk
Information and Statistics Division, NHS in Scotland
Please see Annex B for full address details.

Sources from which data for this product are obtained
Medical and dental staff database

Definitions and Codes Manual
Scottish Executive

To make national standard definitions, codes and data recording rules freely available to the NHSiS.

Delivery: Periodic Release
Frequency: Annually

Available from
Customer help desk
Information and Statistics Division, NHS in Scotland
Please see Annex B for full address details.

GP Directory
Scottish Executive

Publication which contains GP details, GMC number and practice details.

Delivery: Periodic Release
Frequency: Annually

Available from
Customer help desk
Information and Statistics Division, NHS in Scotland
Please see Annex B for full address details.

Sources from which data for this product are obtained
GP and practice database

Health and Personal Social Services Statistics (NI)
Department of Health and Social Services - Northern Ireland

Compendium publication relating to activity, finance and manpower in the whole of the Health and Personal Social Services (NI). Contains health-related data including: hospital services; patient transport; community health; personal social services; family practitioner services; manpower and finance.

Delivery: Ceased publication 1994
Frequency: Annual
Price: Free

Available from
Jenny Orr
Department of Health and Social Services - Northern Ireland
Tel: 028 9052 2580

Sources from which data for this product are obtained
Community Health Services - Northern Ireland; Hospital Inpatient System - Northern Ireland; Mental Health Inpatients System - Northern Ireland; Personal Social Services - Northern Ireland

Health and Personal Social Services Statistics for England
Department of Health

The Health and Personal Social Services publication provides high level summary information on a wide range of health and social care in England, covering the nation's health, health care (primary, community and hospitals), personal social services, workforce and DH expenditure. The publication has 97 pages most of which contain a table, chart and a number of bullet points about a particular topic. Contact names and telephone numbers are provided, together with a full list of statistical publications produced by the Department of Health.

Delivery: Periodic Release
Frequency: Annually
Price: £16.95
ISBN: 0 11 322261 0

Available from
TSO Publications Centre and Bookshops
Please see Annex B for full address details.

Sources from which data for this product are obtained
Ambulance Services - England; Child Protection - England; Children and Young Persons Accommodated in Secure Units - England and Wales; Children Looked After - England; Children Subject to Supervision Orders - England; Children's Daycare Facilities - England; Children's Homes; Community Activity; General Ophthalmic Services - England and Wales; Guardianship Under the Mental Health Act (1983) - England; Hospital Episode Statistics; Inpatient Waiting Lists - England; Patient Care in the Community; Prescription Cost Analysis System; Private Hospitals, Homes and Clinics; Register of the deaf and hard of hearing; Registered blind and partially sighted people; Registers of people with physical disabilities; Residential personal social services for adults; Sexually Transmitted Diseases - England

Health in England 1996
Office for National Statistics; sponsored by The Health Education Authority

A study of health-related knowledge, attitudes and behaviour among adults aged 16-74 living in private households in England.

Frequency: Annually
Price: £30.00
ISBN: 11 691702 4

Available from
TSO Publications Centre and Bookshops
Please see Annex B for full address details.

Health Statistics Wales
National Assembly for Wales

Health Statistics Wales is an annual publication prepared by the National Assembly for Wales. It contains summary text along with graphs and tables that provide information on the health of the population and the range and quality of health care services in Wales. All statistics relate to Wales except where otherwise indicated. Many tables enable comparisons to be made between NHS Trusts or Health Authorities. Others show historical trends for services across Wales. The first edition was published in 1995 replacing four previous National Assembly for Wales publications. This third edition is in bilingual format for the first time. The publication is around 250 pages. It covers the following areas: Population and vital statistics; Lifestyle; Morbidity; Preventive medicine; Family health services; Waiting lists and waiting times; Hospital statistics; Abortions; Psychiatric hospital statistics; Community health services; Patient transport services; Staffing; Finance; Private health care; Health Authority profiles; Regional comparisons; Explanatory notes; NHS Trusts and hospitals in Wales; and Directory of health statistics. Information is presented in tables, charts and text.

Delivery: Periodic Release
Frequency: Annually
Price: £12.00
ISBN: 0 7504 2250 5
ISSN: 1361-3677

Available from
TSO Publications Centre and Bookshops
Please see Annex B for full address details.

Sources from which data for this product are obtained
Adult Screening Programmes - Cervical Cytology (KC53); Census of patients in mental illness and learning disability units in Wales; Chiropody Services - Wales (SBL 618); Community Health Services - Dental Services (KC64); Health Status - Wales; Hospital activity statistics; Hospital Bed Use - Wales; Immunisation & vaccination activity (KC50); Körner return KP90, Informal patients and patients detained under the Mental Health Act 1983; Medical and Dental Staff Census - Wales; NHS day care: availability and use of facilities, England - KH14; Non-Medical Staff Census-Wales; Pathology Laboratories - Cervical Cytology and Biopsies (KC61); Patient Care in the Community - District Nurses and other Nurses (KC55); Patient Care in the Community: CPNs and CMHNS (KC57); Patient Episode Database for Wales (PEDW); Patient Transport Services (KA34) - Wales; Prescriptions - Wales; Sexually Transmitted Diseases - Wales (KC60); Summary of Family Planning Services (KT31); National Assembly for Wales Core Indicators

Health Statistics Quarterly
Office for National Statistics

The quarterly publication covers health information. It is a sister publication to Population Trends. It contains commentary on the latest findings, topical articles on relevant subjects illustrated with colour charts and diagrams, regularly updated statistical tables and graphs, showing trends and the latest quarterly information: on deaths, childhood mortality, cancer survival, abortions, congenital anomalies, morbidity

etc. Coverage: England and Wales, and in many instances United Kingdom as a whole and constituent countries.

Delivery: Periodic Release
Frequency: Quarterly
Price: Annual 4 editions - £75.00 including postage Individual - £20.00
Annual subscription of £135.00 (including postage) for both Health Statistics Quarterly and Population Trends
ISSN: 1665-1645

Available from
TSO Publications Centre and Bookshops
Please see Annex B for full address details.

Sources from which data for this product are obtained
Cancer Registrations - England & Wales; Childhood and Infant Mortality - England and Wales; Congenital Anomalies - England and Wales; Registration of Births - England and Wales; Registration of Deaths - England and Wales; The ONS Longitudinal Study

---

Health Survey for England: The Health of Young People 1995-97
Department of Health

The Health Survey for England comprises a series of annual surveys, of which the 1997 survey is the seventh. Since 1994, the Health Survey for England has been carried out by the Joint Health Surveys Unit of Social and Community Planning Research (SCPR) and the Department of Epidemiology and Public Health at University College, London (UCL).

Since 1995 the surveys have included children aged 2-15 as well as adults. This report is concerned solely with the health and growth of children and young adults aged 2-24, and combines data from the 1995-1997 surveys. Key findings relating to all adults in the 1997 survey are summarised in a separate set of reference tables to be published early in 1999.

The Health Survey series was designed to achieve the following aims:

1. To provide annual data for nationally representative samples to monitor trends in the nation's health.
2. To estimate the proportion of people in England who have specified health conditions.
3. To estimate the prevalence of certain risk factors associated with these conditions.
4. To examine differences between subgroups of the population (including regional populations) in their likelihood of having specified conditions or risk factors.

5. To assess the frequency with which particular combinations of risk factors are found, and in which groups these combinations most commonly occur.
6. To monitor progress towards selected health targets.
7. (From 1995) to measure the height of children at different ages, replacing the National Study of Health and Growth.

Each survey in the series consists of core questions and measurements (for example, anthropometric and blood pressure measurements and analysis of blood and saliva samples), plus modules of questions on specific issues that change periodically. The surveys have involved nurse visits as well as interviews.

The 1997 Survey

In order to increase the number of children available for analysis in the 1997 survey, the design was modified from previous years. In part of the sample the procedure was the same as in the two preceding years: all adults in the selected households were surveyed, and up to two children were surveyed. In the other part of the sample, only children were surveyed, not adults (though a household questionnaire collected a certain amount of information about the household and its members).

'Core' topics, repeated every year for both adults and children, were blood pressure, anthropometry, cigarette smoking, alcohol consumption and self-assessed general health. Saliva samples were obtained from those aged 4-17. Blood samples were obtained from those aged 18-24.

For children, the special topics in 1997 were respiratory conditions (asthma and asthma-related symptoms), lung function, non-fatal accidents, physical exercise and eating habits. The Strengths and Difficulties Questionnaire was completed by parents, describing the behaviour of each surveyed child. A telephone follow-up survey examined children's use of sun protection and the prevalence of sunburn. It also examined parents' and childrens' attitudes toward sun protection.

For those aged 16-24, the special topics in 1997 were respiratory problems, lung function, physical activity and diet. The General Health Questionnaire (GHQ12) was administered to those aged 13 and over.

Frequency: Annual
Price: £70.00
ISBN: 0 11 322266 1

Available from
TSO Publications Centre and Bookshops
Please see Annex B for full address details.

Sources from which data for this product are obtained
Health Survey for England

Informal Carers: Results of An Independent Study Carried Out on Behalf of the Department of Health as Part of the 1995 General Household Survey.
Office for National Statistics

Information collected between April 1995 and March 1996. From a series of questions addressed to those caring for a sick, handicapped or elderly person.

Frequency: Every 5 years
Price: £15.00
ISBN: 0 11 621044 3

Available from
Dr Ann Bridgwood
Office for National Statistics
1 Drummond Gate
London SW1V 2QQ
Tel: 020 7533 5303;
Email: ann.bridgwood@ons.gov.uk

Key Health Statistics 1996 Fact Card
National Assembly for Wales

A small booklet bringing together key health statistics which have been published in more detail in Health Statistics Wales. It is published annually, and provides an easily portable form of reference. The booklet is bilingual and is 20 pages long. Data is presented in a series of tables. Information is provided on the following: Population and vital statistics; Lifestyle; Morbidity; Preventive medicine; Family Health Services; Waiting lists and waiting times; Hospital statistics; Abortions; Psychiatric hospitals statistics; Community health services; Patient transport services; Staffing; Finance; and Private health care.

Delivery: Periodic Release
Frequency: Annually

Available from
Graham Davies
National Assembly for Wales
Statistical Directorate
Crown Building
Cathays Park
Cardiff
Tel: 029 2082 5086; Fax: 029 2082 5350;
Email: graham.davies@wales.gsi.gov.uk

Key Indicators Graphical System
Department of Health

Comparative information for local authorities in England on provision of Social Services.

Contains indicators for: demographic and social profiles, budgets, expenditure, child protection, children looked after, daycare for children; residential day and domiciliary care for elderly people and adults with disabilities; unit cost and local authority staffing. Data for individual local authorities is available on the graphical package allowing the user to view the data and also produce comparative charts. Data is comparable at both local authority and England level.

Frequency: Bi-annually
Price: Full price £20.00

Available from
Jeff Palmer
Room 451C
Department of Health
Skipton House
80 London Road
London SE1 6LH
Tel: 020 7972 5602

Sources from which data for this product are obtained
Child Protection - England; Children and Young Persons Accommodated in Secure Units - England and Wales; Children Looked After - England; Children Subject to Supervision Orders - England; Children's Daycare Facilities - England; Children's Homes; Day and domiciliary personal social services for adults; Guardianship Under the Mental Health Act (1983) - England; Private Hospitals, Homes and Clinics; Register of the deaf and hard of hearing; Registered blind and partially sighted people; Registers of people with physical disabilities; Residential personal social services for adults

Scottish Health Statistics
Scottish Executive

Presents the latest available data and trend statistics on a comprehensive range of health topics to assist planning, policy, performance measurement and research. 40th volume published for 1998 covering health, morbidity, mortality, lifestyle and deprivation.

Delivery: Periodic Release
Frequency: Annually
Price: £25.00 outside NHS, free on website

Available from
Customer help desk
Information and Statistics Division, NHS in Scotland
Please see Annex B for full address details

Sources from which data for this product are obtained
Cancer registration and screening; Notification of an abortion; Population Estimates - Scotland; Record linkage - linked dataset; Sub-national Population Projections - Scotland; Hospital Activity Statistics - Scotland; Workforce; Complaints; Scottish Health Service Costs.

Scottish Key Indicators for Performance (SKIPPER)
Scottish Executive

To provide a comprehensive set of performance indicators for NHSiS. Modules include: cancer, complaints, contracting, cost of care. dental, diagnosis admission rates, fertility, inpatient/outpatient activity, mortality, operations, outcome measures, population, prescription prescribing, primary care provisions, promote / improve health, psychiatric admissions, waiting times.

Delivery: Periodic Release
Frequency: Quarterly

Available from
Customer help desk
Information and Statistics Division, NHS in Scotland
Please see Annex B for full address details

Sources from which data for this product are obtained
Cost book data system

Social Services Statistics for Wales
National Assembly for Wales

An annual publication covering social care services provided by local authorities in Wales. Trend tables for Wales are shown with details by local authority for the latest year. First edition 1999.

Delivery: Periodic Release
Frequency: Annually
Price: £10.00
ISBN: 0 7504 2342 0

Available from
Statistical Publications Unit
National Assembly for Wales
Please see Annex B for full address details

Sources from which data for this product are obtained
Local authority social services returns. Private and voluntary residential / nursing homes.

Use of OPCS Records for Medical Research
Office for National Statistics

Academic report for medical researchers on OPCS (now ONS) medical records. A review of the services provided by ONS to medical researchers wishing to use ONS records. Contains an extensive bibliography of published research work involving the use of ONS records.

Frequency: Ad hoc
Price: £6.25
ISBN: 0 904952 97 5, OPCS (Occasional Paper No 41)

Products

Available from
Beverley Botting
Office for National Statistics
1 Drummond Gate
London SW1V 2QQ
Tel: 020 7533 5195;
Email: bev.botting@ons.gov.uk

See also:
In the Government Statistics Chapter:
International Statistical Classification of
Diseases and Health Related Problems
(ICD-10)
Standard Occupational Classification (SOC)
Volume 1
Standard Occupational Classification (SOC)
Volume 2 (Second Edition)
Standard Occupational Classification (SOC)
Volume 3

4.25 Abortions

Abortion Statistics
Scottish Executive

To provide numbers and rates for age,
locality, parity, statutory ground's and
marital status.

Delivery: Periodic Release
Frequency: Annually
Price: Free

Available from
Customer help desk
Information and Statistics Division, NHS in
Scotland
Please see Annex B for full address details

**Sources from which data for this product are
obtained**
Abortion notifications

**Abortion Statistics Annual
Reference Volume**
Department of Health

Statistics on legal abortions in England and
Wales in the reference year. Contains
detailed statistics on legal abortions in
England and Wales, covering statutory
grounds, gestation weeks, age, parity,
methods of operation, complications, type
of premises, geographical distribution, and
medical conditions. Detailed analysis on
number of abortions by grounds, marital
status, previous live and still born children,
purchaser, gestation weeks, complications,
procedure, duration of stay, area of usual
residence and medical condition.

Delivery: News/Press Release
Frequency: Annually
Price: 1997 annual reference volume - £25.00
ISBN: 0 11 621093 1

Available from
TSO Publications Centre and Bookshops
Please see Annex B for full address details.

**Sources from which data for this product are
obtained**
Abortion Notification Forms (HSA4)

**Legal Abortions Quarterly
Monitor**
Office for National Statistics; sponsored by
Department of Health and National
Assembly for Wales

Provisional abortion statistics for England
and Wales by age and gestation weeks. Data
now published in 'Health Statistics
Quarterly', quarterly monitors discontinued
after 'June quarter 1998'.

Delivery: News/Press Release
Frequency: Quarterly
Price: £20.00

Available from
Nirupa Dattani
Office for National Statistics
1 Drummond Gate
London SW1V 2QQ
Tel: 020 7533 5205; Fax: 020 7533 5635;
Email: nirupa.dattani@ons.gov.uk

**Legal Abortions: Residents of
Regions and Health Authorities
(Report in 'Health Statistics
Quarterly' - Summer Edition)**
Office for National Statistics; sponsored by
Department of Health & National Assembly
for Wales

Number of legal abortions by region and
health authority of residence by age-group,
purchaser and gestation weeks.

Delivery: News/Press Release
Frequency: Annually
Price: £20.00

Available from
Nirupa Dattani
Office for National Statistics
1 Drummond Gate
London SW1V 2QQ
Tel: 020 7533 5205; Fax: 020 7533 5635;
Email: nirupa.dattani@ons.gov.uk

See also:
In this chapter:
Health and Personal Social Services
Statistics for England (4.24)
Health Statistics Quarterly (4.24)
Social Services Statistics for Wales (4.24)

In other chapters:
Birth Statistics - FM1 (See the Population,
Census, Migration and Vital Events chapter)
Conceptions in England and Wales (on Disk)
(See the Population, Census, Migration and
Vital Events chapter)

Population Trends (see the Population,
Census, Migration and Vital Events chapter)

4.26 Ambulance Service

Ambulance Services, England
Department of Health

This Statistical Bulletin summarises
information about the performance of
ambulance services provided by the NHS
in England and includes some information
about earlier years. Results are available for
Regional Office and NHS Trusts. The
bulletin contains key facts, analysis and
commentary, definitions, graphs and
statistical tables.

Delivery: Statistical bulletin - hardcopy and
internet
Frequency: Annually
Price: Free
ISBN: 1 84182 053 9

Available from
Lesz Lancucki
Department of Health
Please see Annex B for full address details

Internet: www.doh.gov.uk/public/amb9899.htm

**Sources from which data for this product are
obtained**
DH Returns KA34 & KA43 (New)

Patient Transport Statistics
Department of Health and Social Services -
Northern Ireland

Data on patient transport services for
Northern Ireland available on request from
an electronic spreadsheet system and from
a bulletin which ceased publication in 1995.
Contains the number and type of ambulance
journeys; activation/response times for
emergency journeys.

Delivery: Ad hoc release
Frequency: Ad hoc
Price: Free

Available from
Jenny Orr
Department of Health and Social Services -
Northern Ireland
Tel: 028 9052 2580

**Sources from which data for this product are
obtained**
Northern Ireland Ambulance Service

Patient Transport Statistics - Annual Statistical Brief to National Assembly for Wales and Ambulance Trust
National Assembly for Wales

Statistical brief produced annually. Summarises information over time about patient transport services provided by the NHS in 6 pages. Mainly contains charts but with a small amount of text. Summarises information about patient transport services provided by the NHS in Wales over time.

Frequency: Annually

Available from
Vivien Trew
National Assembly for Wales
Please see Annex B for full address details

Sources from which data for this product are obtained
Patient Transport Services (KA34) - Wales

Patient Transport Statistics - Quarterly Statistical Brief to National Assembly for Wales and Ambulance Trust
National Assembly for Wales

Statistical brief produced quarterly. Summarises information about patient transport services provided by the NHS in 2 pages. Mainly contains charts but with a small amount of text. Summarises information about patient transport services provided by the NHS in Wales. 2 pages. Mainly contains charts but with a small amount of text.

Frequency: Quarterly

Available from
Vivien Trew
National Assembly for Wales
Please see Annex B for full address details

Sources from which data for this product are obtained
Patient Transport Services (KA34) - Wales

See also:
In this chapter:
Health and Personal Social Services Statistics for England *(4.24)*

4.27 Attitudes to, and experience of, National Health Service (NHS)

All Change? The Health Education Monitoring Survey One Year On.
Office for National Statistics; sponsored by the Health Education Authority

Respondents from the 1996 Health Education Monitoring Survey were interviewed for a second time a year later to measure changes in their health-related knowledge, attitudes and behaviour.

Frequency: Ad Hoc
Price: £30.00
ISBN: 0 11-621065-6

Available from
Dr Ann Bridgwood
Office for National Statistics
1 Drummond Gate
London SW1V 2QQ
Tel: 020 7533 5303;
Email: ann.bridgwood@ons.gov.uk

NHS Complaints Bulletin
Scottish Executive

To provide public accountability on NHS complaints and comparability between Trusts / Boards.

Delivery: Periodic Release
Frequency: Quarterly

Available from
Customer help desk
Information and Statistics Division, NHS in Scotland
Please see Annex B for full address details

Sources from which data for this product are obtained
NHS in Scotland Complaints Return

Women's Experience of Maternity Care, a Survey Manual
Department of Health

Survey manual for maternity services. Describes how to carry out local surveys of the use of maternity services. The Manual, sponsored by the Department of Health and produced by the Social Survey Division of ONS, is designed primarily for use by district health authorities wishing to measure consumers' views of local services. Model questionnaires are provided. The document consists of 183 pages containing information on how to carry out local surveys of women's experience of maternity services.

Delivery: Ad Hoc/One-off Release
Frequency: One-off
Price: £10.50
ISBN: 0 11 691246 4 (series SS 1255)

Available from
TSO Publications Centre and Bookshops
Please see Annex B for full address details.

Sources from which data for this product are obtained
Abortion Notification Forms (HSA4)

See also:
In this chapter:
CRAG Clinical Outcome Indicators *(4.41)*

4.28 Childcare Services

Adoptions Applications in Scotland
Scottish Executive

Statistical Bulletin

Delivery: Periodic Release
Frequency: Occasional
Price: £2.00
ISBN: 0 7480 6487 7
ISSN: 0264 1178

Available from
Sheelagh Harrison
Scottish Executive
Please see Annex B for full address details

Sources from which data for this product are obtained
Statistics of Adoption Applications Survey (SWS FORM A2 & A3)

Child Protection Management Information
Scottish Executive

Statistical Bulletin

Delivery: Periodic Release
Frequency: Annually
Price: £2.00
ISBN: 0 7480 6111 5
ISSN: 0144 5081

Available from
Carol Calvert
Scottish Executive
James Craig Walk
Edinburgh
Tel: 0131 244 5366; Fax: 0131 244 5315;
Email: carol.calvert@scotland.gov.uk

Sources from which data for this product are obtained
Child Protection MIS Survey (SWS FORM CP1, CP2, CP3 & CP4)

Child Protection Register
National Assembly for Wales

An annual publication showing number of children on child protection registers maintained by local authorities in Wales.

Delivery: Periodic Release
Frequency: Annually
Price: Free

Available from
HSA2
Statistical Directorate
National Assembly for Wales
Cathays Park
Cardiff CF10 3NQ
Tel: 029 2082 5041

Sources from which data for this product are obtained
Local authority SSDA 908 returns

Children Accommodated in Secure Units
Department of Health

Statistical summary of the number of children and young persons accommodated in local authority secure units. Contains data on the numbers admitted and discharged in the reported year. Tables include information on age, sex, legal status of child, secure unit and local authority responsible for placing the child. Time series are presented. This publication is approximately 65 pages long. It contains detailed statistics of children and young people accommodated in secure units maintained by local authority Social Services Departments in England and Wales for the year ending 31 March.

Statistics are given on the number of children accommodated at 31 March, the length of their stay and the legal status. Details are also given of admissions and discharges, age on admission, sex, region of accommodation and responsibility, admissions by local authority responsible for children in secure units, number of places available and children accommodated. The publication provides details of the individual secure unit figures. The publication includes a brief summary of the statistics (with charts), an introduction, a commentary on the analysis of the statistics (including bar charts, pi charts and so on), explanatory notes to some of the terms and symbols used in the publication, a list of secure units, the statistical tables which detail the data collected and finally a copy of the return which is sent out to local authorities.

As from the year ending 31st March 1998, this publication has been discontinued. It is now presented as a bulletin on the Department of Health website www.doh.gov.uk/public

Delivery: Periodic Release

Frequency: Annually
Price: Free

Available from
Michael Cornish
Department of Health
Skipton House
80 London Road
London
Tel: 020 7972 5573; Fax: 020 7972 5662;
Email: mcornish@doh.gov.uk

Sources from which data for this product are obtained
Children and Young Persons Accommodated in Secure Units - England and Wales

Children Accommodated in Secure Units year ending 31 March 1998: England and Wales
Department of Health

This is a free statistical bulletin presenting statistics of children and young people accommodated in secure units maintained by local authority social services departments in England and Wales for the year ending 31 March 1998. This is the first year the data has been presented as a statistical bulletin and is 18 pages long. All other details remain the same. The bulletin is also available on the DH web site at: www.doh.uk/public/stats3.htm

Delivery: Periodic Release
Frequency: Annually
Price: Free

Available from
Michael Cornish
Department of Health
Skipton House
80 London Road
London
Tel: 020 7972 5573; Fax: 020 7972 5662;
Email: mcornish@doh.gov.uk

Sources from which data for this product are obtained
Supervision Orders year ending 31 March 1998, England

Children Act Advisory Committee Annual Report
Department of Health; sponsored by Lord Chancellor's Office

Data on judicial proceedings under the Children Act. Contains information on trends in proceedings under the Children Act, with analyses by location together with commentary and recommendations. The Children Act Advisory Committee, established during the passage of the Act to advise Ministers on the Act's operation, presented its first report to the Lord Chancellor on 17 November 1992. That report recorded the experience of the first

year's achievements and problem issues and pointed the way forward with regard to its own work for the following year. Subsequent reports have taken a similar line.

Delivery: Periodic Release
Frequency: Annually

Available from
Lord Chancellor's Office
Lord Chancellor's Department
Please see Annex B for full address details

Children and Young People on Child Protection Registers year ending 31 March 1998, England
Department of Health

This is a priced summary publication, costing £8.00, and it presents data on children and young people on local authority child protection registers for the year ending 31 March 1998, in England. There is also a disk, in Excel spreadsheet format which contains detailed local authority level data, available at £5.00. It is approximately 160 pages long. Extracts of this publication are available on the DH web site at: www.doh.gov.uk/public/stats3.htm

Delivery: Periodic Release
Frequency: Annually
Price: £8.00

Available from
Michael Cornish
Department of Health
Please see Annex B for full address details

Children and Young Persons on Child Protection Registers
Department of Health

Statistical report on the operation of child protection registers. Contains data on the children by age, legal status and the type of risk from which they need to be protected. It covers the number on the register for the reported year and on registrations and deregistrations during the preceding year. Time series are shown for years since 1988-89 and the outcome of child protection conferences are given. This publication is approximately 130 pages long. It contains statistics of children and young people on child protection registers in England for the year ending 31 March. The publication consists of a description of what a Child Protection Register is, a summary of the data and analysis, a commentary on the data collected which includes some charts and graphs, the data collected in the form of tables and a copy of the return that was sent to all local authorities.

Delivery: Periodic Release
Frequency: Annually
Price: £8.00 for paper publication. £5.00 on disc.
ISBN: 1 85839 967 X

Available from
Michael Cornish
Department of Health
Please see Annex B for full address details.

Sources from which data for this product are obtained
Child Protection - England

Children Looked After by Local Authorities
Department of Health

Statistical summary of all children who have been looked after by local authorities. Contains data, in the form of summary tables, on children looked after during the reported year and those starting and ceasing to be looked after during the preceding year by legal status, placement, reason for being looked after and the time spent in local authority care. Limited time series comparisons are available.

This publication is approximately 100 pages long. This publication contains statistics of children looked after by local authorities in England during the year ending 31 March. The figures are based on statistical returns for individual children submitted to the Department of Health by local authorities with social services responsibilities. The publication consists of a summary of the findings, an introduction, a commentary to the data (which includes some charts and graphs), some technical notes, the tables containing the data collected and a copy of the return sent to local authorities.

Delivery: Periodic Release
Frequency: Annually
Price: Free. From year ending 31 March 1998, cost will be £8.00.

Available from
Michael Cornish
Department of Health
Please see Annex B for full address details.

Sources from which data for this product are obtained
Children Looked After - England

Children Looked After in England: 1997/98
Department of Health

This bulletin contains aggregate figures for children looked after by local authorities, by age, sex, legal status, placement and duration. Detailed local authority level tables, along with the bulletin are available

on the internet at 'http://www.open.gov.uk/doh/public/cla9798.htm'. This publication will contain aggregate data and analysis on Children looked after for the year ending 31 March.

Delivery: Periodic Release
Frequency: Annually
Price: Free
ISBN: 1 85839 949 1

Available from
Michael Cornish
Department of Health
Please see Annex B for full address details.

Sources from which data for this product are obtained
Children Looked After - England

Children Under Supervision Orders (Up to 31 March 1998)
Department of Health

Contains detailed statistics on children placed under the supervision of local authorities in England. The data were compiled from the information collected on the Department of Health statistical return SSDA 906, submitted by local authorities. The publication contains statistics relating to numbers of children and young persons under criminal supervision, and children and young persons under supervision orders made under the Children Act 1989. This publication is approximately 90 pages long. It contains detailed statistics on children placed under the supervision of local authorities in England. The publication contains details on the legal background to supervision orders, a commentary (including some charts and graphs), the tables containing the data and a copy of the form sent to all local authorities.

For the year ending 31st March 1998, this publication has been discontinued. It is now presented as a bulletin and is available from the Department of Health website www.doh.gov.uk/public/

Delivery: Periodic Release
Frequency: Ceased after 1998 Bulletin
Price: Free

Available from
Michael Cornish
Department of Health
Please see Annex B for full address details.

Sources from which data for this product are obtained
Children Looked After (SWS FORM CH1) - Scotland; Children Subject to Supervision Orders - England; Residential Care Homes for Children (SWS FORM R1-C)

Children's Homes
Department of Health

This publication contains statistics on children's homes in England at 31 March. The figures are compiled from information on each home submitted either to the Statistics Division of the Department of Health (Branch SD3A) by local authorities on form CH1, or obtained from information provided directly to the Department by voluntary and assisted homes. The statistics cover type of homes, size of homes, age accommodated in the homes, age criteria for admission, facilities in the homes, analysis by local authority of the location of homes, and small unregistered homes used by local authorities. This publication is approximately 40 pages long. It contains statistics on children's homes in England at 31 March. The figures were compiled from information on each home submitted either to the Statistics Division of the Department of Health (Branch SD3A) by local authorities on form CH1 or obtained from information provided directly to the Department by voluntary and assisted homes.

The publication consists of a commentary (including some charts and graphs), notes, the tables containing the data collected, and a copy of the form sent to local authorities.

Delivery: Periodic Release
Frequency: Triennial
Price: Free

Available from
Michael Cornish
Department of Health
Please see Annex B for full address details.

Sources from which data for this product are obtained
Children's Homes

Key Indicators Expert System: Monitoring Services for Children
Department of Health

PC system holding data on each individual local authority. Contains reports on: staffing and resources; demographic indicators; child protection registers; children looked after; court-related activity; children accommodated voluntarily under Section 20 of the Children's Act 1989; and daycare services. The system will produce reports on any local authority Social Services Department.

The Key Indicators Expert System provides for each Local Authority in England: a statistical report covering social factors, resources and services, child protection activity, children looked after and court related work; provides comparisons for each local authority with its family of authorities and England as a whole; and provides commentary on strategic elements of performance in children's services that the statistical profile suggests may warrant further investigation and discussion by the local authority's policy makers, managers and practitioners.

The system provides reports on selected key indicators of children's services for each local authority with social services responsibilities in the year 31 March 19xx. Each report consists of a statistical profile, based on 90 indicators, and an expert commentary, based on comparisons of selected indicators, suggesting areas a local authority might wish to review in the light of its statistical profile. All statistics presented are for the social services authority as a whole. Local investigation of variations between areas within an authority may be prompted.

The variables examined in the statistical profile cover social factors, derived from census and vital statistics data, population characteristics and social need; financial information on budget, standard spending assessment and children's services expenditure; staffing levels; family support services provision (such as respite care and local authority provision and sponsorship of services for under-eights - e.g. day nursery, childminding and playgroups, out of school clubs and holiday schemes; nursery education); child protection register information (e.g. initial conferences; registration and deregistration); youth justice, looked after and supervised children (e.g. emergency interventions, court orders and use of secure accommodation).

For each indicator, the local authority's position is compared to its group (e.g. shire counties, metropolitan districts, or London boroughs) and to England as a whole. These comparisons are based on ranking the indicator. No intrinsic judgements are intended on whether high or low ranks reflect desirable practices or outcomes.

Price: Free

Available from
Michael Cornish
Department of Health
Please see Annex B for full address details

Sources from which data for this product are obtained
Child Protection - England; Children and Young Persons Accommodated in Secure Units - England and Wales; Children Looked After - England; Children Subject to Supervision Orders - England; Children's Daycare Facilities - England; Children's Homes

---

Supervision Orders year ending 31 March 1998, England
Department of Health

This is a free statistical bulletin presenting statistics for children and young persons subject to criminal supervision orders made under the Children and Young Persons Act (CYPA) 1969 in England, for the year ending 31 March 1998. This is the first year that the data has been presented as a statistical bulletin and is 14 pages long. All other details remain the same. This bulletin is also available on the DH web site at: www.doh.gov.uk/public/stats[3].htm

Delivery: Periodic Release
Frequency: Annually
Price: Free

Available from
Olu Sangowawa
Department of Health
Statistics Division
Skipton House
80 London Road
London SE1 6LH
Tel: 020 7972 5710

See also:
In this chapter:
Congenital Anomaly Statistics 1997 *(4.36)*
Health and Personal Social Services Statistics for England *(4.24)*
Key Indicators Graphical System *(4.24)*

In other chapters:
Young Carers and their Families (see the Population, Census, Migration and Vital Events chapter)

4.29 Community Health Services

Chiropody Services
Department of Health

Statistical report summarising data for the chiropody service in England. Contains data on the number of face-to-face contacts, first contacts and initial contacts. Results are available for Regional Office and NHS Trusts. The summary contains covering commentary, definitions and statistical tables.

Delivery: Statistics summary
Frequency: Annually
Price: Free

Available from
Lesz Lancucki
Department of Health
Please see Annex B for full address details

Sources from which data for this product are obtained
DH return KT23

Clinical Psychology Services
Department of Health

Statistical report summarising data for the Clinical Psychology Services in England. Contains data on the number of: face-to-face contacts, first contacts, initial contacts and initial contacts by source of referral. Results are available for Regional Offices and NHS Trusts. The summary contains covering commentary, definitions and statistical tables.

Delivery: Statistical summary - hardcopy
Frequency: Annually
Price: Free

Available from
Lesz Lancucki
Department of Health
Please see Annex B for full address details

Sources from which data for this product are obtained
DH return KT24

Community Health Services
Department of Health and Social Security - Northern Ireland

Community Health statistics for Northern Ireland available on request from a manual database. Contains data on activity in immunisation, child health surveillance, community nursing, cervical cytology, genito-urinary medicine, breast screening, community dental service, infectious disease notifications.

Price: Free

Available from
Fergal Bradley
Department of Health and Social Security - Northern Ireland
Castle Buildings
Stormont
Belfast
Northern Ireland
Tel: 028 9052 2661

Sources from which data for this product are obtained
Community Health Services - Northern Ireland

Community Learning Disability Nursing Activity
Department of Health

Statistical report summarising data for community learning disability nurses. Contains data on the numbers of: face-to-face contacts, first contacts per 10,000 population, initial contacts, initial contacts by referral source. Results are available for Regional Health Authority, Regional Office, NHS Trusts. The summary contains covering commentary, definitions and statistical tables.

Delivery: Statistical summary - hardcopy
Frequency: Annually
Price: Free

Available from
Lesz Lancucki
Department of Health
Please see Annex B for full address details

Sources from which data for this product are obtained
DH Return KC58

Community Maternity Services
Department of Health

Statistical report summarising data for community maternity services in England. Contains data on the number of ante-natal contacts and post-natal contacts with midwives and health visitors. Results are available for Regional Offices and NHS Trusts. The summary contains covering commentary, definitions and 5 statistical tables.

Delivery: Statistical summary - hardcopy
Frequency: Annually
Price: Free

Available from
Lesz Lancucki
Department of Health
Please see Annex B for full address details

Sources from which data for this product are obtained
DH return KC54

Community Psychiatric Nursing Activity
Department of Health

Statistical report summarising data for community psychiatric nursing. Contains data on the numbers of: face-to-face contacts, first contacts per 10,000 population, initial contacts, initial contacts by referral source. Results are available for Regional Offices and NHS Trust. The summary contains covering commentary, definitions and statistical tables.

Delivery: Statistical summary - hardcopy
Frequency: Annually
Price: Free

Available from
Lesz Lancucki
Department of Health
Please see Annex B for full address details

Sources from which data for this product are obtained
DH return KC57

Community Specialist Care Nursing Activity
Department of Health

Statistical report summarising data for Community Specialist Care Nursing Services. Contains data on the number of initial contacts by type of specialist nurse (e.g. MacMillan nurses). Results are available for Regional Offices and NHS Trusts. The summary contains covering commentary, definitions and 2 statistical tables.

Delivery: Statistical summary - hardcopy
Frequency: Annually
Price: Free

Available from
Lesz Lancucki
Department of Health
Please see Annex B for full address details

Sources from which data for this product are obtained
DH return KC59

District Nursing Activity
Department of Health

Statistical report summarising data for District Nursing in England. Contains data on the number of: face-to-face contacts, first contacts per 100 population, initial contacts and initial contacts by source of referral. Results are available for Regional Offices and NHS Trusts. The summary contains covering commentary, definitions and statistical tables.

Delivery: Statistical summary - hardcopy
Frequency: Annually
Price: Free

Available from
Lesz Lancucki
Department of Health
Please see Annex B for full address details

Sources from which data for this product are obtained
DH return KC56

Health Visitors: Professional Advice and Support Programmes (Health Visitors and Other Community Staff Groups - Excluding Maternity)
Department of Health

Statistical report summarising data for Professional Advice and Support Programmes in England. Contains data on the number of: face-to-face contacts, first contacts and contacts by health visitors and other professional excluding maternity groups. Results are available for Regional

Offices and NHS Trusts. The summary contains covering commentary, definitions and statistical tables.

Delivery: Statistical summary - hardcopy
Frequency: Annually
Price: Free

Available from
Lesz Lancucki
Department of Health
Please see Annex B for full address details

Sources from which data for this product are obtained
DH return KC55

Occupational Therapy Services
Department of Health

Statistical report summarising data for Occupational Therapy Services in England. Contains data on the number of: face-to-face contacts, first contacts, initial contacts and initial contacts by source of referral. Results are available by Regional Offices and NHS Trust. The summary contains covering commentary, definitions and statistical tables.

Delivery: Statistical summary - hardcopy
Frequency: Annually
Price: Free

Available from
Lesz Lancucki
Department of Health
Please see Annex B for full address details

Sources from which data for this product are obtained
DH return KT26

Paramedical Statistics
Department of Health and Social Services - Northern Ireland

Paramedical statistics for Northern Ireland available on request from an electronic spreadsheet system (manual system prior to 1993-4). Contains the type and number of contacts by paramedical staff. Regional Information Branch, Department of Health and Social Services, Northern Ireland.

Delivery: Ad hoc release
Frequency: Ad hoc
Price: Free

Available from
Jenny Orr
Department of Health and Social Services - Northern Ireland
Tel: 028 9052 2580

Sources from which data for this product are obtained
Paramedical Services - Northern Ireland

Physiotherapy Services
Department of Health

Statistical report summarising data for Physiotherapy Services in England. Contains data on the number of: initial contacts and initial contacts by source of referral. Results are available by Regional Offices and NHS Trust. The summary contains covering commentary, definitions and statistical tables.

Delivery: Statistical summary - hardcopy
Frequency: Annually
Price: Free

Available from
Lesz Lancucki
Department of Health
Please see Annex B for full address details

Sources from which data for this product are obtained
DH return KT27

Speech Therapy Services
Department of Health

Statistical report summarising data for Speech and Language Therapy in England. Contains data on the number of: face-to-face contacts, initial contacts and initial contacts by source of referral. Results are available by Regional Offices and NHS Trust.

The summary contains covering commentary, definitions and statistical tables.

Delivery: Statistical summary - hardcopy
Frequency: Annually
Price: Free

Available from
Lesz Lancucki
Department of Health
Please see Annex B for full address details

See also:
In this chapter:
Community Care Bulletin *(4.30)*
Community Care Bulletin 1995 *(4.30)*
Health and Personal Social Services Statistics (NI) *(4.24)*
Health and Personal Social Services Statistics for England *(4.24)*
Health in England 1996 *(4.24)*
Health Statistics Wales *(4.24)*
Informal Carers *(4.30)*
(The) Office of Population Censuses and Surveys Survey of Psychiatric Morbidity in Great Britain - Reports 1 to 8 *(4.43)*
Professions Allied to Medicine *(4.33)*
Scottish Health Statistics *(4.24)*

4.30 Community Social Services for Adults

Community Care Bulletin
Scottish Executive

Statistical Bulletin

Delivery: Periodic Release
Frequency: Annually
Price: £2.00
ISBN: 0 7480 7056 7
ISSN: 0144 5081

Available from
Angus MacDonald
Room 52
Scottish Executive
James Craig Walk
Edinburgh EH1 3BA
Tel: 0131 244 3551;
Email: Angus.MacDonald@scotland.gov.uk

Or

Ian Morris
Room 52
Scottish Executive
James Craig Walk
Edinburgh EH1 3BA
Tel 0131 244 3794;
Email: Ian.Morris@scotland.gov.uk

Sources from which data for this product are obtained
Day Services for Adults (SWS FORM D-1B); Financial Provision (SWS FORM F1); Home Care Statistical Return (SWS FORM H1); Lunch Clubs (SWS FORM D3); Material Provision (SWS FORM M1); Meals-on-Wheels (SWS FORM H2); Registered Establishments (SWS FORM RE1 (AH), (AD), (CH), (CD); Registration of Blind Persons and Partially Sighted Persons (SWS FORM SWB); Residential Establishment Census Return (SWS FORM R1); Supported Accommodation (SWS FORM SA-1)

Community Care Bulletin 1995
Scottish Executive

Available from
Andrew Harvey
Scottish Executive
James Craig Walk
Edinburgh
Tel: 0131 244 5431; Fax: 0131 244 5315;
Email: andrew.harvey@so008.scotoff.gov.uk

Community Services Statistics
Department of Health and Social Security - Northern Ireland

Personal social services activity in Northern Ireland available on request from an electronic database. Contains data on residential accommodation, children in care, child abuse, clients in contact with the Board, home help service, and meals-on-wheels service.

Delivery: Hardcopy publication
Frequency: Annual
Price: Free

Available from
Jenny Orr
Department of Health and Social Services - Northern Ireland
Tel: 028 9052 2580

Sources from which data for this product are obtained
Körner Aggregate Returns, Children Order Returns - Northern Ireland

Day and Domiciliary Personal Social Services for Adults, England
Department of Health

Statistical bulletin on services provided to adults at home, at luncheon clubs or day centres in England. Contains data on meals provided and purchased by local authorities, clients served, the number of contact hours of home help/care provided and daycare centres. Results are available for England and at local authority level. This publication holds detailed statistics for Meals services, Day Centre activity and also Home help/care services. The information in this publication is based on the Department of Health statistical returns HH1 (on home help and homes care), MS1 (on the meals service) and DC3 (day centres). These forms were introduced in 1992 in response to the need for information to monitor and evaluate the community care changes.

Delivery: Periodic Release
Frequency: Annually
Price: Free of charge
ISBN: 1 85839 867 3

Available from
David Treacy
Department of Health
Please see Annex B for full address details

Sources from which data for this product are obtained
Day and domiciliary personal social services for adults

Day and Domiciliary Personal Social Services for Adults, Detailed Statistics
Department of Health

Statistical feedback containing detailed statistics on services provided to adults at home, at luncheon clubs or day centres in England. Contains data on meals provided and purchased by local authorities, clients served, the number of contact hours of home help/care provided and daycare centres.

Results are available for England and at local authority level.

Delivery: Periodic Release
Frequency: Annually
Price: To be announced

Available from
David Treacy
Department of Health
Please see Annex B for full address details

Sources from which data for this product are obtained
Day and domiciliary personal social services for adults; Private Hospitals, Homes and Clinics; Register of the deaf and hard of hearing

Informal Carers
Department of Health

Results of an Independent Study carried out by ONS on behalf of the Department of Health as part of the 1995 General Household Survey.

Delivery: Periodic Release
Price: £15.00
ISBN: 11 621044 3

Available from
TSO Publications Centre and Bookshops
Please see Annex B for full address details.

Sources from which data for this product are obtained
1995 General Household Survey

Residential Personal Social Services for Adults, Detailed Statistics on Residential and Nursing Care Homes and Local Authority Supported Residents
Department of Health

This publication provides detailed statistical information on the adult residential and nursing care home and places funded by local authorities. It contains statistics on the total number of residential and nursing care homes, the number of places in these homes and the number of residents supported by local authorities. Data are as at 31 March and are based on returns submitted to the Department of Health by local authorities (in respect of residential care homes) and health authorities (nursing homes registered under Part 2 of the Registered Homes Act 1984).

This publication contains statistics on the total number of nursing care homes, the number of places in these homes and also the number of residents supported by local authorities. Data are for England as at 31 March and are based on returns submitted to the Department of Health by local

authorities (residential care homes) and health authorities (nursing homes registered under Part 2 of the Registered Homes Act 1984).

Delivery: Periodic Release
Frequency: Annually
Price: To be announced

Available from
Gerald Smith
Room 451C
Department of Health
Skipton House
80 London Road
London SE1 6LH
Tel: 020 7972 5585;
Email: GSmith@doh.gov.uk

Sources from which data for this product are obtained
Private Hospitals, Homes and Clinics; Register of the deaf and hard of hearing; Residential personal social services for adults

Residential Personal Social Services for Adults, England
Department of Health

This statistical bulletin provides brief statistical information on the adult residential and nursing care home and places funded by local authorities. It contains statistics on the total number of residential and nursing care homes, the number of places in these homes and the number of residents supported by local authorities. Data are as at 31 March and are based on returns submitted to the Department of Health by local authorities (in respect of residential care homes) and health authorities (nursing homes registered under Part 2 of the Registered Homes Act 1984). Statistics on residential and nursing care homes and on residential and nursing care placements funded by local authorities, England

Delivery: Periodic Release
Frequency: Annually
Price: Free of charge
ISBN: 185839 812 6

Available from
Tracie Kilbey
Department of Health
Skipton House
80 London Road
London
Tel: 020 7972 5582;
Email: tkilbey@doh.gov.uk

Sources from which data for this product are obtained
Residential personal social services for adults

See also:
In this chapter:
Health and Personal Social Services Statistics (NI) *(4.24)*
Health and Personal Social Services Statistics for England *(4.24)*
Key Indicators Graphical System *(4.24)*
Private Hospitals, Homes and Clinics Registered Under Section 23 of the Registered Homes Act 1984 *(4.46)*
Registered Blind and Partially Sighted People *(4.36)*
Social Services Statistics for Wales *(4.24)*
Vacancy Monitoring Report *(4.46)*

4.31 Cost of Healthcare and Social Services

Local Authority Social Work Expenditure
Scottish Executive

Statistical Bulletin

Delivery: Periodic Release
Frequency: Occasional
Price: £2.00
ISBN: 0 7480 0876 4
ISSN: 0144 5081

Available from
Angus MacDonald
Room 52
Scottish Executive
James Craig Walk
Edinburgh EH1 3BA
Tel: 0131 244 3551;
Email: Angus.MacDonald@scotland.gov.uk

Sources from which data for this product are obtained
Local Financial Returns - Scotland

Personal Social Services Current Expenditure in England: 1997-98 (Bulletin)
Department of the Environment, Transport and the Regions

Summary information for local authorities in England on expenditure for Personal Social Services. Sections of the data include: central strategic functions; provision for children and families; elderly people; people with physical disability and/or sensory impairment; people with learning disabilities; people with HIV and AIDS; alcohol or drugs misuse; people with mental health needs; social services management and support services.

Frequency: Annually
Price: Free
ISBN: 1 84182 031 8

Available from
David Ainsley
Room 452C
Department of Health
Skipton House
80 London Road
London SE1 6LH
Tel: 020 7972 5596

Sources from which data for this product are obtained
RO3

Scottish Health Service Cost Book
Scottish Executive

To provide cost information down to speciality and procedure level to Health Boards and Trusts so that they may assess the efficiency of delivery of services compared with their peers.

Delivery: Periodic Release
Frequency: Annually
Price: £50.00

Available from
Customer help desk
Information and Statistics Division, NHS in Scotland
Please see Annex B for full address details

Sources from which data for this product are obtained
Scottish financial returns

Scottish Health Service Cost Book Data Retrieval System
Scottish Executive

To provide a method of analysing costing information from health boards and Trusts and ready transfer to spreadsheets.

Delivery: Periodic Release
Frequency: Annually

Available from
Customer help desk
Information and Statistics Division, NHS in Scotland
Please see Annex B for full address details

Sources from which data for this product are obtained
Scottish financial returns

See also:
In this chapter:
Health and Personal Social Services Statistics for England *(4.24)*
Health Statistics Wales *(4.24)*
Scottish Key Indicators for Performance (SKIPPER) *(4.24)*

4.32 Daycare Facilities for Children

Children's Day Care Facilities (from 1st April 1997)
Department for Education and Employment

Statistical summary on day nurseries, playgroups, childminders, out-of-school clubs, holiday schemes and family centres. Contains data on the numbers of providers and, where appropriate, the places available for children aged under eight for each facility, with local authority provision separately identified. Time series are available, although before 1992 only provision for children under five was recorded. Prior to 1st April 1997 this publication was produced by the Department of Health. Queries relating to this period should be directed to the DoH. This publication is approximately 90 pages long. It contains statistics on day care facilities for children in England at 31 March, compiled from forms submitted by local authorities. The publication contains some background information, a commentary on the data (including some charts and graphs), the tables containing the data, and a copy of the return which was sent out to all local authorities.

Delivery: Periodic Release
Frequency: Annually
Price: Free

Available from
Stephen Cook
Department for Education and Employment
Mowden Hall
Darlington
Co. Durham
Tel: 01325 392765

Children's Day Care Facilities (Up to 31 March 1997)
Department of Health

Statistical summary on day nurseries, playgroups, childminders, out-of-school clubs, holiday schemes and family centres. Contains data on the numbers of providers and, where appropriate, the places available for children aged under eight for each facility, with local authority provision separately identified. Time series are available, although before 1992 only provision for children under five was recorded. As of 1st April 1997 this publication is now produced by the Department for Education and Employment. Queries relating to this period should be directed to the DfEE. It is approximately 90 pages long and contains statistics on day care facilities for children in England at 31 March, compiled from forms submitted by local

authorities to the Statistics Division of the Department of Health (Branch SD3A). It also contains some background information, a commentary on the data (including some charts and graphs), the tables containing the data, and a copy of the return which was sent out to all local authorities.

Delivery: Periodic Release
Frequency: Annually
Price: Free

Available from
Michael Cornish
Department of Health
Please see Annex B for full address details

Sources from which data for this product are obtained
Children's Daycare Facilities - England

Day care services for children: A survey carried out on behalf of the Department of Health in 1990
Department of Health

The Department of Health has lead responsibility within central Government for children's' welfare and development. This includes responsibility for policy on day care services for young children. Current policy is based on variety and parental choice. The Department's main role is to ensure appropriate mechanisms, using legislation as necessary, to regulate standards and issue general guidance. Day care services now have a higher profile than in earlier years, and frequently attract attention from the media.

There are few recent data available about the use of day care services. The last national survey of parents was carried out in 1974. The Department of Health therefore decided to commission OPCS to undertake a survey to find out what services parents used for their children. This information complements the statistical data collected by the Department of Health on day nurseries, playgroups and childminders, and by the Department for Education on the number of pupils in maintained and independent education.

Frequency: One-off
Price: £27.00
ISBN: 0-11-691576-5

Available from
TSO Publications Centre and Bookshops
Please see Annex B for full address details.

Services for Children
Scottish Executive

Statistical Bulletin

Delivery: Periodic Release
Frequency: Annually
Price: £2.00
ISBN: 0 7480 5695 5
ISSN: 0144 5081

Available from
Sheelagh Harrison
Scottish Executive
Please see Annex B for full address details

Sources from which data for this product are obtained
Facilities for the daycare and education of children and Support to the Families Survey (SWS FORM D1-C)

See also:
In this chapter:
Key Indicators Expert System: Monitoring Services for Children *(4.28)*
Key Indicators Graphical System *(4.24)*

Survey of Day Care / Education Provision for Children in Scotland
Scottish Executive

Statistical Bulletin

Delivery: Periodic Release
Frequency: Every 3 years
Price: £2.00
ISBN: 0 7480 5416 2
ISSN: 0144 5081

Available from
Sheelagh Harrison
Scottish Executive
Please see Annex B for full address details

4.33 Demand for, and Supply of, Healthcare staff

Professions Allied to Medicine
Office for National Statistics; sponsored by Department of Health

A follow-up survey from a sample of people identified on the 1991 Census as having qualifications that would enable them to become physiotherapists, remedial gymnasts, radiographers or chiropodists. The report presents data, among other things, on the background characteristics of respondents, details about their current job and if it was not in the public sector what would attract them to work within the public sector.

Delivery: Ad hoc/One-off Release
Price: £20.00
ISBN: 0 11 691684 2

Available from
TSO Publications Centre and Bookshops
Please see Annex B for full address details.

See also:
In this chapter:
Qualified Nurses, Midwifes and Health Visitors *(4.38)*

4.34 Dental Health

Adult Dental Health 1988: United Kingdom
Department of Health

The purpose of the Adult Dental Health Survey 1988 was to establish the state of dental health of adults in 1988 and to compare the results with similar studies carried out in the 1960s and 1970s. The study also enabled a comparison to be made of adult dental health in different parts of the United Kingdom. The report contains results on dental health from over 6,800 adults in the United Kingdom. Data are given on the condition of natural teeth, tooth loss, dentures, dental experiences, attitudes and knowledge, and dental care and dental hygiene. Some comparisons are made with surveys carried out in 1968 and 1978. Results of the corresponding 1998 survey are due to be published by the end of 1999.

Delivery: Periodic Release
Frequency: Decennial
Price: £52.00
ISBN: 0 11 691324 X (series SS 1260)

Available from
TSO Publications Centre and Bookshops
Please see Annex B for full address details.

Sources from which data for this product are obtained
Adult Dental Health 1988; Children's Dental Health in the United Kingdom 1993

Children's Dental Health in the United Kingdom 1993
Department of Health

The specific aims of the Child Dental Health Survey 1993 were to measure the changes, since the previous survey, in dental and oral health of children in the United Kingdom and in each of the four countries of the UK to provide baseline information on such topics as 'the erosion of dental enamel', and 'development defects of the enamel' and to estimate differences between the four countries. Contains results on children's dental health from over 17,000 children aged between five and fifteen in the United Kingdom. Data are given on the condition of primary and permanent teeth, tooth loss, dental treatment and care. Some comparisons

are made between the four UK countries and with the surveys carried out in 1973 and 1983.

Delivery: Periodic Release
Frequency: Decennial
Price: £12.95
ISBN: 0 11 691607 9 (series SS 1350)

Available from
TSO Publications Centre and Bookshops
Please see Annex B for full address details.

Sources from which data for this product are obtained
Adult Dental Health 1988; Children's Dental Health in the United Kingdom 1993; Children's Dental Health Survey - UK

Dental Crowns: Report of a follow up to the 1988 Adult Dental Health Survey
Department of Health

The Adult Dental Health Survey 1988 showed that adults were keeping their natural teeth much longer than had been the case 20 years earlier, and that almost a quarter of adults with natural teeth had at least one tooth that had been restored by the provision of a crown. The Department of Health took this opportunity and commissioned further research among adults in England who said that they had at some time in their lives had at least one tooth crowned.

Frequency: One-off
Price: £6.15
ISBN: 0 11 691594 3

Available from
TSO Publications Centre and Bookshops
Please see Annex B for full address details.

NHS Prescription Items Prescribed by Dentists - Annual Statistical Brief
National Assembly for Wales

Statistical brief produced annually. Summarises information on prescription items prescribed by dentists in Wales in 2 pages of charts and commentary. Summarises information about prescription items dispensed in Wales by dentists.

Frequency: Annually

Available from
Vivien Trew
National Assembly for Wales
Please see Annex B for full address details

Sources from which data for this product are obtained
Prescriptions - Wales

Scottish Dental Practice Board Annual Report
Information and Statistics Division, NHS in Scotland

To provide information on the general dental service activity, including registrations, treatments, fees and number of dentists.

Delivery: Periodic Release
Frequency: Annually

Available from
CST

Sources from which data for this product are obtained
Scottish Dental Payments System

See also:
In this chapter:
Health and Personal Social Services Statistics for England *(4.24)*
Health Statistics Wales *(4.24)*
National Diet and Nutrition Survey: children aged $1^1/_2$ to $4^1/_2$ years. Volume 2: Report of the dental survey *(4.35)*
National Diet and Nutrition Survey: people aged 65 years and over Volume 2: Report of the oral health survey *(4.35)*
Scottish Health Statistics *(4.24)*
Scottish Key Indicators for Performance (SKIPPER) *(4.24)*
Social Services Statistics for Wales *(4.24)*

4.35 Diet and Nutrition

Cooking: Attitudes and Behaviour
Office for National Statistics; sponsored by Dept. of Health

Results from questions asked on the Omnibus Survey carried out by the former OPCS on behalf of the Department of Health in March 1993. The report contains information on how often people prepare their meals and whether frequency of preparing meals is related to confidence in cooking, cooking knowledge, and attitudes towards cooking.

Frequency: Ad hoc,
Price: £5.45
ISBN: 0 11 691609 5 (Omnibus Survey Report 3)

Available from
TSO Publications Centre and Bookshops
Please see Annex B for full address details.

Sources from which data for this product are obtained
The ONS Omnibus Survey - GB

(The) Dietary and Nutritional Survey of British Adults
Department of Health and Ministry of Agriculture, Fisheries and Food (MAFF)

The overall aim of the survey was to provide detailed information on the current dietary behaviour and nutritional status of the adult population living in private households in Great Britain.

Frequency: Ad hoc
Price: £40.00
ISBN: 0-11-691300-2

Available from
TSO Publications Centre and Bookshops
Please see Annex B for full address details.

Food Safety in the Home - A Survey of Public Awareness
Department of Health

Results from questions asked on the Omnibus Survey carried out by the former OPCS on behalf of the Department of Health. In 1990, exploratory questions were included in the ONS Omnibus Survey. An amended set of questions was then repeated five times during the period from 1991 to 1994 (March and November 1991, October 1992, 1993 and 1994). This gave a sample of just over 10,000 respondents aged 16 and over. Additional questions were included in 1993 and 1994 surveys.

Contains information on the public awareness of contamination advice and dangers associated with specific foods.

Delivery: Ad hoc/One-off Release
Frequency: Ad hoc
Price: £10.95
ISBN: 0 11 691678 8

Available from
TSO Publications Centre and Bookshops
Please see Annex B for full address details.

Sources from which data for this product are obtained
The ONS Omnibus Survey - GB

Infant Feeding in 1995
Department of Health

Reports on the latest survey of infant feeding carried out by ONS on behalf of the four UK Health Departments. The report contains detailed information on infant feeding practices in England, Wales and Scotland, plus some key results for Northern Ireland. Changes in infant feeding practice since 1985 are examined.

Frequency: Periodic
Price: £29.95
ISBN: 0 11 620918-6 (series SS 1299)

Available from
TSO Publications Centre and Bookshops
Please see Annex B for full address details.

Sources from which data for this product are obtained
Infant Feeding - UK - 1995

Infant Feeding in Asian Families
Department of Health

This report presents the findings of a survey of Infant Feeding Practices in Asian families living in England. The survey was carried out by the Office for National Statistics (ONS) for the Department of Health in 1996. The Department of Health has commissioned national surveys of infant feeding practices every five years since 1975 but the samples have never included sufficient numbers to allow for separate analyses of any ethnic minority groups. This was a survey of babies born to mothers, who defined themselves as being of Bangladeshi, Indian or Pakistani origin, living in England. The survey also includes a sample of babies born to White mothers living in the same geographical areas as the Asian mothers. The White sample is not nationally representative of the White population.

Frequency: One-off
Price: £40.00
ISBN: 0 11 691693 1

Available from
TSO Publications Centre and Bookshops
Please see Annex B for full address details.

Sources from which data for this product are obtained

National Diet and Nutrition Survey: Children aged $1^1/_2$ to $4^1/_2$ years. Volume 1: report of the diet and nutrition survey
Department of Health and Ministry of Agriculture, Fisheries and Food (MAFF)

The survey is designed to meet the aims of the NDNS programme in providing detailed information on the current dietary behaviour and nutritional status of preschool children living in private households in Great Britain.

Frequency: Ad Hoc
Price: £42.00
ISBN: 0 11 691611 7

Available from
TSO Publications Centre and Bookshops
Please see Annex B for full address details.

National Diet and Nutrition Survey: Children aged 1 ½ to 4 ½ years. Volume 2: report of the dental survey
Department of Health

This dental survey is the first in many years to investigate the dental health of a nationally representative sample of British preschool children. It was carried out as the final component of the National Diet and Nutrition Survey (NDNS) of children aged 1 ½ to 4 ½ years.

Frequency: Ad Hoc
Price: £14.50
ISBN: 0 11 6916125

Available from
TSO Publications Centre and Bookshops
Please see Annex B for full address details.

National Diet and Nutrition Survey: people aged 65 years and over (Volume 1: Report of the diet and nutrition survey)
Ministry of Agriculture, Fisheries and Food and the Department of Health

The National Diet and Nutrition Survey for people aged 65 years and over is part of the wider National Diet and Nutrition Survey (NDNS) programme. The Ministry of Agriculture, Fisheries and Food and the Department of Health established the NDNS programme in 1992. The programme aims to provide a comprehensive cross-sectional picture of the dietary habits and nutritional status of the population of Great Britain. The programme will take eight to ten years to complete and is split into four separate surveys, each on a different age group, conducted at approximately two-yearly intervals.

The NDNS of people aged 65 and over was carried out by Social and Community Planning Research, and is based on a sample of approximately 1,300 people living in institutions in Great Britain.

Quantitative data are collected on food and nutrient intakes (using a weighed record wherever possible), anthropometric measurements, blood pressure, a range of blood and urine analyses, and socio-economic, demographic and lifestyle characteristics. A dental survey and a visual acuity test are also carried out on the sample. The Survey covers Great Britain and data are available for three aggregated standard regions for England, Scotland and Wales.

A pilot study was carried out between January and April 1994 on a smaller sample to test all components of the Survey.

Fieldwork for the main Survey, which began in October 1994, was spread over twelve months to allow for seasonality in eating behaviour. The results were published in two reports in 1998. It is planned to deposit the data in the Data Archive later in 1998.

Frequency: One-off
Price: £63.00
ISBN: 0 11 2430198

Available from
Steven Finch
National Centre for Social Research
35 Northampton Square
London
Tel: 020 7250 1866; Fax: 020 7250 1524;
Email: s.finch@natcen.ac.uk

National Diet and Nutrition Survey: people aged 65 years and over (Volume 2: Report on the oral health survey)
Department of Health

This report presents the findings of a survey of the oral health of 955 adults aged 65 years and over. 753 of whom were living in private households and 202 were living in long-stay accommodation. The survey was carried out over 12 months from January 1995.

Frequency: Ad Hoc
Price: £20.00
ISBN: 0 11 243027 9

Available from
TSO Publications Centre and Bookshops
Please see Annex B for full address details.

See also:
In this chapter:
(The) Health of Adult Britain 1841 - 1994, Decennial Supplement, Volumes 1 and 2 *(4.42)*
Health and Personal Social Services Statistics for England *(4.24)*

4.36 Disability

Chronically Sick and Disabled Persons Act 1970 England
National Health Service Executive Headquarters; sponsored by Department of Health

Booklet presenting data on the number of chronically sick and disabled patients aged under 65 who were admitted to or resident in accommodation normally used wholly or mainly for the care of elderly persons. Booklet presenting data on the number of chronically sick and disabled patients aged under 65 who were admitted to or resident in accommodation normally used wholly or mainly for the care of elderly persons.

Delivery: Periodic Release
Frequency: Annually
Price: Free

Available from
Ian Mills
National Health Service Executive Headquarters
Department of Health
Quarry House
Quarry Hill
Leeds
Tel: 0113 254 5522; Fax: 0113 254 6423;
Email: jclark@doh.gov.uk

Sources from which data for this product are obtained
Chronically Sick and Disabled Persons Act 1970 - Return under Section 17(2), England - SBH179

Congenital Anomaly Statistics 1995 and 1996
Office for National Statistics

Annual review of notifications of congenital anomalies received as part of the England and Wales National Congenital Anomaly System. Contains statistics of notifications of congenital anomalies for England and Wales in the reference year. Data are given for standard regions and regional and district health authorities.

Frequency: Annual
Price: £30.00
ISBN: 0 11 621029 X (series MB3 No 11)

Available from
TSO Publications Centre and Bookshops
Please see Annex B for full address details.

Congenital Anomaly Statistics 1997
Office for National Statistics

Annual review of notifications of congenital anomalies received as part of the England and Wales National Congenital Anomaly System. Contains statistics of notifications of congenital anomalies received as part of the ONS monitoring system for England and Wales in the reference year. Data are given for standard regions, government office regions and regional and district health authorities.

Frequency: Annually
Price: £25.00
ISSN: 011 621 1563 Series MB3 No 12

Available from
TSO Publications Centre and Bookshops
Please see Annex B for full address details.

Sources from which data for this product are obtained
Congenital Anomalies - England and Wales

(The) National Congenital Anomaly System - A Guide for Data Users and Suppliers
Office for National Statistics

Provides detailed guidance about the National Congenital Anomaly System for data suppliers and for data users, for example Public Health Departments and researchers. Contains information about how to notify congenital anomaly cases and how surveillance is carried out.

Frequency: Ad hoc
Price: Free
ISBN: 1 85774 308 3

Available from
Office for National Statistics
Room 2300D
Segensworth Road
Titchfield
Fareham
Hampshire PO15 5RR
Tel: 01328 813297

Sources from which data for this product are obtained
Congenital Anomalies - England and Wales

(The) OPCS Monitoring Scheme for Congenital Malformations
Office for National Statistics

A review by a working group of the Registrar General's Medical Advisory Committee on the objectives and workings of the national system of notifications of congenital malformations. The system as it operated in 1995 is explained in detail and recommendations are made for future improvements to the system.

Frequency: Ad hoc
Price: £6.00.
ISBN: 1 85774 195 1 (ONS Occasional Paper No 43)

Available from
Beverley Botting
Office for National Statistics
1 Drummond Gate
London SW1V 2QQ
Tel: 020 7533 5195;
Email: bev.botting@ons.gov.uk

Sources from which data for this product are obtained
Congenital Anomalies - England and Wales

PPRU Surveys of Disability Report 1: The Prevalence of Disability Among Adults in Northern Ireland
Department of Health and Social Security - Northern Ireland

Latest statistics on disability and related issues in Northern Ireland. Contains data on the estimated rate and prevalence of disability among adults in Northern Ireland, the severity of disability and the characteristics of disabled adults living in private households and communal establishments.

Price: £6.00

Available from
Fergal Bradley
Department of Health and Social Security - Northern Ireland
Castle Buildings
Stormont
Belfast
Northern Ireland
Tel: 028 9052 2661

Sources from which data for this product are obtained
Survey of Disability - Northern Ireland

PPRU Surveys of Disability Report 2: The Prevalence of Disability Among Children in Northern Ireland
Department of Health and Social Security - Northern Ireland

Latest statistics on disability and related issues in Northern Ireland. Contains data on the estimated rate and prevalence of disability among children in Northern Ireland, the severity of disability and the characteristics of disabled children living in private households and communal establishments.

Price: £6.00

Available from
Fergal Bradley
Department of Health and Social Security - Northern Ireland
Castle Buildings
Stormont
Belfast
Northern Ireland
Tel: 028 9052 2661

Sources from which data for this product are obtained
Survey of Disability - Northern Ireland

PPRU Surveys of Disability Report 3: Disability and Employment in Northern Ireland
Department of Health and Social Security - Northern Ireland

Latest statistics on disability and related issues in Northern Ireland. Contains data on the economic activity and employment experience of disabled adults living in private households in Northern Ireland. It also provides information on the effect of disability on those in paid work and those not in paid work, and the Disabled Persons Register.

Price: £6.00

Available from
Fergal Bradley
Department of Health and Social Security - Northern Ireland
Castle Buildings
Stormont
Belfast
Northern Ireland
Tel: 028 9052 2661

Sources from which data for this product are obtained
Survey of Disability - Northern Ireland

PPRU Surveys of Disability Report 4: Disabled Adults in Northern Ireland, Services and Transport
Department of Health and Social Security - Northern Ireland

Latest statistics on disability and related issues in Northern Ireland. Contains data on mobility and use of transport, contact with health and personal social services, use of disability equipment and adaptations, training and leisure activities and informal care and living arrangements.

Price: £6.00

Available from
Fergal Bradley
Department of Health and Social Security - Northern Ireland
Castle Buildings
Stormont
Belfast
Northern Ireland
Tel: 028 9052 2661

Sources from which data for this product are obtained
Survey of Disability - Northern Ireland

(The) Prevalence of Back Pain in Great Britain
Office for National Statistics; sponsored by Department of Health

This is the first report based on data collected as part of the OPCS Omnibus Survey. The questions were commissioned by Department of Health in spring 1993. The report covers the prevalence of lower back pain among adults during the previous twelve months giving results by age and sex, and by region.

Frequency: Ad hoc
Price: £6.15
ISBN: 0 11 691 574 9 (Omnibus Survey Report 1)

Available from
TSO Publications Centre and Bookshops
Please see Annex B for full address details.

Sources from which data for this product are obtained
The ONS Omnibus Survey - GB

Registered Blind and Partially Sighted People
Department of Health

Statistical summary on people registered as blind and partially sighted in England. Contains data by local authority on the numbers registered by selected age groups. Details of additional disabilities are also included. Latest available data relate to March 1994.

Delivery: Periodic Release
Frequency: Every three years
Price: Free of charge

Available from
David Treacy
Department of Health
Please see Annex B for full address details

Sources from which data for this product are obtained
Registers of people with physical disabilities

Register of the Deaf and Hard of Hearing
Department of Health

Statistics on people in England registered as deaf or hard of hearing with local authority Social Services Departments.

Delivery: Periodic Release
Frequency: Every three years
Price: Free of charge

Available from
David Treacy
Department of Health
Please see Annex B for full address details

Registers of People with Physical Disabilities
Department of Health

Delivery: Periodic Release
Frequency: Every three years
Price: Free of charge

Available from
David Treacy
Department of Health
Please see Annex B for full address details

Wheelchairs and Artificial Limbs, England
Department of Health

This book presents the number of wheelchairs, special seating and artificial limbs issued and attendances for assessment, fitting or maintenance of a new or existing artificial limb.

Delivery: Periodic Release
Frequency: Annually
Price: Free
ISBN: 1 85839 796 0

Available from
Ian Mills
Room 4N31
National Health Service Executive Headquarters
Department of Health
Quarry House
Quarry Hill
Leeds LS2 7UE
Tel: 0113 254 5522
Email: jclark@doh.gov.uk

Sources from which data for this product are obtained
Wheelchairs and artificial limbs, England - KO73

See also:
In this chapter:
Community Care Bulletin *(4.30)*
Health and Personal Social Services Statistics for England *(4.24)*

4.37 Drug abuse, Misuse of Alcohol, Smoking

Drinking: Adults' Behaviour and Knowledge in 1998
Department of Health

The report is based on answers to questions included on the ONS Omnibus Survey carried out throughout Great Britain in February, March and April 1998. 28 pages. Includes text, data, tables and charts on alcohol consumption, patterns of drinking, drinking related knowledge and behaviour (knowledge about: 'units' of drink; daily benchmarks; advice on drinking; changes to drinking behaviour).

Price: £8.00
ISBN: 1857743059

Available from
ONS Direct
Please see Annex B for full address details.

Sources from which data for this product are obtained
ONS Omnibus - GB

Drinking: Adults' Behaviour and Knowledge
Department of Health

Results from questions on various aspects of drinking, including behaviour and knowledge, from the Office for National Statistics (ONS) Omnibus surveys in February and March 1997. Relates to Great Britain. Sample size about 3,200. Occasional. 29 pages. Includes text, data, tables and charts on alcohol consumption, patterns of drinking, drinking-related knowledge and behaviour (knowledge about: "units" of drink; daily benchmarks; advice on drinking; changes to drinking behaviour).

Frequency: This is the first report on adult drinking for the DH based on ONS Omnibus Survey data.
Price: £10.95
ISBN: 0 11 620973 9

Available from
TSO Publications Centre and Bookshops
Please see Annex B for full address details.

Robin Boyce
Room 431B
Department of Health
Skipton House
80 London Road
London SE1 6LH
Tel: 020 7972 5553;
Email: rboyce@doh.gov.uk

Sources from which data for this product are obtained
The ONS Omnibus Survey - GB

Products

Drug Misuse Statistics in Scotland
Scottish Executive

To publish data from Scottish Drug Misuse Database and also to provide a source document which includes a summary of all routinely collected data on drug misuse.

Delivery: Periodic Release
Frequency: Annually

Available from
Customer help desk
Information and Statistics Division, NHS in Scotland
Please see Annex B for full address details

Sources from which data for this product are obtained
SMR 22/23

Smoking Among Secondary School Children in 1996: England
Office for National Statistics

A series of biennial surveys, begun in 1982, to estimate the prevalence of cigarette smoking among school children in Great Britain. The surveys are sponsored by the Department of Health, the Scottish Executive Department of Health, and in some years, the National Assembly for Wales. The report contains statistics and analysis on the prevalence of smoking among school children of secondary school age. Details are given of how children obtain their cigarettes, the influence of family and friends, exposure and attitudes to passive smoking and the effects of the health education message. Some comparisons are made with earlier surveys.

Frequency: Biennial
Price: £19.00
ISBN: 0 11 6209453 (England)

Available from
TSO Publications Centre and Bookshops
Please see Annex B for full address details.

Sources from which data for this product are obtained
Smoking Among Secondary School Children 1996 - GB

Smoking Among Secondary School Children in 1996: Scotland
Office for National Statistics

A series of biennial surveys, begun in 1982, to estimate the prevalence of cigarette smoking among school children in Great Britain. The surveys are sponsored by the Department of Health, the Scottish Executive

Department of Health, and in some years, the National Assembly for Wales. The report contains statistics and analysis on the prevalence of smoking among school children of secondary school age. Details are given of how children obtain their cigarettes, the influence of family and friends, exposure and attitudes to passive smoking and the effects of the health education message. Some comparisons are made with earlier surveys.

Frequency: Biennial
Price: £19.00
ISBN: 0 11 620950X (Scotland)

Available from
TSO Publications Centre and Bookshops
Please see Annex B for full address details.

Sources from which data for this product are obtained
Smoking Among Secondary School Children 1996 - GB

Smoking-Related Behaviour and Attitudes
Department of Health

Results from questions on smoking behaviour and attitudes to smoking, included in the Office for National Statistics (ONS) Omnibus surveys in November and December 1997. The report contains some comparisons with results from the ONS Omnibus surveys in November and December 1995 and 1996. Relates to Great Britain. Sample size about 3,700. Occasional. 49 pages. Includes text, data and tables on cigarette smoking prevalence and consumption, dependence, views about giving up smoking, advice from medical people, perceptions of relative risk, awareness of tobacco advertising, views on tobacco advertising, sponsorship of sporting and other events, views about taxation on cigarettes and passive smoking.

Some of the data in this product is disaggregated by gender.

Delivery: Other
Frequency: Ad hoc
Price: £8.00
ISBN: 0 185774 289 3

Available from
TSO Publications Centre and Bookshops
Please see Annex B for full address details.

Sources from which data for this product are obtained
The ONS Omnibus Survey - GB

Statistical Bulletin on Drug Misuse
Department of Health

Statistical bulletin on presenting problem drug misuse in England, that is, people presenting to services with problem drug misuse for the first time, or the first time for six months or more. Includes data by: age; gender; main and subsidiary drugs of misuse; injecting and sharing behaviour; region and Health Authority. Data are from the Department of Health Drug Misuse database, which in turn come from the Regional Drug Misuse Databases. Some data on Great Britain, Wales, and Scotland are included. Bulletin is bi-annual. About 70 pages of text, tables, charts and maps. Some of the data in this product is disaggregated by gender.

Delivery: Periodic Release
Frequency: Bi-annually
Price: Free
ISBN: 1 84182 0067

Available from
Bob Coull
Room 431B
Department of Health
Skipton House
80 London Road
London SE1 6LH
Tel: 020 7972 5550

Sources from which data for this product are obtained
Drug Misuse Database

Statistical Bulletin on Smoking
Department of Health

Statistical bulletin on smoking in England from 1976 to 1996. Contains data on trends in prevalence of smoking, consumption, behaviour and attitudes, economics and health. About 40 pages. Includes text, tables, and charts on: prevalence of adult cigarette smoking by age, gender; NHS Regional Office Area; prevalence of cigarette smoking among secondary school children; types of manufactured cigarettes smoked (in terms of tar yield); behaviour and attitudes, including views about giving up smoking, tobacco advertising & sponsorship, and passive smoking; smoking related deaths, smoking during pregnancy; economic indicators, including indices of relative cigarette prices, and consumer expenditure.

Some of the data in this product is disaggregated by gender.

Delivery: Ad hoc/One-off Release
Frequency: Ad Hoc
Price: Free
ISBN: 1 85839 914 9

Available from
Robin Boyce
Room 431B
Department of Health
Skipton House
80 London Road
London SE1 6LH
Tel: 020 7972 5553;
Email: rboyce@doh.gov.uk

Sources from which data for this product are obtained
Family Expenditure Survey - UK; General Household Survey - GB; Smoking and Misuse of Alcohol

---

Young Teenagers and Alcohol in 1996 Volumes 1 and 2
Office for National Statistics

These reports present the analysis of questions on drinking that were included in the 1996 survey of smoking among secondary school children in England and Scotland. Data biennially from 1988. Expanded in 1990 to provide estimates of consumption of different types of drink. In 1996 it was further expanded to also include more information about the circumstances in which 11-15 year olds drank, plus alcoholic lemonades and similar drinks. To be published biennially in future.

Frequency: Biennial, latest published reports are for 1996
Price: £19.00
ISBN: 011 620949 6 (England) 011 620 9445 (Scotland)

Available from
Eileen Goddard
Office for National Statistics
1 Drummond Gate
London SW1V 2QQ
Tel: 020 7533 5331

Sources from which data for this product are obtained
Smoking Among Secondary School Children 1996 - GB

See also:
In this chapter:
Health and Personal Social Services Statistics for England *(4.24)*
(The) Health of Adult Britain 1841 - 1994, Decennial Supplement, Volumes 1 and 2 *(4.42)*
Health Survey for England: The Health of Young People 1995-97 *(4.24)*

4.38 Employment and Staffing - Healthcare and Social Services

General Household Survey: Voluntary Work 1987
Home Office

Text and statistics from General Household Survey. Contains results from the 1987 General Household Survey showing participation in voluntary work, who volunteers, time spent and types of voluntary work undertaken. Some comparisons with a similar survey, carried out in 1981, are given.

Frequency: Ad hoc
Price: £4.85
ISBN: 0 11 691315 0 (series GHS No 17 Supplement A)

Available from
TSO Publications Centre and Bookshops
Please see Annex B for full address details.

Hospital, Public Health and Community Health Service Medical and Dental Staff in England
Department of Health

Statistical bulletin on medical and dental staff. Contains data for the period which was collected annually as at 30 September from hospitals and the Community Health Service. An annex contains notes to the tables and figures and explains comparability.

Delivery: Periodic Release
Frequency: Annually
Price: Unpriced
ISBN: 1 85839 763 4

Available from
John Bates
Department of Health
Quarry House
Quarry Hill
Leeds
Tel: 0113 25 45878

Sources from which data for this product are obtained
Medical and Dental Workforce Census

Personal Social Services Staff of Social Services Departments at 30 Sept (Bulletin)
Department of Health

Summary information for local authorities in England on staff of Social Services Departments. (Central / strategic / HQ staff; Area office / field work staff; Daycare staff; Residential care staff; Occupational therapists; and Other staff).

Frequency: Annually
Price: Free
ISBN: 1 84182 007 5

Available from
David Ainsley
Room 452C
Department of Health
Skipton House
80 London Road
London SE1 6LH
Tel: 020 7972 5596

Sources from which data for this product are obtained
SSDS 001

Qualified Nurses, Midwifes and Health Visitors
Department of Health

A follow-up survey from a sample of people identified on the 1991 Census as having nursing, midwifery or health visiting qualifications but no longer working in the field. The report presents data, among other things, on the background characteristics of out-of-service respondents, the reason why they no longer worked in these fields and measures that would attract them back into these professions.

Delivery: Ad hoc/One-off Release
Frequency: Ad hoc
Price: £11.30
ISBN: 011 691632 X

Available from
TSO Publications Centre and Bookshops
Please see Annex B for full address details.

Qualified Social Workers and Probation Officers
Department of Health, Scottish Executive and National Assembly for Wales

A follow up survey from a sample of people identified on the 1991 Census as having social work and probation qualifications. The report presents data among other things, on the characteristics and career history of those who work as social workers and probation officers and also information about those who at the time of the Census were not employed in these professions.

Delivery: Ad hoc/One-off Release
Price: £10.25
ISBN: 0 11 691649 4

Available from
TSO Publications Centre and Bookshops
Please see Annex B for full address details.

Quarterly Cost Analysis - Staff Employed in Northern Ireland Health and Personal Social Services
Department of Health and Social Security - Northern Ireland

Delivery: Hardcopy publication
Frequency: Quarterly

Available from
Caroline White
Annexe 2
Castle Buildings
Stormont
Belfast BT5 3UD
Tel: 028 9052 2509;
Email: caroline.white@dhssni.gov.uk

Sources from which data for this product are obtained
Personnel Information Management System (PIMS) - Northern Ireland

Report of the Review Body on Doctors' and Dentists' Remuneration
Office of Manpower Economics

Each report contains recommendations on pay and the results of surveys or relevant enquiries. Contains data on the numbers of doctors and dentists in the National Health Service by grade. Some reports also include the results of surveys of doctors' and dentists' hours of work, pension evaluations or other relevant enquiries. Detailed recommendations of the Review Body are also given, including the salary scales and fee scales.

Frequency: Annual
Price: £14.30 (1999)
ISBN: 0 10 142432 9 (1999)

Available from
TSO Publications Centre and Bookshops
Please see Annex B for full address details.

Sources from which data for this product are obtained
General Medical Practitioners Out-of-hours Work; Research into changes in GMPs work; Research Into Changes in Hospital Consultants Work; Research into the work and responsibilities of hospital consultants; Research into the work and responsibilities of consultants in public health medicine; Research into the workload and intensity of work of hospital consultants.

Review Body for Nursing Staff, Midwives, Health Visitors & Professions Allied to Medicine, Sixteenth Report on Nursing Staff, Midwives & Health Visitors
Office of Manpower Economics

Annual report to the Prime Minister, the Secretary of State for Health, the Secretary of State for Scotland, and the Secretary of State for Wales by the Review Body for Nursing Staff, Midwives, Health Visitors and Professions Allied to Medicine on Nursing Staff, Midwives and Health Visitors.

Frequency: Annually
Price: £12.15
ISBN: 0 10 142402 7

Available from
Leicha Rickards
Office of Manpower Economics
Please see Annex B for full address details

Review Body for Nursing Staff, Midwives, Health Visitors & Professions Allied to Medicine: Sixteenth Report on Professions Allied to Medicine
Office of Manpower Economics

Annual report to the Prime Minister, the Secretary of State for Health, the Secretary of State for Scotland, and the Secretary of State for Wales by the Review Body for Nursing Staff, Midwives, Health Visitors and Professions Allied to Medicine on Professions Allied to Medicine.

Frequency: Annually
Price: £11.20
ISBN: 0 10 142412 4

Available from
Leicha Rickards
Office of Manpower Economics
Please see Annex B for full address details

Staff of Scottish Social Work Departments
Scottish Executive

Statistical Bulletin

Delivery: Periodic Release
Frequency: Annually
Price: £2.00
ISBN: 0 7480 7390 6
ISSN: 0144 5081

Available from
Carol Calvert
Scottish Executive
James Craig Walk
Edinburgh
Tel: 0131 244 5366; Fax: 0131 244 5315;
Email: carol.calvert@scotland.gov.uk

Sources from which data for this product are obtained
Staffing of Social Work Departments (SWS FORM, SSR, SLA1, SLA2, SLA3 & OT1)

Staff of Scottish Social Work Departments 1993
Scottish Executive

Statistical bulletin of the Scottish Executive Home and Health Department. Contains data on staff numbers, training and turnover in Social Work Departments in Scotland.

Frequency: Annual
Price: £2.00
ISBN: 0 7480 1037 8
ISSN: 0144-5081

Available from
TSO Publications Centre and Bookshops
Please see Annex B for full address details.

Sources from which data for this product are obtained

Statistical Bulletin NHS Hospital and Community Health Services Non-Medical Staff in England: 1987-1997
Department of Health

Statistical bulletin relating to non-medical staff employed within the hospital and community health services (HCHS) of the NHS in England. The data was collected through the non-medical workforce census conducted by the Department of Health.

Delivery: Periodic Release
Frequency: Annually
Price: free
ISBN: 1 85839 869 X

Available from
Richard Reed
Department of Health
Quarry House
Quarry Hill
Leeds
Tel: 0113 2545 891; Fax: 0113 2545 924

Workforce and Earnings Benchmarking System (WEBS)
Scottish Executive

Allows users to produce quick and easy comparative statistics, for example skill mix profiles of selected trusts.

Delivery: Periodic Release
Frequency: Bi-annually

Available from
Customer help desk
Information and Statistics Division, NHS in Scotland
Please see Annex B for full address details

Sources from which data for this product are obtained
NAMS; Scottish Payroll System

See also:
In this chapter:
Health and Personal Social Services Statistics for England *(4.24)*
Health Statistics Wales *(4.24)*
Key Indicators Graphical System *(4.24)*
Social Services Statistics for Wales *(4.24)*
Statistics for General Medical Practitioners in England *(4.40)*

4.39 Family Planning

Contraception and Sexual Health, 1997
Department of Health

This report presents the results of a survey on contraception and sexual health that were included on the ONS Omnibus Survey for six months between April 1997 and February 1998. The survey was carried out on behalf of the Department of Health and formed a part of the Office for National Statistics Omnibus Survey, a multi-purpose survey based on a representative sample of adults in Great Britain.

Questions on contraceptive use and sexual health were asked only of women aged under 50 and men aged under 70, so the results in this report are based on 7,560 adults who met this age criterion.

Frequency: One-off
Price: £10.00
ISBN: 1857743121

Available from
TSO Publications Centre and Bookshops
Please see Annex B for full address details.

Sources from which data for this product are obtained
ONS Omnibus Survey - GB

Family Planning Service in Wales - Annual Statistical Brief
National Assembly for Wales

Statistical brief produced annually. Summarises information over time about family planning services provided by clinics and GPs in Wales in 4 pages. Contains charts and text.

Frequency: Annually

Available from
Vivien Trew
National Assembly for Wales
Please see Annex B for full address details

Sources from which data for this product are obtained
Summary of Family Planning Services (KT31)

NHS Contraceptive Services, England
Department of Health

The Statistical Bulletin summarises information about contraceptive services provided by the NHS. It includes data for the Family Planning Clinic Services in England. The bulletin contains data on the number of first contacts with women by age and primary method of birth control, number of first contacts with men and the number of total contacts, first contacts and domiciliary visits. Results are available for Regional Offices and NHS Trust. The bulletin contains covering commentary, definitions, graphs and 12 statistical tables.

Delivery: Statistical bulletin, hardcopy and internet
Frequency: Annually
Price: Free
ISBN: 1 84182 0024

Available from
Lesz Lancucki
Department of Health
Please see Annex B for full address details

Internet: www.doh.gov.uk/public/contra98.htm

Sources from which data for this product are obtained
DH return KT31: Family Planning Services Prescription Analysis; General Household Survey and Omnibus Survey - ONS

See also:
In this chapter:
Health and Personal Social Services Statistics for England *(4.24)*
Health Statistics Wales *(4.24)*
Social Services Statistics for Wales *(4.24)*

4.40 General Medical Practitioners (GPs)

General Practice Research Database (Authorised Users Only)
Department of Health (Medicines Control Agency)

Data are stored in four main sections which are linked together to form the patient's

record. The Patient registration record contains demographic and registration information. The Medical record contains all morbidity / medical events and outcomes, which are recorded using medical code dictionaries (either OXMIS or READ). This also includes referrals by speciality and type of referral. The Therapy record contains all prescribing information (except private prescriptions and Controlled Drugs, but a copy of the latter is recorded on the computer record). Entry of therapy is standardised by the use of the VAMP drug dictionary, mapped to multilex drug codes. Parameters recorded: name, form, strength, dose, PPA (Prescriptions Pricing Authority) code, BNF (British National Formulary) code and size and numbers of packs dispensed. The Prevention record contains information about preventive care, e.g. blood pressure reading, screening, results, weight, height, smoking habit, and other test results. The technical architecture of the database is being redeveloped.

Availability of the data for research is strictly controlled. MCA is bound by an agreement with the donors of the database that the data shall be used only for medical and health research purposes on a non-profit making basis. Users of the data will also have to sign an undertaking agreeing to the conditions for safeguarding confidentiality. Further details about access to the data can be obtained from the address below.

Some of the data in this product is disaggregated by gender.

Frequency: Quarterly to licensees, on request to others
Price: On request: estimates of costs of providing data for research and other purposes will reflect the costs incurred in maintaining and running the database and providing a customer service. MCA is not permitted to make a profit from generating the database but is required to cover the costs of operating the database and service provision.

Available from
General Practice Research Database
Medicines Control Agency
1 Nine Elms Lane
Vauxhall
London SW8 5NQ
Tel: 020 7273 0698;
Email gprd@mca.gov.uk

Sources from which data for this product are obtained
General Practice Research Database - UK

Products

GP Statistics (GP and Practice Profile Statistics)
Scottish Executive

To support manpower planning exercise.

Delivery: Periodic Release
Frequency: Annually

Available from
Customer help desk
Information and Statistics Division, NHS in Scotland
Please see Annex B for full address details

Sources from which data for this product are obtained
GP Database

Key Health Statistics from General Practice 1996 (Series MB6 No. 1)
Office for National Statistics

Key Health Statistics from General Practice 1996 is the second in an annual series of reports using data from the General Practice Research Database (GPRD). It contains analyses derived from anonymised, general practitioner medical records from 288 general practices and over 2 million patients in England and Wales. The analyses presented cover three main areas: prevalence of disease, prescribing of drugs and GP outpatient referrals.

Delivery: Periodic Release
Frequency: Annually
Price: £30.00
ISBN: 1 85774 273 7

Available from
ONS Direct
Please see Annex B for full address details.

Sources from which data for this product are obtained
General Practice Research Database - UK

Key Health Statistics from General Practice, (Studies on Medical and Population Subjects No. 60)
Office for National Statistics

First of a planned series of morbidity reports using data from General Practice. The data in this volume are for 1994, and are contributed by over 400 General Practices in England and Wales which cover 2.9 million patients registered at the end of 1994 - nearly 6 per cent of the population. The data cover England and Wales and, in order that the data can be used for comparisons between geographical areas in England, the data for England are also presented using RHA boundaries as defined on 1 April 1993.

Data are presented in three main areas: prevalence of disease; prescribing of drugs; and GP out-patient referrals to secondary care. Prevalence rates cover most of the key Health of the Nation areas. For most diseases presented these rates relate to patients who are currently, or have recently been treated with medication. Prescription rates of selected types of drugs are by BNF (British National Formulary) chapter and for selected sub-sections of those chapters. Four clinical areas have been selected for more detailed examination of prescribing. Selection is on the basis of the interest expressed in these areas in the medical literature. Referral rates of patients to out-patient departments are presented for major specialities, and for referral rates of selected patient groups to major specialities. These data represent the demand for hospital care generated by GPs on behalf of their patients.

Some of the data in this product is disaggregated by gender.

Frequency: Periodic
Price: £25.00
ISBN: 0-11-691686-9

Available from
ONS Direct or TSO Publications Centre and Bookshops
Please see Annex B for full addresses and contact details.

Sources from which data for this product are obtained
General Practice Research Database - UK

Prescription Cost Analysis
Department of Health

The Prescription Cost Analysis publication is issued annually and provides details of the number of items and the net ingredient cost of all prescriptions dispensed in the community in England. The majority are written by General Medical Practitioners but it also includes prescriptions written by dentists, nurses and hospital doctors, and dispensed in the community. The publication also includes prescriptions written in Wales, Scotland, Northern Ireland and the Isle of Man, but dispensed in England. The prescription items dispensed are listed alphabetically within chemical entity by British National Formulary therapeutic class. Interest in the publication will largely be confined to those requiring data at a very detailed level. The publication has just under 500 pages.

Delivery: Periodic Release
Frequency: Annually
Price: Single copy: £12.00
ISSN: 184 182 0458

Available from
Ann Custance
Room 484D
Department of Health
Skipton House
80 London Road
London SE1 6LH
Tel: 020 7972 5513; Email: acustanc@doh.gov.uk

Sources from which data for this product are obtained
Prescription Cost Analysis System

Statistics for General Medical Practitioners in England
Department of Health

Statistical Bulletin on General Medical Practitioners. Contains data highlighting trends established and show comparisons between fundholding and non-fundholding GPs and also companions between Personal Medical Services (PMS) and general medical services (GMS) doctors. Nineteen pages of text and tables showing Statistics for General Medical Practitioners in England. Latest available data 1988-1998.

Delivery: Periodic Release
Frequency: Annually
Price: free
ISBN: 184182 033 4

Available from
Dr Andy Sutherland
Department of Health
Quarry House
Quarry Hill
Leeds
Tel: 0113 25 45905;
Email: asutherl@doh.gov.uk

Statistics of Prescriptions Dispensed in the Community, England
Department of Health

The statistical bulletin on prescriptions dispensed in the community in England contains data on the trends in numbers and costs of prescriptions over an eleven year period, including analyses by therapeutic group, category of exemption (e.g. children and young people, elderly people) and generic prescribing. The bulletin presents an overview of the total number and cost of prescriptions dispensed in an 11 year period, e.g. 1988 to 1998, in the form of charts, diagrams, and reference tables with commentary. The bulletin has about 35 pages.

Delivery: Periodic Release
Frequency: Annually
Price: Free of charge
ISBN: 1 84182 057 1

Available from
Ann Custance
Department of Health
Skipton House
80 London Road
London
Tel: 020 7551 3; Fax: 020 7972 5661;
Email: acustanc@doh.gov.uk

Sources from which data for this product are obtained
Prescription Cost Analysis System

Statistics of Prescriptions Dispensed in Wales - Annual Report
National Assembly for Wales

Statistical report produced annually. Summarises information on prescription items dispensed in Wales in the most recent year and over time in around 20 pages of charts and commentary. Summarises information about prescription items dispensed in Wales in the most recent year and over time.

Frequency: Annually

Available from
Vivien Trew
National Assembly for Wales
Please see Annex B for full address details

Sources from which data for this product are obtained
Prescriptions - Wales

Statistics of Prescriptions Dispensed in Wales - Annual Statistical Brief
National Assembly for Wales

Statistical brief produced annually. Summarises key information on prescription items dispensed in Wales in the most recent year and over time in 4 pages of charts and commentary. Summarises information about prescription items dispensed in Wales in the most recent year and over time.

Frequency: Annually

Available from
Vivien Trew
National Assembly for Wales
Please see Annex B for full address details

Sources from which data for this product are obtained
Prescriptions - Wales

See also:
In this chapter:
Health and Personal Social Services Statistics for England *(4.24)*
Hospital Waiting List Statistics: England

(Resident Based) *(4.41)*
Residual Medicines *(4.45)*
Scottish Health Statistics *(4.24)*
Scottish Key Indicators for Performance (SKIPPER) *(4.24)*
Waiting Times for First Outpatient Appointments in England *(4.41)*
Waiting Times for First Outpatient Appointments in England: Detailed Statistics *(4.41)*
Workforce and Earnings Benchmarking System (WEBS) *(4.38)*

4.41 Hospital Services (other than for the mentally disordered)

Accident & Emergency: Various Bulletins and Health Briefings
Scottish Executive

Information on waiting times experienced by patients attending A&E departments.

Delivery: Periodic Release
Frequency: Bi-annually

Available from
Customer help desk
Information and Statistics Division, NHS in Scotland
Please see Annex B for full address details

Sources from which data for this product are obtained
Accident & emergency waiting times survey

Bed Availability and Occupancy, England
National Health Service Executive Headquarters; sponsored by Department of Health

This publication is sourced from the KH03 Körner return, "Bed availability and occupancy". The book gives the average daily number of available beds and average daily number of occupied beds by ward type for England, each regional office area and each NHS Hospital Trust in England. A time series is given, by hospital sector, for the average number of available beds in each Trust and aggregated to regional office area and England. Other information is also given covering: residential care beds, beds in wards open during the day only, neonatal intensive care cots, paediatric intensive care beds, and supporting facilities within the Trust.

Delivery: Periodic Release
Frequency: Annually
Price: The cost of the 1996/97 document is £6.00
ISBN: 1 85839 791 X

Available from
Ian Mills
National Health Service Executive Headquarters
Department of Health
Quarry House
Quarry Hill
Leeds
Tel: 0113 254 5522; Fax: 0113 254 6423;
Email: jclark@doh.gov.uk

Sources from which data for this product are obtained
Bed availability and occupancy, England - KH03

CRAG Clinical Outcome Indicators
Scottish Executive

The linked datasets of hospital and death records held at ISD make it possible to trace outcomes after specified episodes of care.

Frequency: Bi-annually

Available from
Customer help desk
Information and Statistics Division, NHS in Scotland
Please see Annex B for full address details

Sources from which data for this product are obtained
Scottish Record linkage - linked dataset

Elective Admissions and Patients Waiting: England
Department of Health

A bulletin containing data and analysis for the hospital waiting list with time series. Data relates to provider figures, that is for patients waiting for admission to NHS hospitals in England.

Analysis is done on national and regional bases, as well as at speciality level. The bulletin was quarterly prior to March 1997 then annual. Two pages of text summarising main points regarding waiting lists, followed by tables of data and then graphs. This publication has now been discontinued. The last bulletin produced was for 31 March 1998.

Delivery: Periodic Release
Frequency: Annually
Price: Free
ISBN: Different for each issue

Available from
Data Management Team
FPA-PA (WT)
NHS Executive
Room 4N34A
Quarry House
Quarry Hill
Leeds LS2 7UE
Tel: 0113 254 5555.

Hospital Activity: Vols. 1 & 2

A report providing aggregate data on bed utilisation and patient throughput at NHS hospital, clinics and units in Wales. Volume 1 contains data on inpatients and day-cases, Volume 2 on outpatients

Available from
Vivien Trew
National Assembly for Wales
Please see Annex B for full address details

Sources from which data for this product are obtained
Hospital Bed Use - Wales

Hospital Episode Statistics CD-ROM
Department of Health

The CD-ROM contains statistical information including length of stay, waiting times and number of episodes occurring for ranges of diagnoses and operating procedures. Information is presented at the national, regional and Health Authority levels of aggregation. The CD-ROM mainly consists of a large number of tables.

Delivery: Periodic Release
Frequency: Annually
Price: CD-ROM: NHS - Free
Academic Institutions and Charities - £100.00 + VAT. Commercial companies - £500.00 + VAT
Above prices refer to financial year 1994-95. Prices may differ for financial year 1995-96.

Available from
Wincen Lowe
Room 430B
Department of Health
Skipton House
80 London Road
London SE1 6LH
Tel: 020 7972 5534

Hospital Episode Statistics Vol 1: Finished Consultant Episodes by Diagnosis and Operative Procedure, Injury, Poisoning by External Causes - England
Department of Health

This is the first of three volumes containing summary tables of Hospital Episode Statistics (HES) data for 1994-95. The tables relate to finished consultant in-patient episodes (Ordinary admissions and day cases) in NHS hospitals in England during 1994-95 and unfinished episodes at 31 March 1995. HES does not include any information on outpatient attendances. This volume contains analyses of finished consultant episodes by diagnosis and by operative procedure. Volume 1 is 306 pages long and mainly consists of tables.

Delivery: Periodic Release
Frequency: Annually
Price: Volume I: £25.00
ISBN: 1 85839 624 7

Available from
Linda Shurlock
Department of Health
Skipton House
80 London Road
London
Tel: 020 7972 5567; Fax: 020 7972 5662

Sources from which data for this product are obtained
Hospital Episode Statistics

Hospital Episode Statistics Vol 2: Finished Consultant Episodes: Administrative Tables - England
Department of Health

This is the second of three volumes containing summary tables of Hospital Episode Statistics (HES) data for 1994-95. The tables relate to finished consultant inpatient episodes (Ordinary admissions and day cases) in NHS hospitals in England during 1994-95 and unfinished episodes at 31 March 1995. HES does not include any information on outpatient attendance's. This volume contains information on finished (and in one case, unfinished) consultant episodes analysed by speciality. The tables on waiting times previously included in Volume 2 are now in Volume 3. Volume 2 is 125 pages long and mainly consists of tables.

Delivery: Periodic Release
Frequency: Annually
Price: Volume 2: £25.00
ISBN: 1 85839 627 1

Available from
Linda Shurlock
Department of Health
Skipton House
80 London Road
London
Tel: 020 7972 5567; Fax: 020 7972 5662

Hospital Episode Statistics Vol 3: Finished Consultant Episodes: Waiting Time - England
Department of Health

This is the third of three volumes containing summary tables of Hospital Episode Statistics (HES) data for 1994-95. This volume covers admissions during the year 1994-95 of waiting list and booked cases. Volume 3 is 332 pages long and mainly consists of tables.

Delivery: Periodic Release
Frequency: Annually
Price: Volume 3: £20.00
ISBN: 1 85839 628 X
ISSN:

Available from
Linda Shurlock
Department of Health
Skipton House
80 London Road
London
Tel: 020 7972 5567; Fax: 020 7972 5662

Hospital Inpatients System (HIS)
Department of Health and Social Services - Northern Ireland

Hospital inpatient activity for Northern Ireland available on request from an electronic database. Contains data such as age, sex, religion, length of stay, diagnosis, hospital, and postcode.

Delivery: Ad hoc release
Price: Free

Available from
Pauline Sheals
Department of Health and Social Services - Northern Ireland
Tel: 028 9052 2925

Sources from which data for this product are obtained
Hospital Inpatients System - Northern Ireland

Hospital Inpatients System (HIS) Standard Analyses
Department of Health and Social Services - Northern Ireland

Tabulated data containing hospital inpatient activity in Northern Ireland available on request. Contains data such as age, sex, religion, length of stay, diagnosis, hospital, and postcode. Hardcopy tables and disks (Lotus Spreadsheets) available

Frequency: Annual
Price: Free

Available from
Pauline Sheals
Department of Health and Social Services - Northern Ireland
Tel: 028 9052 2925

Sources from which data for this product are obtained
Hospital Inpatients System - Northern Ireland

Hospital Statistics
Department of Health and Social Services - Northern Ireland

Tabulated data on hospital inpatients/ outpatients in Northern Ireland. Contains activity details of inpatients and outpatients treated within individual specialties. Data includes available and occupied beds, discharges and deaths, length of stay, numbers of outpatient clinics held, types of referral, etc.

Delivery: Hardcopy publication
Frequency: Annual
Price: Free

Available from
Jim McColgan
Department of Health and Social Services - Northern Ireland
Tel: 028 9052 2566

Sources from which data for this product are obtained
Körner Aggregate Hospital Returns - Northern Ireland

Hospital Waiting List Statistics: England
Department of Health

Detailed information on the number of patients waiting to be admitted to NHS Trusts in England and time waited. Contains data on patients waiting by time waited, type of admission (day case or ordinary) for main contract specialties, and by provider. England table, followed by regional and individual Trust tables.

Delivery: Periodic Release
Frequency: Quarterly
Price: NHS - Free, Others - £10.00
ISBN: Different for each issue

Available from
NHS - NHS Response Line 0541 555455
Others - PO Box 777, London SE1 6XH
(Fax 01623 724524)

Sources from which data for this product are obtained
Inpatient Waiting List Collection by NHS Executive

Hospital Waiting List Statistics: England (Resident Based)
Department of Health

Detailed statistics on waiting lists and times waited for English residents awaiting elective admission to hospital. Contains data on patients waiting by time waited, type of admission (day case or ordinary) for main consultant specialties, and by English Health Authority. England tables, followed by tables for individual Health Authorities. From June 1999 this publication will be produced on a 'responsible population' basis.

Delivery: Periodic Release
Frequency: Quarterly
Price: NHS - Free, Others - £8.00
ISBN: Different for each issue

Available from
NHS - NHS Response Line 0541 555455;
Others - PO Box 777, London SE1 6XH
(Fax 01623 724524)

Sources from which data for this product are obtained
Inpatient Waiting List Collection by NHS Executive

Imaging and Radiodiagnostics, England
National Health Service Executive Headquarters; sponsored by Department of Health

This publication gives details of the number of imaging and radiodiagnostic examinations or tests carried out by imaging departments or other departments in NHS hospitals in England.

Delivery: Periodic Release
Frequency: Annually
Price: The cost of the 1996/97 document is £6.00
ISBN: 1 85839 792 8

Available from
Ian Mills
National Health Service Executive Headquarters
Department of Health
Quarry House
Quarry Hill
Leeds
Tel: 0113 254 5522; Fax: 0113 254 6423;
Email: jclark@doh.gov.uk

Sources from which data for this product are obtained
Imaging and radiodiagnostic examinations or tests, England - KH12

Körner Aggregate Hospital Returns (KARS)
Department of Health and Social Services - Northern Ireland

Hospital services and activity information available on request from an electronic database. Contains hospital data including bed availability and occupancy, patients treated and births. Includes inpatient and outpatient data for the most recent financial year and analysis of trends.

Delivery: Ad hoc release
Frequency: Ad hoc
Price: Free

Available from
Jim McColgan
Department of Health and Social Services - Northern Ireland
Tel: 028 9052 2566

Sources from which data for this product are obtained
Körner Aggregate Hospital Returns - Northern Ireland

Laboratory Statistics
Scottish Executive

To provide information to health boards and trusts. Covers the disciplines of clinical chemistry, clinical genetics, haematology, microbiology and pathology giving a range of statistics on the workload and staffing levels of SHS laboratories.

Delivery: Periodic Release
Frequency: Annually

Available from
Customer help desk
Information and Statistics Division, NHS in Scotland
Please see Annex B for full address details

NHS Day Care Facilities, England
Department of Health

This publication gives details of attendances at NHS day care centres in England. First attendances, reattendances and total attendances at NHS day care facilities, by hospital for the year in question. Time series of first attendances, reattendances and total attendances at NHS day care facilities in England, by patient group. The number of regular day attendees on register and attendances at NHS day care facilities in England and by regional office, by patient group.

Delivery: Periodic Release
Frequency: Annually
Price: Free
ISBN: 1 85839 797 9

Available from
Ian Mills
National Health Service Executive Headquarters
Department of Health
Quarry House
Quarry Hill
Leeds
Tel: 0113 254 5522; Fax: 0113 254 6423;
Email: jclark@doh.gov.uk

Sources from which data for this product are obtained
NHS day care: availability and use of facilities, England - KH14

Products

NHS Maternity Statistics, England: 1989-90 to 1994-95
Department of Health

This statistical bulletin summaries information from the Hospital Episode Statistics (HES) system relating to NHS maternities in the period 1989-90 to 1994-95 and includes some comparisons with similar data from 1985 and earlier years. The bulletin contains key facts, analysis and commentary, definitions, graphs and statistical tables.

Delivery: Statistical bulletin - hardcopy
Frequency: Annually
Price: Free
ISBN: 1 85839 817 7

Available from
Lesz Lancucki
Department of Health
Please see Annex B for full address details

Sources from which data for this product are obtained
DH Hospital Episodes Statistics (Maternity)

NHS Performance (League) Tables
National Health Service Executive Headquarters; sponsored by Department of Health

Overview of how local health services are performing from a patient's point of view - also known as hospital league tables. Contains data by individual hospitals and health authorities on: performance against Patients' Charter standards - waiting times in outpatients clinics, immediate assessment in accident and emergency departments, priority treatment following a cancelled operation; day surgery rates; waiting times for first outpatient appointment; waiting times for admission to hospital; and emergency ambulance response times; screening services; and vaccination and immunisation.

Delivery: Last published in 1998
Frequency: Annually
Price: Free

Available from
Freepost NEA959
Wetherby
West Yorkshire LS23 6YY
Tel: 0800 665544

Sources from which data for this product are obtained
Waiting Time for First Outpatient Appointments - England

NHS Quarterly Review
National Health Service Executive Headquarters; sponsored by Department of Health

Data on particular aspects of NHS performance. Routinely contains information on the volume of patient activity, waiting list and performance against Patients' Charter standards. Published as an insert to the NHS Magazine.

Delivery: Periodic Release
Frequency: Quarterly
Price: Free
ISSN: 1358-7935

Available from
NHS - NHS Response Line 0541 555455; Others - PO Box 777, London SE1 6XH (Fax 01623 724524)

Sources from which data for this product are obtained
Inpatient waiting list, outpatient waiting times. Patient's charter data and activity data collections by NHS Executive.

NHS Wales Hospital Activity
National Assembly for Wales

A quarterly bulletin giving hospital activity information as reported by the Welsh Health Authorities and Trusts. Waiting list figures are also included to provide a comprehensive picture.

Delivery: Periodic Release
Frequency: Quarterly

Available from
Graham Davies
HSA3
Welsh Office
Crown Buildings
Cathays Park
Cardiff CF10 3NQ
Tel: 029 2082 5086;
Email: graham.davies@wales.gsi.gov.uk

Sources from which data for this product are obtained
Welsh Office Core Indicator System

NHS Wales Hospital Waiting Lists
National Assembly for Wales

Delivery: Periodic Release
Frequency: Monthly

Available from
Robin Jones
Room 2-016
National Assembly for Wales
Crown Building
Cathays Park
Cardiff CF10 3NQ
Tel: 029 2082 3625;
Email: robin.jones@wales.gsi.gov.uk

Sources from which data for this product are obtained

NHSIS Activity Quarterly Briefing (Including Waiting Lists)
Scottish Executive

To provide information on trends, and allow comparisons between hospitals and Trusts.

Delivery: Periodic Release
Frequency: Quarterly

Available from
Customer help desk
Information and Statistics Division, NHS in Scotland
Please see Annex B for full address details

Sources from which data for this product are obtained
Inpatient / Outpatient Waiting Lists in Scotland

Northern Ireland Waiting List Statistics
Department of Health and Social Services - Northern Ireland

Departmental bulletin containing data on patients waiting for inpatient treatment and first outpatient appointment for Northern Ireland. Contains details of ordinary admission and day cases awaiting hospital treatment, and of people waiting for their first outpatient appointment. Includes comparisons of changes over time.

Delivery: Hardcopy publication
Frequency: Quarterly
Price: Free

Available from
Pauline Sheals
Department of Health and Social Services - Northern Ireland
Tel: 028 9052 2925

Sources from which data for this product are obtained
Körner Aggregate Hospital Returns - Northern Ireland

Ordinary and Day Case Admissions, England

National Health Service Executive Headquarters; sponsored by Department of Health

This publication is sourced from the KP70 Körner return, "Summary of patient activity return" for every NHS hospital (Trust and directly managed unit) in England. The information is the number of finished consultant episodes undertaken during the year in question, split by speciality and whether the admission was "ordinary" or "day case" in each hospital. Sector statistics are derived by aggregating speciality statistics and time series of activity are shown for each hospital, for each regional office area and for England as a whole.

Delivery: Periodic Release
Frequency: Annually
Price: The cost of the 1996/97 document is £6.00
ISBN: 1 85839 792 8

Available from
Ian Mills
National Health Service Executive Headquarters
Department of Health
Quarry House
Quarry Hill
Leeds
Tel: 0113 254 5522; Fax: 0113 254 6423;
Email: jclark@doh.gov.uk

Sources from which data for this product are obtained
Summary of patient activity return, England - KP70

Outpatients and Ward Attenders, England

Department of Health

This book presents data on the numbers of outpatient attendances, attendances at accident and emergency departments and ward attenders in NHS Hospital Trusts in England. Data are given for individual Trusts, with summary tables for regional office areas and England.

Delivery: Periodic Release
Frequency: Annually
Price: The cost of the 1996/97 book is £8.00
ISBN: 1 85839 793 6

Available from
Ian Mills
National Health Service Executive Headquarters
Department of Health
Quarry House
Quarry Hill
Leeds
Tel: 0113 254 5522; Fax: 0113 254 6423;
Email: jclark@doh.gov.uk

Sources from which data for this product are obtained
Consultant outpatient attendance activity and accident and emergency services activity, England - KH09; Summary of Ward Attenders, England - KH05

Scottish Consultant Review of Inpatient Statistics

Scottish Executive

To provide consultants with feedback and provide comparative national data specific to each clinical speciality.

Delivery: Periodic Release
Frequency: Annually - Only to NHS consultants

Available from
Customer help desk
Information and Statistics Division, NHS in Scotland
Please see Annex B for full address details

Statistical Bulletin: NHS Hospital Activity Statistics, England

Department of Health

England-level information on hospital activity and beds, including: ordinary and day case admissions; finished consultant episodes; average daily number of available and occupied beds and throughput; outpatient attendances; accident and emergency attendances; ward attenders; number of finished consultant episodes by age and sex; average length of stay in hospital, ordinary admissions only; age distribution of acute sector finished consultant episodes; age distribution of patients occupying beds for acute sector, ordinary admissions only; and information on selected diagnoses and operations.

Delivery: Periodic Release
Frequency: Annually
Price: Free
ISBN: 1 85839 947 5

Available from
Ian Mills
National Health Service Executive Headquarters
Department of Health
Quarry House
Quarry Hill
Leeds
Tel: 0113 254 5522; Fax: 0113 254 6423;
Email: jclark@doh.gov.uk

Sources from which data for this product are obtained
Bed availability and occupancy, England - KH03; Consultant outpatient attendance activity and accident and emergency services activity, England - KH09; Summary of patient activity return, England - KP70; Summary of Ward Attenders, England - KH05

Statistical Press Notice: Waiting List Figures

Department of Health

Five page press notice providing headline provisional waiting list figures for Health Authorities and NHS Trusts in England. Bullet points followed by commentary and regional summary tables. Also contains national headline hospital activity figures in June, September, December and March.

Delivery: Periodic Release
Frequency: Monthly

Available from
Data Management Team
FPA-PA (WT)
NHS Executive
Room 4N34A
Quarry House
Quarry Hill
Leeds LS2 7UE
Tel: 0113 254 5555

Sources from which data for this product are obtained
Inpatient Waiting List and Activity collections undertaken by NHS Executive.

Waiting Lists / Times Key Indicators

Scottish Executive

To allow local / central comparison of waiting lists/ times for inpatients, day cases and outpatients to facilitate service planning and staffing.

Delivery: Periodic Release
Frequency: Quarterly

Available from
Customer help desk
Information and Statistics Division, NHS in Scotland
Please see Annex B for full address details

Sources from which data for this product are obtained
Waiting List Return - SMR3

Waiting Times for First Outpatient Appointments in England
Department of Health

A bulletin containing data and analysis for first outpatient attendances in the quarter ending 31 March 1998. Data relates to provider figures, that is for outpatients attending NHS hospitals in England. Analysis is done on national and regional bases, as well as at speciality level. The bulletin is published quarterly.

Delivery: Periodic Release
Frequency: Quarterly
Price: Free
ISBN: Different for each issue

Available from
Data Management Team
FPA-PA (WT)
NHS Executive
Room 4N34A
Quarry House
Quarry Hill
Leeds LS2 7UE
Tel: 0113 254 5555

Sources from which data for this product are obtained
Waiting Time for First Outpatient Appointments - England

Waiting Times for First Outpatient Appointments in England: Detailed Statistics
Department of Health

Detailed information on the waiting times for first outpatient appointments in England. Contains data on the number of patients seen for their first consultant outpatient appointment following referrals by their GP and time waited by main consultant speciality for individual providers.

Frequency: Quarterly
Price: NHS - Free, Others - £11.00
ISBN: Different for each issue

Available from
NHS - NHS Response Line 0541 555455; Others - PO Box 777, London SE1 6XH (Fax 01623 724524)

Sources from which data for this product are obtained
Waiting Time for First Outpatient Appointments - England

See also:
In this chapter:
Health and Personal Social Services Statistics (NI) *(4.24)*
Health and Personal Social Services Statistics for England *(4.24)*
Health Survey for England: The Health of

Young People 1995-97 *(4.24)*
Scottish Health Statistics *(4.24)*
Scottish Key Indicators for Performance (SKIPPER) *(4.24)*

In other chapters:
Digest of Welsh Statistics (see the Government and Public Sector chapter)

4.42 Incidence and Prevention of Disease, Illness and Injury

Agreeing an Accident Information Structure
Department of Health

A one-off report describing a structure for the collection of information on Accidents. Primarily aimed at DH and NHS users, this report should be of use to any agency concerned with the collection or analysis of information on accidents.

Delivery: Ad Hoc/One-off Release
Price: Free

Available from
Vincent Brown
Department of Health
Please see Annex B for full address details

Breast Screening Programme - England
Department of Health

This statistical bulletin summarises information from the computerised call and recall system for breast screening in England including information about earlier years. Results are available for Regional Offices. The bulletin contains key facts, analysis and commentary, definitions, graphs and statistical tables.

Delivery: Statistical bulletin, hardcopy and internet
Frequency: Annually
Price: Free
ISBN: 1 85839 852 5

Available from
Lesz Lancucki
Department of Health
Please see Annex B for full address details

Internet: www.doh.gov.uk/public/bescreen.htm

Sources from which data for this product are obtained
DH returns KC62 and KC63

Cancer 1971-1997
Office for National Statistics

This CD-ROM presents registrations of newly diagnosed cancer cases and of deaths from cancer (publication early 1999). It contains anonymised registrations with person details and tumour characteristics for new cases from 1971 to 1992, together with deaths registered from 1971 to 1997 in England and Wales where cancer was the underlying cause. Also included are dictionaries for the cancer sites and morphology classifications, and mid-year population estimates by region. The new cancer cases and deaths files are in both text (fixed and CSV) and database (Access 95) formats. Also included are estimates of newly diagnosed cases of cancer (as published in ONS Monitor MB1 98/2) for years 1993 to 1997. The three tables present the number of new cases, and both crude and age-standardised incidence rates for the major types of cancer by age and sex.

Frequency: Ad hoc
Price: £100.00 (exc.VAT)
ISBN: 1 85774 297 4

Available from
ONS Direct
Please see Annex B for full address details.

Sources from which data for this product are obtained
Cancer Registrations - England & Wales

Cancer Registration Statistics in Scotland
Information and Statistics Division, NHS in Scotland

To provide a reference document for users of cancer data.

Delivery: Periodic Release

Available from
Customer help desk
Information and Statistics Division, NHS in Scotland
Please see Annex B for full address details

Cancer Registrations in Wales
National Assembly for Wales

Sources from which data for this product are obtained
Cancer Registrations - Wales

Available from
Adrian Crompton
The National Assembly for Wales
Crown Building
Cathays Park
Cardiff
Tel: 029 2082 5033; Fax: 029 2082 5350;
Email: statswales@gtnet.gov.uk

Cancer Statistics - Registration, 1990, England & Wales
Office for National Statistics

Annual reference volume presenting national and regional information for 1990 on cancer incidence. Contains an overview of the cancer registration system and a summary chapter of overall cancer patterns; tables of numbers and rates of new cases of cancer by cancer site, sex, and age group, in England and Wales; regional numbers and rates by cancer site and sex. It also presents the age standardised rates (using the European standard population) for years 1979-1990, by cancer site and sex.

Delivery: Periodic Release
Frequency: Annually
Price: Single copy: £21.95
ISBN: 0 11 691556 0

Available from
TSO Publications Centre and Bookshops
Please see Annex B for full address details.

Sources from which data for this product are obtained
Cancer Registrations - England & Wales

Cancer Statistics - Registration, 1991, England & Wales
Office for National Statistics

Annual reference volume presenting national and regional information for 1991 on cancer incidence. Contains an overview of the cancer registration system and a summary chapter of overall cancer patterns; tables of numbers and rates of new cases of cancer by cancer site, sex, and age group, in England and Wales; regional numbers and rates by cancer site and sex. It also presents the age standardised rates (using the European standard population) for years 1979-1991, by cancer site and sex.

Some of the data in this product is disaggregated by gender.

Delivery: Periodic Release
Frequency: Annually
Price: single copy: £21.95
ISBN: 0 11 620967 4

Available from
TSO Publications Centre and Bookshops
Please see Annex B for full address details.

Sources from which data for this product are obtained
Cancer Registrations - England & Wales

Cancer Statistics - Registration, 1992, England & Wales
Office for National Statistics

Annual reference volume presenting national and regional information for 1992 on cancer incidence. Contains an overview of the cancer registration system and a summary chapter of overall cancer patterns; tables of numbers and rates of new cases of cancer by cancer site, sex, and age group, in England and Wales; regional numbers and rates by cancer site and sex. It also presents the age standardised rates (using the European standard population) for years 1983-1992, by cancer site and sex.

Delivery: Periodic Release
Frequency: Annually
Price: single copy: £30.00
ISBN: 0 11 621091 5

Available from
TSO Publications Centre and Bookshops
Please see Annex B for full address details.

Sources from which data for this product are obtained
Cancer Registrations - England & Wales

Cancer Statistics: 1989 Registrations
Office for National Statistics

Cancer registration statistics. Contains data for England and Wales on those patients who were first diagnosed with cancer in the reference year. Data are given on registrations of newly diagnosed cases of cancer by sex, age and site in the reference year (details at four-digit level of ICD9 are given on microfiche).

Frequency: Annual
Price: £17.70

Available from
TSO Publications Centre and Bookshops
Please see Annex B for full address details.

Sources from which data for this product are obtained
Cancer Registrations - England & Wales

Cancer Survival in England and Wales: 1981 and 1989 Registrations
Office for National Statistics

Survival estimates for the major cancer sites for cancers diagnosed in 1981 and 1989, in England and Wales. Contains tables, charts and text. Table 1 shows crude and relative survival estimates for 1 year and 5 years for selected age groups by cancer site, sex and year of diagnosis. The results in Table 1 are summarised in Figures 1-3. Figure 1 illustrates the results for 1989 and shows sex specific estimates of 5 year relative survival by cancer site. Figures 2(a)-2(p) show comparisons of age and, where appropriate, age and sex adjusted relative survival curves for cancers diagnosed in 1981 and in 1989 for all malignant neoplasms (excluding non-melanoma skin cancer) and for 15 selected cancer sites.

Frequency: Ad Hoc
Price: Single copy: £4.00
ISSN: 0953-3362

Available from
ONS Direct
Please see Annex B for full address details.

Sources from which data for this product are obtained
Cancer Registrations - England & Wales

Cancer Survival Trends in England and Wales, 1971-1995: Deprivation and NHS Region
Office for National Statistics, London School of Hygiene and Tropical Medicine, Cancer Research Campaign

This book presents survival trends since 1971 for almost 60 different cancers in adults and children in England and Wales. The analyses include 2.9 million cancer patients diagnosed during 1971-90 and followed up to the end of 1995. Survival rates for each cancer are presented in a separate chapter. These contain crude and relative survival rates at one, five and ten years after diagnosis for men and women (or boys and girls) diagnosed in the NHS Regions of England and Wales during 1971-75, 1976-80, 1981-85 and 1986-90. Survival rates are also given for each of five deprivation categories, using the Carstairs index. For 14 of the most common cancers, survival rates by sex and deprivation are also presented at regional level. Detailed explanations are given of the data and of the methods used in the analysis.

Comprehensive summary tables show national time trends in relative survival for each cancer (and trends within each NHS Region for 17 of the most common cancers), and survival rates by sex, age at diagnosis, NHS Region and deprivation category. An international comparison of survival is also provided. A CD-ROM is also available (separately from the book). This contains the data sets used in the analyses, plus supporting data - life tables by sex, calendar period, NHS Region and single year of age up to 99; dictionaries of the cancer site and morphology classifications used, and electronic versions of the tables and charts contained in the book.

Frequency: Ad hoc
Price: £130.00
ISBN: 0 11 621031 1

Available from
TSO Publications Centre and Bookshops
Please see Annex B for full address details.

Sources from which data for this product are obtained
Cancer Registrations - England & Wales

Cancer Survival Trends in England and Wales, 1971-1995; Deprivation and NHS Region (CDROM)
Office for National Statistics; London School of Hygiene and Tropical Medicine

This CDROM accompanies the monograph, Cancer Survival Trends in England and Wales, 1971-1995: Deprivation and NHS Region (SMPS No. 61). The monograph forms the most comprehensive analysis of cancer survival trends and patterns ever carried out in Britain. It explores survival trends among almost three million cancer patients diagnosed in England and Wales since the early 1970s, and survival patterns by age, sex, geographic region and socioeconomic status for 58 different cancers in adults and children.

This CDROM contains data, results and tools. Data files of anonymised individual records used for the analyses published in Cancer Survival Trends will enable users to carry out other analyses. All of the survival results for each of 58 cancers (as defined in Cancer Survival Trends) are included. For some cancers, the results on this disk are more detailed than those included in the book. The life tables used to compute relative survival rates are also included, together with dictionaries with descriptions of the cancer sites and morphologies.

Frequency: Ad hoc
Price: £100.00 exc.VAT
ISBN: 1 85774 324 5

Available from
ONS Direct
Please see Annex B for full address details.

Sources from which data for this product are obtained
Cancer Registrations - England & Wales

CDR Weekly Communicable Disease Report
Public Health Laboratory Service

Statistics and commentary on laboratory reports for the reference week. Also contains statistics on notifications of infectious diseases for the particular week. Annual subscription includes four issues of Communicable Disease and Public Health and any supplementary reports such as the quarterly Infectious Diseases in England and Wales.

Frequency: Weekly
Price: £152.00 (£184.00 overseas) per annum
ISSN: 1350 9357

Available from
PHLS Press & Publications
Public Health Laboratory Service
Please see Annex B for full address details

Cervical Cytology
Scottish Executive

To provide feedback on cervical cytology statistics.

Delivery: Periodic Release
Frequency: Quarterly

Available from
Customer help desk
Information and Statistics Division, NHS in Scotland
Please see Annex B for full address details

Sources from which data for this product are obtained
Cervical Cytology Workload Statistics

Cervical Screening Programme - England
Department of Health

This bulletin summarises information from the computerised call and recall system for cervical screening from pathology laboratories on cervical cytology in England including information about earlier years. Results are available for Regional Offices and each pathology laboratory. The bulletin contains key facts, analysis and commentary, definitions, graphs and statistical tables.

Delivery: Statistical bulletin, hardcopy and internet
Frequency: Annually
Price: Free
ISBN: 1 85839 992 0

Available from
Lesz Lancucki
Department of Health
Please see Annex B for full address details

Internet: www.doh.gov.uk/public/cervscr.htm

Sources from which data for this product are obtained
DH returns KC53 and KC61

Cervical Screening Programme, Wales - Annual Report
National Assembly for Wales

Statistical report produced annually. Summarises information from the Cervical Screening Programme in Wales including coverage and result of smears taken in the most recent year in around 15 pages of charts and commentary.

Frequency: Annually

Available from
Vivien Trew
National Assembly for Wales
Please see Annex B for full address details

Sources from which data for this product are obtained
Adult Screening Programmes - Cervical Cytology (KC53); Pathology Laboratories - Cervical Cytology and Biopsies (KC61)

Cervical Screening Programme, Wales - Annual Statistical Brief
National Assembly for Wales

Statistical brief produced annually. Summarises key information from the Cervical Screening Programme in Wales including coverage and results of smears taken in the most recent year in 2 pages of charts and commentary.

Frequency: Annually

Available from
Vivien Trew
National Assembly for Wales
Please see Annex B for full address details

Sources from which data for this product are obtained
Adult Screening Programmes - Cervical Cytology (KC53); Pathology Laboratories - Cervical Cytology and Biopsies (KC61)

Child Health System
Department of Health and Social Security - Northern Ireland

Child health details for Northern Ireland (1971-86) available on request from an electronic database. Contains data such as age, sex, hospital, ICD Code and birth weight.

Price: Free

Available from
Fergal Bradley
Department of Health and Social Security - Northern Ireland
Castle Buildings
Stormont
Belfast
Northern Ireland
Tel: 028 9052 2661

Sources from which data for this product are obtained
Child Health - Northern Ireland

Communicable Disease Statistics 1996
Public Health Laboratory Service

Statistics and commentary on notifiable diseases and deaths for the reference year. Contains statistics on the notifications of cases and deaths from infectious diseases analysed by sex and age for England and Wales and for local authority areas. Limited comparisons are made with the previous ten years. See also CDR quarterly supplements Infectious Diseases in England and Wales. For the editions published from 1974 - 1995 please contact the Stationery Office Publications Centre for availability. Editions published from 1996 onwards can be obtained from PHLS Press & Publications. The 1997 and future editions will have a different format as Communicable Disease Surveillance Centre (CDSC) Annual Reviews.

Delivery: Hardcopy publication
Frequency: Annual
Price: £15.00 plus p/p
ISBN: 00 901144 44 4

Available from
PHLS Press & Publications
Public Health Laboratory Service
Please see Annex B for full address details

Estimates of Newly Diagnosed Cases of Cancer, England and Wales, 1993-1997
Office for National Statistics

Monitor containing estimates of cancer incidence for years 1993-1997 in England and Wales. It presents the numbers and rates of new cases by sex and age group for each year.

Delivery: Periodic Release
Frequency: Annually
Price: Single copy: £4.00
ISSN: 1359-8511

Available from
ONS Direct
Please see Annex B for full address details.

Sources from which data for this product are obtained
Cancer Registrations - England & Wales

(The) Geographical Epidemiology of Childhood Leukaemia and Non-Hodgkin Lymphomas in Great Britain 1966-83
Office for National Statistics

Academic research papers on childhood leukaemia. Contains a series of analyses of data on childhood leukaemia and non-Hodgkin lymphomas occurring in Great Britain during the period 1966-83.

Frequency: Ad hoc
Price: £16.60
ISBN: 0 11 691357 6 (series SMPS No 53)

Available from
TSO Publications Centre and Bookshops
Please see Annex B for full address details.

Health Expectancy and Its Uses
Office for National Statistics; sponsored by Department of Health

Analyses of a series of datasets which reviews existing methods of calculating health expectancy and how they would vary if different definitions were used, to calculate health expectancy and how this would vary by deleting major disease categories.

Delivery: Ad hoc/One-off Release
Price: £14.00
ISBN: 0 11 702005 2

Available from
TSO Publications Centre and Bookshops
Please see Annex B for full address details.

(The) Health of Adult Britain 1841 - 1994, CD-ROM
Office for National Statistics

A CD-ROM supplement to the two volumes of the Decennial Supplement. The Health of Adult Britain 1841-1994. Contains tables of trends in all-cause and cause specific mortality rates, factors known to influence health, and disease incidence and prevalence. Where appropriate each table is linked to definitions of methods, data

sources, references and International Classification of Disease codes. Also included are introductions to, and summaries of the main findings from, each chapter.

Frequency: Decennially
Price: £117.50
ISBN: 1 85774 294 X

Available from
TSO Publications Centre and Bookshops
Please see Annex B for full address details.

Sources from which data for this product are obtained
General Household Survey - GB; Morbidity Statistics from General Practice 1991-92 (MSGP4); Registration of Deaths - England and Wales.

(The) Health of Adult Britain 1841 - 1994, Decennial Supplement, Volumes 1 and 2
Office for National Statistics

Volume 1 contents include mortality, morbidity, and changes in factors which influence health. Topics include: sources for monitoring health and disease; mortality trends 1841-1994; morbidity statistics; socio-economic and demographic trends 1841-1991; trends in diet 1841-1994; alcohol and drug related diseases; smoking related diseases; family and household structure influences on health; environmental changes and health impact; and medical advances. Volume 2 contents include trends in diseases of particular organ systems, and mortality/morbidity in selected population groups. Topics include: communicable diseases; sexually transmitted diseases including HIV/AIDS; cancers; cardiovascular disease; neurological diseases including Alzheimer's disease; asthma/bronchitis/pneumonia; renal diseases; digestive diseases; musculoskeletal disease; accidents; and the health of elderly people.

Frequency: Decennially
Price: £40.00 each or £60.00 for both volumes.
ISBN: Vol.1: 0116916958 Vol.2: 0116916966 Both: 0116209097

Available from
TSO Publications Centre and Bookshops
Please see Annex B for full address details.

Sources from which data for this product are obtained
General Household Survey - GB; Morbidity Statistics from General Practice 1991-92 (MSGP4); Registration of Deaths - England and Wales.

(The) Health of Our Children
Office for National Statistics

Brings together detailed reviews of different child health-related subjects in one volume. Analysis and data covers the following topics: demographic and economic changes to family structures, children's physical development and their health-related behaviour, trends in patterns of childhood morbidity and mortality, the health of ethnic minority children, accidents, respiratory disease, sudden infant deaths, cancer, congenital anomalies, mental health and infectious diseases.

Frequency: Ad hoc
Price: £25.95
ISBN: 0 11 691643 5 (series DS No 11, 1995)

Available from
TSO Publications Centre and Bookshops
Please see Annex B for full address details.

Improving Information on Accidents
Department of Health

A report produced by the Department of Health's Public Health Information Strategy team outlining the Department's requirements for Public Health Information in the field of accidents.

Delivery: Ad Hoc/One-off Release
Frequency: Ad Hoc
Price: Free

Available from
Vincent Brown
Department of Health
Please see Annex B for full address details

Improving Information on Maternity and Child Health
Department of Health

A report produced by the Department of Health's Public Health Information Strategy (PHIS) Team. It makes a careful analysis of the Department's information needs and in relation to this area and identifies a number of shortcomings in the availability of existing information.

Delivery: Ad Hoc/One-off Release
Frequency: Ad Hoc
Price: Free

Available from
Vincent Brown
Department of Health
Please see Annex B for full address details

Improving Information on the Health of Ethnic Groups
Department of Health

A report produced by the Department of Health's Public Health Information Strategy team outlining the Department's requirements for Public Health Information relating to ethnic groups.

Delivery: Ad Hoc/One-off Release
Frequency: Ad Hoc
Price: Free

Available from
Vincent Brown
Department of Health
Please see Annex B for full address details

Incidence of and Mortality from Cancers of the Lung, Skin, Breast and Cervix - England
Office for National Statistics

Presents data on the four cancers for which Health of the Nation targets had been set. Numbers and rates of new cases and deaths, in England and Wales. Data up to 1993 for incidence and 1995 for deaths.

Delivery: Ad Hoc/One-off Release
Frequency: Ad Hoc
Price: £2.00
ISSN: 1359-8511

Available from
ONS Direct
Please see Annex B for full address details.

Sources from which data for this product are obtained
Cancer Registrations - England & Wales

Infant & Perinatal Mortality - Social & Biological Factors
Office for National Statistics

This Monitor presents statistics on stillbirths and infant deaths registered in England and Wales, which have been linked to their corresponding birth records, enabling an analysis of mortality rates by various social and biological factors.

Delivery: Periodic Release
Frequency: Annually
Price: £4.00
ISSN: 0953-4415

Sources from which data for this product are obtained
Childhood and Infant Mortality - England and Wales; Linked Births and Infant Deaths - England & Wales

Longitudinal Study: Socio-Demographic Differences in Cancer Survival 1971-83
Office for National Statistics

Descriptive text and analysis of cancer survival patterns. The first comprehensive analysis of survival patterns for different cancer sites and variations in survival by housing tenure, social class, economic position, marital status and region of residence for the years 1971-83.

Delivery: Ad Hoc/One-off Release
Frequency: Ad hoc
ISBN: 0 11 691289 8

Available from
TSO Publications Centre and Bookshops
Please see Annex B for full address details.

Morbidity Statistics from General Practice - Fourth national study 1991-92
Office for National Statistics

Morbidity data from the fourth National Survey of Morbidity carried out jointly by ONS (formerly OPCS), the Royal College of General Practitioners and the Department of Health. Contains statistics on the reasons, as perceived by the doctor or practice nurse, for which people consult in general practice. These are linked to the socio-economic characteristics of each patient - providing a comparison of the incidence and prevalence of disease among different groups in the community. The results are broadly indicative of reported morbidity in England and Wales as a whole.

Delivery: Periodic Release
Frequency: Decennial
Price: £30.00
ISBN: 0 11 691610 9 (series MB5 No 3)
ISSN:

Available from
TSO Publications Centre and Bookshops
Please see Annex B for full address details.

Sources from which data for this product are obtained
Morbidity Statistics from General Practice - England and Wales; Morbidity Statistics from General Practice 1991-92 (MSGP4)

Morbidity Statistics from General Practice 1991-92 on CD-ROM
Office for National Statistics

Tables and datasets from the report "Morbidity Statistics from General Practice 1991-92". They contain detailed statistics on consulting patterns and disease in the population as seen in general practice, based on a nationally representative sample of half a million patients in England and Wales. Features include: ICD codes at 4-digit level; Socio-economic characteristics; Consultation characteristics; and additional and more detailed tables than in the MSGP4 report. An excellent support aid for epidemiological research, ecological studies, measuring morbidity, general practice planning, and health needs assessment.

For use by academic departments, government/NHS, GP's, health care industry for health research into: Primary care; Morbidity; General Practice workload; General Practice utilisation; Consultation patterns; Health inequalities; Presentation of disease in primary care; Health needs assessment; and Health needs planning.

Delivery: Ad Hoc/One-off Release
Price: £117.50 inc.VAT
ISBN: 1 85774 2605

Available from
ONS Direct
Please see Annex B for full address details.

Sources from which data for this product are obtained
Morbidity Statistics from General Practice - England and Wales

Morbidity Statistics from General Practice 1991-92 Patient Records on CD-ROM
Office for National Statistics

Fully anonymised general practice records of patients who were included in the fourth national morbidity study. The data is presented as a set of relational databases describing contacts, consultations, episodes and socio-economic data which can be linked by patient serial number. The consultation data includes date and place of contact, who consulted, diagnosis by ICD9 and READ codes, type of contact, serious/intermediate/minor consultation classification, episode type (first/new/ongoing). The socio-economic data includes gender, ethnic group, country of birth, age, number of days in study, urban/rural place of residence indicator, housing tenure, social class, marital/cohabiting status, living alone, smoking status, employment status, household type.

For use by academic departments, government departments, NHS, pharmaceutical industry, healthcare industry for research and planning concerned with primary care, morbidity, general practitioner workload, consultation patterns, presentation of disease in general practice, health inequalities and provision of services.

Delivery: Ad Hoc/One-off Release
Price: £117.50 inc.VAT
ISBN: 1 85774 2923

Available from
ONS Direct
Please see Annex B for full address details.

Sources from which data for this product are obtained
Morbidity Statistics from General Practice - England and Wales

NHS Immunisation Statistics, England
Department of Health

The Statistical Bulletin summarises data about the uptake of childhood Immunisations and numbers of vaccinations given in England. Contains data on the number of immunisations against Diphtheria, Tetanus, Polio, Pertussis (whooping cough), Haemophilus, Influenza b, Measles and Tuberculin skin tests by age. Results are available for Regional Office, NHS Trusts and health authority. The bulletin contains covering commentary, definitions, graphs and statistical tables.

Delivery: Statistical bulletin, hardcopy and internet
Frequency: Annually
Price: free
ISBN: 1 85839 981 5

Available from
Lesz Lancucki
Department of Health
Please see Annex B for full address details

Internet: www.doh.gov.uk/public/imunstat.htm

Sources from which data for this product are obtained
DH return KC50 and COVER/KORNER (Coverage of Vaccination Evaluated Rapidly) data collection undertaken by Public Health Laboratory Service - Communicable Disease Surveillance Control (CDSC)

Other Prescribed Diseases - Initial Assessments
Department of Social Security

!00% count of initial assessments of "non respiratory prescribed diseases". From December 1997 this is included in "all prescribed diseases".

Delivery: Periodic Release
Frequency: Quarterly

Available from
Department of Social Security
Benton Park Road
Newcastle upon Tyne
Tel: 0191 225 7661; Fax: 0191 225 3193;
Email: mcgillm@asd11btn.dss-asd.gov.uk

Overview of Sexual Health Information
Department of Health

A report produced by the Department of Health's Public Health Information Strategy team bringing together an overview of information on Sexual Health from disparate sources.

Delivery: Ad Hoc/One-off Release
Frequency: Ad Hoc
Price: Free

Available from
Vincent Brown
Department of Health
Please see Annex B for full address details

(The) Prevalence of Back Pain in Great Britain in 1996
Office for National Statistics; sponsored by Department of Health

The report presents the results from a survey of lower back pain that was carried out in 1996 using the ONS Omnibus Survey and compares them with results of a similar survey carried out in 1993. Questions were included in the months of March, April and June in both years and approximately 6,000 interviews were achieved each year.

The report includes data on the prevalence of lower back pain; the duration of back pain in the 12 months preceding interview; factors perceived to be related to back pain; details of medical help sought; the consequences of back pain and the effects of back pain on respondents' attendance at work.

Price: £12.95
ISBN: 0 11 620968 2

Available from
TSO Publications Centre and Bookshops
Please see Annex B for full address details.

Products

Registrations of Cancer Diagnosed in 1990, England and Wales
Office for National Statistics

OPCS Monitor (MB1 95/1): Provisional cancer registration figures for 1990. Contains summary data for England and Wales on those patients who were first diagnosed with cancer in 1990.

Delivery: Periodic Release
Frequency: Annually
Price: £2.00
ISSN: 1359-8511 OPCS Monitor (MB1 95/1)

Available from
ONS Direct
Please see Annex B for full address details.

Sources from which data for this product are obtained
Cancer Registrations - England & Wales

Registrations of Cancer Diagnosed in 1991, England & Wales
Office for National Statistics

Monitor containing text, tables and charts relating to cancer incidence.

Delivery: Periodic Release
Frequency: Annually
Price: £2.40
ISSN: 1359-8511

Available from
ONS Direct
Please see Annex B for full address details.

Sources from which data for this product are obtained
Cancer Registrations - England & Wales

Registrations of Cancer Diagnosed in 1992, England and Wales
Office for National Statistics

Provisional cancer registration figures for 1992. Contains summary data for England and Wales on those patients who were first diagnosed with cancer in 1992.

Delivery: Periodic Release
Frequency: Annually
Price: £4.00
ISSN: 1359-8511

Available from
ONS Direct
Please see Annex B for full address details.

Sources from which data for this product are obtained
Cancer Registrations - England & Wales

Review of the National Cancer Registration System
Office for National Statistics

Looks at the current working of the National Cancer Registration Scheme and makes various recommendations for improvement to the system.

Frequency: Ad hoc
Price: £5.60
ISBN: 0 11 691301 0 (series MB1 No 17, 1990)

Available from
TSO Publications Centre and Bookshops
Please see Annex B for full address details.

Sources from which data for this product are obtained
Cancer Registrations - England & Wales

Scottish Cancer Intelligence Unit Annual Report
Scottish Executive

To inform NHSiS of the data and information services available in the area of cancer.

Delivery: Periodic Release
Frequency: Annually

Available from
Customer help desk
Information and Statistics Division, NHS in Scotland
Please see Annex B for full address details

Sources from which data for this product are obtained
Cancer Registrations - Scotland; Cancer screening - Scotland

Sexually Transmitted Diseases: New Cases Seen at NHS Genito-Urinary Medicine Clinics
Public Health Laboratory Service - Communicable Disease Surveillance Control (CDSC)

The number of new cases in GUM clinics for England. Covering Sexually Transmitted Diseases by Region and Trust, male and female contacts.

Delivery: Periodic Release
Frequency: Annually
Price: Free
ISBN: 1 85839 458 9
ISSN: 0264 6107

Available from
Mike Catchpole
DHLS: CDSC
Tel: 020 8200 6868

Sources from which data for this product are obtained
DH return KC60 - now available by CDSC

Social Distribution of Cancer
Office for National Statistics

Delivery: Ad Hoc/One-off Release
Price: £9.80
ISBN: 011691212X
ISSN:

Available from
Jillian Smith
Office for National Statistics
1 Drummond Gate
London SW1V 2QQ
Tel: 0207 533 5184; Fax: 0207 533 5103;
Email: jillian.smith@ons.gov.uk

TENDON
Office for National Statistics

Computer-based training package for coding to International Classification of Diseases version 10 (ICD10)

Inter-active self-teaching package. Training modules with examples and exercises.

Frequency: One-off
Price: 1 copy £75.00, Reduction of £25.00 for developing countries
Discounts available for orders of over 50 copies. Network price available upon request.

Available from
WHO Centre
Room 2200
Office for National Statistics
Segensworth Road
Titchfield
Fareham
Hampshire PO15 5RR
Tel: 01329-813458;
Email: lin.shane@ons.gov.uk

Trends in Cancer Survival
Scottish Executive

To describe trends in survival of patients in Scotland with common tumours.

Delivery: Ad hoc/One-off Release

Available from
Customer help desk
Information and Statistics Division, NHS in Scotland
Please see Annex B for full address details

Sources from which data for this product are obtained
Cancer Registrations - Scotland; Cancer screening - Scotland

See also:
In this chapter:
Congenital Anomaly Statistics 1995 and 1996 *(4.36)*
Food Safety in the Home - A Survey of Public Awareness *(4.35)*
General Practice Research Database (Authorised Users Only) *(4.40)*

Health and Personal Social Services Statistics for England *(4.24)*
(The) Health of Adult Britain 1841 - 1994, Decennial Supplement, Volumes 1 and 2 *(4.42)*
Health Statistics Quarterly *(4.24)*
Health Statistics Wales *(4.24)*
Health Survey for England: The Health of Young People 1995-97 *(4.24)*
Key Health Statistics from General Practice 1996 (Series MB6 No. 1) *(4.40)*
Key Health Statistics from General Practice, (Studies on Medical and Population Subjects No. 60) *(4.40)*
(The) OPCS Monitoring Scheme for Congenital Malformations *(4.36)*

In the Labour Market chapter:
Enquiry Point for Health Effects Arising from Occupational Exposure to Non-Ionising Radiation
Enquiry Point for Information on Violence At Work
Enquiry Point for Information on Working Conditions
Enquiry Point for Occupational Acute Poisonings and Injuries from Chemicals
Enquiry Point for Occupational Building-Related Illness
Enquiry Point for Occupational Cancers
Enquiry Point for Occupational Cardiovascular Disease
Enquiry Point for Occupational Hand-Arm Vibration Syndrome
Enquiry Point for Occupational Health Effects Arising from Ionising Radiation Exposure
Enquiry Point for Occupational Health Effects Arising from Lead Exposure
Enquiry Point for Occupational Infections
Enquiry Point for Occupational Musculoskeletal Disorders
Enquiry Point for Occupational Neurotoxic Effects
Enquiry Point for Occupational Noise-Induced Deafness
Enquiry Point for Occupational Pesticide-Related Health Effects
Enquiry Point for Occupational Reproductive Health Effects
Enquiry Point for Occupational Skin Diseases
Enquiry Point for Occupational Stress-Related and Psychosocial Disorders
Enquiry Point for Statistics of Asbestos-Related Cancer
Enquiry Point for Statistics of Enforcement Action by the Health and Safety Executive and Local Authorities Under the Health and Safety at Work Etc. Act 1974
Enquiry Point for Statistics of Occupational Asbestosis
Enquiry Point for Statistics of Occupational Injury

Enquiry Point for Statistics of Occupational Lung Diseases
Health and Safety Commission Annual Report and Accounts 1997/98
Health and Safety Statistics 1997/98
HELA Annual Report of Health and Safety in the Service Industries
National Picture of Health and Safety in Local Authority Enforced Industries
Occupational Health Decennial Supplement
Safety Statistics Bulletin
Self-Reported Working Conditions Survey (SWC)
Statistics of Occupational Injury Within the EU and the USA

4.43 Mental Health Services

Admission of Patients to Mental Health Facilities in Wales (Including Patients Detained Under the Mental Health Act 1983)
National Assembly for Wales

This report gives information on patients admitted to mental health facilities in Wales including admission of patients detained under the Mental Health Act 1983 and other legislation. These data are the first to be published from the new return (KP90) which replaced the KH15, KH16 and KO37 returns in 1996/97. The KP90 provides data on patients detained in NHS facilities as well as private mental nursing homes/hospitals in Wales. The report is 33 pages long.

Section 1 provides information on the total number of patients admitted to both private mental nursing homes and NHS facilities in Wales (this is the first time data has been published for all facilities in Wales). Section 2 provides information on the total number of patients admitted to private mental nursing homes in Wales. Section 3 provides information on the total number of patients admitted to NHS facilities in Wales and for the first time data are published by NHS Trust. Section 4 provides information on historical comparisons of patients admitted to NHS facilities. Over the last 6 years there have been several changes in the way in which data on the use of the Mental Health Act have been collected. This may mean that data are not directly comparable with those published previously.

Delivery: First Release
Frequency: Annually

Available from
Graham Davies
National Assembly for Wales
Statistical Directorate
Crown Building
Cathays Park
Cardiff
Tel: 029 2082 5086; Fax: 029 2082 5350;
Email: graham.davies@wales.gsi.gov.uk

Sources from which data for this product are obtained
Körner return KP90, Informal patients and patients detained under the Mental Health Act 1983

Census of Patients in Mental Handicap Hospitals and Units in Wales
National Assembly for Wales

Available from
Graham Davies
National Assembly for Wales
Statistical Directorate
Crown Building
Cathays Park
Cardiff
Tel: 029 2082 5086; Fax: 029 2082 5350;
Email: graham.davies@wales.gsi.gov.uk

Sources from which data for this product are obtained
Census of patients in mental illness and learning disability units in Wales

Development of Services for People with a Mental Handicap or Mental Illness in Northern Ireland
Department of Health and Social Security - Northern Ireland

A summary of Departmental policy and data in relation to people with a mental disorder. Contains activity, manpower and finance information appropriate to the development of health services and personal social services in the community for people with a mental disorder. Information is also provided on the numbers of inpatients in learning disability and mental illness hospitals analysed by age and length of stay.

Frequency: Annually
Price: £2.55
ISBN: 0 337 07933 1

Available from
TSO Publications Centre and Bookshops
Please see Annex B for full address details.

Sources from which data for this product are obtained
Mental Illness/Learning Disability Patients - Northern Ireland

Guardianship Under the Mental Health Act (1983)
Department of Health

Statistical summary of numbers of new and continuing cases of guardianship under sections 7 and 37 of the Mental Health Act (1983). Contains information from 1984 on numbers of new and continuing cases broken down by main disorder, section of Act and whether guardianship conferred on the local authority or another person, and numbers of cases closed during each year.

Delivery: Periodic Release
Frequency: Annually
Price: Free of charge

Available from
David Treacy
Department of Health
Please see Annex B for full address details

Sources from which data for this product are obtained
Guardianship Under the Mental Health Act (1983) - England

Hospitals and Units for People with a Mental Illness or a Learning Disability in Wales - Census of Patients
National Assembly for Wales

Produced annually. It shows the results of a census of patients resident in hospitals and units for people with a mental illness or a learning disability as at 31 March. The data collected for each patient includes: date of birth; sex; purchaser code; area of residence; date of admission; category of patient; speciality; legal status at census; mental category at census; and ward type at census. Each section contains tables giving data for individual hospitals and units together with some tables of data at an all Wales level.

Delivery: Periodic Release
Frequency: Annually

Available from
Graham Davies
National Assembly for Wales
Statistical Directorate
Crown Building
Cathays Park
Cardiff
Tel: 029 2082 5086; Fax: 029 2082 5350;
Email: graham.davies@wales.gsi.gov.uk

Improving Information on Mental Health
Department of Health

A report by the Department of Health's Public Health Information Strategy team outlining the information required by the Department of Health to support its public health role in mental health.

Delivery: Ad Hoc/One-off Release
Frequency: Ad Hoc
Price: Free

Available from
Vincent Brown
Department of Health
Please see Annex B for full address details

Inpatients Formally Detained in Hospitals Under the Mental Health Act 1983 and Other Legislation - Bulletin
Department of Health

Statistical bulletin concerned with the legal status of inpatients formally detained in hospitals for psychiatric care in England. Contains data for 1987-88 and 1992-93 to 1997-98 on formal admissions to and residents in hospitals by sections of the Acts under which they have been detained. This Bulletin contains information on patients admitted under the Mental Health Act 1983 to NHS hospitals, including the three high security hospitals, and private mental nursing homes in England or who became subject to detention under the Act while in hospital. The Sections of the Act are described in detail in Annex A section A1 of this Bulletin. It also has information for the first time, on the number of patients in hospital at a point in time (31 March). The publication includes data relating to 1997-98 as well as revisions to earlier years.

Delivery: Periodic Release
Frequency: Annually
Price: Free
ISBN: 1 85839 950 5

Available from
Kevin Downey
Department of Health
Please see Annex B for full address details

Sources from which data for this product are obtained
KH15; KH16; KO37; KP90; Mental Health Enquiry (MHE)

Inpatients Formally Detained in Hospitals Under the Mental Health Act 1983 and Other Legislation, NHS Trusts, High Security Hospitals and Private Facilities - Booklet
Department of Health

The aim of this Booklet is to provide information on the uses of the Mental Health Act (MHA) 1983. The Booklet repeats some of the England tables that were published in the Bulletin but its main purpose is to present the data provided by trusts and by Health Authorities (HAs). HAs collate returns for private mental nursing homes in their area. There are also three tables in which the data are presented at Regional Office (RO) area level. Tables on formal admissions to hospital present data on patients detained under the Mental Health Act (MHA) at the point of admission to hospital. Changes from informal status to detention under the Act after admission to hospital are not included in tables on admissions but are presented in tables on changes in status after admission. Tables on use of Part II sections combine information on those detained on admission to hospital with that on those detained after admission to arrive at figures for total uses of these sections. There are also tables showing patients detained at a point in time (31 March); these data were collect for the first time in 1996-97.

Delivery: Periodic Release
Frequency: Annually
Price: Free
ISBN: 1 85839 995 5

Available from
Kevin Downey
Department of Health
Please see Annex B for full address details

Sources from which data for this product are obtained
KH15; KH16; KO37; KP90; Mental Health Enquiry (MHE)

Mental Health Inpatients System (MHIS)
Department of Health and Social Services - Northern Ireland

Mental illness and learning disability inpatient activity and Census data for Northern Ireland available on request from an electronic database. Contains data such as age, sex, religion, length of stay, diagnosis, hospital and postcode.

Delivery: Ad hoc release
Frequency: Ad hoc
Price: Free

Available from
Tony O'Brien
Department of Health and Social Services - Northern Ireland
Tel: 028 9052 2504

Sources from which data for this product are obtained
Mental Health Inpatients System - Northern Ireland

Mental Health Standard Analyses
Department of Health and Social Services - Northern Ireland

Tabulated data of activity and Census information on mental illness/learning disability inpatients. Contains data on admissions, discharge and Census data relating to mental health. These include analyses by age, sex, length of stay, hospital, primary diagnosis, legal status, and board of residence. The latest available publication relates to 1994-95.

Delivery: Hardcopy publication
Frequency: Annual
Price: Free

Available from
Tony O'Brien
Department of Health and Social Services - Northern Ireland
Tel: 028 9052 2504

Sources from which data for this product are obtained
Mental Health Inpatients System - Northern Ireland

Mental Illness/Learning Disability Census Tables
Department of Health and Social Services - Northern Ireland

Census information on mental illness/learning disability inpatients in Northern Ireland. Contains an age by length of stay breakdown for all mental illness/learning disability inpatients.

Delivery: Ad hoc release
Frequency: Annual
Price: Free

Available from
Tony O'Brien
Department of Health and Social Services - Northern Ireland
Tel: 028 9052 2504

Sources from which data for this product are obtained
Mental Illness/Learning Disability Hospitals - Northern Ireland

Non-Fatal Suicidal Behaviour among Prisoners
Department of Health

The report presents the results from secondary analysis of the data on suicide attempts from the ONS survey of psychiatric morbidity among prisoners in England and Wales which was carried out at the end of 1997. In this report, data are presented on the relationship between non-fatal suicidal

behaviour and sociodemographic factors; penal, custodial and criminal characteristics; the presence of psychiatric disorders, life events and social support, and places them in the context of the existing literature.

Frequency: One-off
Price: £15.00
ISBN: 1 85774 329 6

Available from
ONS Direct
Please see Annex B for full address details.

Northern Ireland Psychiatric Census Data
Department of Health and Social Services - Northern Ireland

Departmental bulletin on long-stay and detained mental illness inpatients. Contains a count of Census patients by legal status, age, length of stay, primary diagnosis and year. The latest available publication relates to 1994-95.

Delivery: Hardcopy publication
Frequency: Annual
Price: Free

Available from
Tony O'Brien
Department of Health and Social Services - Northern Ireland
Tel: 028 9052 2504

Sources from which data for this product are obtained
Mental Health Inpatients System - Northern Ireland

(The) Office of Population Censuses and Surveys Survey of Psychiatric Morbidity in Great Britain - Reports 1 to 8
Department of Health, Scottish Home & Health Department. The National Assembly for Wales

The OPCS psychiatric morbidity reports present data on four surveys carried out during 1993 and 1994: a private household survey of 10,000 adults aged 16-64; a supplementary sample of 350 people aged 16-64 with psychosis living in private households identified via GPs and Mental Health Teams and residents of group homes or recognised lodgings who were classified as having schizophrenia or affective psychosis; Institutions - 1,200 people aged 16-64 living in institutions specifically catering for people with mental illnesses; Homeless people - 1,100 people aged 16-64 living in hostels for the homeless and other such institutions.

Reports 1-3 cover: the prevalence of psychiatric disorders amongst people living in private households; physical complaints of people with psychiatric disorders and their use of services; the receipt of treatments; and how people with a neurotic disorder differ from those without one (e.g. their economic activity, social functioning, their use of alcohol, drugs and tobacco). Reports 4-6 cover the prevalence of psychiatric morbidity in different types of institutions and presents data on residents with various disorders and their difficulties with social functioning etc. Report 7: presents data on, among other things, the prevalence of psychiatric disorders, the physical health of the homeless, their economic, social and financial circumstances and their use of alcohol, drugs and tobacco. Report 8: Presents data on the first three surveys and identifies characteristics associated with differences in the circumstances and health related behaviour of adults with psychosis.

Frequency: Ad hoc
Price: Report 1: £17.00
Report 2: £12.00
Report 3: £17.00
Report 4: £16.00
Report 5: £15.00
Report 6: £15.00
Report 7: £21.00
Report 8: £15.00

ISBN: Report 1: 011691 6273
Report 2: 011691 6516
Report 3: 011691 6532
Report 4: 011691 6613
Report 5: 011691 6621
Report 6: 011691 663X
Report 7: 011691 6702
Report 8: 016691 6702

Available from
TSO Publications Centre and Bookshops
Please see Annex B for full address details.

Psychiatric Morbidity among prisoners in England and Wales
Department of Health

The ONS survey of psychiatric morbidity among prisoners in England and Wales was commissioned by the Department of Health in 1997. It provides up-to date baseline information about the prevalence of psychiatric problems among male and female, remand and sentenced prisoners in order to inform policy decisions about services.

Frequency: One-off
Price: £45.00
ISBN: 0-11-621045-1

Available from
TSO Publications Centre and Bookshops
Please see Annex B for full address details.

Substance Misuse among Prisoners in England and Wales
Department of Health

This report presents the results of further analysis of data on substance misuse collected as part of the survey of psychiatric morbidity among prisoners in England and Wales which was carried out at the end of 1997. As well as bringing together information on substance misuse included in the main report of the survey, it includes a range of additional areas of analysis, such as smoking and age of initiation of drug use, which could not be covered in the earlier report.

Frequency: One-off
Price: £15.00
ISBN: 1 85774 330 X

Available from
ONS Direct
Please see Annex B for full address details.

Sources from which data for this product are obtained
Family Expenditure Survey - UK; General Household Survey - GB; Smoking and Misuse of Alcohol

See also:
In this chapter:
Health and Personal Social Services Statistics (NI) *(4.24)*
Health and Personal Social Services Statistics for England *(4.24)*
Health Statistics Wales *(4.24)*
NHS Quarterly Review *(4.41)*
Scottish Health Statistics *(4.24)*
Scottish Key Indicators for Performance (SKIPPER) *(4.24)*
Social Services Statistics for Wales *(4.24)*

4.44 Ophthalmic Services

General Ophthalmic Services Activity Statistics
Department of Health

Report on General Ophthalmic Services statistics on: NHS sight tests, Vouchers, Repairs and replacements and domiciliary visits (SBE 515)

Delivery: Periodic Release
Frequency: Bi-annually
Price: Free

Available from
Sheila M. Dixon
Department of Health
Please see Annex B for full address details

Sources from which data for this product are obtained
General Ophthalmic Services - England and Wales

General Ophthalmic Services Workforce Statistics
Department of Health

Report on the number of ophthalmic opticians (OOs) and ophthalmic medical practitioners (OMPs) who held contracts with Health Authorities to carry out NHS sight tests.

Delivery: Periodic Release
Frequency: Annually
Price: Free

Available from
Sheila M. Dixon
Department of Health
Please see Annex B for full address details

Sources from which data for this product are obtained
General Ophthalmic Services - England and Wales

Ophthalmic Services Statistical Bulletin
Department of Health

Statistical bulletin covering all aspects of ophthalmic statistics. Contains data on sight tests and optional vouchers covering the last ten years, ending March of the same year, and workforce data, collected in December of the previous year. Some financial data are also included.

Delivery: Periodic Release
Frequency: Annually
Price: Free
ISBN: 1 85839 790 1

Available from
Sheila M. Dixon
Department of Health
Please see Annex B for full address details

Sources from which data for this product are obtained
General Ophthalmic Services - England and Wales

Sight Tests Volume and Workforce Survey
Department of Health

Report on number of sight tests, distribution of patient ages and estimated volume compared with previous years survey results; and number and whole time equivalents of Optometrists.

Delivery: Periodic Release
Frequency: Annually
Price: Free

Available from
Sheila M. Dixon
Department of Health
Please see Annex B for full address details

Sources from which data for this product are obtained
Sight Tests Volume and Workforce Survey - GB

Voucher Survey
Department of Health

Report on vouchers redeemed for spectacles. Contains data on the number of vouchers redeemed for spectacles within the voucher value as a proportion of total in the sample.

Delivery: Periodic Release
Frequency: Annually
Price: Free

Available from
Sheila M. Dixon
Department of Health
Please see Annex B for full address details

Sources from which data for this product are obtained
General Ophthalmic Services - Vouchers - GB

See also:
In this chapter:
Health and Personal Social Services Statistics for England *(4.24)*

4.45 Pharmaceutical Services

Community Pharmacies in England and Wales
National Health Service Executive

Statistical Bulletin on Community Pharmacies in England and Wales. This bulletin presents information about community pharmacies in contract with Health Authorities (HAs) in England and Wales to dispense National Health Service (NHS) prescriptions. It is produced on a yearly basis. The data are available for policy development, analysis and monitoring, and for informing the annual negotiations on pharmacy remuneration.

Frequency: Bi-annually
Price: Free
ISBN: 1 84182 062 8

Available from
Marjorie Wilson
National Health Service Executive
Please see Annex B for full address details

Sources from which data for this product are obtained
Pharmaceutical Services form PHS1

General Pharmaceutical Services in England
National Health Service Executive

Statistical Bulletin on general pharmaceutical services in England. This bulletin presents information about general pharmaceutical services (community pharmacies and appliance contractors) within the National Health Service (NHS) in England. It is produced annually. The data are available to be used as a performance management tool for policy development, analysis and monitoring and for informing the annual negotiations on pharmacy remuneration.

Frequency: Annually
Price: Free
ISBN: 1 85839 941 6

Available from
Marjorie Wilson
National Health Service Executive
Please see Annex B for full address details

Sources from which data for this product are obtained
Pharmaceutical Services form PHS1; Prescription Pricing Authority - Chemists' Particulars

---

Residual Medicines
Department of Health

Results from questions asked on the Omnibus Survey carried out by the former OPCS on behalf of the Department of Health during June 1994. The report contains information on the extent to which households had prescribed medicines at home and whether these medicines had been used. Breakdowns include the types of medicines that people had and the characteristics of the user.

Delivery: Ad hoc/One-off Release
Frequency: Ad hoc
Price: £7.20
ISBN: 0 11 691650 8

Available from
TSO Publications Centre and Bookshops
Please see Annex B for full address details.

Sources from which data for this product are obtained
The ONS Omnibus Survey - GB

See also:
In this chapter:
Health and Personal Social Services Statistics for England *(4.24)*

4.46 Private Healthcare, Homes and Hospitals

Private Hospitals, Homes and Clinics Registered Under Section 23 of the Registered Homes Act 1984
Department of Health

Statistical bulletin containing brief statistics on the number of establishments and the total number of beds analysed by the intended use by broad age group and category, bed occupancy, the number of institutions with operating theatres, and an analysis of the nursing staff by grade and whether full or part-time. Data provided for England and Regional Offices of the Department of Health.

Delivery: Periodic Release
Frequency: Annually
Price: Free
ISBN: 1-85839-868-1

Available from
Henry Metcalf
Room 452C
Department of Health
Skipton House
80 London Road
London SE1 6LH
Tel: 020 7972 5584;
Email: HMetcalf@doh.gov.uk

Vacancy Monitoring Report
Scottish Executive

26 page report

Delivery: Other
Frequency: Annually
Price: Free

Available from
Ian Morris
Room 52
Scottish Executive
James Craig Walk
Edinburgh EH1 3BA
Tel: 0131 244 3794;
Email: Ian.Morris@scotland.gov.uk

Sources from which data for this product are obtained
Residential Establishment Census Return (SWS FORM R1); Vacancy Monitoring Return (SWS FORM VM-1)

See also:
In this chapter:
Community Care Bulletin *(4.30)*
Social Services Statistics for Wales *(4.24)*

5 Education and Training

Education and Training statistics are collected, administered and disseminated by a number of separate Departments, Agencies and organisations including the **Office for National Statistics, the Department for Education and Employment, Scottish Executive, Scottish Higher Education Funding Council, the National Assembly for Wales, the Northern Ireland Department of Education, the Northern Ireland Statistics and Research Agency, the Further Education Funding Council, the Higher Education Funding Council, the Higher Education Statistics Agency,** and **the Office of Manpower Economics.** The available statistics embrace a number of subject areas including: the **Demand for/ Supply of Teachers, Funding and Finances of Students, Post School Education, Pre-School Provision, Schools, Teacher Training, Training and Qualifications, Teachers' and Lecturers' Pay.**

The basic data are generated from a number of separate information 'Sources' and the resultant statistics are disseminated through a whole range of statistical 'Analyses' and 'Products', all of which are described in the following chapter. Users looking for a cross-section of UK-wide statistics on **Education and Training** may find the following product useful:

Education and Training Statistics for the United Kingdom (annual publication)

Users interested in a wider range of official statistics including **Education and Training** statistics may like to refer to the following compendia:

On-line Databases (See Chapter 1):
StatBase – StatStore

Hardcopy Compendia (See Chapter 2):
Annual Abstract of Statistics
Britain 2000: The Official Yearbook of the United Kingdom
Regional Trends
Social Trends

Users may also find what they need on the various Departmental Websites. These are listed in Chapter 1.

5

Education and Training - *Sources and Analyses*

5.1 Education - General

Children Receiving Education Elsewhere Than In School
Scottish Executive

Data collected provide information on the numbers of children receiving education outwith school under Section 14 of the Education (Scotland) Act 1980. The data are used as an input to pupil projections and to respond to general requests for statistics on this group of children. Data are disaggregated by age of pupil.

Status: Ongoing
Collection Method: Census
Frequency: Annually
Reference Period: Academic Year
Timeliness: September (collection) - February (available)
Earliest Available Data: 1981-82
National Coverage: Scotland
Disaggregation: Local Authority

Statistician
Sheila Ward
Scottish Executive
Education Statistics; Schools
Tel: 0131 244 0323;
Email: sheila.ward@scotland.gov.uk

See also:
In this chapter:
Annual Monitoring Survey - England *(5.4)*

In other chapters:
British Social Attitudes Survey (BSA) Series *(see the Compendia and Reference chapter)* (The) ONS Longitudinal Study *(see the Population, Census, Migration and Vital Events chapter)*

5.2 Demand for, Supply of, Teachers

Database of Teachers' Records
Department for Education and Employment

The Department for Education and Employment extracts data from the Database of Teacher Records (DTR) maintained by Capita Teachers Pensions.

The DfEE extract of the DTR holds personal, qualification, trailing, salary and service details for those who are or have been in full-time or part-time teachers in maintained schools and others who are or have been members of the Teachers' Superannuation Scheme. Data are held on the personal, qualification and training details of all those who have at some stage completed a course of initial teacher training but have not entered teaching service as described above.

Data are available for full-time teachers, by age, length of service, sex, graduate status, subject of graduation, annual regional staff movements, inflow and outflow, salary scale points, salary bands.

Data from the DfEE DTR extract is used in statistics of Education, Teachers, England and Wales; and in DfEE evidence to the School Teachers Review Body.

Status: Ongoing
Frequency: Annually
Reference Period: 31 March
Timeliness: 18 months
Earliest Available Data: Datasets from 1985
National Coverage: England and Wales

Survey of Teachers and Educational Psychologists = 618G
Department of Education - Northern Ireland

The Department for Education and Employment conducts an annual survey of teachers, lecturers and educational psychologists numbers and teacher vacancies, in Local Education Authority (LEA) maintained institutions.

Data are available separately for full-time, part-time and occasional service teachers, as counts and full-time equivalents, for characteristics by type of institution, temporary teachers, special schools, further education lecturers for adults and educational psychologists.

Teacher vacancies are available by type of school, subject area in secondary schools and level of teacher.

The survey covers all LEAs in England. Final teacher numbers, provisional and final teacher vacancies, and final educational psychologist numbers are available at standard region and LEA level. Provisional teacher numbers are only available at national level.

Provisional figures for teachers numbers are published in the Statistical First Release Teachers in Service, England in April. Provisional numbers for teachers vacancies are published in the Statistical First Release Teacher Vacancies, in May. Data from the 618G survey is combined with Welsh Office equivalent (STAT3) and data on English Government Maintained schools from the Schools Census. 618G data is used in Statistics of Education, Teachers, England and Wales. It is also used for the DfEE evidence to the School Teachers Review Body.

Status: Ongoing
Collection Method: Small sample survey
Frequency: Annual
Reference Period: Third Thursday in January
Timeliness: 3 months
Earliest Available Data: Datasets available from 1993
National Coverage: England

Teacher Flow - Scotland
Scottish Executive

Data are compiled from a survey on teachers joining or leaving employment of the Scottish education authorities. The survey has run since the early 1980s.

Status: Ongoing
Collection Method: Administrative Records
Frequency: Bi-annually
Reference Period: Academic year
Timeliness: March (collected) - June (available) September (collected) - December (available)
Earliest Available Data: 1992-93 (non-archival)
National Coverage: Scotland
Disaggregation: Local Authority

Statistician
Sheila Ward
Scottish Executive
Education Statistics; Schools
Tel: 0131 244 0323;
Email: sheila.ward@scotland.gov.uk

Teachers
Department for Education and Employment

The Department for Education and Employment conducts a survey of teachers, lecturers and educational psychologists numbers and teacher vacancies, in Local Education Authority (LEA) maintained institutions.

Data are available separately for full-time, part-time and occasional service teachers, as counts and full-time equivalents, for characteristics by type of institution, temporary teachers, special schools, further education lecturers for adults, student teachers, etc. and educational psychologists. Teacher vacancies are available by type of school, subject area in secondary schools and level of teacher. The survey covers all LEAs in England and Wales. Final teacher numbers, provisional and final teacher vacancies, and final educational psychologist numbers are available at standard region and LEA level. Provisional teacher numbers are only available at national level.

Earliest Available Data: 1947
National Coverage: England and Wales
Disaggregation: LEAs

Statistician
John Pascoe
Department for Education and Employment
Tel: 020 7925 5426

Products that contain data from this source
Statistics of Education: Teachers in Service, England and Wales; Teacher Vacancies: England (Press Notice); Teachers in Service: England (Press Notice); Written Evidence to the School Teacher's Review Body from the Department For Education: Statistical Tables

Teachers' Records
Department for Education and Employment

The Department for Education and Employment compiles the database of teachers' records (DTR) from data taken from the administrative records of the Teachers Pensions Agency.

The DTR holds personal, qualification, training, salary and service details for those who are or have been full-time or part-time teachers in maintained schools and all others who are or have been members of the Teachers' Superannuation Scheme. Data are held on the personal, qualification and training details of all those who have at some stage completed a course of initial teacher training but have not entered teaching service as described above. Data are available for full-time teachers, by age, length of service, sex, graduate status,

subject of graduation, annual regional staff movements, inflow and outflow, salary scale points, salary bands. Data are published annually in November, about 32 months after the reference date.

Frequency: Annually
Timeliness: About 32 months after the reference date
Earliest Available Data: 1950
National Coverage: England and Wales
Disaggregation: Standard Region

Statistician
John Pascoe
Department for Education and Employment
Tel: 020 7925 5426

Products that contain data from this source
Statistics of Education: Teachers in Service, England and Wales

Teachers Employed by Education Schools
Scottish Executive

Data collected give information on the number of seconded and other teaching staff deployed centrally or mainly outwith schools. The survey also collects data on the number of teachers on reserve/supply lists. The information is used to inform teacher workforce planning work and to meet general requests for information on this topic.

Status: Ongoing
Collection Method: Census
Frequency: Annually
Reference Period: Academic Year
Timeliness: September (collection) - February (available)
National Coverage: Scotland
Disaggregation: Local Authority

Statistician
Sheila Ward
Scottish Executive
Education Statistics; Schools
Tel: 0131 244 0323;
Email: sheila.ward@scotland.gov.uk

5.3 Funding and Finances of Students

Further Education Bursary Statistics
Scottish Executive

This survey provides data on the administration of bursaries by further education colleges for students on further education courses.

Status: Ongoing
Collection Method: Administrative Records
Frequency: Annually
Reference Period: Academic year
Earliest Available Data: 1996-97
National Coverage: Scotland

Statistician
John Landrock
Scottish Executive
Education Statistics; Further Education
Tel: 0131 244 0324;
Email: John.Landrock@scotland.gov.uk

Products that contain data from this source
Further Education Bursary Statistics, 1996-97

Student Awards Agency for Scotland: Student Awards
Scottish Executive; sponsored by Student Awards Agency for Scotland (SAAS)

Provides information about student award holders.

Status: Ongoing
Collection Method: Administrative Records
Frequency: Annually
Timeliness: Available from October, relating to the current academic year.
National Coverage: Scotland

Statistician
Wilma Schofield
Scottish Executive
Education Statistics; Further and Higher Education Statistics
Tel: 0131 244 0297;
Email: wilma.schofield@scotland.gov.uk

Products that contain data from this source
Student Awards 1996-97

Students Eligible for Funding Return
Scottish Higher Education Funding Council

An aggregate return of the full-time equivalent number of students eligible to be counted in the method used by the Scottish Higher Education Funding Council to calculate the allocations from its Main Grant for Teaching. Each SHEFC - funded institution returns its FTE number of students 'eligible for funding' split by funding subject group, level of study and mode of study.

Status: Ongoing
Collection Method: Return made by each SHEFC- funded institution.
Frequency: Annually
Reference Period: Students enrolled at 1 December and forecasts of the enrolments later in the session.
Timeliness: Three to four months.
Earliest Available Data: 1993-94
National Coverage: Scotland

Statistician
Gordon Anderson
Scottish Higher Education Funding Council
Tel: 0131 313 6558

Products that contain data from this source
Facts and Figures; Individual Institutions: Students Eligible for Funding; Students Eligible for Funding

Sources and Analyses

Student Loans - UK
Department for Education and Employment

The Department for Education and Employment compiles data on student loans. Data cover the number of loans, take-up rate, amount of loans, average loans and repayments. Payment data are available by country, gender and type of residence.

Status: Ongoing
Collection Method: Census
Frequency: Annually
Reference Period: Academic and Financial Year
Earliest Available Data: 1990/91
National Coverage: United Kingdom

Statistician
Michael Davidson
Department for Education and Employment
Tel: 01325 392343;
Email: michael.davidson@dfee.gov.uk

Products that contain data from this source
Statistics of Education: Student Support England and Wales - (Volume); Student Support: Statistics of Student Loans in United Kingdom - (Press Notice)

Students Awards - England and Wales
Department for Education and Employment

The Department for Education and Employment conducts a survey on the return of awards to students. It comprises 172 local education authorities in England and Wales and covers awards to all students normally domiciled in the local education authority. Data cover mandatory and discretionary awards and Educational Maintenance Allowances including numbers of awards and expenditure on fees and maintenance. Data collected on mandatory awards includes assessed contributions, rates of grant, status of student and additional allowances.

Status: Ongoing
Collection Method: Census
Frequency: Annually
Reference Period: Academic Year
Earliest Available Data: 1975/76
National Coverage: England and Wales

Statistician
Michael Davidson
Department for Education and Employment
Tel: 01325 392343;
Email: michael.davidson@dfee.gov.uk

Products that contain data from this source
Statistics of Education: Student Support England and Wales - (Volume); Student Awards in England and Wales (Press Notice)

See also:
In this chapter:
Further Education Statistical Record *(5.4)*
Further Education Students - England *(5.4)*

5.4 Post School Education

Annual Monitoring Survey - England
Department for Education and Employment

The Department for Education and Employment conducts a survey for the academic year on student and staff numbers and class contact hours for colleges in further education. Data are available on staff and student hours, average lecturer and student hours, average class size, staff student ratio, exclusions and abatements. Data were collected every academic year until 1993-94.

Status: Ceased completely
Collection Method: Clerical forms
Frequency: Annually
Reference Period: August - July
Timeliness: 10 months after reference period
Earliest Available Data: 1973
National Coverage: England

Statistician
Michael Davidson
Department for Education and Employment
Tel: 01325 392343;
Email: michael.davidson@dfee.gov.uk

Products that contain data from this source
Statistics of Education: Further and Higher Education Student:Staff Ratios 1993-94 England

Community Education Surveys - Budgets
Scottish Executive

The Scottish Education and Industry Department has collected annual data on Community Education Budgets from the 32 Local Authorities (and their predecessors). Along with two companion surveys, the data is intended to assist local and central government plan, develop, promote and evaluate Community Education throughout Scotland. It also serves as a complement to the Scheme of Performance Indicators, which allows for the development of a standardised approach to the professional assessment of the effectiveness and efficiency of a Community Education organisation's performance.

Status: Ongoing
Collection Method: Administrative Records
Frequency: Annually
Reference Period: Financial year
Timeliness: April (collection) - March following year (availability)
Earliest Available Data: 1994-95
National Coverage: Scotland
Disaggregation: Local Authority District (LAD)/ Unitary Authority(Eng)

Statistician
Emma Waddington
The Scottish Executive
Education Statistics; Qualifications and Lifelong Learning
Tel: 0131 244 0313;
Email: emma.waddington@scotland.gov.uk

Products that contain data from this source
Community Education Statistics, 1996-97

Community Education Surveys - Participants
Scottish Executive

The Scottish Education and Industry Department has collected quarterly data on Community Education participants from the 32 Local Authorities (and their predecessors). Along with 2 companion surveys, the data is intended to assist local and central government plan, develop, promote and evaluate Community Education throughout Scotland. It also serves as a complement to the Scheme of Performance Indicators, which allows for the development of a standardised approach to the professional assessment of the effectiveness and efficiency of a Community Education organisation's performance

Status: Ongoing
Collection Method: Administrative Records
Frequency: Quarterly
Reference Period: One week in quarter
Timeliness: July/October/January/April (collection) - March following year (available)
Earliest Available Data: 1994-95
National Coverage: Scotland
Disaggregation: Local Authority District (LAD)/ Unitary Authority(Eng)

Statistician
Emma Waddington
Scottish Executive
Education Statistics; Qualifications and Lifelong Learning
Tel: 0131 244 0313;
Email: emma.waddington@scotland.gov.uk

Products that contain data from this source
Community Education Statistics, 1996-97

Community Education Surveys - Staff
Scottish Executive

The Scottish Executive Education and Industry Department has collected annual data on Community Education staff from the 32 Local Authorities (and their predecessors). Along with 2 companion surveys, the data is intended to assist local and central government plan, develop, promote and evaluate Community Education throughout Scotland. It also serves as a complement to the Scheme of Performance Indicators, which allows for the development of a standardised approach to the professional assessment of the effectiveness and efficiency of a Community Education organisation's performance.

Status: Ongoing
Collection Method: Administrative Records
Frequency: Annually
Reference Period: Financial year
Timeliness: April (collection) - March following year (available)
Earliest Available Data: 1994-95
National Coverage: Scotland
Disaggregation: Local Authority District (LAD)/ Unitary Authority(Eng)

Statistician
Emma Waddington
Scottish Executive
Education Statistics; Qualifications and Lifelong Learning
Tel: 0131 244 0313;
Email: emma.waddington@scotland.gov.uk

Products that contain data from this source
Community Education Statistics, 1996-97

Course and Student Details at Further Education Institutions - Scotland
Scottish Executive

The Scottish Executive Education and Industry Department compiles a survey on courses at Further Education institutions. 43 SOEID - and 2 Local Authority - funded Further Education colleges in Scotland take part in the survey.

Status: Ongoing
Collection Method: Administrative Records
Frequency: Bi-annually
Reference Period: Academic Year
Timeliness: December - April
September - December
Earliest Available Data: 1965 (National Certificate from 1994-95)
National Coverage: Scotland

Statistician
John Landrock
Scottish Executive
Education Statistics; Further Education
Tel: 0131 244 0324;
Email: John.Landrock@scotland.gov.uk

Products that contain data from this source
Further Education Statistics: 1996-97

Examination Results and First Destination of Graduates
Scottish Executive

This survey provides data on the examination results and first destination on graduating of individual students in full-time Higher Education courses at Further Education Colleges.

Status: Ongoing
Collection Method: Administrative Records
Frequency: Annually
Reference Period: Conclusion of academic course
Timeliness: March (collection) - November (available)
Earliest Available Data: 1992-93
National Coverage: Scotland

Statistician
John Landrock
Scottish Executive
Education Statistics; Further Education
Tel: 0131 244 0324;
Email: John.Landrock@scotland.gov.uk

Products that contain data from this source
Further Education Statistics: 1996-97

Finance of Higher Education Institutions
Department for Education and Employment; sponsored by Higher Education Statistics Agency (HESA)

The Higher Education Statistics Agency compiles a survey on the finance of UK higher education institutions. Data are collected from approximately 200 publicly funded institutions. Data are available on income and expenditure accounts, balance sheets, consolidated cash flow statements, research grants and contracts, and capital expenditure. Some longitudinal data are available - term maintenance provision and staff and equipment expenditure. Time series analyses will be made available.

Data are available for England, Scotland, Wales, Northern Ireland and other standard regions derivable from location of institution. The survey is compiled at the end of each calendar year and refers to the previous academic year. Results are published within six months of receipt of the data.

Collection Method: Census
Frequency: Annually
Timeliness: Within six months of receipt of the data
National Coverage: England, Scotland, Wales and Northern Ireland

Statistician
Michael Davidson
Department for Education and Employment
Tel: 01325 392343;
Email: michael.davidson@dfee.gov.uk

Finance Statistics Record (incorporating Aggregate Staff Record)
Higher Education Statistics Agency

The Higher Education Statistics Agency collects data about Finance and Staff in UK higher education institutions. Data are collected from approximately 180 publicly funded institutions. Data are available on income and expenditure, balance sheet information and academic staff load. The data are collected every December and refer to the previous academic/financial year. Results are published within six months of receipt of the data. Data were first collected by HESA in 1994-95.

Status: Ongoing
Collection Method: Administrative Records
Frequency: Annually
Reference Period: 1 August to 31 July
Timeliness: 6 months
National Coverage: United Kingdom

Statistician
Angela Dunn
Higher Education Statistics Agency
Tel: 01242 255577;
Email: AngelaD@hesa.ac.uk

Products that contain data from this source
HE Finance Plus - 1995/96; HE Finance Plus - 1996/97; HE Finance Plus - 1997/98; HESA Online Information Service; Higher Education Management Statistics - Institution Level 95/96; Higher Education Management Statistics - Institution Level 96/97; Higher Education Management Statistics - Institution Level 97/98; Higher Education Management Statistics - Sector Level 94/95; Higher Education Management Statistics - Sector Level 95/96; Higher Education Management Statistics - Sector Level 96/97; Higher Education Management Statistics - Sector Level 97/98; Higher Education Statistics for the UK - 1994/95; Higher Education Statistics for the United Kingdom - 1995/96; Higher Education Statistics for the United Kingdom 1992/93; Higher Education Statistics for the United Kingdom - 1996/97; Higher Education Statistics for the United Kingdom 1997/98; Reference Volume - Resources of Higher Education Institutions - 1994/95; Reference Volume - Resources of Higher Education Institutions - 1995/96; Reference Volume - Resources of Higher Education Institutions - 1996/97; Resources of Higher Education Institutions - 1997/98

First Destination Supplement to Individualised Student Records
Higher Education Statistics Agency

The Higher Education Statistics Agency compiles a survey on the first destinations of students who studied predominantly full-time at UK higher education institutions. Data are collected from approximately 180 publicly funded institutions. Data are available on employment details, standard occupational and industrial classification codes, professional status and unemployment. The data contained in the record may also be linked to the HESA Individualised student record.

Status: Ongoing
Collection Method: Target population
Frequency: Annually
Reference Period: 1 August to 31 July
Timeliness: 6 months
Earliest Available Data: Data were first collected by HESA in 1994-95
National Coverage: United Kingdom

Statistician
Angela Dunn
Higher Education Statistics Agency
Tel: 01242 255577;
Email: AngelaD@hesa.ac.uk

Products that contain data from this source
First Destination of Graduates and Diplomates: 1996; First Destinations of HE Students in UK- (Press Notice); HESA Online Information Service; Higher Education Management Statistics - Institution Level 95/96; Higher Education Management Statistics - Institution Level 96/97; Higher Education Management Statistics - Institution Level - 97/98; Higher Education Management Statistics - Sector Level 94/95; Higher Education Management Statistics - Sector Level 95/96; Higher Education Management Statistics - Sector Level 96/97; Higher Education Management Statistics - Sector Level 97/98; Reference Volume - First Destinations of Students Leaving Higher Education Institutions 1994/95; Reference Volume - First Destinations of Students Leaving Higher Education Institutions 1995/96; Reference Volume - First Destinations of Students Leaving Higher Education Institutions - 1996/97; Reference Volume - First Destinations of Students Leaving Higher Education Institutions 1997/98

Further Education Leavers Survey (FELS) - Northern Ireland
Department of Education - Northern Ireland

Individual-level data are supplied annually by all 17 FE colleges on the qualification outcome for each final year student. Having results data at this level enables analysis to be conducted on subgroups of students; e.g. those in particular age-groups, to feed into the estimation of progress towards the National Targets for Education and Training.

Piloted 1991/92. Annual since then, with no discontinuities.

Status: Ongoing
Collection Method: Census
Frequency: Annually
Reference Period: Academic Year
Timeliness: Results usually available about 1 year after the end of the academic year to which they relate.
Earliest Available Data: 1992/93
National Coverage: Northern Ireland

Statistician
Stephanie Harcourt
Department of Education - Northern Ireland
Corporate Services; Statistics & Research
Tel: 028 9127 9597;
Email: stephanie.harcourt@deni.gov.uk

Further Education Statistical Record (FESR)
Department of Education - Northern Ireland

Individual-level records are returned annually by all 17 colleges on each student enrolled on 1 November, in order to provide a picture of the FE student population, and enrolment trends. Results are presented in a statistical press release.

Status: Ongoing
Collection Method: Census
Frequency: 1 November
Reference Period: Academic Year
Timeliness: June of the academic year to which it relates.
Earliest Available Data: 1991/92
National Coverage: Northern Ireland

Statistician
Stephanie Harcourt
Department of Education - Northern Ireland
Corporate Services; Statistics & Research
Tel: 028 9127 9597;
Email: stephanie.harcourt@deni.gov.uk

Products that contain data from this source
Enrolments on Vocational Courses at Further Education Colleges; Northern Ireland Annual Abstract of Statistics; Regional Trends; Participation in full-time education by 16 and 17 year olds in Northern Ireland; Compendium of Northern Ireland Education Statistics

---

Further Education Statistical Record
Department for Education and Employment

Status: Ceased completely
Collection Method: Magnetic tape
Frequency: Annually
Reference Period: November
Timeliness: 10 months after reference draft.
Earliest Available Data: 1980
National Coverage: England

Statistician
Michael Davidson
Department for Education and Employment
Tel: 01325 392343;
Email: michael.davidson@dfee.gov.uk

Further Education Students - England
Further Education Funding Council

The Further Education Funding Council (FEFC) compiles the Further Education individualised student record (ISR). Data are collected for all students in all further education colleges and for students in other institutions which attract funding from the FEFC. Data are collected in November for an early view of the reference period, July for a complete view and in December for a full view of the previous period including destination and achievement data. The series

covers England and is available at unit postcode levels. Data are collected three times for each teaching year (1 August to 31 July) and published for each collection, usually seven months after the reference date.

Status: Ongoing
Collection Method: Administrative Records
Reference Period: November, July, December
Timeliness: Usually seven months after the reference date
Earliest Available Data: 1994-95
National Coverage: England

Statistician
Colin Stronach
Further Education Funding Council
Tel: 024 7686 3233

Products that contain data from this source
Student Statistics 1994-95: Further Education Colleges in England

---

HESA Aggregate Staff Record
Higher Education Statistics Agency

Status: Ongoing
Collection Method: Census
Frequency: Annually

Statistician
Angela Dunn
Higher Education Statistics Agency
Tel: 01242 255577;
Email: AngelaD@hesa.ac.uk

Products that contain data from this source
HE Planning Plus - 1998; HE Planning Plus - 1999

HESA staff database
Department of Education - Northern Ireland

A census consisting of individual records relating to staff at universities in Northern Ireland, collected annually as part of a UK-wide exercise, to give a detailed picture of staff employed in the higher education sector. Results are reported in 'Resources of Higher Education Institutions' published each year by the Higher Education Statistics Agency (HESA).

Status: Ongoing
Collection Method: Census
Frequency: Annually
Reference Period: Academic Year
Timeliness: By December following the academic year to which it relates.
Earliest Available Data: 1994/95
National Coverage: Northern Ireland

Statistician
Linda Bradley
Department of Education - Northern Ireland
Corporate Services; Statistics & Research
Tel: 028 9127 9395;
Email: linda.bradley.@deni.gov.uk

HESA student database
Department of Education - Northern Ireland

Covers all HE students studying at Higher Education Institutions (HEIs) in UK, and collects a wide range of information to give a picture of students. DENI extracts data on (a) all students domiciled in N. Ireland, and (b) all students studying at HEIs in N. Ireland. Results are presented in DENI statistical press releases.

Status: Ongoing
Collection Method: Census
Frequency: Bi-annually
Reference Period: Academic Year
Timeliness: Student enrolment by late spring of academic year to which it relates. First destinations by June following the students' final academic year. Non-credit bearing courses by December following academic year to which it relates.
Earliest Available Data: 1994/95
National Coverage: United Kingdom

Statistician
Linda Bradley
Department of Education - Northern Ireland
Corporate Services; Statistics & Research
Tel: 028 9127 9395;
Email: linda.bradley.@deni.gov.uk

Products that contain data from this source
First destinations of students gaining qualifications from higher education institutions; Northern Ireland Annual Abstract of Statistics; Regional Trends; Student Enrolments on Higher Education courses; Qualifications Gained from Higher Education Institutions

Higher Education Staff
Department for Education and Employment

The Higher Education Statistics Agency compiles a survey on staff in UK higher education institutions. Data are collected from approximately 200 publicly funded higher education institutions. Analyses of the data are available on many variables including ethnicity and disability, employment details including terms and mode of employment, qualifications, salary and institutional information. Data are available for England, Scotland, Wales, Northern Ireland and other standard regions derivable from location of institution.

Status: Ongoing
Collection Method: Census
Frequency: Annually
Earliest Available Data: 1994-95
National Coverage: England, Scotland, Wales and Northern Ireland

Statistician
Michael Davidson
Department for Education and Employment
Tel: 01325 392343;
Email: michael.davidson@dfee.gov.uk

Higher Education Statistics Agency: Finance Record
Scottish Executive; sponsored by Higher Education Statistics Agency (HESA)

Provides financial information about Higher Education Institutions for the previous financial year.

Status: Ongoing
Collection Method: Administrative Records
Frequency: Annually
Reference Period: Academic year
Timeliness: Available at the end of March following December collection.
Earliest Available Data: 1995
National Coverage: Scotland (part of the UK collection by HESA)

Statistician
Wilma Schofield
Scottish Executive
Education Statistics; Further and Higher Education Statistics
Tel: 0131 244 0297;
Email: wilma.schofield@scotland.gov.uk

Higher Education Statistics Agency: First Destination of Graduates
The Scottish Executive; sponsored by Higher Education Statistics Agency (HESA)

To assess demand for graduates with different qualifications and the patterns of migration of graduates of Scottish Higher Education.

Status: Ongoing
Collection Method: Administrative Records
Frequency: Annually
Reference Period: Graduation
Timeliness: End of April following year of graduation.
Earliest Available Data: 1994-95
National Coverage: Scotland (part of the UK collection by HESA)

Statistician
Wilma Schofield
Scottish Executive
Education Statistics; Further and Higher Education Statistics
Tel: 0131 244 0297;
Email: wilma.schofield@scotland.gov.uk

Higher Education Statistics Agency: Non-Credit Bearing Course Record
Higher Education Statistics Agency (HESA)

To collect information about courses at Higher Education Institutions which do not lead to qualification or credit.

Status: Ongoing
Collection Method: Administrative Records
Frequency: Annually
Reference Period: Academic year
Timeliness: Available at the end of December following September collection.

Earliest Available Data: 1995
National Coverage: Scotland (part of the UK collection by HESA)

Statistician
Wilma Schofield
Scottish Executive
Education Statistics; Further and Higher Education Statistics
Tel: 0131 244 0297;
Email: wilma.schofield@scotland.gov.uk

Higher Education Statistics Agency: Staff Record
Scottish Executive; sponsored by Higher Education Statistics Agency (HESA)

To collect information about academic staff at Higher Education Institutions.

Status: Ongoing
Collection Method: Administrative Records
Frequency: Annually
Reference Period: Academic year
Timeliness: End of January following the July collection.
Earliest Available Data: 1994-95
National Coverage: Scotland (part of the UK collection by HESA)

Statistician
Wilma Schofield
Scottish Executive
Education Statistics; Further and Higher Education Statistics
Tel: 0131 244 0297;
Email: wilma.schofield@scotland.gov.uk

Higher Education Statistics Agency: Student Record
Scottish Executive; sponsored by Higher Education Statistics Agency (HESA)

To monitor Higher Education provision, including the demand for places, the mix of courses available and the profile of students entering Higher Education courses in Scotland. The information is also used in projecting numbers of Higher Education entrants and students, and numbers of student award holders.

Status: Ongoing
Collection Method: Administrative Records
Frequency: Bi-annually
Reference Period: Opening of University Term
Timeliness: End of April (Provisional) October (final data)
Earliest Available Data: 1994-95
National Coverage: Scotland (part of the UK collection by HESA)

Statistician
Wilma Schofield
Scottish Executive
Education Statistics; Further and Higher Education Statistics
Tel: 0131 244 0297;
Email: wilma.schofield@scotland.gov.uk

Sources and Analyses

Products that contain data from this source
Higher Education Student Domicile Statistics, 1996-97

Higher Education Students

Department for Education and Employment; sponsored by Higher Education Statistics Agency (HESA)

The Higher Education Statistics Agency compiles a survey on aggregate numbers of students in UK higher education institutions not covered by the Individualised Student Record. The data are collected from approximately 200 publicly funded UK higher education institutions. Analyses of the data are available on institutional information, course details including level and purpose, enrolments including target groups and enrolment restrictions and student numbers enrolled. Time series analyses will be made available. Data are available for England, Scotland, Wales, Northern Ireland and other standard regions derivable from postcodes.

Status: Ongoing
Collection Method: Census
Frequency: Annually
Earliest Available Data: 1994-95
National Coverage: England, Scotland, Wales and Northern Ireland

Statistician
Michael Davidson
Department for Education and Employment
Tel: 01325 392343;
Email: michael.davidson@dfee.gov.uk

Higher Education Students Early Statistics

Higher Education Funding Council for England

Collection of data on full-time equivalent student load on recognised higher education courses sent out to heads of HEFCE-funded institutions and DENI-funded Universities. These data are collected annually in December and are used to allocate funds for teaching between the institutions. More detailed information on students is available in the HESA student record.

HEFCE's URL http://www.hefce.ac.uk

Status: Ongoing
Collection Method: Census
Frequency: Annually
Reference Period: The academic year in which it is collected.
Timeliness: 3 months.
Earliest Available Data: 1992
National Coverage: England and Northern Ireland

Statistician
Kathy Christie
Higher Education Funding Council for England
Tel: 01179 317366.
Email: k.christie@hefce.ac.uk

Products that contain data from this source
HEFCE - Recurrent Grants

Individualised Staff Record
Higher Education Statistics Agency

The Higher Education Statistics Agency collects data about academic staff employed at UK higher education institutions. Data are collected from approximately 180 publicly funded institutions. Data are available about characteristics of staff whose primary employment function is teaching, research or teaching and research who meet a 25% FTE threshold. The data are collected annually in December and refer to the previous reporting period. Results from the collections are published six months from receipt of the data.

Status: Ongoing
Collection Method: Administrative Records
Frequency: Annually
Reference Period: 1 August to 31 July
Timeliness: 6 months
Earliest Available Data: 1994-95
National Coverage: United Kingdom

Statistician
Angela Dunn
Higher Education Statistics Agency
Tel: 01242 255577;
Email: AngelaD@hesa.ac.uk

Products that contain data from this source
HE Planning Plus - 1998; HE Planning Plus - 1999; HESA Online Information Service; Higher Education Statistics for the UK - 1994/95; Higher Education Statistics for the United Kingdom - 1995/96; Higher Education Statistics for the United Kingdom 1992/93; Higher Education Statistics for the United Kingdom - 1996/97; Higher Education Statistics for the United Kingdom - 1997/98; Reference Volume - Resources of Higher Education Institutions - 1994/95; Reference Volume - Resources of Higher Education Institutions - 1995/96; Reference Volume - Resources of Higher Education Institutions - 1996/97; Reference Volume - Resources of Higher Education Institutions - 1997/98; Research Datapack 9

Individualised Student Record
Higher Education Statistics Agency

The Higher Education Statistics Agency collects data about students studying at UK higher education institutions. Data are collected from approximately 180 publicly funded institutions. Data are available about characteristics of students and their programmes of study, including exam

results. The data contained in the record may also be linked to the HESA First Destinations Supplement (to the Individualised Student Record).

Status: Ongoing
Collection Method: Administrative Records
Frequency: Bi-annually
Reference Period: 1 August to 31 July
Timeliness: 4 months following December collection. 6 months following July collection.
Earliest Available Data: 1994-95
National Coverage: United Kingdom

Statistician
Angela Dunn
Higher Education Statistics Agency
Tel: 01242 255577;
Email: AngelaD@hesa.ac.uk

Products that contain data from this source
Data Report - Students in Higher Education Institutions-95/96; Data Report - Students in Higher Education Institutions-July 1995; Data Report - Students in Higher Education Institutions - 1996/97; HESA Online Information Service; Higher Education Management Statistics - Institution Level 95/96; Higher Education Management Statistics - Institution Level 96/97; Higher Education Management Statistics - Institution Level 97/98; Higher Education Management Statistics - Sector Level 94/95; Higher Education Management Statistics - Sector Level 1995/96; Higher Education Management Statistics - Sector Level 1996/97; Higher Education Management Statistics - Sector Level 1997/98; Higher Education Statistics for the UK - 1994/95; Higher Education Statistics for the United Kingdom - 1995/96; Higher Education Statistics for the United Kingdom 1992/93; Higher Education Statistics for the United Kingdom - 1996/97; Higher Education Statistics for the United Kingdom 1997/98; Reference Volume - Students in Higher Education Institutions - 1994/95; Reference Volume - Students in Higher Education Institutions - 1995/96; Reference Volume - Students in Higher Education Institutions - 1996/97; Reference Volume - Students in Higher Education Institutions 1997/98; Research Datapack 1 - Ethnicity; Research Datapack 2 - Entry Qualifications in HE; Research Datapack 3 - Course Results; Research Datapack 4 - First Destinations; Research Datapack 5 - Disability; Research Datapack 6 - Overseas; Research Datapack 7 - Regional Issues; Research Datapack 8 - Ethnicity in Higher Education; Student Enrolments on HE courses at Publicly Funded HEIs in UK - (Press Notice); Student Enrolments on Higher Education Courses in England and the United Kingdom: Academic Year 1994/95 (Press Notice 107/95); Statistics Focus

Local Authority Funded Further Education for Adults
Department for Education and Employment

The Department for Education and Employment (DfEE) conducts a survey on local authority funded further education for adults. Data are available on the number of students enrolled on local authority funded courses of FE on 1 November by age, sex, mode of attendance and qualification. A count is also taken, over the whole academic year, of course attendances at local authority maintained short-term residential centres for the Further Education Funding Council by age, sex, mode of attendance and qualification.

Status: Ongoing
Collection Method: Census
Frequency: Annually
Reference Period: Snapshot - November each year
Earliest Available Data: 1970
National Coverage: England
Sub-National: Local Authority

Statistician
Ramnik Jain
Department for Education and Employment
Analytical Services
Tel: 020 7273 5987;
Email: ramnik.jain@dfee.gov.uk

Products that contain data from this source
Department for Education and Employment Annual Report; Education Statistics for the United Kingdom; Regional Trends; Social Trends; Statistics of Education: Students in Further and Higher Education

---

Non-credit-bearing Course Record - Aggregate Return
Higher Education Statistics Agency

The Higher Education Statistics Agency collects aggregate data about non-credit-bearing provision at UK higher education institutions. Data are collected from approximately 180 publicly funded institutions. The aim of the record is to provide data about those students not included in the Individualised Student Record. Data are available about numbers of students and their programmes of study.

Status: Ongoing
Collection Method: Administrative Records
Frequency: Annually
Reference Period: 1 August to 31 July
Timeliness: 6 months
Earliest Available Data: 1994/95
National Coverage: United Kingdom

Statistician
Angela Dunn
Higher Education Statistics Agency
Tel: 01242 255577;
Email: AngelaD@hesa.ac.uk

Products that contain data from this source
HE Planning Plus - 1998; HE Planning Plus - 1999

Research Assessment Exercise
Higher Education Funding Council for England

Assessment of research in Higher Education Institution in the UK. Last one carried out in 1996 next planned for 2001. Results available through the Higher Education funding councils' web sites, 'http://www.hefce.ac.uk'. Other data on research staff and HEFCE: research income available from the HESA finance and staff records.

Status: Ongoing
Collection Method: Census
Reference Period: 4 to 5 years.
Timeliness: 8 months.
Earliest Available Data: 1992
National Coverage: United Kingdom

Statistician
Kathy Christie
Higher Education Funding Council for England
Tel: 01179 317366.
Email: k.christie.@hefce.ac.uk

Products that contain data from this source
Research Assessment Exercise: Outcomes

Staff Individualised Records - England
Further Education Funding Council

The Further Education Funding Council (FEFC) compiles the Staff Individualised Record from data obtained for all staff employed in further education sector colleges. The series covers England and data are available at FEFC regional level. Data were collected on a pilot basis from sixth form colleges in July 1994. From November 1994 data are collected annually in July based on a full teaching year (1 August to 31 July).

Status: Ongoing
Collection Method: Administrative Records
Frequency: Annually
Reference Period: 1 full teaching year
Timeliness: 1 year
Earliest Available Data: 1994-95
National Coverage: England

Statistician
Caroline Kempner
Further Education Funding Council
Tel: 024 7686 3228

Products that contain data from this source
Staff Statistics 1994-95 and 1995-96: Further Education Colleges in England

---

Staffing Return
Scottish Executive

The Scottish Executive Education and Industry Department compile a survey on

Further Education staffing. All 43 SOEID- and 2 Local Authority-funded Further Education Colleges in Scotland take part in the survey which gives data on college academic staff.

Status: Ongoing
Collection Method: Administrative Records
Frequency: Annually
Reference Period: Academic Year
Timeliness: August/September (collection) - December (available)
Earliest Available Data: 1994-95
National Coverage: Scotland

Statistician
John Landrock
Scottish Executive
Education Statistics; Further Education
Tel: 0131 244 0324;
Email: John.Landrock@scotland.gov.uk

See also:
In this chapter:
Finance Statistics Record (incorporating Aggregate Staff Record) *(5.4)*
Further Education Bursary Statistics *(5.3)*
GNVQ database *(5.8)*

In other chapters:
British Social Attitudes Survey (BSA) Series *(see the Compendia and Reference chapter)*
Household Survey - Wales *(see the Housing chapter)*
Youth Cohort Study - England and Wales *(see the Labour Market chapter)*

5.5 Pre-School Provision

Facilities for the daycare and education of children and Support to the Families Survey (SWS FORM D1-C)
Scottish Executive; sponsored by Social Work Services Group Statistics Branch

The Scottish Executive carries out the Facilities for the Day Care and Education of Children and Support to the Families Survey, completed every three years. Data are collected on numbers of local authority and registered voluntary day nurseries, pre-school playgroups, registered childminders with numbers of places available, sources of funding, and number of children attending.

Status: Ongoing
Collection Method: Census
Frequency: Every 3 years
Reference Period: as at 17 November (week beginning)
Timeliness: Bulletin produced within 12 months of receipt of data.
Earliest Available Data: 1994
National Coverage: Scotland
Disaggregation: Council Area (Scot)

Statistician
Alan Fleming
Scottish Executive
Social Work Statistics
Tel: 0131 244 3745;
Email: alan.fleming@scotland.gov.uk

Products that contain data from this source
Statistical Bulletin No. SWK/DC1/1996
Statistical Information Note: Social Work
Daycare Services for Children in Scotland,
November 1997.

5.6 Schools

Children with Statements of Special Educational Need
Department for Education and Employment

The Department for Education and
Employment conducts a survey on children
with statements of special educational need.
Data are collected from all 109 local
education authorities in England. Data
covers the number of pupils for whom local
education authorities maintain a statement
and the number awaiting provision, the
number statemented for the first time, those
receiving provision and those awaiting
provision, the number assessed but not
issued with a statement, the number
transferred between mainstream and special
or independent schools and vice versa, and
the number of statements discontinued.

Status: Ongoing
Frequency: Annually
Earliest Available Data: 1984
National Coverage: England
Disaggregation: Local education authority level

Statistician
Stephen Cook
Department for Education and Employment
Analytical Services; Qualifications, Pupil
Assessment and International Division
Tel: 01325 392765

Products that contain data from this source
Statistics of Education: Schools in England

Children with Statements of Special Educational Need - Wales
National Assembly for Wales

An annual survey of all local education
authorities in Wales. Data collected on the
number of pupils for whom LEAs monitor
a statement, and the number for whom a
statement was made for the first time, both
by location (i.e. type of school); the number
assessed but not issued with a statement,
transfers between mainstream and special

or independent schools, and the number of
on-going assessments.

Status: Ongoing
Collection Method: Postal Survey - Census
Frequency: Annual
Reference Period: Census day
Earliest Available Data: 1992
National Coverage: Wales
Disaggregation: LEAs

Statistician
Howell Jones
Education and Training Statistics Unit
Statistical Directorate
National Assembly for Wales
Tel: 029 2082 5060;
Email: hywelm.jones@wales.gsi.gov.uk

Products that contain data from this source
Statistics of Education and Training in Wales:
Schools

Comparative tables of Primary School Performance
Department for Education and Employment;
sponsored by Local Education Authorities

Each Local Education Authority in England
publishes information about the
achievements of eleven-year-olds in the Key
Stage 2 National Curriculum assessment
tests, together with information on pupil
absence and certain background information.

Status: Ongoing
Frequency: Annually
Timeliness: 2 months
Earliest Available Data: 1996
National Coverage: England

Statistician
Catherine Blackham
Department for Education and Employment
QPAI 2; Analytical Services
Tel: 020 7273 4904;
Email: catherine.blackham@dfee.gov.uk

Examination Results - Wales
National Assembly for Wales

The National Assembly for Wales compiles
school and college performance
information. Data are collected from
examination results from all exam boards
in England and Wales by the Welsh Joint
Education Committee (WJEC). The WJEC
also matches the results from the different
boards to individual pupils, and provides the
National Assembly for Wales with summary
tables giving information at the school/
college level. Data are available for Wales
by county, age, gender, examination subject
and grade of results. Results are collected
annually in August and published four
months later.

Status: Ongoing
Collection Method: Comprehensive data
matching
Frequency: Annual
Reference Period: School year
Timeliness: Released in the following Autumn
Earliest Available Data: 1992
National Coverage: Wales
Disaggregation: LEA level

Statistician
Howell Jones
Education and Training Statistics Unit
Statistical Directorate
National Assembly for Wales
Tel: 029 2082 5060;
Email: hywelm.jones@wales.gsi.gov.uk

Products that contain data from this source
College Performance Information: Further
Education Institutions in Wales; Further and
Higher Education and Training Statistics in Wales;
School Performance Information; Statistics of
Education and Training in Wales: Schools

Examination Results of GCSE and GCE
Department for Education and Employment

An annual collection of GCSE/GNVQs and
GCE A/AS/AGNVQs examination results
derived directly from the examination
boards. Data are mainly used in the
compilation of the annual School and
College Performance Tables. They are
available by region, sex, subject entries,
modular subjects and grades. The data cover
England and are available at local education
authority and local education authority
regional level.

Status: Ongoing
Collection Method: Census
Frequency: Annually
Reference Period: The academic year
Timeliness: 2 weeks between the Department
receiving final data and it being released
Earliest Available Data: 1991-92
National Coverage: England
Disaggregation: Local Education Authority
(LEA)

Statistician
Catherine Blackham
Department for Education and Employment
QPAI 2; Analytical Services
Tel: 020 7273 4904;
Email: catherine.blackham@dfee.gov.uk

Products that contain data from this source
GCSE and GCE A/AS Examination Results;
School and College (16-18) Performance Tables

Exclusions Monitoring - Wales
National Assembly for Wales

This is a termly collection from local education authorities in Wales of the number of pupils permanently excluded from school, broken down by type of school

Status: Ongoing
Collection Method: Census
Frequency: Each school term
Reference Period: School term
Timeliness: The following school year
Earliest Available Data: 1995/96
National Coverage: Wales
Disaggregation: Local Education Authority (LEA)

Statistician
Howell Jones
Education and Training Statistics Unit
Statistical Directorate
National Assembly for Wales
Tel: 029 2082 5060;
Email: hywelm.jones@wales.gsi.gov.uk

Products that contain data from this source
Absenteeism, Truancy and Exclusions from Schools in Wales

Information Technology in Schools
Department for Education and Employment

The Department for Education and Employment conducts a survey on information technology in schools. It covers a sample of primary, secondary and special schools, approximately 1,700 in total. Data cover the number, ratios and type of computers and hardware, location and maintenance, expenditure and sources of funding, the use, contribution and support, staff training and use by pupils with special educational needs.

The survey covers England and commenced in 1985. It has been carried out every two years since 1988. Results are published about one year after the survey date.

Collection Method: Survey
Frequency: Every two years
Timeliness: About one year after survey date
Earliest Available Data: 1985
National Coverage: England

Statistician
Stephen Cook
Department for Education and Employment
Analytical Services; Qualifications, Pupil Assessment and International Division
Tel: 01325 392765

Products that contain data from this source
Survey of Information Technology in Schools (Press Notice)

National Curriculum Results for Eleven-Year-Olds
Department for Education and Employment

The Department for Education and Employment compiles data on the attainments of eleven year old pupils in England under the National Curriculum. Results are submitted by schools to the National Data Collection Agency who supply the Department with aggregated and pupil data. Data cover all maintained schools with pupils of the relevant age, and those independent schools who wish to make returns. Data are available on the attainment of eleven-year-old pupils in the Key Stage 2 National Curriculum tests and associated teacher assessment.

Status: Ongoing
Collection Method: Census
Frequency: Annually
Reference Period: May of each Academic Year
Timeliness: 4 months
Earliest Available Data: 1995
National Coverage: England
Disaggregation: Local Education Authority (LEA)

Statistician
Catherine Blackham
Department for Education and Employment
QPAI 2; Analytical Services
Tel: 020 7273 4904;
Email: catherine.blackham@dfee.gov.uk

Products that contain data from this source
Results of the National Curriculum Assessment of eleven-year-olds in England - Key Stage 2

National Curriculum Results for Eleven-year-olds - Wales
National Assembly for Wales

The National Assembly for Wales compiles data on the attainments in the core subjects (English, Mathematics, Science, and in Welsh speaking schools, Welsh) of 11 year old pupils in Wales, i.e. pupils at the end of Key Stage 2 of the National Curriculum. The External Marking Agency supplies aggregated school level results of both NC tests and teacher assessments to the National Assembly.

Status: Ongoing
Collection Method: Census
Frequency: Annual
Reference Period: May
Timeliness: Results are published in the Autumn
Earliest Available Data: 1995
National Coverage: Wales
Disaggregation: LEA

Statistician
Howell Jones
Education and Training Statistics Unit
Statistical Directorate
National Assembly for Wales
Tel: 029 2082 5060;
Email: hywelm.jones@wales.gsi.gov.uk

Products that contain data from this source
National Curriculum Assessment Results in Wales, Key Stage 2
Benchmark Information for Key Stage 2

National Curriculum Results for Fourteen-Year-Olds
Department for Education and Employment

The Department for Education and Employment compiles data on the attainments of fourteen-year-old pupils in England under the National Curriculum. Results are submitted by schools to the National Data Collection Agency who supply the Department with aggregated and pupil data. Data cover all maintained schools with pupils of the relevant age, and those independent schools who wish to make returns. Data are available on the attainment of fourteen-year-old pupils in Key stage 3 National Curriculum tests and associated teacher assessment.

Status: Ongoing
Collection Method: Census
Frequency: Annually
Reference Period: May of each Academic Year
Timeliness: 4 months
Earliest Available Data: 1995
National Coverage: England
Disaggregation: Local Education Authority (LEA)

Statistician
Catherine Blackham
Department for Education and Employment
QPAI 2; Analytical Services
Tel: 020 7273 4904;
Email: catherine.blackham@dfee.gov.uk

Products that contain data from this source
Results of the National Curriculum: Assessment of fourteen-year-olds in England - Key Stage 3

National Curriculum Results for Fourteen-year-olds - Wales
National Assembly for Wales

The National Assembly for Wales compiles data on the attainments in the core subjects (English, Mathematics, Science, and in Welsh speaking schools, Welsh) of 14 year old pupils in Wales, i.e. pupils at the end of Key Stage 3 of the National Curriculum. The External Marking Agency supplies aggregated school level results of both NC tests and teacher assessments to the National Assembly.

Status: Ongoing
Collection Method: Census
Frequency: Annual
Reference Period: May
Timeliness: Results are published in the Autumn
Earliest Available Data: 1995
National Coverage: Wales
Disaggregation: LEA

Sources and Analyses

Statistician
Howell Jones
Education and Training Statistics Unit
Statistical Directorate
National Assembly for Wales
Tel: 029 2082 5060;
Email: hywelm.jones@wales.gsi.gov.uk

Products that contain data from this source
National Curriculum Assessment Results in
Wales, Key Stage 3
Benchmark Information for Key Stage 3 and 4

National Curriculum Results for Seven-Year-Olds
Department for Education and Employment

The Department for Education and Employment conducts a survey on Key Stage 1 in the National Curriculum. Data compiles the attainment of seven-year-old pupils in England under the National Curriculum. Results are submitted by schools to the Local Education Authority who supply the Department with aggregated pupil data. Data cover all maintained primary schools, and those independent schools who wish to make returns.

Status: Ongoing
Collection Method: Census
Frequency: Annually
Reference Period: May of each Academic Year
Timeliness: 4 months
Earliest Available Data: 1995
National Coverage: England
Disaggregation: Local Education Authority (LEA)

Statistician
Catherine Blackham
Department for Education and Employment
QPAI 2; Analytical Services
Tel: 020 7273 4904;
Email: catherine.blackham@dfee.gov.uk

Products that contain data from this source
Results of the National Curriculum: Assessment
of seven-year-olds in England - Key Stage 1

National Curriculum Results for Seven-year-olds - Wales
National Assembly for Wales

The National Assembly for Wales compiles data on the attainments of 7 year old pupils in Wales' i.e. pupils at the end of Key Stage 1 of the National Curriculum, in the core subjects of English (in English speaking schools) on Welsh (in Welsh speaking schools), Mathematics and Science. Pupil level results are submitted by schools for processing to the LEA who supply the Assembly with school level data.

Status: Ongoing
Collection Method: Census
Frequency: Annual
Reference Period: May
Timeliness: Results are published in the Autumn
Earliest Available Data: 1995
National Coverage: Wales
Disaggregation: LEA

Statistician
Howell Jones
Education and Training Statistics Unit
Statistical Directorate
National Assembly for Wales
Tel: 029 2082 5060;
Email: hywelm.jones@wales.gsi.gov.uk

Products that contain data from this source
National Curriculum Assessment Results in
Wales, Key Stage 1
Benchmark Information for Key Stage 1

Placing Requests in Education Authority Schools
Scottish Executive

The data are compiled from a survey on placing requests in education authority schools. Data are available on the number, type and outcome of school placing requests made each year by parents. Data cover Scotland and are available at education authority level.

Status: Ongoing
Collection Method: Census
Frequency: Annually
Reference Period: Academic year
Timeliness: August (collection) - December (available)
Earliest Available Data: 1981-82
National Coverage: Scotland
Disaggregation: Local Authority

Statistician
Sheila Ward
Scottish Executive
Education Statistics; Schools
Tel: 0131 244 0323;
Email: sheila.ward@scotland.gov.uk

Products that contain data from this source
Placing Requests in Education Authority Schools
in Scotland: 1987-88 to 1997-98; Scottish
Abstract of Statistics

Pupil Attendance and Absence
Scottish Executive; sponsored by Scottish Education and Industry Department

The data are compiled from a survey on pupil attendance and absence collected from all 32 Scottish education authorities for the pupils in each of their 3,000 primary, secondary and special schools. Centres of pre-school education, residential schools and independent schools are outwith the scope of this survey.

Status: Ongoing
Collection Method: Census
Frequency: Annually
Reference Period: Academic Year
Timeliness: September (collection) - November (available)
Earliest Available Data: 1993-94
National Coverage: Scotland
Disaggregation: Local Authority

Statistician
Sheila Ward
Scottish Executive
Education Statistics; Schools
Tel: 0131 244 0323;
Email: sheila.ward@scotland.gov.uk

Products that contain data from this source
Attendance and Absence in Scottish Schools 1995
- 97 to 1997/98

Pupils Taking Meals In Education Authority Schools
Scottish Executive

The data are compiled from a census on school meals giving the uptake and the numbers of pupils entitled to free school meals.

Status: Ongoing
Collection Method: Census
Frequency: Annually
Reference Period: Academic year
Timeliness: January (collection) - May (available)
Earliest Available Data: 1971-72
National Coverage: Scotland
Disaggregation: Local Authority

Statistician
Sheila Ward
Scottish Executive
Education Statistics; Schools
Tel: 0131 244 0323;
Email: sheila.ward@scotland.gov.uk

Products that contain data from this source
School Meals In Education Authority Schools,
1996-97: News Release; Scottish Abstract of
Statistics

Qualifications - Scottish Certificate of Education
Scottish Executive; sponsored by Scottish Qualifications Authority

The Scottish Qualifications Authority an annual data set covering the presentations and awards for standard grade, Higher Grade and Certificate of Sixth Year Studies examinations, along with presentations for Short Courses. The data are used to generate the summary information required for Information for Parents, school Standard Tables, and for general analytical purposes. It is also matched to leavers data from the School Census to create a general analysis file of school leavers and their qualifications.

Two versions of the data are produced by the SQA. The first, pre-appeals version received in August is used in the Autumn collation of data for Information for Parents and in the detailed Standard Tables issued to schools and Education Authorities in September. In November, relevant summary figures are also passed back to schools for inclusion in school handbooks, and to Education Authorities for secondary school comparative tables.

Status: Ongoing
Frequency: Annually
Reference Period: Academic Year
Timeliness: Pre-Appeals: August (collection) - September (available); Post-Appeal: November (collection) - December (available)
Earliest Available Data: 1992-93 (first non-archived data set)
National Coverage: Scotland
Disaggregation: LA / Constituency

Statistician
Martin Boyle
Scottish Executive
Education Statistics; Qualifications and Lifelong Learning
Tel: 0131 244 0303;
Email: martin.boyle@scotland.gov.uk

Products that contain data from this source
Scottish School Leavers And Their Qualifications: 1986-87 To 1996-97

School Admission Appeals
Department for Education and Employment

The Department for Education and Employment conducts a survey on the number of appeals lodged by parents against non-admission to the school of their choice. Data are collected from 109 English local education authorities and all grant-maintained schools which would have dealt with their own appeals. Data cover the number of schools which had at least one appeal lodged, the total number of appeals lodged, those withdrawn by parents or settled to mutual satisfaction, the number heard by an appeals committee and the number decided in parents favour, rejected and not decided. The survey is carried out in November and refers to the academic year. Summary results are published about one year after the survey date.

Frequency: November of academic year
Reference Period: Academic year
Timeliness: Summary results are published about one year after the survey date
Earliest Available Data: 1989
National Coverage: England
Disaggregation: Local Education Authority

Statistician
Stephen Cook
Department for Education and Employment
Analytical Services; Qualifications, Pupil Assessment and International Division
Tel: 01325 392765

School Boards
Scottish Executive

The data are compiled from a survey on the status of school boards in each eligible Education Authority primary, secondary and special school, following the regular biennial round of parental elections.

Status: Ongoing
Collection Method: Administrative Records
Reference Period: Biennial elections
Timeliness: May (collection) - September (available)
Earliest Available Data: 1990
National Coverage: Scotland
Disaggregation: Local Authority

Statistician
Sheila Ward
Scottish Executive
Education Statistics; Schools
Tel: 0131 244 0323;
Email: sheila.ward@scotland.gov.uk

Products that contain data from this source
School Boards, May 1999: News Release; Scottish Abstract of Statistics

School Budgeted Running Costs
Scottish Executive

The data are compiled from a survey of all Scottish Education Authorities on the budgeted running costs of each of their 3,000 primary, secondary and special schools.

Status: Ongoing
Collection Method: Census
Frequency: Annually
Reference Period: Academic year
Timeliness: September (collection) - November (available)
Earliest Available Data: 1993-94
National Coverage: Scotland
Disaggregation: Local Authority

Statistician
Sheila Ward
Scottish Executive
Education Statistics; Schools
Tel: 0131 244 0323;
Email: Sheila.ward@scotland.gov.uk

Products that contain data from this source
Scottish Schools: Costs 1996-97 and 1998-99

School Census
Department of Education - Northern Ireland

Tabular information for all nursery and primary schools, and individual pupil-level information for all post-primary schools in N. Ireland, are collected annually in the School Census. In addition to providing a picture of the school population, and information on post-16 participation, the data are used to determine the funding of schools.

Status: Ongoing
Collection Method: Census
Frequency: Annually
Reference Period: Academic year
Timeliness: By spring of academic year to which it relates.
Earliest Available Data: 1986/87 (computerised)
National Coverage: Northern Ireland

Statistician
Ivor Johnston
Department of Education - Northern Ireland
Corporate Services; Statistics & Research
Tel: 028 9127 9677;
Email: ivor.johnston@deni.gov.uk

Products that contain data from this source
Northern Ireland Annual Abstract of Statistics; Participation in full-time Education by 16 and 17 year olds in Northern Ireland; Pupil:Teacher Ratios (PTRs) - Northern Ireland; Regional Trends; Compendium of Northern Ireland Education Statistics

School Census: School Pupil and Teacher Numbers
Scottish Executive

The data are collected as part of the School Census and provide information on pupil and teacher numbers at Education Authority level in Scotland, including information on pupils with special educational needs, class size information and of use classroom assistants. The School Census has been running for over 25 years. The date of the Census moved from January to September in session 1974-75. Collection of the more detailed information about schools and teachers moved from an annual to a biennial basis in session 1987-88. Provisional summary results are published two months after the census in November of each year. More comprehensive results are published in May of each year.

Status: Ongoing
Collection Method: Census
Frequency: Annually
Reference Period: Academic year
Timeliness: September (collection) - from November (available)
Earliest Available Data: 1992-93 (non-archival)
National Coverage: Scotland
Disaggregation: Local Authority

Statistician
Sheila Ward
Scottish Executive
Education Statistics; Schools
Tel: 0131 244 0323;
Email: sheila.ward@scotland.gov.uk

Products that contain data from this source
Education Statistics for the United Kingdom;
Regional Trends; Scottish Abstract of Statistics;
Social Trends; Summary Results of the 1997-98
School Census

School Census: Teachers Employed In Schools
Scottish Executive

Information relating to all teachers in
Education Authority, Grant-Aided and self-
governing independent schools, centres of
pre-school education in Scotland, including
information on teacher's modes of working,
qualifications and subjects taught.

Status: Ongoing
Collection Method: Census
Frequency: 1994-95, 1998-99
Reference Period: Academic year
Timeliness: September (collection) - June
(available).
Earliest Available Data: 1992-93
National Coverage: Scotland
Disaggregation: Local Authority

Statistician
Sheila Ward
Scottish Executive
Education Statistics; Schools
Tel: 0131 244 0323;
Email: sheila.ward@scotland.gov.uk

Products that contain data from this source
Education Statistics for the United Kingdom;
Regional Trends; Scottish Abstract of Statistics;
Social Trends

School Census: The School Curriculum in Publicly Funded Secondary Schools
Scottish Executive

Data are collected as part of the School
Census, providing information on the
number of pupils in each Education
Authority, Grant-Aided and self-governing
school in Scotland by stage, subject, course
and class arrangement. The School Census
has been running for over 25 years. The date
of the Census moved from January to
September in session 1974-75. Collection
of the more detailed information about
schools and teachers moved from an annual
to a biennial basis in session 1987-88.
Results are published about six months after
the end of the reference period.

Status: Ongoing
Collection Method: Census
Reference Period: The week during September
when the Census is carried out
Timeliness: September (collection) - March
(available)
Earliest Available Data: 1993-94
National Coverage: Scotland
Disaggregation: Local Authority

Statistician
Sheila Ward
Scottish Executive
Education Statistics; Schools
Tel: 0131 244 0323;
Email: sheila.ward@scotland.gov.uk

Products that contain data from this source
Education Statistics for the United Kingdom;
Regional Trends; Scottish Abstract of Statistics;
Social Trends

School Leaver Destinations
Scottish Executive; sponsored by Scottish
Education and Industry Department

Data are collected from Careers Service
Companies, Grant-Aided and Independent
Schools about the destinations of pupils who
left school in the previous session. The
information becomes available at mid-
October following the end of the school
session. Careers Service Companies provide
information in respect of each Education
Authority school in their area. In November,
relevant summary figures are passed back
to schools for inclusion in school
handbooks, and to Education Authorities for
secondary school comparative tables.

Status: Ongoing
Collection Method: Administrative Records
Frequency: Annually
Reference Period: End of Academic Year
Timeliness: October (collection) - November
(available)
Earliest Available Data: 1992-93 (first non-
archival data)
National Coverage: Scotland
Disaggregation: Local Authority

Statistician
Martin Boyle
Scottish Executive
Education Statistics; Qualifications and Lifelong
Learning
Tel: 0131 244 0303;
Email: martin.boyle@scotland.gov.uk

Products that contain data from this source
Leaver Destinations From Scottish Secondary
Schools 1994/95 To 1996/97

School Leavers - Scotland
Scottish Executive

The data is compiled from a survey of school
leavers allowing analysis on staying-on-
rates and school leaver qualifications.
Data are collected every January/September
and preliminary survey results are available
about six months following the collection
period. The data are used to monitor trends
in staying on rates and the profile of leaver
cohorts. The information is also matched to
SQA data sets to generate an analysis file of
school leavers by qualifications held; this
in turn is used to monitor trends in school
leaver's qualifications and for incorporating
into projections of potential entrants into
Higher Education.

Status: Ongoing
Collection Method: Census
Frequency: Bi-annually
Reference Period: Term of Leaving
Timeliness: January (collection) - June (available)
September (collection) - January (available)
Earliest Available Data: 1992-93 (non-archival)
National Coverage: Scotland
Disaggregation: Local Authority

Statistician
Sheila Ward
Scottish Executive
Education Statistics; Schools
Tel: 0131 244 0323;
Email: sheila.ward@scotland.gov.uk

Products that contain data from this source
Scottish School Leavers And Their Qualifications:
1986-87 To 1996-97

School Leavers - Wales
National Assembly for Wales

The National Assembly for Wales compiles
data on the intended destinations of pupils.
The returns are completed in the autumn
term, by headteachers of all schools with
pupils of secondary school age. Data are
available on the intended destinations and
qualifications of school leavers. Data are
available for Wales and at county level. The
survey began in September 1992. Previously
similar data was available from School
Examination Survey, carried out in England
and Wales from about 1966. Data are
collected annually and published six months
to a year after collection.

Status: Ceased, last held in 1996
Collection Method: Postal Census
Frequency: Annual
Reference Period: End of school year
Timeliness: 18 months
Earliest Available Data: 1992
National Coverage: Wales
Disaggregation: LEA

Statistician
Howell Jones
Education and Training Statistics Unit
Statistical Directorate
National Assembly for Wales
Tel: 029 2082 5060;
Email: hywelm.jones@wales.gsi.gov.uk

Products that contain data from this source
Statistics of Education and Training in Wales:
Schools

School Leavers' Survey
Department of Education - Northern
Ireland

The Department of Education, Northern
Ireland conducts the School Leavers' Survey
on all school leavers each year. Data are
collected on the qualifications, destinations
of leavers, sex, date of birth, whether entitled
to free school meals, whether holding a
statement of special need, and year group.
The survey enables relationships between
variables to be explored. Results are
reported in a statistical press release. The
survey was carried out every two years from
1979-80 to 1985-86 and annually thereafter.

Status: Ongoing
Collection Method: Census
Frequency: Annually
Reference Period: Academic Year
Timeliness: Around April of academic year after
the one to which it relates.
Earliest Available Data: 1983/84
National Coverage: Northern Ireland

Statistician
Gillian Graham
Department of Education - Northern Ireland
Corporate Services; Statistics & Research
Tel: 028 9127 9379;
Email: gillian.graham@.deni.gov.uk

Products that contain data from this source
Northern Ireland Annual Abstract of Statistics;
Qualifications and destinations of Northern
Ireland school leavers; Compendium of Northern
Ireland Education Statistics

School Performance
Information: Absence
Department for Education and Employment

The Department for Education and
Employment conducts a survey on the
authorised and unauthorised absence in
schools. It is a census of all schools in
England with day pupils of compulsory
school age. Data cover the number of pupils
on roll for at least one session during the
period, the number of pupil sessions, the
number of school sessions missed through
authorised and unauthorised absence and the
number of pupils with at least one authorised/
unauthorised absence. The survey is carried

out each academic year and results are
published about six months after the survey
date.

Collection Method: Survey
Frequency: Each academic year
Timeliness: About six months
Earliest Available Data: 1993
National Coverage: England
Disaggregation: Local Education Authority

Statistician
Stephen Cook
Department for Education and Employment
Analytical Services; Qualifications, Pupil
Assessment and International Division
Tel: 01325 392765

Products that contain data from this source
Secondary School Performance Tables

School Performance
Information: Absence - Wales
National Assembly for Wales

The National Assembly for Wales conducts
a survey on the authorised and unauthorised
absence in schools. It is a census of all schools
in Wales with day pupils of compulsory
school age. Data cover the number of pupil
sessions and the number of school sessions
missed through authorised and unauthorised
absence. The survey is carried out each
academic year and results are published about
six months after the survey date.

Status: Ongoing
Collection Method: Census
Frequency: Annual
Reference Period: School year until Summer
half term
Timeliness: Results available in the following
Autumn
Earliest Available Data: 1993
National Coverage: Wales:
Disaggregation: Local Education Authority

Statistician
Howell Jones
Education and Training Statistics Unit
Statistical Directorate
National Assembly for Wales
Tel: 029 2082 5060;
Email: hywelm.jones@wales.gsi.gov.uk

Products that contain data from this source
Secondary School Performance Tables

School Performance Survey -
Northern Ireland
Department of Education - Northern
Ireland

The Department of Education Northern
Ireland conducts the School Performance
Survey each year, for publication of the
School Performance Tables, which cover all
post-primary schools. Data are collected on

all Year 12, 13 and 14 pupils taking GCSEs,
vocational examinations, AS levels, A levels
and GNVQs. Data are available by number
of pupils in a year, proportion taking exams,
proportion achieving and not achieving
qualifications and school attendance rates.
First run in 1991/92. The sex of pupils has
only been collected since 1995/96. 1991/92
data do not include GNVQ results, and at
A-level only show attainment of 1+A-E.
GNVQ Part 1 results contribute for the first
time in 1996/97, but are subsumed within
the GCSE results.

Status: Ongoing
Collection Method: Census
Frequency: Annually
Reference Period: Academic year
Timeliness: Jan. following academic year to
which it relates.
Earliest Available Data: 1991/92
National Coverage: Northern Ireland

Statistician
Gillian Graham
Department of Education - Northern Ireland
Corporate Services; Statistics & Research
Tel: 028 9127 9379;
Email: gillian.graham@.deni.gov.uk

Products that contain data from this source
Regional Trends; School Performance
Information

School Transport
Scottish Executive; sponsored by Scottish
Education and Industry Department

Information on the number of pupils awarded
free school transport, the number of free pupil
journeys by method of transport and the
criteria used to determine the free transport.

Status: Ongoing
Collection Method: Census
Frequency: Annually
Reference Period: Academic year
Timeliness: September (collection) - February
(available)
Earliest Available Data: 1992-93 (non-archival)
National Coverage: Scotland
Disaggregation: Local Authority

Statistician
Sheila Ward
Scottish Executive
Education Statistics; Schools
Tel: 0131 244 0323;
Email: sheila.ward@scotland.gov.uk

Products that contain data from this source
School Transport, 1997-98: News Release:

School-Business Links
Department for Education and Employment

The Department for Education and
Employment conducts a survey on school-

Sources and Analyses

business links. It covers nearly 900 primary schools and 600 secondary schools. Data cover the type and extent of links schools have with local businesses, including pupils' and teachers' involvement, work experience and other business links. Results are published early in the next calendar year following the academic year of the survey.

Collection Method: Survey
Frequency: Every three years
Timeliness: Early in calendar year following the academic year in question
Earliest Available Data: 1987
National Coverage: England
Disaggregation: Local Education Authority

Statistician
Stephen Cook
Department for Education and Employment
Analytical Services; Qualifications, Pupil Assessment and International Division
Tel: 01325 392765

Schools' Census - England
Department for Education and Employment

The Department for Education and Employment (DfEE) conducts the Schools' Census covering all schools, including maintained (and grant-maintained) nursery, primary, secondary and special schools, non-maintained special schools, Pupil Referral Units and independent schools (including CTCs). Data are collected on pupils (full-time and part-time) by age and sex, number of pupils with special educational needs, number of pupils in nursery classes in primary schools, admissions, teachers, non-teaching staff, classes, lesson time, courses of study of pupils aged 16 and over, school meals and the number of boarding pupils.

Frequency: Annually
National Coverage: England
Disaggregation: Regional and Local Educational Authority

Statistician
Stephen Cook
Department for Education and Employment
Analytical Services; Qualifications, Pupil Assessment and International Division
Tel: 01325 392765

Products that contain data from this source
Education Statistics for the United Kingdom; Facts and Figures; Regional Trends; Social Trends; Statistics of Education: Schools in England; Statistics of Schools in England (Press Notice)

Schools' Census - Wales
National Assembly for Wales

The National Assembly for Wales conducts an annual Schools' Census. The returns are completed by the head teachers of all independent and maintained nursery, primary, secondary, special schools and pupil referral units in Wales. Data are available on pupil and teacher numbers, use of the Welsh language in schools and pupils' ability to speak Welsh (in primary schools), free milk and meals, numbers of pupils with special educational needs and the courses of study of pupils aged 16 and over. The Schools' Census return was previously completed both in the first and second term of the school year. Since 1992-93, a collection has only been made in the second term (January). From 1995 independent schools in Wales have been included in this Census. Data are collected each academic year and published about six months after the end of the reference period.

Status: Ongoing
Collection Method: Census
Frequency: Annual
Reference Period: 2nd Tuesday in January
Timeliness: Min. 5 months
Earliest Available Data: 1976
National Coverage: Wales
Disaggregation: Local authorities

Statistician
Howell Jones
Education and Training Statistics Unit
Statistical Directorate
National Assembly for Wales
Tel: 029 2082 5060;
Email: hywelm.jones@wales.gsi.gov.uk

Products that contain data from this source
Statistics of Education and Training in Wales: Schools
Class sizes in Primary Schools

Violence Against School Staff
Scottish Executive

This new survey was introduced during the summer of 1998, collecting summary information from education authorities on incidents of violence against school staff.

Status: Ongoing
Collection Method: Administrative Records
Frequency: Annually
Reference Period: Academic year
Timeliness: September (collection) - January (available).
Earliest Available Data: 1997-98
National Coverage: Scotland

Statistician
Sheila Ward
Scottish Executive
Education Statistics; Schools
Tel: 0131 244 0323;
Email: sheila.ward@scotland.gov.uk

See also:
In this chapter:
GNVQ database *(5.8)*
National Information System for Vocational

Qualifications (NISVQ) *(5.8)*
School Census *(5.6)*

In other chapters:
Labour Force Survey *(see the Labour Market chapter)*
Youth Cohort Study - England and Wales *(see the Labour Market chapter)*

5.7 Teacher Training / Newly Trained Teachers

Higher Education Statistics Agency: Trainee Teacher Supplement
The Scottish Executive; sponsored by Higher Education Statistics Agency (HESA)

To collect information about students studying teacher training courses at Higher Education Institutions in the UK.

Status: Ongoing
Collection Method: Administrative Records
Frequency: Bi-annually
Reference Period: Academic year
Timeliness: Available from the end of July in the year following November/March collection.
National Coverage: Scotland (part of the UK collection by HESA)

Statistician
Wilma Schofield
The Scottish Executive
Education Statistics; Further and Higher Education Statistics
Tel: 0131 244 0297;
Email: wilma.schofield@scotland.gov.uk

Please see:
In this chapter:
HESA student database *(5.4)*

5.8 Training, Qualifications & National Record of Achievement

1998 Value Added Pilot Matched Key Stage 3 - GCSE/GNVQ Data Sets
Department for Education and Employment

The Department for Education and Employment conducted a pilot project in 1998 to measure the progress schools made between Key stage 3 and GCSE/GNVQ in 1998 on the basis of individual pupils' performance.

205 volunteer secondary schools took part in the pilot, covering nearly 30,000 pupils. The pilot covered England only.

Sources and Analyses

The data was used to publish a value added pilot publication, showing various value-added measures (by gender, different Key Stage 3 starting points etc.) . The data were collected via administrative sources, and schools were given the opportunity to check and amend their data.

Data is available by gender and by region.

Status: Ongoing
Frequency: Annually
Timeliness: 2 months
Earliest Available Data: 1996
National Coverage: England

Statistician
Bridgette Frost
Department for Education and Employment
Level 5C
Caxton House
Tothill Street
London SW1H 9NA
Tel: 020 7273 5498; Fax: 020 7273 5999;
Email: bridgette.frost@dfee.gov.uk

Products that contain data from this analysis
1998 Value Added pilot: Supplement to the Secondary School Performance Tables; GCSE and GCE A/AS Examination results

Continuing Vocational Survey in Enterprises
Department for Education and Employment; sponsored by EC - Eurostat

Measures volumes and costs of training courses provided by non-Governmental employers to employees other than apprentices and recognised trainees in all EC member states. CVTS was part of the action programme for developing continuing vocational training in the EC based on Council Decision 90.267/eec in May 1990. To date there has been only one data collection exercise.

Status: Ceased temporarily
Frequency: Ad hoc
Reference Period: 1993
Timeliness: 2 years
Earliest Available Data: 1994
National Coverage: United Kingdom
Disaggregation: No disaggregation below member state level.

Statistician
Phil Rose
Department for Education and Employment
Employability and Adult Learning; EAL6
Tel: 0114 259 3154;
Email: p.rose@dfee.gov.uk

Products that contain data from this analysis
Employer Provided Training in the United Kingdom - 1993

Continuing Vocational Training Survey
Department for Education and Employment

The Department for Education and Employment is responsible for the European Community Continuing Vocational Training Survey in the UK which covers enterprises with ten or more employees in the private sector (i.e. manufacturing, energy and water supply, construction, banking, finance and insurance, transport and communication and distribution, hotels and catering).
A follow-up survey, CVTS2, will take place in 2000. The CVTS2 project aims to collect similar data as before but will cover most EC member states. Data are collected about the industry and size of establishments, their participation in on or off-the-job training, the costs of training, existence of training plans and training budgets, and the reasons why establishments had not trained any of their staff. The survey was designed to measure the volumes and costs of training courses provided by non-Governmental employers to employees other than apprentices and recognised trainees. The Employee Training Survey in the United Kingdom is an extension of the European Community Training Survey. Data are collected on initial training, in addition to continuing training, and also include more industrial sectors except agriculture, forestry and fishing, the armed forces, households employing domestic staff, and extra-territorial bodies. The survey is carried out on an ad hoc basis and the fieldwork was last conducted in late 1994 and early 1995. The Training in Britain Survey of 1986-87 collected similar data as the extension survey. Results for the extended survey was published in Sept 1996. The title of the publication is "Employer Provided Training in the UK 1993". The design of the study was driven by Eurostat requirements. It was similar to the Training in Britain Survey conducted by the Department in 1987.

Status: Ceased temporarily
Collection Method: Large-scale (Sample) Survey
Frequency: Ad hoc
Reference Period: October - December 1994
Timeliness: Because of links to the wider European study, publication was delayed by two and a half years.
Earliest Available Data: 1993
National Coverage: United Kingdom
Disaggregation: No disaggregation below UK level is possible

Statistician
Phil Rose
Department for Education and Employment
Employability and Adult Learning; EAL6
Tel: 0114 259 3154;
Email: p.rose@dfee.gov.uk

Products that contain data from this source
Employer Provided Training in the United Kingdom - 1993

GNVQ database
Department of Education - Northern Ireland

The Database is collated by Bath University and covers all GNVQs registered at institutions in N. Ireland. It is updated twice each year, and is the only comprehensive source on GNVQ attainment.

Status: Ongoing
Collection Method: Census
Reference Period: 4-monthly periods
Timeliness: Within 3 months of end of academic year.
Earliest Available Data: 1993
National Coverage: Northern Ireland

Statistician
Gillian Graham
Department of Education - Northern Ireland
Corporate Services; Statistics & Research
Tel: 028 9127 9379;
Email: gillian.graham@.deni.gov.uk

Products that contain data from this source
Achievement of General National Vocational Qualifications (GNVQs) in Northern Ireland

GNVQ Student Database
The Department for Education and Employment, the Welsh Office Education Department and the Department of Education Northern Ireland

The GNVQ Student Database supplies comprehensive information on individual student registrations and achievements on GNVQ courses in schools and colleges in England. The database is cumulative, with six monthly additions provided by the three Vocational Awarding Bodies (EdExcel, AQA and OCR).

The database provides information on achievement rates and achievement times for GNVQs and progression rates from one GNVQ level to the next.

Status: Cumulative, with six-monthly updates
Collection Method: Data is collected by the three Vocational Awarding Bodies who submit data twice a year to the contractor. Data is collected from all schools and colleges where students take GNVQs and is a census of all such qualifications.
Frequency: Database updated twice a year
Reference Period: 1992/3 - present
Timeliness: GNVQ data is available on the database around three months after the Awarding Bodies submit the data to the contractor
Earliest Available Data: 1992/93 academic year (pilot basis for GNVQs)
National Coverage: England
Disaggregation: Analyses could be carried out by Local Education Authority or by Government Office Region

Statistician
Mahmoud Rollings-Kamara
Level 5C
Caxton House
Tothill Street
London SW1H 9NA
Tel: 020 7273 5098; Fax: 020 7273 5999;
Email: mahmood.rollings-kamara@dfee.gov.uk

Products that contain data from this source
1998 Value Added pilot: Supplement to the
Secondary School Performance Tables; GCSE
and GCE A/AS Examination Results

Matched Key Stage 3 - GCSE/ GNVQ datasets for all schools in England (1998)
Department for Education and Employment

The Department for Education and
Employment conducted a feasibility study in
1998 to measure the progress schools made
between Key Stage 3 and GCSE/GNVQ in
1998 on the basis of individual pupils'
performance. The data includes information
on all schools in England. The data was used
to investigate the accuracy and timing of
producing matched data for use in the
Secondary Performance Tables. The data was
collected via administrative sources, and has
not been checked by schools.

Data is available by gender and region.

Status: One off study, but similar data will be
used in the future to provide value added
information for School Performance Tables
Collection Method: Census
Frequency: One off
Reference Period: GCSE/GNVQ and Key Stage
3 results (retrospective) for pupils aged 15 who
were on roll at the time of the 1998 Schools
Census
Timeliness: The database was finalised
approximately five months after the GCSE results
were released.
Earliest Available Data: 1998
National Coverage: England
Disaggregation: Government Office Region,
Local Education Authority

Statistician
Bridgette Frost
Department for Education and Employment
Level 5C
Caxton House
Tothill Street
London SW1H 9NA
Tel:020 7273 5498; Fax: 020 7273 5999;
Email: bridgette.frost@dfee.gov.uk

Products that contain data from this source
1998 Value Added pilot: Supplement to the
Secondary School Performance Tables; GCSE
and GCE A/AS Examination results

Modern Apprenticeship Starters and Leavers Database
Department for Education and Employment

Status: Ongoing
Collection Method: Returns from TEC
Frequency: Monthly
Earliest Available Data: 1995 - 96
National Coverage: England and Wales
Disaggregation: Regional and TEC level

Statistician
John Kerr
Department for Education and Employment
Tel: 0114 275 3482;
Email: john.kerr@dfee.gov.uk

Modern Apprenticeships Follow-up Survey - England & Wales
Department for Education and Employment

The Department for Education and
Employment conducts the Follow-up
Survey. Questionnaires are sent to trainees
with a mailable address 6 months after they
have left their apprenticeship. The Survey
covers labour market destinations after
leaving, information on qualifications (those
held before training, those aimed for and
those achieved), and attitudinal questions
which assesses the trainee's time on their
apprenticeship.

Collection Method: Questionnaires
Frequency: Monthly
Reference Period: The data collected relates
to the situation of trainees some six months after
they have left their apprenticeship.
Timeliness: There is a three month interval
between the start of data collection, for each
monthly cohort of leavers, and the release of data.
Earliest Available Data: 1995-96
National Coverage: England and Wales
Disaggregation: Regional and TEC level.

Statistician
John Kerr
Department for Education and Employment
Tel: 0114 275 3482;
Email: john.kerr@dfee.gov.uk

National Information System for Vocational Qualifications (NISVQ)
Department for Education and Employment

The purpose of NISVQ is to monitor the
awards of vocational qualifications made in
each academic year in the UK. NISVQ records
the awards of vocational qualifications by four
of the largest awarding bodies: EdExcel, City
and Guilds, RSA and SQA. It covers NVQ/
SVQs, GNVQ/GSVQs and Other Vocational
Qualifications with a notional level of NVQ
level 1 or above. It also holds information on
candidate age and gender, administering centre
type and location, and subject and occupational
areas of each award.

Status: Ongoing
Collection Method: Administrative Records
Frequency: Quarterly
Reference Period: Quarters ending in
December, March, June and September
Timeliness: Provisional results are available for
internal use in March of the following academic
year. Final results are published in May/June of
the following academic year.
Earliest Available Data: 1991/92
National Coverage: United Kingdom
Disaggregation: Training and Enterprise Council
(TEC) Area (E&W); Standard Statistical Region
(SSR); Training and Enterprise Council (TEC) Area;
Local Enterprise Company (LEC) Area; Local
Education Authority (LEA)

Statistician
Alison Neave
Department for Education and Employment
Qualifications, Pupil Assessment and International
Division
Tel: 0114 259 4979;
Email: alison.neave@dfee.gov.uk

Products that contain data from this source
Labour Market Trends; Vocational Qualifications
in the UK 1996/97

National Traineeships Starters and Leavers Database - England & Wales
Department for Education and Employment

Status: Ongoing
Collection Method: Returns from TEC.
Frequency: Monthly
Earliest Available Data: 1997 - 98
National Coverage: England and Wales
Sub-National: Regional and TEC level.

Statistician
John Kerr
Department for Education and Employment
Tel: 0114 275 3482;
Email: john.kerr@dfee.gov.uk

Qualifications - National Certificate Modules and Group Awards
Scottish Executive

The Scottish Qualifications Authority provide
the Branch with an annual data set covering
individual student uptake and achievement
of National Certificate modules and Group
Awards. The data are used to generate the
summary information required for
Information for Parents, school Standard
Tables, and for general analysis purposes.

Two versions of the data are produced by
the SQA. The first, provisional version of
the file received in July contains all the
relevant data processed at that point.
Information from the provisional file is used
in the autumn collation of data for
Information for Parents and in the detailed
Standard Tables issued to schools and

Education Authorities in September. In November, relevant summary figures are also passed back to schools for inclusion in school handbooks, and to Education Authorities for secondary school comparative tables.

Status: Ongoing
Collection Method: Cohort, Panel or Longitudinal Study
Frequency: Annually
Reference Period: Academic Year
Timeliness: Provisional: July (collection) - August (available); Final: January (collection) - March (available)
Earliest Available Data: 1994-95
National Coverage: Scotland
Disaggregation: Local Authority

Statistician
Martin Boyle
Scottish Executive
Education Statistics; Qualifications and Lifelong Learning
Tel: 0131 244 0303;
Email: martin.boyle@scotland.gov.uk

Skill Needs in Britain
Department for Education and Employment

The Department for Education and Employment is responsible for the Skill Needs in Britain survey. This is a sample survey conducted by IFF Research Ltd of establishments with more than 24 employees in all sectors except agriculture, forestry and fishing. Data are collected on employers' recruitment difficulties (numbers of hard-to-fill vacancies), amount of training funded by employers and information from employers on a number of training issues, e.g. their awareness of training initiatives and skill shortages. Longitudinal data are available from 1990. The survey covers Great Britain and data are available at TEED Regional level. Data have been collected annually since 1989-90 normally between April and July. Results are published by October of the survey year and data are available at Government Office level.

Status: Discontinued
Collection Method: Large-scale (Sample) Survey
Frequency: Annually
Reference Period: Fieldwork May/June
Timeliness: 2-3 months
Earliest Available Data: 1990
National Coverage: United Kingdom
Disaggregation: Government Office Region (GOR)

Statistician
Phil Rose
Department for Education and Employment
Employability and Adult Learning; EAL6
Tel: 0114 259 3154;
Email: p.rose@dfee.gov.uk

Products that contain data from this source
Labour Market Trends; Skills Needs in Great Britain and Northern Ireland 1998; Skills Needs of Small Firms in Britain 1994-1995

Skill Needs of Small Firms in Britain Survey
Department for Education and Employment

The Department for Education and Employment is responsible for the Skill Needs of Small Firms in Britain survey carried out by Public Attitude Surveys Ltd on a sample of establishments with fewer than 25 employees in all sectors (except agriculture, forestry and fishing). Data are collected on employers' recruitment difficulties (numbers of hard-to-fill vacancies), training funded by employers and information from employers on a number of training issues, e.g. their awareness of training initiatives. The survey covers Great Britain and data are available at TEED Regional level. It was first conducted in July and August 1992 and then again from December 1994 to January 1995. First study carried out in 1992. Second study in 1994/5.

Status: Ceased temporarily
Collection Method: Large-scale (Sample) Survey
Frequency: Periodic
Reference Period: December 1994 - January 1995
Timeliness: 2-3 months
Earliest Available Data: 1992
National Coverage: Great Britain
Disaggregation: Government Office Region (GOR)

Statistician
Phil Rose
Department for Education and Employment
Employability and Adult Learning; EAL6
Tel: 0114 259 3154;
Email: p.rose@dfee.gov.uk

Training and Education - Wales
National Assembly for Wales

The National Assembly for Wales compiles a survey on training and education. The survey is carried out as a supplementary sample to the Labour Force Survey. 1,000 individuals are interviewed in each of the seven Training and Education Council (TEC) areas in Wales. It covers training received by individuals, employment status, qualifications and the industry worked in. The main purpose of the survey is to assess the achievement against the National Targets for Education and Training at TEC level.

Reference Period: December 1994 to February 1995
National Coverage: Wales
Sub-National: TEC area level

Statistician
Nick Palmer
National Assembly for Wales
Tel: 029 2082 5868

Products that contain data from this source
1992 Welsh Social Survey: Report on training and education; Welsh Training and Education Survey

Welsh Employer Survey
National Assembly for Wales

The National Assembly for Wales compiles a survey on employer recruitment experiences, training practices and involvement in business development initiatives. It is a telephone survey of 3,000 employer establishments in Wales with two or more people, in all industries except agriculture. Data are available by industrial sector, size and Training and Enterprise Council (TEC) area.

Earliest Available Data: Mid 1980's
National Coverage: Wales

Statistician
Nick Palmer
National Assembly for Wales
Tel: 029 2082 5868

Products that contain data from this source
Welsh Employer Survey

Work-based Training for Adults Follow-up Survey - England and Wales
Department for Education and Employment

The Department for Education and Employment conducts the Follow-up Survey. Questionnaires are sent to trainees with a mailable address 6 months after they left Work-based Training for Adults. The Survey covers labour market destinations after leaving, information on qualifications, and attitudinal questions which assesses the trainee's time on their placement.

Status: Ongoing
Collection Method: Questionnaires
Frequency: Monthly
Reference Period: The data collected relates to the situation of trainees some six months after they have left training.
Timeliness: There is a three month interval between the start of data collection, for each monthly cohort of leavers, and the release of data.
Earliest Available Data: 1988-89
National Coverage: England and Wales
Disaggregation: Regional and TEC

Statistician
John Kerr
Department for Education and Employment
Tel: 0114 275 3482;
Email: john.kerr@dfee.gov.uk

Work-based Training for Adults Starters and Leavers Database - England
Department for Education and Employment

Status: Ongoing
Collection Method: Returns from TECs
Frequency: Monthly
Earliest Available Data: 1988 - 89.
National Coverage: England and Wales
Disaggregation: Regional and TEC.

Statistician
John Kerr
Department for Education and Employment
Tel: 0114 275 3482;
Email: john.kerr@dfee.gov.uk

Work-Related Government Supported Training
Department for Education and Employment

An analysis of Work-Related Government Supported Training. It provides statistics on participation, outcomes, and characteristics of trainees on government supported training. Data is taken from National Trainee Database, TEC Management Information, National Assembly for Wales and Scottish Executive.

Status: Ongoing
Frequency: Quarterly
Earliest Available Data: June 1991
National Coverage: Great Britain
Disaggregation: Government Office Region (GOR); Training and Enterprise Council (TEC) Area (E&W)

Statistician
John Fletcher
Department for Education and Employment
Analytical Services; AS: Employability and Adult Learning
Tel: 0114 259 4317

Products that contain data from this analysis
Government Supported Training - England and Wales

Youth Training Follow-up Survey
Department for Education and Employment

The Department for Education and Employment conducts the Youth Training Follow-up Survey on everybody who leaves the Youth Training programmes. The Survey covers labour market destinations after leaving, information on qualifications (those held before training, those aimed for and

those achieved), and attitudinal questions which assess the trainee's time on their placement.

National Coverage: England & Wales
Disaggregation: TECs, Government Office Regions, England, Wales

Statistician
John Kerr
Department for Education and Employment
Tel: 0114 275 3482;
Email: john.kerr@dfee.gov.uk

Products that contain data from this source
Labour Market Trends

Youth Training Follow-up Survey - England and Wales
Department for Education and Employment

The Department for Education and Employment conducts the Follow-up Survey. Questionnaires are sent to trainees with a mailable address 6 months after they have left Youth Training. The Survey covers labour market destinations after leaving, information on qualifications, and attitudinal questions which assesses the trainee's time on their placement. Data cover England and Wales and are available for TECs in England and Wales, Government Office regions, England, Wales.

Status: Ongoing
Collection Method: Questionnaires.
Frequency: Monthly
Reference Period: The data collected relates to the situation of trainees some six months after they have left training.
Timeliness: There is a three month interval between the start of data collection, for each monthly cohort of leavers, and the release of data.
Earliest Available Data: 1988-89
National Coverage: England and Wales, England, Wales
Disaggregation: TECs, Government Office Regions

Statistician
John Kerr
Department for Education and Employment
Tel: 0114 275 3482;
Email: john.kerr@dfee.gov.uk

Youth Training Starters and Leavers Database - England & Wales
Department for Education and Employment

Status: Ongoing
Collection Method: Returns from TECs.
Frequency: Monthly
Earliest Available Data: 1988-89
National Coverage: England and Wales
Disaggregation: Regional and TEC.

Statistician
John Kerr
Department for Education and Employment
Tel: 0114 275 3482;
Email: john.kerr@dfee.gov.uk

Youth Training Statistics
Department for Education and Employment

The Department for Education and Employment compiles data on the number of starts and participants in Youth Training collected from Training and Enterprise Councils. The series is a count of young people on government training programmes. The data cover England and are available for Training Enterprise Councils in England and Government Office regions.

Earliest Available Data: 1992-93
National Coverage: England

Statistician
John Kerr
Department for Education and Employment
Tel: 0114 275 3482;
Email: john.kerr@dfee.gov.uk

Products that contain data from this source
Labour Market Trends

See also:
In this chapter
Continuing Vocational Training Survey *(5.8)*
Skill Needs in Britain *(5.8)*
Skill Needs of Small Firms in Britain Survey *(5.8)*

In other chapters:
Household Survey - Wales *(see the Housing chapter)*
Labour Force Survey *(see the Labour Market chapter)*
Youth Cohort Study - England and Wales *(see the Labour Market chapter)*

Education and Training - *Products*

5.9 Education - General

Compendium of Northern Ireland Education Statistics
Department of Education Northern Ireland

Data card summarising a wide range of education statistics covering 13 years.

Delivery: Periodic release
Frequency: Annually
Price: Free

Available from
Department of Education Northern Ireland,
Statistics and Research Branch
Please see Annex B for full address details.

Sources from which data for this product are obtained
School Census - Northern Ireland; Further Education Statistical Record - Northern Ireland; School Leavers' Survey; HESA student database; HESA staff database.

Department for Education and Employment Annual Report
Department for Education and Employment

DfEE and OFSTED expenditure plans. Includes an overview of recent achievements and major plans, followed by details of progress towards targets and planned activity by Departmental Objective. Annexes cover the Department's cash plans, LEA expenditure and other information such as participation rates in education. Cash plans give information for five historical years, current year and planned year(s). 1998 report shows only one forward year because of CSR. Primarily of use internally and to education researchers. Text on Department's spending plans and tables with historical and planned figures.

Delivery: Periodic Release
Frequency: Annually
Price: £18.35
ISBN: 0-10-139102-1

Available from
Ranjan Gupta
Room 5B
Department for Education and Employment
Sanctuary Buildings
Great Smith Street
London SW1P 3BT
Tel: 020 7925 6189

Education Across the European Union, Statistics and Indicators, 1998 Edition
Eurostat

This document provides comparable statistics for the 17 countries (the fifteen Member States of the European Union plus Iceland and Norway)

Delivery: Periodic Release
Frequency: Annually
Price: £13.75
ISBN: 92 828 6323 9

Available from
TSO Publications Centre and Bookshops
Please see Annex B for full address details.

Sources from which data for this product are obtained
UNESCO, OECD, Eurostat, Labour Force Survey, the Eurostat demographic database and the European Education Information Network (EURYDICE)

Education and Training Expenditure since 1989-90
Department for Education and Employment

Detailed time series of education and training expenditure from 1989 - 90 up to the latest available year, along with supplementary analyses. Description: Contains data on total expenditure, central government expenditure, local government expenditure, unit public funding per full-time equivalent pupil/student, expenditure on education and training initiatives, distribution of expenditure in schools.

Delivery: Periodic Release
Frequency: Annually
Price: £5.95
ISBN: 0 11 271070 0

Available from
TSO Publications Centre and Bookshops
Please see Annex B for full address details.

Education and Training Statistics for the UK
Department for Education and Employment

The primary source of education and training statistics for the UK as a whole, providing an integrated overview of statistics on education and training in the UK in over 50 tables. Many of the tables allow comparisons to be made over time and also between the four countries. Chapters relate to expenditure; schools; post compulsory education and training; qualifications; destinations, and population. In addition, one chapter is devoted to international comparisons of education and training, containing tables based on the OECD publication "Education at a Glance".

Delivery: Periodic Release
Frequency: Annually
Price: £14.95
ISBN: 0112710506

Available from
Ian Maguire
Department for Education and Employment
Mowden Hall
Darlington
Co. Durham
Tel: 01325 392658

Education Facts and Figures (England)
Department for Education and Employment

Statistical data mainly about education in England for the latest available year and comparable data for earlier years. Contains data on maintained schools, pupils and teachers, independent schools, special education, GCE and GCSE qualifications, national targets for education and training, and post-compulsory education. Hardcopy, Internet

Frequency: Annual
Price: Free

Available from
Department for Education and Employment, Analytical Services
Please see Annex B for full address details.

Education Statistics for the United Kingdom
Department for Education and Employment

The primary source of education statistics for the UK as a whole, allowing comparisons to be made over time and in many of the tables between the four home countries. Contains UK-wide data on population, finance, teaching staff, schools, post-compulsory education, further and higher education and qualifications and destinations. Also contains an annually updated article covering international comparisons and various occasional articles.

Frequency: Annual
Price: £15.00
ISBN: 011 270992 3

Available from
TSO Publications Centre and Bookshops
Please see Annex B for full address details.

Sources from which data for this product are obtained
Local Authority Funded Further Education for Adults; School Census: School Pupil and Teacher Numbers; School Census: Teachers Employed In Schools; School Census: The School Curriculum in Publicly Funded Secondary Schools; Schools' Census - England

Education Statistics for the United Kingdom (Press Notice)
Department for Education and Employment

Statistical data about education in the UK as a whole and comparable data for earlier years. Contains summary UK data on schools, pupils, teachers, post-compulsory participation, further and higher education, non-vocational qualifications attained by school pupils, national targets for education and training, higher education qualifications and education expenditure.

Frequency: Annual
Price: Free

Available from
Department for Education and Employment, Analytical Services
Please see Annex B for full address details.

ISCED Handbook: United Kingdom
Department for Education and Employment

Multi-purpose classification system within which comparable data can be assembled on various features of educational systems and processes. Prepared by UNESCO in 1975 as an instrument suitable for assembling, compiling and presenting statistics of education in different counties on a comparable basis.

Price: Free

Available from
Department for Education and Employment, Analytical Services
Please see Annex B for full address details.

Participation in Education and Training by 16 to 18 Year Olds in England
Department for Education and Employment

Presents the latest statistics on participation in education and training by 16 to 18 year olds. Contains details of participation in education and training by main study aim and institution.

Delivery: Periodic Release
Frequency: Annually
Price: Free

Available from
Anna Isuls
Department for Education and Employment
Caxton House
Tothill Street
London
Tel: 020 7273 5979; Fax: 020 7273 5999;
Email: anna.isuls@dfee.gov.uk

Sources from which data for this product are obtained
HESA student database; Individualised Student Record; Labour Force Survey; School Census

Participation in Education and Training by Young People Aged 16 and 17 in Each Area and Region of England.
Department for Education and Employment

Statistical Bulletin on the rates of 16 and 17 year olds participation in education and training by local area. For each local education authority, TEC area and region percentages of 16 and 17 year olds in 'full-time' and 'part-time' education, and government supported training.

Delivery: Periodic Release
Frequency: Annually
Price: £5.95
ISBN: 0-11-271064-6

Available from
TSO Publications Centre and Bookshops
Please see Annex B for full address details.

Sources from which data for this product are obtained
HESA student database; Individualised Student Record; School Census

Participation in Full-Time Education by 16 and 17 year olds in Northern Ireland
Department of Education Northern Ireland

Statistical Press Release. Tables containing numbers of males and females participating in schools and FE colleges.

Delivery: News/Press Release
Frequency: Annually
Price: Free

Available from
Department of Education Northern Ireland, Statistics and Research Branch
Please see Annex B for full address details.

Sources from which data for this product are obtained
School Census - Northern Ireland; Further Education Statistical Record - Northern Ireland.

Scottish Education Statistics - Annual Review
Scottish Executive

This publication contains a summary of key statistics relating to each sector of education in Scotland. The information has already been published in the bulletins and other publications produced by the Education Statistics Division of the SOEID. The publication appears as part of a package of three flagship publications along with Scottish Education Statistics: Fact Card and Scottish Education Statistics: Guide To Sources.

Delivery: Periodic Release
Frequency: Annually
Price: Single issue: £10.00
ISBN: 0 7480 5850 8
ISSN: 0143-599X

Available from
Martin Boyle
Scottish Executive
Education and Industry Department
Victoria Quay
Edinburgh
Tel: 0131 244 0303; Fax: 0131 244 0354;
Email: martin.boyle@scotland.gov.uk

Scottish Education Statistics: Fact Card
Scottish Executive

At-a-glance pocket breakdown of basic statistics relating to Scottish Education. The Fact Card contains statistics covering: School Numbers; SCE Qualifications; Students in Further Education (excluding non-vocational courses); Students in Higher Education; Students in Further and Higher Education; and Education Finance.

Delivery: Periodic Release
Frequency: Annually

Available from
Martin Boyle
Scottish Executive
Education and Industry Department
Victoria Quay
Edinburgh
Tel: 0131 244 0303; Fax: 0131 244 0354;
Email: martin.boyle@scotland.gov.uk

Scottish Education Statistics: Guide to Sources
Scottish Executive

This publication provides a comprehensive list of the statistical information collected and processed by the Education Statistics Division on behalf of the Scottish Executive Education and Industry Department. The Guide appears as part of a package of three flagship publications comprising Scottish Education Statistics: Annual Review and Scottish Education Statistics: Fact Card.

Delivery: Periodic Release
Frequency: Annually

Available from
Martin Boyle
Scottish Executive
Education and Industry Department
Victoria Quay
Edinburgh
Tel: 0131 244 0303; Fax: 0131 244 0354;
Email: martin.boyle@scotland.gov.uk

Statistical Bulletin
Department for Education and Employment

Youth Cohort Study: The Activities and Experiences of 16 year olds: England and Wales 1996 (June 1997). The most recent bulletin covers the summary findings from Cohort 8 sweep 1 of the Youth Cohort Study of England and Wales. It covers education, labour market and training activities and experiences of young people in the first year following compulsory education. The young people are aged 16/17 at the time of the survey, and where appropriate comparisons are made with earlier Cohorts of the same age. The summary findings are presented in a series of tables, supplemented in some areas by charts. Where appropriate, data is compared with the same age Cohort for previous years. Data is often broken down by sex, ethnic origin or parental socio-economic group. Some of the data in this product is disaggregated by gender.

Frequency: Ad-hoc
Price: £3.50
ISBN: 0-11-271010-7

Available from
Stephanie Morgan
Department for Education and Employment
Moorfoot
Sheffield
Tel: 0114 2593639; Fax: 0114 2593361;
Email: stephanie.morgan@dfee.gov.uk

Youth Cohort Study Information Pack
Department for Education and Employment

Pack containing background information for the Youth Cohort Study. It includes an introduction to the YCS, a schedule of surveys and examples of questionnaires.

Frequency: Ad-hoc

Available from
England and Wales Youth Cohort Enquiries
Department for Education and Employment
Please see Annex B for full address details

Sources from which data for this product are obtained
Youth Cohort Study - England and Wales

Youth Cohort Study Research Reports
Department for Education and Employment

These reports are funded and published by the DfEE but are written by independent research companies using YCS data. Each covers specific topics of relevance to the contemporary policy environment or (more rarely) the design of the survey.

Topical reports using results from the Youth Cohort Study. Other titles have been "Truancy and Youth Transitions" (1995) and "Science and maths in Full time education after 16" (1995). A recent example of a report concerning the design of the survey is "An investigation of the Feasibility of using Different Data collection methods for the YCS" (1996).

The Research Reports differ from the statistical bulletins in that they focus on a single topic. The statistical bulletins provide a summary of key points from (usually) a single survey.

Price: £4.95
ISBN: 0 85522 734 6 for the latest report (Routes at 16)

Available from
England and Wales Youth Cohort Enquiries
Department for Education and Employment
Please see Annex B for full address details

Sources from which data for this product are obtained
Youth Cohort Study - England and Wales

Youth Cohort Study Statistical Bulletin
Department for Education and Employment

Statistical Bulletins are used by DfEE to release statistics on a variety of topics. With the Youth Cohort Study they are used to publish key results from each survey. With the more recent YCS surveys, a statistical bulletin has been used as the initial vehicle for releasing survey results into the public domain. The bulletins differ from the Research Reports in that they provide a summary of key points and (for the most recent ones) report on a single survey. The Research Reports focus on a single topic, which may involve data from more than one survey.

The most recent titles on Youth Cohort Study data are:

Statistical Bulletin 8/97: Youth Cohort Study: the Activities and Experiences of 16 year olds: England and Wales, 1996 (June 1997) ISBN = 0 11 271010 7

Statistical Bulletin 13/98: Youth Cohort Study: the Activities and Experiences of 18 year olds: England and Wales, 1996 (December 1998) ISBN = 0 11 271052 2

Statistical Bulletin 4/99: Youth Cohort Study: the Activities and Experiences of 16 year olds, England and Wales, 1998 (March 1999) ISBN = 0 11 271058 1

Statistical Bulletin: 5/99: Youth Cohort Study: the Activities and Experiences of 18 year olds: England and Wales 1998 (March 1999) ISBN = 0 11 271060 3

Frequency: Ad hoc
Price: £5.95
ISBN: See summary

Available from
England and Wales Youth Cohort Enquiries
Department for Education and Employment
Please see Annex B for full address details

Sources from which data for this product are obtained
Youth Cohort Study - England and Wales

5.10 Demand for, Supply of, Teachers

Statistics of Education: Teachers, England and Wales
Department for Education and Employment

This annual publication gives data on initial teacher training, new entrants, teacher flows, teachers in service, pay, promotions, vacancies and retirement. The main sources are the DfEE extract of the Database of Teacher Records and the 618G survey of teachers and educational psychologists.

Frequency: Annual
Price: £14.95

Available from
Ian Maguire
Department for Education and Employment
Mowden Hall
Darlington
Co. Durham
Tel: 01325 392658

Survey of Vacancies and Recruitment in Schools for the School Teachers' Review Body - September 1998
Office of Manpower Economics

The results of a survey of vacancies and recruitment in schools in September 1998. Contains data on the number of advertised posts, the reason for the vacancy, the number of applications for the post and the number of posts filled. Contains analyses of these factors by school type, region, main teaching subject and level of post.

Delivery: Hardcopy publication
Price: Free

Available from
Office of Manpower Economics
Please see Annex B for full address details

Teacher Vacancies: Statisticial First Release
Department for Education and Employment

Provisional data on the numbers of vacancies for full-time appointments which have been advertised but not filled and the resulting vacancy rates. The press notice contains data on vacancies and vacancy rates in the maintained nursery, primary and secondary sector by region; vacancies and vacancy rates in the maintained nursery and primary sector by region, grade and vacancy rates in the maintained secondary sector by region; and vacancies and vacancy rates in the maintained secondary sector by grade and subject.

Frequency: Annual
Price: Free

Available from
Department for Education and Employment,
Analytical Services
Please see Annex B for full address details.

Sources from which data for this product are obtained
Teachers

Teachers in Service: Statisticial First Release
Department for Education and Employment

Provisional data on the overall numbers of teachers in service in the maintained sector in England. Tables show numbers of teachers in the maintained sector each year by qualification status and type of contract; by nursery, primary and secondary phase; by special schools and education elsewhere and by Government Office Region.

Frequency: Annual
Price: Free

Available from
Department for Education and Employment,
Analytical Services
Please see Annex B for full address details.

Sources from which data for this product are obtained
Teachers

Written Evidence to the School Teacher's Review Body from the Department for Education: Statistical Tables
Department for Education and Employment

Statistical tables relating to the supply, demand and pay of school teachers. Contains tables on the numbers of teachers in service, pupil: teacher ratios and class contact ratios, numbers of initial teacher training students, movements in and out of teaching, class sizes, numbers of non-teaching staff, teacher vacancies, teacher turnover and wastage, numbers of teachers by grade and spine point, and receipt of allowances. Charts are also included showing promotion rates, teachers by length of service, and age profile of the teaching force.

Frequency: Annual
Price: Free

Available from
Teachers Branch
Sanctuary Buildings
Great Smith Street
London SW1P 3BT
Tel: 020 7925 6138.

Sources from which data for this product are obtained
Teachers

Please see:
In this chapter:
Report of the School Teachers' Review Body *(5.16)*
1996 Teachers' Workloads Survey for the School Teachers' Review Body *(5.13)*

5.11 Funding and Finances of Students

Individual Institutions: Students Eligible for Funding
Scottish Higher Education Funding Council

Statistical bulletin showing the number of students eligible to be counted in the method used by the Scottish Higher Education Funding Council to calculate the allocations from its Main Grant for Teaching. The bulletin contains full-time equivalent student numbers by institution, funding subject group, level of provision and mode of attendance.

Delivery: Periodic Release
Frequency: Annually
Price: Free
ISSN: 0969-7187

Available from
Scottish Higher Education Funding Council
Please see Annex B for full address details

Sources from which data for this product are obtained
Students Eligible for Funding return

Mature Students Incomings and Outgoings
Office for National Statistics

Results of a survey on the financial circumstances of mature students. Reports in detail on the characteristics and financial circumstances of mature students (aged 26 or over). The statistics are based on a small-scale study carried out in early 1988 at 60 educational establishments in Great Britain in connection with the Government Student Support Review.

Delivery: Ad Hoc/One-off Release
Price: £11.50
ISBN: 0 11 691269 3

Available from
TSO Publications Centre and Bookshops
Please see Annex B for full address details.

Statistics of Education: Student Support England and Wales - (Volume)
Department for Education and Employment

Final data on student awards. Some data presented in a ten-year time series. Contains data on numbers of awards, expenditure on fees and maintenance, average maintenance, mandatory, discretionary awards and Educational Maintenance Allowances, full-value awards, assessed contributions, average local education authority expenditure, rate of grant for dependent and independent students, full maintenance, partial maintenance and nil maintenance, additional allowances, higher and further education and postgraduate awards.

Delivery: Periodic Release
Frequency: Annually
ISBN: 0-11-271046-8

Available from
Michael Davidson
Department for Education and Employment
Mowden Hall
Darlington
Co. Durham
Tel: 01325 392343;
Email: michael.davidson@dfee.gov.uk

Sources from which data for this product are obtained
Student Loans - UK; Students Awards - England and Wales

Student Awards 1996-97
Scottish Executive

The bulletin provides information on the number of Scottish and European Union students who received awards made by the Scottish Executive Education and Industry Department over sessions 1991-92 to 1993-4 and by the Students Awards Agency for Scotland in 1994-95 to 1996-97, and the cost of these awards.

Delivery: Periodic Release
Frequency: Annually
Price: £2.00
ISBN: 0 7480 6732 9
ISSN: 0143-599X

Available from
TSO Publications Centre and Bookshops
Please see Annex B for full address details.

Sources from which data for this product are obtained
Student Awards Agency for Scotland: Student Awards

Student Awards in England and Wales (Press Notice)
Department for Education and Employment

Provisional grossed national data on student awards for the latest academic year in a ten-year time series. The press notice contains data on the numbers of awards, expenditure on fees and maintenance, average maintenance, mandatory, discretionary awards and Educational Maintenance Allowances.

Delivery: News/Press Release
Frequency: Annual
Price: Free

Available from
Department for Education and Employment, Analytical Services
Please see Annex B for full address details.

Sources from which data for this product are obtained
Students Awards - England and Wales

Student Support: Statistics of Student Loans in United Kingdom - (Press Notice)
Department for Education and Employment

A detailed time series of student loans in higher education in the UK. The press notice contains data on amounts paid out in loans and repaid, number of borrowers taking loans and making repayments, estimated take-up rate of eligible students, and average values of loans issued and total sums borrowed. Data on student loans are completed by the Student Loan Company and passed to the Department for Education and Employment.

Delivery: News/Press Release
Frequency: Annual
Price: Free

Available from
Department for Education and Employment, Analytical Services
Please see Annex B for full address details.

Sources from which data for this product are obtained
Student Loans - UK

Students Eligible for Funding
Scottish Higher Education Funding Council

Statistical bulletin showing the number of students eligible to be counted in the method used by the Scottish Higher Education Funding Council to calculate the allocations from its Main Grant for Teaching. The bulletin contains full-time equivalent student numbers by funding subject groups, levels of provision and modes of attendance.

Frequency: Annual
Price: Free
ISSN: 0969-7187

Available from
Scottish Higher Education Funding Council
Donaldson House
97 Haymarket Terrace
Edinburgh EH12 5IID
Tel: 0131 313 6566.

Sources from which data for this product are obtained
Students Eligible for Funding return

5.12 Post School Education

College Performance Information: Further Education Institutions in Wales
National Assembly for Wales

Statistics concerning further education in

Wales. Contains data on examination results and attendance for all further education institutions in Wales, along with background information on each further education institution.

Frequency: Annual
Price: Free
ISBN: 0 7504 1304 5

Available from
School Performance Division 3, National Assembly for Wales. Tel: 029 2082 6010.

Sources from which data for this product are obtained
Examination Results - Wales

Community Education Statistics, 1996-97
Scottish Executive

This bulletin provides details on the numbers of Community Education Groups and participants, as well as the staff numbers and budgets of statutory Community Education providers in Scotland in the relevant financial year.

Delivery: Periodic Release
Frequency: Annually
Price: Single copy: £2.00
ISBN: 0 7480 6978 X
ISSN: 0143-599X

Available from
TSO Publications Centre and Bookshops
Please see Annex B for full address details.

Sources from which data for this product are obtained
Community Education Surveys - Budgets; Community Education Surveys - Participants; Community Education Surveys - Staff.

Data Report - Students in Higher Education Institutions-96/97 (also available for earlier years)
Higher Education Statistics Agency

This publication describes, in easily assimilable form, including relevant graphics, the characteristics of students in the universities and colleges of the UK in the year of issue. In addition to standard tabulations recording the characteristics of students, a number of specific issues are explored, including the gender balance by subject, overseas student characteristics, and the participation of ethnic minorities. All data is at aggregate (i.e. non-institution) level. This publication provides the most up to date information about the nature of student participation in higher education.

Products

Delivery: Hardcopy publication
Frequency: Annually
Price: £20.00
ISBN: ISBN 1 899840 20 6

Available from
Higher Education Statistics Agency (HESA)
Please see Annex B for full address details.

Sources from which data for this product are obtained
Individualised Student Record

Enrolments and Student Numbers on Further Education Courses at Colleges in the Further and Higher Education Sector
Department for Education and Employment

Details of students enrolled on further education courses in the higher and further education sectors. The press release contains data on type of college, age, sex, mode of attendance and qualification aim.

Delivery: News/Press Release
Frequency: Discontinued
Price: Free

Available from
Department for Education and Employment, Analytical Services
Please see Annex B for full address details.

Enrolments on Vocational Courses at Further Education Colleges
Department of Education - Northern Ireland

Statistical Press Release. Tables containing enrolments by mode of study, level of study, age-group, subject group, and qualification type. Some of the data in this product is disaggregated by gender.

Delivery: News/Press Release
Frequency: Annually
Price: Free

Available from
Jonathan Crook
Statistics and Research Branch
Room 401
Department of Education - Northern Ireland
Rathgael House
Balloo Road
Bangor BT19 7PR
Tel: 028 9127 9403;
Email: jonathan.crook@deni.gov.uk

Sources from which data for this product are obtained
Further Education Statistical Record (FESR)

Examination Results and First Destinations of Higher Education Graduates in Great Britain: 1983-92 (Statistical Bulletin 14/94)
Department for Education and Employment

Data on qualifications obtained and examination results achieved by students on higher education courses at publicly funded institutions in Great Britain. The bulletin contains data on students by first destination, type of institution, subject group, type of employer, gender, type of work, mode of provision, examination result, type of institution, sex, qualification, subject, level of course, first destination of first degree graduates and class of degree.

Delivery: Periodic Release
Frequency: Discontinued
Price: Free
ISSN: 0142-5013

Available from
Department for Education and Employment, Analytical Services
Please see Annex B for full address details.

Facts and Figures
Scottish Higher Education Funding Council

Leaflet giving some key figures about Scottish Higher Education Funding Council funding and the institutions receiving this funding. The leaflet contains data on the kinds of funding provided by the Council, recurrent income of the higher education institutional sector, recurrent funding for each institution, students eligible for funding at each institution, funded places and students by funding subject group, and research assessment exercise (overall sector results).

Frequency: Annual
Price: Free

Available from
Scottish Higher Education Funding Council
Please see Annex B for full address details

Sources from which data for this product are obtained
Schools' Census - England; Students Eligible for Funding return

First Destination of Graduates and Diplomates: 1996
Scottish Executive

Delivery: Periodic Release
Frequency: Annually
Price: £2.00
ISBN: 07480 7036 2
ISSN: 0143-599X

Available from
TSO Publications Centre and Bookshops
Please see Annex B for full address details.

Sources from which data for this product are obtained
HESA First Destination Supplement to Individualised Student Records and SFEFC First Destination Survey from Further Education Colleges

First Destinations of HE Students in UK - (Press Notice)
Higher Education Statistics Agency

Delivery: News/Press Release
Frequency: Annually
Price: Free

Available from
Higher Education Statistics Agency
Please see Annex B for full address details

Sources from which data for this product are obtained
First Destination Supplement to Individualised Student Record

First Destinations of Students Gaining Qualifications from Higher Education Institutions
Department of Education - Northern Ireland

Statistical press release, containing information on students gaining higher education qualifications at UK higher education institutions. Data are presented on (a) Northern Ireland domiciled students, studying anywhere in the UK and (b) all students studying in Northern Ireland. In the tables, destinations of those with first degrees, other undergraduate qualifications, and postgraduate qualifications are shown separately. Destinations are presented in terms of geographical location and activity.

Some of the data in this product is disaggregated by gender.

Delivery: News/Press Release
Frequency: Annually
Price: Free

Available from
Linda Bradley
Department of Education - Northern Ireland
Rathgael House
Balloo Road
Bangor
Co. Down BT19 7PR
Tel: 028 91279395; Fax: 01247 279777;
Email: linda.bradley@deni.gov.uk

Sources from which data for this product are obtained
HESA student database

Funding Allocations 1998-99 (also available for previous years)
Further Education Funding Council

Describes the allocations by the Council of the funds made available to it by Parliament and how the Council arrived at its decisions. The publication contains full listings by college of the funding allocation they received.

Delivery: Periodic Release
Frequency: Annual
Price: Free

Available from
Further Education Funding Council
Please see Annex B for full address details

Further Education Bursary Statistics, 1996-97
Scottish Executive

The bulletin provides details on the administration of bursaries by colleges for students on Further Education courses.

Delivery: First Release
Frequency: Annually
Price: Single copy: £2.00
ISBN: 0 7480 7065 6
ISSN: 0143-599X

Available from
John Landrock
Scottish Executive
Scottish Office Education and Industry Department
Victoria Quay
Edinburgh
Tel: 0131 244 0324; Fax: 0131 244 0354;
Email: john.landrock@scotland.gov.uk

Sources from which data for this product are obtained
Further Education Bursary Statistics

Further Education Statistics: 1996-97
Scottish Executive

Data on students registered in the 43 further education (FE) colleges in Scotland which are directly funded by the Scottish Executive Education Department.

Delivery: Periodic Release
Frequency: Annual
Price: £2.00
ISBN: 0 7480 7163 6
ISSN: 0143-599X

Available from
John Landrock
The Scottish Executive
Scottish Office Education and Industry Department
Victoria Quay
Edinburgh
Tel: 0131 244 0324; Fax: 0131 244 0354;
Email: john.landrock@scotland.gov.uk

Sources from which data for this product are obtained
Course and Student Details at Further Education Institutions - Scotland; Examination Results and First Destination of Graduates

HE Finance Plus - 1997/98 (also available for previous years)
Higher Education Statistics Agency

This CD contains the full finance statistics returned to HESA from virtually all of the United Kingdom's universities and colleges of higher education, including detailed income and expenditure analyses and balance sheet information. The institutional version also contains enhancements specifically for institutional management information purposes. Orders for this CD will only be fulfilled on receipt by post of an official purchase order.

Delivery: CD-ROM
Frequency: Annually
Price: £130.00 + VAT - Institution version
£500.00 + VAT - Commercial Version
ISBN: 1 899840 84 2

Available from
Higher Education Statistics Agency (HESA)
Please see Annex B for full address details.

Sources from which data for this product are obtained
Finance Statistics Record (incorporating Aggregate Staff Record)

HE Planning Plus - 1999 (also available for 1998)
Higher Education Statistics Agency

This CD contains data relating to students for the academic years 1997/98 and 1998/99, academic staff for the academic year 1997/98, finance data for the financial year 1997/98 and non-credit-bearing course data for the academic year 1997/98. Data includes expenditure by cost centre and institution, students by subject, level of study, age, research grants and academic staff by cost centre. Orders for this CD will only be fulfilled on receipt by post of an official order.

Delivery: CD-ROM
Frequency: Annually
Price: £100.00 + VAT - Institution version
£500.00 + VAT - Commercial Version
ISBN: 1 899840 86 9

Available from
Higher Education Statistics Agency (HESA)
Please see Annex B for full address details.

Sources from which data for this product are obtained
Individualised Staff Record; Individualised Student Record: Non-credit-bearing Course Record - Aggregate Return

HEFCE - Recurrent Grants
Higher Education Funding Council for England

Annually produced document summarising HEFCE's allocation of recurrent funding and maximum aggregate student numbers to institutions for the coming academic year. The document is produced in February/March for following academic year starting September/October. One of many documents published by HEFCE for further information see HEFCE URL - http://www.hefce.ac.uk

Delivery: Periodic Release
Frequency: Annually

Available from
HEFCE Publications
Higher Education Funding Council for England
Northavon House
Coldharbour Lane
Bristol BS16 1QD

Sources from which data for this product are obtained
Higher Education Students Early Statistics

HESA Online Information Service
Higher Education Statistics Agency

Delivery: Online database
Price: Free

Available from
Higher Education Statistics Agency website, url: http://www.hesa.ac.uk/holisdocs/home.htm

Sources from which data for this product are obtained
Finance Statistics Record (incorporating Aggregate Staff Record); First Destination Supplement to Individualised Student Records; Individualised Staff Record; Individualised Student Record

Higher Education Institutions: Financial Statistics
Scottish Higher Education Funding Council

Statistical bulletin on income, expenditure and financial indicators for each of the higher education institutions funded by the Scottish Higher Education Funding Council.

The bulletin contains data by institution on recurrent income, recurrent expenditure, grants and fees, financial indicators and a statement of the financial position at the end of the year.

Delivery: Periodic Release
Frequency: Annual
Price: Free
ISSN: 0969-7187

Available from
Scottish Higher Education Funding Council
Please see Annex B for full address details

Higher Education Institutions: Students and Staff
Scottish Higher Education Funding Council

Statistical bulletin on student and staff numbers for each of the higher education institutions funded by the Scottish Higher Education Funding Council. The bulletin contains data on student numbers (head counts and full-time equivalents) by institution, subject, level, mode of attendance, type of course, age group, sex, domicile, entry qualifications, qualification aim, and year of course. Data on academic staff are available by institution, mode, sex and age group.

Frequency: Annual
Price: Free
ISSN: 0969-7187

Available from
Scottish Higher Education Funding Council
Please see Annex B for full address details

Higher Education Management Statistics - Institution Level 1997/98 (also available for previous years)
Higher Education Statistics Agency

When complete, this loose leaf volume will include institutional financial profiles, unit expenditure figures, research statistics, application and admissions profiles, student profiles and student outcome (including first destinations) statistics. It is designed for institutional managers. Sets of loose leaf pages will be issued as the statistics become available, probably in two batches. This publication is still in the development stage and may change from year to year, with additional statistics added in subsequent years. Individual sections of this publication are available.

Delivery: Hard copy publication
Frequency: Annually
Price: £62.00
ISBN: 1 899840 82 6

Available from
Higher Education Statistics Agency (HESA)
Please see Annex B for full address details.

Sources from which data for this product are obtained
Finance Statistics Record (incorporating Aggregate Staff Record); First Destination Supplement to Individualised Student Record: Individualised Student Record

Higher Education Management Statistics - Sector Level 1997/98 (also available for previous years)
Higher Education Statistics Agency

This volume sets out information, in easily assimilable form, about the performance of higher education. Application rates, admission rates, participation rates, unit costs and other indicators are reported for the HE sector as a whole (although not institution level).

Delivery: Hard copy publication
Frequency: Annually
Price: £22.00
ISBN: 1 899840 00 0

Available from
Higher Education Statistics Agency (HESA)
Please see Annex B for full address details.

Sources from which data for this product are obtained
Finance Statistics Record (incorporating Aggregate Staff Record); First Destination Supplement to Individualised Student Record: Individualised Student Record

Higher Education Statistics for the United Kingdom 1997/98 (also available for previous years)
Higher Education Statistics Agency

This volume, prepared in conjunction with the Government Statistical Service contains a number of tabulations describing the higher education sector - applicants, students, staff and finance throughout the sector and some institutional data. The 1992/93 edition describes the sector before the changes introduced by the 1992 Further and Higher Education Acts. The 1994/95 edition updates this by two years and presents all data on a consistent basis for the first time. This Volume includes an explanation of the definitional differences between the data collected up to 1993/94 by the previous different data collection agencies and HESA's own data in 1994/95 and subsequently.

Delivery: Hard copy publication
Frequency: Annually
Price: £32.00
ISBN: 1 899840 74 5

Available from
Higher Education Statistics Agency (HESA)
Please see Annex B for full address details.

Sources from which data for this product are obtained
Finance Statistics Record (incorporating Aggregate Staff Record); First Destination Supplement to Individualised Student Record: Individualised Student Record

Higher Education Student Domicile Statistics, 1996-97
Scottish Executive

The first bulletin in a series drawing together information to present a statistical description of the domicile of students in Higher Education in Scotland.

Delivery: Periodic Release
Frequency: Occasional
Price: £2.00
ISBN: 0 7480 7140 7
ISSN: 0143-599X

Available from
TSO Publications Centre and Bookshops
Please see Annex B for full address details.

Sources from which data for this product are obtained
Higher Education Statistics Agency: Student Record and SFEFC Further Education College Survey

How to Widen Participation: A Guide to Good Practice
Further Education Funding Council

Guide to good practice gathered by the FEFC's Widening Participation Committee. Includes a framework and national baseline for measuring Widening Participation in further education.

Frequency: Annually
Price: £12.95
ISBN: 0-11-361347-4

Available from
TSO Publications Centre and Bookshops
Please see Annex B for full address details.

Sources from which data for this product are obtained
Individualised Student Record

Management Statistics 1995-96: Further Education Colleges in England
Further Education Funding Council

32 management statistics for further education colleges in England. Includes

statistics on students, staffing and finance. Shows range of results by type of college and region.

Frequency: One-off
Price: Free

Available from
The Further Education Funding Council
Please see Annex B for full address details

Mature Students in Higher Education - Great Britain 1982-1992 (Statistical Bulletin 16/94)
Department for Education and Employment

Data and trends for home domiciled, first-year, full-time and part-time mature students at publicly funded institutions in Great Britain. The bulletin contains data on mature students by sex, mode of attendance, sector, level of study, qualification on entry, sector of education, age, sex, associate students, subject of study and Open University students. (Last in series.)

Delivery: News/Press Release
Frequency: Discontinued
Price: Free
ISSN: 0142-5013

Available from
Department for Education and Employment. Analytical Services
Please see Annex B for full address details

Performance Indicators 1996-97: Further Education Colleges in England
Further Education Funding Council

Performance Indicators for 1996-97 and 1995-96 comparators for each further education college in England, together with analysis and interpretation for the college sector as a whole.

Delivery: Periodic Release
Frequency: Annually
Price: £16.95
ISBN: 0-11-361349-0

Available from
TSO Publications Centre and Bookshops
Please see Annex B for full address details.

Sources from which data for this product are obtained
Individualised Student Record

Performance Indicators: Further Education Colleges in England
Department for Education and Employment; sponsored by Further Education Funding Council

Delivery: Hardcopy publication
Frequency: Annual, last published September 1998.
Price: £16.95
ISBN: 011-361352-0
ISSN:

Available from
TSO Publications Centre and Bookshops
Please see Annex B for full address details.

Sources from which data for this product are obtained
Individualised Student Record

Qualifications gained at Higher Education Institutions
Department of Education - Northern Ireland

Statistical press release, containing information on students gaining higher education qualifications at UK higher education institutions. Data are presented on (a) Northern Ireland domiciled students, studying anywhere in the UK and (b) all students studying in Northern Ireland. Tables cover level of qualification obtained, subject group, location of study, degree classification (first degrees only), gender with some of the data disaggregated by mode of study.

Delivery: News/Press Release
Frequency: Annual
Price: Free

Available from
Gillian Graham
Department of Education - Northern Ireland
Rathgael House
Balloo Road
Bangor
Co. Down BT19 7PR
Tel: 028 9279379; Fax: 028 9279777;
Email: gillian.graham@deni.gov.uk

Source from which data for this product are obtained:
HESA student database

Qualifications Obtained by and Examination Results of HE Students at HEIs in UK - (Press Notice)
Higher Education Statistics Agency

Delivery: News/Press Release
Frequency: Annually
Price: Free

Available from
Higher Education Statistics Agency (HESA)
Please see Annex B for full address details

Sources from which data for this product are obtained
Individualised Student Record

Reference Volume - First Destinations of Students Leaving Higher Education Institutions - 1997/98 (also available for previous years)
Higher Education Statistics Agency

This volume includes statistics about the first destinations of graduates, including employment rates, participation in further education and training, etc. A summary tabulation at institution level is included. Tables include base employment codes and aggregations.

Delivery: Hard copy publication
Frequency: Annually
Price: £32.00
ISBN: 1 899840 80 X

Available from
Higher Education Statistics Agency (HESA)
Please see Annex B for full address details.

Sources from which data for this product are obtained
First Destination Supplement to Individualised Student Record

Reference Volume - Resources of Higher Education Institutions - 1997/98 (also available for previous years)
Higher Education Statistics Agency

This volume draws on HESA's collection of data about finance and staff in higher education. Tabulations are included which record and analyse the income and expenditure of universities and colleges (with data shown at institution level) and also about the characteristics of academic staff (including gender balance within academic subject departments, ethnicity, etc.).

Delivery: Hard copy publication
Frequency: Annually
Price: £32.00
ISBN: 1 899840 78 8

Available from
Higher Education Statistics Agency (HESA)
Please see Annex B for full address details.

Sources from which data for this product are obtained
Finance Statistics Record (incorporating Aggregate Staff Record); Individualised Staff Record

Reference Volume - Students in Higher Education Institutions - 1997/98 (also available for previous years)
Higher Education Statistics Agency

This volume puts together statistical data about all aspects of students in higher education. Tabulations cover subjects of study at undergraduate and postgraduate levels. The publication is aimed at those seriously interested in finding out about issues concerning students in higher education: the tabulations are broader but not as extensive as those contained in the Research Datapacks (listed). Some institution level tabulations are provided. From 1995/96 onwards, this publication includes Student FTE information and further PGR/PGT split in certain tabulations.

Delivery: Hard copy publication
Frequency: Annually
Price: £32.00
ISBN: 1 899840 76 1

Available from
Higher Education Statistics Agency (HESA)
Please see Annex B for full address details.

Sources from which data for this product are obtained
Individualised Student Record

Research Assessment Exercise: Outcomes
Higher Education Funding Council for England

Assessment of research in Higher Education Institution in the UK. Last one carried out in 1996 next planned for 2001. Results available through the Higher Education funding councils' web sites hefce url:- 'http://www.hefce.ac.uk'.

Delivery: Periodic Release
Frequency: Periodic (quinquennial)
Price: Free

Available from
Corporate Communications
HEFCE
Northavon House
Coldharbour Lane
Bristol BS16 1QD

Sources from which data for this product are obtained
Research Assessment Exercise

Research Datapack 1 - Ethnicity
Higher Education Statistics Agency

This Datapack contains aggregate (i.e. non-institution level) data about the characteristics of ethnic minority students in higher education, including their subjects of study, gender and age differences, qualifications on entry, etc. Data relates to the 1994/95 academic year.

Frequency: One-off
Price: £120.00

Available from
Higher Education Statistics Agency (HESA)
Please see Annex B for full address details.

Sources from which data for this product are obtained
Individualised Student Record

Research Datapack 2 - Entry Qualifications in HE
Higher Education Statistics Agency

This Datapack provides an extensive range of tabulations covering the qualification background of entrants to courses at different levels in different subjects, together with some institutional tabulations. Data relates to the 1994/95 academic year.

Frequency: One-off
Price: £120.00

Available from
Higher Education Statistics Agency (HESA)
Please see Annex B for full address details.

Sources from which data for this product are obtained
Individualised Student Record

Research Datapack 3 - Course Results
Higher Education Statistics Agency

This pack includes many tabulations detailing the exit qualifications of students leaving higher education in 1994/95, by subject and by institution, including degree classifications. This Datapack includes a complete section on the results of students from ethnic minority groups. It will thus be a valuable resource for those who wish to compare these with the first destinations tabulated in Datapack 4.

Frequency: One-off
Price: £120.00

Available from
Higher Education Statistics Agency (HESA)
Please see Annex B for full address details.

Sources from which data for this product are obtained
Individualised Student Record

Research Datapack 4 - First Destinations
Higher Education Statistics Agency

This pack includes an extensive array of data about the first destinations of 1995 graduates by subject and institution. A complete section of data concerning the employment of students from ethnic minority groups is included. It will be the essential resource for those who wish to study matters concerning graduate employment.

Frequency: One-off
Price: £120.00

Available from
Higher Education Statistics Agency (HESA)
Please see Annex B for full address details.

Sources from which data for this product are obtained
Individualised Student Record

Research Datapack 5 - Disability
Higher Education Statistics Agency

This pack looks at disabled students from entry to higher education through their choices of study programme to completion of those programmes and the resulting qualifications obtained. Some data disaggregations by institution are included. Data on the first destination of graduates and leavers with disabilities are shown in the final section. Data relates to the 1995/96 academic year.

Frequency: One-off
Price: £120.00

Available from
Higher Education Statistics Agency (HESA)
Please see Annex B for full address details.

Sources from which data for this product are obtained
Individualised Student Record

Research Datapack 6 - Overseas
Higher Education Statistics Agency

This datapack aims to provide a comprehensive resource of information relating to students from overseas studying in the UK. Factors such as entry qualifications, study programme characteristics and programme completion performance are included, with disaggregations by country of origin and institution. Data relates to the 1995/96 academic year.

Frequency: One-off
Price: £120.00

Available from
Higher Education Statistics Agency (HESA)
Please see Annex B for full address details.

Sources from which data for this product are obtained
Individualised Student Record

Research Datapack 7 - Regional Issues
Higher Education Statistics Agency

This datapack includes a great deal of source material designed for the analysis of regional influences on higher education in the UK. Many factors will be considered such as the regional origin of students, the migratory flow pattern of students to their chosen site of study, the effect of regional influences on the types of subject and study work or continuing study. Some institutional disaggregations are included.

Frequency: One-off
Price: £120.00

Available from
Higher Education Statistics Agency (HESA)
Please see Annex B for full address details.

Sources from which data for this product are obtained
Individualised Student Record

Research Datapack 8 - Ethnicity in Higher Education
Higher Education Statistics Agency

This datapack aims to re-visit the issue of the Ethnic origin of students in HE as originally addressed in Datapack 1. Data contained in the pack is sourced from the 1996/97 HESA Student Record, providing an update two years later than the information in Datapack 1. This pack will follow a familiar structure including characteristics and demographic information, data on entry qualifications, choices of study programmes and course results. In addition this pack will contain information at institution level.

Delivery: Hard copy publication
Frequency: One-off
Price: £120.00

Available from
Higher Education Statistics Agency (HESA)
Please see Annex B for full address details.

Sources from which data for this product are obtained
Individualised Student Record

Research Datapack 9 - Academic Staff in Higher Education
Higher Education Statistics Agency

This datapack will address the issue of academic staff in higher education institutions. Data will include personal characteristics, demographics and information on nature of contract, etc. Some

data at institution level will be included. Data is sourced from the HESA Individualised Staff Record 1996/97.

Delivery: Hard copy publication
Frequency: One-off
Price: £120.00

Available from
Higher Education Statistics Agency (HESA)
Please see Annex B for full address details.

Sources from which data for this product are obtained
Individualised Staff Record

Scottish Higher Education Statistics 1996-97
Scottish Executive

The bulletin draws together information from two sources to present a statistical description of the main aspects of higher education in Scotland.

Delivery: Periodic Release
Frequency: Annually
Price: £2.00
ISBN: 0 7480 7138 5
ISSN: 0143-599X

Available from
TSO Publications Centre and Bookshops
Please see Annex B for full address details.

Sources from which data for this product are obtained
Higher Education Statistics Agency: Student Record and SFEFC Further Education College Survey

---

Staff Statistics 1996-97 and 1997-98: Further Education Colleges in England (also available for previous years)
Further Education Funding Council

Statistical information on staff numbers and their characteristics in further education colleges in England. Includes teaching and non-teaching staff.

Delivery: Periodic Release
Frequency: Annually
Price: Free

Available from
Further Education Funding Council
Please see Annex B for full address details

Sources from which data for this product are obtained
Academic Staff Individualised Records - England

Statistics of Education: Further and Higher Education Student: Staff Ratios 1993-94 England
Department for Education and Employment

Tables and main findings of the Annual Monitoring Survey and definitions of indicators used. Contains the results of the 1993-94 Annual Monitoring Survey (AMS) and compares the results with those in previous years. Contains data on student: staff ratios, average class size, average lecturer and student hours by type of establishment, levels of education and broad subject areas. (Last of the series.)

Frequency: Annual
Price: £12.00
ISSN: 1354-8603

Available from
Department for Education and Employment, Analytical Services
Please see Annex B for full address details.

Sources from which data for this product are obtained
Annual Monitoring Survey - England

Student Enrolments on HE Courses at Publicly Funded HEIs in UK - (Press Notice)
Higher Education Statistics Agency

Delivery: News/Press Release
Frequency: Annually
Price: Free

Available from
Angela Dunn
Higher Education Statistics Agency
18 Royal Crescent
Cheltenham
Gloucestershire
Tel: 01242 255577;
Fax: 01242 232648; angelad@hesa.ac.uk

Sources from which data for this product are obtained
Individualised Student Record

Student Enrolments on Higher Education Courses
Department of Education Northern Ireland

Statistical press release, giving higher education enrolment figures (a) for all Northern Ireland domiciled students studying in the UK or Republic of Ireland and (b) for all students studying in Northern Ireland. Data presented on (a) Northern Ireland domiciled higher education students studying in the UK and Republic of Ireland and (b) all students studying higher education courses in Northern Ireland. Tables cover mode of study, location of study (for N. Ireland domiciled students), domicile (for

Products

students studying in N. Ireland), level of study, age-group, and subject group with some of the data disaggregated by gender.

Delivery: News/Press Release
Frequency: Annually
Price: Free

Available from
Linda Bradley
Department of Education - Northern Ireland
Rathgael House
Balloo Road
Bangor
Co. Down BT19 7PR
Tel: 028 91279395; Fax: 01247 279777;
Email: linda.bradley@deni.gov.uk

Sources from which data for this product are obtained
HESA student database; Northern Ireland Further Education Statistical Record (FESR)

Student Enrolments on Higher Education Courses in England and the United Kingdom: Academic Year 1994/95 (Press Notice 107/95)
Department for Education and Employment

Details of students enrolled on higher education (HE) courses in England and in HE institutions in the UK. Contains data for students enrolled by sex, mode of attendance, year of study, level of course, country of domicile and subject of course. The Press Notice provides a bridge in the time series between 1993/94 and 1994/95 to take account of changes in data collection.

Delivery: News/Press Release
Frequency: Annually
Price: Free

Available from
Department for Education and Employment, Analytical Services
Please see Annex B for full address details.

Sources from which data for this product are obtained
Individualised Student Record

Student Numbers in Higher Education - Great Britain 1982-83 to 1992-93 (Statistical Bulletin 13/94)
Department for Education and Employment

Data and trends for students in publicly funded higher education institutions in Great Britain. The bulletin contains data on full-time students by country of domicile, type of establishment, subject of study, level of course, mode of attendance, year of study, age, sex, qualifications awarded, and some information for students on vocational/short courses. (Last in series).

Delivery: News/Press Release
Frequency: Annual
Price: Free
ISSN: 0142-5013

Available from
Department for Education and Employment, Analytical Services
Please see Annex B for full address details.

Student Numbers, In-Year Retention, Achievements and Destinations at Colleges in the Further Education Sector and External Institutions in England 1996-97

Further Education Funding Council
Summary statistics on student numbers and their characteristics. 3 releases a year: April - numbers at Nov; December - whole year numbers; July - update on December plus retention and achievements.

Delivery: News/Press Release
Frequency: Periodic
Price: Free

Available from
Further Education Funding Council
Please see Annex B for full address details

Education Colleges in England
Further Education Funding Council

Statistical information on student numbers and their characteristics in further education colleges in England.

Delivery: Periodic Release
Frequency: Annually
Price: Free

Available from
Caroline Kempner
Further Education Funding Council
Cheylesmore House
Quinton Road
Coventry
Tel: 01203 863228; Fax: 01203 863249

Sources from which data for this product are obtained
Further Education Students - England

Students from Abroad in Great Britain 1982 to 1992 (Statistical Bulletin 15/94)
Department for Education and Employment

Data and trends for students from abroad in publicly funded institutions in Great Britain. Contains data on students from abroad by level of study, sex and sector, details on year of study, mode of attendance, level of course, sector of education, subject of study, selected countries of domicile and country of study. (Last of series.)

Delivery: News/Press Release
Frequency: Discontinued
Price: Free
ISSN: 0142-5013

Available from
Department for Education and Employment, Analytical Services
Please see Annex B for full address details.

Students in Higher Education in England (Statistical Bulletin) (Ends 1992/93)
Department for Education and Employment

Statistics and trends for students on higher education courses at publicly funded institutions in England. The bulletin contains data on students by type of institution and level of course, mode of attendance, level of course, sector of education, country of domicile, source of funding, year of study, student FTEs, entry qualifications, age, sex, ethnic groups, exam results, first destinations subject of study, regions and selected individual institutions. (Last of series.)

Delivery: News/Press Release
Frequency: Annual
Price: Free
ISSN: 0142-5013

Available from
Department for Education and Employment, Analytical Services
Please see Annex B for full address details.

Widening Participation in Further Education Statistical Evidence
Further Education Funding Council

Statistical evidence proposed by the FEFC's Widening Participation Committee chaired by Baroness Kennedy of the Shaws in support of recommendations in Learning Works.

Delivery: Ad hoc/One-off Release
Price: £12.95
ISBN: 0-11-361350-4

Available from
TSO Publications Centre and Bookshops
Please see Annex B for full address details.

See also:
In this chapter:
Adult Literacy in Britain *(5.15)*
Education Statistics for the United Kingdom *(5.9)*
Mature Students Incomings and Outgoings *(5.11)*
Statistical Bulletin *(5.9)*

5.13 Schools

1996 Teachers' Workloads Survey for the School Teachers' Review Body
Office of Manpower Economics

The results of a survey of teachers' workloads. Contains data on the hours qualified teachers in maintained primary, secondary and special schools worked in a week in March 1996 (First Report) and in a week in May 1996 (Second Report, which also includes the results of a qualitative exercise) such as the make-up of total hours by detailed and grouped activities, distributions of total hours and of hours spent teaching, and the percentage of hours spent working at weekends or in the evening. Survey previously carried out in 1994.

Delivery: Hardcopy publication
Price: Free

Available from
Office of Manpower Economics
Please see Annex B for full address details

1998 Value Added Pilot: Supplement to the Secondary School Performance Tables
Department for Education and Employment

42 pages of tables with notes and a technical annex. Contains, for pilot schools, background information (address, type of school, number of pupils etc.), GCSE and GNVQ results for pupils aged 15 at the start of the school year, improvement measure since 1995, school progress measure, value added measures based on pupil progress between Key Stage 3 and GCSE/GNVQ (raw indicators, indicators by Key Stage 3 level, indicators by gender), stability measure and coverage.

Frequency: One off publication
Price: free

Available from
Bridgette Frost
Department for Education and Employment
Caxton House
Tothill Street
London
Tel: 020 7273 5498; Fax: 020 7273 5999;
Email: bridgette.frost@dfee.gov.uk

Sources from which data for this product are obtained
1998 Value added pilot matched Key Stage 3 - GCSE/GNVQ datasets

Attendance and Absence in Scottish Schools 1995 - 97 to 1997/98
Scottish Executive

Data on attendance and absence in Scottish schools. Contains summary information on the absence rates of pupils in education authority primary, secondary and special schools in Scotland, session 1997-98. Information is listed for individual schools as well as local authority averages.

Delivery: Periodic Release
Frequency: Annually
Price: free
ISBN: 0 7480 5865 6

Available from
HM Inspector of Schools Audit Unit
Scottish Executive
Please see Annex B for full address details

Sources from which data for this product are obtained
Pupil Attendance and Absence

Benchmark Information for National Assembly for Wales: Key Stage 1
National Assembly for Wales

Delivery: Periodic hardcopy
Frequency: Annually
Price: Free

Available from
School Performance Division 4
National Assembly Education Department
National Assembly for Wales
Please see Annex B for full address details

Sources from which data for this product are obtained
National Curriculum Results for 7-year-olds

Benchmark Information for National Assembly for Wales: Key Stage 2
National Assembly for Wales

Delivery: Periodic hardcopy
Frequency: Annually
Price: Free

Available from
School Performance Division 4
National Assembly Education Department
National Assembly for Wales
Please see Annex B for full address details

Sources from which data for this product are obtained
National Curriculum Results for 11-year-olds

Benchmark Information for National Assembly for Wales: Key Stages 3 and 4
National Assembly for Wales

Delivery: Periodic hardcopy
Frequency: Annually
Price: Free

Available from
School Performance Division 4
National Assembly Education Department
National Assembly for Wales
Please see Annex B for full address details

Sources from which data for this product are obtained
National Curriculum Results for 14-year-olds, and examination results - Wales

Class sizes in Primary Schools
National Assembly for Wales

A statistical release with provisional results from the Schools' Census. Class sizes by Key Stage, Year Group, and LEA.

Delivery: Periodic Statistical Release
Frequency: Annual
Price: free

Available from
Howell Jones
Education and Training Statistics Unit
Statistical Directorate
National Assembly for Wales
Tel: 029 2082 5060;
Email: howell.jones@wales.gsi.gov.uk

Sources from which data for this product are obtained
Schools' Census - Wales

(The) Curriculum in Education Authority Secondary Schools in Scotland 1997-98 News Release
Scottish Executive

Information from the School Census on the timetabled curriculum in Scottish education authority secondary schools at September 1991, 1993 and 1995. This publication can also be found on the Scottish Executive Web Site: "http://www.scotland.gov.uk".

Delivery: News/Press Release
Frequency: Bi-annually

Available from
Andrew Wilson-Annan
Scottish Executive
Victoria Quay
Edinburgh
Tel: 0131 244 0323; Fax: 0131 244 0354;
Email: andrew.wilson-annan@scotland.gov.uk

Enrolments at Schools in Northern Ireland
Department of Education Northern Ireland

Statistical Press Release. Tables containing enrolments by school type, management type, free school meal entitlement, sex and religion.

Delivery: News/Press Release
Frequency: Annually
Price: Free

Available from
Department of Education Northern Ireland,
Statistics and Research Branch
Please see Annex B for full address

Sources from which data for this product are obtained
School Census - Northern Ireland

GCSE GNVQ and GCE A/AS and Advanced GNVQ - England
Department for Education and Employment

Statistical bulletin with tables and charts giving details of examination achievement. Contains data on GCSE attempts and achievements by fifteen-year-old pupils, GCSE achievements for students aged 16+ by individual subject and grade, GCE A/AS achievements, GCE A/AS achievements by subject and grade. Includes a time series of GCSE and GCE A/AS achievement. Mainly tables with some analysis at the beginning.

Delivery: Periodic Release
Frequency: Annually
Price: £5.95
ISBN: 0 11 271064-4

Available from
TSO Publications Centre and Bookshops
Please see Annex B for full address details.

Sources from which data for this product are obtained
Examination Results of GCSE and GCE

GCSE and GCE A/AS Level Performance of Candidates Attempting Two or More GCE A Levels or AS Equivalents
Department for Education and Employment

Statistical bulletin providing a comparison of the GCE A/AS level performance of seventeen-year-old students taking at least two GCE A or AS equivalents with the GCSE performance of the same candidates. Contains data on GCSE and GCE A/AS point scores, GCE A/AS examination results, and GCSE examination results. It provides information for schools, FE colleges, maintained schools, independent schools, and sixth form colleges. The data is presented by science subjects and non-subjects, male and female.

Delivery: Periodic Release
Frequency: Annually
Price: £5.95
ISBN: 0 11 271056-5

Available from
TSO Publications Centre and Bookshops
Please see Annex B for full address details.

Key Stage 1 - Results of the National Curriculum: Assessment of Seven-Year-Olds in England
Department for Education and Employment

Booklet presenting data on results of the Key Stage 1 National Curriculum assessments. Contains attainments of seven-year-old pupils in the National Curriculum tests and associated teacher assessment. A summary of the national results for 7 year olds and showing the information that schools must by law report to parents alongside their school's results has been sent to all schools. Both this booklet and the summary are also available on the Internet.

Delivery: Periodic Release
Frequency: Annually
Price: Free

Available from
Department for Education and Employment
Publication Centre
Please see Annex B for full address details

Sources from which data for this product are obtained
National Curriculum Results for Seven-Year-Olds

Key Stage 2 - Results of the National Curriculum Assessment of Eleven-Year-Olds in England
Department for Education and Employment

Booklet presenting data on results of the Key Stage 2 National Curriculum assessments. Contains attainments of eleven-year-old pupils in the National Curriculum tests and associated teacher assessment. A summary of the national results for 11 year olds and showing the information that schools must by law report to parents alongside their school's results has been sent to all schools. Both this booklet and the summary are also available on the Internet.

Delivery: Periodic Release
Frequency: Annually
Price: Free

Available from
Department for Education and Employment
Publication Centre
Please see Annex B for full address details

Sources from which data for this product are obtained
National Curriculum Results for Eleven-Year-Olds

Key Stage 3 - Results of the National Curriculum: Assessment of Fourteen-Year-Olds in England
Department for Education and Employment

Booklet presenting data on results of the Key Stage 3 National Curriculum assessments. Contains attainments of fourteen-year-old pupils in the National Curriculum tests and associated teacher assessment. A summary of the national results for 14 year olds and showing the information that schools must by law report to parents alongside their school's results has been sent to all schools. Both this booklet and the summary are also available on the Internet.

Delivery: Periodic Release
Frequency: Annually
Price: Free

Available from
Department for Education and Employment
Publication Centre
Please see Annex B for full address details

Sources from which data for this product are obtained
National Curriculum Results for Fourteen-Year-Olds

Leaver Destinations from Scottish Secondary Schools 1994/95 to 1996/97
HM Inspectors of Schools Audit Unit

This report provides basic information on where pupils went after they left Scottish Education Authority, Grant-Aided and Self-Governing secondary schools by the October following each of the 3 school years 1994/95, 1995/96 and 1996/97.

Delivery: Periodic Release
Frequency: Annually
Price: Free
ISBN: 0 7480 5887 7

Available from
HM Inspector of Schools Audit Unit
Scottish Executive
Please see Annex B for full address details

Sources from which data for this product are obtained
School Leaver Destinations Survey, completed by Careers Services and Independent Schools in Scotland

---

National Curriculum Assessment Results in Wales: Key Stage 1
National Assembly for Wales

Booklet presenting results of the end of Key Stage 1 assessments of 7 year olds. Contains results of test and teacher assessments in the core subjects (English, Welsh in Welsh speaking schools, Mathematics and Science) both nationally and for local education authority areas.

Delivery: Periodic hardcopy publication
Frequency: Annual
Price: Free

Available from
School Performance Division 3
National Assembly Education Department
National Assembly for Wales
Please see Annex B for full address details

Sources from which data for this product are obtained
National Curriculum results for 7 year olds - Wales

National Curriculum Assessment Results in Wales: Key Stage 2
National Assembly for Wales

Booklet presenting results of the end of Key Stage 2 assessments of 11 year olds. Contains results of test and teacher assessments in the core subjects (English, Welsh in Welsh speaking schools, Mathematics and Science) both nationally and for local education authority areas.

Delivery: Periodic hardcopy publication
Frequency: Annual
Price: Free

Available from
School Performance Division 3
National Assembly Education Department
National Assembly for Wales
Please see Annex B for full address details

Sources from which data for this product are obtained
National Curriculum results for 11 year olds - Wales

National Curriculum Assessment Results in Wales: Key Stage 3
National Assembly for Wales

Booklet presenting results of the end of Key Stage 3 assessments of 14 year olds. Contains results of test and teacher assessments in the core subjects (English, Welsh in Welsh speaking schools, Mathematics and Science)

both nationally and for local education authority areas.

Delivery: Periodic hardcopy publication
Frequency: Annual
Price: Free

Available from
School Performance Division 3
National Assembly Education Department
National Assembly for Wales
Please see Annex B for full address details

Sources from which data for this product are obtained
National Curriculum results for 14 year olds - Wales

Placing Requests in Education Authority Schools in Scotland: 1987-88 to 1997-98
Scottish Executive Education Department

Presents provisional information on the numbers of placing requests received by Scottish education authorities between 1 August 1997 and 31 July 1998 with comparisons with previous years. This publication can also be found on the Scottish Executive Website: "http://www.scotland.gov.uk".

Delivery: Periodic Release
Frequency: Annually
Price: Free

Available from
Available on the internet

Sources from which data for this product are obtained
Placing Requests in Education Authority Schools

Pupil Projections for Scotland
Scottish Executive Education Department

Projections of pupil numbers in Scotland until 2009. Contains projections of pupil numbers in primary, secondary and special schools in Scotland over the period September 1999 to September 2009. Also shown are projections for the total number of pupils aged four years and over receiving school education.

Frequency: Bi-annually
Price: £2.00
ISBN: 0 7480 4830 8
ISSN: 0143-599X

Available from
TSO Publications Centre and Bookshops
Please see Annex B for full address details.

Pupil: Teacher Ratios (PTRs) - Northern Ireland
Department of Education Northern Ireland

Statistical press release. The release gives comparisons of latest Northern Ireland pupil: teacher ratios with earlier years and contains data on nursery, primary, and secondary schools, by management type and area board. An overall comparison of each school sector with England is given.

Delivery: News/Press Release
Frequency: Annually
Price: Free

Available from
Department of Education Northern Ireland
Statistics and Research Branch
Please see Annex B for full address details

Sources from which data for this product are obtained
School Census

Pupil: Teacher Ratios in Maintained Schools by Local Education Authority in England
Department for Education and Employment

Contains data on overall pupil: teacher ratio, pupil: teacher ratios by type of school and number of full-time equivalent pupils and full-time equivalent teachers in maintained (including grant-maintained) nursery, primary and secondary schools in England. Also contains pupil: teacher ratio figures for Government Office Regions and LEAs.

Delivery: Periodic Release
Frequency: Annually
Price: £3.50
ISBN: 0 11 271019 0

Available from
TSO Publications Centre and Bookshops
Please see Annex B for full address details.

Pupils in Grant-Aided Schools - Northern Ireland
Department of Education Northern Ireland

Statistical bulletin outlining main results of School Census for grant-aided schools. Contains data on pupil enrolments, pre-school age, primary, secondary, grammar, over 16s remaining at school.

Frequency: Annual
Price: Free

Available from
Department of Education (DENI)
Statistics Branch
Rathgael House
Balloo Road
Bangor
Co. Down BT19 7PR
Tel: 01247 279472

Qualifications and Destinations of Northern Ireland School Leavers
Department of Education Northern Ireland

Statistical press release. Tables containing highest level of qualification obtained, and destination (higher education/further education/other), for grammar and non-grammar schools, by sex of pupil and management type. Some of the data in this product is disaggregated by gender.

Delivery: News/Press Release
Frequency: Annually
Price: Free

Available from
Department of Education Northern Ireland
Statistics and Research Branch
Please see Annex B for full address details

Sources from which data for this product are obtained
School Leavers' Survey

School and College (16-18) Performance Tables
Department for Education and Employment

Annual publication of school and college (16-18) performance in geographic regions.

Delivery: Periodic Release
Frequency: Annually
Price: free

Available from
Gillian Blair
Room 5B
Department for Education and Employment
Caxton House
Tothill Street
London SW1H 9NF
Tel: 020 7273 5941;
Email: gillian.blair@dfee.gov.uk

Sources from which data for this product are obtained
Examination Results of GCSE and GCE

School Boards, May 1998: News Release
Scottish Executive Education Department

Reports the summary results of a survey on the status of school boards in Scottish education authority schools in Scotland as at 31 May 1998. Comparisons with the results of similar surveys from 1989-90, 1991-92, 1993-94 and 1995-96 are also given. This publication can also be found on the Scottish Executive Web Site: "http://www.scotland.gov.uk".

Delivery: News/Press Release
Frequency: Every Two Years

Available from
Available on the internet

Sources from which data for this product are obtained
School Boards

School Leavers (National Assembly for Wales Statistical Release)
National Assembly for Wales

Delivery: Statistical Release
Frequency: August until 1997
Price: Free

Available from
Howell Jones
Education and Training Statistics Unit
Statistical Directorate
National Assembly for Wales
Tel: 029 2082 5060;
Email: howell.jones@wales.gsi.gov.uk

Sources from which data for this product are obtained
School Leavers - Wales

School Meals in Education Authority Schools, 1998-99: News Release
Scottish Executive Education Department

Provides a summary of the data gathered from Scottish education authorities in the 1998-99 round of the annual January Census of pupils taking free school meals. This publication can also be found on the Scottish Executive Web Site: "http: www.scotland.gov.uk".

Delivery: News/Press Release
Frequency: Annual

Available from the internet

Sources from which data for this product are obtained
Pupils Taking Meals In Education Authority Schools

School Performance Information
Department of Education - Northern Ireland

Booklet showing enrolment, attendance rate, examination results for each post-primary school in Northern Ireland. The booklet contains, for each post-primary school, total enrolment; attendance rate; proportion of year 12 pupils achieving 1-4 and 5+ GCSE grades A*-C and A*-G; proportion of pupils in the final year of an A level course achieving 3+ grades A-C, 2+ grades A-E, and 1+grades A-E; proportion of pupils in final year of GNVQ Intermediate and Advanced courses achieving the full qualification.

Delivery: News/Press Release
Frequency: Annually
Price: Free

Available from
Department of Education Northern Ireland
Statistics and Research Branch
Please see Annex B for full address details

Sources from which data for this product are obtained
School Performance Survey - Northern Ireland

School Performance Information
National Assembly for Wales

Statistics concerning secondary schools in Wales. Contains data on examination results and attendance for all secondary schools in Wales, along with a background information on the school. There are separate booklets for North, South, South East, South West, Mid and West Wales.

Frequency: Annual
Price: Free

Available from
School Performance Division 3
National Assembly Education Department
National Assembly for Wales
Please see Annex B for full address details

Sources from which data for this product are obtained
Examination Results - Wales

Scottish School Leavers and their Qualifications: 1986-87 to 1996-97
Scottish Executive

This bulletin gives information on all pupils who left Scottish schools during the period 1986-87 to 1996-97. It presents analysis of pupil achievements in the Scottish Certificate of Education examinations and some English examinations (GCSE and A levels).

Delivery: Periodic Release
Frequency: Annually
Price: £2.00
ISBN: 0 7480 7310 8
ISSN: 0143-599X

Available from
TSO Publications Centre and Bookshops
Please see Annex B for full address details.

Sources from which data for this product are obtained
Qualifications - Scottish Certificate of Education; School Leavers - Annual School Census

Scottish Schools: Costs 1995-96 and 1997-98
Scottish Executive

The data provide information on the budgeted school running costs of education authority primary, secondary and special schools in Scotland, for financial years 1995-96 and 1997-98. Costs are given as local authority and national averages and also for individual schools. This publication can also be found on the Scottish Executive Web Site: "http://www.scotland.gov.uk".

Delivery: Periodic Release
Frequency: Annually
Price: Free
ISBN: 0 7480 5888 5

Available from
HM Inspector of Schools Audit Unit
Scottish Executive
Please see Annex B for full address details

Sources from which data for this product are obtained
School Budgeted Running Costs

Secondary School Performance Tables
Department for Education and Employment

Annual publication of secondary school examination performance by region.

Delivery: Periodic Release
Frequency: Annually
Price: free

Available from
Catherine Blackham
Department for Education and Employment
Analytical Services
Caxton House
Tothill Street
London
Tel: 020 7273 4904; Fax: 020 7273 5999

Sources from which data for this product are obtained
School Performance Information: Absence

Statistical Bulletin - National Curriculum Assessments of 7, 11 and 14 Year Olds in England
Department for Education and Employment

National Curriculum assessment results by school types, i.e. maintained, independent and special, size of school, percentage of pupils taking free school meals and percentage of pupils with English as an additional language. This bulletin provides the results of further analyses carried out on the attainments of pupils in England under the National curriculum. It contains results of 1997 tasks/tests and teachers' assessments at each Key Stage. This is the first issue of such a bulletin. It is also an opportunity to consolidate the results published in the 3 individual Key Stage National Curriculum assessment booklets.

Delivery: Periodic Release
Frequency: Annually
Price: £5.95 per booklet

Available from
Catherine Blackham
Department for Education and Employment
Analytical Services
Caxton House
Tothill Street
London
Tel: 020 7273 4904; Fax: 020 7273 5999

Statistics of Education (Volume): Public Examinations GCSE/ GNVQ and GCE /AGNVQ in England
Department for Education and Employment

Annual publication which contains details of GCSE and GCSE A/AS level examination results in England split by region, gender, subject, type of establishment and grade of result. 150 page statistical volume containing data on GCSE and GCE A level and AS examination results of pupils in schools and of students in further education establishments (in England) for each academic year. Mainly tables with some analysis at the beginning.

Delivery: Periodic Release
Frequency: Annually
Price: £14.95
ISBN: 0-11-271068-9

Available from
Gillian Blair
Room 5B
Department for Education and Employment
Caxton House
Tothill Street
London SW1H 9NF
Tel: 020 7273 5941;
Email: gillian.blair@dfee.gov.uk

Statistics of Education and Training in Wales: Schools
National Assembly for Wales

Statistics covering all aspects of the schools sector on Wales. Contains data on education provision for children aged under five; primary education; secondary education; teacher placements and Technical & Vocational Education Initiative (TVEI); teachers; school performance; school leavers; Welsh Joint Education Committee examination results; Welsh; special education; schools services; finance and unit costs; pupil numbers; and participation rates.

Delivery: Hardcopy publication
Frequency: Annual
Price: £10.00
ISBN: 0 7504 2302 1
ISSN: 0968-5588

Available from
Publications Unit
Statistical Directorate
National Assembly for Wales

Sources from which data for this product are obtained
Examination Results - Wales; Local Authority Capital Outturn - Wales; Local Authority Revenue Outturn - Wales; School Leavers - Wales; Schools' Census - Wales.

Statistics of Education: Schools in England
Department for Education and Employment

A Statistical Volume on schools, pupils and teachers with data derived from the Schools' Census. Data are shown at LEA, region and England level. Some time series data are included. It contains pupil (ft and pt) by age and sex, schools by size, denomination, status and type, provision for pupils with Special Educational Needs, provision for pupils under 5 years of age, school meals arrangements, lesson times, teaching staff, non-teaching staff, class sizes, (classes as taught) and courses of study of pupils aged 16 and over. Also includes data on permanent exclusions.

Delivery: Periodic Release
Frequency: Annually
Price: £20.00
ISBN: 0 11 271023 9

Available from
TSO Publications Centre and Bookshops
Please see Annex B for full address details.

Statistics of Schools in England (Press Notice)
Department for Education and Employment

Information on schools, pupils and teachers, derived from returns made by all schools in the Schools' Census. Data are in the form of a time series, figures for the most recent year being provisional. The press notice contains data on pupils by type of school, age and SEN in maintained and non-maintained schools on pupils, teachers and pupil: teacher ratios in maintained and non-maintained schools; on pupils below statutory school age by sex in maintained nursery and primary schools, special schools and independent schools; on class size, class contact ratios and lesson time in maintained primary and secondary schools; on pupils over statutory school age by course of study in maintained secondary schools and independent schools; on non-teaching staff in maintained and special schools; and school meal arrangements in maintained schools.

Frequency: Annual
Price: Free

Available from
Department for Education and Employment, Analytical Services
Please see Annex B for full address details.

Sources from which data for this product are obtained
Schools' Census - England

Summary Results of the September 1998 School Census
Scottish Executive Education Department

This bulletin provides provisional summary results from the September 1999 School Census. The majority of the results relate to publicly funded schools (Education Authority, Grant-Aided and opted out), although some statistics are provided for independent schools. This publication can also be found on the Scottish Executive Web Site: "http://www.scotland.gov".

Delivery: Periodic Release
Frequency: Annually
Price: £2.00
ISBN: 0 7480 7144 X
ISSN: 0143-599X

Available from
TSO Publications Centre and Bookshops
Please see Annex B for full address details.

Sources from which data for this product are obtained
School Census: School Pupil and Teacher Numbers

Survey of Information Technology in Schools (Press Notice)
Department for Education and Employment

A survey report containing data on information technology in schools. The report contains data on the number, ratios and type of computers and hardware, location and maintenance, expenditure and sources of funding, the use, contribution and support, staff training and use by pupils with special educational needs.

Delivery: News/Press Release
Frequency: Every two years
Price: Free
ISBN: 0142-5013
ISSN: ISSN 0142-5013

Available from
Department for Education and Employment, Analytical Services
Please see Annex B for full address details.

Sources from which data for this product are obtained
Information Technology in Schools

1994 Teachers' Workloads Survey for the School Teachers' Review Body
Office of Manpower Economics

The results of a survey of teachers' workloads. Contains data on the hours qualified teachers in maintained primary, secondary and special schools worked in a week in March 1994 (First Report) and in a week in May 1994 (Second Report, which also includes the results of a qualitative exercise) such as the make-up of total hours by detailed and grouped activities, distributions of total hours and of hours spent teaching, and the percentage of hours spent working at weekends or in the evening.

Delivery: Hardcopy publication
Price: Free

Available from
Office of Manpower Economics
Oxford House
76 Oxford Street
London WIN 9FD
Tel: 020 7467 7216

Violence Against School Staff: News Release
Scottish Executive

Reports the summary information from local authorities on incidents of violence against school staff. This News Release can be found on the Scottish Executive website: http://www.scotland.gov.uk

Delivery: News / Press Release
Frequency: Annually

Available from
Kathleen Swift
Scottish Executive
Victoria Quay
Edinburgh
Tel: 0131 244 7529

Sources from which data for this product are obtained
Local Authorities

Welsh Education and Training Statistics Bulletin No.3: Pupils with Statements of Special Educational Needs 1993/94 - 1995/96
National Assembly for Wales

Delivery: Ad hoc hardcopy publication
Frequency: One off
Price: £5.00
ISBN: 0 7504 2182 7

Available from
Publications Unit, Statistical Directorate
National Assembly for Wales
Please see Annex B for full address details

Sources from which data for this product are obtained
Children with statements of special education need - Wales, Schools' Census - Wales

5.14 Teacher Training / Newly Trained Teachers

(The) New Teacher in School: A Survey by HM Inspectors in England and Wales
Department for Education and Employment

Results from a survey on newly trained teachers. Contains data on training, current posts and performance, induction, the nature and type of school, arrangements for appointment and induction, and views of how well the new teachers were equipped for their posts.

Price: £6.50
ISBN: 0 11 350018 1

Available from
TSO Publications Centre and Bookshops
Please see Annex B for full address details.

See also:
In this chapter:
Report of the School Teachers' Review Body *(5.16)*

5.15 Training, Qualifications & National Record of Achievement

Achievement of General National Vocational Qualifications (GNVQs) in Northern Ireland
Department of Education Northern Ireland

Statistical Press Release. Tables containing GNVQ achievements by level, type of institution (school /further education), grade of award and subject.

Delivery: News/Press Release
Frequency: Annually
Price: Free

Available from
Department of Education Northern Ireland, Statistics and Research Branch
Please see Annex B for full address details.

Sources from which data for this product are obtained
GNVQ Database

Adult Literacy in Britain
Office for National Statistics; sponsored by Consortium of Govt. Depts and The Basic Skills Agency.

The report profiles the literacy skills of the population of working age and also describes the characteristics of those with low skills as well as making comparisons with the other countries that took part. The Adult Literacy Survey was carried out in Britain amongst adults aged 16-65 as part of an international programme of surveys known as the International Adult Literacy Survey (IALS). This report contains information on literacy skills by various characteristics, literacy at work and in everyday life and a comparison of literacy skills between a number of countries.

Delivery: Ad hoc/One-off Release
Frequency: Ad hoc
Price: £30.00
ISBN: 0-11-620943-7

Available from
TSO Publications Centre and Bookshops
Please see Annex B for full address details.

Employer Provided Training in the United Kingdom - 1993
Department for Education and Employment

Report of findings of CVTS survey in the UK. Contains information on employers' training behaviour, non-trainers, training exposure, training volumes and costs, and comparison with Training in Britain 1987. Analyses presented by size of business, industrial sector and occupational grades. Mainly text with some tables and charts.

Delivery: Ad Hoc/One-off Release
Price: N/A - available through IFF Research Ltd, 26 Whiskin St, London, EC1R 0BP. (Tel: 020 7837 6363)
ISBN: 0 9516802 6 9

Available from
Phil Rose
Room W625
Department for Education and Employment
Moorfoot
Sheffield S1 4PQ
Tel: 0114 259 3154;
Email: p.rose@dfee.gov.uk

Sources from which data for this product are obtained
Continuing Vocational Survey in Enterprises; Continuing Vocational Training Survey

---

Government Supported Training - England and Wales
Department for Education and Employment

The Press Notice provides information on work-based training for young people and adults. It provides statistics on participation, outcomes and characteristics of trainees on government supported training.

Delivery: News/Press Release
Frequency: Monthly
Price: Free

Available from
John Fletcher
Department for Education and Employment
Analytical Services
Moorfoot
Sheffield
Tel: 0114 259 4317

Sources from which data for this product are obtained
Work-Related Government Supported Training

Skills Needs in Great Britain and Northern Ireland 1998
Department for Education and Employment

A report of a Department for Education and Employment commissioned survey of employers' skills needs, training practices, and awareness and participation in DfEE initiatives. Information on skills gaps and shortages, training and awareness of training and other initiatives in companies with more than 25 employees. Presentation is a mixture of text, tables and charts.

Frequency: Annually - The last in the series
Price: £50.00 - **Available from** IFF Research Ltd, 26 Whiskin St, London, EC1R 0BP. Tel: 020 7837 6363
ISBN: 0 951 6802 85

Available from
TSO Publications Centre and Bookshops
Please see Annex B for full address details.

Sources from which data for this product are obtained
Skill Needs in Britain

Skill Needs of Small Firms in Britain 1994-1995
Department for Education and Employment

A report of a Department for Education and Employment commissioned survey of employers' skills needs and training practices in establishments with less than 25 employees. Presentation is a mixture of text, tables and charts.

Delivery: Other
Frequency: Ah-hoc
Price: £45.00
Available from Public Attitude Surveys, Rye Park House, London Rd, High Wycombe, Bucks. Tel: 01494 532771

Available from
TSO Publications Centre and Bookshops
Please see Annex B for full address details.

Sources from which data for this product are obtained
Skill Needs in Britain

Vocational Qualifications in the UK 1997/98
Department for Education and Employment

This statistical bulletin provides data on NVQs, SVQs, GNVQs, GSVQs and other vocational qualifications awarded in the UK. The publication consists of 20 pages of text, tables and charts. Topics covered are NVQ/SVQs, GNVQ/GSVQs, Other VQs, Awards by level, Awards by age, Awards by gender, Awards by occupational sector, Awards by subject area, and Awards by type of assessment centre. Readers will use the publication to find out how vocational qualifications are broken down and how this break-up has varied since 1991/92. Some of the data in this product is disaggregated by gender.

Delivery: Periodic Release
Frequency: Annually
Price: £5.95
ISBN: 0-11-271066-2

Available from
TSO Publications Centre and Bookshops
Please see Annex B for full address details.

Sources from which data for this product are obtained
National Information System for Vocational Qualifications (NISVQ)

1992 Welsh Social Survey: Report on Training and Education
National Assembly for Wales

An overview of the take-up of and attitudes towards training and further education

Products

amongst the population of working age in Wales. The publication is likely to be of interest to those looking for information about the labour market and the skills of the work-force. This volume is based on information from the 1992 Welsh Social Survey. Although the main survey has been conducted at approximately five year intervals, the questionnaire on training and education was a one-off. Of the 18,600 individuals of working age identified in the households which responded to the main survey, over 16,400 provided responses to the education and training questionnaire. It contains tables, charts and accompanying text covering the qualifications and further, vocational and job-related education and training of the population of working age together with their aims in taking part in education or training and their attitudes toward it. Tables are predominantly analysed by the age, sex, socio-economic group and TEC area of residence of respondents.

Frequency: One-off
Price: £6.00 (including p&p)
ISBN: 0 7504 0687 9

Available from
Publications Unit, Statistical Directorate
National Assembly for Wales
Please see Annex B for full address details

Sources from which data for this product are obtained
Household Survey - Wales

See also:
In this chapter:
Statistical Bulletin *(5.9)*

In other chapters:
Labour Force Survey Quarterly Databases *(see the Labour Market chapter)*
Labour Market Trends *(see the Labour Market chapter)*

5.16 Teachers and Lecturers' Pay

Report of the School Teachers' Review Body
Office of Manpower Economics

The Annual Report by the School Teachers' Review Body to the Prime Minister on such matters relating to the statutory conditions of employment of school teachers (classroom teachers, heads and deputies) in England and Wales as may from time to time be referred to it by the Secretary of State: Report primarily presents recommendations on pay and conditions.

Delivery: Other
Frequency: Annually
Price: £13.00
ISBN: 0 10 142442 6

Available from
Office of Manpower Economics
Please see Annex B for full address details

Teachers' Pay Survey for the School Teachers' Review Body
Office of Manpower Economics

Results of the latest September survey of school teachers' pay. Contains data on the pay of qualified teachers in maintained nursery, primary, secondary and special schools, such as distributions on the pay spine, movements on the pay spine, numbers remaining in post, changes in assessed points scores for classroom teachers, number of points awarded under each assessment criterion, and source of entrants to schools.

Delivery: Hardcopy publication
Frequency: Annually
Price: free

Available from
Office of Manpower Economics
Please see Annex B for full address details

Other products which may be of interest, but are not featured in this book due to lack of details:

1996 Secondary School Staffing Survey - National Assembly for Wales
Further and Higher Education and Training Statistics in Wales - National Assembly for Wales
Statistics of Education: Students in Further and Higher Education - Department for Education and Employment
Welsh Training and Education Survey - National Assembly for Wales

Labour Market

Statistics covering the **Labour Market** are collected, administered and disseminated by a number of separate Departments, Agencies and organisations including the **Office for National Statistics, the Department for Education and Employment, the Office of Manpower Economics, Scottish Executive, the National Assembly for Wales, the Northern Ireland Department of Economic Development, and the Health and Safety Executive.** The available statistics embrace a number of subject areas including: the **Cost of Labour, Demand for/Supply of Labour, Employment and Work, Health and Safety at Work, Labour Relations, Pay and Income from Work, Productivity, Travel to Work, Unemployment and Inactivity.**

The basic data are generated from a number of separate information 'Sources' and the resultant statistics are disseminated through a whole range of statistical 'Analyses' and 'Products', all of which are described in the following chapter. Users looking for a cross-section of UK-wide statistics on the **Labour Market** may find the following products useful:

> **Labour Market Trends** (monthly publication)
> **NOMIS** (on-line database)

Users interested in a wider range of official statistics including **Labour Market** statistics may like to refer to the following compendia:

> On-line Databases (See Chapter 1):
> > **StatBase - StatStore**
> > **StatBase -TimeZone**
> > **DataBank**
> Hardcopy Compendia (See Chapter 2):
> > **Annual Abstract of Statistics**
> > **Britain 2000: The Official Yearbook of the United Kingdom**
> > **Monthly Digest of Statistics**
> > **Regional Trends**
> > **Social Trends**

Users may also find what they need on the various Departmental Websites. These are listed in Chapter 1.

6 Labour Market - *Sources and Analyses*

6.1 Cost of Labour

Compensation of Employees
Office for National Statistics

The Office for National Statistics compiles data on compensation of employees which includes wages and salaries, and employers' social contributions. i) Wages and salaries are estimated annually from an analysis of the PAYE tax deduction cards sent by employers to local tax offices after each financial year. Quarterly figures are estimated by reference to the ONS's index of average earnings, new earnings survey and employment data. The figures for wages and salaries include estimates of income in kind and other benefits of employment and exclude expenses of employment. ii) Employers' social contributions include those made to the National Insurance scheme and to the National Health Service, as well as contributions to private pension schemes. The data are mainly derived from data from the Government Actuaries Department and from the ONS's pension fund inquiries. The data are used by the ONS in the calculation of Gross Domestic Product and in the household sector income account, and by the Treasury and economists elsewhere for economic analysis, modelling and forecasting. Compensation of employees is published quarterly with GDP and is available both unadjusted and seasonally adjusted. An initial estimate is published towards the end of the second month after the quarter to which it refers, with more detailed estimates a month later.

Status: Ongoing
Frequency: Quarterly
Timeliness: Towards the end of the second month after the quarter which the data refers to
Earliest Available Data: 1946 (annually); 1955 (quarterly)
National Coverage: United Kingdom
Disaggregation: Standard Regions

Statistician
Roger Ward
Office for National Statistics
Tel: 020 7533 6002;
Email: roger.ward@ons.gov.uk

Products that contain data from this analysis
Annual Abstract of Statistics; Economic Trends; Economic Trends Annual Supplement; Financial Statistics; Monthly Digest of Statistics; Office for National Statistics Databank / Datastore; Quarterly National Accounts (First Release); UK Output, Income and Expenditure (First Release); United Kingdom Economic Accounts (Quarterly Supplement to Economic Trends); United Kingdom National Accounts - The Blue Book; United Kingdom National Accounts, Sources and Methods

Labour Costs in the EC
Office for National Statistics

The Office for National Statistics conducts the UK Survey of Labour Costs for the European Community. Data are collected by each EC member state on a sample of employers from manufacturing, energy and water, construction, retail and wholesale distribution, hotels and catering, insurance, banking and finance (including building societies and finance houses), business services (including lawyers, accountants, estate agents, employment agencies and architects), and travel agents and tour operators. Firms with fewer than ten employees are excluded. Within the UK the results are used for the National Accounts and for the calculation of labour costs per unit output. Data on labour costs are available by total gross wages and salaries, pension and insurance contributions, redundancy payments, benefits in kind, vocational training costs, services to employees, government subsidies, cost of recruiting staff, voluntary social welfare, and net running cost of company cars. They also cover the average number of employees and the total hours worked. The survey covers Great Britain and Northern Ireland. The Survey was first carried out in 1964 and many changes have occurred. Until 1984 these surveys were carried out every three years but the frequency has now been reduced to every four years. From 1975 firms were held on an establishment basis and in 1981 a sample of smaller companies was approached. UK results are published about eighteen months after the reference period.

Collection Method: Data derived from existing national surveys and administrative data.
Frequency: Every four years
Reference Period: April 1996
Earliest Available Data: 1964
National Coverage: United Kingdom

Disaggregation: 3 digit SIC level, government office region (including N.I) and five different size bands.

Statistician
Derek Bird
Office for National Statistics
Tel: 01928 792614

Products that contain data from this source
Labour Costs (Eurostat), 1988 Volume 1: Principal results; Labour Market Trends

6.2 Demand for/Supply of Labour

Job Centre Vacancies
Office for National Statistics

The Office for National Statistics compiles data on Jobcentre vacancies and placings. The data cover the job-broking activities carried out by Employment Service in Great Britain and the Treasury and Employment Agency in Northern Ireland. Data are collected as a by-product of operational procedures. Data are collected on the stock of unfilled vacancies held by Jobcentres, the number of job vacancies notified to Jobcentres during the month (inflows) and the number filled or cancelled (outflows). Both seasonally adjusted and unadjusted series are available at regional as well as national level. Unadjusted data, however, are also available at various levels by aggregating the data at individual Jobcentre level. The current series run from 1980 onwards. Data are collected every month (apart from the occupational and industry analyses which are available every quarter) and are published about six weeks after the reference date.

Status: Ongoing
Collection Method: Administrative Records
Frequency: Monthly
Reference Period: The "count day" in every month
Timeliness: Data are released about 5 weeks after the "count day" in every month.
Earliest Available Data: From January 1980
National Coverage: United Kingdom
Disaggregation: Down to Government office region (seasonally adjusted) or best-fit county level (unadjusted)

Statistician
Jeremy Schuman
Office for National Statistics
Tel:020 7533 6110;
Email: jeremy.schuman@ons.gov.uk

Products that contain data from this source
Annual Abstract of Statistics; Labour market statistics First Release; Labour Market Trends; Nomis®

6.3 Employment and Work

Annual Employment Survey - Great Britain
Office for National Statistics

The Annual Employment Survey (AES) is conducted by the Office for National Statistics. AES is a sample survey which has run from 1995 to 1998 and replaced the Census of Employment which ran until 1993. The AES is the only source of employment statistics for GB analysed by local area and by detailed industrial classification (gender, full and part time employment splits are also produced). The ONS also provides the benchmark for employment estimates based on the smaller monthly and quarterly surveys (Short-Term surveys). The AES has surveyed a maximum of 125,000 Enterprises covering approximately 500,000 local units. The Annual Employment Survey is due to be superseded by the Annual Business Enquiry from 1998 or 1999.

Status: Ongoing
Collection Method: Sample survey
Frequency: Annually
Reference Period: The survey is a snapshot of Employee Jobs on one date - this date has always been in the first two weeks of September.
Timeliness: Headline figures are usually published within fifteen months of the survey date.
Earliest Available Data: September 1995
National Coverage: Great Britain
Disaggregation: Government Office Regions County, travel to work area, parliamentary constituency, unitary authorities, local authority district, NUTS, ward

Statistician
James Partington
Office for National Statistics
Tel: 01928 792545;
Email: james.partington@ons.gov.uk

Products that contain data from this source
Labour Market Trends; Monthly Digest of Statistics; Nomis®; Regional Trends; AES Results

Census of Employment
Office for National Statistics

The Office for National Statistics conducts the Census of Employment which provides an accurate picture of the level and distribution of employment. The ONS also provides the benchmark for the employment estimates based on the smaller monthly and quarterly surveys (Short-Term Surveys). Data are collected on the number of jobs by local area, detailed industrial activity, sex and whether full or part-time. The Census of Employment covers Great Britain. The Department of Economic Development (Northern Ireland) runs a full Census of Employment and these figures are added to GB for the UK figures. Since 1971 both sample and full Censuses have been conducted. Sample Censuses have covered approximately 300,000 businesses while the full Census in 1993 covered 1.25 million businesses. The Census is conducted every two years in September and results are published 18 to 24 months after the survey date. With effect from September 1995, the Census of Employment has been replaced by the Annual Employment Survey (AES). This is a much smaller annual survey covering approximately 130,000 businesses. The results for the AES are to be published within one year of the Survey date.

Status: Ceased completely
Collection Method: Census
Frequency: Biennial
Reference Period: The first two weeks in the September of a census year
Timeliness: Two years from survey date
Earliest Available Data: 1971
National Coverage: Great Britain and United Kingdom
Disaggregation: Standard Statistical Regions County, Scottish region, travel to work areas, parliamentary constituency, local authority district, ward

Statistician
James Partington
Office for National Statistics
Tel: 01928 792545;
Email: james.partington@ons.gov.uk

Products that contain data from this source
Census of Employment Booklets; NOMIS

Census of Employment - Northern Ireland
Department of Economic Development - Northern Ireland

The Northern Ireland Census of Employment, carried out every two years by the Northern Ireland Department of Economic Development (NIDED), concerns the labour market in Northern Ireland. Under the Statistics of Trade and Employment (NI)

Order 1988, the Census is a full count of the number of employee jobs in all industries except agriculture. Data are available by sex, full or part-time working patterns, industrial activity, and by travel-to-work areas, district council areas and ward. Longitudinal analyses are available from 1971. A Census was carried out annually until 1978; however to reduce costs and the form-filling burden on businesses, it now takes place every two years. Annually from 1971 to 1978 but only every two to three years thereafter. Disaggregated geographical data for Northern Ireland is only available from 1984 onwards.

Status: Ongoing
Collection Method: Census
Frequency: Biennial
Reference Period: First week in September every two years
Earliest Available Data: 1971
National Coverage: Northern Ireland
Disaggregation: District Council Area (Northern Ireland); Parliamentary Constituency; Travel-to-work Area; Ward

Statistician
Martin Monaghan
Department of Economic Development - Northern Ireland
Tel: 028 9052 9421;
Email: martin.monaghan@dedni.gov.uk

Products that contain data from this source
Census of Employment - Northern Ireland Statistics Notice; Northern Ireland Annual Abstract of Statistics

Employment (LFS - Seasonally Adjusted)
Office for National Statistics

Seasonally adjusted employment; UK monthly estimates for 3 month periods derived from the Labour Force Survey and published in the Labour Market Statistics First Release. Monthly series first published April 1998; Available from 1995 onwards. Annual UK estimates available back to Spring 1984 (quarterly from Winter 1994/5). GB - Spring quarter estimates published annually from Spring 1984 and quarterly estimates from Spring 1992.

Status: Ongoing
Frequency: Monthly
Reference Period: Average of 3 months
Timeliness: 6 weeks from end of collection period.
Earliest Available Data: Spring 1984
National Coverage: United Kingdom

Statistician
Sheena Gordon
Office for National Statistics
SED; LFS(OD)
Tel: 020 7533 6140;
Email: sheena.gordon@ons.gov.uk

Sources and Analyses

Products that contain data from this analysis
How exactly is employment measured?; Labour Market Statistics First Release; Labour Market Trends

Hours of Work
Office for National Statistics

The Office for National Statistics compiles data on hours worked per week derived from Workforce in Employment and Labour Force Survey figures. Data are available by industry, region, sex and full or part-time work. Seasonally adjusted figures are available for an aggregated industry split. The data cover the UK and have been collated annually for the period 1984-91 and quarterly from June 1992. This is an experimental series with results published quarterly, with the target that this should be three months after the reference date.

Status: Ongoing
Frequency: Quarterly
Reference Period: The specified count day each quarter for the employee jobs component
Timeliness: 3 months after employee jobs component count day
Earliest Available Data: 1992
National Coverage: United Kingdom
Sub-National: Great Britain
Disaggregation: Government Office Regions

Statistician
James Partington
Office for National Statistics
Tel: 01928 792545;
Email: james.partington@ons.gov.uk

Products that contain data from this analysis
Labour Market Trends

Joint Staffing Watch Survey - England
Department of the Environment, Transport and the Regions; sponsored jointly with the Local Authority Associations

The Department of the Environment, Transport and the Regions and local authority associations compiled data, supplied by local authorities, for the Joint Staffing Watch Survey. The Survey is conducted by the Local Government Management Board (LGMB) on behalf of the Joint Staffing Watch Group, which comprise representatives of both central and local government. Data are available on local authority employment in England by full-time and part-time, manual and non-manual, and service, and at local authority district level. A quarterly Survey was introduced in 1975 and became annual in 1995. Data are collected each June and published three months later. This data collection ceased after the 1998 Joint Staffing Watch Survey.

Status: Ceased completely
Collection Method: Census
Frequency: Annually
Reference Period: Staff Employed at June of each year
Earliest Available Data: 1979
National Coverage: England
Disaggregation: English Shire Counties, English Shire Districts, Metropolitan Districts, London Boroughs, Unitary Authorities, Fire Authorities

Statistician
Mark Chaplin
Department of the Environment, Transport and the Regions
Local Government Finance Policy Directorate; Local Government Finance Statistics Division Branch 3
Tel: 020 7890 4167(GTN 3533);
Email: mark_chaplin@detr.gsi.goc.uk

Products that contain data from this source
Joint staffing Watch (Press Release); Local Government Financial Statistics: England

Labour Survey - England and Wales
Ministry of Agriculture, Fisheries and Food

EC member states are required to collect information for the EC Structure Survey. Most of the data for England and Wales can be met from the June Agricultural and Horticultural Census. Detailed information on labour, not collected in the Census, is collected in the Labour Survey. This is a voluntary survey, conducted by the Ministry of Agriculture, Fisheries and Food (MAFF), based on a sample chosen from the agricultural and horticultural holdings which existed at the last June Census. Data are collected on the status of business, management of the holding, details of the holder, spouse, manager, (by sex, age, time spent on farm work on the holding, time spent on other paid work) other family workers, non-family regular workers, (by sex, time spent on farm work on the holding, time spent on other paid work) casual workers, contract labour and share farming. The Survey covers England and Wales but similar surveys are carried out in Scotland and Northern Ireland with MAFF collating the UK results for the Structure Survey. Data are available at standard region, county and district level. The Structure Survey is carried out every two to three years. It was first conducted in 1966-67 and covered land use, tenure, livestock, cropping, machinery and labour force. Structure surveys, carried out every ten years, usually contain more extensive information than those in the mid-term years, particularly regarding labour data. From 1975 onwards, results are held on a computer databank in the form of standard tables. The main results can take up to three years to publish but some results are released about two years after data are collected.

Status: Ongoing
Collection Method: Large-scale (Sample) Survey
Frequency: Periodic
Reference Period: Around September/October of a Structure Survey year
Timeliness: Approx. 2 years for EC publication.
Earliest Available Data: 1975
National Coverage: England and Wales
Disaggregation: Country; Region (as defined by EC); District (as defined by EC); County

Statistician
Adam Krawczyk
Ministry of Agriculture, Fisheries and Food
Statistics (Census & Surveys); E
Tel: 01904 455319
Email: a.krawczyk@esg.maff.gov.uk

Products that contain data from this source
Eurofarm Tabular Databank System; Farm Structure: Main Results; Farm Structure: Methodology of Community Surveys

Lone Parent Cohort
Department of Social Security

This cohort study is part of the Programme of Research into Low Income Families (PRILIF), conducted by the Policy Studies Institute (PSI) on behalf of the Department. A random, representative sample of lone parents was interviewed in 1991 and again in 1993, 1994, 1995, 1996 and most recently in 1998. PRILIF exists to provide ministers and policy makers accurate and robust information about lone parents. It is particularly used to examine lone parents' relationship with the labour market. It is also used to investigate the impact of policy changes. Data has been gathered from the cohort during 1996 and 1998, results from which will be published. There are no more surveys of the cohort after 1998.

Status: Ceased completely
Collection Method: Household/Person (Sample) Survey
Frequency: Annually
Earliest Available Data: 1991
National Coverage: Great Britain

Statistician
Social Research Branch
Department of Social Security
Tel: 020 7962 8543

Quarterly Employment Survey - Northern Ireland
Department of Economic Development - Northern Ireland

The Quarterly Employment Survey (QES) is carried out by the Northern Ireland Department of Economic Development (NIDED). It is a sample survey covering all public sector bodies, all private sector firms with 25 or more employees, and a representative sample of smaller firms. Data are available by sex, full and part-time employment. The Survey counts the number of jobs rather than the number of persons with jobs. Estimates are provided for the number of employee jobs in all industrial classes, for the periods between Employment Censuses at the Northern Ireland level only. Longitudinal and seasonally adjusted figures are available. The QES has been carried out since September 1978 and was extended in December 1992 to include a full-time/part-time split. Results are published approximately fourteen weeks after each quarter.

Status: Ongoing
Collection Method: Large-scale (Sample) Survey
Frequency: Quarterly
Reference Period: First Monday of each quarter
Timeliness: Three months
Earliest Available Data: September 1978
National Coverage: Northern Ireland

Statistician
Allan Nesbett
Department of Economic Development - Northern Ireland
Tel: 028 9052 9505;
Email: allan.nesbett@dedni.gov.uk

Products that contain data from this source
Northern Ireland Annual Abstract of Statistics; Northern Ireland Labour Market Statistics; Northern Ireland Quarterly Employment Survey – 2 Direct Booklet; Regional Trends

Workforce Jobs (Formerly Workforce in Employment)
Office for National Statistics

Statistics on the number of jobs is mainly collected through postal employer surveys. The total number of Workforce jobs is calculated by summing employee jobs from the Annual Employment Survey (AES), Short-term Employment & Sales Surveys and centralised returns surveys, self-employment jobs (from the LFS), those in HM Forces (from the MoD) and government - supported trainees (from the DfEE). The main part of the estimate is from the employee jobs total, this represents how many jobs there are, it excludes homeworkers and private domestic servants. The Workforce jobs series begins on an annual basis in 1959 and on a quarterly basis from June 1978. Data are available by males and females (GB & UK), full-part and part-time (GB only).

Status: Ongoing
Frequency: Quarterly
Reference Period: Specified dates per quarter for each component
Timeliness: 3 months
Earliest Available Data: June 1978 (SIC 92) for United Kingdom and Great Britain only
National Coverage: United Kingdom and Great Britain
Disaggregation: Civilian Workforce jobs available for Government Office Regions and standard regions

Statistician
James Partington
Office for National Statistics
Tel: 01928 792545;
Email: james.partington@ons.gov.uk

Products that contain data from this analysis
Annual Abstract of Statistics; Economic Trends; Labour Market Trends; Monthly Digest of Statistics; Nomis®; Social Trends; United Kingdom National Accounts - The Blue Book

See also:
In this chapter:
Labour Force Survey (6.5)
Workplace Industrial Relations Survey (6.6)

In other chapters:
EC Farm Structure Survey (see the Agriculture, Fishing, Food and Forestry chapter)
Household Survey - Wales (see the Housing chapter)

6.4 Health and Safety at Work

Asbestosis Register - Great Britain
Health and Safety Executive

The Health and Safety Executive (HSE) compiles the Asbestosis Register to determine the nature and scale of deaths from asbestos-related diseases. Data are collected from the Office for National Statistics and the General Register Office for Scotland through death drafts mentioning 'asbestosis'. Data are available for sex and age. Mentions of lung cancer and mesothelioma on the death draft are also collated. The Register covers Great Britain and has been completed since 1968, although computerised data are only available from 1978. Figures are updated and published annually, the latest available are for 1996. Following reports of the association between asbestos exposure and asbestosis, the advisory panel to Her Majesty's Senior Medical Inspector of Factories recommended the establishment of a national asbestosis register. This register was duly set up in 1967 and has been maintained since then by HSE.

Status: Ongoing
Collection Method: Administrative Records
Frequency: Annually
Reference Period: Calendar year
Timeliness: 2 years
Earliest Available Data: 1967
National Coverage: Great Britain
Disaggregation: Local Authority District (LAD)/ Unitary Authority(Eng)

Statistician
Jacky Jones
Health and Safety Executive
Room 240
Magdalen House
Stanley Precinct
Bootle
Merseyside L20 3QZ
Tel: 0541 545500;
Email: point.publicenquiry@hse.gov.uk

Central Index of Dose Information (CIDI)
Health and Safety Executive

Status: Ongoing
Collection Method: Administrative Records

Statistician
Dorothy Brown
Health and Safety Executive
Tel: 020 7717 6275

Continuing Increase in Mesothelioma Mortality in Great Britain
Health and Safety Executive

Analysis of the mesothelioma register to 1991, including an estimate of the projected number of deaths for the subsequent 25 years.

Status: Ceased temporarily
National Coverage: Great Britain

Statistician
Jacky Jones
Health and Safety Executive
Room 240
Magdalen House
Stanley Precinct
Bootle
Merseyside L20 3QZ
Tel: 0541 545500;
Email: point.publicenquiry@hse.gov.uk

Diseases Reported Under the Reporting of Injuries, Diseases and Dangerous Occurrences Regulations (RIDDOR)
Health and Safety Executive

The Reporting of Injuries, Diseases and Dangerous Occurrences Regulations (RIDDOR) were introduced in April 1986, and have now been replaced by the RIDDOR '95 Regulations (effective from

1 April 1996). The Regulations require employers to report all cases of a defined list of diseases occurring among their employees where: i) they receive a doctor's written diagnosis; and ii) the affected employee's current job involves the work activity specifically associated with the disease. The diseases and their associated occupational conditions are listed in a schedule to the Regulations. This list (based on the DSS list of prescribed diseases but with some exceptions) was revised and extended in the new Regulations, the most significant changes being the addition of specified musculoskeletal disorders (mainly upper limb) and occupational dermatitis. First RIDDOR regulations came into force in 1986. Revised regulations with extended disease coverage in 1996.

Status: Ongoing
Collection Method: Administrative Records
Frequency: Continuously
Reference Period: Annual, years starting 1 April
Timeliness: 6 months
Earliest Available Data: 1986
National Coverage: Great Britain

Statistician
Trevor Benn
Room 239
Magdalen House
Stanley Precinct
Bootle
Merseyside L20 3QZ
Tel: 0541 545500;
Email: point.publicenquiry@hse.gov.uk

Products that contain data from this source
Health and Safety Statistics 1997/98
Health and Safety Commission Annual Report and Accounts 1997/98

Employment Data from Employer Surveys and the Labour Force Survey
Health and Safety Executive

The Health and Safety Executive use employment data from the Office for National Statistics (ONS) to produce rates of workplace injury for employees and the self-employed

Status: Ongoing
Frequency: Quarterly
National Coverage: Great Britain

Statistician
Jacqui Bailey
Health and Safety Executive
Operations Unit; Safety and Enforcement Statistics
Tel: 0541 545500;
Email: point.publicenquiry@hse.gov.uk

Products that contain data from this analysis
Health and Safety Statistics 1997/98; Health and Safety Commission Annual Report of Accounts 1997/98; Safety Statistics Bulletin; National Picture of Health and Safety in Local Authority Enforced Industries

---

Information on Enforcement Action Under the Health and Safety at Work Etc Act 1974 from the Health and Safety Executive and Local Authorities
Health and Safety Executive

Statistics relating to enforcement action taken by HSE and local authorities for breaches of the Health and Safety at Work etc Act 1974 and associated legislation

Status: Ongoing
Collection Method: Administrative Records
Frequency: Continuously
Reference Period: The financial year
Timeliness: Provisional/finalised annual enforcement action statistics are published approximately 6 months/18 months after the end of the financial year respectively
Earliest Available Data: 1974
National Coverage: Great Britain
Disaggregation: Local Authority District (LAD)/ Unitary Authority(Eng)

Statistician
Jacqui Bailey
Health and Safety Executive
Operations Unit; Safety and Enforcement Statistics
Tel: 0541 545500;
Email: point.publicenquiry@hse.gov.uk

Products that contain data from this source
Health and Safety Commission Annual Report and Accounts 1997/98; Health and Safety Statistics 1997/98

Injuries and Dangerous Occurrences Reported Under the Reporting of Injuries, Diseases and Dangerous Occurrences Regulations (RIDDOR)
Health and Safety Executive

HSE compile data on occupational injuries, diseases, and dangerous occurrences based on reports made by responsible persons to HSE and local authorities under the Reporting of Injuries Diseases and Dangerous Occurrence Regulations 1995 (RIDDOR 95). Statistics for the 10 year period 1986/87 to 1995/96 were collected under the Reporting of Injuries Diseases and Dangerous Occurrence Regulations 1985 (RIDDOR 85) and other relevant legislation. RIDDOR 85 was replaced by updated regulations, RIDDOR 95, on 1 April 1996. This caused a discontinuity in the statistical

series for occupational injuries and dangerous occurrences between 1995/96 and 1996/97.

Status: Ongoing
Collection Method: Administrative Records
Frequency: Continuously
Reference Period: The financial year
Timeliness: Provisional/finalised occupational injury and dangerous occurrence statistics are published approximately 6 months/18 months after the end of the financial year respectively
Earliest Available Data: 1986/87
National Coverage: Great Britain
Disaggregation: Local Authority District (LAD)/ Unitary Authority(Eng)

Statistician
Jacqui Bailey
Health and Safety Executive
Operations Unit; Safety and Enforcement Statistics
Tel: 0541 545500;
Email: point.publicenquiry@hse.gov.uk

Products that contain data from this source
Health and Safety Commission Annual Report and Accounts 1997/98; Health and Safety Statistics 1997/98; HELA Annual Report of Health and Safety in the Service Industries; National Picture of Health and Safety in Local Authority Enforced Industries; Occupational Health Decennial Supplement; Safety Statistics Bulletin

---

Lead Workers Under Medical Surveillance
Health and Safety Executive

The Health and Safety Executive (HSE) compiles data on blood-lead levels of workers under surveillance under the Control of Lead at Work Regulations. Data are derived from medical surveillance under the auspices of Regional Offices of the HSE. Data are available on the distribution of maximum measured blood-lead levels of lead workers, and the numbers of workers suspended, by sex in 13 different industrial sectors. Annual returns have been made since introduction of 1980 Control of Lead at Work Regulations, which prescribed certain limits – blood-lead levels above which doctors must consider suspending the worker from working with lead. In 1986 the limit for male workers was lowered, and in 1998 new regulations came into effect which lowered the limits further. These changes have increased the level of detail available in the distribution of blood-lead levels; other than this there are no discontinuities in the statistics.

Status: Ongoing
Collection Method: Administrative Records
Frequency: Annually
Reference Period: Financial year
Timeliness: 18 months
Earliest Available Data: 1981
National Coverage: Great Britain
Disaggregation: HSE administrative regions

Statistician
Alan Spence
Room 246
Magdalen House
Stanley Precinct
Bootle
Merseyside L20 3QZ
Tel: 0541 545500;
Email: point.publicenquiry@hse.gov.uk

Mesothelioma Register - Great Britain
Health and Safety Executive

The Mesothelioma Register is compiled by the Health and Safety Executive. It contains data on occupational ill-health supplied by the Office for National Statistics and the General Registrar's Office for Scotland through death drafts mentioning 'mesothelioma'. Data are available by sex, year of death, site of mesothelioma (pleura, peritoneum, both and unspecified), and occupation. The Register was set up in 1967, but 1968 is the first year of complete data. It covers Great Britain and data are available since 1976 for standard regions, counties and county districts. Results are available to 1996 and are published annually. Following reports of the association between asbestos exposure and mesothelioma, the advisory panel to Her Majesty's Senior Medical Inspector of Factories recommended the establishment of a national mesothelioma register. This register was duly set up in 1967, and has been maintained since then by the HSE.

Status: Ongoing
Collection Method: Administrative Records
Frequency: Annually
Reference Period: Calendar year
Timeliness: Provisional data 2 years
Earliest Available Data: 1968
National Coverage: Great Britain
Disaggregation: Local Authority District (LAD)/ Unitary Authority(Eng)

Statistician
Jacky Jones
Health and Safety Executive
Room 240
Magdalen House
Stanley Precinct
Bootle
Merseyside L20 3QZ
Tel: 0541 545500;
Email: point.publicenquiry@hse.gov.uk

Musculoskeletal Occupational Surveillance Scheme (MOSS)
Centre for Occupational Health, University of Manchester; sponsored by Health and Safety Executive

A database of information from the Muscular Skeletal Occupation Surveillance Scheme held at Manchester University. The

information is provided by Rheumatologists throughout the UK.

Status: Ongoing
Collection Method: Surveillance scheme
Frequency: Monthly
Reference Period: 1997-99
Timeliness: 10 months
Earliest Available Data: First year of reference period - 1997
National Coverage: United Kingdom

Statistician
Prof. Nicola Cherry
Centre for Occupational Health
University of Manchester
Tel: 0161 275 7103

Occupational Physicians Reporting Activity (OPRA) Surveillance Scheme
Centre for Occupational Health, University of Manchester; sponsored by Health and Safety Executive

Status: Ongoing
Collection Method: Surveillance scheme
Frequency: Monthly
Reference Period: 1996 - 97
Timeliness: 10 months
Earliest Available Data: First year of reference period - 1996
National Coverage: United Kingdom

Statistician
Prof. Nicola Cherry
Centre for Occupational Health
University of Manchester
Tel: 0161 275 7103

Occupational Skin Disease Surveillance Scheme (EPIDERM) - UK
Centre for Occupational Health, University of Manchester; sponsored by Health and Safety Executive

The EPIDERM surveillance scheme and its sister scheme OPRA (Occupational Physicians Reporting Activity) are run by the Centre for Occupational Health at Manchester University. Dermatologists have reported cases of occupational skin disease since February 1993 to EPIDERM, and occupational physicians started to report them in May 1994. Since January 1996, occupational physicians have reported to their own scheme OPRA. From 1996 a sampling scheme has been in place for some of the reporters whereby cases are reported for only one month in the reporting year and the results are scaled up to estimate the annual number of cases. The age, sex, post code sector, occupation, industry (from 1996) and suspected causal agent are recorded. Cases of occupational skin disease have been reported by dermatologists since 1993 and by occupational physicians since 1994 for the UK.

Status: Ongoing
Collection Method: Surveillance scheme
Frequency: Monthly
Reference Period: 1993 to 1999
Timeliness: 10 months
Earliest Available Data: First year of reference period - 1993
National Coverage: United Kingdom

Statistician
Prof. Nicola Cherry
Centre for Occupational Health
University of Manchester
Tel: 0161 275 7103

Occupational Surveillance for Audiologists (OSSA)
Centre for Occupational Health, University of Manchester; sponsored by Health and Safety Executive

Status: Ongoing
Collection Method: Surveillance scheme
Frequency: Monthly
Reference Period: 1997-99
Timeliness: 10 months
Earliest Available Data: First year of reference period - 1997
National Coverage: United Kingdom

Statistician
Prof. Nicola Cherry
Centre for Occupational Health
University of Manchester
Tel: 0161 275 7103

Pesticide Incidents Appraisal Panel
Health and Safety Executive

Statistician
Alan Spence
Health and Safety Executive
Health Sciences Division; Epidemiology and Medical Statistics Unit
Tel: 0151 951 4556;
Email: alan.hd.spence@hse.gov.uk

Self-Reported Work-Related Illness Survey 1995 (SWI95)
Health and Safety Executive

Between August 1995 and February 1996, HSE included a set of screening questions in the Labour Force Survey (LFS) to identify individuals who had suffered from some work-related illness in the previous 12 months. A representative sample of households in Great Britain was administered the screening questions which asked about each adult in the household who had ever worked. Any adults identified at the screening stage as having a work-related illness, with consent, were interviewed. In cases where the respondent suffered more than one work-related illness, the survey requested information about each illness. The survey also collected information on working conditions, characterisation of the reported illness, and how the illness was caused or made worse by work. Two further elements were undertaken with consent, the individual's doctor or specialist who treated the illness was contacted to obtain further details of the illness and also a 'control' population were asked the same questions on job conditions to enable features of the job which may be associated with the occurrence of the work-related illness to be identified. The results of the survey are grossed up, using adjustments for age, sex, region of residence and non-response, to obtain estimates of self-reported work-related illness for Great Britain.

Status: Ceased completely
Collection Method: Household/Person (Sample) Survey
Frequency: Quarterly
Reference Period: August 1995 to February 1996
Timeliness: 2 years
Earliest Available Data: 1995
National Coverage: Great Britain
Sub-National: Standard Statistical Region

Statistician
Jacky Jones
Health and Safety Executive
Room 240
Magdalen House
Stanley Precinct
Bootle
Merseyside L20 3QZ
Tel: 0541 545500;
Email: point.publicenquiry@hse.gov.uk

Surveillance Scheme for Infectious Diseases at Work (SIDAW)
Centre for Occupational Health, University of Manchester; sponsored by Health and Safety Executive

Status: Ongoing
Collection Method: Surveillance scheme
Frequency: Monthly
Reference Period: 1996-99
Timeliness: 10 months
Earliest Available Data: First year of reference period - 1996
National Coverage: United Kingdom

Statistician
Prof. Nicola Cherry
Centre for Occupational Health
University of Manchester
Tel: 0161 275 7103

Surveillance Scheme for Occupational Stress and Mental Illness (SOSMI)
Centre for Occupational Health, University of Manchester; sponsored by Health and Safety Executive

Status: Ongoing
Collection Method: Surveillance scheme
Frequency: Monthly
Reference Period: 1999
Timeliness: 10 months
Earliest Available Data: First year of reference period - 1999
National Coverage: United Kingdom

Statistician
Prof. Nicola Cherry
Centre for Occupational Health
University of Manchester
Tel: 0161 275 7103

Surveillance Scheme for Work-Related and Occupational Respiratory Disease Survey (SWORD)
Centre for Occupational Health, University of Manchester; sponsored by Health and Safety Executive

One of the most comprehensive sources of information on occupational respiratory diseases and their likely causes is the Surveillance of Work-related and Occupational Respiratory Disease surveillance scheme known as SWORD. This is a voluntary scheme run by the Centre for Occupational Health at Manchester University, and is funded by the HSE. Under this scheme occupational and specialist chest physicians report new cases of respiratory ill health that they believe to be attributable to the patient's work. Although the scheme has been running since 1989, a major improvement was made to the method of data collection in 1992. This involved some of the physicians being allocated, at random, to report in only 1 of 12 monthly samples, with their reports being scaled up to estimate annual numbers of cases. This change brought about a considerable improvement in participation rates, and so means that figures relating to the period after this date are not comparable to those from before it. From 1996 onwards occupational physicians have reported cases to SWORD via OPRA (Occupational Physicians Reporting Activity).

Status: Ongoing
Collection Method: Surveillance scheme
Frequency: Monthly
Reference Period: 1989 to 1999
Timeliness: 10 months
Earliest Available Data: 1989
National Coverage: United Kingdom

Statistician
Prof. Nicola Cherry
Centre for Occupational Health
University of Manchester
Tel: 0161 275 7103

Work-Related Accidents Survey (Labour Force Survey)
Health and Safety Executive

The Health and Safety Executive commissions questions on accidents and ill-health in the Labour Force Survey. The results give a self-reported view on work-related accidents and illness. In a March to May 1990 'trailer' to the spring Labour Force Survey, adults in a representative sample of households were asked whether they had suffered an accident at work or in connection with their work in the last year. The follow-up questions on positive respondents established the nature of the accident, the job that was thought to have given rise to the accident, and the number of days' absence due to injuries from the accident. A small number of questions also appear annually in the winter quarter of the LFS from 1993-94.

Status: Ongoing
Frequency: Annually
Reference Period: Winter quarter - December to February
Timeliness: 9 months
Earliest Available Data: 1989/90
National Coverage: Great Britain
Sub-National: Sampled

Statistician
Graham Stevens
Health and Safety Executive
Operations Unit; Safety and Enforcement Statistics
Tel: 0541 545 5001;
Email: point.publicenquiry@hse.gov.uk

Products that contain data from this analysis
Health and Safety Commission Annual Report of Accounts 1997/98; Health and Safety Statistics 1997/98

6.5 Labour Force - general

Labour Force Projections
Office for National Statistics

The Office for National Statistics prepares labour force projections for Great Britain each year. The published figures include estimates and projections of the labour force, economic activity rates and the non-institutional resident population aged 16 and over. The estimates for labour force and activity rates are obtained from Labour Force Survey results in the spring quarter. The population projections are based upon the definitive projections of the resident population produced by the Government Actuary's Department in consultation with the ONS, and the General Register Office for Scotland. Projected numbers of full-time students from the Department for Education and Employment and the Scottish Education Department are also used. The projection period reaches to between ten and fifteen years after the base year (currently to 2011). Historic estimates of the labour force and activity rates are available on the current basis from 1984 to 1997, and a series back to 1961 on a slightly different basis has been constructed. National and regional labour force projections are published annually for Great Britain and biennially for standard regions, Northern Ireland and the United Kingdom. More detailed figures are available on request.

Frequency: Annually (Great Britain) or biennially (Other)
National Coverage: United Kingdom

Statistician
Graham Thompson
Office for National Statistics
Labour Market Statistics Division; Labour Force Projections and International
Tel: 020 7533 6118;
Email: graham.thompson@ons.gov.uk

Products that contain data from this analysis
Labour Market Trends; Nomis®; Regional Trends; Social Trends

Labour Force Survey
Office for National Statistics

The GB Labour Force Survey (LFS) is a quarterly sample survey. The questionnaire design, sample selection, and interviewing are carried out by the Social Survey Division of the Office for National Statistics (ONS) on behalf of the Socio-Economic Statistics and Analysis Group of the ONS which analyses and publishes the results. The survey seeks information on respondents personal circumstances and their labour market status during a specific reference period, normally a period of one week or four weeks (depending on the topic) immediately prior to the interview. The LFS is carried out under a European Union Directive and uses internationally agreed concepts and definitions. It is the source of the internationally comparable (International Labour Organisation) measure known as 'ILO unemployment'. ONS publishes full UK LFS results, however, the field work is carried out separately; by ONS for GB and by the Department for Economic Development for Northern Ireland. There are a number of discontinuities in LFS data caused by changes in the way the Survey has been conducted and changes in the definitions of

certain variables. The main breaks occurred in 1984 (when the survey changed from every two years to annual) and 1992 (when the survey became continuous with quarterly publication). Discontinuities are described in the LFS User Guide Volume 1 (1977) 'Background and Methodology' - Section 18.

Status: Ongoing
Collection Method: Household/Person (Sample) Survey
Frequency: Continuously
Reference Period: Headline results are published 12 times a year for the average of 3 consecutive months; full results released for seasonal quarters i.e. March - May; June - August; Sept - November; December - February
Timeliness: 6 weeks after the end of the period to which they refer.
Earliest Available Data: 1979 (biennial - but not using ILO definition of unemployment)1984 (annual)1992 (quarterly)
National Coverage: Great Britain
Disaggregation: GOR, SSR, county, local authority district, unitary authority; Local Authority District (LAD)/Unitary Authority(Eng.); Training and Enterprise Council (TEC) Area (E&W); Local Enterprise Company (LEC) Area (Scotland); County (E&W)/Unitary Authority (Eng.)

Statistician
Frances Sly
Office for National Statistics
Labour Market Division; Labour Market Trends and Quarterly LFS Analysis
Tel: 020 7533 6141;
Email: frances.sly@ons.gov.uk

Enquiries: Labour Market Statistics Helpline
Tel: 020 7533 6094;
Email: labour.market@ons.gov.uk

Products that contain data from this source
Economic Trends; How exactly is employment measured?; International Year Book of Labour Statistics; Labour Force Survey analysis service; Labour Force Survey Historical Supplement; Labour Force Survey Quarterly Supplement; Labour Force Survey User Guide; Labour Force Surveys in the European Union; Labour market statistics First Release; Labour Market Trends; Nomis®; Participation in Education and Training by 16 to 18 year olds in England; Regional Trends; Social Trends; The Data Archive

Labour Force Survey - Northern Ireland
Department of Economic Development - Northern Ireland

A continuous sample survey collecting from each address information on the economic status and activity of all residents aged 16 and over. It is the largest regular household survey in Northern Ireland. Annually in spring of each year from 1984 to 1994. Then continuously on a quarterly basis from winter 1994/95. Rolling monthly data available from December 1997 - February 1998.

Status: Ongoing
Collection Method: Household/Person (Sample) Survey
Frequency: Continuously
Reference Period: 3 month rolling quarters
Timeliness: 2 months
Earliest Available Data: 1984
National Coverage: Northern Ireland
Disaggregation: NUTS III, District Council

Statistician
Owen Johnston
Department of Economic Development - Northern Ireland
Tel: 02890 529585;
Email: owen.johnston@dedni.gov.uk

Products that contain data from this source
Northern Ireland Labour Force Survey - Historical Supplement; Northern Ireland Labour Force Survey - Quarterly Supplement; Northern Ireland Labour Market Statistics; Women in Northern Ireland Factsheet

Northern Ireland Labour Force Survey Religion Report
Northern Ireland Statistics and Research Agency

The Labour Force Survey Religion Report includes information disaggregated by religion on labour force participation rates, reasons for non-participation, unemployment rates, the unemployment differential, length of time seeking work, main methods of job search used by the unemployed, characteristics of those in employment, composition of the major occupational and industrial groupings and the highest level of qualification attained.

Status: Ongoing
Frequency: Annually
Reference Period: Calendar Year
Timeliness: Within one year
Earliest Available Data: 1990
National Coverage: Northern Ireland

Statistician
John Mallon
Department of Finance and Personnel - Northern Ireland
Human Resource Research and Evaluation Branch
Tel: 028 9052 6411;
Email: john.mallon@dfpni.gov.uk

Products that contain data from this source
Labour Force Survey Religion Report

Youth Cohort Study - England and Wales
Department for Education and Employment

The Department for Education and Employment conducts the Youth Cohort Study (YCS) on a sample of young people (aged 16-19) in the year after they are eligible to leave compulsory schooling. Data are collected about their activity status, i.e.

whether they are in a full-time job, full or part-time education, on a training scheme, unemployed or doing something else. Also collected is information about their qualifications (gained and studying for), family background and other socio-economic and demographic data. The survey covers England and Wales and data are available at Standard Regional and Government Office regional level. A sample of around 20,000 young people are followed up over a two-year period.

Respondents are contacted in their first year after the end of compulsory schooling (aged 16/17), and usually followed up one and two years later, aged 17/18 and 18/19. Cohorts started in 1994 and 1996 surveyed young people at age 16/17 and 18/19 only, with a two year gap in between. Data are published as a Statistical Bulletin about a year after the end of the fieldwork.

Status: Ongoing
Collection Method: Person (Sample) Survey
Frequency: Typically biennial
Reference Period: Data are collected in spring (typically March to May)
Timeliness: Approximately one year between close of fieldwork and release of data.
Earliest Available Data: Cohort I sweep I (Spring 1985)
National Coverage: England and Wales
Disaggregation: Standard Statistical Region (SSR); Government Office Region (GOR)

Statistician
Stephanie Morgan
Department for Education and Employment
Youth and Further Education; YFE5
Tel: 0114 2593639;
Email: stephanie.morgan@dfee.gov.uk

Products that contain data from this source
Facts about Women and Men in Wales / Ffeithiau am Fenywod a Dynion yng Nghymru; Labour Market Trends; Social Trends; Youth Cohort Study Information Pack; Youth Cohort Study Research Reports

See also:
In other chapters:
(The) ONS Longitudinal Study(see the Population chapter)

6.6 Labour Relations

Labour Dispute Statistics
Office for National Statistics

The Office for National Statistics compiles labour disputes statistics. Data are derived from a number of sources: the employer or trade union involved, regular centralised returns from certain major industries and public bodies, articles in a selection of national and regional newspapers. Data are available by industry and cause. They exclude disputes which do not result in a stoppage of work, stoppages involving fewer than ten workers or lasting less than one day unless the total number of working days lost in the dispute is 100 or more. Data are available relating to the number of disputes, the number of workers involved and the number of working days lost. The data cover the UK and Government Office regions. Data have been collected on a consistent basis since the late 19th century; annual totals are available from 1891 and monthly data from 1920. Labour disputes data are collected when a dispute occurs. Provisional labour disputes data are published monthly approximately six weeks after the end of the reference month and finalised at the end of the year.

Status: Ongoing
Collection Method: Employed, Trade Unions, press cuttings
Frequency: Monthly
Reference Period: Monthly and annually
Timeliness: End of month
Earliest Available Data: 1891
National Coverage: United Kingdom
Disaggregation: Government Office Region

Statistician
Derek Bird
Office for National Statistics
Tel: 01928 792614

Products that contain data from this source
Annual Abstract of Statistics; Digest of Data for the Construction Industry; Digest of Welsh Statistics; Labour Market Trends; Monthly Digest of Statistics; Regional Trends; The Data Archive; Social Trends

Trade Unionism
Department of Trade and Industry

Under trade union legislation each trade union has to submit a return to the Certification Officer which includes financial information as well as information on the membership. This information is obtained from an annual report produced by the Certification Officer. Data are available on the number of members of each union by sex. They are supplemented by data provided by Northern Ireland Office so that the estimate of trade union membership covers the UK. The series was established in 1892. Data are updated annually and relate to membership figures at 31 December. Results are published approximately eighteen months after the reference date. The Labour Force Survey provides an alternative source of information on union membership.

Status: Ongoing
Collection Method: Administrative Records
Frequency: Annually
Reference Period: Calendar year
Timeliness: 18 months
Earliest Available Data: 1892
National Coverage: United Kingdom

Statistician
Mark Cully
Department of Trade and Industry
Employment Market Analysis and Research (EMAR); ER 4B
Tel: 020 7215 3847
Email: mark.cully@irdv.dti.gov.uk

Workplace Industrial Relations Survey
Department of Trade and Industry; sponsored jointly with the Economic and Social Research Council, the Advisory Conciliation and Arbitration Service, and the Policy Studies Institute

A periodic survey of establishments (workplaces) which examines all aspects of workplace industrial relations. The series began in 1980, with subsequent surveys in 1984, 1990 and 1998. There are around 200 variables which form a consistent time series across the survey series.

Status: Ongoing
Collection Method: Large-scale (Sample) Survey
Frequency: Periodic
Reference Period: Either current or past year
Timeliness: 9 months
Earliest Available Data: 1980
National Coverage: Great Britain
Disaggregation: Government Office Region (GOR)

Statistician
John McQueeney
Department of Trade and Industry
Employment Market Analysis and Research (EMAR); ER 4B
Tel: 020 7215 5926;
Email: john.mcqueeney@irdv.dti.gov.uk

Products that contain data from this source
(The) 1998 Workplace Employee Relations Survey: First Findings
Workplace Industrial Relations in Transition: The ED / ESRC / PSI / ACAS Surveys

See also:
In this chapter:
Labour Force Survey (6.5)

6.7 Pay and Income from Work

Index of Average Earnings - GB
Office for National Statistics

The Office for National Statistics calculates the Index of Average Earnings, based on a sample survey of 8,000 employers on the whole economy, manufacturing industries, service industries and production industries, and also for 26 industry groupings. Data are collected on employee numbers and their total earnings, including pay award arrears, bonuses, commission and overtime payments. Seasonally adjusted data and actual results are available. The Index is used to estimate headline growth in earnings. The survey covers Great Britain, and has been carried out since 1963. The first Index covered mainly production and agriculture. In 1976 coverage was extended to cover service occupations but still excluded business services, higher education and research. These sectors were included from 1989. Provisional and actual figures are published monthly. The provisional figures relate to the previous month and become the confirmed figures in the following month.

Collection Method: Sample survey
Frequency: Monthly
Reference Period: End of month
Timeliness: Approximately 6 weeks from the survey date
Earliest Available Data: 1990 (for whole economy on a 1995 = 100 basis)
National Coverage: Great Britain

Statistician
Derek Bird
Office for National Statistics
Tel: 01928 792614

***

Products that contain data from this source
Labour Market Statistics First Release; Labour Market Trends; Monthly Digest of Statistics; Economic Trends

***

New Earnings Survey - GB
Office for National Statistics

The Office for National Statistics conducts the New Earnings Survey (NES) based on a 1 per cent sample of employees who are members of Pay-As-You-Earn (PAYE) income tax schemes. The Survey concerns the earnings of employees in employment and is designed to represent all categories of employees in businesses of all kinds and sizes. Data are collected on hours worked, industry, occupation, place of work, sex, age and about the levels, distributions and make-up of earnings of employees in all industries and occupations and for the major national collective agreements. The Survey covers Great Britain and data are available for England, Scotland, Wales and all standard regions. Results are also available for the London boroughs, counties of England and Wales and the Scottish Regions. Since 1996, data are available for smaller areas such as Local Authority Districts and Parliamentary Constituencies. Data have been collected for each pay-period in April since 1970 under the Statistics of Trade Act 1947. Results are published in October and at approximately fortnightly intervals through to the middle of December. A UK volume was published for the first time in 1998.

Collection Method: Sample survey
Frequency: Annually
Reference Period: April
Timeliness: 6 months from survey date
Earliest Available Data: 1970
National Coverage: Great Britain
Sub-National: England, Scotland, Wales, Northern Ireland

Statistician
Derek Bird
Office for National Statistics
Tel: 01928 792614

***

Products that contain data from this source
Annual Abstract of Statistics; International Year Book of Labour Statistics; Labour Market Trends; Monthly Digest of Statistics; Regional Trends; Social Focus on Children; Social Trends; Welsh Economic Trends

***

New Earnings Survey - Northern Ireland
Department of Economic Development - Northern Ireland

The New Earnings Survey is carried out in April of each year by the Department of Economic Development and provides a wide range of information on earnings and hours worked by employees in Northern Ireland. The New Earnings Survey is a sample survey of employees who are incorporated in pay-as-you-earn (PAYE) schemes and for whom the Inland Revenue tax offices hold deduction cards. The survey provides details on gross weekly earnings, and the make-up of pay in terms of overtime pay, payments-by-results, Inland Revenue approved profit related pay schemes, other incentive payments and shift and similar premium payments. Information on hourly earnings and hours worked is also available. The survey collects information on the industry, occupation and pension arrangements of all employees included in the sample.

Status: Ongoing
Collection Method: Large-scale (Sample) Survey
Frequency: Annually
Reference Period: April
Timeliness: Data collected April each year and results available October/November of same year.
Earliest Available Data: 1971
National Coverage: Northern Ireland
Disaggregation: Travel-to-work Area; District Council Area (Northern Ireland)

Statistician
Clare Alexander
Department of Economic Development - Northern Ireland
Tel: 028 9052 9525;
Email: clare.alexander@dedni.gov.uk

***

Products that contain data from this source
Northern Ireland Labour Market Statistics; Northern Ireland New Earnings Survey; Northern Ireland New Earnings Survey - Historical Supplement

***

Pay and Working Time - Collective Agreements for Manual Staff
Office for National Statistics

Collection Method: Fax, letter and telephone
Frequency: Monthly amendments
Timeliness: End of month
National Coverage: United Kingdom

Statistician
Derek Bird
Office for National Statistics
Tel: 01928 792614

See also:
In this chapter:
Labour Force Survey (6.5)
Lone Parent Cohort (6.3)
Workplace Industrial Relations Survey (6.6)

6.8 Productivity

Labour Productivity and Unit Wage Costs - UK
Office for National Statistics

The Office for National Statistics produces estimates on labour productivity and unit wage costs. Data are mainly used in economic and labour market analysis. Productivity is the division of output indices by workforce numbers; unit wage costs are estimated by dividing the wage index by the output index, and unit labour costs include additional costs of employment to wages and salaries, such as taxes and NICS. The data cover the UK. They are produced monthly for manufacturing and quarterly for production industries and the whole economy. Data for the economy as a whole are available from 1959. Unit wage costs date from 1970 for monthly and quarterly manufacturing data. Output per head are available from 1978 for the production industries, 1970 for monthly manufacturing figures, and 1950 for quarterly manufacturing data. Timeliness is identical to workforce in employment: whole economy data are published around ten weeks after quarter end, manufacturing around seven weeks after the end of the month.

Frequency: Manufacturing - monthly, whole economy and production industries quarterly
Timeliness: Manufacturing approximately 6 weeks after survey date, whole economy and production industries approximately 10 weeks after survey date.
Earliest Available Data: Whole economy 3rd quarter 1959, manufacturing and production industries 2nd quarter 1978.
National Coverage: United Kingdom
Disaggregation: Whole economy production and manufacturing industries and certain industries within manufacturing industries.

Statistician
Derek Bird
Office for National Statistics
Tel: 01928 792614

Products that contain data from this analysis
Economic Trends; Economic Trends Annual Supplement; Labour Market Trends; Monthly Digest of Statistics; Office for National Statistics Databank / Datastore

---

6.9 Unemployment and Inactivity

Claimant Count
Office for National Statistics

The Office for National Statistics compiles data on the claimant count, derived as a by-product of the Department of Social Security and Department for Education and Employment systems for administering the relevant benefits. These data cover the number of people who are claiming unemployment-related benefits (Jobseeker's Allowance and National Insurance credits) at Employment Service local offices. Data are collected on claimants' postcode, sex, date of birth, age, occupation, and the start and end date of their claim. These details provide information on the number of claimants on a particular day each month, and data on the numbers of people who have started a new claim during the month (inflows) and the number of people who have terminated their claim during the month (outflows). The claimant count covers the UK, and unadjusted data are available down to ward level and at higher levels of aggregation. Claimant count rates

are available down to the level of travel-to-work areas. Unadjusted data are available from 1982, while seasonally adjusted data, adapted to allow for significant discontinuities in the series, are available from 1971 (nationally) and 1974 (regionally). Earlier series covering those registering for work at government offices are available back to the beginning of the century. The count has been affected over time by changes in the rules and procedures governing eligibility for benefits. The consistent series and the post-1988 series relating to UK inflows and outflows, are confined to claimants aged 18 and over, and are seasonally adjusted. Data are collected every month. More detailed information relating to the age of clerically processed claimants, and the duration of their claim, are collected quarterly. Results are published monthly or quarterly about five weeks after the reference date.

Status: Ongoing
Collection Method: Administrative Records
Frequency: Monthly
Reference Period: The "count day" in every month
Timeliness: Data are released about 5 weeks after the "count day" in every month.
Earliest Available Data: January 1971 (nationally) January 1974 (regionally)
National Coverage: United Kingdom
Disaggregation: Down to Government Office Region (seasonally adjusted) or ward level (unadjusted)

Statistician
Jeremy Schuman
Office for National Statistics
Tel: 020 7533 6110;
Email: jeremy.schuman@ons.gov.uk

Products that contain data from this source
Annual Abstract of Statistics; Economic Trends; How exactly is unemployment measured?; Labour Market Statistics First Release; Labour Market Trends; Nomis®; Regional Trends

---

Claimant Count - Northern Ireland
Department of Economic Development - Northern Ireland

Claimant count figures are derived from administrative systems set up for the payment of benefit to unemployed persons. Figures for Northern Ireland are released monthly as part of the Northern Ireland Labour Market Statistics publication.

The following is a list of the major changes since 1980 which affect the consistency of claimant count statistics over time:
February 1994 - introduction of new system for compiling Northern Ireland unemployment statistics. October 1988 - school leavers excluded from the count. Feb/March 1986 -

unemployment figures compiled 3 weeks rather than 1 week after the count date. June 1985 - reconciliation of DED computer records with DHSS Social Security Office manual records. June/Aug 1983 - Budget measures gave males aged 60 and over (a) the long term rate of supplementary benefit without waiting for 1 year and (b) automatic National Insurance credit without signing on. October 1982 - change of basis, from registrants at Employment Services Offices to claimants of benefit in DHSS Social Security Offices.

Status: Ongoing
Collection Method: Administrative Records
Frequency: Monthly
Reference Period: Previous month
Timeliness: One month
Earliest Available Data: January 1971 (seasonally adjusted), June 1983 (unadjusted)
National Coverage: Northern Ireland
Disaggregation: District Council Area (Northern Ireland); Parliamentary Constituency; Travel-to-work Area; NUTS3 Area; Ward (all unadjusted)

Statistician
Sean Donnelly
Department of Economic Development - Northern Ireland
Tel: 028 9052 9311;
Email: sean.donnelly@dedni.gov.uk

Products that contain data from this source
Northern Ireland Labour Market Statistics; Unemployment - Northern Ireland Press Notice (replaced by LMS April 1998)

Claimant Unemployment Cohort (JUVOS Cohort)
Office for National Statistics

The Office for National Statistics compiles statistics on claimant unemployment from which it has established a database of longitudinal information. The database comprises a 5 per cent sample of all claims for unemployment related benefits registered in the national unemployment benefits payments systems (NUBS). The cohort excludes claims paid clerically, since these are handled outside of NUBS. Data collected include sex, date of birth, marital status, usual occupation (defined according to the Standard Occupational Classification (SOC)), occupation sought, the claimant's postcode sector, a code for the claimant's benefit office (includes a regional marker), the claim start date, the claim end date, and an identification number which allows separate claims made by the same individual to be linked. The data cover the UK and are available at standard regional level. Longitudinal information for the UK is available only from early 1994 when data on claimant unemployment in Northern Ireland were first included. The data have been collected since 1983. The cohort is updated monthly by electronic transmission of data, with records being selected from NUBS if a claimant has an appropriate national insurance number. The dataset is provided to an archive twice a year and tables are published quarterly.

Status: Ongoing
Collection Method: Administrative Records
Frequency: Quarterly
Earliest Available Data: 1983
National Coverage: United Kingdom

Statistician
Andrew Machin
Office for National Statistics
Socio Economic Statistics Division; Claimant Count and Vacancies
Tel: 020 7533 6162

Products that contain data from this source
Labour Market Trends; The Data Archive

ILO Unemployment (LFS - Seasonally Adjusted)
Office for National Statistics

Seasonally adjusted unemployment on the ILO (International Labour Organisation) definition; UK monthly estimates for 3-month periods derived from the Labour Force Survey and published in the Labour market statistics First Release. Monthly series first published April 1998; available from 1995 onwards. Annual UK estimates available back to spring 1984 (quarterly from winter 1994/95). GB - spring quarter estimates published annually from spring 1984 and quarterly estimates from spring 1992.

Status: Ongoing
Frequency: Monthly
Reference Period: average of 3 months
Timeliness: 6 weeks from end of collection period
Earliest Available Data: spring 1984

Statistician
Sheena Gordon
Office for National Statistics
SED; LFS(OD)
Iel: 020 7533 6140;
Email: sheena.gordon@ons.gov.uk

Products that contain data from this analysis
Annual Abstract of Statistics; Economic Trends; Guide to Labour Market Statistics First Releases; How exactly is unemployment measured?; Labour Force Survey Quarterly Supplement; Labour Market Statistics First Release; Labour Market Trends; Nomis®; Regional Trends; Social Trends

Seasonally Adjusted Claimant Count Consistent with Current Coverage (SAUCCC Series)
Office for National Statistics

The claimant count has been affected over time by changes in the rules and procedures governing eligibility for benefits. To maintain historical consistency, the seasonally adjusted series has been adapted to allow for significant discontinuities in the series - this means that a consistent series is available from 1971 nationally and 1974 regionally. Earlier series covering those registering for work at government offices are available back to the beginning of the century. The consistent series and post-1988 series relating to UK inflows and outflows are confined to claimants aged 18 and over, and are seasonally adjusted.

Status: Ongoing
Frequency: Monthly
Reference Period: The "count day" in each month
Timeliness: Provisional data are released about 5 weeks after the "count day".
Earliest Available Data: January 1971 (nationally), Jan 1974 (regionally)
National Coverage: United Kingdom
Disaggregation: Government Office Region (GOR)

Statistician
Jeremy Schuman
Office for National Statistics
Tel: 020 7533 6110;
Email: jeremy.schuman@ons.gov.uk

Products that contain data from this analysis
Economic Trends; How exactly is unemployment measured?; Labour market statistics First Release; Labour Market Trends; Nomis®; Regional Trends

See also:
In this chapter:
Labour Force Survey (6.5)
Lone Parent Cohort (6.3)
Northern Ireland Labour Force Survey Religion Report (6.5)
Youth Cohort Study - England and Wales (6.5)

In other chapters:
Lifetime Labour Market Database (see the Household Finances chapter)
Household Survey – Wales (see the Housing chapter)

Labour Market - *Products*

6.10 Abstracts, Compendia, A-Z Catalogues, Directories and Reference Material

Annual Employment Survey - Results
Office for National Statistics

All booklets/diskettes contain data by gender and full/part time status, except size band analysis. All are published annually.

Year 1997 – Part 1: Great Britain and Government Office Region by SIC92 Activity heading (class level). Only available on diskette. Price £25.00.

Year 1997 – Part 2: Counties, Local Authority Districts, Unitary Authorities, TEC/LEC; and Local Units Size band analysis by region. All by SIC92 Broad Industry Group. Only available on diskette. Price £25.00.

Year 1996 – Part 1: Great Britain, Government Office Regions and Standard Statistical Regions by SIC92 activity heading (class level). Price £25.00. ISBN: 1 85774 245 1

Year 1996 – Part 2: Counties, Local Authority Districts, Unitary Authorities, TEC/LEC; and Size band analysis by Region. All by SIC92 Broad Industry Group. Price £25.00. ISBN: 1 85774 246 X.

Year 1995 – Part 1: Great Britain and Standard Statistical Regions by SIC92 activity heading (class level). Price £35.95. ISBN: 1 85774 2273.

Year 1995 – Part 2: Counties, Local Authority Districts by SIC92 Broad Industry Group. Price £35.95. ISBN: 1 85774 229 X.

Year 1995 – Part 3: Other analyses: Government Office Regions and TEC/LECs; Local Unit Size band analysis by Region. All by SIC92 Broad Industry Group. Price £30.00. ISBN: 1 85774 2273.

All are available from
ONS Direct
Please see Annex B for full address details.

Sources from which data for these products are obtained
Annual Employment Survey

Guide to Labour Market Statistics First Releases
Office for National Statistics

Guide to sources of labour market statistics and their use.

Frequency: Ad-hoc
Price: Free

Available from
Labour market statistics enquiries
Please see Annex B for full address details.

Labour Force Survey User Guide
Office for National Statistics

Guidance on the background and methodology of the LFS in seven volumes. Also containing guidance on current and past variables, the LFS questionnaire, LFS classifications and local area data. Vol. 1: Background and methodology. Vol. 2: 1999 LFS Questionnaire. Vol. 3: Details of LFS variables. Vol. 4: LFS Standard Derived Variables. Vol. 5: LFS Classifications. Vol. 6: LFS Local area data. Vol. 7: CFS Variables 1984-91. Vol. 8: Household and Family Data. Vol. 9: Eurostat and Eurostat Derived Variables

Delivery: Ad hoc/One-off Release
Frequency: Annual
Price: Volumes 1,2,5,6,7,8,9: £5.00 each
Volumes 3&4: £10.00 each
Complete set: £50.00

Available from
Barbara Louca
Room B2/10
Office for National Statistics
1 Drummond Gate
London SW1V 2QQ
Tel: 020 7533 6179;
Email: barbara.louca@ons.gov.uk

Sources from which data for this product are obtained
Labour Force Survey

Standard Occupational Classification (SOC) Volume 1
Office for National Statistics

The structure of the Standard Occupational Classification and the definition of its major, minor and unit groups.

Delivery: Other
Frequency: Decennial
Price: £11.40
ISBN: 0 11 691284 7

Available from
Occupational Information Unit
Office for National Statistics
Please see Annex B for full address details

TSO Publications Centre and Bookshops
Please see Annex B for full address details.

Standard Occupational Classification (SOC) Volume 2 (Second Edition)
Office for National Statistics

The coding index to the Standard Occupational Classification. The coding index is an alphabetical list of approximately 23,000 job titles. Each entry is allocated to one of the 371 unit groups of the Standard Occupational Classification

Frequency: Every five years
Price: £15.00
ISBN: 0 11 691647 8

Available from
Occupational Information Unit
Office for National Statistics
Please see Annex B for full address details

TSO Publications Centre and Bookshops
Please see Annex B for full address details.

Standard Occupational Classification (SOC) Volume 2 (Second Edition) - Electronic Version
Office for National Statistics

The electronic file holds the contents of the coding index to the Standard Occupational Classification. This is an alphabetical list of approximately 23,000 job titles. Each entry is allocated to one of the 371 unit groups of the Standard Occupational Classification.

Delivery: Other
Frequency: Every five years
Price: £200.00 for file on diskette (but price subject to use of the contents)

Available from
Occupational Information Unit
Office for National Statistics
Please see Annex B for full address details

Standard Occupational Classification (SOC) Volume 3
Office for National Statistics

Social Classifications and coding methodology. The volume includes the derivation tables for Social Class based on occupation and Socio-economic Groups

Frequency: Decennial
Price: £3.50
ISBN: 0 11 691338 X

Available from
Occupational Information Unit
Office for National Statistics
Please see Annex B for full address details

TSO Publications Centre and Bookshops
Please see Annex B for full address details.

See also:
In other chapters:
Nomis® (see the Websites and Electronic Services chapter)

6.11 Cost of Labour

International Unit Labour Costs for Manufactured Goods
Department of Trade and Industry

Last five years (available) quarterly data of Unit Labour Costs for Manufactured Goods, covering Industrial Countries (excluding Iceland). Data are provided in national currency terms and each country compared with an export-weighted average, in common currency terms.

Delivery: Periodic Release
Frequency: Quarterly

Available from
Trade Statistics enquiries
Room G15
Department of Trade and Industry
10 Victoria Street
London SW1H 0NN
Tel: 020 7215 3287
Email: andy.elliott@esdv.dti.gov.uk

Labour Costs (Eurostat), 1988 Volume 1: Principal Results
Eurostat

This publication is published by Eurostat. Please telephone + 352 4301 34567 for more information.

Frequency: Ad hoc
Price: £13.00
ISBN: 92 826 3888 X

Sources from which data for this product are obtained
Labour Costs in the EC

6.12 Employment and Work

Census of Employment Booklets
Office for National Statistics

Relate only to the 1991-1993 Census and contains data by sex, full-time and part-time employees. The Great Britain and the Regions Booklet contains detailed industry data by SIC activity headings and size of local (data) unit by SIC industry division. The Local Areas in Great Britain Booklet contains data on counties by SIC industry division, local authority districts by SIC industry division, travel-to-work areas (available for 1991 only) by SIC industry division and parliamentary constituency (available for 1991 only) figures for manufacturing, services and all industries.

Delivery: Hardcopy publication
Frequency: Biennial
Price: £30.00

Available from
Employment, Earnings and Productivity Division
Business Statistics Group
Office for National Statistics
Runcorn WA7 2GJ
Tel: 01928 792690

Sources from which data for this product are obtained
Census of Employment

Census of Employment - Northern Ireland Statistics Notice
Department of Economic Development - Northern Ireland

Employee jobs figures for Northern Ireland, Travel to Work Areas, District Councils, Paramilitary Constituencies and Wards by SIC92. Contains employees jobs (split by

gender and whether full-time or part-time) by broad industrial sector and changes by sector from the last Census.

Delivery: News/Press Release
Frequency: Every two years
Price: Free

Available from
Census of Employment
Statistics Research Branch
Netherleigh
Massey Avenue
Belfast BT4 2JP

Sources from which data for this product are obtained
Census of Employment - Northern Ireland

Employment and Unemployment - Aggregates, 1980-1994
Office for National Statistics

Part of Eurostats Population and Social conditions theme (Theme 3), Series 3: Accounts and surveys. This edition provides a comprehensive view of the labour market in the EU. The data were compiled by the statistical offices of the member states as well as in the United States and Japan.

Delivery: Ad hoc/One-off Release
ISBN: 92 827 5968

Available from
Bob Dodds
Please see Annex B for full address details

How Exactly Is Employment Measured?
Office for National Statistics

Small booklet - first edition published April 1998. Explains how ONS measures employment, and the relationship between different sources, including the Labour Force Survey and employer surveys.

Delivery: Ad hoc/One-off Release
Price: Free

Available from
Labour market statistics enquiries
Please see Annex B for full address details.

Sources from which data for this product are obtained
Employment (LFS - seasonally adjusted); Labour Force Survey

Products

International Standard Classification of Occupations 1988 (ISCO-88)
International Labour Office

The standard for presenting information on occupations in a manner which makes international comparisons possible.

Price: £35.10
ISBN: 92 2 106438 7

Available from
Marian Motts
Room 21-24
International Labour Office
5th Floor
Millbank Tower
SW1P 4QP
Telephone No: 020 7828 6401

Joint Staffing Watch Wales (Statistical Release)
National Assembly for Wales

A summary statistical report on the levels of local authority staffing in Wales. Gives details of staff numbers for the major services and totals for each authority.

Frequency: Annual
Price: Free

Available from
Stuart Neil
National Assembly for Wales
Room 2-081
Crown Buildings
Cathays Park
Cardiff
Tel: 01222 823963

Northern Ireland Quarterly Employment Survey
Department of Economic Development - Northern Ireland

Latest statistics on employment in Northern Ireland. Contains the main changes in the number of employee jobs by SIC over the quarter and over the year for a specific reference date. In addition, it includes longitudinal data for the number of employee jobs, self-employment jobs and workforce jobs in Northern Ireland.

Delivery: News/Press Release
Frequency: Quarterly
Price: Free

Available from
Statistics Research Branch
Department of Economic Development
Netherleigh
Massey Avenue
Belfast BT4 2JP

Sources from which data for this product are obtained
Quarterly Employment Survey - Northern Ireland

Women's Attitudes to Combining Paid Work and Family Life

Quantitative survey investigating women's attitudes towards mothers combining paid work and family life, childcare and family friendly working practices. This involved a representative sample of around 1,000 women aged 16 and over across Britain. The sample included: women with children under 16, over 16 and those who were not mothers; employed women; and those specifically choosing not to do paid work.

Frequency: One off survey
Price: Free

Available from
Women's Unit
10 Great George Street
London SW1P 3AE
Tel: 0171 273 8880

See also:
In this chapter:
Guide to Labour Market Statistics First Releases (*6.10*)
Labour Force Survey Historical Supplement (*6.14*)
Labour Force Survey Quarterly Databases (*6.14*)
Labour Market Statistics First Release (*6.14*)
Labour Market Trends (*6.14*)
Northern Ireland Labour Market Statistics (*6.14*)
Workplace Industrial Relations in Transition: the ED/ESRC/PSI/ACAS Surveys (*6.15*)

In other chapters:
1993 Welsh House Condition Survey (Report 1994) (*see the Housing chapter*)
Economic Trends (*see the Economy chapter*)
Eurofarm Tabular Databank System (*see the Agriculture, Fishing, Food and Forestry chapter*)
Farm Structure: Main Results (*see the Agriculture, Fishing, Food and Forestry chapter*)
Nomis® (*see the Websites and Electronic Services chapter*)
United Kingdom National Accounts - the Blue Book (*see the Economy chapter*)

6.13 Health and Safety at Work

Enquiry Point for Health Effects Arising from Occupational Exposure to Non-Ionising Radiation
Health and Safety Executive

Dr. Simon Clarke
Health and Safety Executive
Magdalen House
Stanley Precinct
Bootle
Merseyside L20 3QZ
Tel: 0541 545500;
Email: point.publicenquiry@hse.gov.uk

Enquiry Point for Information on Violence at Work
Health and Safety Executive

Jacky Jones
Room 240
Health and Safety Executive
Magdalen House
Stanley Precinct
Bootle
Merseyside L20 3QZ
Tel: 0541 545500;
Email: point.publicenquiry@hse.gov.uk

Enquiry Point for Information on Working Conditions
Health and Safety Executive

Jacky Jones
Health and Safety Executive
Room 240
Magdalen House
Stanley Precinct
Bootle
Merseyside L20 3QZ
Tel: 0541 545500;
Email: point.publicenquiry@hse.gov.uk

Enquiry Point for Occupational Acute Poisonings and Injuries from Chemicals
Health and Safety Executive

Trevor Benn
Health and Safety Executive
Room 239
Magdalen House
Stanley Precinct
Bootle
Merseyside L20 3QZ
Tel: 0541 545500;
Email: point.publicenquiry@hse.gov.uk

Associated Sources
Reportings of Injuries, Diseases and Dangerous Occurrences Regulations (RIDDOR)

Enquiry Point for Occupational Building-Related Illness
Health and Safety Executive

Suzi Curtis
Health and Safety Executive
Room 246
Magdalen House
Stanley Precinct
Bootle
Merseyside L20 3QZ
Tel: 0541 545500;
Email: point.publicenquiry@hse.gov.uk

Enquiry Point for Occupational Cancers
Health and Safety Executive

Damien McElvenny
Health and Safety Executive
Room 234A
Magdalen House
Stanley Precinct
Bootle
Merseyside L20 3QZ
Tel: 0541 545500;
Email: point.publicenquiry@hse.gov.uk

Enquiry Point for Occupational Cardiovascular Disease
Health and Safety Executive

Dr. Simon Clarke
Room 234A
Health and Safety Executive
Magdalen House
Stanley Precinct
Bootle
Merseyside L20 3QZ
Tel: 0541 545500;
Email: point.publicenquiry@hse.gov.uk

Enquiry Point for Occupational Hand-Arm Vibration Syndrome
Health and Safety Executive

Trevor Benn
Health and Safety Executive
Room 239
Magdalen House
Stanley Precinct
Bootle
Merseyside L20 3QZ
Tel: 0541 545500;
Email: point.publicenquiry@hse.gov.uk

Associated Sources
Industrial Injuries Scheme (Prescribed Diseases)
(Department of Social Security) RIDDOR

Enquiry Point for Occupational Health Effects Arising from Ionising Radiation Exposure
Health and Safety Executive

Damien McElvenny
Health and Safety Executive
Room 234A
Magdalen House
Stanley Precinct
Bootle
Merseyside L20 3QZ
Tel: 0541 545500;
Email: point.publicenquiry @hse.gov.uk

Enquiry Point for Occupational Health Effects Arising from Lead Exposure
Health and Safety Executive

Alan Spence
Health and Safety Executive
Room 246
Magdalen House
Stanley Precinct
Bootle
Merseyside L20 3QZ
Tel: 0541 545500;
Email: point.publicenquiry@hse.gov.uk

Enquiry Point for Occupational Infections
Health and Safety Executive

Dr. Simon Clarke
Health and Safety Executive
Magdalen House
Stanley Precinct
Bootle
Merseyside L20 3QZ
Tel: 0541 545500;
Email: point.publicenquiry@hse.gov.uk

Enquiry Point for Occupational Musculoskeletal Disorders
Health and Safety Executive

Jacky Jones
Room 240
Health and Safety Executive
Magdalen House
Stanley Precinct
Bootle
Merseyside L20 3QZ
Tel: 0541 545500;
Email: point.publicenquiry@hse.gov.uk

Enquiry Point for Occupational Neurotoxic Effects
Health and Safety Executive

Alan Spence
Health and Safety Executive
Room 246
Magdalen House
Stanley Precinct
Bootle
Merseyside L20 3QZ
Tel: 0541 545500;
Email: point.publicenquiry@hse.gov.uk

Enquiry Point for Occupational Noise-Induced Deafness
Health and Safety Executive

Trevor Benn
Health and Safety Executive
Room 239
Magdalen House
Stanley Precinct
Bootle
Merseyside L20 3QZ
Tel: 0541 545500;
Email: point.publicenquiry@hse.gov.uk

Associated Sources
Industrial Injuries (Prescribed Diseases)
(Department of Social Security)

Enquiry Point for Occupational Pesticide-Related Health Effects
Health and Safety Executive

Alan Spence
Health and Safety Executive
Room 246
Magdalen House
Stanley Precinct
Bootle
Merseyside L20 3QZ
Tel: 0541 545500;
Email: point.publicenquiry@hse.gov.uk

Enquiry Point for Occupational Reproductive Health Effects
Health and Safety Executive

Damien McElvenny
Health and Safety Executive
Room 234A
Magdalen House
Stanley Precinct
Bootle
Merseyside L20 3QZ
Tel: 0541 545500;
Email: point.publicenquiry@hse.gov.uk

Enquiry Point for Occupational Skin Diseases
Health and Safety Executive

Damien McElvenny
Health and Safety Executive
Room 234A
Magdalen House
Stanley Precinct
Bootle
Merseyside L20 3QZ
Tel: 0541 545500;
Email: point.publicenquiry@hse.gov.uk

Enquiry Point for Occupational Stress-Related and Psychosocial Disorders
Health and Safety Executive

Dr. Simon Clarke
Health and Safety Executive
Magdalen House
Stanley Precinct
Bootle
Merseyside L20 3QZ
Tel: 0541 545500;
Email: point.publicenquiry@hse.goc.uk

Enquiry Point for Statistics of Asbestos-Related Cancer
Health and Safety Executive

Jacky Jones
Room 240
Health and Safety Executive
Magdalen House
Stanley Precinct
Bootle
Merseyside L20 3QZ
Tel: 0541 545500;
Email: point.publicenquiry@hse.gov.uk

Enquiry Point for Statistics of Enforcement Action by the Health and Safety Executive and Local Authorities Under the Health and Safety at Work Etc. Act 1974
Health and Safety Executive

Statistics of enforcement action taken by HSE and local authorities under the Health and Safety at Work etc Act 1974 are published in the Health and Safety Commission Annual Report and Health and Safety Statistics. Further information is available on request from HSE's Operations Unit.

Delivery: Ongoing
Price: Charges are made according to the time required to compile requested information. This is in line with principals set out in the Code of Practice on Access to Government Information

Available from
Operations Unit
Health and Safety Executive
5th Floor
Daniel House
Trinity Road
Bootle
Merseyside L20 7HE
Tel: 0541 545500;
Email: point.publicenquiry@hse.gov.uk

Sources from which data for this product are obtained
Information on enforcement action under the Health and Safety at Work Etc Act 1974 from the Health and Safety Executive and local authorities

Enquiry Point for Statistics of Occupational Asbestosis
Health and Safety Executive

Jacky Jones
Room 240
Health and Safety Executive
Magdalen House
Stanley Precinct
Bootle
Merseyside L20 3QZ
Tel: 0541 545500;
Email: point.publicenquiry@hse.gov.uk

Enquiry Point for Statistics of Occupational Injury
Health and Safety Executive

The Health and Safety Executive publishes statistics of workplace injury reported by responsible persons under the Reporting of Injuries, Diseases and Dangerous Occurrences Regulations (RIDDOR) in the Health and Safety Commission Annual Report and Accounts, Health and Safety Statistics, and the Safety Statistics Bulletin. Further information is available on request from HSEís Operations Unit.

Delivery: Ongoing
Price: Charges are made according to the time required to compile requested information. This is in line with principles set out in the Code of Practice on Access to Government Information

Available from
Operations Unit
Health and Safety Executive
5th Floor
Trinity House
Stanley Road
Bootle
Merseyside L20 7HE
Tel: 0541 545500;
Email: point.publicenquiry@hse.gov.uk

Sources from which data for this product are obtained
Injuries and dangerous Occurrences reported under the Reporting of Injuries, Diseases and Dangerous Occurrences Regulations (RIDDOR); Employment Data from Employer Surveys and the Labour Force Survey

Enquiry Point for Statistics of Occupational Lung Diseases
Health and Safety Executive

Suzi Curtis
Room 246
Health and Safety Executive
Magdalen House
Stanley Precinct
Bootle
Merseyside L20 3QZ
Tel: 0541 545500;
Email: point.publicenquiry@hse.gov.uk

Associated Sources
Surveillance of Work-Related and Occupational Respiratory Disease (SWORD) Industrial Injuries Disablement Benefit Statistics

Health and Safety Commission Annual Report and Accounts 1997/98
Health and Safety Executive

A Departmental report of the latest statistics available on occupation injuries, ill-health, dangerous occurrences and gas safety. It contains information on the work of the Health and Safety Commission and Executive including legislation, guidance, inspection and enforcement initiatives, research, resource management, and the HSE's performance in improving standards of service.

A summary of the latest statistics available on occupational injuries, ill health, dangerous occurrences, gas safety and enforcement action by HSE is also covered.

Delivery: Periodic Release
Frequency: Annually
Price: £16.50 net
ISBN: 0-7176-1638-X

Available from
HSE Books
Please see Annex B for full address details.

Sources from which data for this product are obtained
Diseases reported under the Reporting of Injuries, Diseases and Dangerous Occurrences Regulations (RIDDOR); Information on enforcement action under the Health and Safety at Work etc Act 1974 from the Health and Safety Executive and local authorities; Injuries and dangerous occurrences reported under the Reporting of Injuries, Diseases and Dangerous Occurrences Regulations (RIDDOR)

Health and Safety Statistics 1997/98
Health and Safety Executive

Health and Safety Statistics is an annual statistical publication accompanying the Health and Safety Commission Annual Report. It contains the latest statistics available on a wide range of topics under the subject of health and safety at work. Health and Safety Statistics is a report of approximately 200 pages containing text tables and charts. It is used by a wide range of people including HSE senior management, MPs, academics, safety organisations and pressure groups.

Delivery: Periodic Release
Frequency: Annually
Price: £16.00 net
ISBN: 0-7176-1636-3

Available from
HSE Books
Please see Annex B for full address details.

Sources from which data for this product are obtained
Information on enforcement action under the Health and Safety at Work etc Act 1974 from the Health and Safety Executive local authorities; Injuries and dangerous occurrences reported under the Reporting of Injuries, Diseases and Dangerous Occurrences Regulations (RIDDOR); Employment data from Employer Surveys and the Labour Force Survey

HELA Annual Report of Health and Safety in the Service Industries
Health and Safety Executive

The annual report of the Health and Safety Executive/Local Authority Enforcement Liaison Committee (HELA) contains summary data on workplace injuries in the service sectors; local authority inspection and enforcement activity; fatal injury case studies; performance of local authorities against priority objectives and information on specific prosecutions and fines. This full colour publication is mainly targeted at local authority Chief Executives and Environmental Health Officers and is around 40 pages in length. It presents information on injuries in local authority enforced industries, along with information on local authority performance in health and safety. Data are presented in text , charts and tables. This publication is part of a package which is published annually and includes the 'National Picture of Health and Safety in the Service Industries'.

Delivery: Periodic Release
Frequency: Annually
Price: Free

Available from
The internet at http://www.open.gov.uk/hse/hsehome.htm

or

HSE Books
Please see Annex B for full address details.

Sources from which data for this product are obtained
Injuries and dangerous occurrences reported under the Reporting of Injuries, Diseases and Dangerous Occurrences Regulations (RIDDOR)

Levels of Reporting of Workplace Injuries by Employers
Health and Safety Executive

Employers are required to report workplace injuries to the Health and Safety Executive

under the Reporting of Injuries, Diseases and Dangerous Occurrences Regulations (RIDDOR). Although all fatal injuries are reported, employers do not report all non-fatal injuries that they should under RIDDOR. Estimates of the level of underreporting for non-fatal injuries are calculated by comparing the level of reported injury with results of the work-related accidents survey. Information is published annually in Health and Safety Statistics

Delivery: Periodic Release
Frequency: Annually
Price: £16.00 net
ISBN: 0 7176 1636 3

Available from
HSE Books
Please see Annex B for full address details.

Sources from which data for this product are obtained
Injuries and dangerous occurrences reported under the Reporting of Injuries, Diseases and Dangerous Occurrences Regulations (RIDDOR); Work-Related Accidents Survey (Labour Force Survey)

National Picture of Health and Safety in Local Authority Enforced Industries
Health and Safety Executive

The National Picture contains detailed statistics on inspection and enforcement activity of local authorities, including number of inspections or visits, staff and prosecution data; data and trends in local authority enforced industries, including breakdowns by severity of injury, industry and kind of accident; and indicators of local authority performance. The National Picture is part of the package which is released with the 'HELA Annual Report of Health and Safety in the Service Industries' and provides more detailed information on accidents and inspection, and enforcement. It is mainly targeted at Environmental Health Officers, is around 60 pages long and includes text, charts and tables.

Delivery: Periodic Release
Frequency: Annually
Price: Free

Available from
The internet at http://www.open.gov.uk/hse/hsehome.htm

or

Operations Unit
Health and Safety Executive
5th Floor
Daniel House
Trinity Road
Bootle
Merseyside L20 7HE

Sources from which data for this product are obtained
Injuries and dangerous occurrences reported under the Reporting of Injuries, Diseases and Dangerous Occurrences Regulations (RIDDOR); Employment data from employer surveys and the Labour Force Survey

Occupational Health Decennial Supplement
Health and Safety Executive; sponsored by Office for National Statistics

A 400 page book containing text, tables and figures describing a decennial update to the overall picture of occupational injuries and ill-health. Summary statistics of occupational injuries and ill-health

Delivery: Periodic Release
Frequency: Periodic
Price: £29.00
ISBN: 0-11-691618-4

Available from
TSO Publications Centre and Bookshops
Please see Annex B for full address details.

Sources from which data for this product are obtained
Injuries and diseases reported under the Reporting of Injuries, Diseases and Dangerous Occurrences Regulations (RIDDOR); Industrial Injuries (Prescribed Diseases) (Department of Social Security); Death registrations; Cancer registrations; Survey of Self Reported Work-Related Illness (SWI90)

Pesticide Incidents Report 1997/98
Health and Safety Executive

Delivery: Hardcopy publication
Frequency: Annual
Price: Free

Available from
Health and Safety Executive
Agriculture and Wood Sector
The Pearson Building
55 Upper Parliament Street
Nottingham NG1 6AN

Sources from which data for this product are obtained
Pesticide Incidents Appraisal Panel

Safety Statistics Bulletin
Health and Safety Executive

Annual bulletin covering occupational injuries to employees and the self-employed, dangerous occurrences and gas safety for Great Britain reported under the Reporting of Injuries, Diseases and Dangerous Occurrence Regulations 1985 and 1995. Figures for the latest year are reported as

Products

well as indications of trends over a number of years. The Safety Statistics Bulletin consists of 8 colour pages of mainly charts and bullet points reporting headline figures. Injury rates per 100,000 workers are reported. It is used by a wide range of people including HSE senior management, MPs, academics, safety organisations and pressure groups.

Delivery: Periodic Release
Frequency: Annually
Price: Free publication

Available from
HSE Books
Please see Annex B for full address details.

Sources from which data for this product are obtained
Injuries and dangerous occurrences reported under the Reporting of Injuries, Diseases and Dangerous Occurrences Regulations (RIDDOR); Employment data from employer surveys and the Labour Force Survey

---

Self-Reported Working Conditions Survey (SWC)
Health and Safety Executive

Presents the main findings from the control population to the 1995 self-reported work-related illness survey. 94 pages of summary statistics, tables and figures with accompanying text describing the results of the control population for the 1995 self-reported work-related illness survey.

Frequency: Ad-hoc
Price: £25.00
ISBN: 0-7176-1449-2

Statistics of Occupational Injury Within the EU and the USA
Health and Safety Executive

Information on the level of workplace injury in Great Britain in comparison with other EU member states and the USA was published in Health and Safety Statistics 1997/98. It builds on the work of Eurostat and member states to produce comparative statistics of workplace injury in the EU

Delivery: Periodic Release
Frequency: Annually
Price: £16.00
ISBN: 0 7176 1636 3

Available from
HSE Books
Please see Annex B for full address details.

Sources from which data for this product are obtained
Injuries and Dangerous Occurrences reported under the Reporting of Injuries, Diseases and Dangerous Occurrences Regulations (RIDDOR)

See also:
In this chapter:
Labour Force Survey Quarterly Databases (6.14)

6.14 Labour Force - general

Great Britain Labour Force Projections
Office for National Statistics

An annual article in Labour Market Trends. Labour Force Projections incorporate information from the Labour Force Survey, national fertility rates and the national population projections. Contains estimates and projections for the labour force, household population and activity rates, by sex and broad age groups. UK projections will be available from 1999. A technical note in the method used to calculate the projections is also included.

Frequency: Annually
Price: Published in Labour Market Trends @ £7.50, annually.

International Year Book of Labour Statistics
International Labour Office

This publication is published by the International Labour Organisation.

Frequency: Annually
Price: £113.40
ISBN: 92-2-007354-4

Sources from which data for this product are obtained
Labour Force Survey; New Earnings Survey - GB

Labour Force Survey Analysis Service
Office for National Statistics

Standard and user-defined analyses from the Labour Force Survey databases.

Delivery: Ad-hoc
Frequency: Quarterly

Available from
LFS Bureau
SPSS MR
67 Maygrove Road
London NW6 2EG
Tel: 020 7625 7222

Sources from which data for this product are obtained
Labour Force Survey

Labour Force Survey and Labour Market Statistics First Release
Office for National Statistics

Labour Force Summary: First results from the quarterly Labour Force Survey. Contains data on the economic activity of those aged 16 and over, those in employment (i.e. employees, self-employed, government employed and training programmes, and unpaid family workers), occupation, industry worked in, job-related training, hours of work, those not in work (under the International Labour Organisation (ILO) definition) and the length of time they had been without a job, redundancies, those economically inactive and the reasons, trade union membership, health, income and demographic characteristics.

Available from
Labour market statistics enquiries
Please see Annex B for full address details.

ONS Press Office
Office for National Statistics
1 Drummond Gate
London
SW1V 2QQ
Tel: 020 7533 6363/6364

Labour Force Survey Historical Supplement
Office for National Statistics

The LFS Historical Supplement contains historical labour market data taken from the Labour Force Survey. The supplement contains data for every Spring from 1984 to 1998 with some data included from the biennial surveys conducted in 1979, 1981 and 1983. Topics covered include: labour market activity, employment, unemployment (ILO), women in the labour market, ethnic groups, regional data.

Delivery: Periodic Release
Frequency: Ad-hoc
Price: Hardcopy £10.00
Electronic £23.50
ISBN: 1 85774 2990

Available from
ONS Direct
Please see Annex B for full address details.

Sources from which data for this product are obtained
Labour Force Survey

Labour Force Survey Historical Supplement Seasonally Adjusted Estimates
Office for National Statistics

To complement the original Labour Force Survey Historical Supplement, the new HS contains 3-month averages monthly from 1992, based on the 1999 Seasonal Adjustment Review. Main tables include UK data for every 3-month period back to March–May 1992. Additional tables cover countries and English regions and headline series for UK and GB for March–May at each year from 1984–1991 (and some series back to 1979). Topics covered include: labour market activity, employment, unemployment, hours worked.

Delivery: Periodic Release
Frequency: Ad-hoc
Price: Hardcopy £10.00
Electronic £23.50

Available from
ONS Direct
Please see Annex B for full address details.

Sources from which data for this product are obtained
Labour Force Survey

Labour Force Survey Quarterly Databases
Office for National Statistics

LFS data for the UK are available for users to analyse on their own PC or via dial-up facilities. There is also an analysis service (see separate entry). Databases are available for spring quarters for 1979-1983 (biennial) and 1984-1991 and every quarter from spring 1992.

Some of the data in this product are disaggregated by gender.

Frequency: Quarterly

Available from
LFS Bureau
SPSS MR
67 Maygrove Road
London NW6 2EG
Tel: 020 7625 7222

Labour Force Survey Quarterly Supplement
Office for National Statistics

Comprehensive results from the quarterly LFS in text, charts and tables. Contains data and trends on: employment and self-employment; full-time and part-time employment; second jobs; employment by age and sex; ILO unemployment by age and sex; economic activity by age and sex; occupations and industry sectors; regional economic activity; average actual weekly hours of work (by industry sector); economic inactivity by age and sex;

economic inactivity by reason including discouraged workers; temporary employees; part-time and self-employed by occupation and industry; average actual weekly hours of work; ILO unemployment by occupation and industry; duration of ILO unemployment; average gross earnings by occupation, industry sector and region; ethnic group economic activity; household population by age and sex; economic activity for countries and larger LADs; long-term unemployed by occupation and industry sector; labour market structure.

Frequency: Quarterly
Price: Annual subscription charge £37.00 (£13.00 for single issue)
ISBN: 0-11-621034-6
ISSN: 1465-8267

Available from
Labour market statistics enquiries or TSO Publications Centre and Bookshops
Please see Annex B for full address details.

Sources from which data for this product are obtained
ILO unemployment (LFS - seasonally adjusted); Labour Force Survey

---

Labour Force Survey Religion Report
Northern Ireland Statistics and Research Agency

The Labour Force Survey Religion Report includes information disaggregated by religion on labour force participation rates, reasons for non-participation, unemployment rates, the unemployment differential, length of time seeking work, main methods of job search used by the unemployed, characteristics of those in employment, composition of the major occupational and industrial groupings and the highest level of qualification attained.

Some of the data in this product is disaggregated by gender.

Delivery: Hardcopy publication
Frequency: Annually
ISBN: 1899203302

Available from
Human Resource Research and Evaluation Branch
Rosepark House
Upper Newtownards Road
Belfast BT4 3NR
Tel: 028 9052 6258; Website: www.nisra.gov.uk

Sources from which data for this product are obtained
Labour Force Survey - Northern Ireland

Labour Market Statistics First Release
Office for National Statistics

A series of monthly ONS publications comprising a UK First Release and one for each GB Government office region. The releases contain the latest employment, unemployment, economic activity & inactivity, claimant count, earnings, productivity and Jobcentre vacancies data.

Delivery: First Release
Frequency: Monthly
Price: Individual copies of ONS releases are available from ONS Press Office at the cost of £3.50.
Annual subscriptions to ONS First Releases cost £42.00

Available from
Labour market statistics enquiries
Please see Annex B for full address details.

ONS Press Office
Office for National Statistics
1 Drummond Gate
London
SW1V 2QQ
Tel: 020 7533 6363/6364

Sources from which data for this product are obtained
Claimant Count; Employment (LFS - seasonally adjusted); ILO unemployment (LFS - seasonally adjusted); Index of Average Earnings - GB; Job Centre Vacancies; Labour Force Survey; Seasonally Adjusted Claimant Count Consistent with Current Coverage (SAUCCC series)

Labour Market Trends
Office for National Statistics

Monthly magazine presenting a wide range of information relating to the labour market. Contains a comprehensive selection of labour market statistics; earnings, employment, labour disputes, Labour Force Survey (LFS), redundancies, Retail Price Index, Government Training and Enterprise Programmes, unemployment and vacancies. Each edition includes special features, ad hoc news items and topical analyses from the LFS.

Delivery: Periodic Release
Frequency: Monthly
Price: Single Issue £9.00
Annual subscription UK £85.00
Annual subscription overseas £116.00
ISSN: 1361 4819

Products

Sources from which data for this product are obtained
Annual Employment Survey - Great Britain; Centralised Returns (Public Sector); Claimant Count; Claimant Unemployment Cohort (JUVOS Cohort); Consumer Price Collection - UK; Employment (LFS - seasonally adjusted); Ethnic Group and Birthplace - GB; Harmonised Index of Consumer Prices; Hours of Work; ILO unemployment (LFS - seasonally adjusted); Index of Average Earnings - GB; Job Centre Vacancies; Labour Costs in the EC; Labour Dispute Statistics; Labour Force Projections; Labour Force Survey; Labour Productivity and Unit Wage Costs - UK; Monthly Short-term Turnover and Employment Survey - Production Industries; National Information System for Vocational Qualifications (NISVQ); New Earnings Survey - GB; Quarterly Short-term turnover and Employment Survey - Service Sector; Regional Selective Assistance Grants to Industry - Scotland; Seasonally Adjusted Claimant Count Consistent with Current Coverage (SAUCCC series); Skill Needs in Britain; Survey of Earnings and Hours of Agricultural and Horticultural Workers; Work-Related Accidents Survey; Workforce jobs (formerly Workforce in Employment); Youth Cohort Study - England and Wales; Youth Training Follow-up Survey; Youth Training Statistics

Local Area Labour Force Survey Data
Office for National Statistics

An annual database comprising of key LFS data with a local area indicator. Earliest year available is 1994-95 using Local Authorities Districts (LADs) as the indicator. Subsequent years include Unitary Authorities as well as LADs as the indicator. The database holds 184,000 records for persons aged 16 and over (60% more than for a single LFS quarter) and 236,000 records in total. The following 12 key variables are available: Age; Sex; Economic-activity; Full-time or part-time employment; Industry Sector; Occupation; Social Class; Ethnicity (selected areas); Educational Status; Qualifications; Job related training from employer; and Geographical indicator (LADs in 1994/95 and LADs/UAs form 1995/96.

Delivery: Periodic Release
Frequency: Annually

Available from
LFS Bureau
SPSS MR
67 Maygrove Road
London NW6 2EG
Tel: 020 7625 7222

Northern Ireland Labour Force Survey
Department of Economic Development - Northern Ireland

Now replaced by Northern Ireland Labour Force Survey - Quarterly Supplement spring 1998. Latest labour force figures are published in monthly Labour Market Statistics. Contains data on the economic activity of the private household population aged 16 and over, employment status of those in employment, unemployment rates, qualification levels of those in employment and the unemployed, age distribution of those in employment and the unemployed, and persons in employment by industry and occupation.

Delivery: First Release
Frequency: Quarterly
Price: Free of charge

Available from
Clare Alexander
Statistics Research Branch
Department of Economic Development
Netherleigh
Massey Avenue
Belfast BT4 2JP
Tel: 028 9052 9525; Fax: 028 9052 9459;
Email: clare.alexander@dedni.gov.uk

Sources from which data for this product are obtained
Labour Force Survey - Northern Ireland

Northern Ireland Labour Force Survey - Historical Supplement
Department of Economic Development - Northern Ireland

Labour Force Historical data from Spring 1984 to Autumn 1997

Delivery: Periodic Release
Frequency: Annually
Price: Free of charge

Available from
Clare Alexander
Statistics Research Branch
Department of Economic Development
Netherleigh
Massey Avenue
Belfast BT4 2JP
Tel:028 9052 9525; Fax: 028 9052 9459;
Email: clare.alexander@dedni.gov.uk

Sources from which data for this product are obtained
Labour Force Survey - Northern Ireland

Northern Ireland Labour Force Survey - Quarterly Supplement
Department of Economic Development - Northern Ireland

Supplementary Labour Force Survey analysis to that contained in monthly Labour Market Statistics publication, of groups within the labour market e.g. those in employment, the unemployed and those economically inactive. In addition to this regular analysis, it also contains ad hoc features of topical interest in the labour market e.g. economic activity of disabled persons, sickness absence and accidents at work.

Delivery: Periodic Release
Frequency: Quarterly
Price: Free

Available from
Owen Johnston
Statistics Research Branch
Department of Economic Development
Netherleigh
Massey Avenue
Belfast BT4 2JP
Tel: 028 9052 9585; Fax: 028 9052 9459;
Email: owen.johnston@dedni.gov.uk

Sources from which data for this product are obtained
Labour Force Survey - Northern Ireland

Northern Ireland Labour Market Statistics
Department of Economic Development - Northern Ireland

Published monthly, this is an integrated labour market publication containing information from the Labour Force Survey, Claimant Count, Employee Jobs, Vacancies & Employment and Training Measures, Index of Production & Manufacturing Productivity and New Earnings Survey.

Delivery: News/Press Release
Frequency: Monthly
Price: Free

Available from
Statistics Research Branch
Department of Economic Development
Room 110
Netherleigh
Massey Avenue
Belfast BT4 2JP
Tel: 028 9052 9399; Fax: 028 9052 9459

Sources from which data for this product are obtained
Claimant Count - Northern Ireland; Labour Force Survey - Northern Ireland; New Earnings Survey - Northern Ireland; Quarterly Employment Survey - Northern Ireland, Index of Production ñ Northern Ireland

Regional Labour Force Projections
Office for National Statistics

Contains estimates and projections of the labour force, household population and activity rates by sex and broad age groups. Shows projections for labour force, household population and activity rates for Standard Statistical Regions. Will show Government Office Regions in 1999.

Frequency: Biennially
Price: Published in Labour Market Trends £7.50

Youth Cohort Study - Statistical Bulletin
Department for Education and Employment

Youth Cohort Study: The Activities and Experiences of 16 year olds: England and Wales 1996 (June 1997). The most recent bulletin covers the summary findings from Cohort 8 sweep 1 of the Youth Cohort Study of England and Wales. It covers education, labour market and training activities and experiences of young people in the first year following compulsory education. The young people are aged 16/17 at the time of the survey, and where appropriate comparisons are made with earlier Cohorts of the same age. The summary findings are presented in a series of tables, supplemented in some areas by charts. For the most recent bulletin in addition to a summary and technical note, the accompanying text is structured to cover the following areas: Careers provision in year 11; Work experience at school; National Record of Achievement; Youth Credits Truancy; Qualifications attainment in year 11; Education and training activities; Full-time education and training; Government supported training; The labour market; and Qualification aims. Where appropriate, data is compared with the same age Cohort for previous years. Data is often broken down by sex, ethnic origin or parental socio-economic group.

Some of the data in this product is disaggregated by gender.

Frequency: Ad-hoc
Price: £3.50
ISBN: 0-11-271010-7

See also:
In this chapter:
Guide to Labour Market Statistics First Releases (6.10)

In other chapters:
Economic Trends (see the Economy chapter)
Nomis® (see the Websites and Electronic Services chapter)

6.15 Labour Relations

Trade Union Membership and Recognition 1996-97: An Analysis of Data from the Certification Officer and the Labour Force Survey
Department of Trade and Industry

This annual article describes data from two alternative sources of information on trade union membership. It contains a detailed commentary on patterns of union membership across various individual and employer characteristics. Also included in this article, is a detailed description of union recognition and collective bargaining coverage. The article is aimed at providing detailed information on trade unions for government officials and a wider academic audience.

Delivery: Periodic Release
Frequency: Annually

Available from
Trade Unions/Labour Enquiries
Room 2103
Department of Trade and Industry
1 Victoria Street
London SW1H 0ET
Tel: 020 7215 5999
Email: stephen.woodland@irdv.dti.gov.uk

(The) 1998 Workplace Employee Relations Survey: First Findings
Department of Trade and Industry; sponsored jointly with the Economic and Social Research Council; Policy Studies Institute/Advisory Conciliation and Arbitration Service

The booklet reports the first findings from the fourth in the series of workplace surveys. Initial results from a survey which involved detailed interviews with over 3,000 managers and around 1,000 worker representatives, as well as completed questionnaires obtained from nearly 30,000 employees.

Delivery: Ad hoc/One-off Release
Price: Free
ISBN: 0 85605 382 1

Available from
DTI Publications
Department of Trade and Industry
151 Buckingham Palace Road
London SW1W 9SS
Tel: 020 7215 6024

Sources from which data for this product are obtained
Workplace Industrial Relations Survey 1998

Workplace Industrial Relations in Transition: the ED/ESRC/PSI/ACAS Surveys
Department of Trade and Industry; sponsored by Employment Department / Economic and Social Research Council / Policy Studies Institute / Advisory Conciliation and Arbitration Service

A detailed description of data from the 1990 Workplace Industrial Relations Survey, including comparisons with data from previous surveys in the series.

Delivery: Ad Hoc/One-off Release
Price: £9.95
ISBN: 1 85521 321 4

Available from
DTI Publications
Department of Trade and Industry
151 Buckingham Palace Road
London SW1W 9SS
Tel: 020 7215 6024

Sources from which data for this product are obtained
Workplace Industrial Relations Survey 1990

See also:
In this chapter:
Labour Force Survey Quarterly Databases (6.14)
Labour Market Trends (6.14)

6.16 Pay and Income from Work

Harmonised Statistics of Earnings - Methodology of National Surveys
Eurostat

This document outlines the methodology used in the national surveys on which the data on harmonised statistics on earnings are based. Definitions, coverage, methods, questionnaire and available series for the Member States.

Frequency: Ad hoc
Price: £7.25
ISBN: 92 826 4110 4

Available from
TSO Publications Centre and Bookshops
Please see Annex B for full address details.

New Earnings Survey - GB (Parts A - F) + UK Volume (from 1998)
Office for National Statistics

This report covers average earnings statistics in Great Britain including gross weekly and hourly earnings and hours worked. Contains data by occupation, industry, age, sex, region and county plus small area data, collective agreements, manual/non-manual workers, full-time/part-time. The results also show the make-up of pay, overtime hours worked, public/private sector earnings and quartiles and deciles. Part A is a summary version of the Survey and Parts B-F give more details of the summary data within Part A. UK volume from 1998. UK Volumes includes Northern Ireland data.

Delivery: Hardcopy publication
Frequency: Annual
Price: Single issue £25.00, annual subscription £120.00, £130.00 if UK included.
ISBN: Part A: 0 11 729637 6.
Part B: 0 11 729638 4.
Part C: 0 11 729639 2.
Part D: 0 11 729640 6.
Part E: 0 11 729641 4.
Part F: 0 11 729642 2.
ISSN: 0262-0553

Available from
ONS Direct
Please see Annex B for full address details.

Sources from which data for this product are obtained
New Earnings Survey - GB

Northern Ireland New Earnings Survey
Department of Economic Development - Northern Ireland

This report covers latest earnings figures for Northern Ireland. Contains latest earnings figures on average weekly and hourly earnings by industry, distribution of earnings, gross weekly earnings by occupation, gross weekly and hourly earnings by area, and Northern Ireland gross weekly and hourly earnings as a percentage of those in Great Britain. Also information on hours worked and the make-up of earnings.

Delivery: Other
Frequency: Annually
Price: Free

Available from
Lorraine Livingston
Statistics Research Branch
Department of Economic Development
Netherleigh
Massey Avenue
Belfast BT4 2JP
Tel: 028 9052 9429; Fax: 028 9052 9459;
Email: jim.doran@dedni.gov.uk

Sources from which data for this product are obtained
New Earnings Survey - Northern Ireland

Northern Ireland New Earnings Survey - Historical Supplement
Department of Economic Development - Northern Ireland

Northern Ireland New Earnings Survey historical data from 1971-1998

Delivery: Ad Hoc/One-off Release
Price: Free

Available from
Lorraine Livingston
Statistics Research Branch
Department of Economic Development
Netherleigh
Massey Avenue
Belfast BT4 2JP
Tel: 028 9052 9429; Fax: 028 9052 9459;
Email: jim.doran@dedni.gov.uk

Sources from which data for this product are obtained
New Earnings Survey - Northern Ireland

Pay and Working Time
Office for National Statistics

Frequency: Amendments published monthly.
Price: £72.00 per annum

Available from
ONS Direct
Please see Annex B for full address details.

Women's Individual Income 1996/7
Women's Unit / Department of Social Security

A series of publications examining individual income statistics from the Family Resources Survey. Individual income refers to the gross weekly personal income of women and men and includes earnings, income from self-employment, investments and occupational pensions/annuities, benefit income and other miscellaneous sources.

Frequency: Annual
Price: Free

Available from
Women's Unit
10 Great George Street
London SW1P 3AE
Tel: 020 7273 8880

See also:
In this chapter:
International Year Book of Labour Statistics (6.14)
Labour Force Survey Quarterly Databases (6.14)

Analysis of Unemployed Claimants
Department of Health and Social Security - Northern Ireland

Statistical bulletin on the number of people out of work in Northern Ireland. Contains data on stock and flow by age, sex, length of unemployment, benefit receipt and amounts in payment, and occupational pension receipt.

Frequency: Quarterly
Price: free

Available from
Fergal Bradley
DHSS - NI
Annexe 2/3
Castle Buildings
Stormont
Belfast
Tel: 028 9052 2661

How Exactly Is Unemployment Measured?
Office for National Statistics

Small booklet - third edition published April 1998. Explains how ONS produces the ILO (International Labour Organisation) definition of unemployment and the count of claimants of unemployment-related benefits.

Delivery: Ad hoc/One-off Release
Price: Free

Available from
Labour market statistics enquiries
Please see Annex B for full address details.

Sources from which data for this product are obtained
Claimant Count; ILO unemployment (LFS - seasonally adjusted); Seasonally Adjusted Claimant Count Consistent with Current Coverage (SAUCCC series)

Jobseeker's Allowance Statistics Quarterly Enquiry
Department of Social Security

Statistical tables on characteristics of Jobseeker's Allowance claimants. Contains data on type and average amount of Jobseeker's Allowance in payment, number and age of claimants, partners and dependants, type and amount of housing costs, income and capital, type and number of premiums and deductions for third parties and length of time in receipt. The report consists of approximately 90 pages of tables, charts and summary text covering key findings. The analysis are mainly used by DSS, policy branches for monitoring and evaluating, and other areas of Analytical Services Division for forecasting future Government expenditure on Social Security.

Delivery: Periodic Release
Frequency: Quarterly
Price: £5.00

Available from
Analytical Services Division
Department of Social Security
The Adelphi
1-11 John Adam Street
London WC2N 6HT

Sources from which data for this product are obtained
Jobseeker's Allowance Quarterly Statistical Enquiry - Great Britain

Unemployment - Northern Ireland Press Notice
Department of Economic Development - Northern Ireland

Press releases of the latest unemployment figures for Northern Ireland (replaced in April 1998 by the Northern Ireland Labour Market Statistics publication). Contains unemployment figures at Northern Ireland, Travel-To-Work Area and local authority district level and the latest vacancy figures for Northern Ireland.

Some of the data in this product is disaggregated by gender.

Delivery: News/Press Release
Frequency: Monthly
Price: Free

Available from
Statistics Research Branch
Please see Annex B for full address details.

Sources from which data for this product are obtained
Claimant Count - Northern Ireland

See also:
In this chapter
Labour Force Survey Historical Supplement (6.14)
Labour Force Survey Quarterly Databases (6.14)
Labour Market Statistics First Release (6.14)
Labour Market Trends (6.14)
Northern Ireland Labour Market Statistics (6.10)

In other chapters:
Economic Trends (see the Economy chapter)
Nomis® (see the Websites and Electronic Services chapter)

Other Products which may be of interest, but are not featured in this book due to lack of details:

Work Organisation and Working Hours, 1983-92 - Office for National Statistics

7 Housing

Statistics covering **Housing** are collected, administered and disseminated by a number of separate Departments, Agencies and organisations including the **Department of the Environment, Transport and the Regions, Scottish Executive, the National Assembly for Wales, the Northern Ireland Department of the Environment**. The available statistics embrace a number of subject areas including: **Clearance and Demolition of Housing, Conversion, Renovation and Repair of Housing, Homelessness, Housing Stock, Letting of Housing, New Housebuilding, Purchases and Sales of Property.**

The basic data are generated from a number of separate information 'Sources' and the resultant statistics are disseminated through a whole range of statistical 'Analyses' and 'Products', all of which are described in the following chapter. Users looking for a cross-section of UK-wide statistics on **Housing** may find the following products useful:

Housing and Construction Statistics (quarterly/annual publications)

Users interested in a wider range of official statistics including **Housing** statistics may like to refer to the following compendia:

On-line Databases (See Chapter 1):
    StatBase - StatStore

Hardcopy Compendia (See Chapter 2):
    Annual Abstract of Statistics
    Britain 2000: The Official Yearbook of the United Kingdom
    Monthly Digest of Statistics
    Regional Trends
    Social Trends

Users may also find what they need on the various Departmental Websites. These are listed in Chapter 1.

7

Housing - *Sources and Analyses*

7.1 Abstracts, Compendia, A-Z Catalogues, Directories and Reference Material

Survey of English Housing
Department of the Environment, Transport and the Regions

The Survey of English Housing (SEH) is a household interview survey with a sample of 20,000 responding households each year. It is a multi-purpose housing survey which provides a comprehensive range of basic information on households and their housing, and full information on the private rented sector. Results are grossed to give estimates for all households. The Survey covers England and data are available for standard and Government Office regions. Data are collected on the type of accommodation, household and personal characteristics, tenure, second homes, moves, repossessions, satisfaction with the accommodation and area, waiting lists for council or housing association housing, owner occupation, social sector tenants, and private renters.

The SEH was launched in April 1993. It updates basic housing information previously collected every 3-4 years in the Labour Force Survey Housing Trailers, and detailed information on the private rented sector from the 1988 and 1990 Private Renters Surveys. From autumn 1994 questions on housing attitudes have been included, mostly on a rotating basis, updating information from the Housing Attitudes Survey carried out for the Department in 1992. Data are collected continuously on a financial-year cycle. Results are published within twelve months of their collection, and the data sets are subsequently placed with the Data Archive.

Status: Ongoing
Collection Method: Household/Person (Sample) Survey
Frequency: Continuously
Reference Period: Financial year
Timeliness: Full annual report usually published within 1 year of end of fieldwork. Starting with 1997/98 Survey, a preliminary bulletin is also published in advance of the main report
Earliest Available Data: 1993/4 financial year
National Coverage: England
Disaggregation: Government Office Region (GOR); Standard Statistical Region (SSR)

Statistician
Jeremy Grove
Department of the Environment, Transport and the Regions
Housing Data and Statistics Division; HDS5
Tel: 020 7890 3301;
Email: hds.huma.hcg.doe@gtnet.gov.uk

Products that contain data from this source
Housing and Construction Statistics Annual Volume; Housing in England; Private Renting in England 1993/94; Regional Trends; Social Focus on Children; Social Focus on Ethnic Minorities; Social Focus on the Unemployed; Social Focus on Women; Social Trends

---

7.2 Clearance and Demolition of Housing

Dwellings Demolished, Closed, Converted and Acquired - Scotland
Scottish Executive

The survey covers tenure of all dwellings demolished and closed and taken out of housing use and reason for demolition. It also counts the change in local authority stock due to all conversions of local authority properties, and the number of dwellings acquired from the private sector. The survey is carried out quarterly, covers Scotland and is available at local authority level.

Status: Ongoing
Collection Method: Census
Frequency: Quarterly
Reference Period: end of March, June, Sept, Dec
Timeliness: 6-8 months
National Coverage: Scotland
Disaggregation: Local Authority

Statistician
Deborah Pegg
Scottish Executive
Economic Advice and Statistics Division; Branch 7: Housing Statistics
Tel: 0131 244 2752.
Email: deborah.pegg@scotland.gov.uk

Products that contain data from this source
Housing Trends in Scotland

Slum Clearance - GB
Department of the Environment, Transport and the Regions

The Department of the Environment, Transport and the Regions, National Assembly for Wales, and Scottish Executive compile data on slum clearance. Data are collected on the number of dwellings demolished (in or adjoining a clearance area, or not in a clearance area) and the number of dwellings closed. The data cover England, Wales and Scotland, and are available for standard regions, Government Office regions, and at county and local authority level within England. Figures have been collected for each financial year since 1980, although some figures are available back to 1946. Results are published annually.

Frequency: Annually
Earliest Available Data: Some figures are available from 1946
National Coverage: Great Britain

Statistician
Henry Small
Department of the Environment, Transport and the Regions
Tel: 0117 987 8076

Products that contain data from this source
Annual Abstract of Statistics; Housing and Construction Statistics Annual Volume; Housing Trends in Scotland; Welsh Housing Statistics

---

Stock Clearance, Compulsory Renovation and Action on Unfit Dwellings
National Assembly for Wales

The National Assembly for Wales carries out an annual survey on stock clearance, compulsory renovation and action on unfit dwellings. Data are available on dwellings demolished or closed, persons displaced as a consequence, action taken to prevent dwellings from becoming unfit and notices served under the Housing Act 1985. Information on demolitions and closures has been available since 1955, although analysis of demolitions by sector has only been available since 1984. The return was changed from a quarterly form to an annual return in April 1991.

Status: Ongoing
Collection Method: Administrative Records
Frequency: Annually
Reference Period: Financial year
Timeliness: Approximately 3 months after the end of the financial year
Earliest Available Data: 1955
National Coverage: Wales
Disaggregation: Unitary Authority

Statistician
Henry Small
National Assembly for Wales
Statistical Directorate; Housing Statistics
Tel: 029 2082 5063;
Email: henry.small@wales.gsi.gov.uk

Products that contain data from this source
A Statistical Focus on Wales; Housing and Construction Statistics Annual Volume; Welsh Housing Statistics; Welsh Social Trends

See also:
In this chapter:
Assistance for Owners of Defective Housing - Wales *(7.3)*
English House Condition Survey (EHCS) *(7.6)*

7.3 Conversion, Renovation and Repair of Housing

Assistance for Owners of Defective Housing - Wales
National Assembly for Wales

The National Assembly for Wales compiled a survey on assistance for owners of defective housing. The survey monitored local authority activity for assistance to owners of defective housing regarding reinstatement grants or property purchase. Data covered Wales and are available at pre-1996 county and local authority district level. Longitudinal analyses are available. The survey was undertaken annually at the end of the financial year. It was introduced in 1984-85 in response to the Housing Defects Act 1984, since consolidated as part XVI of the 1985 Housing Act. The availability of grants through reinstatement or repurchase ceased in November 1994. Collection of data ceased after the financial year 1995-96.

Status: Ceased completely
Collection Method: Administrative Records
Frequency: Annually
Reference Period: Financial year
Earliest Available Data: 1984-85
National Coverage: Wales
Disaggregation: Local authority

Statistician
Henry Small
National Assembly for Wales
Statistical Directorate; Housing Statistics
Tel: 029 2082 5063;
Email: henry.small@wales.gsi.gov.uk

Grant and Group Repair Schemes - Wales
National Assembly for Wales

The National Assembly for Wales carries out a quarterly Census detailing numbers and amounts of approvals and completions of home renovation grants available from local authorities to owners, tenants and landlords. Information has been collected since the 1950's but has changed over time to account for changes in legislation. Major changes occurred following the Housing Defects Act 1984, the Housing Act 1985, the Local Government and Housing Act 1989 and most recently the Housing Grants, Construction and Regeneration Act 1996. The survey covers Wales and is available prior to the 1 April 1996 at local authority level and after this date for unitary authorities. Information on renovation grants in the private sector has been available since the 1950's. Current information dates from 1990 following the introduction of the new grant system detailed in the Local Government and Housing Act 1989 and amended in accordance with the Housing Grants, Construction and Regeneration Act 1996.

Status: Ongoing
Collection Method: Administrative Records
Frequency: Quarterly
Reference Period: January - March, April - June, July - September, October - December
Timeliness: Approximately 3 months after the end of the quarter
Earliest Available Data: 1950's
National Coverage: Wales
Disaggregation: Unitary Authority

Statistician
Henry Small
National Assembly for Wales
Statistical Directorate; Housing Statistics
Tel: 029 2082 5063;
Email: henry.small@wales.gsi.gov.uk

Products that contain data from this source
Digest of Welsh Local Area Statistics; Digest of Welsh Statistics; House Renovation Information Bulletin; Housing and Construction Statistics Annual Volume; Programme for the Valleys Statistical Profile; Quarterly Welsh Housing Statistics; Regional Trends; Social Trends; Welsh Housing Statistics

Grants for Dwelling Repair and Improvement - Northern Ireland
Department of the Environment (NI)

The Department of the Environment (NI) compiles data on repair and improvement grants payable under the Housing (NI) Order 1992 on a financial year basis. The data are supplied by the Northern Ireland Housing Executive, which administers the scheme, and are available at Northern Ireland level for the various types of grant available: renovation, replacement, disabled facilities, repairs, minor works, houses in multiple occupation and common parts.

Status: Ongoing
Collection Method: Administrative Records
Frequency: Annually
Reference Period: Financial Year
Timeliness: Six months
Earliest Available Data: 1993/94 (under current scheme)
National Coverage: Northern Ireland

Statistician:
Brian French
Department of the Environment (NI)
Central Statistics and Research Branch
Tel: 028 9054 0799;
E-mail: brian.french@doeni.gov.uk

Products that contain data from this source
Northern Ireland Housing Statistics

Grants, Group Repair and New Housebuilding (Programme for the Valleys)
National Assembly for Wales

Details activity within the boundary of the Programme for the Valleys area on new housebuilding, grants and group repair. Information on housing activity has been collected separately for the Programme for the Valleys area since April 1990 following the introduction of the scheme in 1988. Historical data was collected on a quarterly basis but, since 1996-97, information has been available only for financial years.

Status: Ongoing
Collection Method: Administrative Records
Frequency: Annually
Reference Period: Financial year
Timeliness: Approximately 3 months after the end of the financial year.
Earliest Available Data: April - June 1990
National Coverage: Wales
Sub-National: Those authorities wholly or partly within the Programme for the Valleys Area.
Disaggregation: Unitary Authority

Statistician
Henry Small
National Assembly for Wales
Statistical Directorate; Housing Statistics
Tel: 029 2082 5063;
Email: henry.small@wales.gsi.gov.uk

Products that contain data from this source
Programme for the Valleys Statistical Profile

House Renovation Grants GB
Department of the Environment, Transport and the Regions

The Department of the Environment, Transport and the Regions, National Assembly for Wales, and Scottish Executive compile data on house renovation grants collected from local authorities. Data are available on grants paid to private owners and tenants under the Housing Act 1985, including grants paid earlier under similar systems starting from 1946 (Scotland). They cover applications and payments of both numbers and total amounts of grant, conversion and improvement grants, intermediate and special grants and repair grants. The series also covers grants paid to private owners and tenants under the Local Government and Housing Act 1989 (for England and Wales only). They show applications and payments of numbers and of total amounts of grant, renovation grants, disabled facilities grants, houses in multiple occupation grants, common parts grants (the four 'main line' grants), and minor works assistance. Mandatory and discretionary grants are taken separately.

Data are collected annually on the sector receiving the grants, the purpose of the minor works assistance grants, the total costs of works for each of the main line grants, and the proportion of grants which fully meet the costs of works. The series covers Great Britain, England, Wales and Scotland. Data are available for standard regions, Government Office regions within England, and at county and local authority district level throughout the UK. Data are available, in their current form, since 1990. Information are available for earlier periods back to 1946. Results are published quarterly, three months after the reference quarter.

Frequency: Quarterly
Timeliness: Three months after the reference quarter
National Coverage: Great Britain

Statistician
Henry Small
Department of the Environment, Transport and the Regions
Tel: 0117 987 8076

Products that contain data from this source
Annual Abstract of Statistics; House Renovation Information Bulletin; Housing and Construction Statistics Annual Volume; Housing Trends in Scotland; Northern Ireland Housing and Construction Bulletin; Regional Trends; Social Trends; Welsh Housing Statistics

Improvement and Modernisation - Scotland
Scottish Executive

The Scottish Executive Development Department collects data on public and private sector improvement activity. The surveys cover Scotland and are available at local authority level. The public sector surveys are carried out quarterly and the private sector survey is carried out monthly.

Status: Ceased temporarily
Collection Method: Census
Frequency: Monthly
Reference Period: end of each month
National Coverage: Scotland
Disaggregation: Local Authority

Statistician
Deborah Pegg
Scottish Executive
Economic Advice and Statistics Division; Branch 7: Housing Statistics
Tel: 0131 244 2752.
Email: deborah.pegg@scotland.gov.uk

Products that contain data from this source
Housing Trends in Scotland

Improvements to Northern Ireland Housing Executive Dwellings
Department of the Environment (NI)

The Department of the Environment (NI) compiles data on improvements to Northern Ireland Housing Executive (NIHE) dwellings on a financial year basis. The data are supplied by NIHE and are available at district council area level.

Status: Ongoing
Collection Method: Administrative Records
Frequency: Annually
Reference Period: Financial Year
Timeliness: Six months
Earliest Available Data: 1983
National Coverage: Northern Ireland
Disaggregation: District council area level

Statistician:
Brian French
Department of the Environment (NI)
Central Statistics and Research Branch
Tel: 028 9054 0799;
E-mail: brian.french@doeni.gov.uk

Products that contain data from this source
Northern Ireland Housing Statistics

Renovation of Local Authority Dwellings
National Assembly for Wales

A quarterly survey that collected information on the renovation of local authority dwellings including home insulation and the right to repair scheme. Information on the renovation of local authority dwellings has been collected since 1984 with changes to data collected made in 1990. A number of data items collected through this survey transferred to the Housing Management and Performance Return at April 1996 when the collection of this form ceased.

Status: Ceased completely
Collection Method: Administrative Records
Frequency: Quarterly
Reference Period: Jan - March, April - June, July - September, October - December
Earliest Available Data: 1984
National Coverage: Wales
Disaggregation: Local authority

Statistician
Henry Small
National Assembly for Wales
Statistical Directorate; Housing Statistics
Tel: 029 2082 5063;
Email: henry.small@wales.gsi.gov.uk

Renovations: Housing Associations - England
Department of the Environment, Transport and the Regions

The Department of the Environment, Transport and the Regions compiles data on renovations completed for housing associations. Data are collected from local authorities and the Housing Corporation. Data are available on the number and costs of converting and improving housing association dwellings. The data cover England and are produced at standard region, Government Office region, county and local authority district level. Figures are available from 1980 and some figures date back to 1966. Results are published quarterly around three months after the reference quarter.

Frequency: Quarterly
Earliest Available Data: 1980
National Coverage: England

Statistician
Henry Small
Department of the Environment, Transport and the Regions
Tel: 0117 987 8076

Products that contain data from this source
House Renovation Information Bulletin; Housing and Construction Statistics Annual Volume

---

Renovations: Local Authorities - England
Department of the Environment, Transport and the Regions

The Department of the Environment, Transport and the Regions collects data on renovations completed for local authorities, collected from the local authorities. Data are collected on the number and costs of both converting and improving local authority dwellings, the number and costs of adapting existing local authority dwellings for the disabled, separating the provision of standard amenities from the general conversion or improvement of these dwellings. The data cover England and are available at standard region, Government Office region, county and local authority district levels. Figures have been produced since 1980, although some date back to 1966. Data are published quarterly, around three months after the reference quarter.

Frequency: Quarterly
Timeliness: Around three months after the reference quarter
Earliest Available Data: 1980
National Coverage: England

Statistician
Henry Small
Department of the Environment, Transport and the Regions
Tel: 0117 987 8076

Products that contain data from this source
House Renovation Information Bulletin; Housing and Construction Statistics Annual Volume

---

Renovations: Tenders Accepted for Local Authorities - England
Department of the Environment, Transport and the Regions

The Department of the Environment, Transport and the Regions compiles data on renovations: tenders accepted for capital works for local authorities, collected from local authorities. Data are available on the numbers of dwellings and total costs for different types of capital works involved in improving local authority dwellings. The works cover structure, doors and windows, roof coverings, rewiring, heating and plumbing, energy efficiency, kitchens and bathrooms, common parts and environmental works, other adaptations, and by age band, numbers of dwellings split between houses, flats up to five stories and flats over five stories, the numbers of dwellings related to the numbers affected by these works. The costs refer to the costs quoted in tenders accepted for this type of work by the local authority during the quarter. Data also include the number of local authority dwellings converted and demolished. The figures cover England and are available at standard region, Government Office region, county and local authority district levels. Information dates back to 1990 and is collected quarterly.

Frequency: Quarterly
Earliest Available Data: 1990
National Coverage: England

Statistician
Henry Small
Department of the Environment, Transport and the Regions
Tel: 0117 987 8076

See also:
In this chapter:
Dwellings Demolished, Closed, Converted and Acquired - Scotland *(7.2)*
English House Condition Survey (EHCS) *(7.6)*
Survey of English Housing *(7.1)*

7.4 Homelessness

Homelessness
National Assembly for Wales

Homelessness data are collected quarterly. Prior to April 1996 information was collected from each of the 37 Welsh local authorities and from 1 April 1996 from the 22 unitary authorities on homelessness enquiries, cases presented, type of household, cause of homelessness and subsequent action taken by the local authority. Data are available on temporary accommodation, applicants in priority cases and applicants homeless but not in priority need. Following a change in legislation data collected from 1997 are for those households for which decisions were taken, households found to be eligible for assistance, unintentionally homeless and in priority need, main reason for loss of last settled home, referrals between authorities, duty accepted, households accommodated and those leaving accommodation.

The monitoring of homelessness statistics was introduced in April 1978 as a result of the Housing (Homeless Persons) Act 1977. Two quarterly returns were collected, one dealing with aggregate district information on households in temporary accommodation, and one with individual case records. In 1984 the two forms were combined into one quarterly form. Following a review by the National Assembly for Wales Housing Consultative Committee in 1986 several new questions and categories were added to the return which were implemented in 1987. Further changes were made in 1992 and again in 1997 following reviews of homelessness legislation. Following the change from local authority boundaries to unitary authority areas at 1st April 1996 the number of quarterly returns made has decreased from 37 to 22.

Status: Ongoing
Collection Method: Administrative Records
Frequency: Quarterly
Reference Period: Jan - March, April - June, July - September, October - December
Timeliness: Approximately 3 months after the end of the quarter
Earliest Available Data: 1978
National Coverage: Wales
Disaggregation: Unitary Authority

Statistician
Henry Small
National Assembly for Wales
Statistical Directorate; Housing Statistics
Tel: 029 2082 5063;
Email: henry.small@wales.gsi.gov.uk

Products that contain data from this source
A Statistical Focus on Wales; Digest of Welsh Statistics; Quarterly Welsh Housing Statistics; Regional Trends; Social Trends; Welsh Housing Statistics; Welsh Social Trends

---

Homelessness - Northern Ireland
Department of the Environment (NI)

The Department of the Environment (NI) compiles data on households presenting and accepted as homeless during each financial year. The data are supplied by the Northern Ireland Housing Executive and are available at district council area level.

Status: Ongoing
Collection Method: Administrative Records
Frequency: Annually
Reference Period: Financial Year
Timeliness: Six months
Earliest Available Data: 1989/90
National Coverage: Northern Ireland

Statistician:
Brian French
Department of the Environment (NI)
Central Statistics and Research Branch
Tel: 028 9054 0799;
E-mail: brian.french@doeni.gov.uk

Products that contain data from this source
Northern Ireland Housing Statistics

Homelessness - Scotland
Scottish Executive

Information is collected on all households applying to the local authority under the homeless persons legislation. As well as details on the applicant households and the reason for them being homeless, information is collected on the classification made by the authority (e.g. priority/non-priority, homeless/potentially homeless etc) and the action taken by the local authority on behalf of each household. In addition to the detailed case returns of all households, summary information is collected on a quarterly basis on the number of applicant households and the number of households in temporary accommodation. Information is available for Scotland and each local authority.

Status: Ongoing
Collection Method: Census
Frequency: Continuously
Timeliness: 8-12 months
National Coverage: Scotland
Disaggregation: Local Authority

Statistician
Deborah Pegg
Scottish Executive
Economic Advice and Statistics Division; Branch 7: Housing Statistics
Tel: 0131 244 2752.
Email: deborah.pegg@scotland.gov.uk

Products that contain data from this source
Operation of the Homeless Persons Legislation in Scotland 1986-87 to 1996-97; Operation of the Homeless Persons Legislation in Scotland 1986-87 to 1996-97 Local Authority Analyses

---

Statutory Homelessness - England
Department of the Environment, Transport and the Regions

The Department of the Environment, Transport and the Regions collects data on households dealt with under the homelessness provisions of the 1985 and 1996 Housing Acts which require local authorities to secure accommodation for homeless households who fall within the priority need categories as defined in the Act. Data are collected from local authorities on the number of households they accept responsibility to secure accommodation for under the terms of the Acts, and the number of such households (and other households awaiting the outcome of enquiries) in bed and breakfast hotels, hostels, women's refuges and in other forms of temporary accommodation. The data cover England and are available at standard region, Government Office region and local authority district level. Data has been

collected since 1978. In 1991 the definition of homeless acceptances was altered to exclude intentionally homeless households. Earlier figures have been estimated on the new basis but are not strictly comparable. A reasonably consistent series is available back to 1978 at national and regional level and by class of authority only. Figures are collected and published quarterly, usually about ten weeks after the end of the quarter.

Status: Ongoing
Collection Method: Administrative Records
Frequency: Quarterly
Earliest Available Data: Around 10 weeks after the end of the quarter
National Coverage: England

Statistician
Chris Woolf
Department of the Environment, Transport and the Regions
Housing Data and Statistics; HDS3
Tel: 020 7890 3324

Products that contain data from this source
Regional Trends; Social Trends

See also:
In this chapter:
Survey of English Housing *(7.1)*

7.5 Housing - General

Allocation of Local Authority Housing - England
Department of the Environment, Transport and the Regions

The Department of the Environment, Transport and the Regions collects data on lettings of local authority housing (in financial years) and on vacant local authority dwellings (at 1 April). Data are collected from local authorities on lettings to existing tenants, new tenants, the homeless, to households displaced by slum clearances and other lettings. The data on vacant dwellings covers reasons for vacancy and time vacant. Data cover England and are available for standard regions, Government Office regions and local authority districts. Figures date back to 1979 at national, regional and local authority level. They are generally available about 6-8 months after the end of the financial year to which they refer.

Status: Ongoing
Collection Method: Administrative Records
Frequency: Annually
Reference Period: Financial years
Earliest Available Data: 1979
National Coverage: England

Statistician
Chris Woolf
Department of the Environment, Transport and the Regions
Housing Data and Statistics; HDS3
Tel: 020 7890 3324

Products that contain data from this source
Housing and Construction Statistics Annual Volume

Calculation of Capital Allocations for All Welsh Local Authorities
National Assembly for Wales

Capital allocations for housing purposes to local authorities are calculated by formulae. Each year the formulae are reviewed and frequently changed. From the allocation for 1999 to 2000, one part of the allocation will be based on bids from local authorities relating to improvements of council dwellings.

Status: Ongoing
Frequency: Annually
Reference Period: Year to September
Timeliness: Information becomes available by the end of the calendar year
Earliest Available Data: 1990-91
National Coverage: Wales
Disaggregation: Unitary Authority

Statistician
Ed Swires-Hennessy
National Assembly for Wales
Statistical Directorate; Housing Statistics
Tel: 029 2082 5087;
Email: ed.swires-hennessy@wales.gsi.gov.uk

Household Estimates
Scottish Executive

Estimates at mid year of the number of households within each local authority in Scotland

Status: Ongoing
Frequency: Annually
Reference Period: Mid-year
Timeliness: 18-20 months
National Coverage: Scotland
Disaggregation: Local Authorities in Scotland

Statistician
Deborah Pegg
Scottish Executive
Economic Advice and Statistics Division; Branch 7: Housing Statistics
Tel: 0131 244 2752.
Email: deborah.pegg@scotland.gov.uk

Products that contain data from this analysis
Housing Trends in Scotland

Sources and Analyses

Household Projections
Scottish Executive

Projections of the numbers of households in the next 14 years

Status: Ongoing
Frequency: Biennial
Reference Period: each year for 14 years ahead
National Coverage: Scotland
Disaggregation: Local Authorities; Structure Plan Areas

Statistician
Deborah Pegg
Scottish Executive
Economic Advice and Statistics Division; Branch 7: Housing Statistics
Tel: 0131 244 2752.
Email: deborah.pegg@scotland.gov.uk

Products that contain data from this analysis
1996-based Household Projections for Scotland; A Statistical Focus on Wales

Housing Action Areas - Scotland
Scottish Executive

The survey consists of an annual progress report on Housing Action areas and the number and type of dwellings included. The survey is carried out annually, covers Scotland and is available at local authority level.

Status: Ongoing
Collection Method: Census
Frequency: Annually
Reference Period: financial year
Timeliness: 6-8 months
National Coverage: Scotland
Disaggregation: Local Authority

Statistician
Deborah Pegg
Scottish Executive
Economic Advice and Statistics Division; Branch 7: Housing Statistics
Tel: 0131 244 2752.
Email: deborah.pegg@scotland.gov.uk

Products that contain data from this source
Dwellings Below the Tolerable Standard (BTS) in Scotland: Estimates by local authorities for April 1996 and details of action on such dwellings

Housing Associations - Northern Ireland
Department of the Environment (NI)

The Department of the Environment (NI) compiles data on activity by Housing Associations in Northern Ireland, including starts and completions of new and rehabilitated dwellings, bedspaces and units of accommodation, average rents, rent arrears, sales of dwellings and the Northern Ireland Co-Ownership Housing Scheme.

The data are supplied by the Department's Housing Associations Branch and the Northern Ireland Co-Ownership Housing Association and are available at Northern Ireland level.

Status: Ongoing
Collection Method: Administrative Records
Frequency: Annually
Reference Period: Financial Year
Timeliness: Six months
Earliest Available Data: 1976
National Coverage: Northern Ireland

Statistician:
Brian French
Department of the Environment (NI)
Central Statistics and Research Branch
Tel: 028 9054 0799;
E-mail: brian.french@doeni.gov.uk

Products that contain data from this source
Northern Ireland Housing Statistics

Housing Investment Program (HIP) Exercise
Department of the Environment, Transport and the Regions

As part of their annual submission to DETR in support of their bid for housing capital resources, local authorities in England complete statistical HIP returns. The HIP Operational Information (Section 1) return (formerly known as HIP1) provides data on housing stock, vacancies, lettings and homelessness, some of which is used in the calculation of the General Needs Index (GNI). [HIP OI Sections 2-4 contains a more descriptive response to management and general housing and is used by Government Regional Offices as part of their performance assessment]. The HIP Annual Plan (formerly HIP2) provides detail about authorities' past, current and proposed capital expenditure programmes, sources of finance and capital receipts. The return also incorporates a section (formerly a separate return HIP3) on authorities' estimates of essential renovation work to their own stock. Returns are due for completion by end June (HIP OI) and end July (HIP AP).

Status: Ongoing
Collection Method: Regular LA Returns to DETR
Frequency: Annual
Reference Period: Financial year
Earliest Available Data: 1978/1979
National Coverage: England
Disaggregation: Local / Unitary Authorities

Statistician
Trevor Steeples
Department of the Environment, Transport and the Regions
Housing Data and Statistics; HDS3
Tel: 020 7890 3324.
Email: trevor_steeples@detr.gsi.gov.uk

Housing Investment Programme (HIP) Allocations
Department of the Environment, Transport and the Regions

HIP allocations are issued to local authorities annually following the HIP exercise (qv), and reflect the Government's assessment of each authority's relative housing need and performance. Need is measured by a mix of key housing indicators within the Generalised Needs Index (GNI), while the authority's qualitative performance is assessed in terms of its housing strategy, management, efficiency and effectiveness. Allocations have three components; the Annual Capital Guideline (ACG) (which does not represent the actual provision of finance, but the level of borrowing permitted for housing capital expenditure); a Grant for private sector renewal activity; and a guideline allocation of Specified Capital Grant, covering disabled facilities grant payments.

Status: Ongoing
Collection Method: Regular LA Returns to DETR
Frequency: Annual
Reference Period: Financial year
Earliest Available Data: 1978/1979
National Coverage: England
Disaggregation: Local / Unitary Authorities

Statistician
Trevor Steeples
Department of the Environment, Transport and the Regions
Housing Data and Statistics; HDS3
Tel: 020 7890 3324.
Email: trevor_steeples@detr.gsi.gov.uk

Housing Needs Indices
Department of the Environment, Transport and the Regions

The statistical index of the relative need for housing capital expenditure by local authorities, used in assessing HIP Allocations (qv) is the Generalised Needs Index (GNI). It is a compound index of individual key indicators covering LA and private sector stock condition, plus the need for new housing provision taking into account various measures of supply and demand. Underlying data is derived from a variety of sources, including the Survey of English Housing, the General Household Survey and the English House Condition Survey. The Housing Needs Index (HNI) is the equivalent index for expenditure by Registered Social Landlords (formerly referred to as housing associations).

Status: Ongoing
Collection Method: Regular LA returns to DETR / Surveys
Frequency: Annual
Reference Period: Financial year
National Coverage: England
Disaggregation: Local Authority/Unitary Authority

Statistician
Trevor Steeples
Department of the Environment, Transport and the Regions
Housing Data and Statistics; HDS3
Tel: 020 7890 3324.
Email: trevor_steeples@detr.gsi.gov.uk

Housing Strategy Operational Plan
National Assembly for Wales

The National Assembly for Wales compiles data on the Housing Strategy Operational Plans. This gives a summary of financial and non-financial information used in the development of strategic and operational plans for each housing authority in Wales.

Status: Ongoing
Collection Method: Administrative Records
Frequency: Annually
Reference Period: Financial year
Earliest Available Data: Approx. 1975-76
National Coverage: Wales
Disaggregation: Unitary Authority

Statistician
Henry Small
National Assembly for Wales
Statistical Directorate; Housing Statistics
Tel: 029 2082 5063;
Email: henry.small@wales.gsi.gov.uk

Products that contain data from this source
Housing Strategy Operational Plan - Wales

Housing Subsidies
National Assembly for Wales

The National Assembly for Wales compiles data on local authority housing revenue accounts and claimed entitlement to housing subsidies. Data are collected on the account as a whole and additional information pertaining to the operation and management of council housing are available on a longitudinal basis. Data for all authorities have been collected from 1990 onwards.

Status: Ongoing
Collection Method: Administrative Records
Frequency: Quarterly
Reference Period: First Advance by April and Second Advance by August of the financial year subsidy is being claimed. Advance Final in September and the Audit Final in January of the year following the financial year subsidy is claimed.
Earliest Available Data: 1990-1991
National Coverage: Wales
Disaggregation: Unitary Authority

Statistician
Ed Swires-Hennessy
National Assembly for Wales
Statistical Directorate; Housing Statistics
Tel: 029 2082 5087;
Email: ed.swires-hennessy@wales.gsi.gov.uk

Products that contain data from this source
Welsh Local Government Financial Statistics

LA Housing Capital Finance
Department of the Environment, Transport and the Regions

Local Authority housing capital expenditure in England collected quarterly (P1A returns) and annually (HIP returns qv.) to inform public expenditure discussions and feed into the national accounts compiled by the Office for National Statistics.

Status: Ongoing
Collection Method: Regular LA returns to DETR
Frequency: Quarterly and Annual
Reference Period: Financial Year and cumulative quarters
Timeliness: 3 - 6 months depending on data quality
Earliest Available Data: Back to 1960s
National Coverage: England
Disaggregation: Local / Unitary Authorities

Statistician
Trevor Steeples
Department of the Environment, Transport and the Regions
Housing Data and Statistics; HDS3
Tel: 020 7890 3324.
Email: trevor_steeples@detr.gsi.gov.uk

Products that contain data from this source
Housing and Construction Statistics Annual Volume

LA Housing Capital Receipts
Department of the Environment, Transport and the Regions

Local authority housing capital receipts in England are collected quarterly (P1A returns) and annually as part of the Housing Investment Programme bidding round (HIP exercise, qv) to inform public expenditure discussions and feed into the national accounts compiled by ONS.

Status: Ongoing
Collection Method: Regular LA returns to DETR
Frequency: Quarterly and Annual
Reference Period: Financial year and cumulative quarters
Timeliness: 3 - 6 months depending on data quality
Earliest Available Data: Back to 1960s
National Coverage: England
Sub-National: Local / Unitary Authorities

Statistician
Trevor Steeples
Department of the Environment, Transport and the Regions
Housing Data and Statistics; HDS3
Tel: 020 7890 3324.
Email: trevor_steeples@detr.gsi.gov.uk

Local Authority Housing Performance Indicators
Department of the Environment, Transport and the Regions

Statistician
Chris Woolf
Department of the Environment, Transport and the Regions
Housing Data and Statistics; HDS3
Tel: 020 7890 3324

Renewal Areas Activity
National Assembly for Wales

An annual survey monitoring the effect of area based renewal and performance in terms of the overall policy intentions and specified aims and objectives set by the local authority. Information collected covers a wide range of housing activity indicators within the renewal area such as demolitions, renovation grants and new building. The return monitors activity under the Local Government & Housing Act, 1989, and the Housing Grants Construction and Regeneration Act, 1996 during a financial year within designated Renewal Areas. The return was introduced from the 1990-91 financial year following new legislation introducing the renewal area scheme. The scheme replaced General Improvement Areas and Housing Action Areas.

Status: Ongoing
Collection Method: Administrative Records
Frequency: Annually
Reference Period: Financial year
Timeliness: Approximately 3 months after the end of the financial year
Earliest Available Data: 1990-91
National Coverage: Wales
Disaggregation: Unitary Authority

Statistician
Henry Small
National Assembly for Wales
Statistical Directorate; Housing Statistics
Tel: 029 2082 5063;
Email: henry.small@wales.gsi.gov.uk

See also:
In this chapter:
Calculation of Stock by Tenure *(7.6)*
English House Condition Survey (EHCS) *(7.6)*
House Condition Survey - Wales *(7.6)*
Household Survey - Wales *(7.6)*
Housing Management and Performance *(7.7)*
Sales and Transfers of Dwellings by Housing Authorities, Quarterly Summary - Scotland *(7.9)*
Sales of Housing Authority Dwellings to Sitting Tenants - Scotland *(7.9)*
Survey of English Housing *(7.1)*

In other chapters:
Household Estimates and Projections (*see the Population, Census, Migration and Vital Events chapter*)
Labour Force Survey (*see the Labour Market chapter*)
(The) ONS Longitudinal Study (*see the Population, Census, Migration and Vital Events chapter*)

7.6 Housing Stock

Calculation of Stock by Tenure
National Assembly for Wales

The information collected from local authorities is used to determine changes in stock and the distribution of stock between tenures.

Status: Ongoing
Frequency: Quarterly
Reference Period: January-March, April-June, July-September, October-December
Timeliness: Approximately 3 months after the end of the quarter
National Coverage: Wales

Statistician
Henry Small
National Assembly for Wales
Statistical Directorate; Housing Statistics
Tel: 029 2082 5063;
Email: henry.small@wales.gsi.gov.uk

Dwelling Stock - Northern Ireland
Department of the Environment (NI)

The Department of the Environment (NI) estimates the level of dwelling stock at 31 December each year from data supplied by the Rate Collection Agency, the Northern Ireland Housing Executive and its own Housing Associations Branch. A breakdown for occupied, vacant and total stock by tenure is available at Northern Ireland level. In addition, data are available for occupied, vacant and total stock at district council area level.

Status: Ongoing
Collection Method: Administrative Records
Frequency: Annually
Reference Period: End of December each year
Timeliness: Nine months
Earliest Available Data: 1987
National Coverage: Northern Ireland
Disaggregation: District council area level

Statistician:
Brian French
Department of the Environment (NI)
Central Statistics and Research Branch
Tel: 028 9054 0799;
E-mail: brian.french@doeni.gov.uk

Dwelling Stock - UK
Department of the Environment, Transport and the Regions

The Department of the Environment, Transport and the Regions, National Assembly for Wales, Scottish Executive, and Department of the Environment - Northern Ireland compile data on dwelling stock. The figures are a constructed series and are based on the Census rather than a direct measure of dwelling stock (apart from Northern Ireland). Data are collected on the number of dwellings, by sector, i.e. owner-occupied, privately rented or rented and provided with job or business, rented from a housing association and finally rented from a local authority or a new town or a Housing Action Trust, and by estimated age of construction (except Northern Ireland). The data cover England, Wales, Scotland and Northern Ireland, and are combined for United Kingdom and Great Britain totals. Data by tenure figures are available at standard region level for England. Total stock figures are also available at county and local authority district level in England. The series are available since 1980, although most figures date back to 1966. Summary figures with tenure details are available from 1910 and total dwelling stock figures from 1801. Data are produced quarterly for England and Wales about fourteen weeks after the reference quarter. Annual results are published for Scotland, Northern Ireland, Great Britain and the United Kingdom.

Frequency: Quarterly (England and Wales) and Annually (Scotland and Northern Ireland)
Timeliness: About fourteen weeks after the reference quarter, for England and Wales
National Coverage: United Kingdom

Statistician
Henry Small
Department of the Environment, Transport and the Regions
Tel: 0117 987 8076

English House Condition Survey (EHCS)
Department of the Environment, Transport and the Regions

DETR carries out the Survey every five years to monitor the condition of the housing stock in England. It is used to monitor housing policies and underpin decisions over need for and allocation of housing resources. The survey is dwelling based and is made up of four parts: (i) A survey of dwellings conducted by building professionals, to provide a description of the stock and an assessment of its current condition; (ii) Interviews with households to determine their characteristics, repair and improvement activity, and attitudes to their homes. The survey also establishes the effectiveness of heating arrangements in the home and fuel consumption; (iii) A postal survey of local authorities and housing associations to identify what action they have taken on their stock, and for local authorities what action they have taken in the private sector; (iv) A survey of current market values to link property prices to condition.

The survey covers England and breakdowns are available by DETR housing region, Government Office region, and some combinations of postcode, ward or local authority areas. Dwellings are randomly selected from a non-clustered sampling frame stratified by tenure, region, dwelling age and (for social housing) dwelling type. The survey is weighted to reflect the sampling strategy and to account for non-response and grossed to provide national estimates. Sampling frame is 25,000 dwellings. Results of each survey are published normally within 18 months of the start of the fieldwork. Conducted every five years since 1966. In any survey year, half the sample (of dwellings) from the previous survey are included, forming the longitudinal component of the survey. The other half of the sample is new for that year. Occupants are not requested to take part in more than two successive surveys.

Data are collected by an interview led questionnaire, an assessment of condition using a detailed surveying form; an assessment of value using photographs and relevant details of property and condition; and a self-completion postal questionnaire for landlords. Data are collected from adult household members; any social landlord. For the 1991-1996 survey, 12,000 dwellings in the longitudinal component of the sample were revisited. The methodology remains broadly consistent although the content of each element of the survey changes to reflect new policy interests. Changes in, for example, the Fitness Standard and in surveyor variability make some types of measures between surveys problematic but where possible data from previous surveys are reworked on a consistent basis to enable 'like with like' comparisons.

Status: Ongoing, next survey 2001
Collection Method: Household interview; property survey; postal survey - large sample survey
Frequency: Every 5 years. Last survey 1996
Reference Period: 5 year period. Last survey 1991 - 1996
Timeliness: Published 18 months after completion of fieldwork
Earliest Available Data: Published reports since 1971; datasets from 1986
National Coverage: England
Sub-National: Regions

Statistician
Terry McIntyre
Department of the Environment, Transport and the Regions
Tel: 020 7890 3523

Products that contain data from this source
English House Condition Survey 1996

House Condition Survey - Wales
National Assembly for Wales

The old Welsh Office conducted several Welsh House Condition Surveys. From 27 April to 30 July 1993 a sample survey was taken covering 6,472 households in Wales. The Survey involved a physical inspection of the properties by building surveyors. Data are available for Wales by state of repair, repair costs and fitness for habitation. Similar surveys were conducted in 1981 and 1986. Unlike the 1986 Survey, the main aim of the 1993 Survey was to produce results for the whole of Wales rather than for individual local authorities. The Survey has been carried out on an ad hoc basis approximately once every five years. The main results of the 1993 Survey were published in September 1994. Equivalent surveys were conducted in 1968, 1973, 1976, 1981 and 1986 but changes in definitions and methodology mean that results from the different surveys are not comparable.

Status: Ceased completely
Collection Method: Household/Person (Sample) Survey
Frequency: Periodic
Reference Period: 1993
Timeliness: Approximately 9 months
Earliest Available Data: 1993
National Coverage: Wales

Statistician
Henry Small
National Assembly for Wales
Statistical Directorate; SD7B
Tel: 029 2082 5063;
Email: henry.small@wales.gsi.gov.uk

Products that contain data from this source
1993 Welsh House Condition Survey (report 1994)

Household Survey - Wales
National Assembly for Wales

The old Welsh Office carried out the Welsh Social Survey between September and December 1992. This was a sample survey which obtained interviews from 12,700 households and some 30,000 individuals. The survey was conducted as part of the 1993 Welsh House Condition Survey. Three questionnaires were used in the interviews: household composition and housing-related issues; Welsh language, education and training; and tenancy arrangements. The Survey covered Wales and data are available at county level. The 1986 Welsh Inter-Censal Survey was the forerunner of the 1992 Survey but covered only housing topics. The survey has been carried out on an ad hoc basis at approximately five yearly intervals. Results for training and education were published in September 1994, the Welsh language section in February 1995 and housing results were published with the Welsh House Condition Survey in September 1994. The survey was conducted in association with the 1993 Welsh House Condition Survey to provide information for sampling purposes and supplementary information about households and their members. An equivalent survey, the 1986 Welsh Inter Censal Survey, was conducted in connection with the 1986 House Condition Survey. A much smaller interview survey was conducted in advance of the 1981 House Condition Survey.

Status: Ceased completely
Collection Method: Household/Person (Sample) Survey
Frequency: Periodic
Reference Period: 1992
Timeliness: Approximately 9 months
Earliest Available Data: 1992
National Coverage: Wales
Sub-National: Programme for the Valleys area

Statistician
Henry Small
National Assembly for Wales
Statistical Directorate; Housing Statistics
Tel: 029 2082 5063;
Email: henry.small@wales.gsi.gov.uk

Products that contain data from this source
1992 Welsh Social Survey: Report on the Welsh Language; 1992 Welsh Social Survey: Report on Training and Education; 1993 Welsh House Condition Survey (report 1994)

Housing Authority Stock - Scotland
Scottish Executive

Annual information is available on the number of local authority dwellings of various types within various age bands.

Information is also collected on the numbers of vacant stock owned by local authorities and Scottish Homes, by type and length of vacancy. The information is collected from all local authorities in Scotland about their stock and from Scottish Homes about the stock which is owned by them and by housing associations.

Status: Ongoing
Collection Method: Census
Frequency: Annually
Reference Period: end of March each year
Timeliness: 6-8 months
National Coverage: Scotland
Disaggregation: Local Authority Scotland

Statistician
Deborah Pegg
Scottish Executive
Economic Advice and Statistics Division; Branch 7: Housing Statistics
Tel: 0131 244 2752.
Email: deborah.pegg@scotland.gov.uk

Products that contain data from this source
Housing Trends in Scotland

Northern Ireland House Condition Survey
Northern Ireland Housing Executive

Every five years, the Northern Ireland Housing Executive (NIHE) conducts the Northern Ireland House Condition Survey, which examines the condition of housing stock in Northern Ireland. Topics covered in the 1996 edition of the report include: the stock and its occupants, the state of repair, unfitness, energy, and environmental conditions. For the most part, the survey findings are comparable with those of the English House Condition Survey.

Status: Ongoing
Collection Method: Large-scale (sample) survey
Frequency: Every five years
Timeliness: Published 18 months after completion of fieldwork
Earliest Available Data: 1974
National Coverage: Northern Ireland
Disaggregation: District council area level, electoral wards (Belfast only)

Statistician:

As the report is not a Government Statistical Service publication, enquiries should be directed to:

The Research Unit
Northern Ireland Housing Executive
2 Adelaide Street
Belfast BT2 8PB
Tel: 028 9024 0588; Fax: 028 9031 8755

Products that contain data from this source
Northern Ireland House Condition Survey, Northern Ireland Housing Statistics

---

Permanent Dwellings Below the Tolerable Standard (BTS) - Scotland
Scottish Executive

Information is collected on the extent of Below Tolerable Standard (BTS) housing in each local authority. Each local authority provides an estimate of the number of BTS dwellings in their area, broken down by tenure, age, type of dwelling and main reason for failing the tolerable standard. Information is also collated on the number of BTS dwellings on which action was taken in the previous year (e.g. statutory action, improvement, demolition). The survey is carried out annually, covers Scotland and is available at local authority level.

Status: Ongoing
Collection Method: Census
Frequency: Annually
Reference Period: At end March each year
Timeliness: 8-12 months
National Coverage: Scotland
Disaggregation: Local Authority

Statistician
Deborah Pegg
Scottish Executive
Economic Advice and Statistics Division; Branch 7: Housing Statistics
Tel: 0131 244 2752.
Email: deborah.pegg@scotland.gov.uk

Products that contain data from this source
Dwellings Below the Tolerable Standard (BTS) in Scotland: Estimates by local authorities for April 1996 and details of action on such dwellings

Special Needs Housing - Scotland
Scottish Executive

The survey covers housing for the elderly by tenure and type of housing, and housing for the disabled by tenure and category. The survey is carried out annually, covers Scotland and is available at local authority level.

Status: Ongoing
Collection Method: Census
Frequency: Annually
Reference Period: end of March each year
Timeliness: 6-8 months
National Coverage: Scotland
Disaggregation: Local Authority

Statistician
Deborah Pegg
Scottish Executive
Economic Advice and Statistics Division; Branch 7: Housing Statistics
Tel: 0131 244 2752.
Email: deborah.pegg@scotland.gov.uk

Products that contain data from this source
Housing Trends in Scotland

Stock Estimates by Tenure
Scottish Executive

Annual estimates of total dwelling stock by tenure in Scotland

Status: Ongoing
Frequency: Annually
Reference Period: end December each year
Timeliness: 12 months
National Coverage: Scotland

Statistician
Deborah Pegg
Scottish Executive
Economic Advice and Statistics Division; Branch 7: Housing Statistics
Tel: 0131 244 2752.
Email: deborah.pegg@scotland.gov.uk

Products that contain data from this analysis
Housing Trends in Scotland

Unfit Dwellings - England
Department of the Environment, Transport and the Regions

The Department of the Environment, Transport and the Regions compiles data for action on unfit dwellings derived from local authorities. Data are collected on dwellings and houses in multiple occupation (HMOs) identified as unfit, reasons why the local authority considers that those dwellings are unfit (as defined by the Housing Act 1985), action completed on unfit dwellings, or action resulting in unfit dwellings being made fit, and action taken by the local authority to prevent dwellings and HMOs becoming unfit. The data cover England and are available for standard regions and Government Office regions. Information is available at county and local authority district level, on request. Figures are available from the start of the new system in 1990 and results are published annually.

Frequency: Annually
Earliest Available Data: 1990
National Coverage: England

Statistician
Henry Small
Department of the Environment, Transport and the Regions
Tel: 0117 987 8076

Products that contain data from this source
Housing and Construction Statistics Annual Volume; Institute of Environmental Health Officers

See also:
In this chapter:
English House Condition Survey (EHCS) *(7.6)*
Housing Management and Performance *(7.7)*
Survey of English Housing *(7.1)*

7.7 Letting of housing

Housing Association New Lettings - England
Department of the Environment, Transport and the Regions

The Housing Corporation is responsible for the CORE survey of housing associations' new lettings. The survey is conducted by the Joint Centre for Scottish Housing Research and covers all major housing associations in England. Data are collected on tenant characteristics, income, savings, receipt of Housing Benefit, receipt of pensions, source of referral, age, sex, reason for housing, whether homeless, tenure, property characteristics and rent levels. The survey covers England and data are available at standard region, Government Office region, Housing Corporation region, county and local authority district level. Data have been collected continuously since 1989. Results are published about three months after the end of the quarter, and six months after the end of the financial year.

Frequency: Continuously
Timeliness: about 3 months
Earliest Available Data: 1989
National Coverage: England
Disaggregation: Local Authority District (LAD)/ Unitary Authority(Eng)

Statistician
David Champion
Department of the Environment, Transport and the Regions
Housing Data and Statistics; HDS2
Tel: 020 7890 3306;
Email: david_champion@detr.gsi.gov.uk

Products that contain data from this source
CORE Annual Statistics; CORE Bulletin (JCSHR); NFHA Research Reports (Nos 19, 20, 23)

Housing Association Statistics - England (HAR10/1, RSR)
Department of the Environment, Transport and the Regions; sponsored by Housing Corporation

The Housing Corporation is responsible for the CORE survey of housing associations' new lettings. The survey is conducted by the National Housing Federation and covers all major housing associations in England. Data are collected on tenant characteristics, income, savings, receipt of Housing Benefit, receipt of pensions, source of referral, age, sex, reason for housing, whether homeless, tenure, property characteristics and rent levels. The survey covers England and data are available at standard region, Government Office Region, Housing Corporation region, county and local authority district level.

Sources and Analyses

Data have been collected continuously since 1989. Results are published about three months after the end of the quarter, and six months after the end of the financial year.

Frequency: Continuously
Timeliness: about 3 months
Earliest Available Data: 1989
National Coverage: England
Disaggregation: Local Authority District (LAD)/ Unitary Authority (Eng)

Statistician
David Champion
Department of the Environment, Transport and the Regions
Housing Data and Statistics; HDS2
Tel: 020 7890 3306;
Email: david_champion@detr.gsi.gov.uk

Products that contain data from this source
CORE Annual Statistics, Core Bulletin (NFHA):
NFHA Research Reports (Nos 19, 20, 23)

Housing Association Statistics - England (HAR10/1, RSR)
Department of the Environment, Transport and the Regions; sponsored by Housing Corporation

The Housing Corporation compiles data on housing associations, collected directly from all registered housing associations. Data comprise of average rents, stock, vacancies, lettings, sales, and development. The series covers England and data are available for Housing Corporation regions, counties and local authority districts. Data covering England have been compiled since 1989; data for 1981-88 cover England and Wales. Figures are collected each year as at 31 March and published nine to ten months after the reference date.

Frequency: Annually
Reference Period: 1 April - 31 March
Timeliness: about 9 months
Earliest Available Data: 1981
National Coverage: England
Disaggregation: Government Office Region (GOR)

Statistician
David Champion
Department of the Environment, Transport and the Regions
Housing Data and Statistics; HDS2
Tel: 020 7890 3306;
Email: david_champion@detr.gsi.gov.uk

Products that contain data from this source
Housing Corporation Source 28 (1997 data)

Housing Management and Performance
National Assembly for Wales

The National Assembly for Wales carries out an annual survey collecting data on the number of dwellings in the Housing Revenue Account (HRA) and the numbers of HRA dwellings that came into management during the year. The survey also monitors key target areas including the control of rent arrears and voids, a measure of local authority maintenance programmes and an assessment as to whether tenants are actively involved in housing management issues. Information is available from 1977 although detailed information on vacant dwellings has only been available since 1985. Further changes were made in June 1990 and again in 1997 for the financial year 1996-97 following the expansion of the return to include greater detail on HRA housing management.

Status: Ongoing
Collection Method: Administrative Records
Frequency: Annually
Reference Period: Financial year
Timeliness: Approximately 3 months after the end of the financial year
Earliest Available Data: 1977
National Coverage: Wales
Disaggregation: Unitary Authority

Statistician
Henry Small
National Assembly for Wales
Statistical Directorate; Housing Statistics
Tel: 029 2082 5063;
Email: henry.small@wales.gsi.gov.uk

Products that contain data from this source
Housing and Construction Statistics Annual Volume; Social Trends; Welsh Housing Statistics

---

Local Authority Rent Arrears - England
Department of the Environment, Transport and the Regions

The Department of the Environment Transport and the Regions collects data on rent arrears of local authorities, collected directly from local authorities. Data are available for cumulative rent arrears, separately for current and former tenants' and on rent arrears arising in the last twelve months. The data cover England and are available for standard regions, Government Office regions and local authority districts. Results are available since 1983 at national level, and from 1987 at regional and local authority level. They are available annually 7-9 months after the end of the financial year to which they refer.

Status: Ongoing
Collection Method: Administrative Records
Frequency: Annually
Reference Period: financial years
Timeliness: 7-9 months after the end of the financial year
Earliest Available Data: 1983 (at national level)
National Coverage: England

Statistician
Chris Woolf
Department of the Environment, Transport and the Regions
Housing Data and Statistics; HDS3
Tel: 020 7890 3324

Local Authority Rents - England
Department of the Environment, Transport and the Regions

The Department of the Environment Transport and the Regions collects data from local authorities on average rents of local authority dwellings at the end of April and for financial years. The figures cover England and are available for standard regions, Government Office regions, and local authority districts. Results date back to 1967 at national level, and to 1987 at regional and local authority level.

Status: Ongoing
Collection Method: Administrative Records
Earliest Available Data: 1967 (at national level) or 1987 (at regional level)
National Coverage: England

Statistician
Chris Woolf
Department of the Environment, Transport and the Regions
Housing Data and Statistics; HDS3
Tel: 020 7890 3324

Products that contain data from this source
Housing and Construction Statistics Annual Volume

Rent Officers - England and Wales
Department of the Environment, Transport and the Regions

The DETR collects rent officer statistics, obtained from the Rent Officer Service. Data are collected on Housing Benefit cases referred by local authorities to the rent officers, and tenancies registered under the Rent Act. Figures for Housing Benefit referrals and registered fair rents are given showing the determined rent and the previous rent-by-rent registration area. The data cover England and Wales and are available for standard regions and Government Office regions. Results have been published quarterly since 1989-90. Other tables are available back to 1970s.

Frequency: Quarterly
Timeliness: up to 6 months after quarter end.
National Coverage: England and Wales
Disaggregation: Counties, London Boroughs

Statistician
David Champion
Department of the Environment, Transport and the Regions
Housing Data and Statistics; HDS2
Tel: 020 7890 3306;
Email: david_champion@detr.gsi.gov.uk

Products that contain data from this source
Housing and Construction Statistics; Housing and Construction Statistics , part 2.

Social Rented Sector Average Rents and Rent Arrears - Northern Ireland
Department of the Environment (NI)

The Department of the Environment (NI) compiles data on social rented sector average rents and rent arrears for tenants of both the Northern Ireland Housing Executive (NIHE) and Housing Associations. They are supplied by NIHE and the Department's Housing Associations Branch and are available at Northern Ireland level.

Status: Ongoing
Collection Method: Administrative Records
Frequency: Annually
Reference Period: Financial Year
Timeliness: Six months
Earliest Available Data: 1993/94
National Coverage: Northern Ireland

Statistician:
Brian French
Department of the Environment (NI)
Central Statistics and Research Branch
Tel: 028 9054 0799;
E-mail: brian.french@doeni.gov.uk

Products that contain data from this source
Northern Ireland Housing Statistics

Social rented Sector Waiting Lists, Allocations and Transfers - Northern Ireland
Department of the Environment (NI)

The Department of the Environment (NI) compiles data on social rented sector waiting lists, allocations and transfers on a financial year basis. The data refer to applicants to either the Northern Ireland Housing Executive (NIHE) or Housing Associations. They are supplied by NIHE and are available at district council area level.

Status: Ongoing
Collection Method: Administrative Records
Frequency: Annually
Reference Period: Financial Year
Timeliness: Six months
Earliest Available Data: 1996/97
National Coverage: Northern Ireland
Sub-National District council area level

Statistician:
Brian French
Department of the Environment (NI)
Central Statistics and Research Branch
Tel: 028 9054 0799;
E-mail: brian.french@doeni.gov.uk

Products that contain data from this source
Northern Ireland Housing Statistics

See also:
In this chapter:
Allocation of Local Authority Housing - England *(7.5)*
English House Condition Survey (EHCS) *(7.6)*
Household Survey - Wales *(7.6)*
Survey of English Housing *(7.1)*

7.8 New housebuilding

Housebuilding - UK
Department of the Environment, Transport and the Regions

The Department of the Environment, Transport and the Regions, National Assembly for Wales, Scottish Executive, and Department of the Environment - Northern Ireland compile data on housebuilding. Data are based on building control records for new dwellings and are derived from local authorities and the National House-Building Council (NHBC). Data are collected on the number of dwellings started, completed and under construction, the activity by private enterprise builders, housing associations, local authorities and new towns, and the rest of the public sector together with total housebuilding, completions in England and in Wales by the numbers of bedrooms for both houses and flats, starts and completions of specialised dwellings for the elderly or the disabled. Data cover England, Wales, Scotland and Northern Ireland and are combined for Great Britain and United Kingdom totals. They are available for standard regions, Government Office regions (within England), and at county and local authority districts level throughout the United Kingdom. Seasonally adjusted data are available for the total England and Great Britain series. The series dates back to 1980, with some figures available back to 1946. Results are published monthly for England, Wales and Great Britain about 25 days after

the reference month, and quarterly for Scotland, Northern Ireland and the United Kingdom.

Frequency: Monthly/Quarterly
Timeliness: About 25 days after the reference month (England and Wales)
National Coverage: United Kingdom

Statistician
Henry Small
Department of the Environment, Transport and the Regions
Tel: 0117 987 8076

Products that contain data from this source
Annual Abstract of Statistics; Economic Trends; Housing and Construction Statistics Annual Volume; Housing Trends in Scotland; Monthly Digest of Statistics; Northern Ireland Housing Bulletin; Northern Ireland Housing Statistics; Regional Trends; Social Trends; Welsh Housing Statistics

New Housebuilding - Northern Ireland
Department of the Environment - Northern Ireland

The Department of the Environment (NI) compiles the new housebuilding (starts) data for each district council area in Northern Ireland. The data are used in the calculation of UK housing starts. Details of all housing starts for the private sector are supplied by the Building Control Offices for each of the 26 district council areas. Data for the social rented sector are provided by the NI Housing Executive and the Housing Associations Branch of the Department of the Environment (NI). The figures are published in the quarterly NI Housing Bulletin, usually in the last week of the third month following the reference quarter. Data are also collected for completions for all sectors but the methods used do not permit figures for the private sector to be produced at district council area. The figures are published in the annual NI Housing Statistics publication. The publication also contains information on a wide range of social rented sector activity, e.g. types of new build, rehabilitations and improvements.

Status: Ongoing
Collection Method: Administrative Records
Frequency: Quarterly for starts; annually for completions
Reference Period: Quarters ending March, June, September & December
Timeliness: 3 months
Earliest Available Data: 1971
National Coverage: Northern Ireland
Disaggregation: District council area level (all starts + social rented completions +NIHE activity)

Statistician
Brian French
Department of the Environment - Northern Ireland
Central Policy and Management Unit; Central Statistics and Research Branch
Tel: 028 9054 0799;
Email: brian.french@doeni.gov.uk

Products that contain data from this source
Northern Ireland Housing Bulletin; Northern Ireland Housing Statistics

New Housebuilding - Scotland
Scottish Executive

The survey covers tenure, type (e.g. sheltered) and number of dwellings for which building has been started and completed in each quarter. The survey is carried out quarterly, covers Scotland and is available at local authority level.

Status: Ongoing
Collection Method: Census
Frequency: Quarterly
Reference Period: end of March, June, Sept and Dec each year
Timeliness: 6-8 months
National Coverage: Scotland
Disaggregation: Local Authority

Statistician
Deborah Pegg
Scottish Executive
Economic Advice and Statistics Division; Branch 7: Housing Statistics
Tel: 0131 244 2752.
Email: deborah.pegg@scotland.gov.uk

Products that contain data from this source
Housing Trends in Scotland

New Housebuilding - Wales
National Assembly for Wales

The National Assembly for Wales carries out a survey on new housebuilding in Wales giving a progress report on dwellings started, under construction and completed by tenures for each local authority in Wales. Historical information by Pre-1996 County on new housebuilding has been published as far back as the inter war years. However, data on newly built dwellings has been collected in a consistent format from 1951 but is only available monthly from 1975. Questions on dwellings designed for elderly and single persons were introduced in 1984 and in 1989 the return changed to include data on information previously collected from district authorities, county councils and police authorities.

Status: Ongoing
Collection Method: Administrative Records
Frequency: Monthly
Timeliness: Approximately 4 weeks after the end of the month
Earliest Available Data: 1951
National Coverage: Wales
Disaggregation: Unitary Authority

Statistician
Henry Small
National Assembly for Wales
Statistical Directorate; Housing Statistics
Tel: 029 2082 5063;
Email: henry.small@wales.gsi.gov.uk

Products that contain data from this source
A Statistical Focus on Wales; Housing and Construction Statistics Annual Volume; Housing and Construction Statistics Part 2 Quarterly; Quarterly Welsh Housing Statistics; Regional Trends; Social Trends; Wales in Figures Fact Card; Welsh Housing Statistics; Welsh Social Trends

See also:
In this chapter:
Grant and Group Repair Schemes - Wales
(7.3)

7.9 Purchases/Sales of Houses and Property

Acquisition of Dwellings
National Assembly for Wales

An annual survey collecting data on: (a) the acquisition of dwellings by local authorities for retention in their own stock; (b) the acquisition of dwellings by local authorities for resale to housing associations; (c) the acquisition of dwellings by local authorities for subsequent sale including low cost home ownership schemes; (d) improvement for sale schemes; and (e) transferable discount schemes. Information on the acquisition of dwellings has been collected since the early 1970's. The current return dates from 1984 with minor revisions being made following a review of Housing Statistics surveys in 1989 and 1995/96.

Status: Ongoing
Collection Method: Administrative Records
Frequency: Annually
Reference Period: Financial year
Timeliness: Approximately 3 months after the end of the financial year
Earliest Available Data: 1984
National Coverage: Wales
Disaggregation: Unitary Authority

Statistician
Henry Small
National Assembly for Wales
Statistical Directorate; Housing Statistics
Tel: 029 2082 5063;
Email: henry.small@wales.gsi.gov.uk

Products that contain data from this source
Welsh Housing Statistics (information used to aid the calculation of stock by tenure)

Building Society Lending for House Purchase - UK (BS4)
Department of the Environment, Transport and the Regions

The Department of the Environment, Transport and the Regions collects data on building society lending for house purchase, derived from the top four building societies. Data are collected on the average house price, the average advance, and the number of transactions at approval and completion stages. The data cover the UK and they have been collected monthly since 1974. Results are published monthly, quarterly and annually, three to four weeks after the reference period. Series runs from 1970s

Status: Ongoing
Frequency: Monthly
Timeliness: 3 weeks after month end
Earliest Available Data: 1974
National Coverage: United Kingdom

Statistician
David Champion
Department of the Environment, Transport and the Regions
Housing Data and Statistics; HDS2
Tel: 020 7890 3306;
Email: david_champion@detr.gsi.gov.uk

Products that contain data from this source
Economic Trends; Financial Statistics; Housing and Construction Statistics Annual Volume; Monthly Digest of Statistics

Council House Sales/Transfers
Department of the Environment, Transport and the Regions

Information on council dwelling sales/transfers by local authorities in England is collected quarterly on the P1B return. The purpose of this form is to monitor progress on sales/transfers; to produce forecasts of future sale/transfer receipts for the annual public expenditure discussions, and in the assessment of possible changes to the framework under which sales/transfers take place. Summary details are published by the Department on a quarterly basis in Housing and Construction Statistics (England totals) and Local Housing Statistics (individual authority data and regional totals). We have collected information on council house sales on the P1B return (and its predecessors) since 1979/80. The right to buy scheme was introduced in October 1980 and regular quarterly sales returns have been received from authorities since that time.

Status: Ongoing
Collection Method: Administrative Records
Frequency: Quarterly
Reference Period: Cumulative within financial year
Timeliness: Three to four months
Earliest Available Data: 1979
National Coverage: England
Disaggregation: By all reporting local/unitary authorities

Statistician
Trevor Steeples
Department of the Environment, Transport and the Regions
Housing Data and Statistics; HDS3
Tel: 020 7890 3324.
Email: trevor_steeples@detr.gsi.gov.uk

Products that contain data from this source
Housing and Construction Statistics
Local Housing Statistics

Council House Transfers
Department of the Environment, Transport and the Regions

Status: Ongoing
Collection Method: Administrative Records
Frequency: Quarterly
Reference Period: Cumulative with financial year
Timeliness: Three to four months
Earliest Available Data: 1979
National Coverage: England
Sub-National: By all reporting local/unitary authorities

Statistician
Trevor Steeples
Department of the Environment, Transport and the Regions
Housing Data and Statistics; HDS3
Tel: 020 7890 3324.
Email: trevor_steeples@detr.gsi.gov.uk

Products that contain data from this source
Housing and Construction Statistics Annual Volume; Local Housing Statistics

---

Mortgage Lending - UK
Department of the Environment, Transport and the Regions

The Department of the Environment, Transport and the Regions compiles data from the Survey of Mortgage Lenders based on a 5 per cent sample survey of mortgage completions. Data are collected on average house price, average advance, age of borrower, average income, first-time buyers, etc. The data cover the United Kingdom, Great Britain, England, Wales, Scotland, Northern Ireland and are available at standard region, Government Office region and county level. The Survey has been conducted monthly since 1968. Results are published quarterly and annually, six weeks after end of the reference quarter.

Frequency: Monthly
Timeliness: 6 weeks after quarter end.
Earliest Available Data: 1968
National Coverage: United Kingdom
Disaggregation: Standard Statistical Region (SSR), Government Office Region (GOR)

Statistician
David Champion
Department of the Environment, Transport and the Regions
Housing Data And Statistics; HDS2
Tel: 020 7890 3306;
Email: david_champion@detr.gsi.gov.uk

Products that contain data from this source
Economic Trends; Housing and Construction Statistics Annual Volume; Housing Finance Quarterly (Council of Mortgage Lenders); Regional Trends; Social Trends; The 5% Sample Survey of Building Society Mortgages (Studies in Official Statistics No 26); The New Survey of Mortgage Lenders (Housing Finance No 16)

Mortgage Possessions - England and Wales
Court Service

The Lord Chancellor's Department collates data on mortgage possession actions taken in the County Courts, compiled by the Court Service from administrative records. Data are available since 1987 and cover England and Wales at standard region, county and individual County Court levels. They are compiled monthly and published on a quarterly basis.

Status: Ongoing
Collection Method: Administrative Records
Frequency: Continuously
Reference Period: Monthly, quarterly, annual and financial year
Timeliness: Published last Wednesday of month following end of quarter.
Earliest Available Data: 1987
National Coverage: England and Wales
Sub-National: Midland & Oxford Circuit
North Eastern Circuit
Northern Circuit
South East (London) Circuit
South East (Provinces) Circuit
Wales & Chester Circuit
Western Circuit
Disaggregation: Individual county courts; Judicial Groups; Judicial Circuits; County Region

Statistician
Sunita Gould
Court Service
Information Management and Analysis Group (IMAGe)
Tel: 020 7210 1773

Products that contain data from this source
Judicial Statistics England and Wales Annual Report; Mortgage Possession Statistics (Press Notice)

Property Transactions
Board of Inland Revenue

Inland Revenue Statistics and Economics Division collects data on sale in the housing and property market. Seasonally adjusted monthly data are available at national level. More detailed data based on a sample are available by region, type of property and value band. The standard monthly series covers England and Wales and is available back to the second quarter of 1977. A consistent quarterly series is available from 1959. Detailed analyses by region and type are only available annually from 1986. The national data are collected monthly and are published on the middle of each month, and relate to sales in the previous month. Annual analyses normally available in May the following year.

Status: Ongoing
Collection Method: Information is obtained from the Stamp Office and HM Land Registry. Aggregate counts for months, sample of administrative forms for annual.
Frequency: Monthly
Reference Period: Monthly for count totals. Annual for detailed analysis including values.
Timeliness: Monthly count figures available about three weeks after end of month. Annual analyses usually available in May.
Earliest Available Data: Monthly from Q2 1977. Quarterly from 1959. Annual analyses from 1986.
National Coverage: England, Wales and Northern Ireland
Sub-National: England, Wales and Northern Ireland (monthly counts only)
Disaggregation: GORs (annual only)

Statistician
Frank Kane
Board of Inland Revenue
Tel: 020 7438 6314

Products that contain data from this source
Economic Trends; Inland Revenue Statistics

Residential Land Prices - England and Wales
Department of the Environment, Transport and the Regions

The DETR collects data on residential land prices, derived from valuation offices. Data are available by average price per hectare, in the land price index and by type of purchaser. The data cover England and Wales and are produced at standard region, Government Office region and county level. Figures date from 1964. The index methodology was changed in 1990 and the series revised back to 1981. Results are published twice a year, six months after the reference period. Current methodology back to 1981.

Frequency: Quarterly
Timeliness: up to 6 months after end of quarter.
Earliest Available Data: 1981
National Coverage: England and Wales
Disaggregation: Government Office Region (GOR)

Statistician
David Champion
Department of the Environment, Transport and the Regions
Housing Data and Statistics; HDS2
Tel: 020 7890 3306;
Email: david_champion@detr.gsi.gov.uk

Products that contain data from this source
Housing and Construction Statistics Annual Volume

Sales and Transfers of Dwellings by Housing Authorities, Quarterly Summary - Scotland
Scottish Executive

Summary information on the numbers of applications and sales of local authority dwellings. The survey is carried out quarterly, covers Scotland and is available at local authority level.

Status: Ongoing
Collection Method: Census
Frequency: Quarterly
Reference Period: End of March, June, September and December each year
Timeliness: 6-8 months
National Coverage: Scotland
Disaggregation: Local Authority

Statistician
Deborah Pegg
Scottish Executive
Economic Advice and Statistics Division; Branch 7: Housing Statistics
Tel: 0131 244 2752;
Email: deborah.pegg@scotland.gov.uk

Products that contain data from this source
Housing Trends in Scotland

Sales and Transfers of Housing Association Dwellings (Other Than to Sitting Tenants) - Scotland
Scottish Executive

Information is collected on all sales and transfers of local authority stock to individuals other than sitting tenants, to housing associations and to private developers. The survey is carried out annually, covers Scotland and is available at local authority level.

Status: Ongoing
Collection Method: Census
Frequency: Annually
Reference Period: Financial Year
Timeliness: 6-8 months
National Coverage: Scotland
Disaggregation: Local Authority

Statistician
Deborah Pegg
Scottish Executive
Economic Advice and Statistics Division; Branch 7: Housing Statistics
Tel: 0131 244 2752
Email: deborah.pegg@scotland.gov.uk

Products that contain data from this source
Housing Trends in Scotland

Sales of Dwellings by the Northern Ireland Housing Executive
Department of the Environment (NI)

The Department of the Environment (NI) compiles data on sales of dwellings by the Northern Ireland Housing Executive (NIHE). These include sales to sitting tenants, sales to non-tenants and sales under the Special Purchase of Evacuated Dwellings (SPED) scheme. Sales to tenants are administered under a similar scheme to Right to Buy. The data are supplied by NIHE and are available at both Northern Ireland and district council area level.

Status: Ongoing
Collection Method: Administrative Records
Frequency: Annually
Reference Period: Financial Year
Timeliness: Six months
Earliest Available Data: 1979/80
National Coverage: Northern Ireland
Disaggregation: District council area level

Statistician:
Brian French
Department of the Environment (NI)
Central Statistics and Research Branch
Tel: 028 9054 0799;
E-mail: brian.french@doeni.gov.uk

Products that contain data from this source
Northern Ireland Housing Statistics

Sales of Housing Authority Dwellings to Sitting Tenants - Scotland
Scottish Executive

Information is collected on all sales of local authority dwellings to sitting tenants. This includes sales under the right to buy and rent to mortgage schemes. The survey is carried out quarterly, covers Scotland and is available at local authority level.

Status: Ongoing
Collection Method: Census
Frequency: Annually
Reference Period: Financial Year
Timeliness: 6-8 months
National Coverage: Scotland
Disaggregation: Local Authority

Statistician
Deborah Pegg
Scottish Executive
Economic Advice and Statistics Division; Branch 7: Housing Statistics
Tel: 0131 244 2752
Email: deborah.pegg@scotland.gov.uk

Products that contain data from this source
Housing Trends in Scotland

Sales of Local Authority Dwellings
National Assembly for Wales

The National Assembly for Wales carries out a quarterly survey concerned with the sale of local authority dwellings under the right-to-buy, rent-to-mortgage and other schemes. Details of disposals of land for housing, disposals of dwellings built and financed by private developers on local authority land, indemnities to building societies and lending to private persons for house purchase and renovation are collected.

Information on sales of local authority dwellings has been available since 1975. In October 1980 on the introduction of Right to Buy legislation a quarterly return was introduced to monitor the progress of Right to Buy applications. This return supplemented the information being collected monthly regarding all completed sales of dwellings. In 1983 the two forms were combined into one quarterly form and since then minor changes have been made to accommodate changes in legislation. The most recent change taking place in December 1993 following revisions due to the Leasehold Reform, Housing and Urban Development Act, 1993.

Status: Ongoing
Collection Method: Administrative Records
Frequency: Quarterly
Reference Period: Jan - March, April - June, July - September, Oct - December
Timeliness: Approximately 3 months after the end of the quarter
Earliest Available Data: 1975
National Coverage: Wales
Disaggregation: Unitary Authority

Statistician
Henry Small
National Assembly for Wales
Statistical Directorate; Housing Statistics
Tel: 029 2082 5063;
Email: henry.small@wales.gsi.gov.uk

Products that contain data from this source
A Statistical Focus on Wales; Digest of Welsh
Statistics; Housing and Construction Statistics
Annual Volume; Quarterly Welsh Housing
Statistics; Regional Trends; Social Trends; Welsh
Housing Statistics; Your Right to Buy Your Home

See also:
In this chapter:
English House Condition Survey (EHCS)
(7.6)
Survey of English Housing *(7.1)*

7

Housing - *Products*

7.10 Abstracts, Compendia, A-Z Catalogues, Directories and Reference Material

Housing and Construction Statistics Annual Volume
Department of the Environment, Transport and the Regions

This report incorporates general national housing and construction statistics for Great Britain, although some figures are for UK, England, Wales, Scotland and Northern Ireland and the regions. Where regional figures are shown for construction statistics they refer to the Standard Statistical Regions, and the housing statistics refer to Government Office Regions. Most tables show how things have changed over the last eleven years. The construction statistics include data on the value of new orders and output; earnings and hours worked; the structure of the industry; material price indices, quantities produced and delivered, and value of overseas trade; and gross domestic fixed capital and government expenditure on construction. The data on housing covers house building starts, under construction and completions; renovations: grants, work carried out, and action on unfit dwellings; slum clearance; stock of dwellings, sales of public sector dwellings, households, population and EC housing; finance: prices, mortgages, arrears, possessions, and local authority revenue accounts; rents and rent regulation; household income, rent and mortgage payments; households by tenure and recent movers.

Frequency: Annually
Price: £30.00

Available from
TSO Publications Centre and Bookshops
Please see Annex B for full address details.

Sources from which data for this product are obtained
Allocation of Local Authority Housing - England; Bricks - GB; Building Societies; Building Society Lending for House Purchase - UK (BS4); Cement - UK; Concrete Blocks - GB; Concrete Roofing Tiles - GB; Construction - New Orders - GB; Construction Output - GB; Dwelling Stock - UK; Fibre Cement Products - GB; Grant and Group Repair Schemes - Wales; House Renovation Grants GB; Housebuilding - UK; Housing Management and Performance; LA Housing Capital Finance; Local Authority Rents - England; Mortgage Lending - UK; New Housebuilding - Wales; Price Index for Public Sector Housing (PIPSH); Price Index of Public Sector Housebuilding; Ready-Mixed Concrete - GB; Renovations: Housing Associations - England; Renovations: Local Authorities - England; Residential Land Prices - England and Wales; Road Construction Tender Price Index - GB; Sales of Local Authority Dwellings; Sand and Gravel - GB; Slate - GB; Slum Clearance - GB; Stock Clearance, Compulsory Renovation and Action on Unfit Dwellings; Survey of English Housing; UK Minerals Industry; Unfit Dwellings - England

Housing and Construction Statistics Part 1 and Part 2 Quarterly
Department of the Environment, Transport and the Regions

Includes general national housing and construction statistics variously on a UK, Great Britain, England, Wales, Scotland or Northern Ireland basis plus some regional figures).

Part 1 contains data on: housebuilding (starts, under construction and completions); estimated time lag from start to completion; specialised dwellings; houses and flats completed by number of bedrooms; mortgages by main institutional sources; building societies: dwelling prices, mortgage advances and commitments, and income of borrowers; and building materials and components: production, deliveries and stocks.

Part 2 contains data on: construction cost and price indices; housing costs and prices; value of output by sector, region and type of work; construction manpower broken down by employees and self-employed and by operatives and administrative, professional, technical and clerical; sales of housing and housing land by local authorities, new towns and housing associations; renovation grants paid; renovation of specialised dwellings for local authorities; stock of dwellings; housing loans by local authorities to private persons and housing associations; dwellings demolished or closed and unfit dwellings made fit; registered rents and housing benefit referrals to rent officers.

Frequency: Quarterly
Price: Annual subscription £75.00 (Part 1)
Annual subscription £75.00 (Part 2)
ISBN: 0 11 729662 7

Sources from which data for this product are obtained
New Housebuilding - Wales

Housing in England
Department of the Environment, Transport and the Regions

The results of the Survey of English Housing carried out for the Department of the Environment, Transport and the Regions. The survey is continuous but the content is revised each April, and results are published annually on a financial year basis.
The information contained within StatBase relates to the latest publication which is Housing in England 1997/98, published in June 1999. Housing in England 1997/98 has been published annually since 1993/94, the first year of the survey. In 1993/4 the results for private renters were published separately as 'Private Renting in England 1993/94' (see separate entry), but since then have been included in the main Housing in England report.

Contains information on the size and composition of the different housing tenures in England together with information on the personal characteristics, income, employment and housing histories of the householders. A variety of more detailed information relevant to particular tenures is also shown, including mortgage payments, mortgage arrears, rents, Housing Benefit, overcrowding, second homes and expectations of buying.

Frequency: Annually
Price: £39.50
ISBN: 011 621234 9

Available from
TSO Publications Centre and Bookshops
Please see Annex B for full address details.

Sources from which data for this product are obtained
Survey of English Housing

Housing Trends in Scotland
Scottish Executive

Key housing data for Scotland with explanatory notes. Contains data on stock of dwellings, new dwelling starts and completions, sales of public authority dwellings, improvement activity and other housing topics.

Frequency: Quarterly
Price: £2.00
ISSN: 0264-1143

Available from
TSO Publications Centre and Bookshops
Please see Annex B for full address details.

Sources from which data for this product are obtained
Dwelling Stock - UK; Dwellings Demolished, Closed, Converted and Acquired - Scotland; House Renovation Grants GB; Housebuilding - UK; Household Estimates; Housing Authority Stock - Scotland; Improvement and Modernisation - Scotland; New Housebuilding - Scotland; Sales and Transfers of Dwellings by Housing Authorities, Quarterly Summary - Scotland; Sales and transfers of housing association dwellings (other than to sitting tenants) - Scotland; Sales of Housing Authority Dwellings to sitting tenants - Scotland; Slum Clearance - GB; Special Needs Housing - Scotland; Stock estimates by tenure

---

Local Housing Statistics
Department of the Environment, Transport and the Regions

Provides for local authorities in England, quarterly statistics on the progress of housebuilding, house renovation, sale of housing land and housing by local authorities, and local authorities action under the homelessness provisions of the1985 and 1996 Housing Acts (subject to availability). Also includes statistics on the construction and renovation of specialised dwellings when available.

Frequency: Quarterly
Price: £17.00

Available from
TSO Publications Centre and Bookshops
Please see Annex B for full address details.

Northern Ireland Housing Bulletin
Department of the Environment - Northern Ireland

Compilation of Northern Ireland housing statistics. Contains data on new house prices, new housing starts, mortgage lending and mortgage possessions.

Delivery: PDF file format and hardcopy publication
Frequency: Quarterly
Price: Free

Available from
Brian French
Department of the Environment - Northern Ireland
Central Statistics and Research Branch
Clarence Court
10-18 Adelaide Street
Belfast BT2 8GB
Tel: 028 9054 0799;
Email: brian.french@doeni.gov.uk

Sources from which data for this product are obtained
Dwelling Stock - UK; House Renovation Grants GB; House Sales and Prices - Northern Ireland; Housebuilding - UK; New Housebuilding - Northern Ireland; Northern Ireland Quarterly Construction Enquiry

---

Northern Ireland Housing Statistics
Department of the Environment - Northern Ireland

Comprehensive Northern Ireland housing statistics. Contains data on housing stock, house condition, energy efficiency, rates bills, planning applications, new housebuilding, repairs and improvements, housing associations, Northern Ireland Housing Executive, homelessness, waiting lists, allocations, transfers, housing benefit, average rents, social rented sector house sales, mortgage lending activity, mortgage possessions, new house sales, housing finance, the private rented sector and household survey statistics.

Frequency: Annual
Price: £10.00

Available from
Brian French
Department of the Environment - Northern Ireland
Clarence Court
10-18 Adelaide Street
Belfast BT2 8GB
Tel: 028 9054 0799;
Email: brian.french@doeni.gov.uk

Sources from which data for this product are obtained
House Sales and Prices - Northern Ireland; New Housebuilding - Northern Ireland

Quarterly Welsh Housing Statistics
National Assembly for Wales

Quarterly data relating to key housing areas. Contains data each quarter on new housebuilding figures including starts, completions and under construction for Wales and by unitary authority; sales of public sector dwellings for Wales; sales of local authority dwellings, claims and completions for Wales; right to buy sales by unitary authority; renovation grant approvals and completions under the Housing Grants, Construction and Regeneration Act 1996 - number and value for Wales and unitary authorities; renovation grant approvals and completions under the Local Government and Housing Act 1989 - number and value for Wales and unitary authorities; homelessness under Part VII of the 1996 Housing Act for Wales and by unitary authority.

Frequency: Quarterly
Price: Free

Available from
Fiona Leadbitter
National Assembly for Wales
Crown Building
Cathays Park
Cardiff CF10 3NQ
Tel: 029 2082 5055;
Email: fiona.leadbitter@wales.gsi.gov.uk

Sources from which data for this product are obtained
Grant and Group Repair Schemes - Wales; Homelessness; New Housebuilding - Wales; Sales of Local Authority Dwellings

---

Scottish Household Survey: First Quarter Bulletin, 1999
Scottish Executive

This bulletin presents the first results from the Scottish Household Survey, a major new continuous survey funded by the Scottish Executive (formerly the Scottish Office). The aim of the survey is to provide representative information about the composition, characteristics and behaviours of Scottish households - both nationally and at a more disaggregate level. Amongst a range of issues, the survey focuses, in particular, on the areas of transport, local government and social inclusion. This first bulletin provides an overview of the type of information collected by the survey and outlines some key findings in each of the main topic areas for the first quarter of 1999.

Frequency: Quarterly
Price: £5.00
ISSN: 1467 7393

Products

Available from
TSO Publications Centre and Bookshops
Please see Annex B for full address details.

Welsh Housing Statistics
National Assembly for Wales

Statistics covering all aspects of housing in Wales. Data are based mainly on returns made to the National Assembly for Wales by the old 37 local authorities and the new 22 unitary authorities. Contains data on dwelling stock, new housebuilding, renovation, clearances, registered social landlords, sales, lettings and vacancies, homelessness, housing finance and rents.

Frequency: Annually
Price: £10.00 inclusive of postage in the UK
ISBN: 0 7504 2246 7
ISSN: 0262 - 8333

Available from
Fiona Leadbitter
National Assembly for Wales
Crown Building
Cathays Park
Cardiff CF10 3NQ
Tel: 029 2082 5055;
Email: fiona.leadbitter@wales.gsi.gov.uk

Sources from which data for this product are obtained
Acquisition of Dwellings; Dwelling Stock - England; Grant and Group Repair Schemes - Wales; Homelessness; Housing Management and Performance; Local Authority Capital Outturn - Wales; Local Authority Capital Payments - Wales; Local Authority Revenue Outturn - Wales; New Housebuilding - Wales; Sales of Local Authority Dwellings; Stock Clearance, Compulsory Renovation and Action on Unfit Dwellings; Registered Social Landlords - Wales; Building Society Mortgages - DETR

7.11 Clearance and Demolition of Housing

Please see:
In this chapter:
English House Condition Survey 1996 *(7.15)*
Housing and Construction Statistics Part 1 and Part 2 Quarterly *(7.10)*
Housing Trends in Scotland *(7.10)*
Welsh Housing Statistics *(7.10)*

7.12 Conversion, Renovation and Repair of Housing

House Renovation Information Bulletin
Department of the Environment, Transport and the Regions

Contains data on house renovations in England, such as renovation grants paid to private owners and all tenants by type of grant, conversions, major repair and other renovations completed for housing associations, conversions and improvements completed for local authorities and new towns.

Frequency: Quarterly
Price: £25.00, annual subscription (included with the Housebuilding Information Bulletin)

Sources from which data for this product are obtained
Grant and Group Repair Schemes - Wales; House Renovation Grants GB; Renovations: Housing Associations - England; Renovations: Local Authorities - England

See also:
In this chapter:
English House Condition Survey 1996 *(7.15)*
Housing and Construction Statistics Annual Volume *(7.10)*
Housing and Construction Statistics Part 1 and Part 2 Quarterly *(7.10)*
Housing Trends in Scotland *(7.10)*
Local Housing Statistics *(7.10)*
Northern Ireland Housing Bulletin *(7.10)*
Quarterly Welsh Housing Statistics *(7.10)*
Welsh Housing Statistics *(7.10)*

7.13 Homelessness

Homelessness Information Bulletin
Department of the Environment, Transport and the Regions

Statistics of households in England found to be homeless under the provisions of the 1985 and 1996 Housing Acts. Contains data on homeless acceptances in total and by priority need group, reason for loss of last settled home, households in temporary accommodation, and type of temporary accommodation.

Delivery: News/Press Release
Frequency: Quarterly
Price: £10.00, Annual subscription

Sources from which data for this product are obtained
Statutory homelessness - England

Operation of the Homeless Persons Legislation in Scotland
Scottish Executive

Characteristics of households in Scotland applying under the homeless persons legislation and details of local authority action. Contains data on the number of applicant households by priority, and number obtaining accommodation by type of accommodation secured.

Frequency: Annually
Price: £2.00
ISSN: 0264-1143

Available from
TSO Publications Centre and Bookshops
Please see Annex B for full address details.

Sources from which data for this product are obtained
Homelessness - Scotland

Operation of the Homeless Persons Legislation in Scotland: Local Authority Analyses
Scottish Executive

Characteristics of households in Scotland applying under the homeless persons legislation and details of local authority action. Contains data on characteristics of applicant households in each district, and action taken by local authorities.

Frequency: Annually
Price: £2.00
ISSN: 0264-1143

Available from
TSO Publications Centre and Bookshops
Please see Annex B for full address details.

Sources from which data for this product are obtained
Homelessness - Scotland

See also:
In this chapter:
Housing in England *(7.10)*
Quarterly Welsh Housing Statistics *(7.10)*
Welsh Housing Statistics *(7.10)*

In other chapters:
(The) Office of Population Censuses and Surveys Survey of Psychiatric Morbidity in Great Britain - Report 7 (see the Health and Care chapter)

7.14 Housing - General

House Property and Inheritance in the UK
Department of the Environment, Transport and the Regions

Research commissioned by the Department of the Environment to investigate the long term consequences of the growth of owner-occupation, in terms of housing inheritance. Estimates of number and value of property inheritances were made from a set of specially-commissioned questions in the General Household Survey.

Frequency: One-off
Price: £25.00
ISBN: 0 11 752913 3

Available from
Jonathan Swan
Room 1/J3
Department of the Environment, Transport and the Regions
Eland House
Bressenden Place
London SW1E 5DU
Tel: 020 7890 3297;
Email: hds.huma.hcg.doe@gtnet.gov.uk

Sources from which data for this product are obtained
General Household Survey - GB

Housing Strategy Operational Plan - Wales
National Assembly for Wales

Contains a summary of financial and non-financial information used in the development of strategic operational plans for each housing authority in Wales.

Delivery: Not published as such - available for inspection. Documents from each Unitary Authority held internally.
Frequency: Annually

Available from
Henry Small
The National Assembly for Wales
Crown Building
Cathays Park
Cardiff CF10 3NQ
Tel: 029 2082 5063;
Email: henry.small@wales.gsi.gov.uk

Sources from which data for this product are obtained
Housing Strategy Operational Plan

Index of Place Names 1997
Office for National Statistics

An electronic gazetteer that pinpoints a comprehensive listing of some 60,000 places in England and Wales within their respective administrative areas. It also includes population figures for those areas which have legally defined boundaries.

Frequency: Annually
Price: £75.00 + VAT
ISBN: 1-85774-264-9

Available from
Kathy Edwards
Office for National Statistics
Segensworth Road
Titchfield
Fareham
Hampshire PO15 5RR
Tel: 01329 813477

Longitudinal Study, Housing Deprivation and Social Change
Office for National Statistics

Delivery: Ad Hoc/One-off Release
Price: £17.00
ISBN: 0116916664

Output Price Indices Information Sheet (2 Sheets Or More)
Department of the Environment, Transport and the Regions

Frequency: Quarterly
Price: £16.00 per year (4 quarters), £27.00 complete index set per year

Available from
Marcella Douglas
Room 3/A4
Department of the Environment, Transport and the Regions
Eland House
Bressenden Place
London SW1E 5DU
Tel: 020 7890 5594
Email: mdouglas@detr-cmi.demon.co.uk

Shared Accommodation in Five Localities
Department of the Environment, Transport and the Regions

Reports on a survey covering three types of 'shares': households in non-self-contained accommodation and families and individuals living in larger households who might potentially want a home of their own. Contains characteristics, circumstances and attitudes to sharing of the three groups studied and draws comparisons between the five different localities.

Frequency: Ad hoc
Price: £12.25
ISBN: 0 11 691593 5

Available from
TSO Publications Centre and Bookshops
Please see Annex B for full address details.

Your Right to Buy Your Home
Department of the Environment, Transport and the Regions

A booklet giving advice to council, new town and housing association tenants on buying their own homes. The publication consists of approximately 40 A5 pages and includes text, graphics and a number of financial examples. The booklet has been designed to be informative and includes sections on the right to buy, rent to mortgage, discount rules, cost of buying, buying flats and maisonettes, getting a mortgage, delays or problems and moving on at a later date.

Delivery: Ad Hoc/One-off Release
Frequency: Ad-hoc
Price: Free

Available from
Henry Small
National Assembly for Wales
Crown Building
Cathays Park
Cardiff CF10 3NQ
Tel: 029 2082 5063;
Email: henry.small@wales.gsi.gov.uk

Sources from which data for this product are obtained
Sales of Local Authority Dwellings

See also:
In this chapter:
Dwellings Below the Tolerable Standard (BTS) in Scotland: Estimates by Local Authorities for April 1996 and Details of Action on Such Dwellings *(7.15)*
Housing and Construction Statistics Annual Volume *(7.10)*
Housing in England *(7.10)*
Housing Trends in Scotland *(7.10)*
Quarterly Welsh Housing Statistics *(7.10)*
1993 Welsh House Condition Survey (Report 1994) *(7.15)*
Welsh Housing Statistics *(7.10)*

In other chapters:
Household Projections for Scotland *(see the Population, Census, Migration and Vital Events chapter)*
Population, Household and Dwellings in Europe - Main Results of the 1990/91 Censuses *(see the Population, Census, Migration and Vital Events chapter)*

7.15 Housing Stock

1993 Welsh House Condition Survey (Report 1994)
National Assembly for Wales

A summary volume containing tables, charts and explanatory text covering the key findings of the 1992 Welsh Social Survey

Products

and the 1993 Welsh House Condition Survey. The publication gives information on the numbers of unfit homes in Wales and estimates of the costs of repair together with information about the dwelling stock and the households who occupy it. The publication is most likely to be of interest to housing practitioners and researchers.

Frequency: Periodic
Price: £7.00 (including p&p).
ISBN: 0 7504 1037 X
ISSN: 0263 - 9629

Available from
Henry Small
Room 2-083
National Assembly for Wales
Crown Building
Cathays Park
Cardiff CF10 3NQ
Tel: 029 2082 5063;
Email: henry.small@wales.gsi.gov.uk

Sources from which data for this product are obtained
House Condition Survey - Wales; Household Survey - Wales

Dwellings Below the Tolerable Standard (BTS) in Scotland: Estimates by Local Authorities for April 1996 and Details of Action on Such Dwellings
Scottish Executive

Statistics on dwellings which are below tolerable standard. Contains data on dwellings below the tolerable standard by district, tenure, age and house type, and action taken.

Frequency: Annually - Currently suspended
Price: £2.00
ISBN: 0 7480 6155 X
ISSN: 0264-1143

Available from
TSO Publications Centre and Bookshops
Please see Annex B for full address details.

Sources from which data for this product are obtained
Housing Action Areas - Scotland; Permanent Dwellings Below the Tolerable Standard (BTS) - Scotland

English House Condition Survey 1996
Department of the Environment, Transport and the Regions

Detailed report on the findings of the 1996 survey. The report provides a national and regional profile of the housing stock and the distribution of different household types across different sectors of the stock. The

report provides an up to date picture of disrepair and unfitness in the stock and how this has changed since 1991. The incidence of poor housing is described together with a profile of household groups who are most likely to live in poor housing or poor living conditions.

Delivery: The report was published in May 1998 and presents results of the survey carried out during 1996. Similar reports have been produced for each of the previous EHCS surveys. Web site went on-line May 1998.
Frequency: Every five years
Price: £50.00 (Summary document available free)
ISBN: 0-11-753458-7

Available from
TSO Publications Centre and Bookshops
Please see Annex B for full address details.

Sources from which data for this product are obtained
English House Condition Survey (EHCS)

Lead Plumbing in Scottish Houses: Estimates by Local Authorities and Other Housing Bodies 1991
Scottish Executive

Statistics showing the number of dwellings by district and by private or public sector with lead plumbing.

Delivery: Ad Hoc/One-off Release
Price: £2.00
ISSN: 0264-1143

Available from
TSO Publications Centre and Bookshops
Please see Annex B for full address details.

Northern Ireland House Condition Survey
Northern Ireland Housing Executive

Every five years, the Northern Ireland Housing Executive (NIHE) conducts the Northern Ireland House Condition Survey, which examines the condition of housing stock in Northern Ireland. Topics covered in the 1996 edition of the report include: the stock and its occupants, the state of repair, unfitness, energy, and environmental conditions. For the most part, the survey findings are comparable with those of the English House Condition Survey.

Delivery: Hardcopy publication
Frequency: Every five years
Price: £15.00
ISBN: 1 85694 027 6

Available from:
Smyth Ryan Ltd
Unit 4, Windsor Business Park
Boucher Road
Belfast
BT12 6HT
Tel: 028 9066 8033; Fax: 028 9068 1668

(The) 1991 Post-Census Survey of Vacant Property (PCVS)
Scottish Executive

Details of the results obtained from the 1991 PCVS. Contains data on vacant and other non-effective dwellings in Scotland at the time of the 1991 Census.

Delivery: Ad Hoc/One-off Release
Price: £2.00
ISBN: 0 7480 0785 7
ISSN: 0264-1443

Available from
TSO Publications Centre and Bookshops
Please see Annex B for full address details.

See also:
In this chapter:
English House Condition Survey 1996 *(7.15)*
Housing and Construction Statistics Annual Volume *(7.10)*
Housing and Construction Statistics Part 1 and Part 2 Quarterly *(7.10)*
Housing in England *(7.10)*
Housing Trends in Scotland *(7.10)*
Northern Ireland Housing Bulletin *(7.10)*
Welsh Housing Statistics *(7.10)*

In other chapters:
1994 Based Household Projections for Wales (1997) *(see the Population, Census, Migration and Vital Events chapter)*
Relative Deprivation in Northern Ireland (PPRU Occasional Paper No 28) *(See the Household Finances chapter)*

7.16 Letting of Housing

CORE Annual Statistics
National Housing Federation

Sources from which data for this product are obtained
Housing Association New Lettings - England

CORE Bulletin
National Housing Federation

From Q2 1999 (April-June) will be produced by the Joint Centre for Scottish Housing Research at St. Andrews and Dundee Universities.

Sources from which data for this product are obtained
Housing Association New Lettings - England

Housing Corporation Annual Report
Housing Corporation

New format means very few useable statistics, some detail on completions and number of RSLs registered. Mainly an account of HC activity in past year.

Frequency: Annually

Sources from which data for this product are obtained
Housing Association Statistics - England (HAR10/1 RSR)

NFHA Research Reports (Nos 19, 20, 23)
National Housing Federation

Sources from which data for this product are obtained
Housing Association New Lettings - England

Private Renting in England 1993/94
Department of the Environment, Transport and the Regions

Report of the private renters component of the 1993/4 Survey of English Housing. In subsequent years these results have been published as part of the main annual report of the survey, 'Housing in England' (see separate entry). Contains information on the size and composition of the private rented sector in England together with information about types of lettings, housing standards, tenant satisfaction, rent and Housing Benefit, income and rent, and housing histories of private tenants.

Delivery: Ad Hoc/One-off Release
Frequency: One-off
Price: £21.00
ISBN: 011 691631 1

Sources from which data for this product are obtained
Survey of English Housing

Well Informed? (Study of the HAR 10/1 Return)
National Housing Federation

Sources from which data for this product are obtained
Housing Association Statistics - England (HAR10/1 RSR)

See also:
In this chapter:
English House Condition Survey 1996 *(7.15)*
Housing and Construction Statistics Annual Volume *(7.10)*
Housing in England (7.10)
1993 Welsh House Condition Survey (Report 1994) *(7.15)*
Welsh Housing Statistics *(7.10)*

7.17 New Housebuilding

Planning Performance Checklist
Department of the Environment, Transport and the Regions

Departmental news release on local planning authorities' performance against the Government's target. Contains data of planning applications decided and percentage decided within eight weeks by individual LPAs, ranked by performance. Also statistics on decisions on applications for householder and minor developments.

Frequency: Every six months
Price: Free

See also:
In this chapter:
Housing and Construction Statistics Annual Volume *(7.10)*
and Part 2 Quarterly *(7.10)*
Housing Trends in Scotland *(7.10)*
Local Housing Statistics *(7.10)*
Northern Ireland Housing Bulletin *(7.10)*
Northern Ireland Housing Statistics *(7.10)*
Quarterly Welsh Housing Statistics *(7.10)*
Welsh Housing Statistics *(7.10)*

In other chapters:
Economic Trends *(see the Economy chapter)*
Output Price Indices *(see the Commerce, Construction, Energy and Industry chapter)*

7.18 Purchases/Sales of Houses and Property

Building Societies Association Monthly Mortgage Lending (Press Release)
The Building Societies Association

Sources from which data for this product are obtained
Building Societies

Housing Equity Withdrawal
Department of the Environment, Transport and the Regions

Research commissioned by the Department of the Environment to investigate the long term consequences of the growth of owner-occupation, in terms of housing inheritance. Estimates of number and value of property inheritances were made from a set of specially-commissioned questions in the General Household Survey.

Delivery: Ad Hoc/One-off Release
Frequency: One-off
Price: Free on request from DETR

Available from
Jonathan Swan
Room 1/J3
Department of the Environment, Transport and the Regions
Eland House
Bressenden Place
London SW1E 5DU
Tel: 020 7890 3297;
Email: hds.huma.hcg.doe@gtnet.gov.uk

Sources from which data for this product are obtained
Family Expenditure Survey - UK; General Household Survey - GB

Housing Finance Quarterly (Council of Mortgage Lenders)
The Building Societies Association

Sources from which data for this product are obtained
Building Societies; Mortgage Lending - UK

Mortgage Possession Statistics (Press Notice)
Lord Chancellors Department

Data on mortgage possession actions taken in the County Courts of England and Wales. Contains data on the number of actions entered, suspended orders and orders made during the quarter compared with the corresponding quarter the year before; trends over the last five years; commentary and explanatory notes. Data are available by court, county and region.

Delivery: First Release
Frequency: Quarterly
Price: Free

Available from
Lord Chancellor's Department Press Office
Selborne House
54-60 Victoria Street
London SW1E 6QW
Tel: 020 7210 8512/13

Sources from which data for this product are obtained
Mortgage Possessions - England and Wales

Mortgage Statistics Northern Ireland (Press Release)
Northern Ireland Court Service

The number of actions for mortgage possession started in Northern Ireland.

Delivery: News/Press Release
Frequency: Quarterly
Price: Free

Available from
Siobhan Morgan
Northern Ireland Court Service
Windsor House
9-15 Bedford Street
Belfast BT2 7LT
Tel: 028 9032 8594

Sources from which data for this product are obtained
Judicial Statistics - Northern Ireland

Negative Equity
Department of the Environment, Transport and the Regions

Research on increases in indebtedness after purchase, and the current circumstances of households with negative equity, using specially commissioned data from the General Household Survey.

Frequency: One-off
Price: Free on request from DETR

Available from
Jonathan Swan
Room 1/J3
Department of the Environment, Transport and the Regions
Eland House
Bressenden Place
London SW1E 5DU
Tel: 020 7890 3297;
Email: hds.huma.hcg.doe@gtnet.gov.uk

Sources from which data for this product are obtained
Family Expenditure Survey - UK; General Household Survey - GB

(The) New Survey of Mortgage Lenders (Housing Finance No 16)
Council of Mortgage Lenders

Delivery: Hardcopy
Price: £25.00

Available from
Margaret Glass
Council of Mortgage Lenders
3 Savile Row
London W1X 1AF
Tel: 020 7440 2229;
Email: margaret glass@cml.org.uk

Sources from which data for this product are obtained
Mortgage Lending - UK

See also:
In this chapter:
English House Condition Survey 1996 *(7.15)*
Housing and Construction Statistics Annual Volume *(7.10)*
Housing and Construction Statistics Part 1 and Part 2 Quarterly *(7.10)*
Housing in England *(7.10)*
Housing Trends in Scotland *(7.10)*
Local Housing Statistics *(7.10)*
Northern Ireland Housing Bulletin *(7.10)*
Northern Ireland Housing Statistics *(7.10)*
Quarterly Welsh Housing Statistics *(7.10)*
Welsh Housing Statistics *(7.10)*

In other chapters:
Economic Trends *(see the Economy chapter)*
Financial Statistics *(see the Economy chapter)*
Judicial Statistics England and Wales Annual Report *(see the Crime and Justice chapter)*

Crime and Justice

Statistics covering **Crime and Justice** are collected, administered and disseminated by a number of separate Departments, Agencies and organisations including the **Home Office, Lord Chancellor's Department, Scottish Executive, Scottish Prison Service, the National Assembly for Wales, the Northern Ireland Office, the Northern Ireland Statistics and Research Agency, the Northern Ireland Court Service, the Royal Ulster Constabulary** and the **Court Service**. The available statistics embrace a number of subject areas including: **Attitudes to, and experience of, Crime, Justice and the Police, Court and Judicial Proceedings, Crimes and Offences, Criminals and Offenders, Firearms registration, Policing and Crime Prevention, Prisons, Prisoners and Parole, Probation and Community Service,** and **Terrorism.**

The basic data are generated from a number of separate information 'Sources' and the resultant statistics are disseminated through a whole range of statistical 'Analyses' and 'Products', all of which are described in the following chapter. Users looking for a cross-section of nationwide statistics on **Crime and Justice** may find the following products useful:

> **Criminal Statistics** (annual publication)
> **Judicial Statistics** (annual publication)
> **Prison Statistics** (annual publication)
> **Probation Statistics** (annual publication)

Users interested in a wider range of official statistics including **Crime and Justic**e statistics may like to refer to the following compendia:

> On-line Databases (See Chapter 1):
> > **StatBase - StatStore**
>
> Hardcopy Compendia (See Chapter 2):
> > **Annual Abstract of Statistics**
> > **Britain 2000: The Official Yearbook of the United Kingdom**
> > **Monthly Digest of Statistics**
> > **Regional Trends**
> > **Social Trends**

Users may also find what they need on the various Departmental Websites. These are listed in Chapter 1.

Crime and Justice - *Sources and Analyses*

8.1 Attitudes to, and experience of, Crime, Justice and the Police

British Crime Survey - England and Wales
Home Office

The Home Office compiles results from the biennial British Crime Survey. The Survey has a sample of about 15,000 people living in private households in England and Wales. Data cover numbers of crimes by offence type and type of victim, fear of crime and crime prevention measures, and on an ad hoc basis, contact and attitudes to the police, drug use, and household fire.

Data are available for England and Wales and are sometimes available at regional level. Northern Ireland and Scotland are covered by separate, more occasional surveys. The series commenced in 1982 and since 1992 has been carried out every two years. Main results on the extent and trends in crime are published in early autumn of the year in which the Survey is conducted. Further publications appear on an ad hoc basis.

Sweeps of surveys in 1982, 1984, 1988, 1992, 1994, 1996 and 1998. Each covers experiences of crime in the previous calendar year. CAPI since 1994. Methodological changes are not thought to have influenced the crime count.

Status: Ongoing
Collection Method: Household/Person (Sample) Survey
Frequency: Periodic
Reference Period: Previous calendar year
Timeliness: Data collected over first 6 months of survey year. Main analysis published about 4 months after collection completed.
Earliest Available Data: 1981
National Coverage: England and Wales
Disaggregation: Government Office Region (GOR), Standard Statistical Region (SSR)

Statistician
Dr Chris Kershaw
Home Office
Tel: 020 7273 3754

Products that contain data from this source
Concern about Crime: Findings from the 1998 British Crime Survey; Regional Trends; Social Trends; The 1996 British Crime Survey - England and Wales; The 1998 British Crime Survey - England and Wales; The Data Archive; Burglary of Domestic Dwellings: Findings from the 1998 British Crime Survey

---

Community Attitudes Survey - Northern Ireland
Northern Ireland Statistics and Research Agency

The Central Survey Unit of the Northern Ireland Statistics and Research Agency conducts a survey on public attitudes and views on crime, law and order and policing issues. The sample is drawn from a list of all private addresses in Northern Ireland, with 2,400 addresses allocated annually on a monthly basis. Data are available on perceived levels of crime, personal fear of crime, reporting of crime, law and order, policing and security issues.

Status: Ongoing
Collection Method: Household/Person (Sample) Survey
Frequency: Annually
Reference Period: January to December
Timeliness: Within 7 months of field exercise
Earliest Available Data: 1992
National Coverage: Northern Ireland
Disaggregation: Regional

Statistician
Kevin Sweeney
Department of Finance and Personnel - Northern Ireland
Central Survey Unit
Tel: 028 9025 2490

Products that contain data from this source
Community Attitudes Survey: The Fifth Report 1998 (September); Community Attitudes Survey: The Fourth Report 1997 (June); Community Attitudes Survey: The Sixth Report (April)

Crime Survey - Northern Ireland
Northern Ireland Office

The Central Survey Unit of the Northern Ireland Statistics and Research Agency carries out a survey on crime. At this stage it is an ad hoc survey with individuals selected from 4,500 addresses in Northern Ireland. Data are available on experiences of personal and household crime, drugs and sexual victimisation, and views of crime policing. The survey was carried out between October 1994 and January 1995, with a reference period from July 1993.

Collection Method: Survey
Frequency: Ad hoc
National Coverage: Northern Ireland

Statistician
Principal Statistician
Northern Ireland Office
Tel: 028 9052 7530

Products that contain data from this source
Preliminary Findings from the Northern Ireland Crime Survey

Crime Survey - Scotland
Scottish Executive

The Scottish Executive Home Department conducted a survey of approximately 5,000 individuals about their experiences of crime, and their perceptions of crime and of policing in 1993 and 1996. Data are available on estimated victimisation rates for specific categories of crime, reporting rates to police, public perceptions of crime and the police. Data cover all Scotland. Previous sweeps of the Survey were carried out as part of the British Crime Survey in 1982 and 1988 (These cover Central and Southern Scotland only).

Status: Ongoing, next sweep in year 2000
Collection Method: Household/Person (Sample) Survey
Frequency: Periodic
Reference Period: Previous calendar year
Timeliness: Within 9 months of field exercise
Earliest Available Data: 1981 (from BCS)
National Coverage: Scotland

Statistician
Fiona Fraser
Scottish Executive
Tel: 0131 244 8275;
Email: fiona.fraser@scotland.gov.uk

Products that contain data from this source
(The) Scottish Crime Survey: First Results: Main Findings from the Scottish Crime Survey.

Police Complaints and Discipline, England and Wales
Home Office

The Home Office collects data for England and Wales on the number of complaints received against the police, and any resulting disciplinary measures as a result of the complaint. Data is published in a statistical bulletin once a year. Data collected by the Research, Development & Statistics Directorate of the Home Office since 1983, prior to which either the Police Policy Directorate or Her Majesty's Inspectorate of Constabularies had responsibility.

Status: Ongoing
Collection Method: Administrative Records
Frequency: Annually
Reference Period: The financial year
Timeliness: up to 6 months
Earliest Available Data: 1972
National Coverage: England and Wales
Sub-National: Full
Disaggregation: Police Force Area

Statistician
David Povey
Home Office
Crime and Criminal Justice Unit
Tel: 020 7273 2711

Products that contain data from this source
Police Complaints and Discipline, England and Wales

See also:
In this chapter:
Notifiable Offences - England and Wales *(8.4)*

8.2 Court and Judicial Proceedings

Appeal Courts - England & Wales
Court Service; sponsored by Lord Chancellors Department

The Lord Chancellors Department collates data on appellate court proceedings from court administrative records. Data are available on applications for leave to appeal and appeals, showing the numbers received, the number and outcome of those dealt with and the number outstanding.

Status: Ongoing
Collection Method: Administrative Records
Frequency: Continuously
Reference Period: Monthly, quarterly, annual and financial year
Timeliness: Published in summer of the following year.
Earliest Available Data: Annual data from 1975
National Coverage: England and Wales

Statistician
Sunita Gould
Court Service
Information Management and Analysis Group (IMAGe)
Tel: 020 7210 1773

Products that contain data from this source
Judicial Statistics England and Wales Annual Report; The Court Service Annual Report; The Court Service Plan

Appeal Courts - Northern Ireland
Northern Ireland Court Service

The Northern Ireland Court Service collect data on Court of Appeal statistics. Data are available by appeals entered, outstanding and disposed of, case outcomes, time taken, intermediate processes and court sittings.

Status: Ongoing
Collection Method: Administrative Records
Frequency: Continuously
Reference Period: Quarter
Timeliness: 3 months
Earliest Available Data: 1983
National Coverage: Northern Ireland

Statistician
Siobhan Morgan
Northern Ireland Court Service
Resource Management Branch
Tel: 020 9032 8594

Products that contain data from this source
Northern Ireland Judicial Statistics

Children Order Proceedings - Northern Ireland
Northern Ireland Court Service

Census of all proceedings in NI under the Children (NI) Order 1995. Data collected since the introduction of the Order in November 1996.

Status: Ongoing
Collection Method: Census
Frequency: Continuously
Reference Period: Quarter
Timeliness: 3 months
Earliest Available Data: November 1996
National Coverage: Northern Ireland
Sub-National: By Court divisions
Disaggregation: Court Venues

Statistician
Siobhan Morgan
Northern Ireland Court Service
Resource Management Branch
Tel: 028 9032 8594

Products that contain data from this source
Northern Ireland Judicial Statistics

Coroners' Courts and Miscellaneous Tribunals - Northern Ireland
Northern Ireland Court Service

The Northern Ireland Court Service collect data on Coroners' Court and miscellaneous tribunal statistics. Data are available by business appearing before the courts, business disposed of and court sittings. Data are available at Coroners' Court area level (composite of district councils).

Status: Ongoing
Collection Method: Census
Frequency: Continuously
Reference Period: Quarter
Timeliness: 3 months
Earliest Available Data: 1983
National Coverage: Northern Ireland
Disaggregation: Court Division

Statistician
Siobhan Morgan
Northern Ireland Court Service
Resource Management Branch
Tel: 028 9032 8594

Products that contain data from this source
Northern Ireland Judicial Statistics

County Courts - England and Wales
Court Service; sponsored by Lord Chancellors Department

The Lord Chancellor's Department collates data on county court civil proceedings in England and Wales. Data are available by the number of proceedings started, dealt with and outstanding, and enforcement proceedings. They are supplemented by a regular sample survey of cases set down for trial in county courts, to obtain information on nature of claim, type of litigant, value of judgement and waiting times.

Data are also available at Judicial Circuit and Judicial Group level, and for individual county courts on request. Data are published annually from 1975 and available in the summer of the following year. Monthly data are available from 1987.

Status: Ongoing
Collection Method: Administrative Records
Frequency: Continuously
Reference Period: Monthly, quarterly, annual and financial year
Timeliness: Published in Summer of following year.
Earliest Available Data: Annually from 1975, monthly from 1987
National Coverage: England and Wales

Sub-National: Midland & Oxford Circuit
North Eastern Circuit
Northern Circuit
South East (London) Circuit
South East (Provinces) Circuit
Wales & Chester Circuit
Western Circuit
Disaggregation: Individual county courts;
Judicial Groups; Judicial Circuits

Statistician
Sunita Gould
Court Service
Information Management and Analysis Group
(IMAGe)
Tel: 020 7210 1773

Products that contain data from this source
Judicial Statistics England and Wales Annual
Report; The Court Service Annual Report; The
Court Service Plan

County Courts - Northern Ireland
Northern Ireland Court Service

The Northern Ireland Court Service collects
data on County Court statistics. Data are
available by cases entered, outstanding and
disposed of, case outcomes, time taken,
intermediate processes and court sittings. The
data are available at County Court Division
level (composite of district councils).

Status: Ongoing
Collection Method: Census
Frequency: Continuously
Reference Period: Quarter
Timeliness: 3 months
Earliest Available Data: 1983
National Coverage: Northern Ireland
Sub-National: Court Divisions

Statistician
Siobhan Morgan
Northern Ireland Court Service
Resource Management Branch
Tel: 028 9032 8594

Products that contain data from this source
Northern Ireland Judicial Statistics

Criminal Appeals - Scotland
Scottish Executive

The Scottish Executive Home Department
collects data from the High Court of
Justiciary on the number, type and outcome
of criminal appeals. All appeals in Scotland
are covered with summary results
published in November following the
calendar year end.

Status: Ongoing
Collection Method: Census
Frequency: Continuously
Reference Period: Calendar year
Timeliness: November following the calendar
year end
Earliest Available Data: 1981
National Coverage: Scotland

Statistician
Sandy Taylor
Scottish Executive
Criminal Justice Division, Civil and Criminal
Statistics 1
Tel: 0131 244 222;
Email: sandy.taylor@scotland.gov.uk

Products that contain data from this source
Criminal Proceedings in Scottish Courts

Criminal Appeals to the Crown Court and Court of Appeal - England and Wales
Home Office

The statistics cover criminal appeals to the
Crown Court against magistrates' courts
convictions and sentences and to the
Criminal Division of the Court of Appeal
against convictions of the Crown Court.
Data cover England and Wales and are
available split by court, sex, offence, leave
to appeal, appeal type (conviction only,
sentence only or both), appeal result and
original and new sentence.

Status: Ongoing
Collection Method: Administrative Records
Frequency: Continuously
Reference Period: Calendar year
Timeliness: Appeals data are usually published
within 15 months of the year end to which the
figures relate. For example the 1996 data were
published in February 1998.
National Coverage: England and Wales
Disaggregation: Crown Court centre for
Crown Court appeals

Statistician
John Frosztega
Home Office
Crime and Criminal Justice Unit; Prosecutions,
sentencing and appeals section
Tel: 020 8760 8283

Products that contain data from this source
Criminal Appeals England and Wales

Criminal Proceedings in Scottish Courts
Scottish Executive

The Scottish Executive Home Department
collects data from the police and courts on
the outcome of criminal proceedings in
Scottish courts. Data are available on the

number of persons proceeded against by main
crime or offence, the type of court
proceedings, age and sex of offender, type of
sentence and length of sentence. Data cover
Scotland and are available at police force area
and court level. Aggregate information is
available from the early part of this century.
Disaggregated information is available for all
years after 1969. Data are collected monthly
and results are published in November
following the calendar year end.

Status: Ongoing
Collection Method: Census
Frequency: Monthly
Reference Period: Calendar year
Timeliness: About 12 months
Earliest Available Data: 1969
National Coverage: Scotland
Disaggregation: Police Force Area; Local
Authority area; Sheriffdoms

Statistician
Sandy Taylor
Scottish Executive
Criminal Justice Division; Civil and Criminal Justice
Statistics 1
Tel: 0131 244 2224;
Email: sandy.taylor@scotland.gov.uk

Products that contain data from this source
Annual Abstract of Statistics; Criminal
Proceedings in Scottish Courts; Regional Trends;
Scottish Abstract of Statistics; Social Trends

Crown Court - Northern Ireland
Northern Ireland Court Service

The Northern Ireland Court Service collect
data on Crown Court statistics. Data are
available by cases entered, outstanding and
disposed of, case outcomes, time taken,
intermediate processes and court sittings.
Data are available at County Court Division
level (composite of district councils).

Status: Ongoing
Collection Method: Census
Frequency: Continuously
Reference Period: Quarter
Timeliness: 3 months
Earliest Available Data: 1983
National Coverage: Northern Ireland
Sub-National: County Court Division

Statistician
Siobhan Morgan
Northern Ireland Court Service
Resource Management Branch
Tel: 028 9032 8594

Products that contain data from this source
Northern Ireland Judicial Statistics

Crown Courts - England & Wales
Court Service; sponsored by Lord Chancellors Department

The Lord Chancellors Department compiles Crown Court proceedings data from the Court Service administrative records. Data are available on Committals for Trial, Cases for Sentence and Appeals received, dealt with and outstanding, pleas, results, waiting times and hearing times.

Status: Ongoing
Collection Method: Administrative Records
Frequency: Continuously
Reference Period: Monthly, quarterly, annual and financial year
Timeliness: Published in summer of following year.
Earliest Available Data: Annually from 1975, monthly from 1986
National Coverage: England and Wales
Sub-National: Midland & Oxford Circuit
North Eastern Circuit
Northern Circuit
South East (London) Circuit
South East (Provinces) Circuit
Wales & Chester Circuit
Western Circuit
Disaggregation: Individual Crown Courts; Judicial Groups; Judicial Circuits

Statistician
Sunita Gould
Court Service
Information Management and Analysis Group (IMAGe)
Tel: 020 7210 1773

Products that contain data from this source
Judicial Statistics England and Wales Annual Report; The Court Service Annual Report; The Court Service Plan

Enforcement of Judgements Office and Court Funds Office - Northern Ireland
Northern Ireland Court Service

The Northern Ireland Court Service collect data on business handled by the Enforcement of Judgements Office and the value of funds held and managed by the Court Funds Office.

Status: Ongoing
Collection Method: Census
Frequency: Annual
Reference Period: Calendar year
Timeliness: 3 Months
Earliest Available Data: 1983
National Coverage: Northern Ireland

Statistician
Siobhan Morgan
Northern Ireland Court Service
Resource Management Branch
Tel: 028 9032 8594

Products that contain data from this source
Northern Ireland Judicial Statistics

Family Proceedings
Court Service; sponsored by The Lord Chancellors Department

The Lord Chancellors Department complies data on family proceedings. Data from family proceedings courts, county courts and the High Court are complied by the Court Service from administrative records and regular sample surveys. Data are available for divorce applications and decrees, adoption applications, public and private law, Children Act applications, injunctions and delays. They cover England and Wales at judicial circuit, group and at individual court level on request.

Data on matrimonial proceedings and selected proceedings involving children in the county court and High Court are available annually from 1975 and monthly from 1987. More detailed information on Children Act proceedings, including quarterly figures for family proceedings courts are available from October 1991.

Status: Ongoing
Collection Method: Administrative Records
Frequency: Continuously
Reference Period: Monthly, quarterly, annual and financial year
Timeliness: Published in summer of following year.
Earliest Available Data: Annually from 1975, monthly from 1987
National Coverage: England and Wales
Sub-National: Midland & Oxford Circuit
North Eastern Circuit
Northern Circuit
South East (London) Circuit
South East (Provinces) Circuit
Wales & Chester Circuit
Western Circuit
Disaggregation: Individual county courts; Judicial Groups; Judicial Circuits; The High Court

Statistician
Sunita Gould
Court Service
Information Management and Analysis Group (IMAGe)
Tel: 020 7210 1773

Products that contain data from this source
Judicial Statistics England and Wales Annual Report; The Court Service Annual Report; The Court Service Plan

High Court - Northern Ireland
Northern Ireland Court Service

The Northern Ireland Court Service collect data on High Court proceedings. Data are available by cases entered, outstanding and disposed of, case outcomes, time taken, intermediate processes and court sittings. Data are available at County Court Division level for appeals from County Court.

Status: Ongoing
Collection Method: Census
Frequency: Continuously
Reference Period: Quarter
Timeliness: 3 months
Earliest Available Data: 1983
National Coverage: Northern Ireland

Statistician
Siobhan Morgan
Northern Ireland Court Service
Resource Management Branch
Tel: 028 9032 8594

Products that contain data from this source
Northern Ireland Judicial Statistics

High Courts - England and Wales
The Court Service

The Lord Chancellor's Department compiles data on civil High Court proceedings in England and Wales, from the High Court's administrative records. Data cover the work of the three Divisions of the High Court - Chancery, Queen's Bench, and Family; the Companies Court, the Patents Court, the Admiralty Court, the Official Referees and the Restrictive Practices Court.

Data are available on the number of proceedings started, dealt with and outstanding, the outcome of cases, and enforcement proceedings. Results are supplemented by a regular sample survey of cases set down for trial in the Queen's Bench Division on the nature of claim, type of litigant, value of judgement and waiting times. Annual figures are available from 1975 and published in the summer of the following year.

Status: Ongoing
Collection Method: Administrative Records
Frequency: Continuously
Reference Period: Monthly, quarterly, annual and financial year
Timeliness: Published in summer of following year.
Earliest Available Data: Annual figures are available from 1975
National Coverage: England and Wales

Statistician
Sunita Gould
Court Service
Information Management and Analysis Group
(IMAGe)
Tel: 020 7210 1773

Products that contain data from this source
Judicial Statistics England and Wales Annual
Report; The Court Service Annual Report; The
Court Service Plan

Judicial Statistics - Northern Ireland
Northern Ireland Court Service

The Northern Ireland Court Service
compiles data on judicial statistics. Data are
collected weekly and monthly and have been
available since 1982, with slight
modifications in detail and coverage since
then. Results are published annually, about
six months after the end of the reference
period.

Status: Ongoing
Collection Method: Census
Frequency: Continuously
Reference Period: Annual
Timeliness: 7 months
Earliest Available Data: 1983
National Coverage: Northern Ireland
Sub-National: Court Divisions
Disaggregation: Court Venues

Statistician
Siobhan Morgan
Northern Ireland Court Service
Resource Management Branch
Tel: 028 9032 8594

Products that contain data from this source
Mortgage Statistics Northern Ireland (Press
Release); Northern Ireland Judicial Statistics

Magistrates' Courts - Northern Ireland
Northern Ireland Court Service

The Northern Ireland Court Service collect
data on Magistrates' Court statistics. Data
are available by business appearing before
the courts and business disposed of, case
outcomes and court sittings. Data are
available at Magistrates' Court venue level
(composite of district councils).

Status: Ongoing
Collection Method: Census
Frequency: Continuously
Reference Period: Quarter
Timeliness: 3 months
Earliest Available Data: 1983
National Coverage: Northern Ireland
Sub-National: Court Divisions
Disaggregation: Court Venues

Statistician
Siobhan Morgan
Northern Ireland Court Service
Resource Management Branch
Tel: 028 9032 8594

Products that contain data from this source
Northern Ireland Judicial Statistics

Magistrates' Courts Time Intervals Survey
Lord Chancellor's Department

Sample survey of time intervals in criminal
cases completed in magistrates' courts.
Geographical scope is England and Wales.
Smallest geographical units that results are
available by are Magistrates' Courts
Committee areas and clerkships. Sample
size is one week each February, June and
October; the first survey being in June 1985.
All surveys cover indictable offences
(including triable either way) while the June
survey also collects information on
summary cases. The information collected
includes date of offence, date of charge or
summons, date of first listing in magistrates'
courts and date of completion. These dates
allow average time intervals for the
following periods to be calculated: offence
to charge or summons, charge or summons
to first listing, first listing to completion, and
offence to completion. Results can be split
by Adult or Youth Court, charge or
summons, offence group, remand status, and
proceedings type, or combinations of these
where sample sizes support this. Numbers
of adjournments are also collected. Results
from the survey are published in Lord
Chancellor's Department Information
Bulletins 3 times a year. Results from the
survey are also used for constructing some
of the magistrates' courts management
information system indicators. The survey
has recently been enhanced to collect
additional information on young offenders,
including persistent young offenders.
Results from the enhanced survey will not
be available before the end of 1999.

Recording changes introduced at the start of
1993 and start of 1994 limited the cases
included in the sample to those with an offence
to charge or summons time of less than 10
years and charge or summons to first listing,
and first listing to completion times of no more
than 1 year. More details are available in the
Information Bulletins on the survey published
by the Lord Chancellor's Department.

Status: Ongoing
Collection Method: Administrative Records
Frequency: Periodic

Reference Period: One week each February,
June and October
Timeliness: Generally 4-5 months
Earliest Available Data: June 1985
National Coverage: England and Wales
Disaggregation: Magistrates' Courts
Committee area; Crown Prosecution Service
area; Police Force area; Region; Magistrates'
Courts clerkship

Statistician
Peter Lumb
Lord Chancellor's Department
Information Management Unit; Statistics Branch
Tel: 020 7210 8602;
Email: plumb@lcdhq.gsi.gov.uk

Products that contain data from this source
Time Intervals for Criminal Proceedings in
Magistrates' Courts

Proceedings and Sentencing in Magistrates' Courts - England and Wales
Home Office

The Home Office compiles data on criminal
court proceedings at magistrates' courts.
Data cover prosecutions, convictions and
types of sentence passed and are available
by age, sex and detailed offence
classification. Data cover England and
Wales and are available by police force area,
commission of the peace area and petty
sessional division. The series dates back to
1893 and is published annually. Provisional
estimates up to and including 1997 were
issued in the following summer, usually
July, however the main form of publication
is usually available in early November.

Status: Ongoing
Collection Method: Administrative Records
Frequency: Continuously
Reference Period: The quarters ending March,
June, September and December
Timeliness: Data are usually published in
November of the following year.
For example figures for magistrates' courts
proceedings and sentencing in 1997 were
published, in detail, in November 1998.
Earliest Available Data: 1893
National Coverage: England and Wales
Disaggregation: Police force area, commission
of the police area and petty sessional division

Statistician
John Frosztega
Home Office
Crime and Criminal Justice Unit; Prosecutions,
sentencing and appeals section
Tel: 020 8760 8283

Products that contain data from this source
Cautions, Court Proceedings and Sentencing
England and Wales; Criminal statistics England
and Wales; Probation Statistics England and
Wales; Home Office Courts Appearance System
(HOCAS); Social Trends

Proceedings and Sentencing in the Crown Court - England and Wales
Home Office

The Home Office compiles data on criminal court proceedings at the Crown Court. Data cover prosecutions, convictions and types of sentence passed and are available by age, sex and detailed offence classification. Data cover England and Wales and are available by police force area, Crown Court circuit and Crown Court centre. The series dates back to 1893 and is published annually. Provisional estimates up to and including 1997 were issued in the following summer, usually July, however the main format of the publication is usually available in early November.

Status: Ongoing
Collection Method: Administrative Records
Frequency: Continuously
Reference Period: Calendar year
Timeliness: Data are usually published in the November of the following year. For example 1997 figures were published, in detail, in November 1998.
Earliest Available Data: 1893
National Coverage: England and Wales
Disaggregation: Police force area, Crown Court circuit and Crown Court centre

Statistician
John Frosztega
Home Office
Crime and Criminal Justice Unit; Prosecutions, sentencing and appeals section
Tel: 020 8760 8283

Products that contain data from this source
Cautions, Court Proceedings and Sentencing England and Wales; Criminal statistics England and Wales; Probation Statistics England and Wales; Home Office Courts Appearance System (HOCAS); Social Trends

Remand Statistics - England and Wales
Home Office

Annual census of administrative records showing police and court remand/bail decisions on those cases which reach criminal court. Data collected from all police force areas in England and Wales.

Status: Ongoing
Collection Method: Administrative Records
Frequency: Continuously
Reference Period: Calendar year
Timeliness: provisional data published 7 months after end of calendar year. Final data published 11 months after end of calendar year.
Earliest Available Data: 1978
National Coverage: England and Wales
Disaggregation: Police force area, court area

Statistician
Jennifer Airs
Home Office
Research and Statistics Directorate; Crime and Criminal Justice Unit
Tel: 020 7273 2809

Products that contain data from this source
Criminal statistics England and Wales (Chapter 8) Prison statistics England and Wales (Table 2.6)

See also:
In this chapter:
Community Service - Scotland (8.9)

8.3 Crime and Justice - General

Police Manpower
Home Office

The Home Office collects data twice yearly (31 March and 30 September) on the number of police officers and civilian staff employed in each of the 43 police force areas in England and Wales. Data on officers is collected by gender, rank and ethnicity. Data on civilian staff is collected by gender and ethnicity. The number of staff joining and leaving each force over the previous six months is collected. Data collected by the Research, Development and Statistics Directorate of the Home Office since 1995, prior to which the Police Policy Directorate had responsibility.

Status: Ongoing
Collection Method: Administrative Records
Frequency: Bi-annually
Reference Period: 31 March and 30 September each year
Timeliness: around 6 months - March figures published annually
Earliest Available Data: 1921
National Coverage: England and Wales
Sub-National: Full
Disaggregation: Police force area

Statistician
David Povey
Home Office
Crime and Criminal Justice Unit
Tel: 020 7273 2711

Products that contain data from this source
Police Service Personnel, England and Wales, Annual Abstract of Statistics, Regional Trends, Social Trends, Focus on London, Digest of Welsh Statistics

8.4 Crimes and Offences (other than Terrorism)

Homicide in Scotland
Scottish Executive

The Scottish Executive Home Department conducts a survey on the homicides recorded by each police force and the outcome of any criminal proceedings. Data are available by age and sex of victim, age and sex of accused, relationship of accused to victim, location of homicide, method of killing by sex of victim, motive for killing each victim, employment status of victim, employment status of accused. Data cover Scotland and are available at police force area level and local authority area. The survey commenced in its current format in 1978. It is carried out annually and the results are published every other year by way of bulletin with a news release in alternate years. Figures are made available within ten months following the calendar year end.

Status: Ongoing
Collection Method: Census
Frequency: Annually
Reference Period: Calendar year
Timeliness: About 10 months after collection
Earliest Available Data: 1978
National Coverage: Scotland
Disaggregation: Police force area

Statistician
Sandy Taylor
Scottish Executive
Criminal Justice Division; Civil and Criminal Justice Statistics 1
Tel: 0131 244 2224;
Email: sandy.taylor@scotland.gov.uk

Products that contain data from this source
Homicide in Scotland; Scottish Abstract of Statistics

Motor Vehicle Offences in Scotland
Scottish Executive

The Scottish Executive Home Department conducts several surveys relating to motor vehicle offences in Scotland. The surveys relate to Police Conditional Offers of fixed penalties, Vehicle Defect Rectification Scheme (VDRS) notices and Procurator Fiscal Conditional Offers of fixed penalties. Data cover Scotland. All three surveys are carried out quarterly and the main results are published around one year after the calendar year end.

Status: Ongoing
Collection Method: Census
Frequency: Quarterly
Reference Period: Calendar year
Timeliness: About 12 months after collection
Earliest Available Data: 1993
National Coverage: Scotland
Disaggregation: Police force area

Statistician
Sandy Taylor
Scottish Executive
Criminal Justice Division; Civil and Criminal Justice
Statistics 1
Tel: 0131 244 2224;
Email: sandy.taylor@scotland.gov.uk

Products that contain data from this source
Motor Vehicle Offences in Scotland; Scottish
Abstract of Statistics

Notifiable Offences - England and Wales
Home Office

The Home Office collects data on the number of Notifiable Offences recorded by each of the 43 police force areas in England and Wales. The statistics provide a measure of the amount of crime with which the police are faced. Broadly the offences include all indictable and triable either way offences, together with a few closely linked summary offences. Data on offences which are detected (or "cleared up") are also collected. Police forces return data quarterly, and data are published half-yearly.

Data collected since 1857. On 1 April 1998 the Home Office issued new guidance rules for classifying and counting notifiable offences to the police. From that date the statistics wherever possible measure one crime per victim. Many of the more serious offences, such as violence against the person and sexual offences have always been counted in that way. However, the fraud, theft and criminal damage categories have not.

Status: Ongoing
Collection Method: Administrative Records
Frequency: Quarterly
Reference Period: Quarters ending March, June, September and December.
Timeliness: up to 6 months - published bi-annually, now for years ending March and September
Earliest Available Data: 1857
National Coverage: England and Wales
Sub-National: Full
Disaggregation: Police Force Area

Statistician
David Povey
Home Office
Crime and Criminal Justice Unit
Tel: 020 7273 2711

Products that contain data from this source
Criminal Statistics England and Wales; Notifiable Offences England and Wales; Annual Abstract of Statistics; Regional Trends; Social Trends; Monthly Digest of Statistics, Key Data; UK in Figures; Digest of Welsh Statistics; Focus on London, Focus on South West; Focus on the East Midlands

Offences Involving Firearms - Scotland
Scottish Executive

The Scottish Executive Home Department conducts a survey on recorded crimes and offences involving firearms from all eight Scottish police forces. Data cover Scotland and are available at police force area and local authority area levels. Data are available on the number of firearms offences, types of firearms used, location of use, etc. The survey is carried out quarterly and the main results are published in the September following the calendar year end.

Status: Ongoing
Collection Method: Census
Frequency: Quarterly
Reference Period: 12 months
Timeliness: About 8-10 months after the end of calendar year
Earliest Available Data: 1978
National Coverage: Scotland
Disaggregation: local authority area

Statistician
Katy Barratt
Scottish Executive
Criminal Justice; Civil & Criminal Justice Statistics
Unit - Branch 2
Tel: 0131 244 2226;
Email: katy.barratt@scotland.gov.uk

Products that contain data from this source
Recorded Crimes and Offences Involving Firearms, Scotland; Regional Trends; Scottish Abstract of Statistics; Social Trends

See also:
In this chapter:
Community Attitudes Survey - Northern Ireland (8.1)
Crown Courts - England & Wales (8.2)
Firearm Certificates - Scotland (8.6)
Proceedings and Sentencing in Magistrates' Courts - England and Wales (8.2)
Proceedings and Sentencing in the Crown Court - England and Wales (8.2)

In other chapters:
Violence Against School Staff (see the Education and Training chapter)

Drug Offenders - UK
Home Office

The Home Office compiles data on drugs and criminal justice. The statistics of drugs offenders are based on returns received directly from HM Customs and the police in Scotland and Northern Ireland, and indirectly (as a subset of the court output and cautioning data collected by CCJU with regard to England and Wales). Data include details of offenders by age, sex, offence, drug involved, police force area, disposal and sentence. Data cover the United Kingdom and are available by police force area.

Data are collected monthly from police forces, and annually (spring) from HM Customs. All data are referenced to a calendar year, and are published in the following autumn or thereabouts.

Status: Ongoing
Collection Method: Administrative Records
Frequency: Monthly
Reference Period: Calendar year
Timeliness: Following autumn after calendar year
Earliest Available Data: 1967 (published 1968)
National Coverage: United Kingdom
Disaggregation: Police force area for police data only; Customs just UK.

Statistician
John Corkery
Home Office
CCJU; RDS
Tel: 020 7273 3266

Products that contain data from this source
Annual Abstract of Statistics; Digest of Welsh Local Area Statistics; Regional Trends; Social Trends

Mentally Disordered Offenders - England and Wales
Home Office

The Home Office compiles data on mentally disordered offenders held under restriction orders in hospital. Data are available by type of hospital, offences, sex, type of mental disorder and type of legal category. Movements into and out of hospital, together with the population in hospital at calendar year end, are published. Data cover England and Wales. They are published about a year after the calendar year to which they relate.

Status: Ongoing
Collection Method: Administrative Records
Frequency: Annually
Reference Period: Calendar year
Timeliness: 9 months in arrears
Earliest Available Data: 1973
National Coverage: England and Wales
Disaggregation: Health trusts in England and Wales; Hospital

Statistician
Dr Chris Kershaw
Home Office
Offenders and Corrections Unit (OCU);
Research and Statistics Directorate (RSD)
Tel: 020 7273 3177;
Email: chris.kershaw@rpu.hmg.ho.gov.uk

Products that contain data from this source
Statistics of mentally disordered offenders in England and Wales 1997

Offenders Index Database
Home Office

The Offenders Index database holds details on over 6 million offenders. The index holds details of all convictions for standard list offences since 1963. Source data for the Index comes from Court Appearance data taken from Home Office records and extra information on CRO number and ethnicity is added from the PNC. The data is used to produce regular information on reconviction rates for offenders who have served different types of sentence, for example, custodial sentence or community penalty. Data from the Index is used in the publications of the unit (see products).

Status: Ongoing
Collection Method: Administrative Records
Frequency: Quarterly
Reference Period: Quarters
Timeliness: 9 months to 1 year
Earliest Available Data: 1963
National Coverage: England and Wales
Sub-National: Courts in England and Wales
Disaggregation: Court or Police Force

Statistician
Dr Chris Kershaw
Home Office
Offenders and Corrections Unit (OCU);
Research and Statistics Directorate (RSD)
Tel: 020 7273 3177;
Email: chris.kershaw@homeoffice.gsi.gov.uk

Products that contain data from this source
Criminal careers of those born between 1953 and 1973

See also:
In this chapter:
Cautions by the Police - England and Wales (8.7)
Proceedings and Sentencing in Magistrates' Courts - England and Wales (8.2)
Proceedings and Sentencing in the Crown Court - England and Wales (8.2)

8.6 Firearms registration

Firearm Certificates - Scotland
Scottish Executive

The Scottish Executive Home Department conducts a survey on the issue of firearm and shotgun certificates under the Firearms Acts 1968 from the eight Scottish police forces. Data are available on the number of applications, renewals, cancellations, revocations of firearms and shotgun certificates issued, the number of registered firearms dealers, and with effect from 1994 the number of visitors' firearm/shotgun permits and European firearms passes and Article 7 authorities issued.

Status: Ongoing
Collection Method: Census
Frequency: Annually
Reference Period: 12 months
Timeliness: About 6-9 months after end of calendar year.
Earliest Available Data: 1980
National Coverage: Scotland
Disaggregation: Police force area

Statistician
Katy Barratt
Scottish Executive
Criminal Justice; Civil & Criminal Justice Statistics Unit - Branch 2
Tel: 0131 244 2226;
Email: katy.barratt@scotland.gov.uk

Products that contain data from this source
Firearm Certificates Statistics ,Scotland

8.7 Policing and Crime Prevention

Cautions by the Police - England and Wales
Home Office

The statistics cover formal police cautions given by, or on the instructions of, a senior police officer. They exclude informal warnings and other informal action, written warnings or cautions issued for motoring offences and warnings or cautions given by non-police bodies, e.g. a department store in the case of shoplifting. Data cover England and Wales and are available by age, sex, ethnicity, offence and police force area.

Status: Ongoing
Collection Method: Administrative Records
Frequency: Continuously
Reference Period: The quarters ending March, June, September, December
Timeliness: Data are usually published annually in November of the following year. For example 1997 figures were published, in detail, in November 1998.
Earliest Available Data: 1959

National Coverage: England and Wales
Disaggregation: Police force area

Statistician
John Frosztega
Home Office
Crime and Criminal Justice Unit; Prosecutions, sentencing and appeals section
Tel: 020 8760 8283

Products that contain data from this source
Cautions, Court Proceedings and Sentencing England and Wales; Criminal statistics England and Wales; Home Office Courts Appearance System (HOCAS)

Notifiable Offences - Northern Ireland
Royal Ulster Constabulary

The Royal Ulster Constabulary compiles crime statistics from details of crimes reported to police which are classed as 'notifiable' under the Home Office's counting rules. Some data on crime are available by number of specific crimes recorded and detected within each of nine classes of crime.

Data cover Northern Ireland and can be obtained at police force area, police region, police division, and police sub-division levels. Statistics on recorded crime are also available for police station areas. At a Northern Ireland level data on recorded crime are available from 1969 onwards. A consistent series of sub-divisional analyses for crime statistics began in 1987. Data are collected continuously and published annually, three months in arrears.

Status: Ongoing
Collection Method: Administrative source
Frequency: Daily
Reference Period: Financial year
Timeliness: 3 months from end of financial year
Earliest Available Data: 1969
National Coverage: Northern Ireland
Sub-National: Full
Disaggregation: Police station area

Statistician
Force Statistician
Central Statistics Unit
RUC Lisnassharragh
42 Montgomery Road
Belfast BT6 9LD
Tel: 028 9065 0222;
Fax: 028 9070 0998

Products that contain data from this source
Northern Ireland Annual Abstract of Statistics; Regional Trends; Royal Ulster Constabulary Chief Constable's Annual Report; Social Trends

Recorded Crime - Scotland
Scottish Executive

The Scottish Executive Home Department conducts a survey on recorded crimes made known and cleared-up. Prior to 1995, information was collected monthly on recorded crimes made known and annually on recorded crimes made known and cleared-up. Information is now collected on a quarterly basis. The main results are published in the April following the calendar year end. In 1994 and 1995 aggregate level information was published in February via a news release, in advance of the main publication in April. There was a break in 1976 due to local government reorganisation.

Status: Ongoing
Collection Method: Census
Frequency: Quarterly
Reference Period: 12 months
Timeliness: About 4-5 months after the end of Calendar year on detailed basis.
Earliest Available Data: From 1971 is readily accessible. Data available for years prior to this in hard-copy.
National Coverage: Scotland
Disaggregation: Local Authority Area; Police Force Area

Statistician
Katy Barratt
Scottish Executive
Criminal Justice; Civil & Criminal Justice Statistics Unit - Branch 2
Tel: 0131 244 2226;
Email: katy.barratt@scotland.gov.uk

Products that contain data from this source
Recorded Crime in Scotland; Regional Trends; Scottish Abstract of Statistics; Social Trends

Seizures of Controlled Drugs - UK
Home Office

The Home Office compiles statistics of seizures of controlled drugs based on returns from the police and HM Customs and Excise. The data are used by the Home Office, the police and other bodies to develop policy on drug misuse, and monitor trends in availability and prevalence of illicit supplies of controlled drugs. The police data cover the United Kingdom and are available by police force area, Customs data is not disaggregated. Data are collected monthly from police forces, and annually (spring) from HM Customs. All data are referenced to a calendar year, and are published annually every autumn.

Status: Ongoing
Collection Method: Administrative Records
Frequency: Monthly
Reference Period: Calendar year
Timeliness: Autumn following year the data refer to.
Earliest Available Data: 1967 (published 1968)

National Coverage: United Kingdom
Disaggregation: Police force area only for police seizures.

Statistician
John Corkery
Home Office
CCJU; RDS
Tel: 020 7273 3266

Products that contain data from this source
Annual Abstract of Statistics; Regional Trends; Social Trends; Digest of Welsh Statistics

See also:
In this chapter:
Notifiable Offences - England and Wales (8.4)
Police Manpower (8.3)

8.8 Prisons, Prisoners and Parole

Parole - England and Wales
Home Office

The Home Office compiles data on considerations and recommendations for the early release of prisoners on parole. Data are available by numbers considered and recommended for parole and rate of recommendation, by length of sentence, by offence type and by length of parole licence granted. Data are collected weekly and published annually.

Frequency: Annual
Earliest Available Data: April 1968
National Coverage: England & Wales

Statistician
Mike Lock
Home Office
Tel: 020 7217 5210

Prison Breaches - Scotland
Scottish Executive

The Scottish Executive Home Department obtains data from administrative sources on the number of breaches of discipline and punishments awarded in the 23 Scottish penal establishments. Data are available by establishment and sex. The data cover Scotland and are available at penal establishment level.

The collection was revised in November 1994 following legislative changes introduced in The Prisons and Young Offenders Institutions (Scotland) Rules 1994. However, prior to this time, similar information was collected for breaches of discipline and punishments awarded under the old rules.

Collection Method: Census
Frequency: Continuously
Reference Period: 12 months, April-March
Timeliness: About 3-4 months after end of financial year
National Coverage: Scotland

Statistician
Katy Barratt
Scottish Executive
Criminal Justice; Civil & Criminal Justice Statistics Unit - Branch 2
Tel: 0131 244 2226;
Email: katy.barratt@scotland.gov.uk

Products that contain data from this source
The Scottish Prison Service Annual Report,

Prison Discipline - England and Wales
Home Office

The Home Office compiles data on offences by prisoners against prison rules and the punishments given. Data are available by type of establishment, sex, type of punishment and are available as rate of offending per 100 prison population. Summary figures have been published since 1952 under the Prison Act, 1952; earlier years under the Prisons Act, 1877. Data are published about eight months after the end of the calendar year and are available since the 1980s.

Frequency: Monthly
Timeliness: Eight months after the end of the calendar year
Earliest Available Data: 1952
National Coverage: England & Wales

Statistician
Mike Lock
Home Office
Tel: 020 7217 5210

Products that contain data from this source
Statistics of Offences Against Prison Discipline and Punishment, England and Wales

Prison Population - England and Wales
Home Office

The Home Office compiles data on the prison population. There are three datasets: prison population, initial receptions into prison and final discharges. These are available by status of prisoner e.g. remand/sentence and by sentence length, offence, ethnic origin, sex, age group. Seasonally adjusted figures are produced. Data cover England and Wales and the prison population is available by prison establishment. Prison population data have been compiled since the last century. Detailed data on the current basis are available since the 1980s.

Earliest Available Data: Detailed data on the current basis are available since the 1980s
National Coverage: England and Wales

Statistician
Philip White
Home Office
Tel: 020 7217 5073

Products that contain data from this source
Prison Statistics England and Wales

Prison Receptions - England & Wales
Home Office

Statistician
Philip White
Home Office
Tel: 020 7217 5073

Prison Receptions - Scotland
Scottish Executive

The Scottish Executive Home Department obtains data from administrative sources on the number of receptions of remand, sentenced and civil prisoners and the number of children held on an unruly certificate to the 23 Scottish penal establishments. Data are available by establishment, age, sex, type of sentence, crime/offence classification and length of sentence. Data cover Scotland and are available at penal establishment level.

Data on remand receptions were historically collected on a monthly basis, and twice a year on civil receptions. Data on sentenced receptions and children held on unruly certificates were collected monthly at a disaggregated level. The information is now received electronically from the Prisoner Records System. The main results are published in the December following the calendar year end.

Status: Ongoing
Collection Method: Census
Frequency: Continuously
Reference Period: 12 months
Timeliness: About 9-12 months after end of calendar year
Earliest Available Data: From 1976 is readily accessible. Data available for years prior to this in hardcopy.
National Coverage: Scotland
Disaggregation: Establishment level

Statistician
Katy Barratt
The Scottish Executive
Criminal Justice; Civil & Criminal Justice Statistics Unit - Branch 2
Tel: 0131 244 2226;
Email: katy.barratt@scotland.gov.uk

Products that contain data from this source
Prison Statistics Scotland; Regional Trends; Scottish Abstract of Statistics; Social Trends; the Scottish Prison Service Annual Report,

Prison Statistics
Scottish Executive

The Scottish Executive Home Department obtains data from administrative sources giving the average daily prison population within and receptions to Scottish penal establishments.

Status: Ongoing
Collection Method: Administrative records
Frequency: Daily
Reference Period: 12 months
Timeliness: Dependant on data.
Earliest Available Data: 1976 (readily accessible)
National Coverage: Scotland
Disaggregation: Establishment level

Statistician
Katy Barratt
Scottish Executive
Criminal Justice; Civil & Criminal Justice Statistics Unit - Branch 2
Tel: 0131 244 2226;
Email: katy.barratt@scotland.gov.uk

Products that contain data from this source
Prison Statistics Scotland; Regional Trends; Scottish Abstract of Statistics; Social Trends; the Scottish Prison Service Annual Report,

8.9 Probation and Community Service

(The) Children's Hearing System Survey - Scotland
Scottish Childrens' Reporter Administration

The Scottish Executive Home Department conduct two surveys on The Children's Hearings System. The Children's Hearings System Survey has collected data continuously since 1975 on children and their reasons for referral to Reporter to the Children's Panel, and on decisions of hearings. Results are published annually.

Frequency: Annually
National Coverage: Scotland

Statistician
Iain Montgomery
Scottish Childrens' Reporter Administration
Tel: 01786 459530

Products that contain data from this source
Referrals of Children to Reporters and Children's Hearings 1993

Community Service (SWS FORM CS1 & CS2)
Scottish Executive

These event based forms give details of referrals for Community Service right through to completion of the hours of service where appropriate. Personal details of offender are given (including relating to previous court appearances) along with details of the relevant court case and sentencing. The referral and termination forms (CS1 and CS2) are linked, where appropriate, by reference number. The CS1 form is being phased out and superseded by the SER1 form. Arrangements made to receive data by computer disk or paper return.

Status: Ongoing
Collection Method: Census
Frequency: Event based unit returned
Timeliness: Information Note produced within 12 months of receipt of data. Provisional tables for use internally, within a few months of receipt of data.
Earliest Available Data: 1980
National Coverage: Scotland
Disaggregation: Council Area (Scot)

Statistician
Jeanie Whyle
Scottish Executive
Social Work Statistics
Tel: 0131 244 5432;
Email: jeanie.whyle@scotland.gov.uk

Products that contain data from this source
Information on Criminal Justice Social Work Services 1993-1997

Community Service - Scotland
Scottish Executive

The Scottish Executive Justice Department conducts Community Service surveys. Data are available on referred offender's personal details, with results of their court appearances and court attended, personal details, reviews/breaches of Probation Order. Data have been collected continuously since 1980 and results are published annually.

Status: Ongoing
Frequency: Annually
Earliest Available Data: Data have been collected continuously since 1980
National Coverage: Scotland

Statistician
Jeanie Whyle
Scottish Executive
Social Work Statistics
Tel: 0131 244 5432;
Email: jeanie.whyle@scotland.gov.uk

Products that contain data from this source
Community Service by Offenders - Scotland

Individual Returns for Reporters, Deputies and Assistants - Scotland
Scottish Childrens' Reporter Administration

The Scottish Executive Home Department conduct two surveys on The Children's Hearings System. Individual returns for Reporters, Deputies and Assistants are collected concerning number of Reporters' staff by region (annually), personal qualifications and job history (every four years). The surveys have been carried out for five years and results are available on request.

Frequency: Annually (by region)
Earliest Available Data: 1994
National Coverage: Scotland

Statistician
Iain Montgomery
Scottish Childrens' Reporter Administration
Tel: 01786 459530

Products that contain data from this source
Referrals of Children to Reporters and Children's Hearings 1993

Offender Services (SWS FORM OA1, OC2 & OP2)
Scottish Executive

These event-based forms cover, in one system, Community Service, Social Enquiry Reports and Probation Terminations. The OA1, OC2 and OP2 forms will thus progressively replace the SER1, CS1, CS2 and SWSP forms. The OA1 gives full details of offender assessments; the OC2 gives community service termination details.

Status: Ongoing
Collection Method: Census
Frequency: Event based unit return
Timeliness: Information note provided within 12 months of receipt of data.
National Coverage: Scotland
Disaggregation: Council Area (Scot)

Statistician
Jeanie Whyle
Scottish Executive
Social Work Statistics
Tel: 0131 244 5432;
Email: jeanie.whyle@scotland.gov.uk

Products that contain data from this source
Information on Criminal Justice Social Work Services 1993-1997

Probation Return (SWS FORM SWSP)
Scottish Executive

These event-based forms give comprehensive information on the Probation process.

Status: Ongoing
Collection Method: Census
Frequency: Event based unit return
National Coverage: Scotland
Disaggregation: Council Area (Scot)

Statistician
Jeanie Whyle
Scottish Executive
Social Work Statistics
Tel: 0131 244 5432;
Email: jeanie.whyle@scotland.gov.uk

Probation Statistics
Home Office

Workload of the Probation Service in England and Wales, published each calendar year. Full coverage by probation area and quarter. Based on administrative data systems of probation areas which have changed over time.

Status: Ongoing
Collection Method: Full coverage of orders and supervisions starting and finishing.
Frequency: Annually
Reference Period: Mainly calendar year with occasional financial year (to March 31)
Timeliness: Estimated results available within four months of end of quarter. Full annual publication available within ten months of end of year.
Earliest Available Data: 1973
National Coverage: England and Wales
Disaggregation: Probation Areas

Statistician
Peter Sheriff
Home Office
Tel: 020 7273 2526

Products that contain data from this source
Probation Statistics England and Wales; Social Trends; Regional Trends; Focus on London

Social Enquiry Reports (SWS FORM SER1)
Scottish Executive

These event-based forms give comprehensive information on the Social Enquiry Report process. Where the sentence is Community Service or Probation, the form will be linked by reference number to a CS2 (Community Service Termination) form or SWSP (Probation Termination) form. The SER1 form will soon remove the need for CS1 forms to be completed. A number of councils use form SER1(s), a variant of the SER1 form. Arrangements made to receive data by computer disk or paper form.

Status: Ongoing
Collection Method: Census
Frequency: Event based unit return
Timeliness: Information note produced within 12 months of receipt of data
National Coverage: Scotland
Disaggregation: Council Area (Scot)

Statistician
Jeanie Whyle
Scottish Executive
Social Work Statistics
Tel: 0131 244 5432;
Email: jeanie.whyle@scotland.gov.uk

Products that contain data from this source
Information on Criminal Justice Social Work Services 1993-1997

See also:
In this chapter:
Proceedings and Sentencing in Magistrates' Courts - England and Wales (8.2)
Proceedings and Sentencing in the Crown Court - England and Wales (8.2)

8.10 Terrorism

Prevention of Terrorism - GB
Home Office

The Home Office compiles data from police forces submissions on individual returns of detentions and examinations of more than one hour of suspected terrorists. Analysis is by police force, detentions, extension of detention, exclusion orders made, where persons removed to, charges under the Acts and other criminal offences, length of detention and length of examination. Data cover Great Britain and are available by police force area. Publication of the data has occurred since 1979. Data are collected on individual returns following a detention or examination under the Act, and are published annually within two months of the end of the calendar year (was quarterly prior to 1993).

Status: Ongoing
Frequency: Monthly
Timeliness: Within two months of the end of the calendar year
Earliest Available Data: Publication of the data began in 1979
National Coverage: Great Britain

Statistician
Prevention of Terrorism Information Line
Home Office
Crime and Criminal Justice Unit
Tel: 020 7273 4126

Terrorist Crime - Northern Ireland
Royal Ulster Constabulary

The Royal Ulster Constabulary compiles Northern Ireland security situation statistics. Data are available on deaths and injuries by year and victim type (e.g. army, civilian); terrorist incidents (shootings, bombs and incendiaries) by year; firearms and explosives finds by year, and persons charged with terrorist offences by year. Data cover Northern Ireland and are available at police force area, police region, police division, and police sub-division levels.

Statistics on deaths and injuries due to the security situation, terrorist incidents, and firearms and explosives finds are available at the Northern Ireland level from 1969 onwards. Data on arrests and charges are available from 1972. Data on paramilitary-style shootings and assaults have been collated from 1973 and 1982, respectively.

A consistent series at current levels of detail and down to sub-divisional level is available from 1990 onwards. Statistics are published annually.

Status: Ongoing
Collection Method: Administrative source
Frequency: Daily
Reference Period: Financial year
Timeliness: 3 months from end of financial year
Earliest Available Data: 1969
National Coverage: Northern Ireland
Sub-National: Full
Disaggregation: Police sub-division

Statistician
Force Statistician
Central Statistics Unit
RUC Lisnassharragh
42 Montgomery Road
Belfast BT6 9LD
Tel: 028 9065 0222;
Fax: 028 9070 0998

Products that contain data from this source
Northern Ireland Annual Abstract of Statistics; Royal Ulster Constabulary Chief Constable's Annual Report; Social Trends

---

Crime and Justice - *Products*

8.11 Abstracts, Compendia, A-Z Catalogues, Directories and Reference Material

A Commentary on Northern Ireland Crime Statistics, 1997
Northern Ireland Office

An annual publication which provides statistics on notifiable offences recorded by the police, offences cleared by the police, court proceedings, sentencing and prison population.

Delivery: Periodic Release
Frequency: Annually
Price: £11.80
ISBN: 0 337 03105 3

Available from
TSO Publications Centre and Bookshops
Please see Annex B for full address details.

Cautions, Court Proceedings and Sentencing England and Wales
Home Office

This is an annual Statistical Bulletin produced by the Research, Development and Statistics Directorate of the Home Office. Its purpose is to provide a summary of the main trends in police cautioning and criminal court proceedings during the previous calendar year prior to publishing. More detailed information is published in the command paper "Criminal statistics, England and Wales" usually in November. The 1997 edition contains 32 pages of text, tables and charts on the following: Offenders cautioned or proceeded against, the latter by type of court; Offenders found guilty and sentenced by type of court; Sentencing by type of disposal; and Proportionate use of custodial sentences and average sentence lengths. In addition to helping formulate Home Office policy the target markets for this publication are magistrates' courts, the Crown Court, other criminal justice agencies, others involved in work concerning the criminal justice system and academia.

Delivery: First Release
Frequency: Annually
Price: Free
ISSN: 0143-6384

Available from
Information and Publications Group
Please see Annex B for full address details.

Sources from which data for this product are obtained
Cautions by the Police - England and Wales; Proceedings and Sentencing in Magistrates' Courts - England and Wales; Proceedings and Sentencing in the Crown Court - England and Wales

Criminal Statistics England and Wales
Home Office

Criminal statistics is an annual command paper usually published in November. Its purpose is to provide statistics on criminal offences recorded by the 43 police forces in England and Wales, and on offenders dealt with by formal police cautions or criminal court proceedings during the previous calendar year. More detailed annual figures are published separately, in four volumes of supplementary tables.

As in previous years, the 1997 volume (268 pages) comprises a commentary, charts and tables covering Notifiable offences recorded by the police; Notifiable offences recorded by the police in which firearms were reported to have been used or stolen; Homicide; Offenders cautioned or found guilty; Court Proceedings; Sentencing; Use of police bail and court remand; Criminal history studies based on the Offenders Index; and International comparisons.

Delivery: Periodic Release
Frequency: Annually
Price: £22.40
ISBN: 010 141622 9

Available from
TSO Publications Centre and Bookshops
Please see Annex B for full address details.

Sources from which data for this product are obtained
Cautions by the Police - England and Wales; Notifiable Offences - England and Wales; Proceedings and Sentencing in Magistrates' Courts - England and Wales; Proceedings and Sentencing in the Crown Court - England and Wales

Digest of Information on the Northern Ireland Criminal Justice System 1992
Northern Ireland Office

Frequency: Periodic
Price: £15.80 (third edition)
ISBN: 0 337 03101 0

Available from
TSO Publications Centre and Bookshops
Please see Annex B for full address details.

Sources from which data for this product are obtained
A commentary on Northern Ireland Crime Statistics, RUC Chief Constable's Annual Reports, Northern Ireland Judicial Statistics, Northern Ireland Prison Service Annual Report

Offenders Index: A User's Guide
Home Office

Detailed instruction on use of the Offenders Index including guidance on interpretation of Index data and a description of the Index.

Delivery: Periodic Release
Frequency: Bi-annually
Price: Free

Available from
Offenders and Correction Unit
Home Office
Please see Annex B for full address details

Offenders Index: Codebook
Home Office: Offenders and Corrections Unit

Demonstrates how to read the code of the Offenders Index, and analyse output.

Delivery: Periodic Release
Frequency: Bi-annually
Price: Free

Available from
Offenders and Correction Unit
Home Office
Please see Annex B for full address details

Royal Ulster Constabulary Chief Constable's Annual Report
Royal Ulster Constabulary

Commentary, graphs and detailed tables of recorded crime, detections, court results and the Northern Ireland security situation. Additional tables for PACE, drugs, and vehicles taken or hijacked.

Contains data on: notifiable offences known and cleared, at Northern Ireland and by police division level; PACE statistics: persons and vehicles searched; vehicles taken or hijacked, by police division; and drug seizures and arrests. Also contains data on: deaths and injuries due to the security situation, 1969 onwards; number of terrorist incidents, 1969 onwards; firearms and explosives finds, 1969 onwards; the number of persons charged with terrorist offences, 1972 onwards; paramilitary-style attacks; complaints statistics.

Delivery: Periodic Release
Frequency: Annual
Price: Free

Available from
Central Statistics Unit
RUC Lisnassharragh
42 Montgomery Road
Belfast BT6 9LD
Tel: 028 9065 0222; Fax: 028 9070 0998

Sources from which data for this product are obtained
Notifiable Offences - Northern Ireland; Terrorist Crime - Northern Ireland

See also:
In this chapter:
Criminal Appeals England and Wales (8.13)
Home Office Courts Appearance System (HOCAS) (8.13)

8.12 Attitudes to, and experience of, Crime, Justice and the Police

(The) British Crime Survey 1996 - England and Wales
Home Office

Data showing the incidence of crime in England and Wales in 1995 and trends since 1981. Data on respondents' concern about crime.

Delivery: First Release
Frequency: Periodic
Price: Free
ISSN: 0143 6384

Available from
Information and Publications Group
Please see Annex B for full address details.

Sources from which data for this product are obtained
British Crime Survey - England and Wales

(The) British Crime Survey 1998 - England and Wales
Home Office

Data showing the incidence of crime in England and Wales in 1997 and trends since 1981. Data on how risks of victimisation vary for different groups.

Delivery: First Release
Frequency: Periodic
Price: Free
ISSN: 0143-6384

Available from
Information and Publications Group
Please see Annex B for full address details.

Sources from which data for this product are obtained
British Crime Survey - England and Wales

Community Attitudes Survey: The Sixth Report 1999 (April)
Northern Ireland Statistics and Research Agency

Tabular information on community attitudes in Northern Ireland. Contains a tabular presentation of a selection of main findings from each of the sections covered in the Community Attitudes Survey.

Delivery: Hardcopy publication
Frequency: Annual
Price: £6.00
ISBN: 1 - 899203 28 1

Available from
Central Survey Unit
Tel: 028 9025 2517

Sources from which data for this product are obtained
Community Attitudes Survey - Northern Ireland

Community Attitudes Survey: The Fifth Report 1998 (September)
Northern Ireland Statistics and Research Agency

Tabular information on community attitudes in Northern Ireland. Contains a tabular presentation of a selection of main findings from each of the sections covered in the Community Attitudes Survey.

Delivery: Hardcopy publication
Frequency: Annual
Price: £6.00
ISBN: 1 - 899203 - 25 5

Available from
Central Survey Unit
Tel: 028 9025 2517

Sources from which data for this product are obtained
Community Attitudes Survey - Northern Ireland

Community Attitudes Survey: The Fourth Report 1997 (June)
Northern Ireland Statistics and Research Agency

Tabular information on community attitudes in Northern Ireland. Contains a tabular presentation of a selection of main findings from each of the sections covered in the Community Attitudes Survey.

Delivery: Hardcopy publication
Frequency: Annual
Price: £6.00
ISBN: 1 899203 06 1

Available from
Central Survey Unit
Tel: 028 9025 2517

Sources from which data for this product are obtained
Community Attitudes Survey - Northern Ireland

Concern about Crime: Findings from the 1998 British Crime Survey
Home Office

Data on Survey respondents' concerns about crime and trends in concern.

Delivery: First Release
Frequency: Periodic
Price: Free
ISSN: 1364 6540

Available from
Information and Publications Group
Please see Annex B for full address details.

Sources from which data for this product are obtained
British Crime Survey - England and Wales

Main Findings from the Scottish Crime Survey
Scottish Office

Overview report presenting the main findings from the Scottish Crime Survey. Contains estimated numbers of crimes committed against individuals, the reporting rate to the police and trend in specific types of crime. Also data on: public attitudes towards the police; the impact of victimisation; and concern about crime.

Delivery: Hardcopy
Frequency: Occasional

Price: £7.00
ISBN: 0 7480 7725I
ISSN: 0950-2254

Available from
Scottish Executive, Central Research Unit
Please see Annex B for full address details

Sources from which data for this product are obtained
Crime Survey - Scotland

Police Complaints and Discipline, England and Wales
Home Office

This statistical bulletin contains an analysis of the complaints made against the police, the outcome of the complaint and disciplinary proceedings for England and Wales as a whole. It contains time series and data in the form of text, tables and charts. It also appears on the Home Office RDS website.

Delivery: Hardcopy publication
Frequency: Annually
Price: Free
ISSN: 0I43 6384

Available from
Research, Development and Statistics Directorate
Information & Publication Group
Home Office
Please see Annex B for full address details

Sources from which data for this product are obtained
Police Complaints and Discipline, England and Wales

Preliminary Findings from the Northern Ireland Crime Survey
Northern Ireland Office

Bulletin containing first results of the Crime Survey carried out in Northern Ireland from 1993 onwards. Contains data on experiences of personal and household crime, drugs, and sexual victimisation, as well as respondents' views on crime policing.

Frequency: Ad hoc
Price: Free

Available from
The Principal Statistician
Royal Ulster Constabulary
Lisnasharragh
42 Montgomery Road
Belfast
Tel: 028 9070 0992

Sources from which data for this product are obtained
Crime Survey - Northern Ireland

(The) Scottish Crime Survey: First Results
Scottish Executive

Findings paper on the initial results from the Scottish Crime Survey. Contains data on the estimated total number of crimes committed against individuals, the reporting rate to police and the trends in specific categories of crime.

Delivery: Hardcopy publication and internet
Frequency: Occasional
Price: Free

Available from
Scottish Executive and Central Research Unit,
Please see Annex B for full address details

Sources from which data for this product are obtained
Crime Survey - Scotland

8.13 Court and Judicial Proceedings

(The) Court Service Annual Report
Lord Chancellors Department

The Court Service carries out the administrative and support tasks for the following courts and jurisdictions: the Court of Appeal; the High Court; the county courts; Crown Courts; the Probate Service; and the Tribunals attached to the Court Service. The annual report reviews the main areas of activity and analyses the progress the Court Service has made towards achieving its aims and objectives. Contains details of the Court Service's performance against six key performance indicators. Also contains other key statistics such as trends in workload and waiting times.

Delivery: Periodic Release
Frequency: Annually
Price: The 1998/1999 Annual Report was priced at £12.10
ISBN: 010 5518468

Available from
Sunita Gould
Court Service
Southside
105 Victoria Street
London
Tel: 020 7210 1773; Fax: 020 7210 1756

Sources from which data for this product are obtained
Appeal Courts - England & Wales; County Courts - England and Wales; Crown Courts - England & Wales; Family Proceedings; High Courts - England and Wales; Insolvency - England and Wales

---

(The) Court Service Plan
The Lord Chancellors Department

The Court Service carries out the administrative and support tasks for the following courts and jurisdictions: the Court of Appeal; the High Court; the county courts; the Probate Service; and the Tribunals attached to the Court Service. It identifies strategic tasks that the Court Service needs to carry out to achieve its objective. It explains how the Court Service has done recently in relation to its targets and sets new targets for next year, making some assessment of likely changes in workload for the next three years

Available from
Sunita Gould
Court Service
Southside
105 Victoria Street
London
Tel: 020 7210 1773; Fax: 020 7210 1756

Delivery: Periodic Release
Frequency: Annually
Price: free

Sources from which data for this product are obtained
Appeal Courts - England & Wales; County Courts - England and Wales; Crown Courts - England & Wales; Family Proceedings; High Courts - England and Wales

---

Criminal Appeals England and Wales
Home Office

This is an annual Statistical Bulletin produced by the Research, Development and Statistics Directorate of the Home Office. Its purpose is to provide a summary of the main trends in criminal appeals, in England and Wales, to the Crown Court against magistrates' convictions and sentences and to the Criminal Division of the Court of Appeal against convictions and sentences of the Crown Court. The 1995 and 1996 edition (combined) contains 32 pages of text, tables and charts. The bulletin covers criminal appeals to the Crown Court against magistrates' convictions and sentences and to the Criminal Division of the Court of Appeal against convictions and sentences to the Crown Court. It details appeals by type of appeal (conviction only, sentence only or both), offence, appeal result and original and new sentence.

Delivery: First Release
Frequency: Annually
Price: Free.
ISSN: 0143-6384

Available from
Information and Publications Group
Please see Annex B for full address details.

Sources from which data for this product are obtained
Criminal appeals to the Crown Court and Court of Appeal - England and Wales

Criminal Proceedings in Scottish Courts
Scottish Executive

Bulletin providing statistics on the number and type of court proceedings in Scotland. Contains data on the number of persons proceeded against, persons with charge proved by crime type, age, sex and disposal.

Delivery: Periodic Release
Frequency: Annual
Price: £2.00
ISBN: 0 7480 7762 6
ISSN: 0264 1178

Available from
TSO Publications Centre and Bookshops
Please see Annex B for full address details.

Sources from which data for this product are obtained
Criminal Proceedings in Scottish Courts

Home Office Courts Appearance System (HOCAS)
Home Office

HOCAS consists of three 3.5 inch floppy disks and a user guide. It gives users access to data on police cautions and court proceedings by offence, type of court and area in electronic form and includes search facilities based on offence and on Act. An automatic setup program is used to install it onto your PC, which is fully documented in the user guide. To use HOCAS EXCEL version 5 and Windows 3.1 or above are required.

HOCAS displays EXCEL tables, from the supplementary volumes of the command paper Criminal statistics, detailing persons cautioned and defendants proceeded against at magistrates' courts and tried at the Crown Court for the calendar year. The figures can be copied and pasted into new spreadsheets for manipulation. The search facilities enable the user to, for example, search for statistics for a particular offence or Petty Sessional Division (for magistrates' courts). It also includes a search facility which links sections of Acts with figures on offences related to those sections.

Data included in the 1996 version, in the form of tables, cover proceedings in magistrates' courts for individual Petty Sessional Divisions; proceedings in magistrates' courts split by offence; defendants tried and/or sentenced at the Crown Court by offence; persons cautioned by offence, sex and age; numbers of persons cautioned by the police; defendants prosecuted at magistrates' courts or tried at the Crown Court and found guilty by detailed breakdown of offence; sex and result.

There is also an Acts and Offences table. This provides a link between sections within Acts and the offences for which figures are available and identifies the correct statistical codes for those offences. The primary use of the table is to link the codes with the data associated with those codes using the search facility.

Delivery: Periodic Release
Frequency: Annually
Price: Free.

Available from
HOCAS hotline
Room 1302
Home Office
Apollo House
36 Wellesley Road
Croydon CR9 3RR
Tel: 020 8760 8235

Sources from which data for this product are obtained
Cautions by the Police - England and Wales; Proceedings and Sentencing in Magistrates' Courts - England and Wales; Proceedings and Sentencing in the Crown Court - England and Wales

Judicial Statistics England and Wales Annual Report
The Lord Chancellor's Department

The Court Service carries out the administrative and support tasks for the following courts and jurisdictions: The Supreme Court, The Court of Appeal; The High Court; The Crown Court & the county courts. The statistics contained within Judicial Statistics relate to the criminal and civil business of those courts in England and Wales for whose administration the Lord Chancellor is responsible. They also cover the work of some associated offices including the Public Trust Office, the Judicial Committee of the Privy Counsel and certain Tribunals. Statistics relating to Northern Ireland courts are available separately from the Northern Ireland Court Service.

Judicial Statistics contains brief descriptions of the function, constitution and jurisdiction of the courts or tribunals concerned together with an explanation of some of the procedures involved. Data concerning the judiciary and taxation of costs and legal aid respectively are also included. In addition, commentary highlighting the major features of the statistics and any notable trends is included.

Delivery: Periodic Release
Frequency: Annually
Price: £27.00 (1998 edition)
ISBN: 0 10 143 7129

Available from
TSO Publications Centre and Bookshops
Please see Annex B for full address details.

Sources from which data for this product are obtained
Appeal Courts - England & Wales; County Courts - England and Wales; Crown Courts - England & Wales; Family Proceedings; High Courts - England and Wales; Insolvency - England and Wales; Mortgage Possessions - England and Wales

Northern Ireland Court Service Annual Report
Northern Ireland Court Service

A report on the activities of the NI Court Service. Contains selected data on all court tiers in Northern Ireland.

Delivery: Periodic Release
Frequency: Annually
Price: £12.50
ISBN: 0 9521715 3 8

Available from
Martin McMullan
Northern Ireland Court Service
Windsor House
9-15 Bedford Street
Belfast BT2 7LT
Tel: 028 9032 8594

Northern Ireland Judicial Statistics
Northern Ireland Court Service

Compendium of statistics describing the court system operations in NI. Contains data on the Court of Appeal, High Court, Crown Court, County Court, Magistrates' Court and other courts, tribunals and the Enforcement of Judgements Office. Tables show cases entered, outstanding and disposed of, analysed by type. Outcomes, intermediate processes and court sittings are also analysed.

Delivery: Periodic Release
Frequency: Annually
Price: £11.00 (1998 Edition)
ISBN: 0 9521715 2 X
ISSN: 1350-3235

Available from
Siobhan Morgan
Northern Ireland Court Service
Court Statistics
Windsor House
9-15 Bedford Street
Belfast
Tel: 028 9089 0206; Fax: 028 9043 9110

Sources from which data for this product are obtained
Appeal Courts - Northern Ireland; Children Order Proceedings - Northern Ireland; Coroners' Courts and Miscellaneous Tribunals - Northern Ireland; County Courts - Northern Ireland; Crown Court - Northern Ireland; Enforcement of Judgements Office and Court Funds Office - Northern Ireland; High Court - Northern Ireland; Judicial Statistics - Northern Ireland; Magistrates' Courts - Northern Ireland

Time Intervals for Criminal Proceedings in Magistrates' Courts
Lord Chancellor's Department

Time intervals between offence, charge or summons, first court listing, and completion for criminal cases in magistrates' courts. Statistical Bulletin consisting of text, charts and tables. Around 12-32 pages depending on issue. Intended for criminal justice system managers, researchers, policy-makers and the general public.

Delivery: Periodic Release
Frequency: Three times a year
Price: Free of charge

Available from
Peter Lumb
Room 9.22
Lord Chancellor's Department
Selborne House
54-60 Victoria Street
London SW1E 6QW
Tel: 020 7210 8602; Email: plumb@lcdhq.gsi.gov.uk

Sources from which data for this product are obtained
Magistrates' Courts Time Intervals Survey

See also:
In this chapter:
Cautions, Court Proceedings and Sentencing England and Wales (8.11)
Criminal Statistics England and Wales (8.11)
Offenders Index: a User's Guide (8.11)

In other chapters:
Children Act Advisory Committee Annual Report (see the Health and Care chapter)
Mortgage Statistics Northern Ireland (Press Release) (see the Housing chapter)

8.14 Crime and Justice - General

Police Service Personnel, England and Wales
Home Office

Statistical bulletin giving details for 31 March each year of the number of police

officers by rank, gender and ethnic origin; the number of civilian staff by gender and ethnic origin; the number of staff joining and leaving over the previous year, by rank and gender. Size 16 pages. It also appears on the Home Office RDS website.

Delivery: Hardcopy publication
Frequency: Annually
Price: Free
ISSN: 0143 6384

Available from
Research, Development and Statistics Directorate
Information & Publication Group
Home Office
Please see Annex B for full address details

Sources from which data for this product are obtained
Police Manpower

8.15 Crimes and Offences (other than Terrorism)

Burglary of Domestic Dwellings: Findings from the British Crime Survey
Home Office

Data showing the incidence of burglary in England and Wales from 1981 to 1997. Also shows how risks of burglary vary for different groups; levels and effectiveness of household security and levels of household insurance.

Delivery: First Release
Frequency: Periodic
Price: Free

Available from
Information and Publications Group
Home Office
Please see Annex B for full address details.

Sources from which data for this product are obtained
British Crime Survey - England and Wales

Homicide in Scotland
Scottish Executive

Bulletin providing statistics on the number of homicides in Scotland. Contains data on the number of homicides, personal characteristics of victims and accused, and court disposals.

Delivery: Periodic Release
Frequency: Every other year
Price: £2.00
ISBN: 0 7480 66519
ISSN: 0264 1178

Available from
TSO Publications Centre and Bookshops
Please see Annex B for full address details.

Sources from which data for this product are obtained
Homicide in Scotland

Motor Vehicle Offences in Scotland
Scottish Executive

Bulletin providing statistics on motor vehicle offences in Scotland. Contains data on offences proceeded against, Vehicle Defect Rectification Scheme offences and fixed penalty offences.

Delivery: Periodic Release
Frequency: Annually
Price: £2.00
ISBN: 0 7480 7790 1
ISSN: 0264-1178

Available from
TSO Publications Centre and Bookshops
Please see Annex B for full address details.

Sources from which data for this product are obtained
Motor Vehicle Offences in Scotland

Notifiable Offences England and Wales
Home Office

This statistical bulletin is the first publication to give details of the amount of crime recorded by the police in England and Wales. It contains offence and clear-up information disaggregated by police force area. Information on offences committed and offences cleared up, presented in the form of text, tables, charts and maps. More detailed information for the calendar year (finance year from 1998/99) appears in the Command Paper, Criminal Statistics - England and Wales Available from The Stationery Office. The bulletin also appears on the Home Office RDS website.

Delivery: Hardcopy publication
Frequency: Bi-annually
Price: Free
ISSN: 0143 6384

Available from
Research, Development and Statistics Directorate, Information and Publications Group
Home Office
Please see Annex B for full address details

Sources from which data for this product are obtained
Notifiable Offences - England and Wales

Recorded Crimes and Offences Involving Firearms, Scotland
Scottish Executive

Bulletin providing statistics on the number and type of offences recorded by the police in which a firearm was alleged to have been used or where a firearm was stolen. Contains data on the number of offences involving firearms by crime, location, how used and type of firearm and age and sex of main accused and victim.

Delivery: Periodic Release
Frequency: Annually
Price: £2.00
ISBN: 7480 7732 4
ISSN: 0264 1178

Available from
TSO Publications Centre and Bookshops
Please see Annex B for full address details.

Sources from which data for this product are obtained
Offences Involving Firearms - Scotland

See also:
In this chapter:
Cautions, Court Proceedings and Sentencing England and Wales (8.11)
Criminal Statistics England and Wales (8.11)

8.16 Criminals and Offenders (other than Terrorists)

Criminal Careers of Those Born Between 1953 and 1973
Home Office

This bulletin gives the latest results of analysis of the criminal histories of offenders born in selected weeks in 1953, 1958, 1963, 1968 and 1973. These figures are now updated annually in the Home Office Criminal Statistics publication. The commentary has been arranged in two parts; participation of the general population in offending is covered first, followed by frequency of offenders. Some of the analyses on frequency of offending show the results for the 1953 cohort only.

Delivery: Periodic Release
Frequency: Annually

Available from
Information and Publications Group
Please see Annex B for full address details.

Sources from which data for this product are obtained
Offenders Index Database

Drug Seizure and Offender Statistics, United Kingdom
Home Office

Statistical Bulletin containing information on drug seizures and drug offenders. Contents include breakdowns on type of seizure; seizures of Class A drugs, Class B drugs, Class C drugs; Age and sex of offenders; Type of offence; Action taken against offenders; Cannabis offences and sanctions; Custodial sentences; Type of drugs; and Confiscation orders

Some of the data in this product is disaggregated by gender.

Frequency: Annually
Price: No charge at present
ISSN: 0143 6384

Available from
Information and Publications Group
Please see Annex B for full address and contact details.

Life Licensees-Reconvictions and Recalls by the End of 1995: England and Wales
Home Office

This bulletin gives the latest results concerning reconvictions and recalls, by the end of 1995, of all persons released on licence from prison since 1972. All those released since 1972 form part of a regularly updated reconviction study created by matching their details against the Offenders Index, a database of criminal histories. Reconviction rates within 2 and 5 years for grave and standard list offences are given together with details of previous history and other characteristics.

Delivery: Periodic Release
Frequency: Every 4 years
Price: Free
ISSN: 01436384

Available from
Information and Publications Group

Reconvictions of Offenders Sentenced or Discharged from Prison in 1994, England & Wales
Home Office

Available from
Information and Publications Group
Please see Annex B for full address details.

Reconvictions of Prisoners Discharged from Prison in 1993
Home Office

This bulletin gives estimates of reconviction rates within 2 years of discharge from custodial sentences in 1993 for all offenders, except fine

defaulters and non-criminal prisoners. Reconviction rates are limited to reconvictions for 'standard list' offences. The bulletin also includes an update on the longer term follow-up of prisoners discharged in 1987. This bulletin now appears as a chapter in the annual Prison Statistics publication.

Delivery: Periodic Release
Frequency: Annually
Price: Free
ISSN: 0143 6384

Available from
Information and Publications Group
Please see Annex B for full address details.

Reconvictions of Those Commencing Community Penalties in 1993
Home Office

Analyses concerning estimates of reconviction rates within two years of the commencement of community penalties in 1993, for all offenders given probation, community service orders or combination orders. Reconviction rates are limited to reconvictions for 'standard list' offences. The bulletin also includes an update on the longer term follow-up of community penalties commencing in 1987. This publication is presently under review.

Delivery: Periodic Release
Frequency: Annually
Price: Free
ISSN: 0143 6384

Available from
Information and Publications Group
Please see Annex B for full address details.

Restricted Patients-Reconvictions and Recalls by the End of 1995: England and Wales
Home Office

Publication giving the latest data and analyses concerning reconvictions and recalls by the end of 1995 of all restricted patients conditionally discharged since 1972. Data on reconvictions were obtained from the Offender Index, a Home Office statistical database of criminal histories. Reconviction rates within 2 and 5 years for standard list offences (including grave offences) are presented together with details of previous history and other characteristics.

Delivery: Periodic Release
Frequency: Every four years
Price: Free
ISSN: 0143 6384

Available from
Information and Publications Group
Please see Annex B for full address details.

Statistics of Mentally Disordered Offenders in England and Wales 1997
Home Office

This bulletin provides information about restricted patients admitted to hospitals between 1987 and 1997 under mental health legislation. It also gives information on the admission to hospital of unrestricted mentally disordered offenders.

Delivery: Periodic Release
Frequency: Annually
Price: Free
ISSN: 0143 6384

Available from
Information and Publications Group
Please see Annex B for full address details.

Sources from which data for this product are obtained
Mentally Disordered Offenders - England and Wales

See also:
In this chapter:
Cautions, Court Proceedings and Sentencing England and Wales (8.11)
Criminal Statistics England and Wales (8.11)
Offenders Index: a User's Guide (8.11)
Prison Statistics England and Wales (8.19)
Reconvictions of Those Commencing Community Penalties in 1993 (8.16)

8.17 Firearms registration

Firearm Certificates Statistics, Scotland
Scottish Executive

Bulletin providing statistics on the issue of firearm and shotgun certificate permits under the Firearms Act 1968. Contains data on certificate applications, number granted and refused by firearm type, and registration of firearm dealers. The bulletin also contains information on Periodic EC and non-EC Visitors' Permits and European Firearms passes.

Delivery: Release
Frequency: Annually
Price: £2.00
ISBN: 0 7480 7571 2
ISSN: 0264 1178

Available from
TSO Publications Centre and Bookshops
Please see Annex B for full address details.

Sources from which data for this product are obtained
Firearm Certificates - Scotland

8.18 Policing and Crime Prevention

Her Majesty's Chief Inspector of Constabulary, Annual Report
Home Office

Summary of Police performance and the findings of HM Inspectorate of Constabulary over a financial year

Delivery: Periodic Release
Frequency: Annually
Price: £18.00 for 1996/97
To be advised of 1997/98
ISBN: To be advised

Available from
TSO Publications Centre and Bookshops
Please see Annex B for full address details.

Recorded Crime in Scotland
Scottish Executive

Bulletin providing statistics on the number and type of crimes and offences recorded by the police in Scotland. Contains data on the number of crimes and offences recorded and cleared-up by the police by crime and police force area. Also details information at a local authority level.

Delivery: Periodic Release
Frequency: Annually
Price: £2.00
ISBN: 0 7480 7792 8
ISSN: 0264 1178

Available from
TSO Publications Centre and Bookshops
Please see Annex B for full address details.

Sources from which data for this product are obtained
Recorded Crime - Scotland

See also:
In this chapter:
Cautions, Court Proceedings and Sentencing England and Wales (8.11)
Criminal Statistics England and Wales (8.11)
Notifiable Offences England and Wales (8.15)
Police Service Personnel, England and Wales (8.14)
Royal Ulster Constabulary Chief Constable's Annual Report (8.11)

8.19 Prisons, Prisoners and Parole

National Prison Survey 1991
Home Office

Results of a survey of prisoners in England and Wales, 1991. Reports on the first national survey of the prison population in England and Wales. It presents socio-economic data on the prisoners, their views on prison regimes and life in prison, and their attitudes on crime and imprisonment.

Frequency: Ad hoc,
Price: £10.00
ISBN: 0 11 691448 3 (series SS 1329)

Available from
TSO Publications Centre and Bookshops
Please see Annex B for full address details.

(The) Prison Population in 1996, England and Wales
Home Office

Statistics on many aspects of prisons and inmates. Contains data on the prison population, reception and discharges by type of prisoner, sentence length, offence, ethnic origin and sex. Includes data on prisoner in police cells, young offenders, females and fine defaulters.

Frequency: Annual
Price: £18.25
ISBN: 0 10 128932 4

Available from
TSO Publications Centre and Bookshops
Please see Annex B for full address details.

Prison Statistics England and Wales
Home Office

Tables, charts and commentary on prison statistics. Contains statistics on type of prisoner, ethnicity and nationality of prisoners, reconvictions and segregation of prisoners.

Frequency: Annual
Price: £18.25
ISBN: 0 10 128932 4

Available from
TSO Publications Centre and Bookshops
Please see Annex B for full address details.

Sources from which data for this product are obtained
Prison Population - England and Wales

Prison Statistics England and Wales. Table 2.6
Home Office

Annual statistics on the prison population in England and Wales containing a table on final outcome (i.e. sentence, acquittal, etc) of those remanded by the court, provisional data which is updated in Criminal Statistics.

Frequency: Released seven months after the end of the calendar year.

Sources from which data for this product are obtained
Remand Statistics - England and Wales

Prison Statistics Scotland
Scottish Executive

Statistical bulletin presenting information on the average daily prison population within and receptions to Scottish Penal establishments. Contains information on average daily prison population by sex, type of custody, age group, type of remand, length of sentence and crime.

Delivery: Periodic Release
Frequency: Annually
Price: £2.00
ISBN: 0 7480 7741 3
ISSN: 0264 1178

Available from
TSO Publications Centre and Bookshops
Please see Annex B for full address details.

Sources from which data for this product are obtained
Prison Receptions - Scotland; Prison Statistics

Projections of Long-Term Trends in the Prison Population to 2005
Home Office

Available from
Philip White
Home Office
Abell House
John Islip Street
London
Tel: 020 7217 5073

(The) Scottish Prison Service Annual Report,
Scottish Executive

Agency report on performance throughout financial year. Contains data on prison population, receptions and breaches of discipline and punishments awarded.

Delivery: Periodic Release
Frequency: Annually
Price: £15.90
ISBN: 0 10 253698 8

Available from
TSO Publications Centre and Bookshops
Please see Annex B for full address details.

Sources from which data for this product are obtained
Prison Breaches - Scotland; Prison Receptions - Scotland; Prison Statistics

Statistics of Offences against Prison Discipline and Punishment, England and Wales
Home Office

Statistics of offences against prison rules and the punishment given. Contains data on adjudication, crime, offences, prison and punishment.

Frequency: Annual
Price: Price not yet available

Available from
TSO Publications Centre and Bookshops
Please see Annex B for full address details.

Sources from which data for this product are obtained
Prison Discipline - England and Wales

Survey of the Physical Health of Prisoners 1994
Office for National Statistics

Results of a survey of prisoners in England and Wales carried out in July 1994. Reports on the first national survey of the physical health of sentenced male prisoners in England and Wales. It presents characteristics of the sample, general health, self-reported morbidity and use of services, health-related behaviour as well as physiological and anthropometric measurements.

Frequency: Ad hoc
Price: £24.00
ISBN: 0 11 691639 7 (series SS 1376)

Available from
TSO Publications Centre and Bookshops
Please see Annex B for full address details.

See also:
In other chapters:
Psychiatric Morbidity among prisoners in England and Wales (see the Health and Care chapter)

Community Service Bulletin
Scottish Executive

Statistical Bulletin

Frequency: Discontinued
Price: £2.00
ISBN: 0 7480 4931 2
ISSN: 0264 1151

Available from
Carol Calvert
The Scottish Executive
James Craig Walk
Edinburgh
Tel: 0131 244 5366; Fax: 0131 244 5315; Email: carol.calvert@scotland.gov.uk

Community Service by Offenders - Scotland
Scottish Executive

Statistical bulletin of the Scottish Executive Home and Health Department. Contains data on Community Service Orders given in Scotland.

Frequency: Annual
Price: £2.00

Available from
TSO Publications Centre and Bookshops
Please see Annex B for full address details.

Sources from which data for this product are obtained
Community Service - Scotland

Information on Criminal Justice Social Work Services 1993-1997
Scottish Executive

Replacement to the Community Service Bulletin

Delivery: First Release
Frequency: Annually

Available from
Carol Calvert
Scottish Executive
James Craig Walk
Edinburgh
Tel: 0131 244 5366; Fax: 0131 244 5315;
Email: carol.calvert@scotland.gov.uk

Sources from which data for this product are obtained
Community Service (SWS FORM CS1 & CS2); Offender Services (SWS FORM OA1, OC2 & OP2); Social Enquiry Reports (SWS FORM SER1)

Probation Statistics, England and Wales
Home Office

Main data on the work of the probation service. Contains data on the probation orders, Community Service orders, combination orders, pre and post-release supervision, staffing, costs, expenditure, Children and Young Persons Act 1969, family court supervision, ethnic monitoring and criminal reports.

Frequency: Annual
Price: Free
ISBN: 1 84082 182 5
ISSN: 0265-573X

Available from
Peter Sheriff
Room 275
Home Office
50 Queen Anne's Gate
London SW1H 9AT
Tel: 020 7273 2526

Sources from which data for this product are obtained
Administrative data from each of the 54 probation areas

Referrals of Children to Reporters and Children's Hearings 1993
Scottish Childrens' Reporter Administration

Statistical bulletin of the Scottish Executive Home and Health Department. Contains data on referrals of children to Reporters and Children's Hearings in Scotland.

Frequency: Annual
Price: £2.00
ISBN: 0 7480 1098 X
ISSN: 0144-5081

Available from
TSO Publications Centre and Bookshops
Please see Annex B for full address details.

Sources from which data for this product are obtained
Individual Returns for Reporters, Deputies and Assistants - Scotland; The Children's Hearing System Survey - Scotland

See also:
In this chapter:
Cautions, Court Proceedings and Sentencing England and Wales (8.11)
Criminal Statistics England and Wales (8.11)
Royal Ulster Constabulary Chief Constable's Annual Report (8.11)

In other chapters:
Qualified Social Workers and Probation Officers (see the Health and Care chapter)

Household Finances

Statistics covering **Household Finances** are collected, administered and disseminated by a number of separate Departments, Agencies and organisations including the **Office for National Statistics, the Department of Social Security, the Inland Revenue, the Northern Ireland Department of Health and Social Services, the Northern Ireland Statistics and Research Agency,** and the **Equal Opportunities Commission.** The available statistics embrace a number of subject areas including: the **Assets and Liabilities of Households and Individuals, Disability within Households, Household/ Personal Expenditure and Taxation, Household and Personal Income, Income from Benefits and Pensions, Occupational, Personal and State Pension Schemes, Social Security Appeals.**

The basic data are generated from a number of separate information 'Sources' and the resultant statistics are disseminated through a whole range of statistical 'Analyses' and 'Products', all of which are described in the following chapter. Users looking for a cross-section of UK-wide statistics on **Household Finances** may find the following products useful:

>**Family Spending** (annual publication)
>**Social Security Statistics** (annual publication)

Users interested in a wider range of official statistics including **Household Finances** statistics may like to refer to the following compendia:

>On-line Databases (See Chapter 1):
>>**StatBase - StatStore**

>Hardcopy Compendia (See Chapter 2):
>>**Annual Abstract of Statistics**
>>**Britain 2000: The Official Yearbook of the United Kingdom**
>>**Monthly Digest of Statistics**
>>**Regional Trends**
>>**Social Trends**

Users may also find what they need on the various Departmental Websites. These are listed in Chapter 1.

9 Household Finances - *Sources and Analyses*

9.1 Abstracts, Compendia, A-Z Catalogues, Directories and Reference Material

Family Expenditure Survey - Northern Ireland
Northern Ireland Statistics and Research Agency

The Northern Ireland Statistics and Research Agency conducts a survey on household expenditure. Each year 1,200 addresses are selected to take part, and a subset of one-fifth of these addresses are included in the UK Family Expenditure Survey. The Northern Ireland FES uses the same questionnaire and procedures as the UK FES. The primary purpose of the Northern Ireland FES is to contribute to UK information on expenditure patterns, from which the weights for the Retail Prices Index can be derived.

Status: Ongoing
Collection Method: Household/Person (Sample) Survey
Frequency: Annually
Reference Period: April to March
Timeliness: within 8 months of field exercise
Earliest Available Data: 1967
National Coverage: Northern Ireland

Statistician
Kevin Sweeney
Department of Finance and Personnel - Northern Ireland
Central Survey Branch
Tel: 028 9025 2490

Products that contain data from this source
Average weekly household expenditure by commodity and service, 1996-97: regional dataset; Family Expenditure Survey (NISRA Monitor); Family Spending; Households with selected durable goods, 1996-97: regional dataset; Northern Ireland Annual Abstract of Statistics; Participation in the National Lottery, 1996-97: regional dataset; Regional Trends; Social Trends; The Data Archive; Selected Housing Costs of Owner Occupiers, 1996-97: regional dataset

---

Family Expenditure Survey - UK
Office for National Statistics

The Family Expenditure Survey (FES) is carried out by the Office for National Statistics and the Northern Ireland Statistics and Research Agency. The FES is primarily a survey of household expenditure on goods and services, and household income. The main purpose of the FES is to provide information on spending patterns for the Retail Prices Index, and as a source of data for estimates of consumers' expenditure in the National Accounts.

The FES is a voluntary sample survey of about 7,000 households in the United Kingdom. In addition to the expenditure and income data, FES collects information on the socio-economic characteristics of the households, e.g. composition, size, social class, occupation, and age of the head of household. Data are available down to GOR (Government Office Region) level.

Status: Ongoing
Collection Method: Household/Person (Sample) Survey
Frequency: Continuously
Reference Period: Financial year (In 1994 the Survey reference period changed from a calendar year to a financial year basis.
Timeliness: Release of data happens as soon as is practically possible every year. Currently an annual database and publication of results are available approx. six and a half months after the end of the survey year.
Earliest Available Data: 1957
National Coverage: United Kingdom
Disaggregation: Government Office Region (GOR)

Statistician
Alyson Whitmarsh
Office for National Statistics
Socio Economic Statistics Division; Family Expenditure Survey
Tel: 020 7533 5761

Products that contain data from this source
Annual Abstract of Statistics; Average weekly household expenditure by commodity and service, 1996-97: regional dataset; Distribution of household income, 1996-97: regional dataset; Economic Trends; Family Expenditure Survey Database; Family Spending; Family Spending CD-ROM; Focus on the East Midlands; Household income: by source, 1996-97: regional dataset; Households Below Average Income Database; Households Below Average Income: A Statistical Analysis 1979 - 1988/89; Households Below Average Income: A Statistical Analysis 1979 - 1990/91; Households Below Average Income: A Statistical Analysis 1979 - 1991/92; Households Below Average Income: A Statistical Analysis 1979 - 1992/93; Households Below Average Income: A Statistical Analysis 1979 - 1993/94; Households Below Average Income: A Statistical Analysis 1979 - 1994/95; Housing Equity Withdrawal; Negative Equity; Participation in the National Lottery, 1996-97: regional dataset; Regional Trends; Social Focus on Children; Social Trends; Statistical Bulletin on Smoking

---

Family Resources Survey
Department of Social Security

The Family Resources Survey (FRS) is a continuous survey which aims to cover private households in Great Britain. Its annual target sample size is 24,000 households (25,000 prior to April 1997). Fieldwork is carried out jointly by the Office for National Statistics and Social and Community Planning Research using computer-assisted personal interviewing. The survey was launched in October 1992 to meet the information requirements of Department of Social Security (DSS) analysts. Households interviewed in the survey are asked a wide range of questions about their circumstances with a focus on areas relevant to DSS policy such as income, including receipt of Social Security benefits, housing costs, assets and savings.

The Family Resources Survey (FRS) was launched in October 1992 but did not build up to its full fieldwork size until April 1993. The target annual sample size between April 1993 and end March 1997 was 25,000, although in the first four years of the survey the achieved sample was higher, exceeding 26,000 households. As more information on response rates has been gathered, target and achieved sample sizes have converged. From April 1997 the target sample size was reduced to 24,000 households.

Status: Ongoing
Collection Method: Household/Person (Sample) Survey
Frequency: Continuously
Reference Period: The financial year
Timeliness: The Family Resources Survey data base is released annually, currently around 12 months after the end of the fieldwork period to which it relates. With changes in responsibilities between the Department of Social Security and the fieldwork contractors, this is expected to improve over the next 2-3 years.
Earliest Available Data: 1993-94
National Coverage: Great Britain
Disaggregation: Government Office Region (GOR); Standard Statistical Region (SSR)

Statistician
Jo Semmence
Department of Social Security
Analytical Services Division; Analytical Services
Division 3E
Tel: 020 7962 8092;
Email: semmencj@asdlondon.dss-asd.gov.uk

Products that contain data from this source
Family Resources Survey 1993-94; Family
Resources Survey 1993-94 - data base; Family
Resources Survey 1994-95; Family Resources
Survey 1994-95 - data base; Family Resources
Survey 1995-96; Family Resources Survey 1995-
96 - data base; Family Resources Survey 1996-
97; Family Resources Survey 1996-97 - data base;
Households Below Average Income Database;
Households Below Average Income: A Statistical
Analysis 1979 - 1993/94; Households in receipt
of benefit: by type of benefit, 1996-97: regional
dataset; Households with different types of
saving, 1996-97: regional dataset; Households
with selected durable goods, 1996-97: regional
dataset; Income Related Benefits - Estimates of
Take-up in 1996/97; Income Related Benefits
Estimates of Take-up in 1994/95; Income Related
Benefits Estimates of Take-up in 1995/96; Income
Related Benefits: Estimates of Take-up in 1993/
94; Regional Trends; Social Focus on Children;
Social Trends; The Data Archive

9.2 Assets and Liabilities of Households and Individuals

Distribution of Personal Wealth - UK
Board of Inland Revenue

The Inland Revenue Statistics and
Economics Division compiles data on the
distribution of personal wealth. Data are
available for aggregate estimates of personal
wealth together with percentage and size
distributions, analyses by asset type, and
derived data including pension rights for
earlier years showing changes in distribution
of wealth and Gini coefficients. The series
covers the United Kingdom and is available
from 1977. Data are collected and published
annually with provisional estimates
published 2-3 years after the end of the year.

Status: Latest year live, others non operational
Collection Method: Sample of inheritance tax
(and Capital Transfer Tax), administrative records
plus other aggregate data.
Frequency: Annually
Reference Period: Calendar year
Timeliness: Provisional estimates available 2-3
years after end of reference period.
Earliest Available Data: 1977
National Coverage: United Kingdom level only

Statistician
Ann White/Kerry Booth
Board of Inland Revenue

Tel: 020 7438 6236;
Email: sed.ir.nwb@gtnet.gov.uk

Products that contain data from this analysis
Economic Trends; Inland Revenue Statistics;
Social Trends

See also:
In this chapter
Family Resources Survey *(9.1)*

9.3 Household and Personal Expenditure and Taxation

Annual costs of tax allowances and reliefs
Board of Inland Revenue

The Inland Revenue Statistics and
Economics Division compiles data on the
annual costs of tax allowances and reliefs.
Data are available on tax expenditures,
structural and mixed reliefs. They cover the
United Kingdom and are available back to
1979-80. They are derived from analysis of
data from a variety of sources; mainly Inland
Revenue administrative data and published
information from other government
departments.

Status: Ongoing
Collection Method: Derived from analyses of
data from a variety of sources; mainly Inland
Revenue administrative data and published
information from other government departments
Frequency: Annually
Reference Period: Financial year
Timeliness: First publication covers the current
year and the next one. When it is updated, it
relates to the current year and the previous one.
Earliest Available Data: 1979-80
National Coverage: United Kingdom
Disaggregation: None

Statistician
Maurice Nettley
Board of Inland Revenue
Tel: 020 7438 7411;
Email: sed.ir.sh@gtnet.gov.uk

Products that contain data from this source
Inland Revenue Statistics; Tax Ready Reckoner
and Tax Reliefs

Tax relief on savings and investment
Board of Inland Revenue

The Inland Revenue Statistics and
Economics Division compiles data on the
take-up and the costs of tax reliefs for
various savings and investment schemes -
including pensions, PEP and TESSA (to be

replaced by ISA), EIS, VCT, approved
employee share schemes and profit related
pay.

Status: Ongoing
Collection Method: Census
Frequency: Annually/quarterly
Reference Period: Tax year
Timeliness: 6-18 months after reference period
Earliest Available Data: From inception of
relevant scheme
National Coverage: United Kingdom

Statistician
Andrzej Walczowski
Board of Inland Revenue
Tel: 020 7438 6231;
Email: sed.ir.nwb@gtnet.gov.uk

Products that contain data from this source
Inland Revenue Statistics

Tax relief for charities
Board of Inland Revenue

The Inland Revenue Statistics and
Economics Division compiles data on the
tax relief associated with charitable giving
and the income of charities.

Status: Ongoing
Collection Method: Census
Frequency: Annually
Reference Period: Tax year
Timeliness: 6 months after reference period
Earliest Available Data: From inception of
relevant scheme
National Coverage: United Kingdom

Statistician
Andrzej Walczowski
Board of Inland Revenue
Tel: 020 7438 6231;
Email: sed.ir.nwb@gtnet.gov.uk

See also:
In this chapter:
Family Resources Survey *(9.1)*

In other chapters:
Consumer Price Collection - UK *(see the
Economy chapter)*

9.4 Household and Personal Income

(The) Effects of Taxes and Benefits on Household Income
Office for National Statistics

An annual article appearing in Economic
Trends that describes and analyses the
effects on the incomes of households of
government taxes and benefits. The analysis
has been undertaken since 1957 but the data

are publicly available only from 1994/95.

Status: Ongoing
Frequency: Annually
Reference Period: Fiscal year
Timeliness: Approximately 5 months after the release of the Family Expenditure Survey data.
Earliest Available Data: 1994/95
National Coverage: United Kingdom

Statistician
Tim Harris
Office for National Statistics
Social & Regional; Income Distribution
Tel: 020 7533 5770;
Email: tim.harris@ons.gov.uk

Income from self employment - UK
Board of Inland Revenue

From 1996-97, the Inland Revenue Statistics and Economics Division has compiled estimates of income from self employment from a database containing data for 10% of all self assessment taxpayers, derived from the tax forms completed by these people and by partnerships in which they are partners. For earlier years estimates were derived from a sample of some 20,000 self employed people included in the Survey of Personal Incomes.

Data are available distinguishing sole traders and partnership. The database contains industry codes. For a sample of 20,000 cases each year, postcodes have been translated into standard geographical areas (down to county level), for which estimates are thereby also available, subject to sample sizes. These estimates are used in the preparation of National and Regional Accounts. The survey is conducted annually. The first formal survey was for 1937-38. There have been annual surveys since 1967-68, with the exception of 1981-82 when no survey was done. It is not possible to provide any analysis prior to 1978-79 as the data no longer exist.

Status: Ongoing
Collection Method: Large-scale (Sample) Survey
Frequency: Annually
Reference Period: Business accounting periods ending in the tax year.
Timeliness: 16 months after the end of the tax year
Earliest Available Data: 1978-79
National Coverage: United Kingdom
Sub-National: County and unitary authority

Statistician
Alan McIntyre
Board of Inland Revenue
Tel: 020 7438 7417;
Email: sed.ir.sh@gtnet.gov.uk

Products that contain data from this source
Inland Revenue Statistics

National Income Statistics Survey - UK
Board of Inland Revenue

Inland Revenue Statistics and Economics Division compiles data on income from employment for inclusion in the National accounts. The data are derived from end of year Pay-As-You-Earn (PAYE) tax documents. Data are available on the amount of pay from employment, tax and national insurance contributions, by industry (SIC92) and sector. Data have been collected annually since 1976-77 and are published about eighteen months after the end of the reference year. Some data are available up to about six months earlier upon request.

Collection Method: Large-scale (Sample) Survey
Frequency: Annually
Reference Period: tax year
Timeliness: 6 months for publication although a few tables are available earlier
Earliest Available Data: published information available back to 1982
National Coverage: United Kingdom
Disaggregation: Regional, county and district level

Statistician
Jude Hillary
Board of Inland Revenue
Tel: 020 7438 7412

Products that contain data from this source
Inland Revenue Statistics; Second Tier Pension Provision

Survey of Personal Incomes - UK
Board of Inland Revenue

The Inland Revenue Statistics and Economics Division carries out a survey on personal incomes. The survey covers a sample of some 80,000 individuals for whom income tax records are held by Inland Revenue tax offices. Data are available for income distributions before and after tax, numbers of taxpayers with income and deductions of various types and the amounts concerned. Some information on tax liabilities and self-employment income is also available. Survey data on self-employment income, income from property, and investment income are used in the preparation of National and Regional Accounts.

Status: Ongoing
Collection Method: Large-scale (Sample) Survey
Frequency: Annually
Reference Period: tax year

Timeliness: 3 months after final file produced although some tables are available earlier upon request
Earliest Available Data: 1978-79
National Coverage: United Kingdom
Disaggregation: Regional, county, metropolitan borough and larger non-metropolitan local authority level

Statistician
Jude Hillary
Board of Inland Revenue
Tel: 020 7438 7412

Products that contain data from this source
Annual Abstract of Statistics; Average total income and average income tax payable: by gender, 1995-96: regional dataset; Distribution of income liable to assessment for tax, 1995-96: regional dataset; Inland Revenue Statistics; Northern Ireland Annual Abstract of Statistics; Regional Trends; Scottish Abstract of Statistics; Social Trends; Welsh Economic Trends

See also:
In this chapter:
Family Expenditure Survey - UK *(9.1)*
Family Resources Survey *(9.1)*

In other chapters:
Data on self assessment taxpayers - UK *(see the Government and Public Sector chapter)*
Expenses and Benefits Survey *(see the Government and Public Sector chapter)*
Household Survey - Wales *(see the Housing chapter)*

9.5   Income from Benefits and Pensions

(The) Abstract of Statistics for Social Security Benefits and Contributions and Indices of Prices and Earnings
Department of Social Security

The Abstract pulls together data from various sources and contains information relating to: retail prices index and uprating factors, earnings data broken down by gender and type of work, net income after housing costs, relativites between benefits, rates of benefits, a comparison of the income received from benefits with average earnings, the rates of National Insurance Contributions and, expenditure on Social Security Benefits.

Status: Ongoing
Collection Method: Various surveys/administrative records
Frequency: Annually
Reference Period: 1998

Timeliness: January
National Coverage: United Kingdom

Statistician
Martin McGill
Department of Social Security
ASD1;ASD1b
Tel: 0191 225 7661;
Email: mcgillm@asd11btn.dss-asd.gov.uk

Products that contain data from this source
The Abstract of Statistics for Social Security
Benefits and Contributions and Indices of Prices
and Earnings

All prescribed diseases - assessments of claims to Industrial Injuries Disablement Benefit
Department of Social Security

A compilation of data of all prescribed diseases - assessments of claims to Industrial Injuries Disablement Benefit.

Status: Ongoing
Frequency: Quarterly
Reference Period: March, June, September, December
Timeliness: 24 weeks
Earliest Available Data: December 1997
National Coverage: Great Britain
Disaggregation: Various

Statistician
Martin McGill
Department of Social Security
ASD1;ASD1B
Tel: 0191 225 7661;
Email: Mcgillm@asd11btn.dss-asd.gov.uk

Products that contain data from this source
All prescribed diseases - assessments of claims
to Industrial Injuries Disablement Benefit

Attendance Allowance - GB
Department of Social Security

The Department of Social Security compiles data on Attendance Allowance, a benefit for people who become disabled. Data are taken from the administrative computer system used for the benefit payment. Attendance Allowance tables contain information about the number of awards made during the quarters ending February, May, August and November. The tables also analyse awards currently in payment at the end of the quarter. The analysis shows the rate of the award, the age of the claimant, length of the award, the main cause of disability and the area of the claimant's residence.

Status: Ongoing
Collection Method: Quarterly scan
Frequency: Quarterly
Reference Period: February, May, August, November

Timeliness: 18 weeks
Earliest Available Data: 1971
National Coverage: Great Britain
Sub-National: County and standard region levels

Statistician
Martin McGill
Department of Social Security
ASD1;ASD1B
Tel: 0191 225 7661;
Email: Mcgillm@asd11btn.dss-asd.gov.uk

Products that contain data from this source
Attendance Allowance Statistics

Child Benefit
Department of Social Security

The Department of Social Security compiles data on Child Benefit based on a 1 per cent sample. Data are available on the number of families and children for whom Child Benefit is claimed, reasons for additions and terminations of Benefit, size of family, position of child in family and details of children under five. Figures based on a 5% sample from November 1998.

Status: Ceased temporarily
Collection Method: Administrative Records
Frequency: Quarterly
Reference Period: Quarters ending March, June, September and December. New quarters are February, May, August and November.
Timeliness: 12 weeks from receipt of data
Earliest Available Data: 1977
National Coverage: Great Britain

Statistician
Martin McGill
Department of Social Security
ASD1;ASD1b
Tel: 0191 225 7661;
Email: mcgillm@asd11btn.dss-asd.gov.uk

Products that contain data from this source
Child Benefit Quarterly Summary of Statistics;
Social Security Statistics

Child Support Agency - GB
Department of Social Security

The Department of Social Security (DSS) and the Child Support Agency (CSA) compile data and analyses on child maintenance. Data are taken from a 5 per cent scan of the Child Support Computer System. The main analyses of CSA cases are: amount of maintenance paid by absent parents, analysed by economic status, earnings and assessment type; amount of maintenance received by the parent/person with care, analysed by economic status and assessment type; general statistics relating to absent parents/persons with care (i.e. sex, marital status and accommodation type).

The CSA came into effect in April 1993. Until March 1995 all scans of the Child Support Computer System captured only a 1 per cent sample. In May 1995 changes to the scan increased the sample size to 5 per cent.

Status: Ongoing
Collection Method: Child Support Agency Statistics
Frequency: Quarterly
Reference Period: Quarters ending February, May, August and November
Timeliness: 10 weeks from end of quarter (receipt of scan)
Earliest Available Data: November 1995
National Coverage: Great Britain
Disaggregation: Government Office Region (GOR)

Statistician
Nigel Brough
Department of Social Security
ASD1;ASD1a
Tel: 0191 225 7391;
Email: broughn@asd11btn.dss-asd.gov.uk

Products that contain data from this source
Child Support Agency Quarterly Statistical
Summary; Social Security Statistics

Child Support Agency Computer System (Northern Ireland)
Department of Health and Social Services - Northern Ireland; sponsored by CSA

Administrative data primarily used by CSA to calculate Maintenance Assessment.

Status: Ongoing
Collection Method: Administrative Records
Frequency: Continuously
Reference Period: 1993-Present
Timeliness: Usually 1 Month
Earliest Available Data: 1993
National Coverage: Northern Ireland
Disaggregation: District Council Area (Northern Ireland); Enumeration District (ED); Postcode District; Postcode Sector; Parliamentary Constituency; Ward

Statistician
Eddie Finn
Department of Health and Social Services - Northern Ireland
Social Security Statistics Branch
Tel: 028 9052 2261;
Email: eddie.finn@dhssni.gov.uk

Products that contain data from this source
Child Support Agency Quarterly Summary of
Statistics (Northern Ireland)

Child's Special Allowance - GB
Department of Social Security

The Department of Social Security compiles data on Special Allowances for Children. Data are a full count of the numbers receiving the Allowance by size of family. Data cover Great Britain. They are available from the introduction of the Allowance in 1957 as a National Insurance benefit for divorced women whose former husband has died. No new claims can be made where the husband died after 5 April 1987. Data are collected annually and published one month after the end of the year.

Status: Ongoing
Collection Method: Census
Frequency: Annually
Reference Period: Calendar year
Timeliness: Two weeks
Earliest Available Data: 1957
National Coverage: Great Britain

Statistician
Martin McGill
Department of Social Security
ASD1;ASD1b
Tel: 0191 225 7661;
Email: mcgillm@asd1lbtn.dss-asd.gov.uk

Products that contain data from this source
Child's Special Allowance and Guardian's Allowance; Social Security Statistics

Cross Benefit Analysis - Population of Working Age on Key Benefits
Department of Social Security

This new series has been developed from existing data on individual benefits to give a more coherent picture of the population of working age on key social security benefits.

Status: Ongoing
Collection Method: 5% sample from various DSS administrative computer systems
Frequency: Quarterly
Reference Period: Quarters ending February, May, August and November
Timeliness: 8 months
Earliest Available Data: May 1995
National Coverage: Great Britain
Disaggregation: Government Office Region & Local Authority District

Statistician
Stuart Grant
Department of Social Security
Analytical Services Division (ASD); ASD1 CBAT
Room B2706, Longbenton, Newcastle Upon Tyne, NE98 1YX
Tel: 0191 225 6048. Fax: 0191 225 7671.
Email: grants@asd1lbtn.dss-asd.gov.uk

Disability Living Allowance - GB
Department of Social Security

The Department of Social Security compiles data on Disability Living Allowance, a benefit for people who became disabled before the age of 65. Data are taken from

the administrative computer system used for the benefit payment. Disability Living Allowance tables contain information about the number of awards made during the quarters ending February, May, August and November. The tables also analyse awards currently in payment at the end of the quarter. The analysis shows the type and rate of the award, the age of the claimant, length of the award, the main cause of disability and the area of the claimant's residence.

Status: Ongoing
Collection Method: Quarterly Scan
Frequency: Quarterly
Reference Period: February, May, August, November
Timeliness: 18 weeks
Earliest Available Data: April 1992
National Coverage: Great Britain
Sub-National: County and standard region levels

Statistician
Martin McGill
Department of Social Security
ASD1;ASD1B
Tel: 0191 225 7661;
Email: Mcgillm@asd1lbtn.dss-asd.gov.uk

Products that contain data from this source
Disability Living Allowance Statistics; Social Security Statistics

Guardian's Allowance - GB
Department of Social Security

The Department of Social Security compiles Guardian's Allowance data. A full count is taken of the numbers receiving Guardian's Allowance by age of child and size of family. Data cover Great Britain and are available since the introduction of the Allowance in 1948 as a National Insurance benefit for children whose parents have died. Data are collected annually and published one month after the end of the year.

Status: Ongoing
Collection Method: Guardians Allowance Microcomputer System- Child Benefit Branch
Frequency: Annually
Reference Period: Calendar year
Timeliness: Two weeks
Earliest Available Data: 1948
National Coverage: Great Britain

Statistician
Martin McGill
Department of Social Security
ASD1;ASD1b
Tel: 0191 225 7661;
Email: mcgillm@asd1lbtn.dss-asd.gov.uk

Products that contain data from this source
Child's Special Allowance and Guardian's Allowance; Social Security Statistics

Housing and Council Tax Benefits - GB
Department of Social Security

The Department of Social Security compiles data on Housing Benefit and Council Tax Benefit. Data are collected on a aggregate basis and on a 1 per cent sample basis. Aggregate data are collected, from each local authority, on the totals of Housing Benefit and Council Tax Benefit recipients, average amounts of Housing Benefit, average eligible rent and a split of claims by tenancy type. Local authorities are also asked to provide detailed information on the selected sample, which includes all the data required to calculate the amount of benefit. Data cover Great Britain and are available by country and Government Office regions. Limited information is available from April 1983. The first set of full tables was produced in May 1988. However, these figures included rate rebates until May 1989 in Scotland and May 1990 in England and Wales. Community Charge Rebate was then shown in tables until May 1993 when Council Tax Benefit was introduced. The data are collected on a quarterly aggregate basis at the end of May, August, November and February and also on a annual 1 per cent sample basis at the end of May. An annual summary is issued in June, a year after the reference period. For the quarterly aggregate counts, data are published three months after the reference period.

Status: Ongoing
Collection Method: Housing Benefit Management Information System.
Frequency: Annual 1% sample plus quarterly 100% caseload counts
Reference Period: Annual sample is for the last working day in May. The quarterly counts are for the last working day in February, May, August and November.
Timeliness: 3 Months for quarterlies and 14 months for annual
Earliest Available Data: 1992
National Coverage: Great Britain

Statistician
Anne Simpson-Hawkins
Department of Social Security
ASD1;ASD1D
Tel: 0191 225 7801;
Email: Simpsona@asd1lbtn.dss-asd.gov.uk

Products that contain data from this source
Annual Housing Benefit and Council Tax Benefit Summary Statistics (and quarterly Update); Housing Benefit and Council Tax Benefit Quarterly Summary Statistics; Social Security Statistics

Incapacity Benefit / Severe Disablement Allowance
Department of Social Security

The Department of Social Security collects data on people claiming benefit due to being incapable of work due to illness or disability. This includes Sickness/Invalidity Benefit and Severe Disablement and Incapacity Benefit. Data are available by age, sex, length of spell of incapacity, marital status of women, contribution conditions, amounts of benefit, dependency position, other benefits in payment, diagnosis, reason not entitled to Statutory Sick Pay, reason for transfer from Statutory Sick Pay and date of entitlement.

Status: Ongoing
Frequency: Annually
Reference Period: June
Timeliness: 12 months
Earliest Available Data: 1948 for Sickness/Invalidity Benefit - 1984 for Severe Disability Allowance - 1995 for Incapacity Benefit
National Coverage: Great Britain
Sub-National: Government Office Region level

Statistician
Martin McGill
Department of Social Security
ASD1;ASD1B
Tel: 0191 225 7661;
Email: Mcgillm@asd1lbtn.dss-asd.gov.uk

Incapacity Benefit / Severe Disablement Allowance (annual)
Department of Social Security

The Department of Social Security collects data on people claiming benefit due to being incapable of work due to illness or disability. This includes Sickness/Invalidity Benefit and Severe Disablement and Incapacity Benefit. Data are available by age, sex, amounts of benefit, dependency position and diagnosis.

Status: Ongoing
Collection Method: Annual rollup of quarterly data plus clerical data
Frequency: Annually
Reference Period: March
Timeliness: 15 months
Earliest Available Data: Data have been collected since May 1995 for Severe Disability Allowance and for Incapacity Benefit
National Coverage: Great Britain
Disaggregation: Government Office Region level

Statistician
Martin McGill
Department of Social Security
ASD1;ASD1B
Tel: 0191 225 7661;
Email: Mcgillm@asd1lbtn.dss-asd.gov.uk

Products that contain data from this source
Social Security Statistics

Incapacity Benefit / Severe

Disablement Allowance (quarterly)
Department of Social Security

The Department of Social Security collects data on people claiming benefit due to being incapable of work due to illness or disability. This includes Sickness/Invalidity Benefit and Severe Disablement and Incapacity Benefit. Data are available by age, sex, amounts of benefit, dependency position and diagnosis.

Status: Ongoing
Collection Method: Quarterly scan
Frequency: Quarterly
Reference Period: February, May, August, November
Timeliness: 3 months
Earliest Available Data: May 95 quarterly
National Coverage: Great Britain
Disaggregation: Government Office Region level

Statistician
Martin McGill
Department of Social Security
ASD1;ASD1B
Tel: 0191 225 7661;
Email: Mcgillm@asd1lbtn.dss-asd.gov.uk

Income Support - Residential Care and Nursing Homes - Great Britain
Department of Social Security

The Department of Social Security conducts the Income Support Quarterly Statistical Enquiry in respect of residential care and nursing home residents. This is a point-in-time survey of the characteristics on Income Support recipients in such accommodation. Information is based on the same 5 per cent sample of recipients used for the main Income Support Quarterly Statistical Enquiry and is collected from the Income Support Computer System and from local offices of the Benefits Agency. Data are available by the number and age of the claimant, sex, type of care and accommodation charges.

Status: Ceased completely
National Coverage: Great Britain
Disaggregation: Standard Regional level (since 1986)

Statistician
Jason Bradbury
Department of Social Security
Analytical Services Division (ASD);ASD1
Tel: 0191 225 7883;
Email: bradburj@asd1lbtn.dss-asd.gov.uk

Income Support Quarterly Statistical Enquiry - GB
Department of Social Security

The Department of Social Security conducts the Income Support Quarterly Statistical Enquiry. This is a point-in-time survey of the characteristics of Income Support recipients. Data are available by number and age of claimants, partners and dependants, sex, type and amount of incomes and length of time in receipt. Also including data regarding claimants in residential care and nursing homes by number and age of claimant, sex, type of care and accommodation charges.

Status: Ongoing
Collection Method: 5% sample of recipients (selected by National Insurance Number).
Frequency: Quarterly
Reference Period: February, May, August and November
Timeliness: 5 Months
Earliest Available Data: 1992
National Coverage: Great Britain
Disaggregation: Government Standard Statistical Region, Local Authority District (LAD) / Unitary Authority (Eng)

Statistician
Jason Bradbury
Department of Social Security
Analytical Services Division (ASD);ASD1
Tel: 0191 225 7883;
Email: bradburj@asd1lbtn.dss-asd.gov.uk

Products that contain data from this source
Annual Abstract of Statistics; Income Related Benefits Estimates of Take-up in 1989; Monthly Digest of Statistics; Regional Trends; Social Security Statistics; Social Trends

Industrial Death Benefit - GB
Department of Social Security

The Department of Social Security compiles data on Industrial Death Benefit from the computer payments file. Data cover the number of Pensions and Child Allowances in payment in Great Britain and are available by age and weekly rate of pension, age of child and recipient of allowance, number of children in the family and age of the youngest or only child. The Benefit was introduced in July 1948 but was abolished for deaths occurring after 10 April 1988 (Widow's Benefit is now paid instead). Tables are published annually about two months after the end of the year. Quarterly tables are also produced which reflect changes occurring during the year.

Status: Ongoing
Collection Method: annual scan
Frequency: Annually
Reference Period: January annually
Timeliness: 4 weeks
Earliest Available Data: 1969
National Coverage: Great Britain

Statistician
Martin McGill

Department of Social Security
ASDI;ASDIB
Tel: 0191 225 7661;
Email: Mcgillm@asd1lbtn.dss-asd.gov.uk

Products that contain data from this source
Industrial Death Benefit; Social Security Statistics

Industrial Injuries - Prescribed Diseases
Department of Social Security

The Department of Social Security compiles data on individuals compensated under the Prescribed Diseases - Industrial Injuries Scheme. The Industrial Injuries Scheme began in 1948. Data are available by year of first assessment, disease, causative agent, percentage disability and sex of the affected worker. Respiratory diseases and deafness are assessed separately. Figures are published annually by HSE in October (DSS publish quarterly figures). Coverage changes periodically due to the addition of new prescribed diseases or by widening the terms of prescription. Discontinuities in benefit rules also affect the ability to make comparisons over time. The major discontinuities were in 1982, when industrial injury benefit was withdrawn (for the generality of claimants) in parallel with the introduction of Statutory Sick Pay. The next major change was the restriction of disablement benefit payments to claimants with 14% or more assessed disability in 1986. Detailed changes consequent on the prescription rules for individual diseases are fairly frequent. They are documented in footnotes to the relevant tables in Health and Safety Statistics.

Status: Ongoing
Collection Method: Administrative Records
Frequency: Quarterly or monthly returns, depending on disease category.
Reference Period: Calendar year for respiratory diseases, benefit years from first week in October for other diseases
Timeliness: 9 months
Earliest Available Data: 1948
National Coverage: Great Britain
Disaggregation: Regional figures available from DSS

Statistician
Martin McGill
Department of Social Security
ASDI;ASDIB
Tel: 0191 225 7661;
Email: Mcgillm@asd1lbtn.dss-asd.gov.uk

Industrial Injuries Disablement Benefit Assessment/Reduced Earnings Allowance
Department of Social Security

IIDB may be paid to people who are disabled because of an industrial accident or prescribed industrial disease. Both benefits may be paid individually. However, they may also be paid together. Assessments current do not refer to recipients as a customer may be in receipt of more than one assessment.

Status: Ongoing
Collection Method: Administrative Records
Frequency: Annually
Reference Period: March
Timeliness: 32 weeks
National Coverage: Great Britain

Statistician
Martin McGill
Department of Social Security
ASDI;ASDIB
Tel: 0191 225 7661;
Email: Mcgillm@asd1lbtn.dss-asd.gov.uk

Products that contain data from this source
Industrial Injuries Disablement Benefit/ Reduced Earnings Allowance /Retirement Allowance Statistics

Industrial Injuries Disablement Benefit/Reduced Earnings Allowance
Department of Social Security

Tabulated data on Disablement Benefit using stock and movements in the current period, rated up from a 10 per cent sample.

Collection Method: Administrative Records
Frequency: Annually

Statistician
Martin McGill
Department of Social Security
ASDI;ASDIB
Tel: 0191 225 7661;
Email: Mcgillm@asd1lbtn.dss-asd.gov.uk

Invalid Care Allowance
Department of Social Security

A 100% count of Invalid Care Allowance claimants and recipients.

Status: Ongoing
Collection Method: Quarterly
Frequency: Quarterly
Reference Period: March, June, September, December
Timeliness: 1 week
Earliest Available Data: 1985
National Coverage: Great Britain
Disaggregation: Various

Statistician
Martin McGill
Department of Social Security
ASDI;ASDIB
Tel: 0191 225 7661;
Email: Mcgillm@asd1lbtn.dss-asd.gov.uk

Products that contain data from this source
Invalid Care Allowance Statistics; Social Security Statistics

---

Jobseeker's Allowance Quarterly Statistical Enquiry - Great Britain
Department of Social Security

The Department of Social Security conducts the Jobseeker's Allowance Quarterly Statistical Enquiry. This is a point-in-time survey of the characteristics and type of payment received by Jobseeker's Allowance claimants. Information is based on a 5 per cent sample of claimants and is collected from the Jobseeker's Allowance Payments System. Data are available by number and age of claimant, partners and dependants, sex, type and amount of incomes and length of time in receipt. The enquiry covers Great Britain including Regions. Validated data based on a 5 per cent sample have been available since November 1996. Prior to this date data on unemployed claimants were included in the Income Support Statistical Enquiry. Data are collected quarterly in February, May, August and November and are published quarterly approximately 6 months after the date to which they relate.

Status: Ongoing
Collection Method: 5% Sample of claimants (selected by National Insurance Number)
Frequency: Quarterly
Reference Period: Quarters ended February, May, August, November
Timeliness: 6 Months
Earliest Available Data: November 1996
National Coverage: Great Britain
Disaggregation: Government Standard Statistical Region, Local Authority District (LAD) / Unitary Authority (Eng.)

Statistician
Jason Bradbury
Department of Social Security
Analytical Services Division (ASD); ASDI
Tel: 0191 225 7883;
Email: bradburj@asd1lbtn.dss-asd.gov.uk

Products that contain data from this source
Jobseeker's Allowance Statistics Quarterly Enquiry; Monthly Digest of Statistics; Social Security Statistics

---

Lifetime Labour Market Database
Department of Social Security

National Insurance Recording System (NIRS) contains details of National Insurance records for over 60 million individuals which are required to calculate entitlement to benefits and retirement pension. The LLMDB is a 1% sample from

NIRS and is extracted primarily to produce information on persons contributing to Second Tier Pensions and details of National Insurance payments or credits and Numbers of Migrant Workers. Key users of the data are the Department of Social Security and the Government Actuaries Department, and it is also of wide interest to external organisations and policy researchers. The LLMDB contains details relating to each tax year from 1975/76 through to 1995/96. Each year the number of years available increases and a project is also being undertaken to transfer information from paper records to the LLMDB for specific age groups for pre 1975 tax years.

Status: Ongoing
Collection Method: Large-scale (Sample) Survey
Frequency: Annually
Timeliness: Ten months after end of tax year
Earliest Available Data: 1975/76
National Coverage: United Kingdom

Statistician
Ann Simpson-Hawkins
Department of Social Security
ASD1;ASD1D
Tel: 0191 225 7801;
Email: Simpsona@asd1lbtn.dss-asd.gov.uk

Products that contain data from this source
Migrant Workers Statistics; Second Tier Pension Provision

Maternity Allowance
Department of Social Security

A 1% sample of awards and disallowances to Maternity Allowance in Great Britain.

Status: Ongoing
Frequency: Annually
Reference Period: April 1997
Timeliness: 4 months
Earliest Available Data: 1948
National Coverage: Great Britain
Disaggregation: Various

Statistician
Martin McGill
Department of Social Security
ASD1;ASD1B
Tel: 0191 225 7661;
Email: Mcgillm@asd1lbtn.dss-asd.gov.uk

Maternity Allowance - Industrial Injuries Disablement Benefit / Reduced Earnings Allowance / Retirement Allowance
Department of Social Security

A 5% sample of awards to Maternity Allowance in Great Britain.

Status: Ongoing

Frequency: Quarterly
Reference Period: February, May, August, November
Timeliness: 3 months
National Coverage: Great Britain

Statistician
Martin McGill
Department of Social Security
ASD1;ASD1B
Tel: 0191 225 7661;
Email: Mcgillm@asd1lbtn.dss-asd.gov.uk

New Claims to Industrial Injuries Disablement Benefit
Department of Social Security

10% quarterly sample of all IIDB claims for accidents and prescribed diseases.

Status: Ongoing
Frequency: Quarterly
Reference Period: March, June, September, December
Timeliness: 18 weeks
Earliest Available Data: June 1995
National Coverage: Great Britain
Disaggregation: Various

Statistician
Martin McGill
Department of Social Security
ASD1;ASD1B
Tel: 0191 225 7661;
Email: Mcgillm@asd1lbtn.dss-asd.gov.uk

Products that contain data from this source
New Claims to Industrial Injuries Disablement Benefit; Occupational Deafness

Occupational deafness
Department of Social Security

All claims to "Occupational deafness" and those referred to an otologist for examination and result of the referral. Monthly return to compile an annual 100% count.

Collection Method: Large-scale (Sample) Survey
Earliest Available Data: 1990

Statistician
Martin McGill
Department of Social Security
ASD1;ASD1B
Tel: 0191 225 7661;
Email: Mcgillm@asd1lbtn.dss-asd.gov.uk

Pension funds quarterly income and expenditure inquiry
Office for National Statistics

Figures from this survey go into quarterly and annual income and expenditure, quarterly transactions in financial assets and annual balance sheets and together with the

annual surveys into the overseas direct investment of insurance companies are used in the income, expenditure and output measures of the gross domestic product, in the sector current, capital and financial accounts, and in the balance of payments current and capital accounts. The data are also required to fulfil international obligations, e.g. to OECD and Eurostat.

Collection Method: Small-scale (Sample) Survey
Frequency: Quarterly
Reference Period: The calendar quarter
Timeliness: 12 weeks after the end of the period.
Earliest Available Data: Press release - "Investment by insurance companies, pension funds & trusts"
National Coverage: United Kingdom

Statistician
Robert Hay
Office for National Statistics
Tel: 01633 812357;
Email: robert.hay@ons.gov.uk

Products that contain data from this source
Financial Statistics; Insurance Companies', Pension Funds' and Trusts Investments (Business Monitor MQ5); Investment by Insurance Companies, Pension Funds and Trusts (First Release); United Kingdom National Accounts - The Blue Book

Retirement Pensions
Department of Social Security

The Department of Social Security compiles data on retirement pensions. A 5 per cent sample is taken of people receiving State Retirement Pensions in Great Britain and overseas. Data is held in a readily accessible archive back to March 1995.

Status: Ongoing
Collection Method: Administrative Records
Frequency: Bi-annually
Reference Period: At 31 March, and at 30 September
Timeliness: Fifteen weeks
Earliest Available Data: 1979
National Coverage: England, Wales, Scotland
Disaggregation: From late 1999, sub-regional disaggregations will be possible.

Statistician
Ann Simpson-Hawkins
Department of Social Security
ASD1;ASD1d
Tel: 0191 225 7801;
Email: simpsona@asd1lbtn.dss-asd.gov.uk

Products that contain data from this source
Retirement Pensions Summary of Statistics

Social Security Benefit Geographical Information System

Sources and Analyses

Department of Health and Social Services

Analysis of Social Security Benefit information by area. Maps available by Ward, District Council, Parliamentary Constituency and Health Board. Analysis also available by Postcode or Enumeration District.

Status: Ongoing
Frequency: Monthly
Reference Period: 1993-1997
Timeliness: Usually 6 months
Earliest Available Data: 1993
National Coverage: Northern Ireland
Disaggregation: Postcode Sector; Health and Social Services Board (Northern Ireland); Parliamentary Constituency; Ward; Postcode District; Enumeration District (ED); Postcode Area

Statistician
Sandy Fitzpatrick
Department of Health and Social Services - Northern Ireland
Social Security Statistics Branch
Tel: 028 9052 2280;
Email: sandy.fitzpatrick@dhssni.gov.uk

Products that contain data from this analysis
Child Support Agency Quarterly Summary of Statistics (Northern Ireland); Disability Living Allowance - Attendance Allowance -Invalid Care Allowance Quarterly Summary of Statistics (Northern Ireland); Disability Working Allowance Quarterly Tables (Northern Ireland); Family Credit Quarterly Tables (Northern Ireland); Unemployed Claimants - Summary Statistics (Northern Ireland)

Social Security Benefit System (Northern Ireland)
Department of Health and Social Services - Northern Ireland

Administrative data collected to determine amount of benefit paid.

Status: Ongoing
Collection Method: Administrative Records
Frequency: Continuously
Reference Period: Varies
Timeliness: Usually 3 Months
National Coverage: Northern Ireland
Disaggregation: Ward; Enumeration District (ED); Postcode District; Postcode Sector; District Council Area (Northern Ireland); Health & Social Services Board Area (Northern Ireland)

Statistician
Sandy Fitzpatrick
Department of Health and Social Services - Northern Ireland
Social Security Statistics Branch
Tel: 028 9052 2280;
Email: sandy.fitzpatrick@dhssni.gov.uk

Products that contain data from this source
Child Support Agency Quarterly Summary of Statistics (Northern Ireland); Disability Living Allowance - Attendance Allowance -Invalid Care Allowance Quarterly Summary of Statistics (Northern Ireland); Disability Working Allowance Quarterly Tables (Northern Ireland); Family Credit Quarterly Tables (Northern Ireland); Unemployed Claimants - Summary Statistics (Northern Ireland)

Social Security Statistics
Department of Social Security

Social Security Statistics is produced annually for the Department of Social Security. The publication is split into sections which cover Social Security Benefits, National Insurance Contributions, Personal Pensions, low income statistics, take up of benefits and appeals and include expenditure tables.

Status: Ongoing
Collection Method: Data produced within the D.S.S.
Frequency: Annually
Reference Period: 31 December
Timeliness: 9 months after end of calendar year
Earliest Available Data: Annual 1972
National Coverage: Great Britain

Statistician
Nigel Brough
Department of Social Security
ASD1;ASD1a
Tel: 0191 225 7391;
Email: broughn@asd1lbtn.dss-asd.gov.uk

Products that contain data from this source
Incapacity Benefit (annual); Incapacity Benefit / Severe Disablement Allowance Statistics (annual); Industrial Injuries Disablement Benefit/ Reduced Earnings Allowance /Retirement Allowance Statistics; Social Security Statistics

Statutory Maternity Pay
Department of Social Security

SMP is paid by an employer when the employee is pregnant and satisfies the class 1 contribution conditions. The tables produced by ASD1B are used for internal purposes only and are based on a 1% Sample of Employers End of Year Summaries (P14's).

Status: Ongoing
Frequency: Annually
Reference Period: April
Timeliness: 3 months
National Coverage: United Kingdom

Statistician
Martin McGill
Department of Social Security
ASD1;ASD1B
Tel: 0191 225 7661;
Email: Mcgillm@asd1lbtn.dss-asd.gov.uk

Statutory Sick Pay - GB
Department of Social Security

Statutory Sick Pay (SSP) is paid by the employer when the employee is sick for a period of more than 3 days and their contributions are fully satisfied. Where an individual has more than one spell of SSP in the period, or is paid SSP by more than one employer in the period they will be counted only once. The tables produced by ASD1B are used for internal purposes only and are based on a 1% Sample of Employers End of Year Summaries (P14's).

Status: Ongoing
Frequency: Annually
Reference Period: September
Timeliness: 4 months
National Coverage: United Kingdom

Statistician
Martin McGill
Department of Social Security
ASD1;ASD1B
Tel: 0191 225 7661;
Email: Mcgillm@asd1lbtn.dss-asd.gov.uk

Tax Benefit Model Tables
Department of Social Security

The Tax Benefit Model tables are designed to illustrate the weekly financial circumstances of a selection of hypothetical local authority and private tenants. The tables are produced annually from a spreadsheet-based model which calculates the interaction between taxes and certain benefits. The publication is divided into two main sections: families whose head is a full-time employee; and families whose head is unemployed and claims Job Seeker's Allowance.

Status: Ongoing
Collection Method: Benefit, tax and National Insurance rates taken from Budget
Frequency: Annually
Reference Period: April 1998
Timeliness: Between November 1980 and April 1993, Tax Benefit Model Tables was published each time there was a significant change to benefit, tax or National Insurance rates. Since April 1993, publication has been each April, reflecting the latest tax, benefit and National Insurance rates taking effect from that month.
Earliest Available Data: November 1980
National Coverage: United Kingdom

Statistician
Martin McGill
Department of Social Security
ASD1;ASD1b
Tel: 0191 225 7661;
Email: mcgillm@asd1lbtn.dss-asd.gov.uk

Products that contain data from this source
Tax Benefit Model Tables

War Pensions
Department of Social Security

A 5% quarterly extract from the War Pensions computer system.

Status: Ongoing
Frequency: Quarterly
Reference Period: February, May, August, November
Timeliness: 2 weeks
Earliest Available Data: November 1996
National Coverage: United Kingdom

Statistician
Martin McGill
Department of Social Security
ASD1;ASD1B
Tel: 0191 225 7661;
Email: Mcgillm@asd1lbtn.dss-asd.gov.uk

Widow's Benefit - GB
Department of Social Security

The Department of Social Security compiles data on Widow's Benefit. A 5 per cent sample is taken of people receiving Widow's Benefit in Great Britain and overseas.

Status: Ongoing
Collection Method: A sample from The Strategy Computer System
Earliest Available Data: 1971
National Coverage: England, Scotland, Wales
Disaggregation: From late 1999, sub-regional disaggregations will be possible.

Statistician
Ann Simpson-Hawkins
Department of Social Security
ASD1;ASD1D
Tel: 0191 225 7801;
Email: simpsona@asd1lbtn.dss-asd.gov.uk

See also:
In this chapter:
Family Resources Survey *(9.1)*

In other chapters:
British Social Attitudes Survey (BSA) Series *(see the Compendia and Reference chapter)*
Lone Parent Cohort *(see the Labour Market chapter)*

9.6 Occupational, Personal and State Pension Schemes

Migrant Workers - UK
Department of Social Security

The Department of Social Security compiles data on migrant workers. A full count is taken of immigrants registering or re-registering for National Insurance by sex, nationality and industry.

Status: Ongoing
Collection Method: Administrative Records
Frequency: Annually
Reference Period: National Insurance Contributions paid in respective of each tax year taken in February, 10 months after the end of each tax year.
Timeliness: Collection is taken 10 months after tax year and information produced 15 months after the end of the tax year
Earliest Available Data: 1975/76
National Coverage: Great Britain, Northern Ireland, United Kingdom
Sub-National: County

Statistician
Anne Simpson-Hawkins
Department of Social Security
ASD1;ASD1D
Tel: 0191 225 7801;
Email: Simpsona@asd1lbtn.dss-asd.gov.uk

Products that contain data from this source
Migrant Workers Statistics

Occupational Pension Schemes - UK
Government Actuary's Department

The Government Actuary's Department conducts the Occupational Pension Schemes Surveys from a sample of occupational pension schemes in the public and private sectors. The data are augmented by the use of data from the General Household Survey. Data are available relating to 1991 on the membership of occupational pension schemes by age, sex and type of scheme, the numbers of pensioners by age, the income and expenditure of schemes, the scheme benefits, employee and employer contributions, appointment of trustees and changes since 1987. The survey relating to 1995 will be published later in 1999.

Status: Ongoing
Collection Method: Large-scale (Sample) Survey
Frequency: Periodic
Reference Period: A calendar year
Earliest Available Data: 1956
National Coverage: United Kingdom

Statistician
Steve Smallwood
Government Actuary's Department
B2
Tel: 020 7211 2667;
Email: steve.smallwood@gad.gov.uk

Products that contain data from this source
Occupational Pension Schemes 1991 - Ninth survey by the Government Actuary

---

See also:
In this chapter:
Family Resources Survey *(9.1)*

9.7 Social Security Appeals

Medical Appeal Tribunals
Department of Social Security

The Department of Social Security compiles data on medical appeals. A full count is taken of appeals heard by Medical Appeal Tribunals relating to awards of Industrial Injuries Disablement Benefit, Mobility Allowance and Severe Disablement Allowance.

Status: Ceased temporarily
Collection Method: Appeals registered with the Independent Tribunal Service
Frequency: Quarterly
Reference Period: Quarters ending 31 March, 30 June, 30 September and 31 December
Timeliness: 13 weeks
National Coverage: Great Britain
Disaggregation: Medical Appeal Tribunal regions

Statistician
Martin McGill
Department of Social Security
ASD1;ASD1b
Tel: 0191 225 7661;
Email: mcgillm@asd1lbtn.dss-asd.gov.uk

Products that contain data from this source
Medical Appeal Tribunal Statistics; Social Security Statistics

---

Social Security Appeal Tribunals - GB
Department of Social Security

The Department of Social Security compiles data on Social Security Appeals. A full count is taken of appeals heard by Social Security Appeal Tribunals relating to awards of most Social Security benefits. Data cover Great Britain and are available for Independent Tribunal Service regions.

Status: Ceased temporarily
Collection Method: Appeals registered with the Independent Tribunal Service
Frequency: Quarterly
Reference Period: Quarters ending 31 March, 30 June, 30 September and 31 December
Timeliness: Thirteen weeks
National Coverage: Great Britain
Disaggregation: Independent Tribunal Service regions

Statistician
Martin McGill
Department of Social Security
ASD1;ASD1b
Tel: 0191 225 7661;
Email: mcgillm@asd1lbtn.dss-asd.gov.uk

Products that contain data from this source
Social Security Appeal Tribunal Statistics; Social Security Statistics

---

Household Finances - *Products*

9.8 Abstracts, Compendia, A-Z Catalogues, Directories and Reference Material

EOC Research Discussion Series
Equal Opportunities Commission

Published reports of research reviews or secondary analysis of data carried out by Equal Opportunities Commission staff or externally commissioned research workers. Each publication contains research on a specific topic. For example, 'Low pay and the National Insurance System: A statistical picture' includes analysis relating to employees earning below the National Insurance Lower Earnings Limit (NILEL). Some of the data in this product is disaggregated by gender.

Frequency: Ad hoc
Price: Please contact the EOC for the current publications list and pricing details.

Available from
Equal Opportunities Commission
Please see Annex B for full address details.

Family Expenditure Survey (NISRA Monitor)
Department of Finance and Personnel - Northern Ireland

Northern Ireland data on expenditure and income in relation to household characteristics. The publication contains data on household characteristics, income, expenditure, and UK regional data.

Delivery: Press Release, hardcopy publication
Frequency: Annual
Price: Free

Available from
Northern Ireland Statistics and Research Agency
Londonderry House
21-27 Chichester Street
Belfast BT1 4SX
Tel: 028 9025 2526

Sources from which data for this product are obtained
Family Expenditure Survey - Northern Ireland

Family Expenditure Survey Database
Office for National Statistics

Database of around 6,400 households each year. Includes details of expenditure, income and household composition. Full documentation included.

Frequency: Annual
Price: Free to academic users through the Data Archive. £1,500.00 to other users.

Available from
Denis Down
Room B2/05
Office for National Statistics
1 Drummond Gate
London SW1V 2QQ
Tel: 020 7533 5760

Sources from which data for this product are obtained
Family Expenditure Survey - UK

Family Resources Survey 1996-97
Department of Social Security

208 page report summarising results from the Family Resources Survey for 1996-97 in which over 25,000 households were interviewed. Chapters cover sample characteristics; income and receipt of Social Security benefits; tenure and housing costs; assets and savings; carers and those needing care; and employment. Similar reports exist for earlier years' Family Resources Surveys.

Delivery: News/Press Release
Frequency: Annually
Price: £30.00
ISBN: 1 84123 047 2

Available from
Corporate Document Services
Department of Social Security
Please see Annex B for full address details.

Sources from which data for this product are obtained
Family Resources Survey

Family Resources Survey 1996-97 - database
Department of Social Security

Hierarchical data set of 25,574 households interviewed as part of the Family Resources Survey (FRS) during 1996-97. Micro data relating to 1996-97 Family Resources Survey. Questionnaire covers household characteristics; sources and amount of income (including receipt of Social Security benefits); tenure and housing costs; assets and savings; carers and those needing care; and unemployment. Similar databases exist for earlier years' Family Resources Surveys.

Frequency: Annually

Available from
The Data Archive
University of Essex
Colchester
Tel: 01206 872001;
Email: archive@essex.AC.UK

Sources from which data for this product are obtained
Family Resources Survey

Family Spending
Office for National Statistics

Household expenditure and income in the UK derived from the Family Expenditure Survey. Each year the publication contains detailed analyses of expenditure on goods and services by households, their income, and the composition, size, type and location of households. Tables also available on floppy disk and CD-ROM.

Delivery: Periodic Release
Frequency: Annually
Price: £35.95 (1997-98)
ISBN: 0 11 621047 8
ISSN: 0965-1403

Available from
TSO Publications Centre and Bookshops
Please see Annex B for full address details.

Sources from which data for this product are obtained
Family Expenditure Survey - Northern Ireland;
Family Expenditure Survey - UK

Family Spending CD-ROM
Office for National Statistics

CD-ROM containing 6 years of information from Family Spending. Consists of tables, charts and descriptive text. Family Spending 1989 to 1994-95 containing detailed analyses of expenditure on goods and services by households, their income, and the composition, size, type and location of households.

Delivery: Ad hoc/One-off Release
Frequency: Ad hoc
Price: £99.00 + VAT Half price for academics
ISBN: 0 11 526507 4

Available from
TSO Publications Centre and Bookshops
Please see Annex B for full address details.

Sources from which data for this product are obtained
Family Expenditure Survey - UK

(A) Guide to ASD Statistical Projects
Department of Social Security

A comprehensive list of ongoing and Ad hoc statistical projects processed within the Department of Social Security's Analytical Services Division. The guide contains details of their frequency, sample size, method of production, data collected, total processing time and month of issue.

Delivery: Periodic Release
Frequency: Annually
Price: Free

Available from
Liz Cowley
Analytical Services Division
Room B2607
Department of Social Security
Benton Park Road
Longbenton
Newcastle upon Tyne NE98 1YX
Tel: 0191 225 7373.

Income Measures for Official Low-Income Statistics: The treatment of Housing Benefit costs and Local Government Taxes (DSS Analytical Note 2)
Department of Social Security

Methodological paper. A methodological paper looking at the treatment of Housing Benefit costs and Local Government taxes in relation to the Households Below Average Income series.

Delivery: Ad hoc/One-off Release
Frequency: One-off

Available from
Frosztega Margaret / Tadd Liz
Room 4/52
Department of Social Security
The Adelphi
1-11 John Adam Street
London WC2N 6HT
Tel: 020 7962 8232;
Email: frosztet@asdlondon.dss-asd.gov.uk

Sensitivity Testing in HBAI: An examination of results (DSS Analytical Note 1)
Department of Social Security

Methodology paper on Households Below Average Income statistics. The income data used in Households Below Average Income statistics are adjusted for the size and composition of the household, a process known as equivalisation, in order to be able to compare the living standards of households of different composition. The weightings used to make these adjustments affect the income attributed to the individuals within the households. This is a methodological paper examining the sensitivity of the results presented in Households Below Average Income statistics to the choice of equivalence scale.

Delivery: Ad hoc/One-off Release
Frequency: One-off

Available from
Frosztega Margaret / Tadd Liz
Room 4/52
Department of Social Security
The Adelphi
1-11 John Adam Street
London WC2N 6HT
Tel: 020 7962 8232;
Email: frosztet@asdlondon.dss-asd.gov.uk

See also:
In this chapter:
Household Incomes and Living Standards: Interpretation of data on very low incomes (DSS Analytical Note 4) *(9.10)*
Households Below Average Income: A Statistical Analysis 1979 - 1996/97 *(9.10)*
Social Security Statistics *(9.11)*
Tax Benefit Model Tables *(9.11)*

9.9 Assets and Liabilities of Households and Individuals

Relative Deprivation in Northern Ireland (PPRU Occasional Paper No 28)

Department of Health and Social Services - Northern Ireland

A research paper containing indices of multiple deprivation. The occasional paper contains relative deprivation scores and rankings for enumeration districts, wards and district council areas in Northern Ireland.

Delivery: Ad hoc/One-off Release
Frequency: Ad hoc
Price: £10.00 Floppy disk: £3.00
ISBN: 1 899203 03 6

Available from
TSO Publications Centre and Bookshops
Please see Annex B for full address details.

See also:
In this chapter:
Family Resources Survey *(9.8)*
Family Resources Survey - database *(9.8)*
Household Incomes and Living Standards: Interpretation of data on very low incomes (DSS Analytical Note 4) *(9.10)*
Households Below Average Income: *(9.10)*

In other chapters:
Economic Trends *(see the Economy chapter)*
Inland Revenue Statistics *(see the Government and the Public Sector chapter)*

9.10 Household and Personal Income

Household Incomes and Living Standards: Interpretation of data on very low incomes (DSS Analytical Note 4)
Department of Social Security

Methodological paper on income and living standards data. The paper investigates the link between household income and living standards in the United Kingdom with particular reference to the official publication Households Below Average Income. The main proposition is that although living standards are in general effectively proxied by household incomes there is reason to believe that, at the very bottom of the income distribution, incomes do not provide a reliable guide to material living standards.

Delivery: Ad hoc/One-off Release
Frequency: One-off

Available from
Frosztega Margaret / Tadd Liz
Room 4/52

Products

Department of Social Security
The Adelphi
1-11 John Adam Street
London WC2N 6HT
Tel: 020 7962 8232;
Email: frosztet@asdlondon.dss-asd.gov.uk

Households Below Average Income Database
Department of Social Security

Micro-data derived from either the Family Expenditure Survey (UK coverage) or the Family Resources Survey (GB coverage) depending on the time period. Detailed information on incomes of individuals within households together with information on household composition, age, sex, marital status and employment status of individuals. Updated annually since 1991/92.

Delivery: Other
Frequency: Annually
Price: Enquiries to Analytical Services Division 3, Department of Social Security

Available from
Frosztega Margaret / Tadd Liz
Room 4/52
Department of Social Security
The Adelphi
1-11 John Adam Street
London WC2N 6HT
Tel: 020 7962 8232;
Email: frosztet@asdlondon.dss-asd.gov.uk

Sources from which data for this product are obtained
Family Expenditure Survey - UK; Family Resources Survey

Households Below Average Income: 1979 - 1996/97
Department of Social Security

Statistics and commentary focusing on the lower part of the income distribution in Great Britain. Also includes some trends in low income households for the United Kingdom based on Family Expenditure Survey data, and an analysis of income dynamics based on the British Household Panel Study. The publication contains data on changes in real income from 1979 for the population as a whole, and by family type and economic status; shares of total income received by individuals below various percentiles of the income distribution, analysed by family type and economic status; and percentages of individuals below various income thresholds analysed by family type and economic status.

Delivery: Periodic Release
Frequency: Annually
Price: £33.00

ISBN: 1 84123 059 6
ISSN: 1359-2254

Available from
Corporate Document Services
Department of Social Security
Please see Annex B for full address details.

Sources from which data for this product are obtained
Family Expenditure Survey - UK; Family Resources Survey

See also:
In this chapter:
Family Expenditure Survey Database *(9.8)*
Family Resources Survey *(9.8)*
Family Resources Survey - database *(9.8)*
Family Spending *(9.8)*

9.11 Income from Benefits and Pensions

(The) Abstract of Statistics for Social Security Benefits and Contributions and Indices of Prices and Earnings
Department of Social Security

This publication shows net income after housing costs for various family types on average earnings since 1978, compares the value of the main state benefits with prices and earnings since 1948, gives rates of National Insurance contributions since 1971, and tabulates expenditure on Social Security benefits since 1948-49. Contains data on retail price Indices - all items, all items except housing, all items except rent, mortgage interest payments and council tax; average earnings indices, average weekly earnings for manual workers and all full-time adults; net income after housing costs for various family types on average, 2/3 and 1/2 average earnings at current and constant prices; rates of benefits, increase over previous rate, equivalent value at constant prices, average real value over the period between upratings, rate as a percentage of average earnings; income from retirement pension, unemployment benefit, sickness benefit and income support compared with average earnings for various family types; rates of national insurance contributions paid by employees on average earnings, by the self-employed and the non-employed; expenditure on social security benefits as a percentage of gross domestic product and in real terms.

Delivery: Periodic Release
Frequency: Annual
Price: £18.00
ISBN: 1 85197 839 9

Available from
Nigel Brough
Analytical Services Division
Room B2710
Department of Social Security
Benton Park Road
Longbenton
Newcastle upon Tyne NE98 1YX
Tel: 0191 225 7391

All Prescribed Diseases - Assessments of Claims to Industrial Injuries Disablement Benefit
Department of Social Security

Text, tables and charts showing a compilation of data covering all prescribed diseases - assessments of claims to Industrial Injuries Disablement Benefit.

Delivery: Periodic Release
Frequency: Quarterly

Available from
Martin McGill
Please see Annex B for full address details.

Sources from which data for this product are obtained
All prescribed diseases - assessments of claims to Industrial Injuries Disablement Benefit

Annual Housing Benefit and Council Tax Benefit Summary Statistics (and quarterly Update)
Department of Social Security

Tables relating to recipients and average weekly amounts of Housing Benefit and Council Tax Benefit. The publication contains data on recipients and amounts received by year, Government Office region, Council Tax valuation band and type of tenant.

Delivery: Periodic Release
Frequency: Annual and Quarterly publication
Price: Free
ISSN: 1359-656X

Available from
Ann Simpson-Hawkins
Department of Social Security
Please see Annex B for full address details.

Sources from which data for this product are obtained
Housing and Council Tax Benefits - GB

Attendance Allowance Statistics
Department of Social Security

DSS compiles data on Attendance Allowance which is for people who are so severely disabled, physically or mentally they need someone with them to help with personal care.

Delivery: Periodic Release
Frequency: Quarterly

Available from
Martin McGill
Please see Annex B for full address details.

Sources from which data for this product are obtained
Attendance Allowance - GB

Child Benefit Quarterly Summary of Statistics
Department of Social Security

Booklet presenting tables and text for recent claims. The Quarterly Child and Child Benefit (Lone Parent) Statistics tables reflect the changes in circumstances, known as 'movements' within a family during the quarters 31 March, 30 June, 30 September and 31 December each year. The Data Source is the Child Benefit Mainframe Computer Records, which show reported changes of circumstances during the relevant quarter. From April 1994, the sample has been reduced from a 4% to a 1% sample. From November 1998 the sample is 5% and following quarters will be February 1999, May 1999, August 1999 and November 1999. No tables are available at the present time.

Delivery: Periodic Release
Frequency: Quarterly
Price: Free

Available from
Martin McGill
Please see Annex B for full address details.

Sources from which data for this product are obtained
Child Benefit

Child Support Agency Quarterly Statistical Summary
Department of Social Security

The Department of Social Security (DSS) and the Child Support Agency (CSA) compile data and analyses on child maintenance. Data are taken from a 5 per cent scan of the Child Support Computer System. The main analyses of CSA cases are: amount of maintenance paid by absent parents, analysed by economic status, earnings and assessment type; amount of maintenance received by the parent/person with care, analysed by economic status and assessment type; general statistics relating to absent parents/persons with care (i.e. sex, marital status and accommodation type). The CSA came into effect in April 1993. Until March 1995 all scans of the Child Support Computer System captured only a 1 per cent sample. In May 1995 changes to the scan increased the sample size to 5 per cent.

Delivery: Hardcopy publication + database for internal interrogation
Frequency: Quarterly
Price: £5.00
ISSN: ISSN 1365-6198

Available from
Analytical Services Division Secretariat
Department of Social Security
Please see Annex B for full address details.

Sources from which data for this product are obtained
Child Support Agency - GB scan which is a 5% extract taken from the Child Support Computer System

---

Child Support Agency Quarterly Summary of Statistics (Northern Ireland)
Child Support Agency

Quarterly publication containing details of the CSA Caseload, Absent Parents and Parents With Care personal and financial details and time series information. Covers Number of cases, Referral Source, Gender, Age, Repartnering, Accommodation, Benefit Status, Maintenance Assessment, Income, Method of Payment and Payment Compliance.

Delivery: Periodic Release
Frequency: Quarterly
Price: £5.00

Available from
Eddie Finn
Department of Health and Social Services - Northern Ireland
Please see Annex B for full address details.

Sources from which data for this product are obtained
Child Support Agency Computer System (Northern Ireland); Social Security Benefit Geographical Information System; Social Security Benefit System (Northern Ireland)

Child's Special Allowance and Guardian's Allowance
Department of Social Security

Booklet presenting tables and text for recent claims. The annual Child Special Allowance and Guardian's Allowance provide an analysis of families and children in receipt of the benefit

Delivery: Periodic Release
Frequency: Annually
Price: Free

Available from
Martin McGill
Please see Annex B for full address details.

Sources from which data for this product are obtained
Child's Special Allowance - GB; Guardian's Allowance - GB

Contributions and Qualifying Years for Retirement Pension
Department of Social Security

Contains analyses of National Insurance Contributions (NIC's) paid or credited, Home Responsibilities Protection and details of number of qualifying years accrued for Retirement Pension.

Delivery: News/Press Release
Frequency: Annually
Price: Free
ISSN: 1462-9984

Available from
Ann Simpson-Hawkins
Department of Social Security
Benton Park Road
Newcastle Upon Tyne
Tel: 0191 225 7801;
Fax: 0191 225 7671;
Email: simpsona@asd11bth.dss-asd.gov.uk

Cross Benefit Analysis - A Quarterly Bulletin on the Population of Working Age on Key Benefits
Department of Social Security

Statistical tables on characteristics of the population of working age on key social security benefits. This shows a more coherent picture of those claimants of working age in the benefit system than can be gained from separate analysis of individual benefits. Includes information on the key characteristics of claimants, such as age, sex, family type, client group, duration of claim and numbers of children.

Delivery: Hardcopy publication
Frequency: Quarterly
Price: Free
ISSN: 1465-0355

Available from
Ian Hertwick
Department of Social Security
Please see Annex B for full address details.

Disability Living Allowance Statistics
Department of Social Security

A compilation of data on DLA which is for people who became disabled before the age of 65 and need help with care and mobility.

Delivery: Periodic Release
Frequency: Quarterly

Available from
Martin McGill
Department of Social Security
Please see Annex B for full address details.

Sources from which data for this product are obtained
Disability Living Allowance - GB

Disability Living Allowance-Attendance Allowance-Invalid Care Allowance Quarterly Summary of Statistics (Northern Ireland)
Department of Health and Social Services - Northern Ireland

Quarterly publication containing details of allowances, decisions on claims, awards by age & sex and main disabling condition.

Delivery: Periodic Release
Frequency: Quarterly
Price: £5.00

Available from
Michelle Martin
Room I Annexe I
Department of Health and Social Services - Northern Ireland
Castle Buildings, Stormont, Belfast, Northern Ireland, BT4 3UD
Tel: 028 9052 2061;
Email: michelle.martin@dhssni.gov.uk

Sources from which data for this product are obtained
Social Security Benefit Geographical Information System; Social Security Benefit System (Northern Ireland)

Disability Working Allowance Quarterly Tables (Northern Ireland)
Department of Health and Social Services - Northern Ireland

Incorporated into Family Credit Quarterly Tables. The tables cover: number of awards, family type, sex, average weekly payment, employment status, gross weekly earnings and qualifying benefit.

Delivery: Periodic Release
Frequency: Quarterly
Price: £5.00

Available from
Eddie Finn
Department of Health and Social Services - Northern Ireland
Please see Annex B for full address details.

Sources from which data for this product are obtained
Social Security Benefit Geographical Information System; Social Security Benefit System (Northern Ireland)

Disability Working Allowance Statistics
Department of Social Security

Statistical tables on characteristics of Disability Working Allowance claimants. Contains data on awards and disallowances. The awards breakdowns are available by country, region, family type, employment status, amount of award, number of children, income and hours worked and qualifying disability benefits. For disallowance breakdowns are available by reason of disallowance. The report consists of approximately 16 pages containing tables and charts.

Delivery: Hardcopy publication + database for internal interrogation
Frequency: Quarterly
Price: £5.00

Available from
Analytical Services Division Secretariat
Department of Social Security
Please see Annex B for full address details.

Sources from which data for this product are obtained
Disability Working Allowance - GB which is a 100% extract taken from the Disability Working Allowance Computer System

---

Family Credit Quarterly Tables (Northern Ireland)
Department of Health and Social Services - Northern Ireland

A quarterly analysis of Family Credit recipients within Northern Ireland. The report also incorporates information on Disability Working Allowance recipients within Northern Ireland. The tables cover: number of cases, office, employment status, family type, family size, amount of average family credit payment, occupation, other benefits, other income, hours worked, earnings, savings, age, age of children and child care costs.

Delivery: Periodic Release
Frequency: Quarterly
Price: £5.00

Available from
Eddie Finn
Department of Health and Social Services
Please see Annex B for full address details.

Family Credit Statistics Quarterly Enquiry
Department of Social Security

Statistical tables on characteristics of Family Credit claimants. Contains data of awards. The award breakdown are available by Country, region, family type, amount of award, number of children in different types of family, age of main earner, age of children and claim assessment details.

Delivery: Periodic Release
Frequency: Quarterly
Price: £5.00

Available from
Analytical Services Division
Please see Annex B for full address details.

Sources from which data for this product are obtained
Family Credit - GB which is a 5% extract taken from the Family Credit Computer System.

Housing Benefit and Council Tax Benefit Quarterly Summary Statistics
Department of Social Security

A leaflet (RR2) giving a guide to Housing Benefit and Council Tax Benefit.

Delivery: Periodic Release
Frequency: Quarterly
Price: Free
ISSN: 1463-8266

Available from
Local DSS Benefits Agency offices
BA Publications
Heywood Stores
Manchester Road
Heywood
Lancashire OL10 2PZ

Sources from which data for this product are obtained
Housing and Council Tax Benefits - GB

Incapacity Benefit (annual)
Department of Social Security

Data are available by amounts and diagnosis. Monthly return to compile an annual 100% count. Data cover Great Britain and are available at Government Office regional levels. Data have been collected since 1948 for Sickness/Invalidity

Benefit, since 1984 for Severe Disability Allowance and since 1995 for Incapacity Benefit. ASD1B Statistics are collected quarterly in May, August, November and February by computer using a 5 per cent sample.

Available from
Tel: 0191 2257661

Sources from which data for this product are obtained
Social Security Statistics

Incapacity Benefit / Severe Disablement Allowance Statistics (annual)
Department of Social Security

The Department of Social Security collects data on people claiming benefit due to being incapable of work due to illness or disability. This includes Sickness/Invalidity Benefit and Severe Disablement and Incapacity Benefit. Data are available by age, sex, length of spell of incapacity, marital status of women, contribution conditions, amounts of benefit, dependency position, other benefits in payment, diagnosis, reason not entitled to Statutory Sick Pay, reason for transfer from Statutory Sick Pay and date of entitlement. Data cover Great Britain and are available at Government Office regional levels. Data have been collected since 1948 for Sickness/Invalidity Benefit, since 1984 for Severe Disability Allowance and since 1995 for Incapacity Benefit. Statistics are collected annually in April, clerically by a 1 per cent sample. The annual statistics are published about fifteen months after the reference period.

Delivery: Periodic Release
Frequency: Annually

Available from
Martin McGill
Department of Social Security
Please see Annex B for full address details.

Sources from which data for this product are obtained
Social Security Statistics

Incapacity Benefit / Severe Disablement Allowance Statistics (quarterly)
Department of Social Security

The Department of Social Security collects data on people claiming benefit due to being incapable of work due to illness or disability. This includes Sickness/Invalidity Benefit and Severe Disablement and Incapacity Benefit. Data are available by age, sex,

amounts of benefit, dependency position, and diagnosis. Data cover Great Britain and are available at Government Office regional levels. Data have been collected since 1948 for Sickness/Invalidity Benefit, since 1984 for Severe Disability Allowance and since 1995 for Incapacity Benefit. Statistics are collected quarterly in May, August, November and February by computer using a 5 per cent sample.

Delivery: Periodic Release
Frequency: Quarterly
ISBN: 1-85197-859-3

Available from
Martin McGill
Department of Social Security
Please see Annex B for full address details.

Income Related Benefits - Estimates of Take-up in 1996/97
Department of Social Security

Content: Estimates of take-up of Housing Benefit, Council Tax Benefit, Income support and Family Credit by both caseload and expenditure for Great Britain. Caseload take-up compares the number of benefit recipients with the number who would be receiving if everyone took up their entitlement for the full period of their entitlement. Expenditure take-up compares the total amount of benefit received with the total amount that would be received if everyone took up their entitlement for the full period of their entitlement. Housing Benefit and Council Tax Benefit figures are given with a family and tenure type breakdown as follows: average weekly amount claimed, average weekly amount unclaimed, the total amount claimed, range of total unclaimed, the expenditure take-up range, the number of recipients, the range of entitled non-recipients, and the caseload take-up range. Income support figures are given with a family type breakdown in the same categories as above. This year the estimates for the family type 'Pensioners' are sub divided into 'Pensioner couples', 'Single females' and 'Single males' and the family type 'Others' is subdivided into 'Other couples', 'Other single females' and 'Other single males'. Estimates of Family Credit take-up are only given in point estimates because the six-month nature of the benefit makes the production of range estimates impossible. Estimates are broken-down into single and couples. This edition also looks into the characteristics of the Entitled Non Recipients, a benefit unit that is entitled to a benefit but is not receiving it.

Delivery: News/Press Release
Frequency: Annually
Price: £15.00
ISBN: 1-84123-068-5

Available from
Corporate Document Services
Department of Social Security
Please see Annex B for full address details.

Sources from which data for this product are obtained
Family Resources Survey, The Family Resources Survey 1996/97, Department of Social Security Administrative Sources, Family Credit Statistical System

Income Support Annual Statistical Enquiry
Department of Social Security

Prior to the Income Support Quarterly Statistical Enquiry, data on caseload characteristics were collected and published annually. Annual publication was replaced in 1993 by quarterly release.

Delivery: Historic hardcopy publication and database for internal interrogation
Frequency: Annual up to 1993

Available from
Jason Bradbury
Department of Social Security
Room B2712
PO Box 2GB
Newcastle-upon-Tyne
Tel: 0191 255 7883;
Email: bradburj@asd11btn.dss-asd.gov.uk

Income Support Statistics - Quarterly Enquiry
Department of Social Security

Statistical tables on characteristics of Income Support recipients. Contains data on total, range and average amounts of income support in payment, number and age of claimant, partners and dependants, type and amount of housing costs, incomes and capital, type and number of premiums and deductions for third parties, and length of time in receipt and distribution of cases by Government Office Region. Also included are data regarding claimants in residential care and nursing homes by number and age of claimant, sex, type of care and accommodation charges.

Delivery: Hardcopy publication and database for internal interrogation
Frequency: Quarterly
Price: £5.00

Available from
Analytical Services Division Secretariat
Department of Social Security
Please see Annex B for full address details.

Industrial Death Benefit
Department of Social Security

Tabulated data on Industrial Death Benefit.

Delivery: Periodic Release
Frequency: Annually

Available from
Martin McGill
Department of Social Security
Please see Annex B for full address details.

Sources from which data for this product are obtained
Industrial Death Benefit - GB

Industrial Injuries Disablement Benefit/ Reduced Earnings Allowance /Retirement Allowance Statistics
Department of Social Security

Tabulated data on Disablement Benefit using stock and movements in the current period, rated up from a 10 per cent sample.

Delivery: Periodic Release
Frequency: Annually

Available from
Martin McGill
Department of Social Security
Please see Annex B for full address details.

Sources from which data for this product are obtained
Industrial Injuries Disablement Benefit Assessment/Reduced Earnings Allowance; Social Security Statistics

Jobseeker's Allowance Statistics Quarterly Enquiry
Department of Social Security

Statistical tables on characteristics of Jobseeker's Allowance claimants. Contains data on type and average amount of Jobseeker's Allowance in payment, number and age of claimants, partners and dependants, type and amount of housing costs, income and capital, type and number of premiums and deductions for third parties and length of time in receipt and distribution of cases by Government Office Region.

Delivery: Hardcopy publication and database for internal interrogation
Frequency: Quarterly
Price: £5.00

Available from
Analytical Services Division Secretariat
Department of Social Security
Please see Annex B for full address details.

Sources from which data for this product are obtained
Jobseeker's Allowance Quarterly Statistical Enquiry - Great Britain which is a 5% data extract

taken from the Jobseeker's Allowance Payment System.

Maternity Allowance Quarterly
Department of Social Security

A 5% sample of awards to Maternity Allowance in Great Britain.

Delivery: Periodic Release

Available from
Martin McGill
Department of Social Security
Please see Annex B for full address details.

New Claims to Industrial Injuries Disablement Benefit
Department of Social Security

10% quarterly sample of all IIDB claims for accidents and prescribed diseases. From December 1997 this is included in "all prescribed diseases".

Delivery: Periodic Release
Frequency: Quarterly

Available from
Martin McGill
Department of Social Security
Please see Annex B for full address details.

Sources from which data for this product are obtained
New Claims to Industrial Injuries Disablement Benefit

Occupational Deafness
Department of Social Security

All claims to "Occupational deafness" and those referred to an otologist for examination and result of the referral. Monthly return to compile an annual 100% count.

Delivery: Periodic Release
Frequency: Annually

Sources from which data for this product are obtained
Occupational Deafness

Occupational Pension Schemes 1991 - Ninth Survey by the Government Actuary
Government Actuary's Department

This report gives information on numbers of pension schemes and pension scheme members and the benefits provided by pension schemes in 1991. It includes financial information on pension schemes.

Delivery: Other
Frequency: Every four years
Price: £7.50
ISBN: 0 11 702582 2

Available from
TSO Publications Centre and Bookshops
Please see Annex B for full address details.

(The) Pensioners' Income Series 1996/97
Department of Social Security

The Pensioners' Incomes Series is an annual publication, which examines trends in the components and level of pensioners' incomes distribution and the position of pensioners within the overall income distribution. It provides analysis for pensioner units, defines as single people over State Pension Age and couples (married or cohabiting) where the male partner is over State Pension Age. It also includes a separate analysis of couples where the male partner is not over the State Pension Age, but the female is. Non-householders are not covered by the series. The 1996/97 edition provides information for 1979, 1989, and from 1994/5 to 1996/7 from the Family Expenditure Survey and from 1994/5 to 1996/7 from the Family Resources Survey.

Delivery: News/Press Release
Frequency: Annually
ISBN: 1 85197 863 1

Available from
Analytical Services Division Secretariat
Department of Social Security
Please see Annex B for full address details.

Sources from which data for this product are obtained
Family Expenditure Survey, Family Resources Survey

Retirement Pensions Summary of Statistics
Department of Social Security

The Department of Social Security compiles data on retirement pensions. The results in this publication are derived from a 5 per cent sample of 'live' cases taken from the Pensions Strategy Computer System (PSCS). Prior to September 1995, the results were based on a 10 percent sample. Please note that all analyses exclude Northern Ireland. All data within the tables are grossed to the total 'live' Retirement Pension caseload for Great Britain and overseas, but excluding Northern Ireland. The data in this publication are, as with any grossed sample results, subject to sampling error. Some of the data in this product is disaggregated by gender.

Delivery: Periodic Release
Frequency: Bi-annually
Price: Free
ISSN: 1464-1364

Available from
Ann Simpson-Hawkins
Department of Social Security
Please see Annex B for full address details.

Sources from which data for this product are obtained
Retirement Pensions

Social Security Statistics
Department of Social Security

Data on recipients of Social Security benefits, amounts claimed, expenditure and National Insurance contributions. Contains data on: family credit, income support, housing benefit, council tax benefit, social fund, retirement pension, unemployment benefit, sickness benefit, invalidity benefit, severe disablement allowance, attendance allowance, disability living allowance, disability working allowance, invalid care allowance, war pensions, industrial injuries disablement benefit, industrial death benefit, workmen's compensation supplementation scheme, child benefit, one parent benefit, widow's benefit, guardian's allowance, child's special allowance, and maternity benefits. Also includes: pensioners' income, medical boarding centres, child support agency, national insurance contributions, personal pensions, low-income statistics, social security appeals, and take-up of income-related benefits

Delivery: Periodic Release
Frequency: Annually
Price: £36.00
ISBN: 0 11 4123067 7

Available from
TSO Publications Centre and Bookshops
Please see Annex B for full address details.

Sources from which data for this product are obtained
Child Benefit; Child Support Agency - GB; Child's Special Allowance - GB; Disability Living Allowance - GB; Disability Working Allowance - GB; Family Credit - GB; Guardian's Allowance - GB; Housing and Council Tax Benefits - GB; Incapacity Benefit / Severe Disablement Allowance (annual); Income Support Quarterly Statistical Enquiry - GB; Industrial Death Benefit - GB; Invalid Care Allowance; Jobseeker's Allowance Quarterly Statistical Enquiry - Great Britain; Medical Appeal Tribunals; Second Tier Pensions - UK; Social Security Appeal Tribunals - GB; Social Security Statistics

---

Social Security Summary Statistics
Department of Health and Social Services

Quarterly publication containing the most recent statistics for a number of Social Security benefits within Northern Ireland. Summary statistics covering Social Security Expenditure, Attendance Allowance, Incapacity Benefit, Disability Living Allowance, Retirement Pension, Family Credit, Child Support Agency, Child Benefit, Job Seekers Allowance, Income Support.

Delivery: Periodic Release
Frequency: Quarterly

Available from
Gordon Brown
Department of Health and Social Services - Northern Ireland
Social Security Statistics Branch
Tel: 028 9052 3339.
Email: gordon.brown@dhssni.gov.uk

Tax Benefit Model Tables
Department of Social Security

Net income for families in work or out of work taking account of deductions from earnings and Social Security benefits received. Contains data on income tax and national insurance contributions, family credit, child benefit, housing benefit, council tax benefit, net income before and after housing costs and marginal deduction rates for a variety of family types living in rented housing at various levels of gross earnings; similar data where the head of the family is unemployed and no longer receiving family credit; levels of gross earnings at which net income in work equals that when unemployed; and replacement ratios, i.e. net income when unemployed and receiving income support/ job seeker's allowance as a percentage of net income when in work.

Delivery: Periodic Release
Frequency: Annually
Price: £5.00
ISBN: 1 85197 875 5

Available from
Susan Abbott
Analytical Services Division
Room B2613
Department of Social Security
Benton Park Road
Longbenton
Newcastle upon Tyne NE98 1YX.
Tel: 0191 225 5512

Sources from which data for this product are obtained
Tax Benefit Model Tables; The Abstract of Statistics for Social Security Benefits and Contributions and Indices of Prices and Earnings

---

Unemployed Claimants - Summary Statistics (Northern Ireland)
Department of Health and Social Services - Northern Ireland

Quarterly publication containing details of claimants, benefit position, sex, reason for non-payment, duration of spell, dependants and amount of Benefit. Some of the data in this product is disaggregated by gender. August 1996 was the last in the series.

Delivery: Periodic Release
Frequency: Quarterly
Price: £5.00

Available from
Helen McClure
Room 1 Annexe 1
Department of Health and Social Services - Northern Ireland
Castle Buildings, Stormont, Belfast, Northern Ireland, BT4 3UD
Tel: 028 9052 2762.
Email: helen.mcclure@dhssni.gov.uk

Sources from which data for this product are obtained
Social Security Benefit Geographical Information System; Social Security Benefit System (Northern Ireland)

See also:
In this chapter:
Family Resources Survey *(9.8)*
Family Resources Survey - database *(9.8)*
Households Below Average Income Database *(9.10)*
Households Below Average Income: *(9.10)*

9.12 Occupational, Personal and State Pension Schemes

Contributions and Qualifying Years for Retirement Pension
Department of Social Security

Publication presenting text and tables on: National Insurance Contributions paid or credited, Home Responsibilities Protection and details of the number of qualifying years accrued towards the basic state Retirement Pension.

Delivery: News/Press Release
Frequency: Annually
Price: Free
ISSN: 1462-9984

Available from
Analytical Services Division 1D
Room B2715
Department of Social Security

Products

Benton Park Road
Longbenton
Newcastle Upon Tyne NE98 IYX.
Tel: 0191 225 7094.

Sources from which data for this product are obtained
Lifetime Labour Market Database

Migrant Workers Statistics
Department of Social Security

Publication presenting tables and text on numbers of non-UK nationals arriving in the UK from abroad, where registered or re-registered for National Insurance purposes.

Delivery: News/Press Release
Frequency: Annually
Price: Free
ISSN: 1358-2119

Available from
Analytical Services Division ID
Department of Social Security
Please see Annex B for full address details.

Sources from which data for this product are obtained
Lifetime Labour Market Database; Migrant Workers - UK

Second Tier Pension Provision
Department of Social Security

Publication presenting text and tables on: Contracting Out Pension schemes; Appropriate Personal Pension schemes; and State Earnings Related Pension scheme

Delivery: News/Press Release
Frequency: Annually
Price: £15.00
ISSN: 1461-7595

Available from
Analytical Services Division ID
Department of Social Security
Please see Annex B for full address details.

Sources from which data for this product are obtained
Lifetime Labour Market Database.

See also:
In this chapter:
Family Resources Survey *(9.9)*
Family Resources Survey - database *(9.8)*
(The) Pensioners' Incomes Series 1993 *(9.11)*

9.13   Social Security Appeals

Medical Appeal Tribunal Statistics
Department of Social Security

Booklet presenting tables and text on recent appeals. The presentation format is main findings with graphs followed by tables. Statistics are collected for all appeals and referrals which have been registered with the Independent Tribunal Service, within each quarter ending 31 March, 30 June, 30 September and 31 December.

Delivery: Periodic Release
Frequency: Quarterly
Price: Free

Available from
Martin McGill
Analytical Services Division
Room B2612
Department of Social Security
Benton Park Road
Longbenton
Newcastle upon Tyne NE98 IYX
Tel: 0191 225 7661.

Sources from which data for this product are obtained
Medical Appeal Tribunals

Social Security Appeal Tribunal Statistics
Department of Social Security

Booklet presenting tables and text on recent appeals. Statistics are collected for all appeals and referrals which have been registered with the Independent Tribunal Service, within each quarter ending 31 March, 30 June, 30 September and 31 December. The publication is abbreviated to 16 pages just to include Great Britain, Scotland and Wales/South Western regions. A further breakdown is available by North East, London North, London South, Midlands, North Western on request.

Delivery: Periodic Release
Frequency: Quarterly
Price: Free

Available from
Martin McGill
Department of Social Security
Please see Annex B for full address details.

Sources from which data for this product are obtained
Social Security Appeal Tribunals - GB

The Economy

Statistics covering the **Economy** are collected, administered and disseminated by a number of separate Departments, Agencies and organisations including the **Office for National Statistics, Her Majesty's Customs and Excise, the National Assembly for Wales, the Department of Trade and Industry, Scottish Executive,** and the **Northern Ireland Department of Economic Development**. The available statistics embrace a number of subject areas including: the **Balance of Payments Accounts, Costs Prices and Inflation, Cyclical Economic Indicators, Input-Output Accounts, International aid and Investment, National Economic Accounts, Overseas Trade in Goods, Overseas Trade in Services, Regional and sub-Regional Accounts..**

The basic data are generated from a number of separate information 'Sources' and the resultant statistics are disseminated through a whole range of statistical 'Analyses' and 'Products', all of which are described in the following chapter. Users looking for a cross-section of UK-wide statistics on the **Economy** may find the following products useful:

> **Economic Trends** (monthly publication)
> **United Kingdom Economic Accounts** (quarterly publication)
> **Economic Trends Annual Supplement** (annual publication)

Users interested in a wider range of official statistics including statistics on the **Economy** may like to refer to the following compendia:

> On-line Databases (See Chapter 1):
> > **StatBase - StatStore**
> > **StatBase -TimeZone**
> > **DataBank**

> Hardcopy Compendia (See Chapter 2):
> > **Annual Abstract of Statistics**
> > **Britain 2000: The official Yearbook of the United Kingdom**
> > **Monthly Digest of Statistics**
> > **Regional Trends**
> > **Social Trends**

Users may also find what they need on the various Departmental Websites. These are listed in Chapter 1.

10 The Economy - *Sources and Analyses*

10.1 Balance of Payments (BoP) Accounts

Balance of Payments Account - UK
Office for National Statistics

The Office for National Statistics compiles these accounts. The object of the balance of payments accounts is to identify and record transactions between residents of the United Kingdom and residents abroad in a way that is suitable for analysing the economic relations between the UK economy and the rest of the world. The transactions may represent resources provided by or to UK residents (i.e. goods and services exported and imported, and the use of investments); transactions in the UK's foreign assets or liabilities; or transfer payments. In principle, transactions are recorded when the ownership of goods or assets changes and when services are rendered. In practice this is not always possible. In the UK balance of payments accounts, transactions are currently classified into the following main groups: current account covers trade in goods, trade in services, income in particular earnings arising from foreign investments and current transfers; capital account: transactions cover transfer of ownership of assets, transfer of funds associated with acquisition or disposal of fixed assets; financial account covers the flows of financial assets and liabilities; and international investment position records the levels of external assets and liabilities.

Status: Ongoing
Frequency: Quarterly
National Coverage: United Kingdom

Statistician
Colin Yeend
Office for National Statistics
Tel: 020 7533 6075

Products that contain data from this analysis
Annual Abstract of Statistics; Economic Trends; Economic Trends Annual Supplement; Financial Statistics; Monthly Digest of Statistics; Office for National Statistics Databank / Datastore; UK Balance of Payments (First Release); United Kingdom Balance of Payments - The Pink Book; United Kingdom Economic Accounts (Quarterly Supplement to Economic Trends); United Kingdom National Accounts - The Blue Book; United Kingdom National Accounts, Sources and Methods

UK Trade on a Balance of Payments Basis
Office for National Statistics

The Office for National Statistics (ONS) converts the Overseas Trade Statistics (OTS) data to a balance of payments (BoP) basis consistent with the National Accounts. BoP data are available from 1988 for trade with the EC and non-EC, and generally from 1970 at world level. BoP data are available at seasonally adjusted current prices for broad commodity and area groups. Volume and price indices are available by commodity group. The ONS also produces seasonally adjusted current price OTS data at a high level of aggregation and certain volume and price indices of OTS commodities. These data are available from 1970.

Status: Ongoing
Frequency: Monthly
Timeliness: Within 8 weeks.
Earliest Available Data: 1970
National Coverage: United Kingdom

Statistician
David Ruffles
Office for National Statistics
Tel: 020 7533 6070;
Email: david.ruffles@ons.gov.uk

Products that contain data from this analysis
Annual Abstract of Statistics; Economic Trends; Economic Trends Annual Supplement; Monthly Digest of Statistics; Monthly Review of External Trade Statistics (Business Monitor MM24); Office for National Statistics Databank / Datastore; UK Trade (First Release); UK Trade in Goods Analysed in Terms of Industries (Business Monitor MQ10); United Kingdom Balance of Payments - The Pink Book; United Kingdom Economic Accounts (Quarterly Supplement to Economic Trends); United Kingdom National Accounts - The Blue Book

See also:
In this chapter:
Overseas Film and Television Industries *(10.8)*
Trade in Services (Annually) *(10.8)*
Trade in Services (Monthly) *(10.8)*
Trade in Services (Quarterly) *(10.8)*

10.2 Costs, Prices and Inflation

Consumer Price Collection - UK
Office for National Statistics

The Office for National Statistics compiles data on consumer prices. Each month around 150,000 price quotations are collected for over 600 items, which make up the Retail Price Index 'basket' of goods. The selection of items to be priced and the weights attached to items and shops are based on the findings of the Family Expenditure Survey (FES). The main use of the data is to calculate the Retail Price Index. This is a measure of price changes used in determining certain state benefits such as pensions, the value of gilts and National Savings certificates, and in assessing liability for capital gains tax. It is also widely used in pay negotiations, sometimes on a contractual basis, and is used by the regulators of privatised industries.

Status: Ongoing
Collection Method: Large-scale (Sample) Survey
Frequency: Monthly
Timeliness: 4 - 5 Weeks
National Coverage: United Kingdom

Statistician
Caroline Lakin
Office for National Statistics
Tel: 020 7533 5840;
Email: caroline.lakin@ons.gov.uk

Products that contain data from this source
A Brief Guide to the Retail Prices Index; Annual Abstract of Statistics; Consumer Trends; Economic Trends; Financial Statistics; Labour Market Trends; Monthly Digest of Statistics; Retail Prices 1914-90; Retail Prices Index (Business Monitor); Retail Prices Index (First Release); Retail Prices Index Technical Manual; RPI Advisory Committee Reports - Methodological Issues Affecting the RPI; Social Trends

Harmonised Index of Consumer Prices
Office for National Statistics

HICPs are calculated in each member state of the European Union for the purposes of European comparisons of consumer price inflation as required by the Maastricht

Treaty. From January 1999, it has been used by the European Central Bank as the measure for its definition of price stability across the Euro area.

Status: Ongoing
Frequency: Index levels and 12-month percentage changes monthly; weights annually
Reference Period: Three days centred around a Tuesday in the middle of the month
Timeliness: The index is published one month after prices are collected.
Earliest Available Data: For the all-items index and its 12 main sub-divisions: index level: January 1988; 12-month percentage changes: January 1989. For the detailed sub-divisions of the HICP: index level: January 1996; 12-month percentage changes: January 1997.
National Coverage: United Kingdom

Statistician
Jim O'Donoghue
Office for National Statistics
Consumer Prices and General Inflation Division
Tel: 020 7533 5818;
Email: jim.o'donoghue@ons.gov.uk

Products that contain data from this analysis
Labour Market Trends; Monthly Digest of Statistics; Retail Prices Index (Business Monitor); Retail Prices Index (First Release)

See also:
In other chapters:
Family Expenditure Survey - UK *(see the Household Finances chapter)*

10.3 Input-Output Accounts

Input-Output Balances - Scotland
Scottish Executive

The Scottish Executive Industry Department compiles data on the relationship between industries, final demand and the labour force. Data provide a detailed and internally consistent picture of the economy for a given time period. They detail the flows of all goods and services, in constant monetary terms, from industry to industry and from producer to consumer. Data are available by what commodities the various industries make, what commodities the various industries purchase and what commodities are purchased from the rest of the world and the rest of the UK. Data are also available on what commodities are exported to the rest of the world and the rest of the UK. The tables cover Scotland and were collected on a ten-yearly basis up until 1989. It is planned that annual updates will be produced from 1992 onwards. 1979, 1989 tables and multipliers produced at SIC80. 1992, 1993

balances only at SIC92. 1994 tables and multipliers at SIC92. 1995 tables and multipliers at SIC92.

Status: Ongoing
Frequency: Annually
Reference Period: annual data
Timeliness: 2 years 6 months
Earliest Available Data: 1979
National Coverage: Scotland

Statistician
Maria Melling
Scottish Executive
Tel: 0131 244 0297

Products that contain data from this analysis
Input-Output Tables and Multipliers for Scotland; The Manufacturing Sector in Scotland (Statistical Bulletin)

Input-Output Tables - United Kingdom
Office for National Statistics

The Office for National Statistics compiles data on input-output supply and use tables. Input-output framework shows a balanced and complete picture of the flows and products of the economy for a year. Data are given at current prices. Analytical input-output tables are also derived from the balances. Analytical tables are compiled and published every five years whereas the Input-Output Supply and Use Tables are published annually. From September 1998 this data will become consistent with the European System of Accounts (ESA 95).

Frequency: Annually
Earliest Available Data: 1961
National Coverage: United Kingdom

Statistician
S. Mahajan
Office for National Statistics
Tel: 020 7533 5954

Products that contain data from this analysis
Economic Trends; Input-Output Tables for the United Kingdom; United Kingdom Input-Output Supply and Use Balances, 1992-1996; United Kingdom National Accounts - The Blue Book

10.4 International Aid and Investment

Statistical Returns to the Development Assistance Committee of OECD
Department for International Development

Production of internationally comparable data on UK aid flows to all recipient countries.

Status: Ongoing
Frequency: Continuously
Reference Period: 1987-1996
Timeliness: Six months
Earliest Available Data: 1970s
National Coverage: United Kingdom
Sub-National: Mainly full, some sampled

Statistician
Elizabeth Robin
Department for International Development
Statistics Department; Statistical Reporting and Support Group
Tel: 01355 843329;
Email: ej-robin@dfid.gov.uk

Products that contain data from this analysis
Statistics on International Development; Development Counts

10.5 National Economic Accounts - Main Aggregates

Consumers' Expenditure
Office for National Statistics

The Office for National Statistics compiles data on consumers' expenditure. The main consumers' expenditure headings are: cars, motorcycles and other vehicles; furniture and floor coverings; other durable goods; food; alcoholic drink and tobacco; clothing and footwear; energy products; other goods; rent, rates and water charges; and other services. Data are available seasonally adjusted and at current and constant prices. Data are also available by region, but only on an annual basis and at current prices. This data are consistent with the European System of Accounts 1995 (ESA 95).

Status: Ongoing
Frequency: Quarterly
Disaggregation: Region

Statistician
Margaret Dolling
Office for National Statistics
NEI; Consumers' Expenditure
Tel: 020 7533 5996;
Email: margaret.dolling@ons.gov.uk

Products that contain data from this analysis
Annual Abstract of Statistics; Consumer Trends; Economic Trends; Economic Trends Annual Supplement; Financial Statistics; Monthly Digest of Statistics; Office for National Statistics Databank / Datastore; Regional Trends; Social Trends; United Kingdom National Accounts - The Blue Book; United Kingdom National Accounts, Sources and Methods

Gross Capital Formation
Office for National Statistics

From September 1998 this data will become consistent with the European System of Accounts (ESA 95).

Status: Ongoing
Frequency: Quarterly
Reference Period: Quarter
Timeliness: Seven weeks
Earliest Available Data: 1948
National Coverage: United Kingdom

Statistician
Uzair Rizki
Office for National Statistics
Tel: 020 7533 5926;
Email: uzair.rizki@ons.gov.uk

Products that contain data from this analysis
Annual Abstract of Statistics; Economic Trends; Economic Trends Annual Supplement; Financial Statistics; Monthly Digest of Statistics; Office for National Statistics Databank / Datastore; Regional Trends; Social Trends; United Kingdom National Accounts - The Blue Book; United Kingdom National Accounts, Sources and Methods

---

National Accounts
Office for National Statistics

The Office for National Statistics combines a very wide variety of data sources to produce economic accounts consistent with the System of National Accounting (SNA) agreed by the United Nations. This overview describes what the major components for output, income and expenditure are and how they fit together. References are made to other chapters in the guide, as appropriate.

Main Approaches
Although National Accounts as a discipline requires understanding of economics and statistics, the basic principles can be described simply. The UK National Accounts set out to quantify three things: 1. goods and services produced; 2. expenditure taking place; 3. income generated. Conceptually the total economic activity quantified through each of these three approaches is identical. In practice, however, statistical problems mean that this rarely occurs. The main aggregates, such as Gross Domestic Product (GDP), therefore need to be derived by combining data from these different approaches. Gross Domestic Product is a measure of total economic activity in this country. It is 'gross' in the sense that it does not deduct the cost of wear and tear, because this is impossible to measure and hard to estimate. It is 'domestic' in the sense that it relates to production in UK territory. There are several other important aggregates, notably Gross National Income. The Gross National

Income includes those overseas activities that generate income for UK nationals, and excludes activities in UK territory that generate income for foreign nationals.

The first approach involves looking at production by industry of output. This approach, called the 'output' or 'production' approach, presents output for different Standard Industrial Classification (SIC 92) categories. Categories of industry comprise `Agriculture' (see Chapter 13), `Production' and `Construction' (see Chapter 14), and `Service' Industries (see Chapters 10 and 15). The most comprehensive and detailed production presentation is given by input-output statistics. The second approach is expenditure analyses which show households and non-profit institutions serving-households expenditure, Government expenditure, capital formation (fixed investment) and charges in inventories. This approach includes the presentation of imports and exports, and of the `Basic Price Adjustment'. This adjustment deducts expenditure on taxes on products (having allowed for subsidies). `Transfer payments' such as taxes and benefits, are not related to production and therefore do not contribute to GDP. Payments related to production are called `primary income'. The third approach gives rise to analyses by category of income. This means wages and salaries for people, and gross operating surplus for corporations and general government enterprises. Gross operating surplus encompasses gross trading profits, rental income, non-trading capital consumption and is measured after deducting holding gains on inventories. The income approach is also used to compile figures for GDP on a regional and county basis. Data are available on an annual basis, at base prices and in current prices only.

Sector Accounts
In the sector accounts the UK economy is divided into institutional sectors. These are the general government, comprising central government and local government; the corporate sector, comprising public and private non-financial and financial companies; and the household sector. The sector accounts also include the rest of the world sector, to show the UK's transactions with the rest of the world, and this is equivalent to the balance of payments.

In the sector accounts, the current and capital accounts show the components of the income measure of GDP by sector, transfers of income between sectors, and the components of the expenditure measure of GDP by sector. The capital account contains transactions relating to capital goods which are used in production and are considered to last for more than one accounting period,

whilst the current account shows income current expenditure and current transfers. Examples of capital goods are buildings, machinery and inventories and in the latest revision of the SNA intangible assets such as computer software are also included. The balance of the current and capital account for each sector shows whether income has exceeded expenditure, or vice versa. This balance is called net lending or borrowing: Sectors with income higher than expenditure have a surplus to invest in financial assets or to reduce borrowing, whilst sectors with expenditure higher than income have a deficit which must be funded by increasing borrowing or selling financial assets. The transactions in financial assets and liabilities are presented in the financial transactions account for each sector, and they show how funds flow from the sectors in surplus to the sectors in deficit. The financial transactions account are compiled from transactions in a standard list of financial instruments, and total financial transactions are, in principal, equal to net lending or borrowing for each sector. Examples of financial instruments are notes and coins, bank lending and company securities. The current, capital and financial transactions accounts together make up a complete transactions account for each sector. The UK National Accounts also include balance sheets showing the value of tangible assets, financial assets, financial liabilities and net wealth for each sector. The financial balance sheet of the rest of the world sector is equivalent to the National balance sheet, showing the external assets and liabilities of the UK.

Status: Ongoing
National Coverage: United Kingdom

Statistician
Jon Beadle
Office for National Statistics
Tel: 020 7533 5938;
Email: jon.beadle@ons.gov.uk

Products that contain data from this analysis
Annual Abstract of Statistics; Economic Trends; Financial Statistics; GDP Preliminary Estimate (First Release); Monthly Digest of Statistics; National Accounts Aggregates Tables A1 and A2; Office for National Statistics Databank / Datastore; Quarterly National Accounts (First Release); UK Output, Income and Expenditure (First Release); United Kingdom Economic Accounts (Quarterly Supplement to Economic Trends); United Kingdom National Accounts - The Blue Book; United Kingdom National Accounts, Concepts, Sources and Methods

---

See also:
In this chapter:
Trade in Services *(10.8)*
Trade in Services (Annually) *(10.8)*
Trade in Services (Monthly) *(10.8)*
Trade in Services (Quarterly) *(10.8)*

10.6 National Economic Accounts - Sector Accounts

Centralised Returns (Public Sector)
Office for National Statistics

Status: Ongoing
Collection Method: Company returns
Frequency: Monthly for production industries and quarterly for agriculture, construction and services
Reference Period: Specified dates in each month / quarter
Timeliness: Monthly, 2 months after collection. Quarterly, 3 months after collection.
Earliest Available Data: June 1978 (SIC 92) Great Britain only
National Coverage: Great Britain
Disaggregation: Government Office Regions and standard regions

Statistician
James Partington
Office for National Statistics
Tel: 01928 792545;
Email: james.partington@ons.gov.uk

Products that contain data from this source
Labour Market Trends; Monthly Digest of Statistics; Regional Trends; United Kingdom National Accounts - The Blue Book

Financial Transactions and Balance Sheets
Office for National Statistics

The Office for National Statistics compiles quarterly financial transactions accounts and balance sheets for each of the institutional sectors of the UK economy, plus the overseas sector, as part of the integrated National Accounts dataset. The financial transactions of the overseas sector are equivalent to the transactions in external assets and liabilities in the balance of payments, and the financial balance sheet of the overseas sector is equivalent to the National balance sheet of the external assets and liabilities of the UK. The compilation and presentation of the financial transactions accounts and balance sheets uses a standard list of financial instruments. For each financial instrument, the sum of all transactions across all sectors is constrained to equal zero, because if one sector acquires a financial asset, then another sector must have sold that asset or incurred an equivalent liability. Similarly, in the financial balance sheets, the level of assets is constrained to be equal to the level of liabilities for each financial instrument. The financial transactions accounts and balance sheets are compiled from a wide variety of data sources, including ONS data collections, the Bank of England and other Government

Departments. Sector balance sheets including end-year estimates of tangible assets as well as financial assets and liabilities are published annually. The first official quarterly estimates of financial transactions were published in 1964 and the first official estimates of balance sheets were published in 1980. From September 1998 this data will become consistent with the European System of Accounts (ESA 95).

Status: Ongoing
Frequency: Quarterly
National Coverage: United Kingdom

Statistician
Alan Hewer
Office for National Statistics
Tel: 020 7533 6029;
Email: alan.hewer@ons.gov.uk

Products that contain data from this analysis
Annual Abstract of Statistics; Economic Trends; Financial Statistics; Office for National Statistics Databank / Datastore; United Kingdom Economic Accounts (Quarterly Supplement to Economic Trends); United Kingdom National Accounts - The Blue Book; United Kingdom National Accounts, Sources and Methods

Household Saving Ratio
Office for National Statistics

The Office for National Statistics compiles the household saving ratio which is household saving expressed as a percentage of total resources which is the sum of gross household disposable income and the adjustment for the change in net equity of households in pension funds (D.8). Household disposable income is the sum of household incomes less UK taxes on income, social and other taxes, contributions and other current transfers, which are all compiled by the ONS. Household saving is what remains of available resources after deducting households' final consumption expenditure, also compiled by the ONS. The estimates of household saving ratio are used by the Treasury and economists elsewhere for economic analysis, modelling and forecasting. The saving ratio is published quarterly with GDP and are available both unadjusted and seasonally adjusted, towards the end of the third month after the quarter to which it refers.

Status: Ongoing
Frequency: Quarterly
Earliest Available Data: 1946 (annually); 1955 (quarterly)
National Coverage: United Kingdom

Statistician
Roger Ward
Office for National Statistics
Tel: 020 7533 6002;
Email: roger.ward@ons.gov.uk

Products that contain data from this analysis
Annual Abstract of Statistics; Economic Trends; Economic Trends Annual Supplement; Financial Statistics; Monthly Digest of Statistics; Office for National Statistics Databank / Datastore; Quarterly National Accounts (First Release); United Kingdom Economic Accounts (Quarterly Supplement to Economic Trends); United Kingdom National Accounts - The Blue Book; United Kingdom National Accounts, Sources and Methods

Income, Capital and Financial Accounts of Non-Financial Corporations
Office for National Statistics

The Office for National Statistics compiles these accounts. The income account includes gross trading profits, rent and other property income, inventory holding gains, income from abroad, payments of dividends and interest, UK taxes on income, and profits due abroad. The capital account takes the resulting undistributed income from the income account and shows capital transfers, gross fixed capital formation, changes in inventories, and acquisitions less disposals of valuables. The net borrowing requirement is an element of the financial account. Key components are the net acquisition of financial liabilities and assets. All data are available quarterly and seasonally adjusted.

Status: Ongoing
Frequency: Quarterly and annually
Timeliness: The quarterly data are released 4 months after the reporting date. The annual data are released 8 months after the reporting date.
Earliest Available Data: 1987 (annual data), 1987 Q1 (quarterly data)
National Coverage: United Kingdom

Statistician
Richard Walton
Office for National Statistics
Tel: 020 7533 6012;
Email: richard.walton@ons.gov.uk

Products that contain data from this analysis
Economic Trends; Economic Trends Annual Supplement; Financial Statistics; Office for National Statistics Databank / Datastore; Quarterly National Accounts (First Release); United Kingdom Economic Accounts (Quarterly Supplement to Economic Trends); United Kingdom National Accounts - The Blue Book; United Kingdom National Accounts, Concepts, Sources and Methods

Mixed Income
Office for National Statistics

The Office for National Statistics compiles data on mixed income which is the distributed and undistributed income of proprietors of unincorporated businesses (farmers, certain professions, and other sole traders) other than partnerships. The data is mainly estimated from details of income assessed for tax under Schedule D, provided by Inland Revenue. The income of farmers is based on data provided by the Ministry of Agriculture, Fisheries and Food. The estimates of income from self-employment are used by the ONS in the calculation of Gross Domestic Product and in the household sector income account, and by the Treasury and economists elsewhere for economic analysis, modelling and forecasting. Mixed income is published quarterly with GDP and is available both unadjusted and seasonally adjusted towards the end of the third month after the quarter to which it refers.

Status: Ongoing
Frequency: Quarterly
Earliest Available Data: 1946 (annually); 1955 (quarterly)
National Coverage: United Kingdom
Disaggregation: Standard Regions

Statistician
Roger Ward
Office for National Statistics
Tel: 020 7533 6002;
Email: roger.ward@ons.gov.uk

Products that contain data from this analysis
Office for National Statistics Databank / Datastore; United Kingdom National Accounts - The Blue Book; United Kingdom National Accounts, Sources and Methods

See also:
In this chapter:
Trade in Services (Annually) *(10.8)*
Trade in Services (Quarterly) *(10.8)*

In other chapters:
Compensation of Employees *(see the Labour Market chapter)*
Family Expenditure Survey - UK *(see the Household Finances chapter)*

10.7 Overseas Trade in Goods

Air Freight - UK Airports
Department of the Environment, Transport and the Regions

The DETR publishes data on the tonnage of freight passing through UK airports and carried by UK airlines. The data are supplied by the Civil Aviation Authority.

Status: Ongoing
Collection Method: Census
Frequency: Monthly
Reference Period: Month / year
Timeliness: 4 months
Earliest Available Data: 1980
National Coverage: United Kingdom

Statistician
Chris Overson
Department of the Environment, Transport and the Regions
Tel: 020 7890 4276

Products that contain data from this source
Annual Abstract of Statistics; Regional Trends; Social Trends

Defence Exports Database
Ministry of Defence

Contains details of Defence exports. Used in preparing Tables 1.11 and 1.13.

Status: Ongoing
Collection Method: Large-scale (Sample) Survey
Frequency: Annually
Reference Period: Government Financial Year

Statistician
Robin Horton
Ministry of Defence
Tel: 020 7218 8326;
Email: triservice@dasa.mon.uk

Imports and Exports Databases
Ministry of Defence; sponsored by HM Customs and Excise

Contains details of UK imports and exports.

Status: Ongoing
Collection Method: Administrative Records
Frequency: Continuously

Statistician
Robin Horton
Ministry of Defence
Tel: 020 7218 8326;
Email: triservice@dasa.mon.uk

Overseas Trade Statistics (OTS) - Visible Trade - UK
HM Customs and Excise

The Overseas Trade Statistics is a count of the UK's visible trade with the European Community and the rest of the world. Data is collected by Her Majesty's Customs and Excise. Trade with the EC is collected through a survey linked to the VAT system (Intrastat) and the remainder is derived from customs declarations. Results are most significantly used by the Office for National Statistics in the formulation of the National Accounts and the current account of the balance of payments. Data are available at EC, non-EC and world level by the Standard International Trade Classification (SITC) and commodity code.

Status: Ongoing
Collection Method: Data is obtained from importers and exporters declarations for Customs purposes and the Intrastat system
Frequency: Continuously
Reference Period: Monthly, quarterly and annually
Earliest Available Data: 1979
National Coverage: United Kingdom as a whole

Statistician
Sandra Tudor
HM Customs and Excise
UK Tariff and Statistical Office
Tel: 01702 367166

Products that contain data from this source
Overseas Trade Statistics (Business Monitors)

Overseas Trade Statistics - Wood Products
Forestry Commission; Using data from Customs & Excise

Quantity and Value of imports and exports of wood products - Divisions 24, 25, 63, 64. Figures for calendar years extracted from OTS publications, adjusted where there are obvious errors.

Status: Ongoing
Collection Method: Extract from publication
Frequency: Annually
Reference Period: the calendar year
Timeliness: 5 months after end of calendar year
Earliest Available Data: 1990
National Coverage: United Kingdom

Statistician
Simon Gillam
Forestry Commission
Policy and Practice Division - Statistics
Tel: 0131 314 6280;
Email: simon.gillam@forestry.gov.uk

Products that contain data from this source
Forestry Commission Facts and Figures; Forestry Industry Yearbook; Forest Product Statistics (UNECE); Forest Products - FAO Yearbook

Return of Port Traffic for the Year
Department of Economic Development - Northern Ireland

The Northern Ireland Department of Economic Development conducts the Trade at the Principal Ports Survey on all main ports and harbours in Northern Ireland. Data are collected on the trade at the ports of Belfast, Larne, Londonderry and Warrenpoint and at smaller ports for which data are presented in aggregate form. They are available for the tonnage of imports and exports (inward and outward traffic respectively) and on foreign and cross-channel unit load carrier traffic (number of containers/vehicles and tonnage carried). Longitudinal data are available from 1957 for the tonnage of inward and outward traffic and from 1976 for unit load carrier traffic. The Survey is carried out annually and published at the end of May each year. Data is also available on agricultural bulk cargo, petroleum imports for consumption in Northern Ireland and coal imports and exports.

Status: Ongoing
Collection Method: Census
Frequency: Annually
Reference Period: Year
Timeliness: Data collected in February for previous year and available in May
Earliest Available Data: 1957
National Coverage: Northern Ireland

Statistician
Clare Alexander
Department of Economic Development - Northern Ireland
Tel: 028 9052 9525;
Email: clare.alexander@dedni.gov.uk

Products that contain data from this source
Trade at Principal Ports - Northern Ireland

10.8 Overseas Trade in Services

Overseas Film and Television Industries
Office for National Statistics

The Office for National Statistics conducts a survey on all identified UK film companies and television broadcasting companies who have overseas transactions. Approximately 600 companies were approached for the 1998 Inquiry. Data are available for receipts and payments in respect of production work, rights, licences, royalties, and any other services rendered. The survey forms part of the invisible component of the UK balance of payments current account.

Status: Ongoing
Collection Method: Large-scale (Sample) Survey
Frequency: Annually
Reference Period: Calendar Year
Timeliness: Eight months
Earliest Available Data: 1964
National Coverage: United Kingdom

Statistician
Martyn Vaughan
Office for National Statistics
Tel: 01633 81 2563;
Email: martyn.vaughan@ons.gov.uk

Products that contain data from this source
Overseas Transactions of the Film and Television Industry (First Release); United Kingdom Balance of Payments - The Pink Book

Overseas Insurances Brokerage - UK
Office for National Statistics

The Office for National Statistics conducts the Inquiry into Insurance Brokerage earned by UK brokers on business written in overseas currencies. Data are used in the compilation of current account credits for the financial and other services part of invisibles in the balance of payments. The Inquiry covers 44 UK insurance company groups. Results are grossed to give estimates for the total population of UK insurance brokers which earn brokerage on business written in overseas currencies. Data are collected on the value in sterling of brokerage earned on business written in US dollars, EC currencies and other overseas currencies.

Earliest Available Data: 1965

Statistician
Philip Gooding
Office for National Statistics
Tel: 01633 812793

Products that contain data from this source
Office for National Statistics Databank / Datastore; UK Balance of Payments (First Release); United Kingdom Balance of Payments - The Pink Book

Overseas Trade in Services
Office for National Statistics

The Office for National Statistics conducts an inquiry into overseas transactions of consultants and companies offering business services. The Overseas Trade in Services Inquiry is a sample survey covering approximately 10,500 UK companies. The results are grossed to provide estimates for the total population. The data are used as part of the UK balance of payments. Data are available by industry, commodity and geographical breakdown. Data are collected on royalties and services and broken down into related and unrelated transactions. A geographical and industrial analysis is produced. The data are used for international comparisons of imports and exports, by various trade associations, and in the UK balance of payments. Information on overseas trade in services data had been collected as part of the Overseas Direct Investment Inquiry. Collection of the miscellaneous other services, including royalties as a separate inquiry, was commenced in 1990 on a quarterly basis and 1991 on a annual basis. Computer services was added to the type of businesses selected for the 1992 Inquiry.

Status: Ongoing
Collection Method: Large-scale (Sample) Survey
Frequency: Annually and quarterly
Reference Period: Calendar year
Timeliness: Six months
Earliest Available Data: 1991 (annual survey); quarter four 1992 (quarterly survey)
National Coverage: United Kingdom

Statistician
Martyn Vaughan
Office for National Statistics
Tel: 01633 81 2563;
Email: martyn.vaughan@ons.gov.uk

Products that contain data from this source
UK Balance of Payments (First Release)
United Kingdom Balance of Payments - The Pink Book UKA1, Economy - UK Trade in Services

Trade in Services
Office for National Statistics

From September 1998 this data will become consistent with the IMF Balance of Payments Manual (5th Edition).

Statistician
Simon Humphries
Office for National Statistics
Balance of Payments and Financial Sector; Trade in Services and External Transfers
Tel: 020 7533 6095;
Email: simon.humphries@ons.gov.uk

Trade in Services (Annually)
Office for National Statistics

Trade in Services measures the export and import of services between the United Kingdom and the Rest of the World. The recording of Trade in Services is consistent with that specified in the International Monetary Fund's Balance of Payments Manual (5th edition). The information is derived from various sources such as quarterly and annual inquiries and government administrative records. Trade in Services are published both at current and constant price, unadjusted and seasonally adjusted. Trade in Services form a component of the Balance of Payments current account and the expenditure measure of GDP. Estimates for Trade in Services are published in the monthly Trade First Release, quarterly Balance of Payments First Release and annual Balance of Payments "Pink Book". Estimates for Trade in Services are also published in the Gross Domestic Product First Release and annual "Blue Book". From September 1998 this data will become consistent with the standards of the IMF Balance of Payments Manual (5th edition). The data are derived from numerous sources. The predominant source of information is the Overseas Trade

Sources and Analyses

in Services inquiry which commenced in 1996. Prior to that the information came from numerous separate inquiries. Government records go back to the 1940's. Data are also supplied by non-government bodies such as the Chamber of Shipping, the Civil Aviation Authority, the Baltic Exchange, the Bank of England and Lloyds of London.

Status: Ongoing
Frequency: Annually
Reference Period: End year
Timeliness: 12 weeks
Earliest Available Data: 1955
National Coverage: United Kingdom
Disaggregation: The Balance of Payments Pink Book separately identifies 58 countries and geographical regions.

Statistician
Simon Humphries
Office for National Statistics
Balance of Payments and Financial Sector; Trade in Services and External Transfers
Tel: 020 7533 6095;
Email: simon.humphries@ons.gov.uk

Trade in Services (Monthly)
Office for National Statistics

Trade in Services measures the export and import of services between the United Kingdom and the Rest of the World. The recording of Trade in Services is consistent with that specified in the International Monetary Fund's Balance of Payments Manual (5th edition). The information is derived from various sources such as quarterly and annual inquiries and government administrative records. Trade in Services are published both at current and constant price, unadjusted and seasonally adjusted. Trade in Services form a component of the Balance of Payments current account and the expenditure measure of GDP. Estimates for Trade in Services are published in the monthly Trade First Release, quarterly Balance of Payments First Release and annual Balance of Payments "Pink Book". Estimates for Trade in Services are also published in the Gross Domestic Product First Release and annual "Blue Book". From September 1998 this data will become consistent with the standards of the IMF Balance of Payments Manual (5th edition). Data are forecast using a small sample of information available monthly.

Status: Ongoing
Frequency: Based on forecasts
Reference Period: Monthly
Timeliness: 7 weeks
Earliest Available Data: 1993m1
National Coverage: United Kingdom
Disaggregation: Monthly Trade in Services is broken down into EU and non-EU countries

Statistician
Simon Humphries
Office for National Statistics
Balance of Payments and Financial Sector; Trade in Services and External Transfers
Tel: 020 7533 6095;
Email: simon.humphries@ons.gov.uk

Trade in Services (Quarterly)
Office for National Statistics

Trade in Services measures the export and import of services between the United Kingdom and the Rest of the World. The recording of Trade in Services is consistent with that specified in the International Monetary Fund's Balance of Payments Manual (5th edition). The information is derived from various sources such as quarterly and annual inquiries and government administrative records. Trade in Services are published both at current and constant price, unadjusted and seasonally adjusted. Trade in Services form a component of the Balance of Payments current account and the expenditure measure of GDP. Estimates for Trade in Services are published in the monthly Trade First Release, quarterly Balance of Payments First Release and annual Balance of Payments "Pink Book". Estimates for Trade in Services are also published in the Gross Domestic Product First Release and annual "Blue Book". From September 1998 this data will become consistent with the Standards of the IMF Balance of Payments Manual (5th edition). The data are derived from numerous sources. The predominant source of information is the Overseas Trade in Services inquiry which commenced in 1996 and from the International Passenger Survey. Prior to that the information came from numerous separate inquiries. Government records go back to the 1940's. Data are also supplied by non-government bodies such as the Chamber of Shipping, the Civil Aviation Authority, the Baltic Exchange, the Bank of England and Lloyds of London.

Status: Ongoing
Frequency: Quarterly
Reference Period: End March, June, September and December
Timeliness: 12 weeks
Earliest Available Data: 1955q1
National Coverage: United Kingdom

Statistician
Simon Humphries
Office for National Statistics
Balance of Payments and Financial Sector; Trade in Services and External Transfers
Tel: 020 7533 6095;
Email: simon.humphries@ons.gov.uk

10.9 Regional and Sub-Regional Economic Accounts

Consumption Expenditure by Households and Non-Profit Institutions Serving Households
Northern Ireland Statistics and Research Agency

The sum of all expenditures by the personal sector (households) on goods and services.

Status: Ongoing
Frequency: Annually
Reference Period: Calendar year
Earliest Available Data: 1989
National Coverage: United Kingdom

Statistician
Dr Paul Donnelly
Northern Ireland Statistics and Research Agency
Regional Reporting and Expenditure Branch
Tel: 028 9052 6933;
Email: paul.donnelly@dfpni.gov.uk

Products that contain data from this analysis
Economic Trends

Gross Domestic Product - Northern Ireland
Northern Ireland Statistics and Research Agency

GDP is the measure of the economic activity taking place in an economic territory. GDP is equivalent to the value added to the economy by this activity. These figures are generated by ONS. The Northern Ireland element of these figures is quality assured by NISRA.

Status: Ongoing
Frequency: Annually
Reference Period: Calendar year
Earliest Available Data: 1989
National Coverage: United Kingdom

Statistician
Dr Paul Donnelly
Northern Ireland Statistics and Research Agency
Regional Reporting and Expenditure Branch
Tel: 028 9052 6933;
Email: paul.donnelly@dfpni.gov.uk

Products that contain data from this analysis
Economic Trends

Regional Accounts
Office for National Statistics

The Office for National Statistics compiles sub-national breakdowns of some of the key national accounts aggregates. Some of these are available at regional level only, whilst others are broken down further to sub-regional levels. All regional accounts estimates are produced on an annual basis and at current prices, and are normally consistent with the most recent Blue Book national estimates.

Sub-national breakdowns

The economic territory of member states of the European Union is broken down into a five-tier hierarchical regional structure, known as the Nomenclature of Units for Territorial Statistics (NUTS). For the UK, NUTS level 1 equates to the nine Government Office Regions (GORs) in England, Scotland, Wales and Northern Ireland. These regions are further broken down into 37 sub-regions at NUTS level 2 and 133 local areas at NUTS level 3. All regional accounts estimates are available at regional level (NUTS level 1), and some are also available at NUTS level 2 and 3.

Gross Domestic Product

Regional GDP data are compiled using the income approach. Estimates are produced for the individual 'income' components, consistent with those published at national level. The total regional GDP figures are also broken down into broad industrial sectors according to SIC(92). Since January 1999, data are being produced according to the European System of Accounts 1995 (ESA95), whilst earlier data were produced according to different definitions. From January 2000 onwards, annual data will be available at basic prices, whilst earlier estimates have been at factor cost, which excluded taxes on production. Sub-regional estimates (NUTS-2 and NUTS-3 levels) of total GDP are also available. Work is underway to produce some industrial breakdowns at these levels.

Household Accounts

Regional and sub-regional estimates of Household Income and Household Disposable Income have been available since 1984. Under ESA95, a more comprehensive set of Household Accounts is being developed. Regional estimates became available in 1999, and sub-regional estimates are being developed. Regional Household Income is broken down into various types of income, such as Compensation of Employees, Property Income, Pensions and Social Security Benefits. Disposable Income is calculated after deducting taxes and Social Security contributions.

Individual Consumption Expenditure

Estimates for Consumption Expenditure are available annually and at regional level only. Figures are published for broad commodity groups, and greater detail (32 categories) is available on request. All estimates are in current prices.

Status: Ongoing
Frequency: Annual
Reference Period: Calendar years
Timeliness: Regional GDP data around a year after the year to which they refer.
Sub-regional GDP data around a year later.
Regional Household Accounts around 18 months after the year to which they relate; sub-regional around a year later.
Earliest Available Data: 1989 on ESA95 basis; various earlier periods on previous basis.
National Coverage: United Kingdom
Sub-National: NUTS levels 1,2 and 3 (see above)

Statistician
Dev Virdee
Regional Accounts Branch
Office for National Statistics
B5/03
1, Drummond Gate
London SW1V 2QQ
Tel: 020 7533 5790;
Email: dev.virdee@ons.gov.uk

Products that contain data from this analysis
Economic Trends; Regional Trends; ONS news releases; datasets

---

UK Regional Overseas Trade Statistics
HM Customs and Excise

HM Customs and Excise collects data on the UK's visible trade with the European Community and the rest of the world. This data is published as the Overseas Trade Statistics - Visible Trade (q.v.). A project is currently underway to produce statistics of overseas trade in goods for 12 regions within the UK. These regions are Scotland, Wales, Northern Ireland and the nine English Government Office regions - Eastern, East Midlands, London, North East, North West, South East, South West, West Midlands and Yorkshire & Humber. Following extensive consultation TSO has produced regional data showing, for each region, the value of overseas trade and the number of importing and exporting companies. Further analysis by partner country and industry group has been produced. TSO is currently discussing these early results with the regions.

Data is obtained from the monthly 'Intrastat' statistical survey of companies that trade with the European Community. This obtains detailed information from some 28,500 companies. Information from companies that trade with the rest of the world is obtained from import and export declarations submitted to HM Customs and Excise at the UK frontier.

It is hoped that publication of UK regional overseas trade statistics will commence, with data for Quarter 3/1999 (1 July to 30 September), during December 1999.

Status: In development
Frequency: Survey and frontier Customs declarations
Reference Period: Monthly
Timeliness: Three months
Earliest Available Data: Third quarter of 1999
National Coverage: UK regions (see above)
Disaggregation: UK regions (see above)

Statistician
Sandra Tudor
HM Customs and Excise, Tariff and Statistical Office
Tel: 01702 367166

See also:
In other chapters:
Family Expenditure Survey - UK *(see the Household Finances chapter)*

10 The Economy - *Products*

Economic Trends
Office for National Statistics

A monthly compendia of statistics and articles on the UK economy including some regional and international statistics. Contains data on UK economic accounts, prices, labour market, output and demand indicators, selected financial statistics, GDP, consumer and wholesale price indices, households final consumption expenditure, final expenditure prices index, visible and invisible trade balance, earnings, and regional and international economic indicators. Includes articles on national accounting, trade, wider economic issues, research and development statistics and international comparisons. From the October 1998 edition, the national accounts data in Economic Trends is consistent with the European System of Accounts (ESA 95).

Frequency: Monthly
Price: Single issue £23.50, annual subscription (including Annual Supplement, United Kingdom Economic Accounts and postage) £380 Single articles £5.00
Electronic database: ONS Sales Desk 020 7533 5678 Fax: 020 7533 5689
Disk: annual subscription £630.00 (in Navidator 'Flat file' format')
ISSN: 0013-0400

Available from
TSO Publications Centre and Bookshops
Please see Annex B for full address details.

Sources from which data for table in this product are obtained
Agricultural Land Prices - England (Table 6.10), MAFF.
Bank lending (Table 6.7, 6.8), BoE.
Building Society Lending for House Purchase (Table 5.4), BSA.
Claimant Count (Table 4.4), ONS.
Construction: New Orders - GB (Table 5.4), DETR.
Construction Count - GB (Table 5.2), DETR.
Consumer Credit (Tables 5.8, 6.6), ONS.
Consumer Price Collection (Table 3.1), ONS.
Inland Energy Consumption (Table 5.9), DETR.

Labour Force Survey (Tables 4.1 - 4.3, 4.5A), ONS.
Monetary Stock and Counterparts (Tables 6.2, 6.3), ONS.
Mortgage lending by all financial institutions (Table 6.10), DETR.
National Accounts ONS.
Aggregates (Table 2.1)
Balance of Payments Account (Table 2.13)
General Government Sector Account (Tables 2.10, 6.4, 6.5)
Gross Domestic Product by category of expenditure (Table 2.2)
Gross Value Added: output measure (Tables 2.8, 2.9, 5.1)
Households' sector Account (Table 2.5, 2.6, 2.10)
Non-financial Corporations Sector Accounts (Tables 2.10, 2.11, 2.12)
Public Sector Accounts (Table 6.5)
Trade on a Balance of Payments basis (Tables 2.13, 2.14), ONS.

Producer Price Collection (Table 3.1, 6.10), ONS
Property Transactions (Table 5.5), IR.
Retail Sales Inquiries - GB (Table 5.8), ONS.
Sterling Exchange Rates (Table 6.1), BoE.
Trade Competitiveness Measures (Table 2.15), ONS.
Workforce Jobs (Table 4.4), ONS.

Economic Trends - Digest of Articles
Office for National Statistics

Digest of key Economic Trends articles from March 1996 to January 1998.

Price: £19.95
ISBN: 1 85774 27 10

Available from
Uzair Rizki
Office for National Statistics
1 Drummond Gate
London
Tel: 020 7533 5926; Fax: 020 7533 5903;
Email: uzair.rizki@ons.gov.uk

Economic Trends Annual Supplement
Office for National Statistics

Economic statistics over a 40-50 year period. The supplement contains long time series of data contained in the monthly Economic Trends plus additional data and detailed methodology. In the 1998 edition the national accounts data in this volume is consistent with the European System of

Accounts (ESA 95). Electronic database: ONS Sales Desk

Frequency: Annual
Price: £28.50
ISSN: 0013-0400

Available from
TSO Publications Centre and Bookshops
Please see Annex B for full address details.

Sources from which data for this product are obtained
Building Society lending for House Purchase (Table 4.4), BSA.
Bank Lending (Tables 5.6, 5.7), BoE.
Claimant Count (Tables 3.7, 3.8), ONS.
Construction: New Orders - GB (Tables 4.2, 4.4), DETR.
Construction Output - GB (Table 4.2), DETR.
Consumer Credit (Tables 5.8, 6.6), ONS.
Consumer Price Collection (Table 2.1), ONS.
Inland Energy Consumption (Table 4.9), DETR.
Labour Force Survey (Tables 3.1 - 3.6), ONS.
Monetary Stock and Counterparts (Tables 5.2, 5.3), ONS.
National Accounts ONS
Aggregates (Table 1.1)
Balance of Payments Account (Tables 1.17 - 1.20)
General Government Sector Account (Tables 1.11, 5.4, 5.5)
Gross Domestic Product by category of expenditure (Table 1.3)
Gross Domestic Product by category of income (Table 1.4)
Gross Value Added: Output measure (Tables 1.9, 1.10, 4.1)
Households' sector Account (Tables 1.6, 1.7, 1.11)
Non-financial Corporations Sector Accounts (Tables 1.12, 1.13, 1.16)
Public Sector Accounts (Table 5.5)
Sterling Exchange Rates (Table 5.1)
Trade on a Balance of Payments basis (Tables 1.17, 1.18, 1.21)

Producer Price Collection (Table 2.1), ONS.
Property Transactions (Table 4.5), IR.
Retail Sales Inquiries - GB (Table 4.8), ONS.

Trade Competitiveness Measures (Table 1.22), ONS.
Workforce Jobs (Tables 3.7), ONS.

MAFF - Ministry of Agriculture, Fisheries and Food
BoE - Bank of England
BSA - Building Societies Association
DETR - Department of the Environment, Transport and the Regions
IR - Inland Revenue
ONS - Office for National Statistics

Financial Statistics
Office for National Statistics

Key financial and monetary statistics of the UK. Contains data on public sector finance, central government revenue and expenditure, money supply and credit, banks and building societies, interest and exchange rates, financial accounts, capital issues, balance sheets and balance of payments. From the October 1998 edition the data in Financial Statistics becomes consistent with the European System of Accounts (ESA 95).

Frequency: Monthly
Price: Monthly, single issue £23.50, annual subscription £280.00 (handbook included)
Electronic database
Available from the ONS Sales Desk
ISBN: 0015-203X
ISSN: 0015-203X

Available from
TSO Publications Centre and Bookshops
Please see Annex B for full address details.

Sources from which data for this product are obtained
Acquisitions and Mergers - UK; Administrative Data on the Official Reserves; Annual survey of financial assets and liabilities; Balance of Payments Account - UK; Borrowing and Lending Inquiry (Monthly) - UK; Borrowing and Lending Inquiry (Quarterly); Building Societies; Building Society Lending for House Purchase - UK (BS4); Capital Issues; Central Government Net Cash Requirement - UK; Central Government Net Cash Requirement on Own Account - UK; Compensation of employees; Consumer Price Collection - UK; Consumers' Expenditure; Current, Capital and Financial Accounts of Non-Financial Corporations; Financial Statistics; Financial Transactions and Balance Sheets; Gross Trading Surplus of Local Authority Trading Enterprises - UK; Household Saving Ratio; Inland Revenue Tax Receipts; Insurance companies balance sheet annual inquiry; Insurance Companies' income and expenditure - quarterly inquiry; Insurance companies' income and expenditure annual inquiry; Insurance companies' transactions in financial assets inquiry; Interest and Exchange Rates; Investment trusts annual return of liabilities and assets; Investment trusts quarterly return of transactions inquiry; Local Authority Direct Net Cash from Central Government - UK; Local Authority Net Cash Requirement - UK; Monetary Stock and Counterparts; National Accounts; National Savings - Financial Statistics; Net Value Added Tax (VAT) Receipts UK; Outstanding Amounts Inquiry (MQBL) - UK; Overseas Direct Investment; Pension fund annual balance sheet inquiry; Pension fund annual income and expenditure inquiry; Pension fund transactions inquiry; Pension Funds - England; Pension funds quarterly income and expenditure inquiry; Property unit trusts annual return of liabilities; Property unit trusts quarterly return of transactions inquiry; Provisional estimates of narrow money;

Public Corporations Net Cash Requirement - UK; Public Corporations' Direct Borrowing from Central Government - UK; Public Sector Net Cash Requirement - UK; Quarterly Profits Inquiry Finance Houses and Other Specialist Consumer Credit Grantors - UK; Quarterly survey of financial assets and liabilities; Receipts of Customs and Excise Taxes other than VAT - UK; Revenue Account Survey - England; Revenue Outturn - England; Securities dealers quarterly return of liabilities and assets and of transactions in securities; Unit trusts annual return of liabilities and assets; Unit trusts quarterly return of transactions inquiry

---

See also:
In this chapter:
Economic Trends *(10.10)*
Economic Trends Annual Supplement *(10.10)*
Quarterly National Accounts (First Release) *(10.15)*
UK Output, Income and Expenditure (First Release) *(10.15)*
United Kingdom Economic Accounts *(10.15)*
United Kingdom National Accounts - the Blue Book *(10.15)*
United Kingdom National Accounts, Sources and Methods *(10.10)*

In other chapters:
Office for National Statistics Databank (see the Websites and Electronic Services chapter)

NACE Rev.1 - Statistical Classification of Economic Activities in the European Communities
Eurostat

NACE Rev. 1 (statistical classification of economic activities in the European Community) is a classification designed for data referring to the unit of activity. It serves as a basis for compiling statistics on the production factors of production (labour, raw materials, energy etc.), fixed capital formation operations and financial operations of these units of activity.

This document contains an introduction, the structure of the classification, explanatory notes and NACE Rev. 1 / NACE 70 conversion keys.

Delivery: Hardcopy publication
Frequency: Ad hoc
Price: £38.00
ISBN: 92 826 8767 8

Available from
TSO Publications Centre and Bookshops
Please see Annex B for full address details.

Regio - Description of Contents of Regional Databank
Office for National Statistics

Available from
Bob Dodds
Office for National Statistics
Please see Annex B for full address details

Scottish Economic Bulletin
Scottish Executive

A wide range of data relating to the Scottish economy, plus detailed articles on specific topics. Contains data on employment, unemployment, production and output, investment and construction, business sector, oil and gas, personal/household income and expenditure.

Frequency: Twice a year
Price: £14.50
ISBN: 0 11 497226 5

Available from
TSO Publications Centre and Bookshops
Please see Annex B for full address details.

Sources from which data for this product are obtained
Index of Production - Scotland; Regional Selective Assistance Grants to Industry - Scotland; Scottish Production Database Labour Force Survey, ONS; New Earnings Survey, ONS; Regional Accounts, ONS; Gross Domestic Product - Scotland; Family Expenditure Survey, ONS; Civilian workforce jobs series, ONS; Claimant count unemployment count, ONS; Annual Employment Survey, ONS.

United Kingdom National Accounts, Sources and Methods
Office for National Statistics

Information on the UK National Accounts, methodology and data sources. It explains in detail the new presentation of the UK National Accounts, the concepts underlying the accounts and the sources and methods used to compile them under the ESA 95 framework.

Frequency: Occasional,
Price: £75.00
ISBN: 0 11 621062 1

Available from
TSO Publications Centre and Bookshops
Please see Annex B for full address details.

Sources from which data for this product are obtained
Balance of Payments Account - UK; Central Government Net Cash Requirement - UK; Central Government Net Cash Requirement on Own Account - UK; Compensation of employees; Construction Stocks - UK; Consumers' Expenditure; Current, Capital and Financial

Accounts of Non-Financial Corporations; Financial Transactions and Balance Sheets; Gross Trading Surplus of Local Authority Trading Enterprises - UK; Household Saving Ratio; Local Authority Direct Net Cash from Central Government - UK; Local Authority Net Cash Requirement - UK; Mixed Income; Motor Traders' Stocks - UK; National Accounts; Production Stocks - UK; Public Corporations Net Cash Requirement - UK; Public Corporations' Direct Borrowing from Central Government - UK; Public Sector Net Cash Requirement - UK; Quarterly Capital Expenditure Inquiry; Retailers' Stocks - UK; Wholesalers' and Dealers' Stocks - UK

(The) United Kingdom National Accounts Methodological Papers
Office for National Statistics

Explanatory material on aspects of the UK system of national accounts. Series started in August 1994. To date three have been published: 1. The measurement of output in the estimation of GDP (August 1994, ISBN). 2. A compiler's guide to the 1993 SNA (February 1995, ISBN). 3. Data sources for the quarterly account.

Frequency: Ad hoc
Price: £12.99
ISBN: 1) 0 903834 81 2 2) 0 90383483 9, 3) 0 90383482 0

Available from
Jon Beadle
Office for National Statistics
1 Drummond Gate
London
Tel: 020 7533 5938;
Email: jon.beadle@ons.gov.uk

Sources from which data for this product are obtained
Index of Production - UK

Welsh Economic Trends
National Assembly for Wales

Welsh Economic Trends was a regular publication prepared by the Welsh Office in collaboration with other government departments. The aim was to bring together a wide range of statistics on the Welsh Economy. It has not been published since 1995. The publication contains data on the working population, skills and training, income and expenditure, earnings and hours, industrial activity, research and development and public expenditure.

Delivery: Periodic Release
Frequency: Annually
Price: £10.00
ISBN: 0-7504-1215-1 (1995 edition)
ISSN: 0262 8309 (1995 edition)

Available from
Alan Jackson
The National Assembly for Wales
Crown Building
Cathays Park
Cardiff
Tel: 029 2082 5088;
Email: alan.jackson@wales.gsi.gov.uk

Sources from which data for this product are obtained
New Earnings Survey - GB; Survey of Personal Incomes - UK

See also:
In other chapters:
Office for National Statistics Databank (*see the Websites and Electronic Services chapter*)

10.11 Balance of Payments (BoP) Accounts

Balance of UK Trade (First Release)
Office for National Statistics

Latest statistics on visible trade classified according to Standard International Trade Classification (SITC). The release contains seasonally adjusted data on the value of visible trade on a balance of payments basis analysed either by commodity or a broad area. Unit value and seasonally adjusted volume indices for commodity groups are also given. Electronic database: ONS Sales Desk

Delivery: First Release
Frequency: Monthly
Price: Annual subscription £48.00

Monthly Review of External Trade Statistics (Business Monitor MM24)
Office for National Statistics

Latest statistics on trade in goods classified according to Standard International Trade Classification (SITC). The monitor contains seasonally adjusted data on the value of trade in goods both on a balance of payments and overseas trade statistics basis, analysed either by commodity or country. Price indices and seasonally adjusted volume indices for commodity groups are also given.

Delivery: Periodic Release
Frequency: Monthly
Price: Annual subscription £180.00

Available from
TSO Publications Centre and Bookshops
Please see Annex B for full address details.

Sources from which data for this product are obtained
UK Trade on a Balance of Payments Basis; UK Overseas Trade Statistics (OTS)

UK Balance of Payments (First Release)
Office for National Statistics

Detailed quarterly balance of payments statistics. The release contains summary of balance of payments accounts and detailed statistics for the current account including trade in goods and services, income current and capital, transfers, transactions in UK external assets and liabilities, and levels of identified assets and liabilities. Current account figures are seasonally adjusted.

Frequency: Quarterly
Price: £12.00 annual subscription

Available from
Colin Yeend
Office for National Statistics
1 Drummond Gate
London
Tel: 020 7533 6075

Sources from which data for this product are obtained
Acquisitions and Mergers - UK; Balance of Payments Account - UK; Overseas Insurances Brokerage - UK

UK Trade (First Release)
Office for National Statistics

Latest monthly statistics on trade in goods classified according to Standard International Classification (SITC) as well as monthly estimates for total trade in services. The release contains seasonally adjusted data on the value of trade in goods on a Balance of payments basis, analysed either by commodity or country. Prices indices and seasonally adjusted volume indices for commodity groups are also given.

Delivery: First Release
Frequency: Monthly
Price: Annual subscription £42.00. Monthly copy £3.50.

Available from
ONS Direct
Office for National Statistics
Please see Annex B for full address details.

Sources from which data for this product are obtained
UK Trade on a Balance of Payments Basis

United Kingdom Balance of Payments - the Pink Book
Office for National Statistics

The Pink Book contains detailed estimates of the UK balance of payments for the last eleven years, including estimates for the current account (trade in goods and services, income and current transfers), the capital account, the financial account and the International Investment Position. A geographical breakdown by 42 countries of the current account is included from 1999. From September 1998 Pink Book data are consistent with the fifth edition of the IMF Balance of Payments Manual.

Frequency: Annual
Price: £39.50
ISBN: 0 11 621060 5
ISSN: 0950-7558

Available from
TSO Publications Centre and Bookshops
Please see Annex B for full address details.

Sources from which data for this product are obtained
Acquisitions and Mergers - UK; Administrative Data on the Official Reserves; Balance of Payments Account - UK; Earnings of UK Insurance Brokers in overseas currencies; Fund Managers and certain other members of IMRO; Overseas Direct Investment; Overseas Direct Investment Income and Flows - UK; Overseas Film and Television Industries; Overseas Insurances Brokerage - UK; Overseas Trade in Services; UK Trade on a Balance of Payments Basis; UK Overseas Trade Statistics (OTS)

See also:
In this chapter:
United Kingdom Economic Accounts (10.17)
United Kingdom National Accounts - the Blue Book (10.17)
United Kingdom National Accounts, Sources and Methods *(10.11)*

In other chapters:
Office for National Statistics Databank (see the Websites and Electronic Services chapter)

10.12 Costs, Prices and Inflation

(A) Brief Guide to the Retail Prices Index
Office for National Statistics

Explanations of inflation figures, basket of goods used, structure of the RPI, price collection, weighting, calculating the index, reference dates, publication.

Frequency: Ad hoc
Price: Free

Guide to Official Statistics

Available from
Dave Sharp
Room D2/13
Office for National Statistics
1 Drummond Gate
London SW1V 2QQ
Tel: 020 7533 5853;
Email: david.sharp@ons.gov.uk

Also available as a downloadable file from the ONS website (www.ons.gov.uk)

Sources from which data for this product are obtained
Consumer Price Collection - UK

Consumer Price Indices (Business Monitor)
Office for National Statistics

The publication contains the Retail Prices Index summary, recent movements, detailed figures for the latest month, main changes in last month, average prices of selected items, other indices, main groups, goods and services, historical series back to 1962, internal purchasing power of the pound, European Union Harmonised Indices of Consumer Prices, pensioner indices, and weights used in the indices.

Delivery: Periodic Release
Frequency: Monthly
Price: Monthly, annual subscription £185.00
Electronic database: ONS Sales Desk
Monthly, annual subscription £780.00 excluding VAT
ISBN: Varies from month to month

Available from
TSO Publications Centre and Bookshops
Please see Annex B for full address details.

Sources from which data for this product are obtained
Consumer Price Collection - UK; Harmonised Index of Consumer Prices

Consumer Price Indices (First Release)
Office for National Statistics

The release contains figures for the RPI, RPIX, RPI excluding housing, RPIY and the Harmonised Indices of Consumer Prices (HICP), detailed breakdown of price indices and percentage changes for groups of items making up the RPI and the HICP, percentage change figures for goods and services.

Delivery: First Release
Frequency: Monthly
Price: Monthly, annual subscription £45.00
Electronic database: ONS Sales Desk
Monthly, annual subscription £320.00 excluding VAT

Available from
ONS Press Office
Office for National Statistics
Please see Annex B for full address details

Sources from which data for this product are obtained
Consumer Price Collection - UK; Harmonised Index of Consumer Prices

Cost of Living Comparisons in the European Union
Eurostat

A publication from Eurostats Economy and Finance theme (Theme 2), Series A: A yearbook and yearly statistics. This booklet contains a comprehensive and authoritative survey of the relative cost of living in different European cities. The figures are for all of the EU capitals (except Luxembourg which is treated as if it were Brussels for staff salary purposes) are given as index numbers, with Brussels always having the value 100.

Delivery: Ad hoc/One-off Release
Frequency: Ad hoc
Price: £7.00
ISBN: 92 826 9923 4

Available from
TSO Publications Centre and Bookshops
Please see Annex B for full address details.

Retail Prices 1914-90
Office for National Statistics

Information about retail prices from the time of the first price collections in 1914. The publication contains all items on the RPI excluding various components, indices for various different groups of items (all taken as far back as possible), pensioner indices, components of expenditure, average weekly expenditures, cost of living index 1914-47.

Delivery: Print on demand
Frequency: Ad hoc
Price: £10.95
ISBN: 0 11 620499 0

Available from
TSO Publications Centre and Bookshops
Please see Annex B for full address details.

Sources from which data for this product are obtained
Consumer Price Collection - UK

Retail Prices Index Technical Manual
Office for National Statistics

The Technical Manual is the definitive explanation of how the Retail Prices Index is produced.

Delivery: Periodic Release
Frequency: Ad hoc
Price: £49.50
ISBN: 0-11-621002-8

Available from
TSO Publications Centre and Bookshops
Please see Annex B for full address details.

Sources from which data for this product are obtained
Consumer Price Collection - UK

RPI Advisory Committee Reports - Methodological Issues Affecting the RPI
Office for National Statistics

Delivery: Hardcopy publication
Frequency: Ad hoc
Price: Variable

Available from
TSO Publications Centre and Bookshops
Please see Annex B for full address details.

Sources from which data for this product are obtained
Consumer Price Collection - UK

See also:
In this chapter:
Economic Trends *(10.10)*

10.13 Input-Output Accounts

Input-Output Methodological Guide
Office for National Statistics

Briefly describing the development and likely future development of UK Input-Output balances with information on the structure of the balance and sources of data used.

Frequency: Ad hoc
Price: £25.00
ISBN: 1-885774-234-6

Available from
ONS Direct
Office for National Statistics
Please see Annex B for full address details.

Input-Output Tables and Multipliers for Scotland
Scottish Executive

The relationships between different sectors in the economy as they combine to produce the total of goods and services in any one year. The publication contains data on domestic output, purchases from domestic production, imports from the rest of the UK and the rest of the world, industry-by-industry domestic flows matrix, The Loentief Inverse, output, employment and income multipliers. Records the intra-industry flows between industries and Final Demand.

Delivery: Periodic Release
Frequency: Annually
Price: £40.00
ISBN: 0 7480 71660

Available from
TSO Publications Centre and Bookshops
Please see Annex B for full address details.

Sources from which data for this product are obtained
Input-Output Balances - Scotland

Input-Output Tables for Scotland (Statistical Bulletin)
Scottish Executive

Summary of input-output tables, with a brief introduction to input-output analysis together with a brief description of its uses. The bulletin contains data on destination of output from Scottish industry, how much of each commodity each industry produces, how much each industry purchases of each commodity, primary inputs and final demands.

Frequency: Occasional
Price: £2.00
ISBN: 0 7480 0987 6
ISSN: 0264-1151

Available from
Scottish Executive Library
Scottish Executive Industry Department
Economic Advice and Statistics Unit
Meridian Court
5 Cadogan Street
Glasgow G2 6AT.

Input-Output Tables for the United Kingdom
Office for National Statistics

Contains the full set of input-output derived tables for one year and some explanatory material on the theory behind input-output.

Delivery: Hardcopy publication (and diskette)
Frequency: Every five years
Price: Hardcopy, £24.95, floppy disk £120.00 +VAT
ISBN: 0 11 620664 0

Available from
TSO Publications Centre and Bookshops
Please see Annex B for full address details.

ONS Direct
Office for National Statistics
Please see Annex B for full address details.

Sources from which data for this product are obtained
Input-Output Balances - United Kingdom

United Kingdom Input-Output Supply and Use Balances, 1992-1996
Office for National Statistics

An essential source for the data underlying Gross Domestic Product - one of the key indicators in the National Accounts - these balances provide a single framework showing the relationships between components of value added, industry inputs and outputs and product supply and demand.

Delivery: Hardcopy and electronically (floppy disk)
Frequency: Annually
Price: Hardcopy £39.50, floppy disk £50.00 + VAT
ISBN: 0 11 621057 5

Available from
TSO Publications Centre and Bookshops
Please see Annex B for full address details.
or
ONS Direct
Office for National Statistics
Please see Annex B for full address details.

Sources from which data for this product are obtained
Input-Output Balances - United Kingdom

United Kingdom Input-Output Supply and Use Tables, 1997
Office for National Statistics

An essential source for the data underlying Gross Domestic Product - one of the key indicators in the National Accounts - these balances provide a single framework showing the relationships between components of value added, industry inputs and outputs and product supply and demand.

Delivery: Periodic Release
Frequency: Annually
Price: Hardcopy £39.50, floppy disk £50.00 + VAT
ISSN: 1468 0718

Products

Available from
TSO Publications Centre and Bookshops
Please see Annex B for full address details.
or
ONS Direct
Office for National Statistics
Please see Annex B for full address details.

Sources from which data for this product are obtained
Input-Output Balances - United Kingdom

See also:
In this chapter:
Sector Classification for the National Accounts (Business Monitor MA23) *(10.10)*
United Kingdom National Accounts - the Blue Book *(10.15)*

10.14 International Aid and Investment

Overseas Direct Investment (Business Monitor)
Office for National Statistics

Available from
Philip Gooding
Office for National Statistics
Government Buildings
Cardiff Road
Newport
Gwent
South Wales
Tel: 01633 812793

Sources from which data for this product are obtained
Overseas Direct Investment; Overseas Direct Investment Income and Flows - UK

Overseas Direct Investment (First Release)
Office for National Statistics

Latest data on investment overseas.

Frequency: Annual
Price: £3.00

Available from
ONS Direct
Office for National Statistics
Please see Annex B for full address details.

Sources from which data for this product are obtained
Overseas Direct Investment; Overseas Direct Investment Income and Flows - UK

10.15 National Economic Accounts - Main Aggregates

Consumer Trends
Office for National Statistics

Details of the consumer's expenditure estimate used in Gross Domestic Product. The publication contains tables with detailed series at current and constant prices. There is commentary on quarterly figures, sections on concepts, methodology and data sources and summary tables with figures dating from 1963. In addition a quarterly article describes the overall economic environment within the consumer sector by pulling together the most important underlying factors. From the October 1998 edition, the data in Consumer Trends will be consistent with the European System of Accounts (ESA 95).

Frequency: Quarterly
Price: Annual subscription £140.00 or £45.00 per copy. Floppy disk and electronic database Available from the Office for National Statistics Sales Desk

Available from
TSO Publications Centre and Bookshops
Please see Annex B for full address details.

Sources from which data for this product are obtained
Consumer Price Collection - UK; Consumers' Expenditure

GDP Preliminary Estimate (First Release)
Office for National Statistics

Estimate of GDP produced three weeks after the end of a quarter. The release contains constant price analyses of output for production industries, service industries, construction and agriculture, in index form and is based upon 1996 information. From September 1998 this data will become consistent with the European System of Accounts (ESA 95).

Frequency: Quarterly
Price: £12.00 annual subscription

Available from
Geoff Reed
Office for National Statistics
1 Drummond Gate
London
Tel: 020 7533 5966

Sources from which data for this product are obtained
National Accounts

Quarterly National Accounts (First Release)
Office for National Statistics

Release produced twelve weeks after the end of the quarter. The release contains estimates and analyses of expenditure at constant and current prices. Also included are estimates of household expenditure; fixed capital formation; charges in inventories; imports and exports of goods and services; household income, expenditure and saving; current and capital for private non-financial corporations; as well as the adjustments made to align income and expenditure estimates to the quarterly output series. The UK National Accounts were moved onto the European System of Accounts (ESA95) - September 1998.

Frequency: Quarterly
Price: Annual subscription £12.00

Available from
Jon Beadle
Office for National Statistics
1 Drummond Gate
London
Tel: 020 7533 5938;
Email: jon.beadle@ons.gov.uk

Sources from which data for this product are obtained
Compensation of employees; Construction Stocks - UK; Current, Capital and Financial Accounts of Non-Financial Corporations; Household Saving Ratio; Motor Traders' Stocks - UK; National Accounts; Production Stocks - UK; Quarterly Capital Expenditure Inquiry; Retailers' Stocks - UK; Wholesalers' and Dealers' Stocks - UK

UK Output, Income and Expenditure (First Release)
Office for National Statistics

National Accounts data produced seven weeks after the end of a quarter. The release contains estimates and analyses of expenditure at constant and current prices, income at current prices, and output at constant prices.

Frequency: Quarterly
Price: £12.00 annual subscription

Available from
Jon Beadle
Office for National Statistics
1 Drummond Gate
London
Tel: 020 7533 5938;
Email: jon.beadle@ons.gov.uk

Sources from which data for this product are obtained
Compensation of employees; Construction Stocks - UK; Household Saving Ratio; Motor Traders' Stocks - UK; National Accounts; Production Stocks - UK; Quarterly Capital Expenditure Inquiry; Retailers' Stocks - UK; Wholesalers' and Dealers' Stocks - UK

Products

United Kingdom Economic Accounts
Office for National Statistics

This quarterly national accounts publication brings together recently published data on national and financial accounts and the balance of payments for the United Kingdom. UK Economic Accounts contains articles incorporating text, charts and tables. These include Key Economic Developments - this brings together a range of economic statistics on the latest quarter and highlights key developments in the economy and articles explaining the data for the latest quarter for National Accounts; UK Economic Accounts - this presents annual and quarterly estimates of national accounts, including balance of payments. Detailed analysis of household expenditure, fixed capital formation, imports and exports of goods and services are shown together with accounts of household sector, companies and general government. Summary financial accounts for each sector are also included. There is an extended section covering the balance of payments.

Delivery: Periodic Release
Frequency: Quarterly
Price: £25.00
ISBN: 0 11 621016 8
ISSN: 1350-4401

Available from
TSO Publications Centre and Bookshops
Please see Annex B for full address details.

Sources from which data for this product are obtained
Similar sources to the Blue Book

United Kingdom National Accounts - the Blue Book
Office for National Statistics

The key annual publication for National Accounts statistics and the essential data source for anyone concerned with macro-economic policies and studies. The Blue Book provides detailed estimates of national product, income and expenditure for the UK. Some tables contain data for the last eighteen years; all tables contain data for the last 9 years. It covers value added by industry, full accounts by sector - including financial and non-financial corporations, central and local government and households - and capital formation.

Frequency: Annual,
Price: £39.50
ISBN: 0 11 621059 1
ISSN: 0267-8691

Available from
TSO Publications Centre and Bookshops
Please see Annex B for full address details.

Sources from which data for this product are obtained
Average Earnings Inquiry; Balance of Payments Account - UK; Borrowing and Lending Inquiry (Quarterly); Central Government Net Cash Requirement - UK; Central Government Net Cash Requirement on Own Account - UK; Centralised Returns (Public Sector); Construction Stocks - UK; Consumer Trends; Current, Capital and Financial Accounts of Non-Financial Corporations; Financial Transactions and Balance Sheets; Gross Trading Surplus of Local Authority Trading Enterprises - UK; Index of Production - UK; Input-Output Balances - United Kingdom; Insurance companies balance sheet annual inquiry; Insurance Companies' income and expenditure - quarterly inquiry; Insurance companies' income and expenditure annual inquiry; Insurance companies' transactions in financial assets inquiry; Investment trusts annual return of liabilities and assets; Investment trusts quarterly return of transactions inquiry; Local Authority Direct Net Cash from Central Government - UK; Local Authority Net Cash Requirement - UK; Mineral Oil and Natural Gas - UK; Monthly Short-term Turnover and Employment Survey - Production Industries; Motor Traders' Stocks - UK; National Accounts; Outstanding Amounts Inquiry (MQBL) - UK; Pension fund annual balance sheet inquiry; Pension fund annual income and expenditure inquiry; Pension fund transactions inquiry; Pension Funds - England; Pension funds quarterly income and expenditure inquiry; Production Stocks - UK; Property unit trusts annual return of liabilities; Property unit trusts quarterly return of transactions inquiry; Public Corporations Employees in Employment - UK; Public Corporations Net Cash Requirement - UK; Public Corporations' Direct Borrowing from Central Government - UK; Public Sector Employment - UK; Public Sector Net Cash Requirement - UK; Quarterly Capital Expenditure Inquiry; Quarterly Short-term turnover and Employment Survey - Service Sector; Retailers' Stocks - UK; Revenue Account Survey - England; Revenue Outturn - England; Securities dealers quarterly return of liabilities and assets and of transactions in securities; UK Trade on a Balance of Payments Basis; Unit trusts annual return of liabilities and assets; Unit trusts quarterly return of transactions inquiry; Wholesalers' and Dealers' Stocks - UK; Workforce jobs (formerly Workforce in Employment)

See also:

In this chapter:
Economic Trends *(10.10)*
Economic Trends Annual Supplement *(10.10)*
Financial Statistics *(10.10)*
United Kingdom National Accounts, Sources and Methods *(10.10)*

In other chapters:
Office for National Statistics Databank (see the Websites and Electronic Services chapter)

10.16 National Economic Accounts - Sector Accounts

National Accounts ESA - Detailed Tables by Sector, 1985-96
Eurostat

This volume presents - insofar as the figures are available - the economic accounts of institutional sectors for Member States of the European Union. The definitions of sectors, accounts and transactions are based on the ESA.

The present edition consists of two statistical parts. Part I compares selected major parameters for Member States while part II is a detailed presentation of the available figures for each country.

Available from
Bob Dodds
Office for National Statistics
Please see Annex B for full address details.

Sector Classification for the National Accounts (Business Monitor MA23)
Office for National Statistics

A division of the economy into institutional sectors with reference to economic organisation as displayed by control/ownership and function (it complements the SIC). The classification brings together particular broad groups of entities within the economy which are similar to one another in general characteristics affecting economic behaviour. The classification embraces in principle all economic units engaging in transactions in goods and services and financial assets. Thus it includes persons and households and overseas concerns as well as corporations and public bodies.

Price: £18.50
ISBN: 0 11 536328 9

Available from
TSO Publications Centre and Bookshops
Please see Annex B for full address details.

10.17 Overseas Trade in Goods

Export Unit Value Indices of Manufactured Goods
Department of Trade and Industry

Last five years (available) quarterly data of export unit value indices for manufactured goods, in the European Union and Norway,

Switzerland, USA, Canada and Japan. Each country compared with an export-weighted average in common currency terms, 1990=100.

Delivery: Periodic Release
Frequency: Quarterly

Available from
Trade Statistics enquiries
Room G15
Department of Trade and Industry
10 Victoria Street
London SW1H 0NN
Tel: 020 7215 3287;
Email: andy.elliott@esdv.dti.gov.uk

External and Intra-European Union Trade: Statistical Yearbook, 1958-97
Eurostat

This yearbook on external and intra-European Union trade sets out to provide long-term trends (1958-97) in the trade of the EU and its Member states. It contains data on the trade flows, broken down by major product group, of the EU with its main trading partners on the one hand and between the Member States on the other.

Delivery: Periodic Release
Frequency: Annually
Price: £20.60
ISBN: 92 828 4778 0

Available from
TSO Publications Centre and Bookshops
Please see Annex B for full address details.

Guide to the Classification for Overseas Trade Statistics OTSG (formerly MA21)
HM Customs and Excise

A guide to the classification used for Overseas Trade Statistics. It provides guidance on Standard International Trade Classification and the correlation with The Combined Nomenclature.

Frequency: Annually
Price: £85.00 per copy
ISBN: 0 11 536306 8

Available from
TSO Publications Centre and Bookshops
Please see Annex B for full address details.
or
Abacus; Business and Trade Statistics Ltd; Dialog Information; MDS Transmodal
Please see Annex B for full address details.

Made in Northern Ireland, Sold to the World
Department of Economic Development - Northern Ireland

Data is available on the sales and export statistics for Northern Ireland companies during the period 1991-92 - 1997-98. There are estimates of total manufacturing, external and export sales, destination of sales, sectoral trends and exports to top ten markets by sectors.

Delivery: Press Release
Frequency: Annually
Price: Free

Available from
Clare Alexander
Statistics Research Branch
Room 110
Department of Economic Development - Northern Ireland
Netherleigh
Massey Avenue
Belfast BT4 2JP
Tel: 028 9052 9525; Fax: 028 9052 9459;
Email: clare.alexander@dedni.gov.uk

Sources from which data for this product are obtained
Northern Ireland Export Survey

Overseas Trade Statistics (OTS)
Office for National Statistics

Latest statistics on the UK's trade with the rest of the world. The monitors contain data on visible trade at Standard International Trade Classification (SITC) and commodity code levels.

Delivery: Hardcopy publication
Frequency: Monthly, quarterly and annually
Price: Various prices
ISBN: Various, see description for details.

Available from
TSO Publications Centre and Bookshops
Please see Annex B for full address details.
or
Abacus; Business and Trade Statistics Ltd; Dialog Information; MDS Transmodal
Please see Annex B for full address details.

Sources from which data for this product are obtained
Overseas Trade Statistics (OTS) - Visible Trade - UK

Overseas Trade Statistics - United Kingdom Trade with the European Community and the the World (formerly MA20)
HM Customs and Excise

Overseas Trade Statistics of the United Kingdom with the world (including data for

countries within the European Community: Intrastat)

Frequency: Annually
Price: £110.00 per copy

Available from
TSO Publications Centre and Bookshops
Please see Annex B for full address details.
or
Abacus; Business and Trade Statistics Ltd; Dialog Information; MDS Transmodal
Please see Annex B for full address details.

Overseas Trade Statistics - United Kingdom Trade with Countries outside the European Community OTS1 (formerly MM20)
HM Customs and Excise

Overseas Trade Statistics of the United Kingdom with countries outside the European Community (Extra EC Trade)

Delivery: Monthly paper publication
Frequency: Monthly
Price: £90.00 per copy, annual subscription £800.00
ISSN: 0436-3574

Available from
TSO Publications Centre and Bookshops
Please see Annex B for full address details.
or
Abacus; Business and Trade Statistics Ltd; Dialog Information; MDS Transmodal
Please see Annex B for full address details.

Overseas Trade Statistics - United Kingdom Trade with the European Community and the World OTS2 (formerly MM20a)
HM Customs and Excise

Overseas Trade Statistics of the United Kingdom with the world (including data for countries within the European Community: Intrastat).

Frequency: Monthly
Price: £45.00 per copy, annual subscription £350.00
ISSN: 1465-4857

Available from
TSO Publications Centre and Bookshops
Please see Annex B for full address details.
or
Abacus; Business and Trade Statistics Ltd; Dialog Information; MDS Transmodal
Please see Annex B for full address details.

Overseas Trade Statistics - United Kingdom Trade with the European Community OTSQ (formerly MQ20)
HM Customs and Excise

Overseas Trade Statistics of the United Kingdom with countries within the European Community (Intra - EC Trade: Intrastat)

Frequency: Quarterly
Price: Single issue £115.00 per copy, annual subscription £380.00
ISBN: 0 11 729920 0

Available from
TSO Publications Centre and Bookshops
Please see Annex B for full address details.
or
Abacus; Business and Trade Statistics Ltd; Dialog Information; MDS Transmodal
Please see Annex B for full address details.

Trade at the Principal Ports
Department of Economic Development - Northern Ireland

Latest statistics on trade at the principal ports in Northern Ireland. Contains data on the changes in inward/outward and unit load carrier traffic at the principal ports in Northern Ireland over the past five years.

Delivery: Periodic Release
Frequency: Annual
Price: Free

Available from
Clare Alexander
Statistics Research Branch
Department of Economic Development
Netherleigh
Massey Avenue
Belfast BT4 2JP
Tel: 028 9052 9525; Fax: 028 9052 9459;
Email: clare.alexander@dedni.gov.uk

Sources from which data for this product are obtained
Exports - Northern Ireland; Trade at Principal Ports- Northern Ireland

UK Trade in Goods Analysed in Terms of Industries (Business Monitor MQ10)
Office for National Statistics

Latest statistics on trade in goods classified according to Standard Industrial Classification (SIC). The monitor contains data on the value of exports and imports on an overseas trade statistics basis analysed by division, group, class and sub-class. Analysis available at four-digit level and above at both current and constant prices on the Office for National Statistics Databank.

Delivery: Periodic Release
Frequency: Quarterly
Price: Annual subscription £70.00

Available from
TSO Publications Centre and Bookshops
Please see Annex B for full address details.

Sources from which data for this product are obtained
UK Trade on a Balance of Payments Basis; UK Overseas Trade Statistics (OTS)

10.18 Overseas Trade in Services

Overseas Earnings from Royalties (First Release)
Office for National Statistics

Overseas trade of royalties and services with tables and supporting text. Contains the main data over time, a geographical breakdown and industrial breakdown for the latest year.

Delivery: First Release
Frequency: Monthly
Price: £3.00

Available from
ONS Direct
Office for National Statistics
Please see Annex B for full address details

Sources from which data for this product are obtained
Overseas Trade in Services

Overseas Transactions of the Film and Television Industry (First Release)
Office for National Statistics

Latest statistics on the overseas transactions of film and television companies. Contains data on overseas transactions of the BBC, independent terrestrial broadcasting, satellite and cable television companies and film production companies.

Delivery: Periodic Release
Frequency: Annual
Price: £3.00

Available from
Martyn Vaughan
Office for National Statistics
Government Buildings
Cardiff Road
Newport
Gwent
South Wales
Tel: 01633 81 2563; martyn.vaughan@ons.gov.uk

Sources from which data for this product are obtained
Overseas Film and Television Industries

See also:
In this chapter:
Economic Trends *(10.10)*
Sector Classification for the National Accounts (Business Monitor MA23) *(10.16)*
UK Balance of Payments (First Release) *(10.11)*
United Kingdom Balance of Payments - the Pink Book *(10.11)*

In other chapters:
Office for National Statistics Databank (see the Websites and Electronic Services chapter)

10.19 Regional and Sub-Regional Economic Accounts

GeoStat Datasets
Office for National Statistics

Available from
Bob Dodds
Office for National Statistics
Please see Annex B for full address details.

Sources from which data for this product are obtained
Regional Accounts

IDB Annual Report - Northern Ireland
Department of Economic Development - Northern Ireland

The IDB Annual Report contains information on the objectives, activity and performance of the Industrial Development Board for Northern Ireland. This includes statistical information on inward investment, assistance offered, jobs promoted, duration & cost of jobs created, potential investor visits, marketing & export development, property & estates, and client company performance.

Delivery: Periodic Release
Frequency: Annually
Price: Free

Available from
Dr Robert Barry
Department of Economic Development - Northern Ireland
IDB House
Chichester Street
Belfast
Tel: 028 9054 5032; Fax: 028 9054 5000;
Email: csu@idb.dedni.gov.uk

Regional Accounts Database
Office for National Statistics

Long run time series of regional accounts data. Available for Government Office Regions and sub-regional areas. Also available for Standard Statistical Regions and counties. Gross Domestic Product by 'income' components; also by industry. Household Accounts by region and type of income; totals by sub-region. Regional Individual Consumption Expenditure by detailed function. All data available as spreadsheets. ASCII tables or hardcopy.

Delivery: Periodic Release
Frequency: Annual data
Price: According to data sub-sets required

Available from
Philip Papaiah
Regional Accounts Branch
Office for National Statistics
1, Drummond Gate
London SW1V 2QQ
Tel: 020 7533 5792;
Email: philip.papaiah@ons.gov.uk

Regional Accounts: Gross Domestic Product
Office for National Statistics

Annual Article in Economic Trends presenting Gross Domestic Product (GDP) for Scotland, Wales, Northern Ireland and English regions, by factors of income and by industry. GDP at sub-regional level.

Delivery: Periodic Release
Frequency: Annual data
Price: According to data sub-sets required

Available from
Philip Papaiah
Regional Accounts Branch
Office for National Statistics
1, Drummond Gate
London SW1V 2QQ
Tel: 020 7533 5792;
Email: philip.papaiah@ons.gov.uk

Regional Accounts: Household Accounts
Office for National Statistics

Economic Trends article presenting figures on Household Incomes by source of income, and Individual Consumption Expenditure by function.

Delivery: Periodic Release
Frequency: Annual data
Price: According to data sub-sets required

Available from
Philip Papaiah
Regional Accounts Branch
Office for National Statistics
1, Drummond Gate
London SW1V 2QQ
Tel: 020 7533 5792;
Email: philip.papaiah@ons.gov.uk

Regional Accounts: Personal Sector
Office for National Statistics

Economic Trends article presenting figures on personal income and household income by source of income; and consumers' expenditure by category for regions. Household income and disposable income at county level.

Delivery: Periodic Release
Frequency: Annually

Available from
Dev Virdee
Office for National Statistics
1 Drummond Gate
London
Tel: 020 7533 5790; Fax: 020 7533 5799;
Email: dev.virdee@ons.gov.uk

Scottish Gross Domestic Product (News Release)
Scottish Executive

Delivery: News/Press Release
Frequency: Annually, quarterly from Summer 1999
Price: Free

Available from
Janice Love
Room 3rd Floor
Scottish Executive
Meridian Court
5 Cadogan Street
Glasgow G2 6AT
Tel: 0141 242 5461;
Email: janice.love@scotland.gov.uk

Sources from which data for this product are obtained
Index of Production - Scotland
Retail Sales Inquiry, ONS

See also:
In this chapter:
Economic Trends *(10.10)*
Regio - Description of Contents of Regional Databank *(10.10)*

Banking and Finance

Statistics covering **Banking and Finance** are collected, administered and disseminated by a number of separate Departments, Agencies and organisations including the **Office for National Statistics, and the Bank of England**. The available statistics embrace a number of subject areas including: the **Bank of England, Banks and Discount Houses, Building Societies, Capital and Financial Markets, Finance and Credit Companies, Finance Leasing, Financial Auxiliaries, Lending to Individuals, Life Insurance and General Insurance Business, Securities Dealers, Self-administered Pension Funds, Unit Trusts and Investment Trusts.**

The basic data are generated from a number of separate information 'Sources' and the resultant statistics are disseminated through a whole range of statistical 'Analyses' and 'Products', all of which are described in the following chapter. Users looking for a cross-section of UK-wide statistics on **Banking and Finance** may find the following products useful:

> **Bank of England: Monetary and Financial Statistics** (monthly publication)
> **Financial Statistics** (monthly publication)
> **Bank of England Quarterly Bulletin** (quarterly publication)

Users interested in a wider range of official statistics including **Banking and Finance** statistics may like to refer to the following compendia:

> On-line Databases (See Chapter 1):
> > **StatBase - StatStore**
> > **StatBase - TimeZone**
> > **DataBank**

> Hardcopy Compendia (See Chapter 2):
> > **Annual Abstract of Statistics**
> > **Britain 2000: The Official Yearbook of the United Kingdom**
> > **Monthly Digest of Statistics**

Users may also find what they need on the various Departmental Websites. These are listed in Chapter 1.

Banking and Finance - *Sources and Analyses*

11.1 Bank of England

Administrative Data on the Official Reserves
The Bank of England

This source is used to produce data on the United Kingdom Official Reserves and Foreign Currency debt. Data is compiled on a monthly basis. The data comes from administrative records.

Status: Ongoing
Frequency: Monthly
Reference Period: One month
Timeliness: Monthly data is published two days after the end - month.

Statistician
Kenny Turnbull
The Bank of England
Tel: 020 7601 3519

Products that contain data from this source
Bank of England: Monetary and Financial Statistics; Financial Statistics; United Kingdom Balance of Payments - The Pink Book

---

Currency Circulation
The Bank of England

The Bank of England compiles data on the note issue outstanding at the previous 28 February, also the value of notes in circulation by denominations and number, of new notes issued by denomination. Data are also available on the notes issued by the Issue Department of the Bank and notes and coin held by the Banking Department, and notes and coin in circulation with the public and held by banks.

Status: Ongoing
Collection Method: Bank of England Returns
Frequency: Weekly and Monthly
Timeliness: Three working days after each Wednesday
Earliest Available Data: 1969 (1998 edition of Bank of England: Statistical Abstract)

Statistician
Amanda Little
The Bank of England
Monetary & Financial Statistics Division
Tel: 020 7601 5468;
Email: mfsd_ms@bankofengland.co.uk

Products that contain data from this source
Bank of England Statistical Abstract Parts 1 and 2; Bank of England: Monetary and Financial Statistics

---

Monetary Stock and Counterparts
The Bank of England

The Bank of England compiles data on the amounts outstanding and changes in monetary stock measures M4 (including retail M4) together with the components and counterparts, including lending to individuals. Sectoral M4 and M4 lending. Divisia components, rates of return, indices and growth rates are also compiled. Data are available seasonally adjusted.

Status: Ongoing
Collection Method: Bank of England Returns
Frequency: Monthly
Timeliness: Reporting day + 14 working days (Provisional Press Release); + 21 working days final.
Earliest Available Data: Quarterly 1964. Monthly 1982 (1998 Editions of Bank of England: Statistical Abstract)

Statistician
Amanda Little
The Bank of England
Monetary & Financial Statistics Division
Tel: 020 7601 5468;
Email: mfsd_ms@bankofengland.co.uk

Products that contain data from this source
Annual Abstract of Statistics; Bank of England: Monetary and Financial Statistics; Economic Trends; Economic Trends Annual Supplement; Financial Statistics; Lending to individuals; Monthly Digest of Statistics; Provisional estimates of M4 and M4 lending and revised estimates of narrow money; Sectoral M4 and M4 lending

---

Provisional Estimates of Narrow Money
The Bank of England

Data for most (but not all) of the components of M0 can be derived from the Bank of England's weekly Bank return, published on Thursday afternoon. Data are available monthly, both unadjusted and seasonally adjusted.

Status: Ongoing
Collection Method: Bank of England returns
Frequency: Monthly
Timeliness: Final Wednesday of month + 3 working days

Statistician
Amanda Little
The Bank of England
Monetary & Financial Statistics Division
Tel: 020 7601 5468;
Email: mfsd_ms@bankofengland.co.uk

Products that contain data from this source
Bank of England: Monetary and Financial Statistics; Financial Statistics

---

See also:
In this chapter:
Transactions with Non-Residents: Interest, Dividends and Other Income (Form BP) (11.2)

11.2 Banks and Discount Houses

Interest Dividends & Other Income by Geographic Location (Form BG)
The Bank of England

This form reports data on income on banks' direct investment earnings, and fee and commission earnings investment/counterparty split by geographic location.

Status: Ongoing
Collection Method: Large-scale (Sample) Survey
Frequency: Annually
Reference Period: Calendar year
Timeliness: Six months
Earliest Available Data: New form: 1998 data published July 1999
National coverage: United Kingdom
Disaggregation: All world countries

Statistician
Kenny Turnbull
The Bank of England
Tel: 020 7601 3519

Levels of Foreign Direct Investment by UK Banks (Form H1(L))
The Bank of England

Form H1 (L) reports data on levels of both inward and outward foreign direct investment by type of instrument. There is a geographic analysis of the data also reported on the Form. Prior to the introduction of this Form for the period Q1 1998, transactions were collected on a triennial basis on Form H1 (Triennial). The earliest data from this Form is 1981.

Status: Ongoing
Collection Method: Bank of England returns
Frequency: Annually
Reference Period: Calendar year
Timeliness: Twelve weeks
Earliest Available Data: 1998
Disaggregation: All world countries

Statistician
Kenny Turnbull
The Bank of England
Tel: 0250 7601 3519

Products that contain data from this source
Bank of England Statistical Abstract; Balance of Payments First Release; Balance of Payments Pink Book; Annual Overseas Direct Investment; Annual Abstract of Statistics; Financial Statistics; Economic Trends Annual Supplement

Portfolio Investment by UK Banks in Securities Issued by Non-Residents (Form P1)
The Bank of England

This form reports data on UK banks portfolio investment. The form collects data on flows but not levels.

Status: Ongoing
Collection Method: Large scale (sample) survey
Frequency: Quarterly
Reference Period: Quarter
Timeliness: Ten weeks
Earliest Available Data: 1988
National coverage: United Kingdom
Disaggregation: None

Statistician
Kenny Turnbull
The Bank of England
Tel: 020 7601 3519

Transactions in Foreign Direct Investment by UK Banks (Form QX (section 7))
The Bank of England

Form QX (section 7) reports data on transactions in both inward and outward foreign direct investment by type of instrument. There is a geographic analysis of the data also reported on the Form. Prior to the introduction of this Form for the period

Q1 1998, transactions were collected on an annual basis on Form H1. The earliest available data from this Form is 1982.

Status: Ongoing
Collection Method: Bank of England returns
Frequency: Quarterly
Reference Period: Quarter
Timeliness: 20 working days after the end of the reference period
Earliest Available Data: 1998
National coverage: United Kingdom
Disaggregation: All world countries

Statistician
Kenny Turnbull
The Bank of England
Tel: 0250 7601 3519

Products that contain data from this source
Bank of England Statistical Abstract; Balance of Payments First Release; Balance of Payments Pink Book; Annual Overseas Direct Investment; Annual Abstract of Statistics; Financial Statistics; Economic Trends Annual Supplement

Dividends and Other Income (Form BP)
The Bank of England

This form reports data on banks' income from business transacted with non-residents.

Status: Ongoing
Collection Method: large-scale (Sample) Survey
Frequency: Quarterly
Reference Period: Quarter
Timeliness: Ten weeks
Earliest Available Data: 1992
National coverage: United Kingdom
Disaggregation: £/Euro/other currencies

Statistician
Kenny Turnbull
The Bank of England
Tel: 020 7601 3519

Products that contain data from this source
Balance of Payments First Release, Pink Book

11.3 Building Societies

Building Societies
Office for National Statistics

The essential function of building societies is to accept savings deposits from members of the public and to extend loans to them, generally for the purpose of purchase or improvement of dwellings. The bulk of such lending is secured on the properties concerned by means of a mortgage agreement. Unlike banks and other financial institutions which carry on similar activities, building societies are structured as mutual (i.e. unincorporated) organisations. Their activities are circumscribed by the Building Societies' Act of 1997, and supervised by

the Building Societies' Commission. A number of larger societies have, in recent years, opted to abandon mutual status either by flotation as independent companies or by acquisitions by banks. There are currently some 70 authorised societies; their total assets at end 1998 amounted to £153.0 billion. Traditionally the societies have been the main providers of finance for the purchase of dwellings in the UK, although banks and centralised mortgage lenders have taken significant shares of this market in recent years. In turn, many of the societies have expanded the range of their products to include current account banking and consumer lending, and have diversified their funding sources to include wholesale deposits and the proceeds of issues of bonds, certificates of deposit and other forms of short-term paper. The Office for National Statistics (ONS) uses and compiles a range of statistics on building societies. Data includes receipts and payments, interest credited, repayments of principal, funds available, advances, net new commitments, net acquisition and end-year holdings of liabilities and assets, net acquisition: cash values of retail share and deposits, commitments and gross advances, interest rates, sources and uses of funds and loans secured. Data are available broken down in a number of ways and some series are seasonally adjusted. The ONS main use of this data is for the National Accounts within which building societies form a sub-sector.

Status: Ongoing
Collection Method: Census
Frequency: Monthly & Quarterly
Reference Period: Monthly
Timeliness: One and a half months.
Earliest Available Data: 1982
National coverage: United Kingdom

Statistician
David Shawyer
Office for National Statistics
Tel: 020 7533 6045;
Email: david.shawyer@ons.gov.uk

Products that contain data from this source
Annual Abstract of Statistics; Bank of England: Monetary and Financial Statistics; Building Societies Association Monthly Mortgage Lending (Press Release); Building Societies Commission: Annual Report; Building Society Yearbook; Compendium of Building Society Statistics; Construction Forecasts; Digest of Welsh Statistics; Economic Trends; Economic Trends Annual Supplement; Financial Statistics; Housing and Construction Statistics Annual Volume; Housing Finance Quarterly (Council of Mortgage Lenders); Monthly Digest of Statistics; Northern Ireland Annual Abstract of Statistics; Scottish Abstract of Statistics

See also:
In other chapters:
Building Society Lending for House Purchase - UK (BS4) (see the Housing chapter)

Sources and Analyses

11.4 Capital and Financial Markets

Capital Issues
The Bank of England

The Bank of England compiles data on various capital issues including bonds and equity issues. Details of these data are compiled from information in the Press and specialist securities publications. A basic analysis is published in a Bank of England press release on the ninth working day of each month: a greater analysis is published monthly in Bank of England: Monetary and Financial Statistics (Bankstats). The published data covers equity and bond issues which raise cash for the issuer (new money). A full definition of the coverage can be found in Bankstats. The Bank of England also collects data on Sterling Commercial Paper and Other Debt Securities (renamed from Medium-Term Notes in April 1997). Data, including a sectoral analysis, are published monthly in Bankstats.

Status: Ongoing
Frequency: Monthly

Statistician
Richard Bennett
The Bank of England
Monetary & Financial Statistics
Tel: 020 7601 4340;
Email: mfsd_fmr@bankofengland.co.uk

Products that contain data from this source
Annual Abstract of Statistics; Bank of England Capital Issues; Bank of England Statistical Abstract Parts 1 and 2; Bank of England: Monetary and Financial Statistics; Financial Statistics

---

Interest and Exchange Rates
The Bank of England

The Bank of England compiles data on a wide range of interest and exchange rates and calculates the Sterling Effective Exchange Rate Indices. The Bank also collects the closing prices of all British Government stocks and derives their yields. Daily data on money market instruments and various FT measures of the London Stock Market are also collected. Data are published daily, monthly and quarterly in Bank of England: Monetary and Financial Statistics (Bankstats), and by the Office for National Statistics in Financial Statistics.

Status: Ongoing
Frequency: Monthly

Statistician
Richard Bennett
The Bank of England
Monetary & Financial Statistics
Tel: 020 7601 4340;
Email: mfsd_fmr@bankofengland.co.uk

Products that contain data from this source
Annual Abstract of Statistics; Bank of England Statistical Abstract Parts 1 and 2; Bank of England: Monetary and Financial Statistics; Financial Statistics

---

Securities Dealers Expenditure Inquiry
Office for National Statistics

This inquiry is undertaken in order to obtain data to measure the contribution to the UK national accounts of this financial institution. It is a component of the "other financial institutions" sector.

Status: Ongoing
Collection Method: Small-scale (Sample) Survey
Frequency: Quarterly
Reference Period: The calendar quarter
Timeliness: 12 weeks after the end of the reporting period
National coverage: United Kingdom

Statistician
Robert Hay
Office for National Statistics
Tel: 01633 812357;
Email: robert.hay@ons.gov.uk

Products that contain data from this source
Financial Statistics

Securities Dealers Quarterly Return of Liabilities and Assets and of Transactions in Securities
Office for National Statistics

This inquiry is undertaken in order to obtain data to measure the contribution to the UK national accounts of this financial institution. It is a component of the "other financial institutions" sector.

Status: Ongoing
Collection Method: Small-scale (Sample) Survey
Frequency: Quarterly
Reference Period: The calendar quarter
Timeliness: 12 weeks after the end of the reporting period.
National coverage: United Kingdom

Statistician
Robert Hay
Office for National Statistics
Tel: 01633 812357;
Email: robert.hay@ons.gov.uk

11.5 Finance and Credit Companies

Finance Houses and Consumer Credit Grantors (Outside the Monetary Sector) and Specialist Finance Leasing Companies and Partnerships Quarterly Inquiry into Capital Expenditure
Office for National Statistics

This inquiry is undertaken in order to obtain data to measure the contribution to the UK national accounts of this financial institution. It is a component of the "other financial institutions" sector.

Status: Ceased
Collection Method: Small-scale (Sample) Survey
Frequency: Quarterly
Reference Period: The calendar quarter
Timeliness: 12 weeks after the end of the reporting period
National coverage: United Kingdom

Statistician
Robert Hay
Office for National Statistics
Tel: 01633 812357;
Email: robert.hay@ons.gov.uk

Fund Managers and Certain Other Members of IMRO
Office for National Statistics

The fund manager's inquiry is needed to measure the industry's earnings from overseas as part of the balance of payments current account. Earliest Available Data: UK Balance of Payments - The Pink Book

Status: Ongoing
Collection Method: Small-scale (Sample) Survey
Frequency: Annually
Reference Period: The calendar year
Timeliness: 9 months after the end of the period
National coverage: United Kingdom

Statistician
Robert Hay
Office for National Statistics
Tel: 01633 812357;
Email: robert.hay@ons.gov.uk

Products that contain data from this source
United Kingdom Balance of Payments - The Pink Book

Monthly Inquiry to Credit Grantors
Office for National Statistics

This inquiry is undertaken in order to obtain data to measure the contribution to the UK national accounts of this financial institution. It is a component of the "other financial institutions" sector. Inquiries to credit grantors are also required to give accurate information on the level of consumer credit issued by non-banks.

Status: Ongoing
Collection Method: Small-scale (Sample) Survey
Frequency: Monthly
Reference Period: the calendar month
Timeliness: 4 weeks after the end or reporting period
Earliest Available Data: Bank of England monthly statistics
National coverage: United Kingdom

Statistician
Robert Hay
Office for National Statistics
Tel: 01633 812357;
Email: robert.hay@ons.gov.uk

Products that contain data from this source
Bank of England Press Release on Lending to Individuals
Financial Statistics

Quarterly Credit Grantors Inquiry
Office for National Statistics

This inquiry is undertaken in order to obtain data to measure the contribution to the UK national accounts of this financial institution. It is a component of the "other financial institutions" sector. Earliest Available Data: Service Sector Monitor SDQ7 "Assets and Liabilities of Finance Houses and Other Credit Companies".

Status: Ceased
Collection Method: Small-scale (Sample) Survey
Frequency: Quarterly
Reference Period: The calendar quarter
Timeliness: 12 weeks after the end of the reporting period.
National coverage: United Kingdom

Statistician
Robert Hay
Office for National Statistics
Tel: 01633 812357;
Email: robert.hay@ons.gov.uk

Products that contain data from this source
Assets and Liabilities of Finance Houses and Other Consumer Credit Grantors (Business Monitor SDQ7)

Quarterly Profits Inquiry Finance Houses and Other Specialist Consumer Credit Grantors - UK
Office for National Statistics

The Office for National Statistics collects data from non-deposit taking finance houses and other specialist consumer credit grantors. The data include net acquisitions and holdings of assets and liabilities - loans and advances; cash and deposits with UK banks and building societies; other current assets; real assets; other assets; borrowing by source; unearned credit charges; and holdings of assets/liabilities (end year). Prior to the first quarter of 1982 assets/liabilities of deposit-taking finance houses and other deposit-taking consumer credit companies were also included. In 1982, many such institutions became authorised institutions under the Banking Act 1979 and more recently 1987, and data for them are included indistinguishably in the banking statistics. Data for the major finance houses, regardless of whether they take deposits or not, are also collected by the Finance and Leasing Association. They provide detail on loans to business and consumers analysed by type and use of credit e.g. hire purchase, leasing, motor credit, retail credit. Data are available monthly and not seasonally adjusted.

Statistician
Robert Hay
Office for National Statistics
Tel: 01633 812357;
Email: robert.hay@ons.gov.uk

Products that contain data from this source
Annual Abstract of Statistics; Assets and Liabilities of Finance Houses and Other Consumer Credit Grantors (Business Monitor SDQ7); Financial Statistics

See also:
In other chapters:
Borrowing and Lending Inquiry (Monthly) - UK (see the Government and the Public Sector chapter)

11.6 Finance Leasing

Asset Finance Annual Income and Expenditure Inquiry
Office for National Statistics

The inquiry is undertaken to obtain data to measure the contribution of the UK National Accounts of the asset finance industry covering non-bank credit grantors, finance lessors and other non bank companies offering forms of asset finance.

Status: Ongoing
Collection Method: Small-scale sample survey
Frequency: Quarterly
Reference Period: The calendar quarter
Timeliness: 9 weeks after the end of the period
National coverage: Great Britain

Statistician
Robert Hay
Office for National Statistics
Tel: 01633 812357;
Email: robert.hay@ons.gov.uk

Products that contain data from this source
The Blue Book

Asset Finance Quarterly Balance Sheet and Transactions Inquiry
Office for National Statistics

The inquiry is undertaken to obtain data to measure the contribution of the UK National Accounts of the asset finance industry covering non-bank credit grantors, finance lessors and other non bank companies offering forms of asset finance.

Status: Ongoing
Collection Method: Small-scale sample survey
Frequency: Quarterly
Reference Period: The calendar quarter
Timeliness: 12 weeks after the end of the period
National coverage: Great Britain

Statistician
Robert Hay
Office for National Statistics
Tel: 01633 812357;
Email: robert.hay@ons.gov.uk

Products that contain data from this source
Financial Statistics

Specialist Finance Leasing Companies and Partnerships Annual Income and Expenditure Inquiry
Office for National Statistics

This inquiry is undertaken in order to obtain data to measure the contribution to the UK national accounts of this financial institution. It is a component of the "other financial institutions" sector.

Status: Ceased
Collection Method: Small-scale (Sample) Survey
Frequency: Annually
Reference Period: The calendar year
Timeliness: 9 months after the end of the reporting period
National coverage: United Kingdom

Statistician
Robert Hay
Office for National Statistics
Tel: 01633 812357;
Email: robert.hay@ons.gov.uk

Sources and Analyses

Specialist Finance Leasing Companies and Partnerships Quarterly Balance Sheet Inquiry
Office for National Statistics

The inquiry is undertaken in order to obtain data to measure the contribution to the UK national accounts of this financial institution. It is a component of the " other financial institutions" sector.

Status: Ceased
Collection Method: Small-scale (Sample) Survey
Frequency: Quarterly
Reference Period: the calendar quarter
Timeliness: 12 weeks after the end of reporting period.
National coverage: United Kingdom

Statistician
Robert Hay
Office for National Statistics
Tel: 01633 812357;
Email: robert.hay@ons.gov.uk

11.7 Lending to Individuals

Please see:
In other chapters:
Building Society Lending for House Purchase - UK (BS4) - (see the Housing chapter)

11.8 Life Insurance and General Insurance business

Earnings of UK Insurance Brokers in Overseas Currencies
Office for National Statistics

The inquiry into overseas earnings of UK insurance brokers is needed to measure the insurance broker's industry's contribution to the UK's balance of payments current account. There is no other source of this information.

Collection Method: Small-scale (Sample) Survey
Frequency: Quarterly
Reference Period: The calendar quarter
Timeliness: 5 weeks after the end of the period
Earliest Available Data: UK Balance of Payments - First Release
National coverage: United Kingdom

Statistician
Robert Hay
Office for National Statistics
Tel: 01633 812357;
Email: robert.hay@ons.gov.uk

Products that contain data from this source
United Kingdom Balance of Payments - The Pink Book and First Release

Insurance Companies Balance Sheet Annual Inquiry
Office for National Statistics

Figures from the survey of quarterly and annual income and expenditure, quarterly transactions in financial assets, annual balance sheets and figures from the annual surveys into the overseas direct investment of insurance companies are used in the income, expenditure and output measures of the gross domestic product, in the sector current, capital and financial accounts, and in the balance of payments current and capital accounts. The data are also required to fulfil international obligations, e.g. to OECD and Eurostat.

Status: Ongoing
Collection Method: Small scale sample survey
Frequency: Annually
Reference Period: The calendar year
Timeliness: 12 months after the end of the period
Earliest Available Data: Press release - "Investment by insurance companies, pension funds & trusts".
National coverage: United Kingdom

Statistician
Robert Hay
Office for National Statistics
Tel: 01633 812357;
Email: robert.hay@ons.gov.uk

Products that contain data from this source
Investment by Insurance Companies, Pension Funds and Trusts (First Release); Insurance Companies', Pension Funds' and Trusts Investments (Business Monitor MQ5); United Kingdom National Accounts - The Blue Book and Financial Statistics

Insurance Companies' Income and Expenditure - Quarterly Inquiry
Office for National Statistics

Figures from the survey of quarterly and annual income and expenditure, quarterly transactions in financial assets, annual balance sheets and figures from the annual surveys into the overseas direct investment of insurance companies are used in the income, expenditure and output measures of the gross domestic product, in the sector current, capital and financial accounts, and in the balance of payments current and capital accounts. The data are also required to fulfil international obligations, e.g. to OECD and Eurostat.

Status: Ongoing
Collection Method: Small-scale (Sample) Survey
Frequency: Quarterly
Reference Period: the calendar quarter
Timeliness: 12 weeks after the end of the period.
Earliest Available Data: Press release - "Investment by insurance companies, pension funds & trusts".
National coverage: United Kingdom

Statistician
Robert Hay
Office for National Statistics
Tel: 01633 812357;
Email: robert.hay@ons.gov.uk

Products that contain data from this source
Investment by Insurance Companies, Pension Funds and Trusts (First Release); Insurance Companies', Pension Funds' and Trusts Investments (Business Monitor MQ5); United Kingdom National Accounts - The Blue Book and Financial Statistics

Insurance Companies' Income and Expenditure Annual Inquiry
Office for National Statistics

Figures from the survey of quarterly and annual income and expenditure, quarterly transactions in financial assets, annual balance sheets and figures from the annual surveys into the overseas direct investment of insurance companies are used in the income, expenditure and output measures of the gross domestic product, in the sector current, capital and financial accounts, and in the balance of payments current and capital accounts. The data are also required to fulfil international obligations, e.g. to OECD and Eurostat.

Status: Ongoing
Collection Method: Small-scale (Sample) Survey
Frequency: Annually
Reference Period: The calendar year
Timeliness: 15 months after the end of the period.
Earliest Available Data: Press release - "Investment by insurance companies, pension funds & trusts".
National coverage: United Kingdom

Statistician
Robert Hay
Office for National Statistics
Tel: 01633 812357;
Email: robert.hay@ons.gov.uk

Products that contain data from this source

Insurance Companies' Transactions in Financial Assets Inquiry
Office for National Statistics

Figures from the survey of quarterly and annual income and expenditure, quarterly transactions in financial assets, annual balance sheets and figures from the annual surveys into the overseas direct investment of insurance companies are used in the income, expenditure and output measures of the gross domestic product, in the sector current, capital and financial accounts, and in the balance of payments current and capital accounts. The data are also required to fulfil international obligations, e.g. to OECD and Eurostat.

Status: Ongoing
Collection Method: Small-scale (Sample) Survey
Frequency: Quarterly
Reference Period: The calendar quarter
Timeliness: 12 weeks after the end of the period.
Earliest Available Data: Press release - "Investment by insurance companies, pension funds & trusts".
National coverage: United Kingdom

Statistician
Robert Hay
Office for National Statistics
Tel: 01633 812357;
Email: robert.hay@ons.gov.uk

Products that contain data from this source
Investment by Insurance Companies, Pension Funds and Trusts (First Release); Insurance Companies', Pension Funds' and Trusts Investments (Business Monitor MQ5); United Kingdom National Accounts - The Blue Book and Financial Statistics

Transactions of UK Insurance Companies with their Overseas Direct Investors and Share Capital
Office for National Statistics

Figures from the surveys of quarterly and annual income and expenditure, quarterly transactions in financial assets, annual balance sheets and figures from the annual surveys into the overseas direct investment of insurance companies are used in the income, expenditure and output measures of the gross domestic product, in the sector current, capital and financial accounts, and in the balance of payments current and capital accounts. The data are also required to fulfil international obligations, e.g. to OECD and Eurostat.

Status: Ongoing
Collection Method: Small-scale (Sample) Survey

Frequency: Quarterly
Reference Period: The calendar quarter
Timeliness: 12 weeks after the end of the period
National coverage: United Kingdom

Statistician
Robert Hay
Office for National Statistics
Tel: 01633 812357;
Email: robert.hay@ons.gov.uk

Transactions of UK Insurance Companies with their Overseas Subsidiaries, Associates, Branches and Agents and Overseas Share Capital and Reserves
Office for National Statistics

Figures from the survey of quarterly and annual income and expenditure, quarterly transactions in financial assets, annual balance sheets and figures from the annual surveys into the overseas direct investment of insurance companies are used in the income, expenditure and output measures of the gross domestic product, in the sector current, capital and financial accounts, and in the balance of payments current and capital accounts. The data are also required to fulfil international obligations, e.g. to OECD and Eurostat.

Status: Ongoing
Collection Method: Small-scale (Sample) Survey
Frequency: Quarterly
Reference Period: The calendar quarter
Timeliness: 12 weeks after the end of the period
National coverage: United Kingdom

Statistician
Robert Hay
Office for National Statistics
Tel: 01633 812357;
Email: robert.hay@ons.gov.uk

11.9 Self Administered Pension Funds

Pension Fund Annual Balance Sheet Inquiry
Office for National Statistics

Figures from the survey of quarterly income and expenditure, quarterly transactions in financial assets and annual balance sheets are used in the income, expenditure and output measures of the gross domestic product, in the sector current, capital and financial accounts, and in the balance of payments current and capital accounts. The data are also required to fulfil international obligations, e.g. to OECD and Eurostat.

Status: Ongoing
Collection Method: Small-scale (Sample) Survey
Frequency: Annually
Reference Period: The calendar year
Timeliness: 12 months after the end of the period
Earliest Available Data: Press release - "Investment by insurance companies, pension funds & trusts".
National coverage: United Kingdom

Statistician
Robert Hay
Office for National Statistics
Tel: 01633 812357;
Email: robert.hay@ons.gov.uk

Products that contain data from this source
Investment by Insurance Companies, Pension Funds and Trusts (First Release); Insurance Companies', Pension Funds' and Trusts Investments (Business Monitor MQ5); United Kingdom National Accounts - The Blue Book and Financial Statistics

Pension Fund Quarterly Income and Expenditure Inquiry
Office for National Statistics

Figures from the survey of quarterly income and expenditure, quarterly transactions in financial assets and annual balance sheets are used in the income, expenditure and output measures of the gross domestic product, in the sector current, capital and financial accounts, and in the balance of payments current and capital accounts. The data are also required to fulfil international obligations, e.g. to OECD and Eurostat.

Status: Ongoing
Collection Method: Small-scale (Sample) Survey
Frequency: Quarterly
Reference Period: The calendar quarter
Timeliness: 12 weeks after the end of the period
Earliest Available Data: Press release - "Investment by insurance companies, pension funds & trusts"
National coverage: United Kingdom

Statistician
Robert Hay
Office for National Statistics
Tel: 01633 812357;
Email: robert.hay@ons.gov.uk

Products that contain data from this source
Investment by Insurance Companies, Pension Funds and Trusts (First Release); Insurance Companies', Pension Funds' and Trusts Investments (Business Monitor MQ5); United Kingdom National Accounts - The Blue Book and Financial Statistics

Sources and Analyses

Pension Fund Quarterly Transactions Inquiry
Office for National Statistics

Figures from the survey go into quarterly income and expenditure, quarterly transactions in financial assets and annual balance sheets are used in the income, expenditure and output measures of the gross domestic product, in the sector current, capital and financial accounts, and in the balance of payments current and capital accounts. The data are also required to fulfil international obligations, e.g. to OECD and Eurostat.

Status: Ongoing
Collection Method: Small-scale (Sample) Survey
Frequency: Quarterly
Reference Period: The calendar quarter
Timeliness: 12 weeks after the end of the period.
Earliest Available Data: Press release - " Investment by insurance companies, pension funds & trusts".
National coverage: United Kingdom

Statistician
Robert Hay
Office for National Statistics
Tel: 01633 812357;
Email: robert.hay@ons.gov.uk

Products that contain data from this source
Investment by Insurance Companies, Pension Funds and Trusts (First Release); Insurance Companies', Pension Funds' and Trusts Investments (Business Monitor MQ5); United Kingdom National Accounts - The Blue Book and Financial Statistics

See also:
In other chapters:
Occupational Pension Schemes - UK (see the Household Finances chapter)
Pension Funds - England (see the Government and Public Sector chapter)

11.10 Unit, Property Unit and Investment Trusts

Investment Trusts Annual Return of Liabilities and Assets
Office for National Statistics

This inquiry is undertaken in order to obtain data to measure the contribution to the UK national accounts of this financial institution. It is a component of the "other financial institutions" sector.

Status: Ongoing
Collection Method: Small-scale (Sample) Survey

Frequency: Annually
Reference Period: The calendar year
Timeliness: 9 months after the end of the period.
Earliest Available Data: Press release - "Investment by insurance companies, pension funds & trusts"
National coverage: United Kingdom

Statistician
Robert Hay
Office for National Statistics
Tel: 01633 812357;
Email: robert.hay@ons.gov.uk

Products that contain data from this source
Financial Statistics; Insurance Companies', Pension Funds' and Trusts Investments (Business Monitor MQ5); Investment by Insurance Companies, Pension Funds and Trusts (First Release); United Kingdom National Accounts - The Blue Book

Investment Trusts Quarterly Return of Transactions Inquiry
Office for National Statistics

This inquiry is undertaken in order to obtain data to measure the contribution to the UK national accounts of this financial institution. It is a component of the "other financial institutions" sector.

Status: Ongoing
Collection Method: Small-scale (Sample) Survey
Frequency: Quarterly
Reference Period: The calendar quarter
Timeliness: 12 weeks after the end of the period
Earliest Available Data: Press release - "Investment by insurance companies, pension funds & trusts".
National coverage: United Kingdom

Statistician
Robert Hay
Office for National Statistics
Tel: 01633 812357;
Email: robert.hay@ons.gov.uk

Products that contain data from this source
Financial Statistics; Insurance Companies', Pension Funds' and Trusts Investments (Business Monitor MQ5); Investment by Insurance Companies, Pension Funds and Trusts (First Release); United Kingdom National Accounts - The Blue Book

Property Unit Trusts Annual Return of Liabilities and Assets
Office for National Statistics

This inquiry is undertaken in order to obtain data to measure the contribution to the UK national accounts of this financial institution. It is a component of the "other financial institutions" sector.

Status: Ongoing
Collection Method: Small-scale (Sample) Survey
Frequency: Annually
Reference Period: The calendar year
Timeliness: 9 months after the end of the period
Earliest Available Data: Press release - "Investment by insurance companies, pension funds & trusts"
National coverage: United Kingdom

Statistician
Robert Hay
Office for National Statistics
Tel: 01633 812357;
Email: robert.hay@ons.gov.uk

Products that contain data from this source
Investment by Insurance Companies, Pension Funds and Trusts (First Release); Insurance Companies', Pension Funds' and Trusts Investments (Business Monitor MQ5); United Kingdom National Accounts - The Blue Book and Financial Statistics

Property Unit Trusts Quarterly Return of Transactions Inquiry
Office for National Statistics

This inquiry is undertaken in order to obtain data to measure the contribution to the UK national accounts of this financial institution. It is a component of the "other financial institutions" sector.

Status: Ongoing
Collection Method: Small-scale (Sample) Survey
Frequency: Quarterly
Reference Period: The calendar quarter
Timeliness: 12 weeks after the end of the period.
Earliest Available Data: Press release - "Investment by insurance companies, pension funds & trusts.
National coverage: United Kingdom

Statistician
Robert Hay
Office for National Statistics
Tel: 01633 812357;
Email: robert.hay@ons.gov.uk

Products that contain data from this source
Investment by Insurance Companies, Pension Funds and Trusts (First Release); Insurance Companies', Pension Funds' and Trusts Investments (Business Monitor MQ5); United Kingdom National Accounts - The Blue Book and Financial Statistics

Unit Trusts Annual Return of Liabilities and Assets
Office for National Statistics

This inquiry is undertaken in order to obtain data to measure the contribution to the UK national accounts of this financial institution. It is a component of the "other financial institutions" sector.

Status: Ongoing
Collection Method: Small-scale (Sample) Survey
Frequency: Annually
Reference Period: The calendar year
Timeliness: 9 months after the end of the period
Earliest Available Data: Press release - "Investment by insurance companies, pension funds & trusts"
National coverage: United Kingdom

Statistician
Robert Hay
Office for National Statistics
Tel: 01633 812357;
Email: robert.hay@ons.gov.uk

Products that contain data from this source
Investment by Insurance Companies, Pension Funds and Trusts (First Release); Insurance Companies', Pension Funds' and Trusts Investments (Business Monitor MQ5); United Kingdom National Accounts - The Blue Book and Financial Statistics

Unit Trusts Quarterly Return of Transactions Inquiry
Office for National Statistics

This inquiry is undertaken in order to obtain data to measure the contribution to the UK national accounts of this financial institution. It is a component of the "other financial institutions" sector.

Status: Ongoing
Collection Method: Small-scale (Sample) Survey
Frequency: Quarterly
Reference Period: The calendar quarter
Timeliness: 12 weeks after the end of the period.
Earliest Available Data: Press release - "Investment by insurance companies, pension funds & trusts".
National coverage: United Kingdom

Statistician
Robert Hay
Office for National Statistics
Tel: 01633 812357;
Email: robert.hay@ons.gov.uk

Products that contain data from this source
Financial Statistics; Insurance Companies', Pension Funds' and Trusts Investments (Business Monitor MQ5); Investment by Insurance Companies, Pension Funds and Trusts (First Release); United Kingdom National Accounts - The Blue Book

Banking and Finance - *Products*

Bank of England Statistical Abstract Parts 1 and 2
The Bank of England

Part 1 contains: Long runs of Money and lending; banks' balance sheets and subsidiary analyses, income, expenditure and direct investment; funding, money markets and other central government financing; issues of securities and short-term paper; interest and exchange rates. Part 2 contains: Long runs of detailed monetary data; breaks in monetary series; further references on monetary and banking statistics in the Bank of England's Quarterly Bulletin, Monetary and financial statistics and elsewhere, diary of events relevant to the interpretation of the monetary statistics since 1960; and outliers etc. modified before the seasonal adjustments are derived.

Frequency: Annually
Price: £20.00 per part (see 'General')
ISBN: Part 1: 1 85730 171 4; Part 2: 1 85730 176 5

Available from
Daxa Khilosia
The Bank of England
Threadneedle Street
London EC2R 8AH
Tel: 020 7601 5353; Fax: 020 7601 3334;
Email: msfd_ms@bankof england.co.uk

Sources from which data for this product are obtained
Capital Issues; Currency Circulation; Interest and Exchange Rates; Monetary Stock and Counterparts; Estimates of Narrow Money

Bank of England: Monetary and Financial Statistics
The Bank of England

Informally known as 'Bankstats'. It consists of money and lending, monetary financial institutions' balance sheets, international business etc of banks operating in the UK, government financing and the money markets (including gilt repo and stock lending), issues of securities and short-term paper, interest and exchange rates and occasional background articles.

Frequency: Monthly
Price: 1998 issues: £8.00 monthly or £80.00 annually (see 'General')
ISSN: 1365-7690

Available from
Daxa Khilosia
The Bank of England
Threadneedle Street
London EC2R 8AH
Tel: 020 7601 5353; Fax: 020 7601 3334;
Email: msfd_ms@bankof england.co.uk

Sources from which data for this product are obtained
Administrative Data on the Official Reserves; Building Societies; Capital Issues; Currency Circulation; Interest and Exchange Rates; Monetary Stock and Counterparts; Provisional estimates of narrow money

Financial Statistics
Office for National Statistics

Key financial and monetary statistics of the UK. Contains data on public sector finance, central government revenue and expenditure, money supply and credit, banks and building societies, interest and exchange rates, financial accounts, capital issues, balance sheets and balance of payments. From the October 1998 edition the data in Financial Statistics becomes consistent with the European System of Accounts (ESA 95).

Frequency: Monthly
Price: Monthly, single issue £23.50, annual subscription £280.00 (handbook included) Electronic database
ISSN: 0015-203X

Available from
TSO Publications Centre and Bookshops
Please see Annex B for full address details.
or
The ONS Sales Desk
Please see Annex B for full address details.

Sources from which data for this product are obtained
Acquisitions and Mergers - UK; Administrative Data on the Official Reserves; Annual survey of financial assets and liabilities; Balance of Payments Account - UK; Borrowing and Lending Inquiry (Monthly) - UK; Borrowing and Lending Inquiry (Quarterly); Building Societies; Building Society Lending for House Purchase - UK (BS4); Capital Issues; Central Government Net Cash Requirement - UK; Central Government Net Cash Requirement on Own Account - UK; Compensation of employees; Consumer Price Collection - UK; Consumers' Expenditure; Current, Capital and Financial Accounts of Non-Financial Corporations; Financial Statistics; Financial Transactions and Balance Sheets; Gross Trading Surplus of Local Authority Trading Enterprises - UK; Household Saving Ratio; Inland Revenue Tax Receipts; Insurance companies balance sheet annual inquiry; Insurance Companies' income and expenditure - quarterly inquiry; Insurance companies' income and expenditure annual inquiry; Insurance companies' transactions in financial assets inquiry; Interest and Exchange Rates; Investment trusts annual return of liabilities and assets; Investment trusts quarterly return of transactions inquiry; Local Authority Direct Net Cash from Central Government - UK; Local Authority Net Cash Requirement - UK; Monetary Stock and Counterparts; National Accounts; National Savings - Financial Statistics; Net Value Added Tax (VAT) Receipts UK; Outstanding Amounts Inquiry (MQBL) - UK; Overseas Direct Investment; Pension fund annual balance sheet inquiry; Pension fund annual income and expenditure inquiry; Pension fund transactions inquiry; Pension Funds - England; Pension funds quarterly income and expenditure inquiry; Property unit trusts annual return of liabilities; Property unit trusts quarterly return of transactions inquiry; Provisional estimates of narrow money; Public Corporations Net Cash Requirement - UK; Public Corporations' Direct Borrowing from Central Government - UK; Public Sector Net Cash Requirement - UK; Quarterly Profits Inquiry Finance Houses and Other Specialist Consumer Credit Grantors - UK; Quarterly survey of financial assets and liabilities; Receipts of Customs and Excise Taxes other than VAT - UK; Revenue Account Survey - England; Revenue Outturn - England; Securities dealers quarterly return of liabilities and assets and of transactions in securities; Unit trusts annual return of liabilities and assets; Unit trusts quarterly return of transactions inquiry

11.12 Bank of England

Analysis of Bank Deposits from and Lending to UK Residents
The Bank of England

Industrial (SIC 92) analysis of deposits with, and borrowing from, banks in the UK by UK residents other than banks and building societies. Contains end-quarterly levels and quarterly flows, distinguishing sterling from other currencies. Deposits include repos. Borrowing covers loans and advances (including reverse repos), finance leasing and acceptances in both sterling and other currencies, and sterling commercial paper held by banks. Facilities data are also shown. Customers are grouped into the following main industrial categories (some of which are analysed further): agriculture, hunting and forestry; fishing; mining and quarrying; manufacturing; electricity, gas and water supply; construction; wholesale and retail trade; hotels and restaurants; transport, storage and communication; real estate, renting, computer and other business activities; public administration and defence; education; health and social work; recreational, personal and community service activities; insurance companies and pension funds; other financial intermediation; activities auxiliary to financial intermediation; and individuals and individual trusts.

Delivery: Press Release
Frequency: Quarterly
Price: Free

Available from
Domestic Banking Statistics Group
Bank of England
Please see Annex B for full address details
or from Bank of England website at http://www.bankofengland.co.uk/mfsd/abi/

Growth Rates of M4 and M4 Lending
The Bank of England

Second release of growth rates of M4 and M4 lending for the month. Release of counterparts to changes in M4 for the month and the previous 12 months and details of sterling repos and reverse repos.

Delivery: Press Release - Paper, internet and wire services
Frequency: Monthly
Price: free

Available from
Domestic Banking Statistics Group
Bank of England
Please see Annex B for full address details.

Sources from which data for this product are obtained
Statistical returns from all authorised banks operating in the United Kingdom
Aggregate building societies data from the Building Societies Commission

---

Official Operations in the Money

Markets
The Bank of England

This provides details of operations by the Bank of England in the money markets; includes repo, outright purchases and late facilities on a daily basis.

Delivery: Periodic Release
Frequency: Monthly

Available from
Stephen Loach
The Bank of England
Threadneedle Street
London EC2R 8AH
Tel: 020 7601 4419; Fax: 020 7601 3300

Other Banks' Balance Sheet
The Bank of England

Aggregate balance sheet of banks in the UK (excluding the Banking Department of the Bank of England from April 1998 and the Issue Department in all periods) analysed by instrument and in part economic sector. Contains end-monthly levels and monthly flows, distinguishing sterling from other currencies (and in turn identifying euro separately). Liabilities identified include sight deposits, time deposits and liabilities under sale and repurchase agreements each analysed by economic sector; CDs and other short-term paper issued; and capital and other internal funds. Assets identified include loans to banks in the UK and to those abroad; and claims under sale and repurchase agreements, advances (other than to banks) and investments each analysed by economic sector. Total liabilities and assets are inflated by acceptances and accruals, whilst within liabilities the net value of derivatives is distinguished from the broadly offsetting profit and loss entries included in capital and other internal funds. Flows do not necessarily equal the difference in successive levels because adjustments are applied to the former to remove the effects of changes in the reporting population, and of exchange rate movements on the sterling value of foreign currency denominated liabilities and assets.

Delivery: Hardcopy publication ('Bank of England: Monetary and Financial Statistics')
Frequency: Monthly
Price: Full price to UK subscribers is £8.00 per copy or £80.00 annually. For concessions and prices for non-resident subscribers please enquire at the contact points below.
ISSN: 1365 7690

Available from
Publications Group
Inflation Report Division, HO-4
Bank of England
Threadneedle Street
London EC2R 8AH
Tel: 020 7601 4030;

Email: mapublications@bankofengland.co.uk
or from Bank of England website at http://www.bankofengland.co.uk/mfsd/ms/

Provisional Estimates of M4 and M4 Lending and Revised Estimates of Narrow Money
The Bank of England

First release of growth rates of M4 and M4 lending and revised estimates of notes and coin and M0 (narrow money) for the month. First release of summary counterparts to changes in M4 for the month and the latest 12 month and details of sterling repos and reverse repos. Growth rates of M4 and M4 lending for latest month and 24 months previous. Level and changes and growth rates in M0 and notes and coin for latest month and 24 months previous.

Delivery: Press Release. Paper, Internet and Wire Services
Frequency: Monthly
Price: Free

Available from
Domestic Banking Statistics Group
Bank of England
Please see Annex B for full address details

Sources from which data for this product are obtained
Monetary Stock and Counterparts
Initial data are from statistical returns from authorised banks
Aggregate data on building societies from the Building Societies Commission

---

Provisional Estimates of Narrow Money
The Bank of England

Data for most (but not all) of the components of M0 can be derived from the Bank of England's weekly Bank return, published on Thursday afternoon. Weekly levels of M0 are available on the Bank of England Website http://www.bankofengland.co.uk/ . First Press Release of growth rates, levels outstanding and changes in notes and coin and M0 (narrow money). Growth rates for latest month and 24 months previous. Levels for present month and 4 months previous. The published level for each month is the average of the levels for all the Wednesdays of the month. Weekly levels available three working days after the Wednesday to which they relate.

Delivery: Press Release. Paper, Internet and Wire Services
Frequency: Monthly
Price: Free

Available from
Bank of England
Please see Annex B for full address details

Sources from which data for this product are obtained
Internal Bank of England data

Sectoral M4 and M4 Lending
The Bank of England

Pre release of three month growth rates of holdings of M4 and Bank and M4 lending by other financial corporations, private non-financial corporations and by the household sector for the quarter.

Delivery: Press Release. Paper, Internet and Wire Services
Frequency: Quarterly
Price: free

Available from
Domestic Banking Statistics Group
Bank of England
Please see Annex B for full address details.

Sources from which data for this product are obtained
Monetary Stock and Counterparts
Initial data are from statistical returns from authorised banks
Aggregate data on building societies from the Building Societies Commission

---

Transactions in Gilt Strips
The Bank of England

This table shows the gilts that are strippable; the amount outstanding for each strippable gilt; and the percentage of the amount outstanding that is actually held in stripped form. Weekly figures are given as the last working day of each week for recent data, and monthly averages for historic data.

Delivery: Periodic Release
Frequency: Monthly

Available from
Stephen Loach
The Bank of England
Threadneedle Street
London EC2R 8AH
Tel: 020 7601 4419; Fax: 020 7601 3300

See also:
In this chapter:
Bank of England Statistical Abstract Parts 1 and 2 (11.11)
Bank of England: Monetary and Financial Statistics (11.11)
Financial Statistics (11.11)

In other chapters:
Economic Trends (see the Economy chapter)

Economic Trends Annual Supplement (see the Economy chapter)

11.13 Banks and Discount Houses

Consolidated Worldwide External Claims of UK-Owned Banks
The Bank of England

Statistics relating to the worldwide consolidated external business of UK-owned banks. Contains data on consolidated external claims and unused commitments of UK-owned banks and their subsidiaries worldwide, analysed by country, sector and maturity.

Delivery: News/Press Release
Frequency: Bi-annually
Price: Free

Available from
Domestic Banking Statistics Group
Bank of England
Please see Annex B for full address details

External Business of Banks Operating in the United Kingdom
The Bank of England

Statistics relating to the external business of banks operating in the UK. Contains data covering external liabilities and claims of UK banks analysed by currency and sector of creditor/ debtor and by country of creditor/debtor; external liabilities and claims in sterling of UK banks - exchange reserves in sterling held by non-resident central monetary institutions and international organisations and banking and money market liabilities to other holders, both analysed by geographical area of creditor; sterling claims, firstly split into loans and money-market instruments, and this is further split into CMI, bank, non-bank, ECGD-guaranteed paper and bills and acceptances, secondly Debt securities, both are also analysed by geographical area.

Delivery: News/Press Release
Frequency: Quarterly
Price: Free

Available from
Domestic Banking Statistics Group
Bank of England
Please see Annex B for full address details

International Banking and Financial Market Developments
The Bank of England; sponsored by Bank for International Settlements, Basle

This is a BIS press release which contains articles and statistical annexes on The International Banking Market; The International Securities Markets; Derivatives Markets and the role of major currencies in emerging foreign exchange markets. Queries concerning the commentary should be addressed to Jean Kertudo (Tel. +41 61 280 8445) or Serge Jeanneau (Tel. +41 61 280 8416). Queries concerning the statistics should be addressed to Rainer Widera (Tel. +41 61 280 8425).

Delivery: News/Press Release
Frequency: Quarterly

Available from
Bank for International Settlements
External Services Section
Centralbahnplatz 2
CH-4002
Basle

(The) Maturity, Sectoral and Nationality Distribution of International Bank Lending
The Bank of England; sponsored by Bank for International Settlements, Basle

This is a BIS press release that contains articles and statistics on the maturity, sectoral and nationality distribution of international bank lending.

Delivery: News/Press Release
Frequency: Bi-annually

Available from
Bank for International Settlements
External Services Section
Centralbahnplatz 2
CH-4002
Basle

Other Banks: Group Detail
The Bank of England

Aggregate balance sheet of banks in the UK (excluding the Banking Department of the Bank of England from April 1998 and the Issue Department in all periods) analysed by nationality groupings, instrument and in part economic sector. Contains end-monthly levels, distinguishing sterling from other currencies (and in turn identifying euro separately). Nationality groupings identified are UK, Other EU, American, Japanese, Other developed and Other. Banks are classified according to the country of their ultimate ownership. UK-registered institutions in which no one institution has a shareholding of more than 50%, and in which at least one shareholder is based outside the UK, are allocated to Other. Liabilities identified include sight deposits, time deposits and liabilities under sale and repurchase agreements each analysed by economic sector; CDs and other short-term paper issued; and capital and other internal funds. Assets identified include loans to banks in the UK and to those abroad; and claims under sale and repurchase agreements, advances (other than to banks) and investments each analysed by economic sector. Total liabilities and assets are inflated by acceptances and accruals, whilst within liabilities the net value of derivatives is distinguished from the broadly offsetting profit and loss entries included in capital and other internal funds.

Delivery: Hardcopy publication ("Bank of England: Monetary and Financial Statistics")
Frequency: Monthly
Price: Full price to UK subscribers is £8.00 per copy or £80.00 annually. For concessions and prices for non-resident subscribers please enquire at the contact points below.
ISSN: 1365-7680

Available from
Publications Group
Inflation Report Division HO-4
Bank of England
Threadneedle Street
London EC2R 8AH
Tel: 020 7601 4030;
Email:mapublications@bankofengland.co.uk
Or from Bank of England website at http://www.bankofengland.co.uk/msfd/ms

Write-offs and Other Revaluations of Loans by Banks
The Bank of England

Comprises write-offs/ons and disposals at a discount or premium to book value of loans, and revaluations of certificates of deposit, commercial paper and bills. Excludes provisions for bad and doubtful debts, changes in the sterling value of foreign currency assets arising from exchange rate movements, and changes in the value of paper resulting from the amortisation of the discount on issue. Total and non-resident data are reported quarterly by all banks with footings of more than £600mn and/or eligible liabilities of more than £60mn; the sectoral analysis of write-offs, etc of lending to UK residents is based on annual data reported by all of these banks and quarterly data reported by those making write-offs, etc totalling more than approximately £50mn in the quarter. Because of the irregular nature of write-offs, etc the figures are not grossed-up to cover smaller banks. The reported aggregates are used to remove the effects of write-offs and other revaluations from the bank lending flows, which are calculated as the difference between amounts outstanding at successive reporting dates, eg write-offs will reduce the stock of lending and so are added to the calculated flows.

Delivery: Hardcopy publication ("Bank of England: Monetary and Financial Statistics")
Frequency: Monthly
Price: Full price to UK subscribers is £8.00 per copy or £80.00 annually. For concessions and prices for non-resident subscribers please enquire at the contact points below.
ISSN: 1365-7590

Available from
Domestic Banking Statistics
The Bank of England
Threadneedle Street
London EC2R 8AH
Tel: 020 7601 3119

Sources from which data for this product are obtained
Publications Group,
Inflation Report Division, HO-4,
Bank of England
Threadneedle Street
London EC2R 8AH
Tel: 020 7601 4030;
Email: mapublications@bankofengland.co.uk
Or from Bank of England website at: http://www.bankofengland.co.uk/mfsd/ms/

Your Guide to the Council of Mortgage Lenders
The Building Societies Association

Delivery: Ad hoc/One-off Release
Frequency: Ad hoc

Available from
Sue Hart
The Building Societies Association
3 Saville Row
London
Tel: 020 7440 2223

See also:
In this chapter:
Bank of England Statistical Abstract Parts 1 and 2 (11.11)
Bank of England: Monetary and Financial Statistics (11.11)
Financial Statistics (11.11)

In other chapters:
Economic Trends (see the Economy chapter)
Financial Statistics (see the Economy chapter)

11.14 Building Societies

Building Societies Commission: Annual Report
The Building Societies Association

Available from
Sue Hart
The Building Societies Association
3 Saville Row
London
Tel: 020 7440 2223

Sources from which data for this product are obtained
Building Societies

Building Society News
The Building Societies Association

Delivery: Periodic Release

Available from
Sue Hart
The Building Societies Association
3 Saville Row
London
Tel: 020 7440 2223

Building Society Yearbook
Charterhouse Communications

Delivery: Hardcopy publication, 73rd edition
Frequency: Annually
Price: £52.25 including postage and package

Available from
Subscriptions Department
Charterhouse Communications
Arnold House
36-41 Holywell Lane
London EC2A 3SF
Tel: 020 7827 5454

Sources from which data for this product are obtained
Building Societies

Compendium of Housing Finance Statistics
Council of Mortgage Lenders

Delivery: Hardcopy or diskette
Frequency: Annual
Price: £75.00 / £150.00 (non-members of CML)
ISBN: 1 872423 34 5

Available from
Margaret Glass
Council of Mortgage Lenders
3 Savile Row
London W1X 1AF
Tel: 020 7440 2229;
Email: margaret.glass@cml.org.uk

Sources from which data for this product are obtained
Mortgage lenders

Mortgage Finance Gazette
Charterhouse Communications

Delivery: Other
Frequency: Monthly
Price: £4.50

Available from
Subscriptions Department
Charterhouse Communications
Arnold House

36-41 Holywell Lane
London EC2A 3SF
Tel: 020 7827 5454

See also:
In this chapter:
Bank of England Statistical Abstract Parts
1 and 2 (11.11)
Bank of England: Monetary and Financial
Statistics (11.11)
Financial Statistics (11.11)
Your Guide to the Council of Mortgage
Lenders (11.13)

In other chapters:
Building Societies Association Monthly
Mortgage Lending (Press Release) (see the
Housing chapter)
Economic Trends (see the Economy
chapter)
Economic Trends Annual Supplement (see
the Economy chapter)
Housing Finance Quarterly (Council of
Mortgage Lenders) (see the Housing
chapter)

11.15 Capital and Financial Markets

Bank of England Capital Issues
The Bank of England

Issues in sterling and other currencies by UK
borrowers including UK company
subsidiaries abroad and sterling issues by
overseas borrowers. Contains
announcements of new issues by: UK
borrowers; overseas subsidiaries of UK
borrowers; overseas borrowers. Issues in
sterling by UK and overseas borrowers and
other currencies by UK borrowers (gross
issues, redemptions and net issues), issues
in sterling by UK and overseas borrowers
and other currencies by UK borrowers (net
issues analysis by sector), net issue analysis
by sector of borrowers - overseas borrowers
overseas subsidiaries of UK borrowers and
amounts raised in all capital markets by UK
borrowers. The series covers only issues
which raise cash for the issuer. They exclude
bonus issues, exchanges of one type of
security for another and issues for
considerations other than cash. Sales of shares
by the Government where no 'new money'
is raised for the companies concerned are
excluded for the same reason. Monthly,
quarterly and annual data from the
beginning of 1986 are available. Key issues
are highlighted on the front page. Both
unadjusted and seasonally adjusted data are
available.

Delivery: Periodic Release
Frequency: Monthly
Price: Free

Available from
Domestic Banking Statistics Group
Bank of England
Please see Annex B for full address details.
Website address: www.bankofengland.co.uk/mfsd/
schedule.htm

Sources from which data for this product are obtained
Capital Issues

See also:
In this chapter:
Bank of England Statistical Abstract Parts
1 and 2 (see 11.11)
Bank of England: Monetary and Financial
Statistics (11.11)
Financial Statistics (11.11)

11.16 Finance and Credit Companies

Assets and Liabilities of Finance Houses and Other Consumer Credit Grantors (Business Monitor SDQ7)
Office for National Statistics

Data on holdings and acquisitions by type
of asset.

Frequency: Quarterly
Price: Annual subscription £80.00
ISSN: 1366 882X

Available from
ONS Direct
Office for National Statistics
Please see Annex B for full address details.

Sources from which data for this product are obtained
Quarterly credit grantors inquiry; Finance Houses
and Other Specialist Consumer Credit Grantors -
UK

See also:
In this chapters:
Financial Statistics (see the Economy
chapter)

11.17 Lending to Individuals

Lending to Individuals
The Bank of England

Press release of growth rates of total lending
to individuals, secured lending and consumer
credit for the month. Growth rates for the
month and 3 previous months and 13 months
data of changes. Secured lending includes
loans approved (Value and Number) and
consumer credit includes credit card credit.

Delivery: Periodic Release
Frequency: Monthly
Price: Free

Available from
Domestic Banking Statistics Group
Bank of England
Please see Annex B for full address details

Sources from which data for this product are obtained
Monetary Stock and Counterparts

See also:
In this chapter:
Bank of England Statistical Abstract Parts
1 and 2 (11.11)
Bank of England: Monetary and Financial
Statistics (11.11)
Financial Statistics (11.11)

11.18 Life Insurance and General Insurance business

Insurance Companies', Pension Funds' and Trusts Investments (Business Monitor MQ5)
Office for National Statistics

This business monitor contains information
on the activities of insurance companies, self
administered pension funds, investment
trusts, unit trusts and property unit trusts.
Estimates of net investment, balance sheet
and income and expenditure statistics are
derived from statistical enquires to these
financial institutions.

Frequency: Quarterly
Price: Annual subscription £70.00
ISBN: 0 11 537383 8
ISSN: 1462-558X

Available from
ONS Direct
Office for National Statistics
Please see Annex B for full address details.

Sources from which data for this product are obtained
Insurance companies balance sheet annual
inquiry; Insurance Companies' income and
expenditure - quarterly inquiry; Insurance
companies' income and expenditure annual
inquiry; Insurance companies' transactions in
financial assets inquiry; Investment trusts annual
return of liabilities and assets; Investment trusts
quarterly return of transactions inquiry; Pension
fund annual balance sheet inquiry; Pension fund
annual income and expenditure inquiry; Pension
fund transactions inquiry; Pension funds quarterly
income and expenditure inquiry; Property unit
trusts annual return of liabilities; Property unit
trusts quarterly return of transactions inquiry;
Securities dealers quarterly return of liabilities and
assets and of transactions in securities; Unit trusts
annual return of liabilities and assets; Unit trusts
quarterly return of transactions inquiry

Investment by Insurance Companies, Pension Funds and Trusts (First Release)
Office for National Statistics

Brings together information on institutions whose primary business is the investment of funds in the financial markets. It covers self administered pension funds, insurance companies, unit and property unit trusts and investment trusts. It contains information on institutions' total net investment in identified financial assets and liabilities such as: gilts, UK company securities, overseas securities; net investment in land, property and ground rents.

Delivery: First Release
Frequency: Quarterly
Price: Annual subscription £12.00. Floppy disk: £280.00 + VAT per annum or £140.00 + VAT for individual copies

Available from
ONS Direct
Office for National Statistics
Please see Annex B for full address details.

Sources from which data for this product are obtained
Insurance companies balance sheet annual inquiry; Insurance Companies' income and expenditure - quarterly inquiry; Insurance companies' income and expenditure annual inquiry; Insurance companies' transactions in financial assets inquiry; Investment trusts annual return of liabilities and assets; Investment trusts quarterly return of transactions inquiry; Pension fund annual balance sheet inquiry; Pension fund annual income and expenditure inquiry; Pension fund transactions inquiry; Pension funds quarterly income and expenditure inquiry; Property unit trusts annual return of liabilities; Property unit trusts quarterly return of transactions inquiry; Securities dealers quarterly return of liabilities and assets and of transactions in securities; Unit trusts annual return of liabilities and assets; Unit trusts quarterly return of transactions inquiry

---

See also:
In this chapter
Financial Statistics (11.11)

In other chapters:
Databank (see the Websites and Electronic Services chapter)
United Kingdom National Accounts, Sources and Methods (see the Economy chapter)

11.19 Self Administered Pension Funds

Please see:
In this chapter:
Financial Statistics (11.11)
Insurance Companies', Pension Funds' and Trusts Investments (Business Monitor MQ5) (11.18)
Investment by Insurance Companies, Pension Funds and Trusts (First Release) (11.18)

In other chapters:
Occupational Pension Schemes 1991 - Ninth Survey by the Government Actuary (see the Household Finances chapter)
Office for National Statistics Databank (see the Websites and Electronic Services chapter)
United Kingdom National Accounts, Sources and Methods (see the Economy chapter)

11.20 Unit, Property Unit and Investment Trusts

Please see:
In this chapter:
Insurance Companies', Pension Funds' and Trusts Investments (Business Monitor MQ5) (11.18)
Investment by Insurance Companies, Pension Funds and Trusts (First Release) (11.18)

12 Commerce, Construction, Energy and Industry

Statistics covering **Commerce, Construction, Energy and Industry** are collected, administered and disseminated by a number of separate Departments, Agencies and organisations including the **Office for National Statistics, the Department of Trade and Industry, the Department of the Environment, Transport and the Regions, Scottish Executive, the National Assembly for Wales, the Northern Ireland Department of Economic Development,** and the **Iron and Steel Statistics Bureau**. The available statistics embrace a number of subject areas including: the **Building and Construction Industry, Building Materials Industry, Business and Commerce, Distribution and Service Trades, Energy/Fuel Production and Supply, Water Supply, Manufacturing and Production Industries, Mineral Extraction, Mining and Quarrying, Motor Vehicle Production, Research and Development Companies**, and the **Telecommunications Industry**.

The basic data are generated from a number of separate information 'Sources' and the resultant statistics are disseminated through a whole range of statistical 'Analyses' and 'Products', all of which are described in the following chapter. Users looking for a cross-section of UK-wide statistics on **Commerce, Construction, Energy and Industry** may find the following products useful:

> **Business Monitors (Various)** (monthly/quarterly/annual publications)
> **Digest of Data for the Construction Industry** (annual publication)
> **Digest of United Kingdom Energy Statistics** (annual publication)

Users interested in a wider range of official statistics including **Commerce, Construction, Energy and Industry** statistics may like to refer to the following compendia:

> On-line Databases (See Chapter 1):
> > **StatBase - StatStore**
> > **StatBase - TimeZone**
> > **DataBank**

> Hardcopy Compendia (See Chapter 2):
> > **Annual Abstract of Statistics**
> > **Britain 2000: The Official Yearbook of the United Kingdom**
> > **Monthly Digest of Statistics**
> > **Regional Trends**

Users may also find what they need on the various Departmental Websites. These are listed in Chapter 1.

12

Commerce, Construction, Energy and Industry - *Sources and Analyses*

12.1 Abstracts, Compendia, A-Z Catalogues, Directories and Reference Material

Annual Business Inquiries - Northern Ireland
Department of Economic Development - Northern Ireland

Annual business inquiries cover retailing, wholesaling and dealing, motor trades, service trades and catering and allied trades. Information is collected on total turnover, stocks, capital expenditure, persons engaged and employment costs.

Status: Ongoing
Collection Method: Large scale sample survey
Frequency: Annually
Reference Period: Year
Timeliness: 1997 data available August 1999
Earliest Available Data: 1995
National Coverage: Northern Ireland

Statistician
Clare Alexander
Department of Economic Development
Northern Ireland
Tel: 028 9052 9525;
Email: clare.alexander@dedni.gov.uk

Products that contain data from this analysis
Northern Ireland Annual Distribution and Service Inquiries

Index of Production - UK
Office for National Statistics

The Office for National Statistics compiles data for the output index which is used as a contribution to the GDP. Data are available on: Mining and quarrying; Manufacturing; and Electricity, gas and water supply. The series covers the UK and began in January 1986. Definitions are covered under the Standard Industrial Classification of Economic Activities 1992 (SIC(92)). Seasonally adjusted data are available. Data are collected quarterly and published two weeks after the end of the quarter.

Status: Ongoing
Frequency: Quarterly
Timeliness: Data published two weeks after the end of the quarter
Earliest Available Data: January 1986
National Coverage: United Kingdom

Statistician
Mark Williams
Office for National Statistics
Tel: 01633 812149

Products that contain data from this source
Annual Abstract of Statistics; Index of Production (First Release); Office for National Statistics Databank / Datastore; The United Kingdom National Accounts Methodological Papers; United Kingdom National Accounts - The Blue Book

Inter-Departmental Business Register
Office for National Statistics

The Inter-departmental Business Register contains records of all UK businesses registered for VAT or PAYE purposes and covers over 99% of UK economic activity. It is continuously updated from administrative sources. The smallest unit held on the register is an individual site (Local Unit). One or more Local Units with their associated legal units (VAT or PAYE) form an Enterprise, the smallest combination of these legal units. A group of enterprises under common ownership form an Enterprise Group. Information for each unit includes name, address, Classification (SIC92), employment, employees, turnover, legal status and country of ownership. The register is primarily used for selecting samples for surveys of businesses and producing analyses of business activity. All data held on the IDBR is treated as 'Restricted Commercial'. Further information can be found in the 'Products and Services' section of the ONS website.

Status: Ongoing
Collection Method: Administrative Records
Frequency: Continuously
National Coverage: United Kingdom
Disaggregation: Postcode Sector

Statistician
John Perry
Office for National Statistics
Central Initiatives Division; Business Registers
Tel: 01633 812212

Products that contain data from this source
Business Start-Up and Closures: VAT Registrations and Deregistrations; Small and Medium Enterprise (SME) Statistics for the UK; Size Analysis of UK Businesses (Business Monitor PA1003); Standard Industrial Classification 1992 by Year; Standard Industrial Classification by Government Office Region and Country by Turnover Sizeband; UK Directory of Manufacturing Businesses CD-ROM; VAT Trade Classification by Year

Quarterly Capital Expenditure Inquiry
Office for National Statistics

The Office for National Statistics conducts a quarterly inquiry into capital expenditure (CAPEX) on a sample of 16,000 businesses in the UK. Grossed results are estimated using the total population of businesses on the Inter-Departmental Business Register and are mainly used in the gross fixed capital formation for the UK National Accounts. Data cover capital expenditure by the private sector across the economy excluding agriculture, extraction of mineral oil and natural gas, air and sea transport, banking, various financial institutions, general government and public corporation expenditure. Data are available by new building works, land and existing buildings, vehicles, and other capital expenditure. Some longitudinal analyses are available. The inquiry began with a voluntary panel in 1955 which gained a statutory position in the first quarter of 1991. Provisional and final results are published eight and twelve weeks respectively after the reference quarter.

Status: Ongoing
Collection Method: Small-scale (Sample) Survey
Frequency: Quarterly
Reference Period: Calendar quarter
Timeliness: Provisional results - 7 weeks after reference quarter
Revised results - 12 weeks after reference quarter
Earliest Available Data: 1973 (some series from 1956)
National Coverage: United Kingdom

Statistician
Wendy Fader
Office for National Statistics
Production Sector Division; ACES Policy
Tel: 01633 812019;
Email: wendy.fader@ons.gov.uk

Products that contain data from this source
Business Investment First Release; Economic Trends; Economic Trends Annual Supplement; Monthly Digest of Statistics; Quarterly National Accounts (First Release); UK Output, Income and Expenditure (First Release); United Kingdom National Accounts - The Blue Book; United Kingdom National Accounts, Sources and Methods

12.2 Building and Construction Industry

Concrete Roofing Tiles - GB
Department of the Environment, Transport and the Regions

The Department of the Environment, Transport and the Regions is responsible for the Concrete Roofing Tiles Inquiry. The Inquiry is conducted by the Office for National Statistics on all the manufacturers. Data are available by the number of square metres produced, delivered and remaining in stock at the end of the quarter for Great Britain only. The Inquiry began in 1948 and is substantially unchanged today. The survey is carried out quarterly with the results being published two months after the end of the reference quarter.

Status: Ongoing
Collection Method: Large-scale (Sample) Survey
Frequency: Quarterly
Timeliness: The survey is carried out quarterly with the results being published two months after the end of the reference quarter.
Earliest Available Data: 1948
National Coverage: Great Britain

Statistician
David Williams
Department of the Environment, Transport and the Regions
Construction Market Intelligence; Statistics Branch 3
Tel: 020 7890 5593;
Email: david_williams@detr.gov.uk

Products that contain data from this source
Housing and Construction Statistics Annual Volume; Monthly Digest of Statistics; Monthly Statistics of Building Materials and Components

Construction Inventories - UK
Office for National Statistics

The Office for National Statistics conducts a quarterly survey on construction inventories. It is a statutory survey covering 1,350 businesses in the construction sector of the economy as defined by section F of the Standard Industrial Classification of Economic Activities 1992 (SIC(92)). The results are grossed to give estimates for the total population of this sector of the economy. The estimates are deflated to constant prices and reflated to current prices. Following deflation, constant and current price estimates are seasonally adjusted. Results from the survey provide essential information on the change in inventories for the National Accounts and are used in the calculation of the expenditure and income measures of Gross Domestic Product (GDP). The survey covers the United Kingdom and was set up in 1992.

Status: Ongoing
Collection Method: Small-scale (sample) survey
Frequency: Quarterly
Reference Period: The quarters ending March, June, September, December.
Timeliness: Provisional results available 8 weeks after reference quarter. Revised results available 4 weeks later.
Earliest Available Data: Quarter 1 - 1992
National Coverage: United Kingdom

Statistician
Wendy Fader
Office for National Statistics
Structural Statistics and Product Analysis Division
Tel: 01633 812019;
Email: wendy.fader@ons.gov.uk

Products that contain data from this source
Economic Trends; Economic Trends Annual Supplement; Monthly Digest of Statistics; Quarterly National Accounts (First Release); Stockbuilding Business Monitor; UK Output, Income and Expenditure (First Release); United Kingdom National Accounts - The Blue Book; United Kingdom National Accounts, Sources and Methods

Construction - New Orders - GB
Department of the Environment, Transport and the Regions

The Department of the Environment, Transport and the Regions (DETR) conducts the Contracts and Orders for New Construction Survey. This is a sample survey covering 5,500 construction firms. Results are grossed to give estimates for the whole of the construction industry above the VAT threshold. Data are available for the value, nature and geographic location of orders for new construction in Great Britain. Aggregate information is available deflated to constant prices, using deflators based on

tender price movements, and in seasonally adjusted form. Seasonally unadjusted cash data are available for England, Scotland, Wales and at county and DETR standard region levels. The Survey has been carried out on a quarterly basis since the late 1950s and on a monthly basis since 1980. The main results of the New Orders Survey are available six weeks after the end of the reference period.

Status: Ongoing
Collection Method: Census
Frequency: Monthly
Timeliness: Six weeks
National Coverage: Great Britain

Statistician
Richard Job
Department of the Environment, Transport and the Regions
Construction Market Intelligence; Statistics branch 1
Tel: 020 7890 5586;
Email: paul_andrews@detr.gov.uk

Products that contain data from this source
Digest of Data for the Construction Industry; Economic Trends; Housing and Construction Statistics Annual Volume; Orders for New Construction Information Bulletin; The State of the Construction Industry

Construction Output - GB
Department of the Environment, Transport and the Regions

The Department of the Environment, Transport and the Regions (DETR) collects returns of construction activity (output and employment). The results are grossed and allowance is made for the 'unrecorded' output of those firms and self-employed workers not on the Department's VAT-based register. Constant price gross output figures are included in the Gross Domestic Product, GDP(O), calculations. The surveys comprise: (i) a sample survey covering 12,000 firms a quarter, with the sample boosted to 30,000 in the third quarter when additional questions are included to provide an analysis of the structure of the industry; (ii) a sample survey of progress on contracts to obtain new work output data by type of work and region; (iii) a complete survey of direct labour departments of public authorities. Data are collected on the value, type and geographic location of output on new construction and repair and maintenance work done each quarter. Seasonally adjusted and deflated data are available. The surveys cover the whole of Great Britain. Seasonally unadjusted cash data are available for England, Scotland, Wales and at DETR standard region level. Data, collected quarterly, are available since 1955. The main results of the output and employment survey are available ten weeks after the end of the reference period. Data, collected quarterly, are available since 1955.

Status: Ongoing
Collection Method: Census
Frequency: Quarterly
Timeliness: Ten weeks
National Coverage: Great Britain

Statistician
Richard Job
Department of the Environment, Transport and the Regions
Construction Market Intelligence; Statistics branch 1
Tel: 020 7890 5586;
Email: rjob@detr-cmi.demon.co.uk

Products that contain data from this source
Digest of Data for the Construction Industry; Economic Trends; Housing and Construction Statistics Annual Volume; Output and Employment in the Construction Industry Information Bulletin; The State of the Construction Industry

Historical Construction Data, Output, Orders, Starts and Completions
Construction Research Ltd; sponsored by Department of the Environment, Transport & the Regions

The purpose of this source is to collect data relating to the volume of contractors' work, the level of new orders placed, the level of housing starts and completions etc. New orders & starts & completions collected monthly, output quarterly. It covers all aspects of the volume of construction work across GB. Its relevance to us is as a historical base upon which to make our forecasts of construction output over the current year plus two.

Status: Ongoing
Collection Method: Large-scale (Sample) Survey
Frequency: Monthly/Quarterly
Reference Period: Each month/Quarters to March, June, Sept, Dec
Earliest Available Data: Year 1955
National Coverage: Great Britain

Statistician
Jacquie Cannon
Construction Research Ltd.
Tel: 020 7379 5339;
Email: cfrjgph@aol.com

Products that contain data from this source
Construction Forecasts

Northern Ireland Quarterly Construction Enquiry
Department of the Environment - Northern Ireland

The NI Quarterly Construction Enquiry is a statutory sample survey, conducted by the Department of the Environment (NI) under Article 5 of the Statistics of Trade and Employment (NI) Order 1988. Its purpose is to collect data necessary for the calculation of the NI Index of Construction, which provides a regular indication of the level of on site construction activity within NI. The NI Index of Construction is an important economic indicator and is used by ONS to feed into the calculation of the output measure of UK gross domestic product [GDP(O)]. Provisional figures are published in both unadjusted and seasonally adjusted formats, in the last week of the fourth month following the reference quarter. The revised figures are published three months later.

Status: Ongoing
Collection Method: Small-scale (Sample) Survey
Frequency: Quarterly
Reference Period: Quarters ending March, June, September & December
Timeliness: 4 months
Earliest Available Data: 1984
National Coverage: Northern Ireland

Statistician
Brian French
Department of the Environment - Northern Ireland
Central Policy and Management Unit; Central Statistics and Research Branch
Tel: 028 9054 0799;
Email: brian.french@doeni.gov.uk

Price Index of Public Sector Housebuilding
National Assembly for Wales

The National Assembly for Wales undertakes a survey on the price index of public sector housebuilding. This index has been developed for England and Wales and is based on returns from English and Welsh local authorities, new towns and housing associations. This quarterly return has been collected by the old Welsh Office since 1980, prior to this date information was collected by the then Department of the Environment.

Status: Ongoing
Collection Method: Administrative Records
Frequency: Quarterly
Reference Period: January - March, April - June, July - September, October - December
Timeliness: Approximately 3 months after the end of the quarter
Earliest Available Data: 1980
National Coverage: Wales
Disaggregation: Unitary Authority; Those authorities that record newbuild activity for the local authority sector

Statistician
Henry Small
National Assembly for Wales
Statistical Directorate; Housing Statistics
Tel: 029 2082 5063;
Email: henry.small@wales.gsi.gov.uk

Public Sector Index (Non-Housebuilding) (PUBSEC)
Department of the Environment, Transport and the Regions

The Department of the Environment, Transport and the Regions compiles the Public Sector Index from bills of quantities - an itemised breakdown of the project cost - of accepted tenders, forwarded from Government Departments. The Index is an indicator of the trend in accepted tender prices for constructing public sector works in Great Britain. It is smoothed, includes scaling factors for location and building function, and adjustment factors are issued for eight groupings of counties covering Great Britain. The series is available back to 1950. Data are collected on an ongoing basis, as and when contracts are awarded and the results are published quarterly.

Status: Ongoing
Frequency: Results are published quarterly
Earliest Available Data: 1950

Statistician
Robert Packham
Department of the Environment, Transport and the Regions
Construction Market Intelligence Division; Statistics Branch 2
Tel: 020 7890 5764;
Email: stats2_cmi@detr.gov.uk

Products that contain data from this source
DETR Public Sector Tender Price Indices; Quarterly Building Price and Cost Indices

Road Construction Tender Price Index - GB
Department of the Environment, Transport and the Regions

The Department of the Environment, Transport and the Regions compiles the Road Construction Tender Price Index from the bills of quantity received by the Highways Agency from its regional offices and from local authorities. Data are available by location, value and road-type factors. A smoothed Index is published for Great Britain and adjustment factors are issued for eight groupings of counties covering Great Britain. Data are collected on an ongoing basis, as and when contracts are awarded, and published quarterly three months after the end of the quarter.

Status: Ongoing
Frequency: Published quarterly
Timeliness: 3 months after end of quarter
Earliest Available Data: 1971
National Coverage: Great Britain

Statistician
Marcella Douglas
Department of the Environment, Transport and the Regions
Construction Market Intelligence Division; Statistics Branch 2
Tel: 020 7890 5594;
Email: stats2_cmi@detr.gov.uk

Products that contain data from this source
Housing and Construction Statistics PT2, and Annual Volume; Quarterly Building Price and Cost Indices; Price Index

State of the Construction Industry Report
Department of the Environment, Transport and the Regions

Status: Ongoing
Frequency: Periodic

Statistician
Jim Woodfine
Department of the Environment, Transport and the Regions
Construction Industry Sponsorship; Construction Industry Sponsorship Branch 1
Tel: 020 7890 5652;
Email: jwoodfine@detr-cis.demom.co.uk

Tender Price Index of Social Housing (TPISH)
Department of the Environment, Transport and the Regions

The Department of the Environment, Transport and the Regions compiles the Tender Price Index of Social Housing (TPISH). The Index is calculated from bills of quantities - an itemised breakdown of the project cost - of accepted tenders, forwarded by housing associations and local authorities. TPISH is an indicator of trends in accepted tender prices for building public sector housing contracts in England and Wales. It is a smoothed quarterly Index and includes adjustment factors for location. Index published for England and Wales only.

Status: Ongoing
Frequency: A smooth quarterly Index is published for England and Wales
Earliest Available Data: The series began in 1968
National Coverage: England and Wales

Statistician
Marcella Douglas
Department of the Environment, Transport and the Regions
Construction Market Intelligence Division; Statistics Branch 2
Tel: 020 7890 5594;
Email: stats2_cmi@detr.gov.uk

Products that contain data from this source
Housing and Construction Statistics Quarterly PT2 and Annual Volume; DETR Quarterly Building Price and Cost Indices

See also:
In this chapter:
Index of Production - UK *(12.1)*

12.3 Building Materials Industry

Bricks - GB
Department of the Environment, Transport and the Regions

The Department of the Environment, Transport and the Regions is responsible for the Bricks Inquiry. The Inquiry is conducted by the Office for National Statistics on all manufacturing sites. Data are available by clay, concrete and calcium silicate bricks, and on the number of bricks produced, delivered and remaining in stock at the end of the month. The survey covers Great Britain and data are published for standard regions. The Inquiry began in 1948 and is substantially the same today. Data are collected monthly. Provisional results for the previous month are published at the end of each month with final results being published a month later. From 1948

Status: Ongoing
Frequency: Monthly
Earliest Available Data: 1948
National Coverage: Great Britain

Statistician
David Williams
Department of the Environment, Transport and the Regions
Construction Market Intelligence; Statistics Branch 3
Tel: 020 7890 5593;
Email: david_williams@detr.gov.uk

Products that contain data from this source
Bricks and Cement (Press Release); Housing and Construction Statistics Annual Volume; Monthly Digest of Statistics; Monthly Statement for Bricks, Cement and Concrete Blocks; Monthly Statistics of Building Materials and Components

Cement - UK
Department of the Environment, Transport and the Regions

The Department of the Environment, Transport and the Regions is responsible for the Cement Inquiry. The Inquiry includes production, deliveries and stocks of cement and production and stocks of clinker. As there are only a few manufacturers, only total UK information is available. The Inquiry began in 1948 and has remained substantially the same ever since. Monthly information is provided by manufacturers. The results for the previous month are published at the end of each month although there is currently an embargo requiring publication to be delayed for a year.

Status: Ongoing
Frequency: Monthly
Earliest Available Data: 1948
National Coverage: United Kingdom

Statistician
David Williams
Department of the Environment, Transport and the Regions
Construction Market Intelligence; Statistics Branch 3
Tel: 020 7890 5593;
Email: david_williams@detr.gov.uk

Products that contain data from this source
Bricks and Cement (Press Release); Housing and Construction Statistics Annual Volume; Monthly Digest of Statistics; Monthly Statement for Bricks, Cement and Concrete Blocks; Monthly Statistics of Building Materials and Components

Concrete Blocks - GB
Department of the Environment, Transport and the Regions

The Department of the Environment, Transport and the Regions is responsible for the Concrete Blocks Inquiry. The Inquiry is conducted by the Office for National Statistics on a monthly sample of the largest manufacturing sites together with a quarterly census of the remaining manufacturing sites. Data are available by production, deliveries and stocks of dense, lightweight and aerated concrete blocks.

The survey covers Great Britain and although site-based, information can only be published for each standard region. The Inquiry began in 1960 but aerated blocks were not separately identified until 1966. Data are collected monthly and quarterly. Provisional results for the previous month are published at the end of each month with final results for each month of the quarter being published two months after the end of the quarter. Inquiry began in 1960 aerated blocks not separately identified until 1966.

Status: Ongoing
Collection Method: Large-scale (Sample) Survey
Frequency: Monthly
Timeliness: Provisional results for the previous month are published at the end of each month with final results for each month of the quarter being published two months after the end of the quarter.
Earliest Available Data: 1960
National Coverage: Great Britain
Disaggregation: Standard Statistical Region (SSR)

Statistician
David Williams
Department of the Environment, Transport and the Regions
Construction Market Intelligence; Statistics Branch 3
Tel: 020 7890 5593;
Email: david_williams@detr.gov.uk

Products that contain data from this source
Housing and Construction Statistics Annual Volume; Monthly Digest of Statistics; Monthly Statement for Bricks, Cement and Concrete Blocks; Monthly Statistics of Building Materials and Components

---

Fibre Cement Products - GB
Department of the Environment, Transport and the Regions

The Department of the Environment, Transport and the Regions is responsible for the Fibre Cement Products Inquiry. The Inquiry is conducted by the Office for National Statistics on all the manufacturers. Data are available by tonnes produced, delivered and remaining in stock at the end of the quarter for Great Britain only. The Inquiry began in 1984. It replaced the previous Inquiry, covering asbestos cement products only, which began in 1948. The Inquiry is carried out quarterly with the results published two months after the end of the reference quarter.

Status: Ongoing
Frequency: Quarterly
Timeliness: The results are published two months after the end of the reference quarter
Earliest Available Data: The inquiry began in 1984
National Coverage: Great Britain

Statistician
David Williams
Department of the Environment, Transport and the Regions
Construction Market Intelligence; Statistics Branch 3
Tel: 020 7890 5593;
Email: david_williams@detr.gov.uk

Products that contain data from this source
Housing and Construction Statistics Annual Volume; Monthly Digest of Statistics; Monthly Statistics of Building Materials and Components

---

Ready-Mixed Concrete - GB
Department of the Environment, Transport and the Regions

The Department of the Environment, Transport and the Regions is responsible for the Ready-Mixed Concrete Inquiry. The Inquiry is conducted by the Office for National Statistics on a quarterly sample of trade association members together with an

annual census of non-members. Data are available for the cubic metres produced during a quarter in Great Britain. The Inquiry began in 1961. The survey is carried out quarterly and results are published two months after the end of the quarter.

Status: Ongoing
Collection Method: Quarterly sample of trade association members together with annual census of non-members
Frequency: Quarterly
Timeliness: Results published two months after the end of the quarter
Earliest Available Data: 1961
National Coverage: Great Britain

Statistician
David Williams
Department of the Environment, Transport and the Regions
Construction Market Intelligence; Statistics Branch 3
Tel: 020 7890 5593;
Email: david_williams@detr.gov.uk

Products that contain data from this source
Housing and Construction Statistics Annual Volume; Monthly Digest of Statistics; Monthly Statistics of Building Materials and Components

---

Sand and Gravel - GB
Department of the Environment, Transport and the Regions

The Department of the Environment, Transport and the Regions is responsible for the Sand and Gravel Inquiry. The Inquiry is conducted by the Office for National Statistics on a sample of the largest 50 per cent of land-won sites together with a census of marine-dredged sites and the results are grossed using the latest available annual Minerals Inquiry. Data are available for the sales (in tonnes) during a quarter of the various types of sand and gravel for Great Britain. An Inquiry began in 1950 and took its present form in 1981. The survey is carried out quarterly. Provisional results are published two months after the end of the quarter with final results being published a month later.

Status: Ongoing
Collection Method: Sample/Census
Frequency: Quarterly
Earliest Available Data: An Inquiry began in 1950 and took its present form in 1981.
National Coverage: Great Britain

Statistician
David Williams
Department of the Environment, Transport and the Regions
Construction Market Intelligence; Statistics Branch 3
Tel: 020 7890 5593;
Email: david_williams@detr.gov.uk

Products that contain data from this source
Housing and Construction Statistics Annual Volume; Monthly Statistics of Building Materials and Components

---

Slate - GB
Department of the Environment, Transport and the Regions

The Department of the Environment, Transport and the Regions is responsible for the Slate Inquiry. The Inquiry is conducted by the Office for National Statistics on a sample of the largest manufacturers. Data are available by tonnes produced, delivered and remaining in stock at the end of the quarter for Great Britain by standard regions and counties for England and Wales and Regions for Scotland. The Inquiry began in 1948 and took its present form in 1990. The survey is carried out quarterly and the results are published two months after the end of the quarter.

Status: Ongoing
Frequency: Quarterly
Timeliness: Two months after end of quarter
Earliest Available Data: The Inquiry began in 1948 and took its present form in 1990.
National Coverage: Great Britain

Statistician
David Williams
Department of the Environment, Transport and the Regions
Construction Market Intelligence; Statistics Branch 3
Tel: 020 7890 5593;
Email: david_williams@detr.gov.uk

Products that contain data from this source
Housing and Construction Statistics Annual Volume; Monthly Statistics of Building Materials and Components

See also:
In this chapter:
Concrete Roofing Tiles - GB *(12.2)*

12.4 Business and Commerce - General

Acquisitions and Mergers - UK
Office for National Statistics

The Acquisitions and Mergers inquiries conducted by the Office for National Statistics (ONS) are designed to measure the timing, value and method of funding of acquisitions and mergers activity involving UK companies. The cross-border inquiry requests information on UK companies' acquisitions and disposals of interests in overseas companies and vice versa, whilst the domestic inquiry collects information on acquisitions and disposals of companies within the UK. The inquiries are conducted on a continuous basis and approaches are made to businesses only when there is a prima facie evidence from the press that they have relevant transactions on which to report. Both the Cross Border and Domestic inquiries are conducted at present on a voluntary basis. The number of companies approached in both varies directly with the level of acquisitions and merger activity. key series available: number of deals; value of deals; method of funding; geographical analysis for the cross border inquiry; and names of the largest ten transactions. Acquisitions and mergers information can help: in research on corporate finance activity; analysis of trends of foreign business activity in the UK and vice versa; preparation of briefing material for delegations travelling abroad; embassies in providing briefing for visiting officials; and research work on particular countries.

Status: Ongoing
Frequency: Continuously when deals are identified, quarterly results compilation.
Reference Period: Date of deal
Timeliness: Weeks
Earliest Available Data: 1986
National Coverage: United Kingdom

Statistician
Philip Gooding
Office for National Statistics
Tel: 01633 812793

Products that contain data from this source
Acquisitions and Mergers (First Release); Financial Statistics; Office for National Statistics Databank / Datastore; UK Balance of Payments (First Release); United Kingdom Balance of Payments - The Pink Book

Annual Survey of Financial Assets and Liabilities
Office for National Statistics

The annual survey into companies' financial assets and liabilities provides estimates of industrial and commercial companies' holdings of, and transactions in, various financial assets and liabilities. These form part of the financial statistics of the company sector in the national accounts and are also used to estimate the liquidity of large industrial and commercial companies. The current statutory surveys replaced a voluntary quarterly inquiry conducted by the DTI. There is no alternative data source for information on holdings of bearer financial instruments.

Status: Ongoing
Collection Method: Small-scale (Sample) Survey
Frequency: Annually
Reference Period: The calendar year
Timeliness: 9 weeks after the end of the period.
National Coverage: Great Britain

Statistician
Robert Hay
Office for National Statistics
Tel: 01633 812357;
Email: robert.hay@ons.gov.uk

Products that contain data from this source
Financial Statistics

Business Counts - UK
Office for National Statistics

The Office for National Statistics compiles data on business counts. This is an annual series using data from the Inter-Departmental Business Register, showing counts of UK businesses by sizeband, geographical location and industrial classification. Similar information at individual site level is also provided for the manufacturing sector. The data cover the UK and are available at economic region and county level in the main publication and local authority district level in the supplement, but can be provided at other levels on request, subject to disclosure constraints. Data have been published since 1971, though the format and content have changed several times since. Supplementary District Tables have been produced since 1990. The data are collected annually, usually around the middle of the year, and published a few months later.

Frequency: Annual
Timeliness: Published a few months after collection
Earliest Available Data: 1971
National Coverage: United Kingdom

Statistician
John Perry
Office for National Statistics
Central Initiatives Division; Business Registers
Tel: 01633 812212

Products that contain data from this analysis
Analysis from the Inter-Departmental Business Register; Size Analysis of UK Businesses (Business Monitor PA1003)

Community Innovation Survey (CIS)
Department of Trade and Industry

The Community Innovation Survey collects data on the innovative characteristics of UK firms. The data include measures of innovation-related expenditure, rates of innovation and factors which have either encouraged or hindered innovation. The first sample survey took place in 1997 and is likely to be repeated every 3/4 years. Similar surveys are being conducted in other EU member states using the same methodology; as a result, it will be possible to benchmark

the performance of UK firms against that of their EU competitors.

Status: Ongoing
Collection Method: Large-scale (Sample) Survey
Frequency: Periodic
Reference Period: 1996
Timeliness: Approx. 9 months after end of survey
Earliest Available Data: 1996
National Coverage: United Kingdom

Statistician
Marc Thomas
Department of Trade and Industry
Technology, Economics, Statistics and Evaluation Directorate; TESE a
Tel: 020 7215 1911;
Email: marc.thomas@tidv.dti.gov.uk

Domestic Acquisitions and Mergers - UK
Office for National Statistics

The Office for National Statistics conducts the Domestic Acquisitions and Mergers Inquiry on the numbers and value of acquisitions and mergers in the UK. Data are primarily used for ICC financial accounts. The Inquiry is voluntary and businesses are only approached when there is evidence from the press that they have relevant transactions on which to report. The number of companies varies with the level of acquisition and merger activity. Data are available on the full legal names of the vendor, acquired and acquiring company, date of the transaction, percentage of shares bought or sold, value of the transaction, and method of funding. Inquiries have been conducted since 1969. The survey is carried out continuously and results are published quarterly, seven weeks after the end of the reference quarter.

Frequency: Continuous
Timeliness: Results are published quarterly
Earliest Available Data: 1969
National Coverage: United Kingdom

Statistician
Philip Gooding
Office for National Statistics
Tel: 01633 812793

Products that contain data from this source
Acquisitions and Mergers (First Release); Office for National Statistics Databank / Datastore

Insolvency - England and Wales
Court Service

The Lord Chancellor's Department collates insolvency proceeding data on company winding-up and individuals' bankruptcy petitions issued in the High Court and

Sources and Analyses

county courts. Data are compiled by the Court Service from administrative records. Data are available from 1987 and cover England and Wales, Judicial Circuit, Judicial Group and individual county court level. Results are compiled monthly and released on a quarterly basis.

Collection Method: Administrative Records
Frequency: Continuously
Reference Period: Quarterly, monthly, annually, financial year.
Timeliness: Published first Friday in second month after end of quarter
Earliest Available Data: Data are available from 1987
National Coverage: England and Wales
Disaggregation: Individual county courts; Judicial Groups; Judicial Circuits; The High Court; County; Region;

Statistician
Sunita Gould
Court Service
Information Management and Analysis Group (IMAGe)
Tel: 020 7210 1773

Products that contain data from this source
Company Winding Up and Bankruptcy Petition Statistics (Press Notice); Judicial Statistics England and Wales Annual Report; The Court Service Annual Report

---

Quarterly Survey of Financial Assets and Liabilities
Office for National Statistics

The quarterly survey into companies' financial assets and liabilities provide estimates of industrial and commercial companies' holdings of, and transactions in, various financial assets and liabilities. These form part of the financial statistics of the company sector in the national accounts and are also used to estimate the liquidity of large industrial and commercial companies. The current statutory surveys replaced a voluntary quarterly inquiry conducted by the DTI. There is no alternative data source for information on holdings of bearer financial instruments.

Status: Ongoing
Collection Method: Small-scale (Sample) Survey
Frequency: Quarterly
Reference Period: The calendar quarter
Timeliness: 9 weeks after the end of the period.
National Coverage: Great Britain

Statistician
Robert Hay
Office for National Statistics
Tel: 01633 812357;
Email: robert.hay@ons.gov.uk

Products that contain data from this source
Financial Statistics

Quarterly Survey of Trading Standards Departments: Numbers of Consumer Complaints
Office of Fair Trading

Quarterly voluntary survey of UK Trading Standards Departments. Data are collected for the numbers of complaints in 59 categories of goods and services, and 9 trading practices. Data collected from June 1974 onwards; reclassification in 1 October 1987, further re-classification from 1st April 1999

Status: Ongoing
Collection Method: Administrative Records
Frequency: Quarterly
Timeliness: Published annually in Annual Report of the Director of Fair Trading, quarterly in Trends in Consumer Complaints.
Earliest Available Data: 1974
National Coverage: United Kingdom

Statistician
Derek Jones
Office of Fair Trading
Consumer Affairs
Tel: 020 7211 8772;
Email: derek.jones@oft.gov.uk

Products that contain data from this source
Annual Report of the Director General of Fair Trading; Fair Trading; Trends in consumer complaints

---

Regional Selective Assistance Grants to Industry - Scotland
Scottish Executive

The Scottish Executive Industry Department compiles data on regional selective assistance (RSA) grants to industry. Data are available on the number and amount of offers of grant accepted, the amount of grant paid out, associated jobs created or safeguarded, and associated total project costs by type of industry, location and whether the firm is UK or foreign owned. Data cover Scotland and are available at travel-to-work area and local authority district level. The series commenced in 1972, but various changes since then in the schemes available, the rules under which they operate, and the definition of the assisted areas mean that direct comparisons between years are not always possible. Data are published annually, six months after the end of the financial year.

Status: Ongoing
Collection Method: Administrative Records
Frequency: Continuously
Reference Period: Financial year
Earliest Available Data: 1972
National Coverage: Scotland
Disaggregation: Council Area (Scot)/District and Islands Area (Scotland); Parliamentary Constituency; Travel-to-work Area; Unitary Authority; Ward

Statistician
Julie Rintoul
Scottish Executive
IA2; Investment Assistance statistics
Tel: 0141 242 5623;
Email: julie.rintoul@scotland.gov.uk

Products that contain data from this source
Labour Market Trends; Overseas Ownership in Scottish Manufacturing Industry; Regional Trends; Scottish Abstract of Statistics; Scottish Economic Bulletin

---

Share Ownership - UK
Office for National Statistics

The Office for National Statistics conducts a survey of share ownership. Until the end 1997 survey, share registers were obtained for a sample of 200 UK companies listed on the London Stock Exchange. A sample of shareholdings (100,000 in total) was analysed from each register and the beneficial owner was coded to one of the institutional sectors of the economy. Data are available on the value of shares held by each sector of the economy at the year end for use in the financial balance sheets of the National Accounts, the sectoral distribution of shares held in the recently demutualised companies and the geographical distribution of shares held overseas. The survey covers the United Kingdom and was carried out annually between 1989 and 1994. The end-1997 survey was published in January 1999. The end-1998 survey is expected to be published in Autumn 1999.

Status: Ongoing
Collection Method: Survey of administrative records
Frequency: Annual: 1989-1994 and 1997 onwards
Reference Period: 31st December
Timeliness: About 9-10 months
Earliest Available Data: Limited data is available from 1963
National Coverage: United Kingdom

Statistician
Ian R Hill
Office for National Statistics
Tel: 020 7533 6019

Products that contain data from this source
Share Ownership - Share Register Survey Report

See also:
In this chapter:
Construction - New Orders - GB *(12.2)*
Construction Output - GB *(12.2)*
Index of Production - UK *(12.1)*

In other chapters:
Continuing Vocational Training Survey (see the Education and Training chapter)

12.5 Distribution and Service Trades

Annual Catering and Allied Trades Inquiry
Office for National Statistics

The Annual Catering Inquiry is a sample survey carried out by the Office for National Statistics covering around 4,200 businesses. The information collected contributes to the compilation of the National Accounts. The survey has been carried out since the mid-1950s.

Status: Ongoing
Collection Method: Large-scale (Sample) Survey
Frequency: Annually
Reference Period: Calendar year
Timeliness: Data is normally made available within 18 months of the end of the reference year. 1996 is the latest data published.
Earliest Available Data: 1950
National Coverage: United Kingdom from 1996 onwards. Great Britain in previous years.

Statistician
Andrew Walton
Office for National Statistics
Distribution and Services Sector Division;
Distribution and Services Inquiry RAP
Tel: 01633 812945;
Email: andrew.walton@ons.gov.uk

Products that contain data from this source
Annual Abstract of Statistics; Sector Review: Catering and Allied Trades

Annual Motor Trade Inquiry
Office for National Statistics

The Annual Motor Trades inquiry is a sample survey carried out by the Office for National Statistics covering about 6,000 businesses. The information collected contributes to the compilation of the National Accounts. The first major inquiry was held in 1950 when a full census was taken as part of the 1950 Census of Distribution. Subsequent inquiries were held in respect of 1962, 1967 and 1972 . In addition simple annual inquiries were held in the remaining years. Over the years the annual inquiry has grown in the range of data collected from a simple inquiry into one collecting a range of information used for the compilation of the National Accounts.

Status: Ongoing
Collection Method: Large-scale (Sample) Survey
Frequency: Annually
Reference Period: Calendar year
Timeliness: Data is normally made available within 18 months of the end of the reference year. 1997 is the latest data published.
Earliest Available Data: 1950
National Coverage: United Kingdom from 1996 onwards. Great Britain in previous years.

Statistician
Andrew Walton
Office for National Statistics
Distribution and Services Sector Division;
Distribution and Services Inquiry RAP
Tel: 01633 812945;
Email: andrew.walton@ons.gov.uk

Products that contain data from this source
Annual Abstract of Statistics; Sector Review: Motor Trades

Annual Property Inquiry
Office for National Statistics

The Annual Property Inquiry is a survey carried out by the Office for National Statistics on around 3,800 businesses. Results are grossed to give estimates for the total population of the sector and used in the production of the National Accounts. The inquiry began in the mid 1950s on an annual basis but its frequency was reduced to biennial as a result of a government scrutiny in 1979. It became annual again in 1989. Up until 1994 data was collected on capital expenditure. From 1995, the range of data was extended to make the inquiry consistent with the other DSS inquiries.

Status: Ongoing
Collection Method: Large-scale (Sample) Survey
Frequency: Annually
Reference Period: Calendar Year
Earliest Available Data: Mid 1950's
National Coverage: United Kingdom from 1996 onwards, Great Britain in previous years

Statistician
Andrew Walton
Office for National Statistics
Distribution and Services Sector Division;
Distribution and Services Inquiry RAP
Tel: 01633 812945;
Email: andrew.walton@ons.gov.uk

Annual Retailing Inquiry
Office for National Statistics

The Annual Retailing Inquiry Survey is carried out by the Office for National Statistics for 10,000 businesses in the United Kingdom. The information contributes to the compilation of the National Accounts. Data are available for employees, total turnover, sales by non-store activity, outlets, questions related to trading in secondhand goods, or from market stalls, roadside pitches and by commodity sales, stocks, purchases and capital expenditure. Periodic censuses of distribution had been conducted since 1950, and these were replaced by a series of annual inquiries in 1976. Results are published within 18 months of the inquiry year.

Status: Ongoing
Collection Method: Sample survey
Frequency: Annually
Reference Period: Calendar year
Timeliness: 18 months after year end of period in question
National Coverage: United Kingdom

Statistician
Andrew Walton
Office for National Statistics
Tel: 01633 812945;
Email: andrew.walton@ons.gov.uk

Products that contain data from this source
Sector Review: Retailing (formerly Business Monitor SDA25)

Annual Service Trades Inquiry
Office for National Statistics

The Annual Service Trades Inquiry is a sample survey carried out by the Office for National Statistics covering around 18,800 businesses. The information collected contributes to the compilation of the National Accounts. The service trades inquiry, covering a limited range of industries, began in the mid 1950s and continued on an annual basis until 1979 when it became biennial. In 1985 with increasing policy interest in the results of the inquiry it again became annual. Until 1985 the inquiry was limited to road transport & ancillary transport services, business services and personal & miscellaneous services. In 1985 many personal & scientific services were added and in 1986, opticians, legal services, private health and education services together with some miscellaneous services. Other services have since been added and most market sector services were covered by the inquiry by 1995.

Status: Ongoing
Collection Method: Large-scale (Sample) Survey
Frequency: Annually
Reference Period: Calendar Year
Timeliness: Data is normally made available within 18 months of the end of the reference year. 1997 data is the latest published.
Earliest Available Data: 1955
National Coverage: United Kingdom from 1996 onwards. Great Britain in previous years.

Statistician
Andrew Walton
Office for National Statistics
Distribution and Services Sector Division;
Distribution and Services Inquiry RAP
Tel: 01633 812945;
Email: andrew.walton@ons.gov.uk

Products that contain data from this source
Sector Review: Service Trades

Sources and Analyses

Annual Wholesaling and Dealing Inquiry
Office for National Statistics

The Annual Wholesaling Inquiry is a sample survey carried out by the Office for National Statistics covering around 6,400 businesses. The information collected contributes to the compilation of the National Accounts. The first full census into wholesaling was carried out in 1950 with simpler inquiries held in 1959 and 1965. Smaller sample inquiries have been carried out since 1965.

Status: Ongoing
Collection Method: Large-scale (Sample) Survey
Frequency: Annually
Reference Period: Calendar Year
Timeliness: Data is normally made available within 18 months of the end of the reference year. 1996 is the latest data published.
Earliest Available Data: 1950
National Coverage: United Kingdom from 1996 onwards. Great Britain in previous years.

Statistician
Andrew Walton
Office for National Statistics
Distribution and Services Sector Division;
Distribution and Services Inquiry RAP
Tel: 01633 812945;
Email: andrew.walton@ons.gov.uk

Products that contain data from this source
Sector Review: Wholesaling

Film, Television and Video Industries - GB
Department for Culture, Media and Sport; sponsored by British Film Institute

The British Film Institute compiles data on the film, television and video industries. The series began in 1993 and world-wide data are available. Data are collected annually and are published in the first half of the year following the reference period.

Collection Method: Database of statistics taken from various sources
Frequency: Annually
Reference Period: It depends on the data origins, but used as basis for annual publication
Timeliness: Released within 6 months of end of reference period.
Earliest Available Data: 1981
National Coverage: Great Britain

Statistician
Paul Allin
Department for Culture, Media and Sport
Analytical Services Unit; Statistics Branch
Room 601
Haymarket House
2-4 Cockspur Street
London SW1A 5DH
Tel: 020 7211 2843;
Email: paul.allin@culture.gov.uk

Products that contain data from this source
BFI Handbook - produced annually

GB Cinema Exhibitors Inquiry
Office for National Statistics

The Great Britain Cinema Exhibitors Inquiry is a quarterly survey carried out by the Office for National Statistics. The information collected is benchmarked against the information collected for cinemas in the Annual Service Trades Inquiry. Data are collected on the number of sites, the number of screens, gross box office takings, and payments for film hire. Data on cinemas was originally collected by the Department of Trade and Industry as part of the administration of the Eady levy (a film exhibition tax used to part finance the British Film Industry). This levy was abolished in 1985 and, with it, the collection of detailed data in the film exhibitors inquiry ceased. It later became apparent that there was a requirement for certain industry specific data on cinemas and in 1987 a quarterly inquiry was introduced to provide data for both the National Accounts and for policy purpose.

Status: Ongoing
Collection Method: Small-scale (Sample) Survey
Frequency: Quarterly
Timeliness: The results of the inquiry are published 11 weeks after the end of the quarter to which the latest figures relate.
Earliest Available Data: Quarter 1 1997
National Coverage: Great Britain

Statistician
Derek Baskerville
Office for National Statistics
Distribution and Services Sector Division;
Distribution and Services Inquiry RAP
Tel: 01633 812945;
Email: derek.baskerville@ons.gov.uk

Products that contain data from this source
GB Cinema Exhibitors (News Release)

Monthly Inquiries into the Distribution and Services Sector
Office for National Statistics

Data is collected on turnover in selected Distribution and Service Industries to provide information on short term movements in measures of GDP(O). Most market sector activities are covered by either the monthly or quarterly inquiries. The collection of short term statistics for Distribution and Services began in 1991. Since then the periodicity of the inquiries to some industries has varied between monthly and quarterly.

Status: Ongoing
Collection Method: Large-scale (Sample) Survey
Frequency: Monthly
Reference Period: Calendar month
Timeliness: The results of the inquiry are published 16 weeks after the end of the quarter to which the latest figures relate.
Earliest Available Data: Quarter 1 1995
National Coverage: Great Britain

Statistician
Derek Baskerville
Office for National Statistics
Distribution and Services Sector Division;
Distribution and Services Inquiry RAP
Tel: 01633 812945;
Email: derek.baskerville@ons.gov.uk

Motor Traders' Inventories - UK
Office for National Statistics

The Office for National Statistics conducts a quarterly survey on motor traders' inventories. It is a statutory survey covering 1,400 businesses in the motor trades sector of the economy as defined by division 50 of the Standard Industrial Classification of Economic Activities 1992 (SIC(92)). The results are grossed to give estimates for the total population of this sector of the economy. The estimates are deflated to constant prices and reflated to current prices. Following deflation, constant and current price estimates are seasonally adjusted. Results from the survey provide essential information on the change in inventories for the National Accounts and are used in the calculation of the expenditure and income measures of Gross Domestic Product (GDP). The survey covers the United Kingdom and was set up in 1992.

Status: Ongoing
Collection Method: Small-scale (sample) survey
Frequency: Quarterly
Reference Period: Quarters ending March, June, September, December
Timeliness: Provisional results available 8 weeks after the reference quarter. Revised results Available 4 weeks later.
Earliest Available Data: Quarter 1 - 1992
National Coverage: United Kingdom

Statistician
Wendy Fader
Office for National Statistics
Structural Statistics and Product Analysis Division
Tel: 01633 812019;
Email: wendy.fader@ons.gov.uk

Products that contain data from this source
Economic Trends; Economic Trends Annual Supplement; Monthly Digest of Statistics; Quarterly National Accounts (First Release); Stockbuilding Business Monitor; UK Output, Income and Expenditure (First Release); United Kingdom National Accounts - The Blue Book; United Kingdom National Accounts, Sources and Methods

---

Quarterly Inquiries into the Distributive and Service Sector - GB
Office for National Statistics

Data is collected on turnover in selected Distribution and Service Industries to provide information on short term movements in measures of GDP(O). Most market sector activities are covered by either the monthly or quarterly inquiries. The collection of short term statistics for Distribution and Services began in 1991. Since then the periodicity of the inquiries to some industries has varied between monthly and quarterly.

Status: Ongoing
Collection Method: Large-scale (Sample) Survey
Frequency: Quarterly
Reference Period: Calendar Quarter
Timeliness: The results of the inquiry are published 16 weeks after the end of the quarter to which the latest figures relate.
Earliest Available Data: Quarter 1 1995
National Coverage: Great Britain

Statistician
Derek Baskerville
Office for National Statistics
Distribution and Services Sector Division;
Distribution and Services Inquiry RAP
Tel: 01633 812945;
Email: derek.baskerville@ons.gov.uk

Quarterly Short-Term Turnover and Employment Survey - Service Sector
Office for National Statistics

Status: Ongoing
Collection Method: Sample survey
Frequency: Quarterly
Reference Period: The specified count day in March, June, September and December
Timeliness: Estimates released 3 months after the count date
Earliest Available Data: June 1978 (United Kingdom only)
National Coverage: United Kingdom and Great Britain
Disaggregation: Government Office Regions and Standard Regions (quarterly)

Statistician
James Partington
Office for National Statistics
Tel: 01928 792545;
Email: james.partington@ons.gov.uk

Products that contain data from this source
Labour Market Trends; Monthly Digest of Statistics; Regional Trends; United Kingdom National Accounts - The Blue Book

Retail Sales Inquiry - GB
Office for National Statistics

The monthly inquiry into retail sales is a sample survey carried out by the Office for National Statistics on 5,000 businesses in Great Britain, including large retailers and a representative panel of smaller businesses. From this survey the Retail Sales Index (RSI) is compiled each month. This is a key indicator in the progress of the economy, and is indirectly used to calculate quarterly consumer spending on retail goods and the output of the retail sector which feed into the compilation of the National Accounts. From January 1992 the RSI expanded and gained compulsory status. The RSI has been rebased using detailed information from the 1995 Annual Retailing Inquiry. The Index has also been reclassified on to the Standard Industrial Classification of economic activities 1992.

Status: Ongoing
Collection Method: Large-scale (Sample) Survey
Frequency: Monthly
Reference Period: Standard period 4 or 5 week months
Timeliness: 10-11 days between collection of data and its release
Earliest Available Data: January 1986
National Coverage: Great Britain
Sub-National: Full

Statistician
Harry Duff
Office for National Statistics
Tel: 01633 812600;
Email: harry.duff@ons.gov.uk

Products that contain data from this source
Economic Trends; Retail Sales Index (First Release); Service Sector: Retail Sales (Business Monitor SDM 28)

Retailers' Inventories - UK
Office for National Statistics

The Office for National Statistics conducts a quarterly survey on retailers' inventories. It is a statutory survey covering 2,000 businesses in the retailing sector of the economy as defined by division 52 of the Standard Industrial Classification of Economic Activities 1992(SIC(92)). The results are grossed to give estimates for the total population of this sector of the economy. The estimates are deflated to constant prices and reflated to current prices. Following deflation, constant and current price estimates are seasonally adjusted. Results from the survey provide essential information on the change in inventories for the National Accounts and are used in the calculation of the expenditure and income measures of Gross Domestic Product (GDP). The survey covers the United Kingdom and was set up in 1955. Data was collected from large

businesses on a monthly basis until the survey became quarterly in June 1980. The retailers' survey was enlarged and made statutory in 1992.

Status: Ongoing
Collection Method: Small-scale (sample) survey
Frequency: Quarterly
Reference Period: The quarters ending March, June, September, December.
Timeliness: Provisional results available 8 weeks after reference quarter. Revised results available 4 weeks later.
Earliest Available Data: 1955
National Coverage: United Kingdom

Statistician
Wendy Fader
Office for National Statistics
Structural Statistics and Product Analysis Division
Tel: 01633 812019;
Email: wendy.fader@ons.gov.uk

Products that contain data from this source
Economic Trends; Economic Trends Annual Supplement; Monthly Digest of Statistics; Quarterly National Accounts (First Release); Stockbuilding Business Monitor; UK Output, Income and Expenditure (First Release); United Kingdom National Accounts - The Blue Book; United Kingdom National Accounts, Sources and Methods

Wholesalers' and Dealers' Inventories - UK
Office for National Statistics

The Office for National Statistics conducts a quarterly survey on wholesalers' and dealers' inventories. It is a statutory survey covering 3,300 businesses in the wholesaling sector of the economy as defined by division 51 of the Standard Industrial Classification of Economic Activities 1992 (SIC(92)). The results are grossed to give estimates for the total population of this sector of the economy. The estimates are deflated to constant prices and reflated to current prices. Following deflation, constant and current price estimates are seasonally adjusted. Results from the survey provide essential information on the change in inventories for the National Accounts and are used in the calculation of the expenditure and income measures of Gross Domestic Product (GDP). The survey covers the United Kingdom and was set up in 1957. The wholesalers' and dealers' survey was enlarged and made statutory in 1991.

Status: Ongoing
Collection Method: Small-scale (Sample) Survey
Frequency: Quarterly
Reference Period: The quarters ending March, June, September and December.
Timeliness: Provisional results available 8 weeks after the reference quarter. Revised results available 4 weeks later
Earliest Available Data: 1957
National Coverage: United Kingdom

Statistician
Wendy Fader
Office for National Statistics
Structural Statistics and Product Analysis Division
Tel: 01633 812019;
Email: wendy.fader@ons.gov.uk

Products that contain data from this source
Economic Trends; Economic Trends Annual Supplement; Monthly Digest of Statistics; Quarterly National Accounts (First Release); Stockbuilding Business Monitor; UK Output, Income and Expenditure (First Release); United Kingdom National Accounts - The Blue Book; United Kingdom National Accounts, Sources and Methods

See also:
In this chapter:
Construction Inventories - UK *(12.2)*
Index of Production - UK *(12.1)*
Quarterly Capital Expenditure Inquiry *(12.1)*

In other chapters:
Overseas Film and Television Industries (see the Economy chapter)

12.6 Energy/Fuel Production and Supply, Water Supply

Domestic Quarterly Fuels Inquiry
Department of Trade and Industry

The Department of Trade and Industry compiles data for monitoring prices and other market developments in the domestic gas and electricity markets.

Status: Ongoing
Collection Method: Census of domestic sector suppliers
Frequency: Quarterly
Reference Period: Quarter
Timeliness: Published annually in July
Earliest Available Data: 1998
National Coverage: United Kingdom

Statistician
Duncan Millard
Department of Trade and Industry
Tel: 020 7215 2720

Products that contain data from this source
Digest of UK Energy Statistics, Energy Trends

DTI Exploration & Appraisal Survey
Department of Trade and Industry

A voluntary survey designed to obtain operators' intentions to drill exploration and appraisal wells on the UK Continental Shelf. In recent years rig availability has become important, and a question on rig types has been added.

Status: Ongoing
Collection Method: Major operators and sample of minor operators
Frequency: Annually
Reference Period: The current year and the next 2 years
Timeliness: Summary usually published in the following: Development of the Oil and Gas Resources of the UK, and May Energy Trends.
National Coverage: UK Continental Shelf
Sub-National: Offshore basins, and rig types

Statistician
Philip Beckett
Department of Trade and Industry
Tel: 020 7215 5260

Products that contain data from this source
Energy Trends; Development of the Oil and Gas Resources of the UK

Energy Production and Consumption - UK
Department of Trade and Industry

The Department of Trade and Industry compiles data on fuel production and use and overseas trade in fuels. Data are derived from the producers or suppliers of the various fuels and HM Custom and Excise. Results form part of the input to the Index of Production. Data are available on production, import, export and use of coal, gas, crude oil, petroleum products, electricity, overseas trade, renewable sources of energy, and fuel consumption figures by classes of consumer (e.g. industry, domestic, transport). Seasonally adjusted and temperature-corrected data are available for the total consumption of each fuel. The data cover the UK and figures for petroleum product deliveries are available for England and Wales, Scotland and Northern Ireland. Data are published quarterly for consumption and overseas trade, and annually between February and May for the same areas at a more detailed level. Monthly results are available for production, imports, exports and use of coal, gas, oil, petroleum products and electricity. Data have been collected since the end of World War II with allowances for changes in the energy markets. Only annual data were published before 1973.

Frequency: Quarterly and annually
Earliest Available Data: Data have been collected since the end of World War II
National Coverage: United Kingdom

Statistician
Michael Janes
Department of Trade and Industry
Tel: 020 7215 5186

Products that contain data from this source
Annual Abstract of Statistics; Digest of United Kingdom Energy Statistics; Economic Trends; Energy Trends; Monthly Digest of Statistics

Fuel Prices - UK
Department of Trade and Industry

The Department of Trade and Industry compiles data on the prices of fuels purchased by industry and domestic consumers, and the retail prices of petroleum products. Data are collected by sample surveys of consumers conducted by the Office for National Statistics. Data are available on the major industrial fuels (i.e. coal, heavy fuel oil, gas oil, electricity, and gas) by level of consumption, and the average prices paid by all the consumers for medium fuel oil, liquefied petroleum gas and hard coke. Seasonally adjusted indices are available for gas and electricity. The data cover the UK, although purchases made by the manufacturing industry only cover Great Britain. Average domestic electricity and gas prices are available for fourteen towns and cities throughout Great Britain. Data on the prices of fuels purchased by industry have been collected in their present form since 1974. In 1988 the sample increased to 1,200 consumers, and the scope of the survey changed to provide the current level of detail. Industrial and domestic price indices have been produced for many years, but comparability between years has been affected by the changes to the collection methods, and by changes to the base years. Data on petrol and Derv have been collected since before World War II, while those for heating oils have been collected since the mid-1970s. Price indices are published quarterly for fuels purchased by industrial and domestic consumers. They are published in both current terms and relative to the Gross Domestic Product (GDP) deflator. The domestic sector indices cover coal, gas, electricity, heating oils and petrol, and motor oil and are also published in both current terms and relative to the GDP deflator. Average tariff-based prices for domestic use of electricity and gas are published annually. Figures for typical retail prices of motor spirit (petrol) and Derv, and for oil products used for domestic heating, are published monthly, with duty rates on petroleum products available annually.

Status: Ongoing
Collection Method: Sample surveys of consumers conducted by ONS
Frequency: Oil products used for domestic heating are published monthly and petroleum products annually
Earliest Available Data: 1974
National Coverage: Great Britain

Statistician
Duncan Millard
Department of Trade and Industry
Tel: 020 7215 2720

Products that contain data from this source
Digest of United Kingdom Energy Statistics;
Energy sectors indicators; Energy Trends

Fuels: Foreign Trade System
Department of Trade and Industry

Volume and value of imports and exports of fuels based upon data provided by ONS. Current system started in 1996.

Status: Ongoing
Collection Method: Returns made to HMC&E
Frequency: Monthly
Reference Period: Quarterly
Timeliness: Available 3 months after reference period end
Earliest Available Data: 1993
National Coverage: United Kingdom
Disaggregation: Split by fuel and by country of origin

Statistician
Lesley Petrie
Department of Trade and Industry
Energy Policy and Analysis unit; Head of Energy Statistics Dissemination and Analysis
Tel: 020 7215 5183;
Email: lesley.petrie@epad.dti.gov.uk

Products that contain data from this source
Energy Trends; Digest of the United Kingdom Energy Statistics

---

Mineral Oil and Natural Gas - UK
Department of Trade and Industry

The Department of Trade and Industry compiles data on the extraction of mineral oil and natural gas. The Inquiry is conducted by the Office for National Statistics on all UK Continental Shelf licence holders, drilling contractors and those providing specialist services to this industry who operate from bases in the UK. Results form part of a direct contribution to the National Accounts. Data are available on the economic activity of companies by sales of oil, NGLs and gas, operating expenditure, capital investment and exploration expenditure. The survey covers the UK Continental Shelf activity of all UK companies registered to 11.10 and 11.20 of the SIC(92) and data are available at regional levels for onshore activity, and at county and Scottish Regional levels. The survey has been carried out quarterly since 1976 and the main results are published two to three months after the end of the reference period.

Status: Ongoing
Collection Method: Census
Frequency: Quarterly
Reference Period: Previous quarter
Timeliness: Provisional results available approximately ten weeks after end of quarter
Earliest Available Data: The survey has been carried out quarterly since 1976
National Coverage: UK, UK Continental Shelf
Disaggregation: Regional, UK Continental Shelf

Statistician
Philip Beckett
Department of Trade and Industry
Tel: 020 7215 5260

Products that contain data from this source
Digest of United Kingdom Energy Statistics; Energy Trends; United Kingdom National Accounts - The Blue Book

---

PIA - Oil Refining and Distribution
Department of Trade and Industry

The UK Petroleum Industry Association (UKPIA) collect data relating to the inland operations of the UK oil industry (i.e. information on the supply, refining and distribution of oil in the UK). The format and coverage of the data is such that it meets most of the needs of both government and the industry itself. As such, it operates by each member of UKPIA providing returns on its refining activities and deliveries of various products to the internal UK market. This information is supplemented whenever necessary to allow for complete coverage within the statistics, with separate exercises carried out on special topics. Although carried out by the oil industry, much of the data is collected at the behest of the UK government. No major discontinuities in the series are known, other than a break in 1995 when a minor part of the system on deliveries of lubricants was enhanced by the inclusion of 12 additional reporting companies.

Status: Ongoing
Collection Method: Census for most areas (all major UK companies covered with supplementary data sources being used on others to produce 100% coverage), with small sample-surveys in some minor areas (e.g. lubricants)
Frequency: Monthly (most major series - e.g. refinery production total deliveries by product), quarterly (e.g. breakdown of deliveries by industrial sector), annual (e.g. breakdown of deliveries by country)
Reference Period: Calendar month and year
Timeliness: For monthly, 1 month from end of reference period to first publication of aggregate results for any months, with more detailed estimates being available after 2 months. For annual series, 7 months from the end of the reference period to publication.
Earliest Available Data: 1960 up to 1980 - limited detail is available other than the published figures. Post 1980 full detail is available.

National Coverage: United Kingdom
Sub-National: Some data available for England, Wales, Northern Ireland and Scotland separately

Statistician
Kevin Williamson
Department of Trade and Industry
Tel: 020 7215 5184

Products that contain data from this source
Press Notice, Energy Trends, Digest of UK Energy Statistics, Energy Report, Development of the Oil and Gas Resources of the UK

PPRS - Oil and Gas Production
Department of Trade and Industry

The Petroleum Production Reporting System (PPRS) is primarily an administrative data collection system in which licensees operating on the UK Continental Shelf are required to make each month to the Department of Trade and Industry on their productions of hydrocarbons. The PPRS is used to report flows, stocks and uses of hydrocarbons from the well-head through to final disposals from a pipeline or terminal. Returns are collected covering field, pipeline and terminal data compiled by relevant reporting units. Each type of return is provided by a single operator, but usually covers the production of a number of companies since frequently operations carried out on the Continental Shelf involve several companies working together. System was introduced in 1975 when exploitation of the URCS reserves of oil and gas started to become significant. New fields have to report to a pre-set format to agreed definitions.

Status: Ongoing
Collection Method: Census
Frequency: Monthly (totals only), Annually (totals broken down by producing fields)
Reference Period: Calendar months and year
Timeliness: For monthly, 1 month from end of reference period to first publication of results for any month. For annual, 4 months from end of reference period to publication.
Earliest Available Data: 1960 - due to confidential nature of the data, limited details is available other than the published totals.
National Coverage: United Kingdom

Statistician
Kevin Williamson
Department of Trade and Industry
Tel: 020 7215 5184

Products that contain data from this source
Press Notice, Energy Trends, Digest of UK Energy Statistics, Development of the Oil and Gas Resources of the UK

Quarterly Fuels Inquiry to Manufacturing Industry in GB
Department of Trade and Industry

The Department of Trade and Industry compiles data on the prices of various fuels purchased by manufacturing industry in GB, for a range of different sized users, in a given quarter. Prior to 1988 only an average price for fuel using a smaller sample of only larger users was available. (The series are not strictly comparable)

Status: Ongoing
Collection Method: A stratified panel survey of over 1200 companies from manufacturing industry.
Frequency: Quarterly
Reference Period: Quarter
Timeliness: Quarterly data is published t+3 months.
Earliest Available Data: 1988
National Coverage: Great Britain

Statistician
Duncan Millard
Department of Trade and Industry
Tel: 020 7215 2720

Products that contain data from this source
Energy Trends, Digest of UK Energy Statistics

Suppliers of Gas
Department of Trade and Industry

The Department of Trade and Industry compiles data on gas consumption. The DTI issues questionnaires to the main gas companies to obtain sales data by sector. Data source changed in 1992 as a result of the opening up of competition following privatisation of the British Gas in 1986.

Status: Ongoing
Collection Method: Census
Frequency: Quarterly and Annually
Reference Period: Quarterly, Calendar year
Timeliness: For quarterly, 4 months from the end of the reference period to publication. For annual, 7 months from end of reference period to publication.
Earliest Available Data: Pre 1960, although data source changed in 1992 as a result of the opening up of competition in gas supply.
National Coverage: United Kingdom

Statistician
Michael Janes
Department of Trade and Industry
Tel: 020 7215 5186

Products that contain data from this source
Energy Trends, Digest of UK Energy Statistics

Survey of Autogeneration and Combined Heat and Power
Department of Trade and Industry

The Department of Trade and Industry compiles data on both autogeneration and CHP from a voluntary survey conducted on their behalf by ONS. ETSU (part of AEA Technology) supplement the CHP data with information gleaned from various sources and compile the data into publishable tables. DTI compile autogeneration statistics from both the ETSU data and the raw ONS data. Over 250 companies are surveyed annually and a sample survey of 80 companies is approached quarterly. CHP data are available only intermittently before 1993

Status: Ongoing
Collection Method: Census (with a lower limit of 250 kWe) for annual; stratified sample for quarterly.
Frequency: Annually and quarterly
Reference Period: Calendar year, calendar quarter
Timeliness: For annual, 7 months, and for quarterly 2 months, from end of reference period to publication.
Earliest Available Data: Some autogenerators data are available back to 1960. Consistent CHP data is available from 1993 with some data available for 1977, 1983, 1988 and 1991.
National Coverage: United Kingdom

Statistician
Michael Janes
Department of Trade and Industry
Tel: 020 7215 5186

Products that contain data from this source
Digest of UK Energy Statistics

Survey of Coal Producers
Department of Trade and Industry

The Department of Trade and Industry compiles data on the production and consumption of coal. The DTI issues questionnaires to the main coal companies to obtain production, stocks, import, export and disposal data. The DTI also collects information on: production from the Coal Authority; coal imports and exports from HCME, and consumption from electricity generators and energy industry. Data source changed in 1994 following the privatisation of the British Coal.

Status: Ongoing
Collection Method: Census (with minimum size cut off)
Frequency: Monthly and Annually
Reference Period: Month, Calendar Year
Timeliness: For monthly, 2 months from end of reference period to publication. For annual, 7 months from end of reference period to publication.

Earliest Available Data: Pre 1960, although data source changed in 1994 following the privatisation of British Coal.
National Coverage: United Kingdom

Statistician
Michael Janes
Department of Trade and Industry
Tel: 020 7215 5186

Products that contain data from this source
Energy Trends, Digest of UK Energy Statistics

Survey of Major Power Producers and Electricity Supply and Distribution
Department of Trade and Industry

The Department of Trade and Industry compiles data on the production and consumption of electricity, fuels used in generation, plant capacities and maximum load met. The DTI sends questionnaires to all major power producers and distributors (currently 33 monthly for generators, of which 10 companies also distribute electricity and 15 monthly for distributors only). 51 annual questionnaires are dispatched. On a monthly basis the DTI also collects import and export data from Northern Ireland Electricity and the National Grid Company. Pumped storage data from First Hydro are collected both monthly and annually. In addition to the above, 6 quarterly questionnaires requesting information on imports of hard coal from third countries are issued. Data sources changed in 1990 when the electricity industry was privatised.

Status: Ongoing
Collection Method: Census of companies meeting the definition which for generators is companies whose prime business is electricity generation.
Frequency: Monthly, Quarterly and Annually
Reference Period: Statistical month, calendar quarter, calendar year.
Timeliness: For monthly and quarterly, 2 months from end of reference period to publication. For annual, 7 months from end of reference period to publication.
Earliest Available Data: Earliest pre 1960, although data source changed in 1990 due to privatisation.
National Coverage: United Kingdom

Statistician
Michael Janes
Department of Trade and Industry
Tel: 020 7215 5186

Products that contain data from this source
Energy Trends, Digest of UK Energy Statistics

Survey of Petroleum Product Prices
Department of Trade and Industry

The Department of Trade and Industry compiles data on the average UK prices of domestic heating and motor fuels. Prior to 1977 only mid month price for January of each year is available.

Status: Ongoing
Collection Method: Census, (with minimum size cut off) of petroleum product suppliers
Frequency: Monthly
Reference Period: Mid month price, this being the price on or around the 15th of the Month
Timeliness: Published t+2 months. Provisional figure of some fuels Published t+1 month
Earliest Available Data: some fuels available from 1954 and majority from 1960
National Coverage: United Kingdom

Statistician
Duncan Millard
Department of Trade and Industry
Tel: 020 7215 2720

Products that contain data from this source
Energy Trends; Digest of UK Energy Statistics

Survey of Renewable Energy
Department of Trade and Industry

The Department of Trade and Industry compiles data on renewable energy used to generate electricity and used to generate heat. ETSU (part of AEA Technology) are contracted to collect and collate the data, and they use a variety of sources including direct questionnaires and information available under the renewables obligations. Because some data are collected on a 3 yearly cycle the number of questionnaires issued varies from year to year. No breaks of series, but as renewable sources have increased confidentiality constraints on the detailed figures have lessened.

Status: Ongoing
Collection Method: Census
Frequency: Annually
Reference Period: Calendar year
Timeliness: For annual, 7 months from end of reference period to publication.
Earliest Available Data: 1989
National Coverage: United Kingdom

Statistician
Michael Janes
Department of Trade and Industry
Tel: 020 7215 5186

Products that contain data from this source
Digest of UK Energy Statistics

Survey of Solid Fuel Producers
Department of Trade and Industry

The Department of Trade and Industry compiles data on the production and consumption of solid fuel other than coal, which covers coke, breeze and manufactured fuels (e.g. briquettes for closed domestic appliances). The DTI issues questionnaires to the main solid fuel producers to obtain production, stocks, import, export and disposal data.

Status: Ongoing
Frequency: Monthly
Reference Period: Month, (published quarter and calendar year)
Timeliness: Data aggregated to quarterly periods and published 2 months from end of the relevant quarterly period to publication.
Earliest Available Data: Pre 1960
National Coverage: United Kingdom

Statistician
Michael Janes
Department of Trade and Industry
Tel: 020 7215 5186

Products that contain data from this source
Energy Trends; Digest of UK Energy Statistics

UK Continental Shelf Capital Investment Intentions Survey
Department of Trade and Industry

A voluntary survey designed to obtain operators' intentions to invest in oil and gas extraction. Summaries were originally published by NEDO. The survey has been simplified in recent years to ease the burden of companies.

Status: Ongoing
Collection Method: Survey of all major operators and sample of minor operators
Frequency: Annually
Reference Period: The current year and the next five years
Timeliness: Summary usually published in December Energy Trends, and the following Development of the Oil and Gas Resources of the UK
Earliest Available Data: December
National Coverage: UK
Sub-National: UK Continental Shelf

Statistician
Philip Beckett
Department of Trade and Industry
Tel: 020 7215 5260

Products that contain data from this source
Energy Trends; Development of the Oil and Gas Resources of the UK

See also:
In this chapter:
Index of Production - UK *(12.1)*
Quarterly Capital Expenditure Inquiry *(12.1)*

12.7 Manufacturing and Production Industries

Annual Business Inquiry (Production and Construction) - UK
Office for National Statistics

The Annual Business Inquiry is carried out by the Office for National Statistics. UK Businesses are sampled according to their employment size and industry sector. Results are used to compile the input-output tables in the National Accounts, rebase the Index of Production, benchmark the stocks and capital expenditure quarterly inquiries and are supplied to Eurostat. Data are available by numbers employed, sales, work done, services rendered, running costs, capital expenditure, and stocks. Data cover the standard regions and estimates can be supplied for counties and districts. The Census began in 1907 and continued at roughly five-year intervals until it became annual in 1970. Census information for this year onwards is available in the Annual Summary Volume.

Status: Ongoing
Collection Method: Large-scale (Sample) Survey
Frequency: Annually
Reference Period: Calendar year but business year data accepted
Timeliness: Provisional results are available 12 months after reference year.
Publication of Revised results available 18 months after reference year.
Earliest Available Data: 1970
National Coverage: United Kingdom
Disaggregation: Government Office Region (GOR)

Statistician
Wendy Fader
Office for National Statistics
Production Sector Division; ACES RAP
Tel: 01633 812019;
Email: wendy.fader@ons.gov.uk

Products that contain data from this source
PACSTAT; Summary Volume - Production and construction (Business Monitor PA1002)

Sources and Analyses

Annual Census of Production
Ministry of Defence; sponsored by Office for National Statistics

Contains details of production expenditure. Used in preparing Tables 1.11 and 1.12.

Status: Ongoing
Collection Method: Census
Frequency: Annually
Reference Period: Government Financial Year

Statistician
Robin Horton
Ministry of Defence
Tel: 020 7218 8326;
Email: triservice@dasa.mon.uk

Annual Census of Production - Northern Ireland
Department of Economic Development - Northern Ireland

An annual inquiry into businesses within Northern Ireland Production Industry. Key variables include Gross Value Added, Net Output, Gross Output, Total Sales and Work Done, Net Capital Expenditure and Employment.

Status: Ongoing
Collection Method: Large-scale (Sample) Survey
Frequency: Annually
Reference Period: Financial Year
Timeliness: 1 Year
National Coverage: Northern Ireland

Statistician
Gillian Seeds
Department of Economic Development - Northern Ireland
Tel: 028 9052 9426;
Email: gillian.seeds@dedni.gov.uk

Products that contain data from this source
Northern Ireland Civil Expenditure on Research and Development during 1996; Summary Volume - Production and construction (Business Monitor PA1002); Annual Business Inquiry Results 1995 - 1997, Northern Ireland; Production and Construction 1995 - 1997 (available from September 1999)

Import Penetration Ratios and Export Sales Ratio - UK
Office for National Statistics

The Office for National Statistics compiles import penetration ratios and export sales ratios. The ratios are derived from the PRODCOM data and the associated trade data collected by HM Customs and Excise. Data are available on ratios calculated relating overseas trade in the goods produced by the different sectors of manufacturing industry to domestic production and apparent consumption of

those goods. Data cover the UK and are compiled both quarterly and annually. Since the introduction of PRODCOM in respect of 1993 the ratios have been calculated at the SIC(92) divisional level and published since 1993 on an annual and quarterly basis.

Status: Ongoing
Frequency: Annual and quarterly
Reference Period: Calendar year or quarters thereof
Earliest Available Data: 1993 (annual data); 1993Q1 (quarterly data)
National Coverage: United Kingdom

Statistician
Debra Prestwood
Office for National Statistics
Product Prices and Sales
Tel: 01633 812029;
Email: debra.prestwood@ons.gov.uk

Products that contain data from this analysis
Annual Abstract of Statistics; Economic Trends; Monthly Digest of Statistics

Index of Production - Northern Ireland
Department of Economic Development - Northern Ireland

The Northern Ireland Index of Production (NI IOP) compiled by the Northern Ireland Department of Economic Development (NIDED), is based on a sample survey of 500 production companies. The Index provides a general measure of changes in production output. Data are available at Northern Ireland level and are seasonally adjusted for all appropriate industrial sectors. The NI IOP has been carried out every quarter since 1949 and has recently been rebased to 1995 = 100. Results are published fifteen weeks after the end of the reference period for a particular quarter. The most recent Press Notice contains quarterly data for 1992 onwards and annual data from 1994 onwards. Historical data on 1995 = 100 is available for all series and data at 2-digit seasonally adjusted series are now available on request subject to confidentiality constraints.

Status: Ongoing
Collection Method: Small-scale (Sample) Survey
Frequency: Quarterly
Reference Period: The quarters ending in March, June, September and December
Timeliness: 15 week cycle, data collection during first twelve weeks, results published 15 weeks after the end of the survey quarter
Earliest Available Data: 1949
National Coverage: Northern Ireland

Statistician
Gillian Seeds
Department of Economic Development - Northern Ireland
Tel: 028 9052 9426;
Email: gillian.seeds@dedni.gov.uk

Products that contain data from this source
Northern Ireland Annual Abstract of Statistics; Northern Ireland Index of Production; Labour Market Statistics Northern Ireland

Index of Production - Scotland
Scottish Executive

The Scottish Executive Enterprise and Lifelong Learning Department compiles data on output in production industries in Scotland. Data are available at constant price indices on a quarterly basis and are seasonally adjusted. The Index data have been published quarterly from 1986 to date. The November 1995 publication was published using the 1992 Standard Industrial Classification (SIC(92)). The index has been published on the 1995=100 base from November 1998. Indices are available at a detailed level either in the annual statistical bulletin, or from the contact address. Rebasing on a five yearly basis - most recently in November 1998 when the index was rebased to 1995=100. Reclassification to Standard Industrial Classification 1992 (SIC92) took place in August 1995, and affects availability of pre-1986 data.

Status: Ongoing
Collection Method: Large-scale (Sample) Survey
Frequency: Quarterly
Reference Period: Quarters ending March, June, September and December
Timeliness: 4 months
Earliest Available Data: 1954 (aggregate on SIC80)
National Coverage: Scotland

Statistician
Hugh McAloon
Scottish Executive
Tel: 0141 242 5497;
Email: hugh.mcaloon@scotland.gov.uk

Products that contain data from this source
Index of Industrial Production and Construction for Scotland (News Release); Index of Industrial Production and Construction for Scotland: Detailed Industry Series (Statistical Bulletin); Scottish Abstract of Statistics; Scottish Economic Bulletin; Scottish Gross Domestic Product (News Release); The Electronics Industry in Scotland (Statistical Bulletin)

Index of Production and Construction - Wales
National Assembly for Wales

The Welsh Index of Production and Construction Survey is compiled by the National Assembly for Wales and provides information on trends in the volume of output of Welsh firms in the production and construction industries. The index draws on data supplied directly to the National Assembly for Wales by Welsh companies as well as the Office for National Statistics' monthly production and PRODCOM inquiries. The volume or value of sales are used to construct the Index, with value data being deflated using price indices. The index dates from 1963 and data on the current SIC(92) industrial classification are available from 1983. Data are published quarterly, around twelve weeks after the quarter to which they relate.

Status: Ongoing
Collection Method: Large-scale (Sample) Survey
Frequency: Quarterly
Timeliness: Published 12 weeks after the quarter
Earliest Available Data: 1st Quarter 1983
National Coverage: Wales

Statistician
Alan Jackson
National Assembly for Wales
Tel: 029 2082 5033;
Email: alan.jackson@wales.gov.uk

Products that contain data from this source
Digest of Welsh Statistics; Welsh Index of Production and Construction

Monthly Sales Inquiries - UK
Office for National Statistics

The Office for National Statistics conducts the Monthly Sales Inquiry (MSI). This is a statutory survey covering 9,300 companies in the UK. Results are grossed to estimate the industry population covering turnover and exports. Data are available for merchanted goods and orders on hand, in some industries. The MSI began in 1958 to measure manufacturing output in engineering sectors. It became statutory in July 1989 in engineering and non-engineering industries and the sample size has gradually been increasing since the 1970s.

Status: Ongoing
Earliest Available Data: 1958
National Coverage: United Kingdom

Statistician
Mark Williams
Office for National Statistics
Tel: 01633 812149

Products that contain data from this source
Engineering Sales and Orders Digest; Engineering Turnover and Orders (First Release); Index of Production (First Release); Machine Tools (First Release); Monthly Digest of Statistics

Monthly Short-Term Turnover and Employment Survey - Production Industries
Office for National Statistics

Status: Ongoing
Collection Method: Sample survey

Frequency: Monthly
Reference Period: The specified count day in every month
Timeliness: Estimates released 2 months after the count date
Earliest Available Data: June 1978 (United Kingdom only)
National Coverage: United Kingdom and Great Britain
Disaggregation: Government Office Regions and Standard Regions (quarterly)

Statistician
James Partington
Office for National Statistics
Tel: 01928 792545;
Email: james.partington@ons.gov.uk

Products that contain data from this source
Labour Market Trends; Monthly Digest of Statistics; Regional Trends; United Kingdom National Accounts - The Blue Book

Northern Ireland Export Survey
Department of Economic Development - Northern Ireland

The Survey of Northern Ireland Exports is carried out by the Northern Ireland Economic Research Centre on behalf of the Northern Ireland Industrial Development Board and Department of Economic Development. It is a sample survey covering 1,133 companies from both the manufacturing and non-manufacturing sectors in Northern Ireland. Only those non-manufacturing companies assisted by the Industrial Development Board or the Local Enterprise Development Unit were covered. Data have been collected on the sales and export statistics for Northern Ireland companies during the period 1991-92 to 1997-98. The Survey has produced estimates of total manufacturing external and export sales, destination of sales, sectoral trends and exports to top-ten markets by sectors. Longitudinal data indicating sales and export statistics are available. Data cover Northern Ireland. The most recent Survey related to three financial years from 1996 to 1998 and results were published in May 1999.

Status: Ongoing
Collection Method: Large-scale (Sample) Survey
Frequency: Annually
Reference Period: Financial year
Earliest Available Data: 1991-2
National Coverage: Northern Ireland

Statistician
Clare Alexander
Department of Economic Development - Northern Ireland
Tel: 028 9052 9525;
Email: clare.alexander@dedni.gov.uk

Products that contain data from this source
Made in Northern Ireland, Sold to the World

Producer Price Index Enquiries
Office for National Statistics

There are 4 individual Producer Price Index enquiries, dealing with UK-made/sold manufactured goods, UK exports of manufactured goods, imports of commodities and manufactured goods and UK-sold corporate services.

Status: Ongoing

Statistician
Andrew Allen
Office for National Statistics
Tel: 01633 813133

Products that contain data from this source
MM17; Aerospace and Electronics Cost Indices (Business Monitor MM19); Producer Price Indices (Business Monitor MM22)

Producer Price Indices - UK
Office for National Statistics

The Office for National Statistics compiles data on producer price indices. Producer prices are a series of economic indicators which measure the price movements of goods bought and sold by manufacturers. A wide collection of representative products is selected and the prices of these fixed sets of goods are collected each month. The movement in these prices is weighted to reflect the relative importance of the products in a chosen year. Index numbers are calculated and available for groups of commodities and for materials purchased by, and output of, broad sectors of industry. Data cover Great Britain and are available at region, county and main city library level. Data are collected and published monthly.

National Coverage: Great Britain
Disaggregation: Region, county and main city library level

Statistician
Ian Richardson
Office for National Statistics
Tel: 01633 812584

Products that contain data from this source
Aerospace and Electronics Cost Indices (Business Monitor MM19); Annual Abstract of Statistics; Economic Trends; Monthly Digest of Statistics; Price Index Numbers of Current Cost Accounting (Business Monitor); Producer Price Index (First Release); Producer Price Indices (Business Monitor MM22); Producer Prices: How They Work; Wholesale Price Index: Principles and Procedures

Sources and Analyses

Production Inventories - UK
Office for National Statistics

The Office for National Statistics conducts a quarterly survey on production inventories. It is a statutory survey covering 7,600 businesses in the mining and quarrying, manufacturing and electricity, gas and water sectors of the economy as defined by sections C, D and E of the Standard Industrial Classification of Economic Activities 1992 (SIC(92)). A statutory monthly survey is also conducted using a subset of a maximum of 100 businesses across twenty manufacturing industries. The collection of monthly data on a voluntary basis began in January 1992, when about 100 businesses were covered across three manufacturing industries. This continued until April 1999, when the survey became statutory, with the existing panel of businesses being replaced with a panel of the top 100 inventory holders across twenty manufacturing industries. The results are grossed to give estimates for the total population of these sectors of the economy. The estimates are deflated to constant prices and reflated to current prices. Following deflation, constant and current price estimates are seasonally adjusted. Results from the survey provide essential information on the change in inventories for the National Accounts and are used in the calculation of the expenditure and incomes measures of Gross Domestic Product (GDP) and in the compilation of the Index of Production (IOP) that in turn forms part of the output measure of GDP. The survey covers the United Kingdom and data was first collected by the Board of Trade in 1953. The series was first benchmarked against the Annual Census of Production in 1958. From quarter three 1990 the voluntary panel of around 2,000 businesses was expanded to 9,000 and the survey made statutory. The number of businesses was cut back to 7,600 in quarter two in 1993.

Status: Ongoing
Collection Method: Small-scale (sample) survey
Frequency: Quarterly
Reference Period: The quarter's ending, March, June, September and December.
Timeliness: Provisional results are available 8 weeks after reference quarter. Revised results available 4 weeks later.
Earliest Available Data: 1953
National Coverage: United Kingdom

Statistician
Wendy Fader
Office for National Statistics
Structural Statistics and Product Analysis Division
Tel: 01633 812019;
Email: wendy.fader@ons.gov.uk

Products that contain data from this source
Economic Trends; Economic Trends Annual Supplement; Monthly Digest of Statistics; Quarterly National Accounts (First Release); Stockbuilding Business Monitor; UK Output, Income and Expenditure (First Release); United Kingdom National Accounts - The Blue Book; United Kingdom National Accounts, Sources and Methods

Products of the European Community (PRODCOM INQUIRY)
Office for National Statistics

The Office for National Statistics compiles a survey on PRODCOM (PRODucts of the European COMmunity), a harmonised system across the EC for the collection and publication of product statistics. It is compiled from UK manufacturers on both an annual and quarterly basis and covers approximately 25,000 businesses annually and 4,500 quarterly. Data are available on the value and volume of UK manufacturers' product sales, merchanted goods, work done, sales of waste products and residues, and all other income. Also total turnover for the industry. PRODCOM began in respect of 1993, classified to the SIC(92), replacing the quarterly sales inquiry (QSI) and annual sales inquiry (ASI), started in 1969 and 1989 respectively. Under PRODCOM there was an increase in both the number of contributors and in the number of products covered. PRODCOM data can be directly matched with the trade data collected by HM Custom and Excise. This is published alongside the PRODCOM data making possible a complete picture of the market for each product. PRODCOM data is used in the construction of input-output balances which are used to reconcile the income, expenditure and output components of Gross Domestic Product (GDP), and in the construction of the Producer Price Index (PPI). Results from the annual survey are currently published from around nine months after the reference year and quarterly data currently becomes available approximately five months after the end of the quarter, with a view to reducing the time to publication as time progresses. PRODCOM began in respect of 1993, classified to the SIC(92), replacing the quarterly sales inquiry (QSI) and annual sales inquiry (ASI), started in 1969 and 1989 respectively.

Status: Ongoing
Collection Method: Large-scale (Sample) Survey
Frequency: Annually and Quarterly
Reference Period: Calendar year or quarters thereof
Timeliness: Currently the annual data is released in stages from around 9 months after the year of data collection.

Earliest Available Data: 1993 (Annual data); 1993 Q1 (Quarterly data)
National Coverage: United Kingdom

Statistician
Debra Prestwood
Office for National Statistics
Product Prices and Sales
Tel: 01633 812029;
Email: debra.prestwood@ons.gov.uk

Products that contain data from this source
Bespoke Requests; PRA 1 to 90 (Product Sales and Trade Annual Reports); PRQ 1 to 35 (Product Sales and Trade Quarterly Reports)

Quarterly Inquiry into Industrial and Commercial Companies, GB Trading Profits
Office for National Statistics

Company profits are a major component of the income measure of gross domestic product. However, definitive annual estimates of non Continental shelf industrial and commercial companies' profits are derived from corporation tax assessments and are not available to sufficient quality until two years after the event. The current statutory quarterly inquiry into companies' GB profits was launched in June 1991 and replaced an Inland Revenue voluntary inquiry which was considered inadequate following investigations recommended by the Pickford Scrutiny Report. There is no alternative data source for these quarterly estimates and the information is sought in a form, which is generally available from companies' own management records.

Status: Ongoing
Collection Method: Small-scale (Sample) Survey
Frequency: Quarterly
Reference Period: The calendar quarter
Timeliness: 7 weeks after the end of the period.
National Coverage: Great Britain

Statistician
Robert Hay
Office for National Statistics
Tel: 01633 812357;
Email: robert.hay@ons.gov.uk

Products that contain data from this source
National Accounts Press Release
Blue Book

Rates of Return for Private Non-Financial Corporations (PNFCs)
Office for National Statistics

The Office for National Statistics compiles rates of return for Private Non-Financial Corporations (PNFCs). These include net and gross rates of return (expressed as percentages) on capital employed by PNFCs.

Underlying data consists of gross operating surplus, capital consumption, net operating surplus, and gross and net average capital employed. Data are produced annually for PNFCs, UK Continental Shelf PNFCs, non-UK Continental Shelf PNFCs and manufacturing PNFCs.

Status: Ongoing
Frequency: Annually
Timeliness: The annual data are released after the Blue Book
National Coverage: United Kingdom

Statistician
Richard Walton
Office for National Statistics
Tel: 020 7533 6012;
Email: richard.walton@ons.gov.uk

Products that contain data from this analysis
Office for National Statistics Databank / Datastore; Profitability of UK Companies (First Release)

Scottish Production Database
Scottish Executive

The Scottish Executive carry out an analysis of the Annual Census of Production for Scotland. Data are available by employment, turnover, sales, expenditure, stocks and capital investment, and are given in current prices. The data cover the whole of Scotland and are available at regional and local enterprise company levels. The earliest data available are for 1983 and are usually published approximately two years after the end of the year to which they relate. See UK Annual Production Inquiry (ABI from 1997)

Status: Ongoing
Collection Method: Large-scale (Sample) Survey
Frequency: Annually
Reference Period: Calendar year
Timeliness: 2 years between end of relevant year and release of Scottish analysis
Earliest Available Data: 1983
National Coverage: Scotland
Disaggregation: LA; LEC

Statistician
Fiona Roberts
Scottish Executive
Tel: 0141 242 5459;
Email: fiona.roberts@scotland.gov.uk

Products that contain data from this source
Scottish Abstract of Statistics; Scottish Economic Bulletin; The Electronics Industry in Scotland (Statistical Bulletin); The Manufacturing Sector in Scotland (Statistical Bulletin)

Scottish Register of Employment
Scottish Executive

The Scottish Executive Enterprise and Lifelong Learning Department compiled data

from a number of sources on numbers of enterprises and employees for units with 11 or more employees. Historical data are available annually from 1950 to 1993. The data covers Scotland. Information is available on UK/non-UK ownership.

Status: Dormant
Collection Method: Hybrid
Frequency: Continuously
Reference Period: Calendar year
Earliest Available Data: 1950
National Coverage: Scotland

Statistician
Hugh McAloon
Scottish Executive
Tel: 0141 242 5497;
Email: Hugh.Mcaloon@scotland.gov.uk

Shipbuilding Inquiry
Department of Trade and Industry

The shipbuilding inquiry is carried out on a quarterly basis in order to complete two OECD Shipbuilding questionnaires, one annual and one quarterly. The inquiry form is sent to all shipbuilding companies in the UK and they have to fill in data on new orders, completions, prospective flag (register) of ship etc. The form asks for value(£m) and volume, in the form of gross tonnage and deadweight. The dataset is of limited wider use because it is collected on the basis that all company data is commercial in confidence and therefore data can only be used at a very aggregated level.

Status: Ongoing
Collection Method: Census
Frequency: Quarterly
Reference Period: quarter/annual
Earliest Available Data: At least since 1960s
National Coverage: United Kingdom

Statistician
Michael Clary
Department of Trade and Industry
Tel: 020 7215 1887;
Email: michael.clary@industry.dti.gov.uk

Steel Statistics Industry (UK)
Iron and Steel Statistics Bureau

Information on production and delivered products to home and export markets based on UK Steel Companies figures

Status: Ongoing
Collection Method: Administrative Records
Frequency: Continuously
National Coverage: United Kingdom

Statistician
Chris Edwards
Iron and Steel Statistics Bureau Industry (UK Information)
Tel: 020 7343 3900;
Email: c.edwards@issb.co.uk

Steel Trade Statistics
Iron and Steel Statistics Bureau

Information based on imports and exports of steel products and materials

Status: Ongoing
Collection Method: Administrative Records
Frequency: Continuously

Statistician
Phil Hunt
Iron and Steel Statistics Bureau
Tel: 020 7343 3916;
Email: p.hunt@issb.co.uk

See also:
In this chapter:
Index of Production - UK *(12.1)*
Northern Ireland Quarterly Construction Enquiry *(12.2)*
Quarterly Capital Expenditure Inquiry *(12.1)*

12.8 Mineral Extraction, Mining, and Quarrying

Minerals Raised Inquiry - GB
Department of the Environment, Transport and the Regions

The Annual Minerals Raised Inquiry (AMRI) is compiled by the Department of the Environment, Transport and the Regions with limited support from the Department of Trade and Industry (DTI). The Inquiry is conducted by the Office for National Statistics on all quarries and mines in Great Britain, excluding deep coal mines. Data are available on the volume of the sales of quarry products. The Inquiry covers the extraction of chalk, clay, crushed rock, dolomite, granite, gypsum, limestone, ore minerals, salt, sandstone, sand and gravel, slate, plus a few minor minerals. DETR is responsible for the construction use of materials whereas DTI is responsible for the industrial use of materials. The Inquiry is site-based. There are some regional and county-level data available. The sand and gravel Inquiry was enhanced in 1954, extended to cover crushed rock in 1972, and took its present form in 1979. The Inquiry is carried out annually, with results published each October after the reference year.

Status: Ongoing
Frequency: Annual
Timeliness: Results are published each October after the reference year
National Coverage: Great Britain

Statistician
David Williams
Department of the Environment, Transport and the Regions
Construction Market Intelligence; Statistics Branch 3
Tel: 020 7890 5593;
Email: david_williams@detr.gov.uk

Products that contain data from this source
Primary Production - Mineral Extraction in Great Britain (Business Monitor PA1007); United Kingdom Minerals Yearbook 1997

UK Minerals Industry
British Geological Survey

The British Geological Survey (Natural Environment Research Council) compiles United Kingdom mineral statistics. Data are obtained from official sources, trade associations and directly from industry and stored in a dataset relating to the production, consumption and trade of minerals in the UK. The data cover the UK and are available at country, planning region (construction minerals), county (construction minerals), British Coal Corporation region, oilfield, and gasfield levels. A consistent series has been maintained since 1973, but earlier statistical data are also available back to 1853. Data are collected throughout the year and published annually, fifteen months after the end of the reference year.

Frequency: Annual
Timeliness: Results are published fifteen months after the end of the reference year
Earliest Available Data: 1973
National Coverage: United Kingdom

Statistician
David Highley
British Geological Survey
Tel: 0115 936 3397

Products that contain data from this analysis
Annual Abstract of Statistics; Development of the Oil and Gas Resources of the United Kingdom; Digest of United Kingdom Energy Statistics; Energy Trends; Housing and Construction Statistics Annual Volume; Monthly Digest of Statistics; Overseas Trade Statistics (Business Monitors); Primary Production - Mineral Extraction in Great Britain (Business Monitor PA1007); United Kingdom Minerals Yearbook 1997; World Mineral Statistics 1992-96

World Mineral Statistics Database
British Geological Survey

The British Geological Survey compiles the World Mineral Statistics database. The database relates to the production and trade of minerals worldwide. Data are shown, as mass or volume, over a five-year period on 65 mineral commodities and approximately 370 sub-commodities. Data cover the world and are available at country or continent level. A consistent series has been maintained since 1978 but a closely similar series dates back to 1913. Mineral statistics are collected throughout the year and published annually, one to two years after the reference year.

Frequency: Annual
Timeliness: Data are published one to two years after the reference year
Earliest Available Data: 1978

Statistician
Greg Chapman
British Geological Survey
Tel: 0115 936 3543

Products that contain data from this analysis
World Mineral Statistics 1992-96

See also:
In this chapter:
Index of Production - UK *(12.1)*

12.9 Motor Vehicle Production

Engine Production Inquiry - UK
Office for National Statistics

The Office for National Statistics conducts the Monthly Engine Production Inquiry on ten UK manufacturers. Data cover engines which are intended for sale to a third party, bought in and subjected to a manufacturing process by the company and intended for resale to a third party, transfers of the above within their UK organisation, and transfers of company's own production to their organisation overseas. The data have been collected since October 1994. They are passed directly on to the Index of Production and published six weeks after the inquiry.

Timeliness: Data published six weeks after the inquiry
Earliest Available Data: 1994

Statistician
Margaret Lane
Office for National Statistics
Production Sector Division; Short Term Employment Estimates
Tel: 01633 81 2072;
Email: margaret.lane@ons.gov.uk

Products that contain data from this source
Index of Production (First Release)

Motor Vehicle Production Inquiry - UK
Office for National Statistics

Data on the production of passenger cars and commercial vehicles are derived from the Motor Vehicle Production Inquiry (MVPI) which surveys the monthly output of 29 UK manufacturers classified to class 34.10 (motor vehicles) of the Standard Industrial Classification (1992). The MVPI is a voluntary inquiry that is conducted jointly by ONS and The Society of Motor Manufacturers and Traders Limited

(SMMT). One of its major roles is as a component of the Index of Production. The First Release contains seasonally and non-seasonally adjusted data for the production of passenger cars and commercial vehicles (total sub-divided into production for the home and export markets). It is published fourteen working days after the close of the survey period.

Status: Ongoing
Collection Method: Small-scale (Sample) Survey
Frequency: Monthly
Reference Period: Calendar month
Timeliness: 5 working days
Earliest Available Data: 1977
National Coverage: United Kingdom

Statistician
Margaret Lane
Office for National Statistics
Production Sector Division; Short Term Employment Estimates
Tel: 01633 81 2072;
Email: margaret.lane@ons.gov.uk

Products that contain data from this source
Motor Vehicle Production (First Release); Motor Vehicle Production and New Registrations (Business Monitor PM3410)

See also:
In this chapter:
Index of Production - UK *(12.1)*

12.10 Research and Development (R&D) Companies

Business Enterprise Research and Development Survey - UK
Office for National Statistics

The Survey of Business Enterprise Research and Development is conducted by the Office for National Statistics. Between 1985 and 1993 there were four yearly large scale surveys. The 1993 Survey was the last large scale survey and since then ONS has moved to a stand alone sample survey based on a continually updated register on R&D performers. Estimates are made for the R&D activity of unsampled and non-responding businesses. The sample and survey results only cover "business enterprises" as defined in the "Frascati" Manual. This excludes government organisations, higher education establishments and charities.

Initial estimates from the survey are published in a First Release in November each year. the detailed final results are published in a Business Monitor (MA14) in January each year and are also used to calculate Gross Research and Development expenditure (GERD) published in the

GERD First Release each March. Figures consistent with the Business Monitor will also be included in the DTI's Office of Science and Technology's publication, Science, Engineering and Technology Statistics, together with detailed figures for R7D activity in Central Government and Higher Education.

Status: Ongoing
Collection Method: Sample Survey
Frequency: Annually
Reference Period: Calendar Year
Timeliness: Data available within 11 months.
Earliest Available Data: 1989
National Coverage: United Kingdom

Statistician
Peter Jones
Office for National Statistics
Overseas and Financial Division; Research, Development and Innovation Statistics
Tel: 01633 813063;
Email: peter.jones@ons.gov.uk

Products that contain data from this source
MA14 Research and Development in UK Business, Business Enterprise Research and Development (BERD (First Release))
Annual Abstract of Statistics; Economic Trends; Gross Domestic Expenditure on Research and Development (GERD (First Release)); Regional Trends; Research and Development Annual Statistics; Main Science and Technology Indicators; Science, Engineering and Technology Statistics 1998

NI Research & Development Survey
Department of Economic Development - Northern Ireland

The first survey began in 1993 and the second was carried out in 1996

Status: Ongoing
Collection Method: Small-scale (Sample) Survey
Frequency: Periodic
Reference Period: 1996
Timeliness: Year
Earliest Available Data: 1993
National Coverage: Northern Ireland

Statistician
Gillian Seeds
Department of Economic Development - Northern Ireland
Tel: 028 9052 9426;
Email: gillian.seeds@dedni.gov.uk

Products that contain data from this source
Northern Ireland Civil and Defence Expenditure on Research and Development during 1996

See also:
In this chapter:
Index of Production - UK *(12.1)*
Quarterly Capital Expenditure Inquiry *(12.1)*

12.11 Telecommunications Industry - Service statistics

BT Quality of Service - UK
Office for Telecommunications (OFTEL)

A quality of service report is collated by the Office of Telecommunications (OFTEL) from statistics provided by BT. This is for use by OFTEL to monitor BT's performance. Data provided by BT covers the UK, and includes network reliability, telephone repair service, provision of service, operator services, public payphones service, and private circuits: provisioning, repair and reliability. BT supplies monthly and six-monthly figures to OFTEL for analysis and investigation. These figures are not released into the public domain, although some are available on BT's web site.

Status: Ongoing
Collection Method: Large-scale (Sample) Survey
Frequency: Monthly
National Coverage: United Kingdom

Statistician
Nick Collins
Office for Telecommunications (OFTEL)
Tel: 020 7634 8851;
Email: ncollins@oftel.gov.uk

See also:
In this chapter:
Community Innovation Survey (CIS) *(12.4)*

12

Commerce, Construction, Energy and Industry - *Products*

12.12 Abstracts, Compendia, A-Z Catalogues, Directories and Reference Material

Analysis from the Inter-Departmental Business Register
Office for National Statistics

Ad hoc analyses of data to customer's specifications. Contains data from the register which can include UK business data at reporting unit, enterprise, enterprise group and local unit level by size, industrial classification, legal status and geographical location.

Delivery: Ad hoc/One-off Release
Frequency: Ad hoc

Available from
Data Analysis Service
Room 1.062
Office for National Statistics
Government Buildings
Cardiff Road
Newport
Gwent
South Wales NP9 1XG
Tel: 0800 731 5761
or
Mike Prestwood
Room 1.023
Office for National Statistics
Government Buildings
Cardiff Road
Newport
Gwent
South Wales NP9 1XG
Tel: 01633 813289

Sources from which data for this product are obtained
Business Counts - UK; Inter-Departmental Business Register

Business Investment First Release
Office for National Statistics

Commentary and tables on investment trends by businesses. Contains capital expenditure data for various sectors of the economy at current prices, constant prices and seasonally adjusted.

Delivery: First Release
Frequency: Twice every quarter
Price: Annual subscription £24.00

Available from
Bob Watson
Room 1.301
Office for National Statistics
Government Buildings
Cardiff Road
Newport
Gwent
South Wales NP9 1XG
Tel: 01633 812059;
Email: bob.watson@ons.gov.uk

Sources from which data for this product are obtained
Quarterly Capital Expenditure Inquiry

Glossary of Business Statistics
Eurostat

This publication contains 418 terms and variables from the field of business statistics and other closely related areas such as company and national accounts, banking and trade. Included in the glossary are also a certain number of general terms from the fields of the environment, tourism, insurance, telecommunications and postal and audiovisual services. All variables from the Council Regulations on structural business statistics and from 'Methodological manual of business statistics, 'General framework' chapter are included in this version. Listing of business statistics terms and their meaning.

Delivery: Ad hoc/One-off Release
Frequency: Ad hoc
Price: £17.50
ISBN: 92 827 9019 3

Available from
Bob Dodds
Office for National Statistics
Please see Annex B for full address details

Size Analysis of UK Businesses (Business Monitor PA1003)
Office for National Statistics

This publication is compiled from the Inter Departmental Business Register (IDBR) which contains information on VAT traders and Paye employers in a statistical register comprising 2 million enterprises, representing nearly 99% of economic activity. The publication contains detailed information on all enterprises in the UK including size, classification and location. This information is also available at local unit (site) level, for the manufacturing sector.

Delivery: Periodic Release
Frequency: Annual
Price: £50.00 for paper publication, £175.00 if required electronically
ISBN: Various
ISSN: 1363 9013

Available from
ONS Direct
Office for National Statistics
Please see Annex B for full address details.

Sources from which data for this product are obtained
Business Counts - UK; Inter-Departmental Business Register

12.13 Building and Construction Industry

Adjustments for Measured Term Contracts - Updating Percentages
Department of the Environment, Transport and the Regions

Percentages and Indices for updating building maintenance and small works contracts. Includes percentages for all "PSA" and two of the "National" Schedules of Rates.

Frequency: Monthly
Price: £60.00 Annual subscription £7.00 single issues
ISSN: 1353 1832

Available from
CRC Publications
Please see Annex B for full address details

Sources from which data for this product are obtained
Building Societies; Historical construction data, output, orders, starts and completions

---

Construction Forecasts
Construction Research Limited

This report serves as a trend analysis marketing tool for contractors, building materials and products companies, investment institutions and others with an interest in GB construction. The report contains volume output forecasts for private housing, public housing, infrastructure, public non-residential building, private industrial and commercial building, and repair and maintenance. It is published four times a year.

Delivery: Periodic Release
Frequency: Quarterly
Price: Annual subscription to the report costs £180.00 for 4 issues (two main editions in Winter and Summer and two updates in Autumn and Spring).
Single copy of the main edition, £90.00.
Updates are only available to subscribers to the report.
ISSN: 0308-079X

Available from
Jacquie Cannon
Construction Research Limited
Princes House
39 Kingsway
London
Tel: 020 7379 5339; Fax: 020 7379 5426;
Email: cfrjgph@aol.com

Sources from which data for this product are obtained
Building Societies; Historical construction data, output, orders, starts and completions

---

Digest of Data for the Construction Industry
Department of the Environment, Transport and the Regions

Construction statistics spanning a wide variety of sources including Government and the industry. Contains floorspace statistics, construction output and new orders, local and central government expenditure, international comparisons, workload of professionals, planning applications, and construction health and safety statistics.

Frequency: Annual,
Price: £45.00
ISBN: 0 11 753465 X

Available from
TSO Publications Centre and Bookshops
Please see Annex B for full address details.

Sources from which data for this product are obtained
Construction - New Orders - GB; Construction Output - GB; Floorspace - England and Wales; Labour Dispute Statistics

---

Orders for New Construction Information Bulletin
Department of the Environment, Transport and the Regions

Press release of the latest monthly estimates and some back data on construction new orders estimates. Contains construction new orders (current price and constant price seasonally adjusted) broken down by sector and, in current prices, by region (quarterly) and type of work.

Delivery: News/Press Release
Frequency: Monthly
Price: £45.00 annual subscription (including postage)

Available from
Richard Job
Department of the Environment, Transport and the Regions
Construction Directorate
Eland House
Bressenden Place
London
Tel: 020 7890 5586; Fax: 020 7890 5639;
Email: pauls_andrews@detr.gov.uk

Sources from which data for this product are obtained
Construction - New Orders - GB

Output and Employment in the Construction Industry Information Bulletin
Department of the Environment, Transport and the Regions

Press release of the latest estimates and some back data on construction output and employment estimates. Contains the construction output (current price/constant price seasonally adjusted) broken down by sector. Also provides estimates of total employment/employees in the construction industry.

Delivery: News/Press Release
Frequency: Quarterly
Price: £20.00 annual subscription (including postage)

Available from
Richard Job
Department of the Environment, Transport and the Regions
Construction Directorate
Eland House
Bressenden Place
London
Tel: 020 7890 5586; Fax: 020 7890 5639;
Email: pauls_andrews@detr.gov.uk

Sources from which data for this product are obtained
Construction Output - GB

Output Price Indices
Department of the Environment, Transport and the Regions

Leaflet of public and private output prices indices from 1970. Contains an 'all-new construction index' and indices for public and private sector new work.

Frequency: Quarterly
Price: £15.00 per year (four quarters), £25.00 complete index set per year

Available from
Marcella Douglas
Department of the Environment, Transport and the Regions
Please see Annex B for full address details

Overseas Construction by British Firms
Department of the Environment, Transport and the Regions

Delivery: News/Press Release
Frequency: Annually
Price: Free of charge

Available from
David Williams
Department of the Environment, Transport and the Regions
Construction Directorate
Eland House
Bressenden Place
London
Tel: 020 7890 5593; Fax: 020 7890 5639;
Email: david_williams@detr.gov.uk

Price Adjustment Formulae for Construction Contracts - Monthly Bulletin of Indices
Department of the Environment, Transport and the Regions

Indices for adjusting construction contracts for cost changes. Includes indices for building works, mechanical and electrical services and civil engineering.

Frequency: Monthly
Price: £110.00 annual subscription
£11.00 single issues
ISSN: 0964-4575

Available from
TSO Publications Centre and Bookshops
Please see Annex B for full address details.

Public Sector Tender Price Indices
Department of the Environment, Transport and the Regions

Leaflet of tender price index for public sector housing and public sector works. Contains indices back to 1980 for variation of price and firm price contracts.

Products

Frequency: Quarterly
Price: £16.00 per year (four quarters), £27.00 complete index set per year

Available from
Marcella Douglas
Department of the Environment, Transport and the Regions
Please see Annex B for full address details.

Sources from which data for this product are obtained
Public Sector Index

Public Sector Tender Price Indices Information Sheet (2 Sheets or More)
Department of the Environment, Transport and the Regions

Construction Industry Indices.

Frequency: Quarterly
Price: £16.00 per year (4 quarters), £27.00 complete index set per year

Available from
Marcella Douglas
Department of the Environment, Transport and the Regions
Please see Annex B for full address details.

Quarterly Building Price and Cost Indices
Department of the Environment, Transport and the Regions

Basic 'tool of the trade' to any quantity surveyor involved in estimating, cost checking and fee negotiation on public sector building projects. Contains public sector tender price indices - roads, housing and works, Construction Output Price Indices, Average building cost indices, projected formula VOP indices and new construction work output price indices are also included.

Frequency: Quarterly
Price: Single issue £18.00, annual subscription £60.00 (including postage)
ISBN: 1353 1821

Available from
CRC Publication
Please see Annex B for full address details
or
TSO Publications Centre and Bookshops
Please see Annex B for full address details.

Sources from which data for this product are obtained
Price Index for Public Sector Housing (PIPSH); Public Sector Index; Road Construction Tender Price Index - GB

Road Construction Tender Price Index
Department of the Environment, Transport and the Regions

Leaflet of road construction tender price index. Contains all-in road index, firm-price and variation of price indices. Regional, value and type of project factors.

Frequency: Quarterly
Price: £16.00 per year (four quarters), £27.00 complete index set per year

Available from
Marcella Douglas
Department of the Environment, Transport and the Regions
Please see Annex B for full address details.

Sources from which data for this product are obtained
Road Construction Tender Price Index - GB

Road Construction Tender Price Indices (2 Sheets or More)
Department of the Environment, Transport and the Regions

Delivery: Other
Frequency: Quarterly
Price: £16.00 per year (4 quarters), £27.00 complete index set per year

Available from
Marcella Douglas
Department of the Environment, Transport and the Regions
Please see Annex B for full address details.

(The) State of the Construction Industry
Department of the Environment, Transport and the Regions

Delivery: Periodic Release
Frequency: Twice-yearly
Price: Free

Available from
Jim Woodfine
Department of the Environment, Transport and the Regions
Construction Directorate
Eland House
Bressenden Place
London
Tel: 020 7890 5652; Fax: 020 7890 5529;
Email: jwoodfine@detr-cis.demon.gov.uk

Sources from which data for this product are obtained
Construction - New Orders - GB; Construction Output - GB

See also:
In this chapter:
Analysis from the Inter-Departmental Business Register *(12.12)*

Size Analysis of UK Businesses (Business Monitor PA1003) *(12.12)*

In other chapters:
Economic Trends (see the Economy chapter)
Housing and Construction Statistics Annual Volume (see the Housing chapter)
Housing and Construction Statistics Part 1 and 2 Quarterly (see the Housing chapter)
Labour Market Trends (see the Labour Market chapter)

12.14 Building Materials Industry

Bricks and Cement (Press Release)
Department of the Environment, Transport and the Regions

Departmental press release of the latest information for bricks and cement.

Delivery: News/Press Release
Frequency: Quarterly
Price: £24.00 annual subscription (1999/2000)

Available from
Terry Hawton
Department of the Environment, Transport and the Regions
Please see Annex B for full address details.

Sources from which data for this product are obtained
Bricks - GB; Cement - UK

Monthly Statement for Bricks, Cement and Concrete Blocks
Department of the Environment, Transport and the Regions

Departmental statement containing the latest information for bricks, cement and concrete blocks.

Delivery: Statement
Frequency: Monthly
Price: £27.00 annual subscription (1999/2000)

Available from
Terry Hawton
Department of the Environment, Transport and the Regions
Please see Annex B for full address details.

Sources from which data for this product are obtained
Bricks -GB; Cement - UK; Concrete Blocks - GB

Monthly Statistics of Building Materials and Components
Department of the Environment, Transport and the Regions

Departmental publication of the latest information for selected building materials. Contains monthly data for price indices, bricks, cement, and concrete blocks. Quarterly data covers concrete roofing tiles, fibre cement products, ready-mixed concrete, sand and gravel, slate, and overseas trade.

Frequency: Monthly
Price: £111.00 annual subscription (1999/2000)
ISSN: 0264-6188

Available from
Terry Hawton
Department of the Environment, Transport and the Regions
Please see Annex B for full address details.

Sources from which data for this product are obtained
Bricks - GB; Cement - UK; Concrete Blocks - GB; Concrete Roofing Tiles - GB; Fibre Cement Products - GB; Ready-Mixed Concrete - GB; Sand and Gravel - GB; Slate - GB

See also:
In other chapters:
Housing and Construction Statistics Annual Volume (see the Housing chapter)
Housing and Construction Statistics Part 1 and Part 2 Quarterly (see the Housing chapter)

12.15 Business and Commerce - General

Acquisitions and Mergers (First Release)
Office for National Statistics

Latest data on domestic and overseas acquisitions and mergers.

Frequency: Quarterly
Price: Annual subscription £12.00

Available from
Philip Gooding
Office for National Statistics
Government Buildings
Cardiff Road
Newport
Gwent
South Wales
Tel: 01633 812793

Sources from which data for this product are obtained
Acquisitions and Mergers - UK; Domestic Acquisitions and Mergers - UK

Annual Report of the Director General of Fair Trading
Office of Fair Trading

Report by the Director General of Fair Trading to the Secretary of State for Trade and Industry under Section 125 of the Fair Trading Act. The aim of the OFT is to promote the economic interests of consumers in the United Kingdom by safeguarding competition, removing trading malpractices and publishing appropriate guidance.

An appendix to this publication contains statistical tables on consumer complaints. Appendix F: Statistical tables on consumer complaints statistics reported to the Office of Fair Trading by Trading Standards Departments and Environmental Health Departments, including relationship between complaints statistics and consumers expenditure.

Frequency: Annually
Price: 1998 report £16.00
ISBN: 0 10 270899 1

Available from
TSO Publications Centre and Bookshops
Please see Annex B for full address details.

Sources from which data for this product are obtained
Quarterly Survey of Environmental Health Departments: numbers of consumer complaints; Quarterly Survey of Trading Standards Departments: numbers of consumer complaints

Business Competitiveness Indicators
Department of Trade and Industry

The Business Competitiveness Indicators provide information covering employment, earnings, gdp, gross value added and company formation and survival rates for England & Wales at county and TEC area level. They are provided on floppy disk specifically for TECs and Government Offices.

Frequency: Bi-annually

Available from
General Enquiries on Regional Statistics
Room G21
Department of Trade and Industry
10 Victoria Street
London SW1H 0NN
Tel: 020 7215 3279/3290;
Email: glenn.everett@esdv.dti.gov.uk

Business Start-Ups and Closures: VAT Registrations and Deregistrations
Department of Trade and Industry

An annual bulletin showing the number of VAT registrations and deregistrations each year since 1980. While not capturing many of the smallest one person businesses, they are a good guide to the pattern of business start-ups and closures across the UK. Useful both for local economic development and for business marketing. Estimates are provided for the UK, regions, counties and local authority districts, all with a broad sector breakdown. The bulletin contains tables showing the number of VAT registrations, deregistrations, and the stock of registered businesses, in each region, country and district. The disk contains the same information for each year since 1980, broken down by broad industrial sector throughout. Data for years before 1994 use the 1980 Standard Industrial Classification and pre-Unitary Authority district boundaries. More detailed sectoral information at the national level is also included.

Delivery: News/Press Release and hardcopy publication with diskette
Frequency: Annually
Price: £25.00 including postage

Available from
Small Firms Statistics Unit
Level 2
Department of Trade and Industry
St Marys House, c/o Moorfoot
Sheffield S1 4PQ
Tel: 0114 259 7538;
Email: ian.dale@SFSH-Sheffield.dti.gov.uk

Sources from which data for this product are obtained
IDBR

Company Winding Up and Bankruptcy Petition Statistics (Press Notice)
Court Service: sponsored by Lord Chancellor's Department

Data on company winding up and creditors' and debtors' bankruptcy petitions issued in the High Court of and county courts of England & Wales. Contains quarterly data on the number of companies winding up and creditors and debtors bankruptcy petitions filed compared with the corresponding quarter the previous year, and trends over the last five years. Data are available by court, county and region.

Delivery: First Release
Frequency: Quarterly
Price: Free

Available from
Lord Chancellor's Department Press Office
Lord Chancellor's Department
Selborne House
54-60 Victoria Street
London SW1E 6QW
Tel: 020 7210 8512/13

Sources from which data for this product are obtained
Insolvency - England and Wales

Facts and Figures from the Inter-Departmental-Business-Register
Department of Economic Development

A booklet on businesses in Northern Ireland containing information on what the IDBR is and what its uses are. Also businesses and employees in Northern Ireland and in each District Council area, comparisons with Great Britain, VAT registrations and deregistrations in the United Kingdom and details on the number of foreign-owned businesses operating in Northern Ireland.

Delivery: Periodic Release
Frequency: Annual
Price: Free

Available from
Ian Gallagher
Statistics Research Branch
Department of Economic Development
Netherleigh
Massey Avenue
Belfast BT4 2JP
Tel: 028 9052 9430; Fax: 028 9052 9459;
Email: ian.gallagher@dedni.gov.uk

Sources from which data for this product are obtained
Inter Departmental Business Register

Insolvency Statistics (Statistical Press Release)
Department of Trade and Industry

Statistical Press Release covering quarterly and annual insolvency statistics for the last 7 years for companies and individuals, in England, Wales and Scotland. Contains company insolvencies in England and Wales (compulsory liquidations and creditors' voluntary liquidations, including seasonal adjustment); personal insolvencies in England and Wales (bankruptcy orders [seasonally adjusted], individual voluntary arrangements and deeds of arrangement); receivership appointments (E&W), administrator appointments (E&W), company voluntary arrangements (E&W); industrial analysis of company insolvencies and of bankruptcies (E&W); ratio of company insolvencies to stock of companies (E&W); sequestrations (equivalent to bankruptcies) in Scotland; and company liquidations in Scotland.

Delivery: News/Press Release
Frequency: Quarterly

Available from
Insolvency Statistics General Enquiries
Room G22
Department of Trade and Industry
10 Victoria Street
London SW1H 0NN
Tel: 020 7215 3291/3305;
Email: adam.gigante@esdv.dti.gov.uk

Overseas Ownership in Scottish Manufacturing Industry
Scottish Executive

Frequency: One-off
ISBN: 07480 6478 8

Available from
Debbie Provan
Room 3rd Floor
Scottish Executive
Meridian Court
5 Cadogan Street
Glasgow G2 6AT
Tel: 0141 242 5604;
Email: debbie.provan@scotland.gov.uk

Sources from which data for this product are obtained
Regional Selective Assistance Grants to Industry - Scotland

Regional Competitiveness Indicators
Department of Trade and Industry

The bi-annual Indicators provide 13 statistics which illustrate the factors determining the regional competitiveness of the English Regions (as defined by the Government Offices) as well as of Scotland, Wales and Northern Ireland. The 56 pages include 26 charts and 35 tables providing information on regional competitiveness and cover economic variables such as GDP per head, productivity, the labour market, education & training, investment, transport infrastructure and property costs. It is aimed to assist those who are responsible for developing regional economic policies and promoting competitiveness such as Regional Development Agencies, Government Offices, TECs and Chambers of Commerce.

Delivery: Periodic Release
Frequency: Bi-annually
Price: £12.00 per year (2 issues)

Available from
General Enquiries on Regional Statistics
Room G21
Department of Trade and Industry
10 Victoria Street
London SW1H 0NN
Tel: 020 7215 3279/3290;
Email: glenn.everett@esdv.dti.gov.uk

Share Ownership - Share Register Survey Report
Office for National Statistics

Trends in share ownership by economic sector of beneficial owner. Contains data on share ownership by sector for the UK economy and the geographical distribution of shares held overseas together with an analysis of the ownership of the recently demutualised companies.

Delivery: Hardcopy publication with associated News Release
Frequency: Annual
Price: £39.50 (for the end 1997 edition)
ISBN: 0 11 621076 1 (for the end 1997 edition)
ISSN: 1465 2752

Available from
TSO Publications Centre and Bookshops
Please see Annex B for full address details.

Sources from which data for this product are obtained
Share Ownership - UK

Small and Medium Enterprise (SME) Statistics for the UK
Department of Trade and Industry

An annual bulletin containing a breakdown of the UK business population, its employment and turnover, by business size. Ten business size classes are used - from those with no employees (owner-only) to those with 500 or more employees. Includes an estimate of the large number of one person businesses not captured by most official sources. Essential for researchers and those offering goods, services or advice to the UK business population. Estimates of the number of businesses, and their aggregate employment and turnover, in each size class. Estimates are shown for the UK economy as a whole, and sector by sector, using the 1992 Standard Industrial Classification. Further tables show the key changes in the make-up of the business population since the previous year, and a breakdown of the business population by size and legal status. In the latest bulletin regional estimates are included for the first time.

Delivery: News/Press Release and hardcopy publication with diskette
Frequency: Annually
Price: £15.00 including postage

Available from
Small Firms Statistics Unit
Level 2
Department of Trade and Industry
St Marys House, c/o Moorfoot
Sheffield S1 4PQ
Tel: 0114 259 7538;
Email: ian.dale@SFSH-Sheffield.dti.gov.uk

Sources from which data for this product are obtained
IDBR and LFS

Small and Medium Enterprise (SME) Statistics for the United Kingdom (Statistical Bulletins)
Department of Trade and Industry

Bulletin on enterprises in the UK. Contains data on the numbers of enterprises in the UK, with analysis of size class, employment and turnover by industry.

Frequency: Annually (twice a year in 1995 and 1997)
Price: £3.00

Available from
Small Firms Statistics Unit
Level 2
Department of Trade and Industry
St Marys House, c/o Moorfoot
Sheffield S1 4PQ
Tel: 0114 259 7538;
Email: ian.dale@SFSH-Sheffield.dti.gov.uk

UK Business in Europe
Office for National Statistics

Economic and business comparisons of EU countries.

Contains a wide range of macro-economics, business sector and business statistics.

Frequency: One-off
Price: £34.95
ISBN: 0 11 620722 1

Available from
TSO Publications Centre and Bookshops
Please see Annex B for full address details.

See also:
In this chapter:
Analysis from the Inter-Departmental Business Register *(12.12)*
Engineering Sales and Orders Digest *(12.18)*
Size Analysis of UK Businesses (Business Monitor PA1003) *(12.12)*
UK Directory of Manufacturing Businesses CD-ROM *(12.18)*

In other chapters:
Financial Statistics (see the Economy chapter)
IDB Annual Report - Northern Ireland (see the Economy chapter)
Judicial Statistics England and Wales Annual Report (see the Crime and Justice chapter)
Labour Market Trends (see the Labour Market chapter)
Nomis® (see the Websites and Electronic Services chapter)

Office for National Statistics Databank (see the Websites and Electronic Services chapter)
UK Balance of Payments (First Release) (see the Economy chapter)
United Kingdom Balance of Payments - the Pink Book (see the Economy chapter)

12.16 Distribution and Service Trades

BFI Handbook - Produced Annually
British Film Institute

Contains statistical information on film and TV to provide a summary on the broadcast media's performance over the year (with some time series information). The Handbook is produced annually, (first one: 1993). Target market would be the industries themselves. The Handbook has 50 pages of general statistics and text on the broadcast media, then deals with reference lists of interest to the industries (such as film company addresses).

Delivery: Periodic Release
Frequency: Annually
Price: £17.99
ISBN: 0 85170 652 5

Available from
GB Film, TV and Video Industries Enquiries
British Film Institute
21, Stephen Street
London W1P 2LN
Tel: 020 7255 1444

Sources from which data for this product are obtained
Film, Television and Video Industries - GB

Distribution and Services Trades
Office for National Statistics

Provides quarterly information on turnover of various Distribution and Service industries at the three digit level of the UK Standard Industrial Classification.

Delivery: News/Press Release
Frequency: Quarterly
Price: £12.00 annual subscription.

Available from
Christine Colling
Room 1.467
Office for National Statistics
Government Buildings
Cardiff Road
Newport
Gwent
South Wales NP9 1XG
Tel: 01633 812180;
Email: chris.colling@ons.gov.uk

(The) Foodservice Industry Report
Office for National Statistics; sponsored in association with the Booker Foodservice Group

This collaborative report pools 1995/96 data made available by both the Booker Foodservice Group and the ONS which is relevant to the UK Catering Industry. It provides market information and an analysis of activities and trends within the food service industry relevant to manufacturers, caterers, hoteliers and food consultants. The report contains a summary of key socio-economic trends, inflation and the Catering Price Index. It also provides an overview by sector - hotels, pubs, restaurants, leisure, snacking, staff restaurants. Further features cover key products used by each sector, the significance of de-skilling for suppliers, and the EC and the impact of packaging directives.

Frequency: One-off
Price: £395.00 (reduced from the original price of £495.00)
ISBN: 0 11 620951 8

Available from
TSO Publications Centre and Bookshops
Please see Annex B for full address details.

GB Cinema Exhibitors (News Release)
Office for National Statistics

Latest statistics on the cinema exhibition sector. Contains data relating to the cinema exhibition sector on number of sites, number of screens, number of admission tickets sold, gross box office takings and payments for film hire.

Delivery: News/Press Release
Frequency: Quarterly
Price: £12.00 annual subscription

Available from
Jon Darke
Room 1.473
Office for National Statistics
Government Buildings
Cardiff Road
Newport
Gwent
South Wales NP9 1XG
Tel: 01633 812959;
Email: jon.darke@ons.gov.uk

Sources from which data for this product are obtained
GB Cinema Exhibitors Inquiry

Northern Ireland Annual Distribution and Service Inquiries
Department of Economic Development

Data from the annual business inquiries covers retailing, wholesaling and dealing, motor trades, service trades and catering and allied trades. Within each of these data is obtained on total turnover, stocks, capital expenditure, persons engaged and employment costs.

Delivery: Periodic Release
Frequency: Annually
Price: Free

Available from
Clare Alexander
Statistics Research Branch
Department of Economic Development
Netherleigh
Massey Avenue
Belfast BT4 2JP
Tel: 028 9052 9525; Fax: 028 9052 9549;
Email: clare.alexander@dedni.gov.uk

Sources from which data for this product are obtained
Annual Business Inquiries: Northern Ireland

Retail Sales Index (First Release)
Office for National Statistics

Retail sales statistics. Contains a first estimate of retail sales index numbers on volume of retail sales seasonally adjusted and value of retail sales not seasonally adjusted for all retailers and the following broad group headings: predominantly food stores, total predominantly non-food stores, non-specialised stores, textile clothing and footwear stores, household goods stores, other stores, and non-store retailing and repair.

Delivery: First Release
Frequency: Monthly
Price: £45.00 annual subscription

Available from
ONS Press Office
Office for National Statistics
Please see Annex B for full address details

Sources from which data for this product are obtained
Retail Sales Inquiry - GB

Sector Review: Motor Trades
Office for National Statistics

Latest statistics on the motor trades sector. Contains data on details of number of businesses turnover and purchases, stocks, capital expenditure, value added, employment costs and taxes and levies.

Delivery: Hardcopy publication - sector review
Frequency: Annually
Price: Single issue £39.50
ISBN: 0 11 621041 9

Available from
TSO Publications Centre and Bookshops
Please see Annex B for full address details.

Sources from which data for this product are obtained
Annual Motor Trade Inquiry

Sector Review: Catering and Allied Trades
Office for National Statistics

Latest statistics on the catering sector. Contains data relating to the catering sector, including number of businesses, turnover, taxes and levies, stocks, capital expenditure, purchases, employment costs and value added.

Delivery: Hardcopy publication - sector review
Frequency: Annually
Price: £39.50
ISBN: 0 11 621042 7

Available from
TSO Publications Centre and Bookshops
Please see Annex B for full address details.

Sources from which data for this product are obtained
Annual Catering and Allied Trades Inquiry

Sector Review: Retailing (Formerly Business Monitor SDA25)
Office for National Statistics

Latest statistics on the retailing sector. Contains data relating to the retailing sector, including number of businesses, total turnover, outlets, taxes and levies, stocks, capital expenditure, purchases, employment costs and value added.

Delivery: Hardcopy publication - sector review
Frequency: Annually
Price: £39.50
ISBN: 0 11 621038 9

Available from
TSO Publications Centre and Bookshops
Please see Annex B for full address details.

Sources from which data for this product are obtained
Annual Retailing Inquiry

Sector Review: Service Trades
Office for National Statistics

Latest statistics on the service trades sector. Contains a wide range of official statistics relating to numerous activities, classified to the service trades sector. It includes the number of businesses, turnover, capital expenditure, purchases, work in progress, employment costs, value added, and taxes and levies.

Delivery: Hardcopy publication - sector review
Frequency: Annually
Price: £39.50
ISBN: 0 11 621043 5

Available from
TSO Publications Centre and Bookshops
Please see Annex B for full address details.

Sources from which data for this product are obtained
Annual Service Trades Inquiry

Sector Review: Wholesaling
Office for National Statistics

Latest statistics on the wholesaling sector. Contains statistics on number of businesses, total turnover, stocks, purchases, employment costs, capital expenditure, value added, and taxes and levies.

Delivery: Hardcopy publication - sector review
Frequency: Annually
Price: £39.50
ISBN: 0 11 621040 0

Available from
TSO Publications Centre and Bookshops
Please see Annex B for full address details.

Sources from which data for this product are obtained
Annual Wholesaling and Dealing Inquiry

Service Sector Retail Sales - SDM 28
Office for National Statistics

Delivery: Periodic Release
Frequency: Monthly
Price: By subscription @ £110.00 per annum
ISSN: 1369-0469

Available from
Harry Duff
Office for National Statistics
Government Buildings
Cardiff Road
Newport
Gwent
South Wales
Tel: 01633 812600;
Email: harry.duff@ons.gov.uk

Sources from which data for this product are obtained
Value of retailers sales by commodity at current prices (not seasonally adjusted)

Service Sector: Retail Sales (Business Monitor SDM 28)
Office for National Statistics

Detailed information on retail sales. Contains tables on the volume of retail sales at 1995 prices (seasonally adjusted), value of retail sales at current prices (not seasonally adjusted), volume of retail sales at 1995 prices (not seasonally adjusted), value of retail sales at current prices (not seasonally adjusted - analysis by detailed kinds of business), and year-to-date value of retail sales at current prices (not seasonally adjusted).

Delivery: Hardcopy publication - Monitor
Frequency: Monthly
Price: £110.00 annual subscription, £15.00 single issue
ISSN: 1369-0469

Available from
ONS Direct
Please see Annex B for full address details.

Sources from which data for this product are obtained
Retail Sales Inquiry - GB

See also:
In this chapter:
Analysis from the Inter-Departmental Business Register *(12.12)*
Size Analysis of UK Businesses (Business Monitor PA1003) *(12.12)*
Stockbuilding Business Monitor *(12.18)*

In other chapters:
Economic Trends (see the Economy chapter)
Economic Trends Annual Supplement (see the Economy chapter)
Labour Market Trends (see the Labour Market chapter)
Quarterly National Accounts (First Release) (see the Economy chapter)
Town Centres: Defining Boundaries for Statistical Monitoring (see the Government Statistics - General chapter)
UK Output, Income and Expenditure (First Release) (see the Economy chapter)
United Kingdom National Accounts - the Blue Book (see the Economy chapter)
United Kingdom National Accounts, Sources and Methods (see the Economy chapter)

12.17 Energy/Fuel Production and Supply, Water Supply

Development of the Oil & Gas Resources of the UK (The Brown Book)
Department of Trade and Industry

More commonly known as the 'Brown Book' this is the pre-eminent source of information for those with a professional or academic interest in the UK's oil and gas resources. Contains information about the upstream industry: including information on the licensing and fiscal regimes governing it, production and remaining reserve levels. There is also detailed information on the UK's offshore environmental regulations.

Delivery: Periodic Release
Frequency: Annually
Price: £45.00
ISBN: 0 11 515463 9
ISSN: 0629 3429

Available from
TSO Publications Centre and Bookshops
Please see Annex B for full address details.

Sources from which data for this product are obtained
DTI Exploration and Appraisal Survey, Mineral Oil and Natural Gas - UK, PIA - Oil Refining and Distribution, PPRS - Oil and Gas Production and UK Continental Shelf Capital Investment Intentions Survey

Digest of United Kingdom Energy Statistics
Department of Trade and Industry

Contains data for latest three years on the production and consumption of overall energy, and separately of coal and other solid /fuels, crude oil, petroleum products, gas and electricity; overseas trade in volume and value terms, in all fuels, and separately in crude oil, petroleum products and coal; estimated values of fuels purchased, average prices paid for fuels, and rates of duty on petroleum products. A limited amount of data are also available for longer periods, mainly back to 1960.

Delivery: Periodic Release
Frequency: Annually
Price: The 1999 edition costs £32.95
ISBN: 0 11 5154639
ISSN: 0307-0603

Available from
TSO Publications Centre and Bookshops
Please see Annex B for full address details.

Sources from which data for this product are obtained
Domestic Quarterly Fuel Inquiry, DTI Exploration and Appraisal Survey, Fuel Prices - UK, Fuels: Foreign Trade System, Mineral Oil and Natural Gas - UK, PIA - Oil Refining and Distribution, Oil and Gas Production, Quarterly Capital Expenditure Inquiry, Suppliers of Gas, Survey of Autogeneration and Combined Heat and Power, Survey of Coal Producers, Survey of Major Power Producers and Electricity Supply and Distribution, Survey of Petroleum Product Prices, Survey of Renewable Energy, Survey of Solid Fuel Producers, and UK Continental Shelf Capital Investment Intentions Survey.

Electricity Prices 1990-98
Office for National Statistics

Part of Eurostats Energy and Industry theme (Theme 4) Series D: Studies and research. This study contains the most recent prices, valid from 1995 to 1997 together with prices for 1990 (base year for comparisons). This study gives for the three price levels concerned prices in national currencies, ECU (average value for January/July) and Purchasing Power Standard (PPS) (annual value as estimates for 1998)

Delivery: Periodic Release
Frequency: Annually
Price: £18.00
ISBN: 92 828 5320 9
ISSN:

Available from
TSO Publications Centre and Bookshops
Please see Annex B for full address details.

Energy Paper 66: Energy Consumption in the UK
Department of Trade and Industry

This publication brings together, for the first time, statistics from a variety of sources to produce a comprehensive review of energy consumption in the UK since the 1970s and contains chapters which look in depth at the various sectors. It contains 133 pages and includes information on the main trends in energy consumption since 1970; an analysis of the factors driving the changes in energy consumption; the impact of increasing activity; increased efficiency; and structural change in the economy. There are detailed sector chapters covering energy use in the industry, the domestic, transport and the services sectors.

Delivery: Ad hoc/One-off Release
Frequency: One-off
ISBN: 0 11 515439 6

Available from
TSO Publications Centre and Bookshops
Please see Annex B for full address details.

Sources from which data for this product are obtained
Domestic Quarterly Fuel Inquiry, DTI Exploration and Appraisal Survey, Fuel Prices - UK, Fuels: Foreign Trade System, Mineral Oil and Natural Gas - UK, PIA - Oil Refining and Distribution, Oil and Gas Production, Quarterly Capital Expenditure Inquiry, Suppliers of Gas, Survey of Autogeneration and Combined Heat and Power, Survey of Coal Producers, Survey of Major Power Producers and Electricity Supply and Distribution, Survey of Petroleum Product Prices, Survey of Renewable Energy, Survey of Solid Fuel Producers, and UK Continental Shelf Capital Investment Intentions Survey.

Energy Prices 1985-98
Eurostat

The aim of this statistical document is to summarise as succinctly as possible the recent price information for all the principal energy sources.

Delivery: Periodic Release
Frequency: Annually
Price: £16.00
ISBN: 92 828 5673 9

Available from
TSO Publications Centre and Bookshops
Please see Annex B for full address details.

(The) Energy Report Volume 1: Transforming Markets
Department of Trade and Industry

Illustrates the direction of the Government's energy policy, including protection of the environment and fuel poverty. There are also sections on environmental and international issues, energy demand trends, maintaining security of supply in a competitive market, and changes to the structure and ownership of the industry. Chapters on each industry set out developments over the last year, including regulatory changes and price movements. Statistical appendices contain data on the production and consumption of energy; estimated values of fuels purchased, average prices paid for fuels, and rates of duty on petroleum products. There are appendices on the role of energy industries in the UK, economy, energy demand, energy prices and also energy related atmospheric emissions. The 1998 edition contained 300 pages.

Delivery: Periodic Release
Frequency: Annually
Price: Price £38.00
ISBN: 0 11 515446 9
ISSN: 0629-3429

Available from
TSO Publications Centre and Bookshops
Please see Annex B for full address details.

Sources from which data for this product are obtained
Domestic Quarterly Fuel Inquiry, DTI Exploration and Appraisal Survey, Fuel Prices - UK, Fuels: Foreign Trade System, Mineral Oil and Natural Gas - UK, PIA - Oil Refining and Distribution, Oil and Gas Production, Quarterly Capital Expenditure Inquiry, Suppliers of Gas, Survey of Autogeneration and Combined Heat and Power, Survey of Coal Producers, Survey of Major Power Producers and Electricity Supply and Distribution, Survey of Petroleum Product Prices, Survey of Renewable Energy, Survey of Solid Fuel Producers, and UK Continental Shelf Capital Investment Intentions Survey.

Energy Sector Indicators
Department of Trade and Industry

The energy sector indicators have been published in response to a set of Indicators of Sustainable Development for the UK that were published in 1996 by the Department of the Environment. This publication contains a full set of energy indicators covering the depletion of fossil fuels, capacity of nuclear and renewable energy sources, energy use by sector and fuel prices.

Delivery: Periodic Release
Frequency: Annually
Price: Free

Available from
EPTAC (Energy Information and Statistics)
Department of Trade and Industry
Please see Annex B for full address details

Sources from which data for this product are obtained
Domestic Quarterly Fuel Inquiry, DTI Exploration and Appraisal Survey, Fuel Prices - UK, PIA - Oil Refining and Distribution, Oil and Gas Production, Quarterly Capital Expenditure Inquiry, Suppliers of Gas, Survey of Autogeneration and Combined Heat and Power, Survey of Coal Producers, Survey of Major Power Producers and Electricity Supply and Distribution, Survey of Petroleum Product Prices, Survey of Renewable Energy, Survey of Solid Fuel Producers, and UK Continental Shelf Capital Investment Intentions Survey.

Energy Trends
Department of Trade and Industry

Statistical bulletin with commentary and tables on production and consumption of fuels in the UK, prices of fuels and overseas trade in fuels. Each issue also has a supplementary article on a particular aspect of energy. Contains data for latest three months on the production and consumption of overall energy, and separately of coal, crude oil, petroleum products, gas and electricity; and quarterly data on overseas trade in volume and value terms, in all fuels, and separately in crude oil, petroleum

products and coal; average prices paid for fuels by manufacturing industry, British Gas and major electricity producers; industrial and domestic fuel price indices; and typical retail prices for motor spirit (petrol), Derv fuel and petroleum products used for domestic heating.

Delivery: Periodic Release
Frequency: Monthly
Price: The 1999/2000 annual subscription in UK was £37.00
ISSN: 0308-1222

Available from
EPTAC (Energy Information and Statistics)
Department of Trade and Industry
Please see Annex B for full address details.

Sources from which data for this product are obtained
Fuel Prices - UK; Mineral Oil and Natural Gas - UK, Domestic Quarterly Fuel Inquiry, DTI Exploration and Appraisal Survey, Fuels: Foreign Trade System, PIA - Oil Refining and Distribution, Oil and Gas Production, Quarterly Capital Expenditure Inquiry, Suppliers of Gas, Survey of Autogeneration and Combined Heat and Power, Survey of Coal Producers, Survey of Major Power Producers and Electricity Supply and Distribution, Survey of Petroleum Product Prices, Survey of Renewable Energy, Survey of Solid Fuel Producers, and UK Continental Shelf Capital Investment Intentions Survey.

Gas Prices 1990-97
Eurostat

This document provides gas prices in national currencies/GJ for a wide range of both domestic and industrial consumers in over 30 locations within the EU, it also contains comparative tables expressed in ECU/GJ and deflated PPS/GJ.

Delivery: Periodic Release
Frequency: Annually
Price: £18.00

Available from
TSO Publications Centre and Bookshops
Please see Annex B for full address details.

UK Energy in Brief
Department of Trade and Industry

This booklet summarises the latest statistics on energy production, consumption and prices and environmental emissions in the United Kingdom. The figures it contains are taken from the latest edition of the "Digest of UK Energy Statistics" . It uses a clear and straightforward format, largely coloured charts and graphs. Although useful for specialists it has been designed with the general reader in mind, whether in business or education. It contains 28 pages.

Delivery: Periodic Release
Frequency: Bi-annually
Price: Available free of charge from the DTI by calling 020 7215 2697. Also available on the INTERNET at http://www.dti.gov.uk/epa.

Available from
EPTAC (Energy Information and Statistics)
Department of Trade and Industry
Please see Annex B for full address details.

Sources from which data for this product are obtained
Domestic Quarterly Fuel Inquiry, DTI Exploration and Appraisal Survey, Fuel Prices - UK, Fuels: Foreign Trade System, PIA - Oil Refining and Distribution, Oil and Gas Production, Quarterly Capital Expenditure Inquiry, Suppliers of Gas, Survey of Autogeneration and Combined Heat and Power, Survey of Coal Producers, Survey of Major Power Producers and Electricity Supply and Distribution, Survey of Petroleum Product Prices, Survey of Renewable Energy, Survey of Solid Fuel Producers, and UK Continental Shelf Capital Investment Intentions Survey.

See also:
In this chapter:
Analysis from the Inter-Departmental Business Register *(12.12)*
Size Analysis of UK Businesses (Business Monitor PA1003) *(12.12)*
Telecommunications Industry - Market Information - UK *(12.22)*
UK Consumption of Raw Materials *(12.18)*

In other chapters:
Economic Trends (see the Economy chapter)
Indicators of Sustainable Development - United Kingdom (see the Environment chapter)
Review of UK Environmental Expenditure (1993) (see the Environment chapter)
United Kingdom National Accounts - the Blue Book (see the Economy chapter)

12.18 Manufacturing and Production Industries

Aerospace and Electronics Cost Indices (Business Monitor MM19)
Office for National Statistics

Price indices for materials, fuel, earnings and combined costs.

Price: Annual subscription £85.00

Available from
TSO Publications Centre and Bookshops
Please see Annex B for full address details.

Sources from which data for this product are obtained
Producer Price Indices - UK

(The) Electronics Industry in Scotland (Statistical Bulletin)
Scottish Executive

Details information on the electronics industry in Scotland, mainly employment, output, productivity and capital investment. Contains data on employment, country of ownership, output, productivity and capital investment by electronics industry sectors, employment shares by country of ownership and capital expenditure by assets.

Delivery: Periodic Release
Frequency: Annual
Price: £2.00
ISBN: 0 7480 0971 X
ISSN: 0264-1151 / 1456 220 X

Available from
TSO Publications Centre and Bookshops
Please see Annex B for full address details.

Sources from which data for this product are obtained
Index of Production - Scotland; Scottish Production Database

Engineering Sales and Orders Digest
Office for National Statistics

Data on engineering sales and orders.

Frequency: Monthly

Available from
Mark Williams
Office for National Statistics
Government Buildings
Cardiff Road
Newport
Gwent
South Wales
Tel: 01633 812149

Sources from which data for this product are obtained
Monthly Sales Inquiries - UK

Engineering Turnover and Orders (First Release)
Office for National Statistics

Latest monthly figures on sales and orders.

Frequency: Monthly
Price: Free

Available from
Mark Williams
Office for National Statistics
Government Buildings
Cardiff Road
Newport
Gwent
South Wales
Tel: 01633 812149

Sources from which data for this product are obtained
Monthly Sales Inquiries - UK

Exports of Northern Ireland Manufacturing Companies 1990
Northern Ireland Economic Research Centre

Available from
Maureen O'Reilly
Northern Ireland Economic Research Centre
46-48 University Road
Belfast
Tel: 028 9026 1800

Index of Industrial Production for Scotland (News Release)
Scottish Executive

Provisional estimates of output in the production industries in Scotland for relevant year and quarter, in index form at constant 1995 prices. Contains output indices in industry sector and production sectors for the relevant year, at constant 1995 prices.

Delivery: News/Press Release
Frequency: Quarterly
Price: Free

Available from
Hugh McAloon
Scottish Executive
Tel: 0141 242 5497;
Email: hugh.mcaloon@scotland.gov.uk
or
TSO Publications Centre and Bookshops
Please see Annex B for full address details.

Sources from which data for this product are obtained
Index of Production - Scotland

Index of Industrial Production for Scotland: Detailed Industry Series (Statistical Bulletin)
Scottish Executive

Annual output indices for 118 industry sectors in Scotland, classified to 1992 Standard Industrial Classification. Contains a very detailed breakdown of industrial output, in index form based on 1995 = 100.

Available from
Hugh McAloon
Scottish Executive
Tel: 0141 242 5497;
Email: hugh.mcaloon@scotland.gov.uk
or
TSO Publications Centre and Bookshops
Please see Annex B for full address details.

Sources from which data for this product are obtained
Index of Production - Scotland

Index of Production (First Release)
Office for National Statistics

Production indices at aggregate and industry level. Contains data on mining, quarrying, manufacturing, electricity, gas and water industries classified to Sections C, D and E of the SIC (92) series. Also at activity heading (four-digit) level covering energy and manufacturing industries classified to Divisions 1-4 of the SIC (92).

Delivery: First Release
Frequency: Monthly
Price: £36.00 annual subscription

Available from
Mark Williams
Office for National Statistics
Government Buildings
Cardiff Road
Newport
Gwent
South Wales
Tel: 01633 812149

Sources from which data for this product are obtained
Brewers, Distillers and Maltsters - UK; Engine Production Inquiry - UK; Glucose and Starch Production - UK; Index of Production - UK; Monthly Sales Inquiries - UK; Raw Sugar - GB; Refined Sugar - GB; Wheat Milled and Flour Production - UK

International Steel Statistics Country Books
Iron and Steel Statistics Bureau

Annual books detailing the steel industry for each country.

Frequency: Annually

Available from
Phil Hunt
Iron and Steel Statistics Bureau
Tel: 020 7343 3916;
Email: p.hunt@issb.co.uk

(The) Manufacturing Sector in Scotland (Statistical Bulletin)
Scottish Executive

Detailed results from the Annual Census of Production which mainly covers employment and financial details on turnover, sales, expenditure, stocks and capital investment. Contains detailed analysis at manufacturing industry level, employment sizebands, Scottish local authorities, and local enterprise companies and compares Scottish and the UK manufacturing industries. Presentation of main aggregated results generated for the Scottish Manufacturing sector from the Scottish Production database incl. Gross output, value added, capital expenditure, labour costs, foreign ownership etc.

Delivery: Periodic Release
Frequency: Annual
Price: £2.00
ISBN: 0 7480 7063 X
ISSN: 0264-1151/1456 220X

Available from
TSO Publications Centre and Bookshops
Please see Annex B for full address details.

Sources from which data for this product are obtained
Scottish Production Database

Machine Tools (First Release)
Office for National Statistics

Latest data on machine tools orders and sales.

Delivery: First Release
Frequency: Monthly
Price: £36.00 annual subscription

Available from
Mark Williams
Office for National Statistics
Government Buildings
Cardiff Road
Newport
Gwent
South Wales
Tel: 01633 812149

Sources from which data for this product are obtained
Monthly Sales Inquiries - UK

MM17 - Price Index Numbers for Current Cost Accounting
Office for National Statistics

The MM17 is a business monitor containing detailed indices for revaluation of assets and stocks, it is a comprehensive guide to capital replacement costs.

Delivery: Hardcopy publication, Databank
Frequency: Monthly
Price: £120.00 per annum

Available from
TSO Publications Centre and Bookshops
Please see Annex B for full address details.

Sources from which data for this product are obtained
Producer Price Inquiry
Retail Price Index

MM19 - Aerospace and Electronic Cost Indices
Office for National Statistics

The Business Monitor MM19 contains combined case indices relevant to the aerospace and electronics industries, for materials and fuels purchased, hourly earnings of adult manual workers, salaries and general expenses. The indices are used by the government and business as an authoritative source of information.

Delivery: Hardcopy publication
Frequency: Monthly
Price: £120.00 per annum

Available from
TSO Publications Centre and Bookshops
Please see Annex B for full address details.

Sources from which data for this product are obtained
Producer Price Inquiry, Average Earnings Inquiry

MM22 Producer Price Indices
Office for National Statistics

Tables 1 to 6, cover manufactured goods and include input & output Producer Price Indices, Import Price Indices, and Export Price Indices. Table 7 contains Price Indices of Corporate Services, which relate to the services provided by UK companies to business (and government) customers in the UK. Coverage of these is continuing to expand.

Delivery: Hardcopy publication, databank
Frequency: Monthly
Price: £230.00

Available from
Producer Price Inquiry, Corporate Services Price Inquiry

Northern Ireland Index of Production
Department of Economic Development - Northern Ireland

Press notice with the latest production and manufacturing indices for Northern Ireland. Contains seasonally adjusted indices for the production industry, manufacturing industry and main manufacturing sectors. A market sector analysis provides indices for the production of investment, intermediate and consumer goods. The Northern Ireland Index of Production is designed to provide a general measure of changes in the output of the production industries.

Delivery: News/Press Release
Frequency: Quarterly
Price: Free

Available from
Michele Manderson
Statistics Research Branch
Room 110
Department of Economic Development - Northern Ireland
Netherleigh
Massey Avenue
Belfast BT4 2JP
Tel: 028 9052 9511

Sources from which data for this product are obtained
Index of Production - Northern Ireland

PACSTAT
Office for National Statistics

A comprehensive CD which allows the manipulation of production and construction data using a variety of selection criteria. Ideal for studying manufacturing as a whole, comparing industry sectors and showing variations in employment, output and sales. Separate Industry results from the Annual Business Inquiry (previously Annual Census of Production & Construction) for latest and previous years. Data on the CD-ROM is multi-dimensional and can be selected in a variety of ways, such as employment sizeband, regional, predefined sets or a chosen combination of variables. Once selections have been made the information can then be viewed in tables, charts or maps.

Delivery: Periodic Release
Frequency: Annually
Price: £350.00 (inc.VAT) per copy
ISBN: 1 85774 274 5

Available from
ONS Direct
Please see Annex B for full address details.

Sources from which data for this product are obtained
Annual Business Inquiry (Production and Construction) - UK

PRA 1 to 90 (Product Sales and Trade Annual Reports)
Office for National Statistics

The Product Sales and Trade AR series are annual reports based on PRODCOM data collected from UK manufacturers by the Office for National Statistics and export and import data supplied by HM Customs and Excise. The reports include data on UK production (manufacturer sales), exports, imports, the balances of trade and net supply to the UK market. Data are shown in both value and volume terms together with average prices for all categories. The 89 AR reports cover around 3,400 products from about 200 industries. The reports are compiled from data obtained by surveying UK manufacturers on an annual basis covering approximately 25,000 businesses. Data are available on the value and volume of UK manufacturers' product sales, merchanted goods, work done, sales of waste products and residues, and all other income. Also total turnover for the industry. Annual PRODCOM began in 1993 (replacing the annual sales inquiry (ASI) started in 1989) and the data is classified to the SIC(92) Industrial Classification), PRODCOM data can be directly matched with the trade data collected by HM Custom and Excise. This is published alongside the PRODCOM data giving a complete picture of the market for each product.

Delivery: Periodic Release
Frequency: Annually
Price: The prices for the individual annual reports range from £50.00 to £90.00. A full set of annual reports is discounted to £2,000.00 (a full set of annual and quarterly reports costs £2,500.00).

ISBN: Various

Available from
UK PRODCOM General Inquiries
Office for National Statistics
Please see Annex B for full address details.

Sources from which data for this product are obtained
PRODucts of the European COMmunity (PRODCOM INQUIRY)

Price Index Numbers of Current Cost Accounting (Business Monitor)
Office for National Statistics

Available from
Andrew Allen
Office for National Statistics
Government Buildings
Cardiff Road
Gwent
South Wales
Tel: 01633 813133

Sources from which data for this product are obtained
Producer Price Indices - UK

PRODCOM: Bespoke Requests
Office for National Statistics

Bespoke customer requests such as individual products, specific aggregates of Prodcom data or specific formats are available. Each request is considered separately. Requests can be ad hoc or regular.

Delivery: Other
Frequency: Ad hoc
Price: The price depends on the individual request and is based on the cost of the Prodcom data and also the resources required to implement the request.

Available from
Debra Prestwood
Office for National Statistics
Government Buildings
Cardiff Road
Gwent
South Wales
Tel: 01633 812029;
Email: debra.prestwood@ons.gov.uk

Sources from which data for this product are obtained
PRODucts of the European COMmunity (PRODCOM INQUIRY)

Producer Price Index (First Release)
Office for National Statistics

A comprehensive selection of data on input and output index series. Contains producer price indices of materials and fuels purchased and output of manufacturing industry by broad sector.

Delivery: Press Release
Frequency: Monthly
Price: Annual subscription £36.00

Available from
ONS Press Office
Office for National Statistics
Please see Annex B for full address details.

Sources from which data for this product are obtained
Producer Price Indices - UK

Producer Price Indices (Business Monitor MM22)
Office for National Statistics

A comprehensive selection of data on input and output index series. Contains producer price indices of materials and fuels purchased, commodities produced in the UK, commodities wholly or mainly imported into the UK and output of manufacturing industry by broad sector.

Price: Annual subscription £215.00

Available from
TSO Publications Centre and Bookshops
Please see Annex B for full address details.

Sources from which data for this product are obtained
Producer Price Indices - UK

Profitability of UK Companies (First Release)
Office for National Statistics

Data on capital employed by Private Non-Financial Corporations (PNFCs). Contains annual, net and gross rates of return (expressed as percentages) on capital used by PNFCs. Sub-sector data are included covering UK Continental Shelf (UKCS) PNFCs, non-UKCS PNFCs and manufacturing PNFCs. Underlying data are provided for the total PNFCs sector and the sub-sectors for gross operating surplus, capital consumption, net operating surplus, and gross and net average capital employed.

Delivery: First Release
Frequency: Annual

Available from
Richard Walton
Zone D3/03
Office for National Statistics
1 Drummond Gate
London SW1V 2QQ

Sources from which data for this product are obtained
Rates of Return for Private Non-Financial Corporations (PNFCs)

PRQ 1 to 35 (Product Sales and Trade Quarterly Reports)
Office for National Statistics

The Product Sales and Trade QR series are quarterly reports based on PRODCOM data collected from UK manufacturers by the Office for National Statistics and export and import data supplied by HM Customs and Excise. The reports include data on UK production (manufacturer sales), exports, imports, the balances of trade and net supply to the UK market. Data are shown in both value and volume terms together with average prices for all categories. The 35 AR reports cover around 1,400 products from about 50 industries. The reports are compiled from data obtained by surveying UK manufacturers on a quarterly basis and covers approximately 4,500 businesses. Data are available on the value and volume of UK manufacturers' product sales, merchanted goods, work done, sales of waste products and residues, and all other income. Also total turnover for the industry. PRODCOM began in 1993 (replacing the quarterly sales inquiry (QSI) started in 1969) and the data is classified to the SIC(92) Industrial Classification), PRODCOM data can be directly matched with the trade data collected by HM Custom and Excise. This is published alongside the PRODCOM data giving a complete picture of the market for each product.

Delivery: Periodic Release
Frequency: Quarterly
Price: The prices for the individual quarterly reports range from £60.00 to £150.00. A full set of quarterly reports are discounted to £1,000.00 (a full set of annual and quarterly reports costs £2,500.00).
ISBN: Various

Available from
UK PRODCOM General Inquiries
Office for National Statistics
Please see Annex B for full address details.

Sources from which data for this product are obtained
PRODucts of the European COMmunity (PRODCOM INQUIRY)

Sector Review - Annual
Office for National Statistics

Data from 30 different statistical inquiry sources are brought together to give a complete picture of specific industry sectors. Includes topics such as production, productivity, employment, imports, exports. Includes information on: employment, imports, exports, productivity, production, etc. Annual titles: Wood products, furniture and other manufacturing. Glass, ceramics and building products; Electrical and optical equipment; Vehicles and other transport; Metals and metal products; Machinery and domestic appliances; Paper, publishing and printing.

Delivery: Periodic Release
Frequency: Annually
Price: Annual reports - £39.50
ISBN: Various

Available from
TSO Publications Centre and Bookshops
Please see Annex B for full address details.

Sector Review - Quarterly
Office for National Statistics

Data from 30 different statistical inquiry sources are brought together to give a complete picture of specific industry sectors. Includes topics such as production, productivity, employment, imports and exports. Quarterly titles include: Food, drink and tobacco; Clothing, footwear and leather goods; Chemicals, rubber and plastic products.

Delivery: Periodic Release
Frequency: Quarterly
Price: £130.00 pa or £40.00 per single copy.
ISBN: Various

Available from
TSO Publications Centre and Bookshops
Please see Annex B for full address details.

Steel Industry UK Customs Tariff & EU Nomenclature
Iron and Steel Statistics Bureau

Guide to the 8 digit tariff codes on products relating to the steel industry.

ISBN: 0 90280006

Available from
Phil Hunt
Iron and Steel Statistics Bureau
Tel: 020 7343 3916;
Email: p.hunt@issb.co.uk

Stockbuilding Business Monitor
Office for National Statistics

Provides details of inventory statistics. A comprehensive publication containing tables, graphs and commentary on quarterly inventory changes within industry sectors at book value and constant prices (seasonally adjusted and unadjusted). Tables illustrating stock to output ratios are also listed. Special articles and features are included in every publication.

Delivery: Periodic Release
Frequency: Quarterly
Price: By subscription at £70.00 per annum or £24.00 per single issue.
ISSN: 1464 - 6641

Available from
Steve Lake or Kevin Buckthought
Room 1.301
Office for National Statistics
Government Buildings
Cardiff Road
Newport
South Wales NP10 8XG
Tel: 01633 812351; Email: steve.lake@ons.gov.uk
Tel: 01633 813121;
Email: kevin.buckthought@ons.gov.uk

Sources from which data for this product are obtained
Construction Inventories - UK; Motor Traders' Inventories - UK; Retailers' Inventories - UK; Wholesalers' and Dealers' Inventories - UK; Production Inventories - UK

Summary Volume - Production and Construction (Business Monitor PA1002)
Office for National Statistics

Annual Business Inquiry (previously Annual Census of Production and Construction) published at SIC(92) two, three and five digit levels. The 200+ page volume (PA1002) contains data on employment, sales, outputs, costs, investments and stocks. Explanatory notes and definitions with data presented in table format. For example, data tables on: Outputs and costs by Group, Sections C-F; Employment and labour costs by Group, Sections C-F; Employment, wages and salaries, output and net capital expenditure by country and standard region by Subsection D.

Delivery: Periodic Release
Frequency: Annually
Price: Summary volume: £75.00.
ISBN: 0 11 536359 9
ISSN: 1463-3736

Available from
ONS Direct
Please see Annex B for full address details.

Sources from which data for this product are obtained
Annual Business Inquiry (Production and Construction) - UK; Annual Census of Production - Northern Ireland

UK Consumption of Raw Materials
Iron and Steel Statistics Bureau

Covering such materials as coal, coke, iron ore, fuels and fluxes used in steel making

Available from
Chris Edwards
Iron and Steel Statistics Bureau
Millbank Tower
21/24 Millbank
London
Tel: 020 7343 3900; Fax: 020 7343 3902;
Email: c.edwards@issb.co.uk

UK Directory of Manufacturing Businesses CD-ROM
Office for National Statistics

Contains the names, addresses and types of business for nearly 7000 UK manufacturers. Ideal for business locations analyses and mailing lists or files.

Delivery: Periodic Release
Frequency: Annually
Price: £95.00 excluding VAT
ISBN: 1 85774 267 2

Available from
ONS Direct
Please see Annex B for full address details.

Sources from which data for this product are obtained
Inter-Departmental Business Register

UK Iron and Steel Annual Statistics
Iron and Steel Statistics Bureau

Information on an annual basis covering all aspects of the UK steel industry.

Delivery: Periodic Release
Frequency: Annually

Available from
Chris Edwards
Iron and Steel Statistics Bureau
Millbank Tower
21/24 Millbank
London
Tel: 020 7343 3900; Fax: 020 7343 3902;
Email: c.edwards@issb.co.uk

UK Production of Finished Steel
Iron and Steel Statistics Bureau

Production figures classified by broad product group

Available from
Chris Edwards
Iron and Steel Statistics Bureau
Millbank Tower
21/24 Millbank
London
Tel: 020 7343 3900; Fax: 020 7343 3902;
Email: c.edwards@issb.co.uk

UK Steel Exports
Iron and Steel Statistics Bureau

Detailed information on steel and raw material exports.

Available from
Phil Hunt
Iron and Steel Statistics Bureau
Tel: 020 7343 3916;
Email: p.hunt@issb.co.uk

UK Steel Imports
Iron and Steel Statistics Bureau

Detailed information on steel and raw material imports

Available from
Phil Hunt
Iron and Steel Statistics Bureau
Tel: 020 7343 3916;
Email: p.hunt@issb.co.uk

UK Steel Production
Iron and Steel Statistics Bureau

Monthly brief on the production of UK crude steel with regional analysis.

Frequency: Monthly

Available from
Chris Edwards
Iron and Steel Statistics Bureau
Millbank Tower
21/24 Millbank
London
Tel: 020 7343 3900; Fax: 020 7343 3902;
Email: c.edwards@issb.co.uk

UK Steel Scrap Consumption
Iron and Steel Statistics Bureau

Available from
Chris Edwards
Iron and Steel Statistics Bureau
Millbank Tower
21/24 Millbank
London
Tel: 020 7343 3900; Fax: 020 7343 3902;
Email: c.edwards@issb.co.uk

UK Steel Stocks
Iron and Steel Statistics Bureau

Available from
Chris Edwards
Iron and Steel Statistics Bureau
Millbank Tower
21/24 Millbank
London
Tel: 020 7343 3900; Fax: 020 7343 3902;
Email: c.edwards@issb.co.uk

Welsh Index of Production and Construction
National Assembly for Wales

Quarterly press release giving the latest seasonally adjusted indices for Welsh production and construction, including mining and quarrying, manufacturing, electricity, gas and water supply. Also includes UK comparisons.

Delivery: News/Press Release
Frequency: Quarterly

Available from
Adrian Crompton
The National Assembly for Wales
Crown Building
Cathays Park
Cardiff
Tel: 029 2082 5033; Fax: 029 2082 5350;
statswales@gtnet.gov.uk

World Steel Exports - All Qualities
Iron and Steel Statistics Bureau

Quarterly Cumulative book on the export trade of 33 major steel producing countries, by product and market.

Frequency: Quarterly
ISSN: 0952-5734

Available from
Phil Hunt
Iron and Steel Statistics Bureau
Tel: 020 7343 3916;
Email: p.hunt@issb.co.uk

World Steel Statistics Monthly
Iron and Steel Statistics Bureau

Information on imports and exports, tonnes and prices on 27 Countries, including production summary

Frequency: Monthly
ISSN: 1359-4249

Available from
Phil Hunt
Iron and Steel Statistics Bureau
Tel: 020 7343 3916;
Email: p.hunt@issb.co.uk

See also:
In this chapter:
Analysis from the Inter-Departmental Business Register *(12.12)*
Northern Ireland Civil and Defence Expenditure on Research and Development During 1996 *(12.21)*
Size Analysis of UK Businesses (Business Monitor PA1003) *(12.12)*

In other chapters:
Economic Trends (see the Economy chapter)
Economic Trends Annual Supplement (see the Economy chapter)
Environmental Protection Expenditure by Industry (1995) (see the Environment chapter)
Northern Ireland Housing Statistics (see the Housing chapter)
Northern Ireland Transport Statistics 1997/98 (see the Transport, Travel and Tourism chapter)
Office for National Statistics Databank (see the Websites and Electronic Services chapter)
Quarterly National Accounts (First Release) (see the Economy chapter)
Review of UK Environmental Expenditure (1993) (see the Environment chapter)
Scottish Gross Domestic Product (News Release) (see the Economy chapter)
UK Output, Income and Expenditure (First Release) (see the Economy chapter)

United Kingdom National Accounts - the Blue Book (see the Economy chapter)
United Kingdom National Accounts, Sources and Methods (see the Economy chapter)
Welsh Economic Trends (see the Economy chapter)

12.19 Mineral Extraction, Mining, and Quarrying

Development of the Oil and Gas Resources of the United Kingdom
Department of Trade and Industry

Available from
Philip Beckett
Department of Trade and Industry
1 Victoria Street
London
Tel: 020 7215 5260

Sources from which data for this product are obtained
UK Minerals Industry

Primary Production - Mineral Extraction in Great Britain (Business Monitor PA1007)
Office for National Statistics

Latest information on minerals extraction. Contains data on the sales of chalk, clays, crushed rock, dolomite, granite, gypsum, limestone, ore minerals, peat, salt, sandstone, sand and gravel, slate plus a few minor minerals; and employment for each quarry type.

Delivery: Hardcopy publication
Frequency: Annual
Price: £25.00
ISBN: 0 11 537074 9

Available from
ONS Direct
Please see Annex B for full address details.

Sources from which data for this product are obtained
Minerals Raised Inquiry - GB; UK Minerals Industry

United Kingdom Minerals Yearbook 1997
Department of the Environment, Transport and the Regions

Annual data on UK minerals production, consumption and trade with an authoritative text commentary on current developments. Statistics are published approximately 15 months after the end of the latest year in

question. Commentary refers to the year that ended 3 months before the date of publication. Data are published for the last five years, i.e. 1992-1996, with longer runs in some cases. Approximately 85 pages of tables, charts maps and text presenting data at different levels of disaggregation, e.g., production of building materials, county data on production, value of minerals produced, data on offshore crude oil and natural gas production by field. Target market is the UK minerals industry, planning organisations at local and national levels and economic analysts.

Delivery: Periodic Release
Frequency: Annually
Price: £35.00
ISBN: 0 85272 292 3

Available from
Greg Chapman
British Geological Survey
Nicker Hill
Keyworth
Nottingham
Tel: 0115 936 3543

Sources from which data for this product are obtained
Minerals Raised Inquiry - GB; UK Minerals Industry

World Mineral Statistics 1992-96
Department of Trade and Industry

Descriptive statistics, published annually of the production and trade throughout the world of mineral commodities and sub-commodities. The book contains tabulated statistics, by mass or volume over a five year period, of 65 mineral commodities and approximately 370 sub-commodities, organised by country. It contains 280 pages of tables, 10 world maps and 5 pages of charts. The target market is the UK and world minerals industry, policy makers, economic analysts, financiers and environmental organisations. Statistics are published approximately 15 months after the end of the latest year shown.

Delivery: Periodic Release
Frequency: Annually
Price: £80.00
ISBN: 0 85272 308 3

Available from
Greg Chapman
British Geological Survey
Nicker Hill
Keyworth
Nottingham
Tel: 0115 936 3543

Sources from which data for this product are obtained
UK Minerals Industry; World Mineral Statistics Database

See also:
In this chapter:
Analysis from the Inter-Departmental Business Register *(12.12)*
Size Analysis of UK Businesses (Business Monitor PA1003) *(12.12)*
Stockbuilding Business Monitor *(12.18)*

In other chapters:
Indicators of Sustainable Development - United Kingdom (see the Environment chapter)
Overseas Trade Statistics (OTS) (see the Economy chapter)
Review of UK Environmental Expenditure (1993) (see the Environment chapter)

12.20 Motor Vehicle Production

Motor Vehicle Production (First Release)
Office for National Statistics

This contains seasonally adjusted and non-seasonally adjusted data for the production of passenger cars and commercial vehicles (total subdivided into production for the home and export markets). It is published fourteen working days after the close of the survey period.

Delivery: First Release
Frequency: Monthly
Price: £36.00 annual subscription

Available from
Electronic Sales Unit
Office for National Statistics
Please see Annex B for full address details.

Sources from which data for this product are obtained
Motor Vehicle Production Inquiry - UK

Motor Vehicle Production and New Registrations (Business Monitor PM3410)
Office for National Statistics

This is a detailed publication containing data for both vehicle production and Registrations Passenger Cars - total and export production by cylinder capacity size. Monthly data for the last 2 years and annual data from 1980. Commercial vehicles - total and export production by vehicle type. Monthly data for the last 2 years and annual data from 1980. Assembly data for commercial vehicles, total and export seasonally adjusted car and commercial vehicle production monthly averages. Motor vehicles registered by taxation class, cylinder capacity; origin; exempt, crown and emergency vehicles. Motor cycles registered by cylinder capacity, goods vehicles registered by gross weight.

Frequency: Monthly
Price: £110.00 annual subscription

Available from
ONS Direct
Please see Annex B for full address details.

Sources from which data for this product are obtained
Motor Vehicle Production Inquiry - UK

See also:
In this chapter:
Index of Production (First Release) *(12.18)*

12.21 Research and Development (R&D) Companies

Gross Domestic Expenditure on Research and Development (GERD (First Release))
Office for National Statistics

Gross expenditure on research and development (GERD) in the UK is the most reliable estimate of national R&D spending and draws together information on R&D spending in the public and private sectors: Business enterprises, Government, Higher education, private non-profit. It is the measure most commonly used for international comparisons and covers all R&D performed in the country concerned irrespective of who pays for it. UK GERD covers all R&D in the UK including that funded from abroad; but excludes R&D performed abroad even if funded from the UK.

Delivery: First Release
Frequency: Annually
Price: £3.00

Available from
ONS Press Office
Office for National Statistics
Please see Annex B for full address details.

Sources from which data for this product are obtained
Business Enterprise Research and Development Survey - UK; Government Research and Development Survey - UK

Main Science and Technology Indicators
Organisation for Economic Co-operation and Development (OECD)

MA14 contains detailed breakdowns of R&D spending and employment across different market sectors from the Survey of Research and Development in UK Businesses. The survey is an annual survey based on a continually updated register of R&D performers. For any business investing in Research and Development, for R&D consultants, and for anyone with an interest in the future of the economy, this is an invaluable and comprehensive guide to Research and Development in the UK today. Initial estimates from the survey are published in a First Release in November each year. Figures consistent with this Business Monitor are included in the Department of Trade and Industry's Office of Science and Technology's publication, Science, Engineering and Technology Statistics, together with detailed figures for R&D activity in Central Government and Higher Education.

Delivery: Hardcopy publication
Frequency: Annually
Price: £25.00
ISBN: 0 11 536357 2

Available from
ONS Direct
Office for National Statistics
Please see Annex B for full address details.

Northern Ireland Civil and Defence Expenditure on Research and Development During 1996
Department of Economic Development - Northern Ireland

Northern Ireland survey into civil and Defence expenditure on research and development in 1996. This data includes key variables on type of R&D expenditure, type of research, sources of funding and employment in R&D.

Delivery: News/Press Release
Frequency: Periodic
Price: Free

Available from
Gillian Seeds
Statistics Research Branch
Room 115
Department of Economic Development - Northern Ireland
Netherleigh
Massey Avenue
Belfast BT4 2JP
Tel: 028 9052 9426

Sources from which data for this product are obtained
Annual Census of Production - Northern Ireland; NI Research & Development Survey

---

Products

Research and Development Annual Statistics
Office for National Statistics; sponsored by Eurostat

Contains up-to-date statistics on R&D and patent applications in the European Union and the EEA. These statistics show the trends and structure of research and development in the European Union.

Frequency: Annual
ISBN: 92 828 4876 0 (published by Eurostat)

Available from
TSO International Sales Agency
Please see Annex B for full address details.

Sources from which data for this product are obtained
Business Enterprise Research and Development Survey - UK; Government Research and Development Survey - UK

Research and Development in UK Business (First Release) (BERD)
Office for National Statistics

Latest data for business enterprise research and development expenditure and employment. Contains data on research and development expenditure performed in the UK. Source of funds and employment are available by civil and defence, and regional breakdowns.

Delivery: First Release
Frequency: Annually
Price: £3.00

Available from
ONS Press Office
Office for National Statistics
Please see Annex B for full address details.

Sources from which data for this product are obtained
Business Enterprise Research and Development Survey - UK

Research and Development in UK Businesses (MA14)
Office for National Statistics

MA14 contains detailed breakdowns of R&D spending and employment across different market sectors from the Survey of Research and Development in UK Businesses. The survey is an annual survey based on a continually updated register of

R&D performers. For any business investing in Research and Development, for R&D consultants, and for anyone with an interest in the future of the economy, this is an invaluable and comprehensive guide to Research and Development in the UK today. Initial estimates from the survey are published in a First Release in November each year. Figures consistent with this Business Monitor are included in the Department of Trade and Industry's Office of Science and Technology's publication, Science, Engineering and Technology Statistics, together with detailed figures for R&D activity in Central Government and Higher Education.

Delivery: Hardcopy publication
Frequency: Annually
Price: £25.00
ISSN: 1463-6115

Available from
ONS Direct
Office for National Statistics
Please see Annex B for full address details.

Sources from which data for this product are obtained
Business Enterprise Research and Development Survey - UK

Research and Development: Annual Statistics, 1998
Eurostat

This document contains statistical information on research and development (government appropriations, research and development personnel, research and development expenditure and patents) together with general and country-specific analyses and methodological explanations.

Delivery: Periodic
Frequency: Annual
Price: £30.00

Available from
TSO Publications Centre and Bookshops
Please see Annex B for full address details.

See also:
In this chapter:
Analysis from the Inter-Departmental Business Register *(12.12)*
Size Analysis of UK Businesses (Business Monitor PA1003) *(12.12)*

In other chapters:
Economic Trends (see the Economy chapter)

12.22 Telecommunications Industry - Service statistics

Telecommunications Industry - Market Information - UK
Office for Telecommunications (OFTEL)

The Office of Telecommunications (OFTEL) publishes information on the UK Telecommunications Industry in a quarterly and annual Market Information report. OFTEL collects data on telecommunications markets from public telecommunications operators and service providers. Data concentrates mainly on fixed telephony services including call revenues and volumes, exchange lines, interconnection disaggregated by type of call and user. Information is also provided on cellular telephone networks. Annual data is **Available from** 1992-93 until 1997/98; quarterly data has been available since April 1994.

Delivery: Periodic Release
Frequency: Quarterly
Price: Quarterly: £15.00
Annually: £30.00

Available from
C.O.I. Tel: 020 7261 8527

13

Transport, Travel and Tourism

Statistics covering **Transport, Travel and Tourism** are collected, administered and disseminated by a number of separate Departments, Agencies and organisations including the **Office for National Statistics, the Department of the Environment, Transport and the Regions, Department for Culture, Media and Sport, Scottish Executive, the National Assembly for Wales, the Northern Ireland Department of the Environment, the British Tourist Authority, the National Tourist Boards of the UK, the Civil Aviation Authority, and the Royal Ulster Constabulary**. The available statistics embrace a number of subject areas including: **Air Transport and Travel, Conference Market, Domestic Tourism, Personal Transport and Travel, Rail Transport and Travel, Road Accidents, Roads, Road Transport and Travel, Sea and Waterborne Transport** and **Travel, Tourist Accommodation, and Transport of UK International Trade.**

The basic data are generated from a number of separate information 'Sources' and the resultant statistics are disseminated through a whole range of statistical 'Analyses' and 'Products', all of which are described in the following chapter. Users looking for a cross-section of UK-wide statistics on **Transport, Travel and Tourism** may find the following products useful:

> **Digest of Tourist Statistics** (annual publication)
> **Transport Trends** (annual publication)
> **Travel Trends** (annual publication)

Users interested in a wider range of official statistics including **Transport, Travel and Tourism** statistics may like to refer to the following compendia:

> On-line Databases (See Chapter 1):
> **StatBase - StatStore**

> Hardcopy Compendia (See Chapter 2):
> **Annual Abstract of Statistics**
> **Britain 2000: The Official Yearbook of the United Kingdom**
> **Monthly Digest of Statistics**
> **Regional Trends**
> **Social Trends**

Users may also find what they need on the various Departmental Websites. These are listed in Chapter 1.

13

Transport, Travel and Tourism - *Sources and Analyses*

13.1	Air Transport and Travel

Air Freight - UK Airports
Department of the Environment, Transport and the Regions

The DETR publishes data on the tonnage of freight passing through UK airports and carried by UK airlines. The data are supplied by the Civil Aviation Authority.

Status: Ongoing
Collection Method: Census
Frequency: Daily
Reference Period: Month / year
Timeliness: 4 months
Earliest Available Data: 1980
National Coverage: United Kingdom

Statistician
Chris Overson
Department of the Environment, Transport and the Regions
Tel: 020 7890 4276

Products that contain data from this source
Annual Abstract of Statistics; Regional Trends; Social Trends, Transport Statistics Great Britain

Air Passengers - UK Airports
Department of the Environment, Transport and the Regions

The DETR publishes data on the numbers of passengers passing through UK airports and the numbers carried by UK airlines. The data are supplied by the Civil Aviation Authority. Data are collected monthly or annually.

Status: Ongoing
Collection Method: Census
Frequency: Daily
Reference Period: Month / year
Timeliness: 4 months
Earliest Available Data: 1980
National Coverage: United Kingdom

Statistician
Chris Overson
Department of the Environment, Transport and the Regions
Tel: 020 7890 4276

Products that contain data from this source
Annual Abstract of Statistics; Regional Trends; Social Trends, Transport Statistics Great Britain

1997 - 1999 Continuous Survey
Civil Aviation Authority

The 1997 -99 Continuous Origin & Destination Survey is conducted at 3 airports throughout the UK - Heathrow, Gatwick and Manchester. It's purpose is to provide ongoing information about air travellers and the determinants of the travel market that can not be collected on a routine basis from the air transport industry. The survey includes questions on journey purpose, final and intermediate surface origins/ destinations, means of transport to and from airports, route flown, country of residence and passenger demographics. The information is used in assessing the type of market served by airports and airlines and consequently for forecasting air transport demand, airport planning and route assessment and segmentation work.

Status: Ongoing
Collection Method: Large-scale (Sample) Survey
Frequency: Daily
Reference Period: 1st Jan 1997 - 31st Dec 1999
Timeliness: Continuous release. (Approximately 3-6 months for sponsors, 10-12 months for others)
Earliest Available Data: 1st Jan 1997
National Coverage: England
Disaggregation: Local Authority District (LAD) / Unitary Authority (Eng.)

Statistician
CAA Passenger Surveys
Civil Aviation Authority
ERG Division 2; Survey Section
Tel: 020 7832 5992;
Email: surveys@caaerg.co.uk

International Passenger Survey - UK
Office for National Statistics

The International Passenger Survey is a sample survey carried out by the Office for National Statistics. Around 250,000 interviews are carried out per year representing 0.2% of all travellers as they enter or leave the UK by the principal air sea and tunnel ports. The data collected includes, country of visit (for UK residents), country of residence (for overseas residents), expenditure, purpose of visit, length of stay, age group, gender, mode of transport, port, the region of the UK visited (for overseas residents), year and quarter of visit. The survey operates continuously throughout the year with results published monthly in the 'First Release Overseas travel and tourism', quarterly in the publication 'MQ6' and annually in the publication 'Travel Trends'. In addition a compact dataset of selected IPS variables called Travelpac is available for basic analysis, with more complicated analyses being available through three marketing agents.

Status: Ongoing
Collection Method: Stratified random sample survey
Frequency: Continuously
Reference Period: Calendar months, quarters and years
Timeliness: Monthly - available 7 weeks after the end of the month. Quarterly - available 5 months after end of quarter. Annually - available around nine to ten months after the end of the year.
Earliest Available Data: Past Publications 1970. Electronically 1993
National Coverage: United Kingdom

Statistician
Iain MacLeay
Office for National Statistics
SED; IPS
Tel: 020 7533 5764;
Email: iain.macleay@ons.gov.uk

Products that contain data from this source
1994-based National Population Projections; 1996-based National Population Projections first release; Digest of Tourism Statistics No 21; Inter-regional migration: Regional Dataset; International Migration (Series MN); International migration: age and sex; International migration: country of last or next residence; International migration: Regional Dataset; International migration: citizenship; MQ6 - Society - Overseas travel and tourism; National Population Projections; Overseas travel and tourism - First Release; Travelpac - Compact Dataset

1992/93 Origin and Destination Survey

Civil Aviation Authority

The 1992/3 Origin & Destination Survey was conducted at 4 airports throughout the UK - Birmingham, East Midlands, Leeds/Bradford and Manchester. It's purpose was to collect information about air travellers and the determinants of the travel market that can not be collected on a routine basis from the air transport industry. The survey included questions on journey purpose, final and intermediate surface origins/destinations, means of transport to and from airports, route flown, country of residence and passenger demographics. The information is used in assessing the type of market served by airports and airlines and consequently for forecasting air transport demand, airport planning and route assessment and segmentation work.

Status: Ceased completely
Collection Method: Large-scale (Sample) Survey
Frequency: Daily
Reference Period: Feb 1992 - Jan 1993
Timeliness: 10 months
Earliest Available Data: 1st February 1992
National Coverage: England
Disaggregation: Local Authority District (LAD) / Unitary Authority (Eng.)

Statistician
CAA Passenger Surveys
Civil Aviation Authority
ERG Division 2; Survey Section
Tel: 020 7832 5992;
Email: surveys@caaerg.co.uk

1994/95 Origin and Destination Survey
Civil Aviation Authority

The 1994/5 Origin & Destination Survey was conducted at 8 airports throughout the UK - Bristol, Cardiff, Exeter, Southampton, Humberside, Newcastle, Norwich and Teesside. It's purpose was to collect information about air travellers and the determinants of the travel market that can not be collected on a routine basis from the air transport industry. The survey included questions on journey purpose, final and intermediate surface origins/destinations, means of transport to and from airports, route flown, country of residence and passenger demographics. The information is used in assessing the type of market served by airports and airlines and consequently for forecasting air transport demand, airport planning and route assessment and segmentation work.

Status: Ceased completely
Collection Method: Large-scale (Sample) Survey
Frequency: Daily
Reference Period: Feb 1994 - Jan 1995

Timeliness: 10 months
Earliest Available Data: 1st February 1994
National Coverage: England
Disaggregation: Local Authority District (LAD) / Unitary Authority (Eng.)

Statistician
CAA Passenger Surveys
Civil Aviation Authority
ERG Division 2; Survey Section
Tel: 020 7832 5992;
Email: surveys@caaerg.co.uk

1994/95 Origin and Destination Survey (Belfast)
Civil Aviation Authority

The 1994/5 Origin & Destination Survey was conducted at both Belfast airports from June 1994 to May 1995. It's purpose was to collect information about air travellers and the determinants of the travel market that can not be collected on a routine basis from the air transport industry. The survey included questions on journey purpose, final and intermediate surface origins / destinations, means of transport to and from airports, route flown, country of residence and passenger demographics. The information is used in assessing the type of market served by airports and airlines and consequently for forecasting air transport demand, airport planning and route assessment and segmentation work.

Status: Ceased completely
Collection Method: Large-scale (Sample) Survey
Frequency: Daily
Reference Period: June 1994 - May 1995
Timeliness: 12 months
Earliest Available Data: June 1994
National Coverage: Northern Ireland
Disaggregation: District Council Area (Northern Ireland)

Statistician
CAA Passenger Surveys
Civil Aviation Authority
ERG Division 2; Survey Section
Tel: 020 7832 5992;
Email: surveys@caaerg.co.uk

1996 Origin and Destination Survey (England)
Civil Aviation Authority

The 1996 Origin & Destination Survey was conducted at 7 airports throughout the UK - Manchester, Birmingham, Luton, Stansted, London City, Heathrow and Gatwick. It's purpose was to collect information about air travellers and the determinants of the travel market that can not be collected on a routine basis from the air transport industry. The survey included questions on journey purpose, final and intermediate surface

origins/destinations, means of transport to and from airports, route flown, country of residence and passenger demographics. The information is used in assessing the type of market served by airports and airlines and consequently for forecasting air transport demand, airport planning and route assessment and segmentation work.

Status: Ceased completely
Collection Method: Large-scale (Sample) Survey
Frequency: Daily
Reference Period: Jan 1996 -Dec 1996
Timeliness: 6 months (database)
11 months (report publication)
Earliest Available Data: 1st Jan 1996
National Coverage: England
Disaggregation: Local Authority District (LAD) / Unitary Authority (Eng.)

Statistician
CAA Passenger Surveys
Civil Aviation Authority
ERG Division 2; Survey Section
Tel: 020 7852 5992;
Email: surveys@caaerg.co.uk

1996 Origin and Destination Survey (Scotland)
Civil Aviation Authority

The 1996 Origin & Destination Survey was conducted at 4 airports throughout the UK - Aberdeen, Edinburgh, Glasgow, and Inverness. It's purpose was to collect information about air travellers and the determinants of the travel market that can not be collected on a routine basis from the air transport industry. The survey included questions on journey purpose, final and intermediate surface origins/destinations, means of transport to and from airports, route flown, country of residence and passenger demographics. The information is used in assessing the type of market served by airports and airlines and consequently for forecasting air transport demand, airport planning and route assessment and segmentation work.

Status: Ceased completely
Collection Method: Large-scale (Sample) Survey
Frequency: Daily
Reference Period: Jan 1996 - Dec 1996
Timeliness: 6 months (database) 11 months (report publication)
Earliest Available Data: 1st Jan 1996
National Coverage: Scotland
Disaggregation: Council Area (Scot)/District and Islands Area (Scotland)

Statistician
CAA Passenger Surveys
Civil Aviation Authority
ERG Division 2; Survey Section
Tel: 020 7832 5992;
Email: surveys@caaerg.co.uk

Punctuality Statistics - Annual Full Analysis
Civil Aviation Authority

Punctuality of passenger aircraft on individual routes at each of the 10 UK airports. Individual airlines are identified and delays are shown with bands of lateness and average delays.

Status: Ongoing
Collection Method: Collected from airports and scheduling committee
Frequency: Monthly
Reference Period: As soon as possible after the end of operating month
Timeliness: Within two months of the month in question
Earliest Available Data: April 1989 for Heathrow, Gatwick, Manchester, Birmingham, Luton and Stansted
National Coverage: England and Scotland
Disaggregation: London, Birmingham, Manchester, Newcastle, Luton, Glasgow, Edinburgh

Statistician
CAA Aviation Data Unit
Please see Annex B for full address details.

Punctuality Statistics - Annual Summary Analysis
Civil Aviation Authority

Punctuality of passenger aircraft on individual routes at each of the 10 UK airports. Individual airlines are identified and delays are shown with bands of lateness and average delays.

Status: Ongoing
Collection Method: collected from airports and scheduling committee
Frequency: Monthly
Reference Period: As soon as possible after the end of operating month
Timeliness: Within two months of the month in question
Earliest Available Data: April 1989 for Heathrow, Gatwick, Manchester, Birmingham, Luton and Stansted
National Coverage: England and Scotland
Disaggregation: London, Birmingham, Manchester, Newcastle, Luton, Glasgow, Edinburgh

Statistician
CAA Aviation Data Unit
Please see Annex B for full address details.

Punctuality Statistics - Monthly Full Analysis
Civil Aviation Authority

Punctuality of passenger aircraft on individual routes at each of the 10 UK airports. Individual airlines are identified and delays are shown with bands of lateness and average delays.

Status: Ongoing
Collection Method: Collected from airports and scheduling committee
Frequency: Monthly
Reference Period: As soon as possible after the end of operating month
Timeliness: Within two months of the month in question
Earliest Available Data: April 1989 for Heathrow, Gatwick, Manchester, Birmingham, Luton and Stansted
National Coverage: England and Scotland
Disaggregation: London, Birmingham, Manchester, Newcastle, Luton, Glasgow, Edinburgh

Statistician
CAA Aviation Data Unit
Please see Annex B for full address details.

Punctuality Statistics - Monthly Summary Analysis
Civil Aviation Authority

Punctuality of passenger aircraft on individual routes at each of the 10 UK airports. Individual airlines are identified and delays are shown with bands of lateness and average delays.

Status: Ongoing
Collection Method: Collected from airports and scheduling committee
Frequency: Monthly
Reference Period: As soon as possible after the end of operating month
Timeliness: Within two months of the month in question
Earliest Available Data: April 1989 for Heathrow, Gatwick, Manchester, Birmingham, Luton and Stansted
National Coverage: England and Scotland
Disaggregation: London, Birmingham, Manchester, Newcastle, Luton, Glasgow, Edinburgh

Statistician
CAA Aviation Data Unit
Civil Aviation Authority
Aviation Data Unit
Tel: 020 7832 5677;
Email: geddesl@caaerg.co.uk

UK Airlines - Annual Operating, Traffic and Financial Statistics
Civil Aviation Authority

UK Airline statistics includes measures such as number of flights, passengers and cargo carried, capacity available and load factors.

Status: Ongoing
Collection Method: Submitted by UK airlines
Frequency: Monthly
Reference Period: As soon as possible after the end of the operating month
Timeliness: Within 3 months of data month
Earliest Available Data: January 1973, hardcopy only until December 1982
National Coverage: United Kingdom

Statistician
CAA Aviation Data Unit
Please see Annex B for full address details.

UK Airlines - Monthly Operating and Traffic Statistics
Civil Aviation Authority

UK Airline statistics includes measures such as number of flights, passengers and cargo carried, capacity available and load factors.

Status: Ongoing
Collection Method: Submitted by UK airlines
Frequency: Monthly
Reference Period: As soon as possible after the end of the operating month
Timeliness: Within 3 months of data month
Earliest Available Data: January 1973, hardcopy only until December 1982
National Coverage: United Kingdom

Statistician
CAA Aviation Data Unit
Please see Annex B for full address details.

UK Airports - Monthly Statements of Movements, Passengers and Cargo
Civil Aviation Authority

Statistical information on activity at some 70 UK airports. Information includes the number of movements, passengers and cargo volumes. Route level passenger volume data is provided for each significant international route.

Status: Ongoing
Collection Method: Submitted by individual UK airports
Frequency: Monthly
Reference Period: As soon as possible after the end of operating month
Timeliness: Within two months of the month in question
Earliest Available Data: January 1973, hardcopy until December 1982
National Coverage: United Kingdom
Disaggregation: Some 70 UK airports

Statistician
CAA Aviation Data Unit
Please see Annex B for full address details.

UK Airports Annual Statements of Movements, Passengers and Cargo
Civil Aviation Authority

Statistical information on activity at some 70 UK airports. Information includes the number of movements, passengers and cargo volumes. Route level passenger volume data is provided for each significant international route. Since 1993 all international data has been split between EC and other international.

Status: Ongoing
Frequency: Annually
Reference Period: Jan 1st - Dec 31st
Timeliness: Three Months
Earliest Available Data: 1973
National Coverage: United Kingdom
Disaggregation: Some 70 UK airports

Statistician
CAA Aviation Data Unit
Please see Annex B for full address details.

See also:
In this chapter:
Administrative System *(13.3)*

13.2 Conference Market

British Conference Market Survey - GB
British Tourist Authority

The British Tourist Authority carries out a survey on conferences. Data are available by volume of activity, type of conference, revenue, conference size and length of conference. The survey covers Great Britain and data are available at regional level. The survey started in the last quarter of 1993 and is carried out annually. Main results are available approximately six months after the reference period.

Status: Ongoing
Frequency: Annually
Timeliness: Six months after the reference period
Earliest Available Data: Last quarter of 1993
National Coverage: Great Britain

Statistician
Linda Rattray
British Tourist Authority
Tel: 020 8563 3011;
Email: lrattray@bta.org.uk

13.3 Domestic Outbound and Inbound Tourism

Administrative System
Civil Aviation Authority

Seasonal analysis of the licensable activity of UK tour operators in the sale of packaged air holidays, and scheduled and charter seat only sales issued bi-annually in January and July compiled from the previous quarterly returns of licence holders of actual passengers carried, and projected passengers carryings for the forthcoming season(s).

Status: Ongoing
Collection Method: Administrative Records
Frequency: Quarterly
Reference Period: Summer and Winter tour operating seasons
Earliest Available Data: April 1991
National Coverage: United Kingdom

Statistician
ATOL
Civil Aviation Authority
Licensing and Finance; ATOL Section
Tel: 020 7832 5620;
Email: onsquery@atol.org.uk

British National Travel Survey - GB
British Tourist Authority

The British Tourist Authority carries out a survey on British holidaymakers and their holidays. It is based on interviews with a sample of adults aged 16 and over representative of the adult population of Great Britain. Data are available on the number of holidays taken, duration of holidays, destinations and expenditure. The survey covers Great Britain and data are available at regional level. It was known as the British Tourism Survey Yearly in the years 1985-88 inclusive. Known as British Tourism Survey during 1985 to 1988

Status: Ongoing
Frequency: Annually
National Coverage: Great Britain

Statistician
Linda Rattray
British Tourist Authority
Tel: 020 8563 3011;
Email: lrattray@bta.org.uk

Products that contain data from this source
Digest of Tourist Statistics No 22 Tourism Intelligence Quarterly

National Parks Visitor Survey
Forestry Commission; sponsored by Consortium led by Countryside Commission

Survey in 1994, in all National Parks of England and Wales, plus New Forest and Broads. Based on questionnaires for roadside and on-site interviews, and for self-completion. Also used data from traffic counters.

Status: Ceased temporarily
Collection Method: Household/Person (Sample) Survey
Frequency: Ad hoc
Reference Period: 1994
Timeliness: 2 years
Earliest Available Data: 1994
Disaggregation: National Parks of England and Wales. Results are for each park.

Statistician
Simon Gillam
Forestry Commission
Policy and Practice Division - Statistics
Tel: 0131 314 6280;
Email:simon.gillam@forestry.gov.uk

Overseas Leisure Visitors Survey - GB
British Tourist Authority

The British Tourist Authority compiles a survey on the opinions of overseas visitors to the UK. The 1994 survey was carried out with a sample of 2,500 overseas visitors. Data are available on the main purpose of visit, whether advance information was obtained or bookings made, the importance of the arts, accommodation, eating out, rail travel, Tourist Information Centres, tourist facilities on Sundays, and Britain's price competitiveness. This survey has been carried out since 1977. The survey is carried out continuously throughout the year. The main results are available approximately six months after the reference period.

Status: Ongoing
Frequency: Annual
Timeliness: Approximately six months after the reference period
Earliest Available Data: 1977
National Coverage: United Kingdom

Statistician
Linda Rattray
British Tourist Authority
Tel: 020 8563 3011;
Email: lrattray@bta.org.uk

Products that contain data from this source
Digest of Tourist Statistics No 22

Regional Tourism
Department for Culture, Media and Sport

The British Tourist Authority compiles data on regional tourism. The principal sources of information used in compiling the information are the UK Tourism Survey and the International Passenger Survey, although regional breakdowns from other sources such as Hotel Occupancy Surveys are included. Data cover the United Kingdom and are available for Tourist Board regions. The series began in 1975, and data are collected annually and published approximately six months after the reference period.

Frequency: Annual
Timeliness: 6 months after reference period
Earliest Available Data: 1975

Statistician
Paul Allin
Chief Statistician

Department for Culture, Media and Sport
Analytical Services Unit; Statistics Branch
6th Floor
Haymarket House
2-4 Cockspur Street
London SW1Y 5DH
Tel: 020 7211 2843;
Email: paul.allin@culture.gov.uk

Products that contain data from this analysis
Regional Tourism Facts 1997

Survey of Visits to Tourist Attractions
Department for Culture, Media and Sport; sponsored by British Tourist Authority / National Tourist Boards

The NTBs collect information on number of visitors, admission charges, revenue, employment and expenditure from the proprietors of tourist attractions. The survey is conducted on an annual basis. Tourist attractions are defined as permanently established excursion destinations, a primary purpose of which is to allow public access for entertainment, interest or education. The attractions must be open to the public without prior booking.

Status: Ongoing
Collection Method: Large-scale (Sample) Survey
Frequency: Annually
Reference Period: Calendar year
Timeliness: Information is available 4 months after the end of the reference year (information published annually in September).
Earliest Available Data: 1976
National Coverage: United Kingdom

Statistician
Paul Allin
Chief Statistician
Department for Culture, Media and Sport
Analytical Services Unit; Statistics Branch
6th Floor
Haymarket House
2-4 Cockspur Street
London SW1Y 5DH
Tel: 020 7211 2843;
Email: paul.allin@culture.gov.uk

Products that contain data from this analysis
Digest of Tourism Statistics No 22; Sightseeing in the UK; Visits to Tourist Attractions

Tourism - Europe
Department for Culture, Media and Sport; sponsored by Eurostat

Tourism data for each member state of the European Union are compiled by Eurostat. Data are available on tourist accommodation, residents and non-residents guest flows in accommodation establishments, accommodation capacity

utilisation, employment in tourist activities, tourist expenditure, trends in certain tourist consumer prices and balance of payments figures. Data for the United Kingdom are available for Tourist Board regions. The series began in 1980. Data are collected annually and are published approximately one year after the reference period.

Status: Ongoing
Frequency: Data series are a mixture of monthly, quarterly and annual.
National Coverage: United Kingdom
Disaggregation: NUTS2 area; NUTS3 area

Statistician
Paul Allin
Chief Statistician
Department for Culture, Media and Sport
Analytical Services Unit; Statistics Branch
6th Floor
Haymarket House
2-4 Cockspur Street
London SW1Y 5DH
Tel: 020 7211 2843;
Email: paul.allin@culture.gov.uk

Products that contain data from this analysis
Tourism - Annual Statistics

Tourism - Worldwide
Department for Culture, Media and Sport

The World Tourism Organisation compiles data on world tourism. Data are collected annually and are available in the year following the reference period.

Frequency: Annually

Statistician
Paul Allin
Department for Culture, Media and Sport
Analytical Services Unit; Statistics Branch
Tel: 020 7211 2843

UK Day Visits Survey
Forestry Commission; sponsored by Consortium led by Countryside Commission and DCMS

Household surveys, run every second year, to ask about leisure day visits from home.

Status: Ongoing
Collection Method: Household/Person (Sample) Survey
Frequency: Biennial
Reference Period: Calendar year
Timeliness: 3 months after year end, for provisional results. Final report up to a year or more later.
Earliest Available Data: 1992 (pilot), 1994 (full year)
National Coverage: Great Britain
Disaggregation: England, Scotland and Wales

Statistician
Simon Gillam

Forestry Commission
Policy and Practice Division - Statistics
Tel: 0131 314 6280;
Email: simon.gillam@forestry.gov.uk

Products that contain data from this source
Forestry Industry Yearbook

(The) UK Tourism Survey
British Tourist Authority

The British Tourist Authority carries out a survey of trips undertaken by UK residents. For the 1993 survey 75,843 interviews were carried out. The survey covers all trips away from home lasting one night or more for holidays, visits to friends and relatives, business, conferences or any other purpose except such things as hospital admissions or school visits. The main results are the number of trips taken, expenditure and nights spent away from home. Data are also available on leisure activities undertaken on the trip, methods of booking or arranging travel, and types of location stayed at. The survey covers the UK and data are available for England, Scotland, Wales, Northern Ireland and at regional level. This survey began in 1989 and replaced the previous domestic tourism survey, the British Tourism Survey Monthly. Since the survey now incorporates methodological improvements and changes, it is not possible to compare 1989 and subsequent domestic tourism data with that of previous years. The survey is carried out continuously, and results are published annually.

Frequency: Continuous
National Coverage: United Kingdom

Statistician
Linda Rattray
British Tourist Authority
Tel: 020 8563 3011;
Email: lrattray@bta.org.uk

Products that contain data from this source
Digest of Tourist Statistics No 21; the UK Tourist: Statistics 1997; Tourism Intelligence Quarterly

United Kingdom Tourism Survey
Department for Culture, Media and Sport; sponsored by National Tourist Boards

An annual survey, first conducted in 1989, comprising of a number of interviews with UK adults (aged 15+) each month across the year. In total around 75,000 to 80,000 people are interviewed. The information gathered relates to domestic and outbound tourism. Questions asked concern destination and purpose of trip, the number of nights spent, type of accommodation, expenditure, transport used, age of tourist, activities pursued, month of trip,

Status: Ongoing
Collection Method: Large-scale (Sample) Survey
Frequency: Annually
Reference Period: Calendar year
Timeliness: Information usually available 4 months after end of reference year. Publication issued July.
Earliest Available Data: 1989
National Coverage: United Kingdom

Statistician
Paul Allin
Department for Culture, Media and Sport
Analytical Services Unit; Statistics Branch
Tel: 020 7211 2843

Products that contain data from this source
Digest of Tourism Statistics No 22; UK Tourist

Visits to Tourist Attractions - UK
British Tourist Authority

The British Tourist Authority compiles an annual survey on visits to tourist attractions. Data are available on number of tourist attractions, number of visits, facilities, capacity of attractions, admission charges, visitor trends, child proportion and employment. The survey covers the UK and data are available for England, Scotland, Northern Ireland and Wales.

Status: Ongoing
Collection Method: Survey
Frequency: Annual
National Coverage: United Kingdom, England, Scotland, Northern Ireland and Wales

Statistician
Linda Rattray
British Tourist Authority
Tel: 020 8563 3011;
Email: lrattray@bta.org.uk

Products that contain data from this source
Heritage Monitor 1998; Scottish Visitor Attraction Survey; Sightseeing in the UK; Sightseeing in the UK 1997; Visitors to Tourist Attractions in Wales; Visits to Tourist Attractions

---

See also:
In this chapter:
International Passenger Survey - UK *(13.1)*

13.4 Personal Transport and Travel

London Area Transport Survey (LATS) 1991
Department of the Environment, Transport and the Regions

The Department of Transport (in partnership with London Research Centre) conducted a survey of travel and transport in London, including a household interview survey consisting of 60,000 households, roadside interviews and traffic counts, and on-mode surveys of public transport users. Data are available on travel behaviour, trip origins and destinations, modes of transport, trip purposes, travel time and distance, travel to work, vehicles, car occupancy, parking, M25 use, public transport ticket types, land use, ethnic groups and disabilities. Data cover London and the neighbouring districts and are available at London borough, ward, postcode district and transport zone levels. The present Survey continues the decennial series begun by the 1962 London Traffic Survey. The 1991 Survey results mainly refer to a typical weekday.

Status: Ongoing
Collection Method: Large-scale (Sample) Survey
Frequency: Ad hoc
Reference Period: 1991 typical weekday
Sub-National: London area
Disaggregation: London borough, ward, postcode district, transport zone

Statistician
Mike Collop
Department of the Environment, Transport and the Regions
Transport Statistics Personal Travel; TSPT3
Tel: 020 7890 3096

Products that contain data from this source
London Area Transport Survey (LATS) 1991; Transport Statistics for London 1998; Transport Statistics Great Britain 1998 edition; Travel in London - London Area Transport Survey 1991

London Journey Times Survey
Department of the Environment, Transport and the Regions

Rolling annual survey to establish typical door-to-door journey times in London using various modes of transport.

Status: Ongoing
Collection Method: Small-scale (Sample) Survey
Frequency: Annually
Reference Period: 3 year rolling programme to cover whole of London
Timeliness: Three months
Earliest Available Data: 1 June 1993
Disaggregation: Sectors of London

Statistician
Chris Morrey
Department of the Environment, Transport and the Regions
Tel: 020 7890 4746

(The) GB National Travel Survey (NTS)
Department of the Environment, Transport and the Regions

The DETR commissions the Office for National Statistics (ONS) to run the NTS with an achieved sample of 3,100-3,400 households per year. This has run continuously since mid 1988. Results are amalgamated into 3-year periods, and published annually on a rolling-year basis. Earlier surveys were carried out on an ad-hoc basis from 1965, although these are not as detailed as or necessarily compatible with later surveys. The survey covers travel in Great Britain, and some data are available at a regional level. The survey details all journeys made over a sample period of seven days, and also includes details of individuals (such as age, working status and driving licence ownership) and households (such as income levels and car availability). It is planned that in future, 'Focus on Personal Travel' will be published every third year, with NTS Bulletins giving updates of the main results in the intervening years. Articles on topics of interest using NTS data will also appear in the annual publication 'Transport Trends'. Ad-hoc surveys in 1960's, 70's and 80's. Last ad-hoc survey 1985/86. Continuous since July 1988. Personal travel factsheets and unpublished data are available from DETR.

Status: Ongoing
Collection Method: Household/Person (Sample) Survey
Frequency: Continuously
Reference Period: 3-year rolling period
Timeliness: Approximately 9 months after end-survey period.
Earliest Available Data: 1972/73 (first electronic database)
National Coverage: Great Britain
Disaggregation: Regional data available

Contact point / Owner
Spencer Broadley
Department of the Environment, Transport and the Regions
Tel: 020 7890 3097

Statistician
Barbara Noble
Department of the Environment, Transport and the Regions
Tel: 020 7890 6594

Products that contain data from this source
Cycling in Great Britain; Focus on London; Focus on Personal Travel; Focus on Roads; Focus on the South West; National Travel Survey; National Travel Survey - Technical Report; National Travel Survey 1994/96; Regional Trends; Scottish Transport Statistics; Social Focus on Children; Social Trends; the Data Archive; Transport Statistics for London 1998; Transport Statistics for Metropolitan Areas 1998; Transport Statistics Great Britain 1998 edition; Transport Trends 1998 edition; Walking in Great Britain; Social Focus on Older People; Welsh Transport Statistics; Travel by Scottish Residents; Personal Travel Factsheets

---

Sources and Analyses

See also:
In this chapter:
Administrative System *(13.3)*
1997 - 1999 Continuous Survey *(13.1)*
1996 Origin and Destination Survey
(Scotland) *(13.1)*
Traffic Speeds on English Trunk Roads
(13.8)
Transport Statistics for London *(13.8)*

13.5   Road Accidents

Road Accident Statistics ("STATS 19" Returns) (Scotland)
Scottish Executive

The Scottish Executive collects road accident statistics for Scotland. The Department of the Environment, Transport and the Regions holds a full dataset for Great Britain. The data cover all injury road accidents (i.e. accidents in which one or more people are injured) which become known to the Police in Scotland. Three types of information are available: (i) Attendant Circumstances of the Accidents - including the severity, number of vehicles and casualties involved, time and location, road class and number, speed limit, weather and road conditions, and carriageway hazards; (ii) Vehicles involved in each accident - includes type, location and manoeuvre at time of accident, and data about the driver (age, sex, and breath test results); (iii) Casualties - age, sex, injury severity and whether a driver, passenger or pedestrian. Data are available at Council and Police Force levels. Returns are received monthly from police forces throughout the year. Summaries of the results for the calendar year are published in early summer of the following year, with more detailed analysis published in the autumn. Data in the current (or very similar) format have been collected since 1979. Some summary information is available for earlier years.

Status: Ongoing
Collection Method: Administrative Records
Frequency: Monthly
Reference Period: Results are published for calendar years
Timeliness: Results for a calendar year are available by the summer of the following year
Earliest Available Data: 1979
National Coverage: Scotland
Disaggregation: Police Force Areas, Council Area (Scot)/District and Islands Area (Scotland)

Statistician
Frank Dixon
The Scottish Executive Development Department

EAS; Transport Statistics
Tel: 0131 244 7254;
Email: frank.dixon@scotland.gov.uk

Products that contain data from this source
Key Road Accident Statistics; Road Accidents Great Britain 1997 - the Casualty Report; Road Accidents Scotland; Road Casualties Great Britain - Final Figures 1997; Scottish Abstract of Statistics; Scottish Transport Statistics

---

Road Accidents Statistics (Stats 19 Returns)
Department of the Environment, Transport and the Regions

The Department of Transport compiles data on personal injury road accidents, resulting casualties and the vehicles involved. Accidents are those which occur on the public highway and which become known to the police within 30 days. Data are available by three main areas: (i) Accidents - including the severity of the accident, the number of vehicles and casualties involved, time and location, road class and number, speed limit, weather and road conditions, and carriageway hazards; (ii) Vehicles - including type, location and manoeuvre at time of accident, and details of the driver (age, sex and breath test results); (iii) Casualties - age, sex, injury severity and whether a driver, passenger or pedestrian. Data are available for Great Britain and England and by regional and county level. Data are collected monthly from police forces throughout the year and the annual accident report in June.

Status: Ongoing
Collection Method: Police records
Frequency: Continuously
Earliest Available Data: Database from 1979
National Coverage: Great Britain
Disaggregation: Government Office Region (GOR); Local Authority District (LAD)/Unitary Authority (Eng.); Local Government Region (Scotland); London Borough; County (E&W)/ Unitary Authority (Eng.)

Statistician
Val Davies
Department of the Environment, Transport and the Regions
Transport Statistics Roads; TSR5
Tel: 020 7890 6387;
Email: dst.detr@gtnet.gov.uk

Products that contain data from this source
Regional Trends; Road Accidents Great Britain 1997 - the Casualty Report; Social Trends; Road Casualties Great Britain. Main Results 1998

Road Accidents - Northern Ireland
Royal Ulster Constabulary

The Royal Ulster Constabulary compiles data on road traffic accidents relating to all road traffic injury accidents reported to the police in Northern Ireland. Data are available on deaths and injuries by road user type, age, sex, month of the year, and on accidents by severity, causation factors, road user responsible, location, road and weather conditions, month of the year and time of day and day of week. The data cover Northern Ireland and are available at police force area, police regions, police divisions, police sub-divisions, and police station area levels. Total accident, death and injury figures for Northern Ireland are available back to 1931. More detailed data are available from 1967 and a consistent series at current levels of detail is available from 1986 onwards. Data are collected continuously and published quarterly two months in arrears.

Status: Ongoing
Collection Method: Administrative source
Frequency: Daily
Reference Period: Financial year
Timeliness: 3 months from end of financial year
Earliest Available Data: 1986
National Coverage: Northern Ireland
Sub-National: Full
Disaggregation: Police station area

Statistician
Force **Statistician**
Central Statistics Unit
RUC Lisnassharragh
42 Montgomery Road
Belfast BT6 9LD
Tel: 028 9065 0222;
Fax: 028 9070 0998

Products that contain data from this source
Royal Ulster Constabulary Chief Constable's Annual Report; Northern Ireland Annual Abstract of Statistics; Northern Ireland Transport Statistics 1997/98; Regional Trends; Road Traffic Accident Statistics, Annual Report (Northern Ireland); Social Trends; Traffic Accident Bulletin (Northern Ireland)

Road Accidents - Wales
National Assembly for Wales

The National Assembly for Wales compiles data on personal injury road accidents. Records are completed by each police force and forwarded to the National Assembly for Wales. Data are available by accident, vehicle and casualty involved including the circumstances of the accident. The results cover Wales at police force and unitary authority level. Results date from 1938 for the number of casualties and 1968 for accidents. Data are collected monthly and are usually published in July and September of each year, the latter containing the more detailed breakdown.

Status: Ongoing
Collection Method: Administrative Records
Frequency: Annual
Reference Period: Calendar year
Timeliness: 9 months (for the more detailed breakdown)
Earliest Available Data: Detailed data is available from 1979
National Coverage: Wales
Disaggregation: Local authority

Statistician
Clive Lewis
National Assembly for Wales
Tel: (+44) 029 2082 3220;
Email: clive.lewis@wales.gsi.gov.uk

Products that contain data from this source
Digest of Welsh Local Area Statistics; Digest of Welsh Statistics; Regional Trends; Road Accidents: Wales; Statistics for Assembly Constituency Areas; Welsh Transport Statistics; Road Casualties in Wales (Statistical Release)

Road Accidents Statistics in English Regions 1996
Department of the Environment, Transport and the Regions

Status: Ceased completely
Collection Method: Police records
Frequency: Continuously
National Coverage: England

Statistician
Val Davies
Department of the Environment, Transport and the Regions
Transport Statistics Roads; TSR5
Tel: 020 7890 6387;
Email: dst.detr@gtnet.gov.uk

Road Safety Monitor
Department of the Environment - Northern Ireland

Survey taps into the attitudes and behaviours of Northern Ireland Drivers. For the past three years this survey has been conducted via the inclusion of a Road Safety module in the Northern Ireland Omnibus Survey. This research continues the series of Road Safety Monitors prepared by Ulster Marketing Surveys from 1984 to 1995.

Status: Ongoing
Collection Method: Household/Person (Sample) Survey
Frequency: Annually
Reference Period: January
Timeliness: 4 months
Earliest Available Data: 1994
National Coverage: Northern Ireland
Disaggregation: Belfast and East and West of Province

Statistician
Anne Jordan
Department of the Environment - Northern Ireland

Central Statistics and Research Branch
Tel: 028 9054 0807;
Email: anne.jordan@doeni.gov.uk

13.6   Roads

National Road Maintenance Condition Survey
Department of the Environment, Transport and the Regions

The survey is jointly sponsored by the Department of Environment, Transport and the Regions (DETR), the Highways Agency and the Local Government Association. The survey has been carried out annually, in England and Wales, since 1977 and covers trends in the visual condition, including footways, for the following road classes: all-purpose trunk roads; urban principal; urban classified; urban unclassified; rural principal; rural classified; and rural unclassified roads in England and Wales. Motorways and concrete roads are excluded from the visual survey. Results show national figures and regional figures by road class. Data showing the structural condition of Motorway, Trunk and Principal roads is available from 1992. The report also includes summary information for maintenance expenditure, motor traffic volumes and road lengths receiving maintenance treatment. Data cover England and Wales and are available at the level of the Department of Transport Regions. The survey started in 1977 and is carried out annually. Results are available in April of the following year.

Frequency: Annually
Timeliness: Results available April the following year
Earliest Available Data: 1977
National Coverage: England and Wales

Statistician
Ed Kafka
Department of the Environment, Transport and the Regions
Transport Statistics Roads; TSR3
Tel: 020 7890 6398

Products that contain data from this source
National Road Maintenance Condition Survey 1997

Road Lengths - Wales
National Assembly for Wales

Status: Ongoing
Collection Method: Survey/forms
Frequency: Annual
Reference Period: As at 1 April
Timeliness: 3 months
Earliest Available Data: 1974

National Coverage: Wales
Disaggregation: by local authority

Statistician
Clive Lewis
National Assembly for Wales
Tel: (+44) 029 2082 3220;
Email: clive.lewis@wales.gsi.gov.uk

Products that contain data from this source
Digest of Welsh Local Area Statistics; Digest of Welsh Statistics; Road Accidents: Wales; Statistics for Assembly Constituency Areas; Welsh Transport Statistics

---

Road Lengths Survey
Department of the Environment, Transport and the Regions; sponsored jointly with Scottish Executive and National Assembly for Wales.

This survey is used to collect details of all types of roads in Great Britain, particularly the lengths of the different classes of roads in the various local authorities throughout the country. The Scottish and Welsh data are collected by the Scottish and National Assembly for Wales.

Status: Ongoing
Collection Method: Paper forms completed by Local Authorities. LAs normally use Geographical Information Systems to provide the data.
Frequency: Annually
Reference Period: Figures relate to lengths as at 1 April of the current year.
Timeliness: Limited data available back to 1909, fuller data available from 1951 and current level of detail available back to 1981. Unsure how data collected prior to 1981.
Earliest Available Data: 1909 (limited)
National Coverage: Great Britain
Disaggregation: Local Authority District (LAD) / Unitary Authority (Eng.)

Statistician
Kerrick Macafee
Department of the Environment, Transport and the Regions
Transport Statistics Roads; TSR2
Tel: 020 7890 6396

Products that contain data from this source
Road Traffic Statistics Great Britain: 1997; 1999 Road Traffic Statistics Report

---

13.7   Road Transport and Travel

Annual Inquiry to PSV Operators
Department of the Environment, Transport and the Regions

Sample survey of public transport operators in GB.

Status: Ongoing
Collection Method: Large-scale (Sample) Survey
Frequency: Annually
Reference Period: Financial year
Timeliness: Five months approximately.
Earliest Available Data: 1986
National Coverage: Great Britain
Disaggregation: London, Counties, Mets

Statistician
Mike Haslam
Department of the Environment, Transport and the Regions
Transport Statistics Personal Transport; TSPT1
Tel: 020 7890 4589

Continuous Survey of Road Goods Transport - UK
Department of the Environment, Transport and the Regions

The Department of the Environment, Transport and the Regions compiles the Continuing Survey of Road Goods Transport. The Survey covers about 350 UK registered heavy goods vehicles (over 3.5 tonnes gross weight) a week. Data are available on the weight and nature of loads carried and the distance transported. Data cover the United Kingdom and are available for Scotland, Wales and Northern Ireland and at county and regional level for England. A survey of road goods transport has been carried out since the early 1970s but in its present form since 1984. The Survey is carried out every week and analysed annually. Main results are available nine weeks after the end of the reference year.

Status: Ongoing
Collection Method: Large-scale (Sample) Survey
Frequency: Weekly
Timeliness: Main results are available nine weeks after the end of the reference year.
Earliest Available Data: 1984
National Coverage: United Kingdom
Disaggregation: County and regional level for England

Statistician
John Garnsworthy
Department of the Environment, Transport and the Regions
Tel: 020 7890 3093;
Email: john_garnsworthy@detr.gsi.gov.uk

Products that contain data from this source
The Transport of Goods by Road in Great Britain 1998: Annual Report of the Continuing Survey of Road Goods Transport

International Road Haulage - UK
Department of the Environment, Transport and the Regions

The Department of Transport compiles the

International Road Haulage Survey. The Survey covers about 80 international road hauliers a week. Data are available on the origin, destination, weight and commodity of every consignment together with details of the sea crossings used. Data cover the United Kingdom and are available by country of origin and destination for Wales and Scotland and regions of England. A survey of road goods transport has been carried out since the early 1980s but only in its present methodological form since 1992. It is a continuous survey carried out at weekly intervals and analysed on an annual basis. Main annual results are available five months after the end of the year.

Status: Ongoing
Collection Method: Sample survey
Frequency: Continuously
Reference Period: Calendar year
Timeliness: 5 months
Earliest Available Data: 1990
National Coverage: United Kingdom
Disaggregation: Country of origin / destination for Wales, Scotland, Northern Ireland and regions of England

Statistician
John Garnsworthy
Department of the Environment, Transport and the Regions
Tel: 020 7890 3093;
Email: john_garnsworthy@detr.gsi.gov.uk

Products that contain data from this source
International Road Haulage by United Kingdom Registered Vehicles - Report on 1996

Light Goods Vehicle Survey - GB
Department of the Environment, Transport and the Regions

The Department of the Environment, Transport and the Regions compiles the Light Goods Vehicle Survey. The survey started in October 1998 and covers about 400 registered light goods vehicles (under 3.5 tonnes gross weight) per week (150 per week from 2000). It follows up similar surveys of small commercial vehicles undertaken by the Department of Transport in 1987 and 1992/3. Vehicle owners are asked to provide, for a single day, information about the reasons for their journeys, type and location (by postcode) of origin and destination, time of day when journeys are made, passenger occupancy, time of day of journeys, and description of goods/equipment carried.

Status: Ongoing
Collection Method: Large-scale sample survey
Frequency: Weekly
Reference Period: October 1998 to present
Timeliness: Main results are available nine weeks after the end of the reference period
Earliest Available Data: 1998 final quarter

National Coverage: Great Britain

Statistician
John Garnsworthy
Department of the Environment, Transport and the Regions
Tel: 020 7890 3093;
Email: john_garnsworthy@detr.gsi.gov.uk

Local Bus Fares Survey
Department of the Environment, Transport and the Regions

Quarterly panel survey of bus operators.

Status: Ongoing
Collection Method: Cohort, Panel or Longitudinal Study
Frequency: Periodic
Reference Period: Quarter
Timeliness: One month.
Earliest Available Data: 1986
National Coverage: Great Britain

Statistician
Mike Haslam
Department of the Environment, Transport and the Regions
Transport Statistics Personal Transport; TSPT1
Tel: 020 7890 4589

Products that contain data from this source
Quinquennial Review Local Bus Fares Survey

London Traffic Monitoring Report 1997
Department of the Environment, Transport and the Regions

Status: Ceased completely
Frequency: Annually
Reference Period: Various, e.g. calendar year or financial year

Statistician
Chris Morrey
Department of the Environment, Transport and the Regions
Tel: 020 7890 4746

Road Goods Vehicles Travelling to Mainland Europe - GB
Department of the Environment, Transport and the Regions

DETR compiles a survey on road goods vehicles travelling to mainland Europe. Data are available on the total number of powered goods vehicles and unaccompanied trailers by country of registration carried on roll-on/roll-off ferries and through the Channel Tunnel. Data cover Great Britain and are available by country of disembarkation and by port group. The survey commenced in the mid 1970s and is carried out quarterly. Results are available about five months after the reference period.

Sources and Analyses

Status: Ongoing
Collection Method: Census
Frequency: Quarterly
Reference Period: Quarterly
Timeliness: 5 months
Earliest Available Data: 1982
National Coverage: Great Britain
Disaggregation: Country of disembarkation. Port group

Statistician
John Garnsworthy
Department of the Environment, Transport and the Regions
Tel: 020 7890 3093;
Email: john_garnsworthy@detr.gsi.gov.uk

Products that contain data from this source
Road Goods Vehicles Travelling to Mainland Europe

Road Traffic Surveys
Department of the Environment, Transport and the Regions; sponsored jointly with Scottish Executive and National Assembly for Wales

The two surveys are used to estimate average traffic flows on various types of road within Great Britain. Manual counts provide limited data (normally 12 hours on one day every three years) at a large number of road sites, whilst the few automatic counters allow interpolation and extrapolation of the manual count data. The resulting information on annual average daily flows on road links is combined with the road length data to give traffic estimates for Great Britain. Limited data available back to 1938. Fuller data, using varying methods, available since 1960. Automatic counters only used since 1992.

Status: Ongoing
Collection Method: Manual counts by enumerators standing by the road and automatic traffic counters.
Frequency: Continuously
Reference Period: Quarterly (summary data) and annual
Timeliness: Quarterly provisional data released on sixth Thursday following the end of a quarter. Summary final figures published with the release of the first quarter provisional figures.
Earliest Available Data: 1938 (limited). 1992 (automatic)
National Coverage: Great Britain
Disaggregation: Some information available at Government Office Region level.

Statistician
Kerrick Macafee
Department of the Environment, Transport and the Regions
Transport Statistics Roads; TSR2
Tel: 020 7890 6396

Road Travel Speeds in English

Urban Areas
Department of the Environment, Transport and the Regions

Survey to monitor road networks performance and effects of congestion in major user areas in England (excluding London).

Status: Ongoing
Collection Method: Small-scale (Sample) Survey
Frequency: Triennial
Timeliness: 3 months.
Earliest Available Data: 1993
National Coverage: England
Disaggregation: Major user areas

Statistician
Chris Morrey
Department of the Environment, Transport and the Regions
Tel: 020 7890 4746

Seatbelt Survey - Northern Ireland
Department of the Environment - Northern Ireland

Survey of Seat Belt Wearing in Northern Ireland. The series which began in 1994 has been conducted biannually in April and October. However from April 1997 the survey has been conducted on an annual basis.

Status: Ongoing
Collection Method: Large-scale (Sample) Survey
Frequency: Annually
Reference Period: Survey carried out during every April
Timeliness: 2 months
Earliest Available Data: April 1994
National Coverage: Northern Ireland

Statistician
Anne Jordan
Department of the Environment - Northern Ireland
Central Statistics and Research Branch
Tel: 028 9054 0807;
Email: anne.jordan@doeni.gov.uk

Traffic Speeds in London
Department of the Environment, Transport and the Regions

Rolling programme of surveys to monitor road networks performance and effects of congestion in London.

Status: Ongoing
Collection Method: Small-scale (Sample) Survey
Frequency: Annually
Reference Period: 3 year rolling programme to cover whole of London and out to the M25.
Timeliness: 3 months

Disaggregation: Central, Inner and Outer sectors of London

Statistician
Chris Morrey
Department of the Environment, Transport and the Regions
Tel: 020 7890 4746

Traffic Speeds on English Trunk Roads
Department of the Environment, Transport and the Regions

Survey to monitor trunk road networks performance and effects of congestion.

Status: Ongoing
Collection Method: Small-scale (Sample) Survey
Frequency: Tri-annually
Timeliness: 3 months
Earliest Available Data: 1995
National Coverage: England

Statistician
Chris Morrey
Department of the Environment, Transport and the Regions
Tel: 020 7890 4746

Vehicle Excise Duty Evasion Studies
Department of the Environment, Transport and the Regions

Statistician
Derek Jones
Department of the Environment, Transport and the Regions
Tel: 020 7271 3738

Vehicle Registrations and Stock - GB
Department of the Environment, Transport and the Regions

Statistics and information on new vehicle registrations and vehicle stock are derived from Driver and Vehicle Licensing Agency records. DVLA run administrative systems to register new vehicles, collect vehicle excise duty (car tax), and maintain appropriate information on the vehicle and its registered keeper. DVLA prepare monthly summaries of new vehicle registrations which are transmitted to the Department of Transport's Statistics Directorate for retention and as the basis of a monthly statistics bulletin. A vehicle information database (VID) containing anonymised details of all vehicle records held at DVLA is also maintained in the Statistics Directorate and updated quarterly. In co-operation with DVLA, the Statistics Directorate also conduct periodic studies of

Sources and Analyses

vehicle excise duty evasion. The most recent were in 1989 and 1994.

National Coverage: Great Britain

Statistician
Derek Jones
Department of the Environment, Transport and the Regions
Tel: 020 7271 3738

Products that contain data from this source
Motor cars currently licensed and new registrations; New Motor Vehicle Registrations Great Britain; Vehicle Excise Duty Evasion in Great Britain; Vehicle Licensing Statistics

Vehicle Speeds in Great Britain 1998
Department of the Environment, Transport and the Regions

Status: Ongoing
Collection Method: Large-scale (Sample) Survey
Frequency: Continuously
Earliest Available Data: 1991
National Coverage: Great Britain

Statistician
Val Davies
Department of the Environment, Transport and the Regions
Transport Statistics Roads; TSR5
Tel: 020 7890 6387;
Email: dst.detr@gtnet.gov.uk

13.8   Sea and Waterborne Transport and Travel

Inland Waterways - Freight Traffic - GB
British Waterways

British waterways compiles data on freight traffic on British Waterway canals and rivers. Data are available on the broad categories of goods carried on a national basis and traffic by the individual waterway on which it is moved. Results have been collected annually for Great Britain since 1972 and are published in June of the following reference year.

Status: Ongoing
Collection Method: Administrative records
Frequency: Continuously
Reference Period: Annually
Timeliness: 6 months
Earliest Available Data: 1972
National Coverage: Great Britain
Disaggregation: Regional

Statistician

Glenn Millar
British Waterways
Tel: 01923 201356;
Email: glenn@canalshq.demon.co.uk

Inland Waterways - Pleasure Boats - GB
British Waterways

British Waterways compiles data on pleasure boats licensed on British Waterways canals and rivers through a computerised licence system. Data are available on the numbers of boat licensed by category of boat (privately owned, hired, powered, unpowered). The data cover Great Britain but are only available on a British Waterways administrative unit basis. Results have been collected since 1968 and are published annually in June of the following year.

Status: Ongoing
Collection Method: Computerised licence system
Frequency: Continuous
Reference Period: Annually
Timeliness: 3 months
Earliest Available Data: 1968
National Coverage: Great Britain
Disaggregation: Regional

Statistician
Glenn Millar
British Waterways
Tel: 01923 201356;
Email: glenn@canalshq.demon.co.uk

Maritime Statistics 1997
Department of the Environment, Transport and the Regions

Maritime statistics incorporate the Department's annual survey of freight traffic through the ports of the UK and world fleet data purchased from Lloyds Maritime Information Services Ltd (LMIS). Annual returns of port traffic are completed by harbour authorities or other wharf operators in about 140 ports, with detailed commodity and unitised (container and roll-on/roll-off) breakdowns for major ports with cargo of at least 2 million tonnes a year. The surveys started in 1965 but database analyses are only available from 1982. Detailed statistics for smaller ports (that is those with less than 2 million tonnes of cargo) are only available until 1994. LMIS world fleet data are analysed to produce detailed statistics of the UK registered fleet and the UK owned fleet. UK registered fleet data are available from 1950 onwards. Revised ship classifications were introduced in 1987 and database analyses of the UK registered and owned fleets using these classifications are available from 1986 onwards.

Status: Ongoing
Collection Method: Administrative Records / Statistical Survey
Frequency: Annually
Reference Period: Previous year
Timeliness: In September after end of period. Provisional ports data in early May.
Earliest Available Data: 1965 (ports); 1950 (fleet)
National Coverage: United Kingdom
Disaggregation: Ports and port groups

Statistician
Stephen Reynolds
Department of the Environment, Transport and the Regions
Transport Statistics Freight; TSF1
Tel: 020 7890 4441;
Email: stephen_reynolds@detr.gsi.gov.uk

Products that contain data from this source
Maritime Statistics 1997

Waterborne Freight Statistics 1997
Department of the Environment, Transport and the Regions

The Department presents statistics compiled in annual surveys of domestic waterborne freight traffic by an external consultant. The consultant uses data from the Department's annual port traffic survey supplemented by enquiries for data from barge and wharf operators, and analyses coastal movements and inland waterways traffic in terms of goods lifted (tonnage) and goods moved (tonne-kilometres). The surveys, which started with 1980, have been carried out by the same consultant. Started in 1980 by the current contractor.

Status: Ongoing
Collection Method: Administrative Records
Frequency: Annually
Reference Period: Previous year
Timeliness: In October after end of period
Earliest Available Data: 1980
National Coverage: United Kingdom
Disaggregation: Port groups and major inland waterways

Statistician
Stephen Reynolds
Department of the Environment, Transport and the Regions
Transport Statistics Freight; TSF1
Tel: 020 7890 4441;
Email: maritimestatistics@gtnet.gov.uk

Products that contain data from this source
Waterborne Freight in the United Kingdom 1997

13.9   Tourist Accommodation

English Hotel Occupancy Survey

Sources and Analyses

(Up to 1995)
British Tourist Authority

The English Tourist Board compiles a survey on hotel occupancy using a panel of 550 hotels. Data are available on bed space and bed occupancy and percentage of overseas visitors. The survey covers England and data are available at Tourist Board level. The survey is carried out monthly and results are published annually.

Frequency: Monthly

Statistician
Linda Rattray
British Tourist Authority
Tel: 020 8563 3011;
Email: lrattray@bta.org.uk

Products that contain data from this source
Digest of Tourist Statistics No 22

Tourist Accommodation - Northern Ireland
Department for Culture, Media and Sport; sponsored by Northern Ireland Tourist Board

The Northern Ireland Tourist Board carries out surveys on tourist accommodation. The surveys cover hotel occupancy, self-catering, guesthouse and bed & breakfast accommodation. Data are available on occupancy rates, the percentage of overseas visitors and the average length of stay. The surveys cover Northern Ireland and are available at regional level. They are carried out and reported monthly, with an overview at the end of each year.

Status: Ongoing
Collection Method: Small-scale (Sample) Survey
Frequency: Monthly
National Coverage: Northern Ireland
Disaggregation: Northern Ireland regions

Statistician
Paul Allin
Chief Statistician
Department for Culture, Media and Sport
Analytical Services Unit; Statistics Branch
6th Floor
Haymarket House
2-4 Cockspur Street
London SW1Y 5DH
Tel: 020 7211 2843;
Email: paul.allin@culture.gov.uk

Products that contain data from this source
Digest of Tourist Statistics No 21; Northern Ireland Survey of Hotel Occupancy Annual Report; Survey of Hotel Occupancy: Northern Ireland

Tourist Accommodation - Scotland
Department for Culture, Media and Sport; sponsored by Scottish Tourist Board

The Scottish Tourist Board compiles surveys on tourist accommodation. The surveys cover hotel occupancy, self-catering, caravan and camping parks accommodation. The surveys cover Scotland and are available at Tourist Board level. The surveys are carried out monthly. Surveys have been commissioned by the Scottish Tourist Board and Highlands and Islands Enterprise since the 1970s. Since 1993 the surveys have been jointly commissioned, but despite this 'merger' distinct surveys are still undertaken for both organisations. The results are available each month and are also published in an annual report shortly after the reference period.

Status: Ongoing
Collection Method: Small-scale (Sample) Survey
Frequency: Monthly
National Coverage: Scotland

Statistician
Paul Allin
Chief Statistician
Department for Culture, Media and Sport
Analytical Services Unit; Statistics Branch
6th Floor
Haymarket House
2-4 Cockspur Street
London SW1Y 5DH
Tel: 020 7211 2843;
Email: paul.allin@culture.gov.uk

Products that contain data from this source
Guest House and B&B Occupancy Survey: Scotland; Hotel Occupancy: Scotland; Scottish Accommodation Occupancy Survey Annual Report; Self catering Occupancy Survey: Scotland; Touring Caravan and Camping Occupancy Survey: Scotland; Tourism in Scotland 1997

Tourist Accommodation - Wales
Department for Culture, Media and Sport; sponsored by Welsh Tourist Board

The Welsh Tourist Board compiles a survey on hotel occupancy. The 1994 survey incorporated a sample of 244 hotels. Data are available on occupancy rates and the percentage of overseas visitors staying in hotels. The survey covers Wales and is available at county level. The survey is carried out monthly. Results are published three months after the reference period.

Status: Ongoing
Collection Method: Small-scale (Sample) Survey
Frequency: Monthly
National Coverage: Wales

Statistician
Paul Allin
Chief Statistician
Department for Culture, Media and Sport
Analytical Services Unit; Statistics Branch
6th Floor
Haymarket House
2-4 Cockspur Street
London SW1Y 5DH
Tel: 020 7211 2843;
Email: paul.allin@culture.gov.uk

Products that contain data from this source
Digest of Tourist Statistics No 21; Wales Serviced Accommodation Occupancy Survey

UK Occupancy Survey
Department for Culture, Media and Sport; sponsored by British Tourist Authority/ National Tourist Boards

A monthly survey of a number of hotels, guest houses and B&Bs in each region is conducted. The survey provides information on room occupancy, bedspace occupancy, nights spent and average length of stay. Started as a UK survey in 1997. Previously, and concurrently, some NTBs have run their own occupancy surveys. No occupancy information for England was collected in 1996.

Status: Ongoing
Collection Method: Large-scale (Sample) Survey
Frequency: Monthly
Timeliness: Results available three months after the end of the survey period.
National Coverage: United Kingdom

Statistician
Paul Allin
Chief Statistician
Department for Culture, Media and Sport
Analytical Services Unit; Statistics Branch
6th Floor
Haymarket House
2-4 Cockspur Street
London SW1Y 5DH
Tel: 020 7211 2843;
Email: paul.allin@culture.gov.uk

Products that contain data from this source
UK Occupancy Survey for Service Accommodation, 1997 Annual Report

13.10 Transport - General

Transport Statistics for London
Department of the Environment, Transport and the Regions

A comprehensive reference source for statistics relating to transport, population and employment patterns in Greater London.

Status: Ongoing
Collection Method: Administrative Records
Frequency: Annually
Reference Period: Either calendar year or financial year, depending on type of data
Timeliness: Various, according to promptness of receipt and conflicting work priorities
Earliest Available Data: 1981
Disaggregation: London Borough level

Statistician
Chris Morrey
Department of the Environment, Transport and the Regions
Tel: 020 7890 4746

Transport Statistics for Metropolitan Areas 1998
Department of the Environment, Transport and the Regions

A comprehensive reference source for statistics relating to transport in the former metropolitan counties.

Status: Ongoing
Collection Method: Administrative Records
Frequency: Annually
Earliest Available Data: 1991
Sub-National: Former metropolitan county level
Disaggregation: District level

Statistician
Chris Morrey
Department of the Environment, Transport and the Regions
Tel: 020 7890 4746

Please see:

In other chapters:
(The) ONS Longitudinal Study *(see the Population, Census, Migration and Vital Events chapter)*

13.11 Transport of UK International Trade

Origin and Destination Survey of United Kingdom International Trade
Department of the Environment, Transport and the Regions

Status: Ceased temporarily
Collection Method: Sample survey
Frequency: Ad hoc
Reference Period: 1996
Earliest Available Data: 1991
National Coverage: United Kingdom
Disaggregation: Some regional results are available

Statistician
Chris Overson

Department of the Environment, Transport and the Regions
Tel: 020 7890 4276

See also:

In other chapters:
Trade in Services (Annually) *(see the Economy chapter)*

13 Transport, Travel and Tourism - *Products*

13.12 Abstracts, Compendia, A-Z Catalogues, Directories and Reference Material

International Comparison of Transport Statistics 1970-1994
Department of the Environment, Transport and the Regions

Contains a series of statistical tables comparing different aspects of transport within and between countries in Europe plus USA and Japan.

Delivery: Ceased completely
Frequency: Annually
Price: £25.00
ISBN: 0 11 551932 7

Available from
TSO Publications Centre and Bookshops
Please see Annex B for full address details.

Northern Ireland Transport Statistics 1997/98
Department of the Environment - Northern Ireland

Comprehensive Northern Ireland transport statistics. Contains data on roads, road transport, road accidents, air transport, rail transport and waterborne transport.

Frequency: Annually
Price: £10.00
ISBN: 1 899824 456
ISSN:

Available from
Anne Jordan
Department of the Environment - Northern Ireland
Please see Annex B for full address details.

Scottish Transport Statistics
Scottish Executive

Provides information on Road transport vehicles, Bus and coach travel, Road freight, Toll bridges, Road network, Road traffic, Injury road accidents, Rail services, Air transport, Water transport, Finance and Personal cross-modal travel. Each section consists of groups of tables and charts on that topic, together with some comments on points shown in the tables, and some notes on the definitions and sources of the statistics. Also includes summary trends in Scottish transport over the past ten years, some longer-term historical series, and some comparisons of the statistics for Scotland and Great Britain.

Delivery: Statistical Volume
Frequency: Annually
Price: £10.00
ISBN: 0 11 497259 1

Available from
TSO Publications Centre and Bookshops
Please see Annex B for full address details.

Sources from which data for this product are obtained
Road Accident statistics ("STATS 19" returns) (Scotland); (The) National Travel Survey (NTS); UK Airports - Annual Statements of Movements, Passengers and Cargo; Annual Inquiry to PSV Operators; Continuous Survey of Road Goods; Transport - UK; International Road Haulage - UK; Road Lengths Survey; Road Traffic Surveys; Vehicle Registrations and Stock - GB; Maritime Statistics; Waterborne Freight Statistics

Transport Statistics for London 1998
Department of the Environment, Transport and the Regions

A comprehensive reference source for statistics relating to transport in London. Contains descriptive text, tables and charts on personal travel, traffic, public transport, aviation, air quality, population and employment.

Delivery: Periodic Release
Frequency: Annual
Price: £10.00
ISBN: 1 851121 35 8

Available from
Chris Morrey
Department of the Environment, Transport and the Regions
Great Minster House
76 Marsham Street
London
Tel: 020 7890 4746

Sources from which data for this product are obtained
London Area Transport Survey (LATS) 1991

Transport Statistics for Metropolitan Areas 1998
Department of the Environment, Transport and the Regions

A comprehensive reference source for statistics relating to transport in the West Midlands, Greater Manchester, Merseyside, South Yorkshire, West Yorkshire and Tyne and Wear. Contains descriptive text, tables and charts on personal travel, traffic, public transport, aviation, air quality, population and employment.

Delivery: Periodic Release
Frequency: Triennial
Price: Free
ISBN: 1 85112 835 2

Available from
Chris Morrey
Department of the Environment, Transport and the Regions
Great Minster House
76 Marsham Street
London
Tel: 020 7890 4746

Transport Statistics Great Britain 1998 Edition
Department of the Environment, Transport and the Regions

24th edition of the Compendium of statistics, including road, rail and air travel for Great Britain.

Delivery: Periodic Release
Frequency: Annually
Price: £29.00
ISBN: 0 11 552172 0

Available from
TSO Publications Centre and Bookshops
Please see Annex B for full address details.

Sources from which data for this product are obtained
London Area Transport Survey (LATS) 1991

Transport Trends 1998 Edition
Department of the Environment, Transport and the Regions

Products

Articles with tables and charts summarising the latest trends in transport in Great Britain today, plus 30 transport indicators.

Delivery: Periodic Release
Frequency: Annually
Price: £29.50
ISBN: 1 11 551987 4

Available from
TSO Publications Centre and Bookshops
Please see Annex B for full address details.

Travel by Scottish Residents: Some National Travel Survey Results
Scottish Executive

Provides information about the trends in the average number of journeys and average distance travelled per person per year, and the average length of journey, by mode of travel and by purpose of the journey. It also provides information about travel patterns by age-group, by sex, by socio-economic group, by working status.

Delivery: Statistical Bulletin
Frequency: Occasional
Price: £2.00
ISBN: 0 7480 8102 X
ISSN: 0264 1178

Available from
TSO Publications Centre and Bookshops
Please see Annex B for full address details.

Sources from which data for this product are obtained
(The) National Travel Survey (NTS)

Welsh Transport Statistics
National Assembly for Wales

Provides information on road lengths, registered and licensed vehicles, road freight, road accidents, motoring offences, usage of difference modes of travel, road traffic volumes on major roads, buses and coaches, sea transport, air transport and a variety of transport related financial statistics including central and local government expenditure on roads and transport. There are some supporting charts and maps as well as a section of detailed notes and definitions.

Delivery: Periodic Release
Frequency: Annual
Price: £10.00
ISBN: 0 7504 2316 1
ISSN: 0267 8160

Available from
Publications Unit, Statistical Directorate
National Assembly for Wales
Please see Annex B for full address details.

Sources from which data for this product are obtained
Road Accidents Wales; Road lengths form (TP1); DETR (e.g. National Travel Survey); Home Office; Bus and Coach Statistics Great Britain; Lloyd's Maritime Information Services Ltd; MAFF; Civil Aviation Authority; returns by local authorities to the National Assembly for Wales (previously the Welsh Office) Statistical Directorate; Transport Statistics GB; Welsh Office Departmental Reports; CIPFA Highways and Transportation Statistics; ONS (incl. Family Expenditure Survey, New Earnings Survey, Census of Employment/Annual Employment Survey), DTI, UK Tourism Survey

---

13.13   Air Transport and Travel

ATOL Business
Civil Aviation Authority

Bi-annual publication presenting an analysis of business under air travel organisers' licences covering passengers carried, revenue earned and average price of air travel, including inclusive packaged conducted in the previous seasons, and anticipated in the future season. It details passengers carried under the top 40 licence holders in total and broken down by main category, in the current season, and projected in the forthcoming season. Tables of passengers numbers, either actual or projected, and analysis of total earning and holiday price by season with some commentary.

Delivery: Periodic Release
Frequency: Bi-annually
Price: Free

Available from
ATOL
Civil Aviation Authority
CAA House
45-49 Kingsway
London
Tel: 020 7832 5620;
Fax: 020 7832 6692;
Email: onsquery@atol.org.uk

CAP 560 - Passengers at the London Area Airports and Manchester Airport in 1987
Civil Aviation Authority

The report contains a summary analysis of the findings of the 1987 Origin and Destination Survey.

Delivery: Ad Hoc/One-off Release
Frequency: One-off

Available from
CAA Passenger Surveys
Please see Annex B for full address details.

CAP 598 - Passengers at the Scottish Airports in 1990
Civil Aviation Authority

The report contains a summary analysis of the findings of the 1990 Origin and Destination Survey.

Delivery: Ad Hoc/One-off Release
Frequency: One-off

Available from
CAA Passenger Surveys
Please see Annex B for full address details.

CAP 610 - Passengers at the London Airports 1991
Civil Aviation Authority

The report contains a summary analysis of the findings of the 1991 Origin and Destination Survey.

Delivery: Ad Hoc/One-off Release
Frequency: One-off
Price: £40.00 per copy

Available from
CAA Passenger Surveys
Please see Annex B for full address details.

CAP 618 - Passengers at Central England Airports in 1992/93
Civil Aviation Authority

The report contains a summary analysis of the findings of the 1992/93 Origin and Destination Survey.

Delivery: Ad Hoc/One-off Release
Frequency: One-off
Price: £40.00 per copy

Available from
CAA Passenger Surveys
Please see Annex B for full address details.

CAP 656 - Passengers at North East Airports in 1994/95
Civil Aviation Authority

The report contains a summary analysis of the findings of the 1994/95 Origin and Destination Survey conducted at Norwich, Teeside, Newcastle and Humberside.

Delivery: Ad Hoc/One-off Release
Frequency: One-off
Price: £40.00 per copy

Available from
CAA Passenger Surveys
Please see Annex B for full address details.

CAP 657 - Passengers at South West Airports in 1994/5
Civil Aviation Authority

The report contains a summary analysis of the findings of the 1994/95 Origin and Destination Survey conducted at Bristol, Southampton. Exeter and Cardiff.

Delivery: Ad Hoc/One-off Release
Frequency: One-off
Price: £50.00 per copy

Available from
CAA Passenger Surveys
Please see Annex B for full address details.

CAP 665 - Passengers at the Belfast Airports in 1994/95
Civil Aviation Authority

The report contains a summary analysis of the findings of the 1994 Origin and Destination Survey conducted at Belfast City and Belfast International Airports.

Delivery: Ad Hoc/One-off Release
Frequency: One-off
Price: £40.00 per copy

Available from
CAA Passenger Surveys
Please see Annex B for full address details.

CAP 677 - Passengers at Birmingham, Gatwick, Heathrow, London City, Luton, Manchester and Stansted Airports in 1996
Civil Aviation Authority

The report contains a summary analysis of the findings of the 1996 Origin and Destination Survey conducted at Birmingham, Heathrow, Gatwick, Luton, London City, Manchester and Stansted.

Delivery: Ad Hoc/One-off Release
Frequency: One-off
Price: £120.00 per copy

Available from
CAA Passenger Surveys
Please see Annex B for full address details.

CAP 678 - Passengers at Aberdeen, Edinburgh, Glasgow and Inverness in 1996
Civil Aviation Authority

The report contains a summary analysis of the findings of the 1996 Origin and Destination Survey conducted at Aberdeen, Edinburgh, Glasgow and Inverness.

Delivery: Ad Hoc/One-off Release
Frequency: One-off
Price: £60.00 per copy

Available from
CAA Passenger Surveys
Please see Annex B for full address details.

Punctuality Statistics - Annual Full Analysis
Civil Aviation Authority

Punctuality of passenger aircraft on individual routes at each of the 10 UK airports. Individual airlines are identified and delays are shown with bands of lateness and average delays. Also available free of charge on the internet at "www.caaerg.co.uk" with effect from 1997 data. Punctuality statistics of airlines travelling to/from the 10 major UK airports

Delivery: Periodic Release
Frequency: Annually
Price: Hardcopy - £50.00 Disk - £50.00 plus vat

Available from
CAA Aviation Data Unit
Civil Aviation Authority
CAA House
45-49 Kingsway
London
Tel: 020 7832 5677;
Fax: 020 7832 6724;
Email: geddesl@caaerg.co.uk

Punctuality Statistics - Annual Summary Analysis
Civil Aviation Authority

Punctuality of passenger aircraft delay split into categories scheduled and charter and delay bands, with examples in detail of specified sample routes. Selected representative sample routes punctuality split by scheduled and charter. Also available free of charge on the internet at "www.caaerg.co.uk" with effect from 1997 data.

Delivery: Periodic Release
Frequency: Monthly
Price: Hardcopy £13.00
 Magnetic £13.00 plus VAT

Available from
CAA Aviation Data Unit
Civil Aviation Authority
CAA House
45-49 Kingsway
London
Tel: 020 7832 5677;
Fax: 020 7832 6724;
Email: geddesl@caaerg.co.uk

Punctuality Statistics - Monthly Full Analysis
Civil Aviation Authority

Punctuality of passenger aircraft on individual routes at each of the 10 UK airports. Individual airlines are identified and delays are shown with bands of lateness and average delays. Currently produced in hardcopy or in magnetic form. Also available free of charge on the internet at "www.caaerg.co.uk" with effect from 1997 data. Punctuality of passenger aircraft on individual routes at each of 10 UK airports. Individual airlines are identified and delays are shown with bands of lateness and average delays.

Delivery: Periodic Release
Frequency: Monthly
Price: Hardcopy - £35.00 each; £350.00 (annual subscription) Disk £34.00 ea. plus VAT; £340.00 plus VAT (annual subscription)

Available from
CAA Aviation Data Unit
Civil Aviation Authority
CAA House
45-49 Kingsway
London
Tel: 020 7832 5677;
Fax: 020 7832 6724;
Email: geddesl@caaerg.co.uk

Punctuality Statistics - Monthly Summary Analysis
Civil Aviation Authority

Punctuality of passenger aircraft delay split into categories scheduled and charter and delay bands, with examples in detail of specified sample routes. Selected representative sample routes punctuality split by scheduled and charter. Also available free of charge on the internet at "www.caaerg.co.uk" with effect from 1997 data. Punctuality Statistics on airlines travelling to/from 10 UK airports - for selected routes only

Delivery: Periodic Release
Frequency: Monthly
Price: Hardcopy - £10.00 ea.; £100.00 annual subscription Magnetic - £7.20 ea.; £72.00 plus vat annual subscription

Available from
CAA Aviation Data Unit
Civil Aviation Authority
CAA House
45-49 Kingsway
London
Tel: 020 7832 5677;
Fax: 020 7832 6724;
Email: geddesl@caaerg.co.uk

1992/3 Survey Database
Civil Aviation Authority

The database includes information on traffic levels, type and characteristics of passengers, surface origins and destinations, surface access, demographics, routes taken, frequency of flyer, ticketing details and choice of airport.

Products

Delivery: Ad Hoc/One-off Release
Frequency: One-off

Available from
CAA Passenger Surveys
Please see Annex B for full address details.

1994/95 Survey Database
Civil Aviation Authority

The database includes information on traffic levels, type and characteristics of passengers, surface origins and destinations, surface access, demographics, routes taken, frequency of flyer, ticketing details and choice of airport.

Delivery: Ad Hoc/One-off Release
Frequency: One-off

Available from
CAA Passenger Surveys
Please see Annex B for full address details.

1996 Survey Database
Civil Aviation Authority

The database includes information on traffic levels, type and characteristics of passengers, surface origins and destinations, surface access, demographics, routes taken, frequency of flyer, ticketing details and choice of airport.

Delivery: Ad Hoc/One-off Release
Frequency: One-off
Price: The complete database with 325,000 records and approximately 90 fields per record costs £155,000. However subsets are available e.g. Western Europe, South East planning region etc. Costs are worked out on a pro rata basis according to the number of records in the subset.

Available from
CAA Passenger Surveys
Please see Annex B for full address details.

1997 -1999 Survey Database
Civil Aviation Authority

The database includes information on traffic levels, type and characteristics of passengers, surface origins and destinations, surface access, demographics, routes taken, frequency of flyer, ticketing details and choice of airport.

Delivery: Periodic Release
Frequency: Quarterly
Price: The complete 1997 database with 150,000 records and approximately 90 fields per record costs £53,000. However subsets are available e.g. Western Europe, South East planning region etc. Costs are worked out on a pro rata basis according to the number of records in the subset.

Available from
CAA Passenger Surveys
Please see Annex B for full address details.

UK Airlines - Annual Operating, Traffic and Financial Statistics
Civil Aviation Authority

Statistical information on activity of some 50 major UK airlines. Information includes number of flights, passengers and cargo carried capacity and fleet utilisation. Passenger volumes are provided for individual domestic routes. Also available free of charge on the internet at "www.caaerg.co.uk" with effect from 1997 data. Statistical information on activity of some 50 major UK airlines

Delivery: Periodic Release
Frequency: Annually
Price: Hardcopy - £18.00 Magnetic - £18.00 plus VAT

Available from
CAA Aviation Data Unit
Civil Aviation Authority
CAA House
45-49 Kingsway
London
Tel: 020 7832 5677;
Fax: 020 7832 6724;
Email: geddesl@caaerg.co.uk

UK Airlines - Monthly Operating and Traffic Statistics
Civil Aviation Authority

Statistical information on activity of some 50 major UK airlines. Information includes number of flights, passengers and cargo carried capacity and fleet utilisation. Passenger volumes are provided for individual domestic routes. Also available free of charge on the internet at "www.caaerg.co.uk" with effect from 1997 data. Statistical information on activity of some 50 UK airlines

Delivery: Periodic Release
Frequency: Monthly
Price: Hardcopy - £6.80 ea.; £68.00 annual subscription Magnetic - £6.20 ea.; £62.00 plus VAT annual subscription

Available from
CAA Aviation Data Unit
Civil Aviation Authority
CAA House
45-49 Kingsway
London
Tel: 020 7832 5677;
Fax: 020 7832 6724;
Email: geddesl@caaerg.co.uk

UK Airports Annual Statements of Movements, Passengers and

Available from
CAA Passenger Surveys
Please see Annex B for full address details.

Cargo
Civil Aviation Authority

Provides current year and time series information on activity at UK Airports. Also available free of charge on the internet at "www.caaerg.co.uk" with effect from 1997 data.

Delivery: Periodic Release
Frequency: Annually
Price: £17.00 for paper copy £17.00 + VAT for magnetic media.

Available from
CAA Aviation Data Unit
Civil Aviation Authority
CAA House
45-49 Kingsway
London
Tel: 020 7832 5677;
Fax: 020 7832 6724;
Email: geddesl@caaerg.co.uk

UK Airports, Monthly Statements of Movements, Passengers and Cargo
Civil Aviation Authority

Provides monthly figures relating to aircraft activity at UK airports. Also available free of charge on the internet at "www.caaerg.co.uk" with effect from 1997 data.

Delivery: Periodic Release
Frequency: Monthly
Price: Paper copy - £7.00 each Magnetic media - £6.20 each plus VAT Yearly subscription - £70.00 for hardcopy; £62.00 plus VAT for magnetic media

Available from
CAA Aviation Data Unit
Civil Aviation Authority
CAA House
45-49 Kingsway
London
Tel: 020 7832 5677;
Fax: 020 7832 6724;
Email: geddesl@caaerg.co.uk

See also:
In this chapter:
Scottish Transport Statistics *(13.12)*
Transport Statistics Great Britain 1998 Edition *(13.12)*
Transport Trends 1998 Edition *(13.12)*

In other chapters:
Indicators of Sustainable Development - United Kingdom (see the Environment chapter)

13.14 Domestic Outbound and Inbound Tourism

Digest of Tourist Statistics No 22
British Tourist Authority

A wealth of facts and figures relating to tourism to, within and from the UK. Contains data on international tourism, domestic tourism, tourism and the economy, sightseeing, hotel numbers and occupancy rates.

Frequency: Annual
Price: £75.00
ISBN: 0 7095 7099 6

Available from
British Tourist Authority
Please see Annex B for full address details

Sources from which data for this product are obtained
British National Travel Survey - GB; English Hotel Occupancy Survey (up to 1995); Overseas Leisure Visitors Survey - GB; The UK Tourism Survey; Tourist Accommodation - Northern Ireland; Tourist Accommodation - Wales

Forest Enterprise Visitor Survey Reports
Forestry Commission; sponsored by Forest Enterprise

Reports on visitor surveys carried out at Forest Enterprise sites throughout GB. One report for each survey. About 15-20 surveys each year since 1995.

Frequency: Annually
Price: Most reports £2.00 each

Available from
Sheila Ward
Room 407
Forestry Commission
231 Corstophine Road
Edinburgh EH12 7AT
Tel: 0131 314 6218;
Email: sheila.ward@forestry.gov.uk

Sources from which data for this product are obtained
Forest Enterprise Visitor Surveys

Forest Visitor Surveys (annual summary reports)
Forestry Commission

Summary report, with one-page summary for each forest visitor survey carried out in the year. Mostly Forest Enterprise visitor surveys, but also results from household surveys, cabin and campsite surveys, etc.

Frequency: Annually
Price: £2.00 for each year's report

Available from
Sheila Ward
Room 407

Forestry Commission
231 Corstophine Road
Edinburgh EH12 7AT
Tel: 0131 314 6218;
Email: sheila.ward@forestry.gov.uk

Sources from which data for this product are obtained
Forest Enterprise Visitor Surveys

Heritage Monitor 1998
British Tourist Authority

A detailed look at ancient monuments, churches and historic buildings from a conservation and tourism viewpoint. Contains data on the numbers of historic buildings and conservation areas, properties open to the public, admission charges and visitor trends. Formerly English Heritage Monitor.

Frequency: Annual
Price: £17.50

Available from
British Tourist Authority
Please see Annex B for full address details

Sources from which data for this product are obtained
Visits to Tourist Attractions - UK; English Churches and Visitors; English Cathedrals and Tourism: Problems and Opportunities

Northern Ireland Survey of Visitor Attractions
Northern Ireland Tourist Board

An overview of the number of visits to the various attractions across the whole of Northern Ireland during the sample year. An analysis of the out-of-state visitors (proportion of non-Northern Ireland residents) usage of attractions, together with analyses of; revenue generated, seasonality, top attractions, visitor profiles ownership and annual trends. Contains data on: number of attractions by attraction type; visitor numbers by visitor type; market share of visitors; revenue from charging attractions by attraction type; seasonality by attraction type; top attractions, forest parks, country parks and gardens; visitor profile, overseas visitor content, child adult ratios; ownership by attraction type, visitors; trend in visitor numbers 1993 to survey year by attraction type.

Delivery: Periodic Release
Frequency: Annually
Price: Free on request

Available from
Iain Bryson
Northern Ireland Tourist Board

St Anne's Court,
59 North Street,
Belfast BT1 1NB
Tel: 028 9023 1221;
Email: i.bryson@nitb.com

Northern Ireland Tourism Facts
Northern Ireland Tourist Board

A summary overview of all visitor and domestic tourism in Northern Ireland during the sample year. Analysis of volume of tourism, revenue, key markets, visitor profiles, seasonality, accommodation, occupancy levels and visitor attractions for both visitor and domestic tourism in Northern Ireland with annual trends.

Delivery: Periodic Release
Frequency: Annually
Price: Free on request

Available from
John McGouran
Northern Ireland Tourist Board
St Anne's Court,
59 North Street,
Belfast BT1 1NB
Tel: 028 9023 1221;
Email: j.mcgouran@nitb.com

Overseas Travel and Tourism - First Release
Office for National Statistics

Monthly estimates of overseas travel and tourism - raw data by month showing number of overseas visitors to the UK from 3 areas of residence: North America, Western Europe and Other Areas; raw data by month showing number of UK residents visits abroad by 3 destinations: North America, Western Europe and Other Areas; raw data by month showing earnings from overseas visits to the UK and the expenditure of UK residents going abroad; seasonally adjusted data of the number of overseas visitors to the UK and their spending and of the number of UK residents going abroad and their expenditure.

Delivery: First Release
Frequency: Monthly
Price: £36:30 by annual subscription

Available from
ONS Press Office
Office for National Statistics
Please see Annex B for full address details.

Sources from which data for this product are obtained
International Passenger Survey - UK

Regional Tourism Facts 1997
British Tourist Authority

A set of ten regional reports detailing tourism facts in graphs, diagrams, tables and text for each English tourism region. Contains data on trips, visits, expenditure, demographic profile, accommodation used, transport used, overseas and domestic visitors, hotel occupancy, employment, and visits to attractions.

Frequency: Annual
Price: £10.00 per region, £90.00 for set of ten

Available from
British Tourist Authority
Please see Annex B for full address details.

Sources from which data for this product are obtained
Regional Tourism; The United Kingdom Occupancy Survey

Scottish Visitor Attraction Monitor
Scottish Tourist Board

The Visitor Attraction Monitor is an annual postal survey of Scottish Visitor Attractions. The report contains details of 981 attractions throughout Scotland.

Frequency: Annually
Price: £15.00 - Please make cheques payable to the: Scottish Tourist Board

Available from
Scottish Tourist Board
23 Ravelston Terrace
Edinburgh EH4 3EU
or
British Tourist Authority
Please see Annex B for full address details

Sources from which data for this product are obtained
Visits to Tourist Attractions - UK

Sightseeing in the UK
National Tourist Boards

Contains various information on the number of visitors to and the admission prices for those UK tourist attractions that received 10,000+ visitors during the year. Produced annually using information from the Survey of Visitors to tourist Attractions. Summary text with charts and photos for the first half of the publication; second half comprises tables.

Delivery: Periodic Release
Frequency: Annually
Price: £22.50 - Sightseeing in the UK 1997

Available from
British Tourist Authority
Please see Annex B for full address details.

Sources from which data for this product are obtained
Survey of visits to tourist attractions; Visits to Tourist Attractions - UK

Sightseeing in the UK 1997
British Tourist Authority

Analysis of the use and capacity of attractions based on a survey of all main tourist sights. Contains data on the number of visitors to attractions, new attractions, opening periods, admission charges, overseas visitors, demand relative to capacity, employment, capital expenditure and revenue trends.

Frequency: Annual
Price: £22.50

Available from
British Tourist Authority
Please see Annex B for full address details.

Sources from which data for this product are obtained
Visits to Tourist Attractions 1997 - UK

Tourism - Annual Statistics
Eurostat

Tourism in the European Union. Contains data on tourist accommodation and guest flows, accommodation capacity, other tourist activities, persons employed in the tourism sector, arrivals of tourists at borders, tourist expenditure and the balance of payments items 'travel' and 'passenger transport'.

Frequency: Annual
Price: 35 ECU
ISBN: 92 826 8622 1

Available from
TSO Publications Centre and Bookshops
Please see Annex B for full address details.

Sources from which data for this product are obtained
Tourism - Europe

Tourism in Europe - Key Figures 1997-98
Eurostat

A synthesis of the most recent and comparable figures collected in European countries on tourism, supply and demand, and on international trade in tourism

Delivery: Ad hoc/One-off Release
Frequency: Annual
Price: 7 ECU
ISSN: 92 828 7295 5

Available from
TSO Publications Centre and Bookshops or ONS Direct
Please see Annex B for full address details.

Tourism in Scotland 1997
Scottish Tourist Board

General publication of statistics relating to tourism in Scotland in 1997. This covers the tourism activities of Scottish adults, and the performance of the Scottish tourism industry in 1997.

Delivery: Periodic Release
Frequency: Annually

Available from
Karen Gladysz-Gryff
Scottish Tourist Board
23 Ravelston Terrace
Edinburgh EH4 3EU
Tel: 0131 472 2391;
Email: karen.gladysz-gryff@stb.gov.uk

Sources from which data for this product are obtained
Tourist Accommodation - Scotland

Tourism Intelligence Quarterly
British Tourist Authority

A quarterly information service which collates and interprets current statistical data. Contains data on expenditure, employment, overseas visitors, UK residents' tourism abroad, mode of travel, tourism within Britain, hotel occupancy, and forecasts of the future market.

Frequency: Quarterly
Price: £90.00
ISSN: 0309-8958

Available from
British Tourist Authority
Please see Annex B for full address details

Sources from which data for this product are obtained
British National Travel Survey - GB; The UK Tourism Survey

Travel Trends - A Report on the 1997 International Passenger Survey
Office for National Statistics

Travel Trends presents the main results from the International Passenger Survey (IPS) which collects information on travel to and from the UK. The 1998 edition concentrates on the findings of the 1997 IPS, but also focuses on the short and long term trends in travel and tourism.

Delivery: Periodic Release
Frequency: Annually
Price: 1998 edition relating to the 1997 IPS £39.50
ISBN: 0 11 621090 7

Available from
TSO Publications Centre and Bookshops or ONS Direct
Please see Annex B for full address details.

Sources from which data for this product are obtained
International Passenger Survey - UK

UK Leisure Day Visits - Summary of the 1996 Survey Findings
British Tourist Authority

Report on a survey carried out in 1996 by Social and Community Planning Research (now National Centre for Social Research) for a number of organisations including DCMS. A further Day Visits Survey is being conducted in 1998.

Frequency: Ad-hoc
Price: £15.00
ISBN: 0 86170 488 6

Available from
Chief Statistician
Department for Culture, Media and Sport
Room 601
Haymarket House
2-4 Cockspur Street
London SW1Y 5DH
Tel: 020 7211 2843

Sources from which data for this product are obtained
Countryside Commission; Countryside Council for Wales; Wales Tourist Board, Scottish Natural Heritage; Scottish Tourist Board; Forestry Commission; British Waterways Board and Environment Agency

---

UK Tourist 1998
National Tourist Boards of the UK (WTB, NITB, STB and ETB)

The aim is to provide information on the tourism undertaken by UK adults in a particular year. It covers both domestic and outbound tourism and provides information on trips, nights spent and expenditure. It is published annually, and is based on the results of the UK Tourism Survey. The information is principally presented in tables, although there is some text and a few charts in a summary at the start of the

publication. Topics covered include nights stayed, accommodation used, age of tourist, purpose of trip, main activity undertaken, transport used, expenditure.

Delivery: Periodic Release
Frequency: Annually
Price: £70.00 (1996 version)
ISBN: 0 85419 5238

Available from
British Tourist Authority
Please see Annex B for full address details

Sources from which data for this product are obtained
United Kingdom Tourism Survey

(The) UK Tourist: Statistics 1998
Sponsored by National Tourist Boards

Statistical information on the volume and value of tourism undertaken by the resident population of the UK. Contains data on the purpose and month of trip, destination, transport, accommodation, leisure activities, use of travel trade, and categories of spending.

Frequency: Annual
Price: £95.00
ISBN: 0 85419 578 5

Available from
English Tourism Council
Mail Order
Thames Tower
Black's Road
Hammersmith
London W6 9EL
Tel: 020 8563 3276

Sources from which data for this product are obtained
The UK Tourism Survey

Visitors to Tourist Attractions in Wales 1997
Wales Tourist Board

Latest statistics on visitor numbers to tourist attractions in Wales. Contains data on visitor numbers to tourist attractions for the current year with three years' historical data.

Delivery: Periodic Release
Frequency: Annual
Price: free

Available from
Imelda Shelley
Research Information Officer
Wales Tourist Board
Brunel House
2 Fitzalan Road
Cardiff CF24 1UY
Tel: 029 2049 9909

Sources from which data for this product are obtained
WTB - Survey of Visits to Tourist Attractions

Visits to Tourist Attractions 1998
National Tourist Boards

Annual publication on number of visitors to UK tourist attractions with more than 10,000 visitors in the year. Tables list number of visitors and admission prices at the various sites. Primarily aimed at the Tourist Industry, and academics, it presents information from the annual Survey of Visits to Tourist Attractions, conducted by the NTBs. There is a brief summary text, followed by many tables, showing the more successful sites by type of attraction, and lists of sites for England, Scotland, Wales and Northern Ireland. More detailed presentation of the Survey information is contained in 'Sightseeing in the UK'. Series goes back until at least 1993.

Delivery: Periodic Release
Frequency: Annually
Price: £19.50 for Visits to Tourist Attractions in 1996.

Available from
English Tourist Board
Mail Order Department
Thames Tower
Black's Road
Hammersmith
London W6 9EL

Sources from which data for this product are obtained
Survey of visits to tourist attractions conducted by the National Tourist Boards, English Heritage, The National Trust, Historical Royal Palaces, CADW and The National Trust for Scotland and Historic Scotland

---

See also:
In other chapters:
BFI Handbook - Produced Annually *(see the Commerce, Construction, Energy and Industry chapter)*

13.15 Personal Transport and Travel

Cycling in Great Britain
Department of the Environment, Transport and the Regions

A report drawing together data on cycling in Great Britain from a number of sources. Topics include cycle traffic (from the Road Traffic Census), characteristics of cyclists (from the National Travel Survey - NTS), cycling to work (from the Census and Labour Force Survey), cycling in London (from the London Area Transport Survey) and accidents involving cyclists (from the Road Accidents Database). The latest report was published in August 1996, using data from the 1993-95 NTS, and 1991 or 1995 data from other sources. Unpublished data are available from DETR.

Frequency: Ad hoc
Price: £20.00
ISBN: 0 11 551864 9

Available from
TSO Publications Centre and Bookshops
Please see Annex B for full address details.
or
Spencer Broadley
Department of the Environment, Transport and the Regions
Please see Annex B for full address details.

Sources from which data for this product are obtained
British Crime Survey - England and Wales; General Household Survey - GB; Labour Force Survey; London Area Transport Survey (LATS) 1991; London Journey Times Survey; The National Travel Survey (NTS)

Focus on Personal Travel
Department of the Environment, Transport and the Regions

Contains data for a three-year survey period from the National Travel Survey (NTS), on journeys made and distance travelled per person per year. These are analysed by personal details (such as age, working status and driving licence holding) and general household details (such as income and car availability). Other sources of data relevant to personal travel are also included. It is planned that 'Focus on Personal Travel' will be published every third year, with NTS Bulletins giving updates of the main NTS data in the intervening years, articles on topics of interest using NTS data will also appear in the annual publication 'Transport Trends'. Chapters in the 1998 edition (covering the 1995-97 survey period) covered personal travel, how and why men and women travel, travel by children, aspects of car ownership and use, trends in public transport usage and travel to work (including data from the Labour Force Survey). A Technical Report, including a copy of the questionnaire and travel diary, notes and definitions and comparisons with other data sources, is published annually by the Office for National Statistics, who carry out the NTS on behalf of DETR. (see separate entry). The latest report was published in November 1998, covering data for 1995-97. Future reports are planned to be published approximately 10 months after the end of each survey period. Personal travel factsheets and unpublished data are available from DETR.

Frequency: Every 3 years
Price: £29.50
ISBN: 0 11 552055 4

Available from
TSO Publications Centre and Bookshops
Please see Annex B for full address details.
or
Spencer Broadley
Department of the Environment, Transport and the Regions
Please see Annex B for full address details.

Sources from which data for this product are obtained
English House Condition Survey (EHCS); Family Expenditure Survey - UK; Labour Force Survey; The National Travel Survey (NTS)

London Area Transport Survey (LATS) 1991
London Research Centre

The database holds results from the 1991 London Area Transport Survey, a household interview survey (of about 60,000 households) reporting travel on weekdays, including origins and destinations of London journeys, modes of transport, and journey purposes. Related databases include results from roadside interview surveys and public transport surveys.

Price: Tabulations priced on request

Available from
Mike Collop
Department of the Environment, Transport and the Regions
Great Minster House
76 Marsham Street
London
Tel: 020 7890 3096;
Fax: 020 7890 2166

Sources from which data for this product are obtained
London Area Transport Survey (LATS) 1991

National Travel Survey
Department of the Environment, Transport and the Regions

Contains data for a three-year survey period from the National Travel Survey (NTS), on journeys made and distance travelled per person per year. These are analysed by personal details, such as age, working status and driving licence holding and general household details (such as income and car availability). It is planned that 'Focus on Personal Travel' will be published every third year, with NTS Bulletins giving updates of the main NTS data in the intervening years. Articles on topics of interest using NTS data will also appear in the annual publication 'Transport Trends'.

The bulletins will mainly consist of updated tables from Chapter 2 of 'Focus on Personal Travel' (see separate entry) which looks at the distance travelled and number of journeys made per person per year, by individual (such as age and sex) and general characteristics (such as income and car availability). A Technical Report, including a copy of the questionnaire and travel diary, notes and definitions and comparisons with other data sources, is published annually by the Office for National Statistics, who carry out the NTS on behalf of DETR. (See separate entry). The latest was published in October 1997, covering data for 1994-96. Previous reports have covered each three-year period from rolling 1989-91 (except 1990-92). Future bulletins are planned to be published approximately 9 months after the end of each survey period. Every third year 'Focus on Personal Travel' will be published instead of the NTS Report, which will include data from the NTS. This was last published in November 1998, covering data for 1995-97, and the next report is planned for 2001, covering the period 1998-2001. Personal travel factsheets and unpublished data are available from DETR.

Frequency: Annually (except every third year)

Available from
TSO Publications Centre and Bookshops
Please see Annex B for full address details.
or
Spencer Broadley
Department of the Environment, Transport and the Regions
Please see Annex B for full address details

Sources from which data for this product are obtained
The National Travel Survey (NTS)

National Travel Survey - Technical Report
Department of the Environment, Transport and the Regions

This report is published annually by the Social Surveys Division of the ONS, who carry out the National Travel Survey (NTS) on behalf of the Department of the Environment, Transport and the Regions (DETR). The 1997 report describes the methodology of the NTS, and is intended as a working reference manual. It describes all of the survey processes and procedures including the sample design, field methodology, data processing and data file production. Details of response rates, sampling errors, comparisons with other sources, and main database variables are included from the 1997 edition. A simpler Technical Report is being published annually, and usually available approximately 3 months after the end of each year's survey period.

Frequency: Annually
Price: £10.00
ISBN: 1 85774 323 7

Available from
Social Survey Division
Office for National Statistics
D1/15
1 Drummond Gate
London SW1V 2QQ
Tel: 020 7533 5500
or
Spencer Broadley
Department of the Environment, Transport and the Regions
Please see Annex B for full address details.

Sources from which data for this product are obtained
The National Travel Survey (NTS)

Travel in London - London Area Transport Survey 1991
London Research Centre

This publication reports a selection of results from the 1991 London Area Transport Survey including an overview of Londoner's travel, use of private vehicles, travel by rail, bus, walking, bicycles, motorcycles and taxis.

Price: £26.00
ISBN: 0 11 701835 X

Available from
TSO Publications Centre and Bookshops
Please see Annex B for full address details.

Sources from which data for this product are obtained
London Area Transport Survey (LATS) 1991

Walking in Great Britain
Department of the Environment, Transport and the Regions

A report drawing together data on walking in Great Britain from a number of sources. Topics include characteristics of walkers (from the National Travel Survey - NTS), walking to work (from the Census and Labour Force Survey), walking in London (from the London Area Transport Survey) and accidents involving pedestrians (from the Road Accidents Database). The latest report was published in June 1998, including data from the 1994-96 NTS, and 1991 or 1996 data from other sources. Unpublished data and a factsheet are available from DETR.

Frequency: Ad hoc
Price: £25.00
ISBN: 0 11 552040 6

Available from
TSO Publications Centre and Bookshops
Please see Annex B for full address details.
or
Spencer Broadley
Department of the Environment, Transport and the Regions
Please see Annex B for full address details.

Sources from which data for this product are obtained
General Household Survey - GB; Labour Force Survey; London Area Transport Survey (LATS) 1991; London Journey Times Survey; The National Travel Survey (NTS); UK Day Visits Survey

See also:
In this chapter:
CAP 598 - Passengers at the Scottish Airports in 1990 *(13.13)*
CAP 610 - Passengers at the London Airports 1991 *(13.13)*
CAP 677 - Passengers at Birmingham, Gatwick, Heathrow, London City, Luton, Manchester and Stansted Airports in 1996 *(13.13)*
CAP 678 - Passengers at Aberdeen, Edinburgh, Glasgow and Inverness in 1996 *(13.13)*
Journey Times Survey 1997: Inner and Outer London *(13.22)*
London Traffic Monitoring Report: 1997 *(13.19)*
Scottish Transport Statistics *(13.12)*
1992/3 Survey Database *(13.13)*
1994/95 Survey Database *(13.13)*
1996 Survey Database *(13.13)*
1997 -1999 Survey Database *(13.13)*
Transport Statistics for London 1998 *(13.12)*
Transport Statistics Great Britain 1998 Edition *(13.12)*
Transport Trends 1998 Edition *(13.12)*

In other chapters:
Indicators of Sustainable Development - United Kingdom *(see the Environment chapter)*

13.16 Rail Transport and Travel

Quarterly Rail Bulletin
Department of the Environment, Transport and the Regions

Quarterly round up of rail (including Freight) statistics.

Delivery: Periodic Release
Frequency: Quarterly
Price: Free

Available from
Lucy de Jong
Department of the Environment, Transport and the Regions
Great Minster House
76 Marsham Street
London
Tel: 020 7890 4129;
Fax: 020 7676 2165

See also:
In this chapter:
Journey Times Survey 1997: Inner and Outer London *(13.19)*
Scottish Transport Statistics *(13.12)*
Transport Statistics Great Britain 1998 Edition *(13.12)*
Transport Trends 1998 Edition *(13.12)*

In other chapters:
Financial Statistics *(see the Economy chapter)*

13.17 Road Accidents

Key Road Accident Statistics
Scottish Executive

Gives the number of accidents, casualties by severity, casualties by type of road, casualties by mode of transport, and child casualties, including trends in recent years.

Delivery: Statistical Bulletin
Frequency: Annually
Price: £2.00
ISBN: 0 7480 8610 2
ISSN: 0264 1178

Available from
TSO Publications Centre and Bookshops
Please see Annex B for full address details.

Sources from which data for this product are obtained
Road Accident statistics ("STATS 19" returns) (Scotland)

Road Accident Statistics in English Regions 1996
Department of the Environment, Transport and the Regions

This gives statistics of road accidents on a local basis for England. It concentrates on accidents as being incidents which may reflect a need for local action and is intended to be of most benefit to traffic engineers, planners and administrators in Local Government Offices for the regions. This is the last edition of this publication.

Delivery: News/Press Release
Frequency: Annually
Price: £15.00
ISBN: 0 11 552012 0

Available from
TSO Publications Centre and Bookshops
Please see Annex B for full address details.

Road Accidents Great Britain 1997 - the Casualty Report
Department of the Environment, Transport and the Regions

Articles and latest statistics on personal injury road accidents. Contains a comprehensive analysis of road accident statistics, including tables and charts.

Frequency: Annual
Price: £17.00
ISBN: 0 11 552068 6
ISSN:

Available from
TSO Publications Centre and Bookshops
Please see Annex B for full address details.

Sources from which data for this product are obtained
Road Accident statistics ("STATS 19" returns) (Scotland); Road Accidents - Great Britain 1996

Road Accidents Scotland
Scottish Executive

Provides a commentary which summarises the key statistics and identifies the most interesting and significant points. This is followed by groups of tables and charts on Accidents, Accident costs, Vehicles involved, Car drivers, Drivers breath tested, drink-drive accidents and casualties. There are notes on the definitions and sources of the statistics.

Delivery: Statistical Volume
Frequency: Annual
Price: £8.00
ISBN: 0 7480 7106 7

Available from
TSO Publications Centre and Bookshops
Please see Annex B for full address details.

Sources from which data for this product are obtained
Road Accident statistics ("STATS 19" returns) (Scotland)

Road Accidents: Wales
National Assembly for Wales

Data on personal injury accidents occurring on Welsh roads. Contains data by severity of injury and type of road user, class of road, speed limit, time of day, driving conditions, and county. A number of sections presenting data on areas of topical interest are included.

Delivery: Periodic Release
Frequency: Annual
Price: £10.00 postage paid within the UK
ISBN: 0 7504 2315 3
ISSN: 0263-9653

Available from
Publications Unit
Statistical Directorate
National Assembly for Wales
Please see Annex B for full address details

Sources from which data for this product are obtained
Road Accident Statistics ('STATS 19' returns), Road Lengths - Wales, Welsh Transport Statistics

Road Casualties Great Britain - Final Figures 1997
Department of the Environment, Transport and the Regions

An annual bulletin pulling together 1996 figures.

Delivery: Periodic Release
Frequency: Annually
Price: Free
ISBN: 1 85112 814 X

Available from
Transport Statistics - Road Safety
Room Zone 1/28
Department of the Environment, Transport and the Regions
Great Minster House
76 Marsham Street
London SW1P 4DR
Tel: 020 7890 3078

Sources from which data for this product are obtained
Road Accident statistics ("STATS 19" returns) (Scotland)

Road Casualties in Wales (Statistical Release)
National Assembly for Wales

Summary of annual road casualties in Wales. Statistics and graphs on road casualties, by severity, broken down by unitary authority.

Delivery: News/Press Release
Frequency: Annual
Price: Unpriced

Available from
Publications Unit, Statistical Directorate
National Assembly for Wales
Please see Annex B for full address details

Sources from which data for this product are obtained
Road Accident Statistics ("STATS 19" returns)

Road Safety Monitor

Survey of Seat Belt Wearing in Northern Ireland. The series which began in 1994 has been conducted biannually in April and October. However from April 1997 the survey has been conducted on an annual basis.

Delivery: Periodic Release
Frequency: Annually

Available from
Anne Jordan
Department of the Environment - Northern Ireland
Please see Annex B for full address details

Road Traffic Accident Statistics, Annual Report (Northern Ireland)
Royal Ulster Constabulary

Commentary, graphs and detailed tables about road traffic accidents and casualties. Includes analyses of persons killed or injured (broken down by road user type, age, sex) and of accidents (by severity, causation factors, road user responsible, location, road and weather conditions, month of the year and time of day and day of week).

Delivery: Periodic Release
Frequency: Annual
Price: Free

Available from
Central Statistics Unit
RUC Lisnassharragh
42 Montgomery Road
Belfast BT6 9LD
Tel: 01232 650222;
Fax: 01232 700998

Sources from which data for this product are obtained
Road Accidents - Northern Ireland

Royal Ulster Constabulary Chief Constable's Annual Report
Royal Ulster Constabulary

Delivery: Periodic Release
Frequency: Annual
Price: Free

Available from
Central Statistics Unit
RUC Lisnassharragh
42 Montgomery Road
Belfast BT6 9LD
Tel: 01232 650222;
Fax: 01232 700998

Sources from which data for this product are obtained
Road Accidents - Northern Ireland

Traffic Accident Bulletin (Northern Ireland)
Royal Ulster Constabulary

Summary of traffic accident statistics for Northern Ireland.

Delivery: Periodic Release
Frequency: Quarterly
Price: Free

Available from
Central Statistics Unit
RUC Lisnassharragh
42 Montgomery Road
Belfast BT6 9LD
Tel: 01232 650222;
Fax: 01232 700998

Sources from which data for this product are obtained
Road Accidents - Northern Ireland

See also:
In this chapter:
Cycling in Great Britain *(13.15)*
Scottish Transport Statistics *(13.12)*
Transport Statistics Great Britain 1998 Edition *(13.12)*
Transport Trends 1998 Edition *(13.12)*
Walking in Great Britain *(13.15)*

In other chapters:
Motor Vehicle Offences in Scotland *(see the Crime and Justice chapter)*

13.18 Roads

National Road Maintenance Condition Survey 1997
Department of the Environment, Transport and the Regions

Report on the annual survey. Contains data on road condition by type of road and type of defect.

Delivery: Periodic Release
Frequency: Annual
Price: Free
ISBN: 1 85112 813 1

Sources from which data for this product are obtained
National Road Maintenance Condition Survey

See also:
In this chapter:
Road Traffic Statistics Great Britain: 1997 *(13.19)*
Scottish Transport Statistics *(13.12)*
Traffic in Great Britain *(13.19)*
Transport Statistics Great Britain 1998 Edition *(13.12)*
Transport Trends 1998 Edition *(13.12)*
Vehicle Speeds in Great Britain 1997 *(13.19)*

In other chapters:
Indicators of Sustainable Development - United Kingdom *(see the Environment chapter)*

13.19 Road Transport and Travel

Annual Inquiry to PSV Operators - Quinquennial Review
Department of the Environment, Transport and the Regions

Review of methodology of the annual survey of bus and coach operators.

Delivery: Ad Hoc/One-off Release
Frequency: Quinquennial
Price: Free
ISBN: 1 85112 822 0

Available from
Paul O'Hara
Department of the Environment, Transport and the Regions
Great Minster House
76 Marsham Street
London
Tel: 020 7271 3734

Bus and Coach Statistics
Scottish Executive

Provides information about the trends in bus and coach services in Scotland, including distances travelled by vehicles, number of bus passenger journeys, fare indices, passenger receipts, public transport support, operating costs, vehicle stock and staffing.

Delivery: Statistical Bulletin
Frequency: Annually
Price: £ 2.00
ISBN: 0 7480 8085 6
ISSN: 0264-1178

Available from
TSO Publications Centre and Bookshops
Please see Annex B for full address details.

Sources from which data for this product are obtained
Annual Inquiry to PSV Operators

Bus and Coach Statistics Great Britain 1996/97
Department of the Environment, Transport and the Regions

Presents bus and coach statistics time series for Great Britain, split into five main geographical areas. Contains data on bus and coach mileage, passenger journeys, fares, passenger receipts, government financial support, operating costs, vehicle stock, and bus and coach staff. Extracts also available on disk. Bus, coach, light rail, national rail, London Underground statistics. Key variables include patronage and fares indices over a long time series, in some tables from 1950.

Delivery: Periodic Release
Frequency: Annual
Price: £20.00
ISBN: 0 11 551975 0

Available from
TSO Publications Centre and Bookshops
Please see Annex B for full address details.

Busdata - 1998 a Compendium of Bus, Coach and Taxi Statistics
Department of the Environment, Transport and the Regions

Presents a wide range of bus, coach and taxi data time series for Great Britain, split into five main geographical areas. Contains data on operator returns, assaults, road accidents, personal characteristics of bus users, vehicle testing and licensing, and travel to work. Extracts also available on disk. Bus, coach, London Underground, metro, light rail, national rail and taxi statistics. Comprising patronage, fares data and other key variables over a long time series (in some cases from 1950).

Delivery: Periodic Release
Frequency: Annual
Price: Free
ISBN: 1 85112 823 9
ISSN:

Available from
Paul O'Hara
Department of the Environment, Transport and the Regions
Great Minster House
76 Marsham Street
London
Tel: 020 7271 3734

Focus on Roads
Department of the Environment, Transport and the Regions

Descriptive text, tables and charts on road traffic volumes and other road data derived from various sources, including the national traffic surveys. Contains 30 pages with the latest annual information on traffic, road lengths, vehicle numbers and other data relating to road travel. Analyses of traffic by vehicle type and road class are given, as well as analyses by month of year, day of week and hour of day. Information on road lengths broken down by class and region are provided and there is information on road conditions and expenditure on roads. There

Products

is also information about vehicle numbers broken down by body type and taxation class ands a section devoted to the environmental aspects of road traffic.

Delivery: First Release
Frequency: Annually
Price: £29.50
ISBN: 0 11 552056 2

Available from
TSO Publications Centre and Bookshops
Please see Annex B for full address details.

International Road Haulage by United Kingdom Registered Vehicles
Department of the Environment, Transport and the Regions

Contains tables on international road haulage. Contains data on goods carried by country of unloading and loading, by commodity, by UK region expressed in terms of number of consignments, tonnes and tonne-kilometres.

Delivery: Hardcopy or electronic tables
Frequency: Annual
Price: Free
ISBN: 0 11 551927 0

Available from
TSF4, 1/28
Department of the Environment, Transport and the Regions
Great Minster House
76 Marsham Street
London SW1P 4DR
Tel: 020 7890 3093.
Email: john_garnsworthy@detr.gsi.gov.uk

Sources from which data for this product are obtained
International Road Haulage - UK

London Traffic Monitoring Report: 1997
Department of the Environment, Transport and the Regions

Descriptive text, tables and charts on traffic in London. Contains data on traffic speeds and traffic flows in the London area, mainly for the years between 1971 and 1994. Average speeds are given separately for peak and off-peak periods, and for different areas within Greater London. Traffic flows crossing a network of cordons and screen lines are given by vehicle type. The total volume of motor traffic on principal, minor and all roads has been included since 1992. This book has now ceased publication.

Delivery: Periodic Release
Frequency: Annual
Price: £16.00
ISBN: 0 11 551935 1

Available from
TSO Publications Centre and Bookshops
Please see Annex B for full address details.

Northern Ireland Road and Rail Transport Statistics Quarterly Bulletin
Department of the Environment - Northern Ireland

Frequency: Quarterly
Price: Free

Available from
Anne Jordan
Department of the Environment - Northern Ireland
Please see Annex B for full address details.

Quinquennial Review Local Bus Fares Survey
Department of the Environment, Transport and the Regions

Review of methodology of quarterly fares panel survey of bus operators. Methodology for the quarterly survey of the bus fares panel.

Delivery: Ad Hoc/One-off Release
Frequency: Quinquennial
Price: Free
ISBN: 1 85112 827 1

Available from
Paul O'Hara
Department of the Environment, Transport and the Regions
Great Minster House
76 Marsham Street
London
Tel: 020 7271 3734

Sources from which data for this product are obtained
Local Bus Fares Survey

Road Goods Vehicles Travelling to Mainland Europe
Department of the Environment, Transport and the Regions

Contains descriptive text, tables and charts on goods vehicles travelling to mainland Europe. Contains data on powered road goods vehicle and unaccompanied trailers by country of disembarkation, by port group, and country of registration of the vehicle.

Delivery: Hardcopy publication
Frequency: Quarterly
Price: Free
ISSN: 0952-1156

Available from
TSF4
Room 109

Department of the Environment, Transport and the Regions
Tollgate House
Houlton Street
Bristol BS2 9DJ
Tel: 0117 987 8484;
Email: lisa_ayers@detr.gsi.gov.uk

Sources from which data for this product are obtained
Road Goods Vehicles Travelling to Mainland Europe - GB

Road Traffic Statistics Great Britain: 1997
Department of the Environment, Transport and the Regions

Descriptive text, tables and charts on road traffic volumes derived from the National Traffic Census. Contains the latest annual estimates of road traffic in Great Britain by road class and by vehicle type. Other sections show how traffic varies by month, day of week and time of day. Time series show how traffic has changed over the last ten years and over the last forty years. While the information presented in this report draws mainly on the results of the National Traffic Census, it also includes information from other sources to provide a picture of road traffic patterns and the road network, how they are changing, what road transport is used for, what it costs and what its effect is on the environment. This book ceased publication in 1997 and has been replaced by the 1999 Road Traffic Statistics Report.

Delivery: Periodic Release
Frequency: Annual
Price: £19.00
ISBN: 0 11 551930 0

Available from
TSO Publications Centre and Bookshops
Please see Annex B for full address details.

Road Travel Speeds in English Urban Areas
Department of the Environment, Transport and the Regions

Descriptive text, tables and charts on vehicle speeds in 24 English towns and cities, ranging in size from the West Midlands conurbation to Peterborough.

Frequency: Triennial
Price: £6.70
ISBN: 0 11 551629 8

Available from
TSO Publications Centre and Bookshops
Please see Annex B for full address details.

Road Travel Speeds in English Urban Areas: 1996/97
Department of the Environment, Transport and the Regions

Frequency: Tri-Annually
Price: £18.00
ISBN: 0 11 552015 5

Available from
TSO Publications Centre and Bookshops
Please see Annex B for full address details.

Seatbelt Survey - Northern Ireland
Department of the Environment - Northern Ireland

Survey of Seat Belt Wearing in Northern Ireland. The series which began in 1994 has been conducted biannually in April and October. However from April 1997 the survey has been conducted on an annual basis.

Delivery: Periodic Release
Frequency: Annually

Available from
Anne Jordan
Department of the Environment - Northern Ireland
Please see Annex B for full address details.

Traffic in Great Britain
Department of the Environment, Transport and the Regions

A short statistics bulletin with some text, tables and charts on the latest traffic figures. Contains 14 pages with the latest quarterly information on road traffic. Limited analyses of traffic by vehicle type and road class are given.

Delivery: Periodic Release
Frequency: Quarterly
Price: One off copies - Free
 Annual Subscription - £27.00
ISSN: 0269 0993

Available from
Kerrick Macafee
Room 1/29
Department of the Environment, Transport and the Regions
Great Minster House
76 Marsham Street
London SW1P 4DR
Tel: 020 7890 6396

Traffic Speeds in Inner and Outer London: 1998
Department of the Environment, Transport and the Regions

Descriptive text, tables, maps and charts on traffic speed in Central and Outer London. Contains data on the network surveyed, the average traffic speeds, the proportion of time vehicles spend at various speeds, and the parking intensity, split by time of day.

Delivery: Periodic Release
Frequency: Periodic
Price: Free
ISBN: 1 85112 838 7

Available from
TSO Publications Centre and Bookshops
Please see Annex B for full address details.

Traffic Speeds on English Trunk Roads 1995
Department of the Environment, Transport and the Regions

Delivery: Periodic Release
Frequency: Periodic
Price: £10.00
ISBN: 0 11 551870 3

Available from
Chris Morrey
Department of the Environment, Transport and the Regions
Great Minster House
76 Marsham Street
London
Tel: 020 7890 4746

(The) Transport of Goods by Road in Great Britain 1998: Annual Report of the Continuing Survey of Road Goods Transport
Department of the Environment, Transport and the Regions

Descriptive text, tables and charts on GB road freight activity. Contains statistics on goods lifted by commodity, length of haul and type of vehicle, goods moved, vehicle kilometres and annual average activity per lorry.

Delivery: Hardcopy publication
Frequency: Annual
Price: £10.00
ISBN: 1 851121 69 2

Available from
Department of the Environment, Transport and the Regions
Publications Sales Centre
Unit 21
Goldthorpe Industrial Estate
Goldthorpe
Rotherham S63 9BL
Tel: 01709 891318;
Fax: 01709 881673

Sources from which data for this product are obtained
Continuous Survey of Road Goods Transport - UK

Vehicle Excise Duty Evasion in Great Britain
Department of the Environment, Transport and the Regions

Text and tables reporting the results of a survey of vehicle excise duty evasions. The survey is conducted every five years throughout Great Britain and is being extended to cover the United Kingdom in the course of the 1999 survey. Data are available by type of vehicle and at regional level.

Delivery: Periodic release
Frequency: 5 yearly
Price: £10.50 in the 1994-95 survey
ISBN: 0 11 551694 8
ISSN:

Available from
Andrew Ledger
Department of the Environment, Transport and the Regions
Tel: 020 7890 6399;
Email: andrew.ledger@detr.gsi.gov.uk

Sources from which data for this product are obtained
Vehicle Registrations and Stock - GB

Vehicle Licensing Statistics
Department of the Environment, Transport and the Regions

Compendium of information covering many aspects of vehicle licensing statistics, including current vehicle stock, new registrations, and goods vehicles, published annually. Contains 27 tables, supported by twelve pages of commentary and charts on the main results, and seven pages of notes and definitions for technical guidance. The tables cover a wide range of topics including vehicle taxation, location of registered keeper, vehicle construction, vehicle age, petrol and diesel propulsion, and international comparisons.

Frequency: Annual,
Price: £13.00
ISBN: 0 11 551715 4

Available from
TSO Publications Centre and Bookshops
Please see Annex B for full address details.

Sources from which data for this product are obtained
Vehicle Registrations and Stock - GB

Vehicle Licensing Statistics: 1998
Department of the Environment, Transport and the Regions

Tables showing licensing details by the GB

Products

vehicle stock as at the end of December 1998. Based on administrative data held by the DVLA, data are presented by body type, by tax class, by year of first registration, by engine size, gross weight.

Delivery: Periodic release, latest being 24/6/1999
Frequency: Annual,
Price: Free

Available from
Andrew Ledger
Department of the Environment, Transport and the Regions
Tel: 020 7890 6399;
Email: andrew_ledger@detr.gsi.gov.uk

Vehicle Speeds in Great Britain 1997
Department of the Environment, Transport and the Regions

Delivery: Periodic Release
Frequency: Annually
Price: Free
ISBN: 1 85112 836 0

Available from
Transport Statistics - Road Safety
Room Zone 1/28
Department of the Environment, Transport and the Regions
Great Minster House
76 Marsham Street
London SW1P 4DR
Tel: 020 7890 3078

See also:
In this chapter:
Cycling in Great Britain *(13.15)*
Scottish Transport Statistics *(13.12)*
Transport Statistics Great Britain 1998 Edition *(13.12)*
Transport Trends 1998 Edition *(13.12)*

In other chapters:
Indicators of Sustainable Development - United Kingdom *(see the Environment chapter)*
Motor Vehicle Offences in Scotland *(see the Crime and Justice chapter)*

13.20 Sea and Waterborne Transport and Travel

Maritime Statistics 1997
Department of the Environment, Transport and the Regions

Statistics of the annual freight traffic of UK ports, and UK and world merchant fleets (replaces the previous publications, Port Statistics and Merchant Fleet Statistics).

Ports - Contains annual freight traffic tonnages for all UK ports; detailed breakdowns of foreign and domestic traffic, bulk commodities, and unitised (container and roll-on/roll-off) traffic for major ports; sea passenger movements; accompanied passenger vehicles; ship arrivals; and historic statistics. Merchant Fleet - Contains data on numbers, gross tonnage and deadweight tonnage of merchant ships in UK owned fleet and UK registered fleet, with analyses by type of ship; world fleet by flag and ship type; and historic statistics.

Delivery: Periodic Release
Frequency: Annually
Price: £30.00
ISBN: 0 11 552080 5

Available from
TSO Publications Centre and Bookshops
Please see Annex B for full address details.

Sources from which data for this product are obtained
Maritime Statistics 1997

Waterborne Freight in the United Kingdom 1997
Department of the Environment, Transport and the Regions

The Department presents statistics on freight traffic moved within the UK by water transport, as compiled by a consultant under contract from the Department. Contains data on traffic carried by both inland craft (barges) and seagoing vessels along the inland waterway system and around the coast of the UK.

Delivery: Periodic Release
Frequency: Annually
Price: Free
ISBN: 1 85112 837 9

Available from
Maritime Statistics Branch
Zone 1/26
Department of the Environment, Transport and the Regions
Great Minster House
76 Marsham Street
London SW1P 4DR
Tel: 020 7890 3087

Sources from which data for this product are obtained
Waterborne Freight Statistics 1997

See also:
In this chapter:
Scottish Transport Statistics *(13.12)*
Transport Statistics Great Britain 1998 Edition *(13.12)*
Transport Trends 1998 Edition *(13.12)*

13.21 Tourist Accommodation

Digest of Tourism Statistics No 22
British Tourist Authority

A summary of information on tourism, taken from a variety of sources (such as the International Passenger Survey, Survey of visits to tourist attractions, UK Tourism Survey). Mainly covers information relating to the UK, but also provides information on international travel.

Delivery: Periodic Release
Frequency: Annually
Price: £75.00

Available from
British Tourist Authority
Please see Annex B for full address details

Sources from which data for this product are obtained
International Passenger Survey - UK; Survey of visits to tourist attractions; United Kingdom Tourism Survey

---

Guest House and B&B Occupancy: Wales
Analysis of B&B and Guest House room and bed occupancy in Wales. Breakdowns by region, grade of establishment, tariff, length of stay, etc.

Delivery: Periodic Release
Frequency: Monthly
Price: On application

Available from
Senior Research Officer
Wales Tourist Board
Brunel House
2 Fitzalan Road
Cardiff CF24 1UY
Tel: 029 2049 9909

Sources from which data for this product are obtained

WTB Serviced Accommodation Occupancy Survey

Hotel Occupancy Survey: Wales
Wales Tourist Board

Analysis of hotel occupancy in Wales, looking at room & bedspace occupancy by region, hotel grade, hotel price etc.

Delivery: Periodic Release
Frequency: Annually / monthly
Price: On application

Available from
Claire Goold
Senior Research Officer
Welsh Tourist Accommodation Enquiries
Wales Tourist Board
Brunel House
2 Fitzalan Road
Cardiff CF24 1UY
Tel: 029 2049 9909

Sources from which data for this product are obtained
WTB Serviced Accommodation Occupancy Survey

Northern Ireland Survey of Guesthouses and Bed & Breakfast Accommodation
Northern Ireland Tourist Board

An overview of the performance of Guesthouses and Bed & Breakfasts in Northern Ireland during the sample year. Assesses patterns of demand for bedrooms and bed spaces throughout the year. Contains comparative trend data on numbers of bedrooms, bed spaces and their utilisation, average length of stay, percentage of overseas visitor content (proportion of non-Northern Ireland residents as a proportion of total arrivals) and occupancy rates.

Delivery: Periodic Release
Frequency: Annually
Price: Free on request

Available from
Iain Bryson
Northern Ireland Tourist Board
St Anne's Court,
59 North Street,
Belfast BT1 1NB
Tel: 028 9023 1221;
Email: i.bryson@nitb.com

Northern Ireland Survey of Hotel Occupancy Annual Report
Northern Ireland Tourist Board

An overview of the performance of the hotel industry in Northern Ireland during survey year. Assesses patterns of demand for bedrooms and bed spaces in the Province's hotels throughout the year. Contains comparative trend data on numbers of hotels, bedrooms, bed spaces and their utilisation, average length of stay, percentage of overseas visitor content (proportion of non-Northern Ireland residents as a proportion of total hotels arrivals) and occupancy rates.

Delivery: Periodic Release
Frequency: Annually / monthly
Price: Free on request

Available from
Iain Bryson
Northern Ireland Tourist Board
St Anne's Court,
59 North Street,
Belfast BT1 1NB
Tel: 028 9023 1221;
Email: i.bryson@nitb.com

Sources from which data for this product are obtained
Tourist Accommodation - Northern Ireland

Northern Ireland Survey of Self-Catering Accommodation Occupancy - Annual Report
Northern Ireland Tourist Board

An overview of the performance of Self-Catering in Northern Ireland during the sample year. Assesses patterns of occupancy throughout the year. Contains comparative trend data on average occupancy, weeks sold, percentage of overseas visitors (proportion of non-Northern Ireland residents), nationality, seasonality, bookings, number of units and total self-catering accommodation stock.

Delivery: Periodic Release
Frequency: Annually
Price: Free on request

Available from
John McGouran
Northern Ireland Tourist Board
St Anne's Court,
59 North Street,
Belfast BT1 1NB
Tel: 028 9023 1221;
Email: j.mcgouran@nitb.com

Scottish Accommodation Occupancy Survey Annual Report
Scottish Tourist Board

The performance of hotels, self-catering accommodation, caravan and camping accommodation. Contains data on bedroom and bed space occupancy rates, percentage of overseas bed occupancy, occupancy by area, hotel size, tariff, location and group membership.

Frequency: Annually
Price: £30.00

Available from
Karen Gladysz-Gryff
Scottish Tourist Board
23 Ravelston Terrace
Edinburgh EH4 3EU
Tel: 0131 472 2391;
Email: karen.gladysz-gryff@stb.gov.uk

Sources from which data for this product are obtained
Tourist Accommodation - Scotland

Scottish Guest House and Bed and Breakfast Occupancy Survey
Scottish Tourist Board

Analysis of Scottish occupancy. Breakdowns by Scottish region, classification of accommodation, size of establishment etc.

Delivery: Periodic Release
Frequency: Annually / Monthly
Price: £40.00 for two accommodation sets, £50.00 for all five sectors.

Available from
Fiona Cunningham
Scottish Tourist Board
Please see Annex B for full address details.

Sources from which data for this product are obtained
Tourist Accommodation - Scotland

Scottish Hotel Occupancy
British Tourist Authority; sponsored by Scottish Tourist Board

Analysis of hotel occupancy in Scotland, by region and grade, size, room tariff and location of hotel.

Delivery: Periodic Release
Frequency: Annually / monthly

Available from
Fiona Cunningham
Scottish Tourist Board
Please see Annex B for full address details.

Sources from which data for this product are obtained
Tourist Accommodation - Scotland

Self Catering Occupancy Survey: Scotland
British Tourist Authority; sponsored by Scottish Tourist Board

Information of unit occupancy of self catering accommodation in Scotland, by region and grade of accommodation.

Delivery: Periodic Release
Frequency: Annually / monthly

Available from
Fiona Cunningham
Scottish Tourist Board
Please see Annex B for full address details

Sources from which data for this product are obtained
Tourist Accommodation - Scotland

Survey of Hotel Occupancy: Northern Ireland
Northern Ireland Tourist Board

Analysis of room and bedspace occupancy in hotels in Northern Ireland, by region, time of year and by type of hotel (location, size, grading).

Delivery: Periodic Release
Frequency: Annually / monthly

Available from
John McGouran
Northern Ireland Tourist Board
St Anne's Court,
59 North Street,
Belfast BT1 1NB
Tel: 028 9023 1221;
Email: j.mcgouran@nitb.com

Sources from which data for this product are obtained
Tourist Accommodation - Northern Ireland

Survey of Tourism Trends in Wales
Wales Tourist Board

Bulletin and an annual management report of the latest statistics on tourism trends in Wales. Contains data on demand levels in self-catering accommodation, caravan parks and attractions.

Frequency: Annual, Monthly bulletin
Price: £10.00

Available from
Claire Goold
Wales Tourist Board
Brunel House
2 Fitzalan Road
Cardiff CF2 1UY
Tel: 029 2049 9909

Touring Caravan and Camping Occupancy Survey: Scotland
Scottish Tourist Board

Information on camping pitch occupancy in Scotland, shown by region, nightly cost of pitch, size and grade of site.

Delivery: Periodic Release
Frequency: Annually / monthly

Available from
Fiona Cunningham
Scottish Tourist Board
Please see Annex B for full address details

Sources from which data for this product are obtained
Tourist Accommodation - Scotland

UK Occupancy Survey for Service Accommodation, 1997 Annual Report
British Tourist Authority

Information on room and bedspace occupancy of hotels, guest houses and B&B's in the UK. Includes special analysis of English RTB's. Information available on average length of stay, origin of visitor, weekday/weekend, size/location/ classification of establishment.

Delivery: Periodic Release
Frequency: Annually
ISBN: 0-854-19-551-3

Available from
Northern Ireland Tourist Accommodation Enquiries
Northern Ireland Tourist Board
St Anne's Court
59 North Street
Belfast BT1 1NB
Tel: 028 9023 1221

Paul Allin
Chief Statistician
Department for Culture, Media and Sport
Room 601
Haymarket House
2-4 Cockspur Street
London SW1Y 5DH
Tel: 020 7211 2843;
Email: paul.allin@culture.gov.uk

Sources from which data for this product are obtained
UK Occupancy Survey

Wales Serviced Accommodation Occupancy Survey 1998
Wales Tourist Board

Bulletin and annual report of the latest statistics on hotel, guest house and B+B occupancy in Wales. Contains data on the monthly usage of hotels, guesthouses and B+B establishments in Wales.

Frequency: Annual, monthly bulletin

Available from
Claire Goold
Senior Research Officer
Wales Tourist Board
Brunel House
2 Fitzalan Road
Cardiff CF2 1UY
Tel: 029 2047 5216;
Email: clairg@tourism.wales.gov.uk

Sources from which data for this product are obtained
Tourist Accommodation - Wales

See also:
In this chapter:
Digest of Tourist Statistics No 22 *(13.14)*

13.22   Transport - General

Journey Times Survey 1997: Inner and Outer London
Department of the Environment, Transport and the Regions

Description of journey times in selected areas of London. A report on average door-to-door journeys times by different modes of transport (car, bicycle and public transport) for short and long trips in inner London and short trips in outer London. The report will analyse changes in journey times for such trips since the previous survey. Has now ceased publication.

Delivery: Periodic Release
Frequency: Annually
Price: Free
ISBN: 1 85112 832 8

Available from
Chris Morrey
Department of the Environment, Transport and the Regions
Great Minster House
76 Marsham Street
London
Tel: 020 7890 4746

MQ6 - Society - Overseas Travel and Tourism
Office for National Statistics

Quarterly business monitor detailing quarterly results from the IPS. Visits to and from the UK by overseas residents and visits abroad by UK residents; overseas earnings and expenditure; visitor nights in the UK by overseas residents and abroad by UK residents; number of visits to the UK by overseas residents by main purpose of visit and area of residence by mode of transport used; number of overseas visits to the UK by country of residence and by mode of travel; overnight visits to the regions of the UK by main area of residence; number of visits abroad by UK residents by main purpose of visit and area visited by mode of travel; number of visits abroad by UK residents by main country visited and by mode of travel; monthly data on overseas visitors to the UK, visits abroad by UK residents and earnings and expenditure data.

Delivery: Periodic Release
Frequency: Quarterly
Price: As at June 1999 £85.00 by subscription for 4 issues.
ISBN: 0-11-537994-0 Qtr 4 1998 edition

Available from
TSO Publications Centre and Bookshops
Please see Annex B for full address details.

Sources from which data for this product are obtained
International Passenger Survey - UK

Travelpac - Compact Dataset
Office for National Statistics

The Travelpac compact dataset is a set of selected variables drawn from the International Passenger Survey (IPS). It provides invaluable information on travel patterns to and from the UK telling you how many people travelled, how they travelled, how long they stayed and how much they spent. Variables include: mode of travel, main purpose of visit, country of residence for overseas visitors, country of visit for UK residents, time of year of travel, age band of traveller, gender, expenditure, nights spent on visit and sample size.

Delivery: Periodic Release
Frequency: Annually
Price: Dataset for 1997 only - £75.00 Dataset for 1993-7 - £150.00
ISBN: 1 85774 256 7

Available from
International Passenger Survey Branch
Room B2/12
Office for National Statistics
1 Drummond Gate
London SW1V 2QQ
Tel: 020 7533 5765

Sources from which data for this product are obtained
International Passenger Survey - UK

See also:
In this chapter:
Overseas Travel and Tourism - First Release *(13.14)*
Scottish Transport Statistics *(13.12)*
Transport Statistics Great Britain 1998 Edition *(13.12)*
Travel Trends - A Report on the 1997 International Passenger Survey *(13.14)*

13.23 Transport of UK International Trade

Origin and Destination Survey of UK International Trade 1996
Department of the Environment, Transport and the Regions

Weight of international trade by inland origins and destinations, by mode of transport and by foreign country. Contains data on UK regions of origin and destination, and inland modes of transport, port areas, sea routes, trade with rest of Europe and air trade.

Delivery: Hardcopy publication
Frequency: Occasional
Price: £12.00
ISBN: 1 85112 145 5

Available from
Department of the Environment, Transport and the Regions
Publications Sales Centre
Unit 21
Goldthorpe Industrial Estate
Goldthorpe
Rotherham S63 9BL
Tel: 01709 891318

Agriculture, Fishing, Food and Forestry

Statistics covering **Agriculture, Fishing, Food and Forestry** are collected, administered and disseminated by a number of separate Departments, Agencies and organisations including the **Ministry of Agriculture, Fisheries and Food, the Forestry Commission, Scottish Executive, the National Assembly for Wales,** and the **Department of Agriculture for Northern Ireland.** The available statistics embrace a number of subject areas including: **Animal and Poultry Diseases, Food Safety, Animal Feed, Arable Crops, Economics of Agriculture, Eggs, Fishing, Food, Beverages and Nutrition, Forestry, Horticulture, Human Resources and Management, Land Prices, Land Use, Rents and Tenures, Livestock and Meat, Milk and Milk Products, Prices, Resources used in Farming, Structure of Agricultural Holdings.**

The basic data are generated from a number of separate information 'Sources' and the resultant statistics are disseminated through a whole range of statistical 'Analyses' and 'Products', all of which are described in the following chapter. Users looking for a cross-section of UK-wide statistics on **Agriculture, Fishing, Food and Forestry** may find the following products useful:

> **Agriculture in the United Kingdom** (annual publication)
> **Forestry Commission Facts and Figures** (annual publication)
> **UK Sea Fisheries Statistics** (annual publication)

Users interested in a wider range of official statistics including **Agriculture, Fishing, Food and Forestry** statistics may like to refer to the following compendia:

> On-line Databases (See Chapter 1):
> > **StatBase - StatStore**

> Hardcopy Compendia (See Chapter 2):
> > **Annual Abstract of Statistics**
> > **Britain 2000: The official Yearbook of the United Kingdom**
> > **Monthly Digest of Statistics**
> > **Regional Trends**

Users may also find what they need on the various Departmental Websites. These are listed in Chapter 1.

14 Agriculture, Fishing, Food and Forestry - *Sources and Analyses*

14.1 Abstracts, Compendia, A-Z Catalogues, Directories and Reference Material

Agricultural and Horticultural Census - Scotland
Scottish Executive Rural Affairs Department

The Scottish Executive Rural Affairs Department conducts a survey on agricultural holdings. Data are available by crops, livestock, labour and machinery. Contains some small discontinuities to statistics on "main" holdings at various points between 1967 and 1976 due to redefinitions of "minor" (or statistically insignificant) holdings

Status: Ongoing
Collection Method: Census
Frequency: Bi-annually
Reference Period: 1st June and 1st December
Timeliness: 4-5 months interval
Earliest Available Data: early 1900's
National Coverage: Scotland
Disaggregation: parishes (subject to disclosure restrictions)

Statistician
Jonathan Davidson
Scottish Executive
Tel: 0131 244 6131

Products that contain data from this source
Agricultural and Horticulture Census, Scotland - June Provisional Results (Press Release); Agricultural Census Summary Sheets by Geographic Area; Agricultural Sample Census - December (Press Release); Economic Report on Scottish Agriculture; Final Results of June Agricultural Census (Press Release); Results of Censuses of Agriculture for Minor Holdings in Scotland, 1987-1996

December Agricultural Survey - England and Wales
Ministry of Agriculture, Fisheries and Food

This is a statutory survey and is a sample of the main agricultural and horticultural holdings in England and Wales selected from recent June Censuses together with some new holdings. The survey complements the June Census data, giving a half-year snapshot of farming. Data are collected on the number of cattle and calves, pigs, sheep and lambs, areas of autumn and winter sown crops, production of hay and silage and fertilizer stocks. A section on vegetables was included for the period 1964-67 and figures for quarried lime were introduced in 1983. Questions on poultry, labour, areas of grass and quarried lime were discontinued in 1996.

Status: Ongoing
Collection Method: Large-scale (Sample) Survey
Frequency: Annually
Reference Period: Survey date in December
Timeliness: 3 -4 months
Earliest Available Data: December 1951
National Coverage: England and Wales

Statistician
Alison James
Ministry of Agriculture, Fisheries and Food
Statistics (Census and Surveys); Branch F
Tel: 01904 455328;
Email: a.james@esg.maff.gov.uk

Products that contain data from this source
December Agriculture Survey (Statistics Notice)

December Agricultural Survey - Northern Ireland
Department of Agriculture - Northern Ireland

The Department of Agriculture for Northern Ireland conducts the December Agricultural Survey based on a sample of 5,000 farms. The Survey provides estimates of agricultural land use and livestock numbers at 1 December. Estimates on hay and silage production are also collected.

Status: Ongoing
Collection Method: Small-scale (Sample) Survey
Frequency: Annually
Reference Period: 1st December
Timeliness: 2 months.
Earliest Available Data: 1931
National Coverage: Northern Ireland

Statistician
Sheila Magee
Department of Agriculture - Northern Ireland
Tel: 028 9052 4427;
Email: sheila.magee@dani.gov.uk

June Agricultural and Horticultural Census - England & Wales
Ministry of Agriculture, Fisheries and Food

Data are collected on land use, land tenure, labour, crops, livestock, and horticulture for all main holdings registered in England and Wales. Currently all of the economically significant holdings are sampled. Economically very small holdings are sampled once in every three years, with the very smallest of these being sampled at a rate of one in ten. Data are available for standard regions, counties and groups of parishes on request.

Status: Ongoing
Collection Method: Large-scale (Sample) Survey
Frequency: Annually
Reference Period: Census date (First weekday in June)
Timeliness: 3 months for provisional results. 7 months for final results.
Earliest Available Data: 1987 (electronic format)
National Coverage: England and Wales
Disaggregation: Government Office Region (GOR); County; Groups of parishes; UK Department

Statistician
Richard Pereira
Ministry of Agriculture, Fisheries and Food
Statistics (Census & Surveys); D
Tel: 01904 455304;
Email: r.pereira@esg.maff.gov.uk

Products that contain data from this source
Frequency Distribution Tables; Regional and County Analyses; Regional Trends; Social Trends; The Digest of Agricultural Census Statistics UK

June Agricultural and Horticultural Census - Northern Ireland
Department of Agriculture - Northern Ireland

The Department of Agriculture for Northern Ireland conducts an Agricultural Census which covers all active farm businesses. The Census provides estimates of agricultural land use, livestock numbers and the number of persons working on farms. Distributions of farms by type and size and of crops and livestock by enterprise size are available.

Status: Ongoing
Collection Method: Postal
Frequency: Annually
Reference Period: 1st June
Earliest Available Data: 1847
National Coverage: Northern Ireland
Disaggregation: District Council Area (Northern Ireland); County

Statistician
Sheila Magee
Department of Agriculture - Northern Ireland
Tel: 028 9052 4427;
Email: sheila.magee@dani.gov.uk

Products that contain data from this source
Agricultural Census Data; Agriculture in the United Kingdom; The Digest of Agricultural Census Statistics UK

14.2 Animal Feed

Animal Compound Feedingstuffs: Sales Value and Volume - GB
Ministry of Agriculture, Fisheries and Food

This monthly survey collects the value and volume of sales from a sample of retail animal feed compounders in Great Britain. There are sufficient volunteers (around 25) to ensure a 60% coverage of all main feed categories. The survey results are used to calculate the cost to the farmer of animal feed.

Status: Ongoing
Collection Method: Voluntary sample of retail animal compound feed manufacturers
Frequency: Monthly
Reference Period: Statistical months (4,4,5 pattern)
Timeliness: Approx. 14 weeks (due to confidentiality reasons)
Earliest Available Data: 1995
National Coverage: Great Britain

Statistician
Steve Walton
Ministry of Agriculture, Fisheries and Food
Commodities and Food; A
Tel: 00 44 (0) 1904 455058;
Email: s.walton@esg.maff.gov.uk

Products that contain data from this source
Agriculture in the United Kingdom; GB Animal Feed Statistical Notice

Animal Feedstuffs - Northern Ireland
Department of Agriculture - Northern Ireland

The Department of Agriculture for Northern Ireland conducts a survey of animal feedstuffs manufacturers in Northern Ireland. Data are collected on the manufacture and exports of various types of animal feedstuffs. The survey has been carried out for over 25 years. Data are collected annually for those producing under 5,000 tonnes a year and monthly for all others.

Status: Ongoing
Collection Method: Postal Census
Frequency: Monthly, Quarterly and Annually
Earliest Available Data: 1979
National Coverage: Northern Ireland

Statistician
Norman Fulton
Department of Agriculture - Northern Ireland
Economics and Statistics Division
Tel: 028 9052 4419;
Email: norman.fulton@dani.gov.uk

Products that contain data from this source
Deliveries of Compound and Other Processed Animal Feedstuffs by Northern Ireland Feedstuff Manufacturers; Usage of Raw Materials of the Production of Animal Feedstuffs and for Delivery as Straights.

Cereals and Animal Feed Stocks Held by Importers and Dealers
Ministry of Agriculture, Fisheries and Food

This is a census survey of stocks of cereals, oilcakes, meals and other animal feedingstuffs ingredients, held by all known importers and dealers in the UK. Companies with a large turnover (stocks in excess of 3 thousand tonne in Dec) are surveyed quarterly whilst smaller companies are surveyed annually. There are approximately 30 companies surveyed quarterly and 120 annually.

Status: Ongoing
Collection Method: Census
Frequency: Quarterly and annual
Reference Period: Jan - Mar, Apr - June, Jul - Sept, Oct - Dec and calendar years
National Coverage: United Kingdom

Statistician
Steve Walton
Ministry of Agriculture, Fisheries and Food
Commodities and Food; A
Tel: 00 44 (0) 1904 455058;
Email: s.walton@esg.maff.gov.uk

Products that contain data from this source

Agriculture in the United Kingdom; Annual Abstract of Statistics; Monthly Digest of Statistics

Composition of Main Livestock Rations - GB
Ministry of Agriculture, Fisheries and Food

This sample survey covers the composition of main livestock rations. It is also known as the Livestock Rations Survey (LRS). About 35 of the companies producing animal compound feedingstuffs in Great Britain participate. Data are available on the composition of raw materials used in animal compound feedingstuffs. The information is used to monitor trends in raw materials usage by individual livestock categories.

Data are collected twice a year. Results for the January-June Survey are published in September and for the July-December Survey in April. (The survey has been suspended pending investigation into the method of data collection and the usefulness of the results).

Status: Suspended pending review
Collection Method: Voluntary sample of compound feed manufacturers
Frequency: Bi-annually
Reference Period: January-June; July-December
Timeliness: Published approx. 12-16 weeks after data collection
Earliest Available Data: 1976
National Coverage: Great Britain

Statistician
Steve Walton
Ministry of Agriculture, Fisheries and Food
Commodities and Food; A
Tel: 00 44 (0) 1904 455058;
Email: s.walton@esg.maff.gov.uk

Products that contain data from this source
Statistical Notices up to December 1995

Grain Fed to Livestock Survey - England and Wales
Ministry of Agriculture, Fisheries and Food

This is a voluntary survey, based on a sample of agricultural holdings which returned livestock and said that they fed straight grain at the most recent June Census. Data are collected on the amounts of grain fed to livestock, the types of grain and the types of livestock.

Status: Ongoing
Collection Method: Small-scale (Sample) Survey
Frequency: Monthly
Reference Period: The month
Timeliness: Within 8 weeks of survey date.
Earliest Available Data: 1986
National Coverage: England and Wales

Statistician

Alison James
Ministry of Agriculture, Fisheries and Food
Statistics (Census and Surveys); Branch F
Tel: 01904 455328;
Email: a.james@esg.maff.gov.uk

Products that contain data from this source
Grain Fed to Livestock (Statistics Notice)

Poultry Feed Production for Units with Large Flocks - GB
Ministry of Agriculture, Fisheries and Food

This GB census survey covers the production of poultry feed by poultry units for their own use. Data are available on the production of poultry compound feedingstuffs and the usage of cereals in this production. The survey was introduced to identify the considerable volume of cereals used by the poultry industry in the production of poultry compound feedingstuffs.

Status: Ongoing
Collection Method: Census
Frequency: Monthly
Reference Period: Statistical months(4,4,5)
Timeliness: 5 weeks after the end of the survey period
Earliest Available Data: July 1994
National Coverage: Great Britain

Statistician
Steve Walton
Ministry of Agriculture, Fisheries and Food
Commodities and Food; A
Tel: 00 44 (0) 1904 455058;
Email: s.walton@esg.maff.gov.uk

Products that contain data from this source
Agriculture in the United Kingdom; GB Animal Feed Statistical Notice

Production of Compound and Other Processed Animal Feedingstuffs - GB
Ministry of Agriculture, Fisheries and Food

This GB census survey covers the production of compound and other processed animal feedingstuffs and the usage of raw materials in their manufacture. Mills are surveyed either monthly or annually according to their level of production. There are approximately 80 companies on the monthly survey and 80 on the annual survey.

Status: Ongoing
Collection Method: Census
Frequency: Monthly and Annual
Reference Period: Statistical months (4,4,5) and calendar years
Timeliness: 5 Weeks after end of survey period.
Earliest Available Data: 1980
National Coverage: Great Britain
Disaggregation: Standard Statistical Region (SSR)

Statistician

Steve Walton
Ministry of Agriculture, Fisheries and Food
Commodities and Food; A
Tel: 00 44 (0) 1904 455058;
Email: s.walton@esg.maff.gov.uk

Products that contain data from this source
Agriculture in the United Kingdom; Annual Abstract of Statistics; Monthly Digest of Statistics; GB Animal Feed Statistical Notice

See also:
In this chapter:
Aggregate Agricultural Account *(14.5)*
Cereals Balance Sheets for Eurostat *(14.5)*
Cereals Production Survey - England and Wales *(14.3)*
Cereals Quarterly Balance Sheets *(14.3)*
Dried Pea and Bean Production Survey - England and Wales *(14.3)*
Dried Pulses Balance Sheets for Eurostat *(14.3)*
Oilseeds Crushed and the Production of Crude Vegetable Oil, Oilcake and Meal - UK *(14.4)*
Overseas Trade in Agricultural Commodities *(14.4)*

14.3 Arable Crops

Cereal Stock Disposal Survey
Scottish Executive

The SEAEFD conducts a survey on cereal stocks. The survey consists of a sample of 640 cereal growers and covers details on the disposal of wheat, barley and oats stocks.

Status: Ongoing
Collection Method: Small-scale (Sample) Survey
Frequency: Monthly
Timeliness: Published annually in August
National Coverage: Scotland
Disaggregation: 4 main agricultural regions of Scotland

Statistician
Tom Whyte
Scottish Executive
Tel: 0131 244 3116

Products that contain data from this source
Economic Report on Scottish Agriculture

Cereal Stocks Held at Ports - UK
Ministry of Agriculture, Fisheries and Food

This quarterly census survey covers cereal stocks held at all grain storage facilities at about 35 UK ports. Data are available on wheat and barley stocks held, either following their import or awaiting their export.

Status: Ongoing

Collection Method: Census
Frequency: Quarterly
Reference Period: Jan - Mar, Apr - June, Jul - Sept, Oct - Dec.
Timeliness: Results published 7 weeks after survey date.
Earliest Available Data: 1992
National Coverage: United Kingdom

Statistician
Steve Walton
Ministry of Agriculture, Fisheries and Food
Commodities and Food; A
Tel: 00 44 (0) 1904 455058;
Email: s.walton@esg.maff.gov.uk

Products that contain data from this source
Agriculture in the United Kingdom; The Agricultural Co-operative and Ports Cereals Stock Surveys (Statistics Notice).

Cereal Stocks Held by Agricultural Co-Operatives - UK
Ministry of Agriculture, Fisheries and Food

This quarterly census survey covers grain stocks held by agricultural co-operatives in the UK. It covers about 30 co-operatives that hold cereals stocks in store. Data are available on the estimated total tonnage of cereals physically in store, excluding intervention grain, grain stored on agricultural holdings and grain stocks associated with any feed mill.

Status: Ongoing
Collection Method: Census
Frequency: Quarterly
Reference Period: Jan - Mar, Apr - June, Jul - Sept, Oct - Dec.
Timeliness: 7 weeks after the end of the survey period.
Earliest Available Data: 1996
National Coverage: United Kingdom
Sub-national: England & Wales, Scotland and Northern Ireland

Statistician
Steve Walton
Ministry of Agriculture, Fisheries and Food
Commodities and Food; A
Tel: 00 44 (0) 1904 455058;
Email: s.walton@esg.maff.gov.uk

Products that contain data from this source
Agriculture in the United Kingdom; The Agricultural Co-operative and Ports Cereals Stock Surveys (Statistics Notice)

Cereal Stocks Survey - England and Wales
Ministry of Agriculture, Fisheries and Food

This is a voluntary survey, based on a sample of holdings returning an area of cereals at the most recent June census or in their administrative returns (for area payments).

Data are available on the quantities of wheat and barley on the farm, and the amounts used on the farm or moved off the farm.

Status: Ongoing
Collection Method: Small-scale (Sample) Survey
Frequency: Quarterly
Reference Period: The quarter ending September, December, March or June
Timeliness: Within 8 weeks of quarter end.
Earliest Available Data: 1966
National Coverage: England and Wales
Disaggregation: Standard Statistical Region until 1996 and thereafter Government Office Region, for September and December surveys only.

Statistician
Alison James
Ministry of Agriculture, Fisheries and Food
Statistics (Census and Surveys); Branch F
Tel: 01904 455328;
Email: a.james@esg.maff.gov.uk

Products that contain data from this source
Cereal Stocks Survey (Statistical Notice)

Cereals Production Survey - England and Wales
Ministry of Agriculture, Fisheries and Food

This is a voluntary survey, based on a sample of holdings returning an area of cereals in the most recent June Census or in their administrative return (for area payments). Data are available on the quantity of cereals produced, the yield per hectare and the area of crop grown, for wheat, barley, oats and from 1998, rye. The survey has been carried out, in its present form, since 1990 and replaced the annual Estimate of Crop Production Survey which ran from 1951 to 1989. From crop year 1997/98, the frequency of collection was reduced to twice a year.

Status: Ongoing
Collection Method: Small-scale (Sample) Survey
Frequency: Twice a year, in August and April
Reference Period: The last harvest
Timeliness: Within 10 weeks of survey date
Earliest Available Data: 1951 harvest
National Coverage: England and Wales
Disaggregation: Standard Statistical Region until 1996 harvest, thereafter Government Office Region

Statistician
Alison James
Ministry of Agriculture, Fisheries and Food
Statistics (Census and Surveys); Branch F
Tel: 01904 455328;
Email: a.james@esg.maff.gov.uk

Products that contain data from this source
Agriculture in the United Kingdom; Cereals Production Survey (Statistics Notice)

Cereals Quarterly Balance Sheets
Ministry of Agriculture, Fisheries and Food

Crop year (July to June) Balance Sheets for each of the main cereal crops are produced on a quarterly basis for the United Kingdom. Each quarter forecasts for the crop year as a whole are made for all parameters i.e. production, stocks, imports, exports and usage. These Balance Sheets are published through the Home-Grown Cereals Authority (HGCA). There are also Balance Sheets produced for Eurostat. These are produced to arrive at an EU Balance Sheet collected on a harmonised basis.

Status: Ongoing
Frequency: Quarterly
Reference Period: Crop Year July to June
Timeliness: Published around the end of October, December, March and June each crop year
Earliest Available Data: 1972
National Coverage: United Kingdom

Statistician
Steve Walton
Ministry of Agriculture, Fisheries and Food
Commodities and Food; A
Tel: 00 44 (0) 1904 455058;
Email: s.walton@esg.maff.gov.uk

Combinable Crops Production and Disposal Survey - Scotland
SERAD

The SERAD conducts an annual survey on combinable crops. The survey consists of a sample of 640 growers and information is collected on total production of triticale, linseed, oilseed rape and combine peas

Status: Ongoing
Collection Method: Small-scale (Sample) Survey
Frequency: Annually
Reference Period: Crop Year
Timeliness: 2-3 months. Published in January.
Earliest Available Data: 1972
National Coverage: Scotland

Statistician
Tom Whyte
Scottish Executive
Tel: 0131 244 3116

Products that contain data from this source
Economic Report on Scottish Agriculture; Scottish Agriculture Output Input and Income Statistics

---

Crop Yields - Northern Ireland
Department of Agriculture - Northern Ireland

The Department of Agriculture for Northern Ireland conducts the crop yield survey on a sample of approximately 200 cereal growing farms. Data are collected on the yields, moisture content, patterns of disposal and sources of seed for the various cereals, oilseed rape and linseed.

Collection Method: Small-scale (Sample) Survey
Frequency: Annually
Timeliness: 3 months
Earliest Available Data: 1986
National Coverage: Northern Ireland

Statistician
Sheila Magee
Department of Agriculture - Northern Ireland
Tel: 028 9052 4427;
Email: sheila.magee@dani.gov.uk

Dried Pea and Bean Production Survey - England and Wales
Ministry of Agriculture, Fisheries and Food

This is a voluntary survey, based on a sample of holdings returning an area of dried peas and beans in the most recent June Census or in their administrative return (for area payments). Data are available on the production of peas for harvesting dry and field beans, yield per hectare and the area of crop sown. Until the 1995 harvest, data was also available on the quantities used on the farm, moved off the farm and remaining on the farm.

Status: Ongoing
Collection Method: Small-scale (Sample) Survey
Frequency: Annually (November)
Reference Period: The last harvest
Timeliness: Within 10 weeks of survey date
Earliest Available Data: 1989 harvest
National Coverage: England
Disaggregation: England only

Statistician
Alison James
Ministry of Agriculture, Fisheries and Food
Statistics (Census and Surveys); Branch F
Tel: 01904 455328;
Email: a.james@esg.maff.gov.uk

Products that contain data from this source
Agriculture in the United Kingdom; Dried Pea and Field Bean Production (Statistics Notice)

Dried Pulses Balance Sheets for Eurostat
Ministry of Agriculture, Fisheries and Food

Annual Balance Sheets are produced for Eurostat for the July to June Crop Year. They cover production, imports, exports, stocks and disposals of each of Peas, Broad and Horse Beans and Lupine Seed.

Status: Ongoing
Frequency: Annually
Reference Period: July to June Crop Year
Timeliness: February after the Crop Year

Statistician
Steve Walton
Ministry of Agriculture, Fisheries and Food
Commodities and Food; A
Tel: 00 44 (0) 1904 455058;
Email: s.walton@esg.maff.gov.uk

Hay/Straw Prices Returns - Scotland
Scottish Executive Rural Affairs Department

The SERAD conducts a survey on the prices of Hay and Straw. The survey consists of a sample of 6 Hay/Straw merchants in Scotland. The data is gathered weekly and is published each week in the Scottish Farmer.

Status: Ongoing
Collection Method: Small-scale (Sample) Survey
Frequency: Weekly
Timeliness: One week
National Coverage: Scotland

Statistician
Tom Whyte
Scottish Executive
Tel: 0131 244 3116

Products that contain data from this source
Scottish Farmer (weekly)

Minor Crops Yield Survey - England and Wales
Ministry of Agriculture, Fisheries and Food

This is a voluntary survey, based on a sample of holdings, chosen either by ADAS or by the Ministry of Agriculture, who were growing the minor crops of interest according to local knowledge or June Census returns. The crops covered (until 1997) are minor cereals (rye, triticale and mixed corn), linseed and minor stockfeeding crops. For 1998 onwards, the survey covered linseed and minor cereals only. Data was obtained on estimated yield with 1998, when the area of crop grown, yield per hectare and quantity produced were collected for linseed.

The survey covers England and Wales. However yield estimates were published at regional level until the 1995 harvest. Until 1997, arable consultants working for ADAS contacted a sample of holdings and supplied the Ministry of Agriculture with yield estimates.

Status: Ongoing
Collection Method: Small-scale (Sample) Survey
Frequency: In October or November each year
Reference Period: The last harvest
Timeliness: Currently several months after survey date
Earliest Available Data: 1985
National Coverage: England and Wales
Disaggregation: England and Wales only since 1995

Statistician
Alison James
Ministry of Agriculture, Fisheries and Food
Statistics (Census and Surveys); Branch F
Tel: 01904 455328;
Email: a.james@esg.maff.gov.uk

Products that contain data from this source
Minor Crops Production (Statistics Notice)

Oilseed Rape Production Survey - England
Ministry of Agriculture, Fisheries and Food

This is a voluntary survey, based on a sample of agricultural holdings returning an area of oilseed rape in the most recent June Census or in their administrative returns (for area payments). Data are available on the quantity of oilseed rape produced, the yield per hectare and the area of oilseed rape sown.

Status: Ongoing
Collection Method: Small-scale (Sample) Survey
Frequency: Annually (August)
Reference Period: The last harvest
Timeliness: Within 10 weeks of survey date
Earliest Available Data: 1988
National Coverage: England

Statistician
Alison James
Ministry of Agriculture, Fisheries and Food
Statistics (Census and Surveys); Branch F
Tel: 01904 455328;
Email: a.james@esg.maff.gov.uk

Products that contain data from this source
Oilseed Rape Production Survey (Statistics Notice)

Overseas Trade in Agricultural Commodities
Ministry of Agriculture, Fisheries and Food; sponsored by MAFF

The Ministry of Agriculture, Fisheries and Food compiles data on import and export figures for agricultural commodities. Data are compiled from HM Customs and Excise data, so as to allow monitoring of trade in (mainly) food, feed and drink.

Status: Ongoing
Frequency: Monthly
Reference Period: Minimum of a calendar month
Earliest Available Data: 1988
National Coverage: United Kingdom

Statistician
Jim Holding
Ministry of Agriculture, Fisheries and Food
Statistics (Commodities and Food); Branch C
Tel: 00 44(0)1904 4555080;
Email: s.j.holding@esg.maff.gov.uk

Products that contain data from this analysis
Agriculture in the United Kingdom; The Ministry of Agriculture, Fisheries and Food Website

Rice Balance Sheets for Eurostat
Ministry of Agriculture, Fisheries and Food

Produced on an Annual Basis for Eurostat for the September to August Crop Year. There is no UK production, so consumption is derived from stock changes and imports and exports.

Status: Ongoing
Frequency: Annually
Reference Period: September to August Crop Year
Timeliness: February following the crop year

Statistician
Steve Walton
Ministry of Agriculture, Fisheries and Food
Commodities and Food; A
Tel: 00 44 (0) 1904 455058;
Email: s.walton@esg.maff.gov.uk

Rye Milled for Human Consumption
Ministry of Agriculture, Fisheries and Food

This is a UK census survey covering the quantity of rye milled for human consumption. There are approximately 5 respondents.

Status: Ongoing
Collection Method: Census
Frequency: Annually
Reference Period: 12 months (collected in July)
Earliest Available Data: 1987
National Coverage: United Kingdom

Statistician
Steve Walton
Ministry of Agriculture, Fisheries and Food
Commodities and Food; A
Tel: 00 44 (0) 1904 455058;
Email: s.walton@esg.maff.gov.uk

Products that contain data from this source
Agriculture in the United Kingdom

Straw Disposal Survey - England and Wales
Ministry of Agriculture, Fisheries and Food

This is a voluntary survey, based on a sample of agricultural holdings returning wheat, barley or oats in the most recent June Census or in their administrative return (for area payments). Data are available on the areas of straw baled and removed, and straw ploughed in or cultivated. Prior to the 1993 harvest, data was also available on the area of straw burned.

Status: Suspended
Collection Method: Small-scale (Sample) Survey
Frequency: Latterly every three years, previously annually
Reference Period: The last harvest
Timeliness: Within 10 weeks of survey date
Earliest Available Data: 1983
National Coverage: England and Wales
Disaggregation: England and Wales only

Statistician
Alison James
Ministry of Agriculture, Fisheries and Food
Statistics (Census and Surveys); Branch F
Tel: 01904 455328;
Email: a.james@esg.maff.gov.uk

Products that contain data from this source
Straw Disposal Survey (Statistics Notice)

Sugar Balance Sheets
Ministry of Agriculture, Fisheries and Food

The Ministry of Agriculture, Fisheries and Food compiles supply and utilisation tables for cereals, oilseeds, pulses and sugar. Data are available on the production of crops grown in the UK, along with area and yield data, UK imports and exports with EU states and with the rest of the world, and UK consumption. For refined sugar, the trade estimates incorporate sugar in various stages of processing.

Status: Ongoing
Frequency: Annually
Reference Period: Crop year
Timeliness: Approx. 9 months
Earliest Available Data: 1972
National Coverage: United Kingdom

Statistician
Steve Walton
Ministry of Agriculture, Fisheries and Food
Commodities and Food; A
Tel: 00 44 (0) 1904 455058;
Email: s.walton@esg.maff.gov.uk

See also:
In this chapter:
Aggregate Agricultural Account *(14.5)*
Agricultural and Horticultural Census - Scotland *(14.1)*

British Survey of Fertiliser Practice *(14.16)*
Cereals and Animal Feed Stocks Held by Importers and Dealers *(14.2)*
Cereals Balance Sheets for Eurostat *(14.5)*
December Agricultural Survey - England and Wales *(14.1)*
EC Farm Structure Survey *(14.17)*
June Agricultural and Horticultural Census - England & Wales *(14.1)*
Minor Holdings Census - England & Wales *(14.12)*
Oilseeds Crushed and the Production of Crude Vegetable Oil, Oilcake and Meal - UK *(14.4)*
Overseas Trade in Agricultural Commodities *(14.4)*

14.4 Arable Crops - Related Industries

Brewers, Distillers and Maltsters - UK
Ministry of Agriculture, Fisheries and Food

This census survey covers cereals usage by brewers, maltsters and distillers. Most mills are surveyed monthly, though those which use less than 2,000 tonnes of barley in a year are surveyed annually. There are approximately 30 mills on the monthly survey and 10 mills on the annual survey. Data are available on stocks, receipts and usage of wheat, maize and barley.

The survey covers the United Kingdom and has been running for several years. Until 1985 two separate surveys were conducted on brewing and distilling but because many of the firms involved operated as both brewers and distillers, the two surveys were amalgamated. Up until 1993 the survey covered Great Britain but since January 1994 UK data have been collected.

Status: Ongoing
Collection Method: Census
Frequency: Monthly and annual
Reference Period: Statistical months (4,4,5 pattern) and calendar year
Timeliness: Approx. 5 weeks
Earliest Available Data: 1990
National Coverage: United Kingdom

Statistician
Steve Walton
Ministry of Agriculture, Fisheries and Food
Commodities and Food; A
Tel: 00 44 (0) 1904 455058;
Email: s.walton@esg.maff.gov.uk

Products that contain data from this source
Agriculture in the United Kingdom; Annual Abstract of Statistics; Brewers, Distillers and Maltsters Usage and Stocks; Index of Production (First Release); Monthly Digest of Statistics

Cereal Breakfast Food Production - UK
Ministry of Agriculture, Fisheries and Food

This census survey covers all known manufacturers of cereal breakfast food (about 10) in the UK. The survey covers the stocks and usage of cereals as raw materials, the production of cereal breakfast foods and the production of cereal by products

Status: Ongoing
Collection Method: Census
Frequency: Monthly
Reference Period: Statistical months (4,4,5 pattern)
Timeliness: Approximately 8 weeks
Earliest Available Data: 1986
National Coverage: United Kingdom

Statistician
Steve Walton
Ministry of Agriculture, Fisheries and Food
Commodities and Food; A
Tel: 00 44 (0) 1904 455058;
Email: s.walton@esg.maff.gov.uk

Products that contain data from this source
Agriculture in the United Kingdom; Annual Abstract of Statistics; Monthly Digest of Statistics

---

Glucose and Starch Production - UK
Ministry of Agriculture, Fisheries and Food

This census survey covers glucose and starch production in the UK. Data are available on the usage of raw materials, stocks of maize grain and the production of glucose and starch. The survey has been running for several years. The survey originally covered the use of maize for the production of glucose and starch but was expanded in 1984 to include the usage of wheat flour, and in 1988 the usage of wheat grain.

Status: Ongoing
Collection Method: Census
Frequency: Monthly
Reference Period: Statistical months (4,4,5 pattern)
Timeliness: About 8 weeks after collection
Earliest Available Data: 1988
National Coverage: United Kingdom

Statistician
Steve Walton
Ministry of Agriculture, Fisheries and Food
Commodities and Food; A
Tel: 00 44 (0) 1904 455058;
Email: s.walton@esg.maff.gov.uk

Products that contain data from this source
Annual Abstract of Statistics; Index of Production (First Release); Monthly Digest of Statistics

Manufacture of Margarine, Solid Cooking Fats and Other Table Spreads - UK
Ministry of Agriculture, Fisheries and Food

This census survey covers the 12 plants in the United Kingdom that produce margarine, solid cooking fats and other table spreads, and the utilisation and stocks of refined oils and animal fats relating to that production.

Status: Ongoing
Collection Method: Census
Frequency: Monthly
Reference Period: Statistical months (4,4,5)
Timeliness: Around 10 weeks after the end of the survey period.
Earliest Available Data: 1994
National Coverage: United Kingdom

Statistician
Steve Walton
Ministry of Agriculture, Fisheries and Food
Commodities and Food; A
Tel: 00 44 (0) 1904 455058;
Email: s.walton@esg.maff.gov.uk

Products that contain data from this source
Annual Abstract of Statistics; Margarine, Other table spreads and solid cooking fat production in the United Kingdom and the refined oils and fats used in their manufacture; Ministry of Agriculture, Fisheries and Food Divisions Faxback Service: Index and Calendar to Statistical Notices (SNs); Monthly Digest of Statistics; The Ministry of Agriculture, Fisheries and Food Website

Oatmeal Millers Receipts, Production and Stocks - UK
Ministry of Agriculture, Fisheries and Food

This census survey collects data on the receipts, production and stocks of UK oatmeal millers. There are currently about 10 oatmeal millers on the survey. Data are available on the total monthly sales of home grown oats for oat milling, the quantity of oats milled and the quantity of oat milling products produced.

Status: Ongoing
Collection Method: Census
Frequency: Monthly
Reference Period: Statistical months (4,4,5 pattern)
Timeliness: About 8 weeks after collection
Earliest Available Data: 1991
National Coverage: United Kingdom

Statistician
Steve Walton
Ministry of Agriculture, Fisheries and Food
Commodities and Food; A
Tel: 00 44 (0) 1904 455058;
Email: s.walton@esg.maff.gov.uk

Products that contain data from this source
Agriculture in the United Kingdom; Annual Abstract of Statistics; Monthly Digest of Statistics

Oilseeds Crushed and the Production of Crude Vegetable Oil, Oilcake and Meal - UK
Ministry of Agriculture, Fisheries and Food

This UK census survey covers oilseeds and nuts crushed and the crude vegetable oils, oilcake and meal produced from the crush.

Status: Ongoing
Collection Method: Census
Frequency: Monthly
Reference Period: Statistical months (4,4,5)
Timeliness: Press notice issued 10 weeks after the end of the survey date.
Earliest Available Data: 1994
National Coverage: United Kingdom

Statistician
Steve Walton
Ministry of Agriculture, Fisheries and Food
Commodities and Food; A
Tel: 00 44 (0) 1904 455058;
Email: s.walton@esg.maff.gov.uk

Products that contain data from this source
Agriculture in the United Kingdom; Annual Abstract of Statistics; Monthly Digest of Statistics; Oilseeds and Nuts crushed in the United Kingdom and the crude vegetable oils, oilcake and meal produced (Press notice)

Output of Refined Vegetable and Marine Oils and Animal Fats by UK Processors
Ministry of Agriculture, Fisheries and Food

This UK census survey covers the usage, production and stocks of vegetable oils, animal fats and marine oils by hardeners and refiners. Data are available on opening and closing stocks and on the partly processed or refined deodorised oils or fats produced.

Status: Ongoing
Collection Method: Census
Frequency: Monthly
Reference Period: Statistical months (4,4,5)
Timeliness: Results are published around 10 weeks after the end of the survey period.
Earliest Available Data: 1994
National Coverage: United Kingdom

Statistician
Steve Walton
Ministry of Agriculture, Fisheries and Food
Commodities and Food; A
Tel: 00 44 (0) 1904 455058;
Email: s.walton@esg.maff.gov.uk

Products that contain data from this source
Annual Abstract of Statistics; Ministry of Agriculture, Fisheries and Food Divisions Faxback Service: Index and Calendar to Statistical Notices (SNs); Monthly Digest of Statistics; The Ministry of Agriculture, Fisheries and Food Website

Raw Sugar - GB
Ministry of Agriculture, Fisheries and Food

This GB census survey collects data on the production of raw sugar from both sugar beet and sugar cane. Data is available on production, deliveries and stocks.

Status: Ongoing
Collection Method: Census
Frequency: Monthly
Reference Period: Statistical months (4,4,5)
Timeliness: Approx. 8 weeks
Earliest Available Data: 1988
National Coverage: Great Britain

Statistician
Steve Walton
Ministry of Agriculture, Fisheries and Food
Commodities and Food; A
Tel: 00 44 (0) 1904 455058;
Email: s.walton@esg.maff.gov.uk

Products that contain data from this source
Agriculture in the United Kingdom; Index of Production (First Release)

Refined Sugar - GB
Ministry of Agriculture, Fisheries and Food

This GB census survey collects data on the production of refined sugar from both sugar beet and sugar cane. Data is available on production, deliveries and stocks.

Status: Ongoing
Collection Method: Census
Frequency: Monthly
Reference Period: Statistical months (4,4,5)
Timeliness: Approx. 8 weeks
Earliest Available Data: 1988
National Coverage: Great Britain

Statistician
Steve Walton
Ministry of Agriculture, Fisheries and Food
Commodities and Food; A
Tel: 00 44 (0) 1904 455058;
Email: s.walton@esg.maff.gov.uk

Products that contain data from this source
Agriculture in the United Kingdom; Index of Production (First Release)

Wheat Milled and Flour Production - UK
Ministry of Agriculture, Fisheries and Food

This UK census survey covers wheat usage and flour production. Most mills are surveyed monthly, though those which produce less than 5,000 tonnes of flour in a calendar year are surveyed annually. There are currently around 60 mills on the monthly survey and around 10 mills on the annual survey. Although the survey covers the UK, data are available at regional level.

Status: Ongoing
Collection Method: Census
Frequency: monthly and annual
Reference Period: Statistical months (4,4,5 pattern) and calendar years
Timeliness: Approx. 5 weeks
Earliest Available Data: 1990
National Coverage: United Kingdom
Disaggregation: SSRs

Statistician
Steve Walton
Ministry of Agriculture, Fisheries and Food
Commodities and Food; A
Tel: 00 44 (0) 1904 455058;
Email: s.walton@esg.maff.gov.uk

Products that contain data from this source
Agriculture in the United Kingdom; Annual Abstract of Statistics; Index of Production (First Release); Ministry of Agriculture, Fisheries and Food Divisions Faxback Service: Index and Calendar to Statistical Notices (SNs); Monthly Digest of Statistics; The Ministry of Agriculture, Fisheries and Food Website; Wheat Milled and Flour Production (Statistics Notice)

See also:
In this chapter:
Aggregate Agricultural Account *(14.5)*
Animal Compound Feedingstuffs: Sales Value and Volume - GB *(14.2)*
Cereals Balance Sheets for Eurostat *(14.5)*
Cereals Quarterly Balance Sheets *(14.3)*
Composition of Main Livestock Rations - GB *(14.2)*
Oils and Fats Balance Sheets for Eurostat *(14.5)*

14.5 Economics of Agriculture

Aggregate Agricultural Account
Ministry of Agriculture, Fisheries and Food

The Ministry of Agriculture, Fisheries and Food compiles data on agricultural accounts and income. Data are available on gross output and input, productivity and on the incomes of those engaged in the industry.

Status: Ongoing
Frequency: Annually
Reference Period: Calendar year
Earliest Available Data: 1973
National Coverage: United Kingdom
Disaggregation: NUTS1 areas; NUTS3 area; Counties

Statistician
Jim Holding
Ministry of Agriculture, Fisheries and Food
Statistics (Commodities and Food); Branch C
Tel: 00 44(0)1904 4555080;
Email: s.j.holding@esg.maff.gov.uk

Products that contain data from this analysis
Agriculture in the United Kingdom; Forecast of UK total income from farming (TIFF); Provisional estimates of UK farm incomes, output and productivity; The Ministry of Agriculture, Fisheries and Food Website

Aggregate Agricultural Account - Northern Ireland
Department of Agriculture - Northern Ireland

The Department of Agriculture for Northern Ireland compiles the Aggregate Agricultural Account (AAA) from a combination of survey data and administratively derived data from numerous sources. The AAA is an annual estimate of the aggregate output, input, gross and net product and income of agriculture.

Status: Ongoing
Collection Method: Various surveys and administratively derived data.
Frequency: Annually
Reference Period: Calendar year
Timeliness: 3 months
Earliest Available Data: 1973
National Coverage: Northern Ireland

Statistician
Ivan Hunter
Department of Agriculture - Northern Ireland
Economics and Statistics; Agricultural Economics
Tel: 028 9052 4675;
Email: ivan.hunter@dani.gov.uk

Products that contain data from this source
Statistical Review of Northern Ireland Agriculture

Aggregate Agricultural Account - Scotland
Scottish Executive

The SOAEFD compiles the Aggregate Agricultural Account (AAA) from a combination of survey data and administratively derived data from numerous sources. The AAA is an annual estimate of the aggregate output, input, gross and net product and income of agriculture.

Status: Ongoing
Collection Method: Various surveys and administratively derived data.
Frequency: Annually
Reference Period: Calendar year
Timeliness: 3 months
Earliest Available Data: 1973
National Coverage: Northern Ireland

Statistician
Tom Whyte
Scottish Executive
Tel: 0131 244 3116

Aggregate Balance Sheets for Agriculture - UK
Ministry of Agriculture, Fisheries and Food

The Ministry of Agriculture, Fisheries and Food (MAFF) compiles the aggregate balance sheets for agriculture. Data are derived from MAFF's Farm Business Survey and June Census and various other sources.

The balance sheets show the level of assets and liabilities of the UK agricultural industry and its net worth. The value of components of both fixed assets (land and buildings, plant, machinery and vehicles, and breeding livestock) and current assets (trading livestock, crops and stores) are estimated, as are long-term and short-term liabilities. Estimates relate to December each year at current prices. For the main aggregates (total assets, total liabilities and net worth) indices in real terms are also derived.

Status: Ongoing
Frequency: Annually
Reference Period: as at end December
Earliest Available Data: 1970
National Coverage: United Kingdom

Statistician
Dr John Walsh
Ministry of Agriculture, Fisheries and Food
Economics (Resource Use); A
Tel: 020 7270 8795;
Email: j.walsh@esg.maff.gov.uk

Products that contain data from this analysis
Agriculture in the United Kingdom; The Ministry of Agriculture, Fisheries and Food Website

Aggregate Bank Advances to Scottish Agriculture
Scottish Executive

The SEAEFD conducts an annual survey on aggregate bank advances. 16 banks/financial institutions are sampled in May to collect information on the bank advances to farming in Scotland and this is subdivided between owner occupiers, tenants, livestock salesmen and contractors. The results are published in a Press Release produced in August/September

Status: Ongoing
Collection Method: Small-scale (Sample) Survey
Frequency: Annually
Reference Period: Financial year
Timeliness: 4 months
Earliest Available Data: mid-70's
National Coverage: Scotland

Statistician
Tom Whyte
Scottish Executive
Tel: 0131 244 3116

Sources and Analyses

Products that contain data from this source
Aggregate Bank Advances to Scottish Agriculture (Press Release); Scottish Agriculture Output Input and Income Statistics

Cereals Balance Sheets for Eurostat
Ministry of Agriculture, Fisheries and Food

Balance sheets are produced for a variety of crops. These are all published on Eurostat's Cronos database and in their 'Crop Production - Half Yearly Statistics' publication.

Cereals Balance Sheets are sent to Eurostat in February for the preceding July to June Crop Year. Eurostat publish such data as soon after receipt from Member States as possible. These Balance Sheets differ from the quarterly Balance Sheets published by the Home-Grown Cereals Authority (HGCA) in that data on 2nd processing products are included. Any comparisons with other Member States should be made by using the Eurostat Balance Sheets, as they are compiled on a consistent basis throughout the EU.

Status: Ongoing
Frequency: Annually
Reference Period: July to June Crop Year.
Timeliness: February after June Crop Year end.

Statistician
Steve Walton
Ministry of Agriculture, Fisheries and Food
Commodities and Food; A
Tel: 00 44 (0) 1904 455058;
Email: s.walton@esg.maff.gov.uk

Farm Accounts - Scotland
Scottish Executive

The survey gives the latest financial results involving the collection of around 550 accounts representing all the main types of full-time farming in Scotland. The survey is carried out every financial year. It is the direct descendant of the 'Investigation of the Profitableness of Farming in Scotland' which was set up in 1928-29.

Status: Ongoing
Collection Method: Small-scale (Sample) Survey
Frequency: Annually
Reference Period: Financial Year
Timeliness: Around eight months
Earliest Available Data: 1986/87
National Coverage: Scotland

Statistician
Robin Haynes
Scottish Executive Rural Affairs Department
Pentland House
Robb's Loan
Edinburgh EH14 1TW
Tel: 0131 244 6132

Products that contain data from this source
Agriculture in the United Kingdom; Economic Report on Scottish Agriculture; Farm Incomes in Scotland

Farm Business Survey - England
Ministry of Agriculture, Fisheries and Food

The Ministry of Agriculture, Fisheries and Food sponsors the collection of data on farm accounts from a sample of around 2,300 farms in England. The sample covers all the major types of farming and the information collected covers physical and financial data for the farm business together with some information on the non-farm incomes of farmers. Data are collected annually for accounting years which end between 31 December and 31 March. The average accounting period ends in mid-February. Results are published in March for each of the major farm types and by business size. Similar surveys are also conducted by the other countries in the United Kingdom.

Status: Ongoing
Collection Method: Cohort, Panel or Longitudinal Study
Frequency: Annual
Reference Period: Farm Accounting year end (February)
Timeliness: Approximately 3 months
Earliest Available Data: 1986/7 as Farm Business Survey, Farm Management Survey dating back to 1936
National Coverage: England and Wales
Disaggregation: Regional Level

Statistician
Roger Price
Room 702
Ministry of Agriculture, Fisheries and Food
Whitehall Place West
London
Tel: 00 44 020 7270 8620.
Email: r.d.s.price@esg.maff.gov.uk
Fax: 00 44 020 7389 9804 / 00 44 020 7270 8558

Products that contain data from this source
Agriculture in the United Kingdom; Farm Incomes in the United Kingdom

Farm Business Survey - Northern Ireland
Department of Agriculture - Northern Ireland

The Department of Agriculture for Northern Ireland conducts the Farm Business Survey on a representative sample of approximately

430 farm businesses. Physical and financial data are collected and income data are available by farm type and business size.

Frequency: Annually
Timeliness: Results published each March
Earliest Available Data: 1936
National Coverage: Northern Ireland

Statistician
Andrew Crawford
Department of Agriculture - Northern Ireland
Tel: 028 9052 4682;
Email: andrew.crawford@dani.gov.uk

Products that contain data from this source
Agriculture in the United Kingdom; Farm Incomes in Northern Ireland 1996/97

Fruit and Vegetable Balance Sheet
Ministry of Agriculture, Fisheries and Food

Balance sheet holds information on Stocks, Production and Trade data required on an annual basis by Eurostat. The figures are published in Eurostats data base - (Cronos) and a Eurostat publication - Crop Production Half-yearly Statistics.

Status: Ongoing
Frequency: Annually

Statistician
Christine Jeannette
Ministry of Agriculture, Fisheries and Food
Statistics (C & F); Branch B
Tel: 01904 455069

Products that contain data from this analysis
Eurostat - European Official Statistics - Sources of Information

Incomes of Agricultural Households Sector
Ministry of Agriculture, Fisheries and Food

The Ministry of Agriculture, Fisheries and Food compiles data on the total incomes of agricultural households. The series combines data from the June Agricultural Census, the Aggregate Agricultural Accounts and the Survey of Personal Incomes.

Status: Ongoing
Frequency: Annually
Reference Period: Calendar year
Earliest Available Data: 1980
National Coverage: United Kingdom

Statistician
Jim Holding
Ministry of Agriculture, Fisheries and Food
Statistics (Commodities and Food); Branch C
Tel: 00 44(0)1904 4555080;
Email: s.j.holding@esg.maff.gov.uk

Products that contain data from this analysis
Agricultural Income, 1996; Income statistics for the agricultural household sector 1996; Manual on the Total Income of Agricultural Households, Eurostat Theme 5 Series A; Total Income of Agricultural Households: Progress in 1993, Eurostat (1994) Theme 5 Series C

Oils and Fats Balance Sheets for Eurostat
Ministry of Agriculture, Fisheries and Food

Crop year (July to June) balance sheets are produced annually for oilseeds, oilcake and vegetable oils and fats. Calendar year balance sheets are produced annually for marine oils & fats, animal oils & fats, vegetable oils and fats and prepared oils and fats (margarine, spreads and solid cooking fats). They cover UK production, imports, exports, stocks and usage.

Status: Ongoing
Frequency: Annually
Reference Period: July to June crop years and calendar years
Timeliness: February after the Crop Year

Statistician
Steve Walton
Ministry of Agriculture, Fisheries and Food
Commodities and Food; A
Tel: 00 44 (0) 1904 455058;
Email: s.walton@esg.maff.gov.uk

See also:
In this chapter:
Agricultural Rent Enquiry - England and Wales *(14.12)*
British Survey of Fertiliser Practice *(14.16)*
Calf Survey - England and Wales *(14.13)*
Crop Yields - Northern Ireland *(14.3)*
EC Farm Structure Survey *(14.17)*
Pig Production - Northern Ireland *(14.13)*
Self Sufficiency in Food *(14.8)*

14.6 Eggs

Egg Packing Station Survey - UK
Ministry of Agriculture, Fisheries and Food

The Ministry of Agriculture, Fisheries and Food (MAFF) conducts a survey on egg packing stations. Data are obtained from a sample panel of 100 egg packing stations on egg throughput and prices, and are available by egg size, egg class and production technique. The sample results are grossed up to provide monthly estimates of eggs packed in the UK, and the average prices at which eggs are sold from producers to packers.

Status: Ongoing
Collection Method: Large-scale (Sample) Survey
Frequency: Monthly
Reference Period: Four and Five week statistical months
Timeliness: 3 weeks
Earliest Available Data: 1992
National Coverage: England and Wales, Scotland, Northern Ireland, United Kingdom

Statistician
Christine Jeannette
Ministry of Agriculture, Fisheries and Food
Statistics (C & F); Branch B
Tel: 01904 455069

Products that contain data from this source
Eggs Statistics Notice

Egg Processing Survey - UK
Ministry of Agriculture, Fisheries and Food

The Ministry of Agriculture, Fisheries and Food conducts a survey on egg processing. Data are collected from a panel of 19 egg processors. Data are available on the number of eggs processed and the amount of egg product produced.

Status: Ongoing
Collection Method: Large-scale (Sample) Survey
Frequency: Monthly
Reference Period: 4 or 5 week statistical months
Timeliness: 3 weeks
Earliest Available Data: 1997
National Coverage: United Kingdom

Statistician
Christine Jeannette
Ministry of Agriculture, Fisheries and Food
Statistics (C & F); Branch B
Tel: 01904 455069

Products that contain data from this source
Eggs Statistics Notice

Eggs Balance Sheet
Ministry of Agriculture, Fisheries and Food

Balance sheet holds information on Production and Trade data required on an annual basis by Eurostat. The figures are published in Eurostat's database - (Cronos)

Status: Ongoing
Frequency: Annually

Statistician
Christine Jeannette
Ministry of Agriculture, Fisheries and Food
Statistics (C & F); Branch B
Tel: 01904 455069

Products that contain data from this analysis
Eurostat - European Official Statistics - Sources of Information

Utilisation and Capacity of Hatcheries - England and Wales
Ministry of Agriculture, Fisheries and Food

The Ministry of Agriculture, Fisheries and Food conducts a survey on the capacity of hatcheries to comply with an EC regulation. Data are available on the number of incubators and maximum number of eggs which could be placed in incubators at any one time. Data cover all registered hatcheries in England and Wales and are available at region level. The survey began in 1975 under EC regulations and is carried out every two years. The survey has not been conducted since 1995. MAFF has asked the EU to clarify the use they make of the data, before conducting the survey again.

Status: Ceased temporarily
Collection Method: Census
Earliest Available Data: 1975
National Coverage: England and Wales
Sub-National: Region

Statistician
Christine Jeannette
Ministry of Agriculture, Fisheries and Food
Statistics (C & F); Branch B
Tel: 01904 455069

See also:
In this chapter:
Aggregate Agricultural Account *(14.5)*
June Agricultural and Horticultural Census - England & Wales *(14.8)*
Minor Holdings Census - England & Wales *(14.12)*
Overseas Trade in Agricultural Commodities *(14.4)*
Production and Marketing of Hatching Eggs and Chicks - England and Wales *(14.13)*
Production and Marketing of Hatching Eggs and Chicks - Scotland *(14.13)*

14.7 Fishing

Fish Farming and Shellfish Farming Businesses Register - England and Wales
CEFAS

The Ministry of Agriculture, Fisheries and Food (MAFF) compiles the fish farming and shellfish farming businesses register. Anyone running a fish farming or shellfish farming business is required to register that business with MAFF.

Data are collected on the name and nature of the business, address and nature of the sites at which it is carried out, species and type of fish or shellfish moved on to the site and from the site for the purpose of stocking other waters.

Status: Ongoing
Collection Method: Administrative Records and Site Visits
Frequency: Bi-annually or annually
Reference Period: May and November each Year
Earliest Available Data: 1985
National Coverage: England and Wales

Statistician
Eric Hudson
Fish Health Inspectorate
The Centre for Environment, Fisheries and Aquaculture Science
Weymouth
Dorset DT4 8UB
Tel:01305 206673/4; Fax: 01305 206602;
Email: fish.health.inspectorate@cefas.co.uk

Fisheries Database
Ministry of Defence; sponsored by MAFF

Contains details of the activities of the English fishing fleet, including the Royal Navy Fishery Protection Squadron.

Status: Ongoing
Collection Method: Administrative Records

Statistician
Robin Horton
Ministry of Defence
Tel: 020 7218 8326;
Email: triservice@dasa.mon.uk

Fisheries - Northern Ireland
Department of Agriculture - Northern Ireland

The Department of Agriculture for Northern Ireland compiles statistics on fisheries. Fisheries statistics are administratively derived by the Fisheries Division. Data are available on fish landings by live weight and value of different and selected species, all fish landed into Northern Ireland ports, all fish landed by Northern Ireland vessels (vessels over 10m overall length classified according to overall length, home port and age), quantities and value of salmon and eel catches, angling permit sales, grants for vessels and aquaculture projects, and production by commercial fish farmers.

The data cover Northern Ireland and are available for Ardglass, Kilkeel, Portavogie and other Northern Ireland ports. The series began in 1966 and results are published annually relating to the previous year.

Frequency: Annually
Earliest Available Data: 1966
National Coverage: Northern Ireland

Statistician
Jack Allister
Department of Agriculture - Northern Ireland
Tel: 028 9052 2376;
Email: jack.allister@dani.gov.uk

Products that contain data from this source
Report on the Sea and Inland Fisheries of Northern Ireland 1996

Fisheries Statistics - Anglers - England and Wales
Environment Agency

The National Rivers Authority (NRA) compiles data on salmonoid and freshwater fisheries. Data are collected from anglers on declared catches and from NRA authorised outlets of fishing licences on the sales of licenses. Data are available for anglers' declared catches of salmon and migratory/sea trout on the numbers and average weight of fish landed by rod and by net, and the number, type and value of rod and net licences sold.

Frequency: Annually
Earliest Available Data: 1989
National Coverage: England and Wales
Sub-National: National Rivers Authority regional and river fishery level

Statistician
Stephen Gledhill
Environment Agency
Tel: 01454 624400

Products that contain data from this source
Fisheries Statistics

Fishing Fleets - UK
Ministry of Agriculture, Fisheries and Food

The Ministry of Agriculture, Fisheries and Food (MAFF) compiles data on the UK fishing fleet. Data are derived from the Registry of Shipping and Seamen, Department of Transport, and the MAFF Vessel File. Data are available on the characteristics of fishing vessels and their status for licensing purposes. Fishing vessels are classified to segments, according to the type of activity they undertake most often.

Status: Ongoing
Collection Method: Administrative Records
Frequency: Annually
Timeliness: Nine months
Earliest Available Data: 1988
National Coverage: United Kingdom
Sub-National: Licensing districts

Statistician
Ian Wood
Ministry of Agriculture, Fisheries and Food
FISH 1; C- Fisheries
Tel: 020 7238 6050;
Email: i.wood@fish.maff.gov.uk

Products that contain data from this source
The English, Welsh and Northern Irish Fishing Vessel List; UK Sea Fisheries Statistics

Number of Fishermen - England and Wales
Ministry of Agriculture, Fisheries and Food

The Ministry of Agriculture, Fisheries and Food (MAFF) compiles data on the number of fishermen from a survey conducted by the Sea Fisheries Inspectorate. The data cover England and Wales and are available at MAFF Sea Fish Inspectorate Districts for 1994; prior to 1994 data are available at country level only. Data have been collected since 1904. Before 1952, figures were based on information supplied by the Registrar General of Shipping and Seamen. Since then they have been supplied by MAFF. From 1966 only commercial fishermen are included. Figures are collected annually in March and published in September. Data are also received from SEAEFD and DANI on the number of fishermen on Scottish and Northern Irish vessels respectively.

Status: Ongoing
Collection Method: Census
Frequency: Annually
Reference Period: April
Timeliness: 9 months
Earliest Available Data: 1938
National Coverage: England and Wales
Sub-National: Licensing districts

Statistician
Ian Wood
Ministry of Agriculture, Fisheries and Food
FISH 1; C- Fisheries
Tel: 020 7238 6050;
Email: i.wood@fish.maff.gov.uk

Products that contain data from this source
UK Sea Fisheries Statistics

Number of Fishermen - Scotland
Scottish Executive

AEFD post offices compile data on the number of fishermen employed on Scottish based vessels, and on the number employed in the first processing of sea fish.

Status: Ongoing
Collection Method: Census
Frequency: Annually
Reference Period: April
National Coverage: Scotland

Statistician
Peter McGill
Scottish Executive
Tel: 0131 244 6437

Products that contain data from this source
See Fisheries Statistics (Scotland)

Sea Fish Landings - Scotland
Scottish Executive

Nearly all white fish are auctioned through markets; vessel, buyer, species, weight, grade and price are all recorded. Copies of these sales notes are sent to AEFD port offices. Pelagic species are usually sold direct to fish processors who provide information equivalent to sales notes on quantities and price. Other arrangements are made to collect information on landings of some shellfish species and transhipments to klondykers. Details of landings abroad by Scottish vessels are provided both by the country in which the landing is made and by the vessels' agents. Data, which are required under EU regulations, are stored on the FIN computer system

Status: Ongoing
Collection Method: Administrative Records
Frequency: Continuously
National Coverage: Scotland and Scottish based vessels abroad

Statistician
Peter McGill
Scottish Executive
Tel: 0131 244 6437

Products that contain data from this source
Sea Fisheries Statistics (Scotland)

Sea Fish Statistics
Scottish Executive

Statistics from logsheets required under EU regulations to be completed by skippers of most fishing vessels for each fishing trip. These logsheets show, inter alia, the date, time and place of departure and arrival, where and when fished and units/weights of catch retained on board. Under the regulations a copy of the logsheet must be submitted to the authorities within 48 hours of landing. Data are stored on the FIN computer system.

Status: Ongoing
Collection Method: Administrative Records
Frequency: Continuously
National Coverage: Scotland and Scottish based vessels landing abroad

Statistician
Peter McGill
Scottish Executive
Tel: 0131 556 8499 x 6437

Products that contain data from this source
Sea Fisheries Statistics (Scotland)

Seafish Landings - UK
Ministry of Agriculture, Fisheries and Food

The Ministry of Agriculture, Fisheries and Food compiles data on the quantity and value of landings of seafish. Under the Common Fisheries Policy, fishermen are required to make returns to the Sea Fisheries Inspectorate in the UK after fishing trips. The data collected include log sheets covering fishing for species subject to Total Allowable Catches (TACs), landing declarations and/or sales notes of the quantities by species landed and their value. Data are available by species, area of capture, port of landing, and fishing organisation.

The information covers the UK, including the Channel Islands and the Isle of Man. Data are also available by territorial department, by administrative district for sea fishing purposes and by port of landing. Information is collected after each fishing trip. Data are published weekly for the landings of quota stocks, and monthly on the quantities and values of species landed, by port. Detailed overall figures are published annually.

Status: Ongoing
Frequency: Annually
Reference Period: Previous year
Timeliness: 9 months
Earliest Available Data: 1993
National Coverage: United Kingdom

Statistician
Ian Wood
Ministry of Agriculture, Fisheries and Food
FISH 1; C- Fisheries
Tel: 020 7238 6050;
Email: i.wood@fish.maff.gov.uk

Products that contain data from this source
Annual Abstract of Statistics; Monthly Digest of Statistics; Monthly Return of Sea Fisheries Statistics England and Wales; Statistics of Fish Landings in England, Wales and Northern Ireland by Port; UK Sea Fisheries Statistics

14.8 Food, Beverages and Nutrition

Manufacture of Regular Coffee, Coffee Essences and Coffee Extracts - UK
Ministry of Agriculture, Fisheries and Food

The Ministry of Agriculture, Fisheries and Food conducts a survey on the usage of raw coffee. Data are collected on the tonnage of raw coffee used in the production of (a) liquid coffee essence, dried coffee extract, dried soluble coffee powder and dry coffee/chicory extract and (b) roasted for regular coffee. Data are also collected on stocks of raw coffee held by manufacturers at the end of the period (excluding stocks of coffee held in public warehouses - see separate survey). The survey has been carried out for over twenty years with the data being used in compiling the published estimates of disposals and stocks of raw coffee. These are published by the ONS in the Monthly Digest and Annual Abstract of Statistics.

Status: Ongoing
Collection Method: Census
Frequency: Quarterly
Reference Period: Quarters
Timeliness: 1 month
National Coverage: United Kingdom

Statistician
Stan Speller
Ministry of Agriculture, Fisheries and Food
Tel: 020 7270 8547;
Email: s.speller@esg.maff.gov.uk

Products that contain data from this source
Annual Abstract of Statistics; Monthly Digest of Statistics

National Diet and Nutrition Survey: People Aged 65 Years and Over (Volume 1: Report of the Diet and Nutrition Survey)
National Centre for Social Research; sponsored by Ministry of Agriculture, Fisheries and Food and the Department of Health

The National Diet and Nutrition Survey for people aged 65 years and over is part of the wider National Diet and Nutrition Survey (NDNS) programme. The Ministry of Agriculture, Fisheries and Food and the Department of Health established the NDNS programme in 1992. The programme aims to provide a comprehensive cross-sectional picture of the dietary habits and nutritional status of the population of Great Britain. The programme will take eight to ten years to complete and is split into four separate surveys, each on a different age group, conducted at approximately two-yearly intervals.

The NDNS of people aged 65 and over was carried out by the National Centre for Social Research, and is based on a sample of approximately 1,300 people living in the community and approximately 400 people living in institutions in Great Britain.

Status: Ceased completely
Collection Method: Household/Person (Sample) Survey
Frequency: One-off
Reference Period: 12 months
Timeliness: 3 years
National Coverage: Great Britain
Disaggregation: Registrar General Standard Regions

Statistician
Steven Finch
National Centre for Social Research
Tel: 020 7250 1866;
Email: s.finch@natcen.ac.uk

Products that contain data from this source
The Data Archive

National Food Survey - Northern Ireland
Department of Agriculture - Northern Ireland

The National Food survey is a continuous survey of household food consumption and expenditure which is carried out throughout the United Kingdom. Although the survey dates back to 1940, Northern Ireland has only been included in the sample since January 1996. The survey provides information on the changing pattern of household food consumption, expenditure and dietary patterns.

Status: Ongoing
Collection Method: Household/Person (Sample) Survey
Frequency: Continuously
Reference Period: Quarter/Year
Timeliness: 3 months
Earliest Available Data: 1996
National Coverage: Northern Ireland

Statistician
Bernie Stuart
Department of Agriculture - Northern Ireland
Tel: 028 9052 4455;
Email: bernie.stuart@dani.gov.uk

National Food Survey - UK
Ministry of Agriculture, Fisheries and Food

The Ministry of Agriculture, Fisheries and Food and the Department of Agriculture for Northern Ireland sponsor the National Food Survey, a survey of food and drink consumption and expenditure by 6,500 households throughout the UK. Results are available on average consumption and expenditure per person per week. Consumption data are also converted to nutritional intakes of energy, protein, fats, sugars and a number of vitamins per person per day.

Status: Ongoing
Collection Method: Household/Person (Sample) Survey
Frequency: Continuously
Timeliness: 10 weeks
Earliest Available Data: 1940's
National Coverage: England, Scotland, Wales, Northern Ireland, Great Britain, United Kingdom
Disaggregation: Government Office Region (GOR)

Statistician
Stan Speller
Ministry of Agriculture, Fisheries and Food
Tel: 020 7270 8547;
Email: s.speller@esg.maff.gov.uk

Products that contain data from this source
Annual Abstract of Statistics; Focus on London; Focus on Northern Ireland; Focus on the East Midlands; Focus on the South East; Focus on the South West; Monthly Digest of Statistics; National Food Survey (Annual Report); National Food Survey GB (Statistical News Release); National Food Survey GB Compendium of Results; Regional Trends; Social Focus on Children; Social Focus on Ethnic Minorities; Social Focus on Families; Social Focus on the Unemployed; Social Focus on Women; Social Trends; The Data Archive

Self Sufficiency in Food
Ministry of Agriculture, Fisheries and Food

Self-sufficiency calculations are based on home production of food and feed as a proportion of both the total supply of all food and feed and of indigenous food and feed.

Status: Ongoing
Frequency: Annually
Reference Period: Calendar year
Earliest Available Data: 1956
Sub-National: UK only

Statistician
Jim Holding
Ministry of Agriculture, Fisheries and Food
Statistics (Commodities and Food); Branch C
Tel: 00 44(0)1904 4555080;
Email: s.j.holding@esg.maff.gov.uk

Products that contain data from this analysis
Agriculture in the United Kingdom; The Ministry of Agriculture, Fisheries and Food Website

Stocks of Human and Pet Food in Public Cold Stores - UK
Ministry of Agriculture, Fisheries and Food

The Ministry of Agriculture, Fisheries and Food conducts a survey on stocks of human and pet food in public cold stores. It is a voluntary survey with up to 126 respondents. Data are available on stocks of dairy products, meat and meat products, poultry and game, fruits and vegetables, and other miscellaneous food products in public cold stores in the United Kingdom.

The survey was started in the 1940s. Data are collected and published monthly.

Status: Ongoing
Collection Method: Census
Frequency: Monthly
Reference Period: Stocks on last Saturday in month
Timeliness: 5-6 weeks after month end
Earliest Available Data: March 1993
National Coverage: United Kingdom

Statistician
Lindsey Clothier
Ministry of Agriculture, Fisheries and Food
Commodities and Food Division; Branch D
Tel: 00 44 (0)1904 455090;
Email: l.j.clothier@esg.maff.gov.uk

Products that contain data from this source
Agriculture in the United Kingdom; Monthly Digest of Statistics; Quarterly Supplies and Total for Domestic Usage of Meat in the UK (Statistical Notice); Stocks in Public Cold Stores (Statistical Notice)

Stocks of Raw Coffee in Public Warehouses - UK
Ministry of Agriculture, Fisheries and Food

The Ministry of Agriculture, Fisheries and Food conducts a survey on stocks of raw coffee in public warehouses. Data are collected on stocks in warehouses, imports not yet landed and stocks in transit to a public warehouse. The survey has been carried out for over twenty years with the data used in compiling the published estimates of total stocks of raw coffee, including that held by manufacturers. These are published by the ONS in the Monthly Digest and Annual Abstract of Statistics.

Status: Ongoing
Collection Method: Census
Frequency: Quarterly
Reference Period: End of quarter
Timeliness: 1 month
National Coverage: United Kingdom

Statistician
Stan Speller
Ministry of Agriculture, Fisheries and Food
Tel: 020 7270 8547;
Email: s.speller@esg.maff.gov.uk

Products that contain data from this source
Annual Abstract of Statistics; Monthly Digest of Statistics

See also:
In this chapter:
Aggregate Agricultural Account *(14.5)*
Stocks of Wine - UK (Wholesalers & Retailers) *(14.10)*

14.9 Forestry

Census of Woodland and Trees
Forestry Commission

The Forestry Commission conducted the Census of Woodland and Trees, at intervals of 15-20 years. The Census combined information for Forestry Commission woodland with data for other woodlands in Great Britain. They used a mix of census and sample data. Data are available for tree species, distribution, volume of timber, forest area and forest type. Censuses were carried out for 1924, 1947, 1965 and 1980. In place of the Census, there is now a National Inventory of Woodland, carried out on a rolling 10-year basis, starting in 1993.

Status: Ceased completely
Collection Method: Mix of sample and census
Frequency: 15-20 year intervals
Reference Period: end-March
Timeliness: 3-5 years
Earliest Available Data: 1924
National Coverage: Great Britain
Disaggregation: Former County (E&W); Former Region (Scotland)

Statistician
Simon Gillam
Forestry Commission
Policy and Practice Division - Statistics
Tel: 0131 314 6280;
Email: simon.gillam@forestry.gov.uk

Products that contain data from this source
Census of Woodland and Trees 1979-82

FASTCo Safety Survey
Forestry Commission; for Forestry and Arboriculture, Safety and Training Council (FASTCo)

Sample survey of forest workers, to assess awareness of safety matters. Surveys conducted in 1991 and 1994.

Status: Ceased temporarily
Collection Method: Small-scale (Sample) Survey
Frequency: Ad hoc
Timeliness: About 3 months
Earliest Available Data: 1991
National Coverage: Great Britain
Sub-National: Four representative areas (2 in England, 1 in Scotland, 1 in Wales)
Disaggregation: None

Statistician
Simon Gillam
Forestry Commission
Policy and Practice Division - Statistics
Tel: 0131 314 6280;
Email: simon.gillam@forestry.gov.uk

Firewood Usage Survey
Forestry Commission

A survey of household usage of firewood, carried out in 1997 using RSGB Omnibus Survey.

Status: Ceased completely
Collection Method: Household/Person (Sample) Survey
Frequency: Ad hoc
Reference Period: 1997
Timeliness: 2 months
Earliest Available Data: 1997
National Coverage: Great Britain
Sub-National: RSGB Omnibus sampling frame
Disaggregation: Standard Statistical Region (SSR)

Statistician
Simon Gillam
Forestry Commission
Policy; Statistics
Tel: 0131 314 6280;
Email: simon.gillam@forestry.gov.uk

Forest Employment Survey
Forestry Commission

The Forestry Commission conducts the Forest Employment Survey, most recently collecting data for 1998. Data are derived from censuses of employment for the Forestry Commission, the largest forest management companies and some wood processors, with sample surveys of private owners and other companies and contractors, and other organisations involved with wood and trees. Data are available by activity and sector

Status: Ongoing
Collection Method: Mix of census and sample
Frequency: Varies - about every 3-5 years
Reference Period: Varies - mostly previous financial year.
Timeliness: Final results published about a year after most data collection.
Earliest Available Data: 1986
National Coverage: England, Scotland and Wales

Statistician
Simon Gillam
Forestry Commission
Policy and Practice Division - Statistics
Tel: 0131 314 6280;
Email: simon.gillam@forestry.gov.uk

Products that contain data from this source
Forest Employment Survey 1993-94

Forest Enterprise Accident Statistics
Forestry Commission; Forest Enterprise

Record of all reportable accidents involving Forestry Commission staff.

Status: Ongoing
Collection Method: Administrative Records
Frequency: Annually
Reference Period: Years ending 31 March
Timeliness: About 4 months
Earliest Available Data: 1986-87 (previously clerical)
National Coverage: England, Scotland and Wales

Statistician
Simon Gillam
Forestry Commission
Policy and Practice Division - Statistics
Tel: 0131 314 6280;
Email: simon.gillam@forestry.gov.uk

Forest Enterprise Forest Fire Statistics
Forestry Commission; Forest Enterprise

Annual number and area of forest fires on Forest Enterprise land (financial years)

Status: Ongoing
Collection Method: Administrative Records
Frequency: Annually
Reference Period: Years ending 31 March
Timeliness: 3 months after financial year end
Earliest Available Data: 1920
National Coverage: Great Britain

Statistician
Simon Gillam
Forestry Commission
Policy and Practice Division - Statistics
Tel: 0131 314 6280;
Email: simon.gillam@forestry.gov.uk

Products that contain data from this source
Forest Fire Statistics (UNECE)

Forest Enterprise Holidays Facilities Inventory
Forestry Commission; Forest Enterprise

Records of numbers and locations of facilities run by Forest Enterprise Holidays - cabins and campsites.

Status: Ongoing
Collection Method: Administrative Records
Frequency: Annually
Reference Period: End-March
Timeliness: Approximately 2 months
Earliest Available Data: 1971
National Coverage: England, Scotland and Wales

Statistician
Simon Gillam
Forestry Commission
Policy and Practice Division - Statistics
Tel: 0131 314 6280;
Email: simon.gillam@forestry.gov.uk

Products that contain data from this source
Forest Enterprise Annual Report & Accounts; Forestry Commission Facts and Figures; Forestry Industry Yearbook

Forest Enterprise Land Acquisitions and Disposals
Forestry Commission; Forest Enterprise

Area and value of land acquisitions and disposals

Status: Ongoing
Collection Method: Administrative Records
Frequency: Annually
Reference Period: Years ending 31 March
Timeliness: 3 months
Earliest Available Data: 1920
National Coverage: England, Scotland and Wales

Statistician
Simon Gillam
Forestry Commission
Policy and Practice Division - Statistics
Tel: 0131 314 6280;
Email: simon.gillam@forestry.gov.uk

Products that contain data from this source
Forest Enterprise Annual Report & Accounts

Forest Enterprise Log Prices
Forestry Commission; Forest Enterprise

Prices of felled softwood logs, sold by Forest Enterprise at tender and auction log sales (but excluding negotiated sales), calculated as total value divided by total volume expressed as "price" index.

Status: Ongoing
Collection Method: Administrative Records
Frequency: Bi-annually
Reference Period: Periods ending March, September
Timeliness: 2 months
Earliest Available Data: 1975
National Coverage: Great Britain

Statistician
Simon Gillam
Forestry Commission
Policy and Practice Division - Statistics
Tel: 0131 314 6280;
Email: simon.gillam@forestry.gov.uk

Products that contain data from this source
Forest Enterprise Timber Price Indices

Forest Enterprise Planting
Forestry Commission; Forest Enterprise

Areas of new planting and restocking by Forest Enterprise

Status: Ongoing
Collection Method: Administrative Records
Frequency: Annually
Reference Period: Years ending 31 March
Timeliness: 3 months
Earliest Available Data: 1920
National Coverage: Great Britain
Sub-national: England, Scotland and Wales

Statistician
Simon Gillam
Forestry Commission
Policy and Practice Division - Statistics
Tel: 0131 314 6280;
Email: simon.gillam@forestry.gov.uk

Products that contain data from this source
Forest Enterprise Annual Report & Accounts; Forestry Commission Facts and Figures; Forestry Industry Yearbook

---

Forest Enterprise Recreation Facilities Inventory
Forestry Commission; Forest Enterprise

Record of number and location of FE recreation facilities, other than cabins and campsites.

Status: Ongoing
Collection Method: Administrative Records
Frequency: Annually
Reference Period: At end-March
Timeliness: Approximately 2 months
Earliest Available Data: 1971
National Coverage: Great Britain
Sub-national: England, Scotland and Wales

Statistician
Simon Gillam
Forestry Commission
Policy and Practice Division - Statistics
Tel: 0131 314 6280;
Email: simon.gillam@forestry.gov.uk

Products that contain data from this source
Forest Enterprise Annual Report & Accounts; Forestry Commission Facts and Figures; Forestry Industry Yearbook

---

Forest Enterprise Standing Sales Timber Prices
Forestry Commission; Forest Enterprise

Prices achieved for conifer standing sales in previous year, broken down by size category.

Status: Ongoing
Collection Method: Administrative Records
Frequency: Bi-annually
Reference Period: Overlapping 12-month periods ending Mar/Sept
Timeliness: 2 months
Earliest Available Data: 1957
National Coverage: Great Britain
Sub-national: England, Scotland and Wales

Statistician
Simon Gillam
Forestry Commission
Policy and Practice Division - Statistics
Tel: 0131 314 6280;
Email: simon.gillam@forestry.gov.uk

Products that contain data from this source
Forest Enterprise Timber Price Indices

Forest Enterprise Sub-Compartment Database
Forestry Commission; Forest Enterprise

Details for each sub-compartment of Forest Enterprise woodland

Status: Ongoing
Collection Method: Administrative Records
Frequency: Annually
Reference Period: At end-March
Timeliness: 3 months
Earliest Available Data: Current data only; summarised extracts exist since 1970 (or earlier)
National Coverage: Great Britain
Disaggregation: Forest Districts

Statistician
Simon Gillam
Forestry Commission
Policy and Practice Division - Statistics
Tel: 0131 314 6280;
Email: simon.gillam@forestry.gov.uk

Products that contain data from this source
Forest Enterprise Annual Report & Accounts; Forestry Commission Facts and Figures

---

Forest Enterprise Timber Harvesting and Sales
Forestry Commission; Forest Enterprise

Area, volume and value of timber harvested/sold each year.

Status: Ongoing
Collection Method: Administrative Records
Frequency: Annually
Reference Period: Years ending 31 March
Timeliness: 3 months
Earliest Available Data: 1920
National Coverage: Great Britain
Sub-national: England, Scotland and Wales

Statistician
Simon Gillam
Forestry Commission
Policy and Practice Division - Statistics
Tel: 0131 314 6280;
Email: simon.gillam@forestry.gov.uk

Products that contain data from this source
Forest Enterprise Annual Report & Accounts; Forestry Commission Facts and Figures

---

Forest Enterprise Visitor Surveys
Forestry Commission; Forest Enterprise

Surveys of visitors to Forest Enterprise sites in GB, about 15-20 each year since 1995. Also continuous surveys of visitors to Forest Enterprise Holidays cabins and campsites.

Status: Ongoing
Collection Method: Household/Person (Sample) Survey
Frequency: Ad hoc
Reference Period: Usually summer
Timeliness: 1 month for provisional results, 6-9 months for final report
Earliest Available Data: 1995 (a few earlier)
National Coverage: Great Britain
Disaggregation: Each survey typically covers visitors to 1, 2 or 3 sites in a Forest District. By site visited, and by home postcode of visitor

Statistician
Simon Gillam
Forestry Commission
Policy and Practice Division - Statistics
Tel: 0131 314 6280;
Email: simon.gillam@forestry.gov.uk

Products that contain data from this source
Forest Enterprise Visitor Survey Reports; Forest
Visitor Surveys (annual summary reports)

Forest Enterprise Visitor Trends
Forestry Commission; Forest Enterprise

Numbers of cars or visitors recorded by
traffic counters, pay & display tickets or
other counters, at Forest Enterprise
locations throughout GB. Monthly totals
reported, starting January 1996. Equipment
problems (and occasionally re-siting of
counters) have affected data consistency
for a number of counters

Status: Ongoing
Collection Method: Administrative Records
Frequency: Monthly
Timeliness: 3-5 months after end of year
Earliest Available Data: 1996
National Coverage: Great Britain
Sub-national: England, Scotland and Wales

Statistician
Simon Gillam
Forestry Commission
Policy and Practice Division - Statistics
Tel: 0131 314 6280;
Email: simon.gillam@forestry.gov.uk

Forestry - Northern Ireland
Department of Agriculture - Northern
Ireland

The Forest Service is an Agency of the
Department of Agriculture for Northern
Ireland and compiles statistics for forestry
in Northern Ireland. Data on state forestry
covers land acquisition/disposal, land use,
buildings, agricultural lettings and leases,
woodland establishment, woodland
improvement and protection, analysis of
harvesting and marketing figures,
recreational statistics, staffing, safety,
workstudy, training, plant health, research
and planning. Data for private planting is
available for grant-aided planting.

Status: Ongoing
Collection Method: Management Information
Frequency: Annually
Timeliness: 6 months
Earliest Available Data: 1975 with some data
available from 1920.
National Coverage: Northern Ireland
Disaggregation: Forest Service Districts;
Planning Branch

Statistician
Stuart Morwood
Department of Agriculture - Northern Ireland
Tel: 028 9052 4154

Products that contain data from this source
Forest Service Annual Report 1997/98

Forestry Employment
Forestry Commission

Annual estimates of forestry employment
were derived by extrapolating data from
surveys of the private sector, which take
place roughly every five years, and adding
figures for employees and contractors used
by the Commission, based on administrative
records. Results are available since the
establishment of the Commission in 1919;
figures for private sector employment have
only been collected since 1986. No
projections have been made since 1993/94
Forest Employment Survey.

Status: Ceased temporarily
Frequency: Annually
Reference Period: End-March
Timeliness: 6 months
Earliest Available Data: 1920 (partial)
National Coverage: Great Britain
Sub-national: England, Scotland and Wales

Statistician
Simon Gillam
Forestry Commission
Policy; Statistics
Tel: 0131 314 6280;
Email: simon.gillam@forestry.gov.uk

Products that contain data from this analysis
Forestry Commission Facts and Figures

Management Grant Areas
Forestry Commission

Areas approved for management grant under
the Woodland Grant Scheme. Information
taken from WGS database, and summarised
for publication in Annual Report.

Status: Ongoing
Frequency: Annually
Reference Period: Years ending 31 March
Timeliness: 4 months
Earliest Available Data: 1992/93
National Coverage: Great Britain
Sub-national: England, Scotland and Wales

Statistician
Simon Gillam
Forestry Commission
Policy; Statistics
Tel: 0131 314 6280;
Email: simon.gillam@forestry.gov.uk

Products that contain data from this analysis
Forestry Commission Annual Report and
Accounts; Forestry Commission Facts and Figures

National Inventory of Woodland - Digital Maps
Forestry Commission

Digital maps, originally based on air
photography, showing all woodlands over
2 hectares. For Scotland, based on Land
Cover of Scotland 1988 (Scottish Executive/
MLURI), updated using FC administrative
records. For England & Wales, based on
interpretation of new air photography,
starting in 1995.

Status: Ongoing
Collection Method: Air photos
Frequency: Decennial
Reference Period: Varies
Timeliness: 1-4 years
Earliest Available Data: 1994 (rolling
programme)
National Coverage: Great Britain
Disaggregation: Any geographic unit, using GIS

Statistician
Simon Gillam
Forestry Commission
Policy and Practice Division - Statistics
Tel: 0131 314 6280;
Email: simon.gillam@forestry.gov.uk

Products that contain data from this source
National Inventory of Woodland & Trees

National Inventory of Woodland - Sample Data
Forestry Commission

Data collected for 1 hectare sample squares.
Cluster sample selected using digital maps,
using stratified sampling scheme, giving 1%
area sample for each size class. Data
recorded on site, using hand-held computers,
for cluster, square, section and element.

Status: Ongoing
Collection Method: Large-scale (Sample)
Survey
Frequency: Decennial
Reference Period: Varies
Timeliness: 1-3 years
Earliest Available Data: 1994 (rolling
programme)
National Coverage: Great Britain
Disaggregation: Any geographic unit, using GIS

Statistician
Simon Gillam
Forestry Commission
Policy and Practice Division - Statistics
Tel: 0131 314 6280;
Email: simon.gillam@forestry.gov.uk

Products that contain data from this source
National Inventory of Woodland & Trees

Planting & Restocking of Woodland
Forestry Commission

Data on new planting and restocking of woodland. Figures are collected on areas for which grants are paid to private woodland owners and internal records of planting undertaken by the Commission.

Enterprise figures are available by administrative district. Planting data have been collected since the establishment of the Forestry Commission in 1919, but for early years did not separate new planting from restocking.

Status: Ongoing
Frequency: Annually
Reference Period: Year ending 31 March
Timeliness: 4 months
Earliest Available Data: 1920
National Coverage: Great Britain
Sub-national: England, Scotland and Wales

Statistician
Simon Gillam
Forestry Commission
Policy and Practice Division - Statistics
Tel: 0131 314 6280;
Email: simon.gillam@forestry.gov.uk

Products that contain data from this analysis
Forestry Commission Facts and Figures; Forestry Industry Yearbook

---

Private Sector Softwood Removals Survey
Forestry Commission

The surveys obtain information from the largest 30-40 companies harvesting timber from private woodlands. The series has been available in its present form since 1993. Previous estimates were compiled by industry associations, from a smaller survey of 5-6 companies.

Status: Ongoing
Collection Method: Census
Frequency: Annually
Reference Period: the calendar year
Timeliness: 2 months for provisional results, 6 months for final report.
Earliest Available Data: 1994
National Coverage: Great Britain

Statistician
Simon Gillam
Forestry Commission
Policy and Practice Division - Statistics
Tel: 0131 314 6280;
Email: simon.gillam@forestry.gov.uk

Products that contain data from this source
Forestry Commission Facts and Figures; Wood Supply & Demand

Private Woodlands Survey
Forestry Commission

The Private Woodlands Survey was carried out by the Universities of Aberdeen and Bangor. It was carried out from April 1989 to March 1992, with results published in 1994. Data are available for Great Britain on the costs of forest operations. Previously, annual surveys on costs of operations, income and expenditure had been carried out by Aberdeen & Oxford Universities, starting 1951/52, using a cohort sample (standard set of traditional estates). Survey discontinued after 1992, because no longer required to determine grant levels.

Status: Ceased completely
Collection Method: Small-scale (Sample) Survey
Reference Period: 1989-1992
Timeliness: 2 years for final report for 1989-1992.
Earliest Available Data: 1951-1952
National Coverage: Great Britain
Sub-national: England, Scotland and Wales

Statistician
Simon Gillam
Forestry Commission
Policy and Practice Division - Statistics
Tel: 0131 314 6280;
Email: simon.gillam@forestry.gov.uk

Products that contain data from this source
Private Woodlands Survey

Public Opinion of Forestry Survey
Forestry Commission

A survey to assess public awareness and opinions of forestry, commissioned by Forestry Commission every second year, using questions in an omnibus survey.

Status: Ongoing
Collection Method: Household/Person (Sample) Survey
Reference Period: Run in February or March
Timeliness: 6 months
Earliest Available Data: 1993
National Coverage: Great Britain
Sub-national: England, Scotland and Wales

Statistician
Simon Gillam
Forestry Commission
Policy and Practice Division - Statistics
Tel: 0131 314 6280;
Email: simon.gillam@forestry.gov.uk

Products that contain data from this source
Public Opinion of Forestry 1997

Round Fencing Manufacturers Survey
Forestry Commission

An annual voluntary survey of 120 - 130 companies asking about purchases of British timber for the manufacture of round fencing material. Data are available for Great Britain and at country level and the results published in the Wood Supply and Demand Report.

Coverage has been improved from 1995, doubling the number of companies surveyed. Now seeking to improve coverage of hardwood fencing.

Status: Ongoing
Collection Method: Census
Frequency: Annually
Reference Period: the calendar year
Timeliness: 2 months for provisional results, 6 months for final report.
Earliest Available Data: 1993
National Coverage: Great Britain
Sub-national: England, Scotland and Wales

Statistician
Simon Gillam
Forestry Commission
Policy and Practice Division - Statistics
Tel: 0131 314 6280;
Email: simon.gillam@forestry.gov.uk

Products that contain data from this source
Wood Supply & Demand

Sawmill Survey - Annual
Forestry Commission

A voluntary survey of all Sawmills using British timber (now around 400 mills) asking about consumption of timber and production of sawnwood. Data are published annually in the Wood Supply and Demand Report, and also used for the report on the full triennial/biennial survey. Methodology changed from 1994, to estimate for each non-respondent instead of applying general rating factors.

Status: Ongoing
Collection Method: Census
Frequency: Annually
Reference Period: the calendar year
Timeliness: 2 months for provisional results, 6 months for final report.
Earliest Available Data: 1980
National Coverage: Great Britain
Sub-national: England, Scotland and Wales.
Disaggregation: Can analyse for smaller areas using address of mill to derive county / region or other area.

Statistician
Simon Gillam
Forestry Commission
Policy and Practice Division - Statistics
Tel: 0131 314 6280;
Email: simon.gillam@forestry.gov.uk

Sawmill Survey - Triennial/ Biennial
Forestry Commission

A voluntary survey of larger Sawmills, carried out every third year from 1987 to 1996, then every second year. This survey collects more detailed information from mills that produce at least 1000m3 sawnwood (at least 5000m3 from 1998). Data are published in the Sawmill Survey Report. Full surveys have been carried out for calendar years 1973, 1977, 1983, 1987, 1990, 1993 and 1996 and 1998.

Status: Ongoing
Collection Method: Census
Frequency: Triennial
Reference Period: the calendar year
Timeliness: 2 months for provisional results, 6 months for final report.
Earliest Available Data: 1973
National Coverage: Great Britain
Sub-national: England, Scotland and Wales.
Disaggregation: Can analyse for smaller areas using address of mill to derive county / region or other area.

Statistician
Simon Gillam
Forestry Commission
Policy and Practice Division - Statistics
Tel: 0131 314 6280;
Email: simon.gillam@forestry.gov.uk

Standing Sales Price Index
Forestry Commission

A Laspeyres Index of standing sales prices, using data broken down by size category. Calculated for GB, and also for Scotland, and England & Wales. Based on quantities for year ending September 1996. First calculated 1997/98, has now replaced FE simple index that does not take account of changes in size mix.

Status: Ongoing
Frequency: Bi-annually
Reference Period: 12-month periods, ending 31 March and 30 September.
Timeliness: 3 months after end of period
Earliest Available Data: 1971
National Coverage: Great Britain
Sub-national: England & Wales, Scotland

Statistician
Simon Gillam
Forestry Commission
Policy and Practice Division - Statistics
Tel: 0131 314 6280;
Email: simon.gillam@forestry.gov.uk

Timber Deliveries to Wood Processing Industries
Forestry Commission

Annual totals for deliveries to wood processing industries, based on sawmill survey, fencing survey and other wood processing industry enquiries.

Status: Ongoing
Frequency: Annually
Reference Period: Calendar year
Timeliness: 5-6 months after end of year.
Earliest Available Data: 1970 (Earlier data may exist)
National Coverage: Great Britain
Sub-national: England, Scotland and Wales (estimates only, for some sectors)

Statistician
Simon Gillam
Forestry Commission
Policy and Practice Division - Statistics
Tel: 0131 314 6280;
Email: simon.gillam@forestry.gov.uk

Timber Price-Size Curves
Forestry Commission

Tables or charts that show the relationship between conifer tree size (volume of timber) and price (per cubic metre) based on Forest Enterprise Standing Sales Timber Prices. Similar information exists for broadleaves.

Status: Ongoing
Frequency: Ad hoc
Reference Period: 1957-1991
Earliest Available Data: 1957-1991
National Coverage: Great Britain

Statistician
Simon Gillam
Forestry Commission
Policy and Practice Division - Statistics
Tel: 0131 314 6280;
Email: simon.gillam@forestry.gov.uk

Timber Production
Forestry Commission

The Forestry Commission compiles data on timber production. Figures are derived from the results of surveys of companies harvesting timber from private woodlands and internal records of the Commission. The series has been available in its present form since 1970.

Status: Ongoing
Frequency: Annually
Reference Period: Calendar year
Timeliness: 6 months after end of year
Earliest Available Data: 1970
National Coverage: Great Britain
Sub-national: England, Scotland and Wales

Statistician
Simon Gillam
Forestry Commission
Policy and Practice Division - Statistics
Tel: 0131 314 6280;
Email: simon.gillam@forestry.gov.uk

Wood Processing Enquiries (Pulp, Wood-Based Panels Etc)
Forestry Commission

Enquiries, mostly sent to industry associations, to obtain figures for the volume of British timber used by these industries. Separate enquiries for pulp exports, pulp industry, particleboard (including OSB), MDF, other fibreboard, wood-wool. Enquiries known to have run since 1970; earlier data may exist. Also enquiries to obtain figures for production by these industries.

Status: Ongoing
Collection Method: Census
Frequency: Annually
Reference Period: Calendar year
Timeliness: 2 months for provisional results, 6 months for final report.
Earliest Available Data: 1975
National Coverage: Great Britain
Sub-National: None at present, seeking England, Scotland and Wales.

Statistician
Simon Gillam
Forestry Commission
Policy and Practice Division - Statistics
Tel: 0131 314 6280;
Email: simon.gillam@forestry.gov.uk

Wood Product Imports & Exports WRME
Forestry Commission

Annual quantities (volumes or weights) of wood products, from overseas trade statistics, converted to wood raw material equivalent using standard conversion factors for each SITC category. Figures for forestry statistics publications are WRME underbark volumes, using factors published in FIYB, but WRME standing volume figures have also been calculated.

Status: Ongoing
Frequency: Annually
Reference Period: Calendar year
Timeliness: 5 months after end of calendar year
Earliest Available Data: 1990
National Coverage: United Kingdom

Statistician
Simon Gillam
Forestry Commission
Policy and Practice Division - Statistics
Tel: 0131 314 6280;
Email: simon.gillam@forestry.gov.uk

Products that contain data from this analysis
Forestry Commission Facts and Figures; Forestry Industry Yearbook

Woodland Areas
Forestry Commission

The Forestry Commission (FC) compiles data on areas of woodland, broken down into FC and private, with each broken down into conifers, broadleaves, coppice, other. Figures are derived by projections of the Census of Woodland and Trees, using administrative records for the area of new planting (by FC or receiving grants paid to private woodland owners), and FC acquisitions and disposals of forest land.

Status: Ongoing
Frequency: Annually
Reference Period: End March
Timeliness: 3 months after reference period
Earliest Available Data: 1977 (some data back to 1919)
National Coverage: Great Britain
Sub-national: England, Scotland and Wales

Statistician
Simon Gillam
Forestry Commission
Policy and Practice Division - Statistics
Tel: 0131 314 6280;
Email: simon.gillam@forestry.gov.uk

Products that contain data from this analysis
Forestry Commission Facts and Figures; Forestry Industry Yearbook

Woodland Grant Scheme Database
Forestry Commission

The Forestry Commission compiles data on woodland areas from administrative data collected through the Woodland Grant Scheme, under which grants are paid to private woodland owners. Data relate to individual WGS applications, but can be aggregated to give data for countries of GB. Additional ad hoc reporting and GIS functionality is now available.

Status: Ongoing
Collection Method: Administrative Records
Frequency: Continuously
Timeliness: 3 months after end of year
Earliest Available Data: 1992 (some data available for earlier years)
National Coverage: Great Britain
Sub-national: England, Scotland and Wales
Disaggregation: Available for smaller areas using GIS functionality

Statistician
Simon Gillam
Forestry Commission
Policy and Practice Division - Statistics
Tel: 0131 314 6280;
Email: simon.gillam@forestry.gov.uk

Products that contain data from this source
Forestry Commission Annual Report and Accounts; Forestry Commission Facts and Figures

Yield Models
Forestry Commission

Tables and graphs showing for each combination of tree species, spacing, thinning regime and age, what is the typical top height and timber volume.

Status: Ongoing
Frequency: Ad hoc
Earliest Available Data: 1975 - 1980 (varies)
National Coverage: Great Britain

Statistician
Simon Gillam
Forestry Commission
Policy and Practice Division - Statistics
Tel: 0131 314 6280;
Email: simon.gillam@forestry.gov.uk

See also:
In this chapter:
EC Farm Structure Survey *(14.17)*

In other chapters:
National Parks Visitor Survey *(see the Transport, Travel and Tourism chapter)*
Overseas Trade Statistics - Wood Products *(see the Economy chapter)*
UK Day Visits Survey *(see the Transport, Travel and Tourism chapter)*

14.10 Horticulture (incl. Potatoes, Hops & Wine)

Cabbages and Cauliflowers - Yields and Prices
Scottish Executive

The SEAEFD conducted a survey on cabbage and cauliflower yields and prices. The survey consisted of a sample of 84 growers and covered Scotland. It was carried

out annually and the reference period was the crop year.

Status: Ceased completely
Collection Method: Small-scale (Sample) Survey
Frequency: Annually
National Coverage: Scotland

Statistician
Tom Whyte
Scottish Executive
Tel: 0131 244 3116

Products that contain data from this source
Economic Report on Scottish Agriculture; Scottish Agriculture Output Input and Income Statistics

Cider Survey - England and Wales
Ministry of Agriculture, Fisheries and Food

The Ministry of Agriculture, Fisheries and Food conducts a survey on the usage of apples and pears grown in the UK. Data are available on total apples and pears tonnages and the split between specific cider, perry and other varieties that have been pressed. The survey covers the United Kingdom and began in the late 1940s.

Status: Ongoing
Collection Method: Small-scale (Sample) Survey
Frequency: Annually
Reference Period: Last Year
Timeliness: 2 Months
Earliest Available Data: 1964
National Coverage: United Kingdom

Statistician
Christine Jeannette
Ministry of Agriculture, Fisheries and Food
Statistics (C & F); Branch B
Tel: 01904 455069

Products that contain data from this source
Basic Horticultural Statistics

Extended Horticulture Survey - Scotland
SERAD

The SERAD conducts a survey on vegetable yields and prices. The survey consists of a sample of 115 vegetable growers and is used to produce average prices and average yields. The survey is carried out every 4 years

Status: Ongoing
Collection Method: Small-scale (Sample) Survey
Reference Period: Crop Year
Timeliness: Approximately 2/3 months
National Coverage: Scotland

Statistician
Tom Whyte
Scottish Executive
Tel: 0131 244 3116

Statistician
Tom Whyte
Scottish Executive
Tel: 0131 244 3116

Statistician
Christine Jeannette
Ministry of Agriculture, Fisheries and Food
Statistics (C & F); Branch B
Tel: 01904 455069

Products that contain data from this source
Economic Report on Scottish Agriculture

Products that contain data from this source
Economic Report on Scottish Agriculture

Products that contain data from this source
Eurostat - European Official Statistics - Sources of Information

Fruit and Vegetables Crops - England and Wales
Ministry of Agriculture, Fisheries and Food

The Ministry of Agriculture, Fisheries and Food compiles data on the production, marketing and prices of fresh fruit and vegetables. Information is supplied by the fifteen Horticultural Crop Intelligence Committees (HCIC) covering field vegetables, fruit and protected crops.

Data are available on area, yield, production, marketing and wastage, average wholesale market prices, and for a small number of crops an estimate of the weighted average 'farm-gate' price. From September 1998 the cumulative percentage marketed figure for each crop has been based on a standard marketing pattern. The figure is based on a monthly average and covers the last four years. The HCIC system was set up in the late 1940s and reports have been produced ever since.

Status: Ongoing
Frequency: Monthly
Reference Period: Crop Year
Timeliness: Monthly Intervals.
Earliest Available Data: 1964

Statistician
Christine Jeannette
Ministry of Agriculture, Fisheries and Food
Statistics (C & F); Branch B
Tel: 01904 455069

Products that contain data from this source
Agriculture in the United Kingdom; Basic Horticultural Statistics

Glasshouse and Protected Crops Survey - Scotland
Scottish Executive Rural Affairs Department

The SERAD conducts a survey of glasshouse and protected crops. The survey consists of a sample of 100 commercial and non-commercial holdings and covers cropping area, cropping method and sales The survey is carried out every 4 years.

Status: Ongoing
Collection Method: Small-scale (Sample) Survey
Reference Period: Crop Year
Timeliness: Approximately 2-3 months
National Coverage: Scotland

Glasshouse Crops Survey - England and Wales
Ministry of Agriculture, Fisheries and Food

The Ministry of Agriculture, Fisheries and Food conducts a statutory survey on the area and production of glasshouse crops. The survey highlights trends in production and the results are used in the calculation of farm incomes. The survey also provides valuable market intelligence for the horticulture industry. The sample is made up of main holdings in England and Wales which reported in the last June Agricultural and Horticultural Census that they had more than 1000 square metres of glasshouse.

Status: Ongoing
Collection Method: Large-scale (Sample) Survey
Frequency: Annually
Reference Period: Previous calendar year
Timeliness: Forms are sent out in mid-January and results are released in April
Earliest Available Data: 1947
National Coverage: England and Wales
Disaggregation: A number of different regional breakdowns could be generated subject to the limitations imposed by the sample size

Statistician
Chris Gibbins
Ministry of Agriculture, Fisheries and Food
Statistics (Censuses and Surveys); H
Tel: 01904 455100;
Email: c.s.gibbins@esg.maff.gov.uk

Products that contain data from this source
Glasshouse Census (Statistics Notice); The Ministry of Agriculture, Fisheries and Food Website

Grape Must Stocks - UK
Ministry of Agriculture, Fisheries and Food

The Ministry of Agriculture, Fisheries and Food conducts a survey on stocks of grape must. The survey is carried out under EC regulation 822/87.

Status: Ongoing
Collection Method: Small-scale (Sample) Survey
Frequency: Annually
Reference Period: Calendar Year
Timeliness: 2 Months.
Earliest Available Data: 1995
National Coverage: United Kingdom

Hardy Nursery Stock Survey - Scotland
SERAD

The SERAD conducts a survey on Hardy Nursery Stock. The survey consists of a sample of over 80 nursery stock growers and collects data on produce area, sales, purchases and stocks. The survey is carried out every 4 years.

Status: Ongoing
Collection Method: Small-scale (Sample) Survey
Reference Period: Calendar Year
Timeliness: Approximately 2-3 months
National Coverage: Scotland

Statistician
Tom Whyte
Scottish Executive
Tel: 0131 244 3116

Products that contain data from this source
Economic Report on Scottish Agriculture

Horticultural Yields and Prices (Soft Fruits) - Scotland
Scottish Executive

The SERAD conducts a survey on soft fruit (including tomatoes) grown in Scotland. The survey consists of a sample of approximately 36 strawberry growers, 14 tomato growers and 1 soft fruit co-operative. It collects information on areas, yields and production.

Status: Ongoing
Collection Method: Small-scale (Sample) Survey
Frequency: Annually
Reference Period: Crop Year
Timeliness: Approximately 2-3 months
National Coverage: Scotland

Statistician
Tom Whyte
Scottish Executive
Tel: 0131 244 3116

Products that contain data from this source
Economic Report on Scottish Agriculture

Mushroom Survey
Ministry of Agriculture, Fisheries and Food

Sources and Analyses

Survey covers the production and sales of mushrooms and it provides an estimate of the output of the mushroom industry. The data is used by SEAEFD & WOAD for agricultural accounts purposes.

Status: Ongoing
Collection Method: Small-scale (Sample) Survey
Frequency: Annually
Reference Period: Last Calendar Year
Timeliness: 6 Weeks
Earliest Available Data: 1993

Statistician
Christine Jeannette
Ministry of Agriculture, Fisheries and Food
Statistics (C & F); Branch B
Tel: 01904 455069

Northern Ireland Orchard Fruit Survey
Department of Agriculture - Northern Ireland

Questionnaires are sent to growers with over 1 hectare of land devoted to orchard fruit. The information is used by Department of Agriculture fruit advisors to provide information on production and yield of fruit trees. This survey is conducted every 5 years.

Status: Ongoing
Collection Method: Postal
Frequency: Quintennial
Reference Period: Crop year
Timeliness: 3 months
Earliest Available Data: 1986
National Coverage: Northern Ireland

Statistician
Sheila Magee
Department of Agriculture - Northern Ireland
Tel: 028 9052 4427;
Email: sheila.magee@dani.gov.uk

Orchard Fruit Survey - England and Wales
Ministry of Agriculture, Fisheries and Food

The Ministry of Agriculture, Fisheries and Food conducts a statutory survey on the area of commercial orchards. Information is collected for a number of different varieties of fruit. The results are used in the calculation of farm incomes and, in recent years, has been used to analyse the effects of EU grubbing grants. The survey also provides valuable market intelligence for the horticulture industry.

In years ending with a 2 or 7, data on the age and density of orchards is collected to meet EU requirements. The sample is made up of main holdings in England and Wales which reported in the June Census that they had a significant area of commercial orchard. The

survey has not been conducted in every year since it was introduced in 1957.

Status: Ongoing
Collection Method: Large-scale (Sample) Survey
Frequency: Annually
Reference Period: 1 June
Timeliness: Forms are sent out in June and results are released in the Autumn.
Earliest Available Data: 1957
National Coverage: England and Wales
Disaggregation: A number of different regional breakdowns could be generated subject to the limitations imposed by the sample size.

Statistician
Chris Gibbins
Ministry of Agriculture, Fisheries and Food
Statistics (Censuses and Surveys); H
Tel: 01904 455100;
Email: c.s.gibbins@esg.maff.gov.uk

Products that contain data from this source
Orchard Fruit Survey (Statistics Notice); The Ministry of Agriculture, Fisheries and Food Website

---

Potato Yields - Northern Ireland
Department of Agriculture - Northern Ireland

The Department conducts the potato yield survey on a sample of approximately 200 farms on which potatoes are grown. Data are collected on the varieties, yields and seeding rates of potatoes. The survey has been carried out each crop year since the mid-1980s. Results are published in December of the crop year.

Status: Ongoing
Collection Method: Small-scale (Sample) Survey
Frequency: Annually
Reference Period: Crop year
Timeliness: 3 months
Earliest Available Data: 1990
National Coverage: Northern Ireland

Statistician
Sheila Magee
Department of Agriculture - Northern Ireland
Tel: 028 9052 4427;
Email: sheila.magee@dani.gov.uk

Stocks of Wine - UK (Producers)
Ministry of Agriculture, Fisheries and Food

The Ministry of Agriculture, Fisheries and Food conducts a survey on stocks of wine. The survey is carried out under EC regulation 822/87. Data is collected on red/rosé and white wines with separate categories for table and quality wines.

Status: Ongoing
Collection Method: Small-scale (Sample) Survey

Frequency: Annually
Reference Period: 12 Month Period
Timeliness: 2 Months
Earliest Available Data: 1995
National Coverage: United Kingdom

Statistician
Christine Jeannette
Ministry of Agriculture, Fisheries and Food
Statistics (C & F); Branch B
Tel: 01904 455069

Products that contain data from this source
Eurostat - European Official Statistics - Sources of Information

---

Stocks of Wine - UK (Wholesalers & Retailers)
Ministry of Agriculture, Fisheries and Food

The survey on stocks of wine is carried out under EC regulation 822/87. Data are collected on red/rosé and white wines with separate categories for table and quality wines. Data cover the UK and are collected and published by Eurostat annually.

Status: Ongoing
Collection Method: Small-scale (Sample) Survey
Frequency: Annually
Reference Period: 12 month period
Timeliness: 2 Months
Earliest Available Data: 1995
National Coverage: United Kingdom

Statistician
Christine Jeannette
Ministry of Agriculture, Fisheries and Food
Statistics (C & F); Branch B
Tel: 01904 455069

Products that contain data from this source
Eurostat - European Official Statistics - Sources of Information

---

Vegetables and Flowers Survey - England and Wales
Ministry of Agriculture, Fisheries and Food

The Ministry of Agriculture, Fisheries and Food conducts a statutory survey on the area of vegetables grown in the open for human consumption and the area of bulbs and flowers grown in the open. The survey highlights trends in production and the results are used in the calculation of farm incomes. The survey also provides valuable market intelligence for the horticulture industry. The sample is made up of main holdings in England and Wales which reported in the last June Agricultural and Horticultural Census that they had at least two hectares of vegetables and flowers.

Status: Ongoing
Collection Method: Large-scale (Sample) Survey

Frequency: Annually
Reference Period: Current growing season
Timeliness: Forms are sent out in January and results are released in April or May
Earliest Available Data: 1971
National Coverage: England and Wales
Disaggregation: A number of different regional breakdowns could be generated subject to the limitations imposed by the sample size.

Statistician
Chris Gibbins
Ministry of Agriculture, Fisheries and Food
Statistics (Censuses and Surveys); H
Tel: 01904 455100;
Email: c.s.gibbins@esg.maff.gov.uk

Products that contain data from this source
The Ministry of Agriculture, Fisheries and Food Website; Vegetables and Flowers Survey (Statistics Notice)

Wine Stocks Balance Sheets
Ministry of Agriculture, Fisheries and Food

Balance sheets on Wine Stocks are required by the Statistical Office of the European Community (SOEC) on an annual basis. They are collected from retailers, wholesalers and producers. The figures are published in the Eurostat database (Cronos), and Eurostat publication Statistical Yearbook.

Status: Ongoing
Frequency: Annually
Reference Period: Crop year basis
National Coverage: United Kingdom

Statistician
Christine Jeannette
Ministry of Agriculture, Fisheries and Food
Statistics (C & F); Branch B
Tel: 01904 455069

Products that contain data from this analysis
Eurostat - European Official Statistics - Sources of Information

See also:
In this chapter:
Aggregate Agricultural Account *(14.5)*
Agricultural Producer Prices - Northern Ireland *(14.13)*
Brewers, Distillers and Maltsters - UK *(14.4)*
EC Farm Structure Survey *(14.17)*
Minor Holdings Census - England & Wales *(14.12)*
Overseas Trade in Agricultural Commodities *(14.4)*

14.11 Human Resources and Management

Agricultural Hired Labour - Northern Ireland
Department of Agriculture - Northern Ireland

The Department of Agriculture for Northern Ireland conducts a survey on a sample of approximately 200 agricultural holdings that employ hired labour. Data are collected on hours, earnings, other employment costs and general characteristics of hired workers. The survey covers Northern Ireland and has been carried out since the early 1980s. Before this, information was obtained from inspections carried out on behalf of the Agricultural Wages Board. Data are published annually.

Status: Ongoing
Collection Method: Small-scale (Sample) Survey
Frequency: Annually
Timeliness: 8 weeks
National Coverage: Northern Ireland

Statistician
Norman Fulton
Department of Agriculture - Northern Ireland
Economics and Statistics Division
Tel: 028 9052 44067;
Email: norman.fulton@dani.gov.uk

Products that contain data from this source
Northern Ireland Annual Abstract of Statistics

Survey of Earnings and Hours of Agricultural and Horticultural Workers
Ministry of Agriculture, Fisheries and Food

The Ministry of Agriculture, Fisheries and Food conducts a statutory survey on the earnings and hours worked by hired workers. The sample size of approx. 5,000 covers a sample of all main holdings in England and Wales which returned at least one standard full time hired worker on the annual Agricultural and Horticultural Census. Data is collected on the sex, age, number of years employed on the holding, type, grade, main duty, pay frequency, earnings, hours, and benefits of hired workers.

Status: Ongoing
Collection Method: Large-scale (Sample) Survey
Frequency: Annually
Reference Period: Around September/October of a survey year
Timeliness: Approx. 3 months (from Survey in October to publication in January)
Earliest Available Data: 1991
National Coverage: England and Wales
Disaggregation: Standard Region level; Country

Statistician
Adam Krawczyk
Ministry of Agriculture, Fisheries and Food
Statistics (Census & Surveys); E
Tel: 01904 455319;
Email: a.krawczyk@esg.maff.gov.uk

Products that contain data from this source
Annual Abstract of Statistics; Earnings and Hours of Agricultural & Horticultural Workers Survey (Statistics Notice); Labour Market Trends

Survey of Hours and Earnings of Agricultural and Horticultural Workers - Scotland
Scottish Executive

The Scottish Executive Rural Affairs Department conducts a annual survey of some 600 holdings, to collect information on weekly hours and earnings of farm workers.

Status: Ongoing
Collection Method: Small scale (sample) survey
Frequency: Annual
Reference Period: Monthly
Timeliness: 2 weeks
Earliest Available Data: 1998
National Coverage: Scotland

Statistician
Tom Whyte
Scottish Executive
Tel: 0131 244 3116

Products that contain data from this source
Economic Report on Scottish Agriculture

See also:
In this chapter:
Aggregate Agricultural Account *(14.5)*
Agricultural and Horticultural Census - Scotland *(14.1)*
December Agricultural Survey - England and Wales *(14.1)*
EC Farm Structure Survey *(14.17)*
European Farm Structure Survey - Scotland *(14.17)*
Forest Employment Survey *(14.9)*
Forestry Employment *(14.9)*
Incomes of Agricultural Households Sector *(14.5)*
June Agricultural and Horticultural Census - England & Wales *(14.1)*
Minor Holdings Census - England & Wales *(14.12)*

In other chapters:
Labour Survey - England and Wales (see the Labour Market chapter)

14.12 Land Prices, Land Use, Rents and Tenures

Agricultural Land Prices - Scotland
Scottish Executive

When agricultural land of over 5 hectares is bought and sold, information is recorded on purchaser's name, seller's name, date of sale, name, area and parish of land sold, current and proposed use and price. This information is passed to the Valuation Office Agency who pass it on to SERAD on a quarterly basis.

Status: Ongoing
Collection Method: Administrative Records
Frequency: Quarterly
Timeliness: Results for each calendar year are published the following May
Earliest Available Data: 1960's
National Coverage: Scotland
Disaggregation: Combinations of parishes on request

Statistician
Jonathan Davidson
Scottish Executive
Tel: 0131 244 6131

Products that contain data from this source
Economic Report on Scottish Agriculture

Agricultural Rent Enquiry - England and Wales
Ministry of Agriculture, Fisheries and Food

The Agricultural Rent Enquiry was a survey conducted by The Ministry of Agriculture, Fisheries and Food until 1995. From 1996 it has been replaced by the Annual Survey of Tenanted Land. The Agricultural Rent Enquiry is a sample survey of over 300 agricultural landlords and agents. In England in 1995 the survey covered 7567 farms comprising 504,451 hectares, all of which were under Full Agricultural Tenancies. This area is about 15% of total rented land in England.

Data are collected on the annual rent prevailing at October each year. Other details collected include size and location of holding, grade of land and whether a rent review is due. Data have been collected since 1959. Since 1972 the Enquiry has been conducted on an individual farm instead of estates basis, which allows more detailed analysis of the data. In 1987 the structure of the Enquiry was altered to improve the range of results and from 1988 separate information for each country has been published.

Status: Ceased completely
Collection Method: large scale sample survey
Frequency: Annually
Reference Period: as at mid October
Timeliness: Rents as at end-October; results published in the Spring around end April.
Earliest Available Data: 1968
National Coverage: England and Wales
Disaggregation: Standard Statistical Region (SSR)

Statistician
Dr John Walsh
Ministry of Agriculture, Fisheries and Food
Economics (Resource Use); A
Tel: 020 7270 8795;
Email: j.walsh@esg.maff.gov.uk

Products that contain data from this source
Agriculture in the United Kingdom; Annual Rent Enquiry; Farm Rents in Wales

Annual Survey of Tenanted Land
Ministry of Agriculture, Fisheries and Food

The Ministry of Agriculture, Fisheries and Food conducts a voluntary survey on annual rents of tenanted land. The sample size of 5,000 covers a sample of all main holdings in England and Wales which completed questions on rented-in land on the annual Agricultural and Horticultural Census. Data is collected on the number and type of agreements, area, length of term, what is rented-in and annual rent and whether this is affected by rent review or a change in the agreement. Data is published by type of tenancy agreement, type of farm and what is included in the agreement. The Ministry has been collecting and publishing annual information on farm rents since 1959, originally as the Annual Rent Enquiry. The Annual Survey of Tenanted Land was first conducted in 1996.

Status: Ongoing
Collection Method: Large-scale (Sample) Survey
Frequency: Annually
Reference Period: Rents applicable at the end of October in each survey year
Timeliness: Approx. 5 months (from survey at end of October to publication in the following March)
Earliest Available Data: 1968
National Coverage: England and Wales
Disaggregation: Type of farm

Statistician
Adam Krawczyk
Ministry of Agriculture, Fisheries and Food
Statistics (Census & Surveys); E
Tel: 01904 455319;
Email: a.krawczyk@esg.maff.gov.uk

Products that contain data from this source
Annual Survey of Tenanted Land (Statistics Notice)

Annual Survey of Tenanted Land - Scotland
Scottish Executive

The SERAD conducts a voluntary survey of 800 tenanted holdings on annual rents. Data is collected on the number and types of agreements, area, length of term, what is rented in and annual rent and whether this is affected by rent review. Data will be published by type of farm and by type of agreement. The Scottish Executive has been collecting and publishing annual information on farm rents since the 1960's, but with no information between 1994-95 and 1997-98. The Annual Survey of Tenanted Land was first conducted in 1998.

Status: Ongoing
Collection Method: Large-scale (Sample) Survey
Frequency: Annually
Reference Period: Rents applicable at the end of October in each survey year
Timeliness: Approx. 8 months
Earliest Available Data: 1974
National Coverage: Scotland
Disaggregation: Type of farm

Statistician
Tom Whyte
SERAD - H.2
Tel: 0131 244 3116;
Email: tom.whyte@scotland.gov.uk

Products that contain data from this source
Economic Report on Scottish Agriculture (1999)

Minor Holdings Census - England & Wales
Ministry of Agriculture, Fisheries and Food

The Ministry of Agriculture, Fisheries and Food conducts a survey of minor holdings. The results feed into the June Agricultural and Horticultural Census. Data are collected on land use, livestock, labour, horticulture and changes in area of holding.

Status: Ongoing
Collection Method: Census
Frequency: 1972, 1979, 1984, 1989 and 1994
Reference Period: Census date (mid-March)
Timeliness: 10 months
Earliest Available Data: 1972
National Coverage: England and Wales

Statistician
Richard Pereira
Ministry of Agriculture, Fisheries and Food
Statistics (Census & Surveys); D
Tel: 01904 455304;
Email: r.pereira@esg.maff.gov.uk

Products that contain data from this source
Minor Holdings Census (Statistics Notice)

Prices of Agricultural Land in England
Ministry of Agriculture, Fisheries and Food

The Ministry of Agriculture, Fisheries and Food compiles statistics and analysis of prices of agricultural land in England, based on data supplied by the Board of the Inland Revenue, which is collected by the Valuation Offices. Analysis is conducted to give average prices by region, size group, tenure, and grade of land. Additional analysis gives a price index of land sales and a weighted average land price. Analysis is conducted quarterly, with additional analysis on an annual basis. The analysis is published quarterly in statistical notices. There is an annual statistical notice published in the summer time, which provides information on average prices for the 12 months to the previous end-September.

Status: Ongoing
Frequency: Quarterly
Reference Period: three months to end quarter; 12 months to end Sept
Timeliness: Interval between collection and release can be variable. The data relating to end Sept 96 was released in July 1997. More importantly there is a time lag between sale and date notified to the Valuation Office, thought to be roughly 9 months.
Earliest Available Data: 1959
National Coverage: England
Disaggregation: Standard Statistical Region (SSR); Government Office Region (GOR)

Statistician
Dr John Walsh
Ministry of Agriculture, Fisheries and Food
Economics (Resource Use); A
Tel: 020 7270 8795;
Email: j.walsh@esg.maff.gov.uk

Products that contain data from this analysis
Prices of Agricultural Land in England

See also:
In this chapter:
Aggregate Agricultural Account *(14.5)*
EC Farm Structure Survey *(14.17)*
June Agricultural and Horticultural Census - England & Wales *(14.1)*
June Agricultural and Horticultural Census - Northern Ireland *(14.1)*

14.13 Livestock and Meat (incl. Poultry)

Autumn Store Sales Returns - Scotland
Scottish Executive Rural Affairs Department

The Scottish Executive Rural Affairs Department conducts a survey on the sales of autumn store calves and lambs. It covers details of sales and prices for calves and lambs.

Status: Ongoing
Collection Method: Administrative Records
Frequency: Weekly
Reference Period: From August until November
Earliest Available Data: 1990
National Coverage: Scotland

Statistician
Tom Whyte
Scottish Executive
Tel: 0131 244 3116

Products that contain data from this source
Scottish Agriculture Output Input and Income Statistics

Bacon and Ham Produced - GB
Ministry of Agriculture, Fisheries and Food

The Ministry of Agriculture, Fisheries and Food conducts a survey on bacon and ham production in Great Britain. There are 16 monthly and 19 annual respondents to the survey. The survey has been running since the late 1940s. It was carried out weekly until the early 1990s, from which point it has been carried out monthly. Results are published two weeks after the end of the reference period.

Status: Ongoing
Collection Method: Census of larger producers only
Frequency: Monthly
Reference Period: Statistical month
Timeliness: Two weeks after relevant month
Earliest Available Data: 1985
National Coverage: Great Britain

Statistician
Lindsey Clothier
Ministry of Agriculture, Fisheries and Food
Commodities and Food Division; Branch D
Tel: 00 44 (0)1904 455090;
Email: l.j.clothier@esg.maff.gov.uk

Products that contain data from this source
Agriculture in the United Kingdom; Monthly Digest of Statistics

Deer Farming Census - Scotland
SERAD

The SERAD conducts a census on deer farmed in Scotland. It covers details of the number of deer at the reference date, the numbers of deer sold and the number sent for slaughter in the previous year. The census covers Scotland and is carried out every two years

Status: Ongoing
Collection Method: Census
Frequency: Every second year
Earliest Available Data: 1997
National Coverage: Scotland

Statistician
Tom Whyte
Scottish Executive
Tel: 0131 244 3116

Products that contain data from this source

England and Wales Slaughterhouse Survey
Ministry of Agriculture, Fisheries and Food

The Ministry of Agriculture, Fisheries and Food conducts a survey on livestock slaughter. Data are collected on the numbers and weights of cattle, sheep and pigs slaughtered. Similar data is collected in Scotland and Northern Ireland. Data for England and Wales are available annually at county level (subject to data confidentiality).

Data are collected from those with the greatest throughput on a weekly basis and from those with a medium throughput on a monthly basis. Data for the smallest slaughterhouses are obtained from an administrative source (the Meat Hygiene Service). Results are published on a weekly basis for the United Kingdom, 12 days after the end of the reference period.

Data on numbers slaughtered and dressed carcass weights are collected in the following categories:

a) Cattle - steers, heifers, young bulls, cows, adult bulls, light calves, heavy calves
b) Sheep - ewes and rams, other sheep
c) Pigs - breeding sows, breeding boars, other pigs

Status: Ongoing
Collection Method: Census of larger units. Administrative data for smallest units
Frequency: Weekly and Monthly
Reference Period: Week ending Saturday for weekly data. Monthly data are for statistical months (5,4,4 weekly pattern)
Timeliness: Weekly data are published 12 days after the survey period.
Earliest Available Data: 1940s
National Coverage: England and Wales

Statistician
Lindsey Clothier
Ministry of Agriculture, Fisheries and Food
Commodities and Food Division; Branch D
Tel: 00 44 (0)1904 455090;
Email: l.j.clothier@esg.maff.gov.uk

Products that contain data from this source
Agriculture in the United Kingdom; Annual Abstract of Statistics; Monthly Digest of Statistics United Kingdom Slaughter Statistics (Statistical Notice)

Sources and Analyses

Meat Balance Sheets
Ministry of Agriculture, Fisheries and Food

Prepared annually for Eurostat (the statistical office of the European Commission). Contains data on production, imports, exports and domestic usage for beef and veal, mutton and lamb, pigmeat, poultry and other meat and offal. Differs to the balance sheets published in the quarterly supplies and domestic usage of meat statistics notice and Agriculture in the United Kingdom due to the use of different trade codes for exports and imports.

Status: Ongoing
Frequency: Annually
Reference Period: calendar years
Timeliness: Prepared every June
National Coverage: United Kingdom
Disaggregation: None

Statistician
Lindsey Clothier
Ministry of Agriculture, Fisheries and Food
Commodities and Food Division; Branch D
Tel: 00 44 (0)1904 455090;
Email: l.j.clothier@esg.maff.gov.uk

Pig Production - Northern Ireland
Department of Agriculture - Northern Ireland

The Department of Agriculture for Northern Ireland assembles pig financial results derived from administrative sources and surveys of animal feed compounders and agricultural markets. Results provide weekly information on the returns and feed costs associated with pig production and data on weaned pig prices.

Status: Ongoing
Collection Method: Small-scale (Sample) Survey
Frequency: Monthly
Reference Period: Monthly
Timeliness: 2 weeks
Earliest Available Data: 1988
National Coverage: Northern Ireland

Statistician
Norman Fulton
Department of Agriculture - Northern Ireland
Economics and Statistics Division
Tel: 028 9052 44067;
Email: norman.fulton@dani.gov.uk

Products that contain data from this source
Pig Financial Results Bulletin - Northern Ireland

Pig Surveys - England and Wales
Ministry of Agriculture, Fisheries and Food

These were originally statutory surveys, carried out to meet EU requirements. A one-off survey was carried out in March 1999, in response to requests from pig producer organisations. They were based on samples taken from holdings returning pigs at the most recent June Census and any new holdings since then. Data were available for the total number of pigs on holdings by breeding pigs, barren sows for fattening, and other pigs, and on the number of pigs kept in outdoor units (selected April only). The April 1995 survey included a special voluntary question on the numbers of pigs kept in stalls or tethers. Data on pigs is also collected as part of the December Agricultural Survey and the June Census.

Status: Ad-hoc
Collection Method: Small-scale (Sample) Survey
Frequency: Formerly April and August each year, now ad-hoc
Reference Period: Survey day
Timeliness: Within 7 weeks of survey date
Earliest Available Data: 1974
National Coverage: England and Wales
Disaggregation: National level only

Statistician
Alison James
Ministry of Agriculture, Fisheries and Food
Statistics (Census and Surveys); Branch F
Tel: 01904 455328;
Email: a.james@esg.maff.gov.uk

Products that contain data from this source
April and August Pig Surveys (Statistics Notice)
March 1999 Pig Survey (Statistics Notice)

Poultry Packing Station Throughput - Scotland
Scottish Executive

The Scottish Executive Agriculture and Fisheries Department conducts a survey on packing station throughputs. Data are collected from 5 poultry packing stations on a monthly basis. Data cover Scotland and are used to calculate an annual value for poultry meat in Scotland.

Status: Ongoing
Collection Method: Small-scale (Sample) Survey
Frequency: Monthly
Timeliness: 2 weeks
Earliest Available Data: 1990
National Coverage: Scotland

Statistician
Tom Whyte
Scottish Executive
Tel: 0131 244 3116

Products that contain data from this source
Scottish Agriculture Output Input and Income Statistics

Poultry Slaughterhouse Survey- England and Wales
Ministry of Agriculture, Fisheries and Food

The Ministry of Agriculture, Fisheries and Food conducts a survey on the throughput of Poultry slaughterhouses, figures are provided on the number of birds processed, by species and total weight.

Status: Ongoing
Collection Method: Small-scale (Sample) Survey
Frequency: Monthly
Reference Period: 4 or 5 week statistical months
Timeliness: 3 weeks
Earliest Available Data: 1996
National Coverage: England and Wales

Statistician
Christine Jeannette
Ministry of Agriculture, Fisheries and Food
Statistics (C & F); Branch B
Tel: 01904 455069

Products that contain data from this source
Poultry and Poultrymeat Statistics Notice

Production and Marketing of Hatching Eggs and Chicks - England and Wales
Ministry of Agriculture, Fisheries and Food

The Ministry of Agriculture, Fisheries and Food conducts a survey on the production and marketing of hatching chicks and eggs. Data are available on the number of eggs set and chicks placed by species and strain of bird. The survey covers hatcheries in England and Wales and was established in its present form under EC regulations in 1973.

Status: Ongoing
Collection Method: Census
Frequency: Monthly
Reference Period: 4 or 5 week statistical months
Timeliness: 3 Weeks
Earliest Available Data: 1995
National Coverage: England and Wales

Statistician
Christine Jeannette
Ministry of Agriculture, Fisheries and Food
Statistics (C & F); Branch B
Tel: 01904 455069

Products that contain data from this source
Poultry and Poultrymeat Statistics Notice

Production and Marketing of Hatching Eggs and Chicks - Scotland
Scottish Executive

The SERAD conducts a survey on the number of hatching eggs and chicks. The survey consists of a sample of 9 hatcheries in Scotland. It is carried out monthly and the results are used in the calculation of Scottish Agriculture Output, Input and Income Statistics.

Status: Ongoing
Collection Method: Small-scale (Sample) Survey
Frequency: Monthly
Earliest Available Data: 1980
National Coverage: Scotland

Statistician
Tom Whyte
Scottish Executive
Tel: 0131 244 3116

Products that contain data from this source
Scottish Agriculture Output Input and Income Statistics

Store Market Reporting - Scotland
Scottish Executive Rural Affairs Depatment

The Scottish Executive Rural Affairs Department conducts a survey on store market throughputs and prices for cattle, sheep and pigs, hay and straw. The survey consists of a sample of 9 markets/auctioneers. Data are available by various categories of store livestock, reporting numbers sold and the value from each category, from which average prices can be calculated.

Status: Ongoing
Collection Method: Small-scale (Sample) Survey
Frequency: Weekly
Earliest Available Data: 1989
National Coverage: Scotland

Statistician
Tom Whyte
Scottish Executive
Tel: 0131 244 3116

Products that contain data from this source
Scottish Agriculture Output Input and Income Statistics
Economic Report on Scottish Agriculture

Survey of Farmed Deer - England and Wales
Ministry of Agriculture, Fisheries and Food

This is a voluntary survey of agricultural holdings returning deer at recent June Censuses. It was run as a census until 1998,

when the survey was altered to only cover the larger deer farms. It began in 1988 and was held again in 1991, 1993 and 1995, with data collected in October when the deer population peaks. For 1998, data was collected in April.

Data are available on the total number of deer farmed by type, age and sex, the fenced area of the holding, movement of the deer and, until 1995, inspection equipment.

Status: Ongoing
Collection Method: Small-scale (Sample) Survey
Frequency: Usually every 2 - 3 years
Reference Period: Survey date or year to survey date
Timeliness: About 3 months after survey date.
Earliest Available Data: 1988
National Coverage: England and Wales
Disaggregation: Standard statistical region until 1995, thereafter government office region

Statistician
Alison James
Ministry of Agriculture, Fisheries and Food Statistics (Census and Surveys); Branch F
Tel: 01904 455328;
Email: a.james@esg.maff.gov.uk

Products that contain data from this source
Farmed Deer Survey (Statistical Notice)

Turkey Census - England and Wales
Ministry of Agriculture, Fisheries and Food

This was a voluntary survey of agricultural holdings which indicated their intention to keep turkeys at the most recent June Census, together with June Census non-respondents who made a positive return to the last Turkey Census. Data were available on the total number of turkeys by age and for breeding and other.

Status: Ceased completely
Collection Method: Census
Frequency: Annually until 1994
Reference Period: Survey date
Earliest Available Data: 1986
National Coverage: England and Wales

Statistician
Alison James
Ministry of Agriculture, Fisheries and Food Statistics (Census and Surveys); Branch F
Tel: 01904 455328;
Email: a.james@esg.maff.gov.uk

Products that contain data from this source
Turkey Census (Statistics Notice)

See also:
In this chapter:
Aggregate Agricultural Account *(14.5)*
Agricultural and Horticultural Census - Scotland *(14.1)*

Agricultural Producer Prices - Northern Ireland *(14.13)*
Animal Compound Feedingstuffs: Sales Value and Volume - GB *(14.2)*
Animal Feedstuffs - Northern Ireland *(14.2)*
Calf Survey - England and Wales *(14.13)*
Composition of Main Livestock Rations - GB *(14.2)*
December Agricultural Survey - England and Wales *(14.1)*
December Agricultural Survey - Northern Ireland *(14.1)*
EC Farm Structure Survey *(14.17)*
Farm Business Surveys *(14.5)*
Grain Fed to Livestock Survey - England and Wales *(14.2)*
Hill and Upland Sheep Pricing Survey - England *(14.13)*
June Agricultural and Horticultural Census - England & Wales *(14.1)*
Minor Holdings Census - England & Wales *(14.12)*
Overseas Trade in Agricultural Commodities *(14.4)*

14.14 Milk and Milk Products

Milk Balance Sheets
Ministry of Agriculture, Fisheries and Food

Prepared annually for Eurostat (the statistical office of the European Commission). Contains data on production, imports, exports and domestic usage for milk products. Different to the balance sheets published in Agriculture in the United Kingdom due to the use of different trade codes for exports and imports.

Status: Ongoing
Frequency: Annually
Reference Period: Calendar years
Timeliness: Prepared every June
National Coverage: United Kingdom

Statistician
Lindsey Clothier
Ministry of Agriculture, Fisheries and Food Commodities and Food Division; Branch D
Tel: 00 44 (0)1904 455090;
Email: l.j.clothier@esg.maff.gov.uk

Products that contain data from this analysis

Production and Stocks of Condensed Milk and Milk Powders - UK
Ministry of Agriculture, Fisheries and Food

The Ministry of Agriculture, Fisheries and Food conducts a survey on the production and stocks of condensed milk and milk powders. The survey covers the United Kingdom and is a long established survey with a history extending over several decades.

Status: Ongoing
Collection Method: Census
Frequency: Monthly
Reference Period: Calendar month
Timeliness: Results published quarterly no later than 9 weeks after the end of the final month
Earliest Available Data: 1987
National Coverage: United Kingdom

Statistician
Lindsey Clothier
Ministry of Agriculture, Fisheries and Food
Commodities and Food Division; Branch D
Tel: 00 44 (0)1904 455090;
Email: l.j.clothier@esg.maff.gov.uk

Products that contain data from this source
Agriculture in the United Kingdom; Monthly Digest of Statistics; The Production of Processed Milk in the UK (Statistical notice)

Raw Milk Utilisation - Northern Ireland
Department of Agriculture - Northern Ireland

The Department of Agriculture for Northern Ireland compiles statistics on the utilisation of raw milk within Northern Ireland. Data on intake, utilisation in the production of various milk products and exports are collected from milk purchasers and processors operating in Northern Ireland. This survey was introduced in January 1995 and is conducted on a monthly basis.

Collection Method: Census
Frequency: Monthly
National Coverage: Northern Ireland

Statistician
Norman Fulton
Department of Agriculture - Northern Ireland
Economics and Statistics Division
Tel: 028 9052 44067;
Email: norman.fulton@dani.gov.uk

Products that contain data from this source
Utilisation of Raw Milk

Survey of Ex-Farm Milk Prices - Scotland
Scottish Executive Rural Affairs Department

The Scottish Executive Rural Affairs Department conduct a survey on ex-farm milk prices. It is a sample of 14 processing plants/co-operatives and covers details on the total volume of milk bought, milk prices and bonuses. The results are used in the calculation of Scottish Agriculture Output, Input and Income Statistics.

Status: Ongoing
Collection Method: Small-scale (Sample) Survey
Frequency: Monthly
Timeliness: Results for Calendar Year Published Annually
Earliest Available Data: 1994
National Coverage: Scotland

Statistician
Tom Whyte
Scottish Executive
Tel: 0131 244 3116

Products that contain data from this source
Scottish Agriculture Output Input and Income Statistics

Utilisation of Milk by Dairies - England and Wales
Ministry of Agriculture, Fisheries and Food

The Ministry of Agriculture, Fisheries and Food conducts a survey on the utilisation of milk by dairies in England and Wales. Data provided are available for whole milk, skim and cream for the following: intake, separation, liquid milk, butter, cheese, cream, condensed/evaporated milk and chocolate crumb, milk powders, yoghurt, other products, sub-sales to other organisations and total disposals.

Status: Ongoing
Collection Method: Census
Frequency: Monthly
Reference Period: Calendar month
Timeliness: Published monthly (11 weeks after the reference period)
Earliest Available Data: November 1994
National Coverage: England and Wales

Statistician
Lindsey Clothier
Ministry of Agriculture, Fisheries and Food
Commodities and Food Division; Branch D
Tel: 00 44 (0)1904 455090;
Email: l.j.clothier@esg.maff.gov.uk

Products that contain data from this source
Agriculture in the United Kingdom; Monthly Digest of Statistics; Utilisation of Milk by Dairies in England and Wales (Statistical Notice)

Utilisation of Milk Survey - Scotland
Scottish Executive Rural Affairs Department

The Scottish Executive Rural Affairs Department conducts a survey on the utilisation of milk. It is a sample of 90 processors and covers details on the volumes of raw milk processed by dairies in Scotland.

Status: Ongoing
Collection Method: Small-scale (Sample) Survey
Frequency: Monthly
Timeliness: Results produced quarterly with about 3 month delay
Earliest Available Data: 1994
National Coverage: Scotland

Statistician
Tom Whyte
Scottish Executive
Tel: 0131 244 3116

Value of Milk Purchased - England and Wales
Ministry of Agriculture, Fisheries and Food

The Ministry of Agriculture, Fisheries and Food conducts a survey on the value of milk purchased in England and Wales. It is a statutory survey of those milk purchasers that purchase more than 200,000 litres of milk each month. Similar surveys are conducted in Scotland and in Northern Ireland.

Data are collected on the amount and value of milk purchased. However, only data on derived milk prices are published. MAFF publishes data on farm gate milk prices (with and without bonus payments) for the United Kingdom only due to confidentiality constraints.

Status: Ongoing
Collection Method: Small-scale (Sample) Survey
Frequency: Monthly
Reference Period: Calendar month
Timeliness: 6 weeks after end of survey period (UK prices only)
Earliest Available Data: November 1994
National Coverage: England and Wales

Statistician
Lindsey Clothier
Ministry of Agriculture, Fisheries and Food
Commodities and Food Division; Branch D
Tel: 00 44 (0)1904 455090;
Email: l.j.clothier@esg.maff.gov.uk

Products that contain data from this source
Agriculture in the United Kingdom; United Kingdom Milk Prices (Statistical Notice)

See also:
In this chapter:
Aggregate Agricultural Account *(14.5)*
Agricultural Producer Prices - Northern Ireland *(14.13)*
June Agricultural and Horticultural Census - England & Wales *(14.1)*
Minor Holdings Census - England & Wales *(14.12)*
Overseas Trade in Agricultural Commodities *(14.4)*

14.15 Prices (including Price Indices)

Agricultural Producer Prices - Northern Ireland
Department of Agriculture - Northern Ireland

The Department of Agriculture for Northern Ireland produces Agricultural Market Reports which provide the latest producer prices for a range of agricultural commodities. Data are derived from surveys of livestock markets, milk purchasers, cereal purchasers, egg and poultry firms, potato merchants and official EU price reporting systems.

Status: Ongoing
Collection Method: Small-scale (Sample) Survey
Frequency: Weekly
Timeliness: <1 week
Earliest Available Data: 1963
National Coverage: Northern Ireland

Statistician
Norman Fulton
Department of Agriculture - Northern Ireland
Economics and Statistics Division
Tel: 028 9052 44067;
Email: norman.fulton@dani.gov.uk

Products that contain data from this source
Agricultural Market Report - Northern Ireland

Calf Survey - England and Wales
Ministry of Agriculture, Fisheries and Food

This survey collects information on the number and price range of bull and heifer rearing calves sold at livestock markets in England and Wales. One use of the information is in the calculation of agricultural prices indices.

Status: Ongoing
Collection Method: Small-scale (Sample) Survey
Frequency: Quarterly
Reference Period: Second week in January, April, July and October
Timeliness: Two weeks
Earliest Available Data: January 1997
National Coverage: England and Wales
Disaggregation: By livestock market for the selected markets

Statistician
Chris Gibbins
Ministry of Agriculture, Fisheries and Food
Statistics (Censuses and Surveys); H
Tel: 01904 455100;
Email: c.s.gibbins@esg.maff.gov.uk

Products that contain data from this source
Agricultural Price Indices (Statistics Notice)

Hill and Upland Sheep Pricing Survey - England
Ministry of Agriculture, Fisheries and Food

This survey collects information on the number of hill and upland sheep sold at livestock markets in Northern England and the total value realised from those sales. One use of this information is in the Autumn Hill Farm Income Review.

Status: Ongoing
Collection Method: Small-scale (Sample) Survey
Frequency: Annually
Reference Period: August to November
Timeliness: Information for all markets available by February of the following year
Earliest Available Data: 1995
Sub-National: northern England
Disaggregation: By livestock market for the selected markets

Statistician
Chris Gibbins
Ministry of Agriculture, Fisheries and Food
Statistics (Censuses and Surveys); H
Tel: 01904 455100;
Email: c.s.gibbins@esg.maff.gov.uk

Suckler Calf Survey - England
Ministry of Agriculture, Fisheries and Food

This survey collects information on the number of suckler calves sold at livestock markets in England and Wales and the price realised from those sales. One use of this information is in the Autumn Hill Farm Income Review.

Status: Ongoing
Collection Method: Small-scale (Sample) Survey
Frequency: Annually
Reference Period: October to November
Timeliness: Information for all markets available by the end of December
Earliest Available Data: 1995
National Coverage: England and Wales
Disaggregation: By livestock market for the selected markets

Statistician
Chris Gibbins
Ministry of Agriculture, Fisheries and Food
Statistics (Censuses and Surveys); A
Tel: 01904 455100;
Email: c.s.gibbins@esg.maff.gov.uk

See also:
In this chapter:
Aggregate Agricultural Account *(14.5)*
Animal Compound Feedingstuffs: Sales Value and Volume - GB *(14.2)*
Value of Milk Purchased - England and Wales *(14.14)*

14.16 Resources used in Farming

British Survey of Fertiliser Practice
Ministry of Agriculture, Fisheries and Food; sponsored by FMA, MAFF and SERAD

This long running annual survey provides information on fertiliser use on the major crops and grass grown in mainland Britain. The main purpose is to estimate average application rates of nitrogen, phosphate and potash used for agricultural crops and grassland. Information is also collected on applications of sulphur fertiliser products, organic manure and lime. The survey is organised and jointly funded by the Fertiliser Manufacturers' Association (FMA), the Ministry of Agriculture, Fisheries and Food (MAFF) and the Scottish Executive Rural Affairs.

Status: Ongoing
Collection Method: Large-scale (Sample) Survey
Frequency: Annually
Reference Period: Cropping year
Timeliness: Fieldwork takes place between May and August, the results of which are published the following Spring/Summer.
Earliest Available Data: 1942
Sub-National: Mainland Britain
Disaggregation: A number of different regional breakdowns could be generated subject to the limitations imposed by the sample size.

Statistician
Chris Gibbins
Ministry of Agriculture, Fisheries and Food
Statistics (Censuses and Surveys); H
Tel: 01904 455100;
Email: c.s.gibbins@esg.maff.gov.uk

Fertilizers - Northern Ireland
Department of Agriculture - Northern Ireland

The Department of Agriculture for Northern Ireland compiles fertilizer statistics based on returns from all fertilizer companies in Northern Ireland. Data are collected on the quantities, nutrient contents and average retail prices of fertilizers delivered to farmers.

Collection Method: Census
Frequency: Monthly
Reference Period: Monthly and Quarterly
Timeliness: 8 weeks
Earliest Available Data: 1979
National Coverage: Northern Ireland

Statistician
Norman Fulton
Department of Agriculture - Northern Ireland
Economics and Statistics Division
Tel: 028 9052 4419;
Email: norman.fulton@dani.gov.uk

Products that contain data from this source
Deliveries of Compounds, Blended and Straight Fertilisers by Northern Ireland Fertiliser Manufactures

Irrigation of Outdoor Crops Survey - England
Ministry of Agriculture, Fisheries and Food

The Ministry of Agriculture, Fisheries and Food conducts a voluntary survey on the irrigation of outdoor crops. The survey highlights changes in the pattern of water use, the amounts being used, the means of delivery and of trends in water storage on farms. The data compiled provides key information on the developments in irrigation, and essential background information for use in policy discussions with the agricultural and horticultural industry and with the National Rivers Authority over the likely demand and availability of water resources to farmers and growers, particularly in times of drought.

The sample is made up of farm holdings in England which took part in the last Irrigation Survey or reported in the June Census that they have irrigated outdoor crops since the last Irrigation Survey.

Introduced in 1963, the survey has generally been held every two to three years. However, following a review of the survey, it was decided that in future it should be conducted only in dry years. Since the present series of questions were introduced in 1982, surveys have been carried out in 1984, 1987, 1992 and 1995. Three of those years, 1984, 1990 and 1995 have coincided with peak years for irrigation. Prior to 1995, all surveys covered both England and Wales. In 1995 the survey was conducted in England only. (Note, in 1992 the area of irrigation in Wales was 1.4 per cent of the total for England and Wales).

Status: Ongoing
Collection Method: Large-scale (Sample) Survey
Frequency: Ad hoc
Reference Period: Calendar year
Timeliness: Results released within eleven months of end of reporting year.
Earliest Available Data: 1963
Sub-National: 1995: England Earlier: England and Wales
Disaggregation: A number of different regional breakdowns could be generated subject to the limitations imposed by the sample size.

Statistician
Chris Gibbins
Ministry of Agriculture, Fisheries and Food
Statistics (Censuses and Surveys); A
Tel: 01904 455100;
Email: c.s.gibbins@esg.maff.gov.uk

Products that contain data from this source
The Ministry of Agriculture, Fisheries and Food Website

See also:
In this chapter:
Aggregate Agricultural Account *(14.5)*
Agricultural and Horticultural Census - Scotland *(14.1)*
December Agricultural Survey - England and Wales *(14.1)*
EC Farm Structure Survey *(14.17)*
European Farm Structure Survey - Northern Ireland *(14.17)*
European Farm Structure Survey - Scotland *(14.17)*
June Agricultural and Horticultural Census - England & Wales *(14.1)*

14.17 Structure of Agricultural Holdings

EC Farm Structure Survey
Ministry of Agriculture, Fisheries and Food

EC member states are required to collect information for the EC Structure Survey. Most of the data for England and Wales can be met from the June Agricultural and Horticultural Census. Detailed information on labour, not collected in the Census, is collected in the Labour Survey. Other sources of data for the Structure Survey include the Mushroom Survey, the Poultry special exercise and IACS set-aside data. The Survey covers the UK with MAFF collating the results for the 4 UK departments.

Data are available at standard region, county and district level. The Structure Survey is carried out every two to three years. It was first conducted in 1966-67 and covered land use, tenure, livestock, cropping, machinery and labour force. Structure surveys, carried out every ten years, usually contain more extensive information than those in the mid-term years, particularly regarding labour data. From 1975 onwards, results are held on a computer databank in the form of standard tables. The main results can take up to three years to publish but some results are released about two years after data are collected. Data is disseminated through hard copy publication, Eurofarm on-line database and New Cronos.

Status: Ongoing
Frequency: Periodic
Reference Period: Calendar year
Timeliness: Approx. 2 years for EC publication.
Earliest Available Data: 1975
National Coverage: United Kingdom
Disaggregation: Country; Regions (as defined by EC); Districts (as defined by EC); County

Statistician
Adam Krawczyk
Ministry of Agriculture, Fisheries and Food
Statistics (Census & Surveys); E
Tel: 01904 455319;
Email: a.krawczyk@esg.maff.gov.uk

Products that contain data from this analysis
Eurofarm Tabular Databank System; Farm Structure: Main Results; Farm Structure: Methodology of Community Surveys

European Farm Structure Survey - Northern Ireland
Department of Agriculture - Northern Ireland

The Department of Agriculture for Northern Ireland conducts a survey of the farm labour force on a sample of 12,000 farms and the data obtained are incorporated into the EU Farm Structure Survey. The Survey covers the status of the occupier, responsibility for management of the farm and details of farm workers. The Survey is used to collect agricultural machinery information approximately every five years.

Status: Ongoing
Collection Method: Large-scale (Sample) Survey
Frequency: 2 - 3 years
Timeliness: 6 months
Earliest Available Data: 1966
National Coverage: Northern Ireland

Statistician
Sheila Magee
Department of Agriculture - Northern Ireland
Tel: 028 9052 4427;
Email: sheila.magee@dani.gov.uk

Products that contain data from this source
Farm Structure 1993 Survey: Analysis of Results (Eurostat); Farm Structure Methodology of Community Surveys (Eurostat)

European Farm Structure Survey - Scotland
Scottish Executive Rural Affairs Department

The Scottish Executive Rural Affairs Department conducts a survey on farm structure. Data are available on agricultural labour and machinery. The survey is carried out every two to three years.

Status: Ongoing
Collection Method: Large-scale (Sample) Survey
Timeliness: 1 and a half years
Earliest Available Data: 1966
National Coverage: Scotland

Sources and Analyses

Statistician
Venetia Radmore
Scottish Executive
Tel: 0131 244 6131

Products that contain data from this source
Farm Structure 1993 Survey: Analysis of Results
(Eurostat)

See also:
In this chapter:
Aggregate Agricultural Account *(14.5)*
Farm Business Surveys *(14.5)*
June Agricultural and Horticultural Census
- England & Wales *(14.1)*
Minor Holdings Census - England & Wales
(14.12)
Pig Surveys - England and Wales *(14.13)*
Survey of Farmed Deer - England and Wales
(14.13)
Turkey Census - England and Wales *(14.13)*

14 Agriculture, Fishing, Food and Forestry - *Products*

14.18 Abstracts, Compendia, A-Z Catalogues, Directories and Reference Material

Agricultural and Horticulture Census, Scotland - June Provisional Results (Press Release)
Scottish Executive

Press Release presenting selected provisional results from June Agricultural Census for agricultural land, livestock and labour.

Delivery: News/Press Release
Frequency: Annually
Price: Free

Available from
Andy Reid
Scottish Executive
Please see Annex B for full address details.

Sources from which data for this product are obtained
Agricultural and Horticultural Census - Scotland

Agricultural and Horticultural Census : 1 June, Final Results for Wales
National Assembly for Wales

Summary results from the Agricultural and Horticultural Census in Wales. Includes agricultural area, land use, livestock and labour estimates.

Delivery: Statistical Release
Frequency: Annually

Available from:
Agricultural Statistics
National Assembly for Wales
Please see Annex B for full address details.

Sources from which data for this product are obtained
June Agricultural and Horticultural Census - England and Wales

Agricultural and Horticultural Census : 1 June, Provisional Results for Wales
National Assembly for Wales

Provisional summary results from the Agricultural and Horticultural Census in Wales. Includes agricultural area, land use and livestock estimates.

Delivery: Statistical Release
Frequency: Annually

Available from:
Agricultural Statistics
National Assembly for Wales
Please see Annex B for full address details.

Sources from which data this product are obtained
June Agricultural and Horticultural Census - England and Wales

Agricultural Census Data
Department of Agriculture - Northern Ireland

Data relating to Northern Ireland farms covering enterprise distribution, farm structure, Less Favoured Areas, district council areas and rural district areas.

Frequency: Annual
Price: £25.00

Available from
Economics and Statistics Division
Room 817
Dundonald House
Upper Newtownards Road
Belfast BT4 3SB
Tel: 028 9052 4855

Sources from which data for this product are obtained
June Agricultural and Horticultural Census - Northern Ireland

Agricultural Census Summary Sheets by Geographic Area: June 1998
Scottish Executive

Regional figures for agricultural land, livestock and labour.

Delivery: Periodic Release
Frequency: Annually
Price: £5.00
ISBN: 0 7480 7775 8

Available from
TSO Publications Centre and Bookshops
Please see Annex B for full address details.

Sources from which data for this product are obtained
Agricultural and Horticultural Census - Scotland

Agricultural Sample Census - December (Press Release)
Scottish Executive

Scotland level information on crops, livestock and labour.

Delivery: News/Press Release
Frequency: Annually
Price: Free

Available from
Andy Reid
Scottish Executive Environment and Fisheries Department
Please see Annex B for full address details

Sources from which data for this product are obtained
Agricultural and Horticultural Census - Scotland

Agriculture Facts and Figures
Scottish Executive

Key Statistics on Scottish Agriculture. Fact card with tables.

Delivery: Periodic Release
Frequency: Annually
Price: No charge

Available from
Scottish Executive Rural Affairs Department
Room 145
Scottish Executive
Pentland House
47 Robbs Loan
Edinburgh EH14 1TY

Also available on the Scottish Executive website at www.scotland.gov.uk

Agriculture: Statistical Yearbook, 1998
Eurostat

This statistical yearbook contains the most important parts from Eurostat's publications on agriculture, forestry and fisheries in abbreviated form.

Frequency: Annual
Price: £10.00
ISBN: 92 825 3720 3

Available from
TSO Publications Centre and Bookshops
Please see Annex B for full address details.

Agriculture in the United Kingdom
Ministry of Agriculture, Fisheries and Food

Publication with summaries, policies and annual statistics of agriculture in the United Kingdom. The publication contains a comprehensive selection of agricultural statistics, agriculture and food in the national economy, structure of the industry, output prices and input costs, commodities, incomes, rent, land prices, balance sheets, farm business and public expenditure.

Delivery: Periodic Release
Frequency: Annually
Price: Approximately £15.00

Available from
TSO Publications Centre and Bookshops
Please see Annex B for full address details.

Sources from which data for this product are obtained
Aggregate Agricultural Account; Aggregate Balance Sheets for Agriculture - UK; Agricultural Census; Agricultural Land Prices - England and Wales; Agricultural Rent Enquiry - England and Wales; Animal Compound Feedingstuffs: Sales Value and Volume - GB; Bacon and Ham Produced - GB; Brewers, Distillers and Maltsters - UK; Cereal Breakfast Food Production - UK; Cereal Stocks Held at Ports - UK; Cereal Stocks Held by Agricultural Co-operatives - UK; Cereals and animal feed stocks held by Importers and dealers; Cereals Production Survey - England and Wales; Dried Pea and Bean Production Survey - England and Wales; England and Wales Slaughter House Survey; Farm Accounts - Scotland; Farm Business Survey - England; Farm Business Survey - Northern Ireland; Farm Business Surveys; Fruit and Vegetables Crops - England and Wales; June Agricultural and Horticultural Census - Northern Ireland; Oatmeal Millers Receipts, Production and Stocks - UK; Oilseeds Crushed and the Production of Crude Vegetable Oil, Oilcake and Meal - UK; Overseas trade in agricultural commodities; Poultry Feed Production for Units with Large Flocks - GB; Production and Stocks of Condensed Milk and Milk Powders - UK; Production of Compound and Other Processed Animal Feeding Stuffs - GB; Raw Sugar - GB; Refined Sugar - GB; Rye Milled

for Human Consumption; Self sufficiency in food; Stocks of Human and Pet Food in Public Cold Stores - UK; Survey of Personal Incomes; Utilisation of Milk by Dairies - England and Wales; Value of Milk Purchased - England and Wales; Wheat Milled and Flour Production - UK

December 1997 Agricultural Survey: Northern Ireland Results
Department of Agriculture - Northern Ireland

This survey provides estimates of cattle, sheep and pigs on farms at the beginning of December. In addition, the survey provides estimates of hay and silage production and sowings of winter cereals.

Delivery: News/Press Release
Frequency: Annually
Price: Free

Available from
Chris Gibbens
MAFF
Foss House
Kings Pool
1-2 Peasholme Green
York YO1 7PX
Tel: 01904 455100

December Agriculture Survey (Statistics Notice)
Ministry of Agriculture, Fisheries and Food

This survey covers a sample of main holdings. The data complements that collected at June, and provides a half-yearly update of the labour and livestock items, reflecting the seasonal pattern in December. Data is also collected on autumn/winter crops of wheat, barley and oilseed rape. Results are published in Statistical Notices - one for England and one for the UK. Results at regional and county level are not produced.

Delivery: Periodic Release
Frequency: Annually
Price: Free

Available from
MAFF Website (see the Websites and Electronic Services chapter), MAFF Faxback Service or Publications Unit (MAFF)
Please see Annex B for full address details.

Sources from which data for this product are obtained
December Agricultural Survey - England

(The) Digest of Agricultural Census Statistics UK
Ministry of Agriculture, Fisheries and Food

The publication contains information from the June censuses for the United Kingdom and constituent countries. This includes

information on land use, livestock, labour and tenure for the last five years and ten years ago; the same information for regions and counties for the current year; and the size patterns of holdings for main items for the current year.

Delivery: Periodic Release
Frequency: Annually
Price: £24.00 (for 1997 edition in hardcopy)
No charge for website version
ISBN: 0-11-243046-5 (1997 edition)

Available from
MAFF Website (see the Websites and Electronic Services chapter) or Publications Unit (MAFF)
Please see Annex B for full address details.

Sources from which data for this product are obtained
June Agricultural and Horticultural Census - England & Wales; June Agricultural and Horticultural Census - Northern Ireland

Farming Fact and Figures, Wales
National Assembly for Assembly

Key statistics on agriculture in Wales. Pocket-size leaflet

Delivery: Periodic Release
Frequency: Annually

Available from:
Statistical Publications Unit
National Assembly for Wales
Please see Annex B for full address details

Sources from which data for this product are obtained
June Agricultural and Horticultural Census - England and Wales

Final Results of June Agricultural Census (Press Release)
Scottish Executive; sponsored by SERAD

Final results from June agricultural census giving Scotland level information on agricultural land, livestock and labour.

Delivery: News/Press Release
Frequency: Annually
Price: Free

Available from
Andy Reid
Scottish Executive Rural Affairs Department
Please see Annex B for full address details.

Sources from which data for this product are obtained
Agricultural and Horticultural Census - Scotland

Products

June Agricultural and Horticultural Census (Statistical Notice)
Ministry of Agriculture, Fisheries and Food

Contains information on land use, tenure, crops, livestock and labour. The figures relate to the position on holdings on the first Monday of June. Provisional results for England are normally published at the end of August and final results in mid-December in the form of a Statistical Notice. Statistical Notices giving provisional and final results for the UK are published in early September and in January of the following year respectively.

Delivery: Periodic Release
Frequency: Bi-annually
Price: Free

Available from
MAFF Website (see the Websites and Electronic Services chapter), MAFF Faxback Service or Publications Unit (MAFF)
Please see Annex B for full address details.

Ministry of Agriculture, Fisheries and Food Faxback Service
Ministry of Agriculture, Fisheries and Food

The faxback services allows you to receive many of the statistical notices produced by MAFF via your fax machine. Details can be obtained by telephoning the faxback helpline on 0870 444 0100.

Available from
Ministry of Agriculture, Fisheries and Food Statistics Division Faxback Service: Index and Calendar to Statistical Notices (SNs) Commodity Surveys (Faxback helpline Tel: 0870 444 0100)

Sources from which data for this product are obtained
Manufacture of Margarine, Solid Cooking Fats and Other Table Spreads - UK; Output of Refined Vegetable and Marine Oils and Animal Fats by UK Processors; Wheat Milled and Flour Production - UK

Minor Holdings Census (Statistics Notice)
Ministry of Agriculture, Fisheries and Food

Contains information on land use, livestock, labour, horticulture and changes in area on minor holdings throughout England.

Delivery: Periodic Release
Frequency: Every five years
Price: Free

Available from
MAFF Website (see the Websites and Electronic Services chapter), MAFF Faxback Service or

MAFF Publications Section
Ministry of Agriculture, Fisheries and Food
Please see Annex B for full address details.

Sources from which data for this product are obtained
Minor Holdings Census - England & Wales

Region and County Tables
Ministry of Agriculture, Fisheries and Food

English and Welsh region and county data in detail from the June Census covering crop (incl. land tenure), livestock, horticulture and labour.

Delivery: Periodic Release
Frequency: Annually
Price: Free

Available from
MAFF Website (see the Websites and Electronic Services chapter) or Publications Unit (MAFF)
Please see Annex B for full address details.

Sources from which data for this product are obtained
June Agricultural and Horticultural Census - England & Wales

Results of Censuses of Agriculture for Minor Holdings in Scotland, 1987-1996
AEFD

Scotland and sub-Scotland level agricultural information for small holdings.

Frequency: Ad-hoc
Price: £2.00
ISBN: 0 748 66106 9
ISSN: 1460 - 7360

Available from
Andy Reid
Scottish Executive
Please see Annex B for full address details.

Sources from which data for this product are obtained
Agricultural and Horticultural Census - Scotland

Socio-Economic Evaluation of Free Advice to Farmers in England by ADAS and FWAG
Ministry of Agriculture, Fisheries and Food

Report by the Countryside and Community Research Unit, Cheltenham.

Available from
MAFF Press Office
Room 21
Whitehall Place (West Block)
London SW1A 2HH
Tel: 020 7270 8441/8065.

Statistical Review of Northern Ireland Agriculture
Department of Agriculture - Northern Ireland

Latest statistics on Northern Ireland agriculture. The review contains a comprehensive picture of Northern Ireland agriculture and includes a wide range of economic and physical data, including details of the aggregate income of the industry; prices; crop areas; livestock numbers; farm structure; and incomes at farm level.

Frequency: Annually
Price: £14.00
ISBN: 1-85527-345-4

Sources from which data for this product are obtained
Aggregate Agricultural Account - Northern Ireland

Survey of Agriculture: 1 December, Results for Wales
National Assembly for Wales

Summary results from the December Survey of Agriculture in Wales. Includes livestock and crop estimates.

Delivery: Statistical Release
Frequency: Annually

Available from:
Agricultural Statistics
National Assembly for Wales
Please see Annex B for full address details.

Sources from which data for this product are obtained
December Agricultural Survey - England and Wales

Welsh Agricultural Statistics
National Assembly for Wales

Contains a wide range of statistics about the agricultural industry in Wales. This includes details of agricultural area, livestock, agricultural holdings, labour, production and marketing, livestock prices, land prices and rents, grants and subsidies, farm structure, less favoured areas and UK comparisons.

Delivery: Hardcopy publication
Frequency: Annually
Price: £10.00
ISBN: 0-7504-2350-1
ISSN: 9 780750 423502

Available from:
Statistical Publications Unit
National Assembly for Wales
Please see Annex B for full address details.

Sources from which data for this product are obtained
June Agricultural and Horticultural Census - England and Wales

14.19 Animal Feed

Deliveries of Compound and Other Processed Animal Feedstuffs by Northern Ireland Feedstuff Manufacturers.
Department of Agriculture - Northern Ireland

Departmental bulletin on deliveries of various types of animal feedstuffs by Northern Ireland feedstuff compounders. Contains data on various types of animal feedstuff deliveries within Northern Ireland and exported by Northern Ireland feed compounders.

Delivery: Periodic Release
Frequency: Monthly, Quarterly and Annual. Within 8 weeks of period covered.
Price: £27.00 (annual subscription) for monthly, quarterly and annual bulletin.
£14.50 (annual subscription) for quarterly and annual bulletin.
£9.50 (annual subscription) for annual bulletin only.

Available from
Norman Fulton
Department of Agriculture - Northern Ireland
Dundonald House
Upper Newtownards Road
Belfast, BT4 3SB
Tel: 028 905244067

Sources from which data for this product are obtained
Animal Feedstuffs - Northern Ireland

GB Animal Feed Statistical Notice
Ministry of Agriculture, Fisheries and Food

Production of animal compound feedingstuffs and on raw materials used in their production. Contains data on the production of 28 different animal compound feedingstuffs by livestock categories and the usage and deliveries of 27 different raw materials relating to their production.

Monthly average prices of animal compound feedingstuffs for the main livestock categories - cattle and calf feed; pig feed; poultry feed; sheep feed. The notice is published monthly and covers GB sales with prices three months in arrears.

Data on production of GB Poultry Compound Feedingstuffs by units with large flocks and the usage of cereals in this production.

Delivery: Periodic Release
Frequency: Monthly and annually
Price: Free

Available from
Janine Horsfall
Ministry of Agriculture, Fisheries and Food
Foss House
Kings Pool
1-2 Peasholme Green
York YO1 7PX
Tel: 00 44 (0) 1904 455067;
Email: j.horsfall@esg.maff.gov.uk
or
Tim Marsh
Ministry of Agriculture, Fisheries and Food
Foss House
Kings Pool
1-2 Peasholme Green
York YO1 7PX
Tel: 00 44 (0) 1904 455061;
Email: t.marsh@esg.maff.gov.uk

Sources from which data for this product are obtained
Animal Compound Feedingstuffs: Sales Value and Volume - GB
Poultry Feed Production for Units with Large Flocks - GB
Production of Compound and Other Processed Animal Feedingstuffs - GB

Grain Fed to Livestock (Statistics Notice)
Ministry of Agriculture, Fisheries and Food

Contains estimates of cereals consumption (wheat, barley, maize, and oats) by livestock. Holdings with more than 50,000 poultry are excluded. A Statistics Notice is published monthly for England and Wales as a whole. No sub-national results are published.

Delivery: Periodic Release
Frequency: Monthly
Price: Free

Available from
MAFF Website (see the Websites and Electronic Services chapter), MAFF Faxback Service or the Publications Unit (MAFF)
Please see Annex B for full address details.

Sources from which data for this product are obtained
Grain Fed to Livestock Survey - England and Wales

Results of the Survey into the Composition of Main Livestock Rations as Used in Great Britain During the Six-Month Period January to June/July to December (Press Notice) (Suspended)
Ministry of Agriculture, Fisheries and Food

Data on the composition of the main animal compound feedingstuffs in Great Britain.

The composition of an average ration is shown for eight main types of animal compound feedingstuffs. The main rations are standard dairy, summer grazing for cattle, pregnant sow, pig rearer, pig finisher, broiler starter, broiler finisher and poultry layer. The percentage of each raw material used in an average ration is shown. There are a total of 37 raw materials which cover cereals, cereal by-products, animal proteins, vegetable proteins and other miscellaneous ingredients. (N.B. This Statistical Notice has been suspended since 1995 and was published bi-annually).
Statistical Notice. Text/tables.

Delivery: Periodic Release
Frequency: Bi-annually
Price: Free

Available from
Janine Horsfall
Ministry of Agriculture, Fisheries and Food
Foss House
Kings Pool
1-2 Peasholme Green
York YO1 7PX
Tel: 00 44 (0) 1904 455067;
Email: j.horsfall@esq.maff.gov.uk

Usage of Raw Materials of the Production of Animal Feedstuffs and for Delivery As Straights.
Department of Agriculture - Northern Ireland

Usage of raw materials in production of animal feedstuff in Northern Ireland. Contains data on the various types of raw materials used in the production of animal feedstuffs in Northern Ireland and the quantities delivered to farmers or distributing merchants in the form of straights.

Frequency: Quarterly and annual, within 8 weeks of period covered.
Price: £27.00 (annual subscription) for monthly, quarterly and annual bulletin.
£14.50 (annual subscription) for quarterly and annual bulletin.
£9.50 (annual subscription) annual bulletin only.

Available from
Norman Fulton
Department of Agriculture - Northern Ireland
Dundonald House
Upper Newtownards Road
Belfast, BT4 3SB
Tel: 028 905244067

Sources from which data for this product are obtained
Animal Feedstuffs - Northern Ireland

See also:
In this chapter:
Agriculture in the United Kingdom *(14.18)*
Ministry of Agriculture, Fisheries and Food Faxback Service *(14.18)*

Products

14.20 Arable Crops

(The) Agricultural Co-Operative and Ports Cereals Stock Surveys (Statistics Notice)
Ministry of Agriculture, Fisheries and Food

Data on grain stocks held at ports and agricultural co-operatives. Contains data on wheat and barley stocks held by agricultural co-operatives, and at ports split between those 'following import' or 'awaiting export'.

Delivery: Periodic Release
Frequency: Quarterly
Price: Free

Available from
Chris Tippin
Ministry of Agriculture, Fisheries and Food
Foss House
Kings Pool
1-2 Peasholme Green
York YO1 7PX
Tel: 0044 (0) 1904 455059;
Email: c.tippin@esg.maff.gov.uk

Sources from which data for this product are obtained
Cereal Stocks Held at Ports - UK; Cereal Stocks Held by Agricultural Co-operatives - UK

Cereal Stocks Survey (Statistical Notice)
Ministry of Agriculture, Fisheries and Food

A quarterly survey of wheat and barley stocks on holdings in England and Wales. Regional results are shown for the September 1997 survey.

Delivery: Periodic Release
Frequency: Quarterly
Price: Free

Available from
MAFF Website (see the Websites and Electronic Services chapter), MAFF Faxback Service or the Publications Unit (MAFF)
Please see Annex B for full address details.

Sources from which data for this product are obtained
Cereal Stocks Survey - England and Wales

Cereals Production Survey (Statistics Notice)
Ministry of Agriculture, Fisheries and Food

Cereals Production Surveys take place 3 times a year, to produce 3 estimates taken in September, December and the following April. Holdings selected for the survey are drawn from those who returned an area of any of the cereals wheat, barley and oats at the previous June census. Results are

published in a Statistical Notice and are for the UK.

Delivery: Periodic Release
Price: Free

Available from
MAFF Website (see the Websites and Electronic Services chapter), MAFF Faxback Service or the Publications Unit (MAFF)
Please see Annex B for full address details.

Sources from which data for this product are obtained
Cereals Production Survey - England and Wales

Dried Pea and Field Bean Production (Statistics Notice)
Ministry of Agriculture, Fisheries and Food

This sample survey is published annually normally in January or February (starting in 1990) for the previous year's harvest of peas and beans. Results show estimates of production of dried peas and field beans for the latest survey together with comparative data for the previous 2 years.

Delivery: Periodic Release
Frequency: Annually
Price: Free

Available from
MAFF Website (see the Websites and Electronic Services chapter), MAFF Faxback Service or Publications Unit (MAFF)
Please see Annex B for full address details.

Sources from which data for this product are obtained
Dried Pea and Bean Production Survey - England and Wales

Minor Crops Production Survey (Statistics Notice)
Ministry of Agriculture, Fisheries and Food

Contains estimates of the production and yield of minor cereals and linseed in England and Wales

Delivery: Statistical Notice
Frequency: Annual
Price: Free

Available from
MAFF Website (see the Websites and Electronic Services chapter)

Publications Unit (MAFF)
Please see Annex B for full address details.

Sources from which data for this product are obtained
Cereals Production Survey
Linseed Production Survey
June Agricultural and Horticultural Census - England and Wales

Straw Disposal Survey (Statistics Notice)
Ministry of Agriculture, Fisheries and Food

Contains information on how straw is disposed of. The results are based on a sample of cereal growing holdings in England and Wales. Three years figures are provided as well as a breakdown for wheat, winter and spring barley, and oats.

Delivery: Periodic Release
Frequency: Periodic
Price: No charge

Available from
MAFF Website (see the Websites and Electronic Services chapter) or Publications Unit (MAFF)
Please see Annex B for full address details.

Sources from which data for this product are obtained
Straw Disposal Survey - England and Wales

See also:
In this chapter:
Agricultural and Horticultural Census: 1 June, Final Results for Wales *(14.18)*
Agricultural and Horticultural Census: 1 June, provisional Results for Wales *(14.18)*
Agricultural and Horticulture Census, Scotland - June Provisional Results (Press Release) *(14.18)*
Agricultural Census Summary Sheets by Geographic Area *(14.18)*
Agricultural Sample Census - December (Press Release) *(14.18)*
Agriculture in the United Kingdom *(14.18)*
Analysis of Holdings *(14.29)*
(The) Digest of Agricultural Census Statistics UK *(14.18)*
Economic Report on Scottish Agriculture *(14.22)*
Eurofarm Tabular Databank System *(14.34)*
Farming Fact and Figures, Wales *(14.18)*
Farm Structure: Main Results *(14.34)*
Final Results of June Agricultural Census (Press Release) *(14.18)*
Frequency Distribution Tables *(14.34)*
Grain Fed to Livestock (Statistics Notice) *(14.19)*
Ministry of Agriculture, Fisheries and Food Faxback Service *(14.18)*
Region and County Tables *(14.18)*
Results of Censuses of Agriculture for Minor Holdings in Scotland, 1987-1996 *(14.18)*
Survey of Agriculture: 1 December, Results for Wales *(14.18)*
Welsh Agricultural Statistics *(14.18)*

14.21 Arable Crops - Related Industries

Brewers, Distillers and Maltsters Usage and Stocks
Ministry of Agriculture, Fisheries and Food

Tables containing quantity of barley, wheat and maize used in the brewing, malting and distilling industry. Also closing stocks of cereals and sales of barley/barley screenings. Data are shown for the current month and the same month the previous year. Also cumulative data (crop year to date).

Delivery: Periodic Release
Frequency: Monthly
Price: Free

Available from
Kath Neild
Ministry of Agriculture, Fisheries and Food
Foss House
Kings Pool
1-2 Peasholme Green
York YO1 7PX
Tel: 00 44 (0) 1904 455066;
Email: k.neild@esq.maff.gov.uk

Sources from which data for this product are obtained
Brewers, Distillers and Maltsters - UK

Margarine, Other Table Spreads and Solid Cooking Fat Production in the United Kingdom and the Refined Oils and Fats Used in their Manufacture
Ministry of Agriculture, Fisheries and Food

Data are shown for the production of soft, other and non-vitaminised margarine, table spreads and solid cooking fats. And the vegetable, marine oils and animal fats used in their manufacture. Data are shown for the current month and the same month the previous year.

Delivery: Periodic Release
Frequency: Monthly and annually
Price: Free

Available from
Alex Clothier
Ministry of Agriculture, Fisheries and Food
Please see Annex B for full address details

Sources from which data for this product are obtained
Manufacture of Margarine, Solid Cooking Fats and Other Table Spreads - UK

Oilseeds and Nuts Crushed in the United Kingdom and the Crude Vegetable Oils, Oilcake and Meal Produced (Press Notice)
Ministry of Agriculture, Fisheries and Food

Contains data on the quantity of nine categories of oilseed crushed and the crude oil, oilcake and meal produced from the crush. Data cover a 13 week period and are shown against those for the equivalent period in the previous year.

Delivery: Periodic Release
Frequency: Monthly and annually
Price: Free

Available from
Alex Clothier
Ministry of Agriculture, Fisheries and Food
Please see Annex B for full address details

Sources from which data for this product are obtained
Oilseeds Crushed and the Production of Crude Vegetable Oil, Oilcake and Meal - UK

Output of Refined, Deodorised Vegetable, Marine Oils and Animal Fats by UK Processing Plants (Press Notice)
Ministry of Agriculture, Fisheries and Food

Shows output of 12 different vegetable, marine oils and animal fats by the UK processors. Data are shown for the current month and the same month the previous year.

Delivery: Periodic Release
Frequency: Monthly and annually
Price: Free

Available from

Alex Clothier
Ministry of Agriculture, Fisheries and Food
Please see Annex B for full address details

Oilseed Rape Production Survey (Statistics Notice)
Ministry of Agriculture, Fisheries and Food

Contains estimates of the area, production and yield of oilseed rape based on a sample of holdings which returned an area of oilseed rape at the previous June Census. A Statistics Notice is published for the UK. Sub-national results are not available.

Delivery: Periodic Release
Frequency: Bi-annually
Price: Free

Available from
MAFF Website (see the Websites and Electronic Services chapter), MAFF Faxback Service or Publications Unit (MAFF)
Please see Annex B for full address details.

Sources from which data for this product are obtained
Oilseed Rape Production Survey - England

Wheat Milled and Flour Production (Statistics Notice)
Ministry of Agriculture, Fisheries and Food

Data on wheat usage and flour production in the United Kingdom. The statistics notice contains data on the quantity of home grown and imported wheat milled, and quantities of eight types of flour produced (e.g. white bread-making flour, self-raising flour). Also includes closing stocks of wheat and flour. Data are shown for the current month and the same month of the previous year. Also cumulative data (crop year to date).

Delivery: Periodic Release
Frequency: Monthly
Price: free

Available from
Kath Neild
Ministry of Agriculture, Fisheries and Food
Foss House
Kings Pool
1-2 Peasholme Green
York YO1 7PX
Tel: 00 44 (0) 1904 455066;
Email: k.neild@esq.maff.gov.uk

Sources from which data for this product are obtained
Wheat Milled and Flour Production - UK

See also:
In this chapter:
Agriculture in the United Kingdom *(14.18)*
Ministry of Agriculture, Fisheries and Food Faxback Service *(14.18)*

14.22 Economics of Agriculture

Aggregate Agricultural Output and Income in Wales
National Assembly for Wales

Details of the levels of output and inputs calculated in line with National Accounts methodology.

Delivery: Statistical Release
Frequency: Annually

Available from:
Economic Advice Division 2
National Assembly for Wales
Cathays Park,
Cardiff CF10 3NQ
Tel: 029 2082 3569;
Fax: 029 2082 5350;
E-mail: stats.pubs@wales.gsi.gov.uk

Economic Report on Scottish Agriculture; 1999 Edition
SERAD

Economics and statistics of farming in Scotland. The report contains data on output, input, income, expenditure, accounts, crops, livestock and labour.

Delivery: Periodic Release
Frequency: Annually
Price: £14.50
ISBN: 0 7480 8229 8

Available from
TSO Publications Centre and Bookshops
Please see Annex B for full address details.

Sources from which data for this product are obtained
Agricultural and Horticultural Census - Scotland; Agricultural Land Prices - Scotland; Agricultural Wages - Scotland; Cabbages and Cauliflowers - Yields and Prices; Cereal Stock Disposal Survey; Combinable Crops Production and Disposal Survey - Scotland; Extended Horticulture Survey - Scotland; Farm Accounts - Scotland; Glasshouse and Protected Crops Survey - Scotland; Hardy Nursery Stock Survey - Scotland; Horticultural Yields and Prices (Soft Fruits) - Scotland

Estimates of Farm Incomes in Wales, Results of the Farm Business Survey
National Assembly for Wales

Records updated estimates of farm incomes in Wales, including lowland as well as hill and upland areas.

Delivery: Statistical Release
Frequency: Annually

Available from:
Economic Advice Division 2
National Assembly for Wales
Cathays Park, Cardiff
CF10 3NQ
Tel: 029 2082 3569;
Fax: 029 2082 5350;
E-mail: stats.pubs@wales.gsi.gov.uk

Sources from which data for this product are obtained
Farm Business Survey

Farm Business Data Book 1998
Department of Agriculture - Northern Ireland

Physical and financial data to assist in preparation of farm business plans. The publication contains farm planning data relevant to Northern Ireland conditions. It covers the major farm enterprises in Northern Ireland and provides information on physical performance, enterprise output, variable costs and gross margins.

Frequency: Annual
Price: £7.50
ISBN: 1-85527-342-X
ISSN: 0956-2869

Available from
Department of Agriculture, Economics and Statistics Division - Northern Ireland
Please see Annex B for full address details

Farm Incomes in Northern Ireland 1996/97
Department of Agriculture - Northern Ireland

Farm incomes by type of farming in Northern Ireland. The publication contains data on farm returns, cost, subsidies, borrowings and investment for the main types of farm businesses. In addition there are sections on enterprise gross margins and fixed costs.

Frequency: Annual
Price: £14.00

Available from
Department of Agriculture, Economics and Statistics Division - Northern Ireland
Please see Annex B for full address details.

Sources from which data for this product are obtained
Farm Business Survey - Northern Ireland

Farm Incomes in Scotland
SERAD

Latest financial results for farms surveyed in Farm Accounts Survey.

Delivery: Periodic Release
Frequency: Annually
Price: £5.00
ISBN: 0 7480 8018 X

Available from
Robin Haynes
Scottish Executive
47 Robbs Loan
Edinburgh, EH14 1TY
Tel: 0131 244 6132

Sources from which data for this product are obtained
Farm Accounts - Scotland

Farm Incomes in the United Kingdom
Ministry of Agriculture, Fisheries and Food

A detailed source of information on the incomes and financial structure of the agricultural industry in each of the four countries of the United Kingdom. The results of the Farm Business Survey in England and Wales and the corresponding surveys in the other countries provide information at the farm level for farm and off-farm incomes, performance measures and assets and liabilities by country, farm types, business size and tenure. These results are supplemented by an indication of the expected movements in farm incomes and by a section showing the gross margins of farm enterprises and how they are changing over time. Additionally, a condensed version of the aggregate agricultural accounts for each country within the UK is included.

Delivery: Periodic Release
Frequency: Annually
Price: £30.00
ISBN: 0-11-243038-4

Available from
MAFF Press Office
Ministry of Agriculture, Fisheries and Food
Nobel House
17 Smith Square
London SW1P 3HX
Tel: 020 7238 5608

Sources from which data for this product are obtained
Farm Business Surveys
Agricultural June Census
Inland Revenue's Survey of Personal Incomes

Forecast of Scottish Total Income from Farming (TIFF)
Scottish Executive

An annual Statistical News Release issued in December of the current year presenting the preliminary TIFF forecast for the year. The release is available from the Scottish Executive website-http://www.scotland.gov.uk

Delivery: News/Press Release
Frequency: Annually
Price: Free

Available from
Tom Whyte
Scottish Executive
47 Robbs Loan
Edinburgh, EH14 1TY
Tel: 0131 244 3116

Sources from which data for this product are obtained
Scottish Aggregate Agricultural Account

Forecast of UK Total Income from Farming (TIFF)
Ministry of Agriculture, Fisheries and Food

An annual Statistical News Release issued in December of the current year presenting the preliminary TIFF forecast for the year. The release is available from the MAFF website - http://www.maff.gov.uk

Delivery: News/Press Release
Frequency: Annually
Price: Free

Available from
Jim Holding
MAFF
Foss House
Kings Pool
1-2 Peasholme Green
York, YO1 7PX
Tel: 01904 455080

Sources from which data for this product are obtained
Aggregate Agricultural Account

Income from Agricultural Activity 1998
Eurostat

This publication focuses on the changes in income from agricultural activity in the Member States and in the EU as a whole for 1998 compared to 1997, with analyses and comments on these changes.

Delivery: Periodic Release
Frequency: Annually
ISBN: 92 827 9590X

Available from
Bob Dodds
Please see Annex B for full address details.

Sources from which data for this product are obtained
Incomes of Agricultural Households Sector

Income Statistics for the Agricultural Household Sector 1996
Ministry of Agriculture, Fisheries and Food; sponsored by European Commission

Proceedings of the Eurostat International Seminar held in Luxembourg on 10 and 11 January 1996.

Delivery: Ad Hoc/One-off Release
Price: ECU 21

Available from
Jim Holding
MAFF
Foss House
Kings Pool

1-2 Peasholme Green
York, YO1 7PX
Tel: 01904 455080

Sources from which data for this product are obtained
Incomes of Agricultural Households Sector

Provisional Estimates of Net Farm Income for Cattle and Sheep Farms, Wales
National Assembly for Wales

Contains the results of the first estimates of farm incomes in the hills and uplands of Wales.

Delivery: Statistical Release
Frequency: Annually

Available from:
Economic Advice Division 2
National Assembly for Wales
Cathays Park, Cardiff
CF10 3NQ
Tel: 029 2082 3569;
Fax: 029 2082 5350;
E-mail: stats.pubs@wales.gsi.gov.uk

Output and Productivity
Ministry of Agriculture, Fisheries and Food

An annual Statistical News Release presenting a commentary on the estimates, including Total Income From Farming (TIFF), with tables for the current year compared with the previous four years showing: outputs, inputs, net product and incomes at current prices; indicators of volume, productivity and incomes; and net farm income by type of farm at current prices and deflated by the retail price index (RPI). The release can be obtained from the MAFF website at http://www.maff.gov.uk.

Delivery: News/Press Release
Frequency: Annually

Available from
Jim Holding
MAFF
Foss House
Kings Pool
1-2 Peasholme Green
York, YO1 7PX
Tel: 01904 455080

Sources from which data for this product are obtained
Aggregate Agricultural Account

Scottish Agriculture Output Input and Income Statistics
Scottish Executive

Data on output, input and incomes of Scottish agriculture. The publication contains data on output of Scottish agriculture, subsidies and grants, at current and constant prices, quantities and prices, and indices.

Delivery: News/Press Release
Frequency: Annually
Price: Free

Available from
Scottish Executive Rural Affairs Department
Room 145
Scottish Executive
Pentland House
47 Robbs Loan
Edinburgh EH14 1TY

Also available on Scottish Executive website: www.scotland.gov.uk

Sources from which data for this product are obtained
Aggregate Bank Advances to Scottish Agriculture; Autumn Store Sales Returns - Scotland; Cabbages and Cauliflowers - Yields and Prices; Combinable Crops Production and Disposal Survey - Scotland; Poultry Packing Station Throughput - Scotland; Production and Marketing of Hatching Eggs and Chicks - Scotland; Store Market Reporting - Scotland; Survey of ex-farm Milk Prices - Scotland

Size and Performance of the Northern Ireland Food and Drinks Processing Sector (Subsector Statistics 1996)
Department of Agriculture - Northern Ireland

Statistics relating to the performance of the food and drinks processing sector in Northern Ireland. The publication contains data on the level of sales, value added and employment for each of the ten sub-sectors within the food and drinks processing sector.

Frequency: Annual
Price: £6.00
ISBN: 1-85527-355-1

Available from
Department of Agriculture, Economics and Statistics Division
Room 817
Dundonald House
Upper Newtownards Road
Belfast BT4 3SB
Tel: 028 9052 4594

See also:
In this chapter:
Agricultural Price Indices (Statistics Notice) *(14.32)*
Agriculture Facts and Figures *(14.18)*
Agriculture in the United Kingdom *(14.18)*
Annual Survey of Tenanted Land (Statistics Notice) *(14.29)*

Products

December 1997 Agricultural survey: Northern Ireland Results *(14.18)*
Eurofarm Tabular Databank System *(14.34)*
Farming Fact and Figures, Wales *(14.18)*
Farm Structure Methodology of Community Surveys (Eurostat) *(14.34)*
Farm Structure: Main Results *(14.34)*
Welsh Agricultural Statistics *(14.18)*

In other chapters:
Indicators of Sustainable Development - United Kingdom *(see the Environment chapter)*

14. 23 Eggs

Eggs Statistics Notice
Ministry of Agriculture, Fisheries and Food

This monthly publication combines the UK egg packing station survey, the UK egg processor survey, the egg laying element of the UK hatcheries survey, together with other MAFF statistics, Intrastat trade data and EU data.

Delivery: Periodic Release
Frequency: Monthly
Price: Free

Available from
Christine Jeanette
MAFF
Foss House
Kings Pool
1-2 Peasholme Green
York, YO1 7PX
Tel: 01904 455069

Sources from which data for this product are obtained
Egg Packing Station Survey - UK; Egg Processing Survey - UK

See also:
In this chapter:
Agriculture Facts and Figures *(14.18)*
Agriculture in the United Kingdom *(14.18)*

14.24 Fishing

(The) English, Welsh and Northern Irish Fishing Vessel List
Ministry of Agriculture, Fisheries and Food

The publication contains data on the characteristics of fishing vessels and their status for licensing purposes on vessels registered in England, Wales and Northern Ireland.

Delivery: Other
Frequency: Annually
Price: £6.00

Available from
Ian Wood
MAFF
Nobel House
17 Smith Square
London, SW1P 3JR
Tel: 020 7238 6050

Sources from which data for this product are obtained
Fishing Fleets - UK

Fisheries Statistics
Ministry of Agriculture, Fisheries and Food; sponsored by Environment Agency

An annual review of salmon and sea trout catches in England and Wales based on anglers' catch returns. The publication contains data on declared rod and net catches of salmon and sea trout by EA region showing a comparison of current year figures with those of the previous five-year mean, historical annual trends in reported catches by region, detailed monthly breakdown of current season's reported catches of salmon and sea trout by region, by river/fishery and by fishing method showing number of fish caught and total weight of catch, and the number and value of rod and net licences sold by EA region.

Delivery: Periodic Release
Frequency: Annually
Price: £3.00

Available from
TSO Publications Centre and Bookshops
Please see Annex B for full address details.

Sources from which data for this product are obtained
Fisheries Statistics - Anglers - England and Wales

Fisheries: Yearly Statistics, 1998
Office for National Statistics

This document contains fishery statistics for the EU Member States and other important countries in this sector. This volume is divided into sections on catches by fishing region, catches of principal species, the fishing fleet and foreign trade in fishery products and covers the period 1987-1996.

Delivery: Periodic Release
Frequency: Annually
Price: £16.45
ISBN: 92 828 5742 5

Available from
TSO Publications Centre and Bookshops
Please see Annex B for full address details.

Monthly Return of Sea Fisheries Statistics England and Wales
Ministry of Agriculture, Fisheries and Food

Summary of information collected from fishermen after fishing trips in UK waters. This document contains data on species of fish caught, area of capture, port of landing and fishing organisation and is intended to provide an up-to-date picture of landings into England and Wales. All the data in the return are provisional and do not reflect final landings for the period concerned.

Delivery: Periodic Release
Frequency: Monthly
Price: £10.00 annual subscription

Available from
Ian Wood
Room 432
Ministry of Agriculture, Fisheries and Food
Nobel House
17 Smith Square
London SW1P 3JR
Tel: 020 7238 6050;
Email: i.wood@fish.maff.gov.uk

Sources from which data for this product are obtained
Seafish Landings - UK

Report on the Sea and Inland Fisheries of Northern Ireland 1996
Department of Agriculture - Northern Ireland

The report contains particulars of the Department's proceedings under the Fisheries Act (NI) 1966 and a statistical account of the fisheries of Northern Ireland. It contains data relating to fish landings, vessels, salmon and eel catches, angling permit sales, grants for vessels and aquaculture, production by commercial shellfish and trout farmers and stocking from the Department's fish farm.

Frequency: Annually
Price: Free
ISBN: 0 337 05354 5

Available from
TSO Publications Centre and Bookshops
Please see Annex B for full address details.

Sources from which data for this product are obtained
Fisheries - Northern Ireland

Sea Fisheries Statistics (Scotland)
Scottish Executive

Statistics on fishing vessels and landings and a vessel list of Scottish based vessels.

Delivery: Periodic Release
Frequency: Annually
Price: £11.00
ISBN: 0 7480 5886 9

Available from
Rob McDonald
Pentland House
Robb's Loan
Edinburgh EH14 1TX
Tel: 0131 244 6441;
Email: patrick.mcdonald@scotland.gov.uk

Sources from which data for this product are obtained
Fishery Statistics; Sea Fish Landings - Scotland

Shellfish News
Ministry of Agriculture, Fisheries and Food; sponsored by Centre for Environment Fisheries and Aquaculture Science

Articles on topics of interest to the shellfish farming and harvesting industry; recent research findings; changes in policy and legislation; annual production figures; monitoring reports.

Delivery: Periodic Release
Frequency: Bi-annually
Price: Free
ISBN: 1363-4720

Available from
Librarian
CEFAS Lowestoft Laboratory
Pakefield Road
Lowestoft,
Suffolk NR33 OHT

Statistics of Fish Landings in England, Wales and Northern Ireland by Port
Ministry of Agriculture, Fisheries and Food

Landings made at ports in England, Wales and Northern Ireland showing species, quantity landed and value.

Frequency: Annually
Price: £6.00

Available from
Ian Wood
Room 432
Ministry of Agriculture, Fisheries and Food
Nobel House
17 Smith Square
London SW1P 3JR
Tel: 020 7238 6050;
Email: i.wood@fish.maff.gov.uk

Sources from which data for this product are obtained
Seafish Landings - UK

UK Sea Fisheries Statistics
Ministry of Agriculture, Fisheries and Food

The volume presents statistics on the fishing industry in the UK and contains data on fishing fleets, number of fishermen and seafish landings.

Frequency: Annually
Price: £25.00
ISBN: 0 11 243045-7

Available from
TSO Publications Centre and Bookshops
Please see Annex B for full address details.

Sources from which data for this product are obtained
Fishing Fleets - UK; Number of Fishermen - England and Wales; Seafish Landings - UK

See also:
In other chapters:
Indicators of Sustainable Development - United Kingdom (see the Environment chapter)

14.25 Food, Beverages and Nutrition

National Food Survey (Annual Report)
Ministry of Agriculture, Fisheries and Food

Annual report of household food consumption and expenditure, presenting the latest results from the National Food Survey for GB with some UK and NI data. The report contains household food consumption and expenditure and nutritional intakes from household food and food eaten out, it also gives some comparisons with data of the preceding year and ten years ago. Text with tables and illustrative graphics.

Delivery: Hardcopy and MAFF Website
Frequency: Annually
Price: £28.00 (1997 edition)
ISBN: 0 11 243044 9

Available from
TSO Publications Centre and Bookshops
Please see Annex B for full address details.

MAFF Website (see the Websites and Electronic Services chapter)

Sources from which data for this product are obtained
National Food Survey - UK

National Food Survey - Northern Ireland 1996
Department of Agriculture - Northern Ireland

This is the second annual report on the National Food Survey (NFS) in Northern Ireland. It covers the period from January to December 1997. The NFS has provided continuous information on household consumption and expenditure in GB since 1950.

Frequency: Annually
Price: £6.00
ISBN: 1 85527 359 4

Available from
Sheila Magee
Room 811A
Department of Agriculture - Northern Ireland
Dundonald House
Upper Newtownards Road
Belfast BT4 3SB
Tel: 028 9052 4427;
Email: sheila.magee@dani.gov.uk

National Food Survey GB (Statistical News Release)
Ministry of Agriculture, Fisheries and Food

Quarterly summary of the National Food Survey results. The release contains household food consumption and expenditure and nutritional intakes from household food.

Delivery: Hardcopy and MAFF Website
Frequency: Quarterly
Price: Free

Available from
TSO Publications Centre and Bookshops
Please see Annex B for full address details.
or
MAFF Website (see the Websites and Electronic Services chapter)

Sources from which data for this product are obtained
National Food Survey - UK

National Food Survey GB Compendium of Results
Ministry of Agriculture, Fisheries and Food

Compendium of tables supplementing the published annual report, the National Food Survey. The compendium contains detailed tables of household food consumption and expenditure and nutritional intakes from household food.

Delivery: Hardcopy
Frequency: Annually
Price: £177.00

Available from
Ministry of Agriculture, Fisheries and Food
National Food Survey Branch
Whitehall Place
London SW1A 2HH

Sources from which data for this product are obtained
National Food Survey - UK

See also:
In this chapter:
Agriculture in the United Kingdom *(14.18)*
Basic Horticultural Statistics *(14.27)*

14.26 Forestry

Census of Woodland and Trees 1979-82
Forestry Commission

FC Bulletin 63, published 1987 describes the methods and results of the most recent (1980) completed survey of woodlands and trees and gives comparisons with previous surveys. For current survey, see "National Inventory of Woodland and Trees". The bulletin contains data on forest type, species type, ownership, standing volume and woodland area.

Frequency: Ad-hoc
Price: £8.50
ISBN: 0 11 7102024

Available from
Forestry Commission
Please see Annex B for full address details

Or:

TSO Publications Centre and Bookshops
Please see Annex B for full address details.

Sources from which data for this product are obtained
Census of Woodland and Trees

Forest Enterprise Annual Report & Accounts
Forestry Commission; Forest Enterprise

Annual Report from Forest Enterprise. First report for 1996-97, following creation of Agency in April 1996. Information was previously included in Forestry Commission Annual Report & Accounts. The report contains statistics for Forest Enterprise (all state forests in GB), some broken down by country or by region.

Frequency: Annually
Price: £12.40
ISBN: 0-10-254-498-0

Available from
TSO Publications Centre and Bookshops
Please see Annex B for full address details.

Sources from which data for this product are obtained
Forest Enterprise Holidays Facilities Inventory; Forest Enterprise Land Acquisitions and Disposals; Forest Enterprise Planting; Forest Enterprise Recreation Facilities Inventory; Forest Enterprise Sub-Compartment Database; Forest Enterprise Timber Harvesting and Sales

Forest Enterprise Timber Price Indices
Forestry Commission; Forest Enterprise

Bi-annual press release by Forest Enterprise, giving indices of average prices of timber sold by FE in previous year.

Delivery: News/Press Release
Frequency: Bi-annually
Price: Free

Available from
Alister Henderson
Forestry Commission
Please see Annex B for full address details.

Sources from which data for this product are obtained
Forest Enterprise Log Prices; Forest Enterprise Standing Sales Timber Prices

Forest Enterprise Visitor Survey Reports
Forestry Commission; Forest Enterprise

Reports on visitor surveys carried out at Forest Enterprise sites throughout GB. One report for each survey. About 15-20 surveys each year since 1995.

Frequency: Annually
Price: Most reports £2.00 each

Available from
Alister Henderson
Forestry Commission
Please see Annex B for full address details.

Forest Fire Statistics (UNECE)
Forestry Commission

Annual forest fire statistics, compiled from UNECE member countries. The publication covers the number of forest fires and total area burned. For UK, figures are for state forests only.

Frequency: Annually
ISSN: 0259-4323

Available from
TSO Publications Centre and Bookshops
Please see Annex B for full address details.

Sources from which data for this product are obtained
Forest Enterprise Forest Fire Statistics

Forest Product Statistics (UNECE)
Forestry Commission

Wood product statistics - production, imports, exports - compiled by UNECE Timber Section from returns by UNECE member countries.

Frequency: Annually
ISSN: 0259-4323

Available from
TSO Publications Centre and Bookshops
Please see Annex B for full address details.

Sources from which data for this product are obtained
Overseas Trade Statistics - Used Products; Wood Processing Industry Enquiries

Forest Products - FAO Yearbook
Forestry Commission

Statistics on production, imports, exports and apparent consumption of wood products, compiled by FAO for all countries (using UNECE data for UNECE members).

Frequency: Annually
ISBN: 92-5-004242-6
ISSN: 0084-3768

Available from
TSO Publications Centre and Bookshops
Please see Annex B for full address details.

Sources from which data for this product are obtained
Overseas Trade Statistics - Wood Products; Wood Processing Industry Enquiries

Forest Service Annual Report 1997/98
Department of Agriculture - Northern Ireland

Data collated on an annual basis for both state and private forestry in Northern Ireland. This report contains information on acquisitions, disposals and planting of forestry land. In addition, it provides information on recreation, conservation, education and timber production and marketing. The tables give details of planting, land utilisation and grants.

Delivery: Periodic Release
Frequency: Annually
Price: Free
ISBN: 1 85527 360 8

Available from
Forest Service
Room 37
Dundonald House
Upper Newtownards Road
Belfast BT4 3SB
Tel: 028 9052 4948

Sources from which data for this product are obtained
Forestry - Northern Ireland

Forest Visitor Surveys (Annual Summary Reports)
Forestry Commission

Summary report, with one-page summary for each forest visitor survey carried out in the year. Mostly Forest Enterprise visitor surveys, but also results from household surveys, cabin and campsite surveys, etc.

Frequency: Annually
Price: £2.00 for each year's report

Available from
Alister Henderson
Forestry Commission
Please see Annex B for full address details.

Sources from which data for this product are obtained
Forest Enterprise Visitor Surveys

Forestry Briefing
Forestry Commission

Briefing on forestry in Britain, originally prepared for new Ministers in May 1997, revised edition March 1998 available to general public. The briefing contains statistics (mostly in charts and maps) and other information about forestry in Britain.

Frequency: Ad-hoc
Price: Free

Available from
Alister Henderson
Forestry Commission
Please see Annex B for full address details.

Forestry Commission Annual Report and Accounts
Forestry Commission

Reports on the Commission's activities during the year and presents the audited accounts. The report contains data on areas under grant schemes, areas for which grants are paid, for new planting and restocking, and management. Previous volumes (up to 1995-96) also included statistics now given in Forest Enterprise Annual Report & Accounts and cover land use, areas thinned and felled, sales and acquisitions, and recreation facilities.

Frequency: Annually
Price: £13.50
ISBN: 0-10-254398-4

Available from
TSO Publications Centre and Bookshops
Please see Annex B for full address details.

Sources from which data for this product are obtained
Management Grant Areas; Woodland Grant Scheme Database

Forestry Commission Facts and Figures
Forestry Commission Leaflet of general forestry statistics.

The leaflet contains statistics on area of woodland, Forestry Commission land use, planting receiving grant aid, new planting, restocking, management grant area, wood production, deliveries of British-grown timber, UK imports & exports of wood products, forestry employment, Forest Enterprise recreational facilities, international comparisons of land use.

Frequency: Annually
Price: Free

Available from
Alister Henderson
Forestry Commission
Please see Annex B for full address details.

Sources from which data for this product are obtained
Forest Enterprise Holidays Facilities Inventory; Forest Enterprise Planting; Forest Enterprise Recreation Facilities Inventory; Forest Enterprise Sub-Compartment Database; Forest Enterprise Timber Harvesting and Sales; Forestry Employment; HGTAC-SSD Enquiries (Pulp, Wood-based Panels etc); Management Grant Areas; Overseas Trade Statistics - Wood Products; Planting & restocking of woodland; Private Sector Softwood Removals Survey; Timber Production; Wood Product Imports & Exports WRME; Woodland areas; Woodland Grant Scheme Database

Forestry Commission Information Notes
Forest Research

A series of leaflets on various research topics. Most contain research findings, from work by Forest Research, including results of tree health surveys. Some have reported results from socio-economic research (e.g. recreation surveys) and timber prices.

Frequency: Ad-hoc
Price: Occasional, single copies free, subscriptions prices vary for all issues

Available from
Forestry Commission
Please see Annex B for full address details.

Sources from which data for this product are obtained
Standing Sales Price Index; Timber Price-Size Curves

Forestry Industry Yearbook
Forestry Industry Council

A compendium of forestry statistics and other information about forestry and wood processing industries. Compiled by Forestry Industry Council, with most statistics provided by Forestry Commission. The yearbook contains statistics on the growing sector, supply and demand, wood processing sector, forestry employment, recreation and international trade.

Frequency: Annual to 1996, then biennial
Price: Free to 1996, then £6.00.

Available from
Alister Henderson
Forestry Commission
Please see Annex B for full address details.

Sources from which data for this product are obtained
Forest Enterprise Holidays Facilities Inventory; Forest Enterprise Planting; Forest Enterprise Recreation Facilities Inventory; HGTAC-SSD Enquiries (Pulp, Wood-based Panels etc); Overseas Trade Statistics - Wood Products; Planting & restocking of woodland; Timber Production; UK Day Visits Survey; Wood Product Imports & Exports WRME; Woodland areas

National Inventory of Woodland & Trees
Forestry Commission

A series of regional reports for Scotland, with county reports for England and Wales to follow 1999-2001, for woodlands of 2 hectares and over. Also summary report for Scotland, and reports on surveys of small woods and trees (to follow). The reports give results for National Inventory of Woodland & Trees, covering GB in a rolling programme 1993-2000.

Frequency: Ad-hoc
Price: £5.00 for each region/county report
ISBN: Various

Available from
Forestry Commission
Please see Annex B for full address details.

Sources from which data for this product are obtained
National Inventory of Woodland - Digital Maps; National Inventory of Woodland - Sample Data

Private Woodlands Survey
Forestry Commission

FC Technical Paper 5, published 1994 gives results of survey of costs of forest operations in GB 1989-92.

Frequency: Ad-hoc
Price: £5.00
ISBN: 0 85538 319 4

Available from
Forestry Commission
Please see Annex B for full address details.

Sources from which data for this product are obtained
Private Woodlands Survey

Public Opinion of Forestry 1997
Forestry Commission

Report giving results of Public Opinion of Forestry 1997 Survey, and comparisons with previous surveys carried out in 1995 and 1993. The report covers: awareness of woodlands in media; general impression of forest management; perceptions of amount of woodland and desire for new woodland; impact of labelling of wood products; awareness of Forestry Commission and other organisations; visits to woodland; desired improvements to woodland recreation; and views on types of woodlands to visit.

Frequency: Biennial
Price: £2.00

Available from
Alister Henderson
Forestry Commission
Please see Annex B for full address details.

Sources from which data for this product are obtained
Public Opinion of Forestry Survey

Revised Forecasts of the Supply & Demand for Wood in the UK
Forestry Commission

FC Technical Paper 19, published 1996. Gives forecasts of UK wood supply and demand to 2050.

Frequency: Ad-hoc
Price: Free?
ISBN: 0 85538 346 1

Available from
Forestry Commission
Please see Annex B for full address details.

Sawmill Survey 1996
Forestry Commission

Report on the triennial sawmill survey of sawmilling activity in 1996, carried out in early 1997. The report covers: GB sawmills, by size category: number of mills, capacity, consumption & production of softwood & hardwood, uses of residues, additional facilities of mills, employment, and survey methodology.

Frequency: Every 3 years 1987-1996, then biennial
Price: £2.00

Available from
Alister Henderson
Forestry Commission
Please see Annex B for full address details.

Sources from which data for this product are obtained
Sawmill Survey - Annual; Sawmill Survey - Triennial

Valuing Informal Recreation on the Forestry Commission Estate
Forestry Commission

Bulletin describing methods and results of estimation of the value of the public benefit from informal recreation in Forestry Commission woodlands, using visitor surveys. The report contains data on techniques that can be used to estimate the value derived from visits, reports the results of recent research and summarises the information available on the number of visitors to woodland.

Frequency: Ad-hoc
Price: £7.50
ISBN: 011 710308 X

Available from
Forestry Commission
Please see Annex B for full address details

or

TSO Publications Centre and Bookshops
Please see Annex B for full address details.

Wood Supply & Demand
Forestry Commission

Estimates of wood production and consumption by wood processing industries, for the latest calendar and previous 10 years. Based on surveys of sawmills and fencing manufacturers and other enquiries for wood processing industries.

Frequency: Annually
Price: £2.00

Available from
Alister Henderson
Forestry Commission

Please see Annex B for full address details

Sources from which data for this product are obtained
Private Sector Softwood Removals Survey; Round Fencing Manufacturers Survey; Sawmill Survey - Annual

See also:
In this chapter:
Eurofarm Tabular Databank System *(14.34)*
Farm Structure: Main Results *(14.34)*
Forest Employment Survey 1993-94 *(14.28)*

In other chapters:
Forest Enterprise Visitor Survey Reports *(see the Transport, Travel and Tourism chapter)*
Forest Visitor Surveys *(Annual Summary Reports) (see the Transport, Travel and Tourism chapter)*
Indicators of Sustainable Development - United Kingdom *(see the Environment chapter)*

14.27 Horticulture (incl. Potatoes, Hops & Wine)

Basic Horticultural Statistics
Ministry of Agriculture, Fisheries and Food

Historic data on the UK horticultural industry over the most recent ten years, both on a calendar and crop-year basis, together with a narrative resume of the previous growing season. The publication contains data on production, area, yield, value of output marketed, average farm-gate price, value per hectare, tonnages and value of imports and exports, and intervention data. Tables on non-edibles relate to area, farm-gate value and value of imports and exports. Information on the production and trade of potatoes and hops is also included.

Delivery: Periodic Release
Frequency: Annually
Price: Free

Available from
Christine Jeanette
MAFF
Foss House
Kings Pool
1-2 Peasholme Green
York, YO1 7PX
Tel: 01904 455069

Sources from which data for this product are obtained
Cider Survey- England and Wales; Fruit and Vegetables Crops - England and Wales

Cider Survey (Press Notice)
Ministry of Agriculture, Fisheries and Food

Survey of home grown apples and pears used in Cider and Perry production. The Survey provides results of the current year Survey together with those for the 1994 to date Surveys. The largest cider and perry producers were contacted for the Cider and Perry Survey and all supplied details of tonnages and prices.

Delivery: Periodic Release
Frequency: Annually
Price: Free.

Glasshouse Crops Survey (Statistics Notice)
Ministry of Agriculture, Fisheries and Food

The results of the survey are published in April or May each year and contains information on the area and production of crops grown in glasshouses. The survey covers holdings with 1000 square metres or more of glasshouse or glasshouse substitute. The results cover holdings that are registered with the Ministry.

Delivery: Periodic Release
Frequency: Annually
Price: Free

Available from
MAFF Website (see the Websites and Electronic Services chapter), MAFF Faxback Service or Publications Unit (MAFF)
Please see Annex B for full address details.

Sources from which data for this product are obtained
Glasshouse Crops Survey - England and Wales

Mushroom Survey (Press Notice)
Ministry of Agriculture, Fisheries and Food

Results of the annual survey of mushroom growers. The report contains data on the production and sale of mushrooms.

Delivery: News/Press Release
Frequency: Annually
Price: Free

Available from
Christine Jeanette
MAFF
Foss House
Kings Pool
1-2 Peasholme Green
York, YO1 7PX
Tel: 01904 455069

Northern Ireland Orchard Fruit Survey 1997

Department of Agriculture - Northern Ireland

This survey was conducted in October and November 1997 when questionnaires were sent to all growers with over one hectare of land devoted to orchard fruit. The information produced is sent to Eurostat for incorporation in EU wide orchard fruit statistics and is also used by DANI fruit advisors to provide information on production and yield of fruit trees.

Delivery: News/Press Release
Frequency: Every 5 years
Price: Free

Available from
Sheila Magee
Room 811A
Department of Agriculture - Northern Ireland
Dundonald House
Upper Newtownards Road
Belfast BT4 3SB
Tel: 028 9052 4427;
Email: sheila.magee@dani.gov.uk

Orchard Fruit Survey (Statistics Notice)
Ministry of Agriculture, Fisheries and Food

Contains information on the tree area of commercial orchards in England and Wales by variety. The survey is carried out every year in June and covers holdings with a significant area of commercial orchard. In years ending in a '2' of '7', information on the age and density of commercial orchards is also collected and published. 3 years results are shown.

Delivery: Periodic Release
Frequency: Annually
Price: Free

Available from
MAFF Website (see the Websites and Electronic Services chapter), MAFF Faxback Service or Publications Unit (MAFF)
Please see Annex B for full address details.

Sources from which data for this product are obtained
Orchard Fruit Survey - England and Wales

Vegetables and Flowers Survey (Statistics Notice)
Ministry of Agriculture, Fisheries and Food

The survey is carried out in January each year and the results, published in April or May contain information on areas cultivated for specific vegetables for human consumption and selected bulbs and flowers grown in the open. Information on crops grown under glass is instead collected and published from the Glasshouse Crops Survey.

Delivery: Periodic Release
Frequency: Annually
Price: No charge

Available from
MAFF Website (see the Websites and Electronic Services chapter), MAFF Faxback Service or Publications Unit (MAFF)
Please see Annex B for full address details.

Sources from which data for this product are obtained
Vegetables and Flowers Survey - England and Wales

See also:
In this chapter:
Agricultural and Horticultural Census: 1 June, Final Results for Wales *(14.18)*
Agricultural and Horticultural Census: 1 June, provisional Results for Wales *(14.18)*
Agricultural and Horticulture Census, Scotland - June Provisional Results (Press Release) *(14.18)*
Agricultural Census Summary Sheets by Geographic Area *(14.18)*
Agricultural Sample Census - December (Press Release) *(14.18)*
Agriculture in the United Kingdom *(14.18)*
Economic Report on Scottish Agriculture *(14.22)*
Eurofarm Tabular Databank System *(14.34)*
Farming Fact and Figures, Wales *(14.18)*
Farm Structure: Main Results *(14.34)*
Final Results of June Agricultural Census (Press Release) *(14.18)*
Frequency Distribution Tables *(14.34)*
June Agricultural and Horticultural Census (Statistical Notice) *(14.18)*
Ministry of Agriculture, Fisheries and Food Faxback Service *(14.18)*
Survey of Agriculture: 1 December, Results for Wales *(14.18)*
Welsh Agricultural Statistics *(14.18)*

14.28 Human Resources and Management

Earnings and Hours of Agricultural and Horticultural Workers (Statistical Notice)
Ministry of Agriculture, Fisheries and Food

Results of the annual survey of agricultural and horticultural workers. The statistical notice contains data on earnings and hours, by different types of workers. Prior to 1998 a more detailed statistical notice was produced, with results from the monthly survey.

Delivery: Periodic Release
Frequency: Annual
Price: Free

Available from
MAFF Publications Section
Room 133a

Products

Ministry of Agriculture, Fisheries and Food
Foss House
Kings Pool
1-2 Peasholme Green
York YO1 7PX
Tel: 01904 455332/455329

Sources from which data for this product are obtained
Survey of Earnings and Hours of Agricultural and Horticultural Workers

Earnings and Hours of Agricultural & Horticultural Workers Survey (Statistics Notice)
Ministry of Agriculture, Fisheries and Food

Up to 1998 this sample survey was conducted monthly and contains estimates of the average weekly earnings and hours of hired workers by type of occupation within agriculture and horticulture. From 1998 the survey has been run annually in the Autumn and results will be available in December.

Delivery: Periodic Release
Frequency: Quarterly
Price: Free

Available from
MAFF Website (see the Websites and Electronic Services chapter)

Sources from which data for this product are obtained
Survey of Earnings and Hours of Agricultural and Horticultural Workers

EU Structure Survey 1997 Northern Ireland Agricultural Labour Force Statistics
Department of Agriculture - Northern Ireland

Statistics on agricultural employment are collected each year in the June agricultural census. However, EU legislation requires the collection of more detailed information, on a comparable basis throughout the European Union, every two or three years. This report contains comparisons with the results of the 1993 and 1995 surveys in Northern Ireland.

Frequency: Every 2 years
Price: £4.00
ISBN: 1-85527-349-7

Available from
Department of Agriculture for Northern Ireland
Economics and Statistics Division
Room 817
Dundonald House
Upper Newtownards Road
Belfast, BT4 3SB
Tel. 028 9052 4594

Forest Employment Survey 1993-94
Forestry Commission

Full description and results of the 1993-94 Forest Employment Survey. It contains detailed analysis of employment in the forestry sector by activity, type of employer and travelling distances.

Delivery: Other
Frequency: Ad-hoc
Price: £2.00

Available from
Alister Henderson
Forestry Commission
Please see Annex B for full address details.

Sources from which data for this product are obtained
Forest Employment Survey

See also:
In this chapter:
Agricultural and Horticultural Census: 1 June, Final Results for Wales *(14.18)*
Agricultural Census Summary Sheets by Geographic Area: June 1998 *(14.18)*
Agricultural Sample Census - December (Press Release) *(14.18)*
Agriculture Facts and Figures *(14.18)*
Agriculture in the United Kingdom *(14.18)*
(The) Digest of Agricultural Census Statistics UK *(14.18)*
Economic Report on Scottish Agriculture *(14.22)*
Eurofarm Tabular Databank System *(14.34)*
Farming Fact and Figures, Wales *(14.18)*
Farm Structure: Main Results *(14.34)*
Final Results of June Agricultural Census (Press Release) *(14.18)*
June Agricultural and Horticultural Census (Statistical Notice) *(14.18)*
Region and County Tables *(14.18)*
Welsh Agricultural Statistics *(14.18)*

14.29 Land Prices, Land Use, Rents and Tenures

Agricultural Land Prices in England (Statistical Release)
Ministry of Agriculture, Fisheries and Food

Statistics on agricultural land transactions from the Inland Revenue land price series. The release contains quarterly, six-monthly and annual land price data by type of property, by tenure, by region and by area size group.

Data are available via the internet: www.maff.gov.uk and faxback: 0908 711 0340

Delivery: News / Press Release
Frequency: Quarterly, six monthly and annually

Available from
Nicole Cadwallader
MAFF
Whitehall Place (West Block)
London, SW1A 2HH
Tel: 020 7270 8542

Sources from which data for this product are obtained
Agricultural Land Prices - England and Wales; Inland Revenue Tax Receipts

Analysis of Holdings
Ministry of Agriculture, Fisheries and Food

This shows the distribution of holdings across size groups and their area. Separate tables are produced for total area, crops and grass and tenure. Results are presented at national, regional and county level.

Delivery: Periodic Release
Frequency: Annually
Price: Free

Available from
MAFF Publications Section
Ministry of Agriculture, Fisheries and Food
Please see Annex B for full address details.

Sources from which data for this product are obtained
June Agricultural and Horticultural Census - England and Wales

Annual Rent Enquiry
Ministry of Agriculture, Fisheries and Food

"Farm Rents in England - Results of Annual Rent Enquiry" is an annual MAFF statistical notice, released in spring of each year from 1959 to 1995. It presents the results of the Enquiry into Farm Rents commissioned by the Ministry's Economics and Statistics Group and conducted by the Agricultural Development and Advisory Service Executive Agency. The report details average rents in England and provides a breakdown by region, size group, land grade; and gives details of rents for those farms due a rent review. The rents shown are those as at mid-October each year.

Delivery: Periodic Release
Frequency: Annually
Price: This product is no longer available, except on special request

Available from
Economic (Resource Use) Division
Room 524
Ministry of Agriculture, Fisheries and Food
Whitehall Place (West Block)
London SW1A 2HH
Tel: 020 7276 8371

Sources from which data for this product are obtained
Agricultural Rent Enquiry - England and Wales

Annual Survey of Tenanted Land (Statistics Notice)
Ministry of Agriculture, Fisheries and Food

Results of the survey on farm rents. The current notice contains charts and tables showing the average rents recorded in the survey for each farm type, type of agreement and coverage of the agreement. Previous notices also contained more detailed results for each region, size group, length of agreement.

Frequency: Annually
Price: Free

Available from
MAFF Publications Section
Ministry of Agriculture, Fisheries and Food
Please see Annex B for full address details.

Sources from which data for this product are obtained
Annual Survey of Tenanted Land

Annual Survey of Tenanted Land, Wales
Results of the Annual Survey of Tenanted Land for Wales including average rents for different types of tenancy agreements.

Delivery: Statistical Release
Frequency: Annually

Available from:
Agricultural Statistics
National Assembly for Wales
Please see Annex B for full address details.

Sources from which data for this product are obtained
Annual Survey of Tenanted Land - England and Wales

Prices of Agricultural Land in England
Ministry of Agriculture, Fisheries and Food

MAFF statistical notice, consisting of one annual plus four quarterly notices. A report on sales of agricultural land in England during the period. The information is derived by the Board of Inland Revenue from returns to its Valuation Offices. Average land prices are of interest to the industry and to government, as values of agricultural capital assets. They can be used as one of a range of indicators of the current state of British Agriculture. The annual publication is released in early summer relating to land sold for the year up to

September in the previous year. The detailed tables give this by region, grouped by tenure; land with or without buildings; and into size bands. It also gives sales by type of vendor and type of purchaser, by region; also by grade and tenure.

Delivery: Periodic Release
Frequency: Quarterly
Price: Current price is £25.00 per annual subscription: covers for 4 quarterly publications plus one annual publication.

Available from
Dr John Walsh
Room 502
Ministry of Agriculture, Fisheries and Food
Whitehall Place (West Block)
London
SW1A 2HH
Tel: 020 7270 8795;
Email: j.walsh@esg.maff.gov.uk

Sources from which data for this product are obtained
Agricultural Land Prices - England and Wales; Prices of Agricultural Land in England

Prices of Agricultural Land in Wales
Latest statistical information on sales of agricultural land and buildings in Wales.

Delivery: Statistical Release
Frequency: Quarterly

Available from:
Agricultural Statistics
Statistical Directorate 6
National Assembly for Wales
Cathays Park,
Cardiff CF10 3NQ
Tel: 029 2082 5052;
Fax: 029 2082 5350;
E-mail: stats.pubs@wales.gsi.gov.uk

See also:
In this chapter:
Agriculture in the United Kingdom *(14.18)*
Economic Report on Scottish Agriculture *(14.22)*
Eurofarm Tabular Databank System *(14.34)*
Farming Fact and Figures, Wales *(14.18)*
Farm Structure: Main Results *(14.34)*
Welsh Agricultural Statistics *(14.18)*

In other chapters:
Economic Trends *(see the Economy chapter)*

14.30 Livestock and Meat (incl. Poultry)

April & August Pigs Surveys (Statistics Notices)
Ministry of Agriculture, Fisheries and Food

These surveys are carried out in accordance with the relevant legislation of the European Community and are based on a sample of those holdings which were keeping pigs at the previous June Census. Results show numbers of pigs analysed over various categories and are published in a Statistical Notice showing England and Wales together and the UK separately. Regional results are not available.

Delivery: Periodic Release
Frequency: Bi-annually
Price: Free

Available from
MAFF Website (see the Websites and Electronic Services chapter), MAFF Faxback Service or Publications Unit (MAFF)
Please see Annex B for full address details.

Farmed Deer Survey (Statistical Notice)
Ministry of Agriculture, Fisheries and Food

Contains information on deer numbers along with movement or deer through the year. The results are based on a survey of all holdings which were recorded as having deer at the time of the last June Census. The results are published in a Statistical Notice for England and its regions and for Wales.

Delivery: Periodic Release
Frequency: Annually
Price: Free

Available from
MAFF Website (see the Websites and Electronic Services chapter), MAFF Faxback Service or Publications Unit (MAFF)
Please see Annex B for full address details.

Sources from which data for this product are obtained
Farmed Deer Survey - England and Wales

Pig Financial Results Bulletin - Northern Ireland
Department of Agriculture - Northern Ireland

Latest statistics on feed costs and return on pig production in Northern Ireland.

Contains data on finished and weaned pig prices and feed costs per pig.

Delivery: Periodic Release
Frequency: Monthly, within 2 weeks of period
Price: £17.50 (annual subscription) for monthly publication

Available from
Norman Fulton
Room 817
Department of Agriculture - Northern Ireland

Dundonald House
Upper Newtownards Road
Belfast BT4 3SB
Tel: 028 9052 44067;
Email: norman.fulton@dani.gov.uk

Sources from which data for this product are obtained
Pig Production - Northern Ireland

Pig Statistics (Statistical Notice)
Ministry of Agriculture, Fisheries and Food

This publication brings together the following sources of statistics relating to pigs: slaughter figures (UK and EU); carcase weights (UK); pigmeat production; trade and supplies (UK); prices (UK and EU); pig populations (UK).

Delivery: Statistics Notice
Frequency: Quarterly
Price: MAFF website - free (www.maff.gov.uk)
Faxback - premium rate telephone call (0906-711-0356)

Available from
Lindsey Clothier
Ministry of Agriculture, Fisheries and Food
Commodities and Food Division; Branch D
Tel: 00 44 (0) 1904 455090;
Email: l.j.clothier@esg.maff.gov.uk

Sources from which data for this product are obtained
Bacon and Ham Produced - GB
England and Wales Slaughterhouse Survey
Stocks of Human and Pet Food in Public Cold Stores - UK
June Census
December Census

Pigs Survey - March (Statistics Notice)
Ministry of Agriculture, Fisheries and Food

Contains estimates of pig numbers in the United Kingdom. These have been derived from the March 1999 pig surveys. These were run as additional surveys by the UK agricultural departments in response to requests from organisations representing pig producers.

Delivery: Statistics Notice
Frequency: One-off
Price: Free

Available from
MAFF Website (see the Websites and Electronic Services chapter) or Publications Unit (MAFF)
Please see Annex B for full address details.

Sources from which data for this product are obtained
March 1999 Pig Surveys

Poultry and Poultrymeat Statistics Notice
Ministry of Agriculture, Fisheries and Food

A monthly publication combining the hatcheries (egg survey and poultry slaughterhouse survey) results together with other MAFF statistics, trade data, and EU data.

Delivery: Periodic Release
Frequency: Monthly
Price: Free

Available from
Christine Jeanette
MAFF
Foss House
Kings Pool
1-2 Peasholme Green
York, YO1 7PX
Tel: 01904 455069

Sources from which data for this product are obtained
Poultry Slaughterhouse Survey- England and Wales; Production and Marketing of Hatching Eggs and Chicks - England and Wales

Quarterly Supplies and Total for Domestic Usage of Meat in the UK (Statistical Notice)
Ministry of Agriculture, Fisheries and Food

Supplies and domestic usage of meat in the United Kingdom. The notice contains six balance sheets (all carcase meat, beef and veal, mutton and lamb, pork, bacon and ham, and poultry meat) which provide data on home fed production, overseas trade, stocks and domestic usage.

Delivery: Statistics Notice
Frequency: Quarterly
Price: Maff Website - free (www.maff.gov.uk)
Faxback - premium rate telephone call:
0906-711-0352 all tables;
0906-711-0353 beef and sheep;
0906-711-0354 pork and bacon and ham
0906-711-0355 total carcase meat and poultry

Available from
Alan Walker
Ministry of Agriculture, Fisheries and Food
Please see Annex B for full address details

Sources from which data for this product are obtained
Stocks of Human and Pet Food in Public Cold Stores - UK
England and Wales Slaughterhouse Survey
Bacon and ham produced - GB

Stocks in Public Cold Stores (Statistical Notice)
Ministry of Agriculture, Fisheries and Food

Stocks of selected commodities in public cold stores in the United Kingdom. The notice contains data showing estimates of stocks of selected dairy products, meat and meat products, fish and fish products, poultry, game, soft fruit, vegetables and other food products in public cold stores in the United Kingdom.

Delivery: Statistics Notice
Frequency: Monthly
Price: MAFF Website - free (www.maff.gov.uk)
Faxback - premium rate telephone call (0906 711 0393)

Available from
Alan Walker
Ministry of Agriculture, Fisheries and Food
Please see Annex B for full address details.

Sources from which data for this product are obtained
Stocks of Human and Pet Food in Public Cold Stores - UK

Summary of Returns Made by Bacon Factories in Great Britain (Statistical Notice)
Ministry of Agriculture, Fisheries and Food

Summary of returns made by bacon factories in Great Britain. The notice contains data for the current year and previous three years on the quantity of bacon and ham produced and the amount produced from imported pigmeat.

Delivery: Statistics Notice
Frequency: Monthly
Price: MAFF Website - free (www.maff.gov.uk)
Faxback- premium rate telephone call (0906 711 0351)

Available from
Alan Walker
Ministry of Agriculture, Fisheries and Food
Please see Annex B for full address details.

Sources from which data for this product are obtained
Bacon and Ham Produced - GB

Turkey Census (Statistics Notice)
Ministry of Agriculture, Fisheries and Food

Contains information on turkey numbers. The turkey census is run irregularly - the last one was in 1994. The results are based on data provided on a voluntary basis by occupiers of agricultural holdings in England and Wales; estimates were made for those not responding, but believed to be rearing turkeys on census day. Minor holdings are excluded.

Delivery: Periodic Release
Frequency: Irregular
Price: Free

Available from
Publications Unit (MAFF)
Please see Annex B for full address details.

United Kingdom Slaughter Statistics (Statistical Notice)
Ministry of Agriculture, Fisheries and Food

Weekly and monthly estimates of the numbers of cattle, sheep and pigs slaughtered for meat in the United Kingdom.

Delivery: Statistics Notice
Frequency: Weekly
Price: MAFF Website - free (www.maff.gov.uk)
Faxback - premium rate telephone call (0906 711 0360)

Available from
Alan Walker
Ministry of Agriculture, Fisheries and Food
Please see Annex B for full address details

Sources from which data for this product are obtained
England and Wales Slaughterhouse Survey

See also:
In this chapter:
Agricultural and Horticultural Census: 1 June, Final Results for Wales *(14.18)*
Agricultural and Horticultural Census: 1 June, provisional Results for Wales *(14.18)*
Agricultural and Horticulture Census, Scotland - June Provisional Results (Press Release) *(14.28)*
Agricultural Census Summary Sheets by Geographic Area *(14.18)*
Agricultural Sample Census - December (Press Release) *(14.18)*
Agriculture Facts and Figures *(14.18)*
Agriculture in the United Kingdom *(14.18)*
December Agriculture Survey (Statistics Notice) *(14.18)*
(The) Digest of Agricultural Census Statistics UK *(14.18)*
Economic Report on Scottish Agriculture *(14.22)*
Eurofarm Tabular Databank System *(14.34)*
Farming Fact and Figures, Wales *(14.18)*
Farm Structure: Main Results *(14.34)*
Final Results of June Agricultural Census (Press Release) *(14.18)*
Frequency Distribution Tables *(14.34)*
June Agricultural and Horticultural Census (Statistical Notice) *(14.18)*
Ministry of Agriculture, Fisheries and Food Faxback Service *(14.18)*
Region and County Tables *(14.18)*
Results of Censuses of Agriculture for Minor Holdings in Scotland, 1987-1996 *(14.18)*
Results of the Survey into the Composition

of Main Livestock Rations as Used in Great Britain During the Six-Month Period January to June/July to December (Press Notice) (Suspended) *(14.19)*
Survey of Agriculture: 1 December, Results for Wales *(14.18)*
Welsh Agricultural Statistics *(14.18)*

14.31 Milk and Milk Products

(The) Production of Processed Milk in the UK (Statistical Notice)
Ministry of Agriculture, Fisheries and Food

Results of the survey into the production and stocks of condensed milk and milk powders.

Delivery: Statistics Notice
Frequency: Quarterly
Price: MAFF Website - free (www.maff.gov.uk)
Faxback - premium rate telephone call (0906 711 0363)

Available from
Alison Bromley
Room 239
Ministry of Agriculture, Fisheries and Food
Foss House
Kings Pool
1-2 Peasholme Green
York YO1 7PX
Tel: 00 44 (0)1904 455092;
Email: a.c.bromley@esg.maff.gov.uk

Sources from which data for this product are obtained
Production and Stocks of Condensed Milk and Milk Powders - UK

United Kingdom Milk Prices (Statistical Notice)
Ministry of Agriculture, Fisheries and Food

Monthly data on farm gate milk prices with and without bonus payments.

Delivery: Statistics Notice
Frequency: Monthly
Price: MAFF Website - free (www.maff.gov.uk)
Faxback - premium rate telephone call (0906 711 0364)

Available from
Alison Bromley
Room 239
Ministry of Agriculture, Fisheries and Food
Foss House
Kings Pool
1-2 Peasholme Green
York YO1 7PX

Tel: 00 44 (0)1904 455092;
Email: a.c.bromley@esg.maff.gov.uk

Sources from which data for this product are obtained
Value of Milk Purchased - England and Wales

Utilisation of Milk by Dairies in England and Wales (Statistical Notice)
Ministry of Agriculture, Fisheries and Food

Availability and usage of milk by dairies. The notice contains data on intake, separation, liquid milk, butter, cheese, cream, condensed/evaporated milk, yoghurt, other dairy products, milk powders, sub-sales to other organisations, stock change and wastage, and total disposals.

Delivery: Statistics Notice
Frequency: Monthly
Price: MAFF Website - free (www.maff.gov.uk)
Faxback - premium rate telephone call (0906 711 0366)

Available from
Alison Bromley
Room 239
Ministry of Agriculture, Fisheries and Food
Foss House
Kings Pool
1-2 Peasholme Green
York YO1 7PX
Tel: 00 44 (0)1904 455092;
Email: a.c.bromley@esg.maff.gov.uk

Sources from which data for this product are obtained
Utilisation of Milk by Dairies - England and Wales

Utilisation of Raw Milk
Department of Agriculture - Northern Ireland

Departmental bulletin on the usage of raw milk in Northern Ireland. The publication contains data on the intake of raw milk from Northern Ireland and elsewhere and traces its utilisation for liquid milk, manufactured milk products and direct exports.

Delivery: First Release
Frequency: Monthly and annual
Price: £27.00 (annual subscription) for monthly and annual publications
£9.50 (annual subscription) for annual bulletin only

Available from
Norman Fulton
Department of Agriculture - Northern Ireland
Dundonald House
Upper Newtownards Road
Belfast, BT4 3SB
Tel: 028 9052 4419

Sources from which data for this product are obtained
Raw Milk Utilisation - Northern Ireland

See also:
In this chapter:
Agriculture Facts and Figures *(14.18)*
Agriculture in the United Kingdom *(14.18)*

14.32 Prices (including Price Indices)

Agricultural Market Report
Ministry of Agriculture, Fisheries and Food

The Agricultural Market Report is produced in two-parts and is available on weekly or monthly subscription. Part I contains information on the prices and quantities of selected cereals, livestock, other agricultural products and feedingstuffs sold during the reference week. Part II contains information on the national average wholesale prices of home grown fruit and vegetables (by class) sold at six major markets in England.

Delivery: Periodic Release
Frequency: Weekly or monthly
Price: Free on the internet. Alternatively, one or both of the reports are available on annual subscription. The reports can be received either every week or every month. To receive one report on a weekly basis the subscription rate is £90.00; for both reports the rate is £120.00. To receive them on a monthly basis the subscription rate is £15.00 per report.

Available from
MAFF Website (see the Websites and Electronic Services chapter)
 or
Jenny Higgins
Room 145
Ministry of Agriculture, Fisheries and Food
Foss House
1-2 Peasholme Green
York YO1 7PX
Tel: 01904 455250;
Email: j.higgins@esg.maff.gov.uk

Agricultural Market Report - Northern Ireland
Department of Agriculture - Northern Ireland

Departmental bulletin of the latest producer prices for a range of agricultural produce. The report contains up-to-date producer price on various categories of livestock, products and crops.

Delivery: Periodic Release
Frequency: Weekly, Quarterly and Annual, within one week of period covered.
Price: £38.00 annual subscription for weekly
£12.50 annual subscription for monthly
£9.50 annual subscription for annual

Available from

Ivan Hunter

Room 817
Department of Agriculture - Northern Ireland
Dundonald House
Upper Newtownards Road
Belfast BT4 3SB
Tel: 028 9052 4675;
Email: ivan.hunter@dani.gov.uk

Sources from which data for this product are obtained
Agricultural Producer Prices - Northern Ireland

Agricultural Price Indices (Statistics Notice)
Ministry of Agriculture, Fisheries and Food

This monthly publication contains indices of the prices received by producers for agricultural products and of the prices paid by producers for inputs used in agricultural production. Both a monthly and annual series are produced. Indices are calculated for a number of individual products/inputs, for groups of products/inputs and for all products/inputs. The data came from a wide range of sources within MAFF, ONS, other public bodies and private sector organisations.

Delivery: Periodic Release
Frequency: Monthly
Price: Free

Available from
Allan Howsam
Room 145
Ministry of Agriculture, Fisheries and Food
Foss House
1-2 Peasholme Green
York YO1 7PX
Tel: 01904 455253;
Email: a.howsam@esg.maff.gov.uk

See also:
In this chapter:
Economic Report on Scottish Agriculture *(14.22)*
Ministry of Agriculture, Fisheries and Food
Faxback Service *(14.18)*

14.33 Resources used in Farming

(The) British Survey of Fertiliser Practice
Ministry of Agriculture, Fisheries and Food

Annual report on fertiliser use on crop farms. Contains information on average application rates of nitrogen, phosphate and potash used for agricultural crops and grassland. Information on applications of sulphur fertiliser products, organic manure and lime is also included. Some information is broken down by month of application and farm type.

Delivery: Hardcopy publication
Frequency: Annual
Price: £32.00
ISBN: 0-11-495885-8

Available from
TSO Publications Centre and Bookshops
Please see Annex B for full address details.
or
For further statistical analyses, contact:
David Heather
Fertiliser Manufacturers' Association
Greenhill House
Thorpe Wood
Peterborough PE3 6GF
Tel: 01733 331303

Sources from which data for this product are obtained
British Survey of Fertiliser Practice

Deliveries of Compounds, Blended and Straight Fertilisers by Northern Ireland Fertiliser Manufactures
Department of Agriculture - Northern Ireland

Departmental bulletin on the deliveries of fertilisers in Northern Ireland. The bulletin contains data on deliveries of compound and straight fertilisers in Northern Ireland by Northern Ireland fertiliser firms.

Frequency: Quarterly and Annual, within 8 weeks of period.
Price: £17.50 (annual subscription) for quarterly and annual bulletin.

Available from
Ivan Hunter
Room 817
Department of Agriculture - Northern Ireland
Dundonald House
Upper Newtownards Road
Belfast
BT4 3SB
Tel: 028 9052 4675;
Email: ivan.hunter@dani.gov.uk

Sources from which data for this product are obtained
Fertilizers - Northern Ireland

Irrigation of Outdoor Crops Survey (Statistics Notice)
Ministry of Agriculture, Fisheries and Food

Contains information on the pattern of water use, the amount of water used, the means of delivery and water storage on farms. The results are based on a sample of holdings which took part in the last survey or reported in the June Census that they have irrigated crops since the last Irrigation Survey. The survey has generally been held every two or three years, but is not only conducted in dry years. Prior to 1995, all surveys covered England and Wales. The 1995 survey was conducted in England only.

Delivery: Statistical Notice
Frequency: Dry years only
Price: Free

Available from
MAFF Website (see the Websites and Electronic Services chapter) or Publications Unit (MAFF)
Please see Annex B for full address details.

Sources from which data for this product are obtained
Irrigation of Outdoor Crops Survey

See also:
In this chapter:
Agriculture in the United Kingdom *(14.18)*
Eurofarm Tabular Databank System *(14.34)*
Farm Structure Methodology of Community Surveys (Eurostat) *(14.34)*
Farm Structure: Main Results *(14.34)*
Grain Fed to Livestock (Statistics Notice) *(14.19)*

In other chapters:
Indicators of Sustainable Development - United Kingdom *(see the Environment chapter)*

14.34 Structure of Agricultural Holdings

Eurofarm Tabular Databank System
Ministry of Agriculture, Fisheries and Food; sponsored by Eurostat

Eurofarm is a database containing data in the form of standard tables from the Farm Structure Survey. Data is available for all EC Member States for all Structure Surveys from 1975 onwards. Access to the database is available at all times and new results are put on as and when they are ready. Standard tables of main results from the Farm Structure Survey. Tables are produced by land use, tenure, livestock, cropping, farm labour, farm machinery and geographical location of holding.

Frequency: On line database

Available from
Michael Rowland
Room 133 B
Ministry of Agriculture, Fisheries and Food
Foss House
Kings Pool
1-2 Peasholme Green
York YO1 7PX
Tel: 01904 455658;
Email: m.rowland@esg.maff.gov.uk

Sources from which data for this product are obtained
EC Farm Structure Survey; Labour Survey - England and Wales

Farm Structure: Main Results
Ministry of Agriculture, Fisheries and Food; sponsored by Eurostat

The main results comprise of standard tables from the Farm Structure Survey. The tables are available for all EU Member States for all Structure Surveys from 1966 onwards. The publication is produced for each Structure Survey, every 2 to 3 years. Tables are produced by land use, tenure, livestock, cropping, farm labour, farm machinery and geographical location of holding.

Delivery: Periodic Release
Frequency: Every 2 to 3 years
Price: ECU 28 (1990)

Available from
Michael Rowland
Room 133 B
Ministry of Agriculture, Fisheries and Food
Foss House
Kings Pool
1-2 Peasholme Green
York YO1 7PX
Tel: 01904 455658;
Email: m.rowland@esg.maff.gov.uk

Sources from which data for this product are obtained
EC Farm Structure Survey; Labour Survey - England and Wales

Farm Structure Methodology of Community Surveys (Eurostat)
Eurostat

Eurostat publication on the methodology of the different Member States contributions to the EC Farm Structure Survey. Contains details of sampling, characteristics collected and organisation of the surveys in the different Member States. Approx 160 pages.

Frequency: Methodologies change approximately every 10 years, publication in line with changes
Price: ECU 40 (1996)

Available from
TSO Publications Centre and Bookshops
Please see Annex B for full address details.

Frequency Distribution Tables
Ministry of Agriculture, Fisheries and Food

These show the distribution of holdings and their areas across item size groups for the main livestock, crop and horticulture items from the June Census. Tables are available

covering England, Wales and regions. Most tables include county data but it is often necessary to amalgamate results, particularly at county level, in order to prevent disclosure of information about individual holdings

Delivery: Periodic Release
Frequency: Annually
Price: Free

Available from
MAFF Website (see the Websites and Electronic Services chapter) or Publications Unit (MAFF)
Please see Annex B for full address details.

Sources from which data for this product are obtained
June Agricultural and Horticultural Census - England & Wales

See also:
In this chapter:
Agriculture in the United Kingdom *(14.18)*
Farm Incomes in the United Kingdom *(14.22)*

Other Products which may be of interest, but are not featured in this book due to lack of details:

Farming Facts and Figures 1997 Fact Card - National Assembly for Wales
Aggregate Bank Advances to Scottish Agriculture (Press Release) - Scottish Executive
Farm Structure 1993 Survey: Analysis of Results (Eurostat) - Ministry of Agriculture, Fisheries and Food
Total Income of Agricultural Households: Progress in 1993, Eurostat (1994) Theme 5 Series C - Office for National Statistics
Fruit & Vegetables Crops England & Wales Monthly Report - Ministry of Agriculture, Fisheries and Food
Farm Rents in Wales - Publication by Welsh Office - Ministry of Agriculture, Fisheries and Food

15 Environment

Statistics covering the **Environment** are collected, administered and disseminated by a number of separate Departments, Agencies and organisations including the **Department of the Environment, Transport and the Regions, the Office for National Statistics, Scottish Executive, the National Assembly for Wales, and the Northern Ireland Department of the Environment**. The available statistics embrace a number of subject areas including: **Air Quality, Designated and Protected Areas, Global Atmosphere, Hazardous Substances, Inland Water Quality and Supply, Marine and Coastal Waters, Land Cover and Land Use, Noise Pollution, Radioactivity, Recovery and Recycling of Materials, Waste,** and **Wildlife.**

The basic data are generated from a number of separate information 'Sources' and the resultant statistics are disseminated through a whole range of statistical 'Analyses' and 'Products', all of which are described in the following chapter. Users looking for a cross-section of UK-wide statistics on the **Environment** may find the following products useful:

>**Digest of Environmental Statistics** (annual publication)
>**Indicators of Sustainable Development - United Kingdom** (biennial publication)

Users interested in a wider range of official statistics including **Environment** statistics may like to refer to the following compendia:

>On-line Databases (See Chapter 1):
>>**StatBase - StatStore**

>Hardcopy Compendia (See Chapter 2):
>>**Annual Abstract of Statistics**
>>**Britain 2000: The Official Yearbook of the United Kingdom**
>>**Regional Trends**
>>**Social Trends**

Users may also find what they need on the various Departmental Websites. These are listed in Chapter 1.

15

Environment - *Sources and Analyses*

15.1 Air Quality

Air Quality Monitoring Network - UK
Department of the Environment, Transport and the Regions

The Department of the Environment, Transport and the Regions (DETR) is responsible for the air quality monitoring survey. Data are collected on the concentrations of ground level ozone, nitrogen oxides (NOx), carbon monoxide (CO), sulphur dioxide (SO2), black smoke, particulates, benzene, lead, trace elements, toxic organic micro pollutants (TOMPS), and hydrocarbons at each site and exceedences against DETR, EC Directive and World Health Organisation (WHO) health criteria are calculated for the latest year for which information is available. Data are collected from monitoring sites located throughout the UK and are available for individual monitoring sites. Continuous automated monitoring gives instantaneous measurements of air pollution concentrations. Non-automated monitoring provides concentration measurements over longer averaging periods, usually daily or monthly. The number of automated monitoring sites is being increased to improve the quality, timeliness and coverage of the information presented.

Status: Ongoing
Collection Method: At monitoring sites in the network
Frequency: Daily, hourly for data on the automated network
Reference Period: Variable, depending on pollutants
Timeliness: Hourly for data on automated network
Earliest Available Data: 1976
National Coverage: United Kingdom
Disaggregation: Monitoring site

Statistician
Dorothy Salathiel
Department of the Environment, Transport and the Regions
Environmental Protection Statistics and Information Management Division; EPSIM 4
Tel: 020 7890 6512;
Email: dorothy_salathiel@detr.gsi.gov.uk

Products that contain data from this source
Air Pollution in the UK (DETR/NETCEN); Digest of Environmental Statistics; National Air Quality Archive: Internet Site; Ozone in the United Kingdom; The UK National Monitoring Network, 1994 (NETCEN); UK Nitrogen Dioxide Survey 1996; UK Smoke and Sulphur Dioxide Monitoring Networks - Summary tables

Environmental Protection - Scotland
SEPA

The Environmental Protection Act 1990 Part I Survey is carried out by the Scottish Executive Agriculture, Environment and Fisheries Department. Data are collected annually on applications for authorisations for 'Part B' industrial processes in Scotland, and are available at Region, district and island council levels.

National Coverage: Scotland

Statistician
John Landrock
Scottish Executive
Tel: 0131 244 0441;
Email: john.landrock@scotland.gov.uk

Products that contain data from this source
Digest of Environmental Protection and Water Statistics to 1994; Environmental Monitoring for Radioactivity in Scotland; Scottish Abstract of Statistics; The New Councils: Statistical Report; the Scottish Environment Statistics

Local Air Pollution Control Statistical Survey
Department of the Environment, Transport and the Regions

The local air pollution control (LAPC) system was established under Part 1 of the Environmental Protection Act 1990. Under this system, operators of certain industrial processes must obtain an authorisation to operate from their local authority. The DETR collects summary data on the administrative life-cycle of LAPC applications for each category of process from all local authorities in England and Wales.

Status: Ongoing
Collection Method: Administrative Records
Frequency: Annually
Reference Period: Year
Earliest Available Data: 1991
National Coverage: England and Wales
Disaggregation: Local Authority District (LAD) / Unitary Authority (Eng)

Statistician
Dorothy Salathiel
Department of the Environment, Transport and the Regions
Environmental Protection Statistics and Information Management Division; EPSIM 4
Tel: 020 7890 6512;
Email: dorothy_salathiel@detr.gsi.gov.uk

Products that contain data from this source
Local Air Pollution Control in England and Wales

National Atmospheric Emissions Inventory - UK
Department of the Environment, Transport and the Regions

The Department of the Environment, Transport and the Regions (DETR) is responsible for the National Atmospheric Emissions Inventory, compiled by the National Environmental Technology Centre (NETCEN). The Inventory covers emissions of sulphur dioxide (SO2), carbon dioxide (CO2), nitrogen oxides (NOx), carbon monoxide (CO), methane (CH4) nitrous oxide (N2O), black smoke, particulates (PM10) volatile organic compounds (VOCs) hydrofluorocarbons, perfluorocarbons and sulphur hexafluoride) hydrogen chloride and heavy metals. The data are published as estimated emissions of each pollutant by UNECE source category, by end user and by type of fuel and also by IPCC source category for greenhouse gases.

Except for emissions of NOx, CO and VOCs from combustion of motor spirit, fuel consumption-related emissions are estimated by applying an appropriate emission factor to statistics on annual fuel consumption. Estimated NOx, CO and VOCs emissions from vehicle exhausts fuelled by motor spirit are usually made using speed-related emission factors and information about road usage and speed distribution in the UK. Data cover the UK and the series are available from 1970 onwards. Data are estimated on an annual basis using other data sources. Inventories are updated annually and any developments in methodology are applied retrospectively to earlier years. Adjustments in methodology are made to accommodate new technical information and to improve international comparability. The published data relate to estimates made to the end of the year before last.

Status: Ongoing
Collection Method: See Summary Description
Frequency: Annually
Reference Period: Year
Timeliness: 15 months after the end of each year
Earliest Available Data: 1970
National Coverage: United Kingdom
Disaggregation: Some urban areas, regional estimates are being developed

Statistician
Dorothy Salathiel
Department of the Environment, Transport and the Regions
Environmental Protection Statistics and Information Management Division; EPSIM 4
Tel: 020 7890 6512;
Email: dorothy_salathiel@detr.gsi.gov.uk

Products that contain data from this source
Digest of Environmental Statistics; National Air Quality Archive: Internet Site; UK Emission of Air Pollutants 1970-1995; UK Greenhouse Gas Emission Inventory 1990-1995 (NETCEN)

15.2 Designated and Protected Areas

Damage to Protected Areas - GB
Department of the Environment, Transport and the Regions

The Department of the Environment compiles data on damage to Sites of Special Scientific Interest (SSSIs) from data collected by the relevant organisations. Data are collected on the number of SSSIs and total area damaged. Data are available by the type of damage, i.e. short-term or long-term, and whether this has resulted in the partial or full loss of the area damaged and the main cause of the damage (agricultural activities, forestry, activities with planning permission, activities by statutory undertakers, recreational activities, miscellaneous activities and insufficient management). Data cover Great Britain and are published annually for the previous financial year.

Frequency: Annual
National Coverage: Great Britain

Statistician
Meg Green
Department of the Environment, Transport and the Regions
Environmental Protection Statistics and Information Management Division; EPSIM 1
Tel: 020 7890 6524;
Email: meg_green@detr.gsi.gov.uk

Products that contain data from this source
Digest of Environmental Statistics; the Scottish Environment Statistics

Designated Protected Areas - UK
Department of the Environment, Transport and the Regions

The Department of the Environment compiles data on designated areas and protected areas. They include the area covered by National Parks, Areas of Outstanding Natural Beauty (AONBs), National Scenic Areas (NSAs) in Scotland and Heritage Coasts. There are also data on the number and area of National Nature Reserves (NNRs), Local Nature Reserves (LNRs), Sites of Special Scientific Interest (SSSIs), Marine Nature Reserves, Special Protection Areas (SPAs), Ramsar Wetland Sites, Environmentally Sensitive Areas (ESAs), Biosphere Reserves and Biogenetic Reserves. Results on designated areas are available by constituent country and by region for England. Data cover the UK with data on National Parks for England and Wales, AONBs for England, Wales and Northern Ireland, NSAs for Scotland, Heritage Coasts for England and Wales, and Preferred Coastal Zones for Scotland.

Frequency: Annual
National Coverage: United Kingdom

Statistician
Meg Green
Department of the Environment, Transport and the Regions
Environmental Protection Statistics and Information Management Division; EPSIM 1
Tel: 020 7890 6524;
Email: meg_green@detr.gsi.gov.uk

Products that contain data from this source
Digest of Environmental Statistics; the Scottish Environment Statistics

15.3 Environment - Cross Media

Environmental Accounts
Office for National Statistics

The Office for National Statistics compiles data for the environmental accounts. These accounts are "satellite" accounts to the main National Accounts. They provide information on the environmental impact of economic activity. The accounts use similar concepts and classifications of industries to those employed in the National Accounts.

The data are derived from a variety of sources, as the accounts present information on the reserves and extraction of oil and gas, the consumption of energy by industrial sectors, emissions of pollutants to the atmosphere, levels of radioactive waste,

revenues from environmental taxes, expenditure on environmental protection and volumes and exports of raw and semi-processed materials. Most data are provided in units of physical measurement (volume or mass), although some are in monetary unit, where this is most relevant or the only available data.

The accounts were first published in May 1998.

Status: Ongoing
Frequency: Periodic
Reference Period: Year
Earliest Available Data: 1987
National Coverage: United Kingdom

Statistician
Rocky Harris
Office for National Statistics
Tel: 020 7533 5196;
Email: rocky.harris@ons.gov.uk

Environmental Expenditure
Department of the Environment, Transport and the Regions

Collection Method: Based on desk research
Frequency: Periodic
Reference Period: Year
Earliest Available Data: 1990
National Coverage: United Kingdom

Statistician
Alan Brown
Department of the Environment, Transport and the Regions
Environmental Protection Statistics and Information Management Division; EPSIM 5
Tel: 020 7890 6513;
Email: alanh_brown@detr.gsi.gov.uk

Products that contain data from this source
A Review of UK Environmental Expenditure (1993)

Environmental Expenditure Surveys - United Kingdom
Department of the Environment, Transport and the Regions

Collection Method: Large-scale (Sample) Survey
Frequency: Periodic
Reference Period: Year
Earliest Available Data: 1994
National Coverage: United Kingdom

Statistician
Alan Brown
Department of the Environment, Transport and the Regions
Environmental Protection Statistics and Information Management Division; EPSIM 5
Tel: 020 7890 6513;
Email: alanh_brown@detr.gsi.gov.uk

Products that contain data from this source
Environmental Protection Expenditure by Industry (1995)

Survey of Public Attitudes to the Environment - England and Wales

Department of the Environment, Transport and the Regions

The Department of the Environment is responsible for a survey on public attitudes to the environment. Data are available on public concern about the environment in general by social class and area. Data are also available for sex, age, the percentage of respondents 'very worried' about each environmental issue comparing past surveys, people's optimism about environmental issues, the allocation of responsibility for environmental issues, how much the British Government and the European Community are doing to protect the environment, the fairest way of finding the money to solve environmental problems, future environmental concerns, knowledge about global warming, knowledge of the major factors contributing to global warming, awareness of individuals' contribution to global warming and personal actions to help the environment. The latest 1996/7 survey is based on a sample of 3,200 adults aged 18 and over from the electoral register in England and Wales. The main fieldwork for the 1996/7 survey was conducted from November 1996 to January 1997. Earlier surveys were conducted in 1986, 89, 93.

Status: Ongoing
Collection Method: Large sample survey
Frequency: Every 3-4 years
Earliest Available Data: 1986
National Coverage: England and Wales

Statistician
John Custance
Department of the Environment, Transport and the Regions
Environmental Protection Statistics and Information Management Division; EPSIM 3
Tel: 020 7890 6514;
Email: john_custance@detr.gsi.gov.uk

Products that contain data from this source
1993 Survey of Attitudes to the Environment; Digest of Environmental Protection and Water Statistics to 1994; Digest of Environmental Statistics

15.4 Global Atmosphere

Please see:
In this chapter:
National Atmospheric Emissions Inventory - UK *(15.1)*

15.5 Hazardous Substances (excluding Radioactivity)

Hazardous Substances Consents Return - England
Department of the Environment, Transport and the Regions

The Hazardous Substances Consents Return (HSC) is collected by the Department of the Environment, Transport and the Regions. The survey is carried out on all hazardous substances authorities (equivalent to local planning authorities) in England. Statistics concern applications for, and decisions on, consent to store hazardous substances. Data are available by individual decision, type and amount of hazardous substance, grid reference of site, speed at which decision was reached, applications for HSC by the authority to the Secretary of State for the Environment, Transport and the Regions enforcement action, and at standard regions, Government Office region, hazardous substances authority, and response group. The number of deemed consents was collected for June to November 1992.

Status: Ongoing
Collection Method: Census
Frequency: Annually
Reference Period: The financial year
Timeliness: 5 months
Earliest Available Data: June 1992
National Coverage: England

Statistician
Guy Ellis
Department of the Environment, Transport and the Regions
Planning and Land Use Statistics; Planning and Development Control Statistics
Tel: 020 7890 5507;
Email: guy-ellis@detr.gsi.gov.uk

Products that contain data from this source
Notes for Completion: Form HSC; Statistics of Applications for Hazardous Substances Consents

15.6 Inland Water Quality and Supply and Marine and Coastal Waters

Bathing Water Quality
Department of the Environment, Transport and the Regions

The Environment Agency, Scottish Environment Protection Agency (SEPA) and the Environment and Heritage Service in Northern Ireland conduct bathing water quality surveys. The Department of the Environment, Transport and the Regions publishes results for the UK. Eleven physical, chemical and microbiological parameters are measured, including total and faecal coliforms, as required under the EC Bathing Water Directive 76/160/EEC. Summary data available include a time series showing the number of identified bathing waters and the number (and percentage) complying with the mandatory coliform standards in the Directive, by region. Information is also available which shows for each bathing water and for each parameter how many of these failed to meet the required mandatory standard. Samples of bathing waters are taken at regular intervals beginning two weeks before, and then during the bathing season, at bathing waters around the UK covered by the directive (496 coastal and 9 inland bathing waters in 1998). The season runs from mid-May to end-September in England and Wales, and from the beginning of June to mid-September in Scotland and Northern Ireland. A minimum of twenty samples are normally taken at each site. Results are published annually.

Status: Ongoing
Collection Method: At identified bathing waters
Frequency: Annually
Reference Period: Summer each year
Timeliness: November in year of collection
Earliest Available Data: 1980
National Coverage: United Kingdom
Disaggregation: Environment Agency Region

Statistician
Dorothy Salathiel
Department of the Environment, Transport and the Regions
Environmental Protection Statistics and Information Management Division; EPSIM 4
Tel: 020 7890 6512;
Email: dorothy_salathiel@detr.gsi.gov.uk

Products that contain data from this source
Bathing Water Quality in England and Wales; Digest of Environmental Statistics; The Environment Agency Website; Scottish Environment Statistics

Contaminant Concentrations in Estuaries and Coastal Waters
Department of the Environment, Transport and the Regions

Status: Ongoing
Collection Method: Sample survey
Frequency: Annually
Reference Period: Year
National Coverage: England and Wales
Disaggregation: Estuaries and Coastal sites around England and Wales

Statistician
Alan Brown
Department of the Environment, Transport and the Regions
Environmental Protection Statistics and Information Management Division; EPSIM 5
Tel: 020 7890 6513;
Email: alanh_brown@detr.gsi.gov.uk

Products that contain data from this source
Digest of Environmental Statistics

Contaminant Inputs to Coastal Waters
Department of the Environment, Transport and the Regions

Collection Method: Direct discharges and estimates based on contaminant concentrations and river flow
Frequency: Annually
Reference Period: Year
Earliest Available Data: 1985
National Coverage: United Kingdom
Disaggregation: Atlantic, North Sea, Channel, Celtic Sea, Irish Sea

Statistician
Alan Brown
Department of the Environment, Transport and the Regions
Environmental Protection Statistics and Information Management Division; EPSIM 5
Tel: 020 7890 6513;
Email: alanh_brown@detr.gsi.gov.uk

Products that contain data from this source
Digest of Environmental Statistics

Drinking Water Quality - England & Wales
Department of the Environment, Transport and the Regions

The Department of the Environment, Transport and the Regions compiles data on drinking water quality. Data are derived from samples of drinking water taken by the Drinking Water Inspectorate. Data are available on the total number of determinations during a calendar year compared with the percentage exceeding the prescribed concentration for a specific parameter, such as coliforms, colour, lead, etc. Regular monitoring of drinking water supplies has been undertaken since the EC Directive on the Quality of Drinking Water came into force, and the Drinking Water Inspectorate has had responsibility since January 1990.

Status: Ongoing
Collection Method: Sampling
Frequency: Annually
Reference Period: Year
Timeliness: 6 months after year end
Earliest Available Data: 1990
National Coverage: England and Wales
Disaggregation: Water company

Statistician
Dorothy Salathiel
Department of the Environment, Transport and the Regions
Environmental Protection Statistics and Information Management Division; EPSIM 4
Tel: 020 7890 6512;
Email: dorothy_salathiel@detr.gsi.gov.uk

Products that contain data from this source
Digest of Environmental Statistics; Drinking Water: A Report by the Chief Inspector, Drinking Water Inspectorate; The Environment Agency Website

Dumping of Waste and Dredgings At Sea
Department of the Environment, Transport and the Regions

Collection Method: Returns from operators
Frequency: Annually
Reference Period: Year
National Coverage: United Kingdom

Statistician
Alan Brown
Department of the Environment, Transport and the Regions
Environmental Protection Statistics and Information Management Division; EPSIM 5
Tel: 020 7890 6513;
Email: alanh_brown@detr.gsi.gov.uk

Products that contain data from this source
Digest of Environmental Statistics

Estuarial Quality
Department of the Environment, Transport and the Regions

Frequency: England and Wales, 5 yearly. Scotland and Northern Ireland, annually.
Reference Period: Year
National Coverage: United Kingdom

Statistician
Alan Brown
Department of the Environment, Transport and the Regions
Environmental Protection Statistics and Information Management Division; EPSIM 5
Tel: 020 7890 6513;
Email: alanh_brown@detr.gsi.gov.uk

Products that contain data from this source
Digest of Environmental Statistics

Freshwater Quality - England and Wales
Department of the Environment, Transport and the Regions

In a series of national surveys, the Environment Agency monitors the chemical quality of rivers, canals and estuaries in England and Wales. In 1990 and 1995, the biological quality of rivers, canals and estuaries was also monitored. The surveys are conducted annually for chemical water quality and quinquennially for biological water quality.

Status: Ongoing
Collection Method: Administrative Records
Frequency: Periodic
Reference Period: Year (3 year average)

Timeliness: September following year end
National Coverage: England and Wales
Disaggregation: River Lengths

Statistician
Dorothy Salathiel
Department of the Environment, Transport and the Regions
Environmental Protection Statistics and Information Management Division; EPSIM 4
Tel: 020 7890 6512;
Email: dorothy_salathiel@detr.gsi.gov.uk

Products that contain data from this source
Digest of Environmental Statistics; Social Trends; The Environment Agency Website; The Quality of Rivers and Canals in England and Wales: 1990 to 1995; The State of the Environment of England and Wales: Fresh Waters

Groundwater Quality - England and Wales
Department of the Environment, Transport and the Regions

The Environment Agency conducts the Groundwater Survey. The Survey monitors the quality of groundwater from boreholes which are used for the abstraction of water for supply to the public and other purposes. Nitrate levels are collected where groundwater sites are known to be experiencing elevated levels of nitrate, and so the results are not representative of all aquifers in England and Wales. Data on pesticides in groundwater have also been collated by the Environment Agency for some of the regions in England and Wales from information supplied by the water companies. The surveys cover England and Wales and nitrate data are presented for named boreholes. The Environment Agency is in the process of establishing a national network of sites to monitor both nitrates and pesticides in groundwater.

Status: Ongoing
Frequency: Annually
Reference Period: Year
Earliest Available Data: 1980 for Nitrates, 1992 for pesticides
National Coverage: England and Wales
Disaggregation: Borehole

Statistician
Dorothy Salathiel
Department of the Environment, Transport and the Regions
Environmental Protection Statistics and Information Management Division; EPSIM 4
Tel: 020 7890 6512;
Email: dorothy_salathiel@detr.gsi.gov.uk

Products that contain data from this source
Digest of Environmental Statistics; The Environment Agency Website

Sources and Analyses

Harmonised Monitoring Scheme - GB
Department of the Environment, Transport and the Regions

The Department of the Environment, Transport and the Regions is responsible for the Harmonised Monitoring Scheme (HMS). The HMS covers about 230 sampling points in Great Britain, mainly sited at the tidal limits of major rivers or at the confluence points of major tributaries. Data are collected for a large range of determinands at river locations including dissolved oxygen, biochemical oxygen demand, ammoniacal nitrogen, nitrates, orthophosphates, the pesticides lindane, dieldrin and aldrin, and the heavy metals zinc, copper, lead, cadmium, nickel, chromium and arsenic. Annual mean concentrations are available for each HMS site together with the annual averages of the site means in each region. In order to give an indication of the range of values at different sites within each region, figures have been published for the maximum and minimum site mean, percentiles, etc. The data cover Great Britain and are available for the Environment Agency regions for England and Wales and SEPA regions for Scotland. Results are published annually with the latest data and summary statistics for previous years.

Status: Ongoing
Frequency: Annually
Reference Period: Year
Timeliness: 9 months after year end
Earliest Available Data: 1975
National Coverage: Great Britain
Disaggregation: Agency Region

Statistician
Dorothy Salathiel
Department of the Environment, Transport and the Regions
Environmental Protection Statistics and Information Management Division; EPSIM 4
Tel: 020 7890 6512;
Email: dorothy_salathiel@detr.gsi.gov.uk

Products that contain data from this source
Digest of Environmental Statistics

Marine Fish Stocks and Catches
Department of the Environment, Transport and the Regions

Status: Ongoing
Frequency: Annually
Reference Period: Year
Earliest Available Data: 1963
Disaggregation: International Council for the Exploration of the Sea (ICES) Regions

Statistician
Alan Brown
Department of the Environment, Transport and the Regions

Environmental Protection Statistics and Information Management Division; EPSIM 5
Tel: 020 7890 6513;
Email: alanh_brown@detr.gsi.gov.uk

Products that contain data from this source
Digest of Environmental Statistics

Marine Water Quality - UK
Department of the Environment, Transport and the Regions

The Department of the Environment, Transport and the Regions compiles data on direct and riverine inputs of contaminants to coastal waters around the UK. The contaminants covered include the metals cadmium, mercury, copper, lead, zinc; the nutrients nitrate, orthophosphate, total nitrogen and total phosphates; the organic compounds lindane and PCBs; and suspended particulate matter. Information is available separately for inputs to the Atlantic, the East Coast, the Channel, the Celtic Sea and the Irish Sea. Data are available for 1985, 1988 and annually from and including 1990. The information is derived from monthly samples taken from all main river systems at points close to but upstream of the tidal limit. All major direct discharges of trade or sewage effluent entering estuaries downstream of the sampling point are also sampled, as are major coastal discharges. Information is also available on oil spills and operational discharges of oil from offshore oil and gas installations, dumping of waste and dredgings at sea, and concentration of contaminants in fish muscle and liver. Results are published annually.

Status: Ongoing
Frequency: Annually (from 1990)
Earliest Available Data: 1985

Statistician
Alan Brown
Department of the Environment, Transport and the Regions
Environmental Protection Statistics and Information Management Division; EPSIM 5
Tel: 020 7890 6513;
Email: alanh_brown@detr.gsi.gov.uk

Products that contain data from this source
Digest of Environmental Statistics

Surveys of Oil Pollution Around the Coasts of the United Kingdom
Department of the Environment, Transport and the Regions

Status: Ongoing
Frequency: Annually
Reference Period: Year
National Coverage: United Kingdom

Statistician
Alan Brown
Department of the Environment, Transport and the Regions
Environmental Protection Statistics and Information Management Division; EPSIM 5
Tel: 020 7890 6513;
Email: alanh_brown@detr.gsi.gov.uk

Products that contain data from this source
Digest of Environmental Statistics

Water Pollution Incidents
Department of the Environment, Transport and the Regions

The Environment Agency collates data on water pollution incidents. Data are available on the number of incidents, and those which have been substantiated since 1990, by type of pollutant for the latest available year. Data are also available on the number of major substantiated water pollution incidents and prosecutions by source, and on substantiated water pollution incidents categorised as major, significant and minor. The data cover all of the UK, except for statistics on major substantiated water pollution incidents and prosecutions, which do not include Northern Ireland, and substantiated water pollution incidents by category, which are for England and Wales only. Water pollution incidents have been reported annually since 1980. Data for Scotland are not available before 1991.

Status: Ongoing
Collection Method: Administrative Records
Frequency: Annually, since 1980
Reference Period: Year
Timeliness: The results are published annually for the year before last.
Earliest Available Data: 1980
National Coverage: United Kingdom
Sub-National: County; Environment Agency region in England and Wales

Statistician
Dorothy Salathiel
Department of the Environment, Transport and the Regions
Environmental Protection Statistics and Information Management Division; EPSIM 4
Tel: 020 7890 6512;
Email: dorothy_salathiel@detr.gsi.gov.uk

Products that contain data from this source
Digest of Environmental Statistics; Social Trends; The Environment Agency Website; Water Pollution Incidents in England and Wales

Water Resources - England and Wales
Department of the Environment, Transport and the Regions

The Environment Agency collects data on water resources for England and Wales. Data are available on the number of abstraction licences in force, new licences determined, and licensed and estimated actual amounts of water abstracted from surface tidal and non-tidal water and groundwater in England and Wales. Data are given by Environment Agency region and by purpose. Estimates of actual abstractions are based on annual returns made by licence holders to the Environment Agency regions and compiled by EA headquarters. Comparable data are not available for Scotland and Northern Ireland. Data are available from 1985, although from 1991 the NRA has made important changes to the format of the survey. Key changes include redefinition of terms, inclusion of new categories, standardisation of methods to take account of non-respondents, and improvements in the allocation of information to appropriate purpose categories.

Status: Ongoing
Frequency: Annually
Reference Period: Year
Earliest Available Data: 1985
National Coverage: England and Wales
Sub-National: Environment Agency region

Statistician
Dorothy Salathiel
Department of the Environment, Transport and the Regions
Environmental Protection Statistics and Information Management Division; EPSIM 4
Tel: 020 7890 6512;
Email: dorothy_salathiel@detr.gsi.gov.uk

Products that contain data from this source
Digest of Environmental Statistics; The Environment Agency Website

Water Resources - Public Water Supply - UK
Department of the Environment, Transport and the Regions

The Office of Water Services (OFWAT) is responsible for public water supply data. Data are available on the amount of water put into the public supply in the UK from 1983. Figures are broken down to show metered and unmetered amounts; unmetered supply includes leakage from the distribution system and miscellaneous uses, such as fire fighting, sewer cleaning, etc. From 1988, figures for metered and unmetered supply are available for each of the water service companies and water supply companies in England and Wales. Since 1990-91, data for England and Wales have been supplied by OFWAT. Although the definitions of metered and unmetered water remain unchanged, the application of these criteria by OFWAT in compiling their data has resulted in more accurate figures.

Status: Ongoing
Reference Period: Year

Earliest Available Data: 1983
National Coverage: England and Wales
Sub-National: Water service and supply companies

Statistician
Dorothy Salathiel
Department of the Environment, Transport and the Regions
Environmental Protection Statistics and Information Management Division; EPSIM 4
Tel: 020 7890 6512;
Email: dorothy_salathiel@detr.gsi.gov.uk

Products that contain data from this source
Digest of Environmental Statistics

Water Resources - Scotland
Scottish Executive

The Water Resources Survey is carried out by the Scottish Executive Environment Department. Information on water resources in Scotland is collated on an annual basis and made available at Scottish water authority level.

Collection Method: Data from Scottish Water Authorities
Frequency: Annually
National Coverage: Scotland
Disaggregation: Water authority

Statistician
John Landrock
Scottish Executive
Tel: 0131 244 0441;
Email: john.landrock@scotland.gov.uk

Products that contain data from this source
Digest of Environmental Statistics; Drinking Water Quality in Scotland; Scottish Abstract of Statistics; the Scottish Environment Statistics; Waterfacts

15.7 Land Cover and Land Use

Countryside Survey - GB
Department of the Environment, Transport and the Regions

The Institute for Terrestrial Ecology and Institute for Freshwater Ecology conducts the Countryside Survey for the Department of the Environment. The Survey was undertaken to record the stock of countryside features, to determine changes and to provide a baseline for comparisons of change. Field surveys and satellite images were used to construct a complete land cover map, to map soil types and to record the length of field boundaries. The Survey also examined the diversity in plant species and freshwater animals through field surveys in 508 separate square kilometres throughout Great Britain. The data cover Great Britain and can be obtained for any area of interest.

Published results are summarised for England, Scotland, and Wales and the four national landscape types: arable, pastoral, marginal upland and upland. The Survey is conducted every six to twelve years over four to six days in each square kilometre. Results are available for 1978, 1984 and 1990, and the sample area has been gradually increasing over the years.

Status: Ongoing
Frequency: Every 5-10 years
Timeliness: Variable according to analyses
Earliest Available Data: 1978
National Coverage: Great Britain
Disaggregation: ITE landcover groups

Statistician
John Custance
Department of the Environment, Transport and the Regions
Environmental Protection Statistics and Information Management Division; EPSIM 3
Tel: 020 7890 6514;
Email: john_custance@detr.gsi.gov.uk

Products that contain data from this source
Comparison of Land Cover Definitions; Countryside Information System; Countryside Survey 1990: Main Report; Digest of Environmental Statistics

Derelict Land - England
Department of the Environment, Transport and the Regions

The Survey of Derelict Land in England (DLS) is the responsibility of the Department of the Environment. The most recent Survey was undertaken by Arups Economics & Planning. Data are available by the type, location and ownership of derelict land, and derelict land reclaimed with its end use, and comparisons between the results of the previous Surveys. They can also be obtained for Government office regions, local authority counties and districts. The Survey is conducted every four to six years. Results are available from 1974 with the most recent Survey results, compiled in March and September 1993, published in two volumes one and two years after the Survey.

Collection Method: Survey
Frequency: Ad hoc
Earliest Available Data: 1974
National Coverage: England

Statistician
Dr Bob Garland
Department of the Environment, Transport and the Regions
Tel: 020 7890 5533

Products that contain data from this source
Digest of Environmental Statistics; The Survey of Derelict Land in England

Floorspace - England and Wales
Department of the Environment, Transport and the Regions

The Department of the Environment (DoE) compiles commercial and industrial floorspace statistics. Floorspace statistics are an annual stock take of commercial and industrial floor area. The data are derived administratively through the Valuation Office Agency's local offices. Data are available for area and number by age, size and type of building. The series covers England and Wales and can be obtained for DoE regions, counties and local authority districts. Floorspace data are collected annually and have been published since 1969. However, no information was published between 1986 and 1994 and information published in 1995 has yet to be updated. There are no plans to do so by the end of 1999.

Status: Ongoing
National Coverage: England and Wales

Statistician
Robert Packham
Department of the Environment, Transport and the Regions
Planning and Land Use Statistics Division
Tel: 020 7890 5764;
Email: stat2_cmi@detr.gov.uk

Products that contain data from this source
Digest of Data for the Construction Industry

Industrial Sites Register - Scotland
Scottish Executive

The Industrial Sites Register is collated by the Scottish Executive Development Department concerning marketable industrial sites and their areas. Data are collected annually for Scotland and are available at council level.

Status: Ongoing
Collection Method: Large-scale (Sample) Survey
Frequency: Annually
Reference Period: Annually on 1st April
Timeliness: Six months (aggregate data only).
Earliest Available Data: 1988
National Coverage: Scotland
Disaggregation: Council

Statistician
John Landrock
Scottish Executive
Tel: 0131 244 0441;
Email: john.landrock@scotland.gov.uk

Products that contain data from this source
Scottish Abstract of Statistics; the Scottish Environment Statistics

Land Use Change - England
Department of the Environment, Transport and the Regions

The Land Use Statistics Division of the Department of the Environment compiles Land Use Change Statistics (LUCS) in England from data recorded by Ordnance Survey. Data are available by land groups including agriculture, forestry, open land and water, minerals and landfill, outdoor recreation, defence (rural uses) and residential, transport and utilities, industry and commerce, community services, vacant land (urban uses). Data are also available for standard regions, Government Offices regions, county and any area defined by grid references. The series began in 1985 covering Great Britain from 1985-92 and England only from 1993. Data are published annually each summer.

Frequency: Annually
Earliest Available Data: 1985
National Coverage: England

Statistician
Dr Bob Garland
Department of the Environment, Transport and the Regions
Tel: 020 7890 5533

Products that contain data from this source
Analysis of Land Use Change Statistics; Digest of Environmental Statistics; Land Use Change in England; Land Use Change Statistics Research Project

Land with Outstanding Planning Permission for Residential Development - England
Department of the Environment, Transport and the Regions

Data on land with outstanding planning permission for residential development are compiled by the Department of the Environment, Transport and the Regions. All district-level local planning authorities (LPAs) in England complete form PS3 with data on the land area for residential development and new dwellings. Data are available since 1987-88 and up until 1995-96 were published annually one year after the reference period. Changes have occurred as a result of changes in data requirement, availability of data from LPAs and survey control quinquennial reviews.

Status: Ongoing
Collection Method: Census
Frequency: Annually
Reference Period: The financial year
Earliest Available Data: 1987-88
National Coverage: England

Statistician
Guy Ellis
Department of the Environment, Transport and

the Regions
Planning and Land Use Statistics; Planning and Development Control Statistics
Tel: 020 7890 5507;
Email: doeplus@gtnet.gov.uk

Products that contain data from this source
Development Control Statistics: England; Housing Land Availability: The Analysis of PS3 Statistics on Land with Outstanding Planning Permission; Monitoring Housing Land Supply: Calibrating Indicators of Constraint; Notes for Completion: Form PS3; Notes for Completion: Forms PS1, PS2, CPS1/2, PS3, Fee1 and Fee2

Mineral Workings Land - England
Department of the Environment, Transport and the Regions

The Survey of Land for Mineral Working is collated on behalf of the Department of the Environment by the mineral planning authorities. Information is based on the area of land within each authority area which is permitted for the extraction of minerals, or for the disposal of wastes derived from mineral extraction. Data are available by mineral type, whether working is in progress or permissions are unimplemented, deep mining, records of land reclaimed, a breakdown of the after-uses of the land, and for mineral planning authorities. The Survey covers England and has been carried out every six years since 1974. Results are published approximately eighteen months after the Survey base date.

Frequency: Every six years
Timeliness: Approximately eighteen months after the survey base date
Earliest Available Data: 1974
National Coverage: England

Statistician
Dr Bob Garland
Department of the Environment, Transport and the Regions
Tel: 020 7890 5533

Products that contain data from this source
Survey of Land for Mineral Working in England 1994

Minerals and Waste Development - Applications and Decisions - England
Department of the Environment, Transport and the Regions

The General Development Control Return CPS1/2 ('county matters') is collected by the Department of the Environment, Transport and the Regions from all county-level planning authorities. The data relate primarily to minerals and waste developments in England. Data are collected on individual decisions, including type, and are available by size of development, enforcement action, grid reference, standard region, Government Office region, local planning authority (LPA), response group, and speed at which the decision was reached by the authority. Data, collected quarterly, are available from April 1989 for county councils and collection was extended to other authorities from April 1992. Some changes have occurred as a result of changes in legislation, availability of data from LPAs and reviews of data requirements. From April 1995 data were also recorded on formal action taken by LPAs against breaches of planning conditions.

Status: Ongoing
Collection Method: Census
Frequency: Quarterly
Reference Period: Quarter
Earliest Available Data: April 1989
National Coverage: England

Statistician
Guy Ellis
Department of the Environment, Transport and the Regions
Planning and Land Use Statistics; Planning and Development Control Statistics
Tel: 020 7890 5507;
Email: guy-ellis@detr.gsi.gov.uk

Products that contain data from this source
Development Control Statistics: England; Notes for Completion: Form CPS1/2; Statistics of 'Country Matters' applications received and decided; Statistics of Planning Applications - England

Planning Application Fees - England
Department of the Environment, Transport and the Regions

The survey of fees received for planning applications is carried out by the Department of the Environment, Transport and the Regions. Local planning authorities in England compile data on the total amount (in £s) received in planning application fees (form Fee1) while 'county matters' authorities compile data on 'county matters' planning application fees (form Fee2). The level of application planning fees is set centrally each year by the Treasury. The survey is compiled quarterly and data are available from January 1991.

Status: Ongoing
Collection Method: Census
Frequency: Quarterly
Reference Period: Quarter
Earliest Available Data: January 1991
National Coverage: England

Statistician
Guy Ellis
Department of the Environment, Transport and the Regions
Planning and Land Use Statistics; Planning and Development Control Statistics

Tel: 020 7890 5507;
Email: guy-ellis@detr.gsi.gov.uk

Products that contain data from this source
Notes for Completion: Forms Fee1 and Fee2

Planning Applications and Decisions - England
Department of the Environment, Transport and the Regions

The General Development Control Returns PS1 and PS2 are compiled from district planning authorities' data by the Department of the Environment, Transport and the Regions. Data on planning applications received and decided are available by size of development, type of development and speed at which decision was reached by the authority. Data are also available on number of departure decisions. delegated decisions, determination applications and formal enforcement action taken by local planning authorities (LPAs) against breaches of planning conditions. Data cover England and are available for standard region, Government Office region, local planning authority, and response groups (developed for DETR use). Results, collated quarterly, have been published from the second quarter of 1979. Changes have occurred as a result of legislation, availability of data from LPAs and reviews of data requirements.

Status: Ongoing
Collection Method: Census
Frequency: Quarterly
Reference Period: Quarter
Earliest Available Data: April 1979
National Coverage: England

Statistician
Guy Ellis
Department of the Environment, Transport and the Regions
Planning and Land Use Statistics; Planning and Development Control Statistics
Tel: 020 7890 5507;
Email: guy-ellis@detr.gsi.gov.uk

Products that contain data from this source
Development Control Statistics: England; Notes for Completion: Forms PS1 and PS2; Notes for Completion: Forms PS1, PS2, CPS1/2, PS3, Fee1 and Fee2; Statistics of Planning Applications - England; Statistics of Planning Enforcement Action by Local Authorities and Appeals Against Enforcement Notices

Urban Areas Analysis
Department of the Environment, Transport and the Regions

Derived from DOE/OPCS Urban areas and Census data. Data analysed geographically by size of urban area, for all England. 1981 and 1991 urban areas were produced by the then DOE in association with the then

OPCS for the purposes of analysing Census data

Status: Ongoing
Frequency: Ad hoc
Reference Period: 1981 and 1991 urban areas
Timeliness: Ad hoc
Earliest Available Data: 1981 urban areas
National Coverage: England

Statistician
Stephen Hall
Department of the Environment, Transport and the Regions
Planning and Land Use Statistics; Census, Demographic, and Town Centre Statistics
Tel: 020 7890 5514;
Email: shall.detr@gtnet.gov.uk

Products that contain data from this analysis
Urban areas analysis

Vacant and Derelict Land - Scotland
Scottish Executive

The Scottish Vacant and Derelict Land Survey is carried out by the Scottish Executive Development Department. Data are available on vacant and derelict land sites in Scotland by area, length of time in this category, contamination, preferred or intended use, and reclamation. Data, collected annually, cover Scotland and can be obtained at regional, district and island council levels.

Collection Method: Large-scale (Sample) Survey
Frequency: Annually
Reference Period: Annually in June
Earliest Available Data: 1990
National Coverage: Scotland
Disaggregation: Local Enterprise Company (LEC) Area (Scotland)

Statistician
John Landrock
Scottish Executive
Tel: 0131 244 0441;
Email: john.landrock@scotland.gov.uk

Products that contain data from this source
Scottish Abstract of Statistics; The New Councils: Statistical Report; the Scottish Environment Statistics

Vacant Land Use - England
Department of the Environment, Transport and the Regions

The National Sample Survey of Vacant Land in Urban Areas of England was carried out by SERRL for the Department of the Environment in March and September 1990. The Survey was based on about 4,000 1:1250 scale maps covering over 10 per cent of urban settlements in England. Estimates of the area of vacant land in urban areas and the percentage of areas covered by vacant land are presented for standard economic regions, former DoE administrative regions, urban programme authorities grouped within region, Inner London, Outer London and broad divisions in the South East and Eastern regions. The results were published in 1992.

National Coverage: England

Statistician
Dr Bob Garland
Department of the Environment, Transport and the Regions
Tel: 020 7890 5533

Products that contain data from this source
Digest of Environmental Statistics; The National Survey of Vacant Land in Urban Areas of England 1990

15.8 Noise Pollution

Complaints About Noise and Action Taken - United Kingdom
Department of the Environment, Transport and the Regions

Collection Method: Census of Local Authorities
Frequency: Annually
Reference Period: Year
National Coverage: Great Britain

Statistician
Alan Brown
Department of the Environment, Transport and the Regions
Environmental Protection Statistics and Information Management Division; EPSIM 5
Tel: 020 7890 6513;
Email: alanh_brown@detr.gsi.gov.uk

Products that contain data from this source
Digest of Environmental Statistics

National Noise Attitude Surveys
Department of the Environment, Transport and the Regions

Collection Method: Large-scale (Sample) Survey
Frequency: Periodic
Earliest Available Data: 1991
National Coverage: Great Britain

Statistician
Alan Brown
Department of the Environment, Transport and the Regions
Environmental Protection Statistics and Information Management Division; EPSIM 5
Tel: 020 7890 6513;
Email: alanh_brown@detr.gsi.gov.uk

Products that contain data from this source
Digest of Environmental Statistics

National Noise Incidence Studies
Department of the Environment, Transport and the Regions

Collection Method: Sample survey
Frequency: Periodic
Reference Period: Year
Earliest Available Data: 1990
National Coverage: England and Wales

Statistician
Alan Brown
Department of the Environment, Transport and the Regions
Environmental Protection Statistics and Information Management Division; EPSIM 5
Tel: 020 7890 6513;
Email: alanh_brown@detr.gsi.gov.uk

Products that contain data from this source
Digest of Environmental Statistics

Noise Pollution - GB
Department of the Environment, Transport and the Regions

The Chartered Institute of Environmental Health Officers (CIEH) and the Royal Environmental Health Institute of Scotland (REHIS) compile data on noise complaints. Data are collected on the number of complaints about noise made to local Environmental Health Officers and are available by source of noise and whether or not the source is controlled by legislation. Data are also collected on the number of noise complaints and prosecutions by source of noise for Great Britain. They include the number of nuisances confirmed and remedied informally and the number of abatement notices served and prosecutions for contravention of these. Data are also presented on complaints about noise from domestic premises received by Environmental Health Officers. The data cover Great Britain. Changes to the basis of the calculation of complaints for England and Wales make data from 1991-2 more realistic, but they are not therefore directly comparable with those for earlier years. Data have been collected on a financial-year basis since 1983-4 for England and Wales, on a calendar-year basis up to 1991 for Scotland and are published in April of the following financial year.

Status: Ongoing
Collection Method: Census of Local Authorities
Frequency: Annually
Reference Period: Year
Timeliness: Results are published in April of the following year
National Coverage: Great Britain

Statistician
Alan Brown
Department of the Environment, Transport and

the Regions
Environmental Protection Statistics and Information Management Division; EPSIM 5
Tel: 020 7890 6513;
Email: alanh_brown@detr.gsi.gov.uk

Products that contain data from this source
Digest of Environmental Statistics

15.9 Radioactivity

Public Exposure to Radioactive Liquid Discharges - GB
Department of the Environment, Transport and the Regions

The Ministry of Agriculture, Fisheries and Food conducts a survey on public exposure to radioactive liquid discharges. Radioactive liquid discharges are monitored and the results are used to estimate the radiation exposure of members of the public who live and work near nuclear sites, i.e. the 'critical group'. Data are available as a time series for the last ten years and show the estimated radiation exposure of critical groups of the public from liquid discharges from sites operated by British Nuclear Fuels plc, AEA Technology, Nuclear Electric plc, Scottish Nuclear Ltd, Amersham International plc, and Albright and Wilson Ltd. The survey is undertaken annually and results are published each April for the latest calendar year available.

Status: Ongoing
Frequency: Annually
Timeliness: Results are published each April for the latest calendar year available
National Coverage: Great Britain
Disaggregation: Nuclear sites

Statistician
Adrian Redfern
Department of the Environment, Transport and the Regions
Environmental Protection Statistics and Information Management Division; EPSIM 1
Tel: 020 7890 6497;
Email: adrian_redfern@detr.gsi.gov.uk

Products that contain data from this source
Digest of Environmental Statistics

Public Exposure to Radon - UK
Department of the Environment, Transport and the Regions

The National Radiological Protection Board (NRPB) conducted a survey on the public exposure to radon in the early 1990s. Data are available on average exposure levels by county and on the estimated proportion of homes which exceed the Radon Action Level in areas which have been designated as Radon Affected Areas. The survey was based on a stratified sample of 2,300 dwellings in the UK to determine the average indoor concentration of radon gas. The survey also enabled identification of the number of houses where radon concentrations exceed 200 Bqm≥ (the level recommended for action to be taken to limit the exposure of householders to high levels of radon). Data are available on each Radon Affected Area, i.e. Northern Ireland, North East Scotland, Cornwall and Devon, Somerset, Northamptonshire and Derbyshire.

Status: Ongoing
National Coverage: United Kingdom
Sub-National: Radon affected areas
Disaggregation: Postcode area

Statistician
Adrian Redfern
Department of the Environment, Transport and the Regions
Environmental Protection Statistics and Information Management Division; EPSIM 1
Tel: 020 7890 6497;
Email: adrian_redfern@detr.gsi.gov.uk

Products that contain data from this source
Board Statement on Radon in Homes (NRPB); Digest of Environmental Statistics; Exposure to Radon in UK Dwellings (NRPB); Natural Radiation Exposure in UK Dwellings (NRPB); the Scottish Environment Statistics

---

Radioactive Discharges - GB
Department of the Environment, Transport and the Regions

The Department of the Environment, Transport and the Regions compiles data on discharges of radioactivity. Radioactive effluent in both liquid and gaseous form is discharged from nuclear installations under authorisation. Data on the amount of both forms of discharge are collected by site operators - British Nuclear Fuels plc, UKAEA, Nuclear Electric plc and Amersham International plc - who are required to measure discharges, sample and analyse the waste, monitor the local environment and supply the results to the regulatory bodies. Data for Scotland are compiled by the Scottish Executive Agriculture, Environment and Fisheries Department. Data cover Great Britain and are available for individual nuclear sites. The monitoring of both atmospheric and liquid discharges from each nuclear site is carried out continuously and data are published annually.

Frequency: Annually
National Coverage: Great Britain

Statistician
Adrian Redfern
Department of the Environment, Transport and the Regions
Environmental Protection Statistics and

Information Management Division; EPSIM 1
Tel: 020 7890 6497;
Email: adrian_redfern@detr.gsi.gov.uk

Products that contain data from this source
Annual Report (Amersham International plc); Annual Report on Radioactive Discharges and Environmental Monitoring at nuclear power stations (Nuclear Electric plc); Annual Report on Radioactive Discharges and Monitoring of the Environment (British Nuclear Fuels plc); Digest of Environmental Statistics; Radioactivity in Surface and Coastal Waters in the British Isles; the Scottish Environment Statistics

---

Radioactive Incident Monitoring Network (RIMNET) - UK
Department of the Environment, Transport and the Regions

The Department of the Environment is responsible for the Radioactive Incident Monitoring Network (RIMNET). RIMNET monitors background gamma radiation at specific sites throughout the UK. Data are available on average gamma radiation doses. The network covers the UK, including Guernsey and Jersey, and data are available for each monitoring site. RIMNET was first introduced in 1988 to monitor the consequences for the UK of nuclear incidents abroad, following the Chernobyl reactor accident in 1986. The system became fully automated in early 1994 and the number of monitoring sites was doubled. In addition, its increased levels of system automation improved the network's analytical, interpretative, display and communications facilities. Data are collected every hour and are available for the latest available quarter.

Status: Ongoing
Collection Method: Automated monitoring sites
Frequency: Quarterly
Earliest Available Data: 1988
National Coverage: United Kingdom
Disaggregation: Monitoring site

Statistician
Adrian Redfern
Department of the Environment, Transport and the Regions
Environmental Protection Statistics and Information Management Division; EPSIM 1
Tel: 020 7890 6497;
Email: adrian_redfern@detr.gsi.gov.uk

Products that contain data from this source
Digest of Environmental Statistics; The National Response Plan and Radioactive Incident and Monitoring Network (RIMNET): Phase 1.

Radioactive Waste Stocks, Arisings and Disposal - GB
Department of the Environment, Transport and the Regions

The Department of the Environment, Transport and the Regions compiles data on radioactive waste stocks, arisings and disposal derived from individual site operators and British Nuclear Fuels plc. Data show the amount of high level (HLW), intermediate level (ILW) and low level (LLW) waste in stock and arising at all nuclear installations in Great Britain. Data are also available on the volume of solid radioactive waste disposed of at Drigg by source. This site receives most of the LLW arising at Sellafield, as well as wastes from other UK nuclear sites and radioactive substances from hospitals, research establishments and industry. The inventories cover Great Britain and data are available for waste arisings at individual nuclear installations. Data were collected annually, usually on 1 January until 1989. Data were subsequently collected in 1991, 1994 and 1998, in 1994 and 1998 on 1 April.

Status: Ongoing
Collection Method: Census of nuclear sites
Frequency: Varied
Reference Period: "Snapshot" taken at one point in time
Earliest Available Data: 1986
National Coverage: Great Britain
Disaggregation: Site

Statistician
Adrian Redfern
Department of the Environment, Transport and the Regions
Environmental Protection Statistics and Information Management Division; EPSIM 1
Tel: 020 7890 6497;
Email: adrian_redfern@detr.gsi.gov.uk

Products that contain data from this source
Digest of Environmental Statistics; UK Radioactive Waste Inventory (Electrowatt)

Radioactivity in Food and the Environment
Department of the Environment, Transport and the Regions

Statistician
Adrian Redfern
Department of the Environment, Transport and the Regions
Environmental Protection Statistics and Information Management Division; EPSIM 1
Tel: 020 7890 6497;
Email: aredfern.epsim@gtnet.gov.uk

15.10 Recovery and Recycling of Materials

Municipal Waste Management Survey - England & Wales
Department of the Environment, Transport and the Regions

Statistician
Meg Green
Department of the Environment, Transport and the Regions
Environmental Protection Statistics and Information Management Division; EPSIM 2
Tel: 020 7890 6524;
Email: meg_green@detr.gsi.gov.uk

Products that contain data from this source
Municipal Waste Management

Waste Recycling - UK
Department of the Environment, Transport and the Regions

Annual figures on the recycling of selected materials in the UK are compiled by a number of non-governmental organisations and presented in the Digest of Environmental Statistics. Data are available from 1984 on the amounts of various scrap metals recovered, imported and exported, and the amount of scrap recycled as a proportion of consumption. The metals included are ferrous scrap, aluminium, copper, zinc and lead. The same data are also available for paper and glass recycling. Figures for glass cover Great Britain only. Data are also given for the number of councils in Great Britain which participate in the British Glass bottle bank scheme, the number of bottle bank sites and kilograms of glass collected per head for each of the territories in the UK. Information on steel can recycling, aluminium can recycling and the recycled content of newsprint feedstock is also available.

Earliest Available Data: 1984
National Coverage: Great Britain

Statistician
Meg Green
Department of the Environment, Transport and the Regions
Environmental Protection Statistics and Information Management Division; EPSIM 2
Tel: 020 7890 6524;
Email: meg_green@detr.gsi.gov.uk

Products that contain data from this source
Annual Iron and Steel Statistics for the UK (Iron and Steel Statistics Bureau); Digest of Environmental Statistics; The National Directory of Recycling Information (Waste Watch); the Scottish Environment Statistics

---

15.11 Waste

Waste Arisings and Disposal - UK
Department of the Environment, Transport and the Regions

The Department of the Environment publishes data on the arisings and disposal

of particular waste streams in the UK. Summary data are provided for each of the territories in the UK where these are available; more detailed data are provided for England, or in some instances England and Wales. The National Assembly for Wales and the Scottish Executive produce separate publications which provide more detailed waste statistics for their area.

The Digest of Environmental Statistics contains information on total sewage sludge arisings for each of the territories of the UK since 1985, and information on sewage sludge disposal since 1990-91. Data compiled from the consignment notes which must accompany all international movements of hazardous waste since 1988 are available. Tables show the imports to and exports from England and Wales of hazardous waste by waste type and country of origin, disposal routes by waste type, and imports by port of entry and by destination Waste Regulation Authority (WRA). Figures for arisings of special waste in the UK since 1986-87 are available; they are compiled by WRAs from the consignment notes which accompany the movement of these wastes. Since 1992-93, more detailed data showing arisings and movements of special waste in England and Wales by standard region and imports from Scotland and Northern Ireland have become available. Data on disposal routes for special wastes by standard region in England and Wales are also available. Data on the number of different types of treatment and disposal facilities are also available for Great Britain.

Earliest Available Data: 1985
National Coverage: Great Britain

Statistician
Meg Green
Department of the Environment, Transport and the Regions
Environmental Protection Statistics and Information Management Division; EPSIM 2
Tel: 020 7890 6524;
Email: meg_green@detr.gsi.gov.uk

Products that contain data from this source
Digest of Environmental Statistics; the Scottish Environment Statistics

---

15.12 Wildlife

Botanical Society Surveys - Great Britain
Department of the Environment, Transport and the Regions

Statistician
John Custance
Department of the Environment, Transport and the Regions
Environmental Protection Statistics and

Information Management Division; EPSIM 3
Tel: 020 7890 6514;
Email: john_custance@detr.gsi.gov.uk

Butterfly Surveys - Great Britain
Department of the Environment, Transport and the Regions

Statistician
John Custance
Department of the Environment, Transport and the Regions
Environmental Protection Statistics and Information Management Division; EPSIM 3
Tel: 020 7890 6514;
Email: john_custance@detr.gsi.gov.uk

Cetacean Strandings - England & Wales
Department of the Environment, Transport and the Regions

Statistician
John Custance
Department of the Environment, Transport and the Regions
Environmental Protection Statistics and Information Management Division; EPSIM 3
Tel: 020 7890 6514;
Email: john_custance@detr.gsi.gov.uk

Common Birds Census - GB
Department of the Environment, Transport and the Regions

The British Trust for Ornithology conducts the Common Birds Census (CBC) and has published Atlases of Breeding Birds. Data are available on population and changes in breeding numbers for the most common British breeding birds for 1991 and on changes in the geographical distribution of bird species by habitat type from 1968 to 1972 and 1988 to 1991. Data cover Great Britain. The Census covers 200 to 300 plots and targets species known to particular habitats, usually woodland or farmland, and a number of other habitats. For the 1988-91 Atlas, a number of methods were used to update and improve population estimates. Data are collected and published annually.

Status: Ongoing
Collection Method: Census
Frequency: Annually
National Coverage: Great Britain

Statistician
John Custance
Department of the Environment, Transport and the Regions
Environmental Protection Statistics and Information Management Division; EPSIM 3
Tel: 020 7890 6514;
Email: john_custance@detr.gsi.gov.uk

Products that contain data from this source
Digest of Environmental Statistics; The New Atlas of Breeding Birds in Britain and Ireland: 1988-91

National Otter Survey - GB
Department of the Environment, Transport and the Regions

The National Otter Surveys are conducted by the Vincent Wildlife Trust. The Surveys examine 600m stretches of river for evidence of otter tracks. If evidence is found, the stretch is counted as a positive survey. Data are collected on the number of stretches of river surveyed, the number with an otter presence and the percentage for each period. Data are available from the major Surveys undertaken in Great Britain 1977-79 and 1984-86, and from an additional Survey conducted in Wales in 1991. Results refer only to stretches of river in England and Scotland which were surveyed in both periods and to stretches in Wales which were surveyed in all three.

National Coverage: Great Britain

Statistician
John Custance
Department of the Environment, Transport and the Regions
Environmental Protection Statistics and Information Management Division; EPSIM 3
Tel: 020 7890 6514;
Email: john_custance@detr.gsi.gov.uk

Products that contain data from this source
Digest of Environmental Statistics

Protected Native Species - GB
Department of the Environment, Transport and the Regions

The Joint Nature Conservation Committee (JNCC) maintains records of protected native species. Data are collected on the numbers of native species which are currently protected under the Wildlife and Countryside Act 1981, compared to the numbers protected in 1981. They are classified either as fully or partially protected and as animals or plants and other organisms. Data cover Great Britain. The data are available from 1981, following the introduction of the Wildlife and Countryside Act, and are published annually.

Frequency: Annually
Earliest Available Data: 1981
National Coverage: Great Britain

Statistician
John Custance
Department of the Environment, Transport and the Regions
Environmental Protection Statistics and Information Management Division; EPSIM 3
Tel: 020 7890 6514;
Email: john_custance@detr.gsi.gov.uk

Products that contain data from this source
Digest of Environmental Statistics; the Scottish Environment Statistics

---

Reptiles and Amphibians in the United Kingdom
Department of the Environment, Transport and the Regions

Statistician
John Custance
Department of the Environment, Transport and the Regions
Environmental Protection Statistics and Information Management Division; EPSIM 3
Tel: 020 7890 6514;
Email: john_custance@detr.gsi.gov.uk

(A) Review of British Mammals - Great Britain
Department of the Environment, Transport and the Regions

Statistician
John Custance
Department of the Environment, Transport and the Regions
Environmental Protection Statistics and Information Management Division; EPSIM 3
Tel: 020 7890 6514;
Email: john_custance@detr.gsi.gov.uk

Scarce Plants - Great Britain
Department of the Environment, Transport and the Regions

Statistician
John Custance
Department of the Environment, Transport and the Regions
Environmental Protection Statistics and Information Management Division; EPSIM 3
Tel: 020 7890 6514;
Email: john_custance@detr.gsi.gov.uk

Seal Stocks - GB
Department of the Environment, Transport and the Regions

The Sea Mammal Research Unit (SMRU) conducts surveys on the status of seals. The surveys monitor changes in the size and status of stocks of grey seals and common seals in Britain. Data are available on the size of different seal stocks for the period 1986-92. The figures quoted for common seals represent estimates of the minimum number in each region. The data cover most of Great Britain and are available for the Inner Hebrides, Outer Hebrides/North Rona, Orkney, Shetland, Farne Islands, Isle of May and South West Britain for grey seals. Common seals are surveyed in the Inner Hebrides/ West Scotland, Outer Hebrides, Orkney, Shetland, east coast of Scotland and the Wash. Surveys of grey seals are conducted annually in the Wash and every two years on the east coast of Scotland and will be conducted every five years elsewhere in Scotland.

Frequency: Between two and five years, depending on location
Earliest Available Data: 1986
National Coverage: Most of Great Britain

Statistician
John Custance
Department of the Environment, Transport and the Regions
Environmental Protection Statistics and Information Management Division; EPSIM 3
Tel: 020 7890 6514;
Email: john_custance@detr.gsi.gov.uk

Products that contain data from this source
Digest of Environmental Statistics

---

15 Environment - *Products*

15.13 Abstracts, Compendia, A-Z Catalogues, Directories and Reference Material

Digest of Environmental Statistics
Department of the Environment, Transport and the Regions

An annual series, formerly entitled Digest of Environmental Protection and Water Statistics (until no 16 1994), which presents data on a wide range of aspects of environmental protection in the UK. Contains data on key trends over time, on geographical variation and on performance in relation to policy targets and commitments, including international commitments. Chapters cover the global atmosphere, air quality, inland water quality and use, coastal and marine waters, radioactivity, noise, waste and recycling, land and wildlife. Every 3-4 years an additional chapter is included summarising the results of the Department's latest survey of public attitudes to the environment.

Delivery: Hardcopy publication (also internet site)
Frequency: Annually
Price: £31.50 (1998 edition)
ISBN: 0 11 753466 8

Available from
TSO Publications Centre and Bookshops
Please see Annex B for full address details.

Sources from which data for this product are obtained
Air Quality Monitoring Network - UK; Bathing Water Quality; Common Birds Census - GB; Complaints About Noise and Action Taken - United Kingdom; Contaminant Concentrations in Estuaries and Coastal Waters; Contaminant Inputs to Coastal Waters; Countryside Survey - GB; Damage to Protected Areas - GB; Derelict Land - England; Designated Protected Areas - UK; Drinking Water Quality - England & Wales; Dumping of Waste and Dredgings at Sea; Estuarial Quality; Freshwater Quality - England and Wales; Groundwater Quality - England and Wales; Harmonised Monitoring Scheme - GB; Land Use Change - England; Marine Fish Stocks and Catches; Marine Water Quality - UK; National Atmospheric Emissions Inventory - UK; National Noise Attitude Surveys; National Noise

Incidence Studies; National Otter Survey - GB; Noise Pollution - GB; Protected Native Species - GB; Public Exposure to Radioactive Liquid Discharges - GB; Public Exposure to Radon - UK; Radioactive Discharges - GB; Radioactive Incident Monitoring Network (RIMNET) - UK; Radioactive Waste Stocks, Arisings and Disposal - GB; Seal Stocks - GB; Survey of Public Attitudes to the Environment - England and Wales; Surveys of Oil Pollution Around the Coasts of the United Kingdom; Vacant Land Use - England; Waste Arisings and Disposal - UK; Waste Recycling - UK; Water Pollution Incidents; Water Resources - England and Wales; Water Resources - Public Water Supply - UK; Water Resources - Scotland

Environment Statistics 1996
Eurostat

Part of Eurostat's Environment theme - Theme 8: Series A - Yearbooks and yearly statistics. This publication covers topics such as climate change, air pollution, water and waste as well as data on land use, energy etc. Maps and graphs are used to illustrate this statistical reference document which is aimed at experts and non-experts alike. (403 pages)

Delivery: Hardcopy publication
Frequency: Annually
Price: £15.00
ISBN: 92 828 07142

Available from
Bob Dodds
Office for National Statistics
Please see Annex B for full address details

Environmental Digest for Wales
National Assembly for Wales

The Environmental Digest for Wales was a regular publication prepared by the National Assembly for Wales bringing together a wide range of data on the Welsh Environment. It has not been published since 1996. Includes data on the population and land, nature conservation, energy, waste, water quality, pollution, nuclear installations and meteorology,

Delivery: Periodic Release
Frequency: Annually
Price: £9.00
ISBN: 0 7504 1205 4 (1996 edition)
ISSN: 0267-310x

Available from
Gaynor Williams
National Assembly for Wales
Crown Building
Cathays Park
Cardiff CF1 3NQ

Indicators of Sustainable Development - United Kingdom
Department of the Environment, Transport and the Regions

This report is one of the first sets of indicators to be constructed by any country to link environmental and developmental concerns. It contains a preliminary set of around 120 indicators, grouped within a framework of 21 families (such as economy, transport use and climate change), developed to measure progress towards sustainable development, to inform about the issues and to stimulate debate contains introductory background text; text and graphics for each indicator.

Delivery: Hardcopy publication (also internet site)
Frequency: Periodic
Price: £25.00
ISBN: 0 11 753174 X

Available from
TSO Publications Centre and Bookshops
Please see Annex B for full address details.

(The) Scottish Environment Statistics
Scottish Executive

Compendium of environmental statistics. Contains data on population, land, land cover, atmosphere, water, conservation, radioactivity and recreation.

Delivery: Periodic Release
Frequency: Bi-annually
Price: £20.00
ISBN: 0 7480 5855 9

Available from
TSO Publications Centre and Bookshops
Please see Annex B for full address details.

Sources from which data for this product are obtained
Damage to Protected Areas - GB; Designated Protected Areas - UK; Environmental Protection

- Scotland; Industrial Sites Register - Scotland; Population Estimates - Scotland; Protected Native Species - GB; Public Exposure to Radon - UK; Radioactive Discharges - GB; Vacant and Derelict Land - Scotland; Waste Arisings and Disposal - UK; Waste Recycling - UK; Water Resources - Scotland; Bathing Water Quality; Vacant and Derelict Land - Scotland

(The) UK Environment

Department of the Environment, Transport and the Regions

Report on the state of the environment in the UK, published in 1992, based on official statistics presented in graphs, tables and maps, supported by explanatory text. Contains data on the environment arranged in chapters: climate, air quality and pollution, the global atmosphere, soil, land use and land cover, inland water resources and abstraction, inland water quality and pollution, the marine environment, coastal erosion flooding and sea level change, wildlife, waste and recycling, noise, radioactivity, environment and health, pressures on the environment, public attitudes, and expenditure on the environment. Selected data available on floppy disk

Delivery: Hardcopy publication (plus diskette)
Frequency: Ad hoc/One-off Release
Price: £14.95
ISBN: 0 11 752420 4

Available from
TSO Publications Centre and Bookshops
Please see Annex B for full address details.

15.14 Air Quality

Air Pollution in the UK (DETR/ NETCEN)
Department of the Environment, Transport and the Regions

Annual Report summarising the results from the UK national automated air pollution monitoring networks.

Delivery: Hardcopy publication
Frequency: Annually
Price: Free
ISBN: 0 7058 1756 3

Available from
DETR UK Air Quality Enquiries
Department of the Environment, Transport and the Regions
Please see Annex B for full address details.

Sources from which data for this product are obtained
Air Quality Monitoring Network - UK

Local Air Pollution Control in England and Wales
Department of the Environment, Transport and the Regions

Statistical bulletin summarising applications for authorisations for 'Part B' industrial processes under Part 1 of the Environmental Protection Act 1990. Contains applications for authorisations, authorisations in force, determination period and enforcement activity. The record is for the period 1991 to 1996.

Delivery: Hardcopy publication
Frequency: Five-yearly
Price: Free
ISBN: 1 85112 017 3

Available from
DETR UK Air Quality Enquiries
Department of the Environment, Transport and the Regions
Please see Annex B for full address details.

Sources from which data for this product are obtained
Local Air Pollution Control Statistical Survey

Ozone in the United Kingdom
Department of the Environment, Transport and the Regions

Fourth report of the UK Photochemical Oxidants Review Group.

Delivery: Hardcopy publication
Frequency: Periodic
Price: Free
ISBN: 1 870393 30 9

Available from
Global Atmosphere Division
Department of the Environment, Transport and the Regions
Ashdown House
123 Victoria Street
London SW1E 6DE
Tel: 020 7890 5232

Sources from which data for this product are obtained
Air Quality Monitoring Network - UK

UK Emission of Air Pollutants 1970-1995
Department of the Environment, Transport and the Regions

Results and comparisons over time of air pollutant monitoring studies.

Delivery: Hardcopy publication
Price: Free
ISBN: 0 7058 1746 6

Available from
DETR UK Air Quality Enquiries
Department of the Environment, Transport and the Regions
Please see Annex B for full address details.

Sources from which data for this product are obtained
National Atmospheric Emissions Inventory - UK

UK Nitrogen Dioxide Survey 1996
Department of the Environment, Transport and the Regions

Analysis of the results from the air quality monitoring survey at sites throughout the United Kingdom.

Delivery: Other
Frequency: Ad hoc

Available from
DETR UK Air Quality Enquiries
Department of the Environment, Transport and the Regions
Please see Annex B for full address details.

Sources from which data for this product are obtained
Air Quality Monitoring Network - UK

UK Smoke and Sulphur Dioxide Network
Department of the Environment, Transport and the Regions

Delivery: Periodic Release
Frequency: Annually
Price: Free
ISBN: 0 7058 1773 3

Available from
DETR UK Air Quality Enquiries
Department of the Environment, Transport and the Regions
Please see Annex B for full address details

Sources from which data for this product are obtained
Air Quality Monitoring Network - UK

See also:
In this chapter:
Digest of Environmental Statistics *(15.13)*
Environment Statistics 1996 *(15.13)*
Indicators of Sustainable Development - United Kingdom *(15.13)*
(The) Scottish Environment Statistics *(15.13)*
(The) UK Environment *(15.13)*

15.15 Designated and Protected Areas

Please see:
In this chapter:
Digest of Environmental Statistics *(15.13)*
Indicators of Sustainable Development -
United Kingdom *(15.13)*
(The) Scottish Environment Statistics
(15.13)
(The) UK Environment *(15.13)*

15.16 Environment - Cross Media

1993 Survey of Attitudes to the Environment
Department of the Environment, Transport
and the Regions

Statistical bulletin of the results of the 1993
Survey of public attitudes to the
environment commissioned by the
Department of the Environment, with
analytical tables and graphs and some
comparisons with the previous Surveys of
1986 and 1989, supported by explanatory
text. Contains data on public attitudes to the
environment based on the results of the
Survey of 1993, such as levels of concern
about various issues, allocation of
responsibility for issues, personal 'green'
actions and knowledge. Also includes
background on the Survey methodology and
on the questionnaire used.

Some of the data in this product is
disaggregated by gender.

Frequency: Approximately every three years
Price: £5.00

Available from
John Custance
Department of the Environment, Transport and
the Regions
Ashdown House
123 Victoria Street
London
020 7890 6514; Fax: 020 8890 6489;
Email: john.custance@detr.gsi.gov.uk

Sources from which data for this product are obtained
Survey of Public Attitudes to the Environment -
England and Wales

Environmental Protection Expenditure by Industry (1995)
Department of the Environment, Transport
and the Regions

Report of a study to advise the Department
of the Environment on protocols and
procedures for the collection of data. The

study aimed to establish the feasibility of
data collection taking account of
methodological and practical
considerations.

Delivery: Hardcopy publication
Frequency: Ad hoc / one off release
Price: £22.00
ISBN: 0 11 753300 9

Available from
TSO Publications Centre and Bookshops
Please see Annex B for full address details.

Sources from which data for this product are obtained
Environmental Expenditure Surveys - United
Kingdom

Review of UK Environmental Expenditure (1993)
Department of the Environment, Transport
and the Regions

Report to the Department of the
Environment of estimates of environmental
expenditure in the UK.

Delivery: Hardcopy publication
Frequency: Ad Hoc/One-off Release
Price: £11.00
ISBN: 0 11 752851 X

Available from
TSO Publications Centre and Bookshops
Please see Annex B for full address details.

See also:
In this chapter:
Digest of Environmental Statistics *(15.13)*
Indicators of Sustainable Development -
United Kingdom *(15.13)*
(The) UK Environment *(15.13)*

15.17 Global Atmosphere

UK Greenhouse Gas Emission Inventory 1990-1995
Department of the Environment, Transport
and the Regions

Frequency: Annually
Price: Free
ISBN: 0 7058 1755 5

Available from
Global Atmosphere Division
Department of the Environment, Transport and
the Regions
Ashdown House
123 Victoria Street
London SW1E 6DE
Tel: 020 7890 5225

Sources from which data for this product are obtained

National Atmospheric Emissions Inventory - UK

See also:
In this chapter:
Digest of Environmental Statistics *(15.13)*
Environment Statistics 1996 *(15.13)*
Indicators of Sustainable Development -
United Kingdom *(15.13)*
UK Emission of Air Pollutants 1970-1995
(15.14)
(The) UK Environment *(15.13)*

15.18 Hazardous Substances (excluding Radioactivity)

Notes for Completion of Hazardous Substances Consents Return
Department of the Environment, Transport
and the Regions

Guidance notes for authorities on how to
complete the statistical return described
below. Contains guidance for authorities on
how to complete this form, with an overview
of why the data are collected, which
authorities should complete them,
definitions of terms used and what should
be included, and references to relevant
legislation.

Frequency: Quarterly
Price: Free

Available from
Ian Rowe
Department of the Environment, Transport and
the Regions
Please see Annex B for full address details

Sources from which data for this product are obtained
Hazardous Substances Consents Return - England

Statistics of Applications for Hazardous Substances Consents
Department of the Environment, Transport
and the Regions

Information bulletin with statistics of
applications received and decided by local
authorities for consent to store hazardous
substances. Contains the number of
applications and decisions by type and
amount of substance, type of decision
(granted/refused, with/without conditions)
and speed of decision.

Frequency: Annual
Price: Free

Available from
Ian Rowe
Department of the Environment, Transport and
the Regions
Please see Annex B for full address details.

**Sources from which data for this product are
obtained**
Hazardous Substances Consents Return - England

See also:
In this chapter:
Digest of Environmental Statistics *(15.13)*
Indicators of Sustainable Development -
United Kingdom *(15.13)*
(The) UK Environment *(15.13)*

15.19 Inland Water Quality and Supply and Marine and Coastal Waters

Bathing Water Directive - Detailed Summary of 1998 Survey Results, United Kingdom
Department of the Environment, Transport
and the Regions

Contains data on the compliance results
(pass or fails) in the United Kingdom with
details by EA region and for each of the 400
odd identified bathing waters showing
number of samples taken and values
obtained for total and faecal coliforms and
for other parameters - transparency, colour,
salmonella, enteroviruses, mineral oils,
surface active substances and phenols.

Frequency: Annual
Price: Free

Available from
Water Quality Division
Department of the Environment, Transport and
the Regions
Ashdown House
123 Victoria Street
London SW1E 6DE
Tel: 020 7890 5336

**Sources from which data for this product are
obtained**
Bathing Water Quality

Contaminants Entering the Sea
Department of the Environment, Transport
and the Regions

A report on contaminant loads (hazardous
substances and nutrients) entering the seas
around England and Wales for 1990-93.
Contains data on trends in the quantities of
specific contaminants entering the seas
around England and Wales showing input
type (riverine or direct input) and catchment

source during the period 1990-93, and trends
since 1985, for 'Black and Grey List' metals.

Delivery: Hardcopy publication
Price: £15.95
ISBN: 0 11 886514 5

Available from
TSO Publications Centre and Bookshops
Please see Annex B for full address details.

**Sources from which data for this product are
obtained**
Marine Water Quality - UK

Drinking Water Quality in Scotland
Scottish Executive

Comments on overall performance of
individual water authorities.

Frequency: Annual
Price: £16.00
ISBN: 0 7480 7179 2

Available from
TSO Publications Centre and Bookshops
Please see Annex B for full address details.

**Sources from which data for this product are
obtained**
Water Resources - Scotland

Drinking Water: a Report by the Chief Inspector, Drinking Water Inspectorate
Department of the Environment, Transport
and the Regions

Information on this publication is available
from 020 7890 6572

Delivery: Hardcopy publication
Frequency: Annually
Price: £33.50
ISBN: 0 11 753 468 4 (1997 report)

Available from
TSO Publications Centre and Bookshops
Please see Annex B for full address details.

**Sources from which data for this product are
obtained**
Drinking Water Quality - England & Wales

Drinking Water Quality Report 1997
Department of the Environment - Northern
Ireland: Water Service

Delivery: Periodic Release
Frequency: Annual
Price: Free

Available from
Water Service
Northland House
3 Frederick Street
Belfast BT1 2NR
Tel: 028 9024 4711; Fax: 028 9035 4888

**Sources from which data for this product are
obtained**
Drinking Water Quality - England & Wales

Pollution Review
SEPA

Information on water pollution events
arising from agricultural practice in
Scotland. Description of pollution events,
table of pollution causes, pollution of
incidents by source, fertiliser use. 8 pages.

Delivery: Periodic Release
Frequency: Annually
Price: Free

Available from
SEPA

(The) Quality of Rivers and Canals in England and Wales: 1990 to 1995
Department of the Environment, Transport
and the Regions

Delivery: Ad hoc/One-off Release
Frequency: Ad hoc

Available from
DETR UK Freshwater Quality Enquiries
Department of the Environment, Transport and
the Regions
Ashdown House
123 Victoria Street
London SW1E 6DE
Tel: 020 7890 6505

**Sources from which data for this product are
obtained**
Freshwater Quality - England and Wales

River Quality in Northern Ireland 1995
Department of the Environment - Northern
Ireland: Environment and Heritage Service

Frequency: Ad hoc
Price: Free

Available from
Environment and Heritage Service
Environmental Protection
Calvert House
23 Castle Place
Belfast BT1 1FY
Tel: 028 9025 4754; Fax: 028 9025 4865

Products

Scottish Bathing Waters
SEPA

Results of bathing water monitoring for compliance with bathing water directive for designated Scottish beaches.

Delivery: Periodic Release
Frequency: Annually
Price: £5.00
ISBN: 1 901322 03 3

Available from
SEPA

Sources from which data for this product are obtained
1998 Bathing Water Quality Report

SEPA: Annual Report and Accounts
SEPA

Report includes "Environmental Review" for Scotland which gives information on water quality classification, pollution incidents and prosecutions brought.

Delivery: News/Press Release
Frequency: Annually
Price: Free
ISBN: 1 901322 09 2

Available from
SEPA

(The) State of the Environment of England and Wales: Fresh Waters
Department of the Environment, Transport and the Regions

Delivery: Other
Frequency: Ad hoc
Price: £35.00
ISBN: 0 11 3101481

Available from
TSO Publications Centre and Bookshops
Please see Annex B for full address details.

Sources from which data for this product are obtained
Freshwater Quality - England and Wales

Water Pollution Incidents in England and Wales
Department of the Environment, Transport and the Regions

An analysis of trends in the number of reported and substantiated water pollution incidents in England and Wales, with details of category of incident, distribution by source of pollution, distribution by type of pollutant, and legal actions taken by the

Environment Agency for pollution incidents. Contains data on the number of reported pollution incidents by EA regions, the number of substantiated pollution incidents by type, by category, by source of pollution, and by type of pollutant, historical trends, the number of legal actions undertaken, successful prosecutions, fines and costs awarded.

Delivery: Hardcopy publication
Frequency: Annual
ISBN: 0 11 310150 3 (1998 publication)

Available from
TSO Publications Centre and Bookshops
Please see Annex B for full address details.

Sources from which data for this product are obtained
Water Pollution Incidents

Waterfacts
Department of the Environment, Transport and the Regions

Data on water works and main assets.

Delivery: Hardcopy publication
Frequency: Annually

Available from
Water UK
1 Queen Anne's Gate
London SW1H 9BT
Tel: 020 7344 1844;
Email: info@water.org.uk

Sources from which data for this product are obtained
Water Resources - Scotland

See also:
In this chapter:
Digest of Environmental Statistics *(15.13)*
Environment Statistics 1996 *(15.13)*
Indicators of Sustainable Development - United Kingdom *(15.13)*
(The) Scottish Environment Statistics *(15.13)*
(The) UK Environment *(15.13)*

15.20 Land Cover and Land Use

Analysis of Land Use Change in England
Department of the Environment, Transport and the Regions

Commentary and results of land use change data collected by Ordnance Survey, in particular, estimates of change to urban uses (especially to residential use) for regions and counties

Delivery: Hardcopy publication
Frequency: Annual
Price: £10.00
ISBN: 1 85112 146 3

Available from
DETR Publications Sales Centre
Unit 8
Goldthorpe Industrial Estate
Goldthorpe
Rotherham S63 9BL
Tel: 01709 891318

Sources from which data for this product are obtained
Land Use Change - England

Annual Survey of Tenanted Land
Department of the Environment, Transport and the Regions

Available from
Dr Bob Garland
Department of the Environment, Transport and the Regions
Eland House
Bressenden Place
London
Tel: 020 7890 5533

Comparison of Land Cover Definitions
Department of the Environment, Transport and the Regions

Report presenting qualitative and quantitative comparisons, important surveys of land use, land cover and habitats used in the United Kingdom. Definitions used are held on the computer programme LUCID. Contains definitions used in the Countryside Survey 1990, Land Cover Map of Great Britain, Land Cover Map of Scotland, MAFF Agricultural Census, DoE Land Use Classification, NCC Phase 1 Habitat Classification, EU CORINE Land Cover and Biotopes Classifications, and UNECE Land Use Classification.

Price: £10.00

Available from
Dr Bob Garland
Department of the Environment, Transport and the Regions
Eland House
Bressenden Place
London
Tel: 020 7890 5533

Sources from which data for this product are obtained
Countryside Survey - GB

Countryside Information System
Institute of Terrestrial Ecology; sponsored by Department of the Environment, Transport and the Regions, and the Natural Environment Research Council

The Countryside Information System (CIS) is a Microsoft Windows-based program for PC's giving easy access to spatial information about the British countryside which can assist policy development at national scales. It combines analyses and presents a comprehensive range of environmental data sets for each one kilometre square of the National Grid in Great Britain. Data supplied with CIS include counties and administrative regions, land cover information from satellite, and national field surveys in 1978, 1984, 1990 and 1998 which document the changes in the ecological characteristics of the British countryside. Other data sets are available such as Designated Areas (e.g. SSSI's), Ordnance Survey topography and geographical reference, and flora and fauna. Details on data available for use in CIS are given in the CIS Environmental Catalogue, a hypertext database regularly updated and downloadable from the World Wide Web at http://mwnta.nmw.ac.uk/ceh/cis/ciscat.htm. The CIS allows users to (1) combine, analyse and present environmental data, (2) characterise geographical regions, (3) select areas with different environmental features and (4) produce maps, tables of statistics and charts.

Delivery: Periodic Release
Price: Single User Licence:
Standard Rate - £1000.00
Concessionary Rate - £500.00 for Charitable Organisations and Educational Institutions
Discounts available for multiple user/network licences

Available from
Timothy Moffat
Institute of Terrestrial Ecology
Monks Wood
Abbots Ripton
Huntingdon
Cambs, UK
PE17 2LS
Tel: 01487 773381;
Email: timothy.moffat@ite.ac.uk

Sources from which data for this product are obtained
Countryside Survey - GB

Countryside Survey 1990: Main Report
Department of the Environment, Transport and the Regions

Main technical report from the Countryside Survey 1990 for Great Britain. Contains data

about the countryside in Great Britain. It includes land cover, linear features, vegetation, freshwater biota and soils. Change statistics are available for 1978, 1984 and 1990.

Delivery: Hardcopy publication
Frequency: Periodic

Available from
Paul Swallow
Department of the Environment, Transport and the Regions
Ashdown House
123 Victoria Street
London
Tel: 020 7890 6502; Fax: 020 7890 6489;
Email: paul.swallow@nfp-gb.eionet.eu.int

Sources from which data for this product are obtained
Countryside Survey - GB

Development Control Statistics: England
Department of the Environment, Transport and the Regions

Comprehensive volume of statistics of planning applications and decisions, data on planning appeals and action against alleged breaches of planning control. Contains data on applications received and decided by local authorities, by type of decision, type and size of development, and speed of decision. Includes historic data at national level, and detailed statistics at local authority level. Also data on action taken against breaches of planning control, appeals against planning decisions and decisions by the Secretary of State for the Environment.

Frequency: Annually
Price: £10.00

Available from
Ian Rowe
Department of the Environment, Transport and the Regions
Please see Annex B for full address details.

Sources from which data for this product are obtained
Land with outstanding planning permission for residential development - England; Minerals and Waste Development - Applications and Decisions - England; Planning Applications and Decisions - England

---

Housing Land Availability: the Analysis of PS3 Statistics on Land with Outstanding Planning Permission
Department of the Environment, Transport and the Regions

Research into the usefulness of statistics on outstanding planning permission for residential development as a means of measuring housing land availability. Contains research commissioned by the Department of the Environment into the relationship between land with OPP and land supply as indicated by other sources on land for housing. Includes proposals for two indicators of housing land availability based on statistics of land with OPP.

Price: £15.00
ISBN: 0 11 752709 2

Available from
TSO Publications Centre and Bookshops
Please see Annex B for full address details.

Sources from which data for this product are obtained
Land with outstanding planning permission for residential development - England

---

Land Use Change in England
Department of the Environment, Transport and the Regions

Statistical bulletin presenting statistics on changes in land use, based on data recorded by Ordnance Survey. Contains a matrix of change for England for the year for which five years of data have been recorded; estimates of change to urban uses, in particular to residential uses at regional and county level; preliminary results for change to residential use for which three years of data has been recorded.

Frequency: Annual
Price: £2.50

Available from
Dr Bob Garland
Department of the Environment, Transport and the Regions
Eland House
Bressenden Place
London
Tel: 020 7890 5533

Sources from which data for this product are obtained
Land Use Change - England

Land Use Change Statistics Research Project
Department of the Environment, Transport and the Regions

Sources from which data for this product are obtained
Land Use Change - England

Available from
Dr Bob Garland
Department of the Environment, Transport and

the Regions
Eland House
Bressenden Place
London
Tel: 020 7890 5533

Monitoring Housing Land Supply: Calibrating Indicators of Constraint
Department of the Environment, Transport and the Regions

Research report on the usefulness of statistics on land with outstanding planning permission as an indicator of the overall supply of land for housing. Contains research into the extent to which routine statistics collected on land with outstanding planning permission for residential development could be used to develop indicators of the overall housing land supply.

Price: £30.00
ISBN: 1 85112 226 5

Available from
Guy Ellis
Department of the Environment, Transport and the Regions
Eland House
Bressenden Place
London
Tel: 020 7890 5507; Fax: 020 7890 5519;
Email: guy.ellis@detr.gsi.gov.uk

Sources from which data for this product are obtained
Land with outstanding planning permission for residential development - England

(The) National Survey of Vacant Land in Urban Areas of England 1990
Department of the Environment, Transport and the Regions

Report presenting the results of a survey of vacant land in urban areas of England carried out in 1990. Contains estimates of area of vacant land in urban areas, and the percentage of areas covered by vacant land presented for standard economic regions, former DoE administrative regions, urban programme authorities grouped within region, Inner London, Outer London and broad divisions of the South East and Eastern regions.

Price: £22.00
ISBN: 0 11 752692 4

Available from
TSO Publications Centre and Bookshops
Please see Annex B for full address details.

Sources from which data for this product are obtained
Vacant Land Use - England

Scottish Vacant and Derelict Land Survey
Scottish Executive

An annual statistical bulletin which presents the results of the annual survey of vacant and derelict land in Scotland. Contains data on vacant and derelict land sites in Scotland by area, length of time in this category, contamination, preferred or intended use, and reclamation.

Statistical Bulletin, also available on the web at www.scotland.gov.uk

Frequency: Annual
Price: £2.00
ISBN: 0 7480 7502 X
ISSN: 0264 1143

Available from
Scottish Executive Publication Sales
The Stationery Office Bookshop
71 Lothian Road
Edinburgh EH3 9AZ
Tel: 0131 228 4181; Fax: 0131 622 7017

Sources from which data for this product are obtained
Vacant and Derelict Land - Scotland

Statistics of 'Country Matters' Applications Received and Decided
Department of the Environment, Transport and the Regions

Information bulletin with statistics on planning applications received and decided by local planning authorities for minerals and waste developments. Contains the number of applications and decisions, by type and size of development, characteristics and type of site, and speed of decision.

Frequency: Annually
Price: Free

Available from
Ian Rowe
Department of the Environment, Transport and the Regions
Please see Annex B for full address details.

Sources from which data for this product are obtained
Minerals and Waste Development - Applications and Decisions - England

Statistics of Planning Applications - England
Department of the Environment, Transport and the Regions

Information bulletin with statistics on planning applications received and decided

by local planning authorities and 'county matters' authorities. Contains the number of applications and decisions, by type and size of development, speed of authority decision, figures on action taken by authorities against breaches of planning control and applications for determination as well as regulation 3 and 4 consents granted by LPAs. Available on World Wide Web at following address http://www.planning.detr.gov.uk/ under the section 'Statistics of Planning Applications'.

Frequency: Quarterly
Price: Free

Available from
Ian Rowe
Department of the Environment, Transport and the Regions
Please see Annex B for full address details.

Sources from which data for this product are obtained
Minerals and Waste Development - Applications and Decisions - England; Planning Applications and Decisions - England

Statistics of Planning Enforcement Action by Local Authorities and Appeals Against Enforcement Notices
Department of the Environment, Transport and the Regions

Information bulletin with statistics on action taken by local planning authorities against breaches of planning control. Contains data on type of action taken (various powers are available to LPAs: enforcement notices, stop notices, breach of condition notices, planning contravention notices, injunctions), and appeals against enforcement notices issued. Last edition published covered 1994/95.

Frequency: Annually
Price: Free

Available from
Ian Rowe
Department of the Environment, Transport and the Regions
Please see Annex B for full address details.

Sources from which data for this product are obtained
Planning Applications and Decisions - England

(The) Survey of Derelict Land in England
Department of the Environment, Transport and the Regions

Information on this publication is available from 020 7276 4704

Available from
Dr Bob Garland
Department of the Environment, Transport and
the Regions
Eland House
Bressenden Place
London
Tel: 020 7890 5533

Sources from which data for this product are obtained
Derelict Land - England

Survey of Land for Mineral Working in England 1994
Department of the Environment, Transport and the Regions

Latest statistics on the land use impact of mineral workings in England.

Available from
Dr Bob Garland
Department of the Environment, Transport and
the Regions
Eland House
Bressenden Place
London
Tel: 020 7890 5533

Sources from which data for this product are obtained
Mineral Workings Land - England

See also:
In this chapter:
Digest of Environmental Statistics *(15.13)*
Indicators of Sustainable Development - United Kingdom *(15.13)*
(The) Scottish Environment Statistics *(15.13)*
(The) UK Environment *(15.13)*

In other chapters:
Digest of Data for the Construction Industry *(see the Commerce, Construction, Energy and Industry chapter)*
Town Centres: Defining Boundaries for Statistical Monitoring *(see the Government Statistics - General chapter)*

15.21 Noise Pollution

Please see:
In this chapter:
Digest of Environmental Statistics *(15.13)*
(The) UK Environment *(15.13)*

15.22 Radioactivity

Environmental Monitoring for Radioactivity in Scotland

Department of the Environment, Transport and the Regions

Statistical bulletin showing levels of radiation monitored in various indicators around nuclear establishments in Scotland.

Frequency: Annual
Price: £2.00
ISBN: 0 7480 0816 0
ISSN: 0264-1143

Available from
TSO Publications Centre and Bookshops
Please see Annex B for full address details.

Sources from which data for this product are obtained
Environmental Protection - Scotland

Exposure to Radon in UK Dwellings (NRPB)
Department of the Environment, Transport and the Regions

Delivery: Hardcopy publication
Price: £10.00
ISBN: 0 85 951379 3

Available from
Adrian Redfern
Department of the Environment, Transport and
the Regions
Ashdown House
123 Victoria Street
London
Tel: 020 7890 6497; Fax: 020 7890 6489;
Email: adrian.redfern@detr.gsi.gov.uk

Sources from which data for this product are obtained
Public Exposure to Radon - UK

Gamma-Radiation Levels Outdoors in Great Britain (NRPB - R191)

Delivery: Hardcopy publication
Frequency: Ad hoc
Price: £5.00
ISBN: 0 85 951 261 4

Available from
TSO Publications Centre and Bookshops
Please see Annex B for full address details.

Sources from which data for this product are obtained
Public Exposure to Radon - UK

Natural Radiation Exposure in UK Dwellings (NRPB)
Department of the Environment, Transport and the Regions

Report of a survey of 2,000 UK dwellings.

Delivery: Hardcopy publication
Frequency: Ad hoc
Price: £10.00
ISBN: 0 85951 260 6

Available from
TSO Publications Centre and Bookshops
Please see Annex B for full address details.

Sources from which data for this product are obtained
Public Exposure to Radon - UK

(The) National Response Plan and Radioactive Incident and Monitoring Network (RIMNET): Phase 1.
Department of the Environment, Transport and the Regions

Available from
Adrian Redfern
Department of the Environment, Transport and
the Regions
Ashdown House
123 Victoria Street
London
Tel: 020 7890 6497; Fax: 020 7890 6489;
Email: adrian.redfern@detr.gsi.gov.uk

Sources from which data for this product are obtained
Radioactive Incident Monitoring Network (RIMNET) - UK

Radioactive Waste Disposals from Nuclear Sites in Scotland
Department of the Environment, Transport and the Regions

Statistical bulletin with summary information on radioactive waste disposals from nuclear sites in Scotland. Contains data on discharges of solid, liquid and gaseous radioactive waste.

Frequency: Annual
Price: £2.00
ISBN: 0 7480 0973 6
ISSN: 0264-1143

Available from
TSO Publications Centre and Bookshops
Please see Annex B for full address details.

Radiation Exposure of the UK Population (NRPB - R263)
Department of the Environment, Transport and the Regions

Comprehensive review of radiation doses in the UK from all sources, both natural and artificial.

Delivery: Hardcopy publication
Frequency: Ad hoc

Price: £10.00
ISBN: 0 85951 364 5

Available from
TSO Publications Centre and Bookshops
Please see Annex B for full address details.

Radioactive Fallout in Air and Rain
Department of the Environment, Transport and the Regions

Delivery: Hardcopy publication
Frequency: Annual
Price: £72.00
ISBN: 070 581 665 6

Available from
Adrian Redfern
Department of the Environment, Transport and the Regions
Ashdown House
123 Victoria Street
London
Tel: 020 7890 6497; Fax: 020 7890 6489;
Email: adrian.redfern@detr.gsi.gov.uk

Radioactivity in Food and the Environment (RIFE)
SEPA; sponsored by MAFF

Gives results of monitoring radioactivity and dose rates. Estimates of dose received by a range of exposure groups. Covers the whole of the UK.

Delivery: Periodic Release
Frequency: Annually
Price: Free
ISSN: 1365 6414

Available from
MAFF Publications Section
Ministry of Agriculture, Fisheries and Food
Please see Annex B for full address details

Radioactivity in Surface and Coastal Waters in the British Isles
Department of the Environment, Transport and the Regions

Reports the results of monitoring the aquatic environment each calendar year.

Price: Free

Available from
Adrian Redfern
Department of the Environment, Transport and the Regions
Ashdown House
123 Victoria Street
London
Tel: 020 7890 6497; Fax: 020 7890 6489;
Email: adrian.redfern@detr.gsi.gov.uk

Sources from which data for this product are obtained
Radioactive Discharges - GB

Radon Atlas of England (NRPB - R290)
Department of the Environment, Transport and the Regions

Presents the results of survey of radon levels in homes in England up to May 1996 as maps.

Delivery: Hardcopy publication
Frequency: Ad hoc
Price: £10.00
ISBN: 0 85951 400 5

Available from
TSO Publications Centre and Bookshops
Please see Annex B for full address details.

Radon in Dwellings in England (NRPB)
Department of the Environment, Transport and the Regions

Companion report to the Radon Atlas of England. Presents the results of radon measurements in English homes available to January 1997. The data are presented by administrative areas and postcode divisions.

Delivery: Hardcopy publication
Frequency: Ad hoc
Price: £10.00
ISBN: 0 85951 4056

Available from
TSO Publications Centre and Bookshops
Please see Annex B for full address details.

Radon in Dwellings in Northern Ireland (NRPB - R308)

Presents the results of radon measurements in homes in Northern Ireland available in early 1999. The results are presented by district council and postcode divisions and as a map.

Delivery: Hardcopy publication
Frequency: Ad hoc

Available from
The Environment and Heritage Service
Calvert House
23 Castle Place
Belfast BT1 1FY
Tel: 028 9025 4773

Radon in Dwellings in Wales (NRPB - R303)

Presents the results of radon measurements

---

in homes in Wales to early 1998. The results are presented by unitary authority and postcode divisions and as a map.

Delivery: Hardcopy publication
Frequency: Ad hoc
Price: £10.00
ISBN: 0 85 951 423 4

Available from
TSO Publications Centre and Bookshops
Please see Annex B for full address details.

UK Radioactive Waste Inventory (Electrowatt Engineering Services Ltd)
Department of the Environment, Transport and the Regions

Report on the Inventory undertaken in 1994. Report DoE/RAS/96.001, UK Nirex No 695. Similar inventories have been produced for 1986, 1987, 1988, 1989 and 1991.

Delivery: Hardcopy publication
Frequency: Every 3 - 4 years

Available from
Radioactive Substances Division
Department of the Environment, Transport and the Regions
Ashdown House
123 Victoria Street
London SW1E CDE
Tel: 020 7890 6289

Sources from which data for this product are obtained
Radioactive Waste Stocks, Arisings and Disposal - GB

See also:
In this chapter:
Digest of Environmental Statistics *(15.13)*
Indicators of Sustainable Development - United Kingdom *(15.13)*
(The) Scottish Environment Statistics *(15.13)*
(The) UK Environment *(15.13)*

15.23 Recovery and Recycling of Materials

Annual Iron and Steel Statistics for the UK (Iron and Steel Statistics Bureau)
Iron and Steel Statistics Bureau

Available from
Chris Edwards
Iron and Steel Statistics Bureau
Millbank Tower
21/24 Millbank
London

Sources from which data for this product are obtained
Waste Recycling - UK

(The) National Directory of Recycling Information (Waste Watch)
Department of the Environment, Transport and the Regions

Available from
Christine Ogden
Department of the Environment, Transport and the Regions
Ashdown House
123 Victoria Street
London
Tel: 020 7890 6524; Fax: 020 7890 6489

Sources from which data for this product are obtained
Waste Recycling - UK

See also:
In this chapter:
Digest of Environmental Statistics (15.13)
Indicators of Sustainable Development - United Kingdom *(15.13)*
Municipal Waste Management *(15.24)*
(The) Scottish Environment Statistics *(15.13)*
(The) UK Environment *(15.13)*

15.24 Waste

Municipal Waste Management
Department of the Environment, Transport and the Regions

Report of the results of an annual survey on the management of municipal and household waste including levels of recycling and recovery, in England and Wales.

Delivery: Periodic Release
Frequency: Annually
Price: £10.00
ISBN: 1 85112 064 5

Available from
Christine Ogden
Department of the Environment, Transport and the Regions
Ashdown House
123 Victoria Street
London
Tel: 020 7890 6524; Fax: 020 7890 6489

Sources from which data for this product are obtained
Municipal waste Management Survey - England & Wales

See also:
In this chapter:
Digest of Environmental Statistics *(15.13)*
Environment Statistics 1996 *(15.13)*
Environmental Protection Expenditure by Industry (1995) *(15.16)*
Indicators of Sustainable Development - United Kingdom *(15.13)*
(The) Scottish Environment Statistics *(15.13)*
(The) UK Environment *(15.13)*

15.25 Wildlife

(The) New Atlas of Breeding Birds in Britain and Ireland: 1988-91
Department of the Environment, Transport and the Regions

Sources from which data for this product are obtained
Common Birds Census - GB

Available from
John Custance
Department of the Environment, Transport and the Regions
Ashdown House
123 Victoria Street
London
020 7890 6514; Fax: 020 7890 6489;
Email: john.custance@detr.gsi.gov.uk

See also:
In this chapter:
Digest of Environmental Statistics *(15.13)*
Indicators of Sustainable Development - United Kingdom *(15.13)*
(The) Scottish Environment Statistics *(15.13)*
(The) UK Environment *(15.13)*

Civic Affairs, Culture, Sport and Leisure

Statistics covering **Civic Affairs, Culture, Sport and Leisure** are collected, administered and disseminated by a number of separate Departments, Agencies and organisations including the **Office for National Statistics, the Home Office, the Department for Culture, Media and Sport, Scottish Executive,** the **General Register Office for Scotland and the Office of Fair Trading.** The available statistics embrace a number of subject areas including: **Consumer Affairs, Cultural Affairs, Elections and the Electorate, the Fire Brigade Service, Gaming and Liquor Licensing, Licensing of Scientific Procedures,** and **Sport and Leisure.**

The basic data are generated from a number of separate information 'Sources' and the resultant statistics are disseminated through a whole range of statistical 'Analyses' and 'Products', all of which are described in the following chapter.Users interested in a wider range of official statistics including **Civic Affairs, Culture, Sport and Leisure** statistics may like to refer to the following compendia:

> On-line Databases (See Chapter 1):
> > **StatBase - StatStore**
>
> Hardcopy Compendia (See Chapter 2):
> > **Annual Abstract of Statistics**
> > **Britain 2000: The Official Yearbook of the United Kingdom**
> > **Regional Trends**
> > **Social Trends**

Users may also find what they need on the various Departmental Websites. These are listed in Chapter 1.

Civic Affairs, Culture, Sport and Leisure - *Sources and Analyses*

16.1 Consumer Affairs

Quarterly Survey of Environmental Health Departments: Numbers of Consumer Complaints
Office of Fair Trading

Quarterly voluntary survey of UK Environmental Health Departments. Data are collected for the numbers of complaints in 59 categories of goods and services, and 9 trading practices. Data collected from June 1974 onwards; reclassification in 1 October 1987.

Status: Ongoing
Collection Method: Administrative Records
Frequency: Quarterly
Timeliness: Published annually in the Annual Report of the Director of Fair Trading.
Earliest Available Data: 1974
National Coverage: United Kingdom

Statistician
Derek Jones
Office of Fair Trading
Consumer Affairs
Tel: 020 7211 8772;
Email: derek.jones@oft.gov.uk

Products that contain data from this source
Annual Report of the Director General of Fair Trading

Television Programmes Complaints - UK
Department for Culture, Media and Sport; sponsored by Broadcast Standards Commission

The Broadcasting Standards Commission compiles data on complaints about television programmes. Data are available on the number of complaints considered, how many were upheld and the area into which a complaint fell. The series covers the United Kingdom and began in 1990.

Status: Ongoing
Collection Method: Administrative Records
Frequency: Monthly
Timeliness: one month after reference period.
National Coverage: United Kingdom

Statistician
Paul Allin
Department for Culture, Media and Sport
Analytical Services Unit; Statistics Branch
Room 601
Haymarket House
2-4 Cockspur Street
London SW1A 5DH
Tel: 020 7211 2843;
Email: paul.allin@culture.gov.uk

16.2 Elections and the Electorate

(The) Electorate - Scotland
General Register Office for Scotland

The General Register Office for Scotland collates information on parliamentary and local government electors on behalf of the Scottish Executive Home Department. Summary information from the electoral registers is supplied by the Electoral Registration Officers. As well as detailing the numbers of people eligible to vote, the data are used in preparing migration estimates. Data are available for Scotland, local authority areas, parliamentary constituencies and electoral wards. Electoral statistics for parliamentary constituencies and local government areas are available from the early 1980s with some summary data available from 1945. Electoral statistics based on the final electoral registers are compiled annually in March.

Status: Ongoing
Collection Method: Administrative Records
Frequency: Annually
National Coverage: Scotland

Statistician
Garnett Compton
General Register Office for Scotland
Tel: 0131 314 4298;
Email: garnett.compton@gro-scotland.gov.uk

Products that contain data from this source
Electoral Registration in 1991; Electoral Statistics (1997); Electoral Statistics - Parliamentary and Local Government Electors (1998); Electoral Statistics 1993 - European Parliamentary Constituencies; General Register Office for Scotland (GRO(S)) Site on the World Wide Web; Scottish Abstract of Statistics

---

Election Expenses
Home Office

The Home Office compiles data on the return of candidates' election expenses following Parliamentary General Elections (but not by-elections); also data relating to postal ballots and number of rejected ballot papers. Data cover the whole of the UK and are available at UK parliamentary constituency levels. Data have been collected and published following every general election since 1885.

Status: Ongoing
Collection Method: Returns from Acting Returning Officers
Frequency: After every general election
Timeliness: No set period; published a.s.a.p.
Earliest Available Data: 1885
National Coverage: Whole of UK
Disaggregation: UK parliamentary constituencies

Statistician
Ann Barber
Home Office
Tel: 020 7273 2712

Products that contain data from this source
Election expenses

European Parliamentary and General Election Expenses - UK
Home Office

The Home Office compiles data on the return of candidates' election expenses following European parliamentary elections and general elections. Data cover the UK and are available at parliamentary or European constituency levels. Data have been collected and published from May 1979 and are collected following every European parliamentary and general election.

Status: Ongoing
Collection Method: Returns from Acting Returning Officers
Frequency: After every European Parliamentary Election (i.e. every five years)
Earliest Available Data: 1979
National Coverage: Whole of UK
Disaggregation: European Parliamentary Constituencies

Statistician
Ann Barber
Home Office
Tel: 020 7273 2712

Products that contain data from this source
European Parliamentary Election Expenses,
United Kingdom

16.3 Fire Brigade Service

Fire - UK
Home Office

The Home Office compiles data on fires attended by local authority fire brigades in the United Kingdom. Reports go back to 1946 but the format for collecting the data has changed over the period resulting in some inconsistencies. From 1994 the report form was improved and there will be some resultant changes in presentation and detail available in the future. Data cover the United Kingdom and are available at fire brigade area level. The data are collected monthly, as individual reports for major fires and monthly totals for secondary fires (mainly outdoor and chimney), and published annually. A summary report is usually available by the middle of the year following the report year, with a full report before the end of the year.

Status: Ongoing
Collection Method: Individual returns and monthly summaries
Frequency: Monthly
Reference Period: Calendar year
Timeliness: 6 to 10 months from the end of the calendar year.
Earliest Available Data: 1946
National Coverage: United Kingdom
Disaggregation: Fire Authority Areas

Statistician
Lorraine Watson
Home Office
Tel: 020 7217 8300

Products that contain data from this source
Fire Statistics United Kingdom

16.4 Gaming and Liquor Licensing

Betting Licensing - Great Britain
Home Office

The data contains details of permits and licences in force, and applications, grants, renewals and cessations of bookmakers' permits and betting office licences in Great Britain, and numbers of appeals against refusal. Data are collected by statute under

paragraph 37 of Schedule 1 to the Betting Gaming and Lotteries Act 1963.

Status: Ongoing
Collection Method: Returns from Justices' Clerks
Frequency: Every three years, the next being in 2000
Reference Period: 12-month period ending 31 May
Timeliness: 4-5 months after the end of the period
Earliest Available Data: 1960
National Coverage: Great Britain
Disaggregation: Counties, Scottish Regions

Statistician
Ann Barber
Home Office
Tel: 020 7273 2712

Products that contain data from this source
Betting Licensing Statistics - Great Britain

Liquor Licensing - England and Wales
Home Office

The Home Office compiles data on liquor licensing. Data cover the number of premises licensed for the retail sale of intoxicating liquor, registered clubs, theatres, special hours certificates, restriction orders, occasional permissions, childrens certificates, and revoked licences. Data cover England and Wales and are available at county and liquor licensing committee (petty sessional division) level. Information is available from the early 20th century, but since 1980 has been collected only every three years.

Status: Ongoing
Collection Method: Returns from Justices' Clerks
Frequency: Every three years, the next being in 2001
Reference Period: 12-month period ending 30 June
Timeliness: 5-6 months after the end of the period
Earliest Available Data: 1905
National Coverage: England and Wales
Disaggregation: Counties

Statistician
Ann Barber
Home Office
Tel: 020 7273 2712

Products that contain data from this source
Liquor Licensing Statistics - England and Wales

Liquor Licensing Statistics Scotland
Scottish Executive

The Scottish Executive Home Department carries out a survey on the numbers of liquor

licenses in force within each District Licensing Board and the number of regular extensions to permitted licensing hours granted to each Licensing Board. Data are available by type of premises. The survey covers Scotland and data are available at District Licensing Board level. Results are published in May or June following the calendar year end.

Status: Ongoing
Collection Method: Census
Frequency: Annually
Reference Period: The calendar year
Timeliness: About 6 months
Earliest Available Data: 1991
National Coverage: Scotland
Disaggregation: Local Authority

Statistician
Sandy Taylor
Scottish Executive
Criminal Justice Division; Civil and Criminal Justice Statistics 1
Tel: 0131 244 2224;
Email: sandy.taylor@scotland.gov.uk

Products that contain data from this source
Liquor Licensing Statistics; Scottish Abstract of Statistics

16.5 Licensing of Scientific Procedures

Scientific Procedures on Living Animals
Home Office

The Home Office is responsible for the control of scientific procedures performed on living animals in accordance with the Animals (Scientific Procedures) Act 1986. Contains data for Great Britain on procedures started in each calendar year, their reason and purpose, species of animals used, and type of establishment.

Status: Ongoing
Collection Method: Returns from project licensees
Frequency: Annual
Reference Period: Calendar year
Timeliness: Returns must be made by end Feb; publication must be by end July
Earliest Available Data: 1877
National Coverage: Great Britain

Statistician
Ann Barber
Home Office
Tel: 020 7273 2712

Products that contain data from this source
Statistics of Scientific Procedures on living animals, Great Britain (annual Command Paper)

See also:

In other chapters:
Judicial Statistics - Northern Ireland *(see the Crime and Justice chapter)*
Magistrates' Courts - Northern Ireland *(see the Crime and Justice chapter)*

16.6 Sports and Leisure Activities

Sports Statistics - UK
Department for Culture, Media and Sport; sponsored by The Sports Council

The Centre for Leisure Research compiles data on sport for the Sports Council. Data are available on participation, provision, organisation and facilities. Studies were published in 1983, 1986 and 1991.

Status: Ongoing
National Coverage: United Kingdom

Statistician
Paul Allin
Department for Culture, Media and Sport
Analytical Services Unit; Statistics Branch
Room 601
Haymarket House
2-4 Cockspur Street
London SW1A 5DH
Tel: 020 7211 2843;
Email: paul.allin@culture.gov.uk

Civic Affairs, Culture, Sport and Leisure - *Products*

16.7 Consumer Affairs

Fair Trading
Office of Fair Trading

Fair Trading is a topical magazine providing information on current OFT activity for anyone with an interest in consumer protection or competition policy. Consumer complaints statistics - quarterly totals broken down by category of goods and services, and broken down by trading practice are presented in appendices to each issue.

Delivery: Periodic Release
Frequency: Quarterly
Price: Free

Available from
Information Branch
Office of Fair Trading
Field House
15 - 25 Bream's Buildings
London EC4Y 1PR

Sources from which data for this product are obtained
Quarterly Survey of Trading Standards Departments: numbers of consumer complaints

Trends in Consumer Complaints
Office of Fair Trading

Quarterly analysis of trends in consumer complaints reported to the Office of Fair Trading by Trading Standards Departments; analysis by goods and services category and by trading practice (type of problem) category. Many bodies record details of the complaints made by individual consumers about goods and services, but the most comprehensive figures available regularly, systematically classified by specific categories of goods and services, and by the trading practice that gave rise to each complaint, are those compiled by local authority trading standards departments and environmental health offices, and other local advisory agencies. These organisations voluntarily submit quarterly returns to the OFT which aggregates the figures and analyses trends. The Office also conducts ad-hoc surveys of consumer dissatisfaction, estimating not only the numbers of complaints but also the numbers of causes for complaint

Delivery: Periodic Release
Frequency: Quarterly
Price: Free

Available from
The Data Manager
Room 630, CAZC
Chancery House
53 Chancery Lane
London WC2A 1SP

Sources from which data for this product are obtained
Quarterly Survey of Trading Standards Departments: numbers of consumer complaints

See also:
In other chapters:
Annual Report of the Director General of Fair Trading *(see the Commerce, Construction, Energy and Industry chapter)*

16.8 Cultural Affairs

Artstat - Digest of Arts Statistics and Trends in the UK
British Tourist Authority; sponsored by Arts Council of England

The publication looks at information relating to the funding of the Arts, income and expenditure of arts organisations, and the attendance and participation of consumers in the arts. The years covered are 1986 to 1996. The purpose of the publication is to be a compendium of the above information, making the access to such data much easier than before. Around 180 pages of mainly tables and text covering information on funding for the arts and museums and libraries, the funding from the National Lottery, the income and expenditure of funded arts organisations and attendance and participation in the arts. The target market is policy markets, researchers, students and people in industry.

Delivery: Periodic Release
Frequency: First available January 1999

Available from
The Arts Council

Sources from which data for this product are obtained
Arts Council of England; Arts Council of Wales (Cyngor Celfyddydau Cymru); Scottish Arts Council, Centre for Leisure and Tourism Studies; Arts Council for Northern Ireland

16.9 Elections and the Electorate

Compiling the Electoral Register
Office for National Statistics; sponsored by Home Office

Contains the results of annual survey, carried out by ONS for the Home Office, on the way the electoral register is compiled and on the kind of statistical information Electoral Registration Officers can provide about their areas. Contains results on: the methods used to compile the electoral register, response to the electoral registration canvass, the effect of the methods used to improve response to the canvass, and the effect of local demographic factors on canvass response rates.

Frequency: Annual (series is now discontinued but the publications are still Available from TSO outlets)
Price: 1997 - £20.00
ISBN: 0 11 620914 3

Available from
TSO Publications Centre and Bookshops
Please see Annex B for full address details.

Electoral Registration in 1991
Home Office

Describes the findings of a survey, commissioned by the Home Office and Scottish Executive, on the coverage and quality of the 1991 electoral registers in Great Britain. The study was carried out in conjunction with the 1991 Census Validation Survey. Contains results on the proportion of people eligible to vote not registered as electors, the proportion of people included on the register and not actually entitled to vote, and the likelihood that eligible people might appear on the register more than once.

Frequency: Ad hoc
Price: £6.85
ISBN: 0 11 691543 9 (series SS 1301)

Products

Available from
TSO Publications Centre and Bookshops
Please see Annex B for full address details.

Sources from which data for this product are obtained
The Electorate - Scotland

Electoral Statistics (1997)
Office for National Statistics

The numbers of electors on the electoral registers for 1997 and, for comparison, 1996. Contains statistics showing the number of parliamentary electors and local government electors including European electors on registers in England, Wales, Scotland, and Northern Ireland.

Delivery: Periodic Release
Frequency: Bi-annually
Price: £18.95
ISBN: 0 11 620989 5 (series EL No 24, 1997)

Available from
TSO Publications Centre and Bookshops
Please see Annex B for full address details.

Sources from which data for this product are obtained
The Electorate - Scotland

Electoral Statistics - Parliamentary and Local Government Electors (1998)
Office for National Statistics

The numbers of electors on the electoral registers for the reference year and, for comparison, the previous year, for the United Kingdom. Contains statistics showing the number of electors in parliamentary constituencies and the number of local government electors on registers in England, Wales, Scotland, and Northern Ireland for the reference year.

Delivery: Periodic Release
Frequency: Annually
Price: £4.00
ISSN: 0953-3451, ONS Monitor (EL 98/1)

Available from
Brett Leeming
Room 2300
Office for National Statistics
Segensworth Road
Titchfield
Fareham
Hampshire PO15 5RR
Tel: 01329 813318

Sources from which data for this product are obtained
The Electorate - Scotland

Electoral Statistics 1993 - European Parliamentary Constituencies
Office for National Statistics

The numbers of electors on the electoral registers for the reference year qualified to vote in the European elections, for the United Kingdom. Contains statistics showing the number of European electors on registers in England, Wales, Scotland, and Northern Ireland for the reference year.

Delivery: Ad Hoc/One-off Release
Frequency: Periodic
Price: £4.00
ISSN: 0953-3451 OPCS Monitor (EL 93/2)

Sources from which data for this product are obtained
The Electorate - Scotland

Election Expenses
Home Office

Data on the return of candidates' election expenses following Parliamentary General Elections (but not by-elections); also data relating to postal ballots and rejected ballot papers.

Delivery: Periodic Release
Frequency: Published after every general election
Price: Fixed by TSO; the publication for the 1997 general election was £17.50
ISBN: 0 10 260599 8 (for 1997)

Available from
TSO Publications Centre and Bookshops
Please see Annex B for full address details.

Sources from which data for this product are obtained
UK Parliamentary General Election expenses

European Parliamentary Election Expenses, United Kingdom
Home Office

Data on the return of candidates' election expenses following elections.

Delivery: Periodic Release
Frequency: Published after every European Parliamentary election
Price: Free
ISSN: 0143-6348

Available from
Information and Publications Group
Home Office
Room 201
50 Queen Anne's Gate
London SW1H 9AT
Tel: 020 7273 2084

Sources from which data for this product are obtained
European Parliamentary and General Election Expenses - UK

16.10 Fire Brigade Service

Fire Statistics United Kingdom
Home Office

Commentary, charts and tables presenting data on fires in 1997. Contains data collected on fires attended by local authority fire brigades throughout the United Kingdom.

Frequency: Annual
Price: Free
ISSN: 0143-6384

Available from
Research, Development and Statistics Directorate
Information & Publication Group
Home Office
50 Queen Anne's Gate
London
SW1H 9AT

Sources from which data for this product are obtained
Fire - UK

National Fire Safety Week and Domestic Fire Safety
Office for National Statistics; sponsored by Home Office

Results from questions asked on the Omnibus Survey carried out by the former OPCS on behalf of the Home Office. Contains the results of questions that sought to monitor the effectiveness of the Home Office domestic fire safety campaign in 1991 and 1992. Questions were also asked about chip pan fires and smoke alarms in the home.

Frequency: Ad hoc
Price: £5.55
ISBN: 0 11 691597 8 (Omnibus Survey Report 2)

Available from
TSO Publications Centre and Bookshops
Please see Annex B for full address details.

Sources from which data for this product are obtained
The ONS Omnibus Survey - GB

16.11 Gaming and Liquor Licensing

Betting Licensing - GB
Home Office

The Home Office compiles data on Betting Licensing in Great Britain. Data are collected by statute under Paragraph 37 of Schedule 1 to the Betting, Gaming and Lotteries Act 1963. Data are available by licenses in force, applications for grants, renewals, cessation and appeals against refusal of applications for grant or renewal. The data cover Great Britain and are available at county and petty sessional division level. Data are published every third October, the next occasion being in 2000.

Delivery: Periodic Release
Frequency: Triennially - next in 2000
Price: Free
ISSN: 0143-6348

Available from
Information and Publications Group
Home Office
Please see Annex B for full address details.

Sources from which data for this product are obtained
Betting Licensing - Great Britain

Liquor Licensing - England and Wales
Home Office

The Home Office compiles data on liquor licences. Data cover the number of premises licensed for the retail sale of intoxicating liquor, registered clubs and theatres, special hours certificates, restriction orders, occasional permissions, and licences revoked. From 1995, information was also collected on children's certificates. Data cover England and Wales and are available at county and Liquor Licensing Committee area level. Information on liquor licensing statistics is Available from the late 19th century and is collected once every three years.

Delivery: Periodic Release
Frequency: Triennially - next in 2001
Price: Free
ISSN: 0143 6348

Available from
Information and Publications Group
Home Office
Please see Annex B for full address details.

Sources from which data for this product are obtained
Liquor Licensing - England and Wales

Liquor Licensing Statistics
Scottish Executive

Bulletin providing statistics on liquor licences in Scotland. Contains data on the numbers of licences in force, regular

extensions to licences and new applications for licences.

Delivery: News/Press Release
Frequency: Annually
Price: £2.00
ISBN: 0 7480 7500 3
ISSN: 0264 1178

Available from
TSO Publications Centre and Bookshops
Please see Annex B for full address details.

Sources from which data for this product are obtained
Liquor Licensing Statistics Scotland

See also:
In other chapters:
Northern Ireland Judicial Statistics *(see the Crime and Justice chapter)*

16.12 Licensing of Scientific Procedures

Statistics of Scientific Procedures Performed on Living Animals
Home Office

Command paper presenting data in accordance with the Animals (Scientific Procedures) Act 1986. Contains data for Great Britain on procedures and their reason and purpose, species of animal, technique used and establishment.

Delivery: Periodic Release
Frequency: Annual
Price: 1997 issue £13.45; 1998 TBA
ISBN: (1997) 010 140252 X; 1998 TBA

Available from
TSO Publications Centre and Bookshops
Please see Annex B for full address details.

Sources from which data for this product are obtained
Return of Procedures

16.13 Sports and Leisure Activities

General Household Survey: Participation in Sport
Office for National Statistics; sponsored by Department of Environment

Describes the method used on the GHS between 1973 and 1986 to collect information about leisure activities and presents results for 1987. Contains analysis

and statistics on participation in sporting activities taken from the 1987 General Household Survey. Chapters on sport have since been included in the main GHS report in 1990, 1993 and 1996 - sponsored by the Sports Council.

Frequency: Ad hoc
Price: £10.00
ISBN: 0 11 620946 1

Available from
TSO Publications Centre and Bookshops
Please see Annex B for full address details.

Sources from which data for this product are obtained
Living in Britain - Results from the 1996 General Household Survey

---

Government and Public Sector

Statistics covering **Government and the Public Sector** are collected, administered and disseminated by a number of separate Departments, Agencies and organisations including the **Office for National Statistics, the Cabinet Office, the Department of the Environment, Transport and the Regions, the Department for International Development, the Department for National Savings, Her Majesty's Treasury, HM Customs and Excise, the Inland Revenue, the Ministry of Defence, Scottish Executive, the National Assembly for Wales, the Northern Ireland Department of Finance and Personnel** and **the Office of Manpower Economics**. The available statistics embrace a number of subject areas including: the **Armed Forces and Defence, Employment in the Public Sector, Local Authorities' Finances, International Aid and Development, National Savings, Northern Ireland - Finances, Public Sector Borrowing, Public Sector Income and Expenditure, Research and Development Expenditure, Tax Revenues, Taxes and Excise Duties.**

The basic data are generated from a number of separate information 'Sources' and the resultant statistics are disseminated through a whole range of statistical 'Analyses' and 'Products', all of which are described in the following chapter. Users looking for a cross-section of UK-wide statistics on **Government and the Public Sector** may find the following products useful:

> **Financial Statistics** (monthly publication)
> **Inland Revenue Statistics** (annual publication)
> **Public Expenditure Statistical Analyses** (annual publication)
> **Public Finance Trends** (annual publication)
> **Statistics on International Development** (annual publication)
> **UK Defence Statistics** (annual publication)

Users interested in a wider range of official statistics including **Government and the Public Sector** statistics may like to refer to the following compendia:

> On-line Databases (See Chapter 1):
> > **StatBase - StatStore**
> > **StatBase - TimeZone**
> > **DataBank**

> Hardcopy Compendia (See Chapter 2):
> > **Annual Abstract of Statistics**
> > **Britain 2000: The Official Yearbook of the United Kingdom**
> > **Monthly Digest of Statistics**
> > **Regional Trends**
> > **Social Trends**

Users may also find what they need on the various Departmental Websites. These are listed in Chapter 1.

17

Government and Public Sector - *Sources and Analyses*

17.1 Armed Forces and Defence

Aerospace Databases
Ministry of Defence: sponsored by Society of British Aerospace Companies.

Contains details of expenditure of British aerospace companies.

Status: Ongoing
Collection Method: Census

Statistician
Robin Horton
Ministry of Defence
Tel: 020 7218 8326;
Email: triservice@dasa.mon.uk

Armed Forces in Northern Ireland Database
Ministry of Defence

Contains details of the Armed Forces in Northern Ireland and of security incidents there.

Status: Ongoing
Collection Method: Administrative Records
Frequency: Continuous
National Coverage: Northern Ireland

Statistician
Robin Horton
Ministry of Defence
Tel: 020 7218 8326;
Email: triservice@dasa.mon.uk

CIPMIS (Civilian Personnel Management Information System)
Ministry of Defence

Contains pay, career and other administrative details of all MoD civilian personnel.

Status: Ongoing
Collection Method: Administrative Records
Frequency: Continuous
Reference Period: Event dates

Statistician
Robin Horton
Ministry of Defence
Tel: 020 7218 8326;
Email: triservice@dasa.mon.uk

DASA Medical Database
Ministry of Defence

Contains details of the health of the UK armed forces.

Status: Ongoing
Collection Method: Administrative Records
Frequency: Continuous

Statistician
Robin Horton
Ministry of Defence
Tel: 020 7218 8326;
Email: triservice@dasa.mon.uk

Defence Bills Authority Databases
Ministry of Defence

Contains details of all bills presented to the MoD.

Status: Ongoing
Collection Method: Administrative Records
Frequency: Continuous
Reference Period: Government Financial Year

Statistician
Robin Horton
Ministry of Defence
Tel: 020 7218 8326;
Email: triservice@dasa.mon.uk

Defence Housing Database
Ministry of Defence

A Defence Housing Executive database that contains details of all MoD housing in the United Kingdom.

Status: Ongoing
Collection Method: Administrative Records
National Coverage: United Kingdom

Statistician
Robin Horton
Ministry of Defence
Tel: 020 7218 8326;
Email: triservice@dasa.mon.uk

Estates and Lands Database
Ministry of Defence

Contains details of lands and foreshores owned or leased by the MoD.

Status: Ongoing
Collection Method: Administrative Records
Frequency: Continuous

Statistician
Robin Horton
Ministry of Defence
Tel: 020 7218 8326;
Email: triservice@dasa.mon.uk

Flight Safety Database
Ministry of Defence

Contains details of MoD aircraft accidents and incidents and of the personnel affected.

Status: Ongoing
Collection Method: Administrative Records
Frequency: Continuous

Statistician
Robin Horton
Ministry of Defence
Tel: 020 7218 8326;
Email: triservice@dasa.mon.uk

Force Structure Database
Ministry of Defence

Contains details of the structure of the front-line and support structure of the three Services.

Status: Ongoing
Collection Method: Administrative Records
Frequency: Continuous

Statistician
Robin Horton
Ministry of Defence
Tel: 020 7218 8326;
Email: triservice@dasa.mon.uk

Home and Special Forces Database
Ministry of Defence

Contains details of incidents of military aid provided to civil ministries during, for example, industrial disputes.

Status: Ongoing
Collection Method: Administrative Records
Frequency: Continuous

Statistician
Robin Horton
Ministry of Defence
Tel: 020 7218 8326;
Email: triservice@dasa.mon.uk

Long Term Costings
Ministry of Defence

Contains details of forecast expenditure against all MoD account codes.

Status: Ongoing
Collection Method: Administrative Records
Frequency: Annually
Reference Period: Government Financial Years

Statistician
Robin Horton
Ministry of Defence
Tel: 020 7218 8326;
Email: triservice@dasa.mon.uk

MoD Central Ledger
Ministry of Defence

Contains details of expenditure against all MoD account codes.

Status: Ongoing
Collection Method: Administrative Records
Frequency: Continuous
Reference Period: Government Financial Year

Statistician
Robin Horton
Ministry of Defence
Tel: 020 7218 8326;
Email: triservice@dasa.mon.uk

MoD Directorate of Commercial Policy Contracts Database
Ministry of Defence

Contains details of all recent and current contracts entered into by the MoD.

Status: Ongoing
Collection Method: Administrative Records
Frequency: Continuous
Reference Period: Government Financial Year

Statistician
Robin Horton
Ministry of Defence
Tel: 020 7218 8326;
Email: triservice@dasa.mon.uk

MoD Service Personnel Databases
Ministry of Defence

Contains pay, career and other administrative details of all MoD Service personnel and reserves.

Status: Ongoing
Collection Method: Administrative Records
Frequency: Continuous
Reference Period: Event dates

Statistician
Robin Horton
Ministry of Defence
Tel: 020 7218 8326;
Email: triservice@dasa.mon.uk

Procurement Plans Database
Ministry of Defence

Contains details of all MoD equipment projects.

Status: Ongoing
Collection Method: Administrative Records
Frequency: Continuously

Statistician
Robin Horton
Ministry of Defence
Tel: 020 7218 8326;
Email: triservice@dasa.mon.uk

Search and Rescue Database
Ministry of Defence

Contains details of aspects of the work of the Search and Rescue services.

Status: Ongoing
Collection Method: Administrative Records
Frequency: Continuous

Statistician
Robin Horton
Ministry of Defence
Tel: 020 7218 8326;
Email: triservice@dasa.mon.uk

Shipping Database
Ministry of Defence: sponsored by Department of the Environment, Transport and the Regions

Contains details of British ships, including the British merchant fleet.

Status: Ongoing

Statistician
Robin Horton
Ministry of Defence
Tel: 020 7218 8326;
Email: triservice@dasa.mon.uk

Stockholdings Databases
Ministry of Defence

Each of the three Services maintain databases containing details of their stockholdings.

Status: Ongoing
Collection Method: Administrative Records
Frequency: Continuous

Statistician
Robin Horton
Ministry of Defence
Tel: 020 7218 8326;
Email: triservice@dasa.mon.uk

UK Defence
Ministry of Defence

The Ministry of Defence compiles data on UK defence. Data are available on expenditure and trade, personnel and resources, and defence services. Data cover the UK and overseas and are available at economic planning region level in the UK and at broad geographic area level overseas. Data are compiled and published every financial year.

Frequency: Annually
National Coverage: United Kingdom

Statistician
Robin Horton
Ministry of Defence
Tel: 020 7218 8326;
Email: triservice@dasa.mon.uk

Products that contain data from this analysis
Defence Statistics Bulletins; UK Defence Statistics

See also:
In other chapters:
Fisheries Database (see the Agriculture, Fishing, Food and Forestry chapter)

17.2 Employment in the Public Sector

Civil Service Personnel: Mandate
Cabinet Office

Database of Civil Service personnel statistics gathered from individual Government Departments / Agencies which is collated, maintained and analysed by Cabinet Office. Data are available by department/agency, permanent and casual staff, sex, full-time and part-time, industrial and non-industrial employees, resignations and recruitment etc. It is collected quarterly, providing estimates of the number of Civil Service staff which are published about six months after the reference period. The database includes most government departments and civil servants and is often combined with civil service Quarterly Staff returns for publication.

Status: Ongoing
Collection Method: Administrative Records
Frequency: Quarterly
Reference Period: 1 January, 1 April, 1 July, 1 October of each year
Timeliness: 6 months
Earliest Available Data: 1975
National Coverage: United Kingdom
Sub-National: Government Office Region (GOR) regularly produced. Other areas can be analysed

Statistician
Linda Murgatroyd
Cabinet Office
Civil Service Corporate Management Command, Central Support: Statistics
Room 128/3
1 Horse Guards Road
London SW1V 1RB
Tel: 020 7270 5420;
Email: lmurgatroyd@cabinetoffice.x.gsi.gov.uk

Products that contain data from this source
Annual Abstract of Statistics; Equal Opportunities in the Civil Service Data Summary: Women, Race, Disability, Age; Cabinet Office Web Site

Civil Service Quarterly Staff Returns
Cabinet Office

The Cabinet Office collects data on the numbers of staff in post from departments/agencies that are not Mandate reliant on both a headcount and full time equivalent basis. Breakdowns are provided by permanent/casual or seasonal, industrial/non-industrial and full time/part time.

Status: Ongoing
Collection Method: Administrative Records
Frequency: Quarterly
Reference Period: Staff in post at 1 January, 1 April, 1 July, 1 October
Timeliness: Approximately 6 months
Earliest Available Data: 1975
National Coverage: United Kingdom
Sub-National: Totals available for Government Regions
Disaggregation: Detailed disaggregation possible, but see entry for Mandate

Statistician
Linda Murgatroyd
Cabinet Office
Civil Service Corporate Management Command, Central Support: Statistics
Room 128/3
1 Horse Guards Road
London SW1V 1RB
Tel: 020 7270 5420;
Email: lmurgatroyd@cabinet-office.x.gsi.gov.uk

Products that contain data from this source
Civil Service Statistics, Civil Service Statistics Key Figures, Civil Service Data Summary: Women, Race, Disability, Age; Annual Abstract of Statistics; Cabinet Office Web Site

Joint Staffing Watch Survey - England
Department of the Environment, Transport and the Regions

The Department of the Environment and local authority associations compiled data, supplied by local authorities, for the Joint Staffing Watch Survey. The Survey was conducted by the Local Government Management Board (LGMB) on behalf of the Joint Staffing Watch Group, which comprise representatives of both central and local government. Data are available on local authority employment in England by full-time and part-time, manual and non-manual, and service, and at local authority district level.

Status: Ceased completely
Collection Method: Census
Frequency: Annually
Reference Period: Staff Employed at June of each year
Timeliness: 9 working days
Earliest Available Data: 1979
National Coverage: England
Disaggregation: English Shire Counties, English Shire Districts, Metropolitan Districts, London Boroughs, Unitary Authorities, Waste Authorities, Fire Authorities

Statistician
Mark Chaplin
Department of the Environment, Transport and the Regions
Local Government Finance Policy Directorate; Local Government Finance Statistics Division Branch 3
Tel: 020 7890 4167;
Email: lgf.doe@dial.pipex.com

Products that contain data from this source
Joint Staffing Watch (Press Release); Local Government Financial Statistics: England

Local Authority Annual Staffing Survey - Scotland
Scottish Executive

The Scottish Executive Development Department compiled data on the full-time equivalent and number of local authority employees. This survey was introduced, from December 1994, to provide detailed information on the number of local authority employees by service and sub-service, covering the period of local government reorganisation in Scotland. Four surveys were planned, with respect to the number of staff in authorities at 31 December each year until December 1997. The surveys were being used to report on changes in the number and structure of local authority staffing over the reorganisation period. They form a key part of the evaluation of the reorganisation. Since the reorganisation was expected to have a disproportionate effect

on numbers of senior staff, the survey distinguished numbers of staff by service in each of four salary bands - designed to cover senior management, middle management, clerical and manual staff. The survey also gathered supplementary information on vacancies, the apportionment of support service staff costs to specific services, and numbers of staff by age and by sex.

Status: Ceased completely
Collection Method: Census
Frequency: Annually
Reference Period: December of each year covered
Timeliness: Summary results published about 6 months after the reference date.
Earliest Available Data: December 1994
National Coverage: Scotland

Statistician
John Landrock
Scottish Executive
Economics Advice and Statistics Division; EAS 5
Tel: 0131 244 7031;
Email: john.landrock@scotland.gov.uk

Products that contain data from this source
First Results of New Annual Local Authority Staffing Survey: (December 1994) (Statistical Bulletin)

Local Authority Joint Staffing Watch - Scotland
Scottish Executive: sponsored by the Convention of Scottish Local Authorities

The Scottish Executive Development Department and The Convention of Scottish Local Authorities compiles data on the number and estimated full-time equivalent number of local authority employees. This information is collected by the Convention of Scottish Local Authorities from all Scottish authorities. It covers number of male and female, full-time and part-time, manual and non-manual staff by main local authority service.

Status: Ongoing
Collection Method: Census
Frequency: Quarterly
Reference Period: Specific dates in June, September, December and March
Timeliness: About 6 months. Target is to reduce this nearer to 3 months.
Earliest Available Data: 1976
National Coverage: Scotland

Statistician
John Landrock
Scottish Executive
Economics Advice and Statistics Division; EAS 5
Tel: 0131 244 7031;
Email: john.landrock@scotland.gov.uk

Products that contain data from this source
Joint Staffing Watch Results (Quarterly Press Release)

Public Corporations Employees in Employment - UK
Office for National Statistics

The Public Corporations Employees in Employment Annual Inquiry is carried out by the Office for National Statistics. Head counts are taken of the employees in each public corporation at 30 June each year. Employees in employment data are available by gender and full-time and part-time staff.

Frequency: Annually
Earliest Available Data: 1988
National Coverage: United Kingdom

Statistician
Jeff Golland
Office for National Statistics
Tel: 020 7533 5987

Products that contain data from this source
Economic Trends; United Kingdom National Accounts - The Blue Book

Public Sector Employment - UK
Office for National Statistics

The Office for National Statistics compiles data on public sector employment. The statistics cover three main areas: (1) Central government, encompassing HM Forces; National Health Service; the Civil Service and other central government areas; (2) Local authorities, including education, social services, construction, police, other local authorities; and local authorities community programme; (3) Public corporations, including nationalised industries, NHS Trusts, and other public corporations.

Earliest Available Data: 1959 (annual), 1974 (quarterly)
National Coverage: United Kingdom
Sub-National: Police force area, Local authority

Statistician
Jeff Golland
Office for National Statistics
Tel: 020 7533 5987

Products that contain data from this source
Economic Trends; General Government Non-Trading Employment Quarterly Employment Briefing; Monthly Digest of Statistics; Office for National Statistics Databank / Datastore; United Kingdom National Accounts - The Blue Book

17.3 England - Local Authorities' Finances

Basic Credit Approvals
Department of the Environment, Transport and the Regions

This booklet sets out the Basic Credit Approvals (BCA) for the coming year issued to local authorities in England. It also gives background to the calculation of the Basic Credit Approvals including: the public spending provision for Basic Credit Approvals for the main blocks of services; the treatment of Capital Challenge allocations; the total Annual Capital Guidelines used in the calculation of Basic Credit Approvals; and the capital ' receipts taken into account'. This paper can be accessed via the internet at http://www.local.detr.gov.uk.

Status: Ongoing
Frequency: Annually
National Coverage: England
Disaggregation: Local Authority

Statistician
Clare Goldschmidt
Department of the Environment, Transport and the Regions
Tel: 020 7890 4076;
Email: clare_goldschmidt@detr.gsi.gov.uk

Capital Estimates Return - England
Department of the Environment, Transport and the Regions

The Department of the Environment, Transport and the Regions collates capital estimate returns from all local authorities in England. Data are collected on local authorities' forecasts of capital expenditure, receipts and use of resources for the following financial year. The forms are despatched beginning of March for return by 1 April.

Status: Ongoing
Collection Method: Census
Frequency: Annually
Reference Period: Financial year
Timeliness: 2 months after return of the forms
Earliest Available Data: 1990/91
National Coverage: England
Disaggregation: Shire Counties, Metropolitan Districts, London Boroughs, Unitary Authorities, Shire Districts, Fire Authorities, Park Authorities, Police Authorities, Probation Authorities, Transport Authorities and Waste Authorities

Statistician
Clare Goldschmidt
Department of the Environment, Transport and the Regions
Tel: 020 7890 4076;
Email: clare_goldschmidt@detr.gsi.gov.uk

Products that contain data from this source
Local Government Financial Statistics: England

Capital Outturn Returns - England
Department of the Environment, Transport and the Regions

The Department of the Environment collates the Capital Outturn Forms (COR1-5) from all local authorities. The COR forms record local authorities' outturn of capital expenditure and receipts. The forms are despatched beginning of May for return by end of July. Until 1996/97 the COR1 covered capital expenditure for details of services such as education, personal social services, transport, housing, art and libraries, sport and recreation, and others. COR2 recorded capital receipts for these groups. The COR3 form recorded further details of capital expenditure for personal social services. COR4 recorded financing of capital payments and the capital account summary, and COR5 recorded data on local authority usable receipts, provision for credit liabilities and credit ceiling. From 1997/98 the COR outturn suite of forms were reviewed and a number of changes introduced. The COR1 and COR2 forms now cover data previously recorded on the old COR1A, COR1B and COR2 forms. The old COR2 form has been abolished, and the receipts data collected, together with expenditure on the new COR1 and COR2 forms. The COR3 form records further details of capital expenditure for personal social services (PSS). COR4 records financing of capital expenditure and capital account summary. COR5 records data on local authority usable receipts, provision of credit liabilities, credit ceiling and value of fixed assets. The data feeds into the National Accounts.

Status: Ongoing
Collection Method: Census
Frequency: Annually
Reference Period: Financial year
Timeliness: 9 to 10 months after collection
Earliest Available Data: 1990/91
National Coverage: England
Disaggregation: Shire Counties, Metropolitan Districts, London Boroughs, Unitary Authorities, Shire Districts, Fire Authorities, Park Authorities, Police Authorities, Probation Authorities, Transport Authorities and Waste Authorities

Statistician
Clare Goldschmidt
Department of the Environment, Transport and the Regions
Tel: 020 7890 4076;
Email: clare_goldschmidt@detr.gsi.gov.uk

Products that contain data from this source
Local Government Financial Statistics: England

Products that contain data from this source
Local Government Financial Statistics: England

Sources and Analyses

Capital Payments Return - England
Department of the Environment, Transport and the Regions

The Department of the Environment collates Capital Payments Returns (CPR) from all local authorities. The forms are despatched at the end of each quarter in June, September, December and March for return a month later in each instance. The data collected on the CPR1 to 3 are cumulative levels of capital expenditure and receipts and forecasts for the whole year. Forecasts of the source of financing are also included. The CPR4 collects capital expenditure and receipts data for the whole year for each service block and the resources used to finance capital expenditure. They are used to provide up-to-date estimates of capital spend and financing for the Public Expenditure review process and for National Accounts.

Status: Ongoing
Collection Method: Census
Frequency: Quarterly
Reference Period: Cumulative totals for the quarters ending in June, September, December and March
Timeliness: 2 to 3 months after return date
Earliest Available Data: 1990/91
National Coverage: England
Disaggregation: Shire Counties, Metropolitan Districts, London Boroughs, Unitary Authorities, Shire Districts, Fire Authorities, Park Authorities, Police Authorities, Probation Authorities, Transport Authorities and Waste Authorities

Statistician
Clare Goldschmidt
Department of the Environment, Transport and the Regions
Tel: 020 7890 4076;
Email: clare_goldschmidt@detr.gsi.gov.uk

Products that contain data from this source
Local Government Financial Statistics: England

Capital Programmes Working Party Local Authority Capital Expenditure (Yr) Final Outturn
Department of the Environment, Transport and the Regions

This report gives detail of the Capital Outturn Returns (COR) from local authorities in England, covering the period 1 April to 31 March. The results are grossed if there are returns missing because authorities have not responded. This paper can be accessed via the internet at http://www.local.detr.gov.uk.

Status: Ongoing
Frequency: Annually
Reference Period: Financial year
National Coverage: England

Statistician
Clare Goldschmidt
Department of the Environment, Transport and the Regions
Tel: 020 7890 4076;
Email: clare_goldschmidt@detr.gsi.gov.uk

Capital Programmes Working Party Local Authority Capital Expenditure (Yr) (No.) Quarter
Department of the Environment, Transport and the Regions

This report gives details of the Capital Payments Return (CPR) covering cumulative totals for each quarter. The analysis is based on returns from local authorities in England and are grossed to allow for missing authorities when needed.

Status: Ongoing
Frequency: Quarterly
National Coverage: England

Statistician
Clare Goldschmidt
Department of the Environment, Transport and the Regions
Tel: 020 7890 4076;
Email: clare_goldschmidt@detr.gsi.gov.uk

Capital Programmes Working Party Local Authority Capital Expenditure and Receipts (Yr) Forecasts from the Capital Estimates Return (CER)
Department of the Environment, Transport and the Regions

This report gives details of local authorities' forecasts of capital expenditure and receipts in (yr), from the Capital Estimates Return (CER). The results are grossed to allow for authorities who did not respond. This paper can be accessed via the internet at http://www.local.detr.gov.uk.

Status: Ongoing
Frequency: Annually
Reference Period: Financial year
National Coverage: England

Statistician
Clare Goldschmidt
Department of the Environment, Transport and the Regions
Tel: 020 7890 4076;
Email: clare_goldschmidt@detr.gsi.gov.uk

Capital Receipts Return - England
Department of the Environment, Transport and the Regions

The Department of the Environment, Transport and the Regions collates the Capital Receipts Returns (CR) from local authorities. They collect the most recent data available on the levels of individual authorities' usable capital receipts. The forms are despatched in the beginning of October for return by the beginning of November. Audited forms are due back by 31 March. Data are used directly in the Receipts Taken Into Account (RTIA) mechanism which is an essential part of the calculation of Basic Credit Approvals.

Status: Ongoing
Collection Method: Census
Frequency: Annually
Reference Period: Previous and current year
Timeliness: Data is used for the BCA exercise which is completed and figures issued by mid December.
Earliest Available Data: 1990/91
National Coverage: England
Disaggregation: Shire Counties, Metropolitan Districts, London Boroughs, Unitary Authorities, Shire Districts and Transport Authorities

Statistician
Clare Goldschmidt
Department of the Environment, Transport and the Regions
Tel: 020 7890 4076;
Email: clare_goldschmidt@detr.gsi.gov.uk

Council Tax and Non-Domestic Rates Collection Data
Department of the Environment, Transport and the Regions: sponsored by ONS

The Department of the Environment, Transport and the Regions compiles the Quarterly Returns of Council Tax (QRC) on billing authorities' receipts of Council Tax, Community Charge arrears, and non-domestic rates. The totals are required for the National Accounts; the monthly breakdown is used to determine the profile of payments of Revenue Support Grant and payments to and from the non-domestic rates pool.

Status: Ongoing
Collection Method: Census
Frequency: Quarterly
Reference Period: Financial Year
Timeliness: 8 weeks from end of reference period
Earliest Available Data: 1990/91
National Coverage: England

Statistician
Ashley Pottier
Department of the Environment, Transport and the Regions
Local Government Finance Policy Directorate; Local Government Finance Statistics Division Branch 4
Tel: 020 7890 4166;
Email: ashley_pottier@detr.gsi.gov.uk

Sources and Analyses

Products that contain data from this source
Council Tax Collection Figures, England (press release); Local Government Financial Statistics: England

Council Taxbase Survey - England
Department of the Environment, Transport and the Regions

The Department of the Environment, Transport and the Regions conducts the Council Taxbase Inquiry. Data are collected about each local authority's Council Taxbase, needed to calculate the amount of Council Tax that each authority could collect, and therefore their entitlement to Revenue Support Grant. The information collected includes the number of dwellings in each band on the Council Tax valuation list; the number in each band that are exempt from Council Taxes; and the number in each band that attract a single person or empty property discount.

Status: Ongoing
Collection Method: Census
Frequency: Annually
Reference Period: mid-October
Timeliness: Limited data published in Council Tax Levels Press Notice 3 months after collection
Earliest Available Data: 1993
National Coverage: England
Disaggregation: London boroughs, Metropolitan Districts, Unitary authorities, Shire Districts

Statistician
Ashley Pottier
Department of the Environment, Transport and the Regions
Local Government Finance Policy Directorate; Local Government Finance Statistics Division Branch 4
Tel: 020 7890 4166;
Email: ashley_pottier@detr.gsi.gov.uk

Products that contain data from this source
Council Tax Levels, England (press release); Local Government Financial Statistics: England

Local Authority Budget - England
Department of the Environment, Transport and the Regions

The Department of the Environment, Transport and the Regions conducts the Budget Requirement Survey. Data are collected about each authority's budget requirement, Council Tax levels and tax collection assumptions. The results are used to determine whether tax capping is required.

Status: Ongoing
Collection Method: Census
Frequency: Annually

Reference Period: Financial Year
Timeliness: Returns are required back by mid March and are published at end March.
Earliest Available Data: 1990/91
National Coverage: England
Disaggregation: London Boroughs, Metropolitan Districts, Unitary Authorities, Shire Counties, Shire Districts, Police Authorities, Fire Authorities

Statistician
Ashley Pottier
Department of the Environment, Transport and the Regions
Local Government Finance Policy Directorate; Local Government Finance Statistics Division Branch 4
Tel: 020 7890 4166;
Email: ashley_pottier@detr.gsi.gov.uk

Products that contain data from this source
Council Tax Levels, England (press release); Local Government Financial Statistics: England

Minimum Revenue Provision - England
Department of the Environment, Transport and the Regions

The Department of the Environment collated Minimum Revenue Provision Returns (MRPR) from local authorities on their adjusted credit ceiling and calculation of minimum revenue provision. Information fed into the capital financing component of Total Standard Spending and the capital financing Standard Spending Assessment control totals. Some of this information is now collected on the Capital Outturn returns.

Status: Ceased completely
Collection Method: Census
Frequency: Annually
Reference Period: 31 July for the previous financial year
Earliest Available Data: 1990
National Coverage: England
Disaggregation: Shire Counties, Metropolitan Districts, London Boroughs, Shire Districts and Miscellaneous Authorities

Statistician
Clare Goldschmidt
Department of the Environment, Transport and the Regions
Tel: 020 7890 4076;
Email: clare_goldschmidt@detr.gsi.gov.uk

Products that contain data from this source
Local Government Financial Statistics: England

Non-Domestic Rates Survey - England
Department of the Environment, Transport and the Regions

The Department of the Environment, Transport and the Regions conducts the Non-Domestic Rates (NNDR) survey on

all local billing authorities. The survey enables billing authorities each year to calculate their provisional, revised and final contributions to the non-domestic rates pool. The information is also used to determine the amount of non-domestic rates which is to be redistributed to local authorities in the forthcoming year and feeds into the National Accounts.

Status: Ongoing
Collection Method: Census
Frequency: Annually
Reference Period: Financial Year
Timeliness: N/A
Earliest Available Data: 1990/91
National Coverage: England
Disaggregation: London boroughs, Metropolitan Districts, Unitary Authorities and Shire Districts

Statistician
Ashley Pottier
Department of the Environment, Transport and the Regions
Local Government Finance Policy Directorate; Local Government Finance Statistics Division Branch 4
Tel: 020 7890 4166;
Email: ashley_pottier@detr.gsi.gov.uk

Products that contain data from this source
Local Government Financial Statistics: England

Pension Funds - England
Department of the Environment, Transport and the Regions

The Department of the Environment, Transport and the Regions compiles data on superannuation from the 80 authorities that run superannuation funds in England. The data are used in the National Accounts. Data are collected on income and expenditure of the superannuation funds, expenditure under the Pensions Increases Acts, and information on members and ex-members of the fund. Data are available at local authority superannuation funds level.

Status: Ongoing
Collection Method: Census
Frequency: Annually
Reference Period: Financial Year
Timeliness: 6 months
Earliest Available Data: 1990/91
National Coverage: England
Disaggregation: Local authorities administering pension funds; Shire counties; Metropolitan Districts, Inner London Boroughs, Outer London Boroughs, other

Statistician
Mark Chaplin
Department of the Environment, Transport and the Regions
Local Government Finance Policy Directorate; Local Government Finance Statistics Division Branch 3
Tel: 020 7890 4167;
Email: mark_chaplin@detr.gsi.gov.uk

Products that contain data from this source
Local Government Financial Statistics: England

Revenue Account Survey - England
Department of the Environment, Transport and the Regions

The Department of the Environment, Transport and the Regions conducts the General Fund Revenue Account (RA) and the General Fund Revenue Account Specific and Special Grants (RA(SG)) surveys. The data are used for the Public Expenditure review process and National Accounts purposes. The RA survey records expenditure paid from the General Fund, including revenue expenditure by individual service, capital charges and capital expenditure charged to the Revenue Account. It also includes income from interest receipts, government grants, non-domestic rates, and the demand/precept on the Collection Fund. The RA(SG) survey records details of government specific and special grants paid into the General Fund.

Status: Ongoing
Collection Method: Census
Frequency: Annually
Reference Period: Financial Year
Timeliness: 2 months after form return date (return date is end of March)
Earliest Available Data: 1990/91
National Coverage: England
Disaggregation: Local Authority

Statistician
Stephen Greenhill
Department of the Environment, Transport and the Regions
LGF; 1
Tel: 020 7890 4157;
Email: stephen_greenhill@detr.gsi.gov.uk

Products that contain data from this source
Local Government Financial Statistics: England

Revenue Outturn - England
Department of the Environment, Transport and the Regions

The Department of the Environment, Transport and the Regions collate Revenue Outturn Forms (RO1-6, TSR1, RS and RG) from local authorities. Data are used for the Public Expenditure review process and National Accounts purposes. The RO1-6 form records details on expenditure paid from the General Fund disaggregated both by service and also by type, e.g. gross expenditure by employee expenses and running expenses, and income by sales, fees and charges, and other income. The TSR1

records expenditure from and income to the Trading Services Revenue Account. The Revenue Summary (RS) form summarises information from the individual RO forms and includes further income and expenditure items, including the demand/precept on the Collection Fund. The RG form records details of specific and special grants paid into the General Fund.

Status: Ongoing
Collection Method: Census
Frequency: Annually
Reference Period: Financial Year
Timeliness: 5 months after return date (return date is end of July)
Earliest Available Data: 1990/91
National Coverage: England
Disaggregation: Local Authority

Statistician
Stephen Greenhill
Department of the Environment, Transport and the Regions
LGF; 1
Tel: 020 7890 4157;
Email: stephen.greenhill@detr.gsi.gov.uk

Products that contain data from this source
Local Government Financial Statistics: England

17.4 International Aid and Development

Statistics on International Development
Department for International Development

The Department for International Development collects data on the British worldwide distribution of aid. Data are compiled from the DFID management information system, Office for National Statistics, Bank of England, ECGD, Foreign and Commonwealth Office and the Commonwealth Development Corporation. Information is currently available on a consistent basis from 1987-88 to 1997-98. Data are produced on a financial-year basis although some are on a calendar-year basis. They are published annually in five-year sets seven to eight months after the end of the financial year, although longer time series are available on request. From 1987-88.

Status: Ongoing
Collection Method: Administrative systems, surveys.
Frequency: Annually
Reference Period: Previous financial year / calendar year plus some historic data.
Timeliness: Nine months
Earliest Available Data: 1987-88
National Coverage: United Kingdom
Sub-National: Full

Statistician
Elizabeth Robin
Department for International Development
Statistics Department; Statistical Reporting and Support Group
Tel: 01355 843329;
Email: ej-robin@dfid.gov.uk

Products that contain data from this source
Statistics on International Development; Development Counts

17.5 Local Government Finance - General

Borrowing and Lending Inquiry (Monthly) - UK
Department of the Environment, Transport and the Regions

The Department of the Environment, Transport and the Regions conducts the Borrowing and Lending Inquiries on local authorities. Data are used as the local authority component in Public Sector Net Cash Requirement estimates.

Status: Ongoing
Collection Method: Small-scale (Sample) Survey
Frequency: Monthly
Reference Period: Transactions during month
Timeliness: 7 working days
Earliest Available Data: 1990
National Coverage: United Kingdom
Disaggregation: London Boroughs, Metropolitan Districts, Unitary Authorities, Shire Counties, Shire Districts, Police Authorities, Fire Authorities, Joint Authorities, Waste Authorities, Welsh Unitaries, Welsh Districts, Scottish Unitaries, Scottish Districts, Northern Ireland Districts

Statistician
Mark Chaplin
Department of the Environment, Transport and the Regions
Local Government Finance Policy Directorate; Local Government Finance Statistics Division Branch 3
Tel: 020 7890 4167;
Email: mark_chaplin@@detr.gsi.gov.uk

Products that contain data from this source
Financial Statistics; Local Government Financial Statistics: England; Public Sector Finances (First Release)

Borrowing and Lending Inquiry (Quarterly) - UK
Department of the Environment, Transport and the Regions

The Department of the Environment, Transport and the Regions conducts the borrowing and lending inquiries on local authorities. Data are used as the local authority component in Public Sector Net Cash Requirement estimates.

Status: Ongoing
Collection Method: Census
Frequency: Quarterly
Reference Period: Transaction during relevant quarter
Timeliness: One month
Earliest Available Data: 1990
National Coverage: United Kingdom
Disaggregation: London Boroughs, Metropolitan Districts, Unitary Authorities, Shire Counties, Shire Districts, Police Authorities, Fire Authorities, Joint Authorities, Waste Authorities, Welsh Unitaries, Welsh Districts, Scottish Unitaries, Scottish Districts, Northern Ireland Districts

Statistician
Mark Chaplin
Department of the Environment, Transport and the Regions
Local Government Finance Policy Directorate; Local Government Finance Statistics Division Branch 3
Tel: 020 7890 4167;
Email: mark_chaplin@@detr.gsi.gov.uk

Products that contain data from this source
Financial Statistics; Local Government Financial Statistics: England; Public Sector Finances (First Release); United Kingdom Economic Accounts; United Kingdom National Accounts - The Blue Book

Gross Trading Surplus of Local Authority Trading Enterprises - UK
Office for National Statistics

The Office for National Statistics compiles data on the gross trading surplus of local authority trading enterprises. The data are used in the compilation of the Gross Domestic Product (GDP) for the National Accounts. The gross trading surplus is the balance of trading receipts over trading expenditure before deducting any provision for depreciation and interest charges. Data cover income from the ownership of property used for government trading activities, but exclude income arising from the ownership and letting of land, buildings and other fixed assets which are taken as rent.

Status: Ongoing
Collection Method: Surveys of local authorities undertaken by DETR
Frequency: Quarterly
Reference Period: Annual
Timeliness: 12 weeks
National Coverage: United Kingdom
Disaggregation: By country

Statistician
Jeff Golland
Office for National Statistics
Tel: 020 7533 5987

Products that contain data from this source
Financial Statistics; United Kingdom National Accounts - The Blue Book; United Kingdom National Accounts, Sources and Methods

Outstanding Amounts Inquiry (MQBL) - UK
Department of the Environment, Transport and the Regions

The Department of the Environment, Transport and the Regions conducts the Outstanding Amounts Inquiry (MQBL) on outstanding amounts at financial year end for longer-term borrowing and investments. The survey covers the United Kingdom and data are available at local authority district level. It was first conducted in April 1991; further ad hoc surveys were carried out in 1993, 1994 and 1997. It provides a benchmark of outstanding amounts of longer-term borrowing and investments at financial year end. Results are available three months after the end of the financial year.

Status: Ongoing
Collection Method: Census
Frequency: Periodic
Reference Period: Amounts Outstanding at the end of the financial year
Timeliness: N/A
Earliest Available Data: 1991
National Coverage: United Kingdom
Disaggregation: London Boroughs, Metropolitan Districts, Unitary Authorities, Shire Counties, Shire Districts, Police Authorities, Fire Authorities, Joint Authorities, Waste Authorities, Welsh Unitaries, Welsh Districts, Scottish Unitaries, Scottish Districts, Northern Ireland Districts

Statistician
Mark Chaplin
Department of the Environment, Transport and the Regions
Local Government Finance Policy Directorate; Local Government Finance Statistics Division Branch 3
Tel: 020 7890 4167;
Email: mark_chaplin@detr.gsi.gov.uk

Products that contain data from this source
Financial Statistics; Local Government Financial Statistics: England; United Kingdom Economic Accounts; United Kingdom National Accounts - The Blue Book

See also:
In this chapter:
Capital Debt Outstanding Returns – Scotland *(17.10)*

17.6 National Savings

National Savings - Financial Statistics
Department for National Savings: sponsored by ONS

The Department for National Savings compiles financial statistics tables from data collected from each of the product divisions and collated by the headquarters of statistical branches. The tables represent monthly statistics on all National Savings products. They show past and present performance per product available by receipts, repayments and interest.

Status: Ongoing
Collection Method: Accounts data, administrative data
Frequency: Monthly
Reference Period: Month
Timeliness: One month
Earliest Available Data: 1970/71
National Coverage: United Kingdom

Statistician
Matthew Tan
Department for National Savings
Statistics Team
Tel: 020 7605 9316

Products that contain data from this source
Financial Statistics; National Savings Press Release

17.7 Northern Ireland - Finances

Capital Receipts and Payments - Northern Ireland
Department of Finance and Personnel - Northern Ireland

The Northern Ireland Statistics and Research Agency compiles accounts on capital receipts and payments. Data are available on capital receipts and capital expenditure of Northern Ireland and earnings on capital advances or investments. They include the Civil Contingencies Fund Account. Accounts cover Northern Ireland and are produced each financial year.

Status: Ongoing
National Coverage: Northern Ireland

Statistician
Kevin Sweeney
Department of Finance and Personnel - Northern Ireland
Central Survey Branch
Tel: 028 9025 2490

Finance Accounts - Northern Ireland
Department of Finance and Personnel - Northern Ireland

The Northern Ireland Statistics and Research Agency compiles finance accounts. They are an account of receipts and issues of the Northern Ireland Consolidated Fund

Frequency: Each financial year
National Coverage: Northern Ireland

Statistician
Kevin Sweeney
Department of Finance and Personnel - Northern Ireland
Central Survey Branch
Tel: 028 9025 2490

Public Income and Expenditure Account - Northern Ireland
Department of Finance and Personnel - Northern Ireland

The Northern Ireland Statistics and Research Agency compiles an account of Public Income and Expenditure of Northern Ireland and receipts and payments not being Public Income and Expenditure.

Frequency: Each financial year
National Coverage: Northern Ireland

Statistician
Kevin Sweeney
Department of Finance and Personnel - Northern Ireland
Central Survey Branch
Tel: 028 9025 2490

Products that contain data from this source
Public Income and Expenditure

17.8 Public Sector Borrowing

Central Government Net Cash Requirement - UK
Office for National Statistics

The Office for National Statistics compiles data on the Central Government Net Cash Requirement (CGBR). Data are obtained from HM Treasury. The CGNCR is the amount, in cash, that the central government needs to borrow from other sectors of the economy in order to finance its total expenditure (including lending to public corporations and local authorities) that is not covered by taxation and other current and capital receipts.

Status: Ongoing
Collection Method: Administrative records and survey of banks
Frequency: Monthly
Reference Period: Month
Timeliness: 12 working days
National Coverage: United Kingdom

Statistician
Jeff Golland
Office for National Statistics
Tel: 020 7533 5987

Products that contain data from this source
Economic Trends; Financial Statistics; Monthly Digest of Statistics; Public Sector Finances (First Release); United Kingdom National Accounts - The Blue Book; United Kingdom National Accounts, Sources and Methods

Local Authority Net Cash Requirement - UK
Office for National Statistics

The Office for National Statistics compiles data on the Local Authority Net Cash Requirement (LANCR). Data are collected from surveys of local authorities, conducted by the Department of the Environment. The LANCR is the amount, in cash, that local authorities borrow in order to finance capital expenditure and smooth their cash flow in anticipation of revenue. Local authorities can borrow only for purposes that have been authorised by Acts of Parliament. Data cover local authorities in the United Kingdom and are collected monthly and quarterly. Results are published each month.

Status: Ongoing
Collection Method: Surveys of local authorities and banks and expenditure
Frequency: Monthly
Reference Period: Month
Timeliness: 12 working days
National Coverage: United Kingdom

Statistician
Jeff Golland
Office for National Statistics
Tel: 020 7533 5987

Products that contain data from this source
Economic Trends; Financial Statistics; Monthly Digest of Statistics; Public Sector Finances (First Release); United Kingdom National Accounts - The Blue Book; United Kingdom National Accounts, Sources and Methods

Public Corporations Net Cash Requirement - UK
Office for National Statistics

The Office for National Statistics compiles data on the Public Corporations Net Cash Requirement (PCNCR). Data are derived from the Bank of England, HM Treasury, the Post Office, and the Department of

National Savings. The PCNCR is the amount, in cash, that public corporations need to borrow from other sectors of the economy.

Status: Ongoing
Collection Method: Surveys of public corporations and banks
Frequency: Monthly
Reference Period: Month
Timeliness: 12 working days
National Coverage: United Kingdom

Statistician
Jeff Golland
Office for National Statistics
Tel: 020 7533 5987

Products that contain data from this source
Economic Trends; Financial Statistics; Monthly Digest of Statistics; Public Sector Finances (First Release); United Kingdom National Accounts - The Blue Book; United Kingdom National Accounts, Sources and Methods

Public Sector Debt
The Bank of England

The Bank of England compiles statistics on central government, general government and public sector debt. Central government debt data are published quarterly in Bank of England: Monetary and Financial Statistics (Bankstats), split by instrument. General government debt (UK and European basis) and public sector debt are published as at end-March each year in the Bank of England's annual Statistical Abstract, along with details of public sector liquid assets. Data on the distribution of the national debt by instrument and sterling national debt by holder are also available in the Abstract. Holdings of British Government Securities are further broken down by economic sector.

Status: Ongoing
Frequency: Quarterly

Statistician
Richard Bennett
The Bank of England
Monetary & Financial Statistics
Tel: 020 7601 4340;
Email: mfsd_fmr@bankofengland.co.uk

Public Sector Net Cash Requirement - UK
Office for National Statistics

The Office for National Statistics compiles data on the Public Sector Net Cash Requirement (PSNCR). Data are derived from HM Treasury, Department of the Environment, Department of National Savings, the Post Office, the Bank of England, and the Building Societies

Commission. The Public Sector Net Cash Requirement indicates the extent to which the public sector borrows from other sectors of the economy and overseas to finance the balance of expenditure and receipts arising from its various activities. The flows which count towards the PSNCR are measured on a cash basis (with a minor exception of interest on National Savings instruments). The PSNCR can be expressed as the sum of three components: the Central Government Borrowing on its Own Account (CGBR(O)), the Public Corporation Borrowing Requirement (PCBR) and the Local Authority Borrowing Requirement (LABR). It can also be defined in terms of the receipts and expenditure of the consolidated public sector accounts.

Status: Ongoing
Frequency: Monthly
Timeliness: 12 working days
National Coverage: United Kingdom

Statistician
Jeff Golland
Office for National Statistics
Tel: 020 7533 5987

Products that contain data from this analysis
Economic Trends; Financial Statistics; Monthly Digest of Statistics; Public Sector Finances (First Release); United Kingdom National Accounts - The Blue Book; United Kingdom National Accounts, Sources and Methods

17.9 Research and Development (R&D) expenditure by Government

Government Research and Development Survey - UK
Office for National Statistics

The Office for National Statistics carry out the Government Research and Development Survey. The Survey collects data on research and development within all Government Departments, excluding local authorities and a small area of central government. Results are used to compile Government Research and Development expenditure (GOVERD) and to calculate Gross Research and Development expenditure (GERD). Data are available by expenditure, employment, source of funds and at regional level for the UK.

Status: Ongoing
Collection Method: Census
Frequency: Annually
Reference Period: Financial Year
Timeliness: Data available within 10 months
Earliest Available Data: 1988-89
National Coverage: United Kingdom

Statistician
Peter Jones
Office for National Statistics
Overseas and Financial Division; Research, Development and Innovation Statistics
Tel: 01633 813063;
Email: peter.jones@ons.gov.uk

Products that contain data from this source
Annual Abstract of Statistics; Economic Trends; Gross Domestic Expenditure on Research and Development (GERD (First Release)); Regional Trends; Research and Development Annual Statistics; Science, Engineering and Technology Statistics 1998; Main Science and Technology Indicators

Research Assessment Exercise
Higher Education Funding Council for England

Assessment of research in Higher Education Institution in the UK. Last one carried out in 1996 next planned for 2001. Results available through the Higher Education funding councils' web sites 'http://www.hefce.ac.uk'. Other data on research staff and research income available from the HESA finance and staff records.

Status: Ongoing
Collection Method: Census
Frequency: Periodic
Reference Period: 4 to 5 years.
Timeliness: 8 months.
Earliest Available Data: 1992
National Coverage: United Kingdom
Disaggregation: Institutional

Statistician
Dr Shekar Nandy
Higher Education Funding Council for England
Tel: 01179 317367

Products that contain data from this source
Research Assessment Exercise: Outcomes

17.10 Scotland - Local Authorities' Finances

Appeals Against Revaluation Values - Scotland
Scottish Executive

The Scottish Executive Development Department compiles data on the number of appeals, number settled and changes in rateable value from these. This is a statistical return from Assessors. It gives information on the number, value, and progress of appeals against rateable values set at the time of revaluation of non-domestic rates. At present, there are only a few outstanding appeals from the 1990 revaluation, and the process of gathering information in relation

to appeals following the 1995 revaluation began in December 1995.

Status: Ongoing
Collection Method: Census
Frequency: Quarterly
Reference Period: Quarter
Timeliness: Results available about 3 months after the end of the quarter.
Earliest Available Data: April-June 1995
National Coverage: Scotland
Disaggregation: Council Area (Scot)/District and Islands Area (Scotland);Valuation Board Area

Statistician
Duncan Gray
Scottish Executive
Economics Advice and Statistics Division; Local Government Finance Statistics
Tel: 0131 244 7031;
Email: duncan.gray@scotland.gov.uk

Capital Debt Outstanding Returns - Scotland
Scottish Executive

The Scottish Executive Development Department collates the Capital Debt Outstanding Return. This is an annual return to the Department from local authorities, used in assessing, for each authority, the level of debt relevant for the loan and leasing charges amount used in distributing aggregate external finance to authorities. Data are available by local authority area and from April 1996 this will be unitary authority area. Information are available in the present form from March 1989 and similar information was collected in Local Financial Returns before this date.

Status: Ongoing
Collection Method: Census
Frequency: Annually
Reference Period: Financial Year
Timeliness: Available about 6 months after the end of the financial year.
National Coverage: Scotland
Disaggregation: Council Area (Scot)/District and Islands Area (Scotland)

Statistician
Duncan Gray
Scottish Executive
Economics Advice and Statistics Division; Local Government Finance Statistics
Tel: 0131 244 7031;
Email: duncan.gray@scotland.gov.uk

Products that contain data from this source
Scottish Local Government Financial Statistics

Capital Payments Returns - Scotland
Scottish Executive

The Scottish Executive Development Department compiles details of authorities'

Sources and Analyses

capital expenditure by type, service, and capital income. This is a series of returns from authorities at various times during the financial year, designed to monitor, forecast and record expenditure. Its primary purpose is to provide information to the Scottish Executive and HM Treasury on which the system of capital controls is administered. The survey provides information on capital expenditure and income for all local authority services. Annual information distinguishes capital expenditure by type of asset and capital income by source.

Status: Ongoing
Collection Method: Census
Frequency: Quarterly
Reference Period: Quarter and Financial Year
Timeliness: Full year detail available around December following the end of the financial year. Quarterly data (much less detailed) available some 3 months after end of quarter.
Earliest Available Data: 1981-82
National Coverage: Scotland
Disaggregation: Local Authority

Statistician
Duncan Gray
Scottish Executive
Economics Advice and Statistics Division; Local Government Finance Statistics
Tel: 0131 244 7031;
Email: duncan.gray@scotland.gov.uk

Products that contain data from this source
Scottish Local Government Financial Statistics

Council Tax and Community Charge Receipts - Scotland
Scottish Executive

The Scottish Executive Development Department compiles data on the total amount of tax (including water charges) billed, rebates granted, and receipts monthly in respect of each financial year. Figures are also collected on total non-domestic rate income. For the Community Charge and Council Tax, the survey provides information on: total tax billed within each Region area (including water charges); total rebates (including transitional relief and Community Charge and Council Tax Benefit) granted; amount collected in each month following the beginning of the financial year to which the bills relate. For non-domestic rates, the survey provides information on the amount collected in each calendar month. There is no distinction of the period of the bill to which the payments relate.

Status: Ongoing
Collection Method: Census
Frequency: Monthly
Reference Period: Month
Timeliness: Generally released quarterly one quarter after the end of the reference period.

Earliest Available Data: First six months of 1989-90 combined
National Coverage: Scotland
Disaggregation: Local Authority Region and island areas

Statistician
Duncan Gray
Scottish Executive
Economics Advice and Statistics Division; Local Government Finance Statistics
Tel: 0131 244 7031;
Email: duncan.gray@scotland.gov.uk

Council Tax Appeals - Scotland
Scottish Executive

The Scottish Executive Development Department compiles data on the number of appeals (mainly against property banding) lodged, number cleared by outcome, number with Valuation Appeals Committees and number outstanding. The statistics give a guide to the speed of settling appeals following the publication of Council Tax bandings in March 1993.

Status: Ceased temporarily
Collection Method: Census
Frequency: Quarterly
Reference Period: Quarter
Timeliness: Available about 1 quarter after reference quarter
Earliest Available Data: Up to December 1993
National Coverage: Scotland
Disaggregation: Local Authority Region and island areas

Statistician
Duncan Gray
Scottish Executive
Economics Advice and Statistics Division; Local Government Finance Statistics
Tel: 0131 244 7031;
Email: duncan.gray@scotland.gov.uk

Council Taxbase - Scotland
Scottish Executive

The Scottish Executive Development Department compiles data on the number of properties within each of eight statutorily defined valuation bands, the number with vacant exemption, and the number with one or two discounts. The primary purpose of the information is to assess the Council Taxbase in each authority area for the purpose of distributing aggregate external finance to each authority. The statistics can also be used to give an indication of numbers of properties, numbers vacant (vacant exemptions plus those receiving two discounts) and numbers with only one adult (those with a single discount). The figures do not give an exact estimate of numbers in these categories since some adults (e.g. students and some disabled adults) are not counted when determining discounts.

Status: Ongoing
Collection Method: Census
Frequency: Annually
Reference Period: Specific date in mid October each year
Timeliness: Available within 1 month of reference date
Earliest Available Data: October 1993
National Coverage: Scotland
Disaggregation: Council Area (Scot)/District and Islands Area (Scotland)

Statistician
Duncan Gray
Scottish Executive
Economics Advice and Statistics Division; Local Government Finance Statistics
Tel: 0131 244 7031;
Email: duncan.gray@scotland.gov.uk

Council Water Charge Base - Scotland
Scottish Executive

The Scottish Executive Development Department collates data on the number of properties in the council water charge base (i.e. connected to domestic water supply), by discounts and exemptions by property valuation band. This is a statistical return from Region/island authorities. It gives information on the water charge base against which the level of water charges is set.

Status: Ceased completely
Collection Method: Census
Frequency: Annually
Reference Period: October each year
Timeliness: Available about 2 months after collection
Earliest Available Data: October 1993
National Coverage: Scotland
Disaggregation: Local Authority district

Statistician
Duncan Gray
Scottish Executive
Economics Advice and Statistics Division; Local Government Finance Statistics
Tel: 0131 244 7031;
Email: duncan.gray@scotland.gov.uk

Final Outturn - Scotland
Scottish Executive

The Scottish Executive Development Department compiles a summary of net expenditure on each authorities' main General Fund services. Separately identifying loan and leasing charges (i.e. debt servicing and leasing charges). The survey is administered by the relevant Scottish Executive local authority finance division.

Status: Ceased completely
Collection Method: Census
Frequency: Annually
Reference Period: Financial Year
Timeliness: About 9 months after the end of the financial year

Earliest Available Data: 1983-84
National Coverage: Scotland
Disaggregation: Local Authority areas (Unitary Authority areas from April 1996)

Statistician
Duncan Gray
Scottish Executive
Economics Advice and Statistics Division; Local Government Finance Statistics
Tel: 0131 244 7031;
Email: duncan.gray@scotland.gov.uk

Local Financial Returns - Scotland
Scottish Executive

The Scottish Executive Development Department compiles detailed information by service and sub-service of elements of authorities' current expenditure and current income. Level of detail varies by service, with the greatest detail collected for education and social work. The survey covers all local authority services, including housing services and trading services. Respondents are asked to ensure that information in the LFRs is consistent with their final accounts. The information is collected under legislation which requires authorities to provide a Local Financial Return to the Secretary of State, and requires the Secretary of State to lay a summary before Parliament. The survey provides detailed information on elements of current expenditure and income for each authority service, together with summary information on local tax income.

Status: Ongoing
Collection Method: Census
Frequency: Annually
Reference Period: Financial Year
Timeliness: CIPFA publish summary details about 12 months after financial year end. Scottish Executive publishes summary material about 18 months after financial year end.
Earliest Available Data: 1945-46
National Coverage: Scotland
Disaggregation: Local Authority areas (Unitary Authority areas from April 1996), Council Area (Scot)/District and Islands Area (Scotland)

Statistician
Duncan Gray
Scottish Executive
Economics Advice and Statistics Division; Local Government Finance Statistics
Tel: 0131 244 7031;
Email: duncan.gray@scotland.gov.uk

Products that contain data from this source
Local Authority Social Work Expenditure; Scottish Local Government Financial Statistics

Non-Domestic Rate Income - Scotland
Scottish Executive

The Scottish Executive Development Department compiles estimates of gross and net non-domestic rate income. This is a return from the Finance Departments of Regional authorities. It gives information, for each year since 1990-91, of the authority's best estimate of gross rate income, discounts, exemptions, etc., leading to an estimate of net non-domestic rate income for the year. Provisional estimates are gathered in June each year, with updated estimates in the autumn. Since grant is paid on the basis of estimates for previous years these must, at some stage, be provided, certified as having been audited. Information is provided separately for local government district areas. From 1996 the statistics will cover new council areas.

Status: Ongoing
Collection Method: Census
Frequency: Periodic
Reference Period: Financial Year
Timeliness: First outturn estimates available about 6 months after end of financial year.
Earliest Available Data: 1989-90
National Coverage: Scotland

Statistician
Duncan Gray
Scottish Executive
Economics Advice and Statistics Division; Local Government Finance Statistics
Tel: 0131 244 7031;
Email: duncan.gray@scotland.gov.uk

Products that contain data from this source
Scottish Local Government Financial Statistics

Non-Domestic Rateable Values - Scotland
Scottish Executive

The Scottish Executive Development Department compiles a statistical return from the Assessor of each of the nine Region and two island areas in Scotland (one Assessor covers the Highlands and Western Isles). It gives information, at April each year, on the total number and rateable value of non-domestic subjects, by type of subject - for about eight types of subject. Information is provided separately for local government district areas. From 1996 the statistics will cover new council areas. Information has been collected in this format since 1989-90. Summary details on domestic and non-domestic rateable values are available from rating review publications back to the 1950's. Data are annual as at 1 April in the relevant year and are available about four months after the end of the reference period.

Status: Ongoing
Collection Method: Census
Frequency: Annually
Reference Period: 1 April each year.
Timeliness: Generally available some 3 months after the reference date.
National Coverage: Scotland
Disaggregation: Council Area (Scot)/District and Islands Area (Scotland)

Statistician
Duncan Gray
Scottish Executive
Economics Advice and Statistics Division; Local Government Finance Statistics
Tel: 0131 244 7031;
Email: duncan.gray@scotland.gov.uk

Products that contain data from this source
Scottish Local Government Financial Statistics

Non-Domestic Water and Sewerage Rateable Values - Scotland
Scottish Executive

The Scottish Executive Development Department collates data on the number and rateable value of subjects by type of subject. This is a statistical return from the Assessor in each of the nine Region and two island areas in Scotland (one Assessor covers the Highlands and Western Isles). It gives information, at April each year on the total number and rateable value of non-domestic subjects, liable for non-domestic water and sewerage rates. (Note that many businesses have metered water supplies and non-domestic water rates are, therefore, a small proportion of total non-domestic rates). Information is provided separately for local government district areas. Details of collection after 1996, if any, have yet to be decided. Information has been collected in this format since 1990-91.

Status: Ceased completely
Collection Method: Census
Frequency: Annually
Reference Period: 1 April each year.
Timeliness: Generally available within 3 months of the reference date.
National Coverage: Scotland
Disaggregation: Local Government Region (Scotland)

Statistician
Duncan Gray
Scottish Executive
Economics Advice and Statistics Division; Local Government Finance Statistics
Tel: 0131 244 7031;
Email: duncan.gray@scotland.gov.uk

Provisional Outturn and Budget Estimates Return - Scotland
Scottish Executive

The Scottish Executive Development Department compiles the Provisional Outturn and Budget Estimates Return. This is an annual Return to the Department from local authorities, used in assessing authorities' budgets against the Secretary of State's criteria for capping the budgets of authorities. The information, which is supplied in the spring, gives estimated net current expenditure in the current financial year and budgeted net current expenditure for the forthcoming financial year, separately distinguishing loan and leasing charges (i.e. debt servicing and leasing charges). The figures relate solely to expenditure on authorities' revenue accounts - i.e. they exclude expenditure on housing and on authorities' trading services. Data are available by local authority area and are available in their present form from the financial year 1975-76. Data are compiled for financial years and are published about six months after the end of the reference year.

Status: Ongoing
Collection Method: Census
Frequency: Annually
Reference Period: Financial Year
Timeliness: data generally available around June following the financial year end.
Earliest Available Data: Financial year 1975-76
National Coverage: Scotland
Disaggregation: Local Authority area; Council Area (Scot)/District and Islands Area (Scotland)

Statistician
Duncan Gray
Scottish Executive
Economics Advice and Statistics Division; Local Government Finance Statistics
Tel: 0131 244 7031;
Email: duncan.gray@scotland.gov.uk

Salaries, Wages and External Interest Receipts - Scotland
Scottish Executive; sponsored by The Office for National Statistics

The Scottish Executive Development Department compiles total salaries and wages of authorities, and income from interest receipts. The information are collected in an annual form, which distinguishes information separately for each quarter in the financial year. The survey is administered by the Local Government Finance Statistics Branch of the Central Statistics Unit and provides information on the total salaries and wages of each local authority and also on interest receipts.

Status: Ongoing
Collection Method: Census
Frequency: Annually
Reference Period: Quarter within the financial year.
Timeliness: Available around 6 months after financial year end.
Earliest Available Data: 1987-88
National Coverage: Scotland
Disaggregation: Local Authority areas (Unitary Authority areas from April 1996); Council Area (Scot)/District and Islands Area (Scotland)

Statistician
Duncan Gray
Scottish Executive
Economics Advice and Statistics Division; Local Government Finance Statistics
Tel: 0131 244 7031;
Email: duncan.gray@scotland.gov.uk

Water and Sewerage Charges - Scotland
Scottish Executive

The Scottish Executive Development Department compiles data on the basis of metered and unmetered water charges and sewerage charges for the forthcoming financial year. This return from Regional authorities gives information on budgets and projected income from various sources (direct charges, Council Tax, council water charge, etc.), showing how the charges set for the forthcoming financial year were derived.

Status: Ceased completely
Collection Method: Census
Frequency: Annually
Reference Period: Financial Year
Timeliness: Generally available about the beginning of the financial year for which charges relate.
Earliest Available Data: 1998-99
National Coverage: Scotland
Disaggregation: Local Government Region (Scotland) and island areas

Statistician
Duncan Gray
Scottish Executive
Economics Advice and Statistics Division; Local Government Finance Statistics
Tel: 0131 244 7031;
Email: duncan.gray@scotland.gov.uk

17.11 Tax Revenues, Taxes and Excise Duties

Annual Costs of Tax Allowances and Reliefs
Board of Inland Revenue

The Inland Revenue Statistics and Economics Division compiles data on the annual costs of tax allowances and reliefs. Data are available on tax expenditures, structural and mixed reliefs. They cover the United Kingdom and are available back to 1979-80. They are derived from analysis of data from a variety of sources; mainly Inland Revenue administrative data and published information from other government departments.

Status: Ongoing
Collection Method: Derived from analyses of data from a variety of sources; mainly Inland Revenue administrative data and published information from other government departments
Frequency: Annually
Timeliness: First publication covers the current year and the next one. When it is updated, it relates to the current year and the previous one.
Earliest Available Data: 1979-80
National Coverage: United Kingdom
Disaggregation: None

Statistician
Maurice Nettley
Board of Inland Revenue
Tel: 020 7438 7411;
Email: sed.ir.sh@gtnet.gov.uk

Products that contain data from this source
Inland Revenue Statistics; Tax Ready Reckoner and Tax Reliefs

---

Capital Gains Computation Samples
Board of Inland Revenue

The Inland Revenue Statistics and Economics Division compiles surveys on the capital gains of individuals (including trusts) and companies. Each sample survey covers either individual capital gains taxpayers for a tax year or companies with disposals in one or more tax years.

The survey covers the United Kingdom and is carried out on an ad hoc basis. Results normally covering the one or more tax years most recently surveyed are available two to three years after the reference period mainly because of time lags in the administration of the tax and in data collection. Tables for individuals are published nearly every year. With the introduction of self assessment it is intended to mount in addition a larger annual sample of individuals but with less detailed information.

Status: Latest – live, earlier not operational
Collection Method: Sample survey of administrative tax records
Frequency: Biannual/annual
Reference Period: Tax Year (Individuals and Trusts), Accounting Period ending in Tax Year (Company)
Timeliness: 2-3 years after reference period
Earliest Available Data: 1985-86 Individuals 1986-87 Companies
National Coverage: United Kingdom level only

Statistician
Bill Elmore
Board of Inland Revenue
Tel: 020 7438 6237

Products that contain data from this source
Economic Trends; Inland Revenue Statistics

Capital Gains Tax Liabilities - Census
Board of Inland Revenue

The Inland Revenue Statistics and Economics Division compiles data on capital gains tax and provides summary information on tax liabilities for individuals (including trusts) for a particular tax year. The series started in 1987-88 and covers the United Kingdom.

The survey covers the United Kingdom and is carried out on an ad hoc basis. Results normally covering the one or more tax years most recently surveyed are available two to three years after the reference period mainly because of time lags in the administration of the tax and in data collection. Tables for individuals are published nearly every year. With the introduction of self assessment it is intended to mount in addition a larger annual sample of individuals but with less detailed information.

Status: Self Asst Ongoing: Assessments – no longer operational
Collection Method: Census of administrative tax records
Frequency: Annual
Reference Period: Tax year
Timeliness: 2 years after reference period
Earliest Available Data: 1987-88 - Assessments; 1996-97 Self Assessment
National Coverage: United Kingdom level only

Statistician
Bill Elmore
Board of Inland Revenue
Tel: 020 7438 6237

Products that contain data from this source
Economic Trends; Inland Revenue Statistics

Corporation Tax: Capital Allowances by Type of Asset and Industry
Board of Inland Revenue

The Inland Revenue Statistics and Economics Division compiles data on the annual levels of capital allowances set against corporation tax. The series is analysed by broad industrial group and type of asset for which the capital allowances were claimed. It covers the United Kingdom.

Status: Ongoing
Collection Method: Analysis of administrative data and large sample survey.
Frequency: Annually
Reference Period: accounting periods ending in each financial year
Timeliness: Three years after reference period.
Earliest Available Data: 1966
National Coverage: United Kingdom
Disaggregation: Type of company and type of asset

Statistician
Jane Whittaker
Board of Inland Revenue
Tel: 020 7438 7624;
Email: sed.ir.sh@gtnet.gov.uk

Products that contain data from this source
Inland Revenue Statistics

Corporation Tax: Company Profits and Computation of Tax Liability
Board of Inland Revenue

The Inland Revenue Statistics and Economics Division compiles data on company profits and corporation tax. Data are available for the derivation of mainstream corporation tax liability from trading and non-trading income and tax reliefs.

Status: Ongoing
Collection Method: Large-scale (Sample) Survey
Frequency: Continuously
Reference Period: Individual company accounting periods
Timeliness: 18 month delay before publication
Earliest Available Data: 1957
National Coverage: United Kingdom
Disaggregation: Broad industry group

Statistician
Richard Balley
Board of Inland Revenue
Tel: 020 7438 6271;
Email: sed.ir.sh@gtnet.gov.uk

Products that contain data from this source
Inland Revenue Statistics

Corporation Tax: Mainstream Corporation Tax Receipts and Reconciliation with Tax Accruals
Board of Inland Revenue

The Inland Revenue Statistics and Economics Division compiles data on corporation tax receipts for advanced and mainstream corporation tax separately. Accrual data fully reconciled with receipts are updated annually for the four most recent years. They have been published annually since the partial imputation system for corporation tax was introduced in 1973-74,

including estimates for the most recent completed year.

Status: Ongoing
Collection Method: Census for payments, sample of accruals
Frequency: Daily for receipts, annual for accruals
Reference Period: Monthly for receipts, annual for accruals
Timeliness: Up to 1 month for receipts, 18 months for accruals
Earliest Available Data: 1973-74
National Coverage: United Kingdom
Disaggregation: None

Statistician
Elizabeth Mellor
Board of Inland Revenue
Tel: 020 7438 7423;
Email: sed.ir.sh@gtnet.gov.uk

Products that contain data from this source
Inland Revenue Statistics

Data on Self Assessment Taxpayers - UK
Board of Inland Revenue

The self assessment tax system, which started for the tax year 1996-97, covers about 8 million people with self employment income, rent income or capital gains; who are higher rate taxpayers; or who have complex tax affairs - and nearly 300,000 personal trusts and estates. The annual tax form collects data on all taxable incomes and gains, on allowances and reliefs and on tax deducted at source (via PAYE, from bank interest, etc), Tax forms are also completed by over 650,000 partnerships. Data on the tax forms returned are captured electronically. Inland Revenue Statistics and Economics Division has access to a database containing these data for a fixed systematic sample of 10% of cases (based on the unique taxpayer reference number), together with data on tax payments and repayments.

Status: Ongoing
Collection Method: electronic from administrative system (10% of SA taxpayers)
Frequency: Annually
Reference Period: tax year
Timeliness: Cumulative, as tax returns data are captured
Earliest Available Data: 1996-97
National Coverage: United Kingdom
Disaggregation: Postcodes held, but not at present coded to geographical areas

Statistician
Alan McIntyre
Board of Inland Revenue
Tel: 020 7438 7417;
Email: sed.ir.sh@gtnet.gov.uk

Products that contain data from this source
Inland Revenue Statistics

Sources and Analyses

Debenture Payments by Companies
Board of Inland Revenue

The Inland Revenue Statistics and Economic Division compiles data on debenture payments by companies from a large sample. Data are available by broad industry group and by derivation of the tax due from amounts paid.

Status: Ongoing
Collection Method: Large-scale (Sample) Survey
Frequency: Quarterly
Reference Period: calendar quarters
Timeliness: 18 month delay before publication
Earliest Available Data: 1957
National Coverage: United Kingdom
Disaggregation: Broad Industry Group

Statistician
Alan McIntyre
Board of Inland Revenue
Tel: 020 7438 7417;
Email: sed.ir.sh@gtnet.gov.uk

Products that contain data from this source
Inland Revenue Statistics

Dividend Payments by Companies
Board of Inland Revenue

Up to the first quarter of 1999 the Inland Revenue Statistics and Economics Division compiled data on dividend payments by companies from a large sample. Data are available by broad industry group and by derivation of advance corporation tax (ACT) due from amounts paid up until the series was discontinued. With the abolition of ACT in April 1999 responsibility for measuring dividend payments was transferred to the Office for National Statistics.

Status: Ongoing
Collection Method: Large-scale (Sample) Survey
Frequency: Quarterly
Reference Period: calendar quarters
Timeliness: 18 month delay before publication
Earliest Available Data: 1957
National Coverage: United Kingdom
Disaggregation: Broad Industry Group

Statistician
Richard Balley
Board of Inland Revenue
Tel: 020 7438 6271;
Email: sed.ir.sh@gtnet.gov.uk

Products that contain data from this source
Inland Revenue Statistics

Expenses and Benefits Survey
Board of Inland Revenue

The Inland Revenue Statistics and Economics Division compiles data on expenses and benefits which is used to inform policy advice on possible Budget measures. Up until 1995-96, the data was collected by doing an annual paper survey of about 9,000 individuals who might have expenses and benefits for whom tax records are held by Inland Revenue tax offices. No data was collected in 1996-97. Data for 1997-98 will be collected electronically for a sample of about 20,000 people with benefits-in-kind reported. It should be available in late summer 1999.

Data are available on many of the common benefits-in-kind including company cars, free level and private medical insurance.

Status: Ongoing
Collection Method: Large-scale (Sample) Survey
Frequency: Annually
Reference Period: tax year
Timeliness: 3 months for publication although some data available earlier
Earliest Available Data: published information available back to 1983-84
National Coverage: United Kingdom
Disaggregation: Government Office Regions (GOR)

Statistician
Jude Hillary
Board of Inland Revenue
Tel: 020 7438 7412

Products that contain data from this source
Inland Revenue Statistics, Report on Expenses and Benefits Survey

Income Taxpayer Numbers and Specimen Income Calculations.
Board of Inland Revenue

Income taxpayer numbers and specimen income tax calculations are generated from an annual survey of personal incomes and projected to the current and future years using a tax model. This covers all UK taxpayers. Fairly consistent series since independent taxation was introduced in 1990-91; differences caused by changes to the personal allowance and the tax band widths.

Status: Ongoing
Collection Method: Household/Person (Sample) Survey
Frequency: Annually
Reference Period: Tax year
Timeliness: Data released on request as soon as it is ready, but is normally published in the Inland Revenue annual publication 'Inland Revenue Statistics' which is available around 3 months after the data is ready.

Earliest Available Data: 1978-79
National Coverage: United Kingdom
Sub-National: All UK nations available separately.
Disaggregation: Regions available based on Government Office Region indicator (13 regions)

Statistician
Sean Whellams
Board of Inland Revenue
Tel: 020 7438 7411

Products that contain data from this source
Inland Revenue Statistics

Inheritance Tax: Transfers on Death/Excise Duties
Board of Inland Revenue

The Inland Revenue Statistics and Economics Division compiles data on inheritance tax. Data are available for transfers on death, lifetime transfers, discretionary trusts, estimates of tax receipts, distribution of estates passing on death, and asset breakdowns by age and sex. The data cover the United Kingdom and are collected continuously. Tax receipt data and distributional analyses are published annually, one and three years respectively after the end of the financial year.

Status: Latest year(s) live, others non operational
Collection Method: Accounts data. Sample of administrative records.
Frequency: Continuous
Reference Period: Tax Year. Monthly for receipts data.
Timeliness: Tax receipt data and distributional analyses are published six months and three years, respectively, after the end of the reference period.
Earliest Available Data: 1986-87 (from date inheritance tax was introduced. Information on its predecessors, capital transfer tax and estate duty, was available prior to this date).
National Coverage: United Kingdom (Estimates of tax receipts available for England & Wales, Scotland & Northern Ireland)

Statistician
Ann White/Kerry Booth
Board of Inland Revenue
Tel: 020 7438 6236;
Email: sed.ir.nwb@gtnet.gov.uk

Products that contain data from this source
Inland Revenue Statistics

Inland Revenue Tax Receipts
Board of Inland Revenue

The Inland Revenue Statistics and Economics Office compiles data on direct tax receipts. They are available from a variety of sources of Inland Revenue administrative data. The figures are produced on a monthly basis by head of tax with further breakdowns by type of tax for income and corporation tax.

Status: Ongoing
Collection Method: Data from various Inland Revenue administrative systems; the figures represent a census.
Frequency: Monthly
Reference Period: Monthly, Quarterly and Annually
Timeliness: Up to one month
Earliest Available Data: 1908-09
National Coverage: United Kingdom
Disaggregation: By head of duty with further breakdowns by type of tax

Statistician
Maurice Nettley
Board of Inland Revenue
Tel: 020 7438 7411;
Email: sed.ir.sh@gtnet.gov.uk

Products that contain data from this source
Agricultural Land Prices in England (Statistical Release); Financial Statement and Budget Report; Financial Statistics; Inland Revenue Statistics; Public Sector Finances (First Release)

Mortgage Interest Relief
Board of Inland Revenue

Inland Revenue Statistics and Economics Division produces analyses of the recipients of mortgage interest relief. These analyses are based on the Family Expenditure Survey with additional information from administrative and commercial sources. Analyses of the Family Expenditure Survey have been produced since 1983-84 and are published about six months after the end of the reference year. Prior to 1983-84 analyses were based on the Survey of Personal Incomes. Published information 1959-60, regional breakdowns back to 1982-83.

Status: Ongoing
Collection Method: Large-scale (Sample) Survey
Frequency: Annually
Reference Period: Financial year
Timeliness: 6 months for publication
Earliest Available Data: 1959-60
National Coverage: United Kingdom
Disaggregation: Government Office Region (GOR)

Statistician
Steve Barry
Board of Inland Revenue
Tel: 020 7438 7385;
Email: sed.ir.sh@gtnet.gov.uk

Products that contain data from this source
Inland Revenue Statistics

National Income Statistics Survey - UK
Board of Inland Revenue

Inland Revenue Statistics and Economics Division compiles data on wages and salaries arising from employment for inclusion in the National Accounts. The data are derived from end of year Pay-As-You-Earn (PAYE) tax documents. Data are available on the amount of pay from employment, tax and national insurance contributions (primary and secondary), by industry (SIC92) and sector.

Collection Method: Large-scale (Sample) Survey
Frequency: Annually
Reference Period: tax year
Timeliness: 6 months for publication although a few tables are available earlier
Earliest Available Data: published information available back to 1982
National Coverage: United Kingdom
Disaggregation: Regional and county level; district level

Statistician
Jude Hillary
Board of Inland Revenue
Tel: 020 7438 7412

Products that contain data from this source
Inland Revenue Statistics; Second Tier Pension Provision

Net Value Added Tax (VAT) Receipts UK
HM Customs and Excise

The Net Value Added Tax Receipts series is compiled by HM Customs and Excise. The data, covering receipts net of repayments, relate to VAT accounted for each month.

Status: Ongoing
Frequency: Monthly
Timeliness: 3 weeks
Earliest Available Data: April 1973
National Coverage: United Kingdom

Statistician
Jill Marson
HM Customs and Excise
Tel: 020 7865 5038

Products that contain data from this source
Annual Report of the Commissioners of Customs and Excise; Financial Statistics; Public Sector Finances (First Release)

Rateable Values of Non-Domestic Properties
Board of Inland Revenue

The Inland Revenue Statistics and Economics Division compiles data on the rateable values of non-domestic properties. Data are available by broad region, property type and value band.

Status: Ongoing
Collection Method: A copy of the changes to the full rating list (i.e. census) is obtained from the Valuation Office Agency.
Frequency: Monthly
Timeliness: Information for 1 April available June the same year. (Annual publication)
Earliest Available Data: 1 April 1995 for the 1995 rating lists.
National Coverage: England and Wales
Disaggregation: Government Office of the Regions, Billing Authorities and postcodes.

Statistician
Frank Kane
Board of Inland Revenue
Tel: 020 7438 6314

Products that contain data from this source
Annual Abstract of Statistics; Inland Revenue Statistics; Local Government Financial Statistics: England; Welsh Local Government Financial Statistics

Receipts and Accruals of Direct Tax from UK Oil and Gas Production
Board of Inland Revenue

The Inland Revenue Statistics and Economics Division compiles data on Government Revenues from Petroleum Revenue Tax (PRT) and Corporation Tax (CT) receipts paid on profits from oil and gas fields. Information is also available for Supplementary Petroleum Duty for the two years payments were received. Accruals data from PRT assessments are compiled. CT accruals, which relate to profits derived from UK oil and gas, are estimated from an annual sample survey.

Status: Ongoing
Collection Method: Census of payments and PRT accruals Sample of CT accruals.
Frequency: Daily for CT receipts, weekly for PRT receipts, half yearly for PRT accruals, yearly for CT accruals.
Reference Period: Monthly for CT and PRT receipts, half yearly for PRT accruals, yearly for CT accruals.
Timeliness: up to 1 month for receipts, 6 months for PRT accruals, 2.5 years for CT accruals.
Earliest Available Data: 1970-71 for CT, 1978-79 for PRT
National Coverage: United Kingdom

Statistician
Peter Smedley
Board of Inland Revenue
Tel: 020 7438 6384

Products that contain data from this source
Inland Revenue Statistics; Development of the Oil and Gas Resources of the United Kingdom

Sources and Analyses

Receipts of Customs and Excise Taxes Other Than VAT - UK
HM Customs and Excise

The Receipts of Customs and Excise Duties series is compiled by HM Customs and Excise. Data cover the receipts of all taxes collected by Customs and Excise. These taxes include duties on hydrocarbon oils, tobacco, beer, wines, spirits, cider, betting and gaming (including lottery), customs duties, agricultural levies, air passenger duty, insurance premium tax, landfill tax and, until 1992, car tax.

Status: Ongoing
Frequency: Monthly
Timeliness: 6 weeks
National Coverage: United Kingdom

Statistician
Jill Marson
HM Customs and Excise
Tel: 020 7865 5038

Products that contain data from this source
Annual Report of the Commissioners of Customs and Excise; Financial Statistics

Survey of Personal Incomes - UK
Board of Inland Revenue

The Inland Revenue Statistics and Economics Division carries out a survey on personal incomes. The survey covers a sample of some 80,000 individuals for whom income tax records are held by Inland Revenue tax offices. Data are available for income distributions before and after tax, numbers of taxpayers with income and deductions of various types and the amounts concerned. Some information on tax liabilities and self-employment income is also available. Survey data on self-employment income, income from property, and investment income are used in the preparation of National and Regional Accounts.

Status: Ongoing
Collection Method: Large-scale (Sample) Survey
Frequency: Annually
Reference Period: tax year
Timeliness: 3 months after final file produced although some tables are available earlier upon request
Earliest Available Data: 1978-79
National Coverage: United Kingdom
Disaggregation: Regional, county, metropolitan borough and larger non-metropolitan local authority district levels

Statistician
Jude Hillary
Board of Inland Revenue
Tel: 020 7438 7412

Products that contain data from this source
Annual Abstract of Statistics; Average total income and average income tax payable: by gender, 1995-96: regional datasheet; Distribution of income liable to assessment for tax, 1995-96: regional datasets; Inland Revenue Statistics; Northern Ireland Annual Abstract of Statistics; Regional Trends; Scottish Abstract of Statistics; Social Trends; Welsh Economic Trends; Agriculture in the United Kingdom

Tax Relief on Savings and Investment
Board of Inland Revenue

The Inland Revenue Statistics and Economics Division compiles data on the take-up and the costs of tax reliefs for various savings and investment schemes - including pensions, PEP and TESSA (to be replaced by ISA), EIS, VCT, approved employee share schemes and profit related pay.

Data cover the United Kingdom and are normally available from the inception of the relevant scheme. With the exception of a few quarterly series, most data are published annually, between 6 and 18 months after the reference period.

Status: Ongoing
Collection Method: Census / sample of administrative returns
Frequency: Annual/quarterly
Reference Period: Tax year
Timeliness: 6-18 months after reference period
Earliest Available Data: From inception of relevant scheme
National Coverage: United Kingdom level only

Statistician
Andrzej Walczowski
Board of Inland Revenue
Tel: 020 7438 6231;
Email: sed.ir.nwb@gtnet.gov.uk

Products that contain data from this source
Inland Revenue Statistics

Tax Relief for Charities
Board of Inland Revenue

The Inland Revenue Statistics and Economics Division compiles data on the tax relief associated with charitable giving and the income of charities. Data cover the United Kingdom and are normally available from the inception of the relevant scheme. Data are published annually, 6 months after the reference period.

Status: Ongoing
Collection Method: Census / Sample of administrative returns
Frequency: Annual
Reference Period: Tax year
Timeliness: 6 months after reference period

Earliest Available Data: From inception of relevant scheme
National Coverage: United Kingdom level only

Statistician
Andrzej Walczowski
Board of Inland Revenue
Tel: 020 7438 6231;
Email: sed.ir.nwb@gtnet.gov.uk

Products that contain data from this source
Inland Revenue Statistics

See also:
In other chapters:
British Social Attitudes Survey (BSA) Series (see the Compendia and Reference chapter)

17.12 Wales - Local Authorities' Finances

Local Authority Budget Requirement - Wales
National Assembly for Wales

The National Assembly for Wales conducts the Budget Requirement Survey. Data are available on the total budgeted revenue expenditure for each local authority for the next financial year together with a broad analysis of the funding of that expenditure and the level of Council Tax set.

Status: Ongoing
Earliest Available Data: 1990-91
National Coverage: Wales
Disaggregation: County, local authority district and police authority levels

Statistician
Stuart Neil
National Assembly for Wales
Tel: 029 2082 3963

Products that contain data from this source
Digest of Welsh Statistics; Welsh Local Government Financial Statistics

Local Authority Capital Forecast - Wales
National Assembly for Wales

The National Assembly for Wales conducts the Capital Forecast Survey. Data are available on the total budgeted capital expenditure for each local authority for the current financial year together with a broad analysis by service.

Status: Ongoing
Earliest Available Data: 1990-91
National Coverage: Wales
Disaggregation: County, local authority district and police authority levels

Statistician
Stuart Neil
National Assembly for Wales
Tel: 029 2082 3963

Products that contain data from this source
Digest of Welsh Statistics; Welsh Local
Government Financial Statistics

Local Authority Capital Outturn - Wales
National Assembly for Wales

The National Assembly for Wales conducts surveys on capital outturn. Data are available on capital expenditure for each local authority for the latest financial year with a detailed analysis by service.

Earliest Available Data: 1990-91 (Similar information is available from 1979-80)
National Coverage: Wales
Disaggregation: County, local authority district and police authority levels

Statistician
Stuart Neil
National Assembly for Wales
Tel: 029 2082 3963

Products that contain data from this source
Digest of Welsh Statistics; Social Services Statistics for Wales; Statistics of Education and Training in Wales: Schools; Welsh Housing Statistics; Welsh Local Government Financial Statistics

---

Local Authority Capital Payments - Wales
National Assembly for Wales

The National Assembly for Wales conducts the Capital Payments Survey. Data are available on the quarterly cumulative capital expenditure for each local authority for the current financial year and the provisional outturn expenditure for the latest year, with a broad analysis by service. Data cover Wales and are available at county, local authority district and police authority levels.

Earliest Available Data: 1990-91 (Partial information is available from 1986-87)
National Coverage: Wales

Statistician
Stuart Neil
National Assembly for Wales
Tel: 029 2082 3963

Products that contain data from this source
Digest of Welsh Statistics; Welsh Housing Statistics; Welsh Local Government Financial Statistics

---

Local Authority Capital Receipts - Wales
National Assembly for Wales

The National Assembly for Wales conducts the Capital Receipts Survey. Data are available on the provisional level of receipts from the disposal of assets for each local authority for the latest financial year with a broad analysis by service.

Earliest Available Data: 1990-91
National Coverage: Wales
Disaggregation: County, local authority district and police authority levels

Statistician
Stuart Neil
National Assembly for Wales
Tel: 029 2082 3963

Products that contain data from this source
Welsh Local Government Financial Statistics

Local Authority Council Tax Dwellings - Wales
National Assembly for Wales

The National Assembly for Wales conducts the Council Tax Dwellings Survey. Data are available on the number of dwellings eligible for the Council Tax in each local authority for the next financial year, analysed by Council Tax band.

Earliest Available Data: 1993-94
National Coverage: Wales
Disaggregation: Local Authority

Statistician
Stuart Neil
National Assembly for Wales
Tel: 029 2082 3963

Products that contain data from this source
Welsh Local Government Financial Statistics

Local Authority General Fund Revenue Account - Wales
National Assembly for Wales

The National Assembly for Wales conducts the Revenue Account Survey. Data are available on the total budgeted revenue expenditure for each local authority for the next financial year together with an analysis by service.

Earliest Available Data: 1990-91
National Coverage: Wales
Disaggregation: County, local authority district and police authority levels

Statistician
Stuart Neil
National Assembly for Wales
Tel: 029 2082 3963

Products that contain data from this source
Digest of Welsh Statistics; Welsh Local Government Financial Statistics

---

Local Authority National Non-Domestic Rates - Wales
National Assembly for Wales

The National Assembly for Wales conducts surveys on the amount of non-domestic rates which local authorities expect to collect or have collected. Provisional calculations are required before the beginning of the financial year and final adjustment calculations are required after the end of the financial year.

Earliest Available Data: 1990-91
National Coverage: Wales
Disaggregation: Local Authority

Statistician
Stuart Neil
National Assembly for Wales
Tel: 029 2082 3963

Products that contain data from this source
Welsh Local Government Financial Statistics

Local Authority Quarterly Return of Charges - Wales
National Assembly for Wales

The National Assembly for Wales conducts the Quarterly Return of Charges Survey. Data are available on the amount of Council Tax, business rates and other income received by local authorities for the previous quarter as well as the amount of wages paid out by the authority.

Earliest Available Data: 1993-94 (Certain equivalent information for earlier years is available from 1988-90)
National Coverage: Wales
Disaggregation: County, local authority district and police authority levels

Statistician
Stuart Neil
National Assembly for Wales
Tel: 029 2082 3963

Products that contain data from this source
Welsh Local Government Financial Statistics

Local Authority Revenue Outturn - Wales
National Assembly for Wales

The National Assembly for Wales conducts surveys on revenue outturn. Data are available on each of the major areas of local government revenue expenditure for each local authority for the most recent financial year

Earliest Available Data: 1990-91
National Coverage: Wales
Disaggregation: County, local authority district and police authority levels

Statistician
Stuart Neil
National Assembly for Wales
Tel: 029 2082 3963

Products that contain data from this source
Digest of Welsh Statistics; Social Services Statistics for Wales; Statistics of Education and Training in Wales: Schools; Welsh Housing Statistics; Welsh Local Government Financial Statistics

---

Local Authority Superannuation Fund - Wales
National Assembly for Wales

The National Assembly for Wales conducts the Superannuation Survey. Data are available on the income and expenditure and number of members of local authority pension funds for the latest financial year.

Earliest Available Data: 1990-91 (Similar information is available from 1979-80)
National Coverage: Wales
Disaggregation: County level

Statistician
Stuart Neil
National Assembly for Wales
Tel: 029 2082 3963

Products that contain data from this source
Welsh Local Government Financial Statistics

---

17 Government and Public Sector - *Products*

17.13 Abstracts, Compendia, A-Z Catalogues, Directories and Reference Material

Modernising Public Services Group
Cabinet Office

In 1998, the Service First Unit in the Cabinet Office commissioned MORI, the market research company, and Birmingham University's School of Public Policy to set up a People's Panel. The Panel consists of 5,000 members of the public randomly selected from across the United Kingdom, and is designed to be a representative cross-section of the population (by gender, age, background, region, etc). Panel members are consulted about how public services are delivered and how that delivery can be improved from the point of view of the user, rather than the system. The Government is committed to publishing all results from the Panel. Summaries of findings are widely distributed periodically, and, along with the full topline results, appear on the Cabinet Office website (www.servicefirst.gov.uk).

Delivery: Periodic Release, hardcopy and via the Internet
Frequency: Periodic
Price: Free

Available from
Paul Greening
Consultation Policy Team
Modernising Public Services Group
Cabinet Office
Horse Guards Road
London SW1P 3AL
Tel: 020 7270 6308;
Email: pgreening@cabinet-office.x.gsi.gov.uk

Or the Service First publications line: 0345 22 32 42

People Count
Ministry of Defence

A newsletter about DASA's work on personnel issues in the Ministry of Defence. The newsletter contains articles illustrating DASA's work, news of recent developments, and telephone contacts for each area of work.

Delivery: Periodic Release
Frequency: Periodic
Price: Free

Available from
Mike Fletcher
Room 120
Ministry of Defence
Northumberland House
Northumberland Avenue
London WC2 5BP
Tel: 020 7218 5143

17.14 Armed Forces and Defence

Defence Statistics Bulletins
Ministry of Defence

The Defence Statistics Bulletins cover: (i) Changes to the statistics of MOD's intramural research and development expenditure; (ii) Changes to the statistics of MOD's research and development expenditure; (iii) Revisions to the statistics of employment dependent on defence expenditure; and (iv) Statistics of exports and imports of defence equipment and of defence balance of payments invisible transactions.

Delivery: News/Press Release
Frequency: When need is agreed.
Price: Free

Available from
Robin Horton
Room 144
Ministry of Defence
Northumberland House
Northumberland Avenue
London WC2 5BP
Tel: 020 7218 8326;
Email: triservice@dasa.mon.uk

Sources from which data for this product are obtained
UK Defence

Report of the Review Body on Armed Forces Pay
Office of Manpower Economics

A report and a supplementary report are published on the pay and allowances of members of the Naval, Military and Air Forces of the Crown. The report contains recommendations on rates of pay and pay-related allowances for most Service personnel, with recommended levels of charges for accommodation and food. The supplementary report recommends levels of pay and additional pay for Service medical and dental officers.

Frequency: Annually
Price: £7.30
ISBN: 010 142422 1

Available from
TSO Publications Centre and Bookshops
Please see Annex B for full address details.

UK Defence Statistics 1998
Ministry of Defence

Annual compendium of defence-related statistics. The latest available statistics on a range of defence activities, grouped under three main headings: finance, personnel, and resources and defence services. Chapter 1 contains statistical trends of Defence expenditure, analysed by purpose (i.e. personnel, equipment etc). Chapter 2 contains trends in the strengths, inflows and outflows of MoD Service and civilian personnel, analysed (for example) by gender, rank/grade, function and ethnic group. Chapter 3 presents statistics of the formation of the armed forces, resources available to the armed forces, Service personnel accommodation and health and on Defence operations.

Delivery: News/Press Release
Frequency: Annually
Price: £12.50
ISBN: 011 - 7728896

Available from
TSO Publications Centre and Bookshops
Please see Annex B for full address details.

Sources from which data for this product are obtained
UK Defence

Products

17.15 Employment in the Public Sector

Civil Service Data Summary 1994: Women, Race, Disability
Cabinet Office

Information on this publication is Available from 020 7270 4775.

Available from
Susan Lain
Cabinet Office
House Guards Road
London
Tel: 020 7270 5719

Sources from which data for this product are obtained
Mandate

Civil Service Statistics
Cabinet Office

Detailed statistics about civil servants, their departments/agencies, location, pay, etc and the staff joining and leaving the Civil Service, with a commentary on trends.

Delivery: Periodic Release
Frequency: Annually
Price: Free
ISBN: 0 7115 03699

Available from
Cabinet Office
Personnel Statistics Branch
Horse Guards Road
London SW1P 3AL
Tel: 020 7270 5744;
Email: psb.gtnet.gov.uk

Sources from which data for this product are obtained
Mandate, Quarterly Staff Returns

Civil Service Statistics - Key figures
Cabinet Office

A folding card summarising in graphical form some of the most-asked-for information about Civil Service personnel statistics

Delivery: Periodic Release
Frequency: Annually
Price: Free
ISBN: 07115 03702

Available from
Cabinet Office
Personnel Statistics Branch
Horse Guards Road
London SW1P 3AL
Tel: 020 7270 5744;
Email: psb.gtnet.gov.uk

Sources from which data for this product are obtained
Mandate, Civil Service Quarterly Staff Review

Civil Service Statistics – Quarterly Summary
Cabinet Office

Latest Staffing figures for departments and the Civil Service in total.

Delivery: Press Notice and summary table
Frequency: Quarterly
Price: Free

Available from
Personnel Statistics Branch: Email: psb.gtnet.gov.uk and Cabinet Office Website: http://www.cabinet-office.gov.uk/civilservice/index/statistics.htm

Sources from which data for this product are obtained
Mandate, Quarterly Staff Review

Equal Opportunities in the Civil Service Data Summary: Women, Race, Disability, Age
Cabinet Office

Provides data on the Civil Service by gender, ethnic origin, and disability together with some analysis by age. Information is provided by gender, ethnic origin, disability and age for both non-industrial and industrial staff on a headcount basis. Typically, analyses involve responsibility levels, gross salary, part-time staff, entrants, promotion rates, average age, and government office regions with male/female breakdowns where possible.

Delivery: Periodic Release
Frequency: Annually
Price: Free

Available from
Haseena Noushad
Cabinet Office
1 Horse Guards Road
London SW1P 3AL
Tel: 020 7270 5734;
Email: hnoushad@cabinet-office.x.gsi.gov.uk

Sources from which data for this product are obtained
Mandate, Quarterly Staff Returns

First Results of New Annual Local Authority Staffing Survey: (December 1994) (Statistical Bulletin)
Scottish Executive

Summary of results from the first of a series of four detailed staffing surveys conducted over the period of local government reorganisation in Scotland. The bulletin contains results of the Local Authority Staffing Survey in a variety of charts and tables. Information on full and part-time staff numbers, costs and characteristics are included.

Price: £2.00
ISBN: 0 7480 4903 7
ISSN: 0264-1143

Available from
The Librarian
Scottish Executive
Victoria Quay
Edinburgh EH6 6QQ

Sources from which data for this product are obtained
Local Authority Annual Staffing Survey - Scotland

Joint Staffing Watch (Press Release)
Scottish Executive

Information on this publication is Available from 020 7276 3003.

Available from
Duncan Gray
Scottish Executive
Victoria Quay
Edinburgh
Tel: 0131 244 7031; Fax: 0131 244 7567;
Email: duncan.gray@scotland.gov.uk

Sources from which data for this product are obtained
Joint Staffing Watch Survey - England

Joint Staffing Watch Results (Quarterly Press Release)
Scottish Executive

Summary information from the Joint Staffing Watch. The release contains information of total full-time staff in current quarter and equivalent quarters from 1975; total full-time staff by service, seasonally adjusted; total full-time staff by service unadjusted; and total full-time, part-time, male, female, manual, non-manual staff by authority.

Frequency: Quarterly
Price: Free

Available from
Mr J. D. Gray
Local Government Finance Statistics
Room 3-J 18
Edinburgh EH6 6QQ

Sources from which data for this product are obtained
Local Authority Joint Staffing Watch - Scotland

Report of the Review Body on Senior Salaries
Office of Manpower Economics

Reports are published annually in respect of the main remit group (Senior Civil Servants; Senior Judiciary; Senior Military) and tri-ennially on aspects of the remuneration, pensions and allowances of members of the Houses of Parliament. The reports on the main remit group contain the recommendations of the Review Body, including salary recommendations. They also have included results of surveys of the earnings of board members and senior executives in the private sector, judges' pre-appointment earnings and earnings of practising lawyers. The reports on parliamentary issues, in addition, have covered, variously, recommendations on salary levels, expenses allowances, pensions and resettlement grants. They have included comparative pensions evaluations and the results of surveys of expenditure on the items covered, by the expenses allowances, members' views on their allowances and the views of MPs' secretaries and research assistants. Comparative data on salaries, allowances and facilities of overseas legislators have also been presented.

Delivery: Periodic Release
Frequency: Annually
Price: £7.30
ISBN: (I) 010 142452 3

Available from
TSO Publications Centre and Bookshops
Please see Annex B for full address details.

See also:
In this chapter:
Local Government Financial Statistics: England *(17.16)*

In other chapters:
Economic Trends *(see the Economy chapter)*
Office for National Statistics Databank *(see the Websites and Electronic Services chapter)*
United Kingdom National Accounts - The Blue Book *(see the Economy chapter)*

17.16 England - Local Authorities' Finances

Council Tax Collection Figures, England
Department of the Environment, Transport and the Regions

Press release detailing council tax and non-domestic rates collection rates by local billing authority.

Delivery: News/Press Release
Frequency: Annually

Available from
Ashley Pottier
Room 5/J5
Department of the Environment, Transport and the Regions
Eland House
Bressenden Place
London SW1E 5DU
Tel: 020 7890 4166;
Email: ashley.pottier@detr.gsi.gov.uk

Sources from which data for this product are obtained
Council Tax and Non-Domestic Rates Collection Data; Council Tax Base Survey, England

Council Tax Levels, England
Department of the Environment, Transport and the Regions

Press release covering council taxes for notifiable (preceptors) and billing authorities.

Delivery: News/Press Release
Frequency: Annually

Available from
Ashley Pottier
Room 5/J5
Department of the Environment, Transport and the Regions
Eland House
Bressenden Place
London SW1E 5DU
Tel: 020 7890 4166

Sources from which data for this product are obtained
Local Authority Budget - England

Local Authority Performance Indicators
Audit Commission

Available from
Worth Houghton
Audit Commission
1 Vincent Square
London

Sources from which data for this product are obtained
Revenue Outturn - England

Local Government Financial Statistics: England
Department of the Environment, Transport and the Regions

Tables and commentary containing a wide variety of local authority financial statistics such as revenue account, capital account, borrowing and investments, Council Taxes, non-domestic rates and government grants.

Delivery: Hardcopy publication; also via internet at http://www.local.detr.gov.uk
Frequency: Annual
Price: £12.00
ISBN: 1 85 112 138 2

Available from
Department and the Environment, Transport and the Regions
Publications Sales Centre
Unit 8
Goldthorpe Industrial Estate
Goldthorpe
Rotherham S63 9BL
Tel: 01709 891318

Sources from which data for this product are obtained

Borrowing and Lending Inquiry (Monthly) - UK; Borrowing and Lending Inquiry (Quarterly); Capital Outturn Returns - England; Capital Payments Return - England; Council Tax and Non-Domestic Rates Collection Data; Council Taxbase Survey - England; Joint Staffing Watch Survey - England; Local Authority Budget - England; Minimum Revenue Provision - England; Non-domestic Rates Survey - England; Outstanding Amounts Inquiry (MQBL) - UK; Pension Funds - England; Rateable Values of Non-Domestic Properties; Revenue Account Survey - England; Revenue Outturn - England

See also:
In this chapter:
Financial Statistics *(17.21)*
Local Government Financial Statistics: England *(17.16)*

In other chapters:
Economic Trends *(see the Economy chapter)*
United Kingdom National Accounts - The Blue Book *(see the Economy chapter)*

17.17 International Aid and Development

Development Counts
A small factsheet produced annually after the publication of 'Statistics on International Development' which contains selected statistics for wider public dissemination.

Delivery: Hardcopy publication
Price: Free

Available from
DFID Public Enquiry Point
Department for International Development
Abercrombie House
Eaglesham Road
East Kilbride
Glasgow G75 8EA

Products

Statistics on International Development
Department for International Development

Data on all aspects of the UK overseas aid programme. The publication is produced annually to provide statistical information on UK external assistance, including comparison with other donors, in accordance with reporting principles set out by the OECD's Development Assistance Committee (DAC). The tables provide details of all external assistance, both bilateral and through multilateral agencies, from all official UK sources. The statistics are presented mainly on a financial year basis, with the exception of the internationally comparable calendar year data based on DAC tables. The 1998 edition mainly contains data for 1993-94 to 1997-98.

Delivery: Hardcopy publication
Frequency: Annual
Price: £10.00
ISBN: 1 86192 008 3
ISSN: 0068-1210

Available from
The Library
Department for International Development
Eaglesham Road
East Kilbride
Glasgow G75 8EA
Tel: 01355 84 3272

Sources from which data for this product are obtained
Statistical returns to the Development Assistance Committee of OECD; Statistics on International Development

17.18 National Savings

National Savings Press Release
Department for National Savings

This release gives a monthly account of National Savings financial results for the previous month. The release contains data relating to National Savings sales and accrued interest, repayments, balances outstanding, contribution of government funding. It provides the press with financial statistics showing how National Savings have performed during the past month, the last three months and also the contribution to government funding that has been made in that period.

Delivery: Press Release
Frequency: Monthly
Price: Free

Available from
The Press Office
Department for National Savings
Charles House
375 Kensington High Street
London W14 8SD
Tel: 020 7605 9433

Sources from which data for this product are obtained
National Savings - Financial Statistics

17.19 Northern Ireland - Finances

Accounts of Capital Receipts and Payments
Department of Finance and Personnel - Northern Ireland

Capital receipts and capital expenditure of Northern Ireland and earnings on capital advances or investments. Also includes the Civil Contingencies Fund Account. The accounts contain data on borrowing by the NI Consolidated Fund from National Loans Fund, Issue of Ulster Savings Certificates, etc., repayment of capital advances to NI Housing Executive, repayment of advances to district councils and other borrowers, repayment of borrowing from NLF, redemption of Ulster Saving Certificates, advances to NI Housing Executive, district councils and other borrowers.

Delivery: Periodic Release
Frequency: Annually (No longer produced, details included in expanded Public Income and Expenditure)
Price: £3.35
ISBN: 0 337 23603 8

Available from
TSO Publications Centre and Bookshops
Please see Annex B for full address details.

Finance Accounts of Northern Ireland
Department of Finance and Personnel - Northern Ireland

Income and expenditure of the Northern Ireland Consolidated Fund. The publication contains data on Northern Ireland share of UK taxes, regional and district rates collected, interest on loans made by the Consolidated Fund, grant-in-aid from UK Consolidated Fund, supply services, interest on sums borrowed, transfer to district councils of district rates, statutory salaries, pensions, capital receipts and issues.

Delivery: Periodic Release
Frequency: Annually
Price: £9.10
ISBN: 0 337 23631 0

Available from
TSO Publications Centre and Bookshops
Please see Annex B for full address details.

Public Income and Expenditure
Department of Finance and Personnel - Northern Ireland

An Account of the Public Income and Expenditure of Northern Ireland in the year ended 31 March, together with the Balance in the Consolidated Fund on 1 April, the Receipts and Payments (not being Public Expenditure) in the year ended 31 March, and the Balance in the Consolidated Fund on that day. Expanded from 1998/99 to include information previously included in Accounts of Capital Receipts and Payments.

Delivery: Periodic Release
Frequency: Annually
Price: £3.70
ISBN: 0 10 142552 X

Available from
TSO Publications Centre and Bookshops
Please see Annex B for full address details.

17.20 Public Sector Borrowing

Financial Statistics
Office for National Statistics

Key financial and monetary statistics of the UK. The publication contains data on public sector finance, central government revenue and expenditure, money supply and credit, banks and building societies, interest and exchange rates, financial accounts, capital issues, balance sheets and balance of payments. From the October 1998 edition the data in Financial Statistics becomes consistent with the European System of Accounts (ESA 95)

Frequency: Monthly
Price: Monthly, single issue £22.50, annual subscription £270.00 (handbook included)
Electronic database: ONS Sales Desk
ISBN: 0015-203X
ISSN: 0015-203X

Available from
TSO Publications Centre and Bookshops
Please see Annex B for full address details.

Sources from which data for this product are obtained
Acquisitions and Mergers - UK; Administrative Data on the Official Reserves; Annual survey of financial assets and liabilities; Balance of Payments Account - UK; Borrowing and Lending Inquiry (Monthly) - UK; Borrowing and Lending Inquiry (Quarterly); Building Societies; Building Society Lending for House Purchase - UK (BS4); Capital Issues; Central Government Net Cash

Requirement - UK; Central Government Net Cash Requirement on Own Account - UK; Compensation of employees; Consumer Price Collection - UK; Consumers' Expenditure; Current, Capital and Financial Accounts of Non-Financial Corporations; Financial Statistics; Financial Transactions and Balance Sheets; Gross Trading Surplus of Local Authority Trading Enterprises - UK; Household Saving Ratio; Inland Revenue Tax Receipts; Insurance companies balance sheet annual inquiry; Insurance Companies' income and expenditure - quarterly inquiry; Insurance companies' income and expenditure annual inquiry; Insurance companies' transactions in financial assets inquiry; Interest and Exchange Rates; Investment trusts annual return of liabilities and assets; Investment trusts quarterly return of transactions inquiry; Local Authority Direct Net Cash from Central Government - UK; Local Authority Net Cash Requirement - UK; Monetary Stock and Counterparts; National Accounts; National Savings - Financial Statistics; Net Value Added Tax (VAT) Receipts UK; Outstanding Amounts Inquiry (MQBL) - UK; Overseas Direct Investment; Pension fund annual balance sheet inquiry; Pension fund annual income and expenditure inquiry; Pension fund transactions inquiry; Pension Funds - England; Pension funds quarterly income and expenditure inquiry; Property unit trusts annual return of liabilities; Property unit trusts quarterly return of transactions inquiry; Provisional estimates of narrow money; Public Corporations Net Cash Requirement - UK; Public Corporations' Direct Borrowing from Central Government - UK; Public Sector Net Cash Requirement - UK; Quarterly Profits Inquiry Finance Houses and Other Specialist Consumer Credit Grantors - UK; Quarterly survey of financial assets and liabilities; Receipts of Customs and Excise Taxes other than VAT - UK; Revenue Account Survey - England; Revenue Outturn - England; Securities dealers quarterly return of liabilities and assets and of transactions in securities; Unit trusts annual return of liabilities and assets; Unit trusts quarterly return of transactions inquiry

Public Sector Finances (First Release)
Office for National Statistics

Latest data on public sector net borrowing, net debt and the net cash requirement

Frequency: Monthly
Price: Annual subscription £36.00

Available from
ONS Direct
Office for National Statistics
Please see Annex B for full address details

Sources from which data for this product are obtained
Borrowing and Lending Inquiry (Monthly) - UK; Borrowing and Lending Inquiry (Quarterly); Central Government Net Cash Requirement - UK; Central Government Net Cash Requirement on Own Account - UK; Inland Revenue Tax Receipts; Local Authority Direct Net Cash from Central Government - UK; Local Authority Net

Cash Requirement - UK; Net Value Added Tax (VAT) Receipts UK; Public Corporations Net Cash Requirement - UK; Public Corporations' Direct Borrowing from Central Government - UK; Public Sector Net Cash Requirement - UK

See also:
In other chapters:
Economic Trends *(see the Economy chapter)*
United Kingdom National Accounts - The Blue Book *(see the Economy chapter)*
United Kingdom National Accounts, Sources and Methods *(see the Economy chapter)*

17.21 Public Sector Income and Expenditure

(The) Foreign and Commonwealth Office Departmental Report: The Government's Expenditure Plans 1998-99
Foreign and Commonwealth Office

This report provides an overview of the work and resources of the whole Foreign and Commonwealth Office (FCO) in the context of a presentation of its expenditure plans to Parliament. The main body of the report includes a number of statistical tables which support the text. The report also includes a number of detailed statistical appendices.

Delivery: Periodic Release
Frequency: Annually
Price: £17.20 (1998 edition)
ISBN: 0-10-139032-7

Available from
TSO Publications Centre and Bookshops
Please see Annex B for full address details.

Pre-Budget Report (November 1998)
Presents revised economic forecasts for the company and public finances, and sets out the direction of Government policy in the run-up to the budget.

Delivery: Hardcopy publication
Frequency: Annual
Price: £25.00
ISBN: 0-10-140762 9

Available from
TSO Publications Centre and Bookshops
Please see Annex B for full address details.

Sources from which data for this product are obtained
Public Expenditure – UK

Public Expenditure Statistical Analyses 1999-2000
HM Treasury

Contains data on public sector spending, including key aggregates and controls on expenditure; figures for central and local government, and for public corporations; spending by economic category and by function; and an analysis of UK spending by region and territory.

Delivery: Hardcopy publication
Frequency: Annual
Price: £15.30
ISBN: 0-10-142182 6

Available from
TSO Publications Centre and Bookshops
Please see Annex B for full address details.

Public Finance Trends: A Statistical Background to Public Spending and Revenues
Office for National Statistics

This is a compendium of previously published data on public finance. It provides explanations of statistical terms, long-run tables, charts and commentary on trends and contains an overview of the public sector and chapters on: general government; central government; local authorities; public corporations; public sector surplus or deficit and outstanding debt; taxation; Social Security

Frequency: Annual
Price: £25.00
ISBN: 0 11 620721 3

Available from
TSO Publications Centre and Bookshops
Please see Annex B for full address details.

See also:
In other chapters:
Sector Classification for the National Accounts (Business monitor MA23) *(see the Economy chapter)*

17.22 Research and Development (R&D) expenditure by Government

Gross Domestic Expenditure on Research and Development (GERD (First Release))
Office for National Statistics

Gross expenditure on research and development in the UK. Gross domestic expenditure on R&D (GERD) is the most reliable estimate of national R&D spending and draws together information on R&D spending in the public and private sectors: Business enterprises, Government, Higher education, private non-profit. It is the measure most commonly used for international comparisons and covers all R&D performed in the country concerned irrespective of who pays for it. UK GERD covers all R&D in the UK including that funded from abroad; but excludes R&D performed abroad even if funded from the UK.

Delivery: First Release
Frequency: Annually
Price: £3.00

Available from
ONS Press Office
Office for National Statistics
Please see Annex B for full address details.

Sources from which data for this product are obtained
Business Enterprise Research and Development Survey - UK; Government Research and Development Survey - UK

Research and Development Annual Statistics
Eurostat

Contains up-to-date statistics on R&D and patent applications in the European Union and the EEA. These statistics show the trends and structure of research and development in the European Union.

Delivery: Hardcopy publication
Frequency: Annual
ISBN: 92 828 4876 0 (published by Eurostat)

Available from
TSO International Sales Agency
Please see Annex B for full address details.

Sources from which data for this product are obtained
Business Enterprise Research and Development Survey - UK; Government Research and Development Survey - UK

Review of UK Environmental Expenditure (1993)
Department of the Environment, Transport and the Regions

Report to the Department of the Environment of estimates of environmental expenditure in the UK.

Delivery: Ad Hoc/One-off Release
Price: £11.00
ISBN: 0 11 752851 X

Available from
TSO Publications Centre and Bookshops
Please see Annex B for full address details.

Science, Engineering and Technology Statistics 1998
DTI, Office of Science and Technology Statistics

SET Statistics is an annual handbook of key science engineering and technology indicators. It covers science, engineering and technology expenditure (including humanities R&D) and employment statistics. Provides a historical analysis of Government financing of Science, Engineering and Technology (SET) activities in the UK. Describes the relationship between the funders and the UK (Government, higher education, business enterprise, charities and overseas). Reports on business enterprise R&D expenditure. Summarises key data on output and employment of science graduates and postgraduates, and other employment data. Shows how the UK compares with major competitor countries.

Delivery: Hardcopy publication, internet
Frequency: Annually
Price: £13.50
ISBN: 0 10 1400 4

Available from
TSO Publications Centre and Bookshops
Please see Annex B for full address details.

Internet address: http://www.gov.uk/ost/setstats99

Sources from which data for this product are obtained
Business Enterprise Research and Development Survey - UK; Government Research and Development Survey - UK

17.23 Scotland - Local Authorities' Finances

Scottish Local Government Financial Statistics
Scottish Executive

Local government financial statistics for Scotland containing data on for example local financial returns, capital payments, capital debt outstanding, non-domestic rateable values and non-domestic rate income.

Price: Annual 1993-94, £5.00
Summary volume 1975-76 to 1978-88, £6.00
ISBN: 0 7480 5089 2
ISSN: 0264-1143

Available from
TSO Publications Centre and Bookshops
Please see Annex B for full address details.

Sources from which data for this product are obtained
Capital Debt Outstanding Returns - Scotland; Capital Payments Returns - Scotland; Local Financial Returns - Scotland; Non-Domestic Rate Income - Scotland; Non-Domestic Rateable Values - Scotland

17.24 Tax Revenues, Taxes and Excise Duties

Annual Report of the Commissioners of Customs and Excise
HM Customs and Excise

Summary of the activities (revenue and non-revenue) of HM Customs and Excise for the year ending 31 March.

Frequency: Annual
Price: £17.45
ISBN: 0 10 129802 1

Available from
TSO Publications Centre and Bookshops
Please see Annex B for full address details.

Sources from which data for this product are obtained
Net Value Added Tax (VAT) Receipts UK; Receipts of Customs and Excise Taxes other than VAT – UK

Economic and Fiscal Strategy Report and Financial Statement and Budget Report (March 1999)
Contains the Government's assessment of the medium-term and budgetary position; and sets out the Government's tax and spending plans, including those for public investment, in the context of its overall approach to social, economic and environmental objectives.

Delivery: Hardcopy publication
Frequency: Annual
Price: £28.00
ISBN: 0 10 262499 2

Available from
TSO Publications Centre and Bookshops
Please see Annex B for full address details.

Sources from which data for this product are obtained
Public Expenditure - UK

Inland Revenue Statistics
Board of Inland Revenue

Annual reference volume of taxes administered by Inland Revenue. Some 150 statistical tables are included with explanatory charts and notes. The publication contains: data on income tax, corporation tax, petroleum revenue tax, inheritance tax, capital gains tax, and stamp duties; tax liabilities and receipts, numbers of taxpayers, tax allowances and reliefs; analyses of personal income, distribution of wealth and taxable benefits in kind and expenses payments; analyses of company income by industrial sector and the enterprise investment scheme; statistics on pensions, employee share schemes and profit related pay, personal savings and equity investments and income of charities; and statistics on non-domestic rating, property transactions and agricultural land prices.

Delivery: Periodic Release
Frequency: Annually
Price: £32.50
ISBN: 0 11 641435

Available from
TSO Publications Centre and Bookshops
Please see Annex B for full address details.

Sources from which data for this product are obtained
Administrative data on employee share schemes, profit related pay, personal pensions, PEPs, TESSAs, charities, and the Enterprise investment scheme; Agricultural Land Prices – England and Wales; Annual Costs of Tax Allowance and Reliefs; Capital Gains Computation Samples; Capital Gains Tax Assessment Suite; Corporation Tax: Capital Allowances by Type of Asset and Industry; Corporation Tax: Company Profits and Computation of Tax Liability; Corporation Tax: Mainstream Corporation Tax Receipts and Income, Allowances and Tax Accruals; Distribution of Personal Wealth – UK; Dividend Payments by Companies; Debenture Payments by Companies; Family Expenditure Survey; Government Revenues from UK Oil and Gas Production; Income Tax administrative data systems; Inheritance Tax: Transfers on Death/During Lifetime; Inland Revenue Tax Receipts; National Income Statistics Survey – UK; Property Transactions – England and Wales; Rateable Values of Non-Domestic Properties; Survey of expense payments and benefits in kind; Survey of Personal Incomes - UK

Public Sector Finances (First Release)
Office for National Statistics

Latest data on the Public Sector Borrowing Requirement (PSBR).

Frequency: Monthly
Price: Annual subscription £36.00

Available from
Jeff Golland
Office for National Statistics
1 Drummond Gate
London
Tel: 020 7533 5987;
Email: jeff.golland@ons.gov.uk

Sources from which data for this product are obtained
Borrowing and Lending Inquiry (Monthly) - UK; Borrowing and Lending Inquiry (Quarterly); Central Government Net Cash Requirement - UK; Central Government Net Cash Requirement on Own Account - UK; Inland Revenue Tax Receipts; Local Authority Direct Net Cash from Central Government - UK; Local Authority Net Cash Requirement - UK; Net Value Added Tax (VAT) Receipts UK; Public Corporations Net Cash Requirement - UK; Public Corporations' Direct Borrowing from Central Government - UK; Public Sector Net Cash Requirement - UK

See also:
In this chapter:
Local Government Financial Statistics: England *(17.16)*

In other chapters:
Economic Trends *(see the Economy chapter)*

17.25 Wales - Local Authorities' Finances

Welsh Local Government Financial Statistics
National Assembly for Wales

An annual statistical compendium, which is presented to Parliament, containing tables, diagrams and explanatory notes on most aspects of local authority finance in Wales. The compendium covers details of revenue and capital income and expenditure, borrowing, grants, Council Tax, non-domestic rates, benefits and local authority staffing. Most tables give figures by authority.

Frequency: Annual
Price: £7.00
ISBN: 0 7504 0738 7
ISSN: 0140-4482

Available from
Publications Unit, Statistical Directorate
National Assembly for Wales
Please see Annex B for full address details

Sources from which data for this product are obtained
Housing Subsidies; Local Authority Budget Requirement - Wales; Local Authority Capital Forecast - Wales; Local Authority Capital Outturn - Wales; Local Authority Capital Payments - Wales; Local Authority Capital Receipts - Wales; Local Authority Council Tax Dwellings - Wales; Local Authority General Fund Revenue Account - Wales; Local Authority National Non-Domestic Rates - Wales; Local Authority Quarterly Return of Charges - Wales; Local Authority Revenue Outturn - Wales; Local Authority Superannuation Fund - Wales; Rateable Values of Non-Domestic Properties

Government Statistics - General

Information about **Government Statistics** in general is made available mainly by the **Office for National Statistics and the Department of Social Security** and mainly covers **Administrative Matters** (embracing, for example, administrative, financial, managerial, policy and professional matters) and **Professional/Statistical Matters** (embracing information about training, methods, qualities and standards, etc).

Users looking for an overview of **Government Statistics** may find the following products useful:

> **Government Statistical Service - Annual Report** (annual publication)
> **GSS Methodology Series**
> **Statistical News** (quarterly publication)

18 Government Statistics - General - Sources and Analyses

18.1 Administrative Matters

Postcode Boundaries - Scotland
General Register Office for Scotland

The General Register Office for Scotland digitises the boundaries of each unit postcode in Scotland and produces fields associated with each postcode such as the grid reference, the 1991 Census output area and the higher areas.

Status: Ongoing
Frequency: Continuously
National Coverage: Scotland

Statistician
Garnett Compton
General Register Office for Scotland
Tel: 0131 314 4298;
Email: garnett.compton@gro-scotland.gov.uk

Products that contain data from this source
Postcode Index - Scotland; Postcode Sector Lineprints; Postcode Unit Counts

See also:
Lifetime Labour Market Database *(see the Household Finances chapter)*

Government Statistics - General - *Products*

(The) Annual Report and Accounts 1997-98
Office for National Statistics

Delivery: Periodic Release
Frequency: Annually
Price: £12.40

Available from
ONS Direct or TSO Publications Centre and Bookshops
Please see Annex B for full address details.

Charging Guidelines for Statistical Products and Services from the Government Statistical Service
Office for National Statistics

Guidance on how charges are set for statistics and statistical services. This pamphlet offers guidance to departments on the setting of charges for statistics and statistical services. First issued in 1984 as 'Government Statistics: Guidelines for Charging', the guidance was revised in October 1995. Charging is the responsibility of individual government departments, subject to boundaries set by government charging policy and legal constraints. Charges for statistical products and services must be set within this general context, and will also be consistent with general departmental charging policies. These guidelines assist departments in determining charges for statistics and statistical services. Most Government Departments and agencies also publish charging policies and tariffs, relating to the specific products and services they provide.

Frequency: Ad hoc
Price: Free

Available from
National Statistics Information and Library Service
Office for National Statistics
Please see Annex B for full address details.

EOC Annual Report
Equal Opportunities Commission

The Annual Report of the Equal Opportunities Commission (EOC). Includes a statistical appendix containing statistics relating to enquiries received by the EOC, requests for assistance, and EOC staff.

Delivery: Periodic Release
Frequency: Annually
Price: Please contact the EOC for the current publications list and pricing details.
ISSN: 1 870358 74 0

Available from
Customer Contact Point
Equal Opportunities Commission
Please see Annex B for full address details.

Geographic Information Systems (GIS) and Mapping Services
Office for National Statistics

This service provides printed maps from electronic data using various geographical aggregations. Maps can be produced up to A0 in size and colours can be chosen.

Delivery: Ad hoc/One-off Release
Price: Prices vary with complexity of data and size of the map produced.

Available from
Alistair Calder
Office for National Statistics
Please see Annex B for full address details.

(The) Government Statistical Service Code of Practice on the Handling of Data Obtained from Statistical Inquiries
Office for National Statistics

GSS guidelines on handling data. This code of practice is concerned with the protection of the confidentiality of information provided in response to government statistical inquiries. A number of Government Departments and agencies supplement this code with more detailed rules relating to the particular information they collect. The code was originally published as a White Paper (Cmnd. 9270) in 1984.

Frequency: Ad hoc
Price: Free
ISSN: None

Available from
National Statistics Information and Library Service
Office for National Statistics
Please see Annex B for full address details.

Geography Products Scotland
General Register Office for Scotland

A booklet giving information and costs for geography products for the current and 1991 Census postcodes in Scotland. The products include the digitised boundaries of 131,776 small user postcodes used in the 1991 Census and the digitised boundaries of Scottish Output Areas from the 1991 Census. Also included are the boundaries of current postcode boundaries. There are also index files relating postcodes and Output Areas to the various higher areas to which they belong and a file giving the Output Area to which each postcode has been assigned.

Frequency: Annually
Price: Free

Available from
Peter Jamieson
Room 1/2/8
General Register Office for Scotland
Ladywell House
Ladywell Road
Edinburgh EH12 7TF
Tel: 0131 314 4254;
Email: peter.jamieson@gro-scotland.gov.uk

(The) Government Social Survey: a History
Office for National Statistics

A history of the immensely varied range of surveys on social and economic topics carried out by the Government Social Survey on behalf of government departments since its origin in 1941. Contains commentary on how the Survey's work has evolved and developed with changes in government over forty years.

Delivery: Ad hoc/One-off Release
Price: £16.00
ISSN: 0 11 691302 9

Available from
TSO Publications Centre and Bookshops
Please see Annex B for full address details.

Products

Government Statistical Service Annual Report
Office for National Statistics

An annual report on the work of the Government Statistical Service. The GSS Annual Report describes the structure and work of the GSS, and gives details of the achievements and future plans in various subject areas. There is a separate report by each subject area covering the work of all parts of the GSS, including the Northern Ireland Departments and the Bank of England, who both work closely with the GSS. It is a useful reference tool with information about statistical publications, contact points for information and Official Statistics Internet pages.

Frequency: Annual
Price: Free

Available from
National Statistics Information and Library Service
Office for National Statistics
Please see Annex B for full address details.

(The) Government Statistical Service Code of Practice on the Handling of Data Obtained from Statistical Inquiries
Office for National Statistics

GSS guidelines on handling data. This code of practice is concerned with the protection of the confidentiality of information provided in response to government statistical inquiries. A number of Government Departments and agencies supplement this code with more detailed rules relating to the particular information they collect. The code was originally published as a White Paper (Cmnd. 9270) in 1984.

Frequency: Ad hoc
Price: Free
ISSN: None

Available from
National Statistics Information and Library Service
Office for National Statistics
Please see Annex B for full address details.

GSS Methodology Series

The GSS Methodology Series is a series of monographs with a substantial methodological content written by people across the Government Statistical Service. The series currently consists of: Software to weight and gross survey data, Report of the Task Force on Seasonal Adjustment, Report

of the Task Force on Disclosure, Gross Domestic Product: Output methodological guide, Interpolating annual data into monthly or quarterly data, Sample design options for an integrated household survey, Evaluating non-response on household surveys, Reducing Statistical Burdens on Business, Statistics on Trade in Goods, The 1997 UK Pilot of the Eurostat Time Use Survey, Monthly Statistics on Public Sector Finances, A review of Sample Attrition and Representativeness in Three Longitudinal Surveys, Measuring and Improving Data Quality, Gross Domestic Product: Output Approach, Report of the Task Force on Weighting and Estimation, Methodological Issues in the Production and Analysis of Longitudinal Data from the Labour Force Survey. See next section for details.

Frequency: Ad hoc
Price: Varies, usually £5.00

Available from
GSS members only:
ONS Library
Room DG/18
Drummond Gate
London SW1V 2QQ
Tel 020 7533 6266

Other customers:
ONS Direct
Office for National Statistics
Please see Annex B for full address details.

National Statistics Updates
Office for National Statistics

National Statistics Updates is the monthly Release Dates diary published by the Office for National Statistics on behalf of the Government Statistical Service and other organisations. The diary features two lists of releases in date order; social statistics and economic statistics.

Delivery: Periodic Release
Frequency: Monthly
Price: Free

Official Statistics: Governance and Consultation
Office for National Statistics

This booklet explains how official statistics are currently governed, and how users - government, Parliament, researchers and the wider community - are consulted. It gives details of the constitutions, terms of reference and contact points for a range of statistical advisory bodies, users' groups and internal management committees.

Frequency: Ad hoc
Price: Free

Available from
National Statistics Information and Library Service
Office for National Statistics
Please see Annex B for full address details.

Official Statistics Code of Practice
Office for National Statistics

Code of practice used by the GSS for official statistics. The Code of Practice sets out the shared good practices that have been built up over many years by statisticians in a wide range of government departments and agencies. Although focused on the work of government statisticians, many of the principles and practices contained within the code are also relevant to others producing official statistics. The code is designed to promote high standards and to maintain public confidence in all official statistics and analyses. It carries a foreword from the Prime Minister. The code sets out twelve key principles for producers of official statistics. It then applies these principles to the main activities involved in producing statistics - from planning through to disseminating - to produce some 50 standards to guide personal behaviour. First published in April 1995, the code will be reviewed regularly, probably for the first time after two years.

Frequency: Ad hoc
Price: Free
ISSN: None

Available from
National Statistics Information and Library Service
Office for National Statistics
Please see Annex B for full address details.

ONS Business Plan 1998-99
Office for National Statistics

Summary of history, aims, resources, business strategy, developments and corporate objectives.

Delivery: Periodic Release
Frequency: Annually
Price: Free

Available from
ONS Direct or TSO Publications Centre and Bookshops
Please see Annex B for full address details.

Statistical News
Office for National Statistics

Describes new developments in British official statistics. Statistical News provides a comprehensive account of new developments in British official statistics and it is designed to help and inform all with an interest in those statistics. Every quarter, Statistical News includes several articles which describe a subject or initiative in depth and shorter items from departments and associated organisations on their latest statistical ventures and plans.

Frequency: Quarterly
Price: £12.00 (Annual subscription £45.00 including postage)
ISSN: 0017-3630

Available from
TSO Publications Centre and Bookshops
Please see Annex B for full address details.

Sources from which data for this product are obtained
Ethnic Group and Birthplace - GB

UK Statistics in the World - GSS International Report 1996-97
Office for National Statistics

Examines why, how and with what effect UK official statisticians work alongside International Organisations and other National Statistical Offices. Members of the Government Statistical Service aim to succeed in influencing statistical developments internationally by understanding the issues, focusing their efforts, participating in decision-making, building alliances, providing technical assistance and learning from others. Selected examples of collaborative work are described.

Delivery: Ad hoc/One-off Release
Frequency: Periodic
Price: Free

Available from
Alwyn Pritchard
Room D4/04
Office for National Statistics
1 Drummond Gate
London SW1V 2QQ
Tell: 020 7533 6204

18.3 Professional / Statistical Matters

Annual Report on Major Regular Social Surveys
Office for National Statistics

In May 1996 the Government Statistical Service Committee on Social Statistics GSS(S) decided that it should receive an annual report on the major continuous or repeat social surveys commissioned by Government, and that these reports would be made publicly available. These reports are to enable members of GSS(S) and others to keep abreast of key developments in the main GSS social surveys, and facilitate a

strategic approach to GSS social survey activity. The latest report summarises key developments in the 1996/97 surveys. The series has been discontinued in view of Statbase becoming available.

The Report is a descriptive guide to Major Regular Surveys, it has 50 A4 pages.

Delivery: Periodic Release
Frequency: Annually (now discontinued)
Price: Available free of charge

Available from
GSS(S) Secretariat
Office for National Statistics
1 Drummond Gate
Room B4/12
London SW1V 2QQ

1991 Census Validation Survey: Coverage Report
Office for National Statistics

This report assesses the coverage of the 1991 Census (i.e. the proportion of the population who were successfully enumerated) as shown by the Census Validation Survey (CVS). Findings are compared to Census results and preliminary estimates of net under-coverage are given. As well as the coverage results, it contains information on the Census Validation Survey methodology, and an account of the way the Census population figures were adjusted to arrive at the official mid-year population estimates made by the Registrar General.

Delivery: Ad Hoc/One-off release
Price: £11.60
ISSN: 0 11 691591 9 (series SS 1334)

Available from
TSO Publications Centre and Bookshops
Please see Annex B for full address details.

1991 Census Validation Survey: Report on Quality
Office for National Statistics

Frequency: Periodic

Available from
TSO Publications Centre and Bookshops
Please see Annex B for full address details.

(The) 1997 UK Pilot of the Eurostat Time Use Survey

This monograph is part of the Government Statistical Service (GSS) Methodology Series. It describes the design and implementation of the pilot survey and makes recommendations for the main stage survey.

Frequency: One off/Ad hoc
Price: £5.00
ISSN: 1 85774 293 1

Available from
GSS members only:
ONS Library
Room DG/18 Drummond Gate
London SW1V 2QQ
Tel 020 7533 6266

Other customers:
ONS Direct
Office for National Statistics
Please see Annex B for full address details.

Computer Assisted Standard Occupational Coding (CASOC)
Office for National Statistics

The Software package was designed to make the coding of occupational information to the Standard Occupational Classification simpler, quicker and more reliable.

Price: £170.00 excluding VAT
ISSN: 0 11 691359 2

Available from
TSO Publications Centre and Bookshops
Please see Annex B for full address details.

European System of Accounts - ESA 1995
Office for National Statistics

Part of Eurostat's 'Economy and Finance' theme Theme 2. The ESA 95 (European system of national and regional accounts) is a joint undertaking by the European Commission, the European Monetary Institute and government statisticians in the EU Member States. It defines the accounting rules and concepts to be used by the Member States to facilitate reliable analyses and comparisons of their economies. This is an excellent tool to help the Community institutions, governments and major economic, social and financial operators in the EU understand and analyse the European economy before taking decisions. (435 pages)

Delivery: Ad hoc/One-off Release
Price: £40.00
ISSN: 92 827 7954 8

Available from
Bob Dodds
Office for National Statistics
Please see Annex B for full address details.

Evaluating Non-Response on Household Surveys
Office for National Statistics

This monograph is part of the Government Statistical Service (GSS) Methodology Series. It assesses non-response bias in 5 ONS surveys by matching 1991 Census records with the survey sample records

Delivery: Ad hoc/One-off Release
Price: £5.00 - Available from ONS Sales Office
Free to GSS members - Available from ONS Library
ISSN: 1 855774 272 9

Available from
GSS members only:
ONS Library
Room DG/18
1 Drummond Gate
London SW1V 2QQ
Tel: 020 7533 6266

Other customers:
ONS Direct
Office for National Statistics
Please see Annex B for full address details.

GDP: Output Methodological Guide
Office for National Statistics

This monograph is part of the Government Statistical Service (GSS) Methodology Series. It describes the output approach for measuring GDP in which GDP is derived as the sum of the net output for all industries. It explains general concepts and aspects of measurement and identifies the indicator series, deflators and weights used in compilation.

Delivery: Ad hoc/One-off Release
Price: £20.00 - Available from ONS Sales Office
Free to GSS members - Available from ONS Library
ISSN: 1 85774 250 8

Available from
GSS members only:
ONS Library
Room DG/18
1 Drummond Gate
London SW1V 2QQ
Tel: 020 7533 6266

Other customers:
ONS Direct
Office for National Statistics
Please see Annex B for full address details.

Gross Domestic Product: Output Approach

This paper provides details of the sources, indicators, deflators and 1995 base weights used to estimate total output (Gross Value Added).

Frequency: One off/Ad hoc
Price: £5.00
ISBN: 1 85774 318 0

Available from
GSS members only:
ONS Library
Room DG/18
Drummond Gate
London SW1V 2QQ
Tel: 020 7533 6266

Other customers:
ONS Direct
Office for National Statistics
Please see Annex B for full address details.

Grossing Up 'An Investigation of Different Methods Applied to Data from the Family Resources Survey'
Department of Social Security

This is an analytical paper which discusses grossing up in the context of the Family Resources Survey (FRS). It details the sort of grossing techniques that have been investigated and describes how these methods differ. It goes on to outline criteria for choosing a grossing system and shows how a choice was made for the FRS. The sensitivity of statistics to this choice is then discussed. Finally, the issue of uncorrected bias in grossed results is explored. This publication is targeted at those who are interested in the methodology used for grossing up the Family Resources Survey and why the particular method is used.

Frequency: One-off

Available from
Ian Davis
Department of Social Security
Analytical Services Division (ASD)
The Adelphi
1-11 John Adam Street
London
Tel: 020 7962 8222; Fax: 020 7712 2001;
Email: davisi@asdlondon.dss-asd.gov.uk

Harmonised Concepts and Questions for Government Social Surveys
Office for National Statistics

This booklet together with its update 'Harmonised Concepts and Questions for Government Social Surveys - update December 1997' (published 1998) reports ongoing work to harmonise survey questions and output categories across a wide range of government surveys. Both publications should be read in conjunction, as the update includes some new concepts, where harmonised concepts have been agreed, as well as a number which have been

changed. Further paper updates are not planned as a project is in train to produce an electronic version of the booklets which will be accessible through the GSS website.

Delivery: Ad hoc/One-off Release
Price: £10.00
ISSN: None

Available from
ONS Direct
Office for National Statistics
Please see Annex B for full address details.

Harmonised Concepts and Questions for Government Social Surveys - Update December 1997
Office for National Statistics

Update to the 1996 version. Wording and definitions for harmonised concepts and questions in government social surveys. Explains the need for harmonisation throughout the Government's many social surveys, and gives the appropriate forms of words and definitions to be used. Further paper updates are not planned as a project is in train at the moment to produce an electronic version of the booklets which will be accessible through the website.

Delivery: Ad hoc/One-off Release
Price: £10.00 including the 1996 version (Two booklets)

Available from
ONS Direct or TSO Publications Centre and Bookshops
Please see Annex B for full address details.

Households Below Average Income Stocktaking: Report of a Working Group 1991
Department of Social Security

This stocktaking exercise looked at HBAI's robustness, methodology, content and presentation. It was carried out by officials; outside analysts were consulted. A technical paper for analysts interested in the reasoning behind the definitions and practices adopted in Households Below Average Income statistics.

Delivery: Ad Hoc/One-off Release

Available from
Frosztega Margaret / Tadd Liz
Room 4/52
Department of Social Security
The Adelphi
1-11 John Adam Street
London WC2N 6HT
Tel: 020 7962 8232;
Email: frosztet@asdlondon.dss-asd.gov.uk

Households Below Average Income: Methodological Review 1996
Department of Social Security

A review of methodological issues related to Households Below Average Income statistics. A technical paper for analysts interested in the reasoning behind the definitions and practices adopted in Households Below Average Income statistics.

Frequency: One-off

Available from
Frosztega Margaret / Tadd Liz
Room 4/52
Department of Social Security
The Adelphi
1-11 John Adam Street
London WC2N 6HT
Tel: 020 7962 8232;
Email: frosztet@asdlondon.dss-asd.gov.uk

Indexes to the UK Standard Industrial Classification of Economic Activities 1992
Office for National Statistics

Indexes to UK SIC(92) listing headings of the SIC and characteristic activities. Contains both an alphabetical and numerical list of a wide range of typical economic activities. One of the 3 UK SIC(92) publications, the Indexes are used as a look-up guide for matching economic activities to SIC codes. Also useful for correlating SIC(92) to SIC(80). Alphabetical and numerical lists of typical economic activities showing the UK SIC(92) class or subclass to which the activity should be classified. The lists also attempt to provide a link to the previous Standard Industrial Classification, SIC(80) although in some cases it was not possible to do so without further information. The link indicated should not, therefore, be taken to be definitive. The publication incorporates 111 new subclasses created since the 1992 edition in response to user demand for a more detailed coding structure. 256 pages

Frequency: Ad-hoc
Price: Hard copy £22.50.
Disk £95.00 + VAT per set (includes main volume and methodological guide)
ISSN: 0 11 620924 0

Available from
ONS Direct (Disk)
Office for National Statistics
Please see Annex B for full address details.

TSO Publications Centre and Bookshops
(Hardcopy)
Please see Annex B for full address details.

International Statistical Classification of Diseases and Health Related Problems (ICD-10)
National Health Service

Classification system used for mortality data. Volume 1: Tabular list, Volume 2: Instruction manual, Volume 3: Alphabetical Index.

Frequency: Ad hoc
Price: Volume 1 £75.00
Volume 2 £22.00
Volume 3 £75.00
ISSN: Various, see summary description.

Available from
TSO Publications Centre and Bookshops
Please see Annex B for full address details.

Interpolating Annual Data to Monthly or Quarterly Data - Michael Baxter
Office for National Statistics

This monograph is part of the Government Statistical Service (GSS) Methodology Series. It describes and evaluates methods for estimating quarterly or monthly figures from data that is only available annually.

Delivery: Ad hoc/One-off Release
Frequency: One-off
Price: £5.00 - Available from ONS Sales Office
Free to GSS members - Available from ONS Library
ISSN: 1 85774 258 3

Available from
GSS members only:
ONS Library
Room DG/18
1 Drummond Gate
London SW1V 2QQ
Tel: 020 7533 6266

Other customers:
ONS Direct
Office for National Statistics
Please see Annex B for full address details.

Measuring and Improving Data Quality

This monograph is part of the Government Statistical Service (GSS) Methodology Series. This is the second report of the GSS(M) Task Force on non-sampling error. It describes the various sources of non-sampling errors, discusses ways to measure the bias and increase in variance, which may result and provides a guide to methods, which can be used to reduce the impact on data quality.

Frequency: One off/Ad hoc
Price: £5.00
ISSN: 1 85774 302 4

Available from
GSS members only:
ONS Library
Room DG/18
Drummond Gate
London SW1V 2QQ
Tel 020 7533 6266

Other customers:
ONS Direct
Office for National Statistics
Please see Annex B for full address details.

Methodological Issues in the Production and Analysis of Longitudinal Data from the Labour Force Survey

This monograph is part of the Government Statistical Service (GSS) Methodology Series. It investigates patterns of non-response and response error in the Labour Force Survey (LFS) and the implications of these for longitudinal analysis of LFS linked samples. A new system of weights is recommended for using linked data from the survey

Frequency: One off/Ad hoc
Price: £5.00

Available from
GSS members only:
ONS Library
Room DG/18
Drummond Gate
London SW1V 2QQ
Tel 020 7533 6266

Other customers:
ONS Direct
Office for National Statistics
Please see Annex B for full address details.

Monthly Statistics on Public Sector Finances

This monograph is part of the GSS Methodology Series. It describes the statistics on public sector borrowing that are compiled for the Treasury and published in ONS's monthly Public Sector Finances First Release. It describes the concepts of net borrowing, net debt and net cash requirement, how these are compiled and the changes made to conform to the new European System of Accounts (ESA95).

Frequency: One off/Ad hoc
Price: £5.00
ISSN: 1 85774 296 6

Available from
GSS members only:
ONS Library
Room DG/18
Drummond Gate
London SW1V 2QQ
Tel 020 7533 6266

Other customers:
ONS Direct
Office for National Statistics
Please see Annex B for full address details.

ONS Occupation Support Service User Guide 1
Office for National Statistics

Mapping of the Standard Occupational Classification (SOC) to the International Standard Classification of Occupations 1988 European Community Version (ISCO 88 COM). Conversion table and file. The mapping was first produced in 1994. The original file on diskette contained codes but a later version was expanded to include the SOC unit group titles.

Frequency: Periodic
Price: Paper Publication £15.00
Disk: £16.50 + VAT

Available from
Occupational Information Unit
Office for National Statistics
Please see Annex B for full address details.

Postcode Index - Scotland
General Register Office for Scotland

An index of about 170,000 live and deleted postcodes showing various fields for each postcode including: council area, health board, constituency, ward, grid reference date of introduction and deletion, delivery point count and 1991 Census residents and households.

Frequency: Bi-annually
Price: £0.04 per postcode. Extracts of postcodes can be purchased for any higher area e.g. Council Area.

Available from
Peter Jamieson
Room 1/G/7
General Register Office for Scotland
Ladywell House
Ladywell Road
Edinburgh
EH12 7TF
Tel: 0131 314 4254;
Email: peter.jamieson@gro-scotland.gov.uk

Sources from which data for this product are obtained
Postcode boundaries - Scotland

Reducing Statistical Burdens on Business
Office for National Statistics

This monograph is part of the Government Statistical Service (GSS) Methodology Series. This paper discusses the nature of statistical burdens on business caused by business surveys and the various methods used to reduce them

Delivery: Ad hoc/One-off Release
Price: £5.00 - available for ONS Sales Office
Free to GSS members - available ONS Library
ISSN: 1 85774 286 9

Available from
GSS members only:
ONS Library
Room DG/18
1 Drummond Gate
London SW1V 2QQ
Tel: 020 7533 6266

Other customers:
ONS Direct
Office for National Statistics
Please see Annex B for full address details.

Report of the Task Force on Disclosure
Office for National Statistics

This monograph is part of the Government Statistical Service (GSS) Methodology Series. Disclosure occurs where information is published which the data providers do not want made public. This paper describes the risks of disclosure with tabular and electronically disseminated data and the steps that can be taken to combat them.

Delivery: Ad hoc/One-off Release
Price: £5.00 - Available from ONS Sales Office
Free to GSS members - Available from ONS Library
ISSN: 1 85774 249 4

Available from
GSS members only:
ONS Library
Room DG/18
1 Drummond Gate
London SW1V 2QQ
Tel: 020 7533 6266

Other customers:
ONS Direct
Office for National Statistics
Please see Annex B for full address details.

Report of the Task Force on Imputation
Office for National Statistics

This monograph is part of the Government Statistical Service (GSS) Methodology Series. Describes imputation methods in the

GSS to deal with item non-response. It describes the general principles of imputation and outlines the main classes of approach. It discusses the main advantages and disadvantages of different approaches.

Delivery: Ad hoc/One-off Release
Price: £5.00 - Available from ONS Sales Office
Free to GSS members - Available from ONS Library
ISSN: 1 85774 248 6

Available from
GSS members only:
ONS Library
Room DG/18
1 Drummond Gate
London SW1V 2QQ
Tel: 020 7533 6266

Other customers:
ONS Direct
Office for National Statistics
Please see Annex B for full address details.

Report of the Task Force on Seasonal Adjustment
Office for National Statistics

This monograph is part of the Government Statistical Service (GSS) Methodology Series. Describes and evaluates the methods currently available for seasonal adjustment. Provides a summary of current practice in GSS and makes recommendations for future work

Delivery: Ad hoc/One-off Release
Price: £5.00 - Available from ONS Sales Office.
Free to GSS members - available ONS Library
ISSN: 1 85774 247 8

Available from
GSS members only:
ONS Library
Room DG/18
1 Drummond Gate
London SW1V 2QQ
Tel: 020 7533 6266

Other customers:
ONS Direct
Office for National Statistics
Please see Annex B for full address details.

Report of the Task Force on Weighting and Estimation

This monograph is part of the Government Statistical Service (GSS) Methodology Series. This report reviews the main approaches used for weighting and grossing data in the GSS. The problems associated with the post stratification approach generally used are discussed. The potential for reducing non-response bias using the calibration method are investigated along with 2 programs available for implementing this procedure.

Frequency: One off/Ad hoc
Price: £5.00
ISBN: 1 85774 331 8

Available from
GSS members only:
ONS Library
Room DG/18
Drummond Gate
London SW1V 2QQ
Tel 020 7533 6266

Other customers:
ONS Direct
Office for National Statistics
Please see Annex B for full address details.

A Review of Sample Attrition and Representativeness in Three Longitudinal Surveys

The report describes the outcome from a review of the statistical aspects of the quality of three longitudinal surveys – the British Households Panel Survey, The 1970 British Cohort Study and the National Child Development Study.

Frequency: One off/Ad hoc
Price: £5.00
ISSN: 1 85774 300 8

Available from
GSS members only:
ONS Library
Room DG/18
Drummond Gate
London SW1V 2QQ
Tel 020 7533 6266

Other customers:
ONS Direct
Office for National Statistics
Please see Annex B for full address details.

Sample Design Options for An Integrated Household Survey
Office for National Statistics

This monograph is part of the Government Statistical Service (GSS) Methodology Series. It considers a number of possible sample designs for a combined survey integrating four major continuous household surveys. It evaluates the advantages and disadvantages of these alternatives in terms of precision and cost.

Delivery: Ad hoc/One-off Release
Price: £5.00 - available for ONS Sales Office Free to GSS members - Available from ONS Library
ISSN: 1 85774 269 9

Available from
GSS members only:
ONS Library
Room DG/18
1 Drummond Gate
London SW1V 2QQ
Tel: 020 7533 6266

Other customers:
ONS Direct
Office for National Statistics
Please see Annex B for full address details.

Software to Weight and Gross Survey Data
Office for National Statistics

This monograph is part of the Government Statistical Service (GSS) Methodology Series. Describes and evaluates the methods available for weighting and grossing survey data and the software for implementing them. The results from tests of the software on two surveys are reported.

Delivery: Ad hoc/One-off Release
Price: £5.00 - Available from ONS Sales Office Free to GSS members - Available from ONS library
ISSN: 1 85774 244 3

Available from
GSS members only:
ONS Library
Room DG/18
1 Drummond Gate
London SW1V 2QQ
Tel: 020 7533 6266

Other customers:
ONS Direct
Office for National Statistics
Please see Annex B for full address details.

Standard Industrial Classification of Economic Activities, Correlation Between SIC(92) and SIC(80) (Business Monitor PO1009)
Office for National Statistics

Tables showing the relationship between the SIC(80) (Standard Industrial Classification of Economic Activities1980) and the SIC(92) (Standard Industrial Classification of Economic Activities 1992) Contains tables covering all activities where either the SIC(80) or the SIC(92) classification have been considered. Also shows the links of the SIC(92) to the United Nations International Standard Industrial Classification of all Economic Activities (ISIC Rev. 3)

Delivery: Hardcopy publication / diskette
Frequency: Ad-hoc
Price: Hardcopy: £26.50
Disk: £26.50 + VAT
ISSN: 0 11 536311 4

Available from
ONS Direct (Disk)
Office for National Statistics
Please see Annex B for full address details.

TSO Publications Centre and Bookshops ((Hardcopy)
Please see Annex B for full address details.

Statistical Quality Checklist
Office for National Statistics

Provides a checklist of questions which should be considered when describing the statistics in a report or publication. It is drafted mainly in the context of survey data but many of the questions relate equally to data from administrative sources.

Frequency: One-off
Price: £5.00
ISSN: 8511 4 238 9

Available from
National Statistics Information and Library Service
Office for National Statistics
Please see Annex B for full address details

Statistics on Trade in Goods

This monograph is part of the Government Statistical Service (GSS) Methodology Series. It describes how statistics on Trade in Goods are compiled by ONS. It describes the data collected by HM Customs and Excise, the adjustments that need to be applied to conform to IMF definitions for Balance of Payments statistics and the division of responsibility between ONS and HM Customs and Excise.

Frequency: One off/Ad hoc
Price: £5.00
ISSN: 1 85774 287 7

Available from
GSS members only:
ONS Library
Room DG/18
Drummond Gate
London SW1V 2QQ
Tel 020 7533 6266

Other customers:
ONS Direct
Office for National Statistics
Please see Annex B for full address details.

(The) Take-up of Income Related Benefits: Inaccuracies in the Estimation of Take-up Rates - (Analytical Note 3)
Department of Social Security

This paper published in 1994 investigates the vulnerability of estimates of benefit take-up to data imperfections and other sources of error. It also presents an analytical framework which allows the effects of errors, singly and in combination, to be quantified. It is targeted at those who are

Products

interested in the motivations and methods for producing take-up estimates in ranges. The publication covers the analytical framework which underpins the production of the take-up ranges, and is presented using text, tables and charts.

Frequency: One-off
ISSN: 1 85197 637 X

Available from
Corporate Document Services
Department of Social Security
Saville House
Trinity Arcade
Leeds LS1 6QW
Tel: 0113 399 4040;
Email: orderline@corpdocs.co.uk

Town Centres: Defining Boundaries for Statistical Monitoring
Department of the Environment, Transport and the Regions

Feasibility Study Report. This research project demonstrates that it is now feasible to generate statistics such as employment, retail sales turnover and floorspace on a consistent basis for all town centres in the UK. Furthermore this can be done using standard Geographic Information Systems, using standard analytical methods applied to existing government data sets. The report investigates the definition of town centres, for statistical purposes, and illustrates the methodology applied to ten case study towns, and generates statistics for each town. A pilot study is now underway to enhance the methodology and apply it to a much larger sample of town centres, as a first step towards national implementation. The intention is for boundaries and statistics to be available for all town centres. These will be used by government, authorities, retailers, property developers, and others to monitor the health of town centres, and to make better informed planning decisions..

Delivery: Ad Hoc/One-off Release
Price: £25.00, Available from The Stationery Office (020 7873 9090)
ISSN: 0 11 753436 6

UK SIC 1992 Methodological Guide
Office for National Statistics

Sets out the rules for classifying statistical units in the UK Standard Industrial Classification of Economic Activities 1992. Also explains the reasons for setting up the UK SIC(92) system and how it is related to other classification systems. The Methodological Guide is an essential reference for anyone who needs to code the economic activities of business government into the UK SIC(92). It is a 25 page text which explains the theory of classifying economic activities. Sets out the rules for classifying statistical units in the UK Standard Industrial Classification of Economic Activities 1992. Also explains the reasons for setting up the SIC(92) system and how it is related to other classification systems.

Delivery: Hardcopy publication / diskette
Frequency: Ad-hoc
Price: Hardcopy: £19.95
Disk: £95.00 (includes UK SIC (92) and Indexes)
ISSN: 0 11 620817 1

Available from
ONS Direct (as part of a 2 disk set comprising UK SIC (92), Indexes to UK SIC (92) and UK SIC (92) Methodological Guide
Please see Annex B for full address details

TSO Publications Centre and Bookshops (hardcopy)
Please see Annex B for full address details.

Economic Activities 1992
Office for National Statistics

The UK Standard Industrial Classification of Economic Activities 1992 - UK SIC(92) - is a system of classification of business establishments and other statistical units by the type of economic activity in which they are engaged. The classification provides a framework for the collection, tabulation, presentation and analysis of data, and its use promotes uniformity. In addition it can be used for administrative purposes by non-government bodies as a convenient way of classifying industrial activities into a common structure.

Delivery: Hardcopy publication / diskette
Frequency: Ad-hoc
Price: Hardcopy: £25.00
disk: £95.00+VAT per set (includes alphabetical and numerical indexes and Methodological Guide)
ISSN: 0 11 620923 2

Available from
ONS Direct (Disk)
Office for National Statistics
Please see Annex B for full address details.

TSO Publications Centre and Bookshops (Hardcopy)
Please see Annex B for full address details.

Weighting for Non-Response
Office for National Statistics

Methodology paper. Office for National Statistics Social Survey researchers' guide to procedures aimed at correcting the effects of non-response during the analysis and presentation of survey results.

Frequency: Ad hoc
Price: £5.00
ISSN: 0 90 495270 3 (series NM17)

Available from
Social Survey Division
Room D1/15
Office for National Statistics
1 Drummond Gate
London
SW1V 2QQ
Tel: 020 7533 5500

Annex A - Classifications

What follows is a list of the main classification systems used within the Government Statistical Service along with, where possible, a contact reference.

Balance of Payments Classification of International Transactions - BPM5

Central Product Classification Version 1 - *CPC Ver 1*
David Knight
Office for National Statistics
Room 1.064
Government Offices
Cardiff Road
Newport
Gwent, NP10 8XG
Tel: 01633 813371, Fax: 01633 812555
E-mail: david.knight@ons.gov.uk

Classification and Coding of Branches of Production for National Account Purposes - *NACE/CLIO (R44)*

Classification of Consumer
Complaints and Consumer Enquiries

(The) Classification of Consumers'
Expenditure by Commodity - *CES*
David Penny
Office for National Statistics
D4/15
1 Drummond Gate
London, SW1P 2QQ
Tel: 020 7533 5998
E-mail: ceb.neid@ons.gov.uk

Classification of Individual Consumption by
Purpose - *COICOP*
David Penny
Office for National Statistics
D4/15
1 Drummond Gate
London, SW1P 2QQ
Tel: 020 7533 5998
E-mail: ceb.neid@ons.gov.uk

Classification of Individual Consumption by Purpose - Household Budgets Survey - *COICOP - HBS*

Classification of Private Non-Profit
Institutions - *COPNI*

Classification of Products by Activity - CPA
David Knight
Office for National Statistics
Room 1.064
Government Offices
Cardiff Road
Newport
Gwent, NP10 8XG
Tel: 01633 813371, Fax: 01633 812555
E-mail: david.knight@ons.gov.uk

Classification of Selected Outlays of Producers by Purpose - *COPP*

Classification of the Subject Area of a
Qualification on *NISVQ*

Classification of Surgical Operations and
Procedures - *OPCS4*
Coding and Classification Help Desk
NHS Information Authority
Woodgate
Loughborough
Leicestershire, LE11 2TG
Tel: 01509 264072, Fax: 01509 211611
E-mail: helpdesk3@nhsccc.exec.nhs.uk

Classifications of the Functions of Government
- *COFOG*
Jeff Golland
Office for National Statistics
D3/24
1 Drummond Gate
London, SW1P 2QQ
Tel: 020 7533 5987, Fax: 020 7533 6023
E-mail: jeff.golland@ons.gov.uk

Combined Nomenclature - *CN*
Gareth Edwards
HM Customs and Excise
Room 5 NC
Alexander House
21 Victoria Avenue
Southend, SS99 1AA
Tel: 01702 366655, Fax: 01702 366596
E-mail: statistics.tso@hmce.gov.uk

Common Procurement Vocabulary - *CPV*
David Knight
Office for National Statistics
Room 1.064
Government Offices
Cardiff Road
Newport
Gwent, NP10 8XG
Tel: 01633 813371, Fax: 01633 812555
E-mail: david.knight@ons.gov.uk

European System of Integrated Economic Accounts - *ESA 1995*

European System of Integrated Social
Protection Statistics - *ESSPROS*

Family Expenditure Survey - *FES*

Foreign Ownership Codes
(Dun & Bradstreet)
Mike Prestwood
Office for National Statistics
Room 1.023
Government Offices
Cardiff Road
Newport
Gwent, NP10 8XG
Tel: 01633 813289, Fax: 01633 812477
E-mail: mike.prestwood@ons.gov.uk

Harmonised Description and Coding System - *HS*

Household Reference Person - a new
derivation designed to replace Head
of Household (HoH) - *HRP*

Input/Output Classifications SIC(92) - *INPUT/OUTPUT*
Sanjiv Mahajan
Office for National Statistics
D3/12
1 Drummond Gate
London, SW1P 2QQ
Tel: 020 7533 5954
E-mail: sanjiv.mahajan@ons.gov.uk

International Statistical Classification of
Diseases and Related Health Problems (Tenth
Revision) - *ICD10*
Lin Shane
Office for National Statistics
Room 2200
Segensworth Road
Titchfield
Fareham
Hampshire, PO15 5RR
Tel: 01329 813458
E-mail: lin.shane@ons.gov.uk

International Classification of Non-Profit Organisations - ICNPO

International Classification of Status of Employment - ICSE

International Standard Classification of Occupations - *ISCO-88*
Tessa Staples
Office for National Statistics
Room 4200W
Segensworth Road
Titchfield
Fareham
Hampshire, PO15 5RR
Tel: 01329 813503, Fax: 01329 813532
Email: occupation.information@ons.gov.uk

International Standard Classification of Occupations (1988) for Use Within the European Community - *ISCO 88(COM)*
Tessa Staples
Office for National Statistics
Room 4200W
Segensworth Road
Titchfield
Fareham
Hampshire, PO15 5RR
Tel: 01329 813503, Fax: 01329 813532
Email: occupation.information@ons.gov.uk

International Standard Industrial Classification of All Economic Activities. Revision 3 - *ISIC Rev.3*
David Knight
Office for National Statistics
Room 1.064
Government Offices
Cardiff Road
Newport
Gwent, NP10 8XG
Tel: 01633 813371, Fax: 01633 812555
E-mail: david.knight@ons.gov.uk

International Statistical Classification of Diseases, Injuries and Causes of Death (Ninth Revision) - *ICD 9*
Lin Shane
Office for National Statistics
Room 2200
Segensworth Road
Titchfield
Fareham
Hampshire, PO15 5RR
Tel: 01329 813458
E-mail: lin.shane@ons.gov.uk

INTRASTAT Classification Nomenclature - *INTRASTAT*

Main Industrial Groupings - *MIG*

(The) Measurement of Scientific and Technological Activities - *FRASCATI*
Peter Jones
Office for National Statistics
Room D.257
Government Offices
Cardiff Road
Newport
Gwent, NP10 8XG
Tel: 01633 813063, Fax: 01633 812855
E-mail: peter.jones@ons.gov.uk

National Statistics Socio-Economic Classification: designed to replace Social Class based on occupation (SC) and Socio-Economic Group (SEG) - *NS-SEC*

Nomenclature De Unitaire Territoire Statistique - *NUTS*

Nomenclature for the Analysis and Comparison of Science Programs and Budgets - *NABS*
Peter Jones
Office for National Statistics
Room D.257
Government Offices
Cardiff Road
Newport
Gwent, NP10 8XG
Tel: 01633 813063, Fax: 01633 812855
E-mail: peter.jones@ons.gov.uk

Nomenclature Generale Des Activities Economiques Dans Les Communautes Europeennes Revision 1 - *NACE Rev.1*
David Knight
Office for National Statistics
Room 1.064
Government Offices
Cardiff Road
Newport
Gwent, NP10 8XG
Tel: 01633 813371, Fax: 01633 812555
E-mail: david.knight@ons.gov.uk

Nomenclature PROCOME 94

ONS Central Postcode Directory - *CPD*

(The) ONS Classification of Local and Health Authorities of Great Britain: Revised for Authorities in 1999
Justine Fitzpatrick
Office for National Statistics
Room B7/08
1 Drummond Gate
London SW1V 2QQ
Tel: 020 7533 5211;
Email: justine.fitzpatrick@ons.gov.uk

ONS Standard Geographic Names and Codes - *OGSS*

Product Groups

Production Communautaire (Products of the European Community) - *PRODCOM*
Debra Prestwood
Office for National Statistics
Room 1.227
Government Offices
Cardiff Road
Newport
Gwent, NP10 8XG
Tel: 01633 813490, Fax: 01633 812229
E-mail: debra.prestwood@ons.gov.uk

Read Clinical Classification - *READ*

Registrar General Standard Region

Social Class Based on Occupation (Formerly Registrar General's Social Class) - *SC*
Tessa Staples
Office for National Statistics
Room 4200W
Segensworth Road
Titchfield
Fareham
Hampshire, PO15 5RR
Tel: 01329 813503, Fax: 01329 813532
Email: occupation.information@ons.gov.uk

Socio-Economic Groups
Tessa Staples
Office for National Statistics
Room 4200W
Segensworth Road
Titchfield
Fareham
Hampshire, PO15 5RR
Tel: 01329 813503, Fax: 01329 813532
Email: occupation.information@ons.gov.uk

Standard Industrial Classification 1968 - *SIC(68)*
David Knight
Office for National Statistics
Room 1.064
Government Offices
Cardiff Road
Newport
Gwent, NP10 8XG
Tel: 01633 813371, Fax: 01633 812555
E-mail: david.knight@ons.gov.uk

Standard Industrial Classification 1980 - *SIC(80)*
David Knight
Office for National Statistics
Room 1.064
Government Offices
Cardiff Road
Newport
Gwent, NP10 8XG
Tel: 01633 813371, Fax: 01633 812555
E-mail: david.knight@ons.gov.uk

Standard International Trade
Classification - SITC

Standard Occupational Classification - *SOC*
Tessa Staples
Office for National Statistics
Room 4200W
Segensworth Road
Titchfield
Fareham
Hampshire, PO15 5RR
Tel: 01329 813503, Fax: 01329 813532
E-mail: occupation.information@ons.gov.uk

Standard Occupational Classification: SOC2000 is designed to replace the current SOC1990 classification - SOC2000

Standard Statistical Regions - *SSR*

Summary Trade Classification - *STC*

System of National Accounts 1993 - *SNA 93*

Trade Classification Number - *TCN*

UK Sector Classifications for National
Accounts - *MA 23*
Katherine Thompson
Office for National Statistics
D3/23
1 Drummond Gate
London, SW1P 2QQ
Tel: 020 7533 5993, Fax: 020 7533 6023
E-mail: katherine.thompson@ons.gov.uk

UK Standard Industrial Classification of
Economic Activities 1992 - *UK SIC(92)*
David Knight
Office for National Statistics
Room 1.064
Government Offices
Cardiff Road
Newport
Gwent, NP10 8XG
Tel: 01633 813371, Fax: 01633 812555
E-mail: david.knight@ons.gov.uk

UN Broad Economic Categories - *BEC*
David Ruffles
Office for National Statistics
D3/19
1 Drummond Gate
London, SW1P 2QQ
Tel: 020 7533 6070, Fax: 020 7533 0207
E-mail: david.ruffles@ons.gov.uk

Urban/Rural Classification
Stehen Hall
Department of Environment Transport and the
Regions
Room 3/J10
Eland House
Bressenden Place
London, SW1E 5DU
Tel: 020 7890 5374

VAT Trade Classification - *VTC*

Annex B - Common Address Details

Throughout the book many entries refer to the same address details for availability. To save space those frequently used common details have been collected together here.

Categories include **TSO Publications Centre and Bookshops, Office for National Statistics** and **Other Addresses**

TSO Publications Centre and Bookshops

London
The Stationery Office
PO Box 276
51, Nine Elms Lane
London SW8 5DT
Tel: 0870 600 5522; Fax: 0870 600 5533
Also the address for 'TSO International Sales Agency'.

London
123 Kingsway
London WC2B 6PQ
Tel: 020 7242 6393; Fax: 020 7242 6412

Birmingham
68-69 Bull Street
Birmingham B4 6AD
Tel: 0121 236 9696; Fax: 0121 236 9699

Bristol
33 Wine Street
Bristol BS1 2BQ
Tel: 0117 926 4306; Fax: 0117 929 4515

Manchester
9-21 Princess Street
Manchester M60 8AS
Tel: 0161 834 7201; Fax: 0161 833 0634

Belfast
16 Arthur Street
Belfast BT1 4GD
Tel: 028 9023 8451; Fax: 028 9023 5401

Edinburgh
71 Lothian Road
Edinburgh EH3 9AZ
Tel: 0870 606 5566; Fax: 0870 606 5588

Cardiff
The Stationery Office Oriel Bookshop
18-19 High Street
Cardiff CF1 2BZ
Tel: 029 2039 5548; Fax: 029 2038 4347

Office for National Statistics

Census Customer Services
Room 4300s
Office for National Statistics
Segensworth Road
Titchfield
Fareham
Hampshire PO15 5RR
Tel: 01329 813800;
Email: census.marketing@ons.gov.uk

Electronic Dissemination Services
(Customer and Electronic Services Unit)
Room B1/05
Office for National Statistics
1 Drummond Gate
London SW1V 2QQ
Tel: 020 7533 5675

Labour Market Statistics Enquiries
Room B3/10
Office for National Statistics
1 Drummond Gate
London SW1V 2QQ
Tel: 020 7533 6094;
Email: labour.market@ons.gov.uk

National Statistics Information and Library Service
Office for National Statistics
Government Buildings
Cardiff Road
Newport
Gwent
South Wales NP10 8XG
Tel: 01633 812973 Fax: 01633 812599
Minicom number: 01633 812399

Occupational Information Unit
Office for National Statistics
Segensworth Road
Titchfield
Fareham
Hampshire PO15 5RR
Tel: 01329 813426;
Email: occupation.information@ons.gov.uk

Bob Dodds
Room D.140
Office for National Statistics
Government Buildings
Cardiff Road
Newport
Gwent
South Wales NP10 8XG
Tel: 01633 813369

ONS Direct
Room D.130
Office for National Statistics
Government Buildings
Cardiff Road
Newport
Gwent
South Wales NP10 8XG
Tel: 01633 812078; Fax: 01633 812762
Email: ons.direct@ons.gov.uk

ONS Press Office
Office for National Statistics
Room DG/19
1 Drummond Gate
London SW1V 2QQ
Tel: 020 7533 6363/6364

UK PRODCOM General Inquiries
Room 1.227
Office for National Statistics
Government Buildings
Cardiff Road
Newport
Gwent
South Wales NP10 8XG
Tel: 01633 813065

Other Addresses

Abacus
Waterloo House
59 New Street
Chelmsford
Essex CM1 1NE
Tel: 01245 252222; Fax: 01245 252244;
Email: abacusuk@aol.com

Ashgate Publishing Ltd
Gomer House
Croft Road
Aldershot
Hampshire GU11 3HR

Distribution Post
Domestic Banking Statistics Group MFSD
HO-5
Bank of England
Threadneedle Street
London EC2R 8AH
Tel: 020 7601 3119;
Email: mfsd-dbs@bankofengland.co.uk
Website: http://www.bankofengland.co.uk/mfsd/cwc/

British Tourist Authority
Mail Order Department
Thames Tower
Black's Road
Hammersmith
London W6 9EL
Tel: 020 8563 3276

Business and Trade Statistics Limited
Lancaster House
More Lane
Esher
Surrey KT10 8AP
Tel: 01372 463121; Fax: 01372 469847;
Email: bt@dial.pipex.com

CAA Aviation Data Unit
Civil Aviation Authority
CAA House 45 - 49 Kingsway
London WC2B 6TE
Tel: 020 7832 5677;
Email: geddesl@caaerg.co.uk

CAA Passenger Surveys
Room T416
Civil Aviation Authority
CAA House 45 - 49 Kingsway
London WC2B 6TE
Tel: 020 7832 5992;
Email: surveys@caaerg.co.uk

CRC Publications
151 Rosebery Avenue
London EC1R 4QX
Tel: 020 7505 6622

Department of Agriculture, Economics and Statistics Division
Annexe B
Dundonald House
Upper Newtownards Road
Belfast BT4 3SB
Tel: 028 9052 4855

Statistics Research Branch
Room 110
Department of Economic Development - Northern Ireland
Netherleigh
Massey Avenue
Belfast BT4 2JP
Tel: 028 9052 9399

Department for Education and Employment
Analytical Services
Mowden Hall
Staindrop Road
Darlington
Co. Durham DL3 9BG
Tel: 01325 392683;
Email: info@dfee.gov.uk

England and Wales Youth Cohort Enquiries
Room W609
Department for Education and Employment
Moorfoot
Sheffield S1 4PQ
Tel: 0114 259 3851;
Email: mark.green@dfee.gov.uk

Department for Education and Employment Publication Centre
P.O. Box 6927
London E3 3NZ
Tel: 020 7510 0150

Anne Jordan
Room 6.09
Department of the Environment - Northern Ireland
Central Statistics and Research Branch
Clarence Court
10-18 Adelaide Street
Belfast BT2 8GB
Tel: 028 9054 0807;
Email: anne.jordan@doeni.gov.uk

DETR UK Air Quality Enquiries
Department of the Environment, Transport and the Regions
Ashdown House
123 Victoria Street
London SW1E 6DE
Tel: 020 7890 6297

Spencer Broadley
Room 1/31
Department of the Environment, Transport and the Regions
Great Minster House
76 Marsham Street
London SW1P 4DR
Tel: 020 7890 3097

Marcella Douglas
Room 3/A4
Department of the Environment, Transport and the Regions
Eland House
Bressenden Place
London SW1E 5DU
Tel: 020 7890 5594;
Email: mdouglas@detr-cmi.demon.co.uk

Terry Hawton
Room 3/A3
Department of the Environment, Transport and the Regions
Eland House
Bressenden Place
London SW1E 5DU
Tel: 020 7890 5578;
Email: Terry_Hawton@detr.gov.uk

Ian Rowe
Room E3/K9
Department of the Environment, Transport and the Regions
Eland House
Bressenden Place
London SW1E 5DU
Tel: 020 7890 5502;
Email: ian_rowe@detr.gsi.gov.uk

Vincent Brown
Room 430B
Department of Health
Skipton House
80 London Road
London SE1 6LH
Tel: 020 7972 5678;
Email: vbrown@doh.gov.uk

Michael Cornish
Room 454 C
Department of Health
Skipton House
80 London Road
London SE1 6LH
Tel: 020 7972 5573;
Email: mcornish@doh.gov.uk

Sheila M. Dixon
Room 490D
Department of Health
Skipton House
80 London Road
London SE1 6LH
Tel: 020 7972 5507/9;
Email: s.dixon@doh.gov.uk

Kevin Downey
Department of Health
Skipton House
80 London Road
London SE1 6LH
Tel: 020 7972 5548

David Treacy
Room 452C
Department of Health
Skipton House
80 London Road
London SE1 6LH
Tel: 020 7972 5589;
Email: DTreacy@doh.gov.uk

Lesz Lancucki
Department of Health
Statistics Division 2B
Room 438B
Skipton House
80 London Road
London SE1 6LH
Tel: 020 7972 5533; Fax: 020 7972 5662;
Email: llancuck@doh.gov.uk

Eddie Finn
Room 1 Annexe 1
Department of Health and Social Services - Northern Ireland
Castle Buildings
Stormont
Belfast
Northern Ireland BT4 3UD
Tel: 028 9052 2261;
Email: eddie.finn@dhssni.gov.uk

Analytical Services Division
Department of Social Security
The Adelphi
1-11 John Adam Street
London WC2N 6HT

Analytical Services Division 1D
Room B2715
Department of Social Security
Benton Park Road
Longbenton
Newcastle upon Tyne NE98 1YX.
Tel: 0191 225 7094

Ann Simpson-Hawkins
Analytical Services Division
Room B2706
Department of Social Security
Benton Park Road
Longbenton
Newcastle upon Tyne NE98 1YX
Tel: 0191 225 7801

Corporate Document Services
Department of Social Security
Saville House
Trinity Arcade
Leeds LS1 6QW
Tel: 0113 399 4040;
Email: orderline@corpdocs.co.uk

Ian Hertwick
ASD1 CBAT
Room B2706
Department of Social Security
Benton Park Road
Longbenton
Newcastle upon Tyne NE98 1YX.
Tel: 0191 225 7336 Fax: 0191 225 7671
Email: hertwici@asd1lbtn.dss-asd.gov.uk

Martin McGill
ASD1B
Room B2612
Department of Social Security
Benton Park Road
Newcastle upon Tyne NE98 1YX
Tel: 0191 225 7661

EPTAC (Energy Information and Statistics)
Bay 1128
Department of Trade and Industry
1 Victoria Street
London SW1H 0ET
Tel: 020 7215 2697;
Email: gillian.purkis@epad.dti.gov.uk

General Enquiries on Regional Statistics
Department of Trade and Industry
Room G21
10 Victoria Street
London SW1H 0NN
Tel: 020 7215 3279/3290;
Email: brian.morris@esdv.dti.gov.uk

Dialog Information
3rd Floor Palace House
3 Cathedral Street
London SE1
Tel: 0800 690 000; Fax: 020 7940 6800;
Email: tony_webb@dialog.com

Customer Contact Point
Equal Opportunities Commission
Overseas House
Quay Street
Manchester M3 3HN
Tel: 0161 833 9244;
Email: info@eoc.org.uk

Alister Henderson
Room 335
Forestry Commission
231 Corstophine Road
Edinburgh EH12 7AT
Tel: 0131 314 6337;
Email: statistics@forestry.gov.uk

Forestry Commission
PO Box 100
Fareham
Hampshire PO14 2SX
Tel: 01329 331345; Fax: 01329 330034;
Email: reception@telelink.co.uk

Further Education Funding Council
Cheylesmore House
Quinton Road
Coventry CV1 2WT

Higher Education Statistics Agency (HESA)
18 Royal Crescent,
Cheltenham GL50 3DA
Tel: 01242 255577

Information and Publications Group
Room 201
Home Office
50 Queen Anne's Gate
London SW1H 9AT
Tel: 020 7273 2084
Email: rds.ho@gtnet.gov.uk

Offenders and Correction Unit
Home Office
50 Queen Anne's Gate
London SW1H 9AT
Tel: 020 7273 4122

Research, Development and Statistics
Directorate
Information & Publications Group
Home Office
50 Queen Anne's Gate
London SW1H 9AT
Tel: 020 7273 2084
Email: rds.ho@gtnet.gov.uk

HSE Books
PO Box 1999
Sudbury
Suffolk CO10 6FS
Tel: 01787 881165; Fax: 01787 313995

Lord Chancellor's Office
Lord Chancellor's Department
Selborne House
54-60 Victoria Street
London SW1E 6QW
Tel: 020 7210 8707

MDS Transmodal
6 Hunter's Walk
Canal Street
Chester CH1 4EB
Tel: 01244 348301; Fax: 01244 348471;
Email: queries@mdst.co.uk

Alex Clothier
Ministry of Agriculture, Fisheries and Food
Foss House
Kings Pool
1-2 Peasholme Green
York YO1 7PX
Tel: 01904 455061;
Email: a.clothier@esq.maff.gov.uk

MAFF Publications Section
Ministry of Agriculture, Fisheries and Food
Room 133a
Ministry of Agriculture, Fisheries and Food
Foss House
Kings Pool
1-2 Peasholme Green
York YO1 7PX
Tel: 01904 455332/455329

Alan Walker
Room 239
Ministry of Agriculture, Fisheries and Food
Foss House
Kings Pool
1-2 Peasholme Green
York YO1 7PX
Tel: 01904 455093;
Email: a.walker@esg.maff.gov.uk

Agricultural Statistics
Statistical Directorate 6
National Assembly for Wales
Cathays Park,
Cardiff CF10 3NQ
Tel: 029 2082 5052; Fax: 029 2082 5350;
E-mail: stats.pubs@wales.gsi.gov.uk

Vivien Trew
Room 2-002
National Assembly for Wales
Cathays Park
Cardiff CF10 3NQ
Tel: 029 2082 5036

Gaynor Williams
National Assembly for Wales
Cathays Park
Cardiff CF10 3NQ

School Performance Division 3
National Assembly Education Department
National Assembly for Wales
Cathays Park
Cardiff CF10 3NQ
Tel: 029 2082 6010

School Performance Division 4
National Assembly Education Department
National Assembly for Wales
Cathays Park
Cardiff CF10 3NQ
Tel: 029 2082 6010

Publications Unit, Statistical Directorate
National Assembly for Wales
Cathays Park
Cardiff CF10 3NQ
Tel: 029 2082 5044;
Email: claire.owen@wales.gsi.gov.uk

Statistical Publications Unit
Statistical Directorate
National Assembly for Wales
Cathays Park
Cardiff CF10 3NQ
Tel: 029 2082 5054; Fax: 029 2082 5350;
E-mail: stats.pubs@wales.gsi.gov.uk

NDAD
National Digital Archive of Datasets
ULCC,
20 Guilford Street
London WC1N 1DZ
Tel: 020 7692 1122;
Email: support@ndad.ulcc.ac.uk

Marjorie Wilson
Room 480D
National Health Service Executive
SD1C
Skipton House
80 London Road
London SE1 6LH
Tel: 020 7972 5502;
Email: mwilson@doh.gov.uk

Customer help desk
Information and Statistics Division,

NHS in Scotland
Trinity Park House
Room B037
South Trinity Road
Edinburgh EH5 3SQ
Tel: 0131 551 8899

Annual Abstract Sales
Northern Ireland Statistics and Research Agency
McAuley House
2-14 Castle Street
Belfast BT1 1SA
Tel: 028 9052 6082;
Email: nisra.rreb@dfpni.gov.uk

Leicha Rickards
Office of Manpower Economics
Oxford House
76 Oxford Street
London W1N 9FD
Tel: 020 7467 7227

Office of Manpower Economics
Oxford House
76 Oxford Street
London W1N 9FD
Tel: 020 7467 7216

PHLS Press & Publications
Public Health Laboratory Service
Communicable Disease Surveillance Centre
61 Colindale Avenue
Colindale
London NW9 5DF
Tel: 020 8200 1295

HM Inspector of Schools Audit Unit
Scottish Executive
Victoria Quay
Edinburgh EH6 6QQ

Sheelagh Harrison
Room 52
Scottish Executive
James Craig Walk
Edinburgh EH1 3BA
Tel: 0131 244 3607;
Email: Sheelagh.Harrison@scotland.gov.uk

Scottish Executive, Central Research Unit
Room JI-O,
Saughton House,
Broomhouse Drive,
Edinburgh EH11 3XA
Tel: 0131 244 2097;
Email: taryn.forrest@scotland.goc.uk

Andy Reid
Scottish Executive Environment and Fisheries Department
Room 28
Pentland House
47 Robb's Loan
Edinburgh EH14 1TY

Scottish Higher Education Funding Council
Donaldson House
97 Haymarket Terrace
Edinburgh EH12 5HD
Tel: 0131 313 6566

Fiona Cunningham
Scottish Tourist Board
Research Section
23 Ravelston Terrace
Edinburgh EH4 3EU
Tel: 0131 332 2433;
Email: fiona.cunningham@stb.gov.uk

Index

Compiled by INDEXING SPECIALISTS,
202, Church Road,
Hove,
East Sussex,
BN3 2DJ

Printed in the UK by The Stationery Office Limited
Dd000777 3/00 19585 493576